THE
TRAVELLER'S
HANDBOOK

A WEXAS PUBLICATION

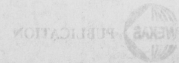

THE TRAVELLER'S HANDBOOK

Edited by
Caroline Brandenburger

Assistant Editor
Carey Ogilvie

Published by
WEXAS Ltd

WEXAS Ltd
45-49 Brompton Road
London SW3 1DE

© WEXAS Ltd, 1980, 1982, 1985, 1988, 1991, 1994

This completely revised and enlarged edition first published in 1994

ISBN 0-905802-05-07-1

Cover designed by Paul Vickers

Printed and bound in Great Britain by
BPC Paperbacks Ltd
A member of
The British Printing Company Ltd

CONTENTS

GETTING THERE BY AIR
Chapter 4

GETTING THERE BY ROAD
Chapter 5

GETTING THERE BY OTHER MEANS
Chapter 6

GREAT JOURNEYS OVERLAND
Chapter 7

YOUR SPECIAL NEEDS
Chapter 8

PAPERWORK AND MONEY
Chapter 9

8

A PLACE TO STAY
Chapter 10

A BASIC GUIDE TO HEALTH
Chapter 11

EQUIPPING FOR A TRIP
Chapter 12

COMMUNICATIONS
Chapter 13

WHEN THINGS GO WRONG
Chapter 14

TRAVEL WRITING AND PHOTOGRAPHY
Chapter 15

AND FINALLY...
Chapter 16

DIRECTORY

12

GETTING THERE BY AIR
Section 4

GETTING THERE BY ROAD
Section 5

GETTING THERE BY OTHER MEANS
Section 6

GREAT JOURNEYS OVERLAND
Section 7

YOUR SPECIAL NEEDS
Section 8

PAPERWORK AND MONEY
Section 9

14

A PLACE TO STAY
Section 10

A BASIC GUIDE TO HEALTH
Section 11

EQUIPPING FOR A TRIP
Section 12

COMMUNICATIONS
Section 13

WHEN THINGS GO WRONG
Section 14

TRAVEL WRITING AND PHOTOGRAPHY
Section 15

AND FINALLY ...
Section 16

WIDE HORIZONS

A foreword by Sir Ranulph Fiennes Bt. OBE DSc.

A great number of people in Britain are proud to announce in their local watering holes that they have never ventured further than a few miles from their home.

An annual visit to Blackpool or Scarborough advances others into a more venturesome category but whether they have gained a sense of achievement over the first less mobile group is debatable. After all, anyone can learn all about Blackpool (or toads in Timbouktou) on the telly without budging from their sitting room. This is a specious point of view, since mere learning is not the same as achieving, which even the most professional devil's advocate (a Bragge or a Dimbleby) would find hard to defend.

The observations of these travellers are enough to convince me that travel is an unbeatable medicine for anyone with depression, narrow horizons, a longing for self-fulfilment or just general malaise.

Joe Simpson, climber extraordinaire, has trod a lonely path on the roof of the world, survived traumatic falls and watched friends die one by one. "For me", he writes, "different memories drift by unexpectedly, made funnier and the more poignant by the passing years... We are still here, playing our silly game of life, forced eventually to forget the sadness and remember the brilliance and the good times. If there are any ghosts they are in my mind, in the haunting echoes of distant laughter, chuckling down from the past."

To Simpson then one of the great advantages of travel is the rich harvest of memories gained that will last him forever (or at least till on the onset of Alzheimer's).

Ffyona Campbell has walked on squelching blisters across most of the world's continents and her books give an insight into her motives as well as her rewards. Fulfilment and achievements are often reflections on an individual traveller's past hang-ups. During one of her mammoth walks, Ffyona wrote, "As I walked every day I carried with me a fear of people who stared and mocked me. By walking round the world, I realised I was the centre of their attention again, but I was using it to make them cast doubt on themselves as they had done so freely and so often to me. This crazed and distorted logic was one of the things I was walking across Australia to understand and reverse."

Housewife Margaret Hobbs titled her first travel book 'Better to Journey'. Having spent a large part of her life holding up the ladder for the rest of her family, she felt it was her turn to "see what was at the top". So she set out to trek the Himalaya and tells a gripping tale of how, in her own words, "we battled with our inner weaknesses and limited physical endurance."

There are a thousand life-enhancing aspects to travel no matter how limited the ambitions of the voyager but, just as a life-long cripple can live a happier life than a jet-setting millionaire, so a narrow-minded, self-centred misery-guts can travel the world and return home as empty and unfulfilled as though he or she had never set out. To coin a travel-worn cliché, 'It's all in the mind'. But only when you've have been there with your eyes and your mind wide open.

INTRODUCTION

'I quite realized,' said Columbus
'That the earth was not a rhombus,
But I *am* a little annoyed
To find it an oblate spheroid.'

E. Clerihew Bentley, 1929

So much of travel is about discovery —personal and actual discovery. Despite the fact that there are few corners of the world now left where man has yet to tread, every traveller setting off, whether on a two-week package to Spain or back-packing round the Far East, feels the frisson, that shiver of excitement at the thought of what may lie ahead.

The Traveller's Handbook aims to guide travellers of every type, from the package holiday-maker to the independent traveller, from the businessman to the expedition worker —through each stage and over each hurdle of the venture. From deciding where to go, to buying an airline ticket or shipping a motorbike. From packing your luggage to surviving in the jungle. From travel by microlight to coping with 'coming home blues'.

The book is divided into two sections: the first part is the 'how-to-do-it' section and the Directory is crammed with thousands of helpful names and addresses relating to the first part of the book. So if Luxury Travel is your taste, read the article on page 96 and then turn to page 692 of the Directory for all the relevant contact addresses.

As the number of travellers world-wide increases year by year, the pressure on the environment increases too. Not only on the surroundings, but on its peoples and cultures. While travelling to these once remote places is so intensely exciting for us, please do remember the respect to which the host people are entitled, and the responsibility with which their environment should be treated.

Happy Travelling!

Caroline Brandenburger
Carey Ogilvie

And thanks to our Editorial Board for all their helpful advice: Sarah Anderson, of The Travel Bookshop; David Prest, of BBC Radio 4; Douglas Schatz, of Stanfords Bookshop; and Valerie Singleton.

WHERE AND WHEN
Chapter 1

PLACES IN VOGUE

by Caroline Brandenburger

Holiday destinations are just as much subject to the vagaries of fashion as anything else. In the 18th century, a young gentleman's Grand Tour inevitably included Paris, Florence, Vienna, even Istanbul. While a hundred years later, English resorts such as Bath, Brighton and Scarborough were considered the apogee of chic.

But travel of this kind was clearly the pastime of the rich and leisured. Mass tourism is a recent, post–War phenomenon and more than 400 million people now travel abroad each year. Some predict that by the year 2000 that figure could reach 650 million.

How has this extreme state of affairs come about? Several potent factors have combined to produce it. In part it is the West's increased general prosperity together with a relative decrease in the cost of travel. Cheaper travel has in turn been fuelled by an heightened awareness of exotic destinations which feature regularly in almost every form of the media. Whether it is the palm–treed beach of a rum advertisement, *Sleepless in Seattle* which brought floods of visitors to a city hitherto not prominent on the tourist circuit, or *Crocodile Dundee's* Kakadu National Park (visitor numbers to this Australian wildlife reserve quadrupled after the film's release), all have contributed to our growing appetite for travel.

A strong need to escape from rising levels of work–induced stress, and a general sense of alienation from normal habitats (statistically those who live in high–rise flats are more likely to go away than those who live in houses) has also helped feed the desire to venture overseas.

The affection for travel is unarguable. But what renders a destination fashionable is another perplexed and much–discussed issue. Cost is obviously a significant element. Scandinavia has not been particularly popular simply because it is more expensive than most West European destinations; whereas less–developed countries such as India are very cheap for the Western visitor, especially now that the cost of long–haul air travel is so accessible. Meanwhile Mediterranean destinations such as Spain, Greece and Turkey promise half–way houses in terms of cost and provide so–called sophisticated leisure amenities at a reasonable price.

In the Sixties and to some extent the Seventies, it was often spiritual and ideological factors that influenced travellers in their choice. The young flocked to India and Nepal to sit at the feet of gurus, smoke pot, and 'explore their inner selves.' Buddhism was also attractive, drawing people further East. The more politically motivated went to Israel to work on a kibbutz and live out, albeit briefly, a form of the socialist ideal. Meanwhile the British middle classes made their way to the Dordogne and Tuscany, drawn by the lure of culture, climate and good food.

The late Seventies and Eighties saw a boom in the number of independent travellers. Thirsty for adventure, they went in hordes to exotic places such as Tibet, Thailand, South America and China. The events of the early Nineties in Eastern Europe have also drawn millions of visitors. *Glasnost, perestroika,* the sudden and dramatic shift into democracy, have meant that countries once so apparently inaccessible are now eagerly sought out by curious Westerners hoping to witness such extraordinary historic change.

So where now? As always, the thirst for unspoilt and naive cultures leads the traveller ruthlessly forth in search of new pastures. Given that Nepal is considered 'out' by the ground-breaking, independent traveller, that Pataya in Thailand is for some the 'Benidorm of the East' and also parts of Kenya, fashionable destinations have become even more esoteric. Far Eastern Russia, Laos, the Galapagos Islands, Polynesia, even Burkino Faso are considered de rigeur for the truly smart traveller; and quasi–scientific expeditions to the Antarctic are particularly popular, especially after the success of David Attenborough's Life in the Freezer, for those who can afford the price of a ticket.

The growth of 'green tourism', a welcome if not entirely altruistic development, has led to an emphasis on the benevolent use of the environment and non resource–consuming activities such as cycling and nature-watching (whale-watching in Greenland is now considered the height of chic).

In the desperate scrabble for unspoiled territory, the traveller is being pushed to the outermost margins of the world. As cruises to the Antarctic become standard, travellers seeking even more esoteric thrills have already put their names down for the first shuttle flights to the moon —all 240,250 miles away!

MORAL DILEMMAS OF TRAVEL

by George Monbiot

The main tourist hotel in Dili, the capital of East Timor, is also an army intelligence headquarters. Until recently, East Timorese political prisoners were tortured by Indonesian soldiers in the basement. Uniformed men are dispatched from its rooms to oversee the execution of dissidents.

Yet the Indonesian government is encouraging tourists to visit East Timor and stay in the hotel. Having killed one third of the occupied country's population, having destroyed the people's homes, their crops and their livelihoods, having invented torture techniques that would make the Gestapo wince, the government has managed to achieve a semblance of normality. The East Timorese are, most of the time, too frightened to protest in public. The rebels still holding out against the government are confined to the remotest places. Bringing tourists into East Timor serves both to assure the rest of the world that nothing is amiss and to legitimize the island's illegal occupation.

So should tourists do as the Indonesian government suggests, and visit East Timor? One's immediate response would be no. But the ethics of tourism, here and elsewhere, are complex: the arguments for going may be as compelling as those for staying away.

Tourists visiting East Timor, or any other country subject to the brutal whims of an intractable dictatorship, can swiftly become accessories to inhumanity. The hotel in Dili, for example, is owned by army officers: everyone who pays for a room there puts money straight into the soldiers' pockets. The ignorance in which most tourists are cocooned is infectious: when they go home and tell their family and friends that the beaches were great or the food was disgusting but say nothing about what is happening there, subtly, unwittingly, they help to blot out the efforts of people trying to draw attention to the atrocities.

On the other hand, for the first fifteen years of its occupation, East Timor languished in obscurity. The government could act without constraint, as there were few investigative journalists and human rights workers, the island was visited only by absurd processions of 'independent observers' who, neither independent nor observant, were steered around the trouble spots by government minders, and concluded that the place was as peaceful as it appeared to be. The presence of tourists may impose restraints on the government's treatment of the population. It provides a cover under which investigators can work. East Timor becomes, to the outside world, a place, rather than just a name.

The dilemma, of course, is not confined to East Timor. Indonesia is one of scores of tourist destinations in which gross abuses of human rights take place. There is probably not a country in the world for which a reasonable argument for a boycott could not be made. The publishing company Lonely Planet is not producing a guide to Norway, on account of its continued harvest of the minke whales. Both Europeans (pointing to our discharges of pollution), and North Americans, (citing our continued presence in Northern Ireland), have called for a tourist boycott of Great Britain. The argument for a boycott of countries already subject to public scrutiny appears to be less clouded than the argument for a boycott of countries left out of the public eye.

At first sight, it would seem that a distinction can be drawn between the ethics of organised tours and the ethics of independent travel. Organised tour operators ensure that their customers are insulated from the unexpected. Nothing is supposed to happen which is not scheduled to happen. Tourists are kept away from trouble spots and seldom interact with anyone, other than those who serve or sell to them. Backpackers, on the other hand, claim to seek out the unexpected. In theory, they are more likely to stumble across atrocities, or meet people who can tell them what is happening. Yet the question is complicated by a further factor, for tourism is not just a means by which oppression can be either masked or exposed. Tourism itself can become an instrument of destruction.

In June 1993 the Burmese town of Pagan was emptied of its inhabitants. The State Law and Order Restoration Council, which intends to make Pagan one of the principal destinations for Visit Myanmar Year (1995) decided to spare tourists the inconvenience and unsightliness of human beings. The townspeople, whose ancestors built the very attraction the tourists will visit, were forcibly evacuated and their homes destroyed. There was no compensation.

Such clearances are a common component of national tourist industries. All over South East Asia, farms, forests, villages, even suburbs, have been destroyed to make way for golf courses. Slums are razed for fear of offending visitors. In many parts of Africa, conservation is used to justify the creation of new parks and reserves for tourism. Their inhabitants are excluded from the lands they have possessed for centuries, re-entering, in Kenya, on pain of death.

It is not just the people's land but also their culture which is expropriated for tourism by unscrupulous governments. During the 1980's, the longhouses of the Asmat people of Irian Jaya, in Indonesia, were destroyed and their traditional ceremonies were proscribed. In 1991, the government launched Visit Indonesia Year. Realizing that tourists want to see how the country's ethnic peoples lived, it instructed the Asmat to rebuild their longhouses and perform ceremonies for the tourists. If they refused, they were beaten or imprisoned. Those who assumed that this meant they could once more start worshipping their ancestors were sadly mistaken: if they performed any ceremonies for their own purposes, they were, again, beaten or imprisoned.

While these are extreme examples, tourism is, wherever it occurs, an extractive industry. It extracts the differences between our land and culture and those of the nations we visit, until they scarcely exist. Remote and romantic beaches become mundane resorts. Remote and remarkable people tailor their culture to suit those who pay for it, until, in the words of the Maasai man, "We have ceased to be what we are; we are becoming what we seem." The exotic, of course, is illusory: as we approach it, it disappears. Tourism, therefore, will never be sated, even when it has penetrated the remotest parts of the world.

While organized tours may be most directly responsible for the muffling of diversity, it is the backpackers who blaze the trail they follow. An independent traveller's destination becomes a mainstream resort within a few years. Indeed, as travel becomes easier and tourists more adventurous, the distinction between the two groups is breaking down: hundreds of tour companies organize journeys which mimic those of independent travellers. Neither category —if they can be categorized — is blameless.

None of the ethical questions tourism raises can be easily answered. Tour organizers have justified their work to me on the grounds that it is a "cultural exchange". Yet what I have seen of their activities suggests that no cultural exchange is taking place. While the visitors get culture, their hosts, if they are lucky, get money. As identity is rooted in place, the tourists have little to offer.

Other people claim that tourism breaks down the barriers between our lives and those of the people we visit. Yet, in most cases, tourists remain firmly behind barriers —be they windows of a coach, the walls of a hotel or the lens of a camera. In many parts of the world, tourism has compounded misunderstanding and hostility: the Egyptian fundamentalists threatening to blow up hotels and the Oxford householders turning their hoses on open-topped buses doubtless have sympathizers all over the world.

Tourism, we are told, brings wealth to local people. All I have seen suggests the opposite —that tourism makes a very few people extremely rich, while impoverishing the majority, who lose their land, their resources and their sense of self and make, if anything, a tiny amount of money.

Even the oldest maxim of all, that travel broadens the mind, is questionable. Tourists are the aristocracy of the New World Order. They are pampered and protected wherever they go, they are treated with deference and never corrected. Indeed, tour companies do their best to provide what the tourists expect the country can reasonably provide. For most tourists, the only surprises will be unpleasant ones, when the reality of the countries they visit pricks the bubble in which they travel. Then the shock of discovery, rather than assuaging fear, tends to enhance it: millions of people return home more convinced that foreigners are dirty, deceitful and dangerous than they were when they left.

Yet it is travelling that shapes many of those who become the social reformers, the human rights activists, the environmental campaigners and investigative journalists without whom every nation on earth would have succumbed to barren dictatorship. These are among the few for whom travel does broaden the mind, for whom exposure to injustice abroad may lift the veil from injustice at home, for whom the conditions suffered by the oppressed of the world, once seen, cannot be tolerated. While they number as tens among the millions, their enlightenment surely means that tourism, for all its monstrosities, cannot be wholly condemned.

COUNTRIES AT WAR

by Andrew Duncan

Since the breaking of the Berlin Wall in November 1989 the world has radically changed. The most significant changes took place in Europe: the Cold War ended; the Warsaw Pact was disbanded; the Soviet Union broke up into twelve independent states; the Baltic states regained their independence; and Czechoslovakia split, peacefully, into the Czech Republic and Slovakia. By the end of August 1994 all Russian troops had withdrawn from central and eastern European countries and the Baltic States. However, garrisons and peace-keeping detachments remained in Belarus, Moldova, Georgia and Tajikistan while in Ukraine the future of the Black Sea Fleet and its Crimean bases remained unsettled. The defeat of communism resulted in a dramatic rise in nationalism; the most drastic example being the break-up of Yugoslavia where parts of Croatia are still controlled by Serbs and the bloody three-way civil war in Bosnia-Hercegovina between Serbs, Croats, and Muslims still, despite many cease fires, peace-talks and international pressure, lingers on.

With the end of the Cold War the possibility of a world war starting in Europe, where the massive armed forces of the Warsaw Pact and NATO faced each other across the barbed wire and minefields of the Iron Curtain, which was more likely to escalate into a global nuclear war, disappeared. While the likelihood of such a war breaking out was always slight, its results would have been catastrophic and so its threat was the most dangerous facing the world.

Throughout the Cold War the two Superpowers felt it necessary to back one side or the other in any minor regional or, more often, civil war. On the other hand the fact that the Superpowers normally took sides in regional conflicts also provided a degree of control and ensured that these conflicts did not get totally out of control, nor spread to direct confrontation between the USA and USSR, and in turn to the two European alliances.

The end of the Cold War saw the end of four long-standing civil wars in Angola, Ethiopia, Mozambique and Nicaragua. Sadly the peace was short lived in the case of Angola where the war rages as bloodily as it ever did before, nor is Nicaragua totally at peace as old adversaries continue to try to settle their differences by force.

The rise of nationalism, religious fanaticism, and the withdrawal of Superpower sponsorship (and control) has contributed to the growing number of conflicts across the world. But sadly the world *is* a violent place and too often its inhabitants resort to violence to solve their problems. There has, for example, been only one year since the end of the Second World War when British troops have not been involved in fighting in some corner of the world. While the world has managed to avoid a major war on a global scale since 1946, and the number of wars between states has much diminished, the number of countries involved in civil war —situations of 'no war' but where violence can erupt without warning or where terrorism can be expected —grows every year. All these situations are included in the global overview which follows.

Some general points must always be borne in mind. Countries are not necessarily safe once a war is over, particularly civil wars. Unexploded bombs and uncleared (sometimes unmarked) minefields may endanger safety for some years. After civil wars, there is often a residue of armed men who take to crime rather than give up the life of excitement (and sometimes prosperity) they experienced as guerrillas. Terrorist attacks are mainly aimed at achieving publicity rather than damaging the state, so terrorists often choose soft targets such as innocent bystanders —including tourists. This last point is a growing phenomenon as recent events in, for example, Egypt and Algeria show.

Europe

Europe is now more dangerous than it has been for many years. While terrorist activities in Northern Ireland (where the United Kingdom has been fighting a guerrilla war against the Irish Republican Army since 1969), in Spain (where Basque separatist group Euskadi ta Askatasuna has attacked government targets since 1962) and from time to time elsewhere in Europe as a result of action by groups such as the Red Brigade, Baader Meinhof, Turkish Kurds, and Italian Mafia, have caused casualties and damaged property they have never yet totally stopped the tourists. But there are now a growing number of 'no go' areas in Europe.

Despite the encouraging progress made early in 1994 towards achieving peace in Bosnia-Hercegovina, the bulk of the former Yugoslavia will be an unwise place to visit for sometime yet. Only in Slovenia is a return to bloodshed unlikely. Elsewhere the hatred engendered by the civil war, or the threat of it in areas such as Vojvodina, Kosovo and Macedonia, will make tourism unwelcome. The civil wars in the southern republics of the former Soviet Union appear to be petering out but it is still unrealistic to expect to travel safely in Moldova, Georgia (where three separate causes of conflict still exist), Armenia or Azerbaijan. Even more dangerous are the eastern provinces of Turkey where the authorities battle with the Kurdistan Workers Party (PKK) and where tens of casualties on both sides are announced each week. The future situation of Ukraine remains unclear and there are growing worries that both the Crimea and the Donbas region where there are also large Russian minorities has receded now that agreement over the withdrawal of Russian troops has been reached.

Northern Africa

There seems to be no end in sight of the long-standing problem of Western Sahara, annexed by Morocco, and the scene of fighting between Polisario guerrillas (based and armed in Algeria) and the Moroccan Army despite a UN monitoring presence.

In Algeria the struggle between the Army-backed government and the Islamic Salvation Front (FIS), which won a surprisingly large victory in the first round of the 1991 elections only to see the second round cancelled and the FIS banned, continues unabated. The FIS has now turned its attention to destroying the economy by targeting both expatriate workers and tourists. France, Spain and the UK have all advised their nationals to leave.

Libya, while refusing to hand over those strongly suspected of causing the Lockerbie air disaster, has agreed to withdraw from the Aouzou strip whose ownership it had been disputing with Chad. The UN still imposes a ban on air travel to Libya.

Western and Central Africa

While the worst of the internal conflicts in the region, the civil war in Liberia appears to be over, hardly any country is free from violence. In Liberia the task of disarming the rival factions and restoring a civil authority still faces the peace-keeping troops sent in by the Economic Community of West Africa States. The most dangerous countries are Burundi and Rwanda where the tribal rivalry between the Tutsi (who normally dominate the governments and armies) and the much more numerous Hutu have resulted in regular massacres of each other. Since the beginning of 1994 violence has been reported, in the following states:- Cameroon, Chad, Congo, Equatorial Guinea, Gabon, Ghana, Senegal, Sierra Leone, Togo and Zaire. A territorial dispute has emerged between Nigeria and Cameroon, while the ethnic fault line between Arab North Africa and Black Africa continues to witness disputes between Mauritania and Senegal and between Tuareg Berber Tribesmen and the government of Mali and Niger.

Southern Africa

The optimism engendered by the end of the civil war in Angola and the withdrawal of Cuban troops was short lived as the rebel movement, Unita, refused to accept the UN monitored election result. The civil war continues at a heightened intensity but this time without the support of the rival sides by outside powers (Cuba, Russia, South Africa and USA).

As apartheid is abandoned in South Africa the incidence of violence increases but now mainly between the followers of the African National Congress, who are likely to win the first multi-national elections, and the Zulu Inkatha movement who are boycotting them. Also guilty of provocation are the white ultra-right wing, the Afrikaner Resistance Movement (ANB), which has vowed to fight for a white homeland.

Only in Mozambique are there good hopes for peace as both government troops and those of the Renamo insurgent movement are exhausted by the civil war and are being disarmed and demobilised by a UN peace-keeping force.

East Africa and the Horn of Africa

Though the situation in Uganda is much improved since the collapse of the guerrilla group known as the Holy Spirit Movement there are still outbreaks of violence mainly along the border with Rwanda but more recently in eastern Uganda where the Karamojong tribe's lack of water has led to the watering of animals backed by guns. In southern Sudan the civil war between the Muslim Arab government and the Christian and Animist population continues unabated. Little or no news emanates from Ethiopia nor from Eritrea which peacefully seceded from Ethiopia. Though starvation has now been avoided in Somalia due to first US and then UN troops escorting aid convoys and feeding centres, no government exists and the war-lords still control their own tribal areas.

The Middle East

Iraq suffered two uprisings immediately after its defeat in the Gulf War. In the south the government continues to harry the remaining rebels who hid in the marshes. In the north the Kurds have developed a homeland cut off from the rest of the country by Iraqi forces. Though only on the fringes of the areas do Iraqi troops provoke conflict but elsewhere both Iranian and Turkish forces from time to time take military action against their own national Kurdish guerrilla groups who have taken refuge over the border.

Egypt is suffering form a growth of violent Islamic fundamentalism which is targeting tourists and other foreigners as much as it does the police forces. Most attacks on tourists take place along the Nile south of Cairo.

Israel still suffers from terrorist attacks mainly from across the northern border with Lebanon but the intruders are more likely to be from Hezbollah or other Islamic extremist groups than from the PLO. Despite apparent progress towards handing over the Gaza strip and an enclave around Jericho to Palestinian autonomy the Intifida, or uprising, continues in the West Bank and Gaza, and Israelis are still attacked within the 1967 borders-mainly in Jerusalem. A new, but not unexpected, phenomenon is the Israeli settlers backlash, the worst instance of which was the massacre of Muslim worshippers at the Tomb of Abraham in Hebron. Though the majority on both sides are eager for peace there are a number of extremists, again on both sides, determined to upset the peace process even if it means resorting to violence. Apart from the West Bank and Gaza, and on occasions Jerusalem, Israel is safe to visit.

Lebanon is slowly returning to normal though the south will remain a no-go area for some years as the authorities are loath to totally disarm the Palestinian groups who have handed over their heavy weapons but are unlikely to confront the Israeli-backed South Lebanese Army. However, the Iranian-backed Hezbollah are still aggressively active. Around Beirut the warring factions have been induced to hand in their heavy weapons and inter-factional violence is no longer a daily event.

The most recent civil war to break out, in May 1994, is that of Yemen. Originally two separate countries the traditionalist Northern Yemen Arab Republic merged with the marxist Southern Peoples Democratic Republic of Yemen in May 1990. However the armed forces were never properly integrated and maintained their original loyalties. The southerners have long claimed that they were being unfairly treated by the far more numerous north. This disagreement culminated in a clash between the northern President and the southern Vice President and the President's attempts to remove his southern rival misfired and civil war broke out between the two still separate armies. It is too early to say how the conflict will end.

Central Asia and the Indian Subcontinent

Although the Soviet Union withdrew its troops from Afghanistan in 1989, peace has not yet returned to the country. The many groups of Mujahedin originally based in eastern Iran and northern Pakistan still oppose the so-called government in Kabul and each other. The main fighting is between the supporters of the President and those of the Prime Minister (two appointments made at the Islamabad peace conference in March 1993) and is concentrated around Kabul.

Afghanistan is also involved in the civil war in Tajikistan where, with Russian military help, the communist-dominated regime narrowly avoided being overthrown by a mixed democratic-Islamic opposition. Over half a million Tajiks were made refugees, and the core of the Islamic movement continues the struggle from Afghan territory.

India and Pakistan still confront each other along the line of the disputed border on the Siachen glacier and over the future of Kashmir; both problems could escalate to war. In Kashmir despite an enormous Indian military presence violence breaks out from time to time and is invariably blamed on Pakistani provocation. Although much international press publicity was given to the Ayodhya incident where a mosque built on a Hindu temple site was destroyed by Hindu extremists, there is really little friction between Hindus and Muslims (or Christians for that matter) who happily live side by side throughout India. However there is a growing security problem in north east India with mainly tribal disorders in Manipur, Nagaland and Assam (the Indian authorities are loathe to allow travel here).

The inter-communal fighting between the Sri Lankan Government and the Tamils still continues despite the intervention of the Indian peace-keeping force and its withdrawal in March 1990. The northern and eastern provinces where the Tamil population lives has witnessed the worst of the violence including atrocities by both sides. Elsewhere in Sri Lanka is safe for tourists though terrorist outrages occur from time to time.

South East Asia

At long last it looks as if the civil war in Cambodia may soon be over. Initially all four parties to the conflict agreed to a cease-fire and a UN-supervised demobilisation process and democratic election. Since then the Khmer Rouge have reneged on their promises but the forces of the new government are slowly but successfully rolling up the opposition. This is having a spill-over effect in the neighbouring border areas of Thailand and Laos. Mines will make parts of Cambodia dangerous for many years.

Indonesia has still not totally subdued the opposition in the former Dutch colony of East Timor and violence erupts from time to time. Nor has Papua New Guinea managed to solve its disputes with the island of Bougainville.

Central America

Central America used to be the area worst affected by revolution and endemic violence but recent years have seen a definite improvement in the situation. In Guatemala the government has reached agreement with four separate guerrilla movements which will lead to a fresh approach to human rights in a country where 100,000 have died and 40,000 'disappeared' since the 1960s. In Nicaragua violence which re-erupted after both Contras and Sandanistas were reconstituted, may subside once Humberto Ortega (brother of the former Sandinsta President) is replaced as head of the Army. Despite UN resolutions, and the arrival of peace-keeping force off-shore, there has been no resolution of the crisis in Haiti and the military still rule the country by force. A new development is the emergence in Mexico of the Zapatista National Liberation Army which seized four towns in the southern province of Chiapas in January 1994.

In Peru there was an encouraging decline in the level of violence due to the actions of the Sendera Luminoso (Shining Path) guerrillas throughout 1993 until September when a new wave of attacks began in December with many taking place in Lima. Drugs are still the basic cause of the high levels of violence which still exist in Colombia despite the death of the leading drug baron Pablo Escobar.

The outlook

Travelling in any of the countries mentioned earlier obviously carries risks. Many of them have little to offer to tourists though some may seem attractive to the young 'back-pack' explorers who are probably those most at risk in these areas.

In many of the countries described, the main centres are relatively, if not entirely safe to visit and probably just as safe as London and safer than Belfast (and for that matter New York where apart from the World Trade Centre bombing there is no terrorism only crime). But it all depends where and when you go and there is no saying truer than "discretion is the better part of valour" when it comes to travelling.

Conflict will continue and may well increase in many parts of the world but for the time being the chance of these conflicts escalating into a major war has dramatically diminished.

An after note

The Consular Department of The Foreign and Commonwealth Office maintains a Travel Advice Unit which keeps up to date advice on travel to some hundred countries where travellers should take care. Apart from warning of civil war, the advice covers violent crime, drug problems and outbreaks of disease. Their telephone number is 071-270 4129. FCO travel advice notices are displayed on BBC 2 (CEEFAX)

WHEN TO GO

by Richard Harrington

Inexperienced travellers may not think too much about when to go before setting off. They know it's always hot in Indonesia and cold in the Arctic. Seasoned travellers, on the other hand, will plan their trip very carefully around certain times of the year.

Airlines, hotels and tour operators all have off–peak seasons when they adjust their prices downwards. Prices are governed by demand rather than by climatic seasons—most Mediterranean countries are at their most idyllic in May when the number of charter flights is at its lowest. However, a great deal of Mediterranean tourism is governed by school holidays so demand is comparatively low during the term. Sometimes one–way traffic distorts the fare structure: for example, westbound fares across the Atlantic are at their lowest when the climate is at its best in many of the destination countries, but the fares are governed by the amount of traffic travelling in the other direction.

Climate (rainfall, humidity, temperature) produces the most obvious type of season. Climates that are no trial to local people may have devastating effects on those ill–adapted souls arriving from more temperate regions.

Hurricanes hardly happen

For reasons still little understood, certain tropical regions of the globe are subject to seasonal monsoon rains, cyclones, hurricanes and tornadoes. For most people, these are non–travel seasons. On the other hand, travel deals may be so attractive in these periods that you may decide to make the trip because you know you could never afford it at any other time. A surfer may choose to travel in the stormiest seasons of the year, knowing that these are usually the times for the biggest and best waves.

There are other types of season too. Big game and birdlife may be more spectacular in certain months. Endemic diseases may be caught more easily at certain times of year. In Arctic Canada and Alaska there are two great torments: an icy wind in winter and mosquitoes in summer. The blessing is that you never get both at the same time.

The going may be physically impossible, or almost so, in certain months. Few have dared to move on the Arctic ice cap during the continuous night of freezing winter. Yachtsmen crossing the Atlantic from west to east avoid a winter crossing on the northern route, and those sailing on the Pacific circuit from North America to Hawaii, Tahiti and New Zealand try to complete the last leg of the voyage before the summer cyclones begin. In the jungles of the African West Coast and of 'Africa's armpit', Cameroon, the Congo, Zaire etc, the going is very rough and extremely unpleasant during the rainy season from May to August. The best time to start a trans–Africa crossing from London would be September/October when the height of the Saharan summer and the rainy season further south have both passed. Autumn and, better still, spring are the best times for a Sahara crossing.

Trekking in Nepal has become so popular that it's worth knowing the best times for it. The best visibility, lowest precipitation, brightest weather, and most tolerable night-time temperatures occur between the end of September and the end of May. Within this period, the best 'subseason' is autumn, from October to mid–December. January and February are very cold, with snow above 3000m, but visibility is good and trekking is still possible. Spring arrives around late February or early March. The monsoon, with its poor visibility, mud and leeches, has its onset about the end of March.

A little–known fact is that since hot air is thinner than cold and hot air rises, the air at altitude will be thinner when hot than when cold. While the heat itself, in high altitude cities like Mexico City, La Paz, Addis Ababa or Nairobi, is unlikely to be overwhelming, the rarefied air may leave you exhausted for several days if you don't take it easy when you get there. If you are susceptible to altitude, winter is probably the best time to go. The heat is also likely to be less overpowering then.

Man, maker of all seasons

Man too creates seasons which affect the traveller, and the Westerner will sometimes find them hard to predict. The festivals of the Orthodox Church do not often coincide with those of the Western churches. The Islamic religious calendar is based upon the lunar month and is therefore out of step with our own progression of months and years. The Kandy Perhera festival in Sri Lanka is one of a number of events whose exact dates are settled by astrologers at inconveniently short notice. So if, for instance, you plan to visit a Muslim country during Ramadan, the month of fasting, bear in mind that the local people will do without food from sun–up to sun–down. Various services will be disrupted or unavailable. Meals will be hard to obtain outside the tourist areas. And you may be woken by whole families noisily eating a meal before dawn puts an end to the revelry. However, a meal shared with an Arab family during Ramadan is a treat to be remembered. In the Haj season, when Muslims from West Africa to Indonesia flock to Mecca on pilgrimage, air services along the necessary routes are totally disrupted for ordinary travellers.

Come and join the dance

In the West Indies, Guyana and Brazil, Carnival is the time of year when the poor are given the chance to forget their worries and feel rich. Cities like Port of Spain in Trinidad and Rio de Janeiro in Brazil have become magnets for tourists but are to be avoided at that time if you have business to do and are not interested in the Carnival itself.

Major festivals in Europe and elsewhere always attract culture–seekers. The centres concerned become impossibly crowded; hotels fill up; airline passengers get 'bumped' off over-booked aircraft; and visitors pay over the odds for everything because all prices in town have been doubled for the duration. So, for certain countries, especially in Central and South America, a look at the festivals calendar should be part of your planning.

If you decide to beat the crowds and travel to a well–touristed area out of season, there is one more thing to watch out for. The weather could be glorious, the swimming perfect, but from one day to the next, everything can close down and you could find yourself without transport, entertainment and even food. There is little benefit to be gained from avoiding the crowds if all museums and places of interest are closed, leaving you a choice of just one place to eat for your entire visit.

Also read a geography book about the place you intend to visit. You may learn things that the tourist brochures and propaganda guidebooks won't tell you for fear of discouraging you.

Checking the seasons will affect your choice of clothes for the trip, the amount of money you take, possibly even the choice of film for your camera. But even knowing all this, the experienced traveller —or even the inexperienced traveller— will often seek consciously to avoid the 'best' time. Climates and seasons present their own challenge. Who can claim to really know India who has not felt the crashing force of the monsoon rains? Or to be acquainted with Islamic culture without experiencing the tension of the month of Ramadan?

CLIMATE AND TRAVEL

by Gilbert Schwartz

Prospective travellers may prepare for their trip carefully, consulting guidebooks, choosing the most desirable accommodation, designing an appropriate itinerary and making thorough preparations in general. But they frequently fail to investigate the most important ingredient affecting the failure or success of the trip —the weather. Well, maybe there isn't much you can do to guarantee good weather but you can do some things to help minimize disappointment.

Be sure to do your homework. Look up reference books on the subject and use them to help select the most favourable times and travel locations. Remember, when interpreting climate information, some statistics are necessary but they could sometimes be misleading. Look for comparisons. Especially compare the prospective location with an area at home or with which you are familiar. For example, San Francisco, California, has a temperature range for July from a maximum average of 18°C to a minimum of 12°C with no precipitation. This becomes more meaningful when it is compared to New York City which has a range of 29°C to 20°C and, on average, 11 days during the month have rain of 0.25cm or more. So, in spite of the fact that California has a reputation for being warm and sunny, if you're planning a trip to San Francisco in the summer, don't forget to take a sweater! The average temperatures are cold and the winds are a brisk 17.5kmph, windier even than Chicago, the 'windy city'.

Sources

Up–to–date weather conditions and forecasts may be obtained from various sources. A current weather map, which is based on information furnished by government as well as private weather services, is the main way of getting a general picture of weather patterns over a large area. These weather maps show conditions around the country at ground level. Elements which are of particular interest to travellers and may be shown on the map include temperature, pressure changes, wind speed and direction, cloud type, current weather, and precipitation.

Of course, the weather information and projected forecasts must be interpreted. You may do well to alter your itinerary and stay clear of areas that project undesirable or threatening weather conditions. Especially keep alert for severe weather conditions such as storms, heavy rains, etc. For example, you should remember when travelling in mountainous regions that flash floods can strike with little or no warning. Distant rain may be channelled into gullies and ravines, turning a quiet stream–side campsite into a rampaging torrent within minutes. Incidentally, there is excellent literature available through the US Government Printing Office prepared by the National Weather Service. The information includes advice on staying safe during lightning, flash floods, hurricanes and tornadoes. Publications containing summaries and other weather data are also available. Write to Superintendent of Documents, **US Government Printing Office, Washington DC 20420,** for a list of publications. In the UK, information on overseas climate and weather is obtainable by telephoning the Weathercall International or the Holiday Weatherline, see Directory for details (page 626).

Basic elements

After you have had an opportunity to review reference materials on climate and sources for weather forecasts, you should become acquainted with the meaning of some basic weather elements and learn how they may affect your travel preparations. Perhaps the most crucial weather element is temperature which is a good indicator of body comfort. The ideal air temperature is around 27°C. Temperatures generally decrease at higher latitudes and at higher elevations, on average by around 1.7°C for every 300m increase in elevation up to 9000m.

Wind, which is air in motion, is another important weather element. Winds are caused by pressure gradients, the difference in pressure between two locations. Air moves from an area of high pressure toward an area of low pressure. The greater the pressure gradient, the faster the wind. Sea breezes form when cool high pressure air flows from the water onshore to the low pressure area created by warm air over the land. On a clear, hot summer day, the sea breeze will begin mid–morning and can blow inland as far as 16 km at wind speeds of 16 to 24kmph. In the evening, the process is reversed. An offshore land breeze blows at a more gentle speed, usually about half the speed of the daytime onshore wind.

A somewhat similar situation occurs in the mountains and valleys. During the daytime, the valley floor and sides and the air above them warm up considerably. This air is less dense than the colder air higher up so it rises along the slopes, creating a 'valley wind'. In the summer, the southern slopes receive more sun, and heat up more which results in valley winds that are stronger than their north slope cousins. At night, the process is reversed and down–slope, 'mountain winds' result from the cold air above the mountain tops draining down into the valley.

Winds are also affected by such factors as synoptic (large area) pressure differences and by day–night effects. The sun produces maximum wind speeds, while at night winds near the ground are usually weak or absent. Wind speed is also influenced by how rough the ground is. Over smooth water surfaces, the wind speed increases very rapidly with increasing altitude and reaches a peak speed at a height of about 180m. Over rough terrain, the wind speed increases more gradually with increasing altitude and does not reach its peak until about 450m.

Comfort

As we all know, wind, temperature and humidity have a bearing on our comfort. To indicate how combinations of these elements affect the weather we experience, two indices should be understood: wind chill factor and temperature/humidity comfort index.

The **wind chill factor** is the cooling effect on the body of any combination of wind and temperature. It accounts for the rate at which our exposed skin loses heat under differing wind–temperature conditions. In a wind of 32kmph, –4°C will feel like –19°C. This effect is called 'wind chill', the measure of cold one feels regardless of the temperature. Chill increases as the temperature drops and winds get stronger —up to about 72kmph, beyond which there is little increase. Thus at 12°C, increasing the wind from 0 to 8kmph reduces temperature by only two degrees, but a change in wind speed from 64 to 72kmph reduces it only 0.5°C.

The wind may not always be caused naturally. For example, someone skiing into the wind may receive quite a chill. If one is moving into the wind, the speed of travel is added to the wind speed; thus if the wind is blowing at 16kmph and one's speed is 24kmph into the wind, the actual air movement against the body is 40kmph. At –9°C this air speed gives a wind chill equivalent to –30°C. This is easily cold enough for exposed parts of the body to sustain frostbite.

A combination of **warm temperatures** *and* **humidity** also has a significant bearing on our comfort, particularly in warmer climates when the higher the relative humidity, the less comfortable we are. This is a result of the corresponding decrease in the rate at which moisture can evaporate from the skin's surface. Since the cooling of the air next to the skin by the evaporation of perspiration is what causes a cooling sensation, a day with 70 per cent relative humidity and 27°C temperature is far less comfortable than one with 25 per cent humidity and 43°C temperature. The THI was developed in order to measure this relative comfort. But remember, where there is low humidity and a high temperature, your comfort can mislead you, for though you feel safe, you may be in danger of burning.

Layman's forecast

Lacking the sophisticated instruments and sources for weather data, you may still be able to project your own forecasts. Become familiar with basic weather elements such as pressure signs, clouds, wind changes, etc. Learn how these indicators change before the weather does. A layman should beware of the climate statistics he sees in many tourist brochures. The climate will almost always be more severe than is evident from the quoted rainfall, temperature and sunshine figures.

All–important humidity figures are usually not given (Bali might be empty of tourists half the year if they were), and temperature figures may be averages over day and night, and well below (or above) actual normal maximum (or minimum) temperatures. Or they may represent averages recorded at 0600 or 1800 hours because these figures will look most attractive to visitors.

Something else you will not find easily is water temperature. Winter sun holidays are now extremely popular. A lot of people do not realize, however, that although the daytime air temperatures may be in the low 20's (°C), water temperatures may only be about 5 to 15°C and swimming without a wet-suit impossible. The sea takes longer to warm up than the land each summer. Conversely it takes longer to cool down in the autumn. Reckon on a lag between sea and land temperatures of about one and a half months. In Tunisia, the sea is a lot cooler in March than in October. On the other hand, by March air and land temperatures are already rising with the beginning of summer. They will reach their highest point in June/July, but the sea will take until August/September to be fully warmed up.

In winter, comfortably warm water is almost a certainty in the tropics, but more doubtful in the subtropics, for which you should find and study year–round water temperatures. You may just decide to go in summer instead, even though it will probably cost more. In short, warm air and warm water don't always go together.

Familiarity with climate information, whether you rely on primary or secondary sources, will go a long way towards permitting you to get the most out of your next trip.

A GUIDE TO SEASONAL TRAVEL

by Paul Pratt and Melissa Shales

Africa

North: The climate here varies widely from the warm and pleasant greenery of a Mediterranean climate in the coastal regions to the arid heat of the deep Sahara. Rains on the coast usually fall between September and May and are heavy but not prolonged. It can get cool enough for snow to settle in the mountainous areas, but temperatures will not usually fall below freezing, even in winter. In summer, temperatures are high (up to around 40°C) but bearable.

The Sahara, on the other hand, is extreme, with maximum summer temperatures of around 50°C and minimum winter temperatures of around 3°C. The temperature can fall extremely rapidly, with freezing nights following blisteringly hot days. What little, if any, rain there is can fall at any time of the year. The desert is also prone to strong winds and dust storms.

West: At no time is the climate in West Africa likely to be comfortable, although some areas and times of the year are worse than others. The coastal areas are extremely wet and humid, with up to 2500mm of rain falling in two rainy seasons (May and June and then again in October). In the north there is considerably less rain, with only one wet period between June and September.

However, the humidity is still high, only lessened by the arrival of the *harmattan*, a hot, dry and dusty north–easterly wind which blows from the Sahara. Temperatures remain high and relatively even throughout the year.

East: Although much of this area is on or near the equator, little of it has an 'equatorial' climate. The lowlands of Djibouti in the extreme east have a very low, uncertain rainfall, creating near-desert conditions plagued by severe droughts. Further down the coast, the high lowland temperatures are moderated by constant sea breezes. The temperatures inland are brought down by high altitude plateaux and mountain ranges to about the level found in Britain at the height of summer. Temperatures are reasonably stable all year round although the Kenya highlands have a cooler, cloudy 'winter' from June to September. There are rainy seasons in most areas in April and May and for a couple of months between July and November, depending on the latitude.

South: The whole area from Angola, Zambia and Malawi southwards tends to be fairly pleasant and healthy, although there are major variations from the Mediterranean climate of Cape Province with its mild winters and warm, sunny summers, to the semi–desert sprawl of the Kalahari and the relatively wet areas of Swaziland, inland Mozambique and the Zimbabwe highlands to the east. In the more northern areas, there is a definite summer rainy season from December to March when the temperatures are highest. On the south coast, there is usually some rain all year round. The west coast, with little rain, has cloud and fog due to the cold Benguela current which also helps keep down the temperature. The best times of the year to visit are April, May and September when the weather is fine but not too hot or humid.

North America
Almost half of Canada and most of Alaska in the north is beyond the Arctic Circle and suffers from the desperately harsh weather associated with this latitude. The ground is tundra and rarely melts for more than a couple of feet and even though summer temperatures are often surprisingly high, the summers are short–lived. Snow and frost are possible at any time of the year, while the northern areas have permanent snow cover. The coast is ice bound for most of the year.

The whole centre of the continent is prone to severe and very changeable weather, as the low–lying land of the Great Plains and the Canadian Prairies offers no resistance to sweeping winds that tear across the continent both from the Gulf and the Arctic. The east is fairly wet but the west has very little rain, resulting in desert and semi–desert country in the south.

Winter temperatures in the north can go as low as –40°C and can be very low even in the south, with strong winds and blizzards. In the north, winter is long–lived. Summers are sunny and often scorchingly hot.

In general, the coastal areas of North America are far kinder than the centre of the continent. The Pacific coast is blocked by the Rockies from the sweeping winds, and in the Vancouver area the climate is similar to that of the UK. Sea breezes keep it cool further south.

Seasons change fairly gradually on the east coast, but the northerly areas still suffer from the extremes of temperature which give New York its fabled humid heatwaves and winter temperatures. New York, in spite of being far further north, is often much hotter than San Francisco. The Newfoundland area has heavy fog and icebergs for shipping to contend with. Florida and the Gulf States to the south have a tropical climate, with warm weather all year round, and winter sun and summer thunderstorms. This is the area most likely to be affected by hurricanes and tornadoes, although cyclones are possible throughout the country.

Mexico and Central America

The best time to visit this area is during the dry season (winter) from November to April. However, the mountains and the plains facing the Caribbean have heavy rainfall throughout the year which is usually worst from September to February. The mountains and plains facing the Pacific have negligible rainfall from December to April.

Central and northern Mexico tend to have a longer dry season and the wet season is seldom troublesome to the traveller as it usually rains only between 4pm and 5pm. The temperature is affected by the altitude. The unpleasant combination of excessive heat and humidity at the height of the wet season should be avoided, if possible, at the lower altitudes.

South America

The climatic conditions of the South American continent are determined to a great extent by the trade winds which, if they originate in high pressure areas, are not necessarily carriers of moisture. With a few regional exceptions, rain in South America is confined to the summer months, both north and south of the Equator. The exceptions are (i) South Brazil and the eastern coast of Argentina and Uruguay; (ii) the southern Chilean coastal winter rainfall region; (iii) the coastal area of northeast Brazil.

The highest rainfall in South America is recorded in the Amazon basin, the coast lands of Guyana and Suriname, the coastlines of Colombia, Ecuador and southwest Chile. Altitude determines temperature, especially in the Andean countries near to the equator: hot —up to 1000m; temperate — 1000 to 2000m; cold —above 2000m.

Ecuador: Dry seasons from June to October. The coast is very hot and wet, especially during the period December to May. The mountain roads can be very dangerous during the wet season owing to landslides.

Peru: During the colder months, June to November, little rainfall but damp on the coast, high humidity and fog. From December to May, travel through the mountains can be hazardous owing to heavy rain which may result in landslides, causing road blockage and long delays.

Bolivia: Heavy rainfall on the high western plateau from May to November. Rains in all seasons to the eastern part of the country.

Chile: Just over the border from Bolivia, one of the driest deserts in the world faces the Pacific coast.

Argentina: The winter months, June to October, are the best time for visiting Argentina. Buenos Aires can be oppressively hot and humid from mid–December to the end of February. Climate ranges from the sub–tropical north to sub–antarctic in Tierra del Fuego.

Paraguay: The best time for a visit is from May to October when it is relatively dry. The heaviest rainfall is from December to March, at which time it is most likely to be oppressively hot and humid.

Brazil: The dry season runs from May to October apart from in the Amazon Basin and the Recife area which has a tropical rainy season from April to July.

The Far East and Southeast Asia

Japan: Japan lies in the northern temperate zone. Spring and autumn are the best times for a visit. With the exception of Hokkaido, the large cities are extremely hot in summer. Hokkaido is very cold in winter. Seasonal vacation periods, especially school holidays, should be avoided if one is going to enjoy visiting temples, palaces and the like in relative comfort.

Korea: Located in the northern temperate zone, with spring and autumn the best times for touring. The deep blue skies of late September/October and early November, along with the warm sunny days and cool evenings, are among Korea's most beautiful natural assets. Though it tends to be rather windy, spring is also a very pleasant time for a Korean visit. There is a short but pronounced wet season starting towards the end of June and lasting into early August. Over 50 per cent of the year's rain falls during this period and it is usually very hot and humid.

Hong Kong: Subtropical climate; hot, humid and wet summer with a cool, but generally dry winter. Typhoon season is usually from July to August. The autumn, which lasts from late September to early December, is the best time for visiting as the temperature and humidity will have fallen and there are many clear, sunny days. Macao has a similar climate but the summers are a little more bearable on account of the greater exposure to sea breezes. There is also an abundance of trees for shelter during the hot summer.

Thailand: Hot, tropical climate with high humidity. Best time for touring is from November to February. March to May is extremely hot and the wet season arrives with the southwest monsoon during June and lasts until October.

Malaysia: There are no marked wet or dry seasons in Malaysia. October to January is the wettest period on the east coast, October/November on the west coast. Sabah has an equable tropical climate; October and April/May are usually the best times for a visit. Sarawak is seldom uncomfortably hot but is apt to be extremely wet. Typhoons are almost unknown in East Malaysia.

Singapore: Like Malaysia, Singapore has no pronounced wet or dry season. The even, constant heat is mitigated by sea breezes. The frequent rain showers have a negligible cooling effect.

The Philippines: The Philippines have a similar climate to Thailand. The best time to travel in the islands is during the dry season, November to March. March to May is usually dry and extremely hot. The southwest monsoon brings the rain from May to November. The islands north of Samar through Luzon are prone to be affected by typhoons during the period July to September. The Visayas Islands, Mindanao and Palawan, are affected to a lesser degree by the southwest monsoon and it is still possible to travel comfortably during the wet season south of Samar Island —long sunny periods are usually interspersed with heavy rain showers.

The Indian Subcontinent

Sri Lanka: The southwest monsoon brings rain from May to August in Colombo and in the southwest generally, while the northeast monsoon determines the rainy season from November to February in the northeast. The most popular time for a visit is during the northern hemisphere's winter.

India: The climate of south India is similar to that of Southeast Asia: warm and humid. The southwest monsoon brings the rainy season to most parts of India, starting in the southwest and spreading north and east from mid–May through June. Assam has an extremely heavy rainfall during monsoon seasons. Generally speaking, the period from November to April is the best time to visit. From April until the start of the southwest monsoon, the northern Indian plains are extremely hot, though the northern hill stations provide a pleasant alternative until the start of the monsoon rains. These places usually have a severe winter.

Nepal: March is pleasant, when all the rhododendrons are in bloom. The monsoon rains begin in April.

Middle East

A large proportion of this area is desert —flat, low–lying land with virtually no rain and some of the hottest temperatures on earth. Humidity is high along the coast and travellers should beware of heat exhaustion and even heat stroke. What little rain there is falls between November and March. To the north, in Iran and Iraq, the desert gives way to the great steppes, prone to extremes of heat and cold, with rain in winter and spring.

Melting snow from the surrounding mountains causes spectacular floods from March to May. The climate is considerably more pleasant in the Mediterranean areas with long, hot, sunny summers and mild, wet winters. The coast is humid, but even this is tempered by steady sea breezes. The only really unpleasant aspect of the climate here is the hot, dry and dusty desert wind which blows at the beginning and end of summer.

Europe

Only in the far north and those areas a long way from the sea does the climate in Europe get to be extreme. In northern Scandinavia and some of the inland eastern countries such as Bulgaria, there are long, bitterly cold winters with heavy snow and, at times, arctic temperatures. In western Europe, the snow tends to settle only for a few days at a time. In Britain, the Benelux countries and

Germany, winter is characterized chiefly by continuous cloud cover, with rain or sleet. In the Alps, heavy snow showers tend to alternate with brilliant sunshine, offering ideal conditions for winter sports. There are four distinct seasons, and while good weather cannot be guaranteed during any of them, all are worth seeing. Summer is generally short, and the temperature varies widely from one year to the next, climbing at times to match that on the Mediterranean. For sun worshippers, the Mediterranean is probably the ideal location, hot for much of the year but rarely too hot or humid to be unbearable. Rain falls in short, sharp bursts, unlike the continuous drizzle to be found further north. Winter is mild and snow rare.

Australasia

Australia: For such a vast land mass, there are few variations in the weather here. A crescent–shaped rain belt follows the coast to provide a habitable stretch around the enormous semi–desert 'outback.' The Snowy Mountains in the east do, as their name suggests, have significant snowfalls, although even here it does not lie long. The east is the wettest part of the country owing to trade winds which blow off the Pacific. The rainfall pattern varies throughout the country: the north and northeast have definite summer rains between November and April; the south and west have winter rains; while in the east and southeast the rains fall year–round. Tropical cyclones with high winds and torrential rain occur fairly frequently in the northeast and northwest. Tasmania, further south and more mountainous, has a temperate climate similar to Britain's.

New Zealand: Although at a different latitude, the great expanse of water around New Zealand gives it a maritime climate similar to Britain's. The far north has a sub–tropical climate with mild winters and warm, humid summers. There are year–round snow fields in the south, and snow falls on most areas in winter. Although the weather is changeable, there is a surprising amount of sunshine, making this country ideal for most outdoor activities. The best time to visit is from December to March, at the height of summer.

Papua New Guinea: The climate here is a fairly standard tropical one –hot and wet all year, although the time and amount of the rains are greatly influenced by the high mountains that run the length of the country. The rains are heavy, but not continuous. While the coast tends to be humid, the highlands are pleasant. ■

FINDING OUT MORE
Chapter 2

WORD OF MOUTH

by Caroline Brandenburger

Once you've decided where you want to go, one of the best and easiest ways of acquiring pertinent and helpful information is simply to talk to other travellers. Start by asking friends if they know any of the destinations you plan to visit; do they know anyone who lives there, or anyone who has spent a significant amount of time there and can share their knowledge and experiences?

If they originate from the country, all the better. They'll be able to give you a very full account. If they are just former visitors, find out how long they spent there —and when they went. Political climates, national moods and economies are all variable elements so you may have to pass what they say through the filter of subsequent events.

Establish what they were doing there. Purely travelling? Working for a volunteer organisation? An executive for a multinational? Obviously try and find someone whose experience most closely matches what you plan for yourself. The executive will probably be supported in some ways by the structure and community of the company, and have different pleasures and stresses to recount from those of an independent traveller living off his wits. But all information will help you to build up a clearer picture of the place you plan to visit.

The first thing you can ask is how they travelled there. By plane, horse, hot air balloon? How did they go about arranging it? What was it like, what were the advantages and disadvantages of that particular mode of travel? And when they arrived, what were their first impressions? What did they find particularly different, delightful, difficult? And, most importantly, what did they wish someone had told them before they went?

On a day–to–day level, find out how to get around, how to negotiate public transport —are there any official or unofficial ways of arranging things which can make the travel more straightforward? There may be some particular pieces of equipment which are absolutely invaluable, or medication you should buy before you travel . And, very important, get some tips on where to stay.

Don't forget to ask about the climate: at what time of the year is it tolerable, insufferable, wonderful? The climate can determine the kind of medical problems you may encounter. Ask your contacts if they fell ill in any way and how they coped.

More specifically, find out where exactly they travelled and if there is a particular route they recommend —or a particular place. And what about the food? How did they get on with it, where did they get it?

Also try and find out if there are any books which will help give you a good introduction to the country, whether it be a factual guidebook, or a novel which captures the spirit of the place.

Whenever you can, get hold of useful addresses from the people you talk to, and above all, contact names of those living in the destination. There is little more transforming to your travels than being able to meet, even stay with local people. It gives a completely different depth and dimension to your trip. Apart from anything, if something disastrous happens, you may well want to get in touch with someone close at hand who knows the local ropes, and who will help out because you're a friend of so–and–so.

If your 'advisor' can also dredge up the name of a diplomatic contact, it could be invaluable in an emergency. One English archaeologist I know only managed to save vital photos of ancient Turkish monuments (the local police thought he was spying) by having cannily deposited them with a British diplomatic contact in Istanbul. You may even want to organize the good old–fashioned introduction —a letter written by someone at home to their contact abroad, telling them you are arriving and would like to be looked after. (Particularly useful for women travelling on their own in an area where they may not feel so confident.)

The more you talk to a wide variety of people, the more in control you'll feel when the time comes to go. And you'll certainly extract infinitely more from the whole experience.

USING TOURIST BOARDS

by Caroline Brandenburger

Tourist boards range in type —from the glossy office in a smart city boulevard run by a fleet of well–groomed staff, to a dingy cubby hole in a backstreet, manned by one forlorn assistant and a cat.

A glance at the annual report of the English Tourist Board reveals a huge, multi–million pound operation involving marketing strategies, development activity and local initiatives. Now that tourism occupies such a significant place in the revenue of so many countries, clearly the role of the tourist board has undergone a radical change.

All this leaves the consumer in some confusion as to what they should expect from a tourist board. What exactly is a tourist board meant to do? Just who is a national tourist board really serving? Officially they represent the tourist industry of that country, while at the same time providing helpful and accurate information to the would–be visitor. Whether it be maps, accommodation brochures, lists of sites of cultural and historical interest, information on facilities for the elderly or disabled, special events, or transport. As the founding statute of the English Tourist Board puts it, the main functions are 'To promote England as a destination,' and 'To encourage the provision and improvement of tourist facilities and amenities within England.'

But do these noble intentions get put into practice? The frustrated consumer who has spent an afternoon trying fruitlessly to get through on the telephone will say that the tourist board is merely an ineffective mouthpiece of the tourist industry. *Condé Nast Traveler* magazine recently conducted a survey in America in which they wrote to the tourist boards of 30 different countries. In their letters, they asked for eight points to be answered, including details of facilities for disabled people. They then monitored how long it took to get replies and how many of those eight points were covered in the replies. Mexico did not reply at all, Argentina took the longest at 96 days, Australia came third with a 33–day delay and India was the quickest, responding in just four days. However, only three countries managed to respond to the eight queries: Germany, Great Britain and Switzerland. Brazil and Thailand tackled just one point, and most tourist boards approached only managed to make a stab at five or six of the queries.

Similarly in London, we tried to telephone eleven offices. The French Tourist Board was consistently engaged, as were those for Thailand and the US. While the Australians provided an answer machine, they did not return our call.

What, then, do tourist boards have to say for themselves? Leslie Agius, former director of the Malta National Tourist Office in London, and past chairman of the ANTOR (Association of National Tourist Office Representatives in the United Kingdom) is frank: "The functions of a national tourist board are various. Some of them may not be immediately apparent to the consumer." But he elaborates: "The most time–consuming task is answering letters. People want to know what facilities there are for, say, the disabled, and we provide that information. The Spanish and French get mail by the sackful every day. On a normal day, we get 200 inquiries, they get 2000. If people complain they don't answer the phone, it's because it's not physically possible."

When Mr Agius listed all the other functions and responsibilities of the tourist board, it seems hardly surprising that travellers do not always get the service they might wish for. There are only so many hours in the day —even for tourist offices. Being the public relations board for an entire country is a large part of it: "We try to get as much publicity as possible, organize press trips, fashion shoots, getting television coverage. It may not be obvious publicity —Jersey used *Bergerac*, Malta used *Howard's Way* and *Antiques Roadshow*. Then there's advertising —we spend a hell of a lot of money advertising in this country. We spend time meeting with the advertising people, the creative people, the graphics people, deciding where to spend money. We bring out brochures —I detected a lot of people from Britain going to Malta on their honeymoon, so we've brought out a brochure on honeymoons. We're in constant discussion with travel agents and tour operators and we take some tour operators to Malta so they can see for themselves exactly what is on offer."

So how can the consumer get the very best from the tourist board of the country they intend to visit? Leslie Agius says adamantly, "The best thing is to write in. Whoever is at the receiving end will have a chance to reflect, think about what you want. If you ring, they are hurried, pressured by other calls. In your letter, be as clear as possible, so that the person at the other end can help as much as possible."

A spokesman for the Association for British Travel Agents gave similar advice for the independent traveller hoping to use the tourist board machinery successfully:

1. Write rather than ring —the lines are often blocked by children ringing up for help with their school projects. Or go in to the office in person. They're usually fairly centrally placed.

2. Be as specific as you can in your request. If, for example, birdwatching is your interest, most tourist boards will at least come up with some sort of relevant literature or contacts for you to pursue when you arrive in your destination.

3. Be realistic about what you expect from them. They can give you advice and information but they won't book your holiday for you. One information–seeker rang the English Tourist Board in London and asked how long it would take to cook a leg of lamb. "We're the *tourist board*," was the rather puzzled response. "Yes," said the caller, "I'm a tourist."

BACKGROUND READING

by Hilary Bradt and Melissa Shales

With all the fuss involved in preparing for a trip, background reading often stays in the background or is neglected altogether. Yet the proper choice of a travel guide can make all the difference between a relaxed, enjoyable trip and one fraught with anxiety and disappointment. Of course, your reading requirements depend on the type of trip you are planning. There's little point in buying a book on the archaeology of Tunisia if all you plan to do in North Africa is lie on a beach; or in buying one of those '$25 a Day books' on how to enjoy cities cheaply if you aim to spend as short a time as possible in cities.

Broadly speaking, guidebooks are designed to inform you of the necessary preparations for your trip, and to guide you on your travels. Travel books aim to entertain, providing useful information in passing.

There has been a vast proliferation in travel publishing since the late 1980s, both in terms of new guides and travel literature. Not only are more and more travellers writing about their experiences, but there are numerous imprints which specialize in reprinting the best of past travel literature. For more popular countries, this means that you can not only read about how you will find them now, but also what they once were, say 100 years ago. This can be a fascinating progression, made even more interesting by the way the traveller's viewpoint has changed.

With offbeat destinations, you may find that the only books available were written 50 or more years ago. And don't ignore coffee table books either. Most do not have a vast amount of information in them, so would probably not be worth buying (especially as they can be incredibly expensive) but leafing through the photographs is an excellent way to get the feel of a place. For most people, background reading involves the use of libraries, both local reference libraries and specialist establishments such as the Royal Geographical Society, the Natural History Museum and universities.

It is much easier to read up on a specific subject than a general one, and those seeking specialist information will have little trouble (even though you will be occasionally surprised to find some out–of–the–way places have no guide books in any shape or form).

It is the first–time travellers, with little knowledge of which publications are aimed at whom, who find the wealth of information on their chosen country or continent bewildering. They are advised to begin by reading an informative and interesting travel book which gives a general feel for the place. Such a book will probably have an annotated bibliography directing the reader to other recommended books. *National Geographic* magazine is an excellent source of background material (although the reality can be a little disappointing after those marvellous photos). Large libraries bind the magazine in six–month batches, plus a separate index, which makes it a simple matter to look up your special interest. Articles from other magazines, such as *Traveller* and *Geographical*, or newspapers are particularly useful for busy people with a thirst for knowledge, and have the added advantage that they can be cut out and taken on the trip. Newspapers are frequently the only source for up–to–date political information —essential if you know there could be trouble. A list of the contents of past issues can often be had on request, especially if accompanied by a stamped, addressed envelope. Articles which appeared only mildly interesting when read at home become quite riveting once you're in the country described.

The same applies to books. Holiday reading matter should be carefully selected, however, and in no sense should it be 'heavy' or it will be left at the hotel while you sit on the beach guiltily reading magazines. Overland travellers with unlimited time will prefer to do much of their reading en route, when they have had the chance to decide which aspects of a country most interest them.

The British Council libraries in capital cities are often useful (although the emphasis is on British culture), and national libraries sometimes have books in English, as do universities. English language bookshops will also have a better selection of titles on that country than can be found at home. And don't neglect to ask other travellers (particularly those heading in the opposite direction) if they have anything to recommend and/or give or swap. The proper selection of a guidebook is as important to the traveller as the choice of luggage or footwear. It should advise and inform, be evocative yet objective, and help you plan your trip and make maximum use of your travel time. The price of books has risen so sharply in recent years that travellers are often reluctant to buy them. Yet most guidebooks cost only as much as a meal in a restaurant and, in contrast, can be thoroughly sampled before buying. Surely books are still among the best bargains available!

A GUIDE TO GUIDES

by Douglas Schatz and Tim Ellerby

With an ever–expanding market of international tourism, there has been a corresponding explosion in the publishing of international travel guides. For the traveller of independent means, or the independent traveller of no means, for coverage of the most common, or uncovering of the uncommon, the question now is one of choice: "Which guide?"

There are 'Blue' guides, 'Red' guides and 'Green' guides. There are guides that promise you 'Insight' or a 'Companion'; guides for 'Visitors' and for 'Travellers'; guides that offer a 'Cultural' experience or a 'Rough' time —or even just 'Survival.' A comparison between the alternatives may be made initially on the general balance of information a guide contains whether it be cultural description or practical reference on accommodation. One can easily compare the relative detail of the information, which is usually reflected in the price of the book, and note should be taken of the publication date (bearing in mind that the research for a guide usually pre–dates publication by six months to a year.

The style of a guide, its prose and presentation, can usually be assessed by its use of maps, indexes or illustrations. The aim, finally, is to match the guide to your individual travel needs and interests. The survey below briefly highlights the distinguishing features of the main travel guides now available —most of which are series of books covering a variety of places in a consistent format. There may not always be more than one choice of guide for a particular destination but, whether there is or not, this may help indicate which is the most appropriate for your travels.

Around the world

The great expansion of the independent travel market in recent years is best reflected in the development of the **Lonely Planet** series of guidebooks. What began in 1975 with two travellers, Tony and Maureen Wheeler, and their self–published guide to *South East Asia on the Cheap*, is now an international company producing nearly 100 titles covering most of the long–haul destinations of the world. With their two main series of guides, Lonely Planet pioneered the practical travel guide for contemporary independent travel. The *Travel Survival Kits*, each of which covers a single country or region, provides all of the touring and practical advice that an independent traveller of any budget requires, including maps, accommodation, transport options, etc. Their larger books covering a whole continent *On a Shoestring* are intended more specifically for budget travellers who are likely to be passing through several countries on the same trip.

Both series are produced in a practical size for the rucksack, with durable bindings that will stand up to the rigours of the road. The guides are updated every two to three years and the range has now been expanded into Europe with all major countries being covered. Lonely Planet also publishes a series of special *Trekking Guides*, as well as pocket phrasebooks for some of the more obscure languages such as Tibetan, Indonesian and Quechua.

Those parts that Lonely Planet has not yet reached, **Rough Guides** more than likely has. The first, *Rough Guide to Greece*, was written in 1982 by a group of English university graduates who saw the need for candid contemporary travel guides. The current *Rough Guides* now cover almost every European country, including the emerging East European destinations, as well as areas of Africa, the USA and Central and South America. The guides contain a mix of basic introductory information, systematic tourist guidance with practical recommendations that tend to favour the low–priced choices, as well as background reading on a country's history and current culture. The books themselves are also very competitively priced —as they should be for their value–conscious readers— and they are updated every two years.

One of the most attractive series of independent travel guides created in recent years is the **Cadogan Guides**, whose style and coverage is strongest for European destinations, but who also publish guides for destinations outside Europe including Morocco, Ecuador, Bali, Mexico, the Caribbean, Central America, Central Asia, and Thailand. The books are elegantly designed, have lively and literate texts, and useful, practical recommendations appropriate for both the independent traveller and luxury tourist alike.

For the better part of this century, the *South American Handbook* has been a bible for independent travellers to that continent. The handbook has now spawned eight companion volumes on the *Caribbean Islands, Mexico & Central America, India, Thailand and Burma, Vietnam, Laos and Cambodia, Indonesia, Malaysia and Singapore, North Africa* and *East Africa*. At an average of 1000 pages each in length, they all possess the same encyclopaedic content as the original, giving background information on politics, history and economics, as well as the most comprehensive travel information available. Unusually they are printed on lightweight paper with hardcover bindings making them robust and yet as light as possible.

If you wish to be led further off the beaten track, then there is no better guide than Hilary Bradt. She founded her own specialist travel imprint, **Bradt Publications**, to produce a series of unique adventure travel guides, beginning with *Backpacking Guides* to the best of South America and Africa, and branching out into more general, practical guidebooks for the less well travelled destinations of the world such as Madagascar, Czechoslovakia and Vietnam.

Moon Handbooks specialize in areas as diverse as the islands of Southeast Asia and the individual states of the USA. These guides are packed with detailed and reliable research on all practical aspects of independent travel, and are enhanced by line maps, drawings and comprehensive descriptive introductions.

On a budget

While all of the books mentioned so far cater for any independent traveller who is seeking value for money, there are two series of guides designed specifically for travellers on a very small budget. The **Let's Go Guides** to Europe and America are written and researched annually by teams of Harvard students, and they contain all of the up–to–date, practical advice required to live cheaply 'on the road.' I recall on my own budget grand tour, tearing out sections of the enormous *Let's Go Europe* when used, and passing the much–needed extracts on to other travellers.

Although also targeted primarily at students, the guides to working and travelling abroad published by **Vacation Work**, contain so many original ideas that anyone would be forgiven for throwing it all in and setting out with these books in hand. For example, the classic guide *Work Your Way Around the World* provides imaginative suggestions on work opportunities around the world, and a guide to *Teaching English Abroad* surveys the possibilities for this popular vocation in more than 20 different countries. Vacation Work also publishes a growing series of *Travellers' Survival Kits* which, not to be confused with Lonely Planet's TSK's, are aimed more directly at budget travellers.

In luxury

Globetrotting does not necessarily mean that you must shoulder a rucksack and work it all out for yourself as you go along, as the success of the lavishly–produced **Insight Guides** testifies. With over 100 titles in the series, covering continents, countries, regions and cities of the world, the *Insight Guide* offers detailed background reading, excellent colour illustrations, clear touring itineraries, and sections of general practical information —all packaged for the "sophisticated traveller". The publishers of the series, APA Productions, is aptly named for each book is a collaborative production of several writers and photographers, and credits are listed for a producer, director, designer and editor, just as with film credits.

Insight's successful formula has spawned a number of virtually indistinguishable clones on the guide book shelves. **Insiders' Guides**, for example, are less substantial, though marginally more practical than the archetypes. The series of **Nelles Guides** look very much like 'baby' Insight Guides, but are a smaller, pocket size and have some good colour maps to complement the texts. The **Odyssey Guides –Introductions to the World** are stylishly designed, written by authors with extensive local experience and include extracts of celebrated travel writing. There are but brief lists of practical information but, as the title of the series implies, these are not handbooks for the independent traveller but introductions to inspire travel dreams.

The two newest additions to the illustrated guidebook market are the exquisite **Eyewitness Guides** by Dorling Kindersley and the **Everyman Guides** both of which illustrate every subject covered in the guide to the extent that you will 'feel familiar' with your surroundings even before you get there.

The **Eyewitness Guides** issued so far cover European cities of culture plus New York and are encylopaedic in approach. Each guide breaks down the city into discrete areas and then leads you through all the cultural features to be found there. In addition to this there is a general introduction to the city and its history plus the main attractions and the guide is completed with a practical section covering such subjects as where to stay and eat, transport, foreign currency and detailed street maps.

The **Everyman Guides** take a similar approach with more space being given to backround history and architecture and other cultural subjects. The main body of the guide then leads you on a complete tour of the city illustrating the sites you will see and giving all necessary details. The last section of each guide lists practical information on such subjects as hotels, restaurants, theatres, museums, transport and much more.

Middle of the road

One of the giants of guide book publishing, with over 100 titles in their list, is the series of **Fodor's Guides**. As conceived by their eponymous American founder, Eugene Fodor, the guides are distinctive for being updated annually, and now cover much of the globe, though the majority are for countries and cities in the western world. Often accused of sanitising travel, Fodor's guides are in fact a useful and dependable resource. They maintain a good balance between their description of sights and the practical information on transport, money and accommodation and restaurants, including recommendations of the latter that cover a range of budgets. Travel may be less of an adventure with Fodor's but is also less likely to go wrong.

Another series of guide books which, like Fodor's, originates in America and bears the name of its founder and editorial master, is Arthur **Frommer's Guides**. The guides are updated every second year, and they cover countries and cities worldwide with an emphasis on Europe. As is suggested by their *Dollarwise* and *So Many Dollars a Day* titles, they concentrate on finding value for money. Though not as detailed as some on sights and culture, they contain very extensive descriptive assessments of hotels, restaurants and nightlife.

The small travel publisher MPC has established its series of **Visitor Guides** with a sensible mix of touring itineraries, tables of highlighted sights, and clear black and white maps. They are handy pocket-sized books, and though their sections of 'Tourist Information' give only general practical advice, they are useful, all–round touring guides.

Probably the most recognizable name in travel guide books lives on in the new generation of **AA/ Baedeker Guides**. Recently reissued in a practical pocket size, the guides contain a comprehensive gazetteer of places to visit, along with a free, fold–out map stored in their plastic cover. There are only minimal listings of practical information but the Baedekers are clear, general purpose tourist guides.

European culture

Famous enough to be identified simply by colour, the **Michelin Red Guides** are an incomparable reference to the hotels and restaurants of Europe, with countless location maps, information on facilities and prices, and of course their famous symbols of recommendation. They are updated annually and, once you master their language, they are hugely informative.

There are basic listings of principal tourist sights in the Red Michelin guides, but more substantial touring information is found in the series of **Green Michelin Tourist Guides**. These contain introductions to the history and art of an area, followed by a remarkably detailed alphabetical survey of places of interest. Their distinctive, tall format, the many maps, the star classification of sights and the clear layout make them easy to use. One of the most impressive features of both the Red and Green Michelin guides is that they are cross–referenced in detail to each other, and to the full range of Michelin maps.

The professed aim of a **Blue Guide** is to give an account of a country or city "without omitting anything...which might appeal to the intelligent visitor." Indeed the long established Blue guides are justly renowned for their comprehensive treatment of the art, architecture and history of their subject. In consequence of the incomparable detail of their scholarship, they can be rather dry to read and also contain little practical travel information. They are, however, the last intelligent word on many European locations.

The perfect European holiday depends on finding just the right **Charming Small Hotels**, and this attractive series of guides published by Duncan Petersen/AA has done just that for Britain, France, Germany, Italy, Spain and Switzerland. Along with the lively descriptions, there is a colour illustration of each recommendation, so you can also see exactly what to expect.

Pocket guides

Where once upon a time there was only Berlitz, now there are four or five choices of pocket–sized travel guides. All of these publishers have rightly recognized that guidebooks that are compact in both format and content will appeal to a great many travellers whose holidays are too brief to warrant reading in depth, or who are simply not inclined to do so. As market leaders, **Berlitz** still produce the largest range of titles. At less than four by six inches, their series of country and city guides are marvels of packaging, containing basic tourist guidance with colour illustrations sufficient for any short package visit. Similarly, the colour–coded phrase books are renowned for organizing language into practical travel phrases for all occasions. **Collins Travellers** are very similar in content to the Berlitz model, though the superficial design of the guides is more contemporary.

AA's **Essential Guides** offer more substantial and personal texts than either of their competitors. The **Insight Pocket Guides** are also written by authors with local experience, but in a more striking style.

Undoubtedly the best pocket travel guides are the **American Express Pocket Guides**, which have recently changed format to a more conventional pocket book size rather than the old 'diary' format. Packed with even more information they contain intelligent and detailed surveys of sights, useful recommendations of accommodation and restaurants, good colour maps, and even walking itineraries.

Literary Guides

Literary guides act as an 'optional extra' —if you don't mind carrying them with you, it can be wonderfully illuminating to read what writers of the past have said about the place you happen to be in at that time. Equally they can prepare you before the trip, or remind you vividly after the event. The best are published by **John Murray,** who have covered Greece, India, Egypt, Rome and Florence amongst others, with a delightful compendium of extracts from writers great and unknown.

Women's Travel

With more women travelling alone or with other women, Virago Press has responded to this particular type of traveller with **The Virago Women's Travel Guide**. Packed with common sense, down-to-earth advice, these guides hope to put in perspective some of the risks run by women travelling alone and allow you to be informed in advance about trouble spots and potential dangers. Each guide will direct you towards areas and activities where you will feel welcome, comfortable and safe and therefore allow you to enjoy your visit to the full. Titles to date focus on the main European cities plus New York and San

Francisco.

The proliferation of guide book publishing goes on apace and this survey is therefore inevitably incomplete. When possible, visit a specialist travel bookseller where you will find the widest range of choice, and possibly even some advice.

CHOOSING MAPS

by Tim Ellerby

In all the hustle and bustle of planning foreign travel it is easy to forget that good mapping of the area you are to visit can be just as useful as a guide book and under some circumstances may even help to get you out of serious trouble. Maps are also an extremely concentrated source of information which can be inexpensive and light to carry. However, perhaps the most important point to make about maps is that with a little application they can take you far beyond your guide book or even local knowledge in pursuit of the unknown and undiscovered.

Having said this, one reason that people do not naturally purchase maps is that they are unsure of how to select and use them. I hope that the following comments will help those who have no previous knowledge to feel confident enough to select the right map and make good use of it. Finally, the serious international traveller should recognise the value of mapping as an aid to advanced planning and that where possible you should purchase your maps in advance because local sources can be surprisingly difficult to locate and unreliable.

The components of a map

The purpose of a map is to provide information about the area covered so that the user can either locate any feature shown or visualize what it would be like to be there so that journeys can be planned or imagined. This information is presented in two ways, through the use of a quoted scale and by employing standard symbols to represent commonly occurring features.

The *scale* of the map is simply a ratio between the original feature on the ground and the size it will appear on the map. It is surprising how many people become confused when presented with scale information and so it is important to understand a few basic points about scale before attempting to select a map. An easy way to remember how this ratio relationship works is to remember that 1:1 is full size. It is easy to see from this that 1:25,000 is a *larger* scale that 1:50,000 by a factor of two. This then helps to resolve the main confusion involving map scales which is the usage of the terms 'large' and 'small' scale. The fundamental relationship is therefore that as the ratio number becomes larger the scale becomes smaller, however in the long run it is far easier to remember a few specific scales from which you can judge for yourself the likely level of detail.

The *symbols* on the map also need a little explaining as they are in effect the cartographer's shorthand. This shorthand is 'decoded' by the use of the *map key* which tabulates all the feature codes and tells you what each one represents. It is also important to realise that whilst location of any feature is accurately portrayed the actual feature itself is purely diagrammatic and not to scale. As an example, roads on motoring maps appear to be far wider than they really are in order to give the maximum clarity and allow junctions and other features to be usefully displayed.

One other consideration regarding both the scale of the map and the symbols used is that there is inevitably a degree of 'selection' of the information that the map attempts to portray so that the map does not become completely cluttered and consequently unreadable. In practice this means that some features will be omitted from the map, something to consider when selecting a map. The decision about what is shown on any given map or series of maps is determined by the cartographer and publisher and is often as much a matter of tradition and style as it is convention or rule.

The choice of scale

If we now move on to some specific map scales we can quickly build up an idea of the sorts of maps to use for a given purpose. Most national surveys were originally based on the scale of 1:50,000 and the British Ordnance Survey was no exception. At this scale it is obvious that a series of maps is needed to cover an area the size of Britain and so a *grid* is used to relate map sheets of equal size to the areas that they cover and to each other. Such grids can be referred to at the map shop or sometimes are available to take away so that you can work on your requirement at home. The 1:50,000 scale is ideal for cycling and slow detailed motoring within a limited area and can also be used by walkers although it is not really ideal. At this scale you will see all the towns, villages and hamlets in a given area together with all roads, tracks, lanes and rights of way. Other features will depend on the style and type of mapping. For walking purposes a map scale of 1:25,000 is ideal where you will see in much more detail all the landmarks and features of the area right down to the field boundaries in some cases. When we move into the urban environment where the number and density of features is very high, scales of 1:10,000, 1:15,000 and 1:20,000 are frequently used and these will allow you to see individual street names and specific building locations. At the other end of the spectrum map scales of 1:100,000 and 1:250,000 (Quarter Million) or even 1:500,000 (Half Million) are regularly used for long–distance motoring and regional touring where the emphasis is on relating one major feature or area to another.

Having established the uses of scale and the importance of symbols on a given map it is useful to look at the types of map which are generally available so that other criteria for selection can be established.

Types of map

For the purposes of the traveller most maps will be either *Topographic* or *Thematic* or possibly a combination of the two. Topographic maps show the general nature of the country, the physical features, the type of terrain, the location of watercourses, forests, marshes, foreshore features and all roads, railways and other lines of communication, and any other significant features be they man-made or natural. In general this type of mapping will have contours (lines connecting points of equal elevation) to indicate the physical relief and as such tends to be a survey map of the Ordnance Survey type.

Thematic maps are more selective in what they show or highlight sometimes to the extent of suppressing more general features. Such themes can be relief, communications, climates, geology, historical features, vegetation, land usage, demography, economic information, tourist information etc. Thus with a geological map whilst the 'base' mapping might show most of the standard features of a topographic map of the same region, the overlaying of geological information will obscure it to the extent that normal navigation is quite difficult. In the same way a tourist map will highlight those features which are considered of importance to the holiday maker such as historical sites, museum, beaches, airports etc. at the expense of comprehensive road layouts, minor villages and physical relief.

This then leaves you with a choice to make in selecting the right map for the job you have in mind. In general a combination of themes or themes plus topography is what the traveller will be looking for and many combine major tourists attractions, communications networks and some physical relief.

There is one final consideration to make if the map that you need covers an area of continental proportions or even the world. If one considers that a map of the whole world represents the surface features of a sphere then it is easy to understand that some approximations have to be applied in order to flatten the features out. This flattening is achieved by the use of a map projection and there are many types of projection and many debates about their relative merits. What is important is that when mapping of this sort is used that you know how to allow for the approximations of the projection when measuring distances or planning routes. In most cases however the map projection is of no relevance to the traveller.

Having decided what is the best scale and what features you want the map to show, you are now ready to compare your criteria with what is available.

Choosing a map

Whilst there is no doubt that many maps are sold each year purely on the basis of their appearance there are a number of points which should be given priority over simply whether it 'looks nice' or not.

First and foremost a map is a graphic representation of information so it is important to establish how accurate that information might be. This can be established in a number of ways but it is fair to say that the publication date is one of the most useful indicators because assuming that an area continues to develop, then the older the map the more information will be missing. Again, as an indicator this rule need not be taken to extremes as some elements of the map only change very slowly such as relief and so if your primary purpose is walking it might not be so critical. In urban and semi-urban areas rates of change to road networks and buildings can be extremely fast, so here you need to be much more critical. Needless to say most map producers are sensitive to such relative rates of change and will revise their urban mapping much more frequently than rural and wilderness coverage. It is also a great mistake to assume that levels of mapping and rates of updating are equal the world over —they are not and so you may have to accept the 'best available' which may date back to the 1960's for some areas. Likewise with scale by no means all areas of the world are mapped at 1:50,000 so again you may be forced to accept a smaller scale than you would ideally choose. The important factor in all of this is that you find a source for your map purchase which can offer reliable advice and explain all the current options available to you.

Unfortunately it is not possible to detail all the main map producers throughout the world and give an appraisal of their relative merits, but I will give a general overview for each of the main continental areas and highlight the sorts of problems you may encounter.

Western Europe

If you are travelling within Western Europe you should have little difficulty in obtaining the mapping you require. In France the national survey **IGN** produces excellent maps at 1:25,000, 1:100,000 and 1:250,000 (but no longer 1:50,000) plus many special sheets. Of particular interest to mountain walkers are the **IGN Top 25** series, the **Didier et Richard** series and **Edition Randonnees Pyreneennes** which are over-printed with the GR routes. For motoring you will find it hard to beat **Michelin** and the town-plan series published by **Blay**. Germany is also well-served by its national survey at the standard scales with some special sheets also being available. For the mountain walker maps produced by **Kompass** are excellent. More general coverage is provided by **Mairs** at a scale of 1:200,000 and **Michelin** at 1:400,000 and good town and city plans are published by **ADAC, Falk** (although their method of folding may take a little getting used to) and **RV Verlag**.

The Benelux countries are again well-covered by their national surveys but good cycling maps for The Netherlands at a scale of 1:100,000 are provided by **ANWB**. General motoring mapping is again provided by **Michelin** and town plans are published by **Falk**, although this time many of the sheets are conventionally folded. The Scandinavian countries all have their own national surveys producing high quality topographical mapping at the standard scales which can be complimented by general coverage produced by commercial publishers.

The **Swiss National Survey** is generally regarded to be exemplary in the accuracy and clarity of its mapping. Produced at the scales of 1:100,000, 1:50,000 and 1:25,000 the maps are a joy to use. Special editions are available with ski routes and walking trails. Again general road maps are published by **Michelin** and a good series of town plans from **Orell Fussli** is also available. Austria's national survey is again a reliable source of mapping but excellent coverage is given by **Kompass, Freytag and Berndt (F&B)** and **Alpenvereinskarte** for the walking and skiing areas.

Moving south to Spain the situation is slightly different. Here the **Spanish Military Survey** is the best source of topographical maps although you will need to check the edition and revision dates carefully. A wide range of scales are available from 1:800,000 down to 1:25,000. Other maps worth considering are the **Editorial Alpina** series which covers the Pyrenees and other mountainous regions at a good walking scale, and a series of provincial maps at 1:200,000 from **MOPT**. **Michelin** and **Geocenter** also produce reliable general mapping for Spain. Over the border in Portugal the situation is very similar with the national survey desperately needing revision. Scales available are 1:200,000, 1:100,000, 1:50,000 and 1:25,000. Commercial mapping from **Michelin**, **Geocenter** and **Hildebrand** provide good route planning and tourist information.

Italy presents some problems to the map user as its national survey is in a rather sorry state and supply situation is very unreliable. Consequently you will have to rely on the commercially produced maps, fortunately there is good coverage from a variety of sources. **TCI** (Touring Club Italiano) the Italian equivalent of the AA provides excellent road maps at 1:200,000 along side the ubiquitous **Michelin** at a scale of 1:400,000. Town plans from **FMB**, **Falk** and **Hallwag** are readily available and the walker is more than adequately catered for by **Kompass**, **IGC**, **Edizioni Multigraphic**, **Mapgraphic Bozen** and **Tabacco** at a variety of suitable scales.

To complete western Europe we need to look at Greece and here we meet our first significant problem. At present the Greek government will not sell survey information of a scale greater than 1:200,000 and then only in the form of an out-of-date provincial series at inflated prices. The result is that you have to rely on the more general mapping of the commercial companies such as **F & B** who produce a good series of maps at 1:200,000. For the Greek islands the 'detailed' mapping on the market is the standard tourist series produced by **Toubi** which are crude in the extreme. A little relief is offered by the **Greek Alpine Club** who have published a number of detailed contour maps of the main mountain regions based on the 'unavailable' 1:50,000 survey. Unfortunately these maps are not all they might be and they certainly should be used with caution. Visitors to Crete will be relieved to discover that an excellent relatively new series of maps at a scale of 1:80,000 is now available, published by **Harms Verlag**.

Eastern Europe

With the break-up of the Soviet Union and an increased freedom to travel through out the former Soviet satellite states the demand for mapping of these countries has grown rapidly. As a result more maps are becoming available from one month to the next and reports of survey mapping being available for the Czech Republic and Hungary have been received. The overall picture however remains very poor. In general you will have to rely on 'western' commercial mapping at the whole country level with some locally produced tourist and walking maps as survey mapping is not available. Worthy of note are four series of maps covering the Czech and Slovak republics at scales of 1:200,000, a map and guide tourist series in 17 sheets, 1:100,000, a contour series in 46 sheets and 1:50,000 contour mapping with tourist information in 29 sheets and 1:50,000 in 3 sheets by **F&B** covering the Tatra Mountains. The walking areas of Poland are reasonably covered by the publisher **PPWK** who also produce town plans. Hungary is covered by a series of tourist maps at a scale of 1:30,000 and 1:20,000 for many of the popular areas. Any intrepid travellers to the former Yugoslavia will find good walking maps available of the Julian Alps published by **Kummerly and Frey (K&F)** and **F&B** as well as general series of sheets at 1:100,000.

Other than the maps mentioned above coverage is best found in the general maps produced by such publishers as **Bartholomew** in the World Travel Series, **Geocenter**, **F&B** and **K&F**.

North America

It may come as a surprise that the United States does not have the highest quality of national survey mapping, however when one considers the vast area covered it is perhaps understandable. Scales available range from 1:25,000 through 1:100,000 up to 1:500,000 and a number of special sheets are also produced for more popular areas. Help is however at hand if you are travelling to any of the National Park areas in the form of the excellent **Trails Illustrated** maps. Printed on waterproof, tear resistant paper and based on **USGS** mapping they are aimed specifically at the back-packer and explorer. For the road user the ubiquitous **Rand McNally** and **Gousha** state and city maps are essential and whilst they may appear crude compared to survey mapping they are surprisingly useable. Other commercial map publishers such as **Hildebrand** and **K&F** produce state and regional maps. Also worth considering are the **National Geographic** Close-up USA maps which cover groups of states and give a great deal of additional information in a very attractive format. Finally, with a land mass the size of the United States it is worth considering looking at State or regional atlases such as produced by **Rand McNally** or **Gousha**.

Moving north to Canada the **Canadian National Survey** serves as the main source of detailed information and is readily available at scales of 1:100,000, 1:50,000 and 1:25,000. Special sheets are produced for some of the national parks which include tourist information. General motoring coverage is available from **Allmaps** and **Rolph-McNally** together with good city plans from **Mapart**.

Central America and Mexico

Survey information for this group of countries is naturally harder to obtain but you should be able to purchase mapping for Mexico, Costa Rica and Panama without too much difficulty. Mapping for Belize is also available from the **Directorate of Overseas Surveys** which is the overseas division of the Ordnance Survey. The remaining countries will be problematic but it is still worth making enquiries as the situation may well change. Other than this you will have to rely on the commercial products from publishers such as **ITM**, **K&F** and **Bartholomew.** If all else fails you might consider **Air Navigation Charts** available at 1:1,000,000 and 1:500,000.

South America

The good news with regards to the South American countries is that survey information is generally available for all destinations, however it may be significantly out of date and very expensive. You should also anticipate a considerable wait if your retailer does not have what you want in stock. Commercial mapping of note comes from **ITM**, **Bartholomew** and **Hallwag**, together with a myriad of locally produced city street plans and motoring maps. Again if you become completely stuck **Air Navigation Charts** may be of some use.

Africa

The African continent presents many problems to the traveller wishing to purchase maps and it is useful to know something of the colonial history of the countries you are visiting when you set out to locate survey information. In general ex-British colonies will still have mapping available from the **DOS (Directorate of Overseas Surveys)**, the overseas division of the British Ordnance Survey. These countries include Kenya, Nigeria, Tanzania, Uganda and The Gambia. South Africa also has an excellent survey department producing maps of a high quality. The rest of Africa is more of a problem and availability will vary with the current political climate. Other countries which sell their survey information at present include Algeria, Ghana, Zimbabwe and possibly Ethiopia. For the remaining areas you will have to rely on either general commercially produced maps or larger surveys such as the 1:2,000,000 **DMA** series or **Air Navigation Charts**.

Middle East

In such areas of turmoil and conflict, survey mapping is inevitably restricted and at present Israel is the only country selling to the general public. Fortunately there is an excellent series of maps produced by **GeoProjects** which covers most of the Middle Eastern states. If more detail is required then you will have to rely on **Air Navigation Charts** as suggested above. Other commercial products worthy of note are produced by **F&B**, **Bartholomew**, **Geocenter** and **K&F**.

Indian Sub-Continent

Despite an immense amount of travel interest in India and its neighbours there is very little in the way of survey mapping available to the general public and even then only by battling with a huge bureaucracy. As a result a number of publishers have produced very good maps for the walking and trekking areas of northern India, Pakistan and Nepal. **Schneider (Nelles)** produce a wonderful series of contour maps covering East and Central Nepal, **Mandala** imported directly from Nepal are a series of dye-line contour which give good overall detail of the main trekking areas of Nepal, **Leomann** produce a series of sketch maps which cover virtually all the accessible parts of the Indian Himalaya and the Karakoram. Other specific sheets are available for the Everest and K2 regions. In addition to this a good series of locally produced regional and city maps are available from **TT Maps** and **Nelles** produce excellent regional relief mapping of the whole of India and Pakistan. Finally a reprint of the **AMS/U502** series at 1:250,000 is available from **Stanfords** which cover the Himalayas and Karakoram region and will serve to fill in the gaps. Coverage for Sri Lanka and Afghanistan is also difficult and **Nelles** or **Geocenter** would be a good choice here. Once again Air Navigation Charts may be worth considering for more remote, less popular regions.

China, Japan and Korea

It will come as no surprise that mapping for any part of China or Korea is hard to come by and so once again we have to use general commercial products such as **Nelles** maps to plan and navigate by. Individual province and city maps are available but often only with Chinese or Korean text. Japan however does have excellent survey mapping but it can be quite an ordeal getting hold of it. Other coverage for Japan is also good and may be bilingual such as from the publishers **JGM**.

South East Asia, Indonesia, Malaysia, Papua New Guinea and the Philippines

This vast area again poses many problems to the traveller who wishes to purchase accurate, detailed mapping but there are a few notable exceptions. Survey mapping in Vietnam, Thailand, the Philippines and Papua New Guinea is generally available although again you may have to wait some time for delivery and coverage may not yet be complete. Other individual islands with a colonial history or which still owe their allegiance to European countries may be mapped by their country of government. Failing all else then **Nelles**, **Bartholomew** and **Geocenter** may come to the rescue again or of course **Air Navigation Charts**.

Australia and New Zealand

Both Australia and New Zealand have excellent survey departments producing a good quality of topographic mapping which can be obtained within a reasonable time frame. The main problem as with the USA is identifying the maps you require from the vast grids. That aside, commercial mapping of a high standard is available from **Bartholomew**, **UBD** and **Gregory's** for Australia and **Hildebrand's**, **Bartholomew** and **Infomaps** for New Zealand.

As a final plea please remember that no shop however large could hold stock of all maps currently available, so if you are venturing off into the unknown and you need to rely on a map please make sure that you order your maps well in advance. Some foreign survey departments can take from six months to two years to respond so give your retailer as much notice as possible otherwise you may be disappointed. ■

WHAT TYPE OF TRAVEL?
Chapter 3

THE CONCERNED TRAVELLER

by Dr David Bellamy

Nomads travel in order to make a living from harsh landscapes, conquerors and business people search for power and resources, holiday-makers to escape the monotony of the workplace. Adventurers, backpackers and grand tourers travel because they have to. Theirs is the quest for knowledge, a quest to be world–wise.

It is somewhat awesome to realize that many areas which were marked as terra incognita on the maps of my youth are now stopovers on regular tour itineraries. So much so that the two-edged sword of tourism now hangs heavily over every aspect of the heritage of this world.

If it had not been for the spotlight which has been turned onto these special regions by grand tourers, past and present, the threat, to coin a phrase, of Costa-Brava-Ization would not be there. Yet it is equally true to say that without those spotlights of interest and concern, much of their heritage could have been lost through apathy and ignorance.

Whatever regrets we weavers of travellers tales may have, I believe the die is now cast. Tourism is the world's fastest growing industry and the only hope for much of our heritage, both natural and people–made, lies within the wise use of its tourist potential.

Fortunately, there is good news from around the world on this front. The infrastructure so long needed along the Costa Brava, is now being put into place. The same is true for the high treks of Nepal, and many African countries are now building on the true value of their big game, live in all its glory.

Unfortunately there is also much bad news, but that is where you all come in, for there is an immense amount of work to be done.

As you lap up the challenge of pushing back the bounds of your personal unknown lands and discovering these pearls of heritage for yourselves, remember they are only there thanks to the natural living systems on which we all depend.

You are the ambassadors of everything that the concerned traveller should be. Set the golden example. Respect local customs, have a care where you leave your footprints, take only photographs, buy only local craft goods made from sustainable resources and always put as much as you can into the local economy.

Thank you for caring.

THE ENVIRONMENTALLY–FRIENDLY TRAVELLER

by Peter Mason

Green tourism, 'responsible tourism' and 'sustainable tourism' are buzz words of the 1990s. Public awareness of all things 'green' has been growing for at least the last five years, with tourism emerging more recently as a focus of attention. As tourist numbers continue to rise and the industry reaches even more parts of the globe, there is increasing concern about its impact on the environment.

This concern is not new. Footpath erosion in the English Lake District and Snowdonia, for example, was the subject of local and national publicity in the early 1970s, and remedial action has been employed here for at least two decades. However, doubts remain about environmentally sensitive areas coping with increasing visitors: environmentalist David Bellamy recently called for restrictions on access to the Lake District claiming it was being 'loved to death.'

In the 1980s, attention focused on other areas of the world where increasing amounts of litter, disturbance to wildlife and pollution of water courses and beaches were attributed to tourism. Piles of pink toilet paper were reputed to have been left at the foot of Everest by mountaineers trekking in Nepal's Sagarmartha National Park; the prehistoric cave paintings of the Dordogne have been closed to the public as a result of damage caused by increasing numbers of visitors, and there have been calls to stop all tourist coaches to Venice because of the relentless pressure on the city's infrastructure. In the Mediterranean, the Greek island of Zakynthos and Turkey's Dalyan Delta were the scenes of bitter disputes between hotel developers, tour operators and environmentalists during the mid 1980s. The subject of the dispute was the loggerhead turtle, an endangered species that has used Zakynthos and Dalyan as breeding sites for millions of years. Not surprisingly, environmentalists argued that tourism development would destroy these sites.

With growing 'green awareness', an uneasy peace seems to have broken out in several 'tourism versus the environment' disputes. But there is little cause for complacency. For too long, tour operators, resort developers and tourists have viewed the earth as a boundless playground rather than a finite and fragile resource.

In the 1970s, 'unpackaged' tourism outside of mainstream, mass travel was considered 'alternative.' One of the first examples of this was established in Senegal and named the Tourism for Discovery Project. The project began in the early 1970s and provided Western visitors with a taste of 'real life' in a West African country. Visitors reached the holiday area by travelling along Senegal's rivers in canoes. They stayed in simple lodges built by local people from traditional materials, ate local foodstuffs and joined in the work and social life of the locals. The concept became popular and visitors to the more 'packaged' Club Méditerranée resort on the Senegal coast began to take canoe trips and stay overnight in traditional village accommodation.

Such an approach, however, was the exception rather than the rule, and concern for the impact of tourism on the environment continued to grow during the

1980s. In 1980, the **World Tourism Association** (WTO), by way of the *Manila Declaration*, demonstrated its awareness of the potential conflict between tourism and conservation. By 1982, the WTO and members of the UN Environment Programme argued in a joint statement for the protection, enhancement and improvement of the various components of the environment to ensure the harmonious development of tourism.

During the late 1980s, the concept of sustainable tourism was developed further. Such tourism would need to achieve the following: sustain the resources for tourism, including both the built and natural resources; sustain the regions where tourism takes place to the extent that local people have both the financial capability and personal willingness to continue living there; and sustain visitors for the long term. More recently, the emphasis has moved to canvassing the opinion of residents in tourist destinations. Their needs have become an important feature of attempts to promote community–led, sustainable tourism.

Preservation of the environment may be seen as the key to ensuring environmentally–friendly tourism. As well as wishing to continue to live in an attractive environment, locals have an interest in preserving the charms which encouraged visitors in the first instance. As the Spanish have discovered to their cost along the country's Mediterranean coastline, if a destination earns a reputation for being ruined by mass tourism, it will quickly lose favour.

Positive action

But what can travellers do to ensure they practise environmentally–friendly tourism? The following general advice applies to most countries of the world:

1. Whenever possible use local public transport, thus saving fuel you would have used in a hire car. In many European countries, North America and some countries of the Third World, trains are electric, which is an excellent reason for selecting this form of transport. Trams are still found in some European cities and they, like trains, are electrically operated, helping to reduce urban atmospheric pollution, highly corrosive for all those beautiful ancient buildings you have come to admire. Even diesel–powered trains and petrol or diesel–operated buses and coaches are a more efficient way to use fuel than private cars.

If public transport is not available or not suitable, try to get together with other like–minded people and hire a minibus. This will not only save you money in comparison with car hire, but will reduce fuel consumption and may well provide a local driver with employment. In many cities it is possible to hire bicycles very cheaply. Bicycles are pollution free and allow access to places impossible to reach by motorized transport. They also have the advantage of travelling at a speed which enables the rider to observe the scenery in detail.

2. When walking through the countryside, particularly environmentally–sensitive areas such as national parks, keep to the marked paths. If you have non–biodegradable rubbish with you —plastic bottles, sweet wrappers and biscuit packets— keep it until you find a suitable receptacle for disposal, or, if permitted, burn the rubbish. Biodegradable rubbish such as fruit peel and vegetable remains should be buried and not just thrown away as some of this waste may adversely affect wildlife.

3. Try to eat local produce, which is usually fresher (particularly in developing countries) and also reduces the need for packaging, refrigeration and transport, all of which consume fuel.

4. When choosing a place to stay, try to select accommodation which is aesthetically in keeping with the local environment and which uses the most efficient form of energy available.

These are specific actions, but an environmentally–minded traveller needs to become aware of the impact of all human activity on the environment, to develop a respect of all living things and an acknowledgement that we share territory with others to the extent that we should treat others as we would like to be treated by them. This may seem rather like a restrictive list of dos and don'ts, but codes of behaviour for visitors have been around for a while. *The Country Code*, produced by the **Countryside Commission**, has been with us for at least two decades and has been telling those who visit rural areas to take their litter home, help keep water clean and protect wildlife, plants and trees.

With the 1980s came a number of tourist codes for Western visitors to developing countries. For example, the Berlin–based group **Tourism with Insight** suggested that visitors to the Third World should use environmentally–friendly transport and generally accept responsibility for the environment in which they travelled.

Recently, the detrimental effects of tourism in the Himalayas has been the cause of growing concern. But the area is also the setting for an innovative development which is being praised as an excellent example of community–led tourism. The scheme, known as **The Annapurna Conservation Area Project** (ACAP), employs a multiple land–use concept of resource management. This involves attempts to reduce environmental damage at the same time as raising visitor awareness and promoting community–based projects. The scheme was established in 1986, originally funded by the **Worldwide Fund for Nature**, and now receives all of its funding from a fee charged to trekkers who enter the ACAP Himalayan mountain environment.

As part of the process of raising visitor awareness ACAP has produced a minimum impact code. The code has three areas of concern:

1. *The need for conservation of resources.* In the context of Nepal this refers particularly to firewood which the code states must be conserved by limiting hot showers, using fuel–efficient stoves or using alternative fuels such as kerosene.

2. *The need to stop pollution.* The code makes specific reference to methods of disposing of non–biodegradable items (which should be deposited in rubbish pits in villages on the trekking trails), biodegradable rubbish (which must be buried) and the use of toilet facilities.

3. *The need to respect Nepali culture.* This means not removing plants, animals or religious artefacts, wearing appropriate dress, (Nepalis are offended by large areas of exposed flesh), avoiding outward signs of physical affection, not giving to beggars (this can contribute to a dependency on tourist hand-outs) and encouraging young Nepalis to be proud of their culture.

The code has only been in operation for a short time, but it has provoked much interest, both within Nepal and internationally. **Tourism Concern** (a major British organization concerned with the impact of tourism) has published a code for the entire Himalayan region. This code, which is based on the ACAP minimum impact code and produced following consultation with representatives from the regions most affected, has been endorsed by tour operators and is intended to be taken as a model for use by all visitors to environmentally–fragile areas.

While there is still an incredibly long way to go in terms of awareness, it is encouraging to note that even some of the largest package-holiday operators endeavour to instruct holiday-makers in environmental matters, by means of videos on the flight in.

Whether you are travelling abroad or in Britain, in a developing country or a Western country, in the countryside or an urban area, the following three reminders may help maintain that awareness and concern that will enable you to be an environmentally–friendly traveller:

Take nothing but photographs
Kill nothing but time
Leave nothing but footprints

And Ecotourism ....?

It would be a considerable omission not to mention the ever-increasing phenomenon of ecotourism in this context. Ecotourism is a new and vibrant strand of the travel industry, but what it actually is covers a considerable spectrum.

Arising from public concern for the world's recourses, it ranges from travel companies who take their clients to contained areas, Club-Med-style, thus lessening the environmental and cultural impact of an influx of Western visitors. To holidays which actively promote environmental awareness, such as a two-week expedition with Earthwatch on a conservation project. In between there is everything from cycling holidays to butterfly-watching. For more information, contact Sustainability, Peoples Hall, Freston Road, London W11 4BD. Tel: 071-243 1277. Also an excellent book written by John Elkington and Julia Hailes of Sustainability called *Holidays that don't cost the Earth* (£5.99) is available at most good bookshops or through Sustainability. Please also see the articles on The Special Interest Traveller and The Expedition Traveller in this chapter.

THE INDEPENDENT TRAVELLER

by Dervla Murphy

Question: *When is a freak not a freak?*
Answer: *When she feels normal*

I was in my late forties before the realization came —very, very slowly, starting as a ridiculous–seeming suspicion that gradually crystallized into an exasperated certainty. Many people think of me as a freak.

From 16 April 1995 all national and international codes change —see page 587 for details.

By middle age one should be well aware of one's public image, given a way of life that makes such an accessory unavoidable. But if what an individual does *feels* normal, and if people are decently reticent about analysing you to your face, it's quite understandable that for decades you see only your self image, vastly as it may differ from the false public image meanwhile gaining credibility.

The freakish thing is, of course, not me, but the modern world —from which I, like millions of other normal folk, need to escape at intervals. Those of us born with the wandering instinct, and not caught in a job trap, can practise the most effective form of escapism: a move back in time, to one of the few regions where it is still possible to live simply, at our ancestors' pace. To describe this as returning to reality would be absurd; for us the modern world is reality. However, escapist travelling does allow a return to what we are genetically fitted to cope with, as we are not fitted to cope with the freakishly hectic, technological present.

Hence the notorious 'pressures', parallelling our marvellous conveniences. We have reduced physical effort to the minimum; everything is 'labour–saving' —transport, communications, entertainment, heating, cooking, cleaning, dressing, marketing, even writing (they tell me) if one uses a repulsive–sounding thing called a 'word processor.' Yet the effort of coming to terms with this effortless world is too much for many of us. So we get ulcers, have nervous breakdowns, take to uppers and/or downers, gamble on the stock exchange —or travel, seriously, for several months at a stretch.

Today's serious travellers are often frustrated explorers who would like to have been born at least 150 years earlier. Now there is nowhere left for individuals to explore, though there may be a few untouched corners (in Amazonia?) accessible only to expeditions. But the modern hi–tech expedition, with its two–way radios and helicopters on call for emergencies, naturally has no appeal for escapist travellers. Among themselves, these lament that their traditional, simple journeys have come to seem —by a cruel twist of the technological spiral— paradoxically artificial. A century ago, travellers who took off into the unknown had to be completely isolated from their own world for months or years on end. Now such isolation is a deliberately–chosen luxury and to that extent, phoney. Had I died of gangrene in the Himalayas or Simiens or Andes, that would have been my own fault (no two–way radio) rather than a sad misfortune.

So the escapist traveller is, in one sense, playing a game. But only in one sense, because the actual journey is for real in a way that the modern expedition, with its carefully prearranged links to home and safety, is not. Whatever happens, you can't chicken out: you are where you've chosen to be and must take the consequences.

Here some confusion arises about courage. There is a temperamental aspect to this issue: optimism versus pessimism —is a bottle half empty or half full? Why should your appendix burst or your bones break abroad rather than at home? Optimists don't believe in disasters until they happen. Therefore they are not fearful and have no occasion to display courage. Nothing puts my hackles up faster than being told I'm brave. This is nonsense —albeit significant nonsense. Where is our effortless civilization at when physical exertion, enjoyed in remote places, is repeatedly mistaken for bravery?

Genuine travellers, far from being brave, are ultra–cautious. That is an essential component of their survival mechanism and one of the dividing lines between them and foolhardy limelight–seekers. Before they start they sus out all foreseeable hazards and either change their route, should these hazards seem excessive and the risk silly, or prepare themselves to cope with reasonable hazards. Thus what looks to outsiders like a daring journey is in fact a safe toddle — unless you have bad luck, which you could have at home. Six times I've broken my ribs; the last time was at home, falling off a ladder. The other times were in Afghanistan, Nepal, Ethiopia, Peru and Madagascar. You could say I have an unhappy karmic relationship with my ribs.

Recently I was asked, "Why is independent travel seen as so much more of an intellectual challenge? And what does it take to cope with it?" That flumoxed me. I have been an escapist traveller for more than 40 years without its ever occurring to me that I was meeting an intellectual challenge. A stamina challenge, usually; an emotional challenge, sometimes; a spiritual challenge, occasionally. But an intellectual challenge? I don't see it. Unless by *intellectual* one means that slight exertion of the grey cells required to equip oneself more or less suitably for the country in view. Yet surely that is a matter of common sense, rather than intellect?

Granted, equipping oneself includes a certain amount of reading; but this, in a literate society, scarcely amounts to an intellectual challenge. I refer only to reading history, not to any sort of heavy sociological or political research —unless of course you happen to fancy that sort of thing, in which case it will obviously add an extra dimension to your journey. Otherwise, for the average traveller, enough of current politics will be revealed en route, should politics be important to the locals; and in those few happy regions where domestic politics don't matter, you can forget about them. But to travel through any country in ignorance of its history seems to me a waste of time. You can't then understand the *why* of anything or anyone. With this view some travellers violently disagree, arguing that all preliminary reading should be avoided, that each new country should be visited in a state of innocence and experienced purely subjectively. The mind on arrival should be a blank page, awaiting one's own vivid personal impressions, to be cherished ever after as authentic and unique. Why burden yourself in advance with loads of irrelevancies about the past and piles of other people's prejudiced interpretations of the present? On that last point I concur; travellers rarely read travel books —unless they have to review them.

Reverting to this odd concept of an intellectual challenge: is the adaptability required of travellers sometimes mistaken for an intellectual feat? That seems unlikely because we're back to temperament: some people slot in easily everywhere. If travellers saw the need to adapt as an intellectual challenge they probably wouldn't slot in anywhere —except perhaps on some pretentious radio chat show.

Maybe the overcoming of language barriers is seen as an intellectual challenge? Yet there could scarcely be anything less intellectual than urgently saying 'P–sssss!' when you must get fast to the nearest earth closet —or at least out of the *tukul*, which has been locked up for the night. The basic need of human beings — sleeping, eating, drinking, peeing— are so basic that they can easily be understood; all our bladders function in exactly the same way. The language barrier unnecessarily inhibits many who otherwise would seek out and relish remote regions. On the practical level, it is of no consequence. I can state this with total assurance, having travelled on four continents using only English and those courtesy phrases of Tibetan, Amharic, Quechua or whatever, that you happen to pick up as you go along. Even on the emotional level, it is not as formidable as it may seem; the human features —especially the eyes— are wonderfully eloquent. In our own society, the extent to which we wordlessly communicate goes unnoticed. In Far Flungery, where nobody within 200 miles speaks a syllable of any European language, one becomes very aware of the range of moods and subtle feelings that may be conveyed visually rather than aurally. However, on the exchange–of–ideas level the barrier is, quite simply, insuperable. Therefore scholar–travellers —people like Freya Stark, Patrick Leigh Fermor, Colin Thubron— consider the learning of Arabic or Albanian or Russian or Mandarin to be as essential as buying a map. And there you have what seems to me (linguistically inept as I am) a bona fide intellectual challenge.

As a label, 'the independent traveller' puzzles me. It verges on tautology; travellers, being inherently independent, don't need the adjective to distinguish them from those unfortunate victims of the tourist industry who, because of sun–starvation on our islands, are happy to be herded annually towards a hot spot where tea and chips are guaranteed and there is no danger of meeting the natives.

I can, however, see that holiday-makers (the category in between travellers and tourists) may validly be divided into 'dependent' and 'independent.' The former, though liking to make their own plans, contentedly follow beaten tracks and book their B&Bs in advance. The latter are often travellers *manqué* for whom unpredictability gives savour to their journey: setting off at dawn with no idea of where one will be by dusk, or who with or what eating. Only a lack of *time* or money prevents them from reaching travellers' territory and usually time is their problem. Travelling can be done on quite a short shoestring, and often must be so done for the excellent reason that the traveller's theatre of operations offers few consumer goods.

Independent holiday-makers are in general much more tolerant and sociable than travellers, whose escapist compulsion causes them to feel their day has been ruined if they glimpse just one other solitary trekker in the far distance, and who break out in spots if they come upon even a vestigial trace of tourism. But that last nightmare contingency is unlikely; the paths of travellers rarely converge, unless one finds oneself within a few miles of somewhere like Machu Picchu and it seems "stupid not to see it." Incidentally, Machu Picchu provided me with my most grisly travel memory —an American helicopter landing amidst the ruins and spewing forth a squeal of excited women whose paunchy menfolk were intent only on photographing them beside the mournful resident llamas. My timing was wrong; you have to get to Machu Picchu at dawn, as I did next day.

The past decade or so has seen the emergence of another, hybrid category: youngsters who spend a year or more wandering around the world in a holiday-making spirit, occasionally taking temporary jobs. Some gain enormously from this experience but many seem to cover too much ground too quickly, sampling everywhere and becoming familiar with nowhere. They have been from Alaska to Adelaide, Berlin to Bali, Calcutta to Cuzco, Lhasa to London. They tend to wander in couples or small packs, swapping yarns about the benefits —or otherwise— of staying here, doing that, buying this. They make a considerable impact where they happen to perch for a week or so, often bringing with them standards (sometimes too low) and expectations (sometimes too high) which unsettle their local contemporaries.

They are the product of cheap air travel, which spawned a 'Let's See the World' cult. Of course one rejoices that the young are free to roam as never before, yet such rapid 'round–the–worlding' is, for many, more confusing than enlightening. It would be good if this fashion soon changed, if the young became more discriminating, allowing themselves time to travel seriously in a limited area that they had chosen because of its particular appeal to them, as individuals.

THE PACKAGED TRAVELLER

by Hilary Bradt

In 1841 Thomas Cook advertised that he had arranged a special train to take a group of temperance workers from Leicester to Loughborough for a meeting some 10 miles away. From this humble beginning has grown a giant tourist industry which has helped the balance of payments in countries all over the world as well as enabling almost everyone to have a taste of 'abroad.' Experienced travellers often scorn package holidays as appealing to the '*If it's Tuesday, this must be Belgium*' mentality, without realizing how much time and money can be saved and how much seen by joining a tour. And now that package tours have expanded into special interest and activity holidays a new world, previously impenetrable to all but the most determined individual, has opened up for the adventurous person in search of the safely exotic.

The most convenient way of booking any sort of package tour is through a travel agent. While you can usually deal directly with the company offering the trip, a good travel agent will save you hours of time and hassle. Not everyone realizes that travel agents earn their income from commissions on sales and not from any charge levied on the customer, so you pay nothing for their services. If your travel agent is a member of ABTA or IATA (International Air Transport Association) or has an Air Tour Operator's Licence (ATOL), you are less likely to become the victim of overbooking or other travel malpractice, and if something does go wrong and it's the company's fault, you do have some recourse.

Do your preparatory brochure reading carefully. If you choose a trip to Greece in mid–summer and can't stand the heat, that's not your travel agent's fault. Nor can he be held responsible for the inefficiencies that are inherent in Third World travel. An honest guide book will warn you of the negative aspects of the countries you are interested in and, likewise, a brochure is more likely to be taken seriously if the picture painted is not too rosy. Beware of advertising jargonese that could be fluffing over the fact that your hotel is a couple of miles from the sea, glimpsed tantalizingly from only one room on the top floor, although recent EC legislation has further strengthened legal penalties for misrepresentation as well as any financial malpractices.

Short haul

Under this heading we can include a two–week break in Turkey, a 'weekend break' in Majorca, or a day's sightseeing in a continental European city. Prices are generally low, as it is this category which covers the vast bulk of package holidays, and there are also plenty of bargains to be had —especially for off–season and late bookings (as a glance at any travel agent's window or the holiday section of the national newspapers or Teletext will show you). Just be careful to check the credentials of any company offering unbelievably cheap trips. Even if they are legitimate, prices are being kept down by lowering the standard of accommodation, using flights that leave at 2am, and offering only self–catering facilities.

Going on a package tour does not necessarily mean travelling in a group. Often the 'package' consists of air tickets and accommodation only, and you are free to explore during the day. And you don't have to stay in the allocated hotel; sometimes the savings on the airfare are such that you can afford to use the hotel for a couple of nights then head off on your own and do some travelling. More and more charter companies are now offering airfares with nominal accommodation thrown in, and with no expectation that you will actually use it.

Even brief sightseeing tours are often well worthwhile for independent travellers. Some of the world's most fascinating places are virtually impossible to get to on your own, and even if easily accessible, sightseeing can be tiring and uninformative without transport or a guide. Tours are easily arranged. Your hotel should be able to recommend a reliable agency, but you can look in the yellow pages of the phone book, or simply walk down the main street until you find one. When setting up your tour, it helps to have some information on the sight or sights you want to visit. Try to meet your guide the day before to make sure he/she is knowledgeable and speaks good English, and if you enjoy walking, make it clear that a tour on foot would be preferable to spending all day on a bus.

Wherever you are going, these short–haul packages come off a mammoth production line, are simple to book and easy to use, leaving you with little else to worry about other than what kind of sun cream to pack. Long–haul and 'adventure' packages are more demanding, mentally, physically and on the pocket, and booking can be more complicated as there are fewer departures and a limited number of places. Far more care should be taken to ensure that you find precisely what you are looking for.

Long haul

Overland journeys lasting several months are traditionally the most popular form of long–haul 'adventure' package for those for whom time is no object, followed closely nowadays by 'Round The World' and itineraries with stopovers in different continents. And for those with less time to spare, plenty of companies offer two or three–week tours which still use the converted trucks which are the hallmark of long overland trips. Dodge three–ton trucks, completely stripped and rebuilt to suit the needs of each company, are the vehicles preferred, being rugged enough to cope with the varied terrain and conditions found on a trans–continental journey. Nights are spent in tents or simple rest houses, and most overlanders cook their own meals on a rota system and eat occasionally in local restaurants.

Most long–haul trips involve journeys through Africa, Asia, South America and, to a lesser extent, Australasia (although this would almost certainly be a key feature of any Round The World air itinerary). The most popular overland routes are London to Kathmandu (open again despite problems in the Middle East and Africa) which offers various possibilities such as the Nile route from Egypt to Kenya, the Sahara from Morocco to French West Africa, Nairobi down to southern Africa, or even North Africa all the way to Cape Town. South America is almost as popular, with a variety of routes.

These are rugged trips and a great test of psychological fortitude as well as physical endurance. Being with the same group of people for several months in often trying. Conditions can be a strain on even the most sociable traveller, so if you suspect your patience may snap after a few weeks, don't try it. A long overland trip can, however, be a bargain in terms of daily expenditure.

Choose your overland company with care. Some have temptingly low prices but unscrupulous employees like the driver I met in Africa: after dropping his group to do some sightseeing, he drove away and sold the truck! No doubt a rare occurrence but you are safer if you use a reputable company or go through an organization which has long experience of dealing with overland companies.

There are of course an increasing number and variety of two–week, long–haul packages for travellers looking for something a little more exotic, but without the time to make all the arrangements. Specialist long–haul operators are your best bet.

THE ADVENTURE TRAVELLER

by Paul Vickers

Adventure travel is a search for and a return to the essentials of travel. It's getting back to basics, the fundamentals. It is an attitude of mind, a philosophy, an openness to the unexpected. Adventure travel is the heat of the tropical sun on your back and your heart pumping as you ride your mountain bike along a dirt track through the jungle; it's saddling up your packhorse on a cold crisp morning as the sun rises over the mountains; it's the first strokes of your paddle in the still clear water as your kyak edges out into the river, knowing there are rapids ahead; it's the sense of achievement as you bivouac on a high pass with a view down the valley of the last few days' trek.

Adventure travel is travel you can experience with all your senses. The heat and the cold, the crunch of snow under your feet, your fingers groping for a handhold on a smooth rock, the crack of an avalanche, the crash of animals in tropical undergrowth. It's the smell of hot saddlery and humid vegetation, the sharp taste of adventure in your mouth, the rush of adrenalin that enables you to do the things you never dreamt of doing. The easier it becomes to travel, the harder it is to be a traveller.

Contemporary travel has become depersonalized and characterless, with fast, easy, lookalike airports, planes and hotels, hermetically–sealed coaches, pre–packaged, in–flight meals and tinned cold drinks. It is easy, safe, dull and totally isolates one from the countries and people one has essentially come in search of. The more critical traveller seeks increasingly the intense, first–hand experiences and emotions of the kind that earlier travellers and the great explorers felt when they first set foot in the uncharted regions of distant lands. There may be no more blank spaces on the map but the adventure traveller can experience the same heightened sense of discovery and achievement by doing it himself in his own way.

The adventure traveller is an individual and as such will seek independent modes of transport that enable him/her to go when he pleases at his own pace — to stop and start at will. Walking and trekking require little more material than a pair of good, well broken–in boots. The further, higher and more extreme the environment you head for, the more gear and experience you need. Riding bicycles, horses, camels and yaks enables you to cover more ground, and in using the indigenous form of transport you bring yourself into contact with the people and participate in their way of life. Familiarity with riding and handling animals is pretty essential for animal–equipped expeditions. Skis, snow shoes, crampons and dog sleighs take some practice but do put mountains, snow– covered country and the frozen wastes within one's reach. Kyaks, canoes and inflatables are the principal craft of river and coastal adventure travel, being small and lightweight, enabling them to be man–handled and carried by the individual or expedition team when necessary.

The adventure traveller can also reach for the sky and travel by microlight or balloon. In 1987 after a one-year bicycle journey from the UK I arrived in Australia. The following week the first microlight to fly from London to Australia flew in as well. We were both discovering the world first-hand in our own particular way!

How to be an adventure traveller

Adventure travel generally requires more thought and planning than most other forms of travel —although equally it can be undertaken at the drop of a hat! If you are travelling alone, you need to think about everything you'll need to be independent and self-sufficient. The lone traveller's approach appeals to some but not others. The loner is perhaps more at risk but on the other hand is perceived as less of a threat to the people he meets on his journey, and is therefore likely to enjoy more contact and hospitality.

If you travel as part of a group, keep it as small as possible, otherwise you can resemble a veritable army on the move, intimidating, slow, noisy and obtrusive. Team dynamics and relationships get increasingly complex as the team gets bigger. Two is ideal, three has the reputation that it risks fragmenting (although personally I have found it works well) and four almost inevitably divides into two units parting company altogether, which can be difficult if you have only one inflatable boat between you!

Beware, travelling puts a great strain on even the best of relationships, long-standing friends can end by splitting up after sharing the confined quarters of a tent and each other's company 24 hours a day for several months! In fact, you are just as likely to get on and succeed with someone you don't know as your best friend.

Sources of information

Talk to like–minded people. It's often inspiring and first–hand information is always the most interesting and up–to–date. If you are unsure of quite what to do or how to do it, other adventurers' stories and advice are most encouraging and supportive. *The Independent Traveller* seminars organized yearly at the Royal Geographical Society are inspirational events devoted to talks, slideshows, films and informal discussion by recently returned adventure travellers. The Globetrotters Club is also a good place to meet fellow travellers and swap ideas and the club's specialist newsletter is full of useful information.

Research and preparation

Thoroughly research your destination, activity and mode of transport. You can never be over–informed, even if your own personal experience is ultimately quite different from what you expected. Climate, terrain, altitude and type of travel are the essential criteria in planning your journey. As it is likely that you will find yourself alone in fairly remote areas, you need to be well prepared for your expedition both mentally and physically. This means an awareness of exactly where you are going and what you are letting yourself in for, as well as a reasonably high level of fitness and some physical preparation and previous experience of the type of travel you plan to undertake. Before launching off into the unknown, practise at home. You can have a great adventure in your own backyard whilst preparing for something more exotic further afield; it also gives you an opportunity to check out your gear and the mental attitude of your colleagues.

Self–sufficiency and independence

If you are going to be off the beaten track, you have to be as self-sufficient as possible, capable of maintaining yourself, your animals and your equipment. Familiarize yourself thoroughly with your equipment, know how to dismantle and reassemble everything before you set out, and carry your own repair and tool kit. Ensure you know what to do in the case of illness or an accident and check your medical kit is comprehensive (how many water–purifying tablets or painkillers might you need?) Always be prepared for the worst. What protection do you require for the weather conditions you could experience? Crossing the Thar desert of Rajasthan by bicycle I needed a dozen litres of water each day, two days' supply was the absolute maximum I could carry and it was boiling hot by the time I came to drink it.

Equipment

He who travels light, travels far. The adventure traveller must travel light as it is he himself who must transport all his equipment. The more you carry, the more encumbered and slow you are. Lightness equals flexibility, enabling you to change your plan, route or mode of transport instantly without problems. Pack your gear three times, ruthlessly pruning out items each time or you'll find yourself leaving a trail of abandoned, expensive equipment across the globe. Carry the absolute minimum that you can safely get away with. I prefer to buy extra clothing when it gets cold and sell it or give it away as it gets warmer —infinitely preferable to carrying it hundreds of miles on the off–chance of needing it again later.

Responsibility and conduct

In remote but inhabited areas that have relatively little contact with the outside world, you will be the focus of interest and attention. You therefore have to be patient, friendly and respectful of local mores and traditions. Your generosity and respect will be reciprocated, often with a measure of hospitality which for those from the materialistic West can be staggeringly generous. Always take something, no matter how small, as a present and token of your appreciation. Picture post cards, badges, flags and sweets make simple light gifts that will be greatly appreciated. If you take people's addresses do write to them, it will mean so much.

Modes of transport

Walking and trekking are the first and most immediate forms of adventure travel, requiring the minimum of equipment. A trekking adventure starts as soon as you leave the tarmac and goes all the way until the mountains become inaccessible without ropes, ice–axes and crampons.

Climbing and mountain travel

Experience is needed, but climbing with a guide or knowledgeable climber will lead you into a new world and ultimately to topping out peaks, one of the most exciting adventures known to man.

Cycling

You don't need to be a great bicycle enthusiast to appreciate the potential of this form of efficient, lightweight and independent travel. With bicycle panniers you have no heavy pack on your back, you cover the ground quickly but at a pace that allows real appreciation and discovery. And you can even cycle right round the world if you've got a couple of years to spare!

Horses, camels and yaks

Animals take a fair bit of handling and you need some experience. Remember they cover less ground than is generally imagined, especially when heavily laden and over long distances (approximately twice a man's daily walking distance, and half a day's cycling distance). For average cross–country rates, count on 40 kilometres a day for a horse. Yaks are slower and can't be taken below 10,000 feet altitude. Camels do need to drink!

Kyaks and inflatables

Select your craft depending on the type of water you will be in. Sea kyaks are bigger, more stable and you can carry enough equipment to be self sufficient for six months. Inflatables are ideal for river descents and white–water rafting.

Ballooning and microlighting

Balloons have flown over mountain ranges and across oceans, microlights across Africa and from the UK all the way down under to Australia. They are highly specialized forms of adventure travel and require a lot of planning and preparation in advance, but they do enable man to fly independently. See page 242 for further information on microlighting.

Adventure travel is primarily a question of independence, determination and confidence. Anyone with an adventurous spirit can do it. The sense of achievement and self–confidence that come from it are quite immeasurable and greatly outweigh the relatively small amount of pain that goes with an enormous degree of pleasure. Don't hesitate, pack this book in your rucksack and go —you will never look back!

THE RESORT TRAVELLER

by Nick Hanna

The idea of spending a holiday on the beach is as old as tourism itself, and each year beach tourism continues to grow as millions flock to coastlines around the globe for their yearly dose of sun, sea and sand. Tourism to the Mediterranean, for instance, has doubled in the past 20 years to 120 million annual visitors and is expected to reach 300 million by the year 2000. As tourism grows, development and pollution are taking an increasing toll on the world's coastlines and beaches.

In the UK, as elsewhere, visitors to beach resorts may find themselves faced with a seaside spoilt by oil, litter, or even raw sewage. Make sure this doesn't happen to you by getting hold of a copy of the Marine Conservation Society's *Good Beach Guide 1994* (Ebury Press, £6.99). As well as giving information about water quality, it also details the most interesting beaches for various activities and includes a 'Golden List' of beaches and Blue Flag beaches (which pass EEC standards). There is also the Heinz Guide to British Beaches 1994 (Vermilion £6.99), covering more than a thousand beaches around Britain and Ireland.

An increasing awareness of the dangers of too much sunbathing, as well as a desire to get more from a holiday than merely slobbing around on a sun lounger, has led to a huge growth in watersports and other beach activities. Whereas a few years ago you'd be lucky to find much more than a rusting pedalo for hire on a Mediterranean beach, now many resorts can offer extensive and sophisticated facilities for everything from windsurfing to parasailing.

Further afield, tropical beach resorts have never been as accessible or as affordable as they are now, with a huge growth in charter flights and long–haul tropical holidays, bringing exotic destinations within reach of even modest travel budgets.

Where to go

For the independent traveller, the **Asia Pacific** region offers the most promising potential for beach hopping —whether you're interested in snorkelling and windsurfing, or simply lazing around under a palm tree. Here follows a brief guide to some of the region's most outstanding beach and island resorts.

The Indian state of **Goa** has numerous fabulous beaches as well as a rich cultural heritage to explore. The hippy legacy is still much in evidence but there is a wide choice of accommodation, ranging from the luxurious Taj Fort Aguada Beach Resort (reservations, tel: 071–242 9964) to simple huts costing a few rupees a night. The season is from October to March/April and charters from the UK are bookable through Inspirations East.

In **Thailand** the combination of culture, nightlife, the ever–hospitable Thai people, superb food and sublime beaches and islands continue to pull in millions of visitors. The country has an incredible variety of islands and beaches to suit almost everyone, from jet set Phuket to laid–back Koh Samui or Koh Phangan. If you're looking for something even more idyllic, book a trip to the Similan Islands, near the Burmese border: an unbeatable combination of virgin beaches and a rich marine environment for divers and snorkellers (further information from Twickers World, (tel: 081-892 3642). Also IHS Travel (tel: 081-905 5252).

Malaysia's main beach resort is Batu Ferringhi on the island of Penang, but the island itself (including the fascinating historical port of Georgetown) is much more appealing than the beach. On Malaysia's east coast Giant Leatherback Turtles come ashore to nest on the beaches at Rantau Aband from May through to September; bookings for the nearby Tanjong Jara resort can be made through Kuoni or Abercrombie & Kent. Further south, the island of Tioman is a well–known budget traveller's retreat, with good snorkelling and jungle walks.

In **The Philippines** there's no doubt that the island of Boracay is one of the world's best. Delightful bamboo and thatch huts nestle under the palm trees, with vanilla–coloured beaches sloping off into the azure depths. Thankfully there are no concrete hotels in sight, but if you don't want to risk taking your chances on finding the perfect beach hut when you arrive, good quality accommodation can be booked through Philippine Airlines. For scuba divers the waters of the South China Seas are at their calmest from January until May, with some of the best diving to be found around Palawan and the beach resort of El Nido (also bookable through PAL).

Like the Philippines, **Indonesia** has literally thousands of islands to choose from. Nonetheless, Bali continues to be the most popular, attracting overland travellers as well as Australian holiday-makers in their thousands, drawn by the smiling people, cheap living, wild nightlife, great surfing, and those body–melting Balinese beach massages. If all that seems too cosmopolitan for your liking, hop over to neighbouring Lombok for a more genuine taste of Indonesia, and to Lombok's triple satellite islands of Gili Air, Gili Meno and Gili Trawangan for some terrific snorkelling. Out–of–the–way beach hotels can be booked through CV Travel (tel: 071-581 0851), and Abercrombie & Kent (tel: 071-730 9600).

Australia has so many beaches it's almost impossible to know where to begin, although one's starting point might be tropical Queensland, where there are 24 island resorts with access to the Great Barrier Reef. If you're looking for unashamed luxury in an island setting, Lizard Island is the place to head for (book though Travelbag or Elegant Resorts); at the other end of the scale, one of the best value islands for divers and snorkellers is Lady Elliott, a coral cay right on the Barrier Reef itself with a friendly, informal atmosphere; a good middle–bracket choice would be Heron Island, also a coral cay, but with somewhat more comfortable facilities. Turtles hatch on both Lady Elliott and Heron from January through to late March. Contact Jetset (tel: 061-953 0920), Austravel (tel: 071-734 7755) or Travelbag (tel: 071-497 0515).

Costs in getting to **South Pacific** beach resorts can be prohibitive, but if you're passing through on a round–the–world ticket (or similar) then **Fiji** has to be the best choice. There are numerous islands with friendly people, good transport links and excellent beaches. By contrast, **Tahiti** doesn't enjoy such a friendly reputation and costs are high. Nonetheless, there is a wide range of accommodation and you can stay in anything from bungalows built on stilts over the lagoon to de luxe establishments such as the Hotel Bora Bora or the Hotel Moana Beach (either of which can be booked through Elegant Resorts, tel; 0244 329671) —you can even camp in beach resorts on fabled islands such as Bora Bora and Moorea. May through to October/November is the best time to visit the South Pacific.

Hawaii has something for everyone: wind–surfing for the experts on Maui; volcano climbing and mountain biking on the Big Island; dramatic scenery on the Garden Isle of Kauia, and, of course, Waikiki Beach and world class surfing on Oahu. During the winter months (November to March) Hawaii is also host to hundreds of Humpback Whales who make the annual 5 to 7000–mile round trip from their summer feeding grounds in Alaska to mate and give birth here. Day trips to view the gentle giants are widely available. Holidays can be booked through Page & Moy (tel: 0533-552551).

THE STUDENT TRAVELLER

by Nick Hanna and Greg Brookes

If you are a student traveller you can take advantage of a comprehensive range of special discounts —both at home and abroad— which enable you to go almost anywhere in the world on the cheap. To qualify for reduced fares to most destinations you need an **International Student Identity Card** (ISIC) which is obtainable from local student travel offices (£5.00) or by post from ISIC Mail Order, Bleaklow House, Howard Town Mills, Mill Street, Glossop SK13 8PT. All full time students are eligible; postal applications should include proof of student status, a passport photo, full name, date of birth, nationality, address and a cheque or postal order for £5.50 payable to ISIC Mail Order. The ISIC card is issued by the Copenhagen–based International Student Travel Confederation (ISTC) who publish a booklet called *The ISIC World Travel Handbook* detailing student discounts worldwide. The ISIC card is recognized all over the world and allows holders reduced rates at many art galleries and other places of cultural and educational interest, as well as reductions on local transport.

Since 1990, when the ISTC signed an agreement with the East European student body, the International Union of Students, the ISIC card entitles you to discounts in Eastern Europe.

The Council of Europe Cultural Identity Card (BP431/R6, F-67006 Strasbourg, France, tel: 010-3388 412621) is available free to postgraduates students, teachers, and a few other categories. It gives reduced or free admission to places of cultural interest in the Vatican and all member countries of the Council of Europe (but not in the country of issue, and only when produced with a passport). The card cannot be used by those travelling for commercial reasons. For application forms and more information, write to the Central Bureau for Educational Visits and Exchange (CBEVE).

There are also a number of travel discount schemes that are not dependent upon student status, although most of these are nevertheless youth schemes for which you cease to be eligible once you reach the age of between 24 and 26. **The Federation of International Youth Travel Organizations** (FIYTO, Bredgade 25H, 1260 Copenhagen, Denmark, tel: 010–45-3333 9600) is made up of 221 organizations throughout the world which specialize in youth travel. A membership card entitles you to a range of concessions similar, although not identical, to those given by ISIC. The card is available to everyone under the age of 26, and is issued with a handbook listing all the concession entitlements.

Accommodation

If you don't fancy spending your travels under canvas, try ISIC's *The World Travel Handbook* for details of accommodation discounts. Probably your best source of information will be the International Youth Hostel Federation which has more than 5000 hostels worldwide. Their directory has now been split into two books, *Europe and the Mediterranean* and *Africa, America, Asia and Oceania,* both are available from any good bookshop.

Slightly more expensive but better equipped, the Young Men's and Young Women's Christian Association hostels are another option for student travellers. *The YMCA Directory* (available for £4 from the National Council of YMCAs, 640 Forest Road, London E17 3DZ) lists all worldwide YMCA hostels. For the women's version, *The World YWCA Directory* (£2.50 includes postage) for travels to Europe, *Pack for Europe* (£1.50 plus 25p postage) contact YWCA, Clarendon House, 52 Cornmarket Street, Oxford OX1 3EJ, tel: 0865 0726110.

With a little initiative, you may be able to negotiate use of student accommodation during vacation time. In West Germany, students can use university catering facilities (*Mensas*) which are decent, reasonably priced and open all year round. Student accommodation is only available during local university vacations.

Travel discounts

Cheap **rail** travel is now dependent chiefly upon age and is generally open to everyone under the age of 26. The popular **Inter–Rail Card** which costs £145, gives you free rail travel within Europe and Morocco for one month, as well as entitling you to discounts on P&O and Sealink. For details of international rail-passes try *The Thomas Cook World Travel Pass Guide* (£2.95).

Eurotrain (52 Grosvenor Gardens, London SW1W 0AG, tel: 071–730 3402) offer low prices to young travellers heading for Europe. If you are under 26 you can take advantage of a selection of European routings (including Eastern Europe) which allow stopovers and two–month ticket validity from as little as £90.

Student and youth discounts are also available for those travelling by **coach**. It pays to compare prices carefully between coach and rail because although coaches are normally considerably cheaper, sometimes the difference can be small and trains are obviously preferable in terms of speed and comfort. Apart from these exceptions, coaches are generally substantially cheaper than trains.

Eurolines (52 Grosvenor Gardens, London SW1, tel: 071–730 8235) runs a daily service to Amsterdam and Paris as well as services to 180 destinations in Europe. A four or five–journey bus pass, lasting two months costs from £98.

Within Britain, National Express (The Coach Travel Centre, 13 Regent Street, London, SW1Y 4LR, tel: 071–730 0202) gives students a 33 per cent reduction on all standard fares (but not on Rapide services) on production of **The Young Person's Coach Card**.

Valuable discounts are also available for **air** travel. Student charters are operated by the major student travel organizations under the umbrella of the Student Air Travel Association. Most of the flights are in the long summer vacation, and are generally open to ISIC card holders under 30 (some are only open to those under 28) together with their spouses and dependent children travelling on the same flight. Again, *The Student Traveller* is a useful source of information, listing Student Travel Offices (STOs) around the world.

Travel offices

Student travel offices are a good source of information for just about every kind of discount: there are nearly 60 of them in Britain, one for every campus or university town. They are coordinated by the **National Association of Student Travel Offices** (NASTO) and staff are often themselves seasoned travellers and can be a mine of information of budget travel in foreign countries. But check out your High Street travel agent as well, and compare prices before making a final decision.

Another source of information on student travel discounts is *The Student Travel Handbook,* produced annually by **STA Travel** (to obtain a free copy contact STA Travel, 74 Old Brompton Road, London SW7, tel: 071–581 1022). Although they started out life as Student Travel Australia, the services offered by STA now cover both hemispheres making them Britain's biggest and most influential student travel operator. They have four offices in London and others throughout Australia, South East Asia, the Far East and the USA.

Also worth checking out is **Campus Travel** (head office: 52 Grosvenor Gardens, London SW1W 0AF, tel: 071–730 8111) who have three offices in London and others in Bristol, Dundee, Glasgow, Liverpool, Manchester and Oxford.

Working and studying abroad

There are several very good references for students who wish to work abroad such as *Working Holidays* published by the **Central Bureau for Education Visits and Exchanges,** and a very useful series of books from Vacation Work publications.

North America is a favourite destination for students who want a working holiday. **The British Universities North America Club** (BUNAC) is a non–profit making organization that exists to give students the chance to get to the States. They've got four programmes in the USA and Canada, one in Australia and one in Jamaica, offering a wide choice of jobs and locations and BUNAC gets you that vital work permit for all of them.

The general work and travel programme *Work America*, allows you a visa so that you can take virtually any summer job you find yourself; the airfare has to be paid in advance —they suggest that bank managers will usually oblige with a loan. Places are limited so it's vital that the lengthy application process is started early. Applicants must be at least 19 and have experience of working with groups of children. Hundreds of opportunities can also be found in BUNAC's *Job Directory*.

If you enjoy the company of children, then they have a BUNACAMP programme which places students in summer camps as counsellors.These are also open to Gap-year students and non-students. The round trip ticket is paid for and you get full board and lodging plus pocket money. Students with specialist skills (music, sports, arts or science) are preferred but more importantly you must be able to deal with children.

Another deal that provides you with airfares full board and lodging and a job is KAMP, the kitchen and maintenance programme. Contact BUNAC at 16 Bowling Green Lane, London EC1 0BD (tel: 071–251 3472).

Camp America (37 Queen's Gate, London, SW7 5HR, tel: 071–589 3223) provides similar facilities with a free flight, free board and work permit all as part of the package. The placement procedure likewise takes a long time, so apply early. There is also **GAP Activity Projects (Ltd)** Tel: 0734 594914, they organize voluntary work overseas for school-leavers who are between school and further training. It has projects in 33 countries around the world for young volunteers, who assist with the teaching of English, and help in schools generally. Volunteers are also needed for social work, caring, conservation and outward bound. For further information write to GAP, 44 Queens Road, Reading, Berkshire RG1 4BB.

To study abroad you must first be sure you can cope adequately with the local language. Organizations such as the Central Bureau and the British Council should be able to help as should the Cultural Attaché at the relevant embassy. If possible ask someone who has just returned for more details about local conditions and lifestyle.

Grants

Ask your university, college, higher education department or local authority if they have any special trust funds for student travel. If it has, it won't be much but every little helps. Two handbooks on grants are *The Directory of Grant*

Making Trusts and *The Grants Register*. Both are expensive but should be in your student or, possibly, your local library. The library noticeboard is also a good place to look for details of bursaries or exchange scholarships which could well lead to a year's studying or travelling upon graduation.

THE EXPATRIATE TRAVELLER

by Doris Dow

Nowadays governments, large organizations and big companies all compete for the expertise and skills they require. More and more people leave their own country to live and work abroad. These expatriates go off with high hopes and expectations but in spite of increased earning power, some are disappointed and frustrated and return home for good. Others adapt well to the challenge of a new life and continue in the expatriate scene for many years, finding it difficult to repatriate.

Contracts

It is important that the terms of the contract are understood and signed by the employer and the employee; if the contract is in another language, a reliable translation should be obtained before signing on the dotted line. Contracts should set out the terms and conditions of employment, including minimum length of contract, working hours and overtime, remuneration, allowances for/provision of accommodation, car, education, medical and dental cover, leave and terminal gratuities/bonuses, dismissal clauses and compassionate leave arrangements.

Many jobs abroad offer what seem to be on paper very large salaries, but the attitude of employers, their willingness to accept responsibility and to offer support when necessary are often worth more than money. **Expats International** (29 Lacon Road, Dulwich, London SE22 9HE, tel: 081–299 4986) is an association for expatriates which not only has a large job advertisement section in its magazine, but will advise on contracts and finance.

Documentation

Before departure, visas, work permits, driving licences, health regulations and other documentation must be attended to. Getting the necessary visas from embassies can entail many visits and long waits, but the first lessons of an aspiring expatriate are quickly learned —the acquisition of tolerance, patience, perseverance and good humour. For those working for a large company or international organization, the documentation is usually done for them.

Preparations for the move

Time spent doing some 'homework' on the country you are going to, its lifestyles, traditions and customs is very worthwhile. Mental preparation is just as important as the practical plans —working and living in a country is quite a different experience from a holiday visit.

Search libraries and bookshops for travel books and up–to–date guides. For Commonwealth countries, there are excellent permanent exhibitions at the **Commonwealth Institute**, Kensington High Street, London, as well as an excellent bookshop. Embassies should also be helpful on specific information on currency, import regulations etc, as well as giving advice on what not to import. Other valuable sources of information are: **The Women's Corona Society**, 35 Belgrave Square, London SW1X 8QB, (tel: 071–235 1230) whose *Notes for Newcomers* series features over 100 countries (£3.50 and £5 per set plus postage) and gives practical details on what to take, education, leisure activities and health etc. **Employment Conditions Abroad**, Anchor House, 15 Britten Street, London SW3 3TY (tel: 071–351 7151) is also another useful source of information.

Finance

Arrangements should be made to continue National Health Insurance contributions, as these are an extremely good investment. All financial aspects of the move should be studied and arranged before departure —tax clearance, financial regulations and exchange controls in your country of destination, investments etc. There are firms and consultancies specializing in this field eg. **The Fry Group,** Crescent House, Crescent Road, Worthing, West Sussex BN11 1RN (tel: 0903-231545)

Despatch and arrival of effects

There are many international firms who specialize in overseas removals. For those who have to make their own arrangements, it is advisable to approach more than one firm for an estimate. When travelling by air, include as many basic essentials as possible in the accompanying luggage so that you are self–sufficient for the first few days (include a few paperbacks to get through lengthy waits and sleepless nights due to jetlag).

Always ensure that personal luggage is locked and insured. Many people find airfreight the quickest, easiest and safest way of consigning goods. Lists of all contents should be available for customs clearance, shipping agents, insurance etc, and two copies of these lists should always be retained. Baggage allowances are usually generous and first entry into a country generally permits duty–free import of personal and household effects.

In many countries there is a ready sale for second–hand possessions at the end of a contract, often at advantageous prices, so it is worthwhile making full use of the allowance. There are only a few instances where what is imported must be taken away again in its entirety. Heavier items for sea freight should be crated and listed —translation into the appropriate language can often hasten customs clearance. Hiring a good local agent who knows the ropes can also be a good investment. Realistic insurance of all effects is essential.

Arrival at destination

If possible, arrange to be met at the airport, and/or have a contact telephone number. Make sure that hotel accommodation has been booked and keep all receipts for later reimbursement. Salary may be delayed so try to have some traveller's cheques to cover this eventuality. A long journey and the shock of new climatic conditions can be depressing until you are acclimatized, so use your common sense and allow yourself time to adjust. Be prepared for long delays at customs and immigration control —patience and good humour will pay dividends here. Don't judge the country by its officialdom! Do not exchange money except through official channels.

Housing

It is unlikely that permanent accommodation will be available immediately, necessitating a few day's or even week's stay in a hotel. Make use of this freedom to get acquainted with local sources of supply etc. To many expatriates, disappointment can begin with housing and furniture, which often does not match up to expectations. Reserve judgement at the beginning, because what may seem a drawback can turn out to be an advantage. There is a big difference in standards between local and expatriate employers, and there is no firm basis for comparison. In oil–rich states, it may well be that expatriate housing is much humbler than that of the nationals. On the other hand, accommodation may be very luxurious and spacious. The less fortunate expatriate should refrain from envious comparisons and, with careful thought and inexpensive ingenuity, make the best of what comes along. Work camps/compounds and high rise flats are all very real challenges to the good homemaker.

Medical care

Primary medical care is sometimes much better than one might expect, easily contacted and near at hand. Further care may be available but, if not, serious cases are flown out for emergency or specialist treatment. Large organizations often have their own hospitals, clinics and doctors. Government contracts usually provide free medical facilities. It is always wise to have a good dental check–up before departure from home. Anybody needing medication on a regular basis should take a good supply to last until an alternative source is established.

Education

Very young children are often well catered for by play groups and nursery schools. For older children there are international schools, company schools, and private or state schools. These vary considerably, but given a good school and parents who take advantage of all there is to offer in the locality, a child will have made a good start. There is often a waiting list and information about schools should be obtained and an early approach made for enrolment well ahead of departure. For those going to outlying areas, it may be necessary to consider correspondence courses eg. **World–Wide Education Service**, (35 Belgrave Square, London SW1X 8QB tel: 071-235 2880).

Many contracts provide for boarding school in the UK and regular holiday visits to parents. As the older child might well lack stimulation and local schooling might be inadequate, early consideration should be given to choosing a boarding school. It is a hard decision to take, but the partings at the end of the holidays are compensated for by the pleasure with which children look forward to travelling out to their parents at the end of term. In some expatriate communities, special events are laid on for the children, they feel special having a home overseas and the experience of travelling alone can make them more responsible, confident and resourceful. The Women's Corona Society also provides an escort service from airport to school trains etc. Children are often used as an excuse for the wife to return home, but for children at boarding school, it can be more important for them to feel that they have a solid family base than to have Mum on the doorstep.

Marriage

The move should be talked over very carefully as it can have a profound effect on a marriage. For busy working parents and weary commuters, expatriate life can be an opportunity to spend more time together as a family, and if both partners are keen, the novelty of the strange environment can be a rewarding experience. I would advise against married men taking single person's contracts or splitting the partnership for long periods of time, as it places too great a strain on communication. Starting again could help rebuild a shaky marriage, but it could also split it apart if an unwilling person is ripped away from everything familiar. So think before you move.

Single men and women

Single (or unaccompanied) men often live in camps which are isolated. They have frequent short leaves, and money to spend. A special interest —sport or hobby— gives them a chance to form stable friendships and does away with propping up the bar for company in their spare time. A single woman usually has to establish a home as well as tackling the job. However, the job, with a real and worthwhile challenge, gives her an advantage over many wives who often find themselves at sea with nothing to do but keep house. A single woman is generally in great demand in a lively social whirl, but this needs to be handled with great care. She is often an object of great interest to the local population who find it difficult to understand that she has no man to tell her what to do, and may receive many offers of marriage because of this.

Wives

While women are generally expected to be supportive of their husbands as they come to terms with a new job, it should also be remembered that they too need support and encouragement as they establish a new home, meet new people and adapt to a different lifestyle. At all times, the rules and regulations and laws of a country must be obeyed. Western women often find the new cultures and traditions difficult to embrace and inhibiting, eg. in a Muslim country, and it is essential to prepare for this. One–day briefing courses for men and women, *Living Overseas*, are run by the Women's Corona Society to counsel on adaptation to a new lifestyle and provide an opportunity to meet someone with current knowledge of their future country of residence. These courses are held at regular intervals, or on request, and cost £100 per person or £150 per couple. A telephone briefing costs £20.

Many women give up careers or interesting part–time jobs to accompany their husbands overseas, and in a number of places, there is no opportunity for them to get a job. Work permits can often be obtained in the teaching or medical professions but not always near to where the husband is posted. If your husband is with a big company, it might be worth asking them about jobs, or otherwise considering the possibilities of working on your own or doing voluntary work.

Careful planning and preparation for the use of leisure time (whether it is a result of having no outside employment or enjoying greater freedom from household duties thanks to servants) is essential to counteract boredom and initial loneliness. There are many hobbies and interests to be resurrected or embarked upon. Join groups with local knowledge eg. archeological, historical, wildlife, photographic, amateur dramatics etc. Involvement in the local scene through clubs and organizations helps understanding and leads to more tolerant attitudes towards cultural differences. Learning the language or taking a correspondence course are just two possible alternatives for the wife determined to make the most of her stay in another country.

There may be a lack of facilities and the posting may entail putting up with a number of uncongenial conditions, but there are so many other rewards to compensate. Expatriates are on the whole friendlier and less inhibited than in their home environment. In hot climates, the sun and outdoor pursuits can often make people seem more attractive and relaxed. Social life is also important as with the exception of big cities, you will frequently have to entertain yourselves. This often provides scope for great ingenuity and many find latent and surprising talents hitherto undeveloped.

In what is often a male–orientated society, it is important for the wife to cultivate her own interests, making sure of an independent identity, rather than identifying too much with her husband's job and position. And with servants, there is more time to experiment, as she is no longer saddled with the day–to–day chores involved in running the house.

Servants

The availability of domestic help brings an easier lifestyle and is recommended for hot and humid climates where your energy will be easily sapped. Many people are diffident about employing servants and don't know how to cope with them. With an initial trial period and the advice of someone who speaks the language and has kept a servant for some time, it is possible for a good relationship to be formed. Settle for a few qualities or skills suitable for the family's needs and be tolerant about other shortcomings. Establish what is wanted and agree time off. A servant who is respected becomes part of the extended family.

Lifestyle

Wherever possible try to respect local customs and laws of behaviour and dress, and be prepared for what might appear odd or rude behaviour. Cultural differences can lead to all sorts of misunderstandings so reserve judgement, take advice from happily established residents and concentrate first on personal relations. Forget efficiency and don't expect things to happen in a hurry. Polite conversation and courtesy are priorities —sincere interest, tolerance and a joke work wonders. Beware of criticizing before you've attempted to understand a situation.

Security

Security can be a problem, but common sense measures, security guards and alarm systems are used in greater or lesser degree according to local hazards. Wilful violence is rare. It is possible for the expatriate to get caught up in political reprisals, but this is fortunately very rare indeed. It is wise to register with the Consular Section of your Embassy or High Commission so they know where to find you in cases of emergency —don't wait until trouble arises as communications can be difficult.

Summary

The expatriate can suffer considerable privation through lack of consumer goods and a low standard of living, or can be handsomely rewarded with higher standards of housing and a hectic social life as well as a worthwhile job. The challenge of helping a country to develop can be very stimulating and even addictive (whatever the conditions encountered) which is why so many expatriates return overseas again and again. Friendships made abroad are often more binding and congenial, through shared experiences, than those made at home, and valuable experience in a job often leads to promotion. The tolerance and understanding of other races and cultures learned through the expatriate experience of shorter or longer duration means that life will forever afterwards be enriched.

THE EXPEDITION TRAVELLER

by Shane Winser

For many, independent travel is a daunting task, and the prospect of joining a group with a pre–determined objective is attractive. Others may feel that they wish to contribute to the peoples or environment in which they travel. The options open to such individuals are enormous: from adventure holidays to community work and scientific fieldwork overseas. The better–known and well–established groups can be found in specialist directories. It may be more difficult to get to know of smaller and/or newly–emerging groups. Almost all will require some sort of financial contribution. Don't be afraid to ask questions either about the organization itself or what your contribution covers. Try and get a feel for the organization, and if you are not happy with its overall aims or the attitudes of the people who run it, don't sign up.

There are many tour operators in Britain and abroad offering adventurous holidays which can be ideal for somebody who wants an unusual holiday. Naturally you pay to join one of these, but the preparation and responsibilities are correspondingly few. For example, the WEXAS *Discoverers* brochure has many such trips; others are advertised in the outdoor magazines and the national press. The useful *Adventure Holidays* (Vacation Work Publications, 9 Park End Street, Oxford OX1 1HJ, tel: 0865-241978) lists holidays by the type of sport or activity. In addition there are many informal groups which set out on adventurous overland journeys. Publications such as *Time Out* and the travel magazines are useful for finding out about these. However, you should beware that the informal group you team up with is not just trying to fund a holiday for themselves. However tempting the trip sounds, don't join up if you don't like or trust the people you are going to have to travel with.

Adventure holidays and genuine expeditions differ in many ways. A scientific expedition will be expected to add to human knowledge, to 'discover' something new. Those joining expeditions will usually be expected to give up considerable time to help with preparations, be whole–heartedly committed to the project's overall aim and objectives, and be capable of working as a skilled member of the team. And that is to say nothing of the efforts required to raise the necessary funds for the expedition.

In Britain, the **Royal Geographical Society** is the principal organization concerned with carrying out scientific expeditions overseas. Through the work of its Expedition Advisory Centre, the society provides information, advice and training to 500 or so groups each year —groups which carry out scientific, adventurous and youth projects abroad. For those who have a clear idea of what they want to do and have already formed themselves into groups, the centre has a number of important services including the annual *Planning a Small Expedition* seminar and the *Expedition Planners' Handbook and Directory*.

Many of the groups helped by the centre are from schools and universities as the principle of outdoor adventure and challenge is widely accepted as an important training ground both for young people and potential managers alike. As a result a number of charitable and commercial organisations now offer expeditions to people of a wide age range. The Expedition Advisory Centre publishes a directory of these entitled *Joining an Expedition*. The directory includes advice on choosing an appropriate project and ideas for raising funds to join projects. Individuals with special skills to offer —doctors, nurses, mechanics, scientists— may be invited to join the register of personnel available for expeditions which is maintained by the centre and used by expedition organizers to recruit skilled individuals.

Two of the longest established expeditionary bodies include the **Brathay Exploration Group**, Brathay Hall, Ambleside, Cumbria LA22 0HP (tel: 05394 33942) which sends out several expeditions each year both in the UK and abroad, with members tending to be between the ages of 17 and 25. **The British Schools Exploring Society** (BSES), 1 Kensington Gore, London SW7 2AR (tel: 071–584 0710) organizes six week–long expeditions for 17 to 20–year–olds during the summer holidays and six, month–long expeditions for those in their 'gap' year between school and university. BSES has always had a strong scientific component to its work and provides useful training for those hoping to go and organise their own expedition.

With public concern for the environment now widespread, a number of other organisations offer a chance to carry out useful fieldwork overseas. Among them are the **British Trust for Conservation Volunteers** (36 St Mary's Street, Wallingford, Oxfordshire OX10 0EU, tel: 0491 39766) which has links with many similar organisations in Europe; the **Field Studies Council Overseas Expeditions** (Montford Bridge, Shrewsbury SY4 1HW, tel: 0743 850164); **Frontier** (77 Leonard Street, London EC2A 4QS, tel: 071-613 2422) run conservation programmes in Tanzania, Uganda and Vietnam; **Trekforce Expeditions** (134 Buckingham Palace Road, London SW1W 9SA, tel: 071-824

8890) organises six-week projects in the remote tropical forests of Indonesia and the **Coral Cay Conservation Programme** (The Ivy Works, 154 Clapham Park Road, London SW4 7DE, tel: 071-498 6248) which recruits qualified divers to help monitor the reefs in a marine reserve off the coast of Belize.

Raleigh International (27 Parsons Green Lane, London SW6 4HZ, tel: 071-371 8585) regularly recruits 17-25 year olds to take part in demanding community projects and conservation programmes lasting up to 12 weeks.

For budding archaeologists, **Archaeology Abroad** (31–34 Gordon Square, London WC1H 0PY) helps directors of overseas excavations find suitable personnel through its bulletins.

Whilst **Earthwatch Europe** (Belsyre Court, 57 Woodstock Road, Oxford OX2 6HU, tel: 0865 311600) matches paying volunteers with scientists who need their help to study threatened habitats, save endangered species and document our changing environmental heritage. Volunteers do not need to have any special skills to join expeditions and anyone aged 16 to 75 may apply once they have become members (£25 annual subscription including a bi–monthly club magazine). Their short two to three–week expeditions cost from £415 (plus travel expenses) and include full board and field expenses.

Those with medical skills to offer might like to contact Health Projects Abroad (HMS President, Victoria Embankment, London EC4Y 0HJ, tel: 071-583 5725) who publish a useful booklet, the *HPA Guide to Voluntary Nursing Overseas* and recruits unskilled volunteers for health-related projects in Tanzania. **The International Health Exchange**, (Africa Centre, 38 King Street, London WC2E 8JT, tel: 071-836 5833) maintains a register of health care professionals wanting to work in developing countries, publishes job vacancies and runs training courses.

It is possible to travel in a group and never make contact with the people of the countries you pass through. **The Experiment in International Living** (Otesga, West Malvern Road, Malvern, Worcs. WR14 4EN, tel: 0684-562577) arranges home-stay programmes for both individuals and groups. Whilst **The Commonwealth Youth Exchange Council** promotes contact between groups of young people of the Commonwealth by funding visits by groups from Britain to an overseas Commonwealth country or vice versa. In order to attract Council funding, the programme must be useful in its own right and involve contact between visitors and hosts, preferably including joint activities. The aim is 'to provide meaningful contact and better understanding between Commonwealth young people' and if possible should lead to a continuing two–way link. Visits must be arranged through an established organization and led by a responsible person. Two–thirds of each group must consist of people aged between 15 and 25 years. Further information is available from the Executive Secretary, CYEC, 7 Lion Yard, Tremadoc Road, SW4 7NQ (tel: 071– 498 6151).

Those wishing to work or study abroad without necessarily joining an expedition should consult **The Central Bureau** , Seymour Mews House, Seymour Mews (off Wigmore Street), London W1H 9PE (tel: 071–486 5101) whose publications are extremely useful. The Bureau, which also has offices in Edinburgh and Belfast, has details of jobs, study opportunities, youth organizations and holidays in some 60 countries. *A Year Off*, published by CRAC Publications, Hobsons Press (Cambridge) Ltd, Bateman Street, Cambridge

CB2 1LZ (tel: 0223 354551) provides information about voluntary service, work camps and summer projects, paid work, au pair work, study courses, scholarships and travel, adventure and expeditions. Aimed at people with time to spare between school and higher education, it discusses the pros and cons of using that year in this special way, giving the views of both students and career experts.

Study Abroad, published by UNESCO, 7 Place de Fontenoy, Paris 75007, France and available from HMSO, PO Box 276, London SW8 5DT, describes some 2600 opportunities for post–secondary study in all academic and professional fields and lists details of scholarships, assistantships, travel grants and other forms of financial assistance available.

Vacation Work Publications of 9 Park End Street, Oxford OX1 1HJ (tel: 0865 241978) publishes many guides and directories for those seeking permanent jobs or summer jobs abroad, unusual travel opportunities, voluntary work and working travel. Often travel for its own sake seems insufficient for those who wish to provide practical help for locals in the country they are to visit.

If you feel that you have both the time and the specialist skills needed to be a volunteer, you should probably start by reading two very helpful directories: *Volunteer Work* (Central Bureau) and/or *The International Directory of Voluntary Work* (Vacation Work). Both books give an outline of the organizations who are willing and able to accept volunteer workers on overseas projects and the skill and commitment required of the volunteer.

At this stage you should be aware that the majority of host countries who welcome volunteers usually require skilled personnel such as nurses, teachers, agronomists and civil engineers. They may be unable to pay even your airfares (although many provide board and lodging) and you may be expected to help for at least one or two years. Remember that during that time you probably won't be travelling but will be based in a poor urban community or remote rural village.

If you feel that you are suitably qualified and have the emotional maturity to be a volunteer you may like to discuss your hopes and ambitions to serve with someone who has already been one. You can contact an ex–volunteer through their own organization: **Returned Volunteer Action**, 1 Amwell Street, London EC1R 1UL (tel: 071–278 0804) which maintains a register of volunteers who have served on projects in many different areas of the world. They may even be able to direct you personally to an organization which is appropriate to both your and their needs. Their information pack *Thinking About Volunteering* is very frank about some of the problems you may face before and after you have been a volunteer. The organization produces a full range of publications so call for more details.

Finding the right organization to suit you can take time, so don't expect to leave next week. The four main agencies who send out volunteers from the UK as part of the British Government's Overseas Aid Programme are: **The International Cooperation for Development (ICD)**, **Skillshare Africa**, **United Nations Association International Service** (UNAIS) and **Voluntary Service Overseas** (VSO). Over 400 volunteers go abroad each year through these organizations, all are over 21 with professional work experience.

If you wish to apply to work for an international aid organization then the

International Recruitment and Index Service of the Overseas Development Administration, Abercrombie House, Eaglesham Road, East Kilbride, Glasgow G75 8EA (tel: 035 52 843414) will be able to advise you through its booklets *Why Not Serve Overseas?* and *Opportunities Overseas with International Organizations*.

THE LUXURY TRAVELLER
by Caroline Brandenburger

The notion of luxury has become one of abused and relative value in recent years (*luxury* loo paper, *luxury* shortbread) but there still remain a few absolutes —many of them to be found in the area of travel. You may choose to travel luxuriously simply because you enjoy luxury or because you feel the rigours of the backpacking trip are beyond you. Sometimes you may combine the two — there is nothing more wonderful than to sink gratefully into the arms of comfort when life has been rather spartan.

Cruising

Cruising can be an exceptionally luxurious way to travel. **The Cruise Advisory Service** (35 Blue Boar Row, Salisbury, Wiltshire SP1 1DA, tel: 0722–335505) is an organization without affiliation to any shipping companies and can provide you with unbiased advice. The advisory service will supply you with a general information pack and, based on its own independent surveys, will give ratings out of 10 for the services of different cruise lines (cabin comfort, food etc). Once you have decided what you want, they will also handle your booking.

One unfailingly popular liner is, of course, the QE2 which journeys regularly from Southampton to New York, as well as following a number of other worldwide routings. Although one of the world's largest passenger ships, the QE2 provides one crew member for every two passengers. The crew will endeavour (within reason!) to satisfy your every whim, whether it be breakfast in bed or a private cocktail party in your stateroom. Facilities range from a designer label–strewn shopping mall to a theatre, four swimming pools, a health club, seven bars and two dance halls.

Nonetheless, the Cruise Advisory Service only rates the QE2 as a Four Star liner (the top rating is Five Star de Luxe). Few companies still provide unadulterated Five Star luxury, but the last surviving cruise companies which do include the Royal Viking Line, Cunard (Sea Goddess 1 and 2), the Seabourn Line, Crystal Cruises and the new Silversea Cruises. Ships like these carry far fewer passengers, and tend to rely on what is now considered old–fashioned attention to detail and service —as well as sumptuously comfortable suites in place of cabins.

Seriously luxurious liners will boast an endless variety of entertainments (multi–gyms, beauty salons, casinos, formal dinners) to keep passengers happy. With Seabourn you can find yourself dining at the Captain's table or al fresco on deck, you can pump iron in the fitness centre or languish in your suite watching videos. Renaissance promises you expert lectures on the local cultures you'll encounter when you put into shore, and after lolling in the ship's library you can luxuriate in the jacuzzi.

Preparations for a Royal Viking cruise may include a shopping spree at Harvey Nichols whose Complimentary Personal Shopping Service offers discounts to Royal Viking passengers cruising for longer than a set period. On board, you'll find herbal massages, tennis and clay–pigeon shooting.

Rail

Whether our impression of luxury train travel has been formed by Agatha Christie's Murder on the Orient Express, or Queen Victoria's blue, velvet–lined personal carriage (now in the London Transport Museum) the reality we generally find is far removed. However, there are a few (and, surprisingly, increasing) opportunities to experience something rather more sumptuous than the Intercity 125 and Traveller's Fare.

A journey on the Venice Simplon **Orient Express** is one way to indulge yourself. The service was discontinued at the end of the 1970s but when two of the carriages came up for sale at Sotheby's in Monte Carlo, they were bought by James Sherwood, President of Sea Containers. He then tracked down more of the carriages, in various states of disrepair and decay, and had them lavishly restored. The wooden panelled interiors and elaborate marquetry now set the scene for the journey from London to Venice (with the option for side trips on the local railway service to cities such as Innsbruck and Cologne). En route you are waited on by gloved attendants, quaff champagne, consume exquisite multiple course meals, and sleep in plush, exquisitely comfortable cabins. If you are feeling slightly less flush, take a day trip! These run to a variety of destinations, ranging from Leeds Castle in Kent, to Bath, Bristol, Chatsworth and Canterbury.

If you are travelling between Cape Town and Pretoria (or vice–versa), as a luxury junkie you can do little better than to ride the **Blue Train**. Cited by experts as the very last of the authentic great trains (it is still part of the national rail system, rather than owned by a private company) it runs for 1600km, during May, June and July only. You travel in a train that is carpeted, air conditioned and boasting well–appointed suites and couchettes, and you will eat splendidly in a dining car which looks out onto the intensely dramatic terrain that characterizes the journey There is also the possibility of a 'steam safari' with **Rovos Rail**, which runs a luxury train through 1000km of the Eastern Transvaal, including a night in a private game reserve. Meanwhile in Zimbabwe, there is the **Zambezi Special**, which runs from Bulawayo to Victoria Falls, through wildlife areas and great forests.

The **Indian–Pacific** travels the huge distance of 4348 km between Sydney and Perth, via Adelaide, and bridges the two oceans of its name. Passing through varied sections of Australian scenery —mountains, wheat fields and rocky plains— you will sip Australian wine in the lounge car to the accompaniment of live music.

'The Palace on Wheels' as the **Rajasthan Express** has been called, is a collection of carriages dating from 1898 to 1937, built to the luxurious specifications of Rajasthan's maharajahs. The train is pulled alternately by diesel engine

From 16 April 1995 all national and international codes change —see page 587 for details.

and steam and begins in Delhi for a seven–day tour of the princely region of Rajasthan. You travel in the regal splendour of velvet-upholstered compartments appointed with brass fittings and eat a choice of Indian or European cuisine while being kept cool under the dining car's numerous spinning fans. Cox and Kings Ltd operate trips which include a stay in Delhi.

In 1992 the Venice Simplon Orient Express extended its network further East with the launch of the **Eastern & Oriental Express**. Travelling from Singapore to Bangkok, the 1243–mile journey takes 42 hours. The carriages, originally built for the New Zealand train, Silver Fern, are decorated with traditional wood carvings, silks and batiks. While local musicians play in the dining cars, fortune tellers predict your future and hostesses who later act as guides, explain the cultural traditions of the region.

Air travel

If time is a factor in your travel plans but you still want to travel with the maximum comfort, you have two options. If you're going to New York, you can travel by **Concorde**. (Anywhere else in the world, pick a good airline and travel business class or first if your budget will stretch that far.) Concorde is not only swift (you arrive five minutes after you leave!) and cuts down the jet lag, but has other advantages too. With its plush grey interior, iced bottles of Mumm champagne and gentleman's club ambience, you can strike deals with captains of industry (Lord Weidenfeld, the publisher, says seven minutes of 'meaningful conversation' on Concorde always does the trick) and star spot at the same time.

As to the best airlines, opinions vary. Different companies attract fans for different reasons. If you are travelling first class, Air France and Cathay Pacific score on the gastronomic front, while Lufthansa's efficiency is superlative and British Airways' attentiveness is refreshing. However, Philippine Airways have rather trounced the competition in one respect by introducing full–length beds in their first class cabins —this really does soften the blow of long–haul trips.

Hotels

The Oriental in Bangkok is probably one of the world's best known luxury hotels. Certainly the grandest in Bangkok, it overlooks the Chao Phyra River and is a combination of old colonial, and plush new marbled extensions. The Oriental has traditionally been a stopping place for royalty, politicians, artists, and numerous writers ranging from Joseph Conrad to Noel Coward and Graham Greene. The hotel's 394 exotically–appointed rooms, decorated with bowls of fresh orchids, are served by a staff of over a 1000.

Venice's **Cipriani** is utterly redolent of luxury. Those who have seen Death in Venice will remember the hero's arrival at the Cipriani by launch, and this is exactly how guests still arrive today. Apart from its extraordinary three–acre site on the Giudecca Island, beautiful gardens and the only swimming pool and tennis court in central Venice, the Cipriani is remarkable for the elegance of its rooms, Venetian glass chandeliers and Empire sofas. At the same time, you can gorge yourself on exquisite pasta and luscious cakes which are made every day by a busy teams of chefs.

The Four Seasons in Hamburg is unusual for having remained a private hotel, and is without doubt the best hotel in Germany. Renowned for its genuine, country–house ambience, it boasts luxuriant wooden panelling, tapestries and excellent antiques offset against impeccable service.

The **Oberoi** in New Delhi is the city's most modern hotel. With its polished, granite lobby, lush gardens and rooms decorated in subtle, eye–soothing colours, you can eat the best French food as well as indigenous cuisine.

London's newest, most lavish hotel is **The Lanesborough** at Hyde Park Corner. With more silk swags per square inch than one might think possible, it is utterly sumptuous and larger-than-life. Hard to believe it used to be St.George's Hospital, budget per room for the interior decor was rumoured to be £2 million.

Villas

Luxury villas can be very pleasantly self–indulgent places to stay. Whether Greece, Portugal or the Caribbean, they can provide you with not only excellent accommodation, but also staff to cook and clean for you, private swimming pools, and the use of a jeep and power boat. **Bears House** in Barbados, for example, comes with a butler, cook, laundress, maid and gardener, four bedrooms with bathrooms en suite, and a huge private pool. Two excellent companies who can help you to find sumptuous villas to stay in are CV Travel (tel: 071-581 0851) and Magic of Italy (tel: 081-748 4999). If you really want to spend time luxuriously and also in seclusion, then an island may be the answer. Mauritius, the Caribbean, the Seychelles all have islands for hire. Abercrombie & Kent (tel: 071-730 9600) can organize this ultimate archipelagic experience for you.

Safaris

The very best safaris are generally to be found in East Africa —Kenya and Tanzania. While other countries, such as Zimbabwe and Botswana, offer luxury safaris, they tend to mean staying in lodges rather than tents. **Safari Consultants** (Orchard House, Upper Road, Little Conard, Suffolk CO10 0NZ, tel: 0787-228494) are able to organize a tailor–made safari to suit your inclinations and requirements. Luxury in the context of a safari, say Safari Consultants, is a maximum of four people per vehicle, large, walk–in tents with proper beds, wash basins, en suite toilets and hot showers, and about 14 staff (excluding guides) to care for eight guests (providing constant iced drinks and three or four–course meals). In other words, every moment that is not spent observing the wildlife is as pampered as they can possibly make it!

THE SPECIAL INTEREST TRAVELLER

by Frank Barrett

The concept of a 'special interest' traveller suggests a weird, eccentric individual wearing plus fours and in determined possession of a butterfly net. His only purpose in travelling is to go to the rainforests of Venezuela in search of something like the lesser crested newt. To talk about 'special interest' travellers seems to suggest that the world is divided into those travellers who have 'special interests' and those who do not. That while the odd–ball with the butterfly–net is up to his waist in a swamp, the rest of us are stretched out on a Spanish beach wading through nothing more treacherous than the latest Jeffery Archer.

The truth is, of course, that potentially we are all special interest travellers. Fewer and fewer of us set off abroad these days with the aim of simply acquiring a sun–tan that disappears in the bath a week after we return.

We travel abroad for many reasons: some go simply from a desire to see the world, others have more specific reasons. It is the people with the more specific reasons that one would probably call the 'special interest' traveller. But while there are many people who are interested in wine, and travel on specific wine tours to Bordeaux or Burgundy, there are many more who on a family holiday to France will find time to visit a vineyard to do a little wine tasting.

Are those in the first category any more of a special interest traveller than those in the second? Although the market for special interest holidays grew dramatically at the end of the 1980's, it is an area that has been hit, not only by the recession but also the EU regulations. However there are still many companies that deal with special interests in hundred of subjects that will have a package available to suit the need of any traveller.

The advantages of buying a specific special interest package from a specialist operator is partly convenience. If you want to visit all the archeological treasures of Turkey, for example, a package tour will relieve you of the trouble of organizing flights, accommodation and transport from place to place. The question of whether it is cheaper to buy such a holiday as a package rather than travelling independently, is up to you to decide. It is hard to make a sensible comparison since it is almost impossible to compare like with like. If your idea of a holiday involves hitchhiking and backpacking, then any tour operator package will probably prove more expensive.

By travelling on a special interest package, you will be travelling with people who share your special interest – this is particularly attractive to single people keen to mix with a crowd. A special interest tour is also likely to have an expert guide who might be able to offer an entry into places not normally open to the individual traveller. As an expert he may also prove to be a source of interesting information, anecdotes, useful history etc.

The only problem about special interest tour operators is finding the one you want. The mainstream travel industry in the UK largely exists to sell bland mass market sun and sand holidays. Travel agents are increasingly 'holiday shops.' Their stock in trade is selling packages to identikit resorts on the Mediterranean. If you want to go walking in the Himalaya, white–water rafting in Colorado, mountain biking in the Alps or take an art tour through Tuscany, they don't want to know. If it's not in a brochure of one of the big operators (and a brochure from their small preferred list of suppliers), they can tell you nothing. The retail trade has become a loose–knit cartel which now only seems to want to promote the biggest and blandest companies, taking almost no account of the changing taste of the public.

Although Britain boasts over 1000 companies offering holidays abroad in one form or another (and more than 700 companies licensed by the Civil Aviation Authority to sell airfare–inclusive charter holidays) most travel agents stock the brochure of no more than 100 companies, and probably fewer than half of these are actually displayed on the agents' shelves.

To find the holidays you want —and the holiday company you need— can require a substantial amount of research. While the normal common–of–garden high street travel agency may not be able to help, there is a new brand of agency which sees itself as a travel adviser rather than simply a travel agent.

If you can't find an agency which will help, you will have to do your own research. The best sources of information to check are the classified advertisement columns of the national newspapers: *The Sunday Times*, *The Observer*, *The Daily Telegraph*, *The Independent* etc.

Another major source of likely leads for special interest holidays will be the special interest magazines. If you are looking for a steam train holiday, for example, check the small ads of the railway magazines read by steam train enthusiasts. Increasingly, many of the specialist magazines now organize their own special interest holidays for readers. Another possible alternative is to consult the relevant tourist offices. Some tourist offices are hopeless; they see their role simply as distributing glossy leaflets and irrelevant brochures; but some are a mine of useful information and advice, such as the Australian Tourist Commission. Many compile lists of tour operators which offer holidays to their countries – with descriptions of the types of holiday they offer, for example, the Falkland Islands Tourist Office sends out a list which includes Major R N Spafford who amongst other things organises tours to the Islands for philatelists —for budding stamp collectors more information can be found in the Directory under Section 3.

It's worth spending some time trying to find a suitable package for one of the important advantages of buying an inclusive package is that it may offer consumer protection in the event of the company going out of business. Many assume that to be sure of protection you have to buy your package from a member of the Association of British Travel Agents. This is not true; you don't have to be an ABTA member to be bonded in this way, although the EU law now requires all tour organisers to offer financial protection and the Civil Aviation Authority has its own bonding arrangements for holders of an Air Tour Organizer Licence (ATOL) —many of whom are not members of ABTA. Similarly it is a requirement of the Association of Independent Tour Operators (AITO) that companies are bonded.

Before you book a package or any sort of travel, therefore, one of the first things you should check is whether your trip is protected; if the tour operator or travel agency were to go out of business, ask the question 'Will I get my money back?' To be absolutely sure of protection, pay by credit card (Access or Visa; not American Express or Diners Club). If the holiday costs more than £100 and the credit payment has been made direct to the tour operator, the credit card company will have to refund the whole amount if the tour operator goes bust.

If you can't find a tour operator that sells the sort of special interest holiday you want, you will have to organize your own trip. The advantages of travelling independently are that you suit yourself rather than a party of other people. If you want to spend more time in a particular place, you can do so; you move at your own pace. You choose the hotels you want, and the means of transport. And if the arrangements are fouled up, you have only yourself to blame. If in the middle of it all, you tire of hunting for the lesser crested newt and you choose to hang up your butterfly net, you can simply retire to your Jeffery Archer novel and sit in the sun. Further information can be found in the Directory.

THE WORKING TRAVELLER
by Susan Griffith

Camels, trains and sailing boats have their peculiar advantages as means of travelling to the far corners of the globe. But there may be times when you will decide to stop for a rest, or choose to absorb the atmosphere in one setting. Working is one way of getting inside a foreign culture, though the kind of job you find will determine the stratum of society which you will experience. The traveller who spends a few weeks picking olives for a Cretan farmer will get a very different insight from the traveller who looks after the children of a wealthy Athenian businessman. Yet both will have the chance to participate temporarily in the life of a culture rather than merely to observe.

Financial considerations are usually the traveller's immediate impetus to look for work. To postpone having to cash the last traveller's cheque, many begin to look around for ways of prolonging their trip. They may find paid work (though few of the jobs which travellers undertake will make them rich) or they may decide to volunteer their labour in exchange for a bed and food —by planting trees on a Lesotho work camp or digging for Biblical remains in Israel.

While the sole ambition of some is to extend their travels, others go abroad specifically in search of highly-paid jobs. This is easier for people with acknowledged qualifications such as nurses and agronomists, divers and pipe–fitters who often do find better-paid opportunities abroad than they would at home. A few might even have their future career prospects in view when they go abroad to teach English as a foreign language or drive a combine harvester. But the majority are trying to put off or escape from career decisions.

Even the unskilled can find jobs which pay high wages. The high minimum wage in Denmark, for example, means that a chambermaid or a strawberry picker can earn enough in a short time to fund long periods of travel. In Japan, the demand for university graduates (of any subject) willing to give English lessons is so great that many foreigners earn an average of US$30 an hour and work as many hours as their stamina will allow. Some Japanese language schools even pay the airfares of teachers whom they recruit abroad. Similarly American organizations pay the airfares of thousands of young people who go to the US each summer to instruct and care for children staying on summer camps (although in this case the advanced airfare is subtracted from the counsellor's total wage which is modest even at the outset). Paid fares are a rarity no matter what job you find. One very helpful organisation is **Vacation Work,** 9 Park End Street, Oxford OX1 1HJ, Tel: 0865 241978, they have a huge amount of experience and information.

Seasonal work

Jobs which are seasonal in nature are those which travellers are most likely to find. Unemployment statistics barely concern themselves with this large and important sector of the economy. In times of recession the number of temporary jobs available may even increase since employers are less eager to expand their regular staff but will need extra help at busy times.

The two categories of employment which appeal most to travellers (and least to a stable working population) are agriculture and tourism. Many farmers from the south of France to the north of Tasmania (with the notable exception of the developing world) cannot bring in their harvests without assistance from outside their vicinity. Similarly the tourist trade in many areas could not survive without a short term injection of seasonal labour.

These economic facts may provide little consolation to the hopeful job–seeker who finds that all the hotels in town are already staffed by local students or that all the fruit is traditionally picked by itinerant Mexicans or Moroccans. Nevertheless, farmers and hotel/restaurant managers remain the best potential sources of employment. It should be noted that work in rural areas normally permits more genuine contact with natives of the country than jobs in tourist resorts where you could find yourself dealing mainly with your fellow countrymen.

English teaching is more specialized and normally requires a nine–month commitment, though there are many countries in the world where it is possible to find work and earn reasonable wages armed only with fluency in the language and a neat appearance. You need only learn the words "English Language School" in the relevant language before you can make use of the Yellow Pages and begin a school–to–school job search. This is unlikely to be productive in countries where English is widely taught and spoken (India, the Netherlands, etc) but can be surprisingly effective in many other countries (Spain, Taiwan, Mexico and so on).

It is not easy to look up 'domestic', 'au pair' or 'live–in' positions in the Yellow Pages. But young women (mainly, but not only, women) who desire the security of a family placement and who may also wish to learn a European language, often choose to work with children for little money. Such positions can be found on the spot or in advance through a relevant agency, notice board or by means of an advertisement.

Volunteering

It would be wrong, of course, to assume that the love (or shortage) of money is at the root of all decisions to work abroad. Paid work in developing nations is available only exceptionally, and yet many arrange to live for next to nothing by doing something positive. For example, enterprising travellers visiting everywhere from Poland to Thailand have been welcomed into the homes of locals who are eager to share long–term hospitality in exchange for informal lessons in English. More structured voluntary opportunities exist worldwide and there are many charities and organizations which can introduce you to interesting projects such as helping a local Indian settlement to build a community centre in Northern Canada, establishing an organic farm near a tribal longhouse in Sarawak or helping in Mother Theresa's Home for Dying Destitutes in Calcutta. There is also the possibility of aid work. With the world continuing to be an unstable place, many war zones or natural disasters areas need aid workers. It is worth contacting the personnel department at the **British Red Cross** tel: **071-235 5454**, or other charities such as **Oxfam** tel: **0865 311 311, Voluntary Services Overseas** tel: **081-780 2266**, and **Save the Children,** (two years overseas experience in a developing country is required) tel: **071-703 5400**. Be warned, this kind of work can be very emotionally challenging, do not undertake it lightly.

Many such organizations require more than a traveller's curiosity about a country; they require a strong wish to become involved in a specific project and, in many cases, an ideological commitment. The fact that few of them can offer any travel or even living expenses deters the uncommitted.

Planning in advance

Some travellers are fortunate enough to fix up a job in advance. This means that they can be reasonably assured of an immediate income once they have arrived. The traveller who sets off without a pre–arranged job has less security, and should take sufficient reserves in case his or her job search fails. In the course of my research, I have met many examples of the fearless traveller who is prepared to arrive in Marseilles, Mexico City or even New York with a few dollars and no guaranteed job prospects. They have remained confident that it will be possible to work their way out of their penury. In most cases they have done just that, though not without experiencing a few moments of panic and desperation. It goes without saying that this situation is best avoided, for it may result in your being forced to take an undesirable job with exploitative conditions, or to go into debt to the folks back home.

There are many organizations, both public and private, charitable and commercial, student and general, which can offer advice and practical assistance to those who wish to fix up a job before leaving home. Some accept a tiny handful of individuals who satisfy stringent requirements; others such as the organizations which recruit voluntary staff for scientific expeditions, accept anyone who is willing to pay the required fee. School and university careers counsellors are often a good source of information, as are newspaper advertisements and the specialist literature.

The work schemes and official exchanges which do exist require a large measure of advance planning. It is not unusual for an application deadline to be six to nine months before the starting date of the scheme.

Red tape

One of the possible advantages of fixing up a job well in advance is that you then have a chance of obtaining the appropriate work permit. Almost every country of the world has legislation to prohibit foreigners from taking jobs from nationals (although citizens of EEC countries can work freely throughout the post–1992 Community). Furthermore, few countries —apart from the newly–welcoming Eastern European countries— will process visas unless applications are lodged outside the country. For example, teachers of EFL (English as a Foreign Language) can usually sort out their visas or at least set the wheels in motion before arrival in Korea, Turkey, Indonesia, Morocco or wherever. This is one area of employment in which governments are relatively generous since locals are not being deprived of jobs.

The support of an employer is virtually always a pre–requisite for conducting a job hunt at a distance. Assuming you are not eligible for one of the special holiday job visas (available in Australia, the US, Canada, Norway, Finland, etc), the ideal arrangement may be to travel to your chosen destination on a tourist visa, persuade an employer to hire you and then leave the country to apply for a work permit. This method has the significant advantage of making it possible for employers to interview you and for you to see the potential work situation at first hand before committing yourself.

Yet it has to be admitted that temporary jobs like cherry–picking and hamburger–making will never qualify you for a work permit. This problem bedevils working travellers and inevitably weakens their position if things go wrong. Sometimes the only recourse which travellers have if they find themselves being exploited is to leave and look for something more congenial. 'Easy come easy go' becomes the motto of many travellers who pick up casual work along their route.

Improving your chances

A number of specific steps will improve your chances either of being accepted on an organized work scheme or of convincing an employer in person of your superiority to the competition. For example, before leaving home you might take a short course in teaching English as a foreign language, cooking, word processing or sailing —all skills which are marketable around the world. If you are very serious, you might learn (or improve) a foreign language or you might simply undertake to get fit.

Contacts, however remote, can be valuable allies. Everyone has ways of developing links with people abroad, even if he or she is not lucky enough to have friends and family scattered around the world. Pen friends, fellow members of travel clubs and foreign students or visitors met in your home town might be able to help you find your feet in a foreign country. Try and publicize your plans as widely as possible since the more people there are aware of your willingness to work, the better the chance of a lead. Once you actually embark, you will be grateful for any extra preparation you have made.

Even if you set off without an address book full of contacts, it is not difficult to meet people along the way. Your fellow travellers are undoubtedly the best source of information on job prospects. Youth hostels can be a gold mine for the job seeker; there may even be jobs advertised on the notice board. Any local you meet is a potential source of help, whether a driver who gives you a lift while hitchhiking or members of a local club which interests you, such as cycling or jazz. The expatriate community might also be willing to help, and can be met in certain bars, at the English–speaking church, at the Embassy library, etc.

Of course, not all jobs are found by word–of–mouth or through contacts. Local English language newspapers like the *Anglo–Portugese News* or the *Bangkok Post* may carry job advertisements appropriate to your situation, or may be a good publication for placing an advert. The most effective method is to walk in and ask. You may have to exaggerate the amount of experience you have had and to display a little more bravado than comes naturally to you.

Persistence, optimism and resilience are essential for such a venture, since on occasion it may be necessary to pester 40 restaurant managers before one will offer you a job as dishwasher, or to visit the offices of an employment agency on many consecutive days before your eagerness will be rewarded. With such determination, it is indeed possible to work your way around the world.

THE BUSINESS TRAVELLER

by David Churchill

The post-recession executive is a very different traveller from the free-spending international jetsetter of the late 1980s. The Gulf War and bitter recession has produced a marked shift in both corporate and individual attitude towards travelling on business. Gone are the hedonistic days when business travellers would only fly in business or first class, stay in five-star luxury hotels (and probably in a suite as well) and treat their charge card as a golden key to having a good time at somebody else's expense.

Tight budgets during the recession have meant that travelling on business has increasingly had to be justified; no longer a perk, it is seen as a crucial part of the marketing mix to win and keep new business. Those travellers who were given the go-ahead to travel during lean times also had to get used to flying at the back of the 'plane and staying in hotels that has fewer stars than they were used to.

Even though the economic position has eased, companies are still keeping a tight rein on travel costs. According to American Express which regularly monitors corporate spending on business travel, the total spent last year by executives away from home came to £19.2bn. While this was the second highest figure recorded by Amex in the six biennial surveys it has undertaken, the highest being the £20bn spent in 1989, in real terms corporate expenditure in this area is still only at the level of the mid-1980s.

Significantly, the responsibility for managing business travel within companies has shifted from *ad hoc* arrangements, usually involving secretaries or as a part-time job for the personnel manager, to the responsibility of purchasing and supply departments who are used to making hard-headed buying decisions. This can make it even more difficult for the individual executive, who has to actually travel to do business on the company's behalf, to arrive in good enough shape to perform at his or her best.

Not surprisingly, suppliers of business travel —notably the airlines, hotels and car rental companies and the business travel agents who manage the travel —are all seeking to woo the business traveller as never before. The frequent flyer scheme pioneered by US airlines and now a feature of virtually all international carriers have, for example, been emulated by the leading international hotel chains which now offer similar programmes for frequent guests. American Express has entered the fray as well with its Membership Miles scheme, giving both airline and hotel points according to how much its charge card is used.

But some of these schemes to woo the business traveller have more than a hint of desperation about them and may, in fact, have overlooked the fact that the psychological profile of the frequent business traveller in the mid 1980s has changed.

For many executives, the joy of travelling at someone else's expense is beginning to pall, giving the reality of modern-day travel and the sheer hassle of getting from city to city. What business travellers worry about most when away from their offices is their lack of control: within their organisation their status is fixed and taken for granted; away from their office, they feel threatened by a lack of recognition and their inability to shape and control events.

These travellers, therefore, are less concerned with the in-flight pampering that features so heavily in airline advertising and are more interested in getting to their destinations on time. This is particularly important on shorter European flights, where even a slight delay can mean missed appointments. Surveys of executive travellers show that the airline schedule and punctuality record are among the most important factors when choosing an airline, not the quality of catering or calibre of airlines business lounges.

Yet it is simply because the airlines have so little effective control over departure and arrival times, due to such vagaries as the weather and intransigence of some air traffic controllers, that they spend millions of such 'gimmicks' as, for example, British Airways's new arrivals lounge at Heathrow's Terminal Four, which provides showers and changing rooms for some arriving business class passengers. As worthwhile as it may be to freshen up on arrival, most business passengers would prefer to be guaranteed of their arrival time instead.

The psychological change in post-recession business travellers, moreover, extends to a reluctance to be away from home and family. An Official Airlines Guide survey of nearly 1,000 frequent flyers found that two-thirds gave as their motivation for travel not their work or careers but helping to provide a better life for their families left behind. "Although travelling on long trips, often with extensive itineraries, their hearts remain at home," the survey suggested.

Hyatt Hotels, in a survey of over 300 regular European business travellers, also found that many preferred to spend more time in their hotel rooms when abroad. The highest accolade they could give a hotel was that it "felt just like home". When asked what extra feature they would like to see in hotel rooms of the future, the top answer was a microwave oven: one participant said that his ideal, even in a hotel while on business would be "to cook beans on toast in my room and be zonked out in front of the television."

It is hardly surprising, therefore, that one of the fastest-growing areas of the hotel business across Europe —it is already big business in the US —are apartment hotels which provide limited catering facilities and more space than average. London recently opened what was claimed to be the first purpose-built apartment hotel in the capital aimed at business travellers: the Orion City apartment hotel, close to the Barbican. Each of the 129 studios and apartments has a kitchenette and there are laundry and business facilities within the hotel building. French hotel group Orion already has similar apartment hotels in Paris and Brussels and plans to open new ones in several other European cities, including Lisbon, Prague, Barcelona and Berlin.

Getting a better deal from business travel, therefore, is increasingly the name of the game. What should the savvy business traveller look out for?

Most attention is now being focused on how to achieve a seamless, efficient service at lowest cost. One sound approach is to make use of a specialist business travel agency, such as the majors (Amex, Thomas Cook, Carlson Wagonlit and Hogg Robinson) or one of the many independent agencies which concentrate on business travel. Most are members of the Guild of Business Travel Agents (tel: 071-222 2744) and have access to consolidated air fares and special deals on hotels and car rental.

An alternative for individual business travellers is the WEXAS Gold Card membership which provides a range of special services and other benefits for the business traveller who does not have —or want to use — a travel agency.

In theory a specialist business travel agency should always be able to get you the best deal but, in practice, poorly informed staff and mistakes with ticketing and bookings do occur. Two pieces of advice: if you find a good travel agent (preferably an individual within an agency) then stick with them; and, remember that the best travel agent is likely to be yourself. While an agent may be able to obtain a corporate hotel rate for you and your company, you may be able to negotiate a better deal directly with a hotel. Depending on the season and availability, a hotel may quote you a better rate than they will offer all year round as a corporate rate.

A good travel agent should also be able to help you with add-on benefits, such as higher grade room or suite and a free breakfast with newspaper. Most hotels are seeking to woo business travellers onto the higher-priced concierge, or club, floors which usually offer complimentary drinks and snacks, are often open all day, and sometimes provide business services. It may be worth paying extra for a room on a club floor if such benefits are important to you.

But no matter how efficient the travel agent, the biggest hassle for business travellers undoubtedly comes on ground at the airport. An increasingly number of airlines (but not British Airways) offer their business and first class passengers a limousine transfer included in the price of their ticket.

For those taking their car to the airport, there are a number of valet parking services available —at a price, unfortunately —but convenient for the last-minute traveller in a rush. Some airlines also allow telephone check-in on the way to the airport, but usually only if there is no hand luggage. BA, for example, has introduced such a service for Concorde passengers and those using its domestic shuttles.

Another tip for Gatwick-bound travellers to avoid check-in queues at the airport is to use the check-in facility at Victoria Station for those using the train. If arriving at Heathrow by Underground with just hand-luggage, there is a special check-in desk at Terminal Four as soon as you come off the escalator.

The most useful development at both Gatwick and Heathrow has been the Fast-Track system, whereby business class passengers are processed through customs and security via a special channel and thus avoid the queues laden with leisure travellers. The Fast-Track system also provides for speedier access to currency booths and duty free and steps are being taken to extend it to other areas of the airport, including car parking.

Heathrow business travellers have also been able to benefit from the fierce competition between major airlines, which has seen them develop increasingly opulent lounges. These range from Virgin Atlantic's 'Clubhouse', complete with miniature train that delivers drinks in the bar, to BA's hotel-style lounges on three floors. Both United and American Airlines have also opened new lounges at the airport.

Increasingly it is on the ground that most efforts are being made to improve service for the business traveller, although the service and comfort in-flight is also continually being upgraded. The key development in long-haul has been the steady erosion of first class cabins, replaced by bigger seats and an improved service in business class. Airlines such as Continental, Air Canada and Northwest have abandoned their first class cabins and price structure, but retained almost equivalent-sized seats for an upgraded business class. This follows the pattern established by Richard Branson's Virgin Atlantic airline, which first introduced the concept of first-class style seats and service at regular business class prices.

Another significant in-flight development has been the introduction of personal video screens which enable a greater range and choice of programming. In addition, most airlines are experimenting with on-board telephone and fax facilities, although these are still some way from being routinely offered on all flights.

For many regular travellers, however, the most important developments in recent years has been the growth of frequent flyer schemes. These originated in the US but have now spread to European airlines. The evidence is mixed about how important these are in the choice of airline and fewer than a third of allocated mileage points are actually taken up. Increasingly, there is concern that such schemes only give a benefit to the individual traveller and not to his or her company, even though it is the company that pays for the flight. While the tax authorities in Britain have so far decided to stay out of the issue of whether frequent flyer programmes are a taxable benefit, the European Commission is looking at the whole subject and may decide to introduce a European-wide ban on them.

Whether or not such schemes are a passing fad —or finally prove too expensive for the airlines to operate —there seems little doubt that the executive traveller will continue to be wooed for his or, increasingly her, business. But, according to surveys of regular travellers, it is a pity that they do not really enjoy the experience as much as they might —business travel, by its very nature, is different from other types of travel in that the traveller is travelling to make money rather than for pleasure.

THE RETREAT TRAVELLER

by Stafford Whiteaker

'Going on retreat' is the alternative holiday that is winning new converts by the thousands across Europe and in the United States. It is a way of recharging your inner resources and getting some peace and quiet in a hectic and demanding world. It is a chance to get away from it all, to think things through, and to reflect on your life and the relationships in it. Monasteries and convents can also provide cheap and safe overnight accommodation, especially if you are a student or under thirty. All this yearning for peace has resulted in the biggest growth in retreats in Europe since the Middle Ages —and America is not far behind where several million people go on retreat *every* weekend. So the choice is wide ranging on both sides of the Atlantic.

Who goes on Retreats?

You do not have to be religious or a Christian or Buddhist to go on a retreat even of you go to a monastery. People of all faiths and those of none go on a retreat. You do not have to know about alternative healing or adhere to any particular life-style to go to a New Age Centre. At a retreat you will meet people of all ages and from every kind of background —student, housewives, grandparents, business people, the rich and the poor.

What is a Retreat?

A retreat is simply the deliberate attempt to step outside your ordinary life and relationships and take time to reflect, rest and be still. It is a concentrated time in which to experience yourself and your relations to others and, if you are fortunate, to feel a sense of the eternal. There is a wide choice from Christian and Buddhist places to New Age and Yoga Centres. Whether you go to a traditional monastery or to a workshop on North American Indian spirituality, the end result should be the same —self-discovery and a new view of life. A retreat may last from a day to many months, but for most people a long weekend is the most suitable length of stay

Almost all places of retreat are Christian, Buddhist or New Age based. The use of a particular approach in the form of spiritual exercises are common. These incorporate every form of examination of conscience, meditation, contemplation, and vocal and mental prayer. Such activities are designed to make the spirit —rather like a body in physical training to become fit —ready and able to get rid of spiritual flab.

In this way for Christians, the spirit may become open to love and to the discovery of God's will. The aim of Buddhism is to show us how to develop our capacity for awareness, love and energy to the point where we become "enlightened" or fully awake to reality. Other religious traditions might say it is to bring consciousness of the unity of all creation and of the eternal. These are enormous goals —but then, why not? Unlike the mind and body, the spirit goes forth with unlimited prospects.

The New Age movement is a collection of many ideas and practices aimed at personal growth. This ranges from alternative healing practices, reincarnation, environmental concern, telepathy, occultism to spiritism. However, many of the New Age idea, techniques and approaches spring from well-established traditions of healing, self-help and self-discovery.

Different kinds of retreats

Retreats divide into two major groups —private retreats in which you go alone as an individual and group retreats which often have a theme and cover a particular topic or approach to spirituality and healing. Many of these are in the form of week or weekend workshops. Some are especially designed to help you unwind. Others are individually structured around a particular system of spiritual exercises, such as those of St Ignatius or based on some defined form of meditation such as *Vipassana*.

The traditional retreat

Traditional weekend retreats are the most popular and likely to run along the following lines if you are to be part of a group. You arrive on Friday evening, settle down in your room, meet the retreat leader and the others. After supper there may be a short discussion about the weekend activities. Then you might go for a walk in the garden or rest. Early to bed is the usual rule but not necessarily early to rise. From the first night, you cease doing much talking unless it is when you gather together for a group discussion, a talk, to learn healing or other aids to well-being, or for prayer or meditation. On Sunday there may be a religious ceremony of some sort, such as Mass if you are in a Catholic monastery. If you go alone and not as part of a group, there will be time to walk, read and just rest. It is all simple, easy and peaceful.

Theme and activity retreats

These offer a wide range of courses and study that combine body and spiritual awareness. The methods used spring from alternative healing practices, group psychology, or are based on rediscovering traditional religious forms of creating spiritual awareness. You enter an activity, such as painting or dance, through which you may gather your feelings, senses and intuition together into a greater awareness of yourself, of others, and of life as part of the cosmic creation. There are a great number of ways to explore this form of retreat. Some are ancient arts and others very much of our own time. Yoga retreats employ body and breathing exercises to achieve greater physical and mental stillness as an aid to meditation and contemplation. Embroidery, calligraphy, and painting retreats focus on awakening personal creativity. Nature and prayer retreats help you to see things freshly, appreciating colour, shape and texture to heighten your awareness of creation at work all around you.

Healing and renewal retreats

Ancient and modern techniques are drawn upon to help achieve this goal in a healing retreat. These may range from discovering the child within you to flotation sessions, nutritional therapy, holistic massage, and aromatherapy. The established churches have regained their awareness of this almost lost aspect of their faith. Now inner healing and healing of the physical body through prayer and the laying on of hands have become prominent features of many Christian ministries.

Renewal retreats

A renewal retreat is usually Christian and is seeking to find a new awareness of the presence of Christ, a deeper experience of the Holy Spirit, and a clearer understanding for the committed Christian of his or her mission in the Church.

Taking the family or going just for the day

For those places that have suitable facilities, a whole family may experience going on retreat together —even the family dog may be welcomed in some places. These retreats need to be well-planned and worked out so that each member of the family from the youngest to the oldest has a real chance to bene-fit from the experience. Buddhist centres and monasteries often have children's *Dahampasala* which is a school study session held each Sunday. Some convents offer creche facilities for Mother & Baby day retreats. Many places have camping facilities or a family annex.

Meditation retreats

These are for the study and practice of meditation from the beginner level to the advanced practitioner. It is a way of opening yourself to an inner level of well-being. There are many kinds of approaches to meditation from the various Buddhist traditions to those of the Christian and Hindu faiths as well as non-religious ones.

The experience of silence

The most ancient retreat of all is the one of contemplation and solitude. Here you live for a few days in that great school of silence in which the legendary hermits and saints of old sought God and made all else unimportant. Silence and stillness are very great challenges in this age of diversion and aggression. Even after a few hours of stillness, an inner consciousness arises and those bound up in busy lives are often surprised at the feelings which surface. This kind of retreat is best done in a monastery or convent where the atmosphere is very peaceful.

Going on retreat

Once you decide to go, select a place which strikes you as interesting and in an area you want to visit, Most places have a brochure of list of activities which includes charges. Write, giving the dates the dates you would like to stay with an alternative, and making it clear whether you are a man or a woman, for some facilities are single gender. You need not declare your faith or lack of it or your age. Enclose a stamped, self-addressed envelope.

How much does it cost?

Retreat costs normally include room and food. They vary little from country to country and are modest by any standard. For example, in Spain expect to pay from 800 to 1,800 pesetas. In Britain the range is £15 to £30 a day per person. Weekends cost between £35 and £125. Many Christian and Buddhist retreat houses refuse to put a price on your stay and will ask only for a donation. Expect most courses and workshop to cost about the same as similar type programmes at colleges or craft centres. If you are a student, over 60, or unwaged, there is usually a special lower rate. In New Age centres where healing therapies and special counselling are on offer, expect to pay a going commercial rate for accommodation, treatments and courses. Such charges can range from £55 a day to over £300 for the weekend plus costs of specific individual treatments. Some places offer camping or caravan facilities or a room with a common kitchen for DIY eating.

Food

Vegetarians and special diets are often catered for in Britain and the United States if you give advance notice. The food in other countries is apt to reflect the national diet and include meat. Self-catering facilities often exist in retreat guesthouses and this is one way around diet problems

A bed for the night

The traditional hospitality of monasteries and convents across Europe remains. If you are young and have little money, knock on the door and say so —you are likely to find warm hospitality, a meal, and a bed for the night. A bit of gardening or cleaning is usually welcomed as a way of repaying such hospitality, bearing in mind that most of these religious communities are poor themselves. Many Continental monasteries do not have rooms for women nor convents rooms for men.

Further information: The Good Retreat Guide by Stafford Whitaker (Rider £11.99) lists over 300 places in Britain, Ireland, France & Spain; National Retreat Association, Liddon House, 24 South Audley Street, London W1Y 5DL (tel: 071-493 3534); the Buddhist Society, 58 Eccleston Square, London SW1 1PH (tel: 071-834 5858) National Council of Hindu Temples, 559 St. Albans Road, Watford, Herts. WD2 6JH (tel: 0923 6784 168); Spanish tourist offices can provide a short list of places in that country. In Italy you can expect to find a place of retreat almost anywhere. French monasteries and convents have made a real effort to cater for the growing numbers who want to go on retreat and many more produce excellent colour brochures. For other countries you will probably need to contact a religious organisation, such as the Catholic church. ■

GETTING THERE BY AIR
Chapter 4

IN CONTROL OF AVIATION

by Philip Ray and Annie Redmile

The world of air travel is littered with the initials of the official bodies which on the face of it control virtually every aspect of flying —ICAO, IATA, FAA, CAA etc. It could well be asked why this particular branch of economic activity should be singled out for special treatment by governments. After all, the international shipping industry is not subject to nearly the same constraints, and a virtually free market exists. But when the governments of the world met in Chicago in 1944 to prepare the way for the post–war pattern of civil aviation, they agreed the fundamental principle, now enshrined in international law, that each nation has sovereignty over its own airspace.

This means that any government has the power to grant or refuse permission for the airline of another country to overfly its territory, to make a technical stop —to refuel, for instance— or to pick up and set down fare–paying passengers. By extension of this principle, governments also lay down the conditions under which foreign airlines may pick up traffic (for instance, by agreeing the routes which can be served, imposing the routes which can be served, imposing restrictions on capacity or approving the fares that can be charged). In practice, all these questions are resolved between governments on a bilateral basis in air ser-vice agreements (ASAs) which are subject to termination by either side after giving notice. The best–known ASA is the Bermuda Agreement which governs air services between the UK and the USA.

Regulation

Nevertheless, every government in the world also exercises regulatory control over its own airline industry to a greater or lesser extent. Perhaps the strongest argument in favour of this is the uncontroversial need to supervise safety stan-dards. Otherwise, it is argued, airlines might cut corners in order to save costs. The main area of current debate and controversy is the extent to which regulato-ry bodies should exercise control over the airlines in terms of the allocation of routes, the entry of new carriers into the market, and the fares charged.

The USA pioneered complete deregulation in 1978, allowing its airlines to open up new routes or move into markets already served by other carriers with-out having to seek approval. Their fares, similarly, are not subject to control. Australia followed suit and liberalized its domestic services in 1990. Canada has also gone almost the whole hog towards complete deregulation. In the UK, the opening up of new domestic routes and the setting of fares have both been liberalized, but limitations on the opening of new services at Heathrow have meant that complete deregulation has so far proved impractical.

Liberalisation is the key word in Europe today and the major breakthrough here came with the introduction of a new intra-community air services agreement known as the 'third package'. The 'third package ' of liberalisation measures took place on 1 January 1993. From that date, there have been common rules for the granting of airline operating licences. Any carriers meeting these criteria are free to set up business and to provide air services with the European Union.

There is also freedom now to set fares but the authorities do have a right to withdraw a fare if they judge it to be unreasonably high or harshly competitive or predatory to the extent that some carriers could be driven out of business as a result.

There have been attempts to stifle the new liberal regimes, with some governments being less responsive and more protectionist than others. The UK and Netherlands governments have however taken a positive approach and lead on liberalisation issues.

Most European countries have one major international flag carrier dominating their scheduled airline network service. The world's airlines suffered huge losses in the early nineties and many of Europe's airlines fared particularly badly. This led to a number of 'state-owned' airlines going to Brussels in an attempt to get approval for 'state-aid' to be awarded. This issue remains highly contentious with a firm body of opinion maintaining that such sponsorship does nothing to encourage fair competition.

Independent airlines such as British Midland and Virgin Atlantic have done much to introduce competition on certain routes and the result has been lower fares to those destinations.

At the heart of the debate is the balance that has to be struck between the need always to give the consumer good value and the equally strong requirement to maintain a strong, healthy airline industry. Regulation in such a world-wide industry is still clearly an essential element and a more detailed look at some of the organisations and bodies responsible for it may be helpful.

International Civil Aviation Organization (ICAO): ICAO is not exactly a household name, and its activities are rarely publicized in the lay press, but it plays an important behind–the–scenes role in laying down standards and controlling the legal framework for international civil aviation. It is based in Montreal and was set up following the Chicago Convention of 1944 which laid the foundations of the international air transport system as we know it today. It is made up of representatives of some 150 governments and its controlling bodies are the Assembly, which normally meets every three years, and the Council, which controls its day–to–day activities.

The organization also lays down standards for air navigation, air traffic control, technical requirements and safety and security procedures. It was also responsible for concluding international agreements on the action needed to deter aircraft hijackings. ICAO works closely with the United Nations and controls assistance development programmes in Third World countries under the

UN Development Programme.

ICAO came into the headlines when it investigated the shooting down of the Korean Airlines Boeing 747 in September 1983. Its report was inconclusive but it led to the calling of an extraordinary session of the Assembly in 1984 which agreed an amendment to the Chicago Convention, for the first time embodying in international law a specific ban on the use of weapons against civil aircraft. On the economic front, ICAO monitors the finances and traffic patterns of the world's airlines and issues research reports from time to time.

International Air Transport Association (IATA): IATA is the trade association which represents more than 98 per cent of the scheduled airline system which carries 825,000 passengers and 25,000 tonnes of freight ever day. Some 140,000 of those passengers on any one day are interlining —in other words using the service of one or more airlines on one trip on one ticket.

IATA provides a range of services to its members including the essential IATA Clearing House and bank settlement plan which makes the international sale and use of airline tickets possible.

Traditionally, IATA airlines used to meet in regular traffic conferences to set fares for the coming season so that all fares within, say, Europe would be increased by a given percentage. Nowadays the system is much more flexible and airlines increasingly file new fares on a unilateral or bilateral basis without any intervention by IATA. However, the association still comes into its own in emergencies such as the Gulf crisis in autumn 1990, when it agreed special across-the-board fare increases to take account of the increased cost of aviation fuel and higher insurance premiums.

Many of IATA's activities are carried out behind the scenes. While ICAO has been agreeing standards at an international level on technical matters like air safety procedures, meteorological services, engineering and so on, it has had to lean heavily on the advice of the airlines via IATA. From the passenger's point of view, the greatest benefit has come from agreements between IATA members on a standard form of airline ticket which enables the passenger to travel round the world with, for example, six different airlines and make only one payment which is then apportioned between the carriers by the IATA Clearing House. It is also IATA which lays down the consumer protection standards for the travel agencies which it appoints to sell international air tickets.

The association has also been active in campaigning against government-imposed increases in user charges (which are ultimately reflected in higher fares) and in fighting for the elimination of airport red tape by encouraging Customs and Immigration authorities to improve the traveller's lot with innovations like the red/green channel system. In 1990 IATA launched an international campaign to create awareness of the problems of congested airports and airspace and to rally public support for government action. This campaign, organised by the Air Transport Action Group (ATAG), has gathered momentum and achieved some success. The work carried out by ATAG continues to be relevant as congestion in the air and on the ground constrains the development of service which in turn inhibits consumer choice.

US Department of Transportation (DoT): With the disbanding of the US Civil Aeronautics Board (CAB) in 1985 and the implementation of complete deregulation, the Federal Department of Transportation's powers are limited. Its most important role is to define and implement policy on international aviation, including the selection of American airlines to operate on specific routes. It also co–operates with the State Department on the negotiation of bilateral air–service agreements with other countries. With the assistance of the Department of Justice, it administers the anti–trust laws with the aim of ensuring that carriers do not reach any restrictive agreements behind the scenes, as well as being responsible for approving or disallowing airline mergers.

Federal Aviation Administration (FAA): Not affected by the demise of the CAB, the FAA deals mostly with airport management, air traffic control, air safety and technical matters. Despite their complete economic freedom, all US airlines still have to conform with FAA safety standards.

Canadian National Transportation Agency (CNTA): Transport policy in Canada went through its biggest period of reform for 20 years as a result of the National Transportation Act which was passed by the Canadian Parliament in 1987. The old Canadian Transport Commission was replaced by a new body, the National Transportation Agency, which operates at arm's length from the Ministry of Transport and whose brief includes not only airlines but also railways, shipping, pipelines and so on.

The new regime also ushered in a virtually complete deregulation of the domestic aviation scene so that airlines are now free to open new routes and introduce new fares without needing approval. However, services in the far north of Canada are still regulated because of the public–service need of maintaining regular air communications in this sparsely–populated area.

The Ministry of External Affairs is responsible for issues of international relations in civil aviation in conjunction with the Ministry of Transport and the National Transportation Agency. Air safety standards and the investigation of air accidents are the responsibility of an autonomous body, the Canadian Transport Accident Investigation and Safety Board, whose brief also covers other methods of transport.

UK Department of Transport (DTp): Control of civil aviation in the UK has shuttled between one ministry and another over the years but now appears to be fairly securely housed in the Department of Transport, which also controls shipping, railways and road construction.

DTp is also responsible for laying down overall policy on the airline industry and airports, usually after consultation with the CAA (see below). The Secretary of State also considers appeals against CAA decisions on new route licences and at one time overruled the authority only rarely. Under the Thatcher Conservative government, however, Transport Secretaries tended to intervene rather more and allow appeals when they felt the CAA was being over–cautious about allowing increased competition.

DTp also handles the international relations aspects of civil aviation and regulates the foreign activities of foreign airlines in the UK in the same way that the CAA controls British carriers. Legally the Transport Secretary has to approve fares charged by foreign airlines, although in practice this vetting is carried out mainly by the CAA.

The Department has powers under the Airports Act 1986 to control airport charges and lay down rules for the distribution of traffic between UK airports, again with advice from the CAA. The investigation of aircraft accidents is carried out by the Air Accident Investigation Branch, staffed by an internationally respected team of inspectors who are independent of political control but work in close liaison with the CAA.

Civil Aviation Authority (CAA): Airline regulatory bodies are usually an integral part of a government ministry but the CAA is unusual in being only an agency of government which operates at arm's length from whichever government is in power. It functions under guidelines laid down by Parliament in the Civil Aviation Act and Airports Act, but this is a fairly loose framework which gives it considerable freedom to develop its own policies without ministers breathing down its neck. At the same time, the authority is an important source of advice to the government on aviation matters, including airport policy.

Broadly, the CAA's role combines those of America's FAA and the former CAB. It has a particularly important function in the monitoring of safety standards —notably in the licensing of airports and aircrew and in the approval and inspection of airlines' operational procedures.The Authority invested million of pounds in new facilities to handle the growth in air travel, the benefits of such an investment are already being felt and average delays at the main London airports had been reduced by the middle of 1994 to only 8 minutes from 28 minutes.

The CAA's economic regulatory functions have changed to a degree since the introduction of the 'third package' of liberalisation measured in Europe (see section on Regulation). It is seldom required to approve or disapprove fares but it still monitors the financial integrity of both the UK's airlines and the leading package tour operators which use air services. The UK airline scene is particularly dynamic, so the Authority often has the difficult task of choosing between two or three applicants for a particular route. The CAA's powers do not extend to foreign airlines which come under the control of the DTp, but the CAA is usually represented in bilateral negotiations on air routes with foreign governments.

Under the 1986 Airports Act, the CAA acquired the important role of regulating charges at the larger airports. Airport operators now have to apply to the CAA for permission to levy charges and the Authority has power to impose conditions so as to ensure that there are no abuses of a monopoly position. Airport charges are also subject to regular review by the Monopolies and Mergers Commission (MMC).

The Authority has a general advisory role to the Government on matters such as noise restrictions, the siting of airports or drafting of rules on the distribution of traffic between airports. It also has the job of enforcing any such rules once they are agreed by government.

UK Office of Fair Trading (OFT): The OFT, a semi–autonomous agency of the Government, acquired new powers relating to civil aviation in 1985 as a backup to the licensing role of the CAA. The Director General of Fair Trading can now investigate and refer to the Monopolies and Mergers Commission any competitive practices on international charter flights. He can also ask the

Commission to investigate potential monopolies on domestic flights or on international charters. The Secretary of State for Trade and Industry has the power to make monopoly references to the MMC on air transport generally, including international scheduled services.

Australian Department of Transport and Communications: Civil aviation in Australia comes under the control of the Department of Transport and Communications. Domestic services were deregulated in October 1990, ending the so–called two–airline policy which had existed since 1947. Under this policy the domestic trunk routes were restricted to the privately–owned Ansett and State–owned Australian Airlines (formerly TAA). Deregulation has led to the removal of controls on pricing and entry to the domestic market, although the regime on international services is still fairly rigid. Qantas, the Australian international flag carrier, is not allowed to handle domestic traffic, although it can carry its own international passengers who make stopovers within Australia. Australia's domestic carrier is now allowed limited access to an international network.

New Zealand Ministry of Transport (MoT): Air transport in New Zealand, excluding air traffic services, is controlled by the Ministry of Transport, which administers the Civil Aviation Act 1990. Air traffic services are now administered by an autonomous, state–owned enterprise, the Airways Corporation. The licensing of international services is undertaken by the Minister of Transport, according to criteria set out in the International Air Services Licensing Act 1947. The Air Services Licensing Authority, which formerly licensed domestic services, was abolished in 1990.

In 1985 the New Zealand Government issued a policy statement rejecting the whole issue of civil aviation deregulation. Instead, it declared its priority as being the creation of an environment for aviation which would maximize the economic benefits to the country, including a concern for tourism as well as for broader foreign policy considerations.

This broad view has led to some liberalisation, including permission for the Australian airline Ansett to set up a domestic airline in New Zealand (Ansett New Zealand). The Government has said that it will review its 1985 policy statement in due course.

AVIATION SAFETY

by David Learmount

It's easy to say that flying is safe; but safe compared with what? Fear of flying is only partly rational, which makes it difficult to persuade the afflicted with the unfeeling logic of statistics. Even when nervous fliers are provided with a comparison which brings the truth of flight safety into easy perspective, the ultimate hurdle is man's innate fear of falling from heights. The latter has never been reduced —let alone eliminated— by pointing out that people don't often fall to their death.

Nevertheless, here is an attempt to put flight safety in perspective. During

1993 the world's air travellers made just over 1.3 billion flights. It was an average year for flight safety compared with the last ten years: there were 33 fatal accidents to civil airliners of all kinds, including the domestic short-hop propeller-powered type. The world total of airline deaths— including statistics from what used to be the Soviet Union was 1,020.

Given the world average, a traveller would have to take 1.25 million flights and travel about 1.25 billion airborne kilometres before facing his or her statistical end. If that means very little to you, read on for your perspective. If it sounds horrifyingly dangerous, read on to discover how you can improve your chances enormously by knowing how to be selective about airline safety.

In the average fatal accident more than half the people on board survive. It has also been shown that frequent air travellers have a better chance of surviving accidents than occasional travellers: this is assumed to be because they know the aeroplane better, panic less, and so can get out faster.

Since you will probably be one of those who survives any accident your flight has, taken the emergency procedures briefing seriously. This is not paranoid, it's pure sense. Look at where all the exits are relative to you and imagine finding your way to them in the dark. Count the seat rows to them if it helps. Read the emergency cards carefully, study the brace position, have your seat belt *firmly* fastened at take-off and landing. Look with particular care at the diagram showing how to open the exit doors, and imagine opening them yourself in the dark. Having done all this, sit back and enjoy your flight.

Airlines specialise in delivering travellers long distance fast and safely. Risk does not increase with distance on an airline flight, whereas it increases almost directly in proportion to distance travelled in a car. According to statistics there is no country in the world where the average car driver could expect to survive 1.25 million journeys if each trip was 1,000km, which is the safety-level offered to airline passengers.

Multiple car journeys of 1000km may sound irrelevant, but the statistics could mean something to the traveller who is considering driving from, say, London to the Cote d'Azure by car: if the purpose is to enjoy the countryside and the local cuisine en route, then drive; if it is to avoid flying for perceived safety reasons, your mathematics is flawed; if you are driving because of an irrational fear of flying, then enjoy the route and good luck.

The world airline safety average, however, is a very rough guide indeed because of enormous regional variations. Actual safety depends heavily on what nationality the airline is,whether the flight is domestic or international, where the flight is taking place, whether the aircraft is jet- or propeller-powered, and what the prevailing weather is like at take-off and landing

The world's most statistically safe flight would be with an Australian airline, on an international flight to an American destination in summer (American summer), using a jet aircraft. More about regional variations later. Conversely, the least safe would be a domestic flight in a country with a 'Third-World' economy (specific details later) in a propeller-driven aeroplane (particularly if the propeller is driven by a piston engine rather than a turbine), in bad weather.

Air travellers at the planning stage sometimes ask whether there is an airline safety league table. Surely, they say, the safe airlines will publicize their achievement, proudly laying claim to their place in the league? In fact, even the safest carriers do not dare to. Airline fatal accidents are so rare that even a single fatal disaster could make the top–of–the–league carrier disappear from the top twenty —and what might that do to the clientele's loyalty? Beside which, the airlines know that high places in league tables do not eliminate basic fear of flying.

How would a league table be drawn up? Should it take into account accidents since flying began? …since jets took over? …during the last 10 or 20 years? Should the accidents taken into account be those in which someone died, or in which everyone on board died, or include also those incidents in which people were injured? And where does the league table put a brand new airline? It is unproven, inexperienced, but has not had an accident yet, so could lay claim to a place high in the league.

These difficulties of definition are among the reasons why airlines themselves steer clear of selling safety. But above all, selling safety clearly implies that there is something to worry about in the first place. Since the airlines, quite reasonably, believe there is not, they do not discuss the matter with the public. Coach companies are not expected to do so, neither are the railways, so why should the airlines?

Probably the best indicator of the safety of any form of travel —if it were possible to get the information— is the size of the operator's insurance premium. If someone has offered you a lift in a car and you want to know how safe a driver he is, ask how much he pays for his motor insurance. The higher it is, the more likely you are to die. Airlines are the same.

It is the plain truth that Third World airlines, and carriers from developing economies generally pay the highest premiums. The Third World airline market does not, it is true, have the same bargaining power with the insurance underwriters that, for example, the US airlines do. But in the end, it is simply accident rates which determine the rate of the premiums. In the USA, airlines will face annual premiums less than 0.5 per cent of the value of their aeroplanes, whereas some carriers from Africa and South America will pay more than three per cent.

Airlines can be crudely graded for air safety by the continent in which they are based: North American airlines as a whole are the most consistently safe; the Middle East has an excellent record for a long time now; western European airlines come third with a high level of safety; Asia, the Indian subcontinent and South East Asia has a mixture of adequate and bad with patches of good; South and Central America is very poor (though better than their road safety); and finally African airlines score lowest for safety, with a few exceptionally good airlines among the bad records.

The disparity is enormous: a South American or African airline is more than ten times as likely to have an accident involving fatalities than a North American, Middle Eastern or Western European one. As for where the accident is most likely to happen, the continents are ranged in the same order but the disparity widens still further, with Africa topping the league by far— at present. Finally the majority of accidents happen to domestic airlines— international carriers have a better record on average.

As for the exceptional nations, Australia is the safest along with the USA and the Middle Eastern nations,and competing for bottom marks are India, China, Korea, Colombia, and Russia.

The safest airline in the world is Australia's Qantas, which has not harmed a soul since the days of wood-and-fabric biplanes in 1937 when it was known by its original name, Queensland and Northern Territories Air Services. But just to show how misleading— even unfair— an airline league table could be, Qantas, with its half-century perfect record, would not be at the top of a ten-year table chart because it is a relatively small airline. Bigger US or European carriers which had a clear record during the last ten years (even though they might have had a fatal accident in the preceding decade) would be higher in the league table than Qantas because they would have operated more accident-free flights in the period under review.

In December 1990, the US magazine *Newsday* carried out an airline safety survey of 140 carriers between 1969 and 1990 using some unusual premises in its calculations. Nevertheless the results again confirmed the well–established truths that the airlines of the world's richer nations tend to have the best records.

Newsday's method was to take not just fatal events against number of flights, but the on–board survival rate in the accidents. This made Swissair safest in the list of those airlines which, during the 22–year period, had had at least one fatal accident. With a single crash in 2,036,000 flights and a 91 per cent survival rate in that event, *Newsday* gives the odds of dying on Swissair at 1 in 22,623,000.

It is statistically extremely shaky to forecast Swissair passengers' (or any other airline passengers') safety in that detail on the basis of a single event in 22 years. It is more accurate simply to say that Swissair is a very safe airline. In that same period the following international airlines had not had any fatal accidents: Qantas, Ansett (Australia), Aer Lingus, Austrian Airlines, Air Madagascar, Air UK, Braathens (Norway), Cathay Pacific (Hong Kong), Finnair, Malaysian Airlines, Sabena (Belgium) and Singapore International.

The biggest safety improvement in aviation's history came with the introduction of jets and turbo–prop engines because the turbines which form the core of both engine types are far more reliable than piston engines. So safety climbed steadily during the late 1950s and in the 1960s as piston–power gradually left the scene. Strangely, there was another upward hike from the Seventies to the Eighties, the reason for which was less clear. But during the last 10 years, flight safety, having reached a high level, seems almost to have frozen.

The industry itself is becoming more concerned with 'human factors'. Pilot error has always played a part in some two-thirds of all serious accidents, so now that aircraft technology has become progressively more refined and less likely to fail with disastrous results, the experts are looking for ways of making pilots safer. Aviation psychologists are studying pilot behaviour on the flight deck, communication between pilots, and the way they handle today's modern, computerized cockpits.

There is some concern that aircrews will begin to feel superfluous in an environment which does all their tactical thinking and flying for them. The pilots' attitude to the task has to be totally different from the way it once was: once the job was to fly the aeroplane; now it is to manage the flight in a progressively more complex and crowded environment. The British Civil Aviation Authority leads the world in the 'human factors' field now, demanding of pilots that they take an examination in task–related behavioural psychology as a part of their commercial pilot's licence–qualifying procedure. The intention is that they are more aware of the kinds of human mistakes their environment can lead them to make.

Obviously there is a search for the reasons why airlines from economically poorer, less sophisticated nations have less good safety records. There is good evidence that they are more likely to cut corners on maintenance and safety regulations than airlines from richer nations —often because government supervision of standards is less stringent. But the accidents themselves are, as in the richer nations, more often caused by pilot error than by aircraft engine, systems or structural failure.

Given the higher Third World accident rates, the implication is that training is less good, or the pilot's attitude towards their job is different, or both. In the end, psychologists have concluded it is largely a cultural matter.

What is it about the Australian culture that makes its airlines so safe? First, discipline is accepted as the basis of cockpit behaviour. Also authority, while respected by Australians, is not put on a pedestal by them —meaning in this context that if the captain makes a mistake the co–pilot will challenge him. There have been many serious accidents in airline history which could have been prevented if the pilot had challenged the captain's actions. For example the Japanese are a disciplined race and meticulous in their attention to technical detail; but culturally it is difficult for a subordinate to challenge authority and this cost Japan Air Lines a fatal accident in 1982.

There are new threats to safety emerging which are modifying the world's safety map. The most dramatic are in the nations of Commonwealth of Independent States, or the former USSR. Although the constituent nations have decided to retain the concept of a central aviation authority for setting and policing standards, the evidence is that it is still a shaky, embryo structure which is paid little respect by the member nations.

All the CIS nations are pledged to maintain International Civil Aviation Organisation standards in their airline operation, and their intent seems genuine. Intentions are not proving good enough, however, with accident rates in the CIS soaring in the early 1990s compared with rates in the late 1980s.

Apart from the CIS's shaky infrastructure, the domestic part of Aeroflot has been dismantled and its role taken by both national airlines of the new independent states and by hundreds of private regional carriers using old Aeroflot equipment. Aircraft are frequently overloaded with people and goods, and safety regulations are breached as a matter of course. It is actually surprising, given the amount of flying that goes on in this massive area, that serious accidents are still fairly rare. Most of the time the rule-breakers get away with their shortcuts.

Aeroflot International, meanwhile maintains an acceptably high safety standard.

In China, with its weird capitalist/communist industrial structure giving it the world's fastest growing economy by far, the civil air transport industry is struggling to keep up an expansion which will provide for the exploding domestic demand. The result is that a safety record which was poor anyway has become worse. China's airlines have the youngest national aircraft fleet in the world, almost all western-built, but pilots cannot be trained fast enough, so average experience levels are going down; the same is true of air traffic controllers and technicians, and meanwhile the airports are becoming inadequate for the task.

Eventually, by putting huge resources into training and infrastructure needs, China will cope with this phenomenal airline expansion and improve its safety standards, but it is not possible to forecast when that will be.

On a smaller scale similar truths apply to other fast-growing economies on the Pacific Rim. Korean airlines are low in the safety league, as are Taiwan's.

India, never above the average, has been positively poor over the last few years. As with everything about India, there does not seem to be a simple reason for the low score, but it has been consistent for a long time now. The country's civil aviation authorities are now clamping down hard on operating standards, so perhaps things can be expected to improve.

Central and South American airlines show safety well below the world average, with Colombia the continent's worst. Its international airline, Avianca, has a poor record by international standards, and its domestic operations, faced with difficult terrain, unpredictable weather among the mountains, and a network of ground navigation aids which have been shown sometimes to be either badly maintained or damaged by terrorists, not surprisingly show a relatively high accident rate.

When considering these 'below average' airlines as a mode of transport in their home countries, the alternative surface transport should be approached critically too. In a country where a cash-strapped economy and a *laissez-faire* culture lets an airline's standards drop, perhaps the same is true of the infrastructure which is supposed to preserve national road and rail safety. It may be true that the national air transport system, while it does not compare well with American or European airline safety standards, is still a relatively safe form of transport in absolute terms. Remember the very high standards with which it is being compared.

Finally, airline and airport security has become very much a part of air travel worldwide. In some parts of the world it is peremptory, but that is often because the perceived risk is low. Lockerbie jolted the airline world into a realisation that the subject of airborne terrorism was a serious one, and airlines and countries at risk usually have an adequate security system now. Hijacking is relatively rare now, but it tends to go in cycles. It will come back again. Meanwhile most hijackings today are not the protest type, but usually amateur efforts by people looking for escape and political asylum. They almost invariably fail.

The only workable advice to passengers afraid of this threat is to decide which airlines are the targets of the active terrorist groups, then to travel with airlines which are not. However, the passengers who take that choice should bear in mind that if they cause the threatened airline's business visibly to suffer they have handed the terrorist his victory, encouraging further terrorism.

UNDERSTANDING AIRFARES

by Philip Ray and Debbie Warne

The world of airline tariffs is an incredibly complex one, but given the help of a well–trained airline reservations clerk or travel agent you can make some substantial savings on your travel by using the various loopholes and legitimate discounts which the system provides.

There are so many permutations of possible fares that, as any travel agent handling complicated itineraries for business executives will tell you, six different airlines will quote six different fares for a particular trip.

To generalize, full–rate First Class and Business Class fares have shown a steady increase over the years but the cost of some promotional discounted fares has been held down, if not actually reduced. And quite apart from the vast range of 'official' fares there are also the special deals offered through the 'bucket shops' —these agents sell cheap seats often without the security of being bonded.

On major international routes like London–New York, some 30 different fares are available depending on the airline you fly with, the time of the year and even, in some cases, the day of the week.

On other routes to the US (London to Los Angeles, for example), it can sometimes be cheaper to take an indirect flight and change at a US airport like New York. Here are the main types of fare available:

First Class

Completely flexible fares; reservations can be changed to an alternative departure date or to another airline. No cancellation charges. Valid one year. For each destination there is an allocated mileage allowance. On a journey such as London to Sydney, you could have stops in Rome, Bangkok and Singapore as it is within the mileage permitted to Sydney. You can exceed this mileage allowance by up to 25 per cent by paying a surcharge. This comes in increments of five per cent. For example, a journey London–Paris–Frankfurt would incur a 10 per cent surcharge. Concorde fares are based on the normal First–Class fare plus a supplement of about 30 per cent.

Holders of first–class tickets qualify for the full range of 'perks', including a generous free baggage allowance (usually 40 kilos) and in some cases free ground transport, special lounges, sleeper seats with plenty of leg–room, lavish in–flight cuisine and VIP treatment both on the ground and in the air.

Business Class/ Full Economy Class

Completely flexible fare with same concessions for mileage deviations as First Class (see above). Business class, which is marketed under a variety of brand names like *Club World*, *Le Club* or *Ambassador Class*, usually offers an enhanced standard of in–flight service and more comfortable seating but sometimes involves a premium of between five and 20 per cent on the normal economy fare. Special facilities like executive lounges, free baggage allowance of up to 32 kilos and dedicated check–in desks are provided for Business Class passengers. Some airlines have now merged their First and Business Class service into one class, for example, Continental Airlines —Business First. Passengers are offered First Class Service at the Business Class fare.

Point–to–point Economy and Business class

Applies mainly to travel between UK and US (and on some routes to the Far

East and southern Africa) and, as the name implies, is valid only for travel between the two points shown on the ticket, i.e. no stop-overs are allowed. This means that no mileage deviation is permitted, nor can the ticket be used for connecting flights with another airline. A similar fare within Europe, known as the Eurobudget, is available at a discount on the full fare but is subject to a cancellation charge of up to 50 per cent.

APEX/SUPER APEX

Stands for *Advance Purchase Excursion*. It has become the airlines' main method of official discounting and is normally available only on a round–trip basis, except to the Far East where one–way Apex fares are available. Must be booked and paid for some time in advance, ranging from seven days to one month depending on destination, and usually a minimum stay abroad is required. No stopovers are permitted and there are cancellation and amendment fees which vary with the destination. Reductions on some long–haul routes can be as high as 60 per cent off the normal full fare.

PEX/SUPER PEX

Stands for *Public Excursion* fare and is similar to Apex, except that there is no restrictive advance–purchase requirement. In Europe your stay must include a Saturday at the destination. Worldwide the minimum stay ranges from seven days to two weeks. There is a penalty of up to 50% for cancellation.

Excursion fares

Available on many long–haul routes, with restrictions on minimum and maximum length of stay. Normally for round–trip travel only but with fewer restrictions than Apex or Pex —for example, flights can be changed. Typical saving on the full economy fare is between 25 and 30 per cent.

Spouse fares

Apply on routes throughout Europe and some long-haul, for example South Africa. If one partner pays the full Business Class or Club Class fare, the other partner can travel at a 50 per cent discount. Tickets to Europe have a maximum validity of one month. No stopovers are permitted and husband and wife must travel together on both the outbound and inbound journeys.

Child and infant fares

An infant under two years of age accompanied by an adult and not occupying a separate seat is carried at 10 per cent of the adult fare. Any additional infants under two years of age occupying a separate seat and accompanying the same adult (and any children aged 2 to 11 inclusive) are carried at half the adult fare. Some fares, do not carry these reductions —for example, many Apex fares allow only a one–third discount for children and certain promotional fares allow no reduction at all.

Student fares

Provided the necessary forms are completed, bona fide students are entitled to a reduction of 25 per cent off the full fare. Students must be aged between 22 and under 31. Student fares are not available on the North Atlantic routes and are becoming less widely used elsewhere because so many other fares like Apex offer bigger reductions.

Youth fares

Available for travel on many routes inside Europe for young people between the ages of 12 and 25. The reduction is 25 per cent off the full fare but, again, a cheaper fare like Apex or Pex is usually available.

Standby fares

Generally available only on routes to the USA (and some UK domestic routes) and even then only in the peak season. Available on day of departure. Akin to the standby fare is the late–booking fare offered to Athens, Malta and Gibraltar. This can be bought up to three months in advance but seat availability is not confirmed until the day before departure.

Round–the–world fares (RTW)

An ingenious method of keeping down your travel costs is the Round–the–World fare offered by combinations of airlines. The first sector of your itinerary usually has to be booked about three weeks in advance and the routing specified, but after that you can reserve your flights as you go along. You usually have to make a minimum number of stopovers and you are not allowed to 'backtrack.' The minimum stay is 14 days and maximum stay from six months to 12 months. You can even buy a First Class or Business Class RTW ticket with some airlines which actually undercuts the normal economy fare.

Advance booking charters

Advance–booking charters (ABCs) still exist across the Atlantic, mainly during the peak summer season, although there are fewer flights nowadays because of the wide variety of attractive fares available on scheduled services. The rules for ABCs are similar to those governing the scheduled airlines' Apex fares. You have to book at least 21 days in advance and you must be away at least seven days. On flights to the US, charters can sometimes provide worthwhile savings on the normal scheduled fares but to Canada charter fares are usually at or about the Super Apex level. Charter services operate from a number of provincial points, which makes them more convenient for many people than scheduled flights.

Charters

Within Europe, there is a well-organized network of charter flights which can give savings of up to 70 per cent off the normal IATA fare. These flights operate not only to top Mediterranean sunspots but also to cities like Geneva and Munich and, for legal reasons, are ranked technically as package tours, so the fare will probably include very basic accommodation. Charters can be booked up to the time of departure but return dates may not be so flexible as on scheduled flights. For instance, you may be able to return only seven days or 14 days after the outward journey.

Scheduled consolidation fares

These are charter–priced seats sold for travel on scheduled flights. They are usually intended to be the basis of inclusive packages but often end up as flight–only tickets sold through bucket shops. These fares are administered by 'consolidators', as they are known in the trade. Their role is to take advantage of special rates for group bookings by making commitments for large blocks of seats which they then make available to travel agents on an individual basis.

Airpasses

Special airpasses are available in a number of countries which enable you to make big savings on domestic travel. Some of the best value is to be had in the US, where all the major airlines offer airpass deals giving virtually unlimited travel on their networks, although you are frequently allowed to make only one stopover per city and there is a ceiling on the number of stopovers you can make. You may be restricted from flying at busy periods. Airpasses have to be bought before arrival in the US. To qualify for some of the best deals you have to travel to the US on a particular airline's trans–Atlantic services. The best plan is to find out which airline has the network which conforms most closely to your preferred itinerary.

A number of other countries with well–developed air services including Australia, Brazil, the Caribbean, India, New Zealand and Thailand also offer airpass schemes.

CHOOSING AN AIRLINE

By Philip Ray and Annie Redmile

Airlines spend huge amounts on advertising to tell us about their exotic in–flight cuisine, their glamorous stewardesses and their swish new aircraft. But surveys conducted regularly among frequent travellers —particularly among those who have to fly on business— tell us that all these 'service' factors are not terribly important when it comes to choosing an airline.

What does count, however, is a particular airline's punctuality record. When Lufthansa did some market research a few years ago, it discovered that punctuality was the most important criterion demanded by business travellers, being mentioned by 98 per cent of the respondents. Close behind were favourable departure times, mentioned by 97 per cent, while separate check–in was demanded by only 78 per cent and a good choice of newspapers by no more than 44 per cent.

Another survey among readers of the Swedish business journal *Svensk Export* produced similar results. Asked to put a priority on the service features which they regarded as most crucial when choosing an airline, 92 per cent cited departure times and 87 per cent regarded punctuality as 'very important.' It seems, therefore, that a lot of airline advertising probably does no more than reinforce a choice which the consumer has already made.

Going direct

Most people prefer a flight which involves few, if any, changes where possible. This can restrict choice of airline as these services are often offered only by carriers such as British Airways and the other national airlines or the US majors.

But the scene is changing and with a choice, for example, of three mainstream London airports alone —Heathrow, Gatwick and Stansted —and London City and London Luton added for good measure, choice is greater than it has ever been. Added to that the increasing number of direct services from airport like Manchester and Birmingham and the traveller is getting a much better deal.

One of the best ways of researching your choice is through the ABC World Airways Guide (or AOAG in the US and some other parts of the world), or the BAA Airport timetable. One possible trap today for unwary travellers is the proliferation of 'code-sharing' deals between airlines. The same flight number does not necessarily mean the same aircraft or even the same airline any more and so it pays to check carefully.

Choice of Airports

London's two airports, Heathrow and Gatwick, have direct flights to such a range of destinations that there is generally no need to fly to a continental airport and change flights there. Passengers living away from the South East may be lucky enough to have access to one of the growing number of direct services from their local airport —particularly Manchester and Birmingham which have expanded their international services considerably. If this is not the case then the alternatives include taking a flight to an airport in mainland Europe —and KLM has done much to encourage this approach, over Schiphol —or to London.

Airline standards

There are hundred of airlines to choose from in the world but it is fair to say that there are those who adopt less rigorous safety standards and maintenance procedures than the major international carriers. Some domestic airlines in South America for instance have pretty poor safety records. There has been growing concern in the aviation industry that the explosion of growth in China's airline industry has affected standards and the profileration of airlines that now operate from the former Soviet Union cause question marks to be placed over a number of carriers where formerly there was only Aeroflot to cause concern.

A number of these airlines compete on price but it can be advisable to pay more and enjoy better comfort and more reliability.

The standards of on–board service offered by carriers from the Far East are probably the highest in the world (service is not a dirty word in Asia) but to generalize, it is probably true to say that the most efficient in terms of punctuality and operational integrity are those of Europe and North America. British Airways, for instance, has had a lot of criticism over the years but it is generally regarded as a world leader in setting high operational and technical standards. Now that its punctuality and service have been vastly improved, it is a force to be reckoned with. Other highly regarded airlines include Virgin Atlantic, Swissair, SAS, Lufthansa, KLM and Japan Air Lines.

Many passengers may be worried about terrorist attacks or hijackings after the events of recent years, although the chances of being involved in an accident of this kind are statistically remote. The most sensible advice is to make a mental note of any airlines or airports which appear to be particularly vulnerable and avoid them. Airlines serving the Middle East are not necessarily bad risks. Israel's national airline, El Al, probably has the most rigorous security standards of any carrier and it was thanks to its own security staff at Heathrow that a catastrophic mid–air bomb explosion was avoided in 1986.

Some Third World Airlines which excel in in–flight service may not be so good on the ground. When travelling in Third World countries, never attempt to make your reservation by phone but visit the airline's office and get them to validate your ticket in front of you. Always check and double–check your reservation —some airlines in out–of–the–way parts of the world do not have computerized reservation systems and mistakes are frequently made.

Charters

The network of charter flights both inside and outside Europe is wider than many people imagine. On international routes within Europe, charters account for more than half the market in terms of passenger kilometres. Most charter flights within Europe carry passengers going on conventional package tours but more and more flights are taking passengers on a 'seat only' basis, albeit with nominal accommodation provided to conform with government regulations.

Some charter flights still operate across the North Atlantic during the summer despite competition from cheap Super–Apex fares offered by the scheduled airlines. The popularity of charters between Europe and North America tends to go in cycles: when the dollar is strong, charters do well because North Americans realize that they can buy a cheap holiday in Europe. Equally, when the dollar is weak, European passengers can find attractive deals on American–originating charters because blocks of seats are often made available to tour operators at knock–down rates. All these North Atlantic charters operate under the ABC (Advance Booking Charter) rules, which mean you have to book at least 21 days before departure. In general, however, there are fewer charters across the Atlantic than there used to be, partly because of the increased range and availability of scheduled services with low fares.

Extras and specials

For many scheduled flights it's possible to request certain special meals such as kosher or vegetarian, and to put in seat requests —for example, window, aisle, smoking or non–smoking etc. If travelling on a long–haul flight, it's a good idea to advise the airline of your contact 'phone number, so that you can be informed on the day of your departure if there is a major delay.

VIP treatment can take the form of better handling on the ground. An airline representative will smooth you through all the hassles of check–in and will escort you to the airline's own VIP lounge. The cabin crew will be informed of your presence and will make every effort to ensure that your flight is a comfortable and enjoyable one. Airlines normally grant VIP treatment to senior government officials and commercially important customers. Some airlines will allow you to use their VIP lounges if you have paid the First Class or full Economy Class fare and your travel agent has cleared this facility with the airline's sales department beforehand.

Other airlines insist that you must be a member of their executive club or 'frequent traveller' club before they grant you admittance, while some carriers merely charge an annual membership fee which allows you to use their executive lounge whether or not you're actually flying with them. But don't expect VIP treatment if you're travelling at a discount rate.

Alternative flights

It is also possible to travel as a courier for a much reduced fare. The courier 'responsibility' tends only to be for one half of the journey and so it is an inexpensive way to get to your destination with just a little work to do on the way.

DISCOUNTS AND DEALS

by Philip Ray and Annie Redmile

The high level of airfares is always fair game as a topic of conversation when frequent travellers get together. It is an even more popular topic for politicians who appear to believe, probably erroneously, that cheap fares are a good vote–catcher. Some fares are certainly high, but it is still possible to fly to most parts of the world for considerably less than the full standard fare, given the assistance of a professional travel agent.

The key word when it comes to the difference between high fares and low fares is 'flexibility.' If you are prepared to be flexible as to the day or time of year when you want to travel and let the airline slot you onto a flight which it knows is likely to have empty seats, you can nearly always find a cheap fare. But this may well mean you have to buy your ticket either several weeks in advance or at the very last minute on a standby basis. Frequently your stay at the destination must include at least one Saturday night —a frequently–criticized requirement which is imposed by airlines to minimize the risk of business travellers trading down from the normal full fare to the cheap rate (on the theory that few business people want to spend a Saturday night away from home). And with most cheap fares, once you have booked your flight, you can usually switch to an alternative service only on payment of a fairly hefty cancellation penalty.

The other side of the flexibility coin is that if you want complete freedom to change or cancel your flight without penalty, you have to pay for the privilege, which means, in practice, the expensive full fare.

Economics

The economics of the wide gap which exists between the highest fare and the lowest are not quite so crazy as might appear at first sight. If business travellers want the flexibility to change or cancel their reservations at short notice, seats will often be empty because the airline has been unable to re–sell them, and the cost of flying that seat still has to be paid for. The price of a fully flexible ticket also has to take account of the 'no–show' factor —those passengers who have a confirmed reservation but do not turn up at the airport and fail to notify the airline that they want to cancel their flight.

So there is an implicit bargain between the airline and the passenger when it comes to a cheap fare. The airline offers a discount in return for a commitment from the passenger (underpinned by a financial penalty) that he or she will actually use that seat.

The most innovative fare concept of recent years was devised by the now sadly defunct British Caledonian. Under its 'Timeflyer' system, the fare was based purely on the time of departure, so that the passenger who wanted to fly at peak times paid the highest fare and anyone who was prepared to travel at a less popular time qualified for the cheaper rate. This system was blocked by some foreign governments but it still survives to the extent that many ultra–cheap fares publicized by airlines are available only on a limited number of off–peak flights.

A similar system operates in some countries on domestic routes, notably in Sweden where SAS and Linjeflyg offer big reductions on off–peak flights throughout the year —and even on peak–time services during the summer when few business executives are flying.

Flexibility

Many business travellers can probably be more flexible about their air–travel schedules and can still save quite a lot of money, provided that they don't mind travelling at the back of the aircraft with the masses.

For example, if you are planning to attend a conference, the date of which is known a long time in advance, you can frequently buy an Apex fare at anything up to half the cost of the full fare. But always bear in mind those heavy financial penalties if you suddenly decide to cancel or change your flight.

Business travellers will also find that it is often worth looking around for a package trip, like those offered by specialist tour operators to tie in with a trade fair. Some travel agencies and tour operators also offer attractive packages to long–haul destinations like Tokyo which provide not only the airfare but also hotel accommodation for a total price which is often less than the normal Business Class fare.

Needless to say, this type of package does not offer the flexibility of the full–fare ticket and you will probably not be able to change your flight if your business schedule overruns.

If you are planning an extensive tour within North America, it is well worth investigating the many airpasses issued by US and Canadian domestic airlines which offer unlimited travel over their networks for a given period (although there are usually some restrictions on routing). For travel to the USA, there are also some remarkably good–value deals on fly–drive trips, with car hire being charged at only nominal rates in many cases.

Some of the best deals for business travellers are to be found in the round–the–world fares offered by a number of airlines which can enable you to plan a complicated itinerary at a knockdown rate.

Frequent–flyer programmes

In the competitive world of aviation, where the frequent traveller is king —or queen —'loyalty programmes ' as the 'frequent-flyer' programmes are classified have become the norm. Passengers collect points or benefits each time they fly with a particular carrier and they redeem them for a free ticket for a partner or for some other benefit.

There was a time that fear of the various tax authorities view on such schemes prevented most airlines outside of the US from offering frequent flyer programme. If they were to offer a scheme it was heavily disguised and travellers had to have a US address.

Competition has forced a more open approach and nearly all airlines have their own schemed today or link in to another carrier's.

There are specialist magazines aimed at frequent travellers such as *Executive Travel* or *Business Traveller* magazine in the UK —which list all the latest offer on airfares and deals.

Bucket shops

The best–known source of discounted air tickets is the so–called 'bucket shop', a phrase which was first coined at a travel industry conference in the early 1970s to denote an outlet specializing in the sale of air tickets at an 'illegal' discount. Such is the power of the media that the term —which was derived from shady activities in the 19th century US stock market— is now universally understood, even by those who have never flown in their lives.

Back in the early 1970s, the world of bucket shops was a pretty sleazy one, based on back rooms in Chinese supermarkets, or in flyblown first–floor offices in Soho. One or two of the early entrepreneurs actually ended up in prison and some of the cheap tickets which found their way into the market place had, in fact, been stolen. One bucket shop which traded as a 'reunion club' ended up owing more than £620,000 to thousands of people who had been saving up to visit relatives abroad, not to mention another £614,000 owed to airlines. The owner of this club was eventually jailed for trading with intent to defraud. He knew that the 'club' could not meet its liabilities and yet he continued to trade for almost a year.

Failures still do occur occasionally but the aura of backstreet sleaze has virtually disappeared. Outlets are being opened in the High Streets of provincial cities by respected companies with long experience of the travel business, and even some of the household names in retail travel are now able to supply discounted tickets. At one time the Association of British Travel Agents (ABTA) officially banned its members from offering 'illegally' discounted airfares, but dropped this rule when the restrictive–practices legislation began to bite on the travel business. Nowadays many 'bucket shops' are members of ABTA and are covered by the association's consumer–protection machinery.

It is worth taking a closer look at the discounting phenomenon and at what makes it 'illegal', if indeed it is. It is an economic fact of life that, on average, the world's scheduled airlines fill only two–thirds of their seats, so there is a very powerful inducement to fill the remaining one–third by any means possible. Assuming that overheads have been covered by the two–thirds paying 'normal' fares (although this is not necessarily a valid assumption), anything earned from one extra passenger means a bigger profit or, more likely, a smaller loss — provided that they can earn some valuable hard currency.

The 'illegality' of discounting stems from the internationally agreed convention that governments can approve airlines using their airspace, and most countries have provision in their legislation which makes the sale of tickets illegal at other than the officially–approved rates. In the UK the legal position is not quite so clear cut. British airlines are regulated by the Civil Aviation Authority and there is specific legislation which lays down heavy penalties against discounting. Foreign airlines, however, are separately controlled by the Department of Transport and, depending on whether there is a specific provision on tariffs in their permits, they may or not be liable to be brought before the courts for discounting.

There is a third class of airline —the so–called 'offline carrier'— which does not actually operate services into the UK but which maintains sales offices here. These airlines can, quite legally, do whatever they want in terms of discounting, because there is no law that can catch them.

All this is somewhat academic in the real world because no British government has ever tried to enforce the law, which suggests that perhaps it is time for it to be repealed. The CAA, too, has rarely refused to sanction a new low fare filed by an airline (although it could intervene if it felt the fare was 'predatory' —in other words, designed to put a competitor out of business). However, the authority has frequently refused applications by airlines to increase their full–price fares.

The passenger's viewpoint

The consumer's dilemma has always been that an element of risk is still attached to the bucket shop market because it is perceived as operating at the fringe of the law. The passenger, it must be stressed, does not commit any offence in buying a bucket shop ticket and, to confuse matters still further, a high proportion of tickets sold in bucket shops are perfectly legitimate anyway —for example, the many round–the–world scheduled fares or cheap European charter flights.

The risk element can be exaggerated. Only a tiny proportion of bucket shop clients suffer financial loss in any year, and there are plenty of satisfied customers who have managed to make substantial savings on their trip. Perhaps word–of–mouth recommendation from a friend is a good way to find a reliable outlet for a discount fare deal.

It is a good sign if a bucket shop has been established for some time in good premises with a street–level office. If possible you should make a personal visit to assess the knowledge of the staff rather than just relying on a telephone call.

Ask as many questions as possible and find out any likely snags such as a protracted stopover en route in an unattractive part of the world; and make sure you know which airline you're flying with.

It is a good indication of a bucket shop's reliability if it holds an Access or Visa appointment because the card firms check the financial integrity of their appointed outlets very thoroughly. Use of a credit card also gives you added security because, under the Consumer Credit Act, the card company becomes liable for provision of the service you have bought in the event of the retailer's failure. It is also a good sign if the office is a member of the Association of British Travel Agents (look for the ABTA sticker on the door) or licensed by IATA (the International Air Transport Association) because you are then protected by the association's financial safeguards.

READING AN AIRLINE TICKET

By Philip Ray and Alex McWhirter

An airline ticket is really a legal contract which specifies and restricts the services that passengers may expect and when they may expect them. On each ticket, the duties and liabilities of both passenger and airline are clearly stated —whether it is a scheduled or a charter flight— and each passenger must be in possession of a ticket for the journey to be undertaken. The Warsaw Convention limits the liability of most airlines in cases of injury or death involving a passenger and also for baggage loss or damage. This agreement is usually explained on the inside cover of the ticket or on a summary inserted in a loose–leaf form.

The format of tickets issued by IATA–appointed travel agents in the UK and a number of other countries has been changed to conform with the requirements of the so–called Bank Settlement Plan (BSP). Instead of having to keep a stock of tickets for each airline with which they deal, agents now have one common stock of 'neutral' tickets, but a special plate is slotted into the ticket validator at the time of issue to indicate which airline is issuing the ticket. The whole BSP operation is essentially aimed at simplifying accounting procedures for both travel agents and airlines. Tickets issued direct by airlines still carry the normal identification.

Flight coupons contain a fare construction box which, on a multi–sector itinerary, indicates how the fare is to be apportioned among the different carriers. Cities are denoted by their three–letter codes, eg LHR is London Heathrow, ROM is Rome, CPH is Copenhagen, LAX is Los Angeles and so on. The fare construction may be shown in FCUs (Fare Construction Units), a universal 'currency' in which fares are frequently expressed. The amount in FCUs is converted into the currency of the country of issue which is shown in the fare box in the left–hand corner. The British pound sterling is shown as UKL so as to distinguish it from other sterling currencies. Where local taxes are to be paid these are also shown, and the final amount to be paid is shown in the total box.

At the bottom of the right–hand side is the 'Form of Payment' box. If you pay for the ticket by cash, it will either be left blank or the word 'cash' will be written in. If it is paid by cheque, the word 'cheque' or abbreviation 'chq' will be used. If the ticket is bought with a credit card, the letters 'CC' will be written followed by the name of the issuing company, the card number and its expiry date. If you have an account with the travel agent the clerk will write 'Non ref', which means that no refund can be obtained except through the issuing office.

In the 'Baggage' section of the ticket, only the 'Allow' column is completed by the agent. This shows the free baggage allowance to which you are entitled. The number of pieces, checked and unchecked weights are completed when the passenger checks in. 'PC' indicates that the piece concept is in operation, as it is on flights to and from North America. There are validity boxes immediately above the cities on your itinerary. These 'not valid before' and 'not valid after' entries relate to promotional fares with minimum/maximum stay requirements and the relevant dates will be shown here. If you have a full–fare ticket where there is no minimum–stay requirement and the maximum is one year, these boxes are frequently left blank.

Immediately to the right of the itinerary there is a column headed 'Fare/Class basis.' The letters most commonly inserted are 'F' for First Class, 'C' for Business Class, or 'Y' for Economy Class. The 'Y' will often be followed by other letters to describe the fare, especially if it is a promotional type. For example, 'YH' would mean a high season fare, 'YZ' a youth fare, 'YLAP' a low season Apex, 'YE' Excursion etc.

Under the 'Carrier' box is the space for the carrier code, eg LH for Lufthansa or BA for British Airways. However, the airline industry has now run out of possible combinations of two–letter codes, and three–letter codes are gradually being introduced. Next follows the flight number and class of travel on that particular flight. Most international flight numbers consist of three figures but for UK domestic flights four figures are frequently used. The date is written as, for example, 04 JUN and not as 4th June, while the time is shown on the basis of the 24–hour clock, eg 14.30 hrs is written instead of 2.30 pm. (The twelve hour clock is still used for domestic travel within the USA).

In the 'Status' box the letters 'OK' must be written if you have a confirmed flight. 'RQ' if the flight has been requested but not yet confirmed, and 'WL' if the flight has been wait–listed. If you haven't decided when you want to travel, the word 'OPEN' is written, spread out across the flight number, date, time and status boxes. Infants, who travel for a 10 per cent fare on international journeys, are not entitled to a seat or baggage allowance so that the reservations entry will be marked 'No seat' and the allowance marked 'nil.' Your ticket is valid for travel only when date–stamped with a travel agency or airline validator which is completed with the clerk's signature or initials.

To help you read your ticket, listings of airline, airport and city codings are given in the Directory.

THE TRAVELLER'S PROTECTION

by David Richardson

The travel industry has an enviable record in protecting customers' money, but when the system breaks down there are inevitably heartbreak stories in the media and the image of the travel industry suffers. This was common-place twenty years ago before financial safegaurds were put in place, but it can still happen today. The vast majority of travellers either continue their arrangements or get their money back if their travel organiser goes bust, but that will be of little comfort if you're one of the unlucky ones.

Package holidays

The package holiday customer enjoys the highest level of financial protection, and it's well worth choosing a package rather than making your own arrangements if you're in the least worried about losing your money. And don't forget, 'package holiday' doesn't mean a chartered flight and a week on the beach in Benidorm. Tour operators are increasingly targeting the independent traveller, and many people trekking in the Himalayas or scuba-diving on the Great Barrier Reef are also on a package.

When Air Europe collapsed in 1991, the traveller who had simply booked his or her own scheduled flight almost certainly lost the money. But the person booking the same flight as part of a package holiday was fully protected through arrangements made by tour operators, who have been regulated and licensed since the early 1970s. New regulations implemented in 1993, as a result of European Community (now European Union) legislation, have widened the gap still further between the cosseted package customer and the independent traveller.

The situation with package holidays by air is straightforward, and the same is true for charter flight passengers buying a seat-only deal rather than a package. All tour operators must have an Air Travel Organiser's Licence (ATOL) issued by the Civil Aviation Authority (CAA), and to get one they must satisfy the CAA that they are financially secure, providing a bond that will be used to reimburse or repatriate customers if they collapse. If the bond proves insufficient, the CAA draws on the Air Travel Trust Fund which was set up by a levy on all package holidays back in the 1970s. Failures have reduced the fund to less than £10 million compared to a high of £20 million, but the Government has pledged to underwrite it and further levy may be made if necessary.

The ATOL system is virtually fail-safe as regards package holidays by air departing from the UK, and has been extended to cover packages using scheduled as well as charter flights. Some companies advertise themselves as 'agents for ATOL holders', and that might be worth checking out with the CAA. If so the ATOL holder must take responsibility for travellers if the agent fails.

The situation regarding package holidays by surface transport is much more complex. Until recently, tour operators using coach or rail transport, cruises or ferries, were not obliged to offer financial protection. Many opted to do so through various trade associations, but this was purely voluntary. But in January 1993 the British government adopted the EC directive on package travel, which introduces a wide range of consumer protection measures including the requirement for all package organisers to protect money. This was no great innovation in the UK, because of the ATOL system and the large number of tour operators providing bonds through trade associations. In some other EU countries, however, public protection lagged far behind the UK. But what may have seemed a good idea to the Eurocrats and MEPs gathered together in Brussels may cause the UK traveller a lot of confusion and give him a false sense of security.

The regulations affect all package travel arrangements sold in the UK, not just for travel to EU countries but worldwide —including holidays taken in the UK itself, incidentally. It is generally considered that the EU wanted to protect the traditional package holiday customer, but in fact the legislation goes much further. Many areas are poorly defined and the British Government has not made things any clearer.

First of all, what is a package? According to the regulation, it is a combination of any two of three elements —transport; accommodation; or other tourist services making up a significant element of a package. The latter is open to interpretation, but could include a theatre ticket, riding lessons, or golf, for example. Even a country hotel in England, including a fishing licence in its weekend rates, could be deemed to be selling a package, with the need to protect any money paid in advance.

This goes far beyond the idea of a traditional holiday package. The British government, when the regulations were debated in Parliament, admitted to having no idea how many package organisers there might be in the UK —its 'educated guess' was between 10,000 and 20,000, when the total number of tour operators belonging to trade associations is less than 1,000. Many of the organisers are coach operators, who are considered to be package travel organisers even if all they do is a one-night trip to Blackpool. Others include social clubs, societies and even individuals, such as the local vicar leading an annual pilgrimage to the Holy Land. 'Occasional' organisers of package travel are exempt from the regulations, but 'occasional' will be defined if and when a case comes to court.

Also unresolved, at the time of writing, was the role of the travel agent in putting together packages. If you ask a travel agent to put together a flight and hotel, it could well be that he will have to provide protection as a package organiser even if the arrangements are not sold at an inclusive price. But business travel packages may not be affected, as most business travellers are on credit and do not pay until their return.

Not surprisingly, the regulations are causing grief in the travel industry and among many other organisations and individuals who had no idea they were considered package travel organisers. But what is causing even more grief, among established tour operators, is that there is no effective way of policing the regulations. A gaping consumer protection loophole is still there.

Organisers of packages using air travel must have an ATOL —that is straightforward. But the government has balked at creating a parallel licensing authority for surface travel operators. They are required to provide evidence to travellers that their money is protected, in one of three ways. Either they can provide a bond, possibly to a trade association which has reserve funds in place; they can insure against the risk of financial failure; or they can place customers' money in a trust account, and not touch it until travel has been completed.

Travellers taking a package by surface transport should look for some evidence that their money is protected —but the only policing authority is local trading standards officers, who by their own admission lack the resources and expertise to do it properly. It is now a criminal offence to operate packages without protecting customers' money, but although the maximum fine is £5,000 the first case to come to court resulted in a fine of only £250. The unlucky traveller caught up in a collapse could try to sue the directors —but if the company has gone bust, the kitty will probably be empty.

As for the future, it is likely that a Labour government would give the legislation more teeth by creating a licensing authority, having attacked the Conservatives' laissez-faire stance and accused them of not implementing the EC directive properly. That would certainly be expensive, but another major collapse could tip the balance. About 40,000 people lost money or holidays when coach holiday company Land Travel went bust in 1992, and although new regulations have since been enacted there is every possibility of the same scenario being repeated.

Further pro-consumer legislation is constantly emanating from Brussels, including the so-called 'distance selling' directive due to be enacted in 1994. If this is taken up in the UK as originally drafted, it could devastate the travel industry. Customers not in direct contact with a travel supplier at the time of booking —such as by telephone or even through a travel agent —would not have to pay until their return, ruining the industry's cash-flow.

Role of the trade associations

The weakness of the new legislation means trade associations continue to have a strong role in protecting travellers' money —especially the Association of British Travel Agents (ABTA), the only one with a strong public profile. Surveys show that the public identify strongly with ABTA because their money is safe, and that remains true although its role is changing.

Your money is still 100 per cent safe if you book with an ABTA tour operator, as ABTA has never reneged on its promise to re-pay customers booking a package holiday with a failed member. This is because ABTA requires all its 600 tour operators to be bonded, either with the CAA through ATOL, or through ABTA itself in the case of surface travel operators. In both cases, back-up funds are in place if bonds prove insufficient.

ABTA will not accept insurance against possible failure, or trust funds, as a substitute for bonding —as allowed by the government for non-ABTA members. It points out that insurance against failure is of no help to travellers stranded abroad after a collapse, while trust accounts are open to abuse. If solicitors can run off with money placed in trust accounts —costing the Law Society millions —then so can travel companies.

ABTA is going through major changes, but its consumer promise remains intact. Before the new regulations it acted as a quasi-licensing authority, and tour operators had to join up if they wanted to sell through ABTA's 7,000 travel agents. But it is no longer a closed shop, and tour operators and agents can leave ABTA if they wish. When dealing with a non-ABTA company, the onus is on the traveller to ensure his money is safe —and if in doubt, contact your local authority trading standards officers for advice.

ABTA will also protect your money if a member travel agent goes bust, whatever kind of travel arrangement you have bought. If you already have your tickets then normally you will be able to continue, but if not then ABTA will reimburse you. This applies to independent travel as well as packages but only when the agent, rather than the travel provider, is the one who goes bust.

Other trade associations also bond their members to protect public money, although it is the CAA which licenses all air packages. These are the Association of Independent Tour Operators, the Bus and Coach Council's Bonded Coach Holidays scheme, the Passenger Shipping Association (Cruises) and the Federation of Tour Operators, formerly known as Tour Operators Study Group. But remember, protection only applies to packages, and not a simple ferry crossing or express coach ticket for example.

The independent traveller

If you book independently rather than a package (depending on the definition of a package which might one day emerge!), your money is much more at risk. But in reality, there are few occasions when a failure will leave you out of pocket.

The main area of risk is scheduled airlines, bringing us back to the Air Europe collapse of 1991. Despite the outcry that followed, neither the British government nor the EU in Brussels have made any moves to protect scheduled airline passengers' money, much to the outrage of the tour operators and travel agents who were bonded up to the hilt. Another British air-line, Dan-Air, came within a whisker of going bust in 1992 before British Airways picked up the pieces.

The risks are definitely increasing as airlines all over the world go private, free of government control but also of government support. Several US airlines are technically bankrupt, but continue to operate under US bankruptcy laws. New private airlines are starting all the time, while new state airlines in the former Soviet Union look particularly unstable.

The British Government has failed to act on a CAA proposal for a levy, partly because it would involve only British airlines' passengers and British Airways objected. As little as £1 added to ticket costs for even a short period would soon build up a substantial protection fund, but there seems no likelihood of this happening in the short-term.

But the risk of a scheduled airline collapsing is small enough for most travellers to accept, and the same is true for ferries and scheduled coach companies who may often help out the passenger if a rival collapses. Car rental companies pose a slightly greater risk, while the position of a private railway company that collapses holding customers' money is unknown —a point to consider as British Rail is privatized. And although hotels go into liquidation all the time, they are nearly always kept open to keep some money coming in.

There is one grey area affecting the independent traveller, and that is the sale of discounted scheduled air tickets. But at last the CAA has decided to take action, and in April 1994 it issued new guidelines which means that most companies selling discounted air tickets, direct to the public or through a travel agent, must acquire an Air Travel Organiser's Licence (ATOL) to protect the public's money

The CAA accepts that some companies will still be able to side-step this requirement, depending on their contractual arrangements with airlines. That means continuing confusion for the public, but the CAA has mounted a major publicity exercise telling the public to look for the ATOL number before booking. When companies are allowed to continue selling discounted fares without ATOL then airlines must agree to fly their customers, even if the discount company goes bust holding the money. But the traveller will be unable to ascertain that at the time of booking, so booking with an ATOL holding company is best. Discount ticket companies operate on low margins and have a habit of going bust, so beware and seek the CAA's advice, if in doubt.

There are, however, two ways of safeguarding independent travel arrangements. The first is through travel insurance, with a growing number of travel insurance policies including a section offering protection (typically of up to £5,000) if a scheduled airline or other travel provider fails. Pay-outs were made in the case of Air Europe, but you need to read the small print. Insurance only pays out if there is no bond in place (as with a package), and if you book with a bonded agent or direct with the travel supplier.

Another way of safeguarding your money is to pay by credit card, which is getting increasingly popular and is much more convenient if booking direct with travel suppliers in foreign countries, who may not even be subject to package travel regulations. Credit card companies are to some extent governed by the Consumer Credit Act to ensure that the service paid for is provided but that, like all legislation, is open to interpretation.

The waters are muddied by the fact that there are now about 40 organisations in the UK issuing credit cards, and their attitude towards refunds may vary. If in doubt ask your bank, building society or whatever, especially for an expensive travel purchase.

Some banks see this as an opportunity to boost card usage, such as Barclays which since 1992 has guaranteed to protect anyone buying a flight or holiday in the UK with Barclaycard, for transactions of over £100 with a ceiling of £30,000. But Barclays accepts no legal liability, and is looking to the travel industry to take primary responsibility.

Credit card companies tell customers to seek refunds from the CAA or ABTA in the first instance, but for non-packaged arrangements there are no bonds in place.

There are probably enough scenarios in this chapter to make even the most resolute traveller wonder if his money is safe, but in general the travel industry's record is good. If you pay in advance for a carpet, a cooker or almost any other consumer goods and the company goes bust, there is no equivalent to the CAA or ABTA to turn to.

But the travel industry is, after all, selling dreams. A ruined holiday is more serious than not getting the carpet you wanted, and the sooner all travel arrangements are fully protected, the better.

MAKING CLAIMS AGAINST AN AIRLINE

by Alex McWhirter and Annie Redmile

Y ou have only to read the correspondence columns in the specialist business travel magazines each month to see what a fashionable occupation it is to complain about airline services. Some people seem to enjoy writing letters of complaint so much that they make a profession of it. They complain at the slightest hiccup and write long letters detailing every flaw, claiming huge sums in compensation and threatening legal action if it is not forthcoming by return.

But the fact is that no matter how much their inefficiency costs you in time, trouble, missed meetings, lost deals and overnight hotel bills, the airlines in many cases are not obliged to pay you anything. They are covered for most eventualities by their *Conditions of Carriage* which are printed on the inside cover of the ticket. However, this is not to say that in an increasingly competitive environment the more enlightened airlines do not take their customers' attitudes seriously. Some airline chief executives take a personal interest in passenger complaints and have frequent 'purges' when they insist on seeing every letter of complaint that comes in on a particular day.

If you have a complaint against an airline which you cannot resolve satisfactorily it is worth contacting the Air Transport Users' Committee (5th Floor, Kingsway House, 103 Kingsway, London WC2B 6QX Tel: 071-242 3882 or Fax: 071-931 4132). The committee is funded and appointed by the Civil Aviation Authority but operates completely independently and, indeed, has frequently been known to criticize some of the authority's decisions. The committee has only a small secretariat and is not really geared up to handle a large volume of complaints, but it has had some success in securing ex gratia payments for passengers who have been inconvenienced in some way.

All the same, the committee likes to receive passenger complaints because it is a useful way of bringing to light some serious problems which can lead to high-level pressure being brought to bear on the airline or airlines involved. Some of the subjects dealt with by the committee in 1990 included European and domestic airfares, passenger safety, the pressure on airport and airspace capacity, overbooking, and baggage problems.

Procedure

Here are some tips which may make complaining to an airline more effective:

1. The first person to write to is the Customer Relations Manager. You can write to the Chairman if it makes you feel better but it makes little difference — unless that happens to be the day that the Chairman decides to have his 'purge.' If you've made your booking through a travel agency, send it a copy of the letter and if the agency does a fair amount of business with that carrier (especially if it is a foreign airline) it is a good idea to ask it to take up the complaint for you.

2. Keep your letter brief, simple, calm and to the point. Remember also to give the date, flight number, location and route where the incident took place. All these details seem obvious but it's amazing how many people omit them.

3. Keep all ticket stubs, baggage claims and anything else you may have from the flight involved. You may have to produce them if the airline requires substantiation of your complaint.

4. If you have no success after all this, write to the Air Transport Users' Council. Send it copies of all the correspondence you've had with the airline and let it take the matter from there.

Lost luggage

Most frequent travellers will at some time have experienced that sinking feeling when the carousel stops going round and their baggage is not on it. The first thing to do if your luggage does not appear is to check with an airline official in the baggage claim area. It could be that your baggage is of a non–standard shape —a heavy rucksack, for example— which cannot be handled easily on the conveyor belt and it will be brought to the claim area by hand. But if your baggage really has not arrived on the same flight as yourself you will have to complete a Property Irregularity Report (PIR) which will give a description of the baggage, a list of its contents and the address to which it should be forwarded.

It is sometimes worth hanging around at the airport for an hour or two because there is always the chance that your baggage may arrive on the next flight. This sometimes happens if you have had to make a tight flight connection and your baggage hasn't quite made it, although the current strict security requirements mean that normally a passenger and his or her baggage must travel on the same flight. But if there is only one flight a day there is no point in waiting and the airline will forward the baggage to you at its expense. In this case, ask the airline for an allowance to enable you to buy the basic necessities for an overnight stay —nightwear, toiletries and underwear for example.

If your baggage never arrives at all, you should make a claim against the airline within 21 days. Airlines' liability for lost luggage is limited by international agreement and the level of compensation is based on the weight of your baggage, which explains why it is filled in on your ticket by the check–in clerk. The maximum rate of compensation at present is US$20 per kilo for checked baggage and US$400 per passenger for unchecked baggage, unless a higher value is declared in advance and additional charges are paid.

The same procedure applies to baggage which you find to be damaged when you claim it. The damage should be reported immediately to an airline official and, again, you will have to fill in a PIR form which you should follow up with a formal claim against the airline.

Overbooking

Losing one's baggage may be the ultimate nightmare in air travel but the phenomenon of 'bumping' must run it a close second. Bumping occurs when you arrive at the airport with a confirmed ticket, only to be told that there is no seat for you because the flight is overbooked. Most airlines overbook their flights deliberately because they know that there will always be a few passengers who make a booking and then don't turn up ('no shows' in airline jargon). On some busy routes like Brussels to London on a Friday evening, some business travellers book themselves on four or five different flights, so that there is a horrendous no–show problem and the airlines can, perhaps, be forgiven for overbooking.

The use of computers has enabled airlines to work out their overbooking factors quite scientifically, but just occasionally things don't quite work out and a few confirmed passengers have to be 'bumped.'

If you are unlucky enough to be bumped or 'denied boarding', to adopt the airline jargon, you will probably be entitled to compensation. A few years ago the Association of European Airlines (AEA) adopted a voluntary compensation scheme based on a 50 per cent refund of the one–way fare on the sector involved, but early in 1991 the European Community agreed new rules which put compensation on a statutory basis. The rules lay down that passengers with a confirmed reservation 'bumped' at an EC airport should receive 150 ecu (about £200) for a short–haul flight or 300 ecu (about £400) for a flight of more than 3500km (2170 miles). These amounts are halved if the passenger can get on an alternative flight within two or four hours respectively. In addition passengers have the right to full reimbursement of their ticket for any part of their journey not undertaken, and can claim legitimate expenses.

Compensation for delays

Whatever the Conditions of Carriage may say, airlines generally take a sympathetic view if flight delays cause passengers to miss connections, possibly entailing overnight hotel accommodation. Our own experience is that most of the better–known scheduled carriers will pull out all the stops to ensure that passengers are quickly re–booked on alternative flights and they will normally pick up the tab for hotel accommodation and the cost of sending messages to advise friends or contacts of the revised arrival time.

The position is not so clear cut when it comes to charter airlines because the extent of their generosity usually depends on whatever arrangement they have with the charterer. But a number of British tour operators have devised delay protection plans which are usually included as part of the normal holiday insurance. Thomson Holidays, for instance, will normally provide meals or overnight accommodation in the event of long flight delays, and if the outbound flight is delayed for more than 12 hours, passengers have the right to cancel their holiday and receive a full refund. If they decide to continue their holiday they receive compensation up to a maximum of £60, in addition to any meals or accommodation which may have been provided. Compensation is also paid on a similar scale if the return flight is delayed.

Injury or death

Airline liability for death or injury to passengers was originally laid down by the Warsaw Convention signed in 1929. The basic principal was that the infant airline industry could have been crippled if it had been forced by the courts to pay massive amounts of compensation to passengers or their relatives for death or injury in the event of an accident.

The trade–off was that the airlines undertook to pay compensation up to a set ceiling irrespective of whether negligence on their part was proved. The limit was set at 250,000 French gold francs, an obsolete currency which is nevertheless still used to this day as the official unit of compensation, and converted into local currencies. In the UK, for instance, the sterling equivalent is currently laid down by statute as £13,633.40 which is generally accepted to be a hopelessly inadequate level of compensation.

The parties of the Warsaw Convention met in Montreal in 1975 and signed four protocols which would have substituted for gold franc the Special Drawing Right (SDR), the international unit of account devised by the International

Monetary Fund, although this still has not be ratified. Progress is being made and a draft voluntary agreement now exists in ECAC recommending that its airlines accept that the limit be raised to 250,00 SDR. ■

GETTING THERE BY ROAD
Chapter 5

OVERLAND BY TRUCK, VAN OR 4 X 4

by Jack Jackson

Travelling overland in your own vehicle gives you independence, freedom to go where you like and when you like, and a familiar bolt-hole away from the milling crowds and the alienation one can feel in a different culture. The vehicle may seem expensive to start with and can involve you in mountains of bureaucracy, but considering the cost of transport and accommodation, it becomes more realistic, particularly as you can escape the bed bugs and dirt that often seem to accompany cheaper accommodation.

Which vehicle?

The choice of vehicle will be a compromise between what can be afforded, what can best handle the terrain to be encountered, and whether spares, fuel, food and water need to be carried, or are readily available en route.

Short wheelbase Land Rovers or Toyota Land Cruisers, Range Rovers and Land Rover Discoverys are ideal in the Tenere Sand Sea, but are impossible to sleep full-length in without the tailgate open and all the fuel, stores and water removed. Moreover, they are heavy on fuel. After a while, one may long for the convenience and comfort of a Volkswagen Kombi, or similar sized panel van!

For a protracted transcontinental or round–the–world journey, you need to consider what sacrifices have to be made to have the advantages of the more cramped vehicles, including the length of time you expect to be on the road, and the degree of home comforts you will want along the way.

If you do not plan to encounter soft sand, mud or snow and your payload is mostly people who, when necessary, can get out and push, then you really only need a two-wheel drive vehicle, provided that it has enough strength and ground clearance.

Where tracks are narrow, overhung and subject to landslides, as in outlying mountainous regions such as the Karakoram, then the only usable vehicles are the smallest, lightweight four-wheel drives, eg, the soft-topped Land Rover 88 or 90, the Suzuki and the Jeep CJ5. These vehicles also give the best performance when traversing soft sand and steep dunes, but their small payload and fuel carrying capacity restrict them to short journeys.

Avoid big American–style conversions. They have lots of room and home comforts like showers, toilets, microwave ovens and storage space; but their large size, fuel consumption, weight, low ground clearance, poor traction, and terrible approach and departure angles, make them unsuitable for any journey off the asphalt road.

If costs were no problem and all spares were to be carried, the ideal vehicle would be a four-wheel drive with a payload of one tonne evenly distributed between all four wheels, a short wheelbase, forward control, high ground clearance, large wheels and tyres, good power to weight ratio and reasonable fuel consumption. The vehicles best fitting this specification are the Mercedes Unimog, the Pinzgauer, the Fiat PC65 and PC75 models and the Land Rover Military 101" one tonne. These are specialist vehicles for best cross country performance and are often soft-topped to keep the centre of gravity low. However, the costs involved in buying, running and shipping such vehicles, would deter all but the very wealthy.

Considering price, availability of spares and working life, the most commonly used vehicles are the long wheelbase Land Rover Defender, the smaller Mercedes Unimogs and the Bedford M type trucks. For two-wheel drives, the VW Kombi and the smaller Mercedes Panel Vans are the most popular. These are big enough to live in and carry food, water, spares, stoves, beds, clothes, extra fuel, sand ladders and two people in comfort. They also remain economical to run, small enough to negotiate narrow bush tracks and light enough to make digging out less frequent and easier.

A high roof vehicle is convenient to stand up in and provides extra storage, but is more expensive on ferries. It also offers increased wind resistance, thus pushing up fuel consumption and making the engine work harder and get hotter. This shortens engine life and increases the risk of mechanical failure.

Trucks

Where heavier payloads are envisaged, such as in Africa where you will often have to carry large quantities of fuel, the most popular four-wheel drive vehicles are the Bedford M type trucks and Mercedes Unimogs. Bedford Trucks are cheap, simple and in some parts crude. They have good cross-country performance when handled sensibly and slowly, but are too heavy in soft sand. They go wrong often, but repairs can usually be improvised, and used spares are readily available. Bedford M Type trucks, are best bought ex-UK military, as are their spare parts.

Ex-NATO Mercedes Unimogs are near to perfect for heavy overland or expedition work. Their cross-country performance is exceptional, and their portal axles give them extra ground clearance, though this also makes them easier to turn over. It is almost impossible to get them stuck in sand but they will stick in mud. Ex-NATO Unimogs usually have relatively small petrol engines, so you need to use the gearbox well, but fuel consumption is good. The standard six-speed, one-range gearbox can be altered to a four-speed, two-range gearbox, which is useful in sand. Four-wheel drive can be engaged at any speed without declutching. Differential locks are standard. The chassis is cleverly arranged to give good weight distribution over all four wheels at almost any angle but gives a bad ride over corrugations.

Mechanically, the Unimog is over-complicated. It doesn't go wrong often, but when it does, it is difficult to work on and needs many special tools. Later models have the clutch set to one side of the transmission, instead of in line with it, making it much easier to change.

Unimogs are best bought from NATO forces in Germany. Spares must be carried with you. Diesel Unimogs are usually ex–agricultural or building contractor and are therefore less well–maintained than forces vehicles.

Land Rovers

Despite some weaknesses, Land Rovers are the most durable and reliable four–wheel drive small vehicles on the market. Their spartan comforts are their main attributes! Most of their recent challengers are too softly sprung and have too many car–type comforts to be reliable in hard, cross–country terrain. There are plenty of spare parts available worldwide and they are easy to work on with most parts bolted on.

The older Series III leaf sprung models, are more durable that the newer "Defender" models and leaf springs are easier to get repaired in the Third World.

The aluminium alloy body does not rust, so the inevitable bent body panel can be hammered back into rough shape and then forgotten. You don't have to be Hercules to change a wheel.

The short wheelbase Land Rover is usually avoided because of its small load–carrying capacity; but in off–road use, particularly on sand dunes, it has a distinct advantage over the long wheelbase models. Hard-top models are best for protection against thieves and safer when rolled, unless you have had a roll cage fitted.

When considering long wheelbase models, it is best to avoid the six-cylinder petrol engine models, including the one tonne and forward control. All cost more to buy, give more than the normal amount of trouble, are harder to find spares for and recoup less on resale.

The six-cylinder engine uses more fuel and more engine oil than the four-cylinder engine and the carburettor does not like dust or dirty fuel which means that it often needs to be stripped and cleaned twice a day in very dusty areas. The electrical fuel pump always gives trouble. The forward control turns over easily, and, as with the Series IIA Land Rovers, rear half-shafts break easily if the driver is at all heavy footed.

It is generally agreed that the four-cylinder models are under–powered, but the increased power of the six-cylinder does not compensate for its disadvantages.

The V8 Land Rover has permanent four-wheel drive, with a lockable central differential. It is an excellent vehicle, but very costly on fuel.

The Land Rover 90 and 110, now renamed *Defender*, are designed for speed, economy and comfort on the newer roads in Africa and Asia. Built on a strengthened Range Rover type chassis and suspension, with permanent four-wheel drive and centre differential lock, stronger gearbox, disc brakes on the front and better doors all around, the vehicle is a vast improvement on earlier models. It is ideal for lightweight safari or personnel carrier use, but for heavy expedition work the coil springs need to be uprated.

In European Union Countries, outside of the UK, 12–seat Land Rovers should be fitted with a tachometer and come under bus regulations.

Range Rovers, Land Rover Discoverys, and other short wheelbase vehicles, are not spacious enough, nor have the load carrying capacity for use on long journeys.

Any hard-top or station wagon Land Rover, is suitable for a long trip. If you buy a new Land Rover in a wet climate, run it in for a few months before setting off on a trip. This allows the wet weather to get at the many nuts and bolts that keep the body together. If these bolts corrode in a little, it will save you a lot of time later. If you take a brand new Land Rover into a hot climate, you will regularly have to spend hours tightening nuts and bolts that have come loose, particularly those around the roof and windscreen.

Early Land Rover diesel engines were not renowned for their reliability. The newer five bearing crankshaft diesel engines are better but still under–powered. Land Rover Ltd still refuses to believe that the Third World requires a large, trouble–free diesel engine, and it is sometimes sensible to fit another engine such as the Isuzu 3.9 litre or the Perkins 4,154.

With the new Tdi, Turbo Diesel engine, Land Rover appears to have fixed the problems of the earlier turbo diesel and most owners are raving about its good fuel economy; but there is still a question mark over its use of a GRP timing belt, in a hot climate

Stretched Land Rovers with 127-inch and now 130-inch wheel base, are available to special order, including crew cab versions.

Modern Land Rovers do not have double-skinned roofs, so a loaded or covered roof rack is useful, to keep the vehicle cooler in sunny climates.

Other 4 x 4s

The latest Land Rover's superb axle articulation and light-weight body give it a distinct advantage in mud, snow and soft sand. If these are not likely to be encountered, then a Toyota Land Cruiser is more comfortable than a Land Rover and is very reliable, though heavy on fuel. Many Toyota models have large overhanging front bumpers, rear steps and running boards which negate off-road performance. The latest coil sprung Toyota Land Cruisers and Nissan Patrols have good performance and comfort but, as with American four-wheel drives, their very large engines are too heavy on fuel.

Despite its Paris/Dakar successes, the Mitsubishi Shogun (called Montero in the USA and Pajero elsewhere), has not proved reliable in continuous Third World use. The Isuzu Trooper is not well designed for true off–road work. Suzukis are just too small. Spares for Japanese vehicles can be a problem to obtain, anywhere in the world. Soft top vehicles are best fitted with a roll cage.

The Range Rover and Mercedes Benz Gelandewagon, have poor load-carrying capacity and their high cost limit their appeal. A new Range Rover is due out in Autumn 1994.

Four-wheel drive versions are available, of most popular pick-up trucks and panel vans. Those most common in Africa are based on the Peugeot 504 and the Toyota Hilux. The Synchro version of the Volkswagen Kombo which has an advanced fluid-coupling four–wheel drive system, is now available but it has poor ground clearance.

Nissan's Pathfinder/Terrano and Toyota's 4 Runner, are car shells mounted in pick-up trucks, they are useful, cheaper solutions, for Third World use.

Two-wheel drive

The Volkswagen Kombi is in use in almost every country outside the Soviet Bloc and China. Anyone who has travelled overland through Africa, Asia, the Americas, or around Australia will agree that the VW is the most popular independent traveller's overland vehicle. Its ability to survive misuse (up to a point), and carry heavy loads over rough terrain economically, whilst providing the privacy of a mobile home, are some of the factors that make it so popular.

The Kombi has a one tonne payload and far more living space in it than a long wheelbase Land Rover or Land Cruiser. It lacks the four-wheel drive capability, but partly makes up for this with robust independent suspension, good ground clearance and engine weight over the driven wheels. With experience and astute driving, a Kombi can be taken to places that will amaze some four-wheel vehicle drivers. The notorious 25km 'sea of sand' between In Guezzam and Assamaka, in the Sahara, has ensnared many a poorly driven 4 x 4, whilst a Kombi has stormed through unscathed! With the use of lengths of chicken wire fencing, as sand ladders, plus some helpful pushing, a Kombi can get through quite soft sand.

The second most popular two-wheel drive vehicle for overlanders is the smaller Mercedes, diesel engined, Panel Van, which is very reliable. Most of the stronger panel vans are suitable for overland use and most are available with a four-wheel drive conversion, at a price. Avoid any vehicle that has only front-wheel drive: when loaded at the rear, these vehicles often lose traction, even on the wet grass of a campsite.

Petrol versus diesel

Weight for weight, petrol engines have more power than diesel engines, but for hard usage in Third World areas, they have several disadvantages. In hot countries there is a considerable risk of fire and the constant problem of vapour lock, which is at its worst on steep climbs, or on long climbs at altitude. Dust, which often contains iron, gets into and shorts out the distributor. High tension leads break down and if much river crossing has to be done, water in the electrics causes more trouble. A further problem is that high-octane fuel is not usually available and low-octane fuel will soon damage a sophisticated engine. However, petrol engines are more easily repaired by the less experienced mechanic.

Avoid any engine with an electronic engine management system. These are not normally repairable if faulty and a flat battery can cause problems with some of these.

Diesel fuel does not have the fire risk of petrol and outside Europe is usually about one third of the price of petrol. It also tends to be more available, as it is used by trucks and tractors.

Diesel engines are heavier and more expensive to buy, but are generally more reliable and need less maintenance, although a more knowledgeable mechanic is required if they do go wrong. An advantage is that extra torque is available at low engine revolutions. This allows a higher gear in the rough, which improves fuel consumption and means less weight of fuel need be carried for a section without fuel supplies —this improves fuel consumption still further. There is also no electrical ignition to malfunction where there is a lot of dust or water. Against this is the fact that diesel engines are noisier than petrol engines, which can be tiring on a long trip, diesel fuel is messy and attacks many forms of rubber.

A second filter in the fuel line is essential to protect the injection pump from bad fuel in the Third World. A water sedimenter is useful, but needs to be well protected from stones and knocks.

Some Japanese diesel vehicles have 24-volt electrical systems.

Tyres

Long–distance travellers usually have to cover several different types of terrain, which makes it difficult to choose just one set of tyres suitable for the whole route. Unless you expect to spend most of your time in mud or snow, you should avoid the aggressive tread, so–called cross–country or all–terrain tyres. These have a large open–cleated tread that is excellent in mud or snow, but on sand they tear away the firmer surface crust, putting the vehicle into softer sand underneath. These open treads also tear up quickly on mixed ground with sharp stones and rocks.

If you expect to spend a lot of time in soft sand, you will need high flotation tyres with little tread pattern, these compress the sand, causing the least disturbance to the firmer surface crust. Today's standard for such work is the Michelin XS, which has just enough tread pattern to be usable on dry roads but can slide about on wet roads or ice. The XS is a soft flexible radial tyre, ideal for low pressure use but easily cut up on sharp stones.

As most travellers cover mixed ground, they need a general truck-type tyre. These have a closed tread with enough tyre width and lugs on the outside of the tread to be good mixed country tyres —although obviously not as good in mud or soft sand. Such tyres when fitted with snow chains, are better than any all–terrain tyres for snow or mud use and, if of radial construction, can be run soft to improve their flotation on sand. The best tyre in this category is the Michelin XZY series

Radial or Cross Ply, Tube or Tubeless

Radial tyres are more flexible and have less heat build–up when run soft, than cross–ply tyres. They also have less rolling resistance, thus improving fuel consumption. For heavy expedition work, Michelin steel-braced radials last longer. With radial tyres you must use the correct inner tubes, preferably by the same manufacturer. Radial and cross–ply tyres should never be mixed.

Radial tyres 'set' in use, so when changed around to even out tyre wear, they should preferably be kept on the same side of the vehicle. A further advantage of radials is that they are easier to remove from the wheel rim with tyre levers when you get a puncture away from help.

Radial tyres have soft side walls that are easily torn on sharp stones, so if you have to drive over such stones, try to use the centre of the tyre, where the tread is thickest.

For soft sand use, radial tyres can be run at 40 per cent pressure at speeds below 10 miles an hour and 75 per cent pressure for mixed terrain below 20 miles per hour. Remember to reinflate to full pressure when you return to firm ground.

Tubeless tyres are totally impracticable for off–road work, so always use tubed tyres and carry several spare inner tubes.

A vehicle travelling alone in bad terrain should carry at least one extra spare tyre, as well as the one on the spare wheel. Several vehicles travelling together can get by with only the tyres on the spare wheels so long as they all have the same types of tyres for interchangeability.

Wide tyres

There is a tendency for 'posers' to fit wide tyres. Such tyres are useful in soft sand and deep snow, but in other situations they negate performance. Worse still, on asphalt roads, hard top pistes or ice, they lower the weight per unit area (= grip), of the tyre on the road, leading to slipping and skidding.

Conversions

An elevating roof or fibreglass 'pop–top' motor caravan conversion has advantages over a fixed-roof van. It is lower on the move, can sleep extra people up top, e.g. children, provide extra headroom while camped and insulates well in tropical heat. Some better designed fibreglass pop–tops do not collect condensation, even when you cook inside them. Some of the disadvantages are that they can be easier to break into, they look more conspicuous and more inviting to thieves than a plain top, and they have to be retracted before a driver, disturbed in the night, can depart in a hurry.

In some vans, the hole cut in the roof weakens the structure of the vehicle. Driving on very bad tracks can cause cracks and structural failures in the body and chassis; failures that would not normally occur if the vehicle spent its life in Europe. Vans such as VW's, the Toyota Hiace, Ford Transit and Bedford CR, should all have roof–mounted support plates added along the elevating roof, to give torsional support. The roof is not an integral part of the structure of the Land Rover so cutting a hole in it does not affect the chassis.

A de–mountable caravan fitted to four-wheel drive pick–up trucks such as the Land Rover, Land Cruiser or Toyota Hi–Lux, could provide a lot more room and comfort, but de–mountables are not generally robust enough to stand up to the off–road conditions of an overland journey. They also add considerably to the height and width of the vehicle and are more expensive than a proper conversion. Moreover, you cannot walk through from the cab to the living compartment.

In deserts, if one doesn't have a motor caravan, sleeping on the roof rack can be a pleasant way of avoiding spiders and scorpions. Fitting the length of the roof rack with plywood makes it more comfortable as well as keeping the vehicle cool in the sun. Special folding tents for roof racks are available, at a price.

Furnishings and fittings

Preferably, camper conversions should have fittings made of marine plywood rather than hardboard, it is stronger, more durable and not prone to disintegration when hot or wet. If your vehicle is finally destined for the US, it must satisfy US Dept of Transport and State Regulations for the basic vehicle and the conversion. The same applies to motor caravans destined permanently for Australia, where equally strict Australian Design Rules, apply to both the vehicle and the conversion.

Most water filtration systems, eg. Katadyn, are portable, though Safari (Water Treatments) Ltd produce a wall–mounted model that can be fitted to a vehicle. On many caravans, the water tank and even a gas bottle, are mounted beneath the floor, where they are most vulnerable off–road.

Front–opening quarter vents in the front doors are sometimes appreciated in warm climates, as are a pair of fans built in for extra ventilation. However, front quarter vents can be attractive to thieves. Fresh air is essential when sleeping inside a vehicle in tropical lands and a roof vent is just not enough to create an adequate draught. Equip open windows with mosquito net and strong wire mesh.

Having up–to–date information along the route can be useful, forewarning of riots, floods, cyclones, earthquakes, revolutions etc. can solve many problems. A short–wave radio will enable you to listen to the BBC World Service, Voice of America and other international stations.

On a long transcontinental journey, one will normally have to do without a refrigerator. (It is often preferable to use the space and weight for more fundamental items like jerry cans or spare parts.) However, if you are carrying large quantities of film or medicines, one could consider a lightweight dry–operating, thermo–electric 'Peltier–Effect' refrigerator by Koolatron Industries, but fit a larger capacity alternator and spare battery, with a split charge system.

Roof racks

These need to be strong to be of any use. Many of those on the market are flimsy and will soon break up on badly corrugated piste. Weight for weight, tubular section is always stronger than box section and it should be heavily galvanized.

To extend a roof rack over or beyond the windscreen for storing jerry cans of water or fuel, is absolute lunacy. The long wheelbase Land Rover for instance, is designed so that most of the weight is carried over the rear wheels. The maximum extra weight allowed for the front axle is the spare wheel and a winch. It does not take much more than this to break the front springs or distort the axle. Anyway, forward visibility is impossible when going downhill with such an extended roof rack. A full–length roof rack can be fitted safely, but it must be carefully loaded, and remember that Land Rover recommend a total roof weight of not more than 90kg. A good full–length roof rack will weigh almost that on its own!

Expect damage to the bodywork and reinforce likely points of stress, in particular the corners of the windscreen. A good roof rack design will have its supports positioned in line with the vehicle's main body supports, and will have its fittings along the back of the vehicle to prevent it from juddering forward on corrugated roads. Without these fittings, holes will be worn in the roof.

Nylon or terylene rope is best for tying down baggage. Hemp rope doesn't last too well in the sun and holds grit which is hard on your hands. Rubber roof rack straps are useful but those sold in Europe soon crack up in the sun. You can use circular strips cut from old inner tubes and add metal hooks to make your own straps. These will stand up to the constant sunlight without breaking. Ratchet straps should not be over–tightened.

Other extras

Stone-guards for lights are very useful, but you need a design that allows you to clean the mud off the lights without removing them (water hoses do not usually exist off the beaten track), and they should not be fitted with self–tapping screws. Such a design is hard to find. Air horns must be fitted in such a location that the horns do not fill with mud, e.g. on the roof or within the body. Horns can be operated by a floor–mounted dip switch. An isolator may be located on the dashboard, to prevent accidental operation of the horn.

For sunny countries, paint chrome windscreen wipers and wing mirrors matt black, to stop dangerous reflections and make sure that you have fresh wind-screen wiper rubbers, for when you return to wet climates.

A good, powerful spotlight fitted on the rear of the roof rack will be invalu-able when reversing and will also provide enough light for pitching a tent. Normal reversing lights will be of no use. Bull Bars, better named Nudge Bars, are usually more trouble than they are worth, may invalidate your insurance and damage the body or chassis if struck with any force.

Finally, whatever type of vehicle you take and however you equip it, you should aim to be as self–sufficient as possible. You should have food to last for weeks not days, clothing to suit the changing climatic and social conditions, and the tools, spare parts and personal ability to maintain your vehicle and keep it going. Without these, and in spite of the occasionally genuinely kind person, you will be conned and exploited to the extent that the journey will be a major ordeal. With adequate care and preparation, your overland journey will be an experience of a lifetime.

OVERLAND BY MOTORBIKE

by Ted Simon

It seems pointless to argue the merits of motorcycles as against other kinds of vehicles. Everyone knows more or less what the motorcycle can do, and atti-tudes to it generally are quite sharply defined. The majority is against it, and so much the better for those of us who recognize its advantages. Who wants to be part of a herd? Let me just say that I am writing here for people who think of travelling through the broad open spaces of Africa and Latin America, or across the great Asian land mass.

Riding in Europe or North America is straightforward, and even the problems posed in Australia are relatively clear cut. As for those fanatics whose notion of travelling is to set the fastest time between Berlin and Singapore, I am all for abandoning them where they fall, under the stones and knives of angry Muslim villages. Here then are some points in favour of the motorcycle for the few who care to consider them. In my view, it is the most versatile vehicle there is for moving through strange countries at a reasonable pace, for experiencing changing conditions and meeting people in remote places.

It can cover immense distances and will take you where cars can hardly go. It is easily and cheaply freighted across lakes and oceans, and it can usually be trucked out of trouble without too much difficulty, where a car might anchor you to the spot for weeks. If you choose a good bike for your purpose, it will be economical and easy to repair, and it can be made to carry quite astonishing amounts of stuff if your systems are right.

Sit up and take notice

In return, the bike demands the highest levels of awareness from its rider. You need not be an expert, but you must be enthusiastic and keep all your wits about you. It is an unforgiving vehicle which does not suffer fools at all. As well as the more obvious hazards of pot holes, maniacal truck drivers and stray animals, there are the less tangible perils like dehydration, hypothermia and plain mental fatigue to recognize and avoid.

The bike, then, poses a real challenge to its rider, and it may seem on the verge of masochism to accept it, but my argument is that by choosing to travel in a way that demands top physical and mental performance you equip yourself to benefit a thousand times more from what comes your way, enabling you quite soon to brush aside the discomforts that plague lazier travellers.

You absolutely must sit up and take notice to survive at all. The weather and temperature are critical factors; the moods and customs of the people affect you vitally; you are vulnerable and sensitive to everything around you; and you learn fast. You build up resistances faster too, your instincts are sharper and truer, and you adjust more readily to changes in the climate, both physical and social. Here endeth the eulogy upon the bike.

After all these generalizations, it is difficult to be particular. There is no one bike for all seasons, nor one for all riders. The BMW is a splendid machine with a splendid reputation for touring, but is *not* infallible, and it *is* expensive. British bikes need a lot of maintenance but they are ruggedly engineered and easily repaired, given the parts of a Punjabi workshop to make them up. Japanese bikes have a shorter useful life, but they work very well, and their dealer networks are incomparable. They are hard to beat as a practical proposition provided you go for models with a tried record of reliability.

On the whole, I would aim for an engine capacity of between 500cc and 750cc. Lightness is a great plus factor. Too much power is an embarrassment, but a small engine will do fine if you don't mean to hump a lot of stuff over the Andes, or carry another person as well.

One's company

I travelled alone almost all the way around the world, but most people prefer to travel in company. As a machine the motorcycle is obviously at its best used by one person, and it is my opinion that you learn faster and get the maximum feedback on your own, but I know that for many such loneliness would be unthinkable. Even so, you need to be very clear about your reasons for choosing to travel in company. If it is only for security then my advice is to forget it.

Groups of nervous travellers chattering together in some outlandish tongue spread waves of paranoia much faster than a single weary rider struggling to make contact in the local language. A motorcycle will attract attention in most places. The problem is to turn that interest to good account. In some countries (Brazil, for example) a motorcycle is a symbol of playboy wealth, and an invitation to thieves. In parts of Africa and the Andes, it is still an unfamiliar and disturbing object. Whether the attention it attracts works for the rider or against him depends on his own awareness of others and the positive energy he can generate towards his environment.

It is very important in poor countries not to flaunt wealth and superiority. All machinery has this effect anyway, but it can be much reduced by a suitable layer of dirt and a muted exhaust system. I avoided having too much glittering chrome and electric paintwork, and I regarded most modern leathers and motorcycle gear as a real handicap. I wore an open face helmet for four years, and when I stopped among people, I always took it off to make sure they saw me as a real person. My ideal was always to get as far away as possible from the advertised image of the smart motorcyclist, and to talk to people spontaneously in a relaxed manner. If one can teach oneself to drop shyness with strangers, the rewards are dramatic. Silence is usually interpreted as stand–offishness, and is almost as much a barrier as a foreign language.

Care and repair

Obviously you should know your bike and be prepared to look after it. Carry as many tools as you can use, and all the small spares you can afford. Fit a capacitor so that you don't need a battery to start. Weld a disc on the swing stand to hold the bike in soft dirt. Take two chains and use one to draw the other off its sprockets. This makes frequent chain–cleaning less painful, something that should be done in desert conditions. Take a tin of Swarfega or Palmit; it's very useful where water is at a premium and for easing off rims. Buy good patches and take them (I like Tip–Top), you won't get them there.

The Schrader pump, which screws into a cylinder in place of the spark plug, is a fine gadget, and one of the best reasons for running on two cylinders. Aerosol repair canisters, unfortunately, do not always work. The quickly detachable wheel arrangement on my old Triumph saved me a lot of irritation too.

Change oil every 2500kms and don't buy it loose if you can avoid it. Make certain your air filter is good enough. Some production models will not keep out fine desert grit, and the consequences are not good. Equally important are low compression pistons to take the strain off and to accept lousy fuel.

I ran on Avon tyres and used a rear tread on the front wheel, which worked well. A set of tyres gave me 19,000kms or more. The hardest country for tyres was India, because of the constant braking for ox–carts on tarmac roads. It was the only places where the front tyre wore out before the rear one because, of course, it's the front brakes that do most of the stopping.

Insurance is a problem that worries many people. Get it as you go along. I was uninsured everywhere except when the authorities made it impossible for me to enter without buying it. This was most definitely illegal and I do not recommend it: if you get clobbered you have only yourself to blame.

Other things I found essential were: a stove, a good, all–purpose knife, some primitive cooking equipment and a store of staples like rice and beans. Naturally you need to carry water too, up to four or five litres if possible. I found the ability to feed myself when I felt like it was a great protection against sickness, as well as an incentive to wander even further off the beaten track. In the end I finished with quite a complex kitchen in one of my boxes, but of course that's just a matter of taste.

Don't...

Finally a few things I learned not to do. Don't ride without arms, knees and eyes covered and watch out for bee swarms, unless you use a screen, which I did not. Don't carry a gun or any offensive weapon unless you want to invite violence. Do not allow yourself to be hustled into starting off anywhere until you're ready; something is bound to go wrong or get lost. Do not let helpful people entice you into following their cars at ridiculous speeds over dirt roads and pot–holes. They have no idea what bikes can do. Always set your own pace and get used to the pleasures of easy riding. Resist the habit of thinking that you must get to the next big city before nightfall. You miss everything that's good along the way and, in any case, the cities are the least interesting places. Don't expect things to go to plan, and don't worry when they don't. Perhaps the hardest truth to appreciate when starting a long journey is that the mishaps and unexpected problems always lead to the best discoveries and the most memorable experiences. And if things insist on going too smoothly, you can always try running out of petrol on purpose.

HIRING A CAR

by Paul Melly and Edwina Townsend

First hire your car... Yes, there are a lot of countries where it is a big advantage to have your own personal transport, especially if you must keep to a tight work schedule or have bulky luggage. Yes, it is relatively easy to book anything from a Fiesta to a limousine for a fair number of the world's destinations, including some which are surprisingly off–beat. Yes, it can be very expensive —and certainly will be if the pre–departure homework is neglected. One journalist acquaintance who thought he knew what travelling was about, managed to burn up over £100 with a day and a half's car hire in Brittany by the time he'd paid all the extras.

The key rule is: don't just read the small print, work out what it actually adds up to. For example, a mileage charge really can rack up the cost, especially if you haven't measured in advance quite how far you will be travelling.

It's no use, after the event, holding a lifelong grievance against the big car hire companies. By and large they do fairly well in providing a comprehensive and reliable service in a wide range of countries, if at a price.

Travelling cheaply

If you want a better deal, you must expect to work for it and be prepared to tramp the back streets looking for a local outfit that is halfway trustworthy —but remember you only get what you pay for! It costs Hertz, Avis, Europcar, Budget and Alamo and the rest a hefty investment to provide that easy–to–book, uniform service across national frontiers and linguistic boundaries. Centralized, computer–based reservation networks don't come free.

If you really want to keep the cost down, perhaps public transport is worth a fresh thought. Shared, long–distance taxis or minibuses are surprisingly fast and cheap in many parts of the Third World and you may have an easier time with police, army or Customs road checks which have a habit of springing up every few kilometres in some countries. If it's not you who is driving, then it's not you – foreign and unfamiliar with the local situations, who has to judge whether it is correct paperwork or a small bribe that is required. Quite apart from the ethical dilemma, there is the practical one: having to pay back–handers is bad, offering them when they are not expected is worse and can get you into far more trouble.

However, it would be stupid to allow such worries to discourage travellers from doing the adventurous thing, and hiring a car can give you the freedom to go where you want at your own pace, stopping in small villages or at scenic viewpoints when it suits you.

The big car hire firms give thorough coverage of much of the developed world and quite a number of tourist and/or business destinations in other regions. But they certainly do not have outlets everywhere and there are many places where you will have to rely on local advice in finding a reliable rental outfit. Advance reservation may well be impossible. In this case, if your time is tight, ask friendly officials in the country's embassy in your home country for suggestions. Most will have a telephone directory for their capital city at least, even if it is a little out of date.

For a few pounds, you can then ring to book in advance, or just to check availability —easier, of course, if the country is on direct dialling. This could well be more effective than asking a small High Street travel agent used to selling Mediterranean package tours to try and arrange something for you. It is also worth contacting agencies which specialize in a particular region of the world.

For most places, it is still definitely worth considering the big hire companies. In recent years they have developed a good range of lower price services to complement the plusher options for those with fat expense accounts. Thanks both to the recession and the growing interest small firms are taking in foreign markets, there are plenty of businessmen who cannot afford to travel five star all the time.

And, though you may be abroad for work, very often you can, with fore–thought, make use of the special packages designed for tourists. Not only are these cheaper, but they also have the advantage of simplicity, being tailored to the needs of leisure visitors who are either not used to or do not want to be bothered with organizing everything for themselves.

Meanwhile, if you are going on holiday, there is something to be learnt from those who have to travel for work, or from their companies. Clearly, big firms have buying power in the car hire market which a private individual does not, but they also pick up a lot of experience.

Here are some useful tips suggested by the travel manager of one multi–national company: read the small print, get your insurance, avoid mileage payments and large cars, and watch out for the chance to save money on the pre–booked deal.

Price in particular, takes some calculation because of the extras which are hard to evaluate exactly. Car hire is sometimes offered per mile or per kilometre, but it is best to go for an unlimited mileage deal, even if the base price is slightly higher. While you cannot be sure how much petrol you will use or how much you will pay for it, at least the local currency cost of hiring the car for, say, six days is fixed.

Legalities

Car hire forms always include some reference to CDW (Collision Damage Waiver) and PAI (Personal Accident Insurance) additional to the cost of renting the vehicle. A customer can be held responsible for a share of loss or damage to the hire vehicle, regardless of who is at fault. But if you accept the CDW clause and pay the daily charge for it, the rental company waives this liability to the financial level advised which varies from country to country and in the US from state to state, provided the customer sticks within the conditions of the hire agreement.

Clearly if you rent a car, you must be insured against damaging it, and, more importantly, any other people or vehicles. But accepting the CDW option can prove an expensive form of protection so explore other possibilities first. For instance your own personal car insurance at home may provide cover, or you may be able to built it into your general travel insurance policy by paying a supplement.

Of particular importance to those contemplating hiring a car in the USA is to remember that the CDW charge is included in the prepayment made includes just the bare minimum amount of cover required by the laws of that state. You will more than likely be asked to top-up this cover but check first what it's going to cost you and what you are paying for.

Again with PAI you will find that most travel insurance policies sold here in the UK include medical expenses and hospital costs. Therefore, before accepting to pay for PAI as an additional extra with the car hire company, check your travel insurance policy as you may be putting yourself to unnecessary extra expense.

Another legal aspect it is vital to check, is whether the hire agreement allows you to drive where you want. This may seem an irrelevant point to make for anyone restricting themselves to a European city for instance, but important should you be visiting a country where you wish to go off the beaten track and drive on unmade roads. The conditions imposed by the car hire companies may insist you stick to metalled roads that may severely limit your freedom. Alternatively if driving off road is allowed you may find an additional supplement is charged.

Driving conditions

Perhaps this is the place to warn that roads in many countries make quite a change from Britain's consistent, if occasionally pot–holed or contra–flowed, tarmac. Clearly a good map, if you can buy one, is indispensable. But it is unlikely to give you the up–to–date or seasonal information you really need before setting out.

Many highways are just dirt or gravel and can become almost impassable at rainy times of year. If they are major trading routes this can be made even worse as huge trucks lurch through the mud cutting deep wheel ruts which fill with water. Maps will not always show the state of the roads, or what they are made of. Of course, in the dry season, such routes may be dusty, but they become much easier to use. In some areas, where the vegetation is fairly stunted, lack of tarmac can make it quite hard to follow the road.

Nor do these warnings go for tropical countries alone: the famed Alaska Hi–way from Dawson Creek in Canada through to Fairbanks is largely gravel surfaced. And many minor roads in Canada turn into muddy bogs, with cars sinking up to their axles in black gumbo when it rains. The worst time of year can be the spring thaw —just when a European visitor might be expecting conditions to get easier!

Meanwhile, if you are likely to drive through mountains, including the relatively domesticated Alps and Pyrenees, make sure your car is equipped with snow tyres or chains, and you know how to them. The Alps may be crossed by motorways and tunnels, but that does not stop winter blizzards. Nor does it stop the local police from making spot checks —and spot fines— on roads where chains or snow tires are obligatory (normally indicated by a sign as you enter the relevant stretch). This advice applies particularly to people who go on business in winter to cities near the mountains and decide to hire a car and pop up the hill for a day's skiing – your tyres may feel OK in downtown Turin, but it's not so sure you'll still feel confident on the nineteenth hairpin bend up to the ski resort, with no room to turn round.

You should also check for road construction projects, especially in the Third World where massive foreign aid spending can make it happen very suddenly on a huge scale. This may sometimes cause a mess, but it can also mean a new hard–top road existed where there was only a mud–track before, opening up fresh areas for relatively easy exploration with a normal hired saloon car. On the other hand, there can be surprising gaps in otherwise fairly good networks.

The basic rule is: before you do something unusual, tell the car hire outlet where you picked up the vehicle and signed it out. And if you should have an accident or break down, telephone the hire firm before paying for expensive repairs. Otherwise you may not be reimbursed. The firm may want to make its own arrangements.

What car?

Deciding what size of car to hire is one of the simplest questions. The main companies use fairly standard makes with which you will be familiar at home, although it is probably safe to say that you are rather more likely to get Japanese makes in Asia, French in West Africa and, not surprisingly, American in the US. But when working out costs, don't forget that larger vehicles are also thirstier.

You should remember this especially when booking in advance —sometimes the rental deal will stipulate that if the car of your choice is not available then the agency will provide one in a higher category for no extra charge. In other words, if you reserve a small car and then turn up to find it isn't there, you may end up with one that uses more petrol —which could be an expensive penalty if you are hiring it for a long trip but the car will probably be more comfortable.

Nor should petrol bills be forgotten when you return the vehicle. Most agreements stipulate that the car is provided with a tankful of petrol and returned also with a full tank. Check that it is full before you take it out and make the final fill–up yourself. This way you will probably pay less than the charges made by the hire company as a refuelling charge is usually added by them to the cost of the petrol itself.

Booking a car in advance is usually worth considering, not only for peace of mind but because you may be able to take advantage of one of the many inclusive deals offered by the major car hire companies. You can choose to either prepay before leaving home in exchange for a prepaid voucher, or alternatively book at a guaranteed rate in the currency of the country you are visiting. These rates can include not only unlimited mileage but also CDW (Collision Damage Waiver), PAI (Personal Accident Insurance) and tax on the completed transaction. This leaves you just the petrol to pay for and any optional extras you may agree to take locally. Bear in mind that these inclusive rates are often for a minimum of a three day rental.

The incidence of extra mandatory charges, which can only be paid locally, is becoming more frequent. For instance there are an increasing number of countries where either a fixed fee, or a percentage of the rental is charged by the local authority for vehicles rented at airport locations. This is passed on to the hirer by the car hire companies. Also, in some US States, Florida immediately springs to mind, there is now a mandatory extra tax levied of approximately $2 per day in addition to the standard charges. in other words, beware of the extras.

If you are not sure whether to rent or not, why not take a prepaid voucher with you for any number of days. Once you are on the spot you can therefore weigh up the possible alternative form of transport and decided whether or not to use it. Most prepaid vouchers, if unused and returned to the outlet where you bought them, will be refunded in full. However, this is not always the case so check before buying. Also be aware that partially used vouchers are often not refundable.

Last of all, but equally important, a deposit is always required by car hire companies at the beginning of any rental. In most cases an imprint of your credit or charge card will suffice. However, you may find that a car rental company may refuse to hire you the car if you cannot produce a credit card. Alternatively, though it is unusual, you may be required to pay the deposit in cash or travellers's cheques.

When you arrive abroad it is always worthwhile asking for tips about reliable local car hire firms; hotel porters are usually a good source of information. Also once at the hire company, before revealing you have a prepaid voucher , why not check if they have any local special offers. Providing your bank balance will stand the cost of the voucher until you return home, and you have sufficient funds to pay again locally, this could be yet another way of making extra savings.

The big groups claim to offer the same level of service, whether it be one of their own offices or a franchise. While you will invariably be provided with the best available wherever you are renting, remember that in some countries new vehicles are scarcer than hen's teeth; the road conditions leave much to be desired and the standards of driving are not quite what you expected to find!

One option for cutting costs and red tape if you are staying somewhere for a lengthy period, or regularly visit the same destination, can be leasing. This is normally provided for conventional business car fleets, but you may find that if you, or a group of people, regularly need a car in one place, a lease could be cheaper. It is also simple because the deal can include repairs and service.

Safety

Of course, the bottom line when you hire a car is safety. Does the vehicle work and can you trust it? Unless you are a natural, or at least a good amateur, mechanic, there isn't much chance of really assessing whether the car is roadworthy. But one can make a few simple checks which are at least a pointer as to how well it's maintained.

Try the steering and test out the brakes by driving a few feet in the hire shop forecourt, and of course listen for any faults in the first mile or two. Have a look at the tyre treads to see if they are still fairly deep and test the lights. If you are in tropical country check the air–conditioning, if any, and in any very cold territory, such as Canada between October and April, be sure it is winterized. Just because the first snow of autumn hasn't survived in the city centre doesn't mean it has melted in the surrounding countryside and suburbs too.

A rather more subtle approach, and probably just as effective, is recommended by the travel manager at a big oil company. Have a look in the rear seat ash trays. If they are stuffed with cigarette butts and rubbish it suggests the hire firm either hasn't had time or can't be bothered to check over the car after the previous customer returned it. Then make sure that any faults such as bumps or scratches are detailed on the hire form before you take the car out. Otherwise you could find yourself held liable when you return it.

It is also a good idea to make sure you are allowed to use the car where you want to. Tell the hire firm if you plan to cross national or state borders, just to make sure the insurance cover extends across the frontier. And remember that while many discount rental deals allow you to drop the car off where you want in the country where you collected it, there is usually a surcharge for leaving it at one of the company's offices in a completely different country.

Getting the right paperwork is also vital. Take photocopies of all hire agreements, insurance etc as well as such basics as an International Driving Permit (see *Documentation for the International Motorist*, Chapter 9). And remember that in many countries travellers are expected to register with the local police on arrival in a town and stop at police posts by the roadside. Often, as a foreigner, you may get less hassle than the locals.

Though when it comes to frontiers, if the border is closed for the night, you will have to wait until morning to cross, even if there is no physical barrier in your way. Otherwise you could have problems when you come to leave and your passport lacks the proper entry stamps. Probably the only reliable way to check whether you're allowed across is to ask the drivers of local bush taxis which may have pulled in to wait for dawn. In the end, when it comes to officialdom, patience and politeness are probably more important than anything else. But first hire your car…

BUYING AND SELLING A CAR ABROAD

by Paul Melly

Who wants to get rid of a car in Jakarta? Well, if you've just spent seventeen weeks driving all the way from London, there's a fair chance that a 'plane, at 17 hours, will seem much the most attractive mode of travel back home. Either way, if you do sell a car or camper van, make sure that anybody who could be affected knows what you've done. Whether you think you still own the vehicle is merely the first stage. The important thing is to be certain that the authorities, both where you bought it and where you sell it, understand the position. What you have to tell them partly depends on where you bought the vehicle and what its status is.

Buying

Traditionally, the favoured market–place for those planning long overland trips, especially Australians and New Zealanders, is a car park near Waterloo Station and the Festival Hall on the South Bank of the Thames in London. On Fridays, Saturdays and Sundays, this is busy with travellers haggling over battered camper vans, many of them various conversions of VW Kombis.

Prices can range from several hundred to several thousand pounds but real bargains are becoming fewer, as dealers begin to muscle in on the market. Many vehicles are actually registered on the continent, with some of the cheapest coming from the Netherlands. Provided the car is not kept in the UK for more than 12 months at a stretch (unlikely if you are buying it specially for a trip) you do not need to incur the costs of UK registration.

However, many of those sold at Waterloo have already done a huge mileage and, although there may be nothing obviously wrong with them, vital parts can be almost worn out, landing you with hefty repair bills soon afterwards.

A more reliable option can be the normal second–hand market: classified adverts, car auctions and so on. *Complete Car Auction* magazine gives information on sales all over the UK together with guideline prices. Of course, a vehicle bought this way will probably be registered in the UK.

Obviously, tyres, brakes and suspension should be checked wherever you buy. But, if a long trip is planned through countries where spares will be hard to get, it is worthwhile investing in a professional mechanical check of the vehicle and the AA, among others, offers this service. After all, even if the seller does provide some kind of guarantee, you're going to have difficulty enforcing it in Kurdistan or Mizoram.

Insurance

Before leaving, it is also essential, if you can, to get full details of the vehicle registration rules for any country you could be passing through. These are often available from tourist offices or embassies. Insurance cover providing for at least local vehicle recovery is also a good idea. If you should have an accident or breakdown and decide to abandon the car altogether, there is much less chance of slipping away unnoticed with your battered suitcases than in the days before computers made police and governments across the world more inquisitive, or at least more efficient at being inquisitive.

Insurance can be expensive, but it probably won't be as expensive as the fine or recovery fee you may end up having to pay a foreign government embassy for leaving them to clear away what was left of your camper van.

The AA and RAC have cooperation deals with their European counterparts, but once you've crossed the Bosphorous, Mediterranean or South Atlantic, you will probably have to turn to someone offering worldwide cover such as Europ Assistance (252 High Street, Croydon CR0 1NF, tel: 081–680 1234).

When you come to sell at the other end, immediately contact the insurers to cancel the balance of insurance time remaining, for which you should get a rebate.

Before leaving you should take two photocopies of all your motoring documents proving insurance registration, ownership, road tax, and if applicable, MOT, together with your passport. You should keep the originals with you, keep one copy in a locked compartment in the vehicle and deposit one copy with the bank or a PO Box number at home where it can be checked out if necessary. This should help you to prove ownership if the police in any country or the insurance authorities require it.

The papers will also be useful when it comes to selling the car – showing that you own it and are therefore entitled to sell.

Selling

When you sell, it is vital to make sure that the transaction is recorded in the presence of a witness who can be easily contacted later if necessary. Motoring journalist Brian Charig recalls the case of the American student who found a garage willing to buy his camper van in India. In this instance the customer asked the manager of the hotel where the student had just paid his bill with an American Express Card (which is traceable) to witness the deal formally. They wanted to be protected in case something went wrong.

Written proof of sale is a safeguard against someone else committing a motoring offence, or even using the car for a serious crime, after you have sold it. You can demonstrate to the local police that it was nothing to do with you. In fact, it is best to tell the police anyway when you sell the car.

One final point: when you sell your car you hope to keep, or spend, all the money you are paid for it, so it is vital to make sure the Contract of Sale stipulates that the local buyer will meet the cost of all taxes, import duties or other official fees involved. When a foreigner sells a vehicle to a local that normally constitutes an import, so be certain that the price you agree is net of all customs dues, sales, tax etc. And before you leave home, check (anonymously) with the embassy of the country where you plan to sell as to how the deal will be viewed by officials. If they record the fact that you bring in a car on your passport or entry document, the people checking you out at the airport Customs or Passport Control may well want to know what you have done with it.

There are one or two legal ways to beat the import duties, which can be as much as 400 per cent of the value of the vehicle. If you have owned the car for at least a year, plan to own it for another two, and it is the first you have imported into that country, you can normally take it in duty free. If the buyer is remaining in the country, they could leave it in your name for the required two years. Only do this, however, if you know the buyer well enough, either personally or by repute, to ensure that they are trustworthy. Or you can legally sell it in the zone between two borders, although this would mean the buyer would have to have access to free passage of a fairly large sum of money across the borders. Or you can sell it to another traveller, diplomat or foreign resident who is, for whatever reason, not bound by local laws. But you may well find that in many countries, such as Zimbabwe, while foreign currency is in desperately short supply, there is no shortage of local currency, and buyers will be queuing, even with the high price demanded by the duties, for vehicles such as Land Rovers in a good state of repair.

Using the money

A further factor to bear in mind, which could influence your choice of country to sell in, is currency status and regulations. Many, but by no means all, Third World countries have a currency which is not internationally exchangeable and a large number of these have controls on what you can take out in both local money and foreign exchange.

So ideally choose a country which has an internationally convertible currency, such as the Singapore Dollar, or the CFA (African franc, underwritten by the Bank of France). That way, if you do take out the payment for the car, you will be able to change it into money you can spend at home such as sterling or dollars. Or you may even be able to buy western currency in a local bank.

If you cannot plan to land up in a hard currency nation, find out what the local exchange control rules are. Otherwise you may find that you cannot take money out in either cash or traveller's cheques, local or foreign currency. Many countries are so short of hard currency they must restrict its use to buying essential imports, and these are unlikely to include fifth hand cars from foreign tourists. Even some countries which do have a convertible currency restrict what funds can be taken abroad.

The simplest answer is to check before you leave what you can buy with the local money —food, souvenirs, and often hotel accommodation, sometimes even air tickets— and spend your takings on the spot. The problem is to guess how much you may be paid for the car. But then, interesting travel is never without its complications.

PS. The career of the amateur currency smuggler is a hazardous one, especially if you aren't much good at telling lies. And customs officers have a talent for mental arithmetic designed to catch you out as you try to persuade them you lived in their country for a week on £3.

SHIPPING A VEHICLE

by Tania Brown and Keith Kimber

To find the best shipping for your vehicle you must know who sails to your destination. Most people begin by looking through the Yellow Pages and contacting shipping agents, but this will never give you a complete list of all the ships using the port. The secret is to locate the industry paper that serves the port and get the latest copy. They appear under a variety of names like *Shipping Times*, *Shipping Schedules* and some less obvious publications such as *The Bulletin* in Panama. Start by asking for them at shipping offices. Most are published weekly and contain a goldmine of information. Listings indicate destinations and arrival/departure dates for all ships in port along with pier and berth numbers that tell you exactly where the ships are located. Also indicated are the shipping line, its local agent and types of cargo carried. The same information is given for ships at sea scheduled to arrive, and there's a directory of agents' telephone numbers and addresses. In some countries this information appears as a weekly supplement to a regular newspaper.

Contact the agents that list sailings to your destination and compare freight costs (always based on volume). The basic freight rate always has three surcharges which follows fluctuating fuel costs; a currency adjustment factor to compensate for exchanging rates; and wharfage charges. Make sure these are included in any quotes you receive. At times the bunker surcharge or currency adjustment factor can be negative values, and represent a discount.

Unconventional channels

Don't only follow conventional channels. The paper will list unscheduled ships using the port mission boats, training ships, all kinds of 'oddball' one–off vessels that might take you on board. They won't have agents at the ports so you'll have to contact the Captain direct. Where port security is minimal and/or corrupt, enter the docks and speak to the Captain personally. Any visual material like photos and maps of your journey are invaluable as an introduction. One good photo can jump the language and cultural barriers and get him interested enough to talk to you. If port security is strict, there is another way. When a ship docks it is immediately connected to a telephone line. Each berth has a different telephone number. In Sydney, for example, the numbers are listed in the telephone directory. Consult your shipping journal for the ship's berth, look up the number and you can speak directly to the ship. If the numbers aren't in the 'phone book, ask at the Shipping and Port Manager's office.

Write to the Captain with your visual material and a covering letter explaining what you are doing and where you want to go. Follow it up two days later to receive his reply. That way he can see what you are doing and you get a chance to speak to him on the 'phone. If he's amenable, ask for a working passage or free shipping for your vehicle, but be prepared to follow up with a realistic offer of payment if his interest starts to wane. If you work your passage as we did, your vehicle is taken free. But we've also received offers from regular shipping lines to take our vehicle unaccompanied to various parts of the world. For this you should approach the Operations Manager or General Manager of the shipping line or its agent. Again, write and interest them in what you are doing. If you are on an expedition, you can generate publicity for them —point this out. If not, don't worry. Offer to give a talk and slide show for the staff in return for free shipping, plus any number of large colour photographs they can use for advertising showing the company logo on your vehicle as you tackle the next desert or jungle. The way you approach them is really more important than what you offer in return. Don't forget, people in poor countries can't always understand the desire for hard travelling and a frugal lifestyle but some dramatic photos of your journey can work wonders.

Packing your vehicle

Your next concern is how the vehicle will travel. Try to avoid crating it if you can. Crating is expensive and involves a lot of back–breaking work. Even in countries where labour is cheap, timber is costly. It's also inconvenient —you can't drive your vehicle to the ship when it's in a crate. If you must crate, visit an import agent to try and obtain a ready–made crate the right size. Un–crated, the vehicle can go 'break–bulk', roll–on/roll–off or containerized. Containerized is the best. The vehicle is protected from theft and the elements, and can't be damaged during loading or unloading —and you can leave all your luggage inside. 'Roll–on/roll–off' services are very convenient. The vehicle is driven onto the ship and stored below deck – just like a regular car ferry. But these only operate on certain routes and your luggage shouldn't be left in the vehicle. 'Break–bulk' means it is carried as it is, either in the ship's hold or on deck surrounded by all the other break–bulk cargo. Countries with weak economies may insist you pay for your freight in US dollars. It's advisable to carry enough US dollars (rather than pounds) for this purpose.

A forwarding agent can do all the paperwork for you although it's cheaper to do it yourself. The best way is to team up with a 'hustler' who works for a forwarding agent. These young lads spend all day pushing paperwork through the system. They know where to find port trust offices, the wharf storekeeper's office, main Customs building, port Customs building, etc, etc; buildings and offices that are usually spaced far and wide across the city. They know how to persuade Customs officers to inspect the vehicle and wharf officers to certify documents. Better still, they know what sort of 'tips' are expected down the line. I've always found them friendly, helpful types, with great sympathy towards anyone on the same side of the counter as themselves pitted against the officials! They've never objected to my tagging along to push my own paperwork through the system. In return, I buy them cold drinks and a good meal each day we're together, and give a few dollars to thank them for their help at the end.

Be well prepared to do your own paperwork. Take a dozen sheets of carbon paper, a handful of paper clips (there will be a lot of copies), a good ball point pen, some large envelopes and a pocketful of small denomination notes in the local currency. Commit your passport number, engine and chassis number, vehicle weight and local address to memory so you can double check details as the officials type them out (this is also good practice for any overland traveller when crossing land borders). Remember if a single digit is incorrect in the serial numbers you will not be entitled to your own vehicle at your destination. People *have* lost their vehicles this way. I also carry a small 'John Bull' type india rubber kit to make up my own rubber stamps. It saves hours filling out forms – especially if you are doing a number of vehicles. It's normal practice to have to buy the forms you use for a nominal sum —either at the port or a stationer's in town. In Western countries the paperwork is often simplified and it's quite easy to do it yourself.

Clean the vehicle thoroughly before shipping (especially under the mudguards where dirt collects) to avoid the cost of it being quarantined or fumigated on arrival. Smear exposed deck cargo with grease or paint it with diesel oil. Grease the disc brakes as well. Don't worry, they will work afterwards. On a motorcycle, remove wing mirrors, the screen and indicators.

Cars should be lashed on deck with chains and bottle screws, not rope which will fray and stretch. If only rope is available look for nylon rope which won't stretch when it gets wet. Motorcycles should be off the centre–stand, wheels chocked front and back and tied to a post using wooden spacers. Look ahead and be prepared to take your own rope. On the *MV Chidambaram* in India we ended up using the guy ropes from our tent and every webbing strap we had to tie our motorcycle securely. Don't leave a vehicle unaccompanied at the dock. Paper work can usually be done two days before sailing, then the vehicle is inspected, cleared by Customs and loaded on board the day it sails. In Third World countries, insist on being allowed to supervise loading. Use rope slings, don't let them use a net. Sling a motorcycle through the back wheel and under the steering head. A car should be lifted using pairs of boards or poles chained together under the wheels. If the correct tackle is unavailable, drive the car into an empty container so it can be lifted on board. If the vehicle must be left on the dockside and loaded in your absence, don't leave any luggage inside, don't leave the key with anyone and lash it to a wooden pallet so they can forklift it to the ship and winch it on board. And don't leave the country before you've seen the vehicles off, in case they don't load it for some reason.

Meet the ship on arrival and confirm your cargo will be unloaded. When we arrived in Malaysia, they told us our bike was destined to continue to Singapore. We had an awful time convincing them they were wrong! The vehicle will then be held in Customs until you complete the paperwork to release it. Insist it goes inside a locked shed. There may be a nominal storage charge but often the first three days are free. Be prepared to be philosophical about accepting some minor damage. Put any dents down to adventure!

Air freight

Motorcyclists can consider airfreight as a viable alternative to shipping. Over short distances, it's often cheaper and sometimes may be the only way of getting somewhere —inland, for example. In a passenger aircraft, the motorcycle lies on its side in the cargo hold, so construct a set of crash bars to support it without damage. It must fly completely dry: no fuel, engine oil, brake fluid, coolant, battery acid or air in the tyres. People worry their battery will be ruined by draining the acid. I've drained mine many times and once left it dry for more than two weeks without any ill effects. It doesn't even lose any charge. But don't use it before refilling with acid! And don't plug the breather hole or the whole thing will explode. A wad of cotton wool over the hole will soak up any acid drops and allow it to breathe. Freight charges are based on weight.

Special notes

Depending on the political situation in Sri Lanka you can sail to Talaimannar by ferry from Rameshwaram Island, India. Vehicles and passengers cross the Pamban Channel by train from Mandapam, the last stop on the mainland. There is no road bridge. Motorcycles are lifted into the goods carriage, cars go on a low loader which costs extra. The ferry moors a quarter of a mile off shore and is loaded by 'lighters' —small wooden boats. Cars go on a flat raft or two lighters tied together, a hair–raising experience. Paperwork takes a full day.

I have met people who have been obliged to spend US$1500 on anti–pollution devices for their cars arriving in California to comply with state laws. This doesn't apply to everyone, but if in doubt, ship to one of the other 49 states. From personal experience, Columbus Shipping Lines take excellent care of vehicles, keeping them regularly washed down with fresh water to reduce the effects of the salty sea air.

On entering Panama, you have to specify where the vehicle will be shipped from. If undecided, specify 'Colon.' When you've organized your shipping, visit the Customs head office at Ancon to make any changes. International motorcyclists in Panama shipping round the Darien Gap can contact the Road Knights Motorcycle Club at Albrook US Air Force Base for advice, use of workshops, and up to two weeks' free accommodation. It will be cheaper to ship cars to Ecuador than Colombia.

Finally, shipping really isn't all that bad. Things always go smoother and quicker than you think and there are always people who will help you out. If you encounter just a quarter of the problems mentioned here you've had an unusually bad trip!

OFF–ROAD DRIVING

by Jack Jackson

Off–road driving techniques vary with the ability and weight of the vehicle, as well as with the driver. Some vehicles have greater capabilities than many drivers can handle and there may often be more than one way of solving a particular problem. So pre–expedition driver training is worthwhile for educating newcomers, to both their own and their vehicle's capabilities.

Alert but restrained driving is essential. A light foot and low gears in four-wheel drive will usually get one through soft or difficult ground situations. Sometimes sheer speed may be better but, if you lose control at speed, you could suffer severe damage or injury. Remember that careful driving in the first instance can save you time, money and effort. Broken chassis, springs, half shafts and burnt-out clutches, are caused by the driver, not the vehicle.

Before you do any off–road driving, look under your vehicle and note the position of its lowest points: exhaust pipes, towing plates, springs, axles, differentials, transfer box and gearbox. These will often be lower than you think and the differentials are usually off–centre. Remember their clearance and position when traversing obstacles that you cannot get around. Do not hook your thumbs around the steering wheel, the sudden twist of the steering wheel when a front wheel hits a stone or rut can easily break your thumb.

Roll up and tie up any mud flaps as high as possible, to stop them being ripped off by humps and rocks.

Make sure that you have good towing eyes for recovery and that your number plates are above bumper level, to avoid damage.

Scouting ahead

Always travel at a sensible speed, keeping your eyes some 20 yards ahead, watching for difficulties. If you are on a track where it is possible that another vehicle may come the other way, have a passenger keep a look out further ahead while you concentrate on negotiating the awkward areas. Travel only at speeds that allow you to stop comfortably within the limit of clear vision. Always travel slowly to the brow of a hump or sharp bend; there may be a large boulder, hole, or steep drop into a river bed beyond it.

Apart from soft sand and snow, most situations where four-wheel drive is needed also require low range, which gives better traction, torque and control. They will normally also require you to stop and inspect the route on foot first, so you will therefore engage low range before starting off again.

On soft sand it is useful to be able to engage low range on the move. On some vehicles this requires plenty of practice of double declutching and the ensuing confidence in being able to do this smoothly will usually save you from getting stuck. For most situations, first gear low range is too low and you might spin the wheels; use second or third gear, except over bad rocks.

When going downhill on a loose surface, it is essential to use four-wheel drive low range with engine braking. Never touch the brakes or declutch, you will lose control. With permanent four-wheel drive systems, remember to engage lock before entering difficult situations.

If you have been in four-wheel drive on a hard surface, when you change back into two-wheel drive or, for permanent four-wheel drive systems, you unlock the centre differential lock; you might find this change and the steering difficult. This is due to wind–up between the axles, which will scrub tyres and damage the drive train. If you are lightly loaded, you can free this wind–up by driving backwards for about 10 yards, whilst swinging the steering wheel from side to side. If on the other hand you are heavily loaded, you will have to free it by jacking up one front wheel clear of the ground; keep clear of the wheel, which may spin violently.

Make use of the rhythm of the suspension, touch the brakes lightly as you approach the crest of the hump and release them as you pass over it; this will stop you from flying. When you come to a sharp dip or rut, cross it at an angle so that only one wheel at a time drops into it. Steer the wheel towards and over the terrain's high points to maintain maximum ground clearance. If you cannot avoid a large or sharp boulder, drive the wheels on one side directly over it, rather than trying to straddle it.

Do not drive on the outside edge of tracks with a steep drop, they may be undermined by water and collapse under the weight. If you have to travel along the deep ruts, try to straddle one of the ruts rather than being in both with your transmission dragging the ground in the centre. Cross narrow river beds at an angle so that you do not get stuck in a dip at 90° with no room left for manoeuvre.

Ground inspection

When on sand, watch out for any changes in colour. If the surface you are driving on is firm and the surface colour remains the same, then the going is likely to be the same. If, however, there is a change in colour, you should be prepared for possibly softer sand. Moving sand dunes and dry river beds produce the most difficult soft sand.

Keep an eye on previous vehicle tracks, they will give you an indication of trouble spots that you might be able to avoid.

All difficult sections should be inspected on foot first. This can save you a lot of hard work getting unstuck later. If you are not sure of being able to see the route or obstacles clearly from the driving seat, get a passenger to stand in a safe place where he or she can see the problem clearly and direct you. Arrange a clear system of hand signal directions with the person beforehand, as vocal directions can be drowned by engine noise.

Sometimes you might have to build up a route, putting stones or sand ladders across drainage ditches or weak bridges, or chipping away high corners, or levering aside large boulders. If you have to rebuild a track or fill in a hole completely, do so from above —rolling boulders down instead of wasting energy lifting them from below. Where possible bind them together by mixing with tree branches or bushes.

In Third World countries, always inspect local bridges before using them. If there are signs that local vehicles cross the river instead of the bridge, then that is the safest way to go.

Stuck fast

If you are stuck in a rut on firm ground, try rocking out by quickly shifting from first to reverse gear, but do not try this on sand or mud as you will only dig deeper. If you cannot rock out, jack up the offending wheel and fill up the rut with stones or logs. A high lift jack makes this much easier and can, with care, also be used to shunt the vehicle sideways out of the rut.

If you need to be towed or winched out, make sure that you have strong towing eyes. Having two of these at the front and two at the back, enables you to spread the load.

If a rock suddenly appears and you cannot stop in time, hit it square on with a tyre, which is more resilient and more easily repaired than your chassis. To traverse large boulders, use first gear low range and crawl over, using the engine for both driving and braking. Avoid slipping the clutch or touching the brakes, or you will lose control.

On loose surfaces, do not change gear whilst going up or downhill for you can lose traction. Always change to a lower gear before you reach the problem to remain in control. If you lose traction going up such a hill, try swinging the steering wheel from side to side —you may get a fresh bite and make the top. If you fail going up a steep hill, make a fast change into reverse, make sure you are in four-wheel drive with the centre differential locked (if you have one) and use the engine as a brake to back down the same way you came up. Do not try to turn round or go down on the brakes.

Always be prepared to stop quickly on the top of a steep hill or sand dune, the way down the other side may be at a completely different angle. Descend steep hills in low range four-wheel drive second or third gear, using the engine as a brake. Do not tackle steep hills diagonally; if you lose traction and slip sideways, you may turn over or roll to the bottom. Only cross slopes if it is absolutely necessary. If you must do so, take the least possible angle and make any turns quickly.

Crossing water

Before crossing water, stop and inspect it first, if possible by wading through. Is the bottom solid or moving? Are there any large holes caused by previously stuck vehicles, which must be filled in or driven round? Is there a sensible angle into it and out on the other side? Is there a current fast enough to necessitate your aiming upstream to get straight across? How deep is it? Will it come above the exhaust, cooling fan or vehicle floor?

Four-wheel drive vehicles should have poppet valves or breather tubes on the axle breathers which will keep out water. If you get stuck in water for several hours, the axle, wheel bearing, swivel pin housing, transfer box and gearbox oils, will need to be changed. Some vehicles have a wading plug that should be screwed into the clutch bell housing when much work is done in water.

If the water comes above the fan, then the fan belt should be disconnected. Though for a short crossing, tying a large plastic bag or sheet across the radiator will suffice. If the water comes above the floor, then you should move any articles that could be damaged by it. Petrol engines should have plenty of ignition sealant around the coil, ignition leads and distributor.

Difficult or deep water should be crossed in low range four-wheel drive, keeping the engine speed high. This keeps enough pressure in the exhaust to stop the back pressure of the water from stalling the engine while the forward speed is not high enough to create a bow–wave and spray water over the electrics. Diesel engines are a great advantage here. If you stall in the water, remove the spark plugs or injector and try driving out in bottom gear on the starter motor. This works over short distances.

On easy crossings, keep the brakes dry by keeping the left foot lightly on the brake pedal. Once out of any water, dry out the brakes by driving a couple of miles this way. Disc brakes are self–cleaning, but drum brakes fill up with water and sediment so should be cleaned regularly. Don't forget the transmission brakes fitted to the best vehicles.

A vehicle stuck in melted glacier water or sea water for more than a couple of hours, will need very thorough washing and several oil changes to get rid of salt and silt. With salt water, electrical connections can be permanently damaged.

Sand

Sandy beaches are usually firm enough for a vehicle between high tide mark and four yards from the sea itself, where there is likely to be an undertow. Beware of the incoming tide, which is often faster than you envisaged and can cut you off from your point of exit. Where there are large puddles or streaming water on a sea beach, beware of quicksand.

The key to soft sand is flotation and steady momentum; any abrupt changes in speed or direction can break through the firmer surface crust, putting the wheels into the softer sand below. Use as high a gear as possible, so that you do not induce wheelspin. If you do not have special sand tyres, speed up as you approach a soft section and try to maintain an even speed and a straight line as you cross the sand. If you find yourself sticking, press down gently on the accelerator. If you have to change down, do it very smoothly to avoid wheelspin. In large soft sand areas, use flotation tyres and/or reduce tyre pressure and drive slowly in four–wheel drive.

Do not travel in other people's tracks, the crust has already been broken and your vehicle's undercarriage will be that much lower, and therefore nearer to sticking to start with. Keeping your eye on other people's tracks will warn you of soft sections, but do not follow them for navigation, as they may be 50 years old.

In general, flat sand with pebbles or grass on its surface, or obvious wind–blown corrugations, will support a vehicle. If in doubt, get out and walk the section first. Stamp your feet. If you get a firm footprint then it should support your vehicle, but if you get a vague oval then it it too soft. If the soft section is short, your can make a track with sand ladders, but if it is long, then low tyre pressures and four–wheel drive will be needed. Bedford four–ton trucks will not handle soft sand without the assistance of sand mats and lots of human pushing power.

Dry river beds can be very soft and difficult to get out of. Drift sand will always be soft. If you wish to stop voluntarily on soft sand, find a place on top of a rise, preferably pointing downhill and roll to a stop instead of using the brakes and breaking the crust.

Most vehicles have too much weight on the rear wheels when loaded and these often break through and dig in, leaving the front wheels spinning uselessly on the surface. A couple of passengers sitting on the bonnet can help for short, bad sections but you must not overload the front continuously or you will damage the front axle.

Sand dunes need proper high flotation sand tyres. You need speed to get up a dune, but must be able to stop on the top, as there may be a steep drop on the other side. Dunes are best climbed where the angle is least, so known routes in opposing directions are usually many miles apart, to make use of the easiest angles. In the late afternoon, when the sun is low, it is difficult to spot sudden changes in dune strata and many accidents occur with vehicles flying off the end of steep drops, so do not travel at this time of day.

Most deserts freeze overnight in the winter months, making the surface crust much firmer. Even if they do not freeze, there is always some dew in the surface crust, making it firmest around dawn, so this is the time to tackle the softest sections.

Local drivers often travel at night, but unless you know the route really well, this will be too dangerous. So start at dawn and then camp around mid–afternoon before the light gets too difficult and the sand is at its softest.

In large dune areas when travelling longitudinally, stay as high up the dunes as possible. Then if you feel your vehicle begin to stick, you can gain momentum by aiming downhill and try again. The bottom of the well between the dunes usually has the softest sand.

Getting unstuck in sand

Once you are stuck in sand, do not spin the wheels or try to rock out, as you will only go in deeper and may damage the transmission. First off–load the passengers and with them pushing, try to reverse out in low range. The torque on the propeller shafts tends to tilt the front and rear axles in opposite directions relative to the chassis. So, if you have not dug in too deep, when you engage reverse you tend to tilt the axles in the opposite direction to the direction involved when you got stuck, thus getting traction on the wheels that lost it before. If you stopped soon enough in the first instance, this technique will get you out. If it does not, the only answer is to start digging and use sand ladders.

It is tempting to do only half of the digging required but this usually fails and you finish up working twice as hard in the end. Self recovery with a winch does not work very well either. Sand deserts do not abound with trees and burying the spare wheel or a stake deep enough to winch you out is as hard as digging the vehicle out anyway. A second vehicle on firm ground, with a winch or tow rope can help, but you will have to dig out the stuck vehicle first. So get down to it and dig!

Long-handled shovels are best —you have to get right under the differentials— small shovels and folding tools are useless. Reconnoitre the area and decide whether the vehicle must come out forwards or backwards. Dig the sand clear of all points that are touching it. Dig the wheels clear and then dig a sloping ramp from all wheels to the surface in the intended direction of travel.

Lay down sand ladders in the ramp, rear wheel only if things are not too bad, all four wheels if things are very bad. Push the ends of the ladders under the wheels as far as possible so that they do not shoot out. A high lift jack can help here. If you are using sand ladders as opposed to perforated steel plates, mark their position in the sand with upright shovels, as they often disappear in use and can be hard to find later. Then, with only the driver in the vehicle and all passengers pushing, the vehicle should come out using low range four-wheel drive.

If the passengers are very fit, they can dig up the sand ladders quickly and keep placing them under the wheels of the moving vehicle. Sometimes, when a ladder is not properly under a rear wheel when a vehicle first mounts it, it can tip up and damage a body panel or exhaust pipe; so an agile person has to keep a foot away on the free end to keep it down. Remember to move *very quickly* once things are safe or you'll get run over!

New sand ladder designs are articulated in the centre or sectioned and tied together, to correct this problem. Do not tie the ladders to the rear of the vehicle in the hope of towing them: they will cause you to bog down again.

Bringing the vehicle out backwards is usually the shortest way to reach firm ground but you will still have to get across or around the bad section. Once out, the driver should not stop again until he has reached firm ground so the passengers may have a long, hot walk, carrying the sand ladders and shovels. With a large convoy, a ramp of several ladders can be made up on bad sections and all hands should help.

Vehicles of one ton or under need only carry lightweight sand ladders. They should be just long enough to fit comfortably between the wheelbase. One vehicle alone needs to carry four; but vehicles in convoy need only carry two each, as they can help each other out. Heavier vehicles need to carry heavy perforated steel plate. It is silly to weigh down lightweight vehicles with this, as one often sees in Africa.

Sand ladders and perforated steel plate bend in use so when you have finished all the soft sections, lay them on hard ground (ends on the ground and the bend in the air) and drive over them to straighten them out.

Salt Flats (Sebkhas, Chotts)

These are like quicksand. You sink quickly and if you cannot be towed out quickly, it can be permanent! In areas known for their salt flats, stick to the track and preferably convoy with another four-wheel drive vehicle. If you are unlucky enough to hit one, try to drive back to firm ground in a wide arc. Do not stop and try to reverse out.

Dirt roads

On dirt roads, watch out for stones thrown up by other vehicles (and in some countries, small boys) which break your windscreen. Do not overtake when you cannot see through the dust of the vehicle ahead. There may be a ditch, or something coming the other way. Use the horn to warn vehicles that you are about to overtake. If you cannot see to overtake, drop back clear of the other vehicle's dust and wait until the track changes direction so that the wind blows the dust to one side, thus providing clear vision. On dirt roads, culverts do not always extend to the full width of the road so watch out for these when overtaking and be especially careful of this in snow.

Avoid driving at night; pot holes, culverts, broken-down trucks, bullock carts and people are hard to see and many trucks drive at speed without lights and then blind you with full beam when spotting you. In many countries there are unlit chains and logs thrown across the roads at night, as checkpoints.

Corrugations

These are parallel ridges and troughs across dirt roads caused by the return spring rates of heavy traffic and, in really bad conditions, can be up to 10 inches deep. They give an effect similar to sitting on a pneumatic drill —for both the vehicle and its occupants! Heavy vehicles have no choice but to travel slowly, but lightweight vehicles often 'iron out' the bumps by finding the right speed to skim over the top of the ruts. This is usually 30 to 40 mph, any faster can be dangerous. Going fast over corrugations increases tyre temperature thus causing more punctures.

Softly sprung vehicles such as the Range Rover, Toyota Land Cruiser and American four-wheel drives, can go faster more comfortably on corrugations, often blowing tyres and, consequently turning over under these conditions, usually with fatal consequences. Short wheelbase vehicles (ie. less than 100 inches) are very unstable on corrugations and often spin and turn over. The only sensible answer is to travel at reasonable speed, make regular stops to ease your growing frustration and be extra vigilant for punctures.

One is often tempted to try travelling beside the corrugations but remember that thousands of other vehicles have tried that before and given up —hence the corrugations. So take it steady and try to be patient.

Third World ferries should be embarked and disembarked in four-wheel drive, to avoid pushing them away from the bank leaving your vehicle in the water.

Mud

Momentum is also the key to getting through mud but there are likely to be more unseen problems underneath mud than in sand. If mud is not too deep, the wheels might find traction on firm ground beneath. So if there are existing tracks and they are not deep enough to ground your transmission in the centre, then such tracks are worth using. Otherwise, slog through in as high a gear as possible —as you would with sand— avoiding any sudden changes of speed or direction.

If the mud is heavy with clay, even aggressive tread tyres will soon clog up. Unless you are using self–cleaning mud tyres, such as dumper truck tyres or terra tyres, you will gain a lot by fitting chains.

High flotation tyres are useful in bogs, but do not help in most muddy situations. Normal width or even narrow width tyres are best, as they can cut through into the firmer ground underneath. Mud is one situation where cross-ply tyres are advantageous.

Muddy areas are likely to be near trees —one area where a winch is useful. If you stick badly, digging out can be very heavy work. It is best to jack up the vehicle and fill in the holes under the wheels with stones, logs or bushes. A high lift jack can make things much easier here, but be careful of it slipping. High lift jacks should always be used on a wide base plate and are less likely to slip if a piece of wood is placed between the jack and the vehicle. Adapters are available to fit high lift jacks into modern Land Rover jacking holes. If there is a lot of water, dig a channel to drain it away. Perforated steel plate can be useful in mud but sand ladders become very slippery.

When you get back on the paved road, clear as much mud as possible off the wheels and propeller shafts for the extra weight will put them out of balance and cause damage. Drive steadily for several miles to clear the tyre treads, or you could skid.

If you are unlucky, you might get the centre of the vehicle's undercarriage stuck on rocks or a tree stump. The answer to this is to jack up one side of the vehicle and build a ramp under the wheels. If you cannot go forwards or backwards, unload the vehicle and use a high lift jack to lever the front and rear ends sideways, one end at a time. This is done by jacking up the vehicle at the centre of the front or rear bumper or chassis and then pushing it sideways off the jack. Beware of injury to yourself and check that the vehicle will not land in an even worse position, before you do it.

Snow and ice

Snow is the most deceptive surface to drive on because it does not always conform with the terrain it covers. If there is a road or track, stay in the middle of it to avoid sliding into ditches or culverts at the side. Drive slowly in four-wheel drive, in as high a gear as possible, and avoid any sudden changes in speed or direction. Use the engine for braking. If you have to use the brakes, give several short pumps to avoid the wheels locking.

Snow chains are better than studded tyres for off–road use and should be either on all four wheels, or on the rear wheels only. Having chains on the front wheels only will put you into a spin if you touch the brakes going downhill. If the vehicle is empty, put a couple of hundredweight sacks over the rear axles. Chains on all four wheels are the only sensible answer to large areas of ice or snow.

If you drive into a drift, you will have to dig out and it is easier to come out backwards. Off–road driving in snow will be easier at night, or in the early morning when the snow is firmest and the mud below it frozen. As with sand, on really deep snow, high flotation tyres are an advantage. If they are fitted with chains, they should be at the correct pressures, not at low pressure for the chains will damage them. Carry a good sleeping bag in case you get stuck and have a long wait for help. Use only the strongest heavyweight chains; having to mend broken chains in frozen conditions is not a pleasant experience.

With some vehicles that have large axle articulation, some older designs of snow chains could sever the brake hoses. So check with your vehicle manufacturer before buying snow chains.

If you start to spin, do not touch the brakes; depress the clutch, then, with all four wheels rolling free, you will regain control.

In very cold conditions, if you have a diesel engine, dilute the diesel fuel with one part of petrol to fifteen parts of diesel, to stop it freezing up (use one to 10 for arctic temperatures). This is illegal in the UK and could damage a modern high speed diesel engine, but often necessary in the Third World.

Convoy driving

When travelling in convoy, it is best for the vehicles to be well spread out so that each has room to manoeuvre, does not travel in another vehicle's dust and has room to stop on firm ground should one or more vehicles get stuck. It is wise to use a system whereby any vehicle which gets stuck, or needs help, has its headlights switched onto mainbeam. This is particularly important in desert situations. All drivers should keep an eye out for headlights in their mirrors, as these can usually be seen when the vehicle cannot.

If the vehicle ahead of you is stuck, you will see this when you catch it up anyway. Thus if a vehicle is stuck, other vehicles stop where possible and return to help —on foot if necessary in conditions such as soft sand.

In a convoy situation, the rear vehicle should have a good mechanic and a good spare wheel and tyre in case of a breakdown. It makes sense, for all convoy vehicles to be using the same type and size of tyres. If the last vehicle in the convoy has a puncture, then the punctured tyre and wheel should be swapped with another vehicle's good one, until it is repaired.

Drivers should keep to the allotted convoy order to avoid confusion and unnecessary searches. In difficult terrain, the convoy leader should make stops at regular intervals, to check that all is well with the other vehicles.

Tips

1. Air conditioning causes the radiator water temperature to rise. One way to create the opposite effect if the radiator temperature is getting too high, is to switch off the air conditioning and to turn on the heating —not very pleasant in tropical heat, but it may save your entire engine from damage.

2. If you deflate the tyres for soft conditions, remember to reinflate them again when you return to firm conditions. Don't deflate tyres too much off–road if the vehicle is heavy.

3. You should know the maximum weight supportable by each wheel at maximum tyre pressure. You should inflate the tyres below the maximum tyre pressure unless GVW is close to tyre maximum. The tyre manufacturers should supply a chart showing optimum pressure, for different loads on different terrain (usually limited to on/off road).

4. Never drive a deflated tyre over sharp rocks.

5. To get the correct tyre pressure, measure pressure when tyres are cold, before use.

6. Remember that the weight of one imperial gallon of petrol is around 4 kgs and the weight of one imperial gallon of water is around 4.5 kgs. These figures are extremely important on a long trip when it comes to calculating GVW without the help of a truck weighing scale. An imperial gallon is about 25 per cent greater in volume than a US gallon.

7. If your radiator is gathering a lot of chaff or insects, you will help cooling by cleaning them off from time to time. You'll also help keep the temperature down by not mounting spare tyres, jerry cans and other pieces of equipment, in front of the radiator grille.

8. Don't mix two different types of engine oil if you can help it.

9. When filling up with engine oil, bring the level up to halfway between the high and low marks on the dipstick and no further.

10. Rotate your tyres every 6500 kms (8000 kms for radials, which should only be changed from front to rear and vice versa on the same side).

11. Special fluids such as automatic gearbox fluid, air conditioning pump fluid, power steering pump fluid and universal brake/clutch fluid, are not generally available in the Third World, so carry them with you.

12. Electrically operated windows regularly fail in off–road conditions and are particularly dangerous when a vehicle has been involved in an accident or has overturned leaving the doors jammed shut. Carry a pointed hammer inside the vehicle to break such windows in this situation.

13. Do not rely entirely on satellite navigation systems (GPS). They are unreliable and so are the batteries that power them.

14. Try to get clearly written guarantees with everything you buy for your travel needs and return the warranty to the manufacturers for registration.

15. Some spares can be purchased on a sale and return basis with a small percentage deducted if returned in good condition.

RUNNING REPAIRS

by Jack Jackson

Before you depart on an overland journey, use your vehicle for several months to run in any new parts properly —this will enable you to find any weaknesses and become acquainted with its handling and maintenance. Give it a thorough overhaul before leaving. If you fit any extras, make sure that they are as strong as the original vehicle. For precise navigation, you should know how accurate your odometer is for the tyres fitted. Larger tyres, e.g. sand tyres, will have a longer rolling circumference.

Once in the field, check the chassis, springs, spring shackles and bushes, steering, bodywork, exhaust and tyres, every evening when you stop for the day. Every morning, when it is cool, check engine oil, battery electrolyte, tyre pressures and cooling water, and fill the fuel tank. Check transmission oils and hydraulic fluids at least every third day. In dusty areas, keep breather vents clear on the axles, gearbox, and check the fuel tank filler cap. Keep an eye on electrical cables for worn insulation which could lead to a fire.

Fit a battery isolation switch. It could save your vehicle in a fire and is an excellent anti-theft device. New models of these will allow enough power through, to run any necessary clocks and memory systems, when disconnected.

Make sure that you carry and use the correct oils and fluids in all systems. De–ionizing water crystals for the battery are easier to carry than distilled water. Remember to lubricate door hinges, door locks, padlocks etc, and remember that in many deserts you need antifreeze in the engine for night temperatures.

Brush all parts clear of sand or dust before working on them. When working under a vehicle, have a groundsheet to lie on and keep things clean, and wear goggles to keep dirt out of your eyes. A small vice fitted to a strong part of the vehicle will aid many repairs. In scrub or insect country you will need to brush down the radiator mesh regularly.

Maintenance

By using several identical vehicles travelling in convoy, you can minimize the weight of spares and tyres to be carried. The idea of using one large vehicle to carry fuel etc., accompanying several smaller, more agile vehicles, does not work out well in practice. The larger vehicle will often be heavily bogged down and the smaller vehicles will have difficulty towing it out, often damaging their drive train in the process. Also the vast difference in general journey speeds and the extra spares needed cause many problems —unless you have a static base camp.

Overloading is the largest single cause of broken-down vehicles and the easiest to avoid. Calculate your payload against the manufacturer's recommendation for the vehicle. Water is 1kg per litre, fuel roughly 0.8kg per litre, plus the container. Concentrate on the essentials and cut back on the luxuries. It could make all the difference between success and failure.

For rough terrain, trailers are not advisable. They get stuck in sand, slip into ditches and overturn on bad tracks. Powered trailers have been known to overturn the prime vehicle. On corrugated tracks, trailer contents become so battered as to be unrecognizable. Trailers are impossible to man–handle in sand or mud and make life difficult if you have to turn around in an awkward situation. They also reduce the efficiency of the front wheels driving and put extra strain on the rear axle.

If you must take a trailer, make sure that it has the same wheels and tyres as the towing vehicle, that the hitch is the strong NATO-type and that the wiring loom is well fixed along the chassis, where it will be protected.

Overturned vehicles

Short wheelbase vehicles have a habit of breaking away or spinning on bends and corrugations, often turning over in the process. So drive these vehicles with extra care. Given the nature of the terrain they cover, overturned vehicles are not unusual on expeditions. Usually it happens at such slow speed that no one is injured, nor even windows broken. First make sure the engine is stopped and battery disconnected. Check for human injury, then completely unload the vehicle. Once unloaded, vehicles can usually be righted easily using manpower, though a second vehicle or winch can make things easier in the right conditions. Once the vehicle is righted, check for damage, sort out all oil levels and spilt battery acid and then turn the engine over several times without the plugs or injectors in place, to clear the bores of oil above the pistons, before running it again.

Punctures

Punctures are the most common problem in off–road travel. Rear wheel punctures often destroy the inner tube, so several spare inner tubes should be carried. Wherever possible, I prefer to repair punctures with a known good tube and get the punctured tube vulcanized properly when I next visit a larger town. However, you should always carry a repair kit in case you use all your inner tubes. Hot patch repair kits do not work well enough on truck-type inner tubes, that are used on four-wheel-drive vehicle wheels.

Michelin radial tyres have the advantage that their beads almost fall off the wheel rim when flat. If you cannot break a bead, try driving over it or using a jack and the weight of the vehicle. If the wheel has the rim on one side wider than the other, only attempt to remove the tyre over the narrowest side, starting with both beads in the well of the wheel. Narrow tyre levers are more efficient than wide ones. Sweep out all sand and grit, file off any sharp burrs on the wheel and put everything back together on a ground sheet, to stop any sand or grit getting in to cause further punctures.

When refitting the tyre, use liquid soap and water or bead lubricant and a Schrader valve tool to hold the inner tube valve in place. Pump the tyre up enough to refit the bead on the rim, then let it down again to release any twists in the inner tube. Pump the tyre up again to rear tyre pressure. If the wheel has to be fitted on the front later, it is easy to let out some air.

Foot pumps have a short life in sand and are hard work. If your vehicle does not already have a compressor, use a sparking plug socket fitting pump if you have a petrol engine, or a 12-volt electric compressor, which can be used with either petrol or diesel engines. Keep all pumps clear of sand. When using electric compressors, keep the engine running at charging speed.

Damaged steel-braced radial tyres often have a sharp end of wire internally, causing further punctures. These should be cut down as short as is possible and the tyre then gaitered, using thicker truck inner tubes. The edges of the gaiter need to be bevelled and the tyre must be at full pressure to stop the gaiter moving about. On paved roads, gaitered tyres behave like a buckled wheel so they are dangerous. Most truck tyres including Michelin XZY, can be re–cut when worn and these re–cuts are useful to use in areas of sharp stones or Acacia thorns, where tyres damage easily. These re–cuts are not legal on light vehicles in the UK.

Wheelbraces get over–worked in off–road use so also have a good socket or ring spanner available to fit the wheel nuts.

In soft sand, use a strong 1ft square metal or wooden plate under the jack when jacking up the vehicle. Two jacks, preferably including a high-lift jack, are often necessary in off–road conditions.

With a hot wheel after a puncture, you may need an extension tube on the wheel brace to undo the wheel nuts; but do not re–tighten them this way or you will cause damage.

If your vehicle spare wheel is stored under the chassis, it can be very difficult to get out when you have a puncture off-road. Store it inside the vehicle or the roof.

Fuel problems

Bad fuel is common; extra fuel filters are useful for everyone and essential for diesel engines. The main problems are water and sediment. When things get bad, it is quicker long term to drain the fuel tank, decant the fuel and clean it out. Always keep the wire mesh filter in the fuel filler in place. Do not let the fuel tank level fall too low as this will produce water and sediment in the fuel lines. With a diesel engine, you may then have to bleed the system. If fuelling up from 40 gallon drums, give them time to settle and leave the bottom inch which will often be water and grit.

If you have petrol in jerry cans in a hot, dry climate, always earth them before opening to discharge any static electricity. Fuel starvation is often caused by dust blocking the breather hole in the fuel tank filler cap. Electric fuel pumps are unreliable; carry a complete spare. For mechanical fuel pumps, carry a reconditioning kit. In hot countries or in low gear at altitude, mechanical fuel pumps on petrol engines often get hot and cause vapour lock. Wrap the pump in bandages and pour water on it to cool it. If this is a constant problem, fit a plastic pipe from the windscreen washer system, to the bandaged fuel pump and squirt it regularly.

Low pressure fuel pipes can be repaired using epoxyresin adhesives, bound by self-vulcanizing rubber tape. High-pressure injector pipes need to be brazed or completely replaced. Carry spares of these and spare injectors. Diesel engine problems are usually fuel or water and you should know how to bleed the system correctly. If this fails to correct the problem, check all pipes and joints, fuel pump and filter seals, for leaks. Hairline cracks in the high pressure injector pipes are hardest to find. Fuel tank leaks repairs best glass reinforced fibre kits.

Electrical problems

These are another constant problem. With petrol engines, it is well worth changing the ignition system to an electronic system without contacts. Carry a spare distributor cap, rotor arm, sparking plugs, points, condenser and coil; all tend to break up or short out in hot countries. Replace modern high-tension leads with the old copper wire type and carry a spare set. Keep a constant check on sparking plugs and contact breaker points. If you are losing power, first check the gap and wear on the points. Spray all ignition parts with Silicone sealant to keep out dust and water. Keep battery connections tight, clean and greased. Replace the battery slip–on connections, with the older clamp–on type. Keep battery plates covered with electrolyte, top up only with distilled water or deionized water. Batteries are best checked with a battery hydrometer. There are special instruments for checking the modern sealed–for–life batteries.

Alternators and batteries should be disconnected before any arc welding is done on the vehicle. Never run the engine with the alternator or battery disconnected. Alternators are not as reliable as they should be. If the diodes are separate, carry spares; if not, carry a complete spare alternator. On some vehicles the red charging warning light on the dashboard is part of the circuit, so carry spare bulbs for all lights. Make sure you carry spare fuses and fan belts.

Regularly check that batteries are well clamped down and that electrical wires are not frayed, or passing over any sharp edges. The risk of electrical fire due to shortening, is very high on rough tracks.

Cold weather

Arctic temperatures are a very specialist situation. Vehicles are stored overnight in heated hangars. When in the field, engines are either left running or else have an electric engine heater, which is plugged into a mains' power supply. Oils are either specialist or diluted to the makers' recommendations. Petrol is the preferred fuel for lighter vehicles, but for heavier uses, diesel vehicles have heaters built into the fuel system and the fuel is diluted with petrol. All fuel is scrupulously inspected for water before being used. Batteries must be in tip–top condition, as they lose efficiency when cold.

General problems and improvisations

Steering locks are best removed; if not, leave the key in them permanently in dusty areas. A spare set of keys should be hidden safely, somewhere under the body or chassis.

When replacing wheel hub bearing oil seals, it is best to replace the metal mating piece also.

Wire hose clips are best replaced with flat metal Jubilee-type clips. Carry spare hoses, although these can be repaired in an emergency with self–vulcanizing rubber tape. Heater hoses can be sealed off with a sparking plug.

Bad radiator leaks can be sealed with epoxy resin or glass-reinforced fibre. For small leaks, add some Radweld, porridge, or raw egg, to the radiator water. Always use a torque wrench on aluminium cylinder heads or other aluminium components.

In sand, always work on a groundsheet and don't put parts down in the sand.

In sand storms, make a protected working area around the vehicle, using groundsheets. If possible, park the vehicle rear on to the wind and cover all windows to stop them being etched by the sand.

Clean the thread of nuts and bolts with a wire brush, before trying to remove them.

If you get wheel shimmy on returning to paved roads, first check for mud, buckled wheels, gaitered tyres and loose wheel bearings. If it is none of these, check the swivel pins, which can usually be dampened by removing shims.

Carry any spare parts containing rubber well away from heat, including the sun's heat on the bodywork.

If you cannot get into gear, first check for stones caught up in the linkage.

If you use jerry cans, carry spare rubber seals. Always carry water in light proof cans, to stop the growth of algae (available ex–military in the UK).

Lengths of strong chain with long bolts plus wood, or tyre levers can be used as splints on broken chassis parts, axles or leaf springs. If you do not have a differential lock and need one in an emergency, you can lock the spinning wheel by tightening up the brake adjuster cam, but only use this system for a few yards at a time.

For emergency fuel tanks, use a jerry can on the roof, with a hose connected to the fuel lift pump. Drive slowly and never let the can get lower than half full.

If one vehicle in convoy has a defunct charging system, swap that vehicle's battery every 100 kilometres.

For repair work at night, or camp illumination, small fluorescent lights have the least drain on the battery.

If the engine is overheating, it will cool down quickest, going downhill in gear, using the running engine as a brake. If you stop with a hot engine then, unless it is showing signs of seizure, keep the engine ticking over fast; this will cool it down quicker and more evenly than if you stop it.

If you switch off an overheating engine, you are likely to get a warped cylinder head.

With air filters, make sure that there are not any pin holes in the rubber connecting hose, between the air filter and the engine inlet manifold.

Roof–mounted air inlet pipes are best avoided, as they tend to break on corrugations.

If you have a partially seized six-cylinder engine, remove the piston and connecting rod involved, disconnect the sparking plug and high tension lead (or the injector if diesel). Close the valves by removing the push rods, or rocker arms if overhead cam. If diesel, feed the fuel from the disconnected fuel injector pipe to a safe place away from the heat of the engine, and drive slowly. If you have a hole in the block, seal it with any sheet metal plus glass-reinforced plastic and self–tapping screws to keep out dust or sand.

In an emergency, you can run a diesel engine on kerosene (paraffin) or domestic heating oil, by adding one part of engine oil to 100 parts of the fuel, to lubricate the injector pump. In hot climates, diesel engine crankcase oils are good for use in petrol engines; but petrol engine crankcase oils should not be used for diesel engines.

Bent track rods should be hammered back as straight as possible, to minimize tyre scrubbing and the possibility of a roll.

With four-wheel drive vehicles, if you break a rear half shaft, you can continue in two-wheel drive, by removing both rear half shafts and putting the vehicle into four-wheel drive. If the front or rear differential is broken, remove both of the half shafts on that axle and the propeller shaft concerned and engage four-wheel drive. If a permanent four-wheel drive jams in the centre differential lock position, remove the front propeller shaft and drive on slowly.

Temporary drain or filler plugs can be whittled from wood and sealed in with epoxy resin.

Silicone RTV compound can be used for most gaskets, other than cylinder head gaskets. Silicone RTV compound or PTFE tape is useful when putting together leaking fuel line connections.

Paper gaskets can be reused if smeared with grease.

If you develop a hydraulic fluid break leak and do not have a spare, travel on slowly, using the engine as a brake. If the leak is really bad, you can disconnect a metal pipe upstream of the leak, bend it over and hammer the end flat, or fit an old pipe to which this has already been done. Rubber hoses can be clamped, using a round bar to minimize damage. If you have a dual system, then the brakes will still work as normal, but if not, you will have uneven braking on only three wheels.

If you lose your clutch, you can still change gear, by adjusting the engine speed, as with double declutching. It is best to start the engine with it already in second gear.

Four-wheel drive vehicles are high off the ground and it is often easier to work on the engine if you put the spare wheel on the ground and stand on it. If your bonnet can be hinged right back, tie it back so that the wind does not drop it onto your head.

Steering relays that do not have a filler hole can be topped up by removing two opposite top cover bolts and filling through one of the holes until oil comes out of the other.

If you burst an oil gauge pressure pipe, remove the 'T' piece, remove the electric pressure sender from it and screw this back into the block. You will then still have the electric low pressure warning light.

MOTOR MANUFACTURERS' CONCESSIONAIRES AND AGENTS

by Colin McElduff

Motor manufacturers have concessionaires and agents throughout the world who are responsible for the importation of vehicles, availability of services and spares etc. Once you have decided on the vehicle to use, you should approach its manufacturer for a list of their representatives in the countries you are visiting so that you are able to evaluate its spares potential.

Today, motor manufacturers are constantly reviewing their viability in terms of production and sales. The effect on universal availability of spares is, however, long term, so the transcontinental motorist derives little immediate benefit. Nevertheless, there is the possibility that the spares of one manufacturer's vehicles will be suitable for another and a careful study of the subject is always worthwhile.

Whatever you do, choose a vehicle with a good spares potential, for it is inevitable that you will be faced with a breakdown at some stage of your journey. Be prepared by finding out your vehicle's weak points and use this as a basis for choosing spares to be taken with you, for you must not rely too much on being able to obtain them en route. When it comes to the crunch, the factors determining spares availability may be divided into three: the assumed, the known, and the unknown. It is unwise to assume that because you have a list of the vehicle's concessionaires and agents, the spares you require will be readily available. They never are, for some of the countries you are visiting may have broken off old ties and now no longer enjoy the expertise and use of equipment so provided in the past. This is often the case in Third World countries. Sometimes the cause of shortages may be the country's balance of payments problems, at other times, just downright political instability.

A great deal is known and can be used to get round the problem of no spares, however, such as using parts designed for another vehicle. To reiterate, check out the manufacturer of your vehicle and obtain a family tree of its affiliations, so that you will have some idea where to direct your search should the need arise. For example, vehicles produced by Vauxhall and Opel have parts common to each other, as also do Ford (UK) and Taunus (Germany) together with Saab, whose V4 engine is used in some Ford models. Rover and BMW now have an affiliation. Because of the intricate spider's web representing connections between manufacturers, it would be confusing to expand on this here, but look into it for your own vehicle.

As always, the unknown is legion, but when in doubt, apply logic. Ask yourself how a local would approach your situation where, for instance, there is little hope of obtaining that urgently needed spare part. The answer? He will cannibalize, and is an expert in doing so. The 'bush' mechanic exists by virtue of his resourcefulness and his ability to adapt under any conditions. He may not know what a concessionaire is, but he does know, as John Steele Gordon puts it in *Overlanding*, how to make the "radiator hose of a 1953 Chevrolet serve as an exhaust pipe for a 1973 Volkswagen and vice versa." ∎

GETTING THERE BY OTHER MEANS
Chapter 6

THE TWO–WHEELED TRAVELLER

by Nicholas Crane

Ever since John Foster Fraser and his buddies Lun and Lowe pedalled around the world in the 1890s, the bicycle has been a popular choice of vehicle for the discerning traveller. It is the most efficient human–powered land vehicle and it is clean, green and healthy.

The standard bicycle is also inexpensive, simple and reliable. Its basic form is similar the world over, with its fundamental parts as available in downtown Manhattan as they are in Douala. With the exception of remote settlements reachable only by foot, most of the world's population are acquainted with the bike. It can never be as symbolic of wealth as a motor vehicle and neither is a bike–rider alienated from his or her surroundings by metal and glass. It's a humble vehicle. It is approachable and it is benign. Bird song and scents are as much a constant companion as voices and faces.

Cycling is slow enough to keep you in touch with life; fast enough to bring daily changes. A fit rider ought to be able to manage an average of 80 to 100 kilometres a day. Pedalling puts you part way between pedestrians and motor cars: a bike can manage a daily distance four times that of a walker and a third that of a car.

Bikes can be carried in 'planes, trains, boats and cars, on bus roofs, taxi–boots; parked in hotel bedrooms and left-luggage stores. They can be carried by hand and taken apart.

But isn't cycling hard work? Sometimes, but for every uphill or head–wind there's a descent or tailwind that's as fun as flying. What happens when it rains? You get wet or stop in a bar. How many punctures do you get? On my last ride (5200 kilometres), two. How do you survive with so little luggage? It's leaving behind the clutter of everyday life that makes bike touring so fun.

Where to go

If you are unsure of your stamina, choose somewhere mild such as East Anglia or northern France for your first trip . Beware of being tricked by the map: it's not always the places with the highest mountains that are the most tiring to ride. Scotland where the roads often follow valley bottoms, is a lot easier than Devon where the roads hurry up and down at ferocious angles. The Fens, Holland and Ganges Delta may be as flat as a pancake but it's this flatness which allows the wind to blow unchecked —exhilarating if it's going your way, but if it isn't…

You may already have a clear idea of where you would like to ride. Hilliness, prevailing winds, temperature, rainfall, whether the roads are surfaced or dirt, are all factors worth quantifying before you leave. Then you must fit the route with the places of interest and accommodation. There may be duller sections of your route which you would like to skip; if so you need to find out in advance whether you can have your bike transported on buses or trains.

You do not have to be an athlete, or even able to run up three flights of stairs without collapsing, to ride a bicycle. It is a rhythmic, low-stress form of exercise. Riding to work or school, or regularly during evenings and weekends, will build a healthy foundation of fitness. If you have never toured before, try a day ride from home (40 kilometres maximum), or a weekend ride.

Once you know how many miles you can comfortably ride in a day, you can plan your tour route. *Always* allow for the first couple of days to be 'easy': set yourself distances which you know you can finish comfortably and this will allow you to adjust to the climate and the extra exercise. It will also let your bike and luggage 'settle in.'

Main roads must be avoided. This means investing in some good maps. As a rule scales of 1:200,000 will show all minor roads. For safe cycling on rough tracks, you'll need maps of 1:50,000 or 1:25,000. Stanfords (12–14 Long Acre, London WC2E 9LP, tel: 071–836 1321) are the best supplier of cycling-scale maps.

The type of accommodation you decide upon affects the amount of luggage you carry, and the money you spend. Camping provides the greatest flexibility but also the greatest weight of luggage. With (or without) a tent you can stay in all manner of places. Farmers will often consent to the use of a field-corner, and in wilderness areas you camp where you choose (leave nothing; take nothing). With two of you, you can share the weight of the tent, cooking gear and so on. If you are using youth hostels, bed-and-breakfast or hotels, you can travel very lightly but your route is fixed by available accommodation.

'Wild camping', where you simply unroll your sleeping bag beneath the stars on a patch of unused land, is free and allows you to carry a minimum of camping gear. Always be careful to check the ownership of the land and bear in mind that you have no 'security' beyond your own ability to be inconspicuous.

The best source of information on the geography of cycle-travel is the **Cyclists' Touring Club** (to join, contact the CTC at Cotterell House, 69 Meadrow, Godalming, Surrey GU7 3HS; tel: 0483-417217).

The bike and clothing

Unlike the purchase of a motorized expedition vehicle, the bicycle need cost no more than a good camera or backpack. Neither need it be an exotic mix of the latest aluminium alloys and hi-tech tyres. John Foster Fraser covered 19,237 miles through 17 countries on a heavy steel roadster fitted with leather bags. Unlike bike frames made from steel, those constructed using carbon-fibre, titanium or even aluminium alloys will be beyond the skills of local blacksmiths to repair. Destinations are achieved through the urge to make the journey, rather than through the colour of the bike frame.

Given the determination to succeed, virtually any type of bicycle will do. The author Christa Gausden made her first journey, from the Mediterranean to the English Channel, on a single–speed shopping bike. My early tours across Europe were made on the heavy ten–speed I had used for riding to school. Spending time and money on your bike does however increase your comfort and the bike's reliability.

For road riding the most comfortable machine is a lightweight 10 or 12–speed touring bike. Gear ratios in the UK and USA are measured somewhat quaintly, in inches —the given figure representing the size of wheel which it would have been necessary to fit to a Penny Farthing to achieve the same effect. *Richard's New Bicycle Book* (and various others) contains detailed gear ratio tables. For normal touring, the lowest gear should be around 30 to 35 inches; the highest, 80 to 90 inches. With these ratios a fit rider ought to be able to pedal over the Pyrenees, while the top gear is high enough to make the most of tail winds.

Good quality wheels and tyres are important. If you can afford it, have some wheels built by a professional wheel–builder, asking him to use top quality pre–stretched spokes and the best hubs and rims. For continental touring it's handiest if the rims are of the size to take the metric 700 C tyres. Some rims will take a variety of tyre widths, allowing your one set of wheels to be shod either with fast, light, road tyres, or with heavier tyres for rough surfaces. Buy the best tyres you can afford. Quality tyres can be expected to run for 8,000 kilometres on a loaded bike ridden over mixed road surfaces.

'Drop' handlebars are more versatile than 'uprights', providing your hands with several different positions and distributing your weight between your arms and backside. Drops also permit for riding in the 'crouch' position —useful for fast riding, or pedalling into head–winds. Drop handlebars come in different widths; ideally they should match the span of your shoulders. The saddle is very much a question of personal preference; try several before deciding. (Note that you should fit a wide 'mattress' saddle if you have upright handlebars, as most of your weight will be on your backside.) Solid leather saddles need treatment with leather oils then 'breaking in' —sometimes a long and painful process but one which results in a seat moulded to your own shape. Also very comfortable are the padded suede saddles which require no breaking in. Since they never change shape, be sure this sort of saddle is a perfect fit before you buy. Steer clear of plastic–topped saddles.

It is very important that your bike frame is the correct size for you. There are several different methods of computing this, but a rough rule of thumb is to sub-tract 25 centimetres from your inside leg measurement. You should be able to stand, both feet flat on the ground, with at least three centimetres between the top tube and your crotch. The frame angles should be between 71 and 73°. The strongest and lightest bike frames are commonly made from Reynolds tubing, most usually of the '531' specification (look for the label). On lighter models it may be 'double–butted.' An option for those with bigger purses is to have a bike frame built to your own specifications and size. Many of the top frame–builders advertise in the magazine *Cycling Weekly* and in *Cycle Touring and Campaigning*, the magazine of the Cyclists's Touring Club.

Generally speaking, the more you spend on your brakes and pedals, the stronger and smoother they will be. Pedals should be as wide as your feet (note that some Italian models are designed for slim continental feet rather than the flat–footed Britisher). Toe–clips and straps increase pedalling efficiency.

Luggage should be carried in panniers attached to a rigid, triangulated carrier which cannot sway. Normally, rear panniers should be sufficient. If you need more capacity, use a low–riding set of front pannier carriers (such as the Blackburn model) and/or a small handlebar bag. Lightweight items, such as a sleeping bag, can be carried on top of the rear carrier if necessary. The guiding rule is to keep weight as low down and as close to the centre of the bike as possible. Never carry anything on your back.

Clothing chosen carefully will keep you warm and dry in temperate climates; cool and comfortable in the heat. Choose items on the 'layer' principle: each piece of clothing should function on its own, or fit when worn with all the others. The top layers should be wind proof, and in cold or wet lands, waterproof too. Goretex is ideal. Close–fitting clothes are more comfortable, don't flap as you ride, and can't get caught in the wheels and chainset. In bright conditions a peaked hat or beret makes life more comfortable, and cycling gloves (with padded palms) will cushion your hands from road vibration. Cleated cycling shoes, as worn by racers, are impossible to walk in and not worth taking; choose shoes with stiff soles (ie. not tennis shoes) which will spread the pressure from the pedals, and which are good for walking too. Specially designed touring shoes can be bought at the bigger bike shops.

The Touring Department of the CTC publish technical information sheets on equipping bike and rider.

Mountainbikes

If you're planning to venture off the beaten track, on rough roads and tracks, a mountainbike will provide strength and reliability. Mountainbikes evolved in California from hybrid *clunkers* during the '70s, first arriving in Britain *en masse* in 1982. Since then, mountainbikes have become lighter, swifter and stronger. For tarmac riding, a mountainbike is still heavier, harder work and slower than a lightweight touring bike. The mountainbike's fatter tyres create greater rolling resistance and the upright riding position offers greater wind resistance. The additional weight requires more pedalling effort on hills but on dirt roads and trails mountainbikes are in their element: easy to control, with excellent traction and superb resistance to vibration, knocks and crashes.

Mountainbikes generally come with 18 to 21 gears, with a bottom gear of around 25 inches. (In practice five or so of these gears are always unusable because of the sharp angle which the chain is forced to make when it is running on the largest front chainring and smallest rear sprocket —and vice versa). Mountainbike brakes are generally more powerful than those on road bikes and their heavy–duty ribbed tyres are virtually puncture proof. Lighter tyres with smoother tread patterns and higher pressures can be fitted for road–riding. For sheer toughness, a mountainbike is impossible to beat, but you pay for this toughness by pedalling more weight in a less efficient riding position.

Buying secondhand

Buying secondhand can save a lot of money —if you know what to look for. Touring bikes and mountainbikes are advertised regularly in the classified

columns of the bi-monthly magazine of the CTC, the monthly cycling magazines, and in *Cycling Weekly*. Before buying, check that the frame is straight,
first by sight, and then by (carefully!) riding no–hands. If the bike seems to veer
repeatedly to one side, the frame or forks are bent. Spin the wheels and check
they are true. Wobble all the rotating parts; if there is a lot of 'play', the bearings
may be worn. Above all, only buy from somebody you feel is honest.

On the road

The greatest hazard is other traffic. Always keep to your side of the road, watching and listening for approaching vehicles. In Asia and Africa, buses and trucks
travel at breakneck speeds and expect all to move from their path. Look out too
for carts and cows, sheep, people, pot holes and ruts —all of which can appear
without warning.

Dogs deserve a special mention. Being chased up–hill by a mad dog is the
cyclist's nightmare. I've always found the safest escape to be speed, and have
yet to be bitten. If you are going to ride in countries known to have rabies, consider being vaccinated before departure. It goes without saying that you should
check with your GP that you have the full quota of inoculations (including
tetanus) suited for your touring area.

Security need not be a problem if you obey certain rules. Unless you are going
to live with your bike day and night, you need a strong lock. Always lock your
bike to an immovable object, with the lock passing round the frame and rear
wheel. For added security, the front wheel can be removed and locked also.
Before buying, check that the lock of your choice is big enough for the job. Note
that quick–release hubs increase the chance of the wheels being stolen. Always
lock your bike in a public place, and if you're in a cafe or bar, keep it in sight. In
most Third World countries, it is quite acceptable to take bicycles into hotel
bedrooms; elsewhere, the management can usually be persuaded to provide a
safe lock–up.

The CTC sells travel insurance and bicycle insurance policies.

Expedition cycling

Bikes have been ridden, carried and dragged in some ridiculous places: across
the Darien Gap, through the Sahara and up Kilimanjaro. They have been pedalled round the world, many times. And they have been used as a sympathetic
means of transport into remote, little–visited corners of the globe. The step up
from holiday touring in Europe to prolonged rides to the back–of–beyond
requires sensible planning. Choice of bicycle and equipment will have great
bearing on the style of the ride. If you want to be as inconspicuous as possible,
the best machine will be a local black roadster. Such a bike will probably need
constant attention, but pays off handsomely in its lack of western pretension. I
once pedalled across the African Rift Valley on a bike hired from a street market
in Nairobi; the bike fell apart and had to be welded and then rebuilt, but the ride
was one of the most enjoyable I've ever had.

For serious journeys defined by a set goal and a time limit, you need a
well–prepared, mechanically perfect machine. If much of the riding is on dirt
roads, a mountainbike may well be the best bet. If you can keep your weight

down, a lightweight road–bike will handle any road surface too. On the *Journey to the Centre of the Earth* bike ride across Asia with my cousin Richard, our road bikes weighed 10kg each, and our total luggage came to 8kg each. We carried one set of clothes each, waterproofs and a sleeping bag, picking up food and water along the way. Our route included a crossing of the Himalayas, and then a south to north traverse of the Tibetan Plateau and Gobi Desert. Objectivity obliges me to note that I've seldom come across other cyclists travelling this light; most voicing the opinion that they'd rather carry their cooking stove, pans, food, tent, and extra clothes.

The Expeditionary Advisory Centre (whose home is at the Royal Geographical Society, 1 Kensington Gore, London SW7 2AR; tel; 071-581 2057) publish an excellent manual called 'Bicycle Expeditions', the new edition having been revised by a man who pedalled across Russia.

Spares

Lightness gives you speed. One spare tyre and one spare inner tube, and a few spokes are the basic spares. Rear tyres wear faster than front ones, so switch them round when they are part worn. For rides of over 5000 kilometres, in dry or gritty conditions, a replacement chain will be necessary too. In 'clean' conditions a good–quality, regularly lubricated chain will last twice that distance. The tool kit should include a puncture repair kit, appropriate Allen keys, chain–link remover, freewheel block remover, small adjustable wrench and cone–spanners for the wheel–hubs. Oil, grease and heavy tools can be obtained from garages and truck drivers along the route.

Saving weight saves energy. Look critically at your equipment, and have some fun cutting off all unnecessary zips, buckles, straps, labels. Discard superfluous clothing and knick–knacks. Make sure there are not unnecessary pieces of metal on the bike (such as wheel guides on the brakes).

It is useful to know what the absolute maximum is that you can ride in one day, should an emergency arise. On a loaded bike ridden on tarmac when fully fit, this could be as much as 200 to 300 kilometres, but it will vary from person to person. With a constant air–flow over the body, and steady exertion, a cyclist loses body moisture rapidly —particularly in hot climates where it's possible to become seriously dehydrated unless you drink sufficient liquid. You need a minimum of one–litre carrying capacity on the bike; whether you double or treble this figure depends on how far from habitation you are straying. In monsoon Asia I've drunk up to 13 litres a day.

You may have surmised from all this that there are as many different ways of making an enjoyable bicycle journey as there are stars in the sky. I've yet to meet two cyclists who could agree on what equipment to carry.

I have already mentioned *Richard's New Bicycle Book*, which is published by Pan, and which has for years provided the answers to all those oily technical questions. Richard Ballantine has now produced a more specific work, called *Richard's Bicycle Repair Manual*, published by Dorling Kindersley.

HITCHHIKING

by Simon Calder

Why hitch? Hitchhiking as an art, or science, is almost as old as the motor car. Originally the concept was largely synonymous with hiking. You started walking, and if a car came along you put out your hand; mostly you ended up hiking the whole way. From this casually optimistic pursuit, hitching has evolved into a fast, comfortable form of travel in some parts of the world. Elsewhere it remains one big adventure.

Hitching has many virtues. It is the most environmentally–sound form of motorized transport, since the hitcher occupies an otherwise empty space. Socially it can be rewarding, enabling you —indeed obliging you— to talk to people whom you would not normally meet. Financially it is highly advantageous: hitching allows you to travel from A to B for free or next–to–nothing, whether A is Aberdeen or Auckland, and B is Birmingham or Bucharest.

Yet standing for hours at a dismal road junction with the rain trickling morosely down your neck as heartless motorists stream past, is guaranteed to make you question the wisdom of trying to thumb a ride. And placing yourself entirely in the hands of a complete stranger can be harrowing. Some travellers dislike the degree of dependence upon others that hitchhiking engenders. Hitchhiking can also be enormously lonely. Expect the elation of getting the ideal lift to be tempered with stretches of solitude and frustration and bear in mind that motorists rarely give lifts out of pure philanthropy. Your role may be to keep a truck driver awake with inane conversation, to provide a free English lesson or to act as a sounding board for a life history. But no two rides are ever the same. Techniques and conventions of hitchhiking vary considerably around the world, most notably the divergence between fast, money–saving hitching in the West and the slower and more chaotic practices of lift–giving in less developed countries.

The West and the developed world

In Europe, North America and Australasia, hitching can be an almost mechanically precise way of travelling. The main criteria are safety and speed. To enable a motorist to decide whether or not to pick you up, he or she must be able to see you and stop safely. The driver must evaluate whether he or she can help you, and if you would enhance the journey. Make yourself as attractive as possible by looking casual, but clean. Hitching in a suit raises driver's suspicions (normal dress for an average hitcher being denim). Looking as though you've been on the road for a year without a wash is equally counter–productive. So freshen up, choose a suitable stretch of road, smile and extend your arm. The actual gesture is a source of possible strife. In most parts of Europe and North America, the raised thumb is understood to be an innocent gesture indicating that a lift is needed. Elsewhere it represents one of the greatest insults imaginable. A vague wave in the general direction of the traffic is safest.

Never accept a lift with anyone who is drunk, high or otherwise gives you cause for concern (eg by squealing to a halt in a cloud of burning rubber after crossing six lanes of traffic to pick you up). Turning down a ride is easier said than done, especially if you have been waiting for six hours on a French auto-route and night is falling, but try to resist the temptation to jump into a van full of dubious characters. If you find out too late that you've accepted a dodgy ride, feign sickness and ask to be let out. It sometimes works.

Some offers should be turned down simply because they are not going far enough. Hitching right through Germany from the Dutch border to the Polish frontier can be done in a day, but it is best achieved by using discrimination in your choice of lifts. Refuse a ride which would take you only 20km to the next town. By hopping from one autobahn service area to another, you can cover ground phenomenally quickly.

All kinds of gimmicks can help you get rides more easily. The most effective device is a destination sign. Road systems in developed countries are often so complex that a single road may lead to several different directions. The only commonly enforced law on hitching is the one forbidding hitching on motor-ways, freeways or autopistas. By using a sign you minimize the risk that the driver who stops will want to drop you at an all–motorway junction such as those on London's M25 or the Boulevard Peripherique in Paris. Make your destination request as modest or as bold as you wish – from London you could inscribe your sign 'Dover' or 'Dar Es Salaam', but always add 'Please'.

Sophisticated hitchers concentrate their attention on specific cars. The real expert can spot a Belgian number plate at 100 metres. He or she will refuse lifts in trucks (too slow), and home in on the single male driver, who is easily the most likely provider of a lift. So good is the hitching in Germany that if you vowed to accept only lifts in Mercedes, you would still get around happily. Neighbouring France, in contrast, is hell for hitchers, as is much of southern Europe and Scandinavia.

Hitchers fare well in the newly liberated nations of eastern Europe, especially Poland. It has a Social Autostop Committee —effectively a ministry for hitch–hiking— which provides incentives for motorists to pick up hitchers.

Having taken Lou Reed and Jack Kerouac's advice, and hitchhiked across the USA, I would hesitate to recommend the experience to anyone. While the chances of being picked up by an oddball or religious fanatic in Europe are tiny, in the States almost every lift–giving motorist is weird and not necessarily friendly. New Zealand could not be more different nor less threatening: if you need a place to stay, just start hitching around nightfall, and a friendly Kiwi will almost certainly offer you a ride and a room. In Australia, the hitcher is the object of greater abuse than anywhere else, with insults (and worse) hurled from car windows alarmingly often.

One exception to the hitching lore of the developed world is Japan. Western hitchhikers are picked up, usually very quickly, by one of the extremely consid-erate local drivers. In the absence of any other information, he or she will assume that you want to go to the nearest railway station. But upon learning that your final destination is hundreds of miles away in, say, Kyoto, the driver may feel duty bound to take you all the way there.

Japan is one place where women can feel comfortable hitching alone. The conventional wisdom is that women should never hitch alone. Single women hitchhikers are all too often victims of male violence. Nevertheless, women continue to hitch alone, and get around without problem; some maintain that safety is largely a question of attitude: if you are assertive and uncompromising, you survive.

If 'real' hitching does not appeal, ride–sharing agencies exist in many countries. The idea is simply that travellers share expenses, and often the driving, and pay a small fee to the agency that arranges the introduction. Be warned, however, that there is no guarantee that a driver you contact in advance will not turn out to be a psychopath or a drunk as you hurtle through the Rocky Mountains or central Australia.

The concept of hitching can be extended to boats and 'planes. Hitching on water can involve anything from a jaunt along a canal in Europe to a two–month voyage to deliver a yacht from the Canary Islands to Florida. And in countries where private flying is popular, rides on light aircraft have been successfully procured.

Less–developed countries

At the other extreme are the dusty highways of Nigeria or Nicaragua. In the Third World, the rules on hitching are suspended. Almost any vehicle is a possible lift–provider, and virtually every pedestrian is a potential hitchhiker. Amid such good–natured anarchy, hitching is tremendous fun.

You have to accept any form of transport from a horse and trap upwards. To make the most of opportunities, it helps to be adept at riding side–saddle on a tractor engine, or pillion on a moped for one.

Purists who regard paying for petrol as contrary to the ideals of hitchhiking, and dismiss the idea of asking a driver for a ride as capitulation, can expect a miserable time in the Third World. Definitions of what constitutes a bus or a taxi, a truck or a private car, are blurred. Sometimes the only way to reach a place is by hitching, and local motorists may exploit their monopoly position accordingly.

El Salvador's transport system has been devastated. Everyone hitches, and you are expected to pay the equivalent of the fare on the [notional] bus. The same applies in large swathes of Latin America, Africa and south Asia. Unless you have insurmountable moral objections or a serious cash–flow crisis, you should always offer something for a ride. More often than you might expect, the ride will cost nothing more than a smile. In Indonesia, for example, the Western hitchhiker is a curiosity, to be taken [temporarily] home and paraded in front of friends and relations as an exotic souvenir. You too can become an instant celebrity.

Cuba has massive transport problems, some of which are solved by an intriguing form of mass hitch–hiking. Little old ladies and large young louts join forces to persuade passing trucks to stop, or pile into a Lada saloon driven by a grumbling member of the bourgeoisie.

In such places hitching is at its simplest and most effective. Thumbing a ride enables you to see corners of the world which might otherwise remain hidden, and to meet people whom you would surely pass by. And, in the final analysis, there are worse ways to travel than being chauffeur–driven.

OVERLAND BY PUBLIC TRANSPORT

by Chris Parrott

It's not everyone who has the resources to plan, equip and insure a full–scale Range Rover expedition across one of the less developed continents, although it's the sort of thing we all dream about. One possible answer is to travel with an overland company, but here the drawback is that you can neither choose your travelling companions nor your itinerary. You can, however, do it all more cheaply on your own, by public transport. Generally speaking, wherever overland companies take their trucks, public transport goes too. And often public transport goes where overland companies cannot: over the snow–bound Andes to Ushuaia in Tierra del Fuego, across Siberia to the Pacific.

Of course, Damascus to Aleppo is not quite the same as getting on a coach to Washington DC at the New York Greyhound Terminal, nor does 'First Class' imply in Bolivia quite what it does on the 18.43 from Paddington to Reading.

A schedule of surprises

The Damascus to Aleppo bus is an ancient Mercedes welded together from the remains of past generations of Damascus/Aleppo buses, and propelled in equal proportions by a fuming diesel engine, the Will of Allah, and the passengers (from behind). It makes unscheduled stops while the driver visits his grandmother in Homs, when the driver's friend visits the Post Office in the middle of nowhere, and when the whole bus answers the call of nature – the women squatting on the left, and the men standing on the right (the French normally display more cool at moments like this).

First Class in Bolivia means hard, upright seats, already full of people and chickens spilling over from Second Class; whimpering children; no heating, even in high passes at night in winter; passageways blocked by shapeless bundles and festering cheeses; impromptu Customs searches at 4am; and toilets negotiable only by those equipped with Wellingtons and a farmyard upbringing. Trains rarely arrive or depart on time, and the author has experienced a delay of 26 hours on a journey (ostensibly) of eight hours. But these trains are nothing if not interesting.

The secret of the cheapness of this means of travelling lies in the fact that it is *public*, and therefore the principal means by which the public of a country moves from place to place. It follows that if the standard of living of the majority of people is low, so will the cost of public transport be low. A 20–hour bus ride from Lima to Arequipa in Southern Peru can cost as little as $20; a 20–hour bus ride in Brazil from Rio de Janeiro to the Paraguayan border costs about $40; whilst a 20–hour bus ride through France or Germany would cost twice as much. It all depends on the ability of the local population to pay. Of course there are disadvantages to travel by public transport:

1. Photography is difficult at 70mph, and though most drivers will stop occasionally, they have their schedules to keep to.
2. You may find that all transport over a certain route is fully booked for the week ahead, or there is a transport strike.
3. You may find that your seat has been sold twice. In circumstances like this,

tempers fray and people begin to speak too quickly for your few words of the local language to be of much use.

Efficiency of reservation arrangements varies from one part of the world to the next. The following may serve as a general guide to travelling in the undeveloped parts of the world.

Booking

Whenever you arrive in a place, try and find out about transport and how far ahead it is booked up. It may be, for example, that you want to stay in Ankara for three days, and that it's usually necessary to book a passage four days in advance to get to Iskenderun. If you book on the day you arrive, you have only one extra day to wait; if you book on the day you intended leaving, you have four days to kill. This is a basic rule and applies to all methods of transport.

Routing

Try to be as flexible as possible about your routing and means of transport. There are at least six ways to get from La Paz in Bolivia to Rio de Janeiro in Brazil. Check all possible routes before making a final decision.

Timing

Don't try and plan your itinerary down to the nearest day – nothing is ever that reliable in the less developed world (or the developed world for that matter). You should allow a 10 to 20 per cent delay factor if, for example, you have to be at a certain point at a certain time to catch your plane home.

Possessions

Baggage is often snatched at terminals. Be sure, if you are not travelling within sight of your bags, that they have the correct destination clearly marked, and that they do actually get loaded. Breakfast in New York, dinner in London, baggage in Tokyo happens all too often. Arriving or leaving early in the morning or late at night you are particularly vulnerable to thieves. This is the time when you must be most on your guard. Never leave anything valuable on a bus while you have a quick drink, not even if the driver says the bus door will be locked.

Borders

Prices rise dramatically whenever your route crosses a national frontier. Usually it's cheaper to take a bus as far as the frontier, walk across and then continue your journey by the local transport in the new country. 'International' services are always more expensive, whether airlines, buses, trains or boats. (The author recalls that a donkey ride to the Mexican frontier cost him 20 pesos but to have crossed the international bridge as far as the Belize Immigration Office, an extra 40 metres, would have increased the cost to 40 pesos).

Fare and medium

Each particular medium of transport has its own special features. Trains are generally slower than buses, and the seats may be of wood. There is often no restriction on the number of seats sold, and delays are long and frequent. However, slow trains make photography easier, and the journeys are usually more pleasant than on buses if not too crowded. It's often worth going to the station a couple of days before you're due to depart and watching to see what happens. It will tell you whether you need to turn up two hours early to be sure of a seat.

Buses reflect the sort of terrain they cross. If the roads are paved and well maintained, the buses are usually modern and in fair condition. If the journey involves unmade mountain roads, your bus and journey are not going to be very comfortable.

If you are travelling through bandit country —or a country where political stability conforms to the Third World stereotype— the company may be a consolation when the whole bus is stopped and robbed by bandits or searched by transit police (robbed too, some say).

If you're in your own vehicle or hitchhiking, it is somehow far more demoralizing. You probably lose the same things or have your Tampax broken in half by over–zealous soldiers in search of drugs, but it affects you less if you're just part of a coach load.

Urban transport

One of London's biggest failures has been its inability to provide a cheap mass transit system within the city. Other Western industrialized capitals seem to have managed it to a greater or lesser extent, but the Third World has really got the problem licked —for the locals at least. Most urban dwellers in the Third World own no car; they have to travel by public transport— by train, rickshaw, underground and so on.

The networks are labyrinthine in their complexity, the services are frequent and the fares cheap. Everyone uses the system. Which generates which, I don't know, but it works. The problem is that there is rarely any information available for the traveller. He or she is meant to go by taxi or limousine. Buy yourself a city map, jump on a bus and explore. It's a great way of seeing the city cheaply with no censorship, and spending next to nothing in the process.

Boats

This, if you're lucky, could mean an ocean–going yacht that takes passengers as crew between, say, St.Lucia and Barbados, a cement boat from Rhodes to Turkey, or an Amazon river steamer. With a little help from your wallet, most captains can be persuaded to accept passengers. A good rule is to take your own food supply for the duration of the trip and a hammock if there is no official accommodation.

Cargo boats ply the rivers Amazon, the Congo and Ubangi in Zaire, the Niger in Mali, the White Nile in the Sudan, the river Gambia and Ecuador's river Guaya, where an all–night crossing costs next to nothing.

'Planes

In areas where 'planes are the only means of communication, they are often very cheap or even free. Flying across the Gulf of Aden to Djibouti, for example, costs as little as sailing. A good trick is to enquire about privately owned 'planes at mission schools (in Africa) or at aeroclubs. Someone who is going 'up country' may be only too pleased to have your company.

Similarly, in parts of South America, the Air Forces of several countries have cheap scheduled flights to less accessible areas, though, of course, one must be prepared for canvas seats and grass runways.

TRAVEL BY TRAIN

by Keith Strickland

"I have seldom heard a train go by and not wished I was on it," wrote Paul Theroux at the start of "The Great Railway Bazaar," his account of a train journey from London to Tokyo. Commuters on the London Underground or the New York Subway might not share this sentiment, but trains are more than just a means of getting from A to B.

At one extreme, they give the traveller an insight into the everyday life of the countries they serve. To see and experience India away from the main tourist attractions, there is no better way than to take the train. Railway stations themselves are a microcosm of Indian life. The homeless and beggars may spend their whole time cooking, drinking, washing and sleeping on platforms. Then there are the tradesmen —*chai–wallahs*, book–sellers, stall–holders— and, of course, the crowds.

At the other end of the spectrum, the traveller can enjoy five-star luxury on wheels. South Africa's Blue Train from Cape Town to Johannesburg has gold–tinted windows, haute cuisine and en suite accommodation.

You can take a train for a one–off trip, or you can spend your whole holiday on one. Sometimes there is no alternative form of transport —unless you are a mountain climber, the only way of ascending the Jungfrau in Switzerland is by rail.

Wherever you want to go, some planning is essential. In parts of the world, trains run much less frequently than in the UK. The famous line through the Khyber Pass in Pakistan use to have only one a week. If you missed it, you would have to wait seven days for the next! (Unfortunately, this meagre service is 'temporarily' suspended). Even in the USA passenger trains are much scarcer than we British are used to.

The most comprehensive guides to train times are *Thomas Cook's European Timetable* and *Overseas Timetable* (available from Thomas Cook Publications, PO Box 227, Peterborough PE3 6SB). The latter includes road services and shipping as well as railways. Both concentrate on major routes. For minor lines, one must consult local timetables. The best known is *Newman's Indian Bradshaw* which contains every passenger train on the 35,000 miles of India's rail network.

Sometimes, there is no way of getting advance information. In parts of South America, the timetable consists of nothing more sophisticated than a handwritten poster at the local station.

Tickets

Three things need to be said:

1. No railway administration likes ticketless travellers. You may get away without paying in places like India, especially if you enjoy riding on the carriage roof, but in many countries fines are stiff. The same goes for riding first class with a second class ticket.

2. Train travel can be incredibly cheap particularly in the Third World. If you want relative comfort and space, use first class accommodation (if it's available) —you won't have to raise a mortgage.

3. Rover tickets offering unlimited travel within a geographical area are real value for money. Lovers of India know of the Indrail pass. Students and those under 26 years of age have long enjoyed cheap travel in Europe, and there is an all–European rail pass for the over–26s. Major travel companies will have details. So will British Rail's international travel centre at Victoria Station, London, (tel: 071-834 2345) but the efficiency of its telephone service leaves much to be desired.

Luggage

Travel light. It's amazing when looking at pictures of Victorian travellers to see the massive trunks they took with them. What did they pack? The station porter may be a rare species in Britain but flourishes elsewhere —at a price. Even so, a mass of luggage is an encumbrance on a train. Pack essentials only. Choose according to the length of the journey and the climate of the country.

Security

Petty theft is a fact of life almost everywhere. Unattended luggage is easy game. Remember that in the Third World the value of a camera may equate to several months' average wage. Keep money and other valuables on you. If you have to leave baggage, make sure it is locked and try to chain it to some immovable object such as the luggage rack. Also make sure you have adequate insurance.

Food

On long train journeys, find out in advance if food and drink are likely to be available. On–board catering should be indicated in the timetable, though standards and prices vary enormously. South African dining cars offer superb food and wine at modest prices. France is disappointing: food on the high–speed TGV is a no more than average aircraft–style meal. Catering on the Trans–Siberian Express is, by most people's accounts, hardly bearable.

Don't overlook the possibility of station restaurants, but in the Third World, western stomachs should be wary of platform vendors. Their wares look colourful but can have devastating effects. Treat local drinks with caution. Peru has its own version of Coke —green Inca Cola— as nauseating to look at as to drink. *Chai* (sweet milky tea) is the safest drink in India. Every station has its *chai-wallah*.

From 16 April 1995 all national and international codes change — see page 587 for details.

Health

The first item in my personal medical kit is a bottle of eye drops – essential for countries where trains are still pulled by steam engines. Sooner, rather than later, the inevitable smuts will be acquired! Other than this, there are no special health hazards associated with trains. But a long journey is not the best way to pass the time if you are unlucky enough to be ill, and on–board toilet facilities are pretty primitive in many places. So it's important to take the health precautions necessary for the country you are visiting.

Sleeping

There's no experience quite like sleeping on a train. Again, if you plan to do this, plan ahead. Find out from the timetable if sleeping facilities are available, and if so, what they are. There may be a sleeping compartment with fresh sheets, its own loo, and an attendant. Couchettes are popular in some countries (beware, the sexes are not always segregated). In India and Pakistan, sleeping accommodation means a bed–roll spread out on an ordinary compartment seat.

Whatever the facilities, a supplementary fee and advance reservation are almost always essential, though greasing the palm of the conductor often works wonders in countries where backhanders are a way of life. In the Indian sub–continent, the more important stations have retiring rooms where a bed can be rented for the night.

Class of travel

How to travel: First or Second Class? Express or slow train? By day or by night? The answers depend on the time and money you have at your disposal, and on the aims of the journey. Do you want to be cosseted from the outside and pampered with luxury? Do you prefer to mix with local people? It's entirely up to you; the choice is enormous. But remember one golden rule: the more comfort you want, the more you'll have to pay, and the greater will be the likelihood of having to make reservations in advance of your journey. Conversely, second class travel is cheaper, does not need to be booked ahead, but will inevitably be more crowded. Incidentally, some countries have more than two classes. India has six, though you won't necessarily find them all on the same train.

Suggested routes

Starting at the top of the market, the **Blue Train** has already been mentioned. In the same class is the **Orient Express** from London to Venice. Can there be a more romantic way to arrive than by this train of restored luxury carriages? In India, the **Rajasthan Express** or 'Palace on Wheels' takes a week on its circuit of Rajasthan. Guests live and sleep in carriages which once belonged to princes. (See also the Luxury Traveller in chapter 3)

These trains are designed specifically for the tourist trade. But the long–distance train survives in every day use in many parts of the world. **The Trans Siberian Express** runs daily from Moscow eastwards to the Pacific Coast. One can still cross the USA by rail, though not as one continuous journey. Trains travel vast distances in both India and China. The **Indian–Pacific** traverses the complete width of Australia, from Sydney to Perth. And there is no better way of getting to the Victoria Falls than by the overnight train from Bulawayo with its teak–panelled sleeping cars.

From an engineering point of view, the most remarkable line is the **Central Railway of Peru**. From Lima, loops and zig–zags take the tracks to 15,500 feet above sea level – the highest point in the world reached by a passenger train. The conductor dispenses oxygen to those in need!

There are not many railwayless countries, and the possibilities for train travel are limitless. Don't just stick to the well–known routes. Branch out and see what you discover. The most memorable journey is often the least expected. Tucked away in a remote, mountainous region of Peru are the towns of Huancayo and Huancavelica. The train takes all day to go from one to the other, stops every-where and is full of people going to market with their produce and livestock. There are tunnels, steep gradients, river gorges and all the while the Andes form a stunning backcloth. A humble line; an extraordinary and exhilarating experience.

Special interests

To many, railways are a hobby; some would say an addiction. Every aspect of railway history and operation has been studied in great detail; but it is the steam locomotive which commands the most devotion. Steam has an atmosphere all of its own. One can see it, hear it, smell it and taste it. Steam buffs travel the world to experience its thrill.

China is the enthusiasts' mecca. With cheap labour and plentiful coal sup-plies, China was still building steam engines in the late 1980s, and there are probably 10,000 at work on the country's railways. Next comes **India**. Most mainline trains are now diesel or electric hauled, but steam locos can be found all over the sub–continent.

Elsewhere the number of countries where steam is in everyday use is dwin-dling fast. **Poland** and the former **East Germany** are the only European ones. Further afield are **Zimbabwe**, **Pakistan** and parts of **South America**.

There is a compensating increase in museum and preserved railways, but to the purist these are no substitute for the real thing: he or she wants to search out every last steam location, however remote or obscure. Visits to places like Cuba or Vietnam are best made in organized groups. Specialist travel operators for the serious enthusiast include: **TEFS Travel**, 77 Frederick Street, Loughborough LE11 3TL (tel: 0509 262745). And in America: **Trains Unlimited**, 235 West Pueblo Street, Reno, Nevada 89509 (tel: 836 1745); **Explorers Travel Club**, 223 Copper Mill Road, Wraysbury TW19 5NN (tel: 0753-681999).

Reading material

Trains are places for meeting people. You will rarely be on your own. It's only in England that strangers never converse. Nevertheless, make sure you put a good book in your luggage. Every journey has a dull moment.

Books about railways are legion. Fodor's *Railways of the World* provides a general introduction. Of books on rail travel in individual countries, the best is

India by Rail published by Bradt. There is also *France by Rail*, by Simon Vickers and *Italy by Rail*, by Tim Jepson (both published by Hodder & Stoughton). Paul Theroux's *The Great Railway Bazaar* remains the most readable account of one man's journey. Even my own *Steam Railways around the World* (Alan Sutton Publishing).

Above all, buy a timetable. It is a mine of information. My Pakistan Railways timetable tells me the cost of a bed in the retiring rooms at Karachi; breakfast on the Shalimar Express consists of "a choice of two eggs, two toasts with butter and jam, pot of tea", and I can find out the colour of staff uniforms in station tea–rooms. If I want to take a rickshaw with me as part of my luggage, it will be deemed to weigh 150kg and charged accordingly. And I duly note the solemn warning: "Passengers are requested in their own interest not to light or allow any other passenger to light any oil stove or any other type of fire in the passenger carriages as this practice is not only fraught with dangerous consequences but is also a penal offence under the Railways Act."

And look at the names of the trains. Whose imagination fails to be stirred by the *Frontier Mail*, the *Himalayan Queen*, or the *Assam Mail*? Trains are not some sort of travel capsule. They seem natural —a part of the landscape almost. They certainly reflect the characteristics and atmosphere of the countries and communities through which they run, in a way air travel, cruise ships or air–conditioned road coaches can never do.

Flanders and Swann put it rather differently in one of their songs: "If God had meant us to fly, he would never have given us railways."

SAILING

by Robin Knox–Johnston

Sailing beneath a full moon across a calm tropical sea towards some romantic destination is a wonderful dream, but to make it become a reality requires careful preparation, or the dream can turn into a nightmare.

The boat you choose should be a solid, robust cruiser. There is no point in buying a modern racing yacht as it will have been designed to be sailed by a large crew of specialists and will need weekly maintenance. The ideal boat for a good cruise should be simple, with a large carrying capacity, and easy to maintain. Bear in mind that it is not always easy to find good mechanics or materials abroad, and most repairs and maintenance will probably be done by the crew.

It is important to get to know the boat well before sailing so that you will know how she will respond in various sea states and weather conditions. This also enables one to make out a proper check list for the stores and spares that will need to be carried. For example, there is no point taking a spare engine, but the right fuel and oil filters, and perhaps a spare alternator, are advisable. Try and standardize things as much as possible. If the same size of rope can be used for a number of purposes, then a spare coil of that rope might well cover nearly all your renewal requirements.

Electronics

There is a huge array of modern equipment available and these 'goodies' can be tempting. It pays to keep the requirement to a minimum to reduce expense and complexity. Small boat radars are now quite cheap and can be used for navigation as well as keeping a look–out in fog. The Decca Navigation system is due to be extended, but the date is as yet unspecified. However, the new Global Positioning System (GPS) is now in service and, about the same price as Loran or Decca, does now give very accurate positions with a worldwide coverage. There is a worldwide system of Radio Direction Beacons and a receiver for these stations is not that expensive although the range is not great. All these 'Black Boxes' are only aids to navigation however, and the knowledge of how to use a sextant and work out a position from the reading is essential.

Radio communications are now everywhere and are important for the boat's safety. Short range, Very High Frequency (VHF), is in use worldwide for port operations and for communications between ships at sea. It is best to buy a good, multi–channel set and make sure that the aerial is at the top of the mast as the range is not much greater than the line of sight, so the higher the aerial, the better. For long range communications, there is a worldwide maritime communications network using Single Side Band in the medium and high frequency bands. There are now easy–to–operate SSB sets at quite reasonable prices —with patience I have managed to contact the UK from the Caribbean with only 150 watts of output.

Before sailing it is advisable to study the Radio Telephone procedure and if possible take the operator's examination which is organized in Britain by the Royal Yachting Association. The Admiralty publishes lists of frequencies for all Radio Communications and Direction Finding stations worldwide. An alternative is to qualify as an Amateur Radio Operator or 'ham.' There are hundreds of thousands of enthusiastic hams all over the world and an increasing number of special maritime networks which will arrange regular schedules if requested.

Meteorology plays an important part in any voyage and the rudiments of weather systems, and how they are going to affect the weather on the chosen route, is essential knowledge for anyone making any voyage. Weather forecasts are broadcast by most nations but it is possible to buy a weatherfax machine which prints out the weather picture for a selected area and costs about the same as an SSB radio set.

The crew

The choice of crew will ultimately decide the success or otherwise of the venture. They must be congenial, enthusiastic and good work sharers. Nothing destroys morale on board a boat more quickly than one person who moans or shirks their share of shipboard duties. Ideally the crew should have previous sailing experience so that they know what to expect, and it is well worth while going for a short shakedown sail with the intended crew to see if they can cope and get on well. Never take too many people, it cramps the living quarters and usually means there is not enough work to keep everyone busy. A small but busy crew usually creates a happy purposeful team.

Beware of picking up crew who ask for passage somewhere at the last minute.

For a start, you will not know their background and you will only find out how good or bad they are once you get to sea, which is too late. In many countries, the Skipper of the boat is responsible for the crew, and you can find that when you reach your destination. Immigration will not allow the marine 'hitch–hiker' ashore unless they have the fare or ticket out of the country to their home. If you do take people on like this, make sure that they have money or a ticket and I recommend that you take the money as security until they are landed. I once got caught out in Durban with a hitchhiker who told me I would have to give him the airfare back to the US. However, he 'accidentally' fell into the harbour, and when he put his pile of dollars out to dry, we took the amount required for his fare. Never hesitate to send crew home if they do not fit in with the remainder. The cost will seem small in comparison to a miserable voyage.

Provisions

Always stock up for the longest possible time the voyage might take, plus 10 per cent extra. The system that I use for calculating the food requirement is to work out a week's worth of daily menus for one person. I then multiply this figure by the number of weeks the voyage should take plus the extra, and multiply that figure by the number of crew on board.

Always take as much fresh food as you can. Root vegetables will last at least a month if kept well aired and dry, greens last about a week. Citrus fruit will last a month. Eggs, if sealed with wax or Vaseline, will last a couple of months. Meat and fish should not be trusted beyond a day or two unless smoked, depending on the temperature. Flour, rice and other dry stores will last a long time if kept in a dry, sealed container.

The rest of the provisions will have to be canned, which are of good quality in Europe, the US, South Africa, Australia and New Zealand, but not so reliable elsewhere. Code all the cans with paint, then tear off the labels and cover the whole tin with varnish as protection against salt water corrosion and stow securely in a dry place on–board. Freeze dried food is excellent, but you will have to take extra water if you do use it.

When taking water on board, first check that it is fresh and pure. If in doubt, add Chloride or Lime to the water tanks in the recommended proportions. Very good fresh water can be obtained from rain showers. The most effective method is to top up the main boom, so that the sail 'bags' and the water will flow down to the boom and along the gooseneck where it can be caught in a bucket. There are a number of de–salination plants on the market. If the budget allows this could be worthwhile in case the water tanks go foul and rain water is hard to come by.

Safety

The safety equipment should be up to the Offshore Racing Council's minimum standards. Ensure that the life raft has been serviced before sailing, and that everyone on board knows how to use their life–jackets and safety harnesses. A number of direction–finding and recovery systems have been developed recently for picking up anyone who falls overside, and this drill should be practised before the start of the voyage.

Paperwork and officialdom

Before setting out on a long voyage, make sure that someone at home, such as a member of the family or your solicitor, knows your crew list, their addresses and your intended programme —and keep them updated from each port. Make sure your bank knows what you are planning, and that there are enough funds in your account for emergencies. It is better to arrange to draw money at banks en route rather than carry large sums on board.

It is always wise to register the boat. Not only is this proof of ownership and nationality, but it also means that your boat comes under the umbrella of certain international maritime agreements.

A Certificate of Competence as a Yachtmaster is advisable. Some countries (eg. Germany) are starting to insist on them. The crew must have their passports with them, plus required visas for countries such as the USA, Australia and India. More countries are demanding visas these days and it is advisable to check with the embassies or consulates for details. You should also check the health requirements and make sure that the crew have the various up–to–date inoculation or vaccination certificates. It is always advisable to have tetanus jabs.

Finally, before setting out, obtain a Clearance Certificate from Customs. You may not need it at your destination, but if you run into difficult officials, it will be helpful.

On arrival at your destination, always fly your national flag and the flag of the country you have reached on the starboard rigging and the quarantine flag (Q). If the Customs and Immigration do not visit the boat on arrival, only the Skipper need go ashore to find them and report, taking the Registration Certificate, Port Clearance, crew passports and any other relevant papers.

Foreign officials, particularly in less developed countries, can be extremely rude and peremptory. Always be polite, even if you sometimes have to grit your teeth. If you get into serious difficulties ask for assistance from the local national Consul.

Smuggling and piracy

Smuggling is a serious offence and the boat may be confiscated if smuggled items are found on board, even if the Skipper knows nothing about the offending items. There are certain areas where smuggling and piracy have become common and, of course, it is largely in the same areas that law enforcement is poor. The worst areas are the Western Caribbean, the North Coast of South America, the Red Sea and the Far East. There have also been a number of attacks on yachts off the Brazilian coast. The best protection is a crew of fairly tough–looking individuals, but a firearm is a good persuader. Never allow other boats to come alongside at sea unless you know the people on board, and if a suspicious boat approaches, let them see that you have a large crew and a gun. Call on VHF Channel 16, as this might alert other boats, and if the approaching vessel is official, they are probably listening to that channel. When in a strange port, it is a good rule never to allow anyone on board unless you know them or they have an official identity card.

If you do carry a firearm, make sure you obtain a licence for it. Murphy's Law says that if you carry a rifle, you will never have to use it —it is what the law says if you don't carry one that causes concern!

RIVER TRAVEL
by John and Julie Batchelor

Wherever you want to go in the world, the chances are that you can get there by river. Indeed, the more remote your destination, the more likely it will be that the only way of getting there, without taking to the air, will be by river. This is particularly true of tropical regions where, throughout the history of exploration, rivers have been the key that has opened the door to the interior. It is still the case that for those who really want to penetrate deep into a country, to learn about a place and its peoples through direct contact, the best way to do so is by water. River travel splits neatly into three categories: public transport, private hire and your own transport.

Public transport

Wherever there is a large navigable river, whether it be in Africa, South America, Asia or even Europe, you will find some form of river transport. This can range from a luxury floating hotel on the Nile to a dug-out canoe in the forests of Africa and South America. And between these extremes, all over the world there can be found the basic work-a-day ferries which ply between villages and towns carrying every conceivable type of commodity and quite often an unbelievably large number of people.

Let's start by examining travel on an everyday ferry. First you must buy your ticket. The usual method is to turn up at the waterfront, find out which boat is going in your direction and then locate the agent's office. With luck, this will be a simple matter, but on occasion even finding out where to purchase your ticket can be an endless problem. Don't be put off. Just turn up at your boat, go on board and find someone, preferably someone in authority, to take your money. You'll have no difficulty doing this, so long as you do not embarrass people by asking for receipts.

Board the boat as early as possible. It is probable that it will be extremely crowded, so if you are a deck passenger you will need to stake out your corner of the deck and defend it against all comers. Make sure of your sleeping arrangements immediately. In South America this will mean getting your hammock in place, in Africa and the Far East making sure you have enough space to spread out your sleeping mat. Take care about your positioning. If you are on a trip lasting a number of days do not place yourself near the one and only toilet on board. By the end of the journey the location of this facility will be obvious to anyone with a sense of smell. Keep away from the air outlet from the engine room unless you have a particular liking for being asphyxiated by diesel fumes. If rain is expected, make sure you are under cover. On most boats a tarpaulin shelter is rigged up over the central area. Try to get a spot near the middle as those at the edges tend to get wet. Even if rain is unlikely it is still a good idea to find shade from the sun. For those unused to it, sitting in the tropical sun all day can be unpleasant and dangerous.

Go equipped. There may be some facilities for food and drink on board, but in practice this will probably only mean warm beer and unidentified local specialities which you might prefer not to have to live on. Assume there will be nothing. Take everything you need for the whole journey, plus a couple of days just in case. On the Zaire river, for instance, it is quite common for boats to get stuck on sand banks for days on end. And don't forget the insects. The lights of the boat are sure to attract an interesting collection of wildlife during the tropical night, so take a mosquito net.

Occasionally, for those with money, there may be cabins, but don't expect too much of these. If there is supposed to be water, it will be only intermittent at best, and there certainly won't be a plug. The facilities will be very basic and you are almost certain to have the company of hordes of cockroaches who will take particular delight in sampling your food and exploring your belongings. Occupying a cabin on a multi–class boat also marks you out as 'rich' and thus subject to attention from the less desirable of your fellow passengers. Lock your cabin door and do not leave your window open at night. In order to do this you will also have to go equipped with a length of chain and padlock. On most boats the advantages of a cabin are minimal.

Longer journeys, especially on African rivers, tend to be one long party. Huge quantities of beer are drunk and very loud music plays through the night. It is quite likely that you will be looked on as a guest and expected to take an active part in the festivities. It's a good way of making friends, but don't expect a restful time.

Given these few common-sense precautions, you will have a rewarding trip. By the time you have reached your destination you will have many new friends and will have learned a few essential words of the local language, all of which make your stay more pleasant and your journey easier.

Private hire

In order to progress further up the river from the section navigable by larger boats, you will have to look around for transport to hire. This may be a small motor boat, but is more likely to be a dug–out canoe with an outboard motor. When negotiating for this sort of transport, local knowledge is everything: who's reliable and who owns a reliable boat or canoe. With luck, your new–found friends from the first stage of your journey will advise you and take care of the negotiations over price. This is by far the best option. Failing that, it is a question of your own judgement. What you are looking for is a well–equipped boat and a teetotal crew. In all probability such an ideal combination doesn't exist —at least we have never found it. So we are back to common sense.

Look at the boat before coming to any agreement. If possible try to have a test run just to make sure the motor works. Try to establish that the boatman knows the area you want to go to. If he already smells of drink at 10 in the morning, he may not be the most reliable man around. This last point could be important. If you are returning the same way, you will need to arrange for your boatman to pick you up again at a particular time and place. The chances of this happening if he is likely to disappear on an extended drunken binge once he has your money is remote in the extreme. Take your time over the return arrangements. Make sure that everyone knows and understands the place, the day and the time that they are required to meet you. Don't forget that not everyone can read or tell the time. If you have friends in the place, get them to check that the boatman leaves when planned. Agree on the price to be paid before you go and do not pay anything until you arrive at the destination. If the part of the deal is that you provide the fuel, buy it yourself and hand it over only when everyone and everything is ready for departure. Establish clearly what the food and drink arrangements are as you may be expected to feed the crew.

Once you are on your way, it is a question again of common sense. Take ready–prepared food. Protect yourself from the sun and your equipment from rain and spray. If you are travelling by dug–out canoe, it will be a long uncomfortable trip with little opportunity for stretching your legs. Make sure you have something to sit on, preferably something soft, but don't forget that the bottom of the canoe will soon be full of water.

Once you have arrived at your destination, make sure that you are in the right place before letting the boat go. If the boatman is coming back for you, go over all the arrangements one more time. Do not pay in advance for the return if you can possibly avoid it. If the boatman has the money, there is little incentive for him to keep his side of the bargain. If absolutely necessary, give just enough to cover the cost of the fuel.

Own transport

After exhausting the possibilities of public transport and hire, you must make your own way to the remote head–waters of your river. You may have brought your own equipment, which will probably be an inflatable with outboard motor or a canoe. If you have got this far, we can assume that you know all about the requirements of your own equipment. Both inflatables and rigid kayaks are bulky items to transport over thousands of miles so you might consider a collapsible canoe which you assemble once you have reached this part of the trip. We have not used them personally but have heard very good reports on them in use under very rigorous conditions.

Your chances of finding fuel for the outboard motor on the remote head–waters of almost any river in the world are negligible. Take all you need with you. Your chances of finding food and hospitality will depend on the part of the world you are exploring. In South America, you are unlikely to find any villages and the only people you may meet are nomadic Indians who, given present circumstances, could be hostile. You will have to be totally self–sufficient. In Africa the situation is quite different. Virtually anywhere that you can reach with your boat will have a village or fishing encampment of some description. The villagers will show you hospitality and in all probability you will be able to buy fresh vegetables, fruit and fish from the people. Take basic supplies and enough for emergencies but expect to be able to supplement this with local produce.

Another alternative could be to buy a local canoe, although this option is fraught with dangers. Without knowing anything about mechanics, buying a second–hand canoe is as tricky as buying a second–hand car. You can easily be fobbed off with a dud. We know of a number of people who have paddled off proudly in their new canoe only to sink steadily below the surface as water seeped in through cracks and patches. This is usually a fairly slow process so that by the time you realize your error you are too far away from the village to do anything about it. A word or two about dug–out canoes: these are simply hollowed–out tree trunks and come in all sizes. The stability of the canoe depends on the expertise of the man who made it. They are usually heavy, difficult to propel in a straight line, prone to capsize, uncomfortable and extremely hard work. The larger ones can weigh over a ton which makes it almost impossible for a small group to take one out of the water for repairs. Paddling dug–outs is best left to the experts. Only if you are desperate – and going downstream — should you entertain the idea.

Travel etiquette

When travelling in remote areas anywhere in the world, it should always be remembered that you are the guest. You are the one who must adjust to local circumstances and take great pains not to offend the customs and traditions of the people you are visiting. To refuse hospitality will almost always cause offence. Remember that you are the odd one out and that it is natural for your hosts to be inquisitive and fascinated by everything you do. However tired or irritable you may be, you have chosen to put yourself in this position and it is your job to accept close examination with good grace. Before travelling do take the trouble to research both the area you intend to visit and its people. Try to have some idea of what is expected of you before you go to a village. If you are offered food and accommodation, accept it. Do not be squeamish about eating what is offered. After all, the local people have survived on whatever it is, so it is unlikely to do you very much damage.

No two trips are ever the same, thank goodness! The advice we have tried to give is nothing more than common sense. If you apply this to whatever you are doing, you will not go far wrong. Just remember that what may be impossible today can be achieved tomorrow… or the next day. Don't be in a hurry. There is so much to be enjoyed. Take your time… and good luck!

CRUISING

by Tony Peisley

More than four million cruise holidays are now taken every year, most of them by North Americans, but in the last couple of years, the British have overtaken the Germans to become second in the cruising league, taking about 260,000 cruise holidays in 1993.

The key word is 'holiday', because ocean–going travel is almost exclusively about leisurely travel for its own sake. Not a race from A to B with the destination the object of the trip, rather than simply one of its highlights.

The jumbo jet put paid to liner travel. The first jet crossed the Atlantic in 1959 and by the mid–1970s the jumbos had become the only way to cross as far as most travellers were concerned. All bar the QE2 of the major transatlantic liners were put out of business and it was the same story on other popular seagoing journeys from the UK to Australia, South Africa and the Middle East.

Some liners (and cruise lines) couldn't or wouldn't adapt to changing times and they disappeared from the scene. Others just changed tack and decided to slow down the journey, add ports of call, and return to base every week or fortnight. Although there were 'cruises' like this in the Mediterranean as far back as the 1930s, it was in the Caribbean in the '70s that cruising holidays really came into their own.

The Caribbean is still the world's most popular destination and it is the cruise lines' competitive pricing of Caribbean cruise packages that has done most to stimulate renewed interest in cruises among British passengers. But the range of cruise destinations has never been wider and new places are being added to itineraries all the time.

There are lots of different cruises and lots —150–plus— of different cruise ships, but certain rules do apply when booking a cruise, any cruise:

1. Make sure you're getting good advice. Many travel agents know little about cruising and some will book you a ship that you won't enjoy, rather than own up to their lack of knowledge.

2. If you are a first–time cruiser, ask about cruises designed for 'new–comers.' Several lines, including P&O, Cunard, and Royal Viking Line, now offer these. On such cruises, first–timers will have their own dedicated check–in desk to take the hassle out of what can seem a confusing embarkation procedure to the uninitiated: welcome gifts (champagne, flowers, chocolate etc) in the cabins; designated tables in the on–board restaurant exclusive to first–time passengers; and either simplified tipping procedures or no tipping at all.

3. If you are travelling with children, ask about the facilities on board. On some ships there is far more done to entertain children than on others. Some positively discourage children from their cruises while others have sophisticated entertainment programmes just for children, with designated 'hosts' or 'counsellors' to organize them on board and also at ports of call. This is particularly true of lines in the Caribbean during the traditional summer holiday months. Princess Cruises have good children's programmes, while Norwegian Cruise Line have just revamped theirs following a deal with Universal Studios that means there'll be film stars and shows on board. A good choice for families is Premier, and the world's biggest cruise liners, Carnival.

4. It is the same story if you are disabled or intend cruising with somebody who is: some lines/ships are very much better than others, although, as so many new ships are being built these days, there has been much more chance to incorporate more facilities for disabled passengers in new ships than to convert older ships built at a time when the interests of the disabled were very low on anyone's priority list. Some common sense is also required here on the part of the disabled passenger and his/her companions. There is no point in not telling the whole truth about the level of disability, as ship's staff are much better able to cope when fully advised of any walking or other problems in advance. Also, however well–equipped a ship and helpful the staff, they can only have a limited effect on the on–shore part of the holiday. If there are severe walking difficul-

ties, then enjoyment of a cruise to, say, the Galapagos is going to be limited as much of it is to be gained from clambering in and out of small boats and yomping across rocks and other unfriendly terrain.

5. If you are not a good sailor (or think you won't be), there are various remedies, including wrist–bands or patches to wear behind the ear, which you can either get from your doctor or chemist before you go, or from the ship's doctor (it's usually cheaper ashore). But it does make sense to choose a larger ship (above 20,000–ton for sure, and above 35,000–ton for preference). And try to stick to an area that isn't prone to bad weather ie. the Caribbean rather than the Canaries in winter, and never the Atlantic at any time of the year. The vast majority of ships now have stabilizers, which not surprisingly improve the ship's stability through the seas, so opt for one of those. But stabilizers cannot make a force 10 into a flat–calm, so be advised. Cabins on higher decks are usually more expensive, those on lower decks (especially amidships) give the smoothest ride.

Outside of these general guidelines of what to look for when it comes to booking a cruise, choosing one to suit comes down to personal taste, and this is where a few cruise myths need to be debunked.

The first is that only old people go on cruises or that the average age of cruise passengers is deceased! Some cruises —usually the very expensive or the very long (three weeks plus)— do attract mainly people in the 55 to 75 age bracket, as they are the passengers with the most disposable time and income. But, overall, the average age is nearer 40. It is below 30 on short cruises from Florida to the Bahamas, and in the mid–30s for one–week Caribbean cruises, which are, after all, the most popular of all cruises at the moment. Discos and health spas are now as important a part of a ship's attractions as the more traditional cruising entertainments: bingo, cabaret, and deck sports.

This leads us to another myth: that cruise ships are just like floating holiday camps. They never really were: British camps had to ensure their guests were organized every minute of the day to take their minds off the often indifferent weather and poor quality food and accommodation they were enduring; while ships, with one or two dishonourable exceptions, were usually better appointed and cruised where the sun shone. The simple difference has always been that there has never been any feeling that passengers *must* join in the many cruise ship on–board activities to enjoy themselves or to make an 'atmosphere.' Many people just find a corner, read a book, sunbathe, swim in the pool and wouldn't dream of joining the dancing, bridge, aerobic or macrame classes that run through a typical day on board. They are just as typical and made just as welcome as the joiners–in.

Perhaps the most enduring myth, though, can be blamed on all those old Somerset Maugham cruise tales which told of the rich and/or snobbish old fogeys permanently in DJs and evening dresses. Round–the–clock formality disappeared when one–class ships replaced two and three–class liners. Only the QE2 still has a first and second class and then only on its transatlantic runs, she cruises one–class like the rest.

The norm nowadays is for ships to have a couple of formal days during the week (for Captain's welcome and farewell dinners). On those evenings, depending on the ship (rule of thumb: the more expensive, the more formal) some passengers will wear DJ/long evening dresses, while others will simply wear suits and smart dresses. For the rest of the cruise, jacket and tie or just shirt and slacks for the men, and anything other than swim–suits or shorts for the women, is in order for dinner. During the day, casual wear (designer or other-wise) is de rigeur with most ships offering on–board buffet breakfasts and lunches, as well as the slightly more formal dining room affairs.

The quality of food will, of course, depend on the ship —you get what you pay for— but the quantity is assured. Although in these more health conscious days, late night snacks have replaced the gargantuan midnight buffet on some (but not all) ships. There are also usually low calorie alternatives to the main menus. Unfortunately the food faddism that has gone hand–in–hand with health–awareness has led to much blander–tasting food being the norm on cruise ships, particularly in the Caribbean, where the majority of passengers are American.

On the other hand, while Americans are not fazed at all by the cruise tradition of tipping cabin stewards and table waiters at the end of the cruise, the British have never taken to it —so much so that one line, Cunard, has adopted a sepa-rate system on its Caribbean ships whereby the American passengers tip as nor-mal, but the British pay theirs as part of the cruise price. One or two other lines have a no–tipping policy for all their passengers, but still the majority have retained tipping. The recommended levels vary according to the cost of the cruise, but an average would be £2.50 per passenger, per day for each of the cabin steward and the table waiter and £1.50 per day for the busboy.

It is, though, one of the definite attractions of a cruise that there are very few extras once the brochure price has been paid: just those tips, drinks on board (watch out for ships where service charges are automatically added to drinks' bills and make sure you don't tip twice!), and shore excursions. All the enter-tainment on board is included —except casino bets.

Most ships also operate a signing system so that bills can be paid (by credit card usually) at the end of the cruise. Shore excursions can also be paid for by credit card, so there is no need to take wads of money or travellers' cheques in most cases. Those that you do take should be in the on–board currency —usual-ly dollars or sterling, check with your agent or in the brochure.

With a dozen or so new ships being built every year (more than 30 are current-ly being built at a cost of more than £2000m over the next three years) the gener-al standard of on–board accommodation and public facilities has come on in leaps and bounds during the past three or four years. A typical cabin on a medi-um–priced ship will have its own colour TV, individually–controlled air–condi-tioning, direct–dial telephone, as well as its own bathroom with shower/wc.

The larger ships now have entire shopping malls or decks on board, while some of the smaller ones have their own watersports marina extendible from the stern. There is also good news for people who don't like flying: a resurgence in demand for cruises that leave and return to British ports.

Most companies selling Caribbean cruises package them with a week in Florida, and there are some good deals (from Costa Line, for one) where a week's room in Florida and a week's car hire only costs an extra 100 or so on the price of the cruise. Prices are also being kept down by lines using charter instead of scheduled flights. Cunard is doing this for cruises out of San Juan and Fort Lauderdale.

Another interesting development is the return of the sailing ships. Windstar started it with its sail–assisted ships offering high–priced cruises in the South Pacific, Caribbean and Mediterranean; Club Med followed suit with a larger but similar style ship at a more middle–range price for passengers, combining it with a week ashore at a Club Med village. And from 1991 a fully–fledged sailing ship cruise was on offer from new line Star Clippers with its authentic tall ships.

The major cruise destinations are the Caribbean, Mediterranean, Alaska, the Baltic/Scandinavia, the Far East, the Mexican Riviera (including Acapulco), and South America, in that order. There are also cruises that transit the Panama Canal between the Caribbean and the US West Coast.

So–called adventure or expedition cruise lines are also increasingly popular – and adventurous. Destinations include the North West Passage and Antarctica. These are usually small ships with even smaller inflatable boats which can take passengers right amongst the ice floes and wildlife.

In mainstream cruising, ship sizes vary considerably from small, yacht–like ships carrying 100 passengers to huge, mini–city ships carrying upwards of 2000 passengers. The on–board differences are fairly obvious but, in brief, if you are looking for masses of entertainment, shops, and potential new friends, choose the leviathans; if peace and quiet, personal service, and top–class food are the criteria, small is beautiful. A couple of final tips on choosing the right cruise:

1. Travel agents displaying the PSARA sign, belong to the Passenger Shipping Association Retail Agent training scheme. This means that at least some of the staff have taken courses specifically designed to increase their knowledge of ships and cruising.

2. *The Berlitz Complete Handbook to Cruising* by Douglas Ward, which is up–dated every couple of years, has plenty of information on different ships.

TRAVEL BY FREIGHTER

by James and Sheila Shaw

Travel by ocean–going freighter has been on the rise again following its near elimination in the early 1980s. Conversion to container ships by many of the world's steamship companies and rising costs forced most firms to curtail the carrying of passengers on working cargo vessels through the late 1970s. Fortunately, a number of operators are now making space for passengers again. Behind this movement lie high demand and a willingness by travellers to pay higher fares than before. Nevertheless, many people still consider travel on a working cargo ship to be one of the great adventures of life —and a very good buy for the money.

Such travel, however, is not for everyone; what is adventure for one may be inconvenience for another. Travel agents are quick to point out that cargo dictates the operation of freighters, and few such vessels travel on a set schedule.

Consequently a ship's departure may be delayed for days, it may have to wait off–shore instead of going immediately into a berth, and an expected port of call may be eliminated or a new port added after the voyage is under way. For these reasons freighter travellers must have an abundance of time, patience, flexibility and stamina. Most today are retired people in their 60s or 70s with financial means to afford such travel and the time to pursue it. But this does not rule out freighter travel for everyone else! There are a number of companies that offer either short duration round–trip voyages or that operate their ships on such a tight schedule that they can be successfully incorporated into holiday plans. Where there's a will there's a way.

Finding out

One of the quickest ways to find out what freighter trips are available, and how much they will cost, is to visit a travel agent or library and browse through a recent issue of the *ABC Passenger Shipping Guide* (Reed Travel Group, Dunstable, Beds. LU5 4HB, UK, tel: 0582–600111). This is a monthly listing of all the companies in the world offering passenger transportation by sea, except for very short ferry runs or excursion boats. It lists passenger–carrying freighter services by geographic area and gives a complete breakdown of voyage itineraries, durations, ships, fares and sailing frequencies. Also given are the passenger capacity and tonnage of each vessel and the name of the operating company and their worldwide agents.

Once a decision has been made as to a particular shipping line or the intended area of travel, the next move should be to talk with a reputable travel agent who specializes in freighter travel. These people are likely to have travelled on or visited many of the ships in question and they should be familiar with the companies involved. This is almost essential with freighter travel as cargo lines are not as adept at handling passengers and their many requests as a cruise line or full time passenger line might be. An agent will be able to ask the right questions and get the right answers. Important points to consider will be the registration of the ship and the nationality of the crew and officers (this will determine what language is spoken), the location of the passenger accommodation as compared to its public rooms and dining room (some ships require the use of several staircases and are not equipped with lifts), the availability of laundry facilities and deck chairs on board, and the existence of a bar and 'slop chest' where passengers can purchase alcohol, cigarettes and sundry items during the voyage.

There are very few 'break–bulk' cargo vessels left on the high seas in this modern age. Break–bulk vessels were the ships that loaded all sorts of bales and crates into their holds and spent days in port, giving their passengers more than enough time to get a good look around. Today, more often than not, the freighter traveller's choice of ships will be limited to a container ship or a roll–on/roll–off vessel, both designed with the intent of spending as little time in port as possible. A travel agent familiar with freighters will also have a good idea of how long each vessel will usually spend in port. Agents can also arrange sightseeing excursions in ports of call, including excursions that leave the ship in one port and rejoin it in another. This is one way interior points can be visited when the stay is short.

Accommodation

Cabins aboard most present–day freighters are large, much larger than comparably priced cabins on cruise liners. Unlike cruise liners, however, passengers cannot always choose their cabin in advance. Because of the abnormally long booking schedule of a cargo ship, some passengers may have booked years in advance. The best cabins in any given price range are usually awarded automatically to those who make their reservations first. A travel agent or the shipping company should be able to provide a diagram showing the layout of the cabins on a particular ship. Remember that the forward–looking windows on a container vessel will be blocked from view when the ship is carrying a full load.

Once reservations for a freighter ship have been secured, the waiting process begins. Apart from a few lines which sail on a set schedule, most freighters sail only when all cargo is aboard. This can be held up for a variety of reasons, including late arriving cargo, industrial disputes, weather and mechanical problems. The intending passenger must put up with this and realize that several nights may have to be spent in a motel near the port (at his or her expense) until the go ahead to board the ship is finally received. Even finding the ship can be an adventure in itself as many of the large container terminals are now located far from urban areas. The ship's agent in the port should be contacted for advice and assistance in boarding.

Once aboard, the passenger's welcome may be a waiting officer, completely ambivalent crew, or no one at all. Quite often, and particularly in a ship's home port, the vessel will be virtually empty of crew until just before sailing. This is one reason why passenger boarding times are sometimes delayed until the last hour. If an officer or steward is not present upon boarding, it is best to ask for the Captain. Even if the vessel's crew is non–English speaking, the Captain, Radio Officer and usually the first mate will have some command of English.

Life on board

If there is some time between boarding and the ship's scheduled departure, a quick inspection of the cabin and galley should be made to determine if anything should be purchased before you set sail. A better grade of toilet paper, face tissues, special laundry soaps, aspirin, cigarettes, alcohol and snack items are the things that most passengers usually wish they had brought abroad. A freighter's scheduled departure time will be noted on a board placed at the gangway, but it is wise to confirm this with the Captain before leaving on any trips back to town.

Life aboard a freighter at sea can be very relaxing, one reason why there is such demand for this type of travel. The hustle and bustle found on cruise ships is completely lacking, and, as there is usually little or no organized entertainment, there are few decisions to make. Some of the newer cargo ships now carry small swimming pools and gyms. These will be shared with the ship's crew and/or officers. Passengers should check to see if there are regulation or set times governing their use. Meal times are set and should be observed. A ship's crew has 'time on' and 'time off' while at sea and a steward may have to work his own 'off time' to serve someone who is late for a meal. On many American ships the dinner is unusually early, sometimes as early as 4.30pm because of union regulations. Food on freighters is normally good, but this depends entirely on the cook and the provisions that the ship is allowed to take on board.

Safety at sea is an important issue today and passengers will be required to follow set regulations determined by the ship's country of registration and its Master. Cooperation in following the rules is to everyone's advantage. A lifeboat drill is usually given during the first day at sea. If by some chance it is not, a passenger should make certain of life–jacket location, which is usually in the cabin closet, and his or her muster station. As freighters tend to get a bit untidy while loading and discharging cargo, it becomes important to watch one's footing and one's head while the ship is in port. Grease and cables may be lying on the deck and cargo rigging in a lowered position —and be careful on the docks too. A ship's decks are usually cleared of debris once she returns to sea. As tanks may have been cleaned or plumbing work done in port, it is a good idea to allow water to run from tap and shower heads before using. *Always* test the water temperature on older ships before using as it may come straight from the boilers.

Quite often passengers will be asked to surrender their passports or travel documents to the Captain during the course of the voyage. This is normal and allows for smoother immigration procedures at the vessel's various ports–of–call. A few countries, such as Saudi Arabia, will restrict passengers to the ship in port unless they have visas. In other ports it may not be advisable to go ashore because of local political or health problems. The ship's agent, who will usually be the first person to board the ship once it ties up, should be able to recommend shore–based excursion operators. These people, as well as hawkers of souvenirs and money changers, may swarm aboard the ship in certain ports. It is highly advisable to check with the Captain or agent before doing business with any of these people. In most instances the Captain or steward will be able to furnish or change small amounts of the local currency and advise passengers on transportation from and to the docks. If you leave the ship in a foreign port it's helpful to have the ship's name and location written down in a form understandable to a native taxi–driver —in case you lose track of time and need to return to the ship hastily.

Entertainment

While the Captain may be a continual source of information during the voyage he should not be over–taxed. In port he will be busy with agents, immigration and customs people and salesmen as soon as the ship docks. At sea he can be called to the bridge at any time and for long periods. If his office or cabin door is closed respect his privacy and contact another of the ship's crew to ascertain if the Captain is up or not. Often he will be sleeping during the day after a long night on the bridge while you slept undisturbed. Some Captains enjoy joining passengers at meals; others dine in their cabins. One well–known Asian firm stopped carrying passengers on its freighters because the Chinese Captains didn't like making small talk at the dinner table. Socializing is not part of the Captain's job, be sensitive to this.

A Captain who enjoys having passengers aboard his ship is easy to recognize. He will usually extend an invitation to join him on the bridge at one time or another. For some this is a high point of the voyage, a time in which technical questions can be posed. The bridge usually becomes off limits in very rough weather, when navigating confined or congested waters and when a pilot is aboard. Don't abuse your Captain's kind invitation. Similarly, an interested passenger may be invited to the engine room by the Chief engineer or one of the engineering officers. Whether on the bridge or down below it is wise to wear good, rubber soled shoes. New ships, especially those which have steel decks rather than wood, are extremely dangerous when there is the least bit of water or oil about.

Dress aboard freighters is usually very informal. However, some passengers dress up for one or two dinners, particularly if the Captain is hosting a cocktail party or reception. On at least one British line it is now custom to dress formally for dinner. A travel agent or the steamship company's ticketing office will be able to advise in this matter as well as furnish information regarding mail, baggage, tipping and safe–keeping facilities on board. In regard to the latter it is important to keep cabin doors locked while in port and valuables should be entrusted to the Captain's safe. The sudden loss of money, jewellery or travel papers can quickly ruin what would otherwise have been a very enjoyable voyage.

An excellent way to find out other people's reactions to a certain ship or line and day–to–day life at sea is to subscribe to one or two newsletters printed for freighter travel enthusiasts. The first is *Freighter Travel News* printed each month by the Freighter Travel Club (PO Box 12693 Salem, OR, 97309, USA). The second is *TravLtips*, a monthly publication produced by TravLtips, (PO Box 1008, Huntington, NY, 11753, USA). Both offer passenger voyage reports each month and current information on up–coming sailings.

Working your passage

As for working one's passage, there is little opportunity for this type of travel on freighters in the 1990s. Crews have been drastically reduced on most ships and unions are strictly against the employment of unremunerated labour. These days, there is a much higher chance of obtaining a working passage on a private yacht than a commercial cargo vessel. Unfortunately, the best places for finding such passages are at mid–voyage points such as Panama and Tahiti, where other crew members may have become disillusioned with yacht travel and returned home by air. As with the freighters of old, it is a case of contacting the Captain and telling one's story. Tenacity is often the ingredient that will spell success.

TRAVEL BY CAMEL

by René Dee

In this mechanized and industrial epoch, the camel does not seem to be an obvious choice of travelling companion when sophisticated cross–country vehicles exist for the toughest of terrains. Add to this the stockpile of derisory and mocking myths, truths and sayings about the camel and one is forced to ask the question: why use camels at all?

Purely as a means of getting from A to B when time is the most important factor, the camel should not even be considered. As a means of transport for scientific groups who wish to carry out useful research in the field, the camel is limiting. It can be awkward and risky transporting delicate equipment and specimens. However, for the individual, small group and expedition wishing to see the desert as it should be seen, the camel is an unrivalled means of transport.

Go safely in the desert

From my own personal point of view, the primary reason must be that, unlike any motorized vehicle, camels allow you to integrate completely with the desert and the people within it —something it is impossible to do at 80 kmph enclosed in a 'tin can'. A vehicle in the desert can be like a prison cell and the constant noise of the engine tends to blur all sense of the solitude, vastness and deafening quiet which is so intrinsic to the experience.

Travel by camel allows the entire pace of life to slow down from a racy 80kmph to a steady 6.5kmph, enabling you to unwind, take in and visually appreciate the overall magnificence and individual details of your surroundings. Secondly, camels do, of course, have the ability to reach certain areas inaccessible to vehicles, especially through rocky and narrow mountain passes, although camels are not always happy on this terrain and extreme care has to be taken to ensure they do not slip or twist a leg. They are as sensitive as they appear insensitive.

Thirdly, in practical terms, they cause far fewer problems where maintenance, breakdown and repairs are concerned. No bulky spares or expensive mechanical equipment are needed to carry out repairs. Camels do not need a great deal of fuel and can exist adequately (given that they are not burdened with excessively heavy loads) for five to 10 days without water. Camels go on and on and on and on until they die; and then one has the option of eating them, altogether far better-tasting than a Michelin tyre.

Lastly, camels *must* be far more cost effective if you compare them directly with vehicles, although this depends on whether your intended expedition/journey already includes a motorized section. If you fly direct to your departure point, or as near as possible to it, you will incur none of the heavy costs related to transporting a vehicle, not to mention the cost of buying it. If the camel trek is to be an integral portion of a motorized journey, then the cost saving will not apply as, of course, hire fees for camels and guides will be additional.

In many ways, combining these two forms of travel is ideal and a very good way of highlighting my primary point in favour of transport by camel. If you do decide on this combination, make sure you schedule the camel journey for the very end of your expedition and that the return leg by vehicle is either minimal or purely functional for I can guarantee that after a period of 10 days or more travelling slowly and gently through the desert by camel, your vehicle will take on the characteristics of a rocket ship and all sense of freedom, enquiry and interest will be dulled to the extreme. An overwhelming sense of disillusion and disinterest will prevail. Previously exciting sights, desert towns and Arab civilization, will pall after such intense involvement with the desert, its people and its lifestyle.

First steps

For the individual or group organizer wanting to get off the beaten track by camel, the first real problem is to find them and to gather every bit of information possible about who owns them. Are they for hire, for how much, what equipment/stores/provisions are included (if any) and, lastly, what are the guides/owners capable of and are they willing to accompany you? It is not much good arriving at Tamanrasset, Timbouctou or Tindoug without knowing some, if not all, of the answers to these questions. Good pre–departure research is vital but the problem is that 90 per cent of the information won't be found from any tourist office, embassy, library or travel agent. Particularly if you're considering a major journey exclusively by camel, you'll probably have to undertake a pre-liminary fact–finding recce to your proposed departure point to establish contacts among camel owners and guides. It may well be that camels and/or reliable guides do not exist in the area where you wish to carry out your expedition.

I would suggest, therefore, that you start first with a reliable source of information such as the Royal Geographical Society, which has expedition reports and advice which can be used as a primary source of reference including names and addresses to write to for up–to–date information about the area that interests you. Up–to–date information is without doubt the key to it all. Very often this can be gleaned from the commercial overland companies whose drivers are passing through your area of interest regularly and may even have had personal experience of the journey you intend to make.

Equally important is the fact that in the course of their travels, they build up an impressive collection of contacts who could well help in the final goal of finding suitable guides, smoothing over formalities and getting introductions to local officials, etc. Most overland travel companies are very approachable so long as you appreciate that their time is restricted and that their business is selling travel and not running an advisory service.

In all the best Red Indian stories, the guide is the all–knowing, all–seeing person in whom all faith is put. However, as various people have discovered to their cost, this is not always so. Many so–called guides know very little of the desert and its ways. How then to find someone who really does know the route/area, has a sense of desert lore and who preferably owns his best camel? I can only reiterate that the best way to do this is through personal recommendation.

Having found him, put your faith in him, let him choose your camels and make sure that your relationship remains as amicable as possible. You will be living together for many days in conditions which are familiar to him but alien to you, and you need his support. Arrogance does not fit into desert travel, especially from a *nasrani*. Mutual respect and a good rapport are essential.

Pack up your troubles

Once you've managed to establish all this and you're actually out there, what are the do's and don'ts and logistics of travel by camel? Most individuals and expeditions (scientifically orientated or not) will want, I imagine, to incorporate a camel trek within an existing vehicle–led expedition, so I am really talking only of short–range treks of around 10 to 15 days' duration, and up to 400km. If this is so, you will need relatively little equipment and stores, and it is essential that this is kept to a minimum. Remember that the more equipment you take, the more camels you will need, which will require more guides, which means more cost, more pasture and water, longer delays in loading, unloading, cooking and setting up camp and a longer wait in the morning while the camels are being rounded up after a night of pasturing.

Be prepared also for a very swift deterioration of equipment. In a vehicle you can at least keep possessions clean and safe to a degree, but packing kit onto a camel denies any form of protection —especially since it is not unknown for camels to stumble and fall or to roll you over suddenly and ignominiously if something is not to their liking, such as a slipped load or uncomfortable saddle. My advice is to pack all your belongings in a seaman's kit–bag which can be roped onto the camel's side easily, is pliable, hard-wearing and, because it is soft and not angular, doesn't threaten to rub a hole in the camel's side or back-bone. (I have seen a badly–placed baggage saddle wear a hole the size of a man's fist into an animal's back.)

If rectangular aluminium boxes containing cameras or other delicate equip-ment are being carried, make sure that they are well roped on the top of the camel and that there is sufficient padding underneath so as not to cause friction. Moreover, you'll always have to take your shoes off while riding because over a period of hours, let alone days, you could wear out the protective hair on the camel's neck and eventually cause open sores.

Water should be carried around in goat–skin guerbas and 20–litre round metal bidons which can again be roped up easily and hung either side of the baggage camel under protective covers. Take plenty of rope for tying on equipment, sad-dles etc., and keep one length of 15 metres intact for using at wells where there may be no facilities for hauling up water. Don't take any sophisticated tents either; they will probably be ruined within days and anyway are just not neces-sary.

I have always used a piece of cotton cloth approximately six metres square, which, with two poles for support front and rear and with sand or boulders at the sides and corner, makes a very good overnight shelter for half a dozen people. Night in the desert can be extremely cold, particularly of course in the winter, but the makeshift 'tent' has a more important role during the day when it pro-vides shelter for the essential two–hour lunch stop and rest.

The day's schedule

Your daily itinerary and schedule should be geared to the practical implications of travelling by camel. That is to say that each night's stop will, where possible, be in an area where pasture is to be found for the camels to graze. Although one can take along grain and dried dates for camels to eat, normal grazing is also vital. The camels are unloaded and hobbled (two front legs are tied closely together), but you will find they can wander as much as three or four kilometres overnight and there is only one way to fetch them: on foot. Binoculars are extremely useful as spotting camels over such a distance can be a nightmare. They may be hidden behind dunes and not come into view for some time.

Other useful equipment includes goggles for protection in sandstorms, pre-scription sunglasses and, of course, sun cream. Above all, take comfortable and hard-wearing footwear for it is almost certain that you will walk at least half the way once you have become fully acclimatized. I would suggest that you take Spanish felt boots or something similar, which are cheap, very light, give ankle support over uneven terrain and are durable and very comfortable.

The one disadvantage of boots by day is that your feet will get very hot, but it's a far better choice than battered, blistered and lacerated feet when one has to keep up with the camel's steady 6.5kmph. Nomads wear sandals, but if you take a close look at a nomad's foot you will see that it is not dissimilar to the sandal itself, ie. as hard and tough as leather. Yours resembles a baby's bottom by comparison, so it is essential that you get some heavy walking practice in before hand with the boots/shoes/sandals you intend to wear. If your journey is likely to be a long one, then you could possible try sandals, as there will be time for the inevitable wearing–in process with blisters, as well as stubbed toes and feet spiked by the lethal acacia thorn.

For clothing, I personally wear a local, free–flowing robe like the *gandoura*, local pantaloons and *cheche*, a three metre length of cotton cloth which can be tied round the head and/or face and neck for protection against the sun. You can also use it as a rope, fly whisk and face protector in sandstorms. In the bitter cold nights and early mornings of winter desert travel, go to bed with it wrapped around your neck, face and head to keep warm.

If local clothing embarrasses and inhibits you, stick to loose cotton shirts and trousers. Forget your tight jeans and bring loose–fitting cotton underwear. Anything nylon and tight–fitting next to the skin will result in chafing and sores. Do, however, also take some warm clothing and blankets, including socks and jumpers. As soon as the sun sets in the desert, the temperature drops dramatically. Catching cold in the desert is unbearable. Colds are extremely common and spread like wildfire. Take a good down sleeping bag and a groundsheet.

Your sleeping bag and blankets can also serve as padding for certain types of camel saddle. In the Western Sahara you will find the Mauritanian butterfly variety, which envelops you on four sides. You're liable to slide back and forth uncomfortably and get blisters unless you pad the saddle. The Tuareg saddle is commonly used in the Algerian Sahara. This is a more traditional saddle with a fierce–looking forward pommel which threatens man's very manhood should you be thrown forward against it. In Saudi Arabia, female camels are ridden and seating positions are taken up behind the dromedary's single hump rather than on or forward of it.

Culture shock

Never travel alone in the desert, without even a guide. Ideal group size would be seven group members, one group leader, three guides, eleven riding camels and three baggage camels. The individual traveller should take at least one guide with him and three or four camels.

Be prepared for a mind–blowing sequence of mental experience, especially if you are not accustomed to the alien environment, company and pace, which can lead to introspection, uncertainty and even paranoia. Travel by camel with nomad guides is the complete reversal of our normal lifestyle.

Therefore it is as important to be mentally prepared for this culture shock as it is to be physically prepared. Make no mistake, travel by camel is hard, physically uncompromising and mentally torturing at times. But a *Meharee* satisfactorily accomplished will alter your concept of life and its overall values, and the desert's hold over you will never loosen.

TRAVEL BY PACK ANIMAL

by Roger Chapman

The donkey is the most desirable beast of burden for the novice and remains the favourite of the more experienced camper —if only because the donkey carries all the traveller's equipment, leaving them free to enjoy the countryside unburdened. Although small and gentle, the donkey is strong and dependable; no pack animal excels him for sure–footedness or matches his character. He makes the ideal companion for children old enough to travel into the mountains or hills, and for the adult who prefers to travel at a pace slow enough to appreciate the scenery, wildlife and wilderness that no vehicle can reach.

The rock climber, hunter, fisherman, scientist or artist who has too much gear to carry into the mountains may prefer to take the larger and faster mule, but if they are sensible, they will practice first on the smaller and more patient donkey. The principles of pack–animal management are the same, but the mule is stronger, more likely to kick or bite if provoked, and requires firmer handling than the donkey. The advantage of a mule is obvious. Whereas a donkey can only carry about 50kgs (100lbs), the mule, if expertly packed, can carry a payload of 100kgs (200lbs). Although both are good for 15 miles a day on reasonable trails, the donkeys will have to be led on foot, whereas mules, which can travel at a good speed, require everyone to be mounted —unless their handlers are fast hikers.

Planning

To determine the number of animals needed before an expedition or holiday, the approximate pack load must be calculated. The stock requirement for a 10–day trip can be calculated by dividing the number of people by two, but taking the higher whole number if the split does not work evenly. Thus, a family of five would take three donkeys. It is difficult to control more than 10 donkeys on the trail, so don't use them with a party of 20 or more unless certain individuals are prepared to carry large packs to reduce the number of animals. Mules are usually led by a single hiker or are tied in groups of not more than five animals led by a man on horseback. This is the 'string' of mules often mentioned in Westerns; each lead rope passes through the left–hand breech ring of preceding animal's harness and is then tied around the animal's neck with a bow–line. One or more horses are usually sent out with the pack mules because mules respect and stick close to these 'chaperones.'

Whichever method you decide to use, don't prepare a detailed itinerary before your journey; wait and see how you get on during the first few days, when you should attempt no more than eight to 10 miles (12 to 16kms) a day. Later you will be able to average 12 to 15 miles (20 to 24kms), but you should not count on doing more than 15 miles (24kms) a day although it is possible, with early starts and a lighter load, if you really have to.

Campers who use pack animals seldom restrict themselves to the equipment list of a backpacker. There is no need to do so, but before preparing elaborate menus and extensive wardrobes, you would do well to consider the price of hiring a pack animal. The more elaborate, heavy equipment, the more donkeys or mules there are to hire, load, unload, groom and find pasture for. In selecting your personal equipment you have more freedom —a 'Karrimat', or a larger tent instead of the small 'Basha'— but it should not exceed 12kgs (924lbs) and should be packed into several of those small cylindrical soft bags or a seaman's kit–bag. You can take your sleeping bag as a separate bundle and take a small knapsack for those personal items such as spare sweaters, camera, first aid kit and snacks required during the day. But there are some special items you will require if you are not hiring an efficient guide and handler: repair kit for broken pack saddles and extra straps for mending harness. An essential item is a 100lbs spring scale for balancing the sacks or panniers before you load them on the pack animals in the morning. Remember too that each donkey/mule will be hired out with a halter, lead rope, tow 'sacks', a pack cover, and a 30ft pack rope. In addition, there will be pickets and shackle straps, curry combs, froghooks, canvas buckets, tools and possibly ointment or powders to heal saddle sores.

Animal handling

The art of handling pack animals is not a difficult one, but, unfortunately you cannot learn it entirely from a book. With surprisingly little experience in this field, the novice soon becomes an expert packer, confident that he can handle any situation which may arise on the trail and, above all, that he has learnt the uncertain science of getting the pack animal to do what he wants it to do. The donkey is more responsive than the mule and is quick to return friendship, especially if he knows he is being well packed, well fed and well rested. The mule tends to be more truculent, angry and resentful until he knows who is in charge. Therefore, an attitude of firmness and consideration towards the animal is paramount.

Perhaps the easiest way to learn the techniques of handling pack animals is to look at a typical day and consider the problems as they arise:

Collecting in the morning: Pack animals can either be let loose, hobbled or picketed during the night. The latter is preferable as even a mule which has its front legs hobbled can wander for miles during the night searching for suitable grass. If the animal is picketed, unloosen the strap around the fetlock which is attached to the picket rope and lead him back to the campsite by the halter. If the animals are loose, you may have to allow a good half hour or so to catch them. Collect the gentle ones first, returning later for the recalcitrant animals. Approach each cautiously, talking to him and offering a palmful of oats before grabbing the halter.

Tying up and grooming: Even the gentlest pack animal will need to be tied up to a tree or post before packing. The rope should be tied with a clove hitch at about waist height. Keep the rope short, otherwise the animal will walk round and round the tree as you follow with the saddle. It also prevents him stepping on or tripping over the rope. It is advisable to keep the animals well apart, but not too far from your pile of packed sacks or panniers.

Often, donkeys in particular, will have a roll during the night, so they require a good work–over with the brush or curry comb to remove dust or caked mud. Most animals enjoy this, but you musn't forget that one end can bite and the other end can give a mighty kick. Personally, I spend some time stroking the animal around the head and ears, talking to him before I attempt to groom him. Ears are very good indicators of mood. If the ears are upright he is alert and apprehensive, so a few words and strokes will give him confidence; soon the ears will relax and lie back. If the ears turn and stretch right back along his neck, then there is a good chance you are in for trouble. The first time he nips, thump him in the ribs and swear at him. He will soon learn that you do not appreciate this kind of gesture.

Your main reason for grooming is to remove caked dirt which may cause sores once the animal is loaded. Remove this dirt with a brush and clean rag and, if there is an open wound, apply one of the many antiseptic ointments or sprinkle on boric acid powder which will help dry it up. Finally, check each hoof quickly to see that no stone or twig has lodged in the soft pad. Lean against the animal, then warn him by tapping the leg all the way down the flank, past the knee to the fetlock, before lifting the hoof; otherwise you will never succeed. If there is a stone lodged between the shoe and the hoof, prise it out with a frog hook.

Saddling and loading: Animals are used to being loaded from the left or near side. First you fold the saddle blanket, place it far forward then slide it back into position along the animal's back so that the hair lies smooth. Check that it hangs evenly on both sides, sufficient to protect the flanks from the loaded sacks. Stand behind the mule or donkey —but not too close— and check it before you proceed further. Pick up the pack saddle (two moulded pieces of wood jointed by two cross–trees) and place it on the saddle blanket so it fits in the hollows behind the withers. Tie up the breast strap and rear strap before tying the girth tight. Two people will be required to load the equipment in the soft canvas sacks onto the saddle pack, but it is essential to weigh the sacks before you place them on the cross–trees; they should be within 2 kgs of each other. If the saddle is straight, but one sack is lower than the other, correct the length of the ear loops.

On the trail: Morning is the best time to travel, so you must hit the trail early, preferably before 7am. At a steady 2 kms an hour, you will be able to cover the majority of the day's journey by the time the sun is at its hottest. This will allow you to spend a good three hours' rest–halt at midday before setting off once more for a final couple of hours before searching for a camp–site. Avoid late camps, so start looking by 4pm.

During the first few days you may have some trouble getting your donkeys or mules to move close together and at a steady pace. One man should walk behind each animal if they are being led and if there are any hold ups, he can apply a few swipes of a willow switch to the hind–quarters. It is a waste of time to shout at the animals or threaten them constantly as it only makes them distrustful and skittish. The notorious stubbornness of the mule or donkey is usually the result of bad handling in the past. Sometimes, it is a result of fear or fatigue, but occasionally it is sheer cussedness or an attempt to see how much he can get away with. The only occasion when I could not get a mule moving was travelling across some snow patches in the mountains of Kashmir. Eventually, after losing my temper and lashing him with a switch, I persuaded him to move slowly across the icy surface and disappear into a snow hole. It took my companion and me three hours to unload him, pull him out and calm him down before we could re–pack. I learned a good lesson from my lack of awareness of the innate intelligence of the mule.

Understanding: There is no problem with unpacking which can be done quickly and efficiently. Just remember to place all the equipment neatly together so it is not mixed up. Keep individual saddles, sacks and harnesses close enough together to cover with the waterproof cover in case of rain. Once unloaded, the donkeys can be groomed, watered and led off to the pasture area where they are to be picketed for the night.

Not long ago, I took my wife and two young daughters on a 120–mile journey across the Cevennes mountains in south–east France. We followed Robert Louis Stevenson's routes which he described in his charming little book *Travels With a Donkey*. We took three donkeys —two as pack animals and one for the children to take turns in riding— on a trail which had not changed much over the past hundred years. It made an ideal holiday, and we returned tanned, fitter, enchanted by the French countryside and aware that it was the character of our brave little donkeys which had made our enjoyment complete.

The speed with which the children mastered the technique of pack animal management was encouraging because it allowed us to complete our self–imposed task with enough time to explore the wilder parts of the mountains and enjoy the countryside at the leisurely pace of our four–footed companions. We also took a hundred flies from one side of the Cevennes to the other, but that is another story.

TRAVEL BY HORSE

by Robin Hanbury–Tenison

If the terrain is suitable, then riding a horse is the ultimate method of travel. Of course, in extreme desert conditions, or in very mountainous country, camels, donkeys or mules may be more appropriate. The previous two sections, by René Dee and Roger Chapman describe these methods clearly and they also give a great deal of excellent practical advice which is equally applicable to horses and which should be read by anyone planning a long–distance ride. This is especially the case if the decision is to take a pack animal or animals, since the care of these is as important as that of the animal you are riding yourself.

But for me the prime purpose of riding is the freedom which it can give to experience fully the sounds, smells and sights of the landscape through which I am passing; to divert on the spur of the moment so as to meet local people or look closer at interesting things; to break the tedium of constant travel by a short gallop or a longer canter in the open air, surely the closest man or woman can come to flying without wings.

One way to achieve this freedom is to have a back–up vehicle carrying food for both horses and riders, spare clothes, kit and all the paraphernalia of modern life such as film, paperwork and presents. Often it may not be necessary to meet up with the support team more than once or twice a week, since it is perfectly possible to carry in saddle–bags enough equipment to survive for a few days without overloading your horse. In this way an individual, couple or group can live simply, camping in the open or in farm buildings. If a rendezvous is pre–arranged, the worries of where to stop for the night, whether there will be grazing for the horses and what sort of accommodation and meal awaits at the end of a long day in the saddle is removed.

Fussing about this can easily spoil the whole enjoyment of the travel itself and it is well worth considering carefully in advance whether sacrificing the ulti-mate vagabondage of depending solely on equestrian transport for the serenity of mechanical support is worth it. It does, however, involve a certain amount of expense, although this may be less in the long run than being at the mercy of whatever transport is available locally in an emergency, and most significantly, as with ballooning, it depends on having someone who is prepared to do the driving and make the arrangements.

The alternative is to use time instead of money and resolutely to escape from a fixed itinerary and desire to cover a pre–determined distance each day. This is quite hard to do, since we all tend today to think in terms of programmes and time seems to be an increasingly scarce commodity.

Where to go

After half a lifetime spent on other types of exploratory travel through tropical rainforests and deserts, I came to long distance riding more by accident than design. My wife and I needed some new horses for rounding up sheep and cattle on our farm on Bodmin Moor in Cornwall and we bought two young geldings in the Camargue where the legendary white herds run free in the marshes. Riding them home across France we discovered that the footpaths are also bridle–paths and there is an excellent and well–marked network of *sentiers de grande ran-donnée*. Thanks to this we were able to avoid most roads and instead ride across country. It was an idyllic and addictive experience during which we rode some 1000 miles in seven weeks. Leaving the horses to graze each night in grassy fields, for which we were never allowed to pay, we either camped beside them or stayed in remote country inns so far off the beaten track that the prices were as small as the meals were delicious. This was an unexpected bonus of riding: the need to arrange accommodation around a daily travelling distance of no more than 30 miles or so —and that, in as straight a line as possible, took us to villages which did not appear on even quite detailed maps but where the culi-nary standards were as high as only the French will insist on everywhere.

Later, we were to ride 1000 miles along the Great Wall of China. There we had to buy and sell three different pairs of horse and my suspicions were con-firmed that horse dealers the world over tend to be rogues. We were luckier with our mounts on similar subsequent rides in New Zealand and Spain, but with horses nothing is certain and it is essential to be constantly on guard for the unexpected. However, this only serves to sharpen the senses and when something really wonderful happens, like reaching a wide, sandy beach on the coast, riding the horses bareback out into huge breakers and teaching them to surf, then you know it has been worthwhile.

This piece is meant to be full of practical advice and information, but I am hesitant to give it where horses are concerned. People are divided into those who are 'horsy' and those who are not. The former know it all already and do not need my advice. The latter (and I include myself among them, in spite of having spent much of my life around horses) have to rely on common-sense and observation. It is, on the whole, far better to fit in with local conditions than to try and impose one's ideas too rapidly. For example, we learned to appreciate the superb comfort of the Camargue saddles which we acquired for our ride across France and we took them with us on all our subsequent rides. But in both China and Spain, I found that mine did not suit the local horse I was riding and, to preserve its back, I had to change to a local model, which was much less comfortable for me but much better for the horse.

And it is the horses' backs which should be the most constant concern of all on long–distance rides. Once a saddle sore develops it is very difficult to get rid of and prevention is far the best cure. To begin with it is wise to use a horse whose back is already hardened to saddle use. Scrupulous grooming and regular inspection of all areas where saddle or saddle–bags touch the horses is essential. Washing helps, if water is available and a sweaty back should be allowed to dry as often as possible, even if it does mean unsaddling during a fairly brief stop when one would rather be having a drink and a rest oneself. A clean, dry saddle cloth is essential (felt, cotton or wool) so find out what the horse is used to.

There are many local cures for incipient sores. I have found surgical spirit good, though it will sting if the skin is at all sore or sensitive. Three tablespoons of salt to a pint of water will help harden the skin if swabbed on in the evening, but complete rest is the best treatment. The same goes for girth galls, although these should be avoided if the girths are tightened level and a hand run downwards over the skin to smooth out any wrinkles. A sheepskin girth cover is a good idea too, as it prevents pinching. If it is absolutely essential to ride a horse with a saddle sore, the only way to prevent it getting worse is to put an old felt *numnah* under the saddle with a piece cut out so as to avoid pressure on the affected part.

It is also vital to keep checking the feet, ideally every time you rest and dismount. Stones lodge easily between the frog and the shoe and soon cause trouble if not removed. Small cuts and grazes can be spotted and treated with ointment or antiseptic spray at the same time and a hand passed quickly up and down each leg can give early warning of heat or other incipient problems. Once again the best general cure is usually to take the pressure off horse and rider by resting, if necessary for a day or two.

While putting on a new set of shoes is a skilled business which should not be attempted by the amateur, it is invaluable to have enough basic knowledge of shoeing to be able to remove a loose shoe or tighten it by replacing missing nails from a supply of new ones, which should always be carried in the saddle–bag. I have had to do this with a Swiss Army knife and a rock but it is much better to carry a pair of fencing pliers since these are essential in an emergency if your horse should get caught up in wire.

Your own footwear is also important on a long ride, since it is often necessary to walk leading your horse almost as much as you ride. Riding boots which protect your calves from rubbing on the saddle are useful, especially at the start and if you are using an English or cavalry saddle, but you must be able to walk in them. With a Western type of saddle and once your legs have settled down, it is better to wear comfortable walking shoes or trainers. Leather chaps, which can be found at most country shows, are also invaluable. The protection they give to legs both against rubbing and from passing through bushes easily outweighs the heat and sweat they may generate in a hot climate.

Choosing your horse

As Christina Dodwell says in *A Traveller on Horseback,* a valuable horse is more likely to be stolen and what you need is 'a good travelling horse.' Tschiffely, on the most famous of all long distance rides, from Buenos Aires to Washington in the 1920s, had two Argentinian ponies already 15 and 16 years old when he acquired them. He covered 10,000 miles in two and a half years, covering about 20 miles a day on the days he rode, but making many long stops and side trips.

Tim Severin started out on his ride to Jerusalem on a huge Ardennes Heavy Horse as used on the First Crusade. In spite of suffering from heat exhaustion it reached Turkey before being replaced with a more suitable 13 hand local pony. The ideal horse for covering long distances in comfort is one possessing one of the various 'easy' inbred gaits which lie between a walk and a trot. We were lucky enough to use 'amblers' in New Zealand. These had been bred to have the pace, a two beat gait in which the legs on either side move together giving an impression a bit like the wheels of a steam engine. Once we learned to relax into the unfamiliar rhythm and roll a little from side to side with the horse, we found it wonderfully comfortable and the miles passed effortlessly and fast. However, even then we seldom averaged more than 4 mph (7 kmph). Unless you are setting out to break records or prove a point, the object of a long distance ride should be the journey itself not the high performance of your mount. The close relationship which develops between horse and rider is one of the bonuses of such a journey and as long as your prime concern is your horse's welfare before your own you won't go far wrong.

On a horse it is uniquely possible to let an intelligent creature do most of the thinking and all of the work, leaving you free to enjoy and absorb your surroundings. Birds are not afraid to fly near and be observed; the sounds of the countryside are not drowned by the noise of a motor or the rasping of one's own breath; and if you are lucky enough to have a congenial companion, conversation can be carried on in a relaxed and pleasant way. Notes can even be taken en route without the need to stop or the danger of an accident, especially if you carry a small portable tape recorder. This helps greatly in taking down instant impressions for future inclusion in books and articles which are surely the chief justification of pure travel. Photographic equipment can be readily to hand in saddle–bags, and much more can be carried. Above all, those you meet along the way, whether they be fellow travellers, farmers or remote tribes people, are inclined to like you and respond to your needs.

LONG DISTANCE WALKING

by Nicholas Crane

We are all bipeds. We are all *experts* at walking. Legs require no skills to use or licence to operate. They're built in, cost us nothing to use and are greener than any other means of transport. Legs! Stick 'em in a couple of boots and they'll do thousands of miles without so much as a service. Marvellous things.

Legs have been a recent discovery for me. For years I've been travelling on bicycles, occasionally boats and under pressure, some kind of motorised transport. Horses are fine, but are limited to particular types of terrain. Legs are versatile. You can vary your mode of transport on a whim. Rides in trains or haycarts, buses and boats are all possible complements to a foot-journey.

At walking pace you become part of the infinitely complex matrix which is the countryside. After a while, animals and birds tend not to take flight at your approach. Strangers stop to chat, flattered that you are exploring their neighbourhood at a civilised, respectful pace. On foot you pose no threat and appear to have nothing to hide.

My life as a leg-advocate began with my decision to walk across Europe, following the mountain ranges of the continent from Cape Finisterre in Spain to the Black Sea. This 10,000-kilometre hike took me one and a half years, and was the greatest adventure of my life. I learnt a lot from that walk and I hope that the notes below will be helpful to you. I must however ask you to remember that I am a newcomer to long-distance walking (my only other hikes have been a youth hostelling trip in the Peak District with my mother, a one-week hike in Wales, and another week in the Greek mountains) and so my 'tips' are based on a limited number of extremely vivid experiences, rather than a lifetime's worth of gnarly miles.

I'd like to divide this into two sections: principle and practicalities.

First, principles

When I began my trans-European walk I made the basic mistake of being so excited that I forgot to rest. I walked for 18 days non-stop through sierras of northern Spain. It did not occur to me to take a break until my right leg swelled up like a balloon and reduced me to an agonised hobble. After that I made it a rule that I must stop every 5 to 7 days for at least one day's rest. I learnt that being conscious of incipient ailments will prevent them from becoming problems. Blisters, muscle strain and back-pain can be avoided by being continually aware of how your body-as-machine is functioning.

Interestingly, the Roman, who were experts at thousand-mile marches, walked to a system of three days on, one day off, a routine which they found to be ideal for legions crossing continents. One other authority I'd like to mention is Christopher Whinney, who once walked from London to Rome and who subsequently set up the walking-holiday company Alternative Travel Group. After prolonged trial and error, Christopher found that —just like the Romans —his groups remained the most happy and cohesive if they took every fourth day as a rest day.

Ultimately of course, you must find your own best rhythm. There is no golden mean for everyone. If you walk one day and take two off, that's fine if it's bringing the best rewards from the journey. On several occasions on my European amble, I spent a week or so in one place, or made wide detours from my planned route, and on a couple of occasions walked *backwards* to visit places I'd missed the day before. There is no magic distance which should be covered each day; a fit walker with a medium-sized pack can cover say 20 or 30 kilometres in one day with no trouble. Sometimes I've walked over 50 kilometres in one day, but as a result have been wrecked the following day.

To round off this rhythm section, I'll just add that I'm not a believer in training. If you want to try a long-distance walk, just go. Take it easy and use the first days (or weeks) to get fit.

So much for the rhythm. Now, where to go? Because walking is the slowest form of travel, you do need to choose a route which brings variety on an almost hourly basis. Either you choose a landscape which is choc-a-bloc with physical changes, or you learn to spot the interest in what to many would seem a dull landscape. An interest in flora and fauna, history, geomorphology, agricultural implements, mountain cultures ... whatever (the list is endless) will turn a walk into a fascinating treasure trail. Some landscapes hand the walker hourly interest on a plate. Rambling in mountains; following the courses of rivers; following coastlines are all 'themes' which will, through the natural lie of the land, create a change of view with every hour. Also in this category is the long-distance footpath, way-marked and 'themed' to provide interest, for example the pilgrims' Camiño de Santiago, across northern Spain.

The one area of essential knowledge which is required before embarking upon a long walk in wilderness areas is navigation. This means being able to use a compass accurately and in gales and mists. It also means being able to read maps and to master 'dead-reckoning' —the ability to estimate how much time it will take to cover a certain compass-bearing. It is essential to know how to do this before walking in mountains.

There are some terrains —and I'm thinking of mountains—which are potentially dangerous for inexperienced walkers. It is important not to be lulled into a sense of false security by believing that superior equipment is a substitute for old-fashioned savvy. Had I not spent 25 years messing about trying to climb mountains in Scottish winter white-outs, I would not have survived my trans-European wander. To walk safely in mountains, it is essential that you feel confident using a map and compass in zero visibility and gale force winds on precipitous ridges. This is unlikely ever to happen, all being well, but it is a possibility and you need to be ready to cope. This kind of knowledge can be built up over time, in the company of more experienced companion, on the hills of Wales, the Pennines, the Lake District or Scotland. The most testing ground I've ever found for navigation in mist was Dartmoor.

Saving weight has the dual benefit of making the walking less strenuous and of reducing the clutter of everyday life to a minimum of essentials. I cut my comb in half, trim the edges of maps and keep my hair short, not because these minor weight reductions are going to be noticeable individually, but because each minimalization reminds me daily not to overload my rucksack with unnecessary stores. Carrying a half-kilo of jam unopened from one town to the next is a waste of effort. And while a shortage of water is to be avoided at all costs (dehydration is dangerous), it is worth remembering than one litre of liquid really does weigh one kilogram. It pays to think ahead; to ask locals where the next spring or tap can be found rather than load up like a camel.

So, on to practicalities

It is not worth getting obsessive about equipment, beyond the one rule of minimal weight and maximal safety. There are however a number of items of equipment whose suitability to your needs will affect your enjoyment of the walk.

The single most important item is footwear. The first decision to make is between running/training shoes or boots. The former do not need wearing in; are far lighter than boots and have a 'softer' feel. Boots offer ankle support; a leather construction which breathes better than man-made fibres; an element of water-proofness and grippy treads for steep or uneven surfaces. Again, it is down to personal preference; when my cousins Richard and Adrian made their foot-traverse of the Himalayas in 1982, they wore running shoes; when I made my European mountain hike ten years later, I wore boots. After much experimentation I settled on the British-designed 'Brasher Boot', which combines running-shoe technology with the construction of traditional leather boots. Brasher Boots are lightweight and comfortable

Footwear more than any other item of walking equipment has the power to determine whether a hike is hellish or heavenly. A perfect fit is critical. My method for selecting the correct size (taught to me by Chris Brasher, the Olympic gold medallist runner and designer of the Brasher Boot) is to push my foot forward as far as possible in the unlaced boot or shoe. There should be space to fit a finger down the gap between my own heel and the inside of the boot/shoe. Footwear which is slightly too tight is the most common cause of foot problems. No matter how good the footwear, extraneous factors such as wet weather or extreme heat can cause sores and blisters. On extended hikes, washing feet daily prevent infection. over-long toenails collide with the front of the boot or shoe during descents and, after a period of excruciating discomfort, will turn black then fall off. During my hike I lost a total of ten toenails, to no noticeable disadvantage. They seem fairly superfluous.

Foot problems can be largely circumvented by giving these put-upon appendages considered thought at least three times a day. At the end of a day's walk, I wash my feet, even if doing so mean using precious supplies of drinking water. With practice, it is possible to wash two feet in half a litre of water, tipped in a trickle from a mug. In winter, feet can be cleaned by running very fast on snow, but the subsequent pain as they thaw is dramatic. Washing feet in the evening means that they spend the night bacteria-free in the sleeping bag, thus encouraging the healing of any sores.

In the morning I inspect each toe and every point of wear on each foot. I always pierce blisters the moment they appear, using the tip of a sewing needle, sterilised in the flame of a cigarette lighter. Blisters are more likely to appear when the skin has been softened by water-logged footwear or sweat. Morning is also the time to clip toenails, which left unattended, can wear holes in adjacent toes and abrade the ends of socks.

At midday, half-way through a day's hike, I de-boot for lunch, giving my feet the chance to bask in ultra-violet and my boots the opportunity to air. This pleasurable diversion has to be forsaken if lunch is being taken in a bar or restaurant.

Toe technology is a limited field, but the one device which I have found particularly useful is the 'Scholl's Toe Separator'. This is a small wedge of foam rubber which can be inserted into the gap between two quarrelling digits. For anyone prone to pronation (walking on the outside of your feet), a toe divider inserted between the two smallest toes on each foot will prevent the little toe being rolled under the ball of the foot and gradually eroded.

While I'm dealing with leg-matters, I'll briefly mention knees. After feet, these are the rambler's least reliable component. Aches (and damage) most frequently occur as a result of long descents or stumbles. I have no idea whether there is any physiological sense in this, but my own technique on long descents is to take exaggeratedly short steps, keeping my knees bent. Walk thus, the legs act like car shock-absorbers. The shorter strides also allow greater control and more precise placement of every footstep. It is easier to be thrown off balance while carrying a loaded rucksack, and the knees are frequently the weak link which hit the ground first, or which suffer violent twisting. An accident can be caused by a minor misplacement of the foot: the boot skating on a tiny, unseen pebble, or glancing off a curl of turf, or a heel skidding on a coin-sized spot of ice.

Many walker protect their knees by using a walking aid. There are three alternatives. A conventional walking stick is the least expensive and in most mountainous areas can be bought locally. A hi-tech equivalent favoured by many Himalayan mountaineers for their multi-day treks to the foot of their climb, is the telescopic ski-stick. When not in use, the three sections retract and can be strapped to the side of the rucksack. Finally there is the combined umbrella/walking stick (see below).

After boots, the rucksack is the next most critical item of equipment. Like footwear, the rucksack should be carefully chosen to fit the wearer. A waist belt is essential, as is a chest strap. A properly-fitting rucksack divides the load between the shoulder straps and the waist-belt. Rucksacks of the same capacity can range widely in weight. In the Karrimor range for example, the 45-litre capacity ultra-light 'KIMM II' model weighs only 450 grams, while the high-specification 'Alpiniste 45' (also 45 litres) weighs 1,200 grams. After various experiments, I now find that it is worth carrying the extra grams to guarantee that a rucksack is comfortable. Rucksacks with non-adjustable backs are substantially lighter than the more sophisticated adjustable models. A zip compartment at the foot of the rucksack can be useful for stowing a tent, where it can be kept separate from the rest of the luggage; sensible since it will sometimes be wet.

Clothing should be worn on the 'layering' principle. Each item should be selected so that it can be worn either on its own, or as a part of a series of layer. The ideal layering system allows you to wear every item of clothing in your rucksack, simultaneously and comfortably, or individually. A typical layering system for the top part of the body might work thus: thermal vest, cotton shirt, fleece jacket, Goretex jacket.

Individual items of clothing should be chosen for their light weight, comfort and insulation properties. On my legs I usually wear poly-cotton trousers, which dry quickly and, with the 'poly' for extra strength, tend to last longer than all-cotton trousers. The most comfortable walking trousers I have ever used were made from Ventile, a very fine weave of cotton, which is both windproof and has an almost silk-like feel. My shirts are always 100% cotton. Here the poly element is less important since a shirt gets less of a hammering than trousers. With a rucksack semi-permanently glued to the shirt, natural fibres are easier on the skin. I favour shirts with two breast pockets for carrying my compass and money. If possible, the shirt should have double shoulders, to cope with the wear of the rucksack straps.

For summer walking I usually wear Marks and Spencer wool/nylon mix ankle socks, which are durable and which dry overnight after being washed. For extra insulation in the winter, the 'Thor-Lo' brand, with their differentially-padded panels, are comfortable and warm (and expensive).

A foot-trick of which I am rather proud is my practice of carrying a spare set of 'footbeds' (the insoles which fit onto the floor of the boot). When my boots get wet, I start the next day with the spare, dry pair of footbeds, thus thwarting the misery of early-morning rising damp.

I always carry an 'emergency layer' such as a second fleece jacket, or a sleeping bag (which, wrapped around the torso beneath a waterproof jacket, works like a duvet). I have an 'emergency rule' which is that one set of thermal underwear is kept inside my sleeping bag, which is kept inside a plastic bag, inside the rucksack. Under no circumstances are the sleeping bag or underwear allowed to get wet. This means that in a crisis I always have a complete set of warm, dry insulation.

The item I feel most particular about is my hat, which should have a brim to keep the sun (the ultra-violet is intense at higher altitudes) from the eyes and the back of the neck. French berets are virtually indestructible but cast shade on only one part of the head at a time. More suitable is the Basque beret, with its greater diameter. Best of all though is the lightweight travelling trilby, which can be rolled up like a cornet when not in use, whilst on the head, its generous brim works well as a cranial parasol. The best trilby I have found is made by Herbert Johnson of New Bond Street, London. It should be noted that the trilby does not perform well in high wind. I always carry supplementary headwear, in the form of a very lightweight thermal balaclava. And of course my waterproof jacket (whether Ventile or Goretex) has an integral hood. Reducing heat loss from the head is one of the most efficient methods of maintaining overall body temperature.

The other item essential for head protection is a pair of sunglasses. In mountains some walkers prefer the glasses which have leather side-pieces fitted, which cut out lateral glare. Walking on snow with unprotected eyes can cause 'snow-blindness', both painful and damaging to the eyes.

The only item of equipment which I duplicate is my compass. Without one of these I am lost, literally and philosophically. I use liquid-filled, Swedish-made 'Silva' compasses. The 'Type 3' model is carried in my breast pocket, tied by cord to the button-hole. The much smaller 'Type 23' model, which weighs only 15 grams and is supplied in a modified form to the pilots' survival packs in the seats of Tornado aircraft, is kept in reserve, in my rucksack.

Without maps, long-distance walking can be erratic. Every popular mountain area in western Europe is mapped at a scale of 1:50,000 or, even better, 1:25,000. No other series however is comparable for accuracy or clarity to our own Ordnance Survey, so Britons heading overseas must prepare for a lesser quality of cartography. The best source for walking maps in Britain is Edward Stanford, 12-14 Long Acre, London WC2E 9LP. For hiking in Eastern Europe, the best source is the shop Fretytag & Berndt, Kohlmarkt 9, Vienna 1010, Austria (tel: 533 20 94) and the Bundesamt fur Eich-und Vermessungswesen at Krotenthallergasse 3, Vienna 1080, who sell the old maps of the Austro-Hungarian Empire. The sense of history imparted by these beautifully-drawn maps compensates for the fact that most users will spend 90% of the time completely lost. I relied on them for walking 3,000 kilometres through the Carpathians. They were invaluable.

There is an inverse relationship between the number of days you've been hiking, and the number of tent-pegs remaining to erect your nightly home. Pegs disappear in long grass, drop down rabbit holes, or get used as a tea-stirrer then left on a tree-stump. Peg loss can be reduced by reciting BBC-man Brian Hanrahan's famous Falklands quote: "I counted them all out; I counted them all back", when inserting pegs in the evening and retrieving then next morning.

I've often noticed how that red-handled talisman, the Swiss Army knife, is more treasured than it is used. At the top of the Victorinox range of penknives is the 'Swiss Champ', whose 29 features (among them a hacksaw, a reamer and a ballpoint pen) would be useful for hiker who think that they might be called upon to construct a bi-plane using nothing but driftwood and the contents of their rucksack. I carry the smallest, lightest in the range, the two-bladed 'Pocket Pal'. I use the larger blade for cutting food and the smaller blade for less hygienic roles such as emergency chiropody.

I would not go walking without an umbrella. Furled, it can be used for parrying dog-attacks or beating back briars. Driven spike first into the ground, it is handy for drying socks. Reversing the umbrella and holding the spike converts it into a harvesting tool for out-of-reach blackberries. In the open mode, it is both rain and snow shelter, a sun shade and during exposed picnics, a handy wind-break, My favourite umbrella was obtained when I visited the 'Que Chova' (it means 'What Rain!' in Calician) umbrella factory in Santiago de Compostela, one of the wettest places in Europe. The best mountaineering umbrellas are made by James Smith & Son (53 New Oxford Street, London) whose hickory-shafted model is strong enough to serve as a walking stick, and unlike the metal-shafted models, does not act as a lightening conductor when strapped to a rucksack. A good mountaineering umbrella has 8 ribs; it is a fallacy that 10- and 16-rib umbrellas are tougher; the extra ribs create variable shrinkage in the umbrella's fabric, and thus encourage wear and tear.

After some experimentation, I have settled on the Parker 'Vector' fountain pen, which costs less than a round of beer and is available throughout Europe (on the Continent, it is a favourite among French schoolchildren, an indication more of its durability than its writing quality). Such a pen is more suitable than a ballpoint, whose ink become treacly at low temperatures and leaks in the heat; fancy fibre-tips are expensive and have to be thrown away once they have run dry —not a very green option. In sub-zero temperatures, the conventional ink in my fountain pen will thaw from frozen after a few minutes compression under an armpit. Ten spare Parker cartridges bunched in an elastic band lasted me about 1,000 kilometres of note-making and postcard writing.

Diet is not a facet of everyday life which many long-distance walkers are likely to be able to control to any great extent. You eat what you can find (I do not carry food from home, since part of the interest of travelling is in discovering the local food). But on extended walks, dietary deficiencies can lead to a lowering of the body's defences against bugs and a reduction of its capacity to heal wounds. During my 507-day hike across Europe I lived largely on bread and sardines, bread and pork fat, and bread and jam —the staples generally available in mountain villages. During the same period I ate 1,014 tablets of Vitamin B Complex, Vitamin C and zinc. I was never ill and wounds healed within 3 or 4 days, without the use of antiseptic.

I'll round off this fairly random checklist of my tips with the thought that the best way of finding out about long-distance walking is to start with a short walk and not to stop.

THE MICROLIGHTING TRAVELLER

By Christina Dodwell

To travel long distance by microlight aircraft is sometimes harder to organise logistically than to carry out. It took me nearly three months to sort out the route and obtain the necessary permits for my four-month microlight flight through West Africa.

The most obvious essential is to fit the journey to the prevailing winds; travel is hard enough without wasting fuel in headwinds. My best advice about winds come from the Locust Control Unit whose London office has extensive reference windcharts. The Met. Office in Bracknell were also helpful.

The second controlling factor of the route was the terrain which had to offer plenty of open landing areas; we had no back-up ignition system. Our fuel tank size was increased to 49 litres, and we used an average of 12 litres per hour in flight. We were fortunate that Mobil sponsored us and agreed to stash sealed jerrycans for us at intervals along our route. The alternative of using a support vehicle would mean following roads.

The type of fuel at roadside petrol stations was very low octane and in remote places was contaminated by transportation in unclean containers. In the mountains of Cameroon, petrol was being sold in old Coke bottles.

When route and timing are known you should apply for flight clearances. This is done by letter/fax or telex to the CAA or relevant authority of each country en route, and in due course they should each give you a clearance number. While travelling you must put that number on all flight plans. If the country is a military state or dictatorship, you also need a Military Clearance Number. Although I had received mine for Nigeria, I was arrested on arrival because the number was not on government-headed paper. It took 24 hours to sort out.

Nowadays one can use a Clearance Agent to arrange all these clearances. A recommended one is Mike Gray of Overflight International, tel: 0682-842311. For those who wish to organise their own clearances, there is an excellent free advice and access to addresses from AIS Briefing Services (part of the CAA), tel: 081-745 3447, open 7 days a week. The contacts are Barry Davidson and Mike Blackband. They will give all the necessary 'info' on rules, regulations and how to apply. Also they sell the CAP 555 which lists the entry and exit requirements of every country. They strongly recommend that microlight pilots carry ELT (electronic locator transmitter) and navigate with GPS (global positioning system). GPS didn't exist in West Africa in my days but I am assured there is now world coverage. We did have an ELT disaster signal but a curious person pulled out its pin the day before the journey began, leaving it exhausted.

When flying in ultra inhospitable regions (as I found out mid-Sahara) one is obliged by law to have or hire a support vehicle, and the aircraft must carry fuel and water for a minimum of about five days.

In parts of Europe, the regulations against microlights have recently tightened and they are banned from certain major airports. It would be simpler to enter such a country by road with microlight in tow and assemble it there. This requires only a courtesy call as a visitor asking to fly in their airspace, plus flight plan. For all advice on procedures, contact AIS (above) and also the very helpful Department of Transport whose International Aviation Section 1B, tel: 071-276 5397, is run by Hugh Hopkins.

If a microlight does not have the fuel capacity to reach an international airport as the first stop, you can get permission to stop and re-fuel, and to check-in with any immigration and custom post; must have Customs, doesn't need an airport. Report to the local Chief of Police.

As to the practical side, it wasn't until we began our journey in Cameroon that we learnt our compass was calibrated to northern latitudes; unusable in the tropics; and the only tropical compasses for sale were brass maritime heavies. The most basic things have a way of growing complicated. Luggage, camping gear, tools of lightweight aluminium, and spare parts were loaded into panniers strapped outside the cockpit, plus spare wheel and spare propeller, while water cans and oil were stowed under the seats and sleeping bags were securely tied to the trike's mast.

If things fall off, they usually get sucked into the propeller. I remember Mik Coyne saying when they threw cereal packets out of a microlight for promotional photography, the packets were drawn into the propeller and chipped it badly. Our propeller had chunks torn out of it on several occasions, usually by sticks and stones whirled up on landing and taking off. But we glued the chunks back into place, or refilled the gap with wood carved to shape. Also I had to stitch patches on the wing when it was torn by thorns. Others have trouble from thorns in tyres, for which Richard Meredith Hardy recommended putting strips of carpet between tyre and tube.

My microlight was a standard Pegasus XL, which has an all-up weight capacity of 390 kg, inclusive of trike, wing, two people and everything. When we overloaded by 30 kg we had a total engine failure at 50 ft while taking off, and we fell to the ground like a stone. But nothing broke. At normal full weight there were no adverse effects except for heavier fuel consumption (up to 19 litres an hour in take-off) and a longer take-off and landing run. Perhaps it made us more stable in the air, though on occasions when we were tossed into negative gravidity the stress was appaling and I was surprised that nothing snapped. It was a sturdy machine.

In fact the dangers were few but naturally we had a lot of narrow escapes, particularly when landing on roads with unforeseen traffic. Our worst was a steeply banked road where we landed after dark with no lights, only to find a truck with no lights driving towards us. Sandstorms were not much of a problem, you can usually jump over them. They grow bigger as they approach but you can judge the size. Our standard type was 2 miles wide and 2,000 ft tall. Flight rules say that when storms blow up you must land and secure your aircraft; often it would have been too dangerous to land and there was nothing to tie the wing to, so we stayed airborne. One time a storm grew so big we couldn't find its top and at 4,000 ft we were being pushed backwards by the strength of the wind. Windspeed increases with height, it was futile to go higher and we decided to try flying low down in the storm; it wasn't fun.

Thermal pillars used to start bouncing off the desert by 11am. By midday they were uncomfortable. The only practical times for flight were a few hours morning and evening. If you arrive at an airport after sunset, approx 6pm, you will be charged for landing lights which tends to be expensive.

When taking off near towns or villages with no airstrip, there is a danger of causing harm to people. In their delight the crowds go crazy and, not wanting you to leave, they dash forward to try and grab your moving wing-tips, or rush behind the propeller where a whirled up stone can kill. Sometimes it's worth asking the local police or headman to hold crowds behind the aircraft. Don't allow people to form a corridor during take-off since they'll run into your path.

The horrors were equalled by the moments of pure joy; bad usually equals good; I loved the aerial perspective and being able to see how things fit together. We could pick out the shape of tombs and ancient fortresses that would be invisible from the ground, and we were free to land wherever looked interesting: some weirdly eroded rocks turned out to have caves with wall inscriptions, and some bone fragments led to the discovery of a dinosaur skeleton. It all combines to make a memorable way to travel.

THE MOUNTAINEERING TRAVELLER

by Chris Bonington

It doesn't matter how brilliant the adventure, how talented the team, if a vital piece of equipment is missing, or the food or fuel has run out, not only could the expedition fail to achieve its objective, but lives could be put at risk. Sound logistic planning ensures having the right supplies to achieve the objective and survive, hopefully in relative comfort and with enjoyment.

The principles are the same for any type or scale of expedition or journey, though the size of the party and the nature of the objective obviously must affect the complexity of the logistics. Since my own expertise is in mountaineering, I shall use the planning of a mountaineering expedition as my model, but the principles behind this could be transposed to almost any venture.

It is important to start by deciding exactly what the objective is to be —this might sound very obvious but it is amazing how many people become confused about precisely what they are trying to achieve and end up with a set of conflicting objectives, which in turn make it difficult, if not impossible, to prepare a workable plan. There could, for instance, be a conflict between trying to introduce a group of youngsters of different nationalities to the mountains and tackling a very difficult unclimbed peak.

Having clarified the aim, the next step is to formulate an outline plan of how to achieve it. In the case of a mountain objective the first consideration is the style of climbing proposed to tackle it. There are two approaches: alpine style —packing a rucksack at the bottom of the peak and then moving in a continuous push to the top, bivouacking or camping on the way —or siege style —establishing a series of camps up the mountain, linked by fixed rope on difficult ground. The latter inevitably demands a larger team, more gear and more complex logistics. These have to be worked out in detail, from the number of camps needed, the quality of rope to be fixed if the ground looks steep, the cooking gear needed for each tent, and then the amount of food and fuel necessary to feed the climbers and/or porters while they force the route and ferry loads.

It pays to start the calculations with a summit bid of, say, two people from a top camp of one assault tent and then work back down the mountain. As a rule of thumb, estimate a camp every five hundred metres which represents a reasonable distance for a load carry. Loads of around fifteen kilos can be carried comfortably up to seven thousand metres, but the higher you get the lighter the load should be. It is also important to allow adequate rest periods, so that the team doesn't burn itself out. Using a spread sheet on a computer makes the calculations easier and the various 'what if?' scenarios can then be played out

Planning in this detail at an early stage, automatically supplies information about the size of the team needed and the kind of skills required. This will help choose a team that is not only the right size but also the right composition. This may not appear to come under the heading of logistics but it most certainly does, for without the right people to carry out the tasks in hand, the best laid plans and logistics fall apart. From this point of view in choosing a team it is essential to have a good balance between people who are capable of taking on organisational or management roles and those with skills to attain the objective —in the case of a climbing expedition, talented climbers, or for a scientific one, people with the right scientific qualifications and knowledge. It is also important that the team is compatible, that the brilliant expert — climber, canoeist or scientists — will work effectively for the team as a whole.

The foundations of the expedition are laid in this initial planning phase and are then built into the organisational stage in the home country when everything is being assembled. If vital items of food or equipment are left out, shipping arrangements mishandled, or perhaps most important of all, there is a shortfall in the amount of money to pay for the enterprises, it could be condemned to failure before even setting out. In this organizational phase it is important for the leader to delegate responsibility effectively, in the first instance ensuring that the right person has been given the right job, giving briefs of what is required and the deadlines to be reached and finally leaving them to get on with it, but having a reporting-back system so that if there are any critical problems, the leader can take any necessary action. This role should be one of support rather than interference.

Sound budgeting and raising sufficient funds is obviously a key task in this preparatory phase. In getting sponsorship it is also very important to be realistic over what is promised, so that not only can the promises be fulfilled but, equally important, the commitments to a sponsor do not prejudice achieving the end objective or the way the expedition is conducted.

It pays to build some slack into the schedule to allow for delays and crises. In 1970 when I went to the South Face of Annapurna we sent all the expedition gear by sea, scheduled to arrive in Bombay a fortnight before we were due to reach Nepal by air. The ship carrying it broke down off Africa and was over a month late, giving us a major crisis at the very beginning of the expedition. We got round it with the help of an Army expedition going to the north side of Annapurna. They allowed us to send some gear out with their air freight and loaned us some excellent army Compo rations. This kept us going until the main gear caught up with us but it caused a lot of unnecessary worry and delay. Even today when most expeditions use air freight for their baggage, gear can be lost, delayed in customs or sent to the wrong place, so it pays to allow plenty of time, particularly for clearing customs.

When packing, keep in mind at which stage of the trip the different items of food or gear will be used and also how they are going to be carried to the base of operations. Put together all the items not needed until base camp. The gear and food for use on the approach march needs to be separate and accessible. It is best carried in lockable containers and it pays to get a set of padlocks with a uniform key so that any team member can get access to communal equipment.

It saves a lot of time and hassle if containers are kept to a weight that can be carried by local porters or pack animals and protected sufficiently robustly to withstand rough treatment and exposure to the weather. It is best to distribute similar items in different loads, so that if a single box goes missing the total supply of a vital piece of equipment is not lost —all the oxygen masks, or for that matter, all the matches. The other vital task is to list everything and mark all the boxes clearly with some form of identification that gives no clue of the contents to the casual observer.

Remember that certain items can not be sent by air. It is irresponsible and dangerous to try to smuggle such items through. Gas cylinders can be sent by cargo plane, but must be specially packed. The air freight agent can give advice on these matters.

Once at the roadhead life becomes much more simple. At last everyone is together and hopefully all the gear and food is there with you. It is just a matter of keeping the porters happy —not always easy —and keeping tabs on gear and loads. To make this easier, on some expeditions, I have issued each porter with a numbered plastic disk to coincide with the number of the load and then taken a Polaroid photo of him holding his disk and load.

An approach march can be a leisured delight or a nightmare, depending on the behaviour of the porters. Very often problems with the porters are outside your control, since so much depends on the local situation, the attitude of the liaison officer and the conduct of the *naik* or overseer who might have extracted a large commission from the porters in return for employment. It is very difficult to advise on any specific reaction other than to stay cool, to listen carefully and to bargain effectively.

And then to base camp. The objective —in my case, a mountain —is in sight and some might think that this is where the real challenge begins. However, the eventual success or failure will have been strongly influenced by everything that has been done in the preparatory phase and the approach. If the expedition has been planned out in detail, all the essential gear packed away in the containers that have come straight through to base camp is now available ready for use. Provided team members are fit and relaxed and happy, they certainly have a much better chance of success, or at least of having a good try at achieving the objective and enjoying themselves at the same time.

In the case of a mountain, particularly one that is unclimbed, the first priority, having made base camp comfortable, is to make a thorough recce, to check out if the actual terrain corresponds with what pictures and maps you have managed to get hold of, and whether the plan of campaign needs changing or adjusting. A plan should always be flexible. It is possible to change and adapt it to circumstances, but it must be a well-thought out plan in the first place. On the South West Face of Everest in 1975, we had completed a detailed plan using a computer model back in Britain, but made frequent changes during the course of the expedition. However, with the original plan which acted as a solid foundation, we could never have climbed the South West Face as quickly and smoothly as we did.

It is all too easy, when the weather is good, to believe it will last forever. Each fine day needs to be regarded as the last one you'll get on the expedition. Equally when the weather is bad, it is also easy to slip into lethargy. It is just as important to be poised to take advantage of a clearance.

We all want to achieve success, to reach our objective, but I believe it is important to remember that the journey is as important as the final objective. The way that journey is carried out not only determines the eventual outcome, but equally important, how you are going to feel about it in the future. If the logistics are right, if everyone works well together as a team, with each individual being prepared to sacrifice personal ambition for the good of the group as a whole, being aware of the needs of others and helping where necessary, the venture has achieved complete success. Sound planning from the very beginning provides the foundations of that success. ■

GREAT JOURNEYS OVERLAND
Chapter 7

OVERLAND THROUGH AFRICA

by Warren Burton

It is no wonder that the vastness of Africa's landmass, unknown and untamed, has presented the ultimate challenge to the European for centuries. Its size was only realised by sea-faring explorers who began charting the coastlines during the 17th and 18th centuries. The search into its hidden interior was to start. That it contains the world's largest desert, the longest river, represents just part of Africa's statistics. But little is really known about it, though the Great Rift Valley contains the evidence of the origins of mankind. The records of exploration undertaken by Livingstone, Burton and Speke still, today, inspire many to take on Africa's challenge.

Crossing the Sahara to Central Africa

Hardly a year goes by when some part of Africa is considered a 'no-go' region. The Sahara is no exception and despite its usual barriers —the extremes of heat, lack of roads, closed frontiers —it is now the Sahara's own internal unrest which stands in the way, at the time of writing, (March 1994). The established and rather traditional route that has been followed for some 25-30 years, is now very questionable.

In the past (and we hope these options will return), journeys either started from Morocco crossing the Atlas Mountains into Algeria, or alternatively sailing from Italy entering at Tunis. Either route takes you south on the 'Trans Sahara Highway' to the oasis towns of Ghardaia, El Golea, In Salah and finally Tamanrasset, at the base of the mighty Hoggar Massif. More adventurous overlanders, with well-equipped 4-WD vehicles and ample supplies of fuel/water, opted for the dramatic and somewhat tortuous route east via the Tassili plateau and extraordinary rock formations around Djanet. Here, found in caves, are 3000-year old rock inscriptions, records of Sahara life before the expanding sands engulfed much of its vegetation. Desert tracks marked occasionally by oil drums then lead you south to Tamanrasset and the ever-elusive 'Highway'. The Sahara has its own way of dealing with development —no sooner do the Algerian and Nigerian governments lay a few more kilometres of bitumen, then along comes a typical desert 'flash flood' which can destroy years of work in a few hours.

A less popular but practical alternative, again with a suitable vehicle (carrying long range fuel/water supplies), was to travel directly south from Bechar to

Reggane, to follow the Tanzerouft route in Mali. Either way, the present political unrest and rise of Islamic fundamentalism in Algeria renders the country unsafe and therefore these routes are unviable. Regrettably this has followed a long period of unrest in the south of the Sahara, on the frontier lands of Algeria, Niger and Mali. During 1991 and 1992 unruly factions of Tuareg seeking autonomy and self control, set about attacking and robbing any vehicle entering the region. Several incidents led to travellers being robbed of their vehicles and belongings, with isolated reports of shootings. Alternative routes had to be found. Crossing Libya into Chad is out of the question, so all attention was focused on a route through the former Spanish Sahara (now administered by Morocco) into Mauritania. However, whilst overlanders have obtained permits from the Moroccan authorities, the Mauritanian Government have never really acknowledged this and permission to enter from Morroco is often refused.

Still, it can be done —but you are *strongly* advised to investigate this route thoroughly first. Whilst many still attempt and succeed crossing Africa without 4WD, it is still wise to do so, and particularly as this alternative route certainly presents some tough days of soft sand in northern Mauritania.

Carnet de Passage documents are required for your vehicle once you leave Morocco and most, if not all, countries in Africa are now very wised up to the requirements of vehicle insurance.

Visas are required to enter Mauritania and you are advised to obtain these in Europe (Bonn, Paris or Madrid) as it is reported that they are almost impossible to obtain in Rabat, Morocco. It is also best to obtain visas for Mali whilst in Europe —thus avoiding the risk of not being able to obtain them before exiting Mauritania. Most other visas can be obtained en route in neighbouring countries. Up-to-date medical advice should also be sought before departure, because health risks in Africa are ever present and especially the risks of malaria, which is now on the increase, particularly in Sub-Sahara and West Africa.

The route through Morocco should certainly go via the imperial city of Fes renowned for its huge walled Medina. Then crossing the High Atlas to Todra Gorge and the edge of the Grand Erg Occidental with its 'sea of sand dunes'. Marrakech still retains its mystic aura, and is your last 'semi-civilised' centre, before heading south to the coastal sands of the Western Sahara. Following the Atlantic coast via Layounne you arrive in Dakhla, the formal exit point from Morocco. Here at least a day of tedious paperwork and form-filling enables you to join a twice-weekly 'convoy' south to the frontier post at La Gouria. A short but tricky desert crossing brings you into Mauritania at Nouadhibou —a strange town, servicing the rail link and port which is essential to the export of the country's phosphate reserves.

Mauritania is an Islamic Republic and thus prohibits the import of alcohol, so it is wise to consume or dispose of this prior to entry. Furthermore overland travel has only recently arrived on Mauritania's doorstep —so one should tread lightly and savour the rather timid reception you may receive, though early reports state that generally local folk are very friendly and helpful.

Formalities are slow on entry and you must obtain a '*Laissez Passe*' (permit) to travel south to Nouakchott. For the more adventurous and with the 'recommended' assistance of a local guide, try the route directly south with plenty of sand-matting. You then have to catch the low tide in order to drive the last 150 kms along the beach into Nouakchott.

A relatively new bitumen road takes you east to Nema before joining some rough tracks south into Mali and on to Bamako.

Borders have opened with Mauritania and Senegal, so a route encompassing all of West Africa can be considered, but check for the rainy season —it can make many routes impassable.

If time permits then Mali presents a wealth of culture, history and tradition, much of which is found around Mopti and Djenne in the lands of the Songhai. A little east is the Bandiagara Escarpment, the home of the Dogon people, with their traditional lifestyle in evidence. South from here you cross into Burkina Faso (formerly Upper Volta), through Ouagadougou and on to Niger. Niamey, its capital, though offering little of interest, does provide the opportunity to obtain several visas before heading off to Nigeria. The popular route now is to Kano in northern Nigeria— time out to service vehicles and restock for Central Africa and Zaire. Then into northern Cameroon and the spectacular route through the Kapsiki Mountains.

The alternative is to head south from Ougadougou to the Ivory Coast, Ghana, Togo, Benin and southern Nigeria. This route will provide more varied insight into West Africa but will obviously add considerable time to your journey. From Nigeria you will enter Cameroon by the southern route visiting Doula and Yaounde, the capital, en route to the Central African Republic. Whilst visas are readily available to enter Gabon and the Republic of Congo, any route further south appears doubtful. Angola has reverted to a state of unrest and civil war and southern Zaire is politically split by power struggles to decide who controls the country.

Back on the traditional overland trail takes you into Central African Republic via Bouar to Bangui, the sleepy, but shifty colonial capital renowned for its French patisseries —make the most of them, you won't find too many in Zaire.

Zaire to East Africa

The route east through Central Africa Republic to southern Sudan, Juba, then south to Kenya, has really been 'out of bounds' for some years now. The continuance of civil war with the North shows no let up, much to the suffering of the local Dinka and Nuer tribes people who roam these lands.

So far, and for the foreseeable future, the only route 'open' to East Africa is through Zaire. Whilst Zaire continues to struggle under President Mobutu, its ruler for almost 30 years, the country somehow functions despite itself. Corruption is rife, fuel and food shortages are common, and the 'roads' deteriorate by the year. Hence one is warned to go prepared with a vehicle in sound state (very little in the way of spares or assistance is available on the way). Certainly reserve food and fuel supplies are a must.

There are presently two entry points into Zaire from Central Africa, both involving a ferry crossing of the rivers that from the frontiers. Entering at Zongo (across the river from Bangui) will take you southeast via Gemena to Lisala and the Zaire River. Here there may be the opportunity to board a barge or one of the river ferries travelling upstream to Kissangani, (formerly Stanleyville during the colonial days of the Belgium Congo). The overland route follows north of the river via Bumba, Buta and then south to Kisangani.

Either way progress is slow. The ferries and barges constantly run aground on shifting sand bars, whereas the road will inevitably be worse for wear especially during and after the long rainy season (July to November).

The other alternative is to travel further east in the Central African Republic, viewing the awesome Kembe Falls, en route to Bangassou. Having crossed the Mbomou River you join a 'secondary road' (more like a track) south to Bondo then to Buta - makeshift 'bridges' on this route are very suspect and should always be checked.

Into eastern Zaire via the Ituri Forests and the home of the Pygmies, then you are at a point where the option is to either cross Uganda, or to travel further south through the Virunga National Park and enter Rwanda. Here on the densely forested slopes of the Virunga volcanoes is the home of the much threatened Mountain Gorilla. Their plight was much publicized by the movie 'Gorillas in the Mist'. Protection projects operated in Zaire, Rwanda, and more recently Uganda, have helped to safeguard their environment and partially protect them from ever-present poachers. The projects are funded by charging a fair price to travellers wishing to hike with guides into the forest to view these wonderful gentle giants comfortable in their mountain habitat. However at the time of writing, Rwanda is out of bounds due to the civil war, and the whole area should be avoided.

Were you to exit Zaire directly into Uganda, a route taking you through Murchinson Falls National Park, you will be well rewarded. Here you are at the meeting points of the Victoria and Albert Niles, as they form the mighty White Nile and the start of its long slow route to the Mediterranean. Uganda, once the 'Jewel of Africa', has had a long road to recovery following the horrific periods of rule by Amin and Abote, which left this friendliest of countries in rack and ruin. Uganda's people offer you wonderful hospitality, definitely include it on your route.

From Kampala there are several choices of route, either directly into Kenya and through the rift valley and its lakes of Baringo, Naivasha and Nakuru to Nairobi. Or take the southernly route round Lake Victoria directly into Tanzania and on to Mwanza. By doing this you can then visit the game–filled plains of the Serengeti, discover the Oldovia Gorge then climb to the rim of the Ngorongoro Crater. This natural haven for wildlife can be visited by descending in a landrover, locally chartered at the parks wildlife headquarters.

From here you descend into Tanzania's rift valley, via Lake Manyara and the Masai tribelands to Arusha sitting at the base of Mt Meru. Time is well spent exploring the game reserves of Kenya, the Indian Ocean coast from Lamu to Malindi and the old Arab trading port at Mombassa. South via the slopes of Kilimanjaro, Africa's highest peak where, with the support of local guides and porters, one can make a non-technical climb to its snow-capped summit of 19,000ft.

The Rift Valley to the Cape

Recent political changes in South Africa and the structured move to abolish Apartheid, have eased travel to the south dramatically. Gone are the days of questioning border controls, intent on stalling your progress south through Tanzania, Zambia and Botswana, knowing full well that your destination was ultimately South Africa. Now very few visas are even required to travel through this section, the only real challenge is deciding on your route and preferences.

The popular journey is south via Dar es Salaam and with time out to visit the exotic spice island of Zanzibar. Here life is dramatically different to that of the mainland. Then by joining the 'Tanzam Highway' one actually enters the eastern fork of the Great Rift Valley that leads you down into Malawi to the characteristic fishing villages dotted along the shores of its beautiful lake. To Lilongwe, Malawi's peaceful capital, then entering Zambia, your choice is either to head south via Lake Kariba into Zimbabwe and Harare. Or to head for Livingstone and the thundering Victoria Falls on the frontier of Zimbabwe and Zambia. Here activities include white-water rafting, birds eye flights over the falls and would you believe, bungy jumping off the bridge joining the frontiers.

There are many variations of routes from here to the Cape, but most now prefer crossing Botswana, including an excursion into the waterways of the Okavango Basin. The 'islands' of the delta are a haven for wildlife and birds. Then a route through the Caprivi Strip into Namibia, the unique Etosha Pans and the vast mountainous sand dunes that fall dramatically into the Atlantic. The rugged shoreline is littered with skeletons of shipwrecks for which the coastline is notorious. Sealife havens can be visited when you travel south via Walvis Bay and Luderitz. The Fish River Canyon is a must before leaving Namibia to cross the Orange River into South Africa. Several days' drive brings you to the end of an incredible journey —and Cape Town, overlooked by its distinctive Table Mountain, is an ideal place to end.

Cairo to the Cape

Regrettably with southern Sudan being a 'no go' zone, the route directly south from Egypt up the Nile to Khartoum, Kosti, Juba and into Kenya is still not possible. However recent reports have it that the Sudan and Ethiopian Governments are warming to the idea of travellers taking the little-used route from Wad Madani to the gorges of the Blue Nile into Ethiopia and Lake Tana. Addis Ababa perched on the 'wall' of the Great Rift Valley now offers a viable route south through the lakes and desert lands bordering on Kenya. This is harsh country experiencing extreme temperatures, yet it is now at least part of an overland route which has not been possible for some 20 years.

AROUND SOUTH AMERICA

by Chris Parrott

'The Gringo Trail' (not to be confused with the Inca trail) is what everyone calls the most frequently travelled route through and around South America. *Gringo* is derived either from 'Green go home' in the days when the US Army used to wear green uniforms, or from *Greigo*, the Spanish word for Greek.

Despite assurances in the guide books that the term is widely used in friendly reference to anyone with a pale complexion, it is definitely not a complimentary form of address. If you need confirmation, watch how a blond Argentine reacts to being called *Gringo*.

The trail begins in whichever gateway happens to be the cheapest to fly into from Europe or the USA. Let's start in the north, in Colombia. The coast here boasts beautiful golden beaches, clear water and crystal streams cascading down from the 5800m summits of the Sierra Nevada. To the south is the big industrial port of Barranquilla and then Cartagena, an impressively fortified town dating from 1533, through which, for nearly 300 years, gold and treasures were channelled from throughout the Spanish colonies. Passing through the hot swampland and then inland up the attractive forested slopes of the Cordillera Occidental, the traveller emerges on a high plateau where Bogota is sited, at 2620m. The Gold Museum has over 10,000 examples of pre–Columbian artefacts. An hour away are the salt mines of Zipaquira, inside which the workers carved an amazing 23m high cathedral.

South from Bogota are the Tequendama Falls, the splendid valley of the Magdalena river and, high up on the Magdalena Gorge, the village of San Agustín. Here, hundreds of primitive stone statues representing gods of a little–known ancient Indian culture, guard the entrances to tombs. The road then loops back over high moorland to Popayan, a fine city with monasteries and cloisters in the Spanish style. The tortured landscape near here has been said to resemble "violently crumpled bedclothes." And so the road crosses into Ecuador. Just north of Quito, the equator, *La Mitad Del Mundo*, cuts the road a few hundred meters from the grand stone monument built to mark the meridian. Quito itself is at 2700m, ringed by peaks, amongst them the volcanoes of Pinchincha. It has much fine colonial architecture including, according to *The South American Handbook*, 86 churches, many of them gleaming with gold.

The Andes

Travellers then cross the Andes, passing from near–Arctic semi–tundra, through temperate forest, equatorial jungle and down to the hot total desert of the Peruvian coast, punctuated by oases of agricultural land where irrigation has distributed the melt–waters from the Andes over the littoral. Here too the ancient empires of the Chavin, Mochica, Nazca and Chimu people flourished. Ruined Chan–Chan, near Trujillo, was the Chimu capital; nearby Sechin has a large square temple, 3500 years old, incised with carvings of victorious leaders and dismembered foes.

A popular detour here is to turn inland at the fishing port of Chimbote and head for the Callejon de Huaylas. The route passes through the spectacular Canóon del Pato, where the road is literally drilled through the rock wall of the canyon, with 'windows' looking down to the roaring maelstrom of the Santa river below.

The Callejon de Huaylas valley runs along the foot of the Cordillera Blanca; here the 1970 earthquake buried the town of Yungay under an avalanche of mud. The towns of Caraz and Juaraz make good centres for walking and trekking in the Cordillera, and the road south across the mountains has spectacular views of the snowcapped Cordillera Blanca.

The coast near Lima is picturesque and rich in fish and birdlife, owing to the

Humboldt Current. Lima itself has both shanty towns (*barrios*) and affluent suburbs, parks and fine beaches. Well worth seeing are the National Museum of Anthropology and Archaeology, the Gold Museum at Monterrico on the outskirts of town, and the Amano private museum.

South from Lima

From Lima, there are two routes south. One branches into the mountains (the pass reaches 4800m) through the zinc smelting town of La Oroya, to Huancayo. The road continues through Ayacucho and Abancay to Cuzco, and though Lima, Cuzco looks a relatively short distance on the map, it actually represents about 50 hours of continuous travel overland. The other route follows the fast coast road through the desert past the wine centre of Ica to Nazca with its vast and little–understood lines, on to Arequipa. There are several cut–off routes — from Pisco or Nazca, for example, or you can take the train in a grand circle from Arequipa to Cuzco.

One thing that is certain: any route in Peru that crosses the Andes is tortuous, time–consuming, and stunningly spectacular. Cuzco sits in a sheltered hollow at 3500m. This was the capital of the Inca Empire. Inca stonework forms the base of many of the Spanish buildings and the ancient city layout survives to this day.

Overlooking Cuzco's red roofs is the ruined fortress of Sacsahuaman. Nearby too are the ruins of Pisac and Ollantaitambo and, reached by train only, down the valley of the Urubamba (further up–stream, this is called the Vilcanota), the 'Lost City of the Incas', Machu Picchu. This magnificent ruined city sited nearly 500m above the river was overgrown with jungle until its discovery in 1911. There are several legends which add to the mystery of the lost city. One states that after the sacking of Cuzco, the Virgins of the Sun fled to this city, whose existence was unknown to the Spanish. Others say that the Incas themselves had erased all mention of the city from their oral histories, retribution for some, now forever–censored, local uprising long before Pizarro and his men set foot in Peru.

From Cuzco, the road crosses the watershed of the Andes to the dry and dusty Altiplano, a high treeless plateau stretching from here across much of the Bolivian upland. Here lies Lake Titicaca, at 3810m the world's highest navigable lake, blazing a deep blue because of ultra–violet rays. On the floating reed islands of the lake live the Uru–Aymara Indians. Across the border in Bolivia are the ruins of Tiahuanaco, relic of an ancient race; the main feature is the carved 'Gate of the Sun.' La Paz lies in a valley just below the rim of the Altiplano, the city centre lying at approximately 3500m.

La Paz and beyond

From La Paz, there are three possible routes, depending on the size of the circuit that you intend making:

1. Eastwards through the relatively low–lying city of Cochabamba to Santa Cruz, then on by rail to Corumba on the Brazilian border, from where you can head for São Paulo or the Iguaçu Falls. The road from Santa Cruz to Corumba and any of those from Bolivia to Paraguay are suitable for four–wheel–drive

only.

2. Southwards via Cochabamba to Sucre and the mining town of Potosi to Villazón on the Argentine border and points south. NB: Uk passport holders no longer need visas for Argentina.

3. Southwards to Arica in northern Chile. The roads gradually peter out over the salt pans and quicksands that stretch over this region —a region that should only be traversed in the dry season (May to November) and then with very great care. The road passes through the very beautiful Lauca National Park, and then continues (for the most part tar–sealed) through the Atacama desert, the farm–lands and vineyards of central Chile to the so–called 'Little Switzerland' of mountainous southern Chile.

There is no road in Chile south of Puerto Montt, and the most usual point of crossing the border south of Santiago is that near Osorno to reach Bariloche, now a fashionable ski resort in Argentina. This route may not be passable in winter (June to October). The road from Santiago to Mendoza via Uspallata is kept open all year round, though in winter the road uses the railway tunnel and does not pass the famous Christ of the Andes statue. Travel south from Bariloche frequently takes you over unmade roads in the foothills of the Andes through the beautiful Argentine lake district to Viedma and Calafate. Here the lakes are fed by melt–waters from the Patagonian ice cap, and 'arms' of the lakes are sometimes blocked by tongues of glacial ice. The scenery around Lago Argentino, for example, is some of the most spectacular anywhere in the world. Roads here are passable at most times of year, though from June to October, four–wheel drive is advisable.

Alternatively you can combine the Pan American highway with local ferries via the island of Chiloe and the Chonchi to Chaiten ferry. You can also travel east out of Puerto Montt using the local *Balsa* or ferries crossing the numerous rivers and fjords on the way to Chaiten. The road continues down to Cochrane but ferry services stop during winter. Bear in mind that periodically, heavy rains cause landslides which end all hope of travel.

The South

It is possible to reach South America's southernmost tip, Tierra del Fuego, by ferry from near Rio Gallegos, or from Punta Arenas across the border in Chile. In winter it is impossible to cross the mountains by road to reach the small town of Ushuaia on Tierra del Fuego's south coast, but there are regular flights throughout the year from nearby Gallegos and Rio Grande.

A worthwhile excursion from Punta Arenas (Chile) is to Puerto Natales and the famous Torres del Paine National Park; a must for mountaineers, and an unforgettable experience for anyone who thinks that those etchings by early explorers always made mountains look ridiculously precipitous.

The fast, straight east coast road through temperate scrubland takes you north again via Comodoro Rivadavia, and Puerto Madryn with its Welsh–speaking colony, to Bahia Blanca and Buenos Aires. This cosmopolitan city of nearly 10 million inhabitants lies on the estuary of the River Plate, a few hours by ferry from Montevideo in Uruguay.

Most travellers tend to bypass the rolling cattle–grazed plains of Uruguay in favour of the roads northwards, either through Santa Fé and Resistencia to Asunción, or direct to Iguaçu via Posadas and the Misiones province. Ferries are now almost extinct but new bridges (Ponte President Tancredo Neves between Argentina and Brazil, and the Friendship Bridge, between Brazil and Paraguay) make the journey quicker —if less interesting. There are also three bridging points across the Parana River between Buenos Aires and Asunción. The first is at Zarate; the second is the tunnel from Santa Fé to Rosario; and the third is the bridge between Resistencia and Corrientes.

There is a good fast road from Asunción to Foz do Iguaçu where the frontier is crossed by bridge. Car and passenger ferries from Foz de Iguaçu (Pôrto Meira) in Brazil to Puerto Iguaçu (or Iguassu) in Argentina, make it possible to visit these spectacular falls from both sides of the river.

Plantations of Brazil

The dense forest that once spread across Brazil from Iguaçu to Rio and beyond is gradually making way for coffee and soya bean plantations, though there is a particularly special stretch of road between Curitiba and São Paulo, since the new road follows the Serra do Mar coastal range. Carriageways are often separated by several kilometres as east–bound traffic goes around one side of a jungle–clad mountain, while westbound takes the high road.

From São Paulo there are two routes to Rio —one through Santos and Angra dos Reis along a beautiful coast road; the other the fast motorway, along the ridge of the mountains via the steel town of Volta Redonda. Rio is a focus; from here routes divide once more:

1. The north–east coast road through Salvador, Recife and Fortalaza to Belém at the mouth of the Amazon. Many travellers feel that this route, passing through the regions first settled by Portugal and her slaves four centuries ago, is the real Brazil.

2. North west via Belo Horizonte and the old mining towns of Minas Gerais province, such as Ouro Preto, Congonhas, Tiradentes and Mariana. This route leads to that oasis of modernity, that ultimate in planned cities, Brasilia.

There are several routes up to the Amazon basin from Brasilia, the fastest and easiest of which is direct to Belém via Anapolis. On this road there is a cut–off at Estreito, along the Transamazónica Highway to Altamira and Santarem.

Alternatively you can follow the newer road west to Cuiabá , and then take the Transamazónica north to Santarém. At both Belém and Santarém there are river steamers to Manaus though, for anyone with their own vehicle to ship, car ferries are few and far between. A more practical route in this instance is that to the west, to Cuiabá and Pôrta Velho, and then north along the new road via Humairá to Careiro on the south bank of the Amazon opposite Manaus. From here there are three ferries daily across to Manaus.

In the days when Brazil held a monopoly of rubber supplies, Manaus built a splendid (and recently restored) opera house for the best mezzosopranos in the world, and the rubber barons lit their cigars with 1000 *millreis* notes. Most of that glitter has faded, though edifices built of stone imported from Britain are still to be seen.

From here, riverboats ply the Rio Negro and the Rio Branco, tributaries of the Amazon, and they provide a break from overlanding and a convenient, if primitive, way of visiting remote villages. North from Manaus the authorities have 'subdued' the Indians who for years threatened white lives on the road to Boa Vista, and the route is now passable in safety.

Angel Falls

The road between Boa Vista and the gold mining town of El Dorado (Venezuela) winds through spectacularly beautiful country passing the sheer–sided 'lost world' of Mount Roraima at the junction of the three countries. Side trips can be taken to the world's highest waterfall, Angel Falls (979m), either from El Dorado or from Puerto Ordaz (now part of the new city of Ciudad Guayana).

After crossing the Orinoco, you'll soon reach Caracas, having completed almost a full circle of the continent. If you've still not seen enough, there's a route eastwards that is definitely not on the Gringo Trail. It is not possible, owing to border disputes, to cross the frontier from Venezuela to Guyana.

From Boa Vista (Brazil) however, there is a road of sorts to the frontier and a fordable river into Lethem. In the dry season, it's possible to drive all the way to Georgetown, and from there along the coast to the Corentyne River. Getting across that and into Nieuw Nickerie in Suriname will cause problems for those with their own vehicles, though there is an infrequent ferry. In fact, it's possible to drive all the way to Cayenne in French Guiana, though the road is little more than a sand track in places, and there are a number of rivers that have to be crossed by ferry.

Saint Laurent lies just over the river from Suriname, in French Guiana, and the remnants of both this penal colony and the better–known one of the Isles de Salut are beginning to prove something of a tourist attraction. Devil's Island is part of the Isles de Salut Group, but is hard to reach.

At Cayenne, the road ends, though it is possible to fly either direct to Belém at the mouth of the Amazon or to Saint Georges just across the river from the Brazilian river port of Oiapoque, from where a road runs all the way to Macapa. There are ferries from Belém from there, and that puts you back on the route southwards to Rio either along the northeastern coast, or south to Brasilia. In fact, you could just keep circling and recircling the continent in ever decreasing circles, clockwise and anticlockwise. It's a very dizzying part of the world in every respect!

THE CLASSIC OVERLAND THROUGH ASIA

by Warren Burton

The journey across Asia must still be considered the original of all overland routes. History provides us with sketchy accounts of the great overland journeys by Alexander, Hannibal, and Marco Polo. Those routes can still be taken to India and beyond, despite recent conflicts such as the Gulf War and continuing tribal conflict in Afghanistan. There is always a way through. The Middle East has continued to present some instability, yet there has always been a safe alternative to follow. With the Revolution in Iran almost 15 years ago, the country is no longer the bureaucratic and logistical struggle that prevailed during those few years of turmoil. Visas are available to all, except holders of USA passports, and in spite of being issued only a 7-day Transit Visa, one can extend these up to 21 days with relative ease whilst in Iran. However, following the Gulf War in 1991, and despite promises to the Kurds from the Western Powers, unrest has erupted in Southeast Turkey (Turkish Kurdistan). Yet again the suppressed and isolated Kurds struggle for autonomy and the Turkish Government's answer to this— send in the Army! So this region should most definitely be avoided.

With the continued breakup of former Yugoslavia, the most direct route to Istanbul following the E5 is not recommended. By diverting through Hungary, Romania and Bulgaria one can still arrive in Turkey (and Asia) without travelling too many more miles. Certainly you will see countries which have experienced considerable change since the breakup of the Eastern Bloc.

However the crossing of Asia remains a bureaucratic challenge, so you must go prepared with the correct vehicle documentation, most importantly a *Carnet de Passage* and your vehicle *Registration Document*, both correct in every detail —border officials can be very uncompromising. Furthermore almost all nationalities now require a visa for all countries east of Turkey. These must be obtained *before* departure as they *cannot* be issued on entry and are often not obtainable in neighbouring countries.

Istanbul East

Istanbul, where Europe meets Asia, is the perfect place to slow down, and finalise your plans and timings. The city is well serviced and although it is not the capital of Turkey, most countries on your route have diplomatic representation here. Istanbul is also an ideal meeting place for travellers heading east and you may be fortunate to meet some who have come west-bound— recent information from them is always the most up-to-date source.

The most direct route to Iran and beyond, is to travel via Ankara (the capital) then rising on to the Anatolian Plateau through Sivas, Erzincan, Erzurum to Dogubayazit (last stop in Turkey). This region has been affected recently by the Kurdish unrest, therefore you should check with local authorities before leaving Ankara. In any case, do not drive at night and stay in towns rather than camping.

The alternative longer route and by far the most rewarding is to head south from Istanbul via the Gallipoli Peninsular, crossing the Dardanelles to Canakkale. Then the choice is yours, but why not visit Troy, Bergama, Kusadasi (and Epheseus), then east to Pamukkale before crossing the mountains to the south coast. Several days can then be spent lazing on the beaches and coves of Olu Deniz, before following the dramatic coastal route from Fethiye via Kas to Antalya, Side and Anamur. This route is not only scenically spectacular but dotted with ancient Roman sites, Crusader castles and coastal villages of typical Turkish character.

Having virtually travelled the entire length of the south coast, Adana is the crossroads. South to Syria and a diversion to the Middle East (see below) or north across the Taurus Mountains to Cappadocia (and the environs of Goreme). and on north to rejoin the 'main road' at Sivas.

Diverting into the Middle East

If time and money permits then certainly consider visiting Syria and Jordan. More recent conflicts and friction between neighbours restrict you to where you can travel, but the situation is ever changing. The Israel/Palestine peace process could well change the entire area —even Syria and Israel are at last talking to each other over conference tables.

Visas are required for both Syria and Jordan which should be obtained before you leave Europe. You do not require any other special paperwork for your vehicle, but be patient on the Syrian borders, they can be very autocratic and time–consuming.

From Adana head, south to the coastal town of Iskenderun and then cross into Syria at the Baba el Hawa border and on to Allepo, which has the largest medieval citadel in the world and the largest bazaar/souq in the Middle East. Further south are the water wheels at Hama, and from there to Homs and then Damascus, Syria's bustling capital. Cross the Jordanian border at Dar'a then to Amman, the capital. The city has little of interest but the site of Jerash to the north is well worth a visit.

Jordan surprises many travellers, the people (65 per cent of the population being Palestinian) are extremely friendly and hospitable, but also the country is geographically stunning and historically dramatic. A route via the Dead Sea takes you along the King's Highway from Madaba to Keraka and Petra, the hidden city of Nabateans. Several days here would not be wasted before heading south to the Aqaba on the Red Sea.

One can complete a circuit by returning to Amman along the Desert Highway, it is highly recommended to do an excursion en route to Wadi Rum, (famous in the days of Lawrence of Arabia). Take a local Bedouin guide and you will travel through some of the most spectacular desert scenery to be seen anywhere in the Middle East.

From Amman it is possible to take an excursion to the 'West Bank', but you require a special permit and you are not permitted to take your own vehicle. Fortunately, border controls between Jordan and Israel do not stamp your passport, however, on return from Jordan you must ensure that you have no evidence of Israeli goods, souvenirs etc —otherwise you will run into great difficulty attempting to re-enter Syria.

At the time of writing (March 1994) a route into Iraq is not advisable. Furthermore, you are still not permitted to travel overland through Saudi Arabia.

On re-entering Syria from Jordan and returning to Damascus you should consider the route northeast to the remote desert ruin of Palmyra —the Roman city built on the ancient Greek site dating back to 1000BC. Your route could then take you via Lake Assad on the Euphrates, returning via Allepo to re-enter Turkey. Again, due to the present Kurdish unrest the region east and northeast of Gaziantep and Diyarbakir is best avoided, most certainly any route around

Lake Van is out of bounds.

Iran to India

The only practical entry point to Iran from Turkey is the border of Barzagan. Before entering, in order to conform with Islamic dress codes, you must, if female, equip yourself with a *chadoor,* a long loose-fitting gown that will cover your head, shoulders and covering the distinguishing shape of your body. This must be worn in public. Furthermore alcohol is strictly forbidden, so drink it all before the border. Having said all this, the border control, although slow, is usually very civil and again as long as everything is in order, then all should run smoothly.

The direct and most travelled route goes via Tabriz, Zanjan then south to Esfahan via Hamadan avoiding Tehran —unless of course you want to tackle the worst traffic jams in Asia. Esfahan is the cultural centre of Iran, and still houses some of the most valuable craft workshops and bazaars of the Middle East. The Shah Abbas Mosque is spectacular with the turquoise blue ceramics covering its domes and minarets.

A day's drive south to Shiraz, the garden city renowned for its hospitality, and the nearby ruin of Persepolis. This 2500-year old site was built by the Persian King, Darius the Great, only to be destroyed by Alexander the Great around 300 BC.

You now follow the old southern trade routes across Dasht-e-Lut, via Kerman and Zahedan. The way is marked with Caravansari and desert fortresses, one in particular at Bam is still very intact.

Afghanistan though very near, is definitely out of bounds to overland travel for the foreseeable future. Therefore crossing the Baluchistan desert into Pakistan is the only viable route. However, this is a very sensitive region and one should proceed with caution, avoiding any night-driving and 'camping out'. You should also avoid any form of disagreement or conflict, no matter who might be at fault. Folk are 'touchy' in this area, most are armed, so be diplomatic and you should have no problems.

The rather chaotic border post at Mijaveh/Taftan is usually straight forward and travellers are often welcome to sleep overnight at the Pakistan Customs post.

Attempts are being made to complete the construction of a bitumen road through the desert to Quetta —though it's a long process and the constant affects of drifting sand and seasonal flash floods seem to hinder progress.

Quetta is very much a frontier town and a real crossroads for traders and 'smugglers'. Whilst the town has very little architectural character, the people, who congest the streets and markets, replace what is missing —Afghani, Baluchi and Pathans all mingle in this mountain oasis to make a colourful bazaar of trade (and not all of it legal!).

Following nomad routes into the Indus river valley, Pakistan's lifeline, you head north via Multan to Lahore. However, if time and resources are still available, Northern Pakistan is a must, especially during the months (May to September).

The frontier region of west Pakistan bordering on Afghanistan is tribal and restricted. Therefore if you are going to visit the north, follow the Indus Valley via Dera Ismail Khan to Khot and then Peshawar. On reaching Peshawar you then have the choice of exploring the Northwest Frontier or taking the Grand Trunk Road —which the British built from Kabul to Calcutta.

From Peshawar the Hindu Kush and the Swat valley can be explored. Further north, Chitral and the Kalash Valleys inhabited by the Kafirs —possible descendants of Alexander the Great. The North West Frontier is inhabited by people with cultures so established that you would never believe that time moves on.

To Islamabad from Peshawar the route crosses the Indus river overlooked by the mighty Attock Fort, then to Rawalpindi and Islamabad, Pakistan's satellite capital. From Islamabad it is possible to do another excursion, this time north to the Hunza valley and the Karakorams. Although the land border is open over the Khunjerab Pass to China and Xinjiang Province, it is only possible to do this using local public transport. The Chinese authorities still make it very difficult to obtain permission to enter with foreign-registered vehicles. Though to go by public transport provides an alternative via Kashgar and Urumqi following the ancient Silk Route through the land of Ghengis Khan to Beijing and Shanghai.

However, continuing from Islamabad, south again, into the heart of the Punjab to Lahore, with its Moghul Red Fort and Shalimar Gardens: Lahore is a bustling thriving city —to the overlander with your own vehicle, it is an ideal centre to make any repairs before entering India.

From Lahore the Grand Trunk Road takes you the short distance to the Wagah/Attari Road border with India. Here strict times of opening and 'bureaucracy personified' welcome you to India. You will very soon see and feel the change.

India and beyond

This fascinating country of diverse culture, terrain, language and religion, with its 850 million people creating the largest democracy in the world, predominately Hindu, still has the largest Muslim population in the world. The history and sights provide the overlander with a unique journey whether taking a direct route to Nepal or following the Grand Trunk Road to its end, at Calcutta.

The first stop into India, is the wealthy Punjab State, and Amritsar —the centre of the Sikh religion. The holy shrine to their faith is the Golden Temple which welcomes visitors and pilgrims alike. Now to Delhi —from here the choice is yours!

During autumn, winter and early spring the colourful desert state of Rajasthan makes a rewarding diversion. Some head further south to Goa and its beaches or further still to the 'hill stations' of the south.

During the summer months, to avoid the heat and rain of the monsoon, the Himalayan foothills offer some respite. Simla, the Kulu valley and Darhamsala are wonderful spots to relax.

Following the overland route, one cannot miss Agra and the Taj Mahal, the highlight of any journey to India. East to Varanasi on the Ganges and one of the holiest places for the Hindu faith, with early morning cremations on the historical Ghats. Not only is Varanasi sacred to the Hindu, the Muslim faith of India hold the city dear in their religion. Nearby, at Sarnath, is the site where Buddha gave his first sermon.

The traditional route of the past 25 years or so take most overlanders to the Himalayan Kingdom of Nepal and to Kathmandu. Once the hidden-away capital of a relatively private kingdom, it is now the busy tourist centre servicing climbing, trekking, and rafting expeditions. Nepal will always be the welcome rest at the end of a long journey, its friendly people, scenery and climate provide a welcome contrast to finish a trip or take a break, if venturing on further.

However, for those who wish to continue, during the summer months many cross the passes of the Himalaya onto the Tibetan plateau and in through the back door of China. However, entry is still restricted to organised tour groups, and again it is not possible to enter with foreign-registered vehicles. The other alternative of Bangladesh and on to Myanmar is still not possible, yet times are changing —recent reports state the opening of some land borders between Myanmar (Burma) and Thailand.

There may yet be the opportunity of a complete land route to Singapore, and (with a few sea crossings) on to Sydney.

OVERLAND THROUGH SOUTHEAST ASIA

by Myfanwy Vickers

The principle of an overland trip is that it is as good to travel as to arrive. Most guidebooks will jump you from site to site, city to city, beautiful beach to ancient temple, and tell you little if anything about the stretches in between. But precisely because of this, it is here that you will find the vital heart of the country.

Overland travel, in my view, is best undertaken independently, by self–propelled means: not only do you have total freedom of movement, but your pace is adjusted to that of the life going on around you. If you travel by train, bus, jeep or any other local means, you still have the opportunity either to take a side road or to get out mid–way to do some exploring. Failing this, so–called independent travel can hover close to the tour: you meet the same people on the same route in the same places, and the mystique of the exotic somehow eludes you.

The choices available are more or less the same in every country, but part of the fun is the variety of transport on offer throughout Southeast Asia. Not only buses and trains, which may bear little resemblance to that which goes under the same name back home, but trucks and jeeps, taxis and *tuk–tuks*, *bemos* and *becaks*, rickshaws and trishaws, pony and traps. For the weary traveller, a ride around town in a bicycle rickshaw which resembles an open–air armchair on wheels, decked out with bells and bunting, is a luxury hard to beat – and this despite the constant stream of commercial invitations at your ear ("Batik? Statues? Sarongs? My cousin's factory? Cheap rates!"). What is more, it will probably only cost you about 30p an hour.

Nevertheless, travel on public transport can be less than fun. Simply buying a ticket can be a chaotic and frustrating experience. You might be forgiven for mistaking the process for some other pursuit, like a treasure hunt or mystery tour —or even an oblique way of inflicting punishment on those foolish enough to be visiting the place. This, coupled with the principle of not setting off until the vehicle is filled to three times its capacity, can be a maddening experience for the Anglo–Saxon. Once aboard, you have not just your fellow passengers to contend with, but baskets and boxes, goats and birds (caged and uncaged), babies and elbows, airlessness, cramp, perhaps the distorted wail from an amplifier in your ear, and a permanently worrying sense that you have paid over the odds for something which is heading in the wrong direction and provides nowhere for your feet. There is, perhaps, little more frightening than travel in an Indonesian public bus, the cab's holy shrine swaying as it bears down, avenger–like, on yet more passengers on a bend in the road —its apparent intent to carry people off into the next world becoming, on occasion, all too grim a reality.

In such a situation, try telling yourself that it is all part of 'the experience'. Not only the ability to be assertive when necessary, but an inexhaustible sense of humour, are great assets. But with time on your hands, you can give yourself space to recover from the rigours of travelling.

Most tourists fly into Bangkok and head north to trek in Chiang Mai, proceeding south to the beaches. Avoid this trail if you can. For those of you arriving overland from India and Nepal, Thailand is a blessing for travel is easy. When I was there on a bicycle, barely a day passed without a vehicle stopping to offer me a ride; hitchhikers should not have a problem. Thailand's public transport system is increasingly modern and efficient —*and* it keeps pretty good time!

The four trunk routes of the State railway run to the north, north east, east and south; long–distance trains have sleeping cars and/or air–conditioned coaches. Slower than buses, they are safer and, as with all trains everywhere, you have the added advantage of not being pinned to your seat.

Both State and private buses are cheap and uncomfortable, and tend to be accident prone; this is not unusual in Asia and many travellers still use them. Whilst private buses are in some ways more civilized, you may find that curtains sealing off the view while a video of 'Life in Rural Thailand' blares through the bus is something of a horror. Do not accept food or drink: whole coach–loads of people have awoken from a peculiarly deep sleep to find all their belongings gone.

Reputable rental companies such as Hertz and Avis operate out of Bangkok and Chiang Mai and there is the usual panoply of taxis, *tuk–tuks* and *bemos*. Travel by motorbike or bicycle is easy, and increasingly seems the only way to see parts of the country that are not well–trodden by others. Mae Hong Son, long cut off by mountains, is being promoted as one of the last undeveloped areas for trekking, but when you learn that Thai Airways flies from Bangkok and twice daily from Chiang Mai, you begin to see why the in–between bits become almost essential. Head out to the north east, a dry plateau known as 'Isaan', meaning 'vastness', before the hordes.

Overland travel is interrupted by Burma (Myanmar): you are not allowed to enter through any of its five land borders and unless you attempt to ford a river, you are forced to take to the air. Vast areas of the country are out of bounds to visitors, and any bikes will be temporarily impounded. With the ongoing troubles, regulations have tightened up. Check on the latest before departure. With restrictions to your movements and your time (seven days) it may be that you are best advised to resort to internal flights. However, despite the machinations of the state–run Tourist Myanmar to thwart your every move, it is just feasible (if you plan your time efficiently in advance) to see the open areas within the week. If you feel anxious about fitting it all in, you could fall back on a Tourist Myanmar package.

Trains in Myanmar are cheap, but the only rail route authorized for use by tourists is the 14–hour Yangon (Rangoon) to Mandalay. Cheap buses run everywhere. Jeeps run randomly, leaving when they are full. Hiring is expensive, and if you stray off limits you may waste time being stopped. Bicycle trishaws and pony traps can be hired for the day —but you may end up walking some of it out of compassion. Ferries are excellent for getting around, the twelve–hour trip down the Irawaddy from Mandalay to Pagan being the one package worth doing through the official channels.

A possible itinerary (suggested by Frances Capel in the Cadogan guide) makes the most of your time and concentrates on Pagan: Night train from Yangon to Mandalay, explore Mandalay, fly to Pagan (boat if in season). Explore Pagan and Mount Popa, then fly to Heho; bus to Yaunghwe for boat tour of Lake Inle. Bus to Thazi for night train to Yangon and get off two hours short of Yangon to explore Pegu in the early morning, catching a later train out.

The 13,000 islands making up the Indonesian archipelago are all slightly different when it comes to transport! Only Java and Sumatra, for example, have a railway —consult a specialist guidebook for details. Java and Bali are now well served with new roads, but getting off the beaten track in Indonesia means just that: the road may be hard to locate! Parts of the so–called Trans Sumatran highway are like a battlefield, pitted with pot–holes and scattered with boulders. Wooden bridges built for buffalo carts now take heavy goods traffic; the lorries have a system of grinding to a virtual halt at the bridge, throwing themselves into top gear, and then lurching across with engines roaring, as if taking the bridge by surprise might somehow forestall its collapse. Roads in the less developed southeastern islands, Nusa Tenggara, are even bumpier and liable to have been flooded and washed away in the rainy season (November to March). Here, outlying areas are served by an irregular public transport system, and you are better off going under your own steam.

In Kalimantan, however, dense jungle, a sparse population and a natural network of waterways make rivers the main arteries. If they are not navigable, travel is virtually impossible except by air. Take outboard motor boats, longboats, dug–outs, ferries and water taxis. In Irian Jaya, you will need a spirit of adventure and a sharp implement for cutting your way through tangled vegetation.

Whilst the Philippines boast very cheap internal flights, these get heavily booked, so be prepared for a wait. Overland travel here is quite hard work, and whilst boats are a must, bear in mind that only the luxury end will be relaxing. Every type of tub and ferry is available; ask at the port if you get no joy in the office. Be wary of travelling in bad weather, however: safety precautions are nil and people regularly drown in shipping accidents. Unique to the Philippines is the *jeepney*, an ex–US Jeep festooned with flashing lights, garishly painted cut–out characters, bells and baubles. Shout and gesticulate when you want to get out.

Although most current guide books will tell you it is not possible to travel independently overland in Indo–China, it is. However, unlike Malaysia and Singapore, where travel is self–explanatory and far from alien, these countries are only just opening up, after long periods of devastation, and there are things you need to know.

Vietnam has an extensive network of decrepit, crammed and exhausting buses. Trains are more reliable, but can average as little as 15 kms an hour! Thanks to the war efforts of the Americans, the roads are not bad, and you can always hire a car with driver.

In Laos, secure yourself an inter–province pass from the Department of Commerce before doing anything else —without one you can be arrested and deported. Then investigate flights: Laos is incredibly mountainous, it has no railway, and the roads are abysmal even by Asian standards. Tortuous dirt roads will defeat you utterly between June and September (rainy season). The major towns are linked by air, and rivers form some of the country's main thoroughfares.

Tourists are forbidden to travel on buses in Cambodia and huge areas are without roads anyway. Again, ferries provide a useful service, and the railway functions despite frequent delays. For those keen to economize at any price, the front two cars of any train are free—they may act as a detonator to mines on the track... A limited number of flights on set routes are available, and others are added when there is sufficient demand.

Everything about transport in Indo–China reinforces the point I made at the outset: self–propelled means are the most effective! People are already walking and mountainbiking in Indo–China; I do urge you, with undisguised bias, to try it! It is often, paradoxically, less tiring than mechanical means, and it has an uncanny way of making everything seem more wonderful. You are grateful, perhaps, for small mercies when you finally arrive. But appreciating the little things, and the everyday, is what overland travel is all about. ∎

YOUR SPECIAL NEEDS
Chapter 8

TRAVELLING ALONE

By Nicholas Barnard

The noise and movement of an elderly Land Rover negotiating a footpath within dense bush was no foil to the impact of the tales of swamp life I was being subjected to. "Of course, you realise that the crocodiles are the least of your worries," the great white pot–bellied hunter paused, wrenched the wheel this way and that, before continuing with great deliberation, "no, the crocodiles will have what is left of you after the hippo have chewed up your dug–out." The "Hip–po", previously a happy word of the nursery and cartoon, was instantly dismembered by his accent to create a clear onomatopoeic vision of a wobbly dug–out snapping in the jaws of the snarling leander. Turning to look at me in the bright moonlight, my congenial host shared with me a calabash of pertinent information. "As for the snakes for which this part of Africa is famous —don't worry, there may be a snake bite kit in the back, but if there is, what use will it be to you? Moments after most snake bites you will be completely paralysed and the polers will be standing around watching you die, for none speak or read a word of English."

By the time we reached fishing camp near the Angolan border at dawn, I believed that I had come to terms with the prospect of travelling alone for at least eight days in such taciturn company; but dying alone in their presence was an untenable thought. To endure that journey down the Okavango to the Kalahari was an early and rigorous introduction to the art of travelling alone, to the condition of being able to survive alone.

Between the concept of travelling alone and the reality of the journey, there exists a gulf that will be bridged by painful as well as pleasing experience. From country to country and culture to culture, the act of travelling alone exposes the myths and expectations of a singular path. No manner of preparation and solitariness will disguise the fact that, from leaving a homeland, one is inescapably foreign and obtrusive. How the citizens of each culture will react to this small–time intrusion will make or break the experience of travelling alone. The solitary habit may help the desire to achieve inconspicuousness or it may increase the attention received: within one land one may know just how lonely a journey may be in the close company of others and yet again, how intrusive a train compartment of strangers may prove. Dependent upon the age and sex of the would–be loner, the choice of destination certainly needs careful thought.

Travelling alone enjoys a different status within the varied regions of the world. Successful solitude may be found in the most unlikely destinations or modes of transport. Without exception, it is very difficult to travel alone outside Europe and North America. Consider how easy it is to take a railway or a bus journey across Europe in delicious isolation from the friendliness of the companions of the carriage. To ignore a possible foreigner is acceptable in those parts —in Southern Asia it is unthinkable. If you want isolation from the land and its people when travelling the Subcontinent, take the First Class air conditioned wagon or the Air India flight. There you will be forced to endure the foppish company of the politician, the government official or the corporation executive. I take the clamour of second–class reserved and share the ever–proffered tiffin with the broad–beamed smiles of the families in my compartment —and even answer all the questions I am able concerning the greatness of Tottenham Hotspur, Ian Botham and Mrs Thatcher. Indeed, I have come to relish, to look forward to these casteless ceremonies of intimate hospitality so alien to my first desire to be alone, and despite seeking to be that sentinel of isolation with my open and over–thumbed leaden volume of social history I never fail to pack, never finish and always discard at a faraway hotel for a more appreciative reader.

The obtrusiveness of being foreign has, seemingly, considerable demerits. Escaping to the Omayid mosque from the demographic froth of the most wonderful Damascine bazaar, I passed through the firingis gate to behold for the first time that temple of temples to monoaetheism. Bewitched, I entered the cathedral–lofty prayer hall and sat near the tomb of John the Baptist (for reassurance, I suppose) and observed the interplay of women and children, men and boys at prayer and at play. The all–pervading sense of tranquillity was an unparalleled experience and it was wise to have drunk so deeply, so rapidly, for my peace was to be cast aside by the introduction of a student of agriculture eager to exercise his World Service English. It was not the interruption that was so galling, but the fact that he was so charming, so genial and good —characteristics that precluded any beastly dismissiveness on my part. As ever, so gentle a meeting converted solitude to a shared and unforgettable experience of being led with gusto to the hidden tombs, chapels and by–ways of ancient and old Damascus.

Being foreign and a woman alone in certain cultures is an unenviable circumstance. Certain countries are simply not enjoyable to visit for the single woman, whether for the mis–match of the religious, cultural and social mores with our own. Chittagong, like so many conurbations of Muslims the world over, is not a forum for the proselytising of worthy feminine liberal sentiments. The paucity of any kind of foreigners drew undesirable companionship, as mosquitoes to the ear. Boarding a bus I was approached by an English girl and her train of admirers. After so long in the company of well–wrapped women I was as shocked and confused by the state of her lack of clothing as the gathered young Bangladeshis. The crowd was divided in sentiment —from the full–scale stoning party to lascivious indulgence— and I was delighted when the bus pulled out of the station. I had to ask about her dress and I should have known that I was wasting my time. Fixing me with a stare that took my eyes permanently away from her partly–dressed bodice, she stated her view with a certain clarity: "Of course I realise what I should wear. These people simply will have to learn." I forfeited my 45p all–night bus ride and got off before the perimeter of the city.

The personal qualities needed for successful solitary travel are multifarious. Sitting at this desk to map out the requisite facets of character, I wrote: "Foresight, diligence, flexibility and humour." With a smile I scribbled over these worthy notions and thought of my most memorable expeditions. Many of my journeys were undertaken in a parlous mental condition, for from the experience of travel I was seeking solutions. It is this balance of being able to allow the outside world to influence one's inward–beseeching world that makes a solitary expedition worthwhile. Take a reserve of worthy notions and a good health insurance policy, for there is nothing more miserable and frightening than to be ill or damaged on the road alone.

What I appreciate about travelling alone are the extremes of experience so often encountered. The sense of solitude in a tropical land will be acutely felt in the early evening after eating —when the darkness falls like a shutter and the hours before sleep are many. A bright–beamed small torch is essential, for the lighting in inexpensive hotels is never failingly diabolical. The slim volumes of my favourite poets are dog–eared from browsing and memorising, and a capacious hip flask of fine whisky is always a soothing companion. By contrast, one may be transported without warning from a cycle of long evenings of quiet thoughtfulness to a night of wayward indulgence. The invasion of my private oceanside guest house in Cochin by a group of exuberant and friendly New Zealanders resulted in days of parties that became nights with new–found companions, complete with the exhausting surfeit of conversation.

Without companions the pace and direction of travel may vary to one's will. About to depart for the Amazon, I sat within a Quito hotel eating a silent breakfast seeking not to overhear the siren conversations in English amidst the guttural clutter of the local Spanish. From such precocious eavesdropping, I gleaned an introduction to a Galapagos ornithological enthusiast. His vision was an immediate inspiration: "You haff walked a jungle before?", he swung the questions with the directness of a large Swedish wood axe, "Well, you haff seen enough. Go to the Galapagos. If you like wildlife and most important, the birds, then there is no decision!" So inspired I ditched an elaborate and painstakingly calculated schedule of buses and aeroplanes and flew west to the Pacific. He was right, there is no decision.

If you had no notion of writing a journal, the action of travel in would–be solitude is the finest inspiration. Not only is there so much more time and space for the quiet dissemination and recording of days past, but the act of mute concentration over a pen and paper will deter all but the most callous interloper of personal privacy.

Whereas the lack of company may be a boon for privacy and quietitude, the security of companionship is often sorely missed. That the urban centres of the world are hotbeds of energetic and endemic crime is obvious. The need for vigilance when alone is a source of debilitating fear for many and so it is best to avoid taking a visible array of baggage that may create so much desire. I feel safest travelling light and take less and less each journey, looking to pack what is worthless to both parties or (as necessary with a camera, travellers cheques and cash) securely covered by a reliable traveller's insurance policy.

No manner of personal privations, however, will dampen my enthusiasm for the act of travelling alone. The diverse range of memories I carry from such journeys are legion. From anguish to exhilaration, fulfilment to the most intense and destructive frustration that only alien bureaucracy will create, I may recall the extremes of experience with a shudder of a smile. It is ironic that what makes this practice of attempted solitude so consuming and addictive is the participation of others. Leaving home without a companion is an excellent beginning, for without a partner or friends one may be a susceptible witness to the openness of the human condition that is simple friendship. Of the greatest pleasures of travel, the new–found and often sweetly ephemeral companionship of others is my source of guiding inspiration and steadfast joy.

FINDING A TRAVELLING COMPANION

by John Pullen

Finding a travelling companion is not always easy, especially for anything longer than the usual two or three–week journey. Even if one has a very wide circle of friends it can be difficult to find someone who has both the time and the money, and who is also interested in going to the same area and is compatible enough as a companion for a considerable length of time. After all, not everyone fancies the idea of bumping across arid deserts in a Land Rover for days on end in blistering heat, or cycling up a 20–mile mountain pass and then hurtling down the other side at 40 to 50mph through hairpin bends.

The less adventurous may find that their friends are not too keen to wander round art galleries for hours, and even those who indulge in that most popular of all holiday pastimes, frying on a beach, can find that all of their friends are otherwise engaged.

Of course, many people just rely on meeting someone on the same package tour, but packaged trips often consist of couples and the few singles in the party may not have much in common. This can sometimes result in a rather lonely holiday and a feeling of being the odd one out.

Why have a companion anyway? Why not just jaunt off by yourself and rely on meeting up with someone en route? A lot of travellers are happy to do this and some find they really prefer it, but in actual fact many who travel alone for the first time have a miserable time, quite a few problems and swear they will never do it again.

Apart from being lonely, there are other more practical reasons for travelling with a companion. One of the most common of these is the expense of travelling alone. Most hotels charge a considerable supplement for a single room which can add significantly to the cost of a holiday and to add insult to injury, singles not only pay more but they get the worst rooms, inferior service in restaurants and generally seem to take second place. For the backpacker, life also becomes easier for two, as the weight of the tent, cooking equipment etc is little if any more for two people, and the weight can be shared. An even more important consideration is security. A single person is much more likely to be mugged, conned or subject to the attentions of some unwelcome strangers. In the event of an accident there may be no one to go for help, to get proper medical attention or, if necessary, contact home. There are in fact, dozens of circumstances which can arise while travelling abroad (especially in less developed parts of the World) where for the less experienced traveller a companion should be regarded as essential.

Having made the decision that you need a travelling companion, the next problem is how to find one. There are two main methods: advertise or join a travellers' introduction service. Which is the best method? There is no simple answer, each has its advantages. Advertising can be the cheapest method if one meets someone suitable from the first advert, but it can become expensive if repeated adverts become necessary. Also, with many magazines, there is a considerable delay between placing the ad and its appearance.

Nevertheless, provided there is adequate time in which to find someone it can be very effective. It is better to give a Box Number rather than a phone number. Anyone really serious is prepared to write. Give plenty of information in the ad. It may cost a little more but it saves a lot of wasted time in the long run.

The following information should be included: destination or route and a brief description of the type of trip, departure date, duration of journey, age and sex of companions required, and the sort of personality you prefer for a companion, ie. adventurous, practical, sense of humour etc. Arrange your first meeting on neutral ground ie in a pub near your own home, or if very promising, be prepared to go half way to meet someone. If you decide you would like to proceed further, arrange other meetings in order to get to know the person better and do some weekend trips to see if you really do get on OK for more than an hour or two. If the trip is likely to be arduous, spend a long weekend partaking in that activity, walking, climbing, cycling, sailing etc. Remember there is nothing worse than going off for a long trip and finding your companion is an incessant moaner whenever things get difficult, or that he/she has any particularly irritating habits and is in some way so incompatible as to ruin a trip for which you may have been saving for years.

The other method of finding a travel companion is to use an agency which specializes in offering this service. Initially it may appear to be slightly more expensive than advertising but a good agency will guarantee that you receive a minimum number of introductions to persons travelling to the area in which you are interested, and of the age range and sex of companion you require. Your details will also go out to other members for a whole year if required, plus you get a list of names as soon as you join with no waiting for publications dates.

CHOOSING TRAVELLING COMPANIONS

by Nigel Winser

    "I *would say that this matter of relationships between members… can be more important than the achievement of the stated objective, be it crossing a desert or an ocean, the exploration of a jungle or the ascent of a mountain peak"*, John Hunt.

"Bill always takes his boots off inside the tent and Ben has yet to cook a decent meal… yackety yack, moan, moan." A familiar and typical cry, triggered by lack of privacy and repetitive food. Add to the melting pot such problems as financial mismanagement, change of itinerary, ill health and a stolen rucksack, and you may realize that you have not given as much thought to the choice of your travelling companions as you should.

While the fire remains hot there is little you can do about it, so it is worth thinking about before you depart. All travelling groups will have storms, so don't kid yourself that they won't happen to you. But perhaps you can weather them without breaking up the party.

I am not concerned here with choosing specialist members of a scientific team for an expedition. That is up to the leader of the group. The more specialized the positions, the more specific the qualifications required. My own experience is with more formal expeditions, but any travellers, from those on a budget package to overlanders, will run up against many of the same problems, and should be able to learn from the techniques used by countless expeditions around the world.

Expedition leaders are fortunate to be able to draw on the experiences of many past ventures as well as long–term projects in Antarctica where all nations have studied personnel selection and interview techniques in detail. It is lucky we all don't have to go through such interviews because you and I probably wouldn't make it.

Common sense

In theory, choosing your companions is common sense. You are looking for good–humoured individuals who, by their understanding and agreement of the objectives, form a close bond and so create a functional and cohesive team. It also helps if you like each other.

People go on journeys to satisfy ambitions, however disparate. The more you understand everyone else's ambitions, the better you will be at assessing the bonds that maintain the group. But it is not that easy. A common problem arises when, for instance, en route you require someone to do a job such as repair a vehicle. Suddenly your good friend has to be moulded into a mechanic, a role for which he or she may or may not be fit. The other solution is to have in your party a mechanic whom you have never met but who has to be moulded into a 'good friend'. There are no black–and–white guidelines here. If any virtues were to be singled out to aid your decision, high tolerance and adaptability would be two.

So, with no fixed guidelines, how can you begin to choose your companions? The single factor most likely to upset the group on a journey will be that an individual does not satisfy his or her own reasons for going. Fellow members of the party will be directly or indirectly blamed for preventing such satisfaction.

Travelling itself acts as a catalyst to any dispute and provocations and pressures may build up to intolerable levels. Any bonds that have formed will be stretched to the limit as individuals continually reassess their expectations.

It is assumed that differing personality traits are to blame here. While there are, of course, exceptions, I do not believe that personality clashes are sufficient to account for groups breaking up. I see them as symptoms of disorder within the group, and a lack of cohesion owing to ill–matched objectives —the original cause. It is worth mentioning here that the 'organization' of the trip will come under fire whenever difficulties arise; and while no one wants to lose the freedom of individual travel, the machinery of group travel (shared kitty, agreed itinerary, overall responsibility) should be well oiled.

Practical tips

From a practical point of view, you may like to consider the following tips, which apply as much to two hitchhikers as to a full–blown expedition:

1. Get to know one another before you go. If necessary, go to the pub together and get slightly pickled, then see if you can get on just as well in the morning.
2. Discuss openly with all members of the group the overall objectives of the trip and see how many members of the group disagree. Are all members of the group going to be satisfied with the plans as they stand?
3. Discuss openly the leader's (or the main organizer's, if there is one) motivation in wanting to undertake this particular journey. Is he or she using the trip to further selfish ambitions? If these are made clear beforehand so much the better, particularly if the others are not connected with the hidden objective.
4. Discuss and plan to solve the problems which will certainly crop up. The regular ones are poor health, stolen goods, accidents, insurance, itinerary. If everyone knows where they stand before the chips are down, the chance of remaining a group improve.
5. If possible, have the team working together before departure, particularly if there has been an allocation of duties. To know where you fit in is important.
6. If there is to be any form of hierarchy, it must be established before leaving and not enforced en route. If everyone can be made to feel that he or she is an integral part of the group and the group's interdependence, you will all stay together throughout the journey and have a rewarding and enjoyable experience.

THE WOMAN TRAVELLER

by Isabella Tree

❝The art of travelling is learning to behave like a chameleon❞. So said a woman friend of mine on her second year around the world and I don't believe a truer word was ever spoken. Blending into the background is not only a prerequisite to understanding and observing a different culture, it also keeps you out of trouble.

Indecent exposure

For women in particular, how you behave and especially how you dress can be construed as camouflage or an open invitation; it can make you one of the crowd or a moving target. This may be an unfair state of affairs but it's a fact of life and in someone else's country one is in no position to rail against it.

Call it ignorance or misdirected feminism, but, many women make the mistake of travelling in a 'no compromise' frame of mind. They wear shorts and bra tops in Marrakech and Istanbul, G-strings in Goa and Phuket, and nothing at all in the Mediterranean. I know and you know that this does not mean they are 'loose women', but it does show a distinct lack of respect for local custom and the sensitivities of the men, and women, of the country.

Dress is the first line of defence and the most immediate symbol of respect. If you get that wrong you are starting your travels with a glaring disadvantage.

Of course codes of dress differ wildly from country to country. In Southern Africa and part of the Indian subcontinent short sleeves and hemlines not far below the knee are fully respectable. In Iran and strict Muslim countries, the body must be totally covered, usually by a black *chador* which drapes you completely from head to foot. A woman not wearing a veil risks flogging or imprisonment, although as a foreigner you are likely to be let off with a caution and forced to cover up.

There are legally enforced dress codes at home as well, though they're so familiar we may take them for granted. But it serves to show that though conventions may differ, they are universal. In London, or Paris or New York, you would be a fool for walking the street topless, let alone racing across a cricket pitch, and not expecting to be arrested. In rainforest tribal communities from Sumatra to the Amazon, on the other hand, bare breasts are *de rigeur*.

A culture's standard of dress has a lot to do with what parts of the body are considered sensuous or provocative. In China the feet are still thought erotic, while in many countries direct eye contact can be as promiscuous as the offer of a spare key to your hotel room. In Papua New Guinea you can bare your breast to the world, but your thighs must be covered at all times. Not only that, but the space between your legs is so sexually suggestive that trousers can be as much of a turn-on as wearing nothing at all.

It pays to be prepared for the dress sense of your destination before you head off for a pre-holiday splurge in the high street, but clearly this is not always possible. As a general rule it can be said that tight and skimpy clothes are inappropriate for most countries outside Europe and the States, and that generous, loose-fitting clothes are not only more comfortable to travel in, but less controversial.

If you don't want to wear dresses and skirts, you can't do better for propriety's sake, especially in tropical heat, than the kind of cool, cotton pyjamas worn by Chinese or Kashmiri women, or a Moroccan *jalaba*. However, in places like Burma, Thailand and Vietnam, particularly in the cities, this may be too casual. Asian women taken a great deal of trouble with their appearance however poor their background, and while torn jeans and a tattered T-shirt may seem relaxed and inoffensive to the Westerner, it can seem dirty and disrespectful in Bangkok or Singapore.

If conventions are strict on the street they are doubly so in places or worship. I once met a French woman who had been stoned in Turkey —one of the most relaxed of the Muslim countries, for being dressed inappropriately in a mosque. In Greece you may be provided with frumpy, elasticated skirts to hide your trousers or miniskirt when entering an Orthodox Church. You may even be asked to cover your head. Never enter even a remote chapel on a beach in anything else than full daily dress. You may get away with it, but the distress you will cause a worshipper who stumbles on you wearing a bikini in the crypt is indefensible. In all these cases, a simple length of wrap-around cotton, like an Indian lungi or a sarong, or an African kanga or kakoi, is a handy extra to have with you.

The Hands-off approach

Perhaps the most persistent and aggravating problem a woman has to deal with, particularly if she is travelling alone, is male harassment. Satellite TV and black market videos have a lot to answer for. In Third World countries Madonna and Sam Fox are seen as the archetypal western woman; while the steamier side of Swedish exports, now providing a boom business for the black market in Asia, gives the impression that American or European women have an indiscriminate and insatiable appetite for sex. Black western women fare even worse than blondes because they are considered 'exotic'.

The sad truth is that you can be dressed modestly and impeccably on a bus in Lima or Tangiers and still feel a hand on your bum. Ironically it is often in Catholic or Muslim countries, where impropriety is most despised, that local men feel they can take liberties with foreigners. Most self-defence experts advise; "Never create a 1:1 confrontation". "Get your hands off my bum, you filthy expletive" can exacerbate the situation, even incite a violent response. The best solution is to make a scene and enlist the support of other passengers. "Did you see what that man did to me?" creates a sense of moral outrage and people, when directly appealed to, will be more eager to leap to your defence. The same attitude that implies Western women are 'loose', can work as an effective antidote to harassment when the groper, having been sprung, is hounded out of the bus and given a going-over by the other male passengers.

The first rule of self-defence, in general, is awareness. Be alert, listen to the advice of locals and fellow travellers, develop a street sense, try not to be in the wrong place at the wrong time. Good judgement is every traveller's personal responsibility and chances are, if you find yourself alone, late at night, being pursued up a dark alley, you could have avoided being there in the first place.

It is politically incorrect nowadays to suggest that women should ever play a 'passive' role, or —heaven forbid —that they could court disaster. But avoidance and weak-minded submissiveness are two completely different things, and the distinction is one that is crucial to survival, especially in foreign countries where the threat is an unknown quantity. Hitchhiking alone has to be put out of the question.

A woman is rarely a physical match for a man. And even if she is a black-belt in the martial arts, it would be unwise to launch into front kicks and elbow strikes if the man confronting her is just after money. Hand over the wallet and have done with it. Your pursuer may be armed, crazy or drunk and there is no need ever to find out if it can be avoided.

Most confrontational scenarios must be played by ear to a great extent, but there are a few universal rules: Don't turn a scary situation into a dangerous one if you can help it. Don't panic, don't show fear and don't allow the person accosting you to get the upper hand. Try to gain the psychological advantage by throwing him of his balance. In most cases a man who is attempting to intimidate a woman believes himself invulnerable and a strong show of resistance will unnerve him enough to make him back down. Never be persuaded to try and resolve the situation by moving to another place, like a car, a hotel room or someone else's house.

If you do find yourself in a dangerous, enclosed situation, try to anticipate the aggressor's next move and plan ahead for it. You may only get one chance to defend yourself —the earlier the better — and you won't want to miss it. As the innocent one in confrontation you have the advantage of surprise, but if you are forced to strike back physically, make sure it is a crippling blow that gives you a chance to escape. The last thing you want is to provoke a more serious physical attack. As one London-based martial arts master recommends: "There is only one thing better than a kick in the balls —and that's two kicks in the balls."

If you are worried about your ability to gauge dangerous situations and to defend yourself if they get out of hand, a few classes in the basic strategies of awareness and self-defence before you travel can boost your confidence immeasurably.

Warm receptions

Stay alert and these 'worse case scenarios' should never arise. I've travelled most of my life, some of it on my own, and though I'm certainly no Kate Adie, I've been caught up in anti-British demonstrations in Peru, tear-gassed in Czechoslovakia and Papua New Guinea, been ambushed by tribal warriors in Indonesia, and never had a hand laid on me in earnest.

Appreciation of the dangers should never stop you from sharing in the action, or making friends. One of the great advantages of being a woman is that men and woman find you more approachable. Sometimes the offers of hospitality and kindness can be overwhelming. And any woman who has travelled with a child or a baby can regale you with stories of such warmth and tenderness that it melts the heart and restores all your faith in human nature. These are the moments one travels for and that stay with you for ever.

Contraception and feminine hygiene

Contraception is often difficult to come by abroad and should be acquired before you leave home. Time changes should be taken into consideration if you take a low dosage contraceptive pill. Stomach upsets and diarrhoea may also reduce or neutralise the effectiveness of oral contraception.

Condoms are not as freely available, especially to women, as they should be, and packets that you do find in clinics or chemists in areas off the beaten track may be past their sell-by-date and the rubber may break or corrode. Always take condoms with you, however remote the possibility of sex. AIDS and other sexually-transmitted diseases are, thanks to the ease and popularity of travel, a universal threat.

Women should be aware that the physical stress of travel, jet-lag and time difference can all upset the biological clock and throw even the most regular period out of kilter. Sanitary towels and tampons are also often difficult to buy abroad, especially in the Third World. A form of Tampax, with plastic or cardboard applicator, is perhaps the most hygienic and convenient to take with you, as on some occasions you may find it difficult to find clean water and soap to wash your hands. If you do prefer to take the more discreet-sized tampons without applicators, carrying a sachet of disinfectant wipes to clean your hands which will guard against the transmission of germs.

Be sensitive about cultural attitudes to menstruation. In some places, especially tribal areas, men are really frightened of the powers a woman has when she is menstruating. Some cultures believe it is contaminating, and will not allow you to touch or even walk near their food. Of course, they need never know, but be extra careful to dispose of sanitary towels and tampons in these situations.

In brief conclusion, don't be a loud tourist, keep an open mind, stay cool and be wise, and travelling, especially if you are a woman, will be a fulfiling and exciting adventure.

THE TRAVELLING BUSINESSWOMAN

by Trisha Cochrane

Fifteen years ago, women who travelled on business were almost completely unheard of. In those bad old days, the travel industry could perhaps be excused for concentrating on those customers who provided the vast majority of their income, ie business *men*. Hotels and airlines fell over themselves to compete for their custom; trouser presses in hotel rooms proliferated and any woman on the scene seemed to be viewed as some sort of accessory to the nearest man.

During the late 1980s, however, a very different story emerged. As women's role in business has advanced, so has their need to be mobile, and women now make up between 20 and 30 per cent of all business travellers in the UK. Across the Atlantic, numbers are even higher and women there often outnumber the men. One Englishwoman living in New York feels that the US is years ahead in its attitudes to women, partly because of the Equal Opportunity Laws, and partly because there are enough astute business people there to realize that business women represent an enormous future market.

Only time will tell whether the same will be true in the UK. Hotels and airlines are certainly beginning to shake up their ideas, but for many women who travel, it is all taking much too long.

Again and again I hear the same old stories: the automatic assumption that as a woman you are some kind of second class citizen, apparently incapable of making decisions or paying your own bills; the hotel restaurants and bars where women are seated at the worst tables and then ignored, or must suffer pick–up attempts if they want a drink in the bar (no wonder that around 50 per cent of women end up eating in their rooms); the facilities and services which seem to be directed at men's needs only (why are there never any skirt hangers in hotel wardrobes) and the lack of security which leaves women fearful for their safety when they should be under the secure protection of a reputable travel company. Clearly a change of attitude is required. It is only right that women should receive the same respect from airline and hotel staff as their male colleagues, and that they should be able to travel freely and comfortably without hassle.

Of course, attitudes cannot be changed overnight but the fact that there are now so many women travelling means that some hotels and airlines are beginning to sit up and take notice. Creating awareness is a good first step, and once the attitudes are right, relevant facilities and security provisions should follow.

In the meantime, however, there has been some confusion within the travel industry as to whether special services and facilities should be laid on for women. Some hotels provide 'ladies' rooms' complete with hair dryers, irons/ironing boards, skirt hangers, women's magazines, cotton wool, shower caps, and so on. All well and good, but in fact women rarely ask for any special treatment themselves, believing most of these items should be provided automatically. (The trouser press is now a standard feature in hotel rooms whereas an iron and ironing board is a rarity).

Customers' needs may vary due to a number of factors—age, sex, culture etc— but at the same time a hotel or airline should provide what it is being paid for: comfort, protection from burglary or assault, and facilities which will depend on price and location. It is pointless tailoring these to fit one type of customer only —ie pin–stripe man.

More serious is the question of security which many women find quite inadequate. Public areas are often poorly lit and unpatrolled (particularly in airports, car parks and railway stations). And hotels seem to regard room numbers as public property: some staff display a surprising lack of discretion by announcing the room number for all in the vicinity to hear. It is all too common for women to find themselves being hassled either on the internal phone system or with unwelcome visits to their room.

If you are staying at a hotel and you do receive nuisance phone calls, ring reception immediately and ask them to screen all future calls —good hotels do this as a matter of course. And if there is a knock at your door, the general rule is not to open it unless you are expecting someone. In any case, always use the spy hole and security chain if available and, if you are at all worried, ring reception to ask for assistance or to insist that they move you to another room. Get hold of a 'Door Guard', a keyless security lock which will prevent anyone from entering your room once you are inside.

Request a room near the lifts or stairwell —not at the end of a darkly lit corridor— and you may refuse a room on the ground floor in certain situations. If you feel unsafe, ask to be accompanied, although in some circumstances you may not always wish to trust the staff! Always make your feelings known to the management; I cannot stress strongly enough that you must complain about any problems, and whilst some hotels are completely clueless, many will take your complaints very seriously.

If possible, try and pick a hotel that is in a safe area, not bang in the middle of the local red light district. If your travel agent can't help you, get a recommendation from a friend or colleague or network with other women who travel. The Women's Travel Advisory Bureau can help you with this sort of information (tel: 0386-701082).

At the same time check the general safety, especially for women, in that area or country. Is it safe to go out at night? Is there a problem with bag snatching and pick–pockets? It is important to be sensitive to others' culture and thus avoid any misunderstandings —how you dress can be particularly important in some countries. Find out how the country you are visiting views both local and foreign women.

Sources of such information can be a problem, but again, network with women who have been there, or read a good travel guide. The *Economist Guides* are recommended for their political, economic and cultural background information. And **Employment Conditions Abroad** (Anchor House, 15 Britten Street, London SW3 3TY, tel: 071–351 7151) produce detailed *Country Outlines*. Courses on cultural awareness for the business traveller which can help you to conduct business successfully are run by Going Place (tel: 081-949 8811). A useful book on this subject is *Mind Your Manners: Culture Clash in the European Single Market* (John Mole, Industrial Society Press).

Although security is a problem, harder to articulate and therefore more difficult to pin–point are the attitudes of management and staff towards their guests or passengers. The assumption that a woman is in a somehow subservient position to a man can be so ingrained that I have reluctantly come to the conclusion that some 'offenders' do not even realize that their behaviour is a cause for concern. The ubiquitous image in advertising and promotional material of a pretty woman serving a pin–striped man does not help matters and can be a good indicator of that company's attitude towards women.

Customer service training within the travel industry should address these issues and include positive role models of women. A typical example of such outdated assumptions was related to me by a senior manager working for a British bank. Staying at a hotel in Leeds, she went down to the dining room and ordered the set menu. A few minutes later another solitary diner came in and ordered the same set menu. The meal was served promptly —but to him. Embarrassed, she enquired why she, who had arrived first, been seated first, and ordered first, should be last to be served 'Oh, we didn't think you'd mind,' said the waitress. 'After all, he probably has something important to do after lunch.'

Other problems in restaurants can arise when women are hosting business lunches or dinners with male guests; it is invariably the man who is presented with the wine to taste and the bill to pay. A pre–emptive strike is often needed here. Try and use a restaurant where you are known; make a point of talking to the *maitre d'* and ensuring that you are remembered. If using a restaurant for the first time, book the table in your name and explain that you will be hosting the meal. Remember how men behave: you will not get good service, male or female, if you do not act confidently. If all else fails, keep your sense of humour. I remember one occasion when everything went well until the end of the meal; I signed the credit card voucher which was taken away… and then returned to my (male) guest.

If you hate eating on your own in a hotel, remember that most men do not like it either. And although it is easier for them to find a dinner companion, you could also keep a look out for other lone women —you never know who you might meet, and part of the interest of travelling is the different types of people you do come across. Some hotels will even set aside a travellers' table where people can eat together if they wish.

Most experienced businesswomen agree that self–confidence is the key to success. Good preparation is the essence of survival for any travelling —and that includes mental preparation as well. Even if it is a pretence, it is worth learning to look confident in order to receive good service. Adaptability, stamina, a sense of humour, and a positive attitude are also important qualities. You can get a great deal out of travelling on business but you are more likely to cope and enjoy yourself if you view a trip with enthusiasm rather than trepidation.

Assertiveness training is always a good starting point. Being assertive means knowing that you have a right to be on that plane when you are told it has been overbooked. The right to be seated properly in a restaurant, and to expect an attentive service when you are paying for it. The key to assertive behaviour is to state what you want, clearly and calmly, and if necessary to repeat it until they realize that you will not go away. Some good books are *A Woman in Your Own Right:Assertiveness and You* (Anne Dickson, Quartet) and *Beating Aggression: A Practical Guide for Working Women* (Diana Lamplugh,Weidenfield & Nicholson).

There are also plenty of assertiveness training courses, many of which are designed with businesswomen in mind. One company offering such courses is **Monadnock International Ltd** (2 The Chapel, Royal Victoria Patriotic Building, Fitzhugh Grove, London SW18 3SX, tel: 081–871 2546).

In fact, people don't often expect women to complain (many women would rather 'not make a fuss') but if you do, they should take notice of you. If all else fails, tell them you handle all the travel arrangements for your multi–national company and that you will personally ensure that they never get a booking again! Remember that you or your company are paying for good service and you deserve to receive it. And never forget to exercise that most important of consumer rights: choice.

Finally, and at the risk of sounding like your mother, beware of strange men! When away on business, even supposedly trusted colleagues can become strange men; a friend of mine was propositioned not by the stranger in the lift but by someone that she knew. Good books to read are the Virago Women's City Guides.

TRAVELLING WITH CHILDREN

by Rupert and Jan Grey

The difference between travelling with children and travelling without is not unlike crossing the Sahara on foot as opposed to in a Land Rover: you go much slower, it is much harder work, but it is (arguably) much more fun. Given the choice, we always take ours with us for they open doors that were previously closed. Parenthood is an international condition and the barriers erected by race and language fall away in the presence of children. Of equal importance for the travelling parent is the opportunity to experience, with and through their children, the newness of their world, their innocence and their instinctive fear of the unknown. The reactions of children are not yet blunted by the passage of years and the compromises of adulthood, and a journey to the jungles of the equator or the forests of the north can be one of discovery, between, as well as by parent and child.

Children require explanations, and their passion for knowledge is as infectious as their imagination is vivid. The dark recesses of a cave in the heart of

Borneo were, for ours, the home of dragons and crocodiles, long since mourned by conservationists which lurked in the darkening shadows over the river. The reality of adulthood suddenly became rather boring. So, of course, is changing nappies. In many parts of the world the locals will regard you with amazement; they will probably have never seen disposable nappies and for children over six months they regard them as superfluous in any event. Nappies clothes, children's games and books are items which suddenly become indispensable, and the notion of travelling light becomes a part of your past along with many other aspects of pre–children life.

Preparation

Eric Shipton, so he said, used to plan his expeditions on the back of an envelope. Not with children, he didn't. Detailed organization and preparation is not an optional extra. It is vital. What you take will depend on the age and individual requirements of your children. If they have a passion for pure wool Habitat ducks, as our eldest daughter did the first time we took her to Malaysia at the age of two and a half, take it. Take a second one just in case the first one gets lost. It will probably be your most crucial item of equipment.

Your choice of clothes will of necessity be dictated by the climate; cotton clothes with long legs and sleeves are best for the tropics, and for fair–skinned children a sun hat (also made of cotton) is essential —particularly if travelling on water.

While children generally adapt to heat better than adults, the younger ones are much more vulnerable to cold. Warm clothing should be in layers and easily washable, and if you put children still in nappies into ski suits you will need the patience of Job.

No less important than choosing the right equipment is packing it in the right way. There will be a '*rucksack that is only opened at night* '(all things necessary for sleeping), the '*rucksack that you have beside you at all times*'(which has a few nappies, drinks, a couple of children's books games, the teddy, guide books etc) a '*rucksack just for nappies*', a '*rucksack just for toys*', a '*rucksack just for clothes*' and to give them a sense of participation, one little tiny rucksack for each of the children containing a couple of nappies a piece (it is bound to get lost).

As important as sorting out your equipment is preparing the children. This calls for a lot of topical reading and storytelling spread over several weeks or months before departure. The object of the exercise here is twofold: firstly to instill a sense of adventure and anticipation, and secondly as a sort of advance warning that life is going to be very different. If you are about to expose your children to a radically different culture, and extreme of climate, fly them through eight different time zones into a world of extraordinary insects, holes in the ground for lavatories and a completely unfamiliar diet, it is an advance warning that they will need. You won't, for you will probably have already been there. The demands on your children will be far greater than on you.

The children should help in the preparations. Erect the mosquito nets for them to play in, let them pack and unpack the rucksacks, read them the story of how the elephant got his trunk (Kipling) or show them pictures of how the Eskimo catch their fish, and tell them all about aeroplanes.

Flights

There are only two classes of air travel: with children and without. The former is a nightmare and the latter (in relative terms) nirvana.There are airlines that go out of their way to cater for children and those who merely tolerate them. This is a field all of its own. Bear three rules in mind: do not rely on the airline to supply nappies; the best seats are behind the bulkhead between the aisles, and book them well in advance along with the cradle that hitches to the bulkhead (the children may not like it but it is useful for stowing toys and books). Give them a boiled sweet before each descent and take–off and if they want to run about the aircraft let them. They can't fall off, they can't get lost and they might make some friends. If they cause mayhem, it is easy to pretend they're not yours.

In the field

Tired children are grumpy, and the grump–factor escalates in direct proportion to the number of time–zones you cross. The longer you allow for their sleeping patterns to get back to normal the better, particularly if, like ours, they are not too good at going to bed in the first place. If travelling to Southeast Asia, for example, find somewhere peaceful to spend a three or four–day adjustment period in one place before engaging in any major adventures.

The usual routine for independent travellers who have a month at their chosen destination is to see as much as possible. This does not work with children. Whatever plans you fancy by way of an itinerary, the most critical ingredient is flexibility. The yardstick of a successful journey is no longer the scaling of a mountain, the descent of a river, or a visit to the Taj Mahal.

It is ensuring that laughter predominates over tears, that children get enough sleep, don't get too bored for too long and eat food they find edible with reasonable regularity. The Taj Mahal will leave them completely unmoved, but the goldfish (or whatever lives in those fountains that appear in the foreground of all the photographs of the Taj) will keep them going for hours.

It is no good thinking that your children ought, for the good of their cultural souls, learn to enjoy chowmien or boiled monkey's testicles. You will have plenty of problems without inviting arguments over food, so keep packets of dried mince and Safeway's noodles in the *rucksack that you have beside you at all times*. A little bit of what they fancy will do them good, and more to the point, what does them good does you better.

This principle, indeed governs the whole journey and it is not one that is easy to contend with for fathers who are accustomed to seeing their children in the evenings and at weekends, nor for parents who have developed an efficient pre–children system for surviving and enjoying life on the road. Forget the stories about local babysitters; they might be on hand in Marbella but they are pretty scarce in Borneo. Even if you found someone you could trust, the children already have enough novelties to contend with.

The trick, as with all expeditions, is to select targets that will motivate the expedition members and build your plan around them. A two or three–day river journey, for example, is excellent value for children of almost any age; a dug-out canoe, a little bit of slightly exciting white water, a log cabin or long-house, a couple of fishing rods, the prospect of sighting a crocodile or a bear and a campfire under the stars are all good ingredients for success.

Sightseeing should not be on the agenda at all. If parent must go to a museum, select it with reference to the running-around space. Driving long distances will only be a success if done for one day at a time and punctuated regularly with diversions, the excitement of which can be built up as the journey progresses.

Disasters

There will be several of these, even for the most circumspect and cautious of parents. The first one to avoid is losing your child at the airport, particularly at Terminal 3, Heathrow. We managed this very successfully when Katherine was two and a half. She was there, and then all of a sudden, she was not. Thirty minutes later, after public announcements and private panics, she appeared through the legs of the crowd bearing a plate of chocolate cakes. She seemed quite unmoved by the experience. We both vowed that this would be our last international journey with children.

The second disaster, which is less easy to avoid, is illness. This happened to Katherine within about four hours of the first disaster. She developed tonsillitis on the plane, which was then grounded in Abu Dhabi on the grounds that she had a contagious disease and there being no doctor available to suggest otherwise. We were not popular with the other 373 passengers on board.

The acquisition of a little basic knowledge, ie when to worry and get moving fast, and when to hold a hand and mutter sweet nothings, is the best that a parent can do. Aside from bellyache, your children are not more likely to be ill in Singapore or the Sahara than in Brighton or Benidorm. (A helpful book is *Travellers' Health; How to stay healthy abroad*, by Richard Dawood, published by OUP £7.99).

The third disaster is injury. As a general guideline, the louder they scream, the more likely they are to be all right. A bit of sticking plaster and a lot of cuddles usually suffice to mend the wound, and an exhaustive supply of both is recommended. Katherine, on this occasion aged four and a half, disappeared through the split-bamboo floor of a longhouse in Borneo in front of our very eyes. Directly below were the longhouse pigs. Her howls of protest, which were sweet music to us, put the pigs into a panic instead, and the subsequent rescue programme was further hampered by the fact that we were both stark naked, being engaged at the time in having what passes in longhouses for a bath. Equanimity was eventually restored by a combination of *Thomas the Tank Engine*, an unlimited supply of cuddles and quite a few bits of elastoplast. The following practical tips may help to avoid or mitigate these disasters:

1. If your child knows his/her name and address you are less likely to lose him/her permanently.
2. Watch out for monsoon drains. In the wet season, your child may be swept away and drowned, and in the dry season there are things in them that it would be better that your child did not eat or roll in.
3. Small children freeze more quickly than large children, so watch them carefully when the temperature drops.

4. Children dehydrate much more quickly than adults. Watch their level of fluid intake, particularly on long flights, in hot climates and, most of all, if they contract a fever or any illness that involves diarrhoea or vomiting. Get him/her to take water mixed with sugar and a little salt. The juice of an orange will make it more palatable.

5. If your child contracts a temperature over 103F find a doctor fast. If you are in a foreign capital, the British Embassy will help. Members of the expatriate community are often a good source of information about good doctors.

6. Select your medicine bag carefully before you go, preferably in consultation with your family doctor.

7. Children do not like malaria tablets. They will be more palatable if buried in a piece of fruit and nut chocolate with the aid of a penknife (thus disguising the pill as a nut). Even then, watch them carefully. Our youngest, aged one and three quarters when we took her to Borneo, used to tuck them in her cheek and spit them out anything up to an hour later when we were not looking. The other trick was to feed them to the nearest dog. We must have left a trail of malaria–free dogs behind us on our progress around Asia!

8. Sun cream is a vital commodity.

Hotels

Travelling with children is a great deal more strenuous than travelling without them. This is partly because children are an exhausting business anyway, but mainly because the routine of home life, which provides a measure of defence for beleaguered parents, is banished by the unpredictability of life on the road. This is where hotels come in: expensive ones —the sort that have a laundry service, room service, clean bathrooms for grubby children and a bar for distressed parents. A swimming pool with reclining chairs in the shade for Mum and Dad to take it in turns to sleep is an added bonus.

It may sound extravagant, but this is money well spent. It is only in this kind of circumstance that parents on holiday with their children have a chance to find some peace and even a little time on their own.

Age of children

There are no rules about this. The best time to start, from the children's point of view, is when they start to enjoy the world about them. There is not much point before they can walk, and better still to wait until they are out of nappies, at least during the day. At the other end of the scale, when they reach their mid–teens they will be thinking in terms of becoming independent travellers themselves, so you have about 12 to 14 years to show them the world. No time to waste.

THE PREGNANT TRAVELLER

by Dr Richard Dawood

Paradoxically, some of the hazards of travel during pregnancy have increased in recent years. This is partly due to the continuing spread of drug–resistant malaria, and also arises from the fact that countries with poor medical care have become increasingly accessible to the adventurous traveller.

Good ante–natal care has brought about a dramatic reduction in the complications of pregnancy, and travel has become almost too easy —it is often taken for granted. Perhaps the first hazard that the pregnant woman faces is a psychological one; pregnancy is not the ideal time for adventurous travel, but there is a widespread belief that travel to any country should be possible and that the fact of pregnancy should not be allowed to get in the way.

The early weeks of pregnancy are an important time to be at one's home base. It is necessary to begin planning ante–natal care, and to arrange routine blood tests and ultrasound scans. Morning sickness is common, and as a result many women have no particular interest in travel at this stage. Early pregnancy is also a time when miscarriage is relatively more common. Travel itself does not increase the risk of miscarriage, but the consequences in a country where medical facilities are poor could be serious. If bleeding is severe, blood transfusion may be necessary. In many poor countries the risk of AIDS from unscreened blood transfusions is high, and facilities for surgery (including supplies of sterile medical instruments) may be difficult to obtain. Poor medical treatment may have serious consequences for future pregnancies.

Towards the later stages of pregnancy, premature delivery becomes a possibility. It is not generally feasible to predict which pregnancies are at risk. Survival of a premature baby depends upon immediate access to sophisticated neonatal intensive care facilities, and the greater the prematurity the more important this becomes. Even when such facilities are available they may be extremely expensive, and the cost of neonatal intensive care may not be covered by travel insurance. Severely premature babies may not be able to travel for several weeks, adding further to the cost. Facilities for skilled medical care during delivery, surgical facilities and access to adequate blood transfusion facilities may again be a problem.

Aeroplanes do not make good delivery suites, and while air travel does not in itself induce labour, long flights should be avoided during late pregnancy; in any case, most airlines do not accept passengers beyond the 32nd week of pregnancy.

Chief hazards

Two direct hazards of travel deserve mention. The first is the fact that there is an increased tendency for blood to clot in the veins of the legs: deep vein thrombosis. This tendency is accentuated by dehydration and prolonged immobility, both of which are common during long air journeys. The preventive measures are simple; drink plenty of fluids, stand up and walk around the aircraft cabin at least every two hours during a flight. The same applies to travel by road; make a rest, and stretch your legs at least every one to two hours on a long journey.

The second hazard has received much attention over the last two years and relates to exposure to radiation. It has long been known that exposure to cosmic radiation at normal flying altitudes (35,000 feet) is more than 100 times greater than at ground level. There has been increasing concern about the effect of low–dose radiation and calculations show that it is possible for frequent flyers to build up a significant radiation exposure. Solar flares —bursts of energy on the surface of the sun— account for periodic increases in such exposure, and occur in unpredictable patterns. The radiation exposure for a return trip between London and New York is roughly equivalent to the exposure from a single chest x–ray (0.1 milliSievert); a return flight between London and Los Angeles would clock up 0.16 mSv. Calculations on the extent of harm associated with radiation exposure are generally based on exposure to much larger doses —for example such as occurred at Hiroshima.

It is difficult to be sure how such results extrapolate to lower doses and it is conceivable that low doses may be relatively more harmful. It is also difficult to document the effects, and to know whether subtle changes such as differences in intelligence or minor defects can be attributed to such exposure rather than nature.

For this reason, it has been suggested that pregnant women should avoid unnecessary long distance flights during the early, most vulnerable stages of pregnancy. Because Concorde flies at higher altitudes, radiation exposure might be expected to be higher; this is balanced by the shorter flying time, and overall exposure is generally reduced.

Vaccinations involving a live virus should be avoided during pregnancy: these include the oral polio vaccine, and the vaccines for measles, rubella and yellow fever. If a yellow fever vaccination certificate is necessary for travel, a medical certificate should be able to circumvent the requirement. Protection against polio can be provided using a killed, injectable vaccine. Vaccines that commonly cause a fever, such as diphtheria and the injectable typhoid vaccine should be avoided during pregnancy and the BCG vaccine should not be given.

Drug-resistant malaria continues to spread, and there are now relatively few parts of the world where chloroquine and paludrine —the two safest drugs for use in pregnancy —provide reliable protection. Mefloquine (Lariam) is a newer antimalarial drug that is now widely used for travellers to resistant areas, but there are parts of the world —especially in the region of the Thai/Cambodian border —where resistance to mefloquine is common. Mefloquine has not been in use long enough for a clear picture to have emerged regarding its safety for use in pregnancy; there is certainly no clear evidence of a risk, but caution is still advisable, especially during early pregnancy.

The particular problem with malaria in pregnancy —particularly in women visiting malarial areas as compared with local inhabitants, is that malaria attacks tend to be considerably more severe. There is a high risk of death or of losing the baby. Chloroquine and Paludrine are considered safe during pregnancy. Insect repellents and other anti–insect measures (mosquito netting, suitable clothing, insecticide sprays, etc) should also be used assiduously to reduce the number of mosquito bites. However, there is a strong case to be made for avoiding all unnecessary travel to malarial areas during pregnancy —particularly to areas with drug resistant malaria.

Other tropical or infectious diseases tend to affect pregnancy only indirectly, such as causing dehydration or a high fever, both of which put the foetus at risk. Great care should be taken to avoid diseases such as Dengue fever (by use of anti–insect measures) and to observe careful food and water hygiene measures.

If travel during pregnancy is considered essential, it is important to find out as much as possible about local medical care – names and addresses of doctors, hospitals, and facilities for neonatal intensive care should anything go wrong. It is also important to take particular care to insure adequate insurance cover for both mother and child.

Experts consider that the most suitable time for an overseas trip during pregnancy—provided that there have been no complications or other problems— is after the majority of the ante–natal tests have been completed and the main risks of miscarriage are over, but before the foetus becomes viable and would need neonatal intensive care facilities if born prematurely. This period lies between the 18th and 24th week of pregnancy, though high risk countries should definitely be avoided throughout the pregnancy.

THE OLDER TRAVELLER

by Cathy Braithwaite

A rough orange dirt track in the scorching Maasai Mara. In a small van, five travel journalists —the young and intrepid type— clutch their seats, knuckles white, jaws set, staring straight ahead, hating every minute of the bouncy, five–hour journey.

"These roads are just too bumpy, too uncomfortable. This is ridiculous – you can't possibly call this a holiday," complains one just as another van carrying two elderly but beaming tourists bounces by.

Lesson one: remember journalists have tender bottoms and mature travellers can be a darn sight more adventurous! In fact, these days, senior citizens think nothing of tackling the most demanding challenges, and relish new experiences at an age when they have the time and money. And this is the essence of the growing market for older travellers: time and money.

The retired can travel when and for as long as they choose. No jobs to groaningly return to; no children to force through school gates. You can break the journey up into manageable sections, pausing for periods of rest when necessary.

This is good news for any travel operator or airline. It's hardly a problem to sell travel in the high season but it's a different story off–peak, which is when the buying power of older travellers really comes into its own.

The benefits of off–peak travel are many and varied: you can holiday when temperatures are kinder (avoiding the searing heat), when there are fewer crowds, lower prices and beaming smiles from travel industry staff delighted by your off–peak business.

All you, the traveller, have to do is decide is where, how and when to go. There need not even by a 'why'. Your horizons are impressive and while your age may prove a restriction with some operators and car hire companies (usually for travellers aged over 65), you will doubtless be spoilt for choice.

Whether you are a fit older person who can happily cope with a two–week camp and trek holiday in the Himalayas, or if a lack of stamina precludes a two–month tour of Australia's outback or a six–month journey around the world, if you recognize your limitations and are realistic about your expectations, it is possible to make travel in retirement safe and exhilarating.

Destinations

Today even the most remote corners of the world are accessible and it is tempting to embark on the most unusual and exciting journey you can find. First establish what you seek from your holiday. Then weigh up your own ability to cope. Don't fool yourself; there is no shame in admitting that a whirlwind tour of six South American countries in 30 days would be too much for you. It is far worse to arrive at the start of what would be the experience of a lifetime, only to realize your holiday has turned into a test of endurance. The maxim 'different strokes for different folks' is never more applicable than in the context of older people and travel. What to one person is tame and unadventurous is to another the most daring project they've ever contemplated. But whether you are the type who would take out a mortgage to buy the latest walking boots, or you follow the 'have time table, will travel' school of travelling, building your own itinerary maximizes your choice. You can choose how to travel, when and where to overnight, whether or not to spend a couple of days at a stopover, and you can make the whole experience as demanding or relaxed as you wish.

Preparation

While it is romantic and inspiring to think of intrepid 85–year–olds throwing more knickers than shirts into a bag and wandering wherever the whim leads, life is so much easier if you take a few basic precautions.

Explore visa requirements and apply as much in advance as possible. Passport regulations can also differ. If you suffer from a medical condition, make sure the destination you visit easily meets your needs. Also invest in insurance which will cover all eventualities including the cost of repatriation. Not all insurance policies include this, so do check. You may need to shop around for a policy that will cover a traveller of advancing years but they do exist!

See your doctor well before you embark on your trip. He'll be able to advise and arrange vaccinations and will ensure you are prescribed for any regular medicinal needs during your time overseas. Doctors can normally only prescribe a limited quantity under the NHS but your GP may be able to make an exception or advise you of what is available at your intended destination/s. The countries you visit may also impose restrictions on certain medicinal drugs and it is always a good idea to carry notification of any significant medical condition you suffer from.

Health

The older you are, the longer it takes to recover from an illness or broken bone. So it is common sense to preclude predicaments such as being stuck in a Nepalese hospital with a leg in plaster because you were convinced you could imitate that mountain goat —and failed. Assess your level of fitness before you decide where to travel.

Up–to–date information on the health problems of the country you plan to visit is available from clinics across the UK. Contact the **British Airways Travel Clinics** on 071–831 5333 for your nearest clinic, or try the **Medical Advisory Service for Travellers Abroad** (MASTA) on 071–631 4408. It is also sensible to have a full medical check–up before you leave.

For a free copy of the Department of Health leaflet *The Traveller's Guide to Health* (ref T4) see your doctor, travel agent, local post office or call 0800–555 777. Remember, you will not enjoy your holiday if you are constantly tired. And if you feel tired, rest. Pushing yourself to the limit all day every day, will only see the excitement of being in a new place, witnessing a different culture, pall.

Services for older people

There are now a number of travel companies which provide holidays specifically for older travellers. Most offer packages but there is an increasing demand for holidays which combine the advantages of package deals (easy travel arrangements, the support of large organizations should you need help) with independence once you reach your destination.

A number of specialist operators now cater for older travellers. Forty years ago **Saga** pioneered holidays exclusively for over–60s, long before anyone else realized the market potential. The company has since moved on a continent or two from UK seaside hotel holidays. Saga includes travel insurance in the cost of all overseas travel and also offers a free visa service.

Other companies offering package holidays tailored to the needs of older people include Thomson's *Young at Heart*, Cosmos' *Golden Times*, Enterprise's *Leisurely Days*.

Practicalities

No matter how dauntless you are, nothing makes for a grouchier traveller than the lack of life's little comforts. So take small inflatable cushions to rest that weary head, cartons of drink to quench that thirst when you are nowhere near civilization, use luggage with wheels or spread the load over a couple of soft–pack bags.

And if you're the type who would consider the ultimate travel experience ruined by a lack of milk, let alone tea, check that in the destination of your choice they also appreciate such basics!

THE BUDGET TRAVELLER

by Pat Yale

Often born of necessity, budget travel nevertheless has an appeal all of its own. After all, even if 'shoestringing' it through the United States leaves you feeling like the beggar at the banquet, in developing countries it often allows you to explore your surroundings in a way that luxury holiday-making makes impossible.

Advance planning

Travelling cheaply involves meticulous advance planning. Start by pinpointing those parts of the world where budget travel is realistic by finding out which are accessible overland, which can be reached by discounted air tickets, where the cost of living is low and where you can work your keep. Then mug up details to ensure you've got it right. Many of the likeliest places will be developing countries of the southern hemisphere but there are always exceptions: the Comoros Islands sit off the coast of Africa but prices may be higher than you expect because of imported goods and visiting South Africans; China offers some marvellous bargains but if you stay where the authorities prefer it may cost more than you anticipated. Conversely Japan sounds prohibitively expensive but teaching English can ease the pain. Even Scandinavia can be brought within a tight budget if you're prepared to camp, hitch and carry staple foods brought from home.

The cost of paperwork for the route you fancy could be a determining factor; UK passport holders will find West African journeys particularly expensive. Forget countries with wars unless you're prepared to risk unexpected extra flight costs and hefty insurance premiums etc.

Next pick the cheapest travel times. Most airlines and ferry companies offer peak, shoulder and low season prices, and any travel agent can tell you the earliest and latest dates to qualify for the best prices. Book as early as possible to ensure you get a seat, bearing in mind that events like Rio's February Carnival lead to a run on cheap tickets. Remember too that prices are rarely guaranteed until you have paid in full. Watch for special offers, particularly when airlines start new services, and try to reduce the cost of reaching expensive smaller airports by flying to the nearest tourist centre and continuing your journey overland.

National tourist offices can supply free maps and advice on where to go, but for information on how to travel and where to stay, budget travellers must depend on guidebooks, particularly those published by **Lonely Planet**, **Rough Guide** and **Vacation Work** (borrow from your library until you're sure of your route). To guard against unpleasant surprises make sure you are using the latest edition and then check the inflation rate in the country you're visiting. Lonely Planet publishes a quarterly newsletter full of useful tips from recent travellers. *TNT* and *Globe* magazines are also useful sources of up–to–date information.

High street travel agents sometimes keep details of shipping routes, train times and so on, but the budget end of the market is rarely their forte. Try student and independent travel specialists like **Campus Travel**, **WEXAS**, **STA** and **Trailfinders** for help with a variety of enquiries from experienced consultants. Alternatively tap into the experience of specialists such as **South American Experience** (47 Causton Street, London SW1P 4AT, tel: 071–976 5511) and the **Africa Travel Shop** (4 Medway Court, Leigh Street, London WC1H 9QX, tel: 071–387 1211).

Bucket shops selling rock–bottom airfares advertise in Time Out and TNT. The prices quoted will apply to the low season, so ring round for precise fares for your journey. Never part with any money until you know your flight number which can be double–checked by contacting the airline to confirm your name is on their reservation list.

Cheap flights are usually on Eastern European or Third World carriers, few of them offering luxury, some with better safety records than others. They may also involve long stopovers en route in places like Bucharest and Karachi, so check flight times carefully.

From 16 April 1995 all national and international codes change — see page 587 for details.

Courier companies may even provide you with a free flight if you're prepared to travel smartly and forfeit your baggage allowance. *The Insider's Guide to Air Courier Bargains* (£11.95 plus £1 postage) is an excellent reference for budget travellers with the time to take advantage of this more unorthodox form of air travel. Contact ASAP Publications on 0494 520600 for a copy. High Street agents are still your best bet for bargain charter flights to Mediterranean destinations. Don't automatically dismiss packages since some offer unbeatable value for money; for example, **New Millennium Holidays'** (tel: 021-711 2232) Polish coach tours are so cheap that it would be hard to undercut them. It's worth checking mainstream brochures for special deals, usually highlighted at the front. Lone women and first–time travellers may prefer the security of group travel and companies like **Encounter Overland** (tel: 071-370 6951), **Exodus Expeditions** (081-675 5550), **Guerba** (0373-826689) and **Dragoman** (0728-861133) offer long–haul trips to Asia, Africa and South America.

By the time you've added the cost of food kitties, etc. to the basic brochure price they may not seem particularly cheap in comparison with some of the deals offered in the classified ads but it's worth remembering that you're paying extra for their expertise to get you out of potentially costly and frightening fixes. A cheap tour which falls behind schedule so you have to renew all your visas is likely to be a false economy.

Even if you prefer travelling alone, having a companion can reduce accommodation costs by eliminating single supplements. Members of the *Globetrotters Club* can use the 'Mutual Aid' columns of the club magazine *Globe* to advertise for travelling companions or you can put a card up on the board at the *Travellers' Bookshop,* 25 Cecil Court, London WC2N 4EZ. However, on the popular overland routes there are regular meeting points where it's easy to find fellow travellers.

However great the temptation, it's never wise to scrimp on health precautions before you leave. Budget travellers who eat from street stalls and sleep in flea–pits are especially likely to come into contact with contaminated food and drink and the sort of conditions in which diseases breed. Never economize on compulsory vaccinations since you risk forcible inoculation at the border with a needle which may have seen more than one arm. Some people blithely leave home without insurance which is hardly surprising given the quotations for longer term policies. But even if you can live with the prospect of robbery, to fall ill without the means to pay for treatment could be disastrous. **Endsleigh** (97–107 Southampton Row, London WC1B 4AG, tel: 071–436 4451) offer competitive prices for long–term travellers and their policies even cover so–called war zones such as Nicaragua. **WEXAS** (45 Brompton Road, London SW3 1DE, Tel: 071-589 3315) also offer good insurance schemes. When travelling in Europe make sure you take Form E111 (if you are an EEC citizen) from the DSS for reciprocal free treatment in EC countries.

Taking a self–defence course can be a good investment since cheap accommodation isn't always in the safest parts of towns. A language class could also represent money well spent: those who can make themselves understood not only have the best chance of making friends and finding out what's really going on but are also less likely to get ripped off. Travellers to Central or South America should plan a stop in Antigua (Guatemala) to take advantage of its beautifully–sited, bargain–priced language schools.

When deciding how much money to take, the cost of carrying it should also be a consideration. It's worth supplementing travellers' cheques with some local currency to tide you over until you can get to a bank —even though it means paying two lots of commission (exchange rates are rarely good at borders). If you are travelling to the Americas, always take dollar cheques. Otherwise don't be talked out of sterling: what you'll gain in avoiding exchange rates is unlikely to justify the extra charge for currency cheques. Carrying a credit card is a sensible safeguard, provided you can get one free and merit a high enough credit limit to cover your flight home. Carry your money in a variety of forms, stored in a variety of places to reduce the chance of losing everything at once.

Using black markets can cut your costs but needs advance planning; most black marketeers only want cash, preferably in large dollar bills. Bear in mind the risk of being robbed or shipped to the police and get wise to local cons by listening into the traveller's grapevine. Sudan now has the death penalty for currency racketeering…don't be tempted.

Full–time students are eligible for the **International Student Identity Card** (ISIC) which offers discounts on transport, museum entrance fees, etc. These are available from student travel offices which also sell **The Under-26 Youth Card** for a small fee. Despite increasing efforts to prevent forgery of these cards, there are still places like Banglamphu in Bangkok where it's easy to acquire them whether or not you're eligible.

While you're away

The cheapest ways of travelling are, of course, walking, cycling and hitching. Walking limits the scope of what you can do, and cycling is for enthusiasts — particularly outside Europe—but anyone can hitch provided they take elementary precautions like standing somewhere safe and dressing in a way that makes their intentions clear. However, in parts of the world where transport is thin on the ground, locals negotiate the fare for 'lifts' in advance to avoid argument. Travellers to the USA can use the marvellous 'driveaway' car system which lets you drive someone else's car for them from A to B just for the price of the petrol.

Rail, bus and airpasses may restrict you to using one form of transport but can reduce travel costs considerably. One of the all–time best buys, the **Inter Rail** card, offers one month's free travel in West and Eastern Europe and Morocco. For a supplementary charge, Inter–Railers also get the freedom of Europe's ferries. Most European countries have rail rovers as do India, Malaysia, Australia, Canada, New Zealand and Japan. Airpasses are popular in the USA (some also cover the Caribbean, Canada and Mexico), Australasia and, increasingly, in parts of Asia.

Even if you don't buy passes you can still keep transport costs down. Anyone under 26 can buy Eurotrain or Route 26 rail tickets which offer up to 50 per cent discounts on individual routes or for fixed circuits. Those over 26 may have to sacrifice speed for economy, particularly in Europe where the fastest trains often carry supplementary fares (for trains to avoid, check *Thomas Cook's International Timetable*). Travellers to the USA and Canada are also eligible for discounted sector airfares, especially when these have been purchased in the country of origin. Many South American airfares are low enough to fit tight budgets and flying from one side of Australia to the other could save you days of strenuous and not necessarily very exciting bus travel. Never buy tickets, even for local journeys, without checking competitor's prices and asking about discounts for return travel or multiple journeys. Watch out for special promotions, particularly the 'Visit...Years' when reduced fares on all forms of transport are sometimes offered to tourists.

Keep living costs down by eating and drinking whatever the locals do. In developing countries you can often fill up cheaply on staples like rice, noodles and chapatis. Always avoid eating in restaurants frequented by coach parties; a *paella* down a Barcelona side street will cost much less than one eaten in the Ramblas; an ice–cream in a Sintagma cafe in Athens could set you back the price of a night's accommodation.

With endless time, most places can be reached more cheaply without the cost of a middleman. If time is pressing you should still shop around before settling for organized excursions, treks etc, especially in centres like Kathmandu and Chiang Mai where there are lots of competing operators. By staying in hostels/hotels popular with other travellers you'll soon get wind of the best deals.

However tight your budget, allow for unexpected extras like airport taxes (sometimes payable only in hard currency). And make sure you're wise to local offences for which fines are levied: in Singapore these include failure to flush a public lavatory and leaving food in an eat–as–much–as–you–like restaurant.

Occasionally you can spin out your funds by selling something, if rarely for what you originally paid; in Bangkok's Banglamphu district almost any backpacking gear has its price. In countries like Myanmar (Burma) you can usually sell your duty free alcohol and tobacco allowance without any problems. Where you can get reliable information about local shortages you can also buy items in one country to sell in another —provided you take Customs regulations into account. The desperate can sometimes sell blood or semen as well but how wise it is to cut things as fine as this —especially in poorer, developing countries— is debatable. Never, under any circumstances, consider carrying drugs, gems or gold across borders: even without the death penalty, as in Malaysia, a jail sentence is hardly the best way to end your travels.

THE DIABETIC TRAVELLER

by Robin Perlstein

Holidays and travel should be something to look forward, but it is important to plan ahead —even more so if you have diabetes and you want your journey (and blood sugars) to run smoothly.

Vaccination

Some countries do insist on certain immunizations for visitors, so it is wise to check in advance what (if any) vaccinations are required. There are no vaccinations contra–indicated because you have diabetes but be aware that some may affect blood sugar level control in the hours or days following.

Identification and customs

It is sensible to wear some form of identification bracelet/necklace indicating you are diabetic —especially if taking insulin. It is wise to have a letter from your doctor stating you have diabetes and its mode of treatment or a British Diabetic Association photo Identification card. This is very important if you are taken ill while away or if you have any problems going through Customs. However, it is not essential to declare insulin/medicines/ syringes, as these are personal medical requirements.

Insurance

The cost and availability of medical services differs from country to country. Some countries have a reciprocal health care agreement with the UK and so emergency medical treatment is free or available at a reduced cost. Many countries provide no free medical services and all treatment and medical supplies must be paid for. This can be very costly and it is vital you take out adequate medical insurance.

Insurance policies that will reimburse you if you need to be flown home in an emergency are also advisable, and ensure that holiday insurance packages do not exclude pre–existing illnesses such as diabetes.

Illness

Being ill is unpleasant and can spoil a holiday especially if you are unwell in a country where foods are different and hygiene standards dubious. Knowing what to do regarding your medication and food intake is essential and so discuss this with your diabetes nurse specialist before you leave. Find out about anti–diarrhoea medication, motion sickness tablets as well as basic food hygiene. Having the name and address of the local Diabetes Association may also be of assistance if you are taken ill.

Medical supplies

It is very important to take enough medical supplies (insulin, syringes etc.) so that valuable time and money is not wasted. For some items, your GP can only write a prescription for three months and so if you are holidaying for an extended period of time, consulting a doctor in the place you are visiting may be necessary. Many insulins and/or oral hypoglycaemics available in the UK are available in other countries. The manufacturers of most products can also give an idea of worldwide availability. Having the generic and brand name of medication is helpful as brand names often differ in other countries.

Remember that in some countries in Europe, 40 or 80 units per ml strength insulin is still used rather than U100. If you have to use U40 insulin the simplest thing to do is ask for U40 syringes at the same time. If U100 syringes are used for U40 insulin much *less* insulin will be taken than needed, and conversely if U100 insulin is used with U40 syringes *too much* insulin will be taken.

If you have any concerns about your pending travel, you should see your

Diabetes Nurse Specialist before you travel. Blood glucose control should be reviewed as well as general health, and a rough plan may need to be mapped if you are crossing time zones.

On the journey

Whether travelling by train, plane or automobile, you should take food with you in case of delays or extensions to journey times. Include quick–acting carbohydrates such as sugar and glucose tablets and the longer–acting variety: biscuits, fruit, sandwiches, etc. If you are prone to travel sickness, you may also need to take motion sickness tablets prior to your journey.

If driving, remember you should test blood sugars before getting into the car, and eat regularly. Testing blood sugars every two hours over long journeys to avoid hypoglycaemia is essential (if on sulphonylureas or insulin).

Long periods of sitting relatively motionless may lead to a rise in blood sugars. It is preferable to have sugars running a little high than low, as hypos can be very dangerous when driving and very embarrassing and inconvenient when on buses and trains. Remember though that you may be quite active at the beginning and end of a trip, ie. when rushing to get to the station, packing the car and lifting luggage.

Airline and shipping companies are usually helpful about arranging for special diets and will provide information on meal times. Most travellers find they can manage on the standard meals provided, especially if carrying extra food for emergencies.

Packing for the trip

Insulin should be packed in your hand luggage, as flying altitudes can cause baggage in the hold to freeze; what is more, checked luggage might be lost or delayed. It is wise to have all essential items such as your insulin, blood glucose meter, etc. kept close or at least split between yourself and a travelling companion.

Insulin storage

Remember that extremes of temperature (hot or cold) can lead to a drop in activity of insulin rendering it less effective. At home, most insulin is probably kept in the refrigerator and can be stored in this way for up to two years or more (depending on the expiry date). Keeping the vials of insulin out of the refrigerator will not automatically mean it is unusable: insulin activity will remain stable for about one month at 25°C (normal room temperature). So long as temperatures are not extreme, the activity of the insulin should not be altered.

If there are no refrigerators available while travelling, vials should be kept in a cool, dark place avoiding hot spots such as the glove box or back shelf of the car. There are a number of insulin carriers available which have a frozen water container acting as a coolant. Freezer facilities must be available to make use of these and vials must not be in contact with the frozen blocks.

Alternatives include placing the insulin in a plastic sandwich box to keep it cool. Wide–necked vacuum flasks and polystyrene containers are a useful and cheaper option. If you are concerned that the activity of the insulin may have been affected, check its appearance: short acting insulins should remain clear, while longer acting insulins should appear cloudy, but with no odd pieces or lumps present.

Climate

Take sensible precautions in extremes of temperatures such as using a good sunscreen and maintaining a high fluid intake in hot climates; conversely, in cooler weather wear warm socks and comfortable shoes to protect your feet. Remember also that some blood glucose test strips will over–read in very warm climates, and under–read in colder climates.

Activity

Generally, holidaymakers are more active than normal, taking long walks, trying out new sports etc. Alternatively some might do less, missing out on usual daily activities and taking time to lie on the beach and relax. It is important that blood sugars are regularly monitored and recorded as this information will prove useful for future travel.

Food

Remember that a holiday is a time to sample new and different foods. Many people are daunted by the prospect of selecting from menus and eating food they are unaccustomed to while travelling. Yet, food in most places consists of the same basic ingredients: fruit, vegetables, meats and usually plentiful supplies of starchy foods such as rice, potatoes, bread and pastas.

An increase in the amount of alcohol consumed is a common occurrence while on holiday but remember it can lower blood sugars if taking certain tablets or insulin. Therefore, it is wise to eat when drinking or even wiser to drink lower or no alcohol alternatives. Remember to drink plenty of water, but if unsure of the purity of the local water supply, drink bottled water only.

Holiday check–list

Ensure you have had all the required vaccinations
Diabetic ID Card
Doctor's letter
Take adequate travel insurance (which does not exclude diabetes) is imperative
Make sure you have thought about how to deal with becoming ill while away
Take the name of the local Diabetes Association if travelling to a foreign country
Take sufficient supplies (approximately twice as much as required normally) of: Insulin, syringes, oral hypoglycaemic agents (generic and trade name), blood glucose meter and spare batteries, testing strips, lancets, needle clipper, any other medication, glucose gel, glucose tablets/sweets, Glucagon, tissues and longer–acting carbohydrate foods (biscuits/bread/fruit)
Useful foreign phrases
Currency of the foreign country being visited (to purchase food/drinks on arrival).

Insulin storage containers —if you feel the climate/circumstances warrant it
Pack a good sunscreen and comfortable socks and shoes for walking
Record Book

For more information contact the British Diabetic Association, 10 Queen Anne
Street, London W1M 0BD, tel: 071–323 1531. The BDA produces general trav-
el information for diabetics as well as information specific to certain countries.
See the Directory for more helpful names and addresses.

THE VEGETARIAN TRAVELLER

by Andrew Sangar

What does a vegetarian do when invited by a smiling, rough–and–ready
truck–driver in Eastern Turkey to join his family for dinner in a small village at the end of a long dusty track?

In many ways, limitations on what you eat, what you do and where you will
go are anathema to the traveller. An open mind and a willingness to adapt make
a much better approach. However, we all carry a few ethical ideas in our mental
rucksack, and some of these principles are worth keeping. After all, we preserve
our own moral standards when at home —even if the 'locals' don't agree with
us— so it's reasonable to do the same when abroad.

For vegetarians, this isn't easy. It's not just the food, but attitudes. In most
parts of the world, vegetarians are regarded as mere harmless foreign lunatics.
Certain countries do have vegetarians of their own: they generally have either
opted to give up meat for health reasons, or they are enjoined to do so on religious grounds. Some in Europe (mainly Holland and Germany) have a political
commitment to avoiding meat because of the waste of resources which it
entails. Few outside the Anglo–Saxon world have any sympathy with the notion
(or have even come across it) that wantonly killing animals is actually wrong.
Indeed, if they were to hear it, most would fiercely oppose the idea.

A problem arises when your morality is totally at odds with that of the people
around you —especially when your views are seen as a Western luxury or as an
absurd ethnocentricity.

Culture and circumstances impose a diet which is right for a given people. So
it can sometimes be wise (if all you want is food and no arguments) to offer the
most acceptable explanation for your own vegetarianism. Among friends, this
may not be necessary. In everyday encounters, however, you'll get the best out
of people if you can either claim to be 'on a diet', possibly under medical supervision, or dress up personal ethics as part of some religious persuasion. Above
all, *don't try to persuade people that they too should give up meat.*

On the road it's essential to be flexible. Even meat–eating travellers may be
faced with food (sheeps' eyes, for example) which they find hard to swallow.
My approach is simply to avoid meat and fish as much as possible. Usually it *is*
possible, and with no greater hardship than a rather monotonous diet at times.

In Greece, for example, a vegetarian must be happy with lots of delicious
horiatiki salad, fresh bread and oily vegetables; or in France, some marvellous
four–course meals in which the main dish is always omelette; or in a dozen other

countries, meals consisting entirely of snacks or a succession of starters. Some countries are easier than others. In Italy where pasta usually comes before the main course, it usually is the main course for vegetarians. Mercifully, Italy is one of those places where nobody bats an eyelid at such eccentricities, and pasta comes in a score of different forms with a dozen different meatless sauces. Meatless pizzas are everywhere, and it's worth adding that many Italian cheeses, such as gorgonzola, are made commercially without animal rennet.

In north west Europe, eating habits are decidedly meaty, or fishy (especially in Scandinavia). But there are so many vegetarians that almost all cities and a good number of provincial towns have eating places catering for meat–free consumers. Holland and Germany, like Britain, have thousands of such establishments. Further east in Europe, there's a different problem —a lack of anything much to eat *except* meat (accompanied by potatoes and cabbages, and followed by lard–rich sticky cakes). This is not invariably the case. Czechoslovakia, or at least its capital Prague, seems now to enjoy an abundance of produce of all kinds.

One of the best parts of the world for vegetarian travellers is the Middle East. Israel, above all, is a land of meat–free snacks and meals. All sorts of cultural reasons account for this. Many Jews are vegetarian, but in any case Jewish dietary laws prohibit the mixing of meat and milk within six hours of each other. This has led to a proliferation of 'dairy' restaurants in which nothing on the menu (not even the cheese) contains any meat products. Note though that dairy restaurants do serve fish.

Israelis particularly like salads, even for breakfast, eaten with yoghurt–like milk products. More salad at lunch time or in the evening is accompanied by fried, meat–free items such as *falafel* (like meatballs made of chickpeas), *blintzes* (filled rolled pancakes), *latkes* (fried grated potato) and *borekas* (little filled savoury pastries). Some of these have been brought from Eastern Europe, others are native Middle Eastern dishes, reflecting the differing origins of the refugees who make up Israel's population.

In neighbouring Arab countries (not the Maghreb, though), and in Turkey, several of the same delicious snacky dishes can be found. A traditional Arab *mezze* (a meal consisting of many small items served all at once) can be made of such dishes, although in the Islamic world it is hard indeed to get anyone to accept that you truly don't want any meat.

That's not particular to Islam. In much of fervently Christian South America, meat is the be–all and end–all of cookery. While I was in Brazil, a crisis involving farmers led to meat shortages which actually sparked off riots —even though nothing else was in short supply. There I managed happily mainly on salads, fruit and bread. North America has followed a similar path, despite closer historic links with north west Europe. True, there is a glossy American magazine called *Vegetarian Times*, and hundreds of 'veggie' eateries on the hip West Coast (some Canadian cities with even stronger British ties have vegetarian restaurants), but on the whole North America is hooked on meat, and the only alternative seems to be a cheese sandwich.

It's perhaps reminiscent of holidaymakers who go abroad loaded with the familiar foods of home, but don't be too proud to put some emergency rations in your luggage. I have staved off hunger on countless occasions —and in every continent— with a small bag of muesli, mixed with milk powder. It can be turned into a nourishing, tasty and filling snack just by adding water. If there's milk, yoghurt or fruit juice on hand, so much the better.

The one country where vegetarianism is really normal, and meat–eaters in the minority is India. Hindus are supposed to steer clear of all meat (including eggs) but yoghurt is eaten in abundance. Most Hindu eating places at the poorer end of the scale are completely vegetarian, as are the smarter (but entirely un–Western) Brahmin restaurants. Travellers tend to find themselves in a different class of establishment, quasi–European in a dignified, old fashioned way, as if the days of Raj were still not quite forgotten. Railway stations, for example, usually have a good dining room divided into meat and vegetarian sections. Many hotels do likewise. Moslem or Christian regions, say Kashmir or Goa, are less reliable. But similarly, beyond India, pockets of Hinduism provide resources throughout southeast Asia.

The places where vegetarianism is best known, and often quite well catered for, tend to be those countries formerly under British influence. Australia — which also benefits from Middle Eastern and Indian immigration— is an obvious example. And it's not for patriotic reasons that I commend British Airways to vegetarian travellers. They are more aware of what vegetarians want and more serious about providing it than just about any other of their competitors. When booking, you can opt for lacto–vegetarian, vegan or Oriental vegetarian in–flight meals. Other airlines capable of providing (rather than just promising to provide) a decent meatless meal include Air India, El Al and Swissair.

But to return to earth. I accepted the Turkish truckdriver's invitation. A goat was slaughtered and served, with no accompaniment but bread. I picked reluctantly at the meat, hoping no one would notice. While we men ate and the women peeked from the kitchen door, the severed head of the animal gazed at us horribly from the end of the table. Rough drinks were poured and we toasted mutual understanding.

THE DISABLED TRAVELLER

by Quentin Crewe

My doctor, when a patient asks whether it is wise for him or her to travel, nearly always says, "Yes, it will do you good".

He takes the view that, unless it is obviously impossible or plainly dangerous any patient who wants to go will be happier going. Only twice in his long career has he lost a patient. He still reckons that it was a good way for them to go and they might just have well died if they had stayed at home.

This is the principle I have always worked on. I live my life in a wheelchair, as I have muscular dystrophy, but I have been round the world many times. I have been blown up by a land mine in Mauritania, nearly drowned in Niger, robbed by bandits in Brazil, lost in the Saudi Arabian desert, embraced by a snake in Kenya, threatened by a bear in India, but I am still here, as John Major has been known to say.

Disability takes many forms. What is true for one person does not necessarily apply to the next one, but my hope is that as many disabled people as possible will, as it were, have a go. They will have many agreeable surprises. Who for instance would guess that Bogota is one of the best cities in the world for wheelchairs, almost every pavement carefully ramped. It is a pleasure to wander around, but I would carry a little mugging money with you.

Obviously, the easiest way to travel is by car and I must admit that most of my major journeys have been by road, including 24,000 miles round South America in a Toyota Landcruiser, which involved 1000 miles floating down the Amazon river for five days and nights on a barge, sleeping on the deck, under some lorries.

Crossing to the Continent will presumably be easier when the Eurotunnel is working, but the ferries are helpful. I have found that, if I ask politely and firmly enough, the captains of hovercrafts will let me stay in the car for the crossing. This might be nerve-wracking for claustrophobics, though they do give one a life-jacket.

Air is my next preferred method of travel. This has improved immensely in the last few years. On the whole, I do not warn anyone of my situation when I buy a ticket, taking the view that disabled people should be able to do things on the spur of the moment, like everyone else. I just turn up at the airport and leave it to them. I have found that if one goes to a travel agent and alerts them, they create problems and ask for doctor's certificates to say one is fit to travel.

I have seldom had trouble. Once some years ago in Tunis, I was asked to sign an indemnity saying that if there were a crash and I impeded someone's escape I would be liable. It seemed a reasonable chance to take. Forgetting my own rules, not long ago in India I went myself into the airline office. They asked for a doctor's certificate. There was a doctor in the same street. For a few rupees, he wrote a certificate to my dictation.

In more remote places, the airport may not have one of those narrow chairs for getting disabled people to their seats and up and down aircraft steps. On the other hand, in remote places, there are usually strong, helpful people ready and eager to carry you on and off the plane. If this could hurt you, it is worth checking beforehand. I have often been carried off upside down with all my change falling out of my pocket to the delight of the helpers. If you are flying with your own chair it is important to make sure they have put it in the hold. Taking off from Beirut once, I looked out of the window to see my chair sitting abandoned on the runway.

A major drawback to air travel is the impossibility of getting to the toilets. Fortunately air travel is de-hydrating and it is amazing what, with the help of a friend, can be achieved discreetly, by a man at least, under a rug, as I dare say members of the 'mile high club' would testify. Otherwise a G.P. could give advice about incontinence aids.

Before arrival, it is essential to check that the pilot has radioed ahead to ask for help to be ready at your destination.

Rail travel in Britain used to mean a chilly ride in the guard's van. British Rail have changed all that, but unlike the airlines it is well to warn them ahead, especially when there is a question of taking a seat out to make room for your chair.

Additional information for Disabled Travellers

by Carey Ogilvie

The world has become so accessible in the last twenty years or so, no one blinks an eye lid if, on the spur of the moment, you go to France for the weekend. The ease with which we are able to travel the world improves annually. With more people travelling, the industry fights for our custom, airlines negotiate new routes, operators offer more and more irresistible deals and with the abundance of guide books and information, the world is our oyster. However it has not been the same for disabled travellers. Although there are numerous organisations and charities which have offered help and advice, it is only recently that the attitude has changed within the tourist industry. As with most changes in any industry, it has been market forced. There are 14 million disabled persons in Europe.

Success as a disabled traveller often depends on attitude of mind and great things can be achieved, though you may not always find that the system works for you. Still, these are some organisations that are around to help you (an ever increasing number).

The two most useful contacts other than **RADAR** are **Tripscope** (mentioned later) and the **Holiday Care Service** (2 Old Bank Chambers, Station Road, Horley, Surrey RH6 9HW, tel: 0293 774535). The latter has been instrumental in the changes of attitude within the industry. Holiday Care Service is a registered charity, and was established in 1981, since then it has been going from strength to strength. Three years ago with Judith Chalmers, their Vice Chairman, they set up the Holiday Care Awards to encourage a better reception for disabled travellers, to recognise companies that offer superior facilities and to raise the profile of disabled travel. Holiday Care Service publishes 14 regional guides on accommodation which are accessible for the wheelchair user, all of which can be booked through them at discounted prices.

Cars

Travelling by car is probably the easiest way of travelling, especially if it's your own car. Discounts abound with many of the ferry companies giving concessions, contact the **Disabled Motorist Federation** (tel: 0743 761889) or the **Disabled Drivers' Motor Club** (tel: 08912 4724). **The Disabled Drivers' Association** is also worth contacting for advice and information (tel: 058041 449). For those who want to have the freedom of travelling in their own vehicle, but don't own one, help is at hand. **The Rod Surrage Appeal Fund**, based in Guildford (tel: 0483 233640) has 5 adapted mini-buses, they can be hired either on a self-drive basis or with a driver. All can carry wheelchair users and are fitted with tail-lifts for easy access, perfect for the family holiday. **Hertz** have adapted cars available for hire in most international cities, contact Hertz (UK) Ltd, Radnor House, 1272 London Road, London SW16 (tel: 081-679 1777)

Buses and Trains

Although this is improving, public transport for the disabled passenger can depend on a sense of humour and a great deal of patience. However there is a wealth of advice and help on offer. Perhaps the most informative is **Tripscope,** The Courtyard, Evelyn Road, London W4 5JL (tel: 081-994 9294). The service is free, and although they are not a travel agent and therefore can not arrange your bookings, their suggestions pave the way. **The Department of Transport** publish a guide called 'Door to Door', this is also useful for the initial planning.

London Transport are slowly getting their act together. Although wheelchairs are no longer banned from the Underground, the tube is still inaccessible, unlike the Metro in Amsterdam. However, London can still be crossed without lining the pocket of a black cab. **The Unit of Disabled Passengers** set up by London Transport in 1984, publish a series of leaflets detailing facilities available, tel: 071-918 3312. Stationlink offers an hourly shuttle service linking all the main-line railway stations, this is free to holders of the British Rail Disabled Persons Card, but can take hours to get from one station to another —not ideal. Airbus routes between Heathrow and Central London are equipped with hydraulic lifts.

As for British Rail, it is improving but is a long way from being perfect. I am afraid there are still those stations that, if you are in a wheelchair and on the wrong platform, it seems to be tough luck. However they do have a leaflet 'British Rail and Disabled Travellers' giving general advice and information and, if given advance warning, will try to do everything to make your journey more pleasant. They also issue the 'Disabled Persons Railcard' which can entitle you to at least a third off all rail travel.

In Europe there is also room for improvement, with the exception of the new Eurostar trains. In some countries, there can be the problem of higher trains and lower platforms, not very user-friendly. It is therefore advisable to contact the UK offices of the relevant railways. Norway leads the way in Europe with specially adapted coaches for wheelchair users, with hydraulic lifts and accessible toilets, advance ticket purchase is necessary though, contact NSR, 24 Cockspur Street, London SW1Y 5DA, (tel: 071-930 6666)

As with trains anywhere in the world check on the width of the corridors, most I am afraid are too narrow for the standard wheelchair.

Flying

There are two schools of thought on this one. Do you alert the airline and find out all you can about the facilities at the airport, or like Quentin Crewe do you turn up and let them do the organising. If you prefer to do the former, 'Care in the Air', published by the **Air Transport Users Committee** (ATUC) gives general advice for disabled air passengers. It is available from ATUC, 5th Floor, 103 Kingsway, London WC2B 6QX (tel: 071-242 3882. **The Disabled Living Foundation,** 380-384 Harrow Road, London W9 2HU (tel: 071-289 6111) produce a booklet in conjuction with British Airways called 'Flying High' (£2.50 including P&P), this practical guide takes the reader through the flight from booking to returning home.

Organised Tours

There are numerous companies organising tours for disabled travellers, some are mixed ability tours, other solely for the handicapped, some are charities and others work on a commercial basis, the opportunities however, are endless. One of the most inspiring charities is **Across,** they organise tours and pilgrimages for the severely disabled in their Jumbulances. They started in 1972 with a transit van to Lourdes, they now have 10 Jumbulances and as well as weekly trips to Lourdes, they also organise tours to parts of Europe and the Holy Land. For more information contact Across Trust, Bridge House, 70/72 Bridge Road, East Moslesey, Surrey KT8 9HF (tel 081-783 1355)

Cruising has become more and more popular with wheelchair users, and as ships get refurbished more facilities are being offered. **Page and Moy Ltd** (tel 0533 524444) produce a leaflet called 'Cruising and the Disabled Traveller' and they can advise which ship and cruise would suit your needs.

For the more adventurous, **Oxventure,** 28 Beech Road, Wheatley, Oxford OX9 1UR (tel: 0865 875598) runs adventure holidays to Nepal, which normally include two or three disabled people. These mixed ability adventure trips included white water rafting and safari by elephant back. John Havers who runs Oxventure can also give advice for other mixed ability expeditions.

For those who are bored with this world, there is a club that can show you another ... **Going Down** is a diving club run by Leon Golding. He teaches diving to mixed ability groups in this country and then organises diving expeditions to the Red Sea, Canaries and various destinations in the Mediterranean. He can be contacted at 46 Hill Drive, Hove, Sussex BN3 6QL (tel: 0273 566616). Another sporting holiday on offer is skiing. As they say at the **Uphill Ski Club,** "Why shouldn't you have a wheel chair at the top of a mountain?". The club was founded over 18 years ago and is committed to providing winter sporting activities for people with a wide range of disabilities including, CP, spinabifida, epilepsy, learning difficulties, head injuries and sensory handicaps. The enjoyment and the morale boost felt by the skiers is illustrated by their letters, "I hope that more disabled people will, in the future, be able to experience the exhilaration that we were lucky enough to feel". For further information contact 12 Park Crescent, London W1N 4EQ (tel: 071-636 1989).

Useful Books

With more and more disabled people travelling, that ever present market force has produced a new wealth of information. However some of the most informative guides have been around for years, for example **RADAR** publishes 2 books annually, 'Holidays in the British Isles' and 'Holidays and Travel Abroad'. As is to be expected they are a mine of information: being totally independent, they are unbiased in their advice. Both the RAC and AA publish their own guides, both are informative and packed full with useful names and addresses. One of the most encouraging books is 'Nothing Ventured' edited by Alison Walsh, it was published in 1991, but is still available in most good bookshops. The book is a collection of tales by disabled travellers all over the world, not only is the book inspiring but at the end of each country are useful travel notes. A second edition is in the pipeline. Alison Walsh has been an inspiration to many, she has written an excellent booklet to accompany the BBC Holiday Programme, which is a must for any disabled traveller, send a large self-addressed envelope with a 43p stamp to Disabled Traveller, PO Box 7, London W3 6XJ.

New books include the 'Smooth Ride Guides', the first edition on Australia and New Zealand was published in April 1994, the second on the USA is hitting the bookshops in March 1995.

As Alison Walsh writes "There is no such thing as a holiday which is unsuitable for disabled people: everything depends on the degree of disability and the attitude of the traveller..." For further contacts please see the directory and happy travelling. ■

PAPERWORK AND MONEY
Chapter 9

TRAVEL INSURANCE

by Malcolm Irvine

One of the most important aspects of planning a major trip abroad is your insurance, but it is frequently overlooked until the last minute, or costed inaccurately into the travel budget.

Personal

The first and most important thing to determine is that you are buying the correct insurance for your particular activities and involvements. It is much better to deal with a professional insurance broker than make the mistake of buying a mundane travel insurance policy from your local High Street travel agent. A policy designed for a few weeks in the sun on the Costa Brava is of no help to you if you end up as a stretcher case in deepest Africa in need of immediate air evacuation. Don't be afraid to ask for an explanation of the insurance policy that you are purchasing, or written confirmation that it is suitable for your purposes.

A major travel insurance scheme underwritten at Lloyd's of London, and aimed principally at long periods of travel on a worldwide basis, gathered the following statistics in 1993. Almost 40 per cent of claims paid related to baggage and personal effects, 35 per cent to medical expenses and 25 per cent to cancellation. The average claim came to £240 and the highest single claim paid under that particular contract was for £103,000 worth of medical expenses.

It is most common nowadays to purchase an inclusive policy where the sums insured for the various sections of cover have been tailored to suit 99 per cent of travellers. A breakdown of such an inclusive policy would be as follows:

Medical expenses: This must surely be considered the most important of all forms of insurance —one can replace lost belongings but one cannot replace one's health or body. Over the last few years, inflation and the more general availability of expert medical attention have resulted in a large increase in the cost of medical care. The need for adequate cover is therefore essential.

At the time of writing in 1994, we would recommend an absolute minimum sum insured of £500,000, and it is quite common for a higher figure to apply, perhaps £2m. Make sure your cover is total, rather than giving specified maximum amounts for any individual section such as ambulances, hospital beds, surgery, etc. A high sum insured is of no help to you if you can only spend a limited part of it on any one aspect of your treatment.

If you are in a remote area and any form of complicated or specialist medical treatment is needed, then it is likely that you will either be repatriated, or moved to a country where suitable treatment is available. Whereas air ambulances are used regularly to bring holidaymakers back to the UK from Western European resorts at a cost of about £6000 per time, the situation can be totally different in far-flung parts of the world. An accident in Nepal, for example, might mean a short helicopter flight to a light aircraft landing strip, followed by a light aircraft flight to an international airport. Loss adjusters would then charter a section of an intercontinental jet with full medical backup facilities to bring someone all the way back to the UK.

Logistically this is the normal procedure for making arrangements promptly and as an example, the above case could involve expenditure from as little as £15,000 if it were a case of, say, a badly broken limb, needing just one medical attendant as an escort and half a dozen seats on the intercontinental jet. On the other hand, if a full medical team were needed and an entire section of a jet were necessary, the cost would escalate to some £60,000.

Nowadays, all travel insurance includes a 24–hour emergency service, but do bear in mind it can only be put into effect if you make contact with the UK, or if a hospital or embassy does so on your behalf. Whilst air evacuation from most areas following an accident or illness would be covered, do bear in mind that 'search and rescue expenses' would not be covered unless you had specified them and paid an additional premium.

Do be careful if relying on private medical insurance from the UK since it is only within the last few years that such schemes have been extended on a worldwide basis, and even then, many of the policies have gaps in cover, and expenses would almost certainly be limited as to how much can be spent in any single aspect of treatment. It is unlikely that ambulance charges, repatriation expenses, etc., would be covered, but this may be available on payment of an additional premium.

Personal accident insurance: This is normally included within a travel insurance policy, but although the sum insured for total disablement, loss of an eye or a limb is likely to be anything up to £50,000, the death benefit is often limited to £5000 or £10,000. This can be increased on payment of an additional premium for those travellers with family responsibilities who are particularly concerned.

Whilst it is reassuring to know that there is a benefit payable under the Personal Accident section of the travel insurance this is not generally considered to be that important since any person who is concerned about such matters would probably have a life policy operative on a permanent basis. It is surprising how many people worry about an accident while in another country yet do not consider the possibility that they could just as easily be involved in an accident in their normal country of residence. Unless the activities that you are going to be involved in are particularly hazardous, there is arguably no more reason to think you will have an accident overseas than at home.

Cancellation or curtailment: This covers irrecoverable deposits or payments made in advance where a journey has to be cancelled or curtailed for some good reason such as the traveller's own ill health or that of a relative or travelling companion. The sum insured obviously has to relate to the type of pre–payments that are being made —as a general rule it's about £3000. If you only have air tickets, the cancellation charges and consequently the amount that might be lost, are sometimes quite low, but look at it from the worst possible point of view. An airline may make just a 10 per cent cancellation charge if you notify them that you cannot use the seat and they consequently re-sell it, but what would happen if you were to become ill two hours before departure, and, in airline jargon, become a 'no show'? In such circumstances, the entire value of your ticket might be lost altogether. It is now possible under a few travel insurance schemes to include cancellation risks in the event of war, invasion, civil commotion etc. This could certainly be relevant in Third World countries particularly if flights and ground arrangements have been booked separately. You may find that you cannot fly, but the ground arrangements are going ahead (perhaps a trekking tour), or visa versa where the ground arrangements have been cancelled due to civil unrest, but the airline are quite happy to fly and will not give a refund.

Personal liability: This gives protection for compensation payable for injury, loss or damage to other people or their property. However, it excludes risks which should more properly be covered by a separate insurance such as Third Party motor insurance. It is included within most travel policies, the indemnity limit is normally £1m.

Strikes and delay: This section relates to industrial action, breakdown or adverse weather conditions which cause delay on the first outward or first return leg of the journey. As a rule, compensation of £25 per day is payable for a maximum of three days, but only after an initial 12-hour delay. Alternatively, on the outward journey only total abandonment claims are possible.

Baggage and personal money

Generally, a limit of £1250 is available per person, but most policies will be subject to a non-extendible limit for valuable items. The correct procedure for photographic equipment, etc., is to have it insured permanently in your place of residence on an 'all risks' basis which will normally operate throughout the world for a period of three months and sometimes longer. This limit can always be extended if necessary.

Travel insurance is meant to cover those risks which are not already insured in your home country, and if you have valuables which you have been happy not to insure at home, then you may have to continue like that while you are away.

If you are on an expedition and have supplies and scientific equipment with you, there may be difficulty in obtaining insurance cover. Do check that the insurance includes items which you might be sending in advance as freight and, for certain areas, check whether you need *Carnet de Passage* documents.

It is a condition of insurance that one acts as if uninsured. For some unknown reason, many travellers tend to adopt a careless attitude when overseas, and do things they would not think of doing at home such as leaving valuable photographic equipment on a beach while bathing, or abandoning all their worldly goods on the luggage rack of a train while going for a cup of tea. All insurers have adopted the same attitude, which is simply that if a client can't act with a reasonable degree of common sense, insurers will not deal with claims. In particular this applies to valuable items where it is now a condition that they are kept about one's person at all times. Theft from unattended motor vehicles is often excluded.

Money and documents

The personal money section of a travel insurance policy normally covers actual cash for an amount of, say, £250 but cover will also extend to include traveller's cheques, documents, etc. However, if the loss of traveller's cheques is reported in the correct manner, there is no monetary loss and it is a condition that such action is taken. Most policies will cover the additional expenses involved — perhaps telex charges to notify a bank or additional accommodation expenses incurred while waiting for replacement funds to be sent, or a new passport to be issued.

Within the money section, most insurances will also include air tickets, and whereas money cover is normally limited to £200, air tickets are insured for a much higher amount on the more specialised policies for long–haul travellers. Some airlines will provide replacement tickets without any difficulty, but there are a few that will insist on full payment being made for replacements, with a refund unavailable for as long as 18 months afterwards. It is almost unheard of for a thief to try and use an airline ticket, but a handful of carriers insist on waiting before accepting the position.

Vehicle insurance

Once outside the European area, vehicle insurance does present certain difficulties and it is certainly not possible to arrange a single comprehensive insurance policy as we know it in the UK. This is due to the varying liability or Third Party insurance legislation in different parts of the world. Vehicle insurance can be understood by the following equation: *Third Party liability plus Accident Damage, Fire and Theft = Comprehensive.*

Within the European 'Green Card' area, a single comprehensive insurance policy can be arranged —either as a one–off policy on a short–period basis, or as an extension of an existing policy. At the time of writing, the Green Card area includes all of Europe plus Morocco, Tunisia, Turkey, Iran and Iraq. However, few insurers are prepared to give cover in the more outlying parts of Europe.

Third party liability: This will need to be arranged locally at each border, which can in itself present problems. In some parts of the world, such as Algeria, insurance is nationalized and there is a reasonably efficient method of selling it to travellers. The cost is relatively low —about £30 for one month— but the cover given is also low by European standards, often as low as £10,000. In Europe liability limits are generally from £1m upwards.

Theoretically, Third Party insurance is a legal requirement in virtually every country in the world, but there are several who are totally indifferent as to whether travellers have it or not. If it is not automatically offered at the border, it is strongly recommended that you seek it out. However limited, it does at least give you some measure of protection and the cost will certainly be low by our standards.

Because of difficulties with liability claims in the USA, the legal requirements there are surprisingly low by UK standards. If you are hiring a vehicle in the States it is possible to purchase additional liability before departure from the UK, thus topping up the contract of hire insurance to a more realistic level.

Warning:
1. Cover is not readily available at some borders. In many areas it includes bodily injury claims only, which means you may have to pay the cost of damage to other people's property yourself.
2. Although liability limits are absurdly low by European standards, there is no other means of arranging this cover.
3. It is not uncommon to hear of relatively large amounts being demanded for local certificates (one can only guess whether the premium is passed on to the insurance company).

Accidental damage, fire and theft: As you will see from the equation earlier, this is the other half of a comprehensive insurance policy and simply covers damage to one's own vehicle as the result of an accident, fire or theft. It is in no way connected with liability risks and is available from Lloyd's of London on a worldwide basis. Compared with insurance premiums in the United Kingdom this cover will appear costly, since in nearly all claims underwriters have to pay out for repairs with very little chance of recovering their outlay, even if you were not at fault. Whatever the circumstances, it is surprising how many witnesses will suddenly appear to claim that the local driver was blameless and the visitor totally at fault!

This insurance is very strongly recommended on valuable vehicles. In the event of an accident occurring, contact the local Lloyd's agent. Repairs would then be completed by the most suitable repairer. In many cases, temporary repairs are carried out at the time and full repairs left until the vehicle returns home. As a general rule, repairs are authorized very quickly, since the insurers are aware of the inconvenience that any delays might cause and because the insurers are responsible for the cost, irrespective of liability in the accident. Please consider the *Carnet de Passage* implications, as mentioned below.

Carnet indemnity insurance: This is arranged in conjunction with *Carnet de Passages* documents issued by the Automobile Association and is the alternative to having to provide a large bank guarantee if you do not have the financial means to do so. Before issuing the *Carnet,* the AA will require a financial guarantee equal to the highest possible duties payable on the vehicle in the countries you intend to visit. Generally, this figure is about twice its UK value, although for India and some South American and East African countries the figure can be considerably higher. *Carnet* indemnity insurance for India is available on a selective basis due to the abnormal volume of claims originating from that area. If you are a genuine traveller with a Land Rover, motor caravan or similar vehicle, then cover can be arranged. The standard premium is calculated at 5 per cent of the indemnity figure. However, the premium is on a sliding scale and for larger amounts reduces down as low as one per cent. In addition, the AA will require a service charge of about £60 and refundable deposit of £250. Similar facilities are available from the RAC, but the AA do arrange the bulk of *carnets* issued. It is important that you understand the serious implications if the *carnet* documentation is not discharged by the local authorities when you leave the country, or in the unlikely event that the vehicle is totally destroyed by fire or accident, or stolen. A subsequent claim, sometimes a year or two later, could be made against you unless you have the documentation discharged correctly.

Life assurance

As a general rule, life assurance cover is not taken out specifically for overseas travel, since most people who have family responsibilities will already have a policy in force. Life assurance policies are not normally subject to exclusions but if your journey is of a hazardous nature, it would be as well to give written details to the life office concerned and ask for their written confirmation that they accept the position. They may impose an additional premium just for the period you are away but the amount involved is generally quite low and it is worth the peace of mind that it gives to know that your cover is fully operative.

Arranging insurance and claims

As I've said before, I would recommend the advice of an experienced, professional insurance broker for anything other than the totally standard European holiday. Be sure to outline your proposed activities, and if you are buying a standard policy, ask for written confirmation that it is suitable for your needs.

If you are booking through one of the specialist agencies that deals with overland or long–haul travel, they will almost certainly have a tailor-made policy available. A normal High Street agency clerk, however, may have little knowledge of the type of insurance you are looking for.

As far as vehicle insurance is concerned, a proposal form will need to be completed and you must disclose all material facts relating to both your own driving experience and that of any other person who might be driving the vehicle. It is much better to spend some time giving all the information about yourself and your requirements to the insurer than finding, after an accident, that there is a gap in the cover.

Pre–existing medical conditions are not normally excluded from travel insurance nowadays, there is simply a warranty that if you are already receiving treatment, you must be travelling with the approval of your GP —bearing in mind the duration and type of journey. In addition, if you are receiving on–going medication, then you must make arrangements at your own expense to replenish supplies or take sufficient with you. It is only in the event of the condition suddenly becoming worse that underwriters would need to be involved and accept responsibility for costs.

As far as claims are concerned, do be patient. Contrary to popular belief, insurers do like paying claims. However, they do require certain information and if it is not available, there will be inevitable delays in dealing with paperwork. Any expenditure will need to be supported by a written statement from the local police authorities, airline or government agency.

If possible, claims should be left until you return home. Under no circumstances should you send original documentation by post from overseas, since it can easily go astray. Unless you have incurred large expenditure for which you require reimbursement while you are still away, it is much better to leave things until you return when you can collate everything and present your claim in a concise manner. Most claims can be dealt with in about two weeks, but if you happen to lose a valuable item, don't be surprised if the insurers insist on seeing a receipt, valuation or some other documentation relating to the original purchase.

Most claims will be subject to an excess (normally £35 for personal claims) and is imposed by insurers simply because the cost of dealing with small claims can sometimes be more than the value of the claim itself. Vehicle insurance claims will generally be subject to a much higher excess, probably £250, which is imposed in order to keep the premiums to a reasonable level and to cut out claims for the inevitable minor scratches or dents that will occur on any long journey.

VISAS

by Ralph Whitmarsh

The subject of visas is an everchanging scene. Not only are the rules and regulations frequently being revised, but the way the Embassies and High Commissions impart the information to the public and process the visa applications is constantly being altered. And often, not to the benefit of the traveller.

Such is the world today that there is a steady drift of people trying to leave their country and rebuild their lives elsewhere, either due to wars, famine or persecution. This is putting an increasing strain on the immigration policies of various governments, and the regulations dictating whether you may enter a country visa-free are always being reviewed. Whilst the situation for UK passport holders is reasonably static, there are many other nationalities resident in the UK who no doubt may read these pages, and who may be subject to a different set of rules.

The ever increasing desire to travel and the spontaneity with which travel can be organised has little impact on the authorities who issue passports and the required visas. Some countries have closed their UK provincial consulates, thus putting an additional strain on the hard pressed London-based staff, guaranteeing long queues especially at peak travel times of the year. The Spanish, however, insist that you apply to the consulate closest to your place of residence. This all adds up to the fact that whilst you can virtually arrange a round-the-world itinerary in a matter of minutes, if your documents are not in order, you cannot travel. So some thought has to be given to the matter of your passport and the possible need to obtain visas for the countries you wish to visit.

Efficiency and bureaucracy

The cost to a Government of maintaining an Embassy or High Commission overseas is enormous, and most, if not all, are conscious of the need to reduce costs, or raise extra revenue. Some have introduced premium rate telephone lines for the public to use when wishing to make an enquiry; others have installed an automated switchboard, which is fine if you know the extension number you want. You may have to listen to a long message before reaching the information you are seeking; sometimes your question may not be answered at all. These means of imparting information to the caller enable the Embassy or High Commission to reduce the number of staff (or hopefully redeploy them to issue visas), and raise revenue from the premium rate telephone line.

It is necessary to do your research regarding visas early in your travel planning process, for, according to where you are going, your reasons for visiting a country, and your nationality, the issuing time can vary from a matter of hours to weeks. The reader must appreciate the role of the Embassy of High Commission and the staff working there. You are very much in their hands as to whether a visa is granted or not, and any Consular Official has the authority to reject an application if he or she thinks fit. If a rejection takes place, it may only require an extra supporting document such as a bank statement to resolve the matter. Beware though, the Americans and Indians actually endorse the passport when an application is rejected whereupon a fresh application needs to be submitted, the paperwork for which has to persuade the Embassy to reverse their previous decision.

Understanding

It is necessary to appreciate that when entering an Embassy you are entering the territory of another country, and frustrating though it may be after you have spent much time in the queue, you need to be polite and tolerant with the Consular Official who, after all, is only carrying out the checks and procedures imposed by his Government. You may need to remind yourself that British Embassies abroad may be just as daunting a place to other nationals. The opening hours are limited to enable the staff to issue the visas once the public have left the promises, but for those people residing some distance from London accessibility is difficult and can be costly if you have to stay overnight in London. Postal applications are treated as non urgent by the Authorities and your envelope may remain in the mail bag for some weeks before it is opened and dealt with by the Embassy or High Commission. It is unrealistic to expect them to spend time searching for your application amongst hundreds of others.

In addition one has to be aware of the public holidays recognised by these Authorities. Not only do they close on UK public holidays but on their own as well. This obviously disrupts the issuing process and after a few days of closure, the sudden demand can be very high. Be aware of the holy month of Ramadan when appropriate Embassies change their hours of business and at the end of this period they close altogether. Be aware also of the Chinese New Year dates and other important religious festivals.

Your passport

Obviously before you can leave these shores you require a 10-year passport. The MRP (machine readable passport) is available in two versions, one costing £18, and the other, with additional pages costing £27 at the time of writing. Many countries require a minimum of six months' validity remaining on the passport when you either enter or leave their territory, so first of all check your passport's date of expiry. Make sure the passport has one blank page for each visa required, as well as sufficient space for entry and exit stamps. Some Embassies will only issue a visa on a right-hand page.

Ensure your passport is signed. Again, many authorities, the Indian High Commission among them, will not grant a visa on an unsigned passport. Some Embassies grant visas, the validity of which exceeds the validity of the passport, but others restrict the visa validity to coincide with the passport expiry date.

Take great care of your passport not only when you are travelling, but also in between journeys. Keep it secure, as a UK passport can command a price of many hundreds of pounds on the black market.

Visa requirements

There is much to consider here. Business or tourism? How many entries and for how long? The United States have over 20 different categories of visas reflecting different reasons for travel - but only one application form. The Saudis have four different forms covering varying reasons for travel. Non UK-passport holders may find their application referred with a delay of about four weeks if they are not a permanent resident of the UK.

Most visas are valid from the date of issue, frequently for three months. Some, for example, Russia, are valid from the date you enter the country. In this example the entry and exit dates are clearly stated on the visa and you cannot enter Russia before, or leave after the date quoted. It is therefore necessary to plan when to apply for a visa to avoid a situation where it expires before you even arrive in the country. Other countries issue visas which may be valid for twelve months and allow multiple entries with no restrictions.

You will need to make allowances in your financial calculations for the purchase of the visas you require. The majority cost under £25, but some are granted free of charge. There are some for which you will have to pay considerably more, particularly if your reason for travel is business. The price may also vary according to your nationality and the costs are agreed between Governments. To these costs must be added the charges incurred in actually getting the paperwork to the Embassy —are you going to employ the services of an agent who specialises in visa procurement, or are you going to spend a lot of your time making trips to the Embassies and waiting in queues?

Some countries, for example, Rwanda, Burundi, Mali and Mauritania have no representation in London.Their nearest Embassy is in Paris and this fact can only add to the cost and logistics of acquiring the visa.

Many nationals have for a few years now been able to travel to the United States for a maximum of 90 days without a visa, providing they meet the criteria set down on the 'waiver' form. However, if you have incurred a conviction you must declare this and apply for a visa. The Australian Working Holiday visa for those under 26 years of age is valid for thirteen months and is an attractive proposition, as a period of holiday can be combined with work in order to help finance additional travel.

Beware of an Israeli stamp in your passport should you wish to visit the Arab countries in the Gulf area. Ask the Israeli entry and exit controls to stamp a loose leaf document. A South African stamp in the passport is not the problem it used to be, as South Africa is gaining acceptability in the world.

Ready to go?

Check your visa for accuracy and to ensure it covers you for your plans. Mistakes are frequently made due to the pressure of work loads in Embassies and even the computer-issued visas are only as accurate as those who input the data. If taking family members who are on your passport —husband or wife or children under 16 —ensure that the visa issued covers them as well, or that a separate one has been issued. Some visa applications forms, for example, India, Australia, and Egypt include space for all those included on the one passport, but some other countries require one form to be completed per person. Remember that children who have reached 16 years of age require their own passport.

Visa trends

In recent years we have witnessed the breakup of the USSR; the Iron Curtain has come down; Czechoslovakia has become two separate countries,and Yugoslavia has fragmentated into pieces. In South America, Argentina and Brazil do not require a visa from UK nationals, but tourists to Venezuela will require a tourist card obtainable from the airline on which you are arriving in the country (check this when booking your seat).

Although the Commonwealth of Independent States (USSR) has become more accessible, the documents required for a visa has changed little, viz, either an invitation from the company being visited, if travelling on business, or confirmation of your accommodation if travelling as a tourist. Poland, Hungary, Czech and Slovak Republics no longer require a visa from UK passport holders, but visitors to Bulgaria and Romania still need a visa. Those requiring a German visa must show the Embassy proof of medical insurance cover: an E111 from the Post Office, if you are a UK resident and registered under the National Health Service, is sufficient.

The requirements for entering France and Spain on a non-UK passport are complicated, and surprisingly Australian passport holders require a visa for both countries, although they are issued free of charge if married to an EEC passport holder and the partner's passport is produced for the Embassy together with the original marriage certificate.

India is an ever-popular destination and the High Commission offer a tourist visa valid for a 30 day stay providing you arrive in India within 30 days of the issue date of the visa. At £3 it is excellent value, but do not apply by post as you will probably not receive your passport back in time. Taiwan has relaxed visa requirements for periods of stay up to 14 days depending on nationality. Whilst still in the Far East, UK nationals can stay in Thailand for fifteen days as a tourist providing you are in possession of air tickets with confirmed bookings in and out of the country. A two-month stay is allowed in Indonesia visa-free, provided entry and exit is made through designated air and sea ports. Residing with friends and relatives during the visit is not allowed and not all nationals are permitted this 60 day stay visa-free. China require to see a visa for all visitors, as do

Vietnam and Myanmar (Burma), which are now being visited in greater numbers.

Finally, even though you have got all your visas, an immigration official has the power to deny you entry to his or her country if they so wish, and they are not obliged to state their reasons. The United States is perhaps the most formidable in this respect so it is always sensible to have an onward or return ticket with you, altogether with proof of sufficient funds to support yourself, and additional evidence that you have good reason to return to your country of residence from the USA.

PERMITS, REGISTRATIONS AND RESTRICTED AREAS

by Jack Jackson

Travel in the Third World used to be easy for Westerners, with few restrictions and little in the way of police checks, paperwork or permissions, to hold travellers back. Europe, in those days, offered more barriers to travellers, with frequent customs and police enquiries.

Nowadays, the position is reversed. In most Third World countries the hindrances to free travel grow yearly, in number and variety. Ambiguous taxes are demanded at borders and airports. The legality of these may be questionable, but the man behind the desk is all–powerful so the traveller does not have any choice. Many countries where monetary systems are unstable and which therefore have flourishing black markets, now require travellers to complete a currency declaration on entry, detailing all monies, jewellery, cameras, tape recorders, etc. This is checked on departure against bank receipts for any money changed. Some countries, eg. Algeria, are very thorough in their searches of departing travellers.

With groups, border officials naturally try to cut down massive form filling, by completing just one form for the group leader. This can make life very difficult later, if one person in a group wishes to change money at a bank, or wishes to leave the group, but does not have their own individual form and cannot immediately produce the group form, of the leader to vouch for him. Individual forms should always be obtained if possible.

Deliberate delays

Some countries purposely delay the issue of permits in capital cities, so that travellers will spend more money there. As most travellers are limited for time, a straightforward Tourist Tax would be more acceptable.

Registration

In many places the law requires that you register with the police within twenty four hours of arrival. Often a fee is charged for this. Usually, if you are staying at a hotel, the registration is done for you by the hotel and the costs are included in your room charges; but if you are in a very small hotel, camping or staying with friends, you will either have to do it yourself, or pay someone to do it for you. As this often entails fighting through a queue of several hundred local people, at the

Immigration Office, with the chance that you have picked the wrong queue anyway— *baksheesh* for a hotel employee to do it for you is a good investment.

Most of these countries also require that you register with the police in each town in which you stop. In some cases eg. South Sudan, you may even have to report to the police in every town or village through which you pass. In smaller places the registration is usually much easier.

Permission from central government may be necessary to travel outside major cities. Usually, for this permission you go to the Ministry of the Interior, but if a Tourist Office exists, it is wise to check there first. Any expedition or trekking party will have to do this anyway. This system is not always just 'red tape', if there is local strife it may be for traveller's safety.

Restricted areas

Most countries have restricted or forbidden areas somewhere. Much of Africa and Asia has large areas of desert or semi–desert. Restrictions on travel in these areas are formulated by the government for travellers' safety and take account of such obvious things as ensuring travellers have good strong vehicles, are carrying plenty of water and fuel and are spending the nights in safe places.

Unfortunately, officials in these out–of–the–way places tend to be the bad boys of their profession. Forced to live in inhospitable places, they are usually very bored and often turn to drink and drugs. When a party of Westerners suddenly turns up, they see this as a chance to show their power, get their own back for the old colonial injustices, hold the travellers up for a day or more, charge them *baksheesh*, turn on a tape recorder and insist on a dance with each of the girls and suggest they go to bed with them. If there is a hotel locally, they may hold them up overnight so as to exact a percentage from the hotel keeper. Unfortunately, your permit from the central government means nothing here. These people are a law unto themselves. Some have been known to insist visas from nationals of a country who do not require one. This often requires that you go back to the nearest capital city, where incredulous officials may, or may not, be able to sort things out. The police in Djanet (Algerian Sahara), really have it tied up. You can not get fuel to leave, without their permission and to get that you have to spend a lot of money with the local tourist organisation and hotel as well as fork out *baksheesh* to the police themselves.

Local officials also have a habit of taking your government permit from you and then 'losing' it. This makes life difficult both there, and with local officials later on, in other areas. It is best to carry ten or more photocopies of the original government permission (photocopying machines are always available in capital cities) and never hand over the original. Let officials see the original if necessary, but always give them a photocopy instead.

If you are travelling as a group, most officials and most hotels will want a group list from you. Carry a dozen or more copies of a group list made up of names, passport numbers, dates of issue of passports, dates of expiry of passports, dates of issue of visas, numbers of visas and occupations.

Fortunately new passports no longer quote occupations; but where these are asked for, never mention: photographer, journalist, writer or member of the armed forces, unless you are travelling in such a capacity officially.

Photographic permits

Some countries, eg Sudan, Mali and Cameroon, require that you obtain a photographic permit. These are usually only available in the capital, so overland travellers will have problems, until they can get to the capital and obtain one.

As with currency declarations, officials obviously like to save work by giving one permit per group; but it is best to have one per person. I have known several instances where big–headed students have made 'citizens' arrests' of travellers taking photographs, who then had to spend a couple of hours at the police station waiting for their group leader with the photo permit to be located! Possession of a photo permit does not necessarily mean that you can take photos. It is usually best to enquire with the local police first. In some areas where photography is forbidden, local guides may goad you on, to take photographs. Beware of the situation, they are likely to blackmail you for money or other gifts, afterwards.

In theory, you should be able to find out about documents and permit requirements, from the consulate in your country of origin, but in the Third World countries this can never be relied on, as local officials make their own rules. Information from source books such as this one and recent travellers are your best guide.

Before issuing visas, most countries will require at least two clear pages left in your passport and the passport to be valid for at least 6 months after your date of entry into the country concerned. Some countries will also require proof that you have suitable funds available and return or onward ticket. You may also require a letter of introduction from your won government, or a sponsor if on business or working. If you are travelling overland or on an extended continuous journey, visas for later destinations may become out of date before you reach those destinations. So enquire whether or not you can get such visas, whilst en route.

Some Third World countries may hold your passport for 6 weeks or more, whilst searching their archives, before issuing a visa. If you have to travel somewhere else during this period, UK citizens can obtain a temporary second passport. *Never* carry both passports on the same journey!

Many countries will not issue visas to anyone whose passport contains Israeli or South African stamps. If you visit either of these countries, ask them not to stamp your passport. If your passport does contain any of these stamps, get a new passport as soon as possible. Business passports with their larger number of pages, can cause problems in the Third World. If you have had many visas for the same country, local immigration officers may start questioning you as to why you keep coming. For the Third World the standard size passport is preferable and the new type EC passport is smaller and more convenient to carry under clothing, for safety.

Do as much as you can before you leave home. Carry plenty of passport–sized photographs and be prepared for delays, harassment, palms held out and large doses of the unexpected.

DOCUMENTATION FOR THE INTERNATIONAL MOTORIST

by Colin McElduff

The following advice is directed principally towards motorists from the UK and should be used as a general guide only, as each and every case produces its own requirements dependent on the countries concerned and the circumstances and regulations prevailing at the time.

As many travellers neglect documentation —some of which should be obtained well in advance of departure— list all that is known to be relevant to your trip and make enquiries as to the remainder. I have included only those documents specifically related to vehicles. Details on personal documentation are to be found elsewhere in this book. For most overland trips you will need the following:

1. Driving Licence
2. Insurance —Third Party and/or:
3. International Motor Insurance Certificate (Green Card)
4. International Registration Distinguishing Sign (GB, etc)
5. Vehicle Registration Certificate. Depending on your country of departure and those through which you will be travelling, you may additionally need your birth certificate, extra passport photographs and:
6. Bail Bond
7. *Carnet* ATA
8. *Carnet Camping*
9. *Carnet de Passages en Douane*
10. Letter of Authority to use borrowed, hired or leased vehicle
11. VE103—Hired/Leased Vehicle Certificate
12. International Certificate for Motor Vehicles
13. International Driving Permit (IDP)
14. Motoring Organization Membership Card
15. Petrol Coupons

Driving licence

Most countries will allow you to drive for six months on your national driving licence. After this you must have an IDP or take a local test. In Italy a translation of the visitor's National Driving Licence is required if the National Licence is the older UK all green colour licence. This may be obtained from motoring organizations. Motorists in possession of an IDP do not require a translation. It is probably also useful to have a translation if travelling in Arab countries. In some countries car-hire companies require an IDP to be produced.

Third Party Insurance

This is essential to cover claims relating to death of or bodily injury to third parties as a result of the vehicle's use. When travelling in countries outside the scope of the 'Green Card' – which is generally outside Europe – Third Party insurance should be taken out at the first opportunity on entering the country.

International Motor Insurance Certificate (Green Card)

Whilst a Green Card is technically no longer necessary in EEC countries, it is extremely unwise to visit these countries without it as it remains readily acceptable as evidence of insurance to enable a driver to benefit from international claim–handling facilities. In any case, a Green Card is required in all European countries outside the EEC. It should be obtained from the insurance company that is currently insuring your vehicle.

International registration distinguishing sign

This sign is mandatory and should be of the country in which your vehicle is registered, thus identifying your registration plates.

Vehicle Registration Certificate

This is an essential document to take. However, further proof of ownership or authority to use the vehicle may sometimes be required.

Bail bond

For visitors to Spain, it was always a wise precaution to obtain a Spanish Bail Bond from the vehicle insurers since the driver involved in an accident could have been required to lodge a deposit with the local Spanish Court and failure to meet that demand could result in imprisonment for the driver and detention of the vehicle until funds became available. Now that Spain is in the EEC, this requirement is no longer technically applicable, but many insurers will still issue a Bail Bond at nil cost for anybody who wants to play doubly safe.

Carnet ATA

This is a customs document valid for 12 months which facilitates the entry without payment of customs duties, etc on professional equipment, goods for internal exhibition and commercial samples, temporarily imported into certain countries —a list of which may be obtained from the London Chamber of Commerce and Industry (69 Cannon Street, London EC4, tel: 071–248 4444) or through one of their many offices throughout the UK.

Carnet Camping

An international document jointly produced by the three international organizations dealing with camping and caravanning —the Fédération Internationale de l'Automobile, the Fédération Internationale de Camping et Caravanning and the Alliance Internationale de Tourisme. It serves as an identity document and facilitates entry to sites under the wing of these organizations —sometimes at reduced rates. In addition, the document provides personal accident cover up to a specified sum for those names on it. You should approach a motoring organization for this document.

Carnet de passages en douane

This is an internationally recognized customs document. If acceptable to a country, it will entitle the holder to import temporarily a vehicle, caravan, trailer, boat, etc, without the need to deposit the appropriate customs duties and taxes. The issuing authority of the *carnet* is made directly responsible for the payment of customs duties and taxes if the *carnet* is not discharged correctly, ie if the owner violates another country's customs regulations by selling the vehicle illegally. Consequently, any substantial payment will be recovered from the *carnet* holder under the terms of the signed issuing agreement.

Motoring organizations are issuing authorities and will provide issue documents upon receipt of a bank guarantee, cash deposit or an insurance indemnity from an agreed firm of brokers to cover any liability. The sum required is determined by the motoring organization, taking into consideration the countries the vehicle will enter (destinations are declared when the application for the *carnet* is made).

Normally the amount of the bond required as security is related to the maximum import duty on motor vehicles required in the countries to be visited, which can be as high as 400 per cent of the UK value of the vehicle.

In the case of a bank guarantee, you need to have collateral with the issuing bank or funds sufficient to cover the amount required to be guaranteed. These funds cannot be withdrawn until the bank's guarantee is surrendered by the motoring organization. This is done when the *carnet* is returned correctly discharged. The procedure is for the bank manager to provide a letter of indemnity to the motoring organization, normally the motoring organization's specially printed documents.

If you have insufficient funds or security to cover the bond, you may pay an insurance premium (the AA and the RAC have their own nominated insurance companies with which they have carnet indemnity agreements) and the company will act as guarantor. There are certain points to watch, however. The car must usually be registered in the country where the *carnet* is issued. In some cases (at the discretion of the issuing club or association) being a citizen of the country where the *carnet* is issued as an alternative —even though the car has been registered elsewhere. In all cases, membership of the issuing club is a requirement.

A *carnet* is required for most long transcontinental journeys and should be obtained regardless of the fact that some of the countries on the itinerary do not require it. To be without one where it *is* required usually means being turned back if you have insufficient funds to cover the customs deposit for entry.

A *carnet de passages en douane* is valid for 12 months from the date of issue and may be extended beyond the expiry date by applying to the motoring organization in the country you are visiting at the point of expiry. The name of the motoring organization is shown in the front cover of the *carnet*. An extension should be noted on every page and not just inside the cover in order to avoid difficulties at border checks. When a new *carnet* is required, the application must be made to the original issuing authority. *Carnets* are issued with five, 11 or 25 pages, depending on the number of countries to be visited, and a nominal fee is charged accordingly to cover administration. Each page contains an entry voucher (*volet d'entrée*), exit voucher (*volet de sortie*) and a counterfoil (*souche*). When the vehicle, etc leaves the country, the customs officer endorses the exit part of the counterfoil and detaches the appropriate exit voucher, thus discharging the *carnet*. If you have not taken care to have this done, the validity of the *carnet* may be suspended until this is rectified.

Certificate of Authority for borrowed or hired vehicle

This is required when a vehicle is borrowed or hired and should bear the signature of the owner. This must be the same as on the Registration Certificate which must also be taken. A motoring organization will provide a 'Vehicle on Hire/Loan' certificate, VE103.

International certification for motor vehicles

In countries where the British Vehicle Registration Certificate is not accepted, this document is required and is issued by a motoring organization.

International Driving Permit

An IDP is required by the driver of a vehicle in countries that do not accept the national driving licence of the visiting motorist. It is issued on request by motoring organizations for a small fee and is valid for 12 months from the date of issue. An IDP can only be issued in the country of the applicant's national driving licence.

Motoring organization membership card

Most countries have a motoring organization which is a member of the Alliance Internationale de Tourisme (AIT) or the Federation Internationale de l'Automobile (FIA) and provides certain reciprocal membership privileges to members of other motoring organizations.

Petrol coupons

These are issued to visiting motorists in some countries either to promote tourism or where there are restrictions on the residents' use of petrol. Motoring organizations can advise which countries issue petrol coupons.

MONEY PROBLEMS —THE ILLEGAL SIDE

by Jack Jackson

Fifteen years ago it used to be common for dealers on black markets in Third World countries, to offer money at three or more times the official rate. Nowadays however, most such countries have black-market rates of only 10-20 per cent higher than the normal rate. Buyers should always weigh up the risk before dealing, remembering that in black-market operation the traveller, just as easily as the dealer, can end up in prison.

In countries recently ravaged by war or *coup d'etat*, black markets usually continue to thrive at good rates.

Dollar mania

Black markets usually operate best in ports; where money can be easily smuggled out and goods back in.Where, with the help of *baksheesh* to customs officers, nobody in government pay needs to know, or admit to knowing. However, a new quasi–black market is operated by expatriate technicians working in oil fields or on international aid or construction programmes. These people are usually paid part of their salary in local currency, which is more than they need to live on. Such people are usually keen to get rid of some of it in exchange for US dollars, at a good rate to the buyer. In much of Islamic Africa and the poorer Middle Eastern countries, you will also find Egyptian, Syrian, or Palestinian teachers, employed in smaller villages, who are very keen to convert their local salary into US dollars.

Another method of dealing, common in countries where businessmen do not feel safe and cannot get their money out legally, is for a businessman or hotel owners to 'lend' you funds locally which you repay in hard currency into a relative's bank account in the West. Those who travel regularly often arrange this in advance before leaving; but local businessmen will often take a risk on unfamiliar travellers, if they are reasonably dressed and staying in recognized (though smaller) hotels, because their own local currency is worthless to them.

Even in large, top quality hotels, cashiers will often take payment in hard currency at near black-market rates, if the customer pays them outside the manager's normal working hours.

Travellers should particularly avoid street dealings, as they are more likely to be short changed, given bad notes, or robbed.

On–the–spot black-market deals nowadays, are always for cash and mostly for US dollars. A few countries with strong links and trade with the UK or Germany will trade in pounds sterling or deutschmarks, but other currencies, even strong ones such as the Swiss franc of Dutch guilder, will find few black market buyers. Deutschmarks go down well in Turkey, pounds sterling in Pakistan, India, and Nepal but elsewhere, the US dollar is the prime requirement.

Normally, larger denomination notes fetch a higher rate, as they are easier to smuggle out. Avoid the older $100 bills which do not have 'In God We Trust' written on them: even though they may not be forgeries, most dealers will not touch them. Also avoid English £50 notes which may be unknown to smaller dealers.

There is no longer any problem attached to taking money out of the UK, so it is best to buy dollars there before you leave. The old tricks with sterling travellers' cheques are no longer required!

Declaration forms

Many countries with black market problems insist on a declaration of all money and valuables on entry, and then check this against bank receipts on exit. Remember that you may be searched, both on entry and exit and any excess funds will be confiscated.

If you want to take in some undeclared money to use on the black market, you should understand the risks. Obviously you must change a reasonable amount of money legally at a bank and keep receipts, so that you will be able to explain what you have lived on during your stay. You will also need these receipts if you are going to try and change local currency back into hard currency when you leave. It is usually inadvisable to try, since most countries make it very difficult for you to do this, despite their literature claiming that you can.

The local officials —who probably don't read the literature— like to remove your excess local money and keep it for themselves. The bank clerk who tells you he cannot change your money is often in on the act. He informs custom officials how much money you have and they, acting on his tip–off, search you as you leave. On the plus side, allowing customs or money declaration officials to remove a reasonable amount of money from you at the point of departure, may minimize further red tape.

Currency declaration forms are taken very seriously in some countries eg. Algeria and you must have an explanation for any discrepancy. Make sure that the amount written, agrees with the amount in figures. If any money which is entered on your form is stolen, get a letter giving details, from the police or you may have trouble when you come to leave the country.

Some countries, eg. Sudan, and Yemen, get around some of the black market by making you pay for hotels in hard currency, at the local business rate, which is often lower than the official tourist rate and much lower than the black-market rate. In such hotels you can usually get away with paying for meals with black-market cash, so long as you pay for it at the time. If you sign a restaurant bill to be paid for later, then you will be charged in hard currency. Corrupt hotel staff may refuse to accept cash payment in the restaurant, in which case you will be better off taking your custom to restaurants outside the hotel.

International airline tickets will always be charged for in hard currency plus a premium ordered by IATA, to cover currency fluctuations. Hence, such tickets are much cheaper in Europe. Internal air tickets can usually be bought with black money but you may have to pay a local ticketing agent to do it in his name.

Beware of black market currency quotations by normally acceptable press, such as up-market Sunday papers, *Newsweek* and the BBC. These quote from local correspondents who have to be careful of what they say for fear of deportation.

Street trading

Black market dealers are usually found where budget travellers are most likely to be —in smaller hotels, bars, shops selling tourist items; in very small towns, try the pharmacy.

In the main streets of a city of port, street traders will chase you and, assuming you don't know the correct rate, will start with a very low rate. It is usually worth bargaining to see how high you can go —and then approach safer places such as small hotels to check the real rate. Street trading is very risky. You should never show that you have a lot of money, as there is a high chance that you will be short–changed, have money stolen from the bundle by sleight of hand, see all your money grabbed and run off with, or meet one of those dealers who has a crooked, profit–sharing partnership with the police.

In general, show only the amount of money you want to exchange and keep all other money out of sight, beneath your clothes.

Refuse any approaches to buy your passport or traveller's cheques. This kind of trading is becoming so common, that embassies delay issuing fresh passports to travellers who, may or may not, have genuinely lost their own. Getting traveller's cheques replaced in the Third World can take months, as can funds wired to banks or American Express offices. Never rely on receiving hard currency transferred in this way, you are likely to be forced to accept local currency.

Black-market rates fluctuate with both inflation and availability. Rates will increase dramatically in the Islamic world when the time for the annual pilgrimage to Mecca (the Haj) approaches, and decreases rapidly when the pilgrims return, or when a lot of 'up-market' travellers are in town, or a cruise ship or fleet ship is in port. Dealing out of season usually commands a better rate.

Central London banks often carry an excess of Arab currency and one of their branches may be happy to off load a weak currency at a good rate. It is always worth checking whether this is so, before you buy; but remember that the bank notes may no longer be legal currency. Wherever you are, always check that you have not been short–changed. Bank cashiers try this regularly in the Third World.

Many people end up changing money on the black market, just because it can take up to two hours to go through legal channels, in some countries. Currently it is difficult to know which way the black markets of eastern European states and the Commonwealth of Independent States, are heading. Before the fall of the iron curtain, they were amongst the strictest regulators, due to having worthless currencies. Now, some of these states have burgeoning economies, but others are returning to their old ways. Many of them are technically bankrupt, have rampant inflation, pay their employees with unredeemable money and are changing their currencies. So you must be careful not to be given out-of-date banknotes. On a recent visit to Uzbekistan, when I legally changed US$4, I was given a wad of newly-printed 'monopoly money' four inches thick.

The best way to travel in countries like this, or those with high rates of inflation, is to carry a large number of small denomination UDS dollar bills, change a little at a time as you go along and where possible, pay for everything in US dollars, so that you do not collect worthless change. UK banks do not like holding US$1 bills, so give them plenty of warning when ordering currency.

Begging

Begging is probably the world's second oldest profession. In the Muslim and Hindu world, giving a percentage of one's income to the poor, is considered a legal form of paying tax. However, with the increase of mass, up-market tourism, begging is becoming an increasingly popular way of making a living —not only among the obviously poor people of the Third World but also among Western hippies and some better dressed, professional confidence tricksters, who claim to be refugees. This form of begging is now common on the London Underground

In some countries, beggars are very persistent, knowing full well that wearing you down produces results. Mere persistence may not be too hard for you to repel, but worst of all are the young children (often blind or with deformed limbs) who are guaranteed to arouse your pity. What you may not realize however, is that the child may have been intentionally deformed or blinded by its parent or 'master' in order to make a successful beggar. The child is almost certainly encouraged by the family or ringleader, to beg and may be their chief source of income, since the child beggar can perhaps earn more in a day, than his father working in the fields or factory. Remember that a child who is out begging is necessarily missing school. An adult with no education or experience, other than begging, tends to be less successful than a child beggar . What are their options? Crime, if they are fit, destitution if crippled. Begging is obviously easier than work, but to give money is to contribute to a vicious circle. By withholding money you may help to eradicate these appaling practices.

MONEY PROBLEMS —THE LEGAL SIDE

by Harry Stevens and Melissa Shales

I belong to that generation whose first real experience of foreign travel was courtesy of HMG —when European towns were teeming with black marketeers trying to prove to every young serviceman that 200 British cigarettes were really worth 200 or even 300DM. Traveller's cheques and banks hardly existed and credit cards, like ballpoint pens, had not yet been invented. Consequently, my trust in ready cash as the essential ingredient for trouble–free travelling is no doubt due to this early conditioning.

Cash is, of course, intrinsically less safe to carry than traveller's cheques, especially when these are fully refundable when lost (this is not always the case, particularly if a 'finder' has cashed them in before the loss has been reported.

Nowadays, I carry all three: traveller's cheques, credit cards, and cash; but only a slim book of traveller's cheques, which I hold in reserve in case I do run out of cash —and for use in countries which do not allow you to bring in banknotes of their own currency. If travelling in Europe, it is also worth applying for a Eurocheque book and card which allows you to write cheques on the continent as you would at home. This could mean that you don't have to go to the trouble of getting foreign exchange before departure —particularly convenient for short trips. However, the cash I carry always includes a few low denomination dollar bills useful for 'emergency' tips, or taxi fares in almost any country.

Small change

There are a number of cogent reasons for equipping yourself with the currency of the country you are about to visit before you get there:

1. Even on the 'plane you may find you can make agreeable savings by paying in some currency other than sterling.

2. Immediately on arrival it may be difficult, or even impossible, to change your money and in any case, you may be doubtful as to whether you are being offered a good rate of exchange.

3. Yes, the immediate problem of tipping a porter, making a 'phone call and paying for a taxi or airport bus must be solved long before reaching your hotel. And when you do eventually get there, this does not necessarily solve your problem as not all hotels exchange traveller's cheques for cash (and not necessarily at any time of day or night) and if they do, the vexed question of the rate of exchange arises once more.

Many countries do not allow unrestricted import or export of their currency —and in a number of countries for 'unrestricted' read 'nil'!— so one has to exchange traveller's cheques or hard cash on arrival (there is usually a small exchange rate advantage in favour of the cheques). In addition, if you plan to visit several countries, it is usually best not to keep bank notes of a currency no longer required on that journey (although I do hold on to small change and some low denomination notes, if there is a likelihood of a next time). Every such exchange results in a loss but the sums involved are usually not large and one can console oneself with the thought that the next taxi ride will help to recoup it. Remember to keep a record of all financial transactions, particularly in sensitive countries, as you may well be asked to account for everything before you are allowed to leave.

Nest eggs

If you are planning to be away for a long time, and possibly travel through many countries, there is one other way to ensure that you don't have to carry too much with you and risk losing it all in some remote village. Before you leave home, set up a number of accounts along the way through banks affiliated to your own and arrange for money to be wired over to you at regular intervals. Ask the foreign section of your bank to advise you on the best way of doing this.

It is a simple–sounding operation, but as with most aspects of travel, reality is infinitely more complex, each transaction taking weeks longer than claimed and your money being misplaced en route or misfiled on arrival. The bureaucracy alone could make the whole exercise too difficult to be worthwhile, never mind the fact that you are having to place an immense amount of trust in bank staff who may be corrupt. It is probably not worthwhile unless you are planning to spend some considerable time in the country. Whatever you decide to do, don't rely on having money waiting for you —keep an emergency fund for survival while you are trying to wring your money out of them.

Even if you haven't set up accounts along the way, ask your bank for a list of affiliated banks in the countries you will be visiting. In an emergency, you can be asked for money to be wired out from home to any bank, but if you can choose one that is already in contact, it should make life considerably easier. Always ask for a separate letter, telex or fax confirming that the money has been sent and specify that it should be sent to SWIFT (express).

Be careful not to wire more money than you will need into countries with tight export restrictions. No one will mind the sterling coming in, but they may well object to leaving again, and if not careful you could find yourself with a nest egg gathering dust in a country you are never likely to visit again. ■

A PLACE TO STAY
Chapter 10

CHOOSING THE RIGHT HOTEL

by Susan Grossman

In the old days a bed for the night used to be all a traveller would expect when he booked into a hostelry. These days most would be horrified if they weren't also offered a mini bar and satellite TV, let alone somewhere to park the car and a restaurant serving decent food. Of course, hotels vary the world over and most travellers know exactly what they want and shop around until they find it.

City hotels

Not surprisingly, city hotels are often different from those in rural areas and holiday resorts. Given the choice, most people generally want their hotel to be within walking distance of the main sites. Since cities are noisy places, they also usually want a quiet room or at least one that is double glazed. If you haven't booked, most European cities have a tourist office that will help locate hotels with a vacancy.

Some will make a booking for you and there is usually an office in the main railway station or at the airport, though it is best to get the address from the national tourist board in London before you set off, and have enough local currency on you to pay for the phone call or booking fee that the office may charge.

Don't judge a hotel by its star rating. Every country has a different hotel rating system, so a two-star hotel in France, for example, will bear little resemblance to a similarly accredited hotel in Eastern Europe. Extra stars don't necessarily mean extra comfort either, they may simply refer to whether the hotel has a lounge, or whether you can get a cup of tea at 3am, something which may not be important to you at all.

Cheap hotels in cities tend to be near railway stations or have some other disadvantage, like being by the port or in the heart of the red light district. If you don't fancy climbing upstairs to get to your room at the top, check if the hotel has a lift; smaller hotels often don't. City hotels often don't have dining rooms, which is not necessarily a disadvantage since it is often not only cheaper but a distinct advantage to take breakfast and indeed other meals at a neighbouring cafe. In Italy, for example, a cup of *espresso* and a doughnut from a small *pasticeria* round the corner can be a much more attractive way in which to start the day than the stale coffee and plastic toast and jam on offer in the hotel dining room.

En route

If you are driving abroad, either as a complete holiday or en route to your destination, you may well need a hotel as a stopover or a break from driving. The later in the day you leave it, the less chance you have of finding one when you want it. In towns, it is worth parking the car and walking up back streets to find a hotel, rather than relying on those on the main through routes. If you can't get into a hotel in the town of your choice, the receptionist at a hotel belonging to a chain may 'phone ahead for you.

In France, the en suite facilities may confuse you. The French tend to find bidets more important than toilets, which may well be down the corridor rather than in the bedroom. Towels are often wafer–thin, even in the best establishments, but certainly in the cheaper ones; it is also best to take your own soap.

Hotels outside Europe

British travellers are often surprised at the different style of hotels worldwide, particularly those in hot climates. Hotels in the Caribbean, for example, rarely exceed three stories and accommodation is often low-lying, simple bungalows scattered in the grounds. The central area housing the sitting area and dining room may well have a roof that is open to the elements, attracting a variety of flying visitors when the lights go on in the evening. It is often important to ask whether there are mosquito nets over the windows or nets over the beds, and air conditioning certainly adds to the comfort as well as keeping insects out.

Double beds

In the States you won't have any problem getting a double bed, you'll probably get two. On the Continent, in holiday resorts, they're pretty hard to find. It is worth looking up the word in the dictionary if you want to ask for a double bed when you book in —in Italy, for example, it is called a *lit matrimoniale*.

The guidebooks

Hotel guidebooks, on the whole, make confusing reading. But what most readers do not appreciate is that around two–thirds of all guidebooks only include hotels that pay to be there. The ratings vary too. All sorts of intriguing and often contradictory criteria are taken into account in the overall rating, from the provision of shoe–cleaning facilities to whether the hotel can provide a cooked breakfast in bed. Some hotel guidebooks have a confusing array of symbols from which you have to pick out the facility you find most important. In England there is no statutory registration scheme and no 'official' grading system. In France, all hotels have to be registered with their local *Prefecture*. If they want to be graded, it costs them nothing, but hefty increases in VAT not long ago, for higher rated hotels have meant that a large number of French four–star hotels have asked to be downgraded to three!

Hotels that get picked for their food in one guidebook, may be totally overlooked in another. The best guidebook from which to assess whether the food is any good is the *Red Michelin*. In Britain, the *Good Food Guide* is essential reading alongside the *Good Hotel Guide*.

Hotel chains

Hotels that belong to hotel chains aren't all bad, but some are dreadful. The worst are owned by anonymous corporations who install piped musak, patterned carpets, plastic flowers and disinterested staff, and fill their bedrooms with disillusioned travelling businessmen. In these hotels, if you want tea, you have to make it yourself from a little kettle and sachets in the room, if you want your shoes cleaned another sachet will provide the polish. Some hotel chains are, of course, better than others, but hotels that are expensive are not necessarily any better than those that are not.

Family-owned and run

Fewer hotels these days are family-owned and run, though in the Mediterranean you may find five generations of the same family in a typical Italian *pensione*. In Britain, many top country house hotels are family-owned and run. These properties, often inherited, would otherwise have gone to the tax man, and have been kept on as private hotels.

British country house hotels

In Britain country house hotels are spending thousands and often millions of pounds on adding leisure centres and sports facilities. Often open to non residents as well as to residents of the hotel, these facilities are usually free to guests. As well as a swimming pool, many have well–equipped gymnasiums with instructors prepared to assess fitness or programme a specific range of exercises.

There are usually saunas and steam rooms too. In addition, the more up–to–date leisure centres come with a whole range of staff ready to massage and wax legs as well as offer a variety of alternative therapies from aromatherapy to reflexology. Hotels with these leisure centres need not be expensive as use of the facilities is usually free to guests (though individual treatments are often extra). Special low–cost weekend breaks are also worth enquiring about.

Travelling with children

If you've got young children, the important criteria are the same the world over. Nevertheless, on the Continent they take a lot more kindly to young children than they do in Britain —thinking nothing of putting an extra bed into your room, providing small portions at meal times and having someone on hand willing to baby–sit.

In Britain, hoteliers generally take a dim view of children and are often keener on dogs. A significant number ban children altogether, something completely unheard of abroad. Some hotels ban children from the dining room or insist that they eat earlier than adult guests. What many fail to understand is that the average toddler does not take kindly to being left alone in a hotel bedroom while you go down to dinner.

Some hotels allow children (up to 16 in some cases) to share your room for nothing. The large hotels chains, like Trusthouse Forte, often adopt this policy. However, this is not always as beneficial as it might sound. The bedroom in which the hotel is prepared to put another bed may be so small that you find yourselves leap–frogging over each other down to breakfast.

If you are looking for a suitable hotel for a young family, it is worth finding out a number of things before you make a booking. If you need a cot for a young baby, for example, bear in mind that on the Continent they may not have the same standards as we have in Britain. Cots provided by overseas hotels are often too dangerous to put the baby in. It is worth checking whether the gaps in the bars are too wide, or whether your healthy bouncing baby will end up in a heap on the floor.

And finally…

The worst hotel experiences usually occur when you have arrived too late in the day to make a choice and you end up staying somewhere ghastly. As George Bernard Shaw said: "The great advantage of a hotel is that it's a refuge from home life." Sometimes home life can be infinitely more desirable.

SELF–CATERING

by Caroline Brandenburger

Self–catering need not be the chain and ball round the ankle that some might imagine. It is a particularly good idea if you're travelling with children, and it can act as base where you only occasionally use the kitchen. You can come and go as you like, without incurring the wrath of the management, spend as much or as little time there as you want —and it can be fairly cheap.

Another advantage is the enormous range of accommodation to choose from —villa, castle, flat, log cabin, house boat— in all parts of the world. In Britain you can stay in anything from a National Trust thatched cottage set deep in a forest to a stone pineapple folly, the wing of a stately home or a seaside bungalow. In France it might be a chateau, in Italy a Tuscan farmhouse and in Spain try a villa equipped with its own private swimming pool.

Not surprisingly, the price and value for money varies enormously. Your holiday home can be private and secluded or part of a large complex of identical properties. If it's the former, you'll probably need a car, just so you can get to the nearest shops, restaurant, pub or beach. If it's the latter, there may be facilities on site, a swimming pool, a tennis court, launderette —even discos and restaurants in particularly organized self–catering complexes.

Another thing to think about if you're planning to self–cater abroad, is that food prices may be higher than you're used to, in which case you should account for this in your budget. Thomas Cook recently conducted a survey of comparative food prices in different countries, and found that, for example, eggs were more expensive in Corfu than in Britain, and tea was more than double British prices in Portugal. Wine, however, was cheaper everywhere! Nevertheless, it is worth remembering that one of the great pleasures of being abroad is buying in local markets, browsing in intriguing food shops, and sampling the different fare.

How you equip yourself is dependent on each individual property. Many are privately owned so there are no hard and fast rules, but often linen will be provided, and sometimes even microwaves, dishwashers, high chairs, cots and board games for rainy days. If the brochure is not clear and you have particular requirements, then check before you go. Don't risk spoiling your enjoyment by being bereft of that vital garlic crusher or clock radio.

To find out how you can book self–catering accommodation, both here and abroad, get in touch with the appropriate Tourist Board. If they don't actually have lists of companies operating in this field, they should certainly be able to point you in the right direction. The big shipping companies such as P&O, Sealink and Brittany Ferries offer self–catering packages, and a decent travel agent should know exactly what's available.

One of the most commonly–used sources of self–catering accommodation is private advertisements in the classified sections of national and local newspapers and magazines. If you are booking through a private individual, it is even more important that you find out exactly what facilities are on offer —both at the property and in the vicinity— and that you are very clear about terms and conditions relating to utility costs and damage.

What to find out before you book

1. Accommodation: number and type of bedrooms, beds, bathrooms, living areas; cooking facilities, garage, heating, bed linen, cots.
2. How far is the property from the nearest shops, restaurants, bars, town or village? If you are in an isolated area with limited shopping facilities, prices are likely to be high.
3. How far from the beach, recreational facilities for adults and/or children, places of interest? It's all very well finding yourself an idyllically secluded cottage if you are after seclusion, but a disaster if you have teenage children chafing at the bit for the company of their peers.
4. Hazards for young children: an unfenced garden? An unattended pool or nearby pond or river, main road?
5. Hidden extras, are utilities included in the cost, is the electricity run on a metre, how is this measured, is there a deposit, what are the conditions under which you lose this deposit?
6. Is the property serviced by maids, cooks or baby- sitters?

What to take

Trial and error has taught most of us what to take on a self–catering holiday and our shopping list will also depend on the destination — you are hardly likely to take your favourite wine to France, but you might pop a jar of Branston Pickle in your suitcase. Nevertheless, we usually manage to forget some vital article.

Even if you do arrive with some vital implement missing, the best advice is to try not to get too worked up about it. After all, this is a holiday, and the intention is not to try and transpose all your domestic habits to the Dordogne. A self–catering holiday will not necessarily offer a restful break (someone has to do the washing up) but it can offer the privacy and flexibility which, even with the best will in the world, is sometimes lacking in a hotel holiday.

TIMESHARE AND HOME EXCHANGE

by Michael Furnell and Diana Hanks

The majority of people believe that timesharing is something new which has only developed over the last 15 years or so, but in fact it is not really a new concept because as far back as the last century, villagers were time–sharing water in Cyprus where there was no piped supply.

Property timeshare is believed to have been initiated in the 1960s when certain French developers of ski apartments experienced difficulties in selling their leisure accommodation outright and decided to offer for sale the ownership of weekly or fortnightly segments at the same time each year for ever.

The idea spread to other parts of Europe including Spain. On the Costa Blanca a British company, which was building apartments in Calpe, offered co–ownership of two–bedroomed flats in the main shopping street near the sea. Prices were as little as £250 per week's usage in the summer in perpetuity. Winter periods were even cheaper at £180 for a month, and easy terms were available on the payment of a £50 deposit with the balance payable at £4.50 per month over three years.

The Americans soon recognized this form of holiday home ownership and in the early stages converted condominiums, motels and hotels —unviable in their original form— into time–share units. Often these had rather basic facilities and it is only in recent years that developers in Florida and elsewhere have realized that top–quality homes with luxury facilities are the key to successful multi–ownership.

It was not until 1976 that timesharing was launched in Britain. The first site was in a beautiful loch–side location in the Highlands of Scotland. This was a luxury development with excellent sporting facilities and prices were set from about £5000 per week.

How it works

The aim of timesharing is to provide luxury quality homes for which a once–only capital sum is paid at today's prices. Future holidays are secure without the need for hotel bills or holiday rents —just an annual sum to cover maintenance expenses.

Timeshare is sold by several different methods at prices from as little as £1500 (low season, one bedroom) to £22,000 and over (peak season, three bedrooms, highest quality resort) for deluxe accommodation and on–site leisure facilities.

About 132,000 European families bought timeshare in 1993, spending a total of £1.2bn. There are now over 800 European resorts (3500 worldwide), over 2.5 million owners worldwide and at least 90 resorts in the UK itself. In Europe some 800,000 families are timeshare owners of which about 400,000 live in the UK.

When a freehold is purchased, as in Scotland, the period of time which you buy is yours to use 'forever', and you may let, sell, assign or leave the property to your heirs in your will. In England and Wales, the law only permits ownership for a maximum of 80 years, but in many other parts of the world, ownership in 'perpetuity' is possible.

An alternative is membership of a club which grants the right to a club member to use specified accommodation in a specified property for either specified weeks in the timeshare calendar, or 'floating time' in the high/medium/low season time band (choosing which weeks annually for a stated number of years is an alternative scheme). Hence the assets of the property ie buildings, lands and facilities are conveyed (or leased) to custodian trustees, (often a bank or other institution) which holds the property for the benefit of the club members. The rights of all owners collectively are regulated by the Club Constitution. This legal structure works well in the UK and, with modifications, in developments overseas.

The formation of a public limited company with the issue of ordinary shares which vary in price according to the season chosen for occupation and apartment size is another form of holiday ownership, although not strictly timeshare. Each share provides one week's occupancy for a set number of years, usually 20 or 25 years. The properties are then sold in the open market and the proceeds divided among the shareholders.

One company uses capital contributed by participants to purchase land and build holiday homes in various parts of Europe. Each member is entitled to holiday points which can be used for a vacation of a week or more in a chosen development at any time of year.

Another provides for the sums paid by participants to be converted into a single–premium insurance policy. Part of that premium is invested in fixed–interest securities and another portion is used to acquire properties (over 400 in about 20 locations). 'Bondholders' pay a user charge to cover the maintenance cost of the property for each week's holiday taken, and are given a 'points per week' basis depending on the accommodation's size, location and season chosen. Investors are permitted to encash their bonds (whose price is quoted daily in the financial press) at any time after two years. A capital sum is repaid upon death of the Bondholder —the amount determined by the age at which the holder took out the insurance policy. Such bond schemes are subject to legal regulations which are not applicable to the timeshare concept.

Golden rules

The Golden Rules to be remembered when buying a timeshare home are:

1. Purchase from a well established developer or selling agent who already has a reputation for fair dealing and offering really successful schemes.

2. The location of the property is vital, so be sure to select a well–situated development with adequate facilities and a quality atmosphere. Be sure that it appeals to the family as well as yourself so that you are all able to enjoy regular visits. If you are likely to want to resell in the future, the location will prove even more important.

3. Remember that the UK Timeshare Act 1992, which came into force on 12th October 1992, provides for simply a 14 day mandatory cooling off period for those who are in the UK when they sign a purchase agreement (the actual location of the timeshare resort is irrelevant). The Act does not apply to purchases made. even though you are a UK resident, when you buy whilst overseas,

Portugal also has a 14–day cooling off period but other countries in Europe do not at present. An EU Directive on timeshare, which inter alia will provide for a mandatory ten–day cooling off period in the member states, may not produce national legislation outside the UK and Portugal before 1997.

4. Check carefully the annual maintenance costs and be sure you know what they cover. Part of the yearly charges should be accumulated in a sinking fund by the management company to cover replacements, new furnishings and regular major redecorations.

5. If all the amenities promised by the sales staff are not already in existence, get a written commitment from the vendors that they will be completed, and when.

6. Ascertain the rights of owners if the builder or management company gets into financial difficulties, and ascertain if it is possible for the owners to appoint a new management company if they are not satisfied with the service of the original one. The *Constitution* and the *Management Agreement* are the two documents to show to a specialist lawyer to determine that title is safeguarded and occupation rights protected.

7. Find out about the timeshare concept and the wide variety of resorts available in Europe by reading up on the subject. Compare resorts to find the most suitable. Is it one of the two exchange networks, RCI or Interval International? Find out if the vendor owns the property, and if they do not, discover who holds the freehold and if there is any mortgage on the property. Before signing any documents check if a 'cooling off' period (in which one can have a change of mind) is written into the purchase agreement: at present there is no such statutory right. A solicitor can check the wording of agreements relatively easily, but it will be a considerably greater task —and thus more expensive— to consider the occupation rights granted, the nature of the developer's title, details of any mortgages or encumbrances on the timeshare property, the granting of correct local planning permission, the legal structure of the scheme in the context of that country's property laws, the effects of jurisdiction, the safeguards for monies paid for an unbuilt or incomplete property and the arrangements at the termination of the period of lease.

8. Talk to an existing owner wherever possible before purchasing.

9. The experts believe that any timeshare scheme should have a minimum of 10 units to be viable. If it is too small, amenities may be lacking and each owner's share of management costs may be excessive.

10. Are payments held in trust pending the issue of title documents, or a licence to use, and has a trustee been appointed to hold the master title deeds?

11. A solicitor should scrutinize the documentation and perform independent checks regarding payments held in trust pending the issue of title documents, club membership certificates and a licence to use. Is the Trustee reputable?

12. If you wish to have the flexibility to swap worldwide, the timeshare resort should be affiliated to one of the two international exchange resorts, Resort Condominiums International (RCI) or Interval International, its smaller competitor. Check any claim to affiliation.

Investment

Timesharing is not a conventional money–making investment in property, although some owners who purchased time in the earliest schemes have enjoyed substantial capital appreciation over the past ten years. Essentially, you are investing in leisure and pleasure but you cannot expect inflation–proof holidays. What you are buying is vacation accommodation at today's prices. Expenditure on travel, food and entertainment is still likely to rise in future years according to the rise of inflation.

Exchange facilities

It was recognized long ago that after a few years, many timeshare owners may want a change of scene for annual holidays, and as a result, organizations were established to arrange exchange facilities for timesharing owners. There are exciting possibilities for owners wanting to swap their seaside apartment in, say, England's West Country, for a contemporary–style bungalow in Florida or an Andalucian *pueblo* in Spain. Today there are two major exchange organizations operating in the UK and between them they offer an immense variety of timeshare accommodation in many holiday destinations. Both had their origins in America and now have their offices in England.

RCI, the largest established exchange organization, had 1.7 million timeshare owners registered on its exchange system at the close of 1993, and 2,600 resorts available in 70 countries worldwide. Interval International had about 500,00 members registered and over 1,200 resorts offered.

There is normally an annual membership fee payable by each family wishing to join the exchange system. The developer usually pays this for each family for the first two or three years as a purchase inducement. In addition, a modest fee (£61) is due when an exchange is successfully organised.

Orderly growth

There is a single professional timeshare trade body in the UK, The Timeshare Council (23 Buckingham Gate, London SW1E 6LB, tel: 071–821 8845). TTC has been set up to represent all legitimate interests in the industry including developers, marketers, resale companies, trustees, finance houses, owners' groups, with an independent Executive Chairman. It also aims to monitor consumer protection issues, and the orderly growth of the industry. It gives free advice to owners at its member resorts, and makes a small charge for conciliation where owners belong to non–member resorts. TTC's Rules broadly follow the recommendations set out in the Office of Fair Trading's report on timeshare published in summer 1990. It is lobbying the European Parliament for european controls to be exercised through an EU Timeshare Directive, possibly to be passed in late 1994.

An encouraging aspect for the future well–being of the timeshare industry is the active participation of well–known building firms who all have their own developments in the UK, Spain or Portugal, lending respectability to an area renowned for its appaling press and dubious operators.

In an attempt to educate the public to buy timeshare wisely, to avoid commitment without prior checks through the trade body or professional advisers, the

UK Department of Trade and Industry has now up–dated its leaflet *Your Place in the Sun; or is it?* The new leaflet is available from the DTI or Citizen's Advice Bureaux as well as TTC.

Home exchange

Many British home owners fancy the idea of exchanging their home with another family in Europe or elsewhere for a fortnight or a month, in order to enjoy a 'free' holiday (apart from transport costs). Although the idea is attractive, there are many problems to be overcome unless you arrange the swap with friends. A number of relatively small organizations have been established to arrange holiday home exchanges, but few of them have been successful. A new American publication, *The Vacation Home Exchange and Hospitality Guide* (£8.95 plus £1 postage, ASAP Publications, Prospect House, Downley House, Downley Common, High Wycombe, Bucks HP13 5XQ), is a helpful introduction to home exchange and the various organizations worldwide who can help. The Worldwide Home Exchange Club (45 Hans Place, London SW1X 0JZ, tel: 071–589 6055) is a subscription–based organization which publishes directories of available properties.

Ideally, a swap should be with a like–minded family or group of a similar size, so both will feel at home, and will look after the property well. The various organizations work in two ways. Some simply publish a directory listing the property, with size, location and basic features, and leave it to the individual to make contact and iron out all the details of the arrangement. Others work more like a dating agency, visiting the property, taking down its (and your) details, together with what you are looking for, whether you are prepared to lend your car, feed cats, water plants etc. They will then cross–match you with another suitable scheme member. This obviously costs more but, from the amount of hassle saved, is probably worthwhile.

Alternatively you can advertise in a suitable publication. The journal of a university in the area you want to go to is a good idea. Academics often spend a summer attached to a foreign university, and if you're lucky there may be someone planning to come and work at whatever establishment is near you.

Whichever method you use, make sure that every eventuality has been covered and agreed in writing, that your insurance cover is full and up to date, and that neighbours or friends are primed before you leave. Put away anything you are worried about and leave detailed notes about how the washing machine works, what the rabbit eats, where the nearest transport is, and all possible numbers needed in case of an emergency. At the end of your time in someone else's home, be sure that you leave it sparkling, replace anything damaged or broken, or leave the money for them to do so, and generally behave in the way you hope they are also behaving. Some people have become hooked on home–swapping as a way of travelling, and do so at least once a year, loving the opportunity to live within a real community and meet the 'natives' while away. Others, who have had more sobering experiences, swear never to try again. It is a more risky business than a normal holiday in a purpose–built hotel, but the rewards can, if you're lucky, be infinitely greater. You just have to be prepared to take the risk. See the Directory for useful names and addresses.

ON A LIMITED BUDGET

by Pat Yale

After transport, accommodation is likely to burn the biggest hole in budget travellers' pockets. Luckily this is one area where economies can still be made. The cheapest accommodation is, of course, completely free and there's not much of it.

In a few parts of the world it's fine to sleep on the beaches. However, not only are the rules subject to unexpected change and the whim of the local police, but beach bums are deprived of necessities such as washrooms, making this an unsatisfactory way to pass more than the odd emergency night. Those with a tent may find local farmers prepared to let them use their fields and facilities but such ad hoc arrangements tend to depend on negotiating skills.

Some Indian and African Sikh temples also offer free accommodation. Don't expect luxury —one large bed may serve for any number of visitors. Nevertheless staying in a temple can be a magical experience, offering the chance to find out about the religion at the same time. Visitors must abide by prohibitions on smoking, drinking and eating on the premises, but will often be included when the post–service sweetmeats are being handed out. While there is rarely an official fee, most temples appreciate a 'donation' and may keep a visitor's book indicating what is expected.

'Networking' can also result in free accommodation. Members of the Globetrotters Club (BCM Roving, London, WC1N 3XX) or of Servas (77 Elm Park Mansions, London, SW10 0AP) can sometimes stay with fellow members in other countries. Home owners can even swap their homes with others in a similar situation (see above).

Travellers who hitch or use public transport may also find themselves invited to stay with people they meet on the way. This can be the perfect way to find out about a place but in developing countries may mean staying in houses without running water or toilets, and where conventions, particularly concerning women, may be very different from those at home. The tradition of hospitality to strangers, especially in Muslim countries, is still strong and may mean someone going without to provide for the guest.

It pays to be aware of local customs: in some countries anything a guest admires must be given to them, in others, refusing food can cause offence. Clearly women must be especially careful about accepting offers of hospitality, particularly in Islamic countries where such offers will invariably come from men. If you think you would like to take up offers of hospitality, squeeze suitable thank–you presents into your backpack—pictures of London, British coins, malaria pills and biros often do the trick.

Organized camping is the next best option, particularly in Europe and North America where there are lots of well–equipped sites. The main snag, unless you have a vehicle, is having to carry the tent and cooking equipment. However, companies like Robert Saunders, Vango and Lichfield sell tents weighing less than three kilograms.

Camp–sites are frequently in the middle of nowhere: in developing countries you may find that by the time you've added the cost of getting to and from them to the site fee, it is cheaper to stay in a budget hotel. Staying in hostels can minimize accommodation costs while also ensuring you meet other travellers. There are more than 5000 International Youth Hostel Federation hostels and most are open to members of all ages, with priority going to younger members at busy times. Although you can usually take out temporary membership on the spot it is often cheaper to join before leaving home.

Despite their name, YMCA/YWCA hostels are not usually any more overtly religious or restrictive than other hostels. In the UK guests are still expected to work for their keep; elsewhere this custom has been quietly dropped. Many hostels now offer central heating, cooking facilities and relative privacy. However, most still close during the day, segregate the sexes and impose evening curfew. In Third World countries, some serve as long–stay accommodation for the homeless. In Europe expect noisy school parties.

If you want to stay in cheaper hotels you must normally rely on guidebooks and recommendations; travel agents and tourist offices rarely keep details of budget accommodation, although Campus Travel shops stock *Sleep Cheap* guides to popular destinations like Bangkok. If you haven't got a guidebook, the best hunting ground is likely to be near bus and railway stations (for a good night's sleep make sure you get a room at the back of the building).

In Europe the 'pension' equivalents of British bed and breakfasts generally omit the breakfast. As with the more expensive hotels, some pensions are subject to tourist board inspection, ensuring reasonable standards. Travel agents usually charge for booking hotels, however cheap. Instead get the address from a telephone book in the library reference section. If possible write in the relevant language, and enclose a Post Office international reply paid coupon. If you prefer to phone but would find this difficult, British Telecom's translation service can work out cheaper than paying an agent to make your booking. To cut down communication costs, use central reservation offices for cheaper hotel chains such as Travelodge.

Finding budget accommodation in the United States can be difficult and package deals often offer excellent value. The US Tourism Administration has details of companies which can make bed and breakfast bookings. Groups of three or four people can reduce costs by sharing twin rooms which often have two double beds. Avoid unpleasant extra costs by carefully observing the latest check–out times, and never make 'phone calls from your room.

In developing countries, rooms costing only a couple of pounds a night may only be furnished with a bed and chair. Where dormitories are more popular than individual rooms, some will not accept women travellers. Even when they do, the same rooms double as children's nurseries, guaranteeing sleepless nights. Before accepting a very cheap room, check that the fan works, that the door locks properly, that the window will close and is fitted with mosquito–protection where appropriate, that there are no peep-holes in partition walls, that the walls reach right to the ceiling and that there are no tell–tale signs of bed bugs, ants or other insects. Then check the state of the toilets and the water supply (in Islamic countries the *hammams* or public baths make private baths and showers less important).

Try and pair up with someone else before booking in to avoid being charged a single supplement. Train travellers can evade accommodation costs if they're prepared to sleep sitting up in frequently crowded conditions. Within Europe you'll get a better night's sleep at a reasonable price by opting for a couchette, a sort of fold–down shelf–bed which comes much cheaper than a true sleeping berth. Bear in mind that not everyone can sleep through a train's stopping and starting and that ticket collectors often time their visits for the early hours. Outside Europe some sleeping cars offer an experience not to be missed. Nairobi to Mombasa sleepers, for example, have fold–down sinks and dining cars of near-Orient Express splendour. Their route also ensures that you wake up with the Tsavo National Park drifting past your bedroom window.

Taking a campervan or caravan with you obviously eliminates accommodation costs. However, few budget travellers can afford the initial outlay, the extra ferry fares and the high cost of petrol. Nevertheless, package deals to the United States which include a campervan offer excellent value for money.

A cautionary note on false economy. In some parts of the world, hotel prices are ludicrously low in comparison with the UK. In Udaipur (India) it's possible to stay in the usual £1–a–night pit; however, you could also stay in the fairy–tale Lake Palace Hotel, an ex–Maharajah's palace, for a fraction of what it would cost at home. Likewise in Yangon (Rangoon) you can find a cheap room or upgrade to the fading colonial Strand. With Raffles in Singapore having been resurrected in a new guise with London–style prices, it's worth snapping up the real bargains that still remain to be had.

HOW TO SECURE A GOOD HOTEL DEAL

by Alex McWhirter

Even though they may have secured a good air fare deal, many travellers continue to pay over the odds for their hotel accommodation. Far too many executive and leisure guests realise that hotel normal or 'rack' rates are now virtually obsolete and that it pays to shop around. That wasn't the case 10 or 15 years ago when most business travellers would have paid either the rack or a negotiable corporate rate. But nowadays, leaving aside trade fair times or those destinations where hotel capacity is restricted, the number of guests paying rack rate can be counted on the fingers of one's hand. Even corporate rates are now less popular because most hotels are undercutting them with a deal of one sort or another in order to fill their empty rooms.

However, the corporate rate is a good starting point for most business people. In general, it provides a saving of between 10 and 25% on the rack price. And it can be an easy rate to access —some properties will provide their corporate rate to any bona fide business person, although in general you may have to book a certain number of room nights to qualify.

For this reason, individual travellers seeking corporate rates and who travel to a variety of destinations will be better off by joining WEXAS (£39.58 for Blue Card membership) or the Club Reserve (membership is free of charge) operated by London's Gray Dawes Travel. Another suggestion would be to join IAPA (International Airline Passengers Association) which costs £45. (IAPA is based at Croydon, Surrey). Collectively, these firms use their members' clout to negotiate discounts of between 10 and 50% with hotels all over the world. These savings are greater than individual travellers or small to medium-sized firms could ever hope to achieve. For example, Club Reserve quotes a rate of £110 at London's four star SAS Portman Hotel (rack rate £170) and Bfr 4,400 (as against the rack price of Bfr 8,800) at the Sheraton Hotel adjoining Brussels Airport which is handy for visiting the dozens of multi-national firms who are located in the nearby Zaventum and Woluwe business parks. In Hong Kong, the Club Reserve price for the luxury Ritz Carlton is just HK$1,395 compared to HK$2,250.

However, often the best deal of all can be secured on your behalf by the firm you are visiting. In the Gulf or the Far East, for example, local banks and trading houses often have financial stakes in the city's better hotels. So if your meetings are with one of those firms, remember to ask them to book your room because their clout can secure you an unbeatable rate. The same can apply closer to home in the former Eastern Bloc. When I was in Warsaw recently, LOT Polish Airlines secured me a rate of US$75 a night at the five star Marriott hotel, a property in which LOT has equity. This was an excellent deal for not only was I there at a busy time (when I wouldn't normally expect to be offered such a low rate) but LOT's price handsomely undercut the US$140-$170 corporate rate along with the rack rate of over $200.

Off-season rates are another option for the budget-minded guest. Suitable for both executive and leisure guests, they are offered by most four– and five–star chain hotels when business travel is slack. In other words, from around June to September and from December to March (with some regional variations depending on holiday times and business customs) you can expect to save 60% on rack rates. In some cases the hotel will offer a flat discount, in others it will 'dress up' the rate with added-value amenities such as airport transfers, breakfast, free valet service, early check-in/late check-out and so on. In Summer 1993, for example, virtually every top hotel chain around the world (including Britain's posh Savoy Group) had a deal of one sort or another. You could have booked Hyatt's four star Lowndes hotel in London's Belgravia for £105 (£180 normally) or stayed at one of the Savoy properties in the capital for £145. Two chains, namely Scandinavia's SAS Hotels and Swiss company Swissotel which have properties in Europe, the Far East and the USA simply cut rates by 50% across the board and threw in a further night free for guests staying four nights. In addition, both chains were providing senior citizens with age-related discounts so that a 70 year old guest had 70% knocked off his or her bill while one aged 75 years saves 75% and so on.

Last winter (1994) the deals were more selective but equally generous. London's Edwardian group were offering 33% discounts (from £153 to £99 a night in the case of the Edwardian Heathrow) and throwing in breakfast plus a third night free. French chain Meridien sliced 33% off its rate while Inter-Continental's 'Global Business Options' scheme (which later extended to August 1994) provided an upgrade to suite accommodation for guests paying rates similar to rack or corporate prices. At the time of writing there was every indication that these rooms sales would again be offered in winter 1994 and in summer 1995. Available year round are the special rate available from airline stopover packages. These reward passengers with hefty discounts both on hotel accommodation and ground arrangements across an airline's network. Which ever package you choose depends largely on your final destination and where you wish to stopover but long-distance airlines like British Airways, Cathay Pacific, Malaysia, Singapore Airlines (SIA) and Thai International operate stopover rates throughout their networks. The deals are generous because an airline has enormous clout with hoteliers, particularly at its home base. SIA, for example, booked 200,000 into Singapore hotels in 1992 hence its stopover rate at five star properties like the Hilton or Pacific is £72 compared to £125 normally. But, unlike the normal rate, SIA's price includes return airport-hotel transfers, breakfast, sightseeing, service/tax and discount shopping vouchers - extra inflating the normal room rate to £169. So in other words, SIA's package price represents a saving of 60% on the cost of booking the arrangements separately. Emirates Air of Dubai is another carrier with good value packages at its home base. Dubai's five star Royal Abjar costs between US$55 and US$88 (savings of 50% on the normal price) when booked through Emirates while a Mercedes can be hired for the same price as it costs to rent a small hatchback in Europe.

Another good bet are the 'business' packages marketed by several airlines. Japan Airlines, for example, provides UK-originating First and Business class passengers with 50% discounts at top hotels in Tokyo and Osaka for stays of up to four nights. Passengers pay Yen 17,500 at Tokyo's famous five–star Imperial or Yen 15,000 at the four–star New Otani.

Take advantage of Apex and weekend rate. Several chains including Marriott and SAS Hotels have copied the airlines' advance purchase Apex rates. Guests prepared to book say, 14 days ahead, automatically save one-third on the rack price at all SAS Hotels. Similar savings are offered at Marriott properties in Europe and the US. The drawback is that Apex room rates have steep penalties should you change or cancel.

Always request the weekend rate should your stay include a Friday, Saturday or Sunday night. Most four– and five–star hotels at business locations now cut rates by up to 50% at weekends, a time when executives prefer to stay at home. Finally, as long as there are more rooms than guest to fill them, the world hoteliers will always be accommodating on price. So it pays to shop around for the best deal.

HOTELS FOR BUSINESS TRAVELLERS

by Philip Ray and Carol Wright

Regular business travellers have often complained —with a good deal of justification sometimes— about the high level of scheduled air fares. But it is an undeniable fact that when they have reached their destination, those same travellers have frequently quite happily paid the full 'rack' rate in a five–star hotel.

Research has shown that hotel costs (including meals and drinks) can often account for more than 60 per cent of the total travel bill on a typical business trip, so it is just as important to control this element of expenditure as it is to find ways of saving money on airfares.

The comparison between airfares and hotel rates is, perhaps, not entirely a fair one because the fares in many parts of the world are the result of cartel–type agreements which do not necessarily reflect true market rates. Hotels, though, normally operate in a competitive environment and would clearly reduce their rates if they were unable to fill their rooms. In the dynamic capitalist environment of some Far Eastern destinations, hotel rates are notoriously prone to the laws of supply and demand. In recent years there has been a tremendous surge in the construction of new hotels in Singapore, for example, leading to over–capacity and massively reduced room rates.

In many parts of the world, though, the rates at hotels used by business travellers are distinctly on the high side. This is partly a function of location and high city–centre rents, because the typical business traveller usually wants to stay in a centrally–sited hotel. There is also the question of prestige, particularly in the USA, because you may not be so highly regarded by your business contacts if you decide to stay in an unfashionable hotel on the outskirts of town. Just like the airlines, hoteliers are particularly anxious to secure the patronage of frequent business travellers, firstly because of the high rates which they —or, more accurately— their companies pay, and also because they produce year–round business in contrast to the holiday-maker who travels only during a limited period of the year and is highly budget conscious.

Before you book, it's worth checking with a leading convention firm or magazine as to whether there is a convention taking place at your chosen destination. The Non–Aligned Conference has closed all up–market hotels to individual travellers in both Delhi and Harare in recent years and governments have even cancelled firm bookings to fill hotels with conference delegates. In any case, there is nothing worse than being the single traveller among hearty name–labelled hordes. I once stayed at the 1407–bedroomed Grand Hyatt in New York along with 1300 lady masons. It took a half–hour supervised queue to get to an elevator. Service, whether in a room or restaurant, disappears when a convention is on.

Perks

For clients paying the full room rate —or even a premium rate in some cases— many of the world's major hotel groups have come up with 'Executive' or 'Gold Card' clubs which offer a variety of added–value benefits. Some provide entire floors of superior–standard rooms with a full–time manager to look after their special requests and possibly valet and butler service as well. More and more are also providing an executive club room with separate entrance, bar, magazines and games. Pre–registration, speeded–up check–in and check–out, late check–out and free use of health clubs are other typical facilities.

SAS International, a subsidiary of the Scandinavian airline, SAS, has capitalized on its airline links by introducing airline check–in desks in the lobby of most of its hotels so that business travellers can check in for their homeward flight in the morning and then go off on a day's round of appointments without having to carry their luggage around all day.

Most of the major chains also include business facilities for clients with secretaries, telex, interpreters and even sometimes radio pagers. Separate facilities for non–smokers are also often available.

The future in hotels, as predicted by the President of the Holiday Inn chain, is a computer terminal in each room from which dining table, menu and wines can be selected and ordered by remote control. Bathrooms will all contain whirlpool and steam baths in addition to a shower and tub, and hotel rooms will be linked to airline reservations and luggage transferred automatically to rooms from the plane (some hope here).

Women travelling alone get less than welcoming reactions from some hotels, particularly in Japan where they refuse to believe you travel alone, and in Britain where often you are thought to be someone 'not quite nice.' American hotels will site women near the elevator; noisy, but it saves long night time walks along dim corridors.

A survey by Best Western found that women want good lighting, mirrors and security more than the hair driers, magazines and flowers which are normally the mark of a 'woman's room'. More hotels are now putting in club floors for women travelling alone. The New Otani in Japan has a separate floor for mothers with small children with special baby foods and a nursery.

Which hotel?

Best value hotels are found where governments are keen to encourage visitors to spread out and see more of their country. The demise of the maharajahs helped India have a set of uniquely sumptuous palace hotels. Sri Lanka has kept up the old raj rest house system for tourists and in Spain and Portugal old manor houses have been turned into *paradors* and *pousadas*, beautiful, characterful stop–over places at low prices with local food.

Airport hotels are, on the whole, places to be avoided, drawing to themselves the dreariness and characterless practicality of airports. They can be worthwhile, however, if you need a room for a day on a stopover, so you can have a wash and a rest, or if you need somewhere for business meetings. They are geared to short stays and odd arrival and check–out times and will be far more likely to accommodate you than the most interesting, city centre hotels.

As a general hotel principle, small is beautiful. In anything under 50 rooms, more attention and character are to be expected.

Incentives and discounts

Most large hotel chains (Sheraton, Marriott, Hyatt, Inter–Continental and Hilton, to name a few) operate schemes to reward customer loyalty with extra privileges or special rates —or a combination of both. These incentives change constantly, with regular improvements now that more and more chains have jumped on the bandwagon. The principal aim of such schemes is to ensure repeat business but, for a regular traveller, they can also offer a good source of reasonable rates and welcome perks.

In order to join a frequent–stay club, you are usually expected to pay an administration charge (US$25 to US$100), although Pan Pacific has a Loyalty Club (PCI) which is completely free. Points are also usually awarded for every night you stay in your favoured hotel chain, although in some cases the amount you spend at the hotel and associated companies will earn you additional points.

These points may be redeemed against gifts, similar to the Barclaycard scheme, and if you exceed the pre–set number of points you are automatically 'upgraded' and offered even more perks and/or discounts.

Typically, most schemes offer an automatic upgrade to superior accommodation (if available), extended check–out times, welcome gifts, express and early check–in and often guaranteed rooms with advance reservations. These perks and incentives, although not necessarily always of monetary value, do make life easier for the hectic, travelling businessman or woman.

Despite the proliferation of 'goodies' offered by the hotel chains, financial directors who have to try and control their executives' travel costs are more likely to be impressed by a reduction in room rates than a free morning newspaper, so when evaluating the various club schemes, it is best to look for the ones which give the most favourable reductions.

Most major hotel groups are prepared to offer discounts or 'corporate rates' to business organizations which give them a reasonable amount of business, typically a minimum of 100 room–nights in a year. With careful planning by your company's business travel manager —if you have one, or a professional business travel agent if you don't— it is possible to negotiate discounts of up to 20 per cent with many leading chains. Even if you are not a regular customer, it is always worth asking for a corporate discount and seeing what happens.

There is a lot to be said for using one of the specialist travel agencies handling business travel who have tremendous buying power. Even if your own company is unlikely to provide insufficient business to a particular hotel group to qualify for corporate rates, it is often possible to pick up a similar deal through one of these agencies on a one–off basis and sometimes to do even better. Their discounts can be as much as 50 per cent. Members of WEXAS (45–49 Brompton Road, Knightsbridge, London, SW3 1DE, tel: 071–589 3315) can use their membership cards to obtain corporate rates at 28 major hotel chains worldwide.

If your company decides to organize its own hotel bookings, it is essential that you take advantage of all the special rates and deals which are available. One frequently hears stories about companies enjoying preferential rates with a particular hotel group which are not taken advantage of by staff because information about deals has not been passed on.

Within the UK, it is also often worth checking the brochures of the many mini–break operators, because some of them offer packages to important business centres, with or without rail travel, at prices which offer huge reductions over the normal hotel rate.

A SAFE HOTEL STAY

by Samantha Lee

One of the first recorded hotel fires took place at Kerns Hotel in Lancing, Michigan, on November 12, 1934. Thirty five people lost their lives. Just over a decade later in 1946, one of the worst fires occurred when 119 people perished —again in the States but this time in Georgia.

As recently as 1986, on New Year's Eve, 96 unfortunate souls met their maker as a result of a huge conflagration at the Hotel Dupont Plaza in Puerto Rico. After the disaster it was found that the building, upon which no expense had been spared in the luxury department, had been totally unprepared for an emergency of any description. Safety precautions were so inadequate as to be almost non–existent. The hotel had no evacuation plan and no staff training in emergency procedures. There was no smoke detection system to alert the occupant to danger, exits from the Casino were woefully sparse and the hotel boasted a number of unprotected vertical, horizontal openings.

Such a fire could never happen in Britain. Fire regulations in the UK are tight and strictly enforced but worldwide travellers would do well to remember that not all countries are quite so well–organized.

In 1989 *Which?* magazine repeated a survey into fire safety precaution in holiday hotels which they had originally carried out 10 years previously. The survey revealed that little had changed in the preceding decade.

Which? reported that many hotels lacked even the most basic fire safety provisions and hoteliers displayed a frightening ignorance of or disregard for fire safety measures.

In Europe, Greece and Spain were singled out for particular censure with 10 out of 11 hotels rated 'poor'('poor' means that in a serious fire many —or all— of the hotel's occupants might not get out).

The 1977 Fire Precautions Act states that every hotel with space to sleep more than six people must have a Safety Certificate. This certificate requires that the hotel have protected escape routes, fire doors, a fire alarm system and portable fire extinguishers.

The Trust House Forte chain have, in addition, made it a policy one to install smoke detectors in all their hotels —both at home and abroad. As an added precaution, there is also a system whereby the Night Porter checks the hotel from top to bottom every two hours between 11pm and 7am. He carries a key which he inserts into a time clock at strategic points around the route. This 'keying–in' procedure is recorded on a type which the Manager then checks the following day.

If a hotel or hotel chain has poor safety standards, some big companies such as Shell have a policy of banning them for company personnel. Wherever possible it is advisable to stay in a hotel with sound fire safety regulations but it is also important to remember that not all fires are caused by negligence. One cannot always anticipate the arsonist or indeed an incendiary bomb planted by a terrorist group. The bottom line is that like the good old Boy Scouts, it is better to take ultimate responsibility into your own hands and be prepared.

After a long and gruelling journey, searching out the nearest hotel fire exits is probably not going to be your number one priority but it should be. A few minutes 'casing the joint' before you order up the G and T or slip into the pre–prandial bath, could mean the difference between life and death should the unthinkable occur.

If fire breaks out, two factors govern your chances of escape: hotel design and available fire safety equipment (extinguishers, fire doors, safety lighting, escape signs and smoke alarms).

You can't do much about hotel design at this stage but remember that smoke, rather than the fire itself is the major killer, and that if the hotel has a large open–plan ground floor with wide unprotected stairways leading upwards, then smoke will move quickly, and easily permeate the upper reaches of the building. If there are no alternative stairways and exits from the ground floor dining rooms, bars and discos seem cramped or inadequate, you might want to lift your bags off the bed and find yourself another place to lay your weary head.

If the hotel seems to have covered these points adequately, you might move on to a few responsible measures of your own. Most people caught in a life–threatening situation for which they are not prepared will panic. With good reason, since trying to find the nearest Fire Exit when the smoke is already filtering under the door will not maximize your chances of survival. Below are a few sensible precautions which will:

On arrival

Check the ground floor layout and identify escape routes. Read the fire emergency instructions in your room and find the fire exit, making sure that it is clear and obstruction–free (if not notify the management and complain). Walk the route counting the number of doors from your room to the exit (an aide memoir should the lighting fail or smoke obscure the view). Note the location of fire alarm call points and fire fighting equipment in the vicinity of your room. Familiarize yourself with the layout of your room and the way to the door (particularly important if you've arrived late, after a large and liberally liquid dinner). Find out what (if anything) lies outside the window and keep your valuables next to the bed for easy access. Don't smoke in bed and never ignore a fire alarm

In case of fire

Report the outbreak immediately, either by phoning reception or by breaking a fire alarm. Don't attempt any fire–fighting heroics unless you are an off–duty fireman. Close the door of the room where the fire is located (to restrict the spread of flames and poisonous fumes) and use the nearest exit to leave the building but don't use the lift. Don't open any closed doors without first feeling them for heat (there may be a fire directly behind them). If your escape route is filled with smoke, keep low, on your hands and knees where air quality and visibility will probably be better. Stay close to the wall to avoid disorientation. On leaving the hotel, report to your evacuation point so that people know you are safe and won't risk their lives unnecessarily looking for you.

If you are cut off by fire try to contact the reception and report the situation. Close the door of the room. Run the bath to soak bedding curtains, carpets etc, and block up any cracks with wet towels. Fill the wastepaper bin with water to fight any outbreak of fire in the room and go to the window to attract attention. If possible open the window to vent smoke from the room where necessary. Do not break the glass since you may have to close the window to prevent smoke from below blowing in.

Jumping from even a second floor window is not advisable and with this in mind you might like to specify in advance that you want a room on the first floor!

HOSTELLING

by John Carlton, Diane Johnson and Kent Redding

Youth hostels are ideal for the budget traveller, offering an extensive network of accommodation around the world of a reasonable standard and at very affordable prices. Hostels are designed primarily for young people, but there is now no age limit and they are used by the 'young at heart' of all ages. Youth hostel facilities are provided by a club run not for profit, but to help young people travel. They aim to encourage a knowledge and love of the countryside as well as an appreciation of other cultures, thereby promoting international friendship.

Each country runs its own hostels independently (usually by committees from within its membership) but the national Youth Hostel Associations of every nation is linked through the International Youth Hostel Federation. The IYHF lays down recommended standards for member associations worldwide.

Theoretically, membership of the YHA is compulsory for all travellers wishing to use the facilities, but this rule is not so stringently applied in some countries outside Europe. However, membership is worthwhile, even as a precautionary measure. In England and Wales, the annual subscription is currently £3 for five to 17–year–olds, £9 for 18 and over and £19 for a family membership (two adults and all children aged under 17) —life membership costs £120. A similar small fee is the norm elsewhere. You can join the YHA at association offices (and sometimes at a hostel) outside your country of residence, but it usually costs more.

Facilities

As a member you can stay in any of over 5000 hostels in more than 60 countries worldwide. A youth hostel will provide a bed in a dormitory of varying size, and will normally have anything from four to 100 beds. There are toilet and washing facilities and a communal room where members can meet. In most countries, members will find facilities to cook their own food. Cooking utensils and crockery are provided, but not always cutlery. In some countries, cheap meals cooked by the warden or staff in charge are available.

One familiar feature of youth hostel life is the sheet sleeping bag —a sheet sewn into a bag with a space for a pillow. Any traveller intending to use the hostels should have one, although at some hostels there are sheets which may, or indeed, must be hired to protect the mattresses. Most hostels provide blankets and consider that these are adequately protected by the traveller's own sheet sleeping bag. In this respect, as in others, Youth Hostel customs vary from country to country.

A full list of the world's youth hostels can be obtained from information centres. Ask for the *International Handbook* (two volumes, *Europe and the Mediterranean* and *Africa, America, Asia and Australia*, priced £5.99 or £6.55 including postage and package). As well as listing the addresses and facilities of each hostel, the handbook summarizes the local regulations for age limits, youth hostel facilities for families, etc. However, all the information given is subject to correction as circumstances change during the year and, of course, prices will inevitably rise in time.

Europe

Europe (including many countries in Eastern Europe, but not Russia) is well covered by hostels and the wide variation in their characteristics reflects the local culture of each country. Hostels in the British Isles are perhaps now unique in expecting a small domestic duty from members before departure, but this does help to emphasize to members that they are part of a self–helping club. This idea is less apparent in some countries where the youth hostel is often run as a service by the local municipality (with the agreement of the National Association concerned) and relations between members and staff are strictly commercial.

The club atmosphere is also stronger in France, Holland and Greece. For 'real' hostel atmosphere, try Cassis, situated in an isolated position on the hills overlooking the *calanques* of Marseilles, 30km from the city. In Germany, where the youth hostel movement started in 1909, hostels are plentiful —mostly large, well–appointed buildings, but lacking members' cooking facilities and largely devoted to school parties. Scandinavian hostels are also usually well appointed, many having family rooms, and therefore more emphasis on family hostelling.

Africa

In North Africa, there are hostels in Morocco, Tunisia, Libya, Egypt and Algeria. These too reflect the local culture. Try calling at Asne, a hostel in a Moroccan village 65km south of Marrakesh on the edge of the High Atlas mountains. Here the warden has three wives and will talk to you with great charm in French.

The Kenyan YHA has nine hostels, two of which are on the coast. One is at Malindi and the other at Kanamai (about 25km north of Mombassa) in an idyllic setting amongst the coconut palms a few yards from a deserted white sandy beach. The Nairobi hostel is a meeting place for international travellers and at Nanyuki the hostel is close to one of the routes up Mount Kenya. Kitale hostel, near the Ugandan border, is part of a farm with accommodation for eight people and the one room serves as dormitory, dining and common room.

The rest of Africa is devoid of hostels until one reaches the south. At the last count, Lesotho had one hostel, Mazeru, which is well worth a visit. Local young Basutos use the property as a youth centre, so travellers have a chance to meet them.

Middle East and Asia

Israel's YHA consists of some 27hostels —the smallest, in the heart of the old city of Jerusalem, having 70 beds. All provide meals, and many have family rooms, but the members' kitchens are poor. Orphira hostel in southern Sinai boasts superb snorkelling and diving close to hand. Syrian hostels are small and reasonably equipped and many hostellers travelling to or from India meet in Damascus. There are 19 very well equipped hostels in Saudi Arabia, but only one or two are as yet open to women.

There is a good network in Pakistan, mostly well kept, and there are also a number of Government rest houses open to hostellers, as are some schools in certain areas during school holidays. Indian hostels tend to be mainly in schools and colleges and are therefore only open for short periods of the year, although there is a large permanent hostel in Delhi. Some hostels do not provide any kind of bedding, even mattresses. Sri Lanka has several hostels including one in Kandy and one in Colombo. Here, too, Government rest houses and bungalows provide alternative accommodation at a reasonable price.

The Philippines, South Korea, Malaysia and Thailand all have some hostels of which the Malaysian properties are particularly well organized. In Thailand, some hostels listed in the International Handbook appear not to exist. The two Bangkok hostels, however, certainly do. None of the six Hong Kong hostels is in the city itself. A hostel has recently been opened in New Caledonia under the auspices of the French Association.

Japan has the most extensive network of hostels outside Europe, numbering some 600. There are two kinds —Western–style with the usual bunk beds, and Japanese–style with a mattress rolled out on the floor. Television is a common feature. Several hostels are on the smaller islands of the country such as Awaji, an island in the Inland Sea. Japanese food is served in most hostels —a bowl of rice, probably served with raw egg, fish and seaweed, and eaten with chopsticks.

Australasia and America

Australia has over 100 hostels, mostly in New South Wales, Queensland and Western Australia. Distances between them are great. The smaller, more remote hostels, do not have a resident warden and the key has to be collected from neighbours.

New Zealand has hostels throughout the country. They are fairly small and simple, with no meals provided, but have adequate cooking facilities. Many are in beautiful country, such as the hostel near Mount Cook.

The Canadians still give preference to those arriving on foot or by bike over motorists. They also run a number of temporary city hostels in the summer. There are not many hostels in North America, considering the size of the continent but there are a few hostels in some of the biggest cities. (In the USA, a city hostel will often turn out to be a YMCA offering rooms to YHA members at reduced rates.) The majority are found in isolated areas of scenic interest not always accessible by public transport. There are, however, chains of hostels in New England, Colorado and the Canadian Rockies. A feature of the United States hostel scene is the 'Home Hostel' service where accommodation is offered to members in private houses.

In Central and South America, youth hostelling has not yet caught on seriously, although there are a few hostels in Mexico, Peru, Argentina, Chile, Brazil, Costa Rica, Uruguay and Colombia. Although in poorer countries you can find accommodation which is as cheap as the local youth hostel, members have the advantage of being able to look up an address in advance at points all over the world. They can then stay at the local branch of their own 'club' finding (albeit minimal) common standards of accommodation, and be sure of meeting and exchanging experiences with fellow travellers. See Directory for details.

CAMPING

by Anthony Smith, Jack Jackson, Melissa Shales and Martin Rosser.

Travelling light

Anthony Smith:

The first real camping I ever did was on a student expedition to Persia. There I learned the principle of inessential necessities. We were travelling by truck and could therefore pile on board everything we might possibly need. The truck could transport it all and we only had the problem of sorting through the excess whenever we needed something. Later we travelled by donkey and, miraculously, the number of necessities diminished as we realized the indisputable truth that donkeys carry less than trucks. Later still, after the donkey drivers had failed to coerce higher rates of pay from very empty student pockets, we continued on foot.

Amazingly, the number of necessities decreased yet again as a bunch of humans realized they could carry far less than donkeys and much, much less than trucks. The important lesson learned was that happiness, welfare and the ability to work did not lessen one iota as the wherewithal for camping decreased in quantity. It could even have been argued that these three blessings increased as less time was spent in making and breaking camp.

This lesson had to be learned several times over. Sometime later I was about to travel from Cape Town to England by motorbike. As I wished to sleep out, provide my own meals and experience a road network that was largely corrugated dirt, I found no difficulty in compiling a considerable list of necessities. We must have all made these lists (of corkscrews, tin openers, self–heating soup) and they are great fun, with a momentum that is hard to resist. "Why not a spare tin opener?" "And more medicine and another inner tube?" "Isn't it wise to take more shirts and stave off prickly heat?" Fortunately the garage that sold me the bike put a stop to such idiotic thinking. I had just strapped on a sack containing the real essentials (passport, documents, maps, money and address book) when a passing mechanic told me that any more weight would break the machine's back. (It was a modest machine.) Thus it was that I proceeded up the length of Africa without a sleeping bag, tent, groundsheet, spare petrol, oil, tools, food or even water, and never had cause for regret concerning this lack of wealth. Indeed I blessed the freedom it gave me. I could arrive anywhere, remove my one essential sack and know that nothing, save the bike itself, could be stolen. To have possessions is to be in danger of losing them. Better by far to save the robbers their trouble and start with nothing.

Kippered hammock

A sound tip is to do what the locals do. If they sleep out with nothing more than a blanket, it is probable that you can do likewise. If they can get by with a handful of dates at sunset, it is quite likely that you too can dispense with half a hundred-weight of dried egg, cocoa, vitamin tablets, corned beef, chocolate —and self–heating soup. To follow local practice and then try to improve on it can, however, be disastrous. Having learned the knack of sleeping in a Brazilian hammock as if it were in bed, I decided one thunderous night to bring modern technology to my aid. I covered myself with a space blanket to keep out the inevitable downpour.

Unfortunately, while I was asleep, the wretched thing slipped round beneath me and I awoke to find my body afloat in the pool of water it had collected. Being the first man to drown in a hammock is a poor way of achieving immortality. I looked over at my Indian travelling companion. Instead of fooling around with sublethal blankets, he had built a fire longitudinally beneath his hammock. Doubtless kippered by the smoke, but certainly dry, he slept the whole night through.

Planning and adventure

One trouble with our camping notions is that we are confused by a lingering memory of childhood expeditions. I camp with my children every year, and half the fun is not quite getting it right. As all adventure is said to be bad planning, so is a memorable camping holiday in which the guys act as trip wires, the air mattress farts into nothingness and even the tent itself falls victim to the first wind above a breeze.

Adults are therefore imbued with an expectation that camping is a slightly comic caper, rich with potential mishap. Those who camp a lot, such as wildlife photographers, have got over this teething stage. They expect camping to be (almost) as smooth and straightforward a business as living in a house. They do their best to make cooking, eating, washing and sleeping no more time–consuming than it is back home. The joy of finding grass in the soup or ants in the pants wears off for them on about the second day. It is only the temporary camper, knowing he will be back in a hotel (thank God) within a week, who does not bother to set things up properly.

Surviving natural hazards

I like the camping set–up to be as modest as possible. I have noticed, however, though that others disagree, welcoming every kind of extra. A night spent beneath the stars that finishes with the first bright shafts of dawn is hardly punishment, but some seem to think it so, and concentrate on removing as much of the natural environment as possible.

I remember a valley in the Zagros mountains where I had to stay with some colleagues. I had thought a sleeping bag would be sufficient and placed mine in a dried–up stream which had piles of sand for additional comfort. Certain others of the party erected large tents with yet larger flysheets (however improbable rain was at that time of year). They also started up a considerable generator which bathed the area in sound and light. As electricity was not a predominant feature of those wild regions, considerable numbers of moths and other insects, idling their way between the Persian Gulf and the Caspian Sea, were astonished at such a quantity of illumination and flew down to investigate. To counter their invasion, one camper set fire to several of those insect repellent coils and the whole campsite was shrouded in noxious effluent. Over in the dried–up stream I and two fellow spirits were amazed at the camping travesty down the way. We were even more astonished when, after a peaceful night, we awoke to hear complaints that a strong wind had so flapped at the fly sheets that no–one inside the tent had achieved a wink of sleep.

The most civilized camping I have ever experienced was in the Himalayas. The season was spring and tents are then most necessary both at the lower altitudes (where it rains a lot) and at the higher ones (where it freezes quite considerably). Major refreshment is also necessary because walking in those mountains is exhausting work, being "always up", as the locals put it, "except when its down." We slept inside sleeping bags on foam rubber within thick tents. We ate hot meals three times a day. We did very well —but we did not carry a thing. There were 36 porters for the six of us, the numbers falling as we ate into the provisions the men carried for us. I laboured up and down mighty valleys, longing for the next refreshment point and always delighted to see the ready–erected tents at each night's stopping place.

Personally, I was burdened with one camera, the smallest of notebooks and nothing more. The living conditions, as I have said, were excellent but what would they have become if I had been asked to carry everything I needed myself? It is at this point, when neither donkeys nor incredibly hardy mountain men are available, that the camper's true necessities are clarified. For myself, I am happy even to dispense with the toothbrush if I have to carry the thing all day long.

Fixing a tent

Jack Jackson: If you aren't worried about weight, and you are not constantly on the move, you might as well make yourselves as comfortable as possible, which can mean virtually building a tented village. Large groups will find it very useful to have a mess tent where the party can all congregate during bad weather and for meals.

On hard, sunbaked ground in hot countries, pegs normally supplied with tents are of little use, so have some good, thick, strong ones made for you from 60mm iron (or use 15cm nails). As wooden mallets will not drive pegs in, carry a normal claw hammer —you can also use the claw to pull the pegs out again. In loosely–compacted snow, standard metal pegs do not have much holding power, so it is useful to make some with a larger surface area from 2.5cms angle alloy. Even this does not solve all the problems because any warmth during the day will make the pegs warm up, melt the snow around them, and pull out causing the tent to fall down. The answer is to use very big pegs or ice axes for the two main guys fore and aft and then, for all the other guys, dig a hole about 25 cms deep, put the peg in horizontally with the guy line around its centre and compress fresh snow down hard on the peg with your boots to fill the hole.

Vango now offer a special 'tent anchor' for snow and soft sand; it is not any better in snow than the method described above, but is good in soft sand. Four of these would normally be all you would carry per tent.

If you sleep without a tent, you need a mosquito net in some areas. There are several types on the market, the ex–army nets which have the advantage of needing only one point of suspension, a camera tripod or ice axe will do for this if there is not a vehicle or tent nearby. However commercial manufacturers have now produced lighter and more compact nets and special impregnation kits are available which enhance the effectiveness of the net.

Since tents take heavy wear, carry some strong thread and a sailmaker's needle for repairs plus some spare groundsheet material and adhesive. Tents which are to be carried by porters, on donkeys or on a vehicle roof rack are best kept in a strong kit bag or they will soon be torn. If it is not a windy area, a 'space blanket' covering the reflecting side of the tent will help keep the tent cool during the day.

A site for sore eyes

Melissa Shales: If a large group of you are travelling together in the more civilized parts of the world, you won't have the option of just choosing a suitable area to camp, particularly if you want to explore the towns. In many countries, or in National Parks, it is actually illegal to camp outside the official sites. These, however, are often a very good option, far cheaper and cleaner than inexpensive hotels. Some motels have camp sites attached which allow you the option of using their restaurant facilities, swimming pools etc. The Caravan Club of Great Britain (East Grinstead House, East Grinstead, West Sussex RH19 1HA, tel: 0342 326944) is a useful source of information about good sites in Europe (for tented camping as well as caravanning) and also runs various small sites around the UK. Contact the club for details about their publication *Continental Sites Guide* (£13).

If there is an option, aim for a smaller site first. During the height of the tourist season, the larger ones tend to get very crowded, to the point where guy ropes are overlapping and you can hear the conversation in the tent next door. Some have hard stands which, while conveniently clean, are exceptionally hard unless you are travelling with the full paraphernalia of air beds etc. They also become horribly sterile areas that destroy virtually the entire ethos of camping. Avoid them if possible.

Many of the better sites will either have barbecues or special sites for fires. You will rarely be allowed to have a fire wherever you choose. The caretaker will often be able to supply wood if you ask in the morning. Check the toilets and washing facilities before you book in. Unless very small, when all you can expect is a primitive or chemical toilet and a stand–pipe, there should be showers and laundry facilities and a plentiful supply of hot water. In some countries, such as Zimbabwe, the sites will even have servants attached who will do your washing, sweep out the tent, run errands and build your fires for a small fee.

As with hotels, there are listings, and even star ratings in many places. If you want to go to what is obviously a highly rated site, visit the only one in the area, or are travelling in high season try and book first.

Camping on the hoof

Martin Rosser: It's not the expense of campsites that I object to, but having to put up with the others that are crammed in around you. I camp to find peace and solitude, to commune with nature. How to do that on a canvas conurbation is beyond me. As for facilities, I can and do bathe in the woods and prefer it to slopping around in an overcrowded concrete shower block.

If you make the decision to camp freely, you have to decide whether to ask the landowner for permission or remain discreetly out of sight. Which you do will depend solely on the circumstances. I am aware that trespassing campers have an awesomely bad reputation, so I prefer just to get on with it quietly. Nine times out of ten I am not discovered and leave everything as it was except for a piece of flattened grass. I doubt if anyone is the wiser. If you are discovered, your best defence is the clean and tidy way you are camping, so that it can be readily seen that nothing has, is, or will be damaged. It helps if you can greet the person without guilt (I have only once received more than a general caution to take care and that once was well deserved —we had left a cooking fire unattended).

When you come to select a spot, remember to avoid all extremes. If the climate you are in is hot, seek shade; if the land is marshy, look for high, well drained ground. Don't leave selecting your sight to the last minute, stopping in late twilight and having to choose within a small area. From late afternoon on you should keep an eye open and be prepared to stop a little short of your planned destination —or backtrack a mile or so if need be. A bad night's sleep or wet and damaged gear are well worth avoiding.

The selection of a resting place that is not to be final involves experience: here I can do little more than outline the general do's and don't's. After that, bitter experience starts to take over. I rarely camp with a tent, preferring a bivi–bag, which makes my choice of spot very versatile. Generally, I select a spot protected by trees or in a sheltered dip. The patch need not be bigger than 8 by 4ft for me and my gear. I have even slept on substantial slopes —the record being 45°. I avoid all low–lying wetlands (and even streams in summer) because flying bloodsuckers enrage me to the point of sleeplessness. In areas I know are going to be extra bad, I try to find ground high enough to have a constant stiff breeze. This is the most sure way I have of deterring the Scottish midge or the Australian mosquito.

For those who carry tents, the rules are slightly different. The ground you are after has to be as flat as possible and with as few rocks etc. Take a leaf out of the London taxi driver's book who knows the exact dimensions of his cab. Just as he is able to slide his cab into the most unlikely looking gaps, you too should know where and, more importantly, where not to pitch. Sleeping in a tent, you have less to worry about on the insects front, but you should be more wary of falling branches and the like. Tents are far easier to damage than bivouac sheets, and more expensive to repair or replace. If you have the opportunity, face the tent doors eastwards. That way you don't have to get up, or even fully wake up, to watch the dawn break. For the rest, just apply common sense. Don't pitch a tent with its only door facing into a gale, and don't camp in a dry river bed when the rains are due, although it has to be said that dry river beds are very comfortable in the right season —flat floor, and plenty of firewood to hand.

The reason I prefer bivouacing is that is forces you to take greater notice of the terrain that surrounds you. You become more versatile in your camping and more ready to sleep anywhere. I have slept in derelict buildings and under bridges whilst experiencing the low life; up trees; in caves; and I once found a sea cliff with a horizontal crack running three feet high and over ten feet deep. Sleeping in there was an experience and a half as it was 60 feet above a rocky shore on which the waves crashed all night.

A friend went onto greater things and slept behind a waterfall (and once in the down turned shovel of an ancient and abandoned mechanical digger). So if there is a moral to this tale of where to camp: use your common sense; break all the rules in the boy scout manual —but sensibly; and finally to be adventurous and try new ways. Even if you carry a tent you don't have to use it. ■

A BASIC GUIDE TO HEALTH
Chapter 11

HEALTH PLANNING

by Drs Nick Beeching and Emma Woolfenden

The most carefully planned holiday, business trip or expedition may be ruined by illness, much of which is preventable. It is logical to put as much effort into protecting your health while abroad as you have into planning your itinerary and obtaining the necessary equipment and travel papers. Unfortunately, it is not in the best commercial interests of travel companies to emphasize the possible health hazards of destinations that are being sold to potential customers: most holiday brochures limit health warnings to the minimum legal requirements, and some travel agents are woefully ignorant of the dangers of travel to more exotic climates. I have recently treated a travel agent for life–threatening malaria caught on the Kenyan coast. He had not taken malaria prophylaxis, despite the long and widespread recognition of the dangers of malaria in this area.

Happily, travellers' health problems are usually more mundane. Fatigue from overwork before a business trip or much–needed holiday, the stress of travel itself, exposure to new climates and overindulgence in rich food, alcohol and tobacco all contribute to increased vulnerability to illness. Short–lived episodes of diarrhoea affect up to 50 per cent of travellers, and up to one fifth of tourists on some Mediterranean package holidays will have mild respiratory problems such as head colds, flu–like illnesses or, rarely, more severe pneumonias such as Legionnaires' disease. Sunburn or heat exhaustion are common, and accidents associated with unfamiliar sports such as skiing are an obvious hazard. The commonest cause of death among expatriates is road traffic accidents —not exotic infections.

Pre–travel health check–list

Starting three months before you travel, consult your family doctor and specialist agencies as necessary to:

1. Obtain information about specific health problems at your destinations
2. Consider current health, medical and dental fitness for travel and current medications
3. Obtain adequate health insurance (and form E111 if travelling to an EC country)

4. Check again that health insurance is adequate
5. Plan and obtain necessary immunizations and malaria prophylaxis
6. Plan and obtain other medications and first aid items and any necessary documentation
7. Consider need for first–aid training course

Information sources

The depth of preparation required before travel clearly depends on the general health of the individual and on his or her destination(s). Since the last edition of this handbook in 1991 accessible information on health for travellers has improved considerably and the following sections in this chapter are only intended to provide a brief outline of steps to be considered.

Travellers to areas outside Europe, North America or Australasia are advised to invest in a copy of *Travellers' Health: How to Stay Healthy Abroad* (3rd edition OUP, £7.99) by Dr Richard Dawood —a guide which contains a wealth of information on all aspects of travel medicine. This is updated by regular features in *TRAVELLER* magazine (published by WEXAS), and is particularly recommended for those planning to work abroad or embarking on prolonged overland trips or expeditions in remote areas.

British travellers should obtain the booklet *Health Advice for Travellers Anywhere in the World*, prepared by the Department of Health and the Central Office of Information (booklet T4). This contains details of the documentation required for entitlement to free medical care and can be obtained from Post Offices, GP surgeries and vaccination centres or by telephoning the Health Literature Line (Freephone 0800 555 777). The leaflet is also updated daily on Prestel, page 50063.

When travelling outside Europe, it is wise to obtain information about compulsory immunization requirements from the appropriate Embassy, Consulate or High Commission of each country that you plan to visit. However, do not expect their personnel to be able to give you general medical advice, and their information is not always as up to date as it should be.

British travellers to exotic locations should also consult their District Public Health Department or one of the centres of specific expertise listed in the Directory (Section 11) for the latest information on immunization requirements and malaria prophylaxis. Those planning to work abroad should try and contact an employee of the company to ensure that adequate provision for medical and dental care is provided within their contract. If necessary, they should also consider taking out health insurance in addition to company policies.

Your medical and dental health

If in any doubt about possible hazards of travel because of a pre–existing medical condition, consult your family doctor. People with heart or chest problems, recurrent blood clots in the legs or lungs, recent strokes, uncontrolled blood pressure, epilepsy, psychiatric disorders or chronic sinus or ear problems may be at risk when flying.

Late pregnancy is a contra indication to flying, diabetics taking medication will need special advice and the disabled will have specific requirements that may need to be notified to airline and airport authorities (see Chapter 8). People with chronic health problems or women who are obviously pregnant should ask their doctor to complete a standard airline form certifying their fitness for flying. This form should be obtained from the airline concerned.

Adequate supplies of all routinely–prescribed medications, including oral contraceptives, should also be obtained before departure. For short trips within Europe, these will be provided as NHS prescriptions. Those planning longer stays abroad should determine the availability of their medication overseas or take adequate supplies (you may need to pay for these on private prescription). It is also strongly recommended that you obtain a certificate from your doctor detailing the drugs prescribed, including the correct pharmacological name, as well as the trade name. This will be necessary to satisfy customs officials and you may need to obtain certified translations into appropriate languages. Some drugs readily obtainable in the UK are viewed with great suspicion elsewhere (codeine, for example, is considered a controlled drug in many countries, and tranquillizers such as diazepam can cause problems). Single women working in Saudi Arabia should take adequate supplies of oral contraceptives and will need a certified Arabic translation of the certificate stating that the contraceptives have been prescribed for their personal use.

Those with recurring medical problems should also obtain a letter from their family doctor detailing the condition(s) —the letter can then be shown to doctors abroad if emergency treatment becomes necessary.

People with surgically implanted devices are also advised to carry a doctor's certificate to show security officials. Artificial hip replacements frequently set off metal detection security alarms at airports, as do indwelling intravenous (eg. *Portacath*) central venous lines. People with cardiac pacemakers are unlikely to run into problems due to electrical interference from British or North American airport metal detectors, but should try to avoid going through them and arrange instead for a personal body check by security officials.

Expatriates taking up a contract abroad will often have to submit to a detailed medical examination as a condition of employment. Many countries insist on a negative HIV–antibody test before allowing foreigners to work. Some, including the USA, will not allow any known HIV positive individual to enter the country, despite advice from the World Health Organization (WHO) that such regulations are ineffective as a means of controlling the spread of HIV infection.

HIV–positive travellers should consult their medical specialist and local support groups about specific travel insurance problems and the advisability of travel. Individuals with specific chronic health problems such as epilepsy, diabetes or long term steroid treatment, should obtain a 'Medic–alert' bracelet or similar, which is more easily located in a medical emergency than a card carried in a pocket.

Dental health is often taken for granted by British citizens who get a rude shock when faced with bills for dental work overseas. Those embarking on prolonged travel or work abroad, or planning to visit very cold areas, should have a full preventative dental check up before leaving.

Spare spectacles, contact lenses and contact lens solutions should also be obtained before travelling. If you are planning a vigorous holiday or expedition (eg. skiing, hill–walking etc) you will need to begin an appropriate fitness regime long before departure.

Insurance

Falling ill while abroad can be very expensive. Partial exemption from medical charges only applies in certain circumstances —primarily in EC countries. Those travelling to the EC should obtain the booklet *Health Advice for Travellers Anywhere in the World* (T4, as mentioned before). This contains the form CM1 which must be completed in order to obtain the important E111 form which you should carry with your travel documents to be eligible for benefit in all EC countries (except Denmark, Gibraltar, the Irish Republic and Portugal which do not require form E111).

The EC will allow eligible citizens of any member country to get urgent treatment free, or at a reduced cost, during temporary stays. Continuing treatment for a pre–existing illness, eg asthma, high blood pressure, etc., may not fall within the definition of urgent treatment and may not attract these benefits. What is more, these arrangements do not apply if you are working or living in another EC country. In these circumstances you should write to the DSS Contributions Agency, Overseas Branch Newcastle upon Tyne, NE98 1YX seeking information on your rights to health care in another EC country.

In some EC countries (eg. France, Belgium and Luxembourg) you will only be covered for approximately 70 per cent of treatment and the remainder may be costly. You may also have to pay the full cost initially and then claim back the 70 per cent share. For these reasons, travellers should consider taking out private insurance to cover that part of the cost they may have to meet themselves.

Outside the EC, some countries offer emergency care either free or for a part fee only. This concession may apply only in public health hospitals and not in private clinics. It is also often necessary to show your National Health Service medical card as well as your UK passport. Details of reciprocal health agreements for all countries are listed in DSS leaflet NI38, available from local DSS offices or the DSS Overseas Branch. Specific leaflets giving details of health care in individual countries can also be obtained from the DSS Overseas Branch.

Elsewhere, the cost of consultation, medicines, treatment and hospital care must be paid by the patient. As this could be financially crippling, full health insurance is a wise precaution (see Chapter 9 for more details). If you are taken gravely ill or severely injured in the USA, the final medical bill may seem astronomical.

Discuss the adequacy of your cover with your travel agent, especially if high technology medical care may be needed. Those working or travelling abroad for extended periods and those taking part in hazardous expeditions, should ensure that travel insurance has adequate allowance for emergency evacuation to a country with good medical facilities.

If you incur medical expenses, present your policy to the doctor and ask him/her to send the bill direct to your insurance company. Many doctors demand cash (and the level of their fees may alarm you) so keep a reserve of traveller's cheques for this purpose. Insist on a receipt and the insurance company will reimburse you on your return.

Do not expect to find the same medical standards as those of your home country during your wanderings. Some practitioners routinely include expensive drugs for the simplest of conditions; multi–vitamin therapy, intravenous injections and the inevitable suppositories may also be given unnecessarily to run up a bigger bill. Be prepared to barter diplomatically about this, to offer those drugs you are carrying for treatment if appropriate, and even to shop around for medical advice.

Immunizations

Immunizations may be necessary to prevent illnesses that are common in many countries but which are rarely encountered in Western Europe, North America or Australasia. In the UK you can get most vaccinations through a general practitioner or a specialized vaccination centre (see Directory, Section 11). Some will be free of charge, but the majority will have to be paid for privately. The exact requirements for a traveller will depend on his or her lifestyle, intended destinations and personal vaccination history, but should be considered at least two to three months before departure.

Modern immunizations are remarkably safe and well–tolerated. However, some vaccines contain traces of penicillin or neomycin and allergy to these antibiotics should be declared. Some vaccines are prepared in eggs and serious allergy to eggs will preclude some inoculations. Patients with chronic illness, particularly immune deficiency due to steroid treatment, cancer chemotherapy or HIV infection, should not receive most vaccines containing live organisms (such as oral polio vaccine), while pregnancy is also a contraindication for several vaccines.

International regulations cover the *minimum* legal requirements for a few vaccinations, particularly yellow fever which has to be administered in a designated centre and recorded on a specific internationally–recognized certificate. Many countries have idiosyncratic certificate requirements — cholera vaccinations, for example— and the situation will change if an epidemic is in progress, hence the need for up–to–date information before you travel.

If in doubt about the need for International Certificates for yellow fever or cholera, it may be wise to obtain one before travel rather than being forced to accept vaccination (using needles of dubious origin and sterility) on arrival at your destination.

It is equally important that the traveller has adequate protection against infections such as hepatitis A, polio and tetanus, even though proof of this will not be required by immigration officials at your destination. All travellers should have up–to–date tetanus immunizations, and travellers outside Europe, North America and Australasia should ensure that polio immunization is adequate. Children should have received all their childhood immunizations, and children who are going to live in the tropics should have early immunization against tuberculosis (BCG).

The following list summarizes information on the most commonly required vaccinations. For a guideline of requirements for each country see the Geographical Section, starting page 589. The information below is in alphabetical order.

Cholera: A profuse diarrhoeal illness which poses little risk to the majority of travellers, and which is acquired from contaminated food or water. There have recently been large epidemics in much of South America and regions of Central Africa and the Indian Subcontinent. Limited protection (about 50 per cent) is by vaccination which ideally consists of two injections at least 10 days apart. Some countries still insist on a cholera vaccination certificate which is only valid for six months and can be provided after one injection.

Diphtheria: Still common in many parts of the tropics although rarely a hazard for Western tourists. There have recently been epidemics in several member states of the former USSR. Most travellers will have received adequate immunization in childhood (the 'D' in DPT), but may require a booster. Older adults may not have had the vaccine and will need a full course of three doses separated by a month each.

Hepatitis A: A water–borne virus infection that poses a *significant* health hazard for travellers to all parts of the tropics. The illness has an incubation period of three to six weeks and causes lethargy and jaundice which may last for several weeks. The illness is often very mild in children aged less than 5, and often goes completely unnoticed in this age group, so some adults will already have immunity even if they never had jaundice.

There are two options for protection. The old–fashioned immunization with a gammaglobulin injection just prior to travel provides reasonable protection for up to six months, after which a repeat will be needed if still travelling. This is still a suitable option for the 'one off' traveller going on a short trip, but supplies of gammaglobulin are erratic and time should be allowed to ensure that the immunization is available.

Frequent travellers, or those planning to stay abroad for more than six months, should consider having the new vaccine ('Havrix'). Two doses separated by two to four weeks give excellent protection, which lasts for several years if a third booster dose is given six to twelve months later. The vaccine is expensive and frequent travellers should ask for a blood test first to see if they are already immune to hepatitis A. Newer versions of 'Havrix' are now being marketed, providing equal protection with only one dose.

Hepatitis B: A common infection in the tropics and countries bordering the Mediterranean, hepatitis B is caused by a virus that is transmitted by sex or an infusion of contaminated blood (see the article on sex and drugs in this chapter). Hepatitis B shows similar symptoms to those of hepatitis A but sometimes is more severe and may lead to lasting liver damage. It is preventable with safe and highly effective injections given at three intervals, ideally with the second and third injections following at one and six month intervals after the first. More rapid protection can be provided by giving the third dose two months after the first, but this has to be boosted by a fourth dose at one year if protection is to last for several years.

The vaccination is recommended for health workers and those working in refugee camps and similar environments, as well as for people planning to live in the tropics for more than six months. It should also be considered by all adults who might have sexual contact with travellers (other than their regular partner) or anyone living in areas where the infection is prevalent. A course of three injections costs approximately £35.

Japanese encephalitis: A rare virus infection causing severe encephalitis (inflammation of the brain) primarily in rural areas of Asia, especially during the rainy season. A moderately effective vaccine is obtainable only through specialist vaccination clinics and usually restricted to those wandering off the beaten track for prolonged periods.

Malaria: No vaccine available, see the article on malaria in this chapter for details about prevention.

Meningococcal meningitis: Epidemics recur in many parts of Sub–Saharan Africa (mainly in the dry season) and an epidemic which began in Nepal moved to many other countries via the 1987 Haj pilgrimage to Mecca. The Saudi Arabian authorities now require Haj pilgrims to provide certificates of vaccination against the infection, and a safe and effective vaccine against strains A and C of the organism is now available. This vaccine does not protect against strain B of the meningococcus which is the commonest strain found in the UK. The vaccine is not normally required by tourists unless travelling to an area with a current epidemic, or unless you plan to work in a region (especially in hospitals or schools) where the infection is common.

Poliomyelitis (polio): This viral infection, which causes untreatable meningitis and paralysis, is still a problem in all parts of the tropics and can be prevented by vaccination. Most adults have been immunized but should receive a booster if this has not been done in the past 10 years. Vaccination is usually given by mouth using a 'live' polio virus variant that provides protection but does not cause illness. Patients with immune suppression can receive injections of killed organisms instead (the 'Salk' vaccine).

Rabies: This virus infection of animals is found in most countries apart from the UK and Australia and New Zealand. It is untreatable once symptoms have developed. Avoid contact with all dogs or cats while abroad, or with any animal that behaves strangely. Vaccination before travel is safe but is usually reserved for those working with animals or those planning expeditions or employment in remote areas (see the following article on health problems abroad for action to be taken if bitten).

Smallpox: This vaccination is no longer required following the successful worldwide eradication of smallpox.

Tetanus: This severe illness can follow even minor trauma that introduces soil through the skin (eg. thorn injuries). Vaccination effectively prevents this and a booster dose will be needed for adults who have not been immunized in the last 10 years. Routine childhood immunization did not begin in the UK until 1961 and older adults may need a full course of immunization if they have missed out on this. Any contaminated wounds received while abroad should be cleaned and medical consultation sought concerning the need for antibiotics and additional vaccination.

Tuberculosis: Although this bacterial infection is widespread in the tropics, it does not pose a major hazard for most travellers. Most British (but not North American) adults, and children aged over 13, will have already been immunized against TB (BCG vaccination). Those embarking on prolonged travel or employment abroad should consult their doctor about their TB immune status. Pre–employment medical examinations usually include this.

Typhoid: This bacterial infection is acquired from contaminated food, water or milk in any area of poor sanitation outside Europe, North America or Australasia.

Typhoid vaccination is not necessary for most short–stay tourists, but should be considered by all planning prolonged or remote travel in areas of poor hygiene. The old–fashioned TAB (typhoid and paratyphoid A and B vaccine) is no longer used, as there are now several alternatives.

The older vaccine (two injections) provides moderate protection for about three years, after which a single booster dose is required. The vaccine commonly causes a sore arm and fever, especially in those who have had the vaccine before. The side-effects may be lessened if the vaccine is given in the skin tissues (intradermal injection). A new injected vaccine ('Typhim Ci') appears to give equivalent protection after one dose only, but is more expensive.

The third alternative is a course of capsules ('Ty 21a') containing a live vaccine strain, taken by mouth over several days. This may appeal to those with a phobia of needles, but the course is expensive and, must be taken strictly according to the manufacturer's instructions, and only provides immunity for one year after which it will need to be repeated. It cannot be taken at the same time as oral polio vaccine or any antibiotic, or within 12 hours after taking mefloquine. As with other live vaccines, it is not recommended for pregnant women.

Yellow fever: This virus infection, causing a lethal hepatitis, is transmitted by mosquitoes and is restricted to parts of Africa and South and Central America. It can be prevented by a highly effective and safe vaccine, the certificate for which is valid for 10 years, starting 10 days after vaccination. Vaccination and the International Certificate can only be given at World Health Organization approved centres —in Britain this has now been extended to include many general practitioners.

Simple first aid

Individual requirements vary greatly and most travellers do not need to carry enormous bags of medical supplies. This section covers a few health items that the majority of travellers should consider. Those going to malarious areas should read the advice given on malaria in this chapter, and those going to areas without ready access to medical care should read the article on health problems abroad for further suggestions for their kit bag.

First–aid training is appropriate for travellers to remote areas and those going on prolonged expeditions which might include a medical officer. As the medical needs of expeditions vary so much, an expedition kit bag list has not been included in this edition of the handbook. Expedition leaders should consult their own organization or one of the specialist agencies for advice.

Painkillers: I always carry soluble aspirin (in foil–sealed packs) which is an excellent painkiller and reduces inflammation associated with sunburn (just be careful about the water you dissolve it in!). Aspirin should not be given to children aged less than 12 and I also take paracetamol syrup for my young children. Both paracetamol and aspirin reduce fever associated with infections.

Adults who cannot tolerate aspirin because of ulcer problems, gastritis or asthma, should instead take paracetamol (not paracetamol/codeine preparations). To avoid potential embarrassment with customs officials, stronger painkillers should only be carried with evidence that they have been prescribed.

Cuts and grazes: A small supply of waterproof dressings (eg, *Bandaids*) is useful together with a tube of antiseptic cream such as *Savlon* —especially if travelling with children.

Sunburn: British travellers frequently underestimate the dangers of sunburn and should take particular care that children do not get burnt. Protect exposed areas from the sun, remembering the back of the neck. Sunbathing exposure times should be gradually increased and use adequate sunblock creams (waterproof if swimming), particularly at high altitude where UV light exposure is higher. Sunburn should be treated with rest, plenty of non–alcoholic drinks, and paracetamol or aspirin. Those who burn easily, may wish to take a tube of hydrocortisone cream for excessively burnt areas.

Motion sickness: If you are liable to travel sickness, try to sleep through as much of the journey as possible and avoid reading. Avoid watching the horizon through the window and, if travelling by boat, remain on deck as much as possible.

Several types of medication give potential relief from motion sickness when taken before the start of a journey, and sufferers should experiment to find out which suits them best. Antihistamines (eg, *Phenergan*) are popular, especially for children, but should not be taken with alcohol. Adults should not drive until all sedative effects of antihistamines have worn off. Other remedies include *Kwells* (hyoscine tablets), *Dramamine* (dimenhydrinate) and *Stugeron* (cinnarazine). *Scopoderm* patches, only available on prescription, release hyoscine through the skin for up to three days. Hyoscine taken by mouth or by skin patch causes a dry mouth and can cause sedation.

Constipation: The immobility of prolonged travel, dehydration during heat acclimatization and reluctance to use toilets of dubious cleanliness all contribute to constipation. Drink plenty of fluids and try to eat a high fibre diet. Those who are already prone to constipation may wish to take additional laxatives or fibre substitutes (eg, *Fybogel*).

Diarrhoea: Although this is a common problem, it is usually self–limiting and most travellers do not need to carry anti–diarrhoea medication with them (see the article on diarrhoeal illness). Diarrhoea reduces absorption of the contraceptive pill and women may wish to carry supplies of alternative contraceptives in case of this.

Female problems: Women who suffer from recurrent cystitis or vaginal thrush, should consult their doctor to obtain appropriate antibiotics to take with them. Tampons are often difficult to buy in many countries and should be bought before travelling. Periods are often irregular or may cease altogether during travel but this does not mean that you cannot become pregnant.

Insect bites: Insect bites are a nuisance in most parts of the world and also transmit a variety of infections, the most important of which is malaria. Personal insect repellents will be needed by most travellers and usually contain DEET (diethyltoluamide). Liquid formulations are the cheapest but less convenient to carry. Lotions and cream are available and sprays are the easiest to apply but are bulky to carry. Sticks of repellent are easier to carry and last the longest.

All these should be applied to the skin and to clothing adjacent to exposed areas of skin, but should not be applied around the eyes, nose and mouth (take particular care with children).

When abroad, try to reduce the amount of skin available to biting insects by wearing long sleeves, trousers or skirts. If a mosquito net is provided with your bed, use it. Permethrin–impregnated mosquito nets are effective and can be purchased before travel to malarious areas. 'Knock–down' insecticide sprays may be needed, and mosquito coils are easy to carry. Electric buzzers (that imitate male mosquito noises) are useless and candles and repellent strips (containing citronella) are not very effective. The bewildering variety of insect repellents and devices were comprehensively reviewed in the July 1991 issue of *Which?* (pages 398 to 401), and further advice can be obtained from your local chemist. Since then, a new insect repellent has been marketed by MASTA, called 'Mosiguard Natural'. This is made from a blend of eucalyptus oils and is said to be as effective as repellents based on DEET, and certainly more suitable for people who are sensitive to DEET.

If bitten by insects, try to avoid scratching which can introduce infection, particularly in the tropics. *Eurax* cream or calamine lotion can relieve local irritation, and antihistamine tablets may help those that have been bitten extensively.

Antihistamine creams should be used with caution as they can cause local reactions, and I prefer to use weak hydrocortisone cream on bites that are very irritating. Hydrocortisone cream should only be used if the skin is not obviously broken or infected. Increasing pain, redness or swelling or obvious pus suggest infection, and medical attention should be sought.

HIV prevention: Most HIV infections are acquired sexually (see article on sex and drugs in this chapter). All adults should consider taking a supply of condoms. Travellers to countries with limited medical facilities should consider taking a supply of sterile needles and syringes so that injections required abroad are not given with re–usable needles of doubtful sterility.

Personal supplies of syringes and needles can make customs officials very suspicious, and condoms are not acceptable in some countries —particularly the Middle East and Eire.

To avoid problems at the border, it is worth buying these items as part of a small HIV/AIDS prevention pack which are available from most of the medical equipment suppliers listed in Section 11 of the Directory. Larger 'HIV prevention packs' that may include blood product substitutes, are rarely worth carrying.

On your return

On returning from a long trip, most travellers will experience some euphoria and elation, as well as family reunions and the interested enquiries of friends. After this, as relaxation, and possibly jet lag set in, a period of apathy, exhaustion and weariness can follow. Recognize this and allow a few quiet days if it is feasible. There are usually many pressures at this stage, especially if equipment is to be unpacked and sorted, photographs processed, etc.

Another pressure for most people is the none too welcome thought of returning to the mundane chores involved in earning one's daily bread. If your travels have been challenging, then a couple of recovery days will probably make you work more efficiently thereafter and cope more expeditiously with the thousands of tasks which seem to need urgent attention.

After a time of excitement and adventure, some will go through a period of being restless and bored with the simple routine of home and work. They may not be aware of this temporary change in personality but their families certainly will be. Having pointed out this problem, we cannot suggest any way of overcoming it except perhaps to recommend that everyone concerned try to recognize it and be a little more tolerant than normal. This may not be a sensible time to take major decisions affecting career, family and business.

Some will be relieved to arrive in their hygienic homes after wandering in areas containing some of the world's nastiest diseases. Unfortunately, the risk of ill health is not altogether gone as you may still be incubating an illness acquired abroad —incubation for diseases such as hepatitis or malaria could take a few months or in the extreme case of rabies, a few years.

After your return, any medical symptoms or even just a feeling of debility or chronic ill health must not be ignored —medical help should be sought. Tell your physician where you have travelled (in detail), including brief stopovers. It may be that you are carrying some illness outside the spectrum normally considered. Sadly this has been known to cause mistaken diagnosis so that malaria, for example, has been labelled as influenza with occasionally fatal consequences.

Tropical worms and other parasites, enteric fevers, typhus, histoplasmosis (a fungal disease breathed in on guano, making cavers particularly vulnerable), tuberculosis, tropical virus diseases, amoebic dysentery and hepatitis may all need to be treated. For these illnesses to be successfully treated, many patients will need expert medical attention.

Routine tropical disease check ups are provided by some companies for their employees during or after postings abroad. They are not generally required by other travellers who have not been ill while abroad or after their return. People who feel that they might have acquired an exotic infection or who have received treatment for infection abroad, should ask their doctor about referral to a unit with an interest in tropical diseases. Most health regions have a suitable unit and more specialist units are listed in the Directory.

All unprotected sexual encounters while travelling carry high risks of infection with various sexually transmitted diseases in addition to HIV and hepatitis B. A post–travel check up is strongly advised, even if you have no symptoms. Your local hospital will advise about the nearest clinic —variously called genito-urinary medicine (GUM) clinics, sexually–transmitted disease (STD) clinics, sexual health clinics, VD clinics or 'special' clinics. Absolute anonymity is guaranteed, and no referral is needed from your general practitioner.

After leaving malarial areas, many will feel less motivated to continue their antimalarial drugs. It is strongly recommended that these be taken for a minimum of 28 days after leaving the endemic area. Failure to do this has caused many travellers to develop malaria some weeks after they thought they were totally safe. This is more than a nuisance: it has occasionally been fatal.

Fortunately, the majority of travellers return home with nothing other than pleasant memories of an enjoyable interlude in their lives.

TRAVEL STRESS

by Hilary Bradt

The scene is familiar: a crowded bus station in some Third World country; passengers push and shove excitedly; an angry and discordant voice rings out, "But I've got a reserved seat! Look, it says number 18, but there's someone sitting there!" The foreigner may or may not win this battle, but ultimately he will lose the war between 'what should be' (his expectations) and 'what is' (their culture) —becoming yet another victim of stress.

It is ironic that this complaint, so fashionable among businessmen, should be such a problem for many travellers who believe they are escaping such pressures when they leave home. But by travelling rough, they are immediately immersing themselves in a different culture and thus subjecting themselves to a new set of psychological stresses.

The physical deprivations that are inherent in budget travel are not usually a problem. Most travellers adjust well enough to having a shower every two months, eating beans and rice every day and sleeping in dirty, lumpy beds in company with the local wildlife. These are part of the certainties of this mode of travel. It is the uncertainties that wear people down: the buses that double–book their seats, usually leaving an hour late but occasionally slipping away early; the landslide that blocks the road to the coast on the one day of the month that a boat leaves for Paradise Island; the inevitable *mañana* response; the struggle with a foreign language and foreign attitudes.

Culture shock

It's this 'foreignness' which often comes as an unexpected shock. The people are different, their customs are different, and so are their basic values and moralities. Irritatingly, these differences are most frequently exhibited by those who amble down the Third World Corridors of Power controlling the fate of travellers. But ordinary people are different too and believers in Universal Brotherhood often find this hard to accept —as do women travelling alone. Many travellers escape back to their own culture periodically by mixing with the upper classes of the countries in which they are travelling —people who were educated in Europe or America and are westernised in their outlook. Come to think of it, maybe this is why hitchhikers show so few signs of travel stress: they meet wealthier car owners and can often lapse into a childlike dependence on their hosts.

Fear and anxiety

At least hitchhikers can alternate between blissful relaxation and sheer terror, as can other adventurous travellers. Fear, in small doses, never did anyone any harm. It seems a necessary ingredient to everyday life; consciously or unconsciously, most people seek out danger. If they don't rock climb or parachute jump, they drive too fast, refuse to give up smoking or resign from their safe jobs to travel the world. The stab of fear that travellers experience as they traverse a glacier, eye a gun–toting soldier or approach a 'difficult' border is followed by a feeling of exhilaration once the perceived danger has passed.

A rush of adrenaline is OK. The hazard is the prolonged state of tension or stress, to which the body reacts in a variety of ways: irritability, headaches, inability to sleep at night and a continuous feeling of anxiety. The budget traveller is particularly at risk because money shortages provoke so many additional anxieties to the cultural stresses mentioned earlier. The day–to–day worry of running out of money is an obvious one, but there is also the fear of being robbed (no money to replace stolen items) and of becoming ill. Many travellers worry about their health anyway, but those who can't afford a doctor, let alone a stay in hospital, can become quite obsessional. Yet these are the people who travel in a manner most likely to jeopardise their health. Since their plan is often 'to travel until the money runs out', those diseases such as hepatitis with a long incubation period will manifest themselves during the trip. Chronic illnesses like amoebic dysentery undermine the health and well–being of many budget travellers, leaving them far more susceptible to psychological pressures. Even the open–endedness of their journey may cause anxiety.

Tranquillizers

Now I've convinced you that half the world's travellers are heading for a nervous breakdown rather than the nearest beach, let's see what can be done to ease the situation (apart from bringing more money). There are tranquillizers. This is how most doctors treat the symptoms of stress since they assume that the problems causing the anxiety are an unavoidable part of everyday life. Travellers should not rule them out (I've met people who consume Valium until they scarcely know who they are), but since they have chosen to be in their situation, it should be possible to eliminate some of the reasons.

They can begin by asking themselves why they decided to travel in the first place. If the answer is that it was 'to get away from it all', journeying for long distances seems a bit pointless —better to hole up in a small village or island and begin the lotus–eating life. If the motive for travel is a keen interest in natural history, archaeology or people, then the problems inherent in getting to their destination are usually overridden in the excitement of arriving. However, those who find the lets and hindrances that stand between them and their goal too nerve–wracking (and the more enthusiastic they are, the more frustrated they'll become) should consider relaxing their budget in favour of spending more money on transportation, etc, even if it does mean a shorter trip.

The average overlander, however, considers the journey the object and will probably find that time on the road will gradually eliminate his anxieties (like a young man I met in Ecuador: he was forever thinking about his money, but when I met him again in Bolivia, he was a changed man, relaxed and happy. "Well," he said, in answer to my question, "You remember I was always worrying about running out of money? Now I have, so I have nothing to worry about!"

If a traveller can learn the language and appreciate the differences between the countries he visits and his own, he will come a long way towards understanding and finally accepting them. His tensions and frustrations will then finally disappear.

But travellers should not expect too much of themselves. You are what you are, and a few months of travel are not going to undo the conditioning of your formative years. Know yourself, your strengths and weaknesses, and plan your trip accordingly. And if you don't know yourself at the start of a long journey, you will by the end.

CULTURE SHOCK

by Adrian Furnham

Nearly every traveller must have experienced culture shock at some time or other. Like jet lag it is an aspect of travel which is both negative and difficult to define. But what precisely is it? When and why does it occur? And, more importantly, how can we prevent it or at least cope with it?

Although the experience of culture shock has no doubt been around for centuries, it was only 25 years ago that an anthropologist called Oberg coined the term. Others have attempted to improve upon and extend the concept and have come up with alternative jargon such as 'culture fatigue,' 'role shock' and 'pervasive ambiguity.'

Strain

From the writings of travellers and interviews with tourists, foreign students, migrants and refugees, psychologists have attempted to specify the exact nature of this unpleasant experience. It seems that the syndrome has six facets. Firstly, there is strain caused by the effort of making necessary psychological adaptations —speaking another language, coping with the currency, driving on the other side of the road, etc. Secondly, there is often a sense of loss and a feeling of deprivation with regard to friends, possessions and status. If you are in a place where nobody knows, loves, respects and confides in you, you may feel anonymous and deprived of your status and role in society, as well as bereft of familiar and useful objects. Thirdly, there is often a feeling of rejection —your rejection of the natives and their rejection of you.

Travellers stand out by their skin, clothes, and language. Depending on the experience of the natives, they may be seen as unwanted intruders, an easy rip–off, or friends.

A fourth symptom of culture shock is confusion. Travellers can become unsure about their roles, their values, their feelings and sometimes about who they are. When a people lives by a different moral and social code from your own, interaction for even a comparatively short period, can be very confusing. Once one becomes more aware of cultural differences typical reactions of surprise, anxiety, even disgust and indignation occur. The way foreigners treat their animals, eat food, worship their god, or perform their toiletries often cause amazement and horror to naive travellers. Finally, culture shock often involves feelings of impotence due to not being able to cope with the new environment.

Little England

Observers of sojourners and long–term travellers have noted that there are usually two extreme reactions to culture shock: those who act as if they 'never left home' and those who immediately 'go native.' The former chauvinists create 'little Englands' in foreign fields, refusing to compromise their diet or dress, and like the proverbial mad dogs, insisting on going out in the midday sun. The latter reject all aspects of their own culture and enthusiastically do in Rome as the Romans do.

Most travellers, however, experience less dramatic but equally uncomfortable reactions to culture shock. These may include excessive concern over drinking water, food, dishes and bedding; fits of anger over delays and other minor frustrations; excessive fear of being cheated, robbed or injured; great concern over minor pains and interruptions; and a longing to be back at the idealised home "where you can get a good cup of tea and talk to sensible people."

But, as any seasoned traveller will know, often one begins to get used to, and even learns to like the new culture. In fact writers have suggested that people go through a number of phases when living in a new culture. Oberg, in his original writings, listed four stages: the 'honeymoon' which is characterised by enchantment, fascination, enthusiasm and admiration for the new culture as well as cordial (but superficial) relationships. In this stage people are generally intrigued and euphoric. Many tourists never stay long enough to move out of the honeymoon period. The second phase heralds crisis and disintegration. It is now that the traveller feels loss, isolation, loneliness and inadequacy, and tends to become depressed and withdrawn. This happens most often after two to six months of living in the new culture.

The third phase is the most problematic and involves reintegration. At this point people tend to reject the host culture, becoming opinionated and negative partly as a means of showing their self–assertion and growing self–esteem. The fourth stage of 'autonomy' finds the traveller assured, relaxed, warm and empathic because he or she is socially and linguistically capable of negotiating most new and different social situations in the culture.

And finally the 'independent' phase is achieved —characterised by trust, humour and the acceptance and enjoyment of social, psychological and cultural differences.

U–curve

For obvious reasons, this independent phase is called the 'U–curve' hypothesis. If you plot satisfaction and adaptation (x axis) over time (y axis), you see a high point beginning, followed by a steep decline, a period at the bottom, but then a steady climb back up. More interestingly, some researchers have shown evidence not of a U–curve but a 'W–curve', ie once travellers return to their home country, they often undergo a similar re–acculturation, again in the shape of a U.

Hence a 'double U' or W–curve.

Other research has shown similar intriguing findings. Imagine, for instance, that you are going to Morocco for the first time. You are asked to describe or rate both the average Briton and the average Moroccan in terms of their humour, wealth, trustworthiness etc. both before you go and after you return. Frequently it has been found that people change their opinions of their own countrymen and women more than that of the foreigners. In other words, travel makes you look much more critically at yourself and your culture than most people think. And this self–criticism may itself be rather unhelpful.

The trouble with these stage theories is that not everyone goes through the stages. Not everyone feels like Nancy Mitford when she wrote: "I loathe abroad, nothing would induce me to live there… and, as for foreigners, they are all the same and make me sick." But I suspect Robert Morley is not far from the truth when he remarked: "The British tourist is always happy abroad so long as the natives are waiters."

Then there is also the shock of being visited. Anyone who lives in a popular tourist town soon becomes aware that it is not only the tourist but also the native who experiences culture shock. Of course, the amount and type of shock that tourists can impart to local people is an indication of a number of things, such as the relative proportion of tourists to natives, the duration of their stay, the comparative wealth and development of the two groups and the racial and ethnic prejudices of both.

Of course not everybody will experience culture shock. Older, better educated, confident and skillful adults (particularly those who speak the language) tend to adapt best. Yet there is considerable evidence that sojourners, like foreign students, voluntary workers, businessmen, diplomats and even military people become so confused and depressed that they have to be sent home at great expense. That is why many organizations attempt to lessen culture shock by a number of training techniques. The foreign office, the British Council and many multi–nationals do this for good reason, learning from bitter experience.

Training

For a number of reasons, information and advice in the form of lectures and pamphlets, etc, is very popular but not always very useful . The 'facts' that are given are often too general to have any clear, specific application in particular circumstances. Facts emphasise the exotic and ignore the mundane (how to hail a taxi, for example,). This technique also gives the impression that the culture can be easily understood; and even if facts are retained, they do not necessarily lead to accommodating behaviour.

A second technique is 'isomorphic training.' This is based on the theory that a major cause of cross–cultural communication problems comes from the fact that most people tend to offer different explanations for each other's behaviour. This technique introduces various episodes that end in embarrassment, misunderstanding or hostility between people from two different cultures. The trainee is then presented with four or five alternative explanations of what went wrong, all of which correspond to different attributions of the observed behaviour. Only one is correct from the perspective of the culture being learned. This is an interesting and useful technique but depends for much of its success on the relevance of the various episodes chosen.

Perhaps the most successful method is 'skills training.' It has been pointed out that socially inadequate or inept individuals have not mastered the social conventions of their own society. Either they are unaware of the rules and processes of everyday behaviour or, if aware of the rules, they are unable or unwilling to abide by them. They are therefore like strangers in their own land. People newly arrived in an alien culture will be in a similar position and may benefit from simple skills training.

This involves analysing everyday encounters such as buying and selling, introductions, refusal of requests. You will also observe successful culture models engaging in these acts and will practise yourself, helped in the learning process by a video tape of your efforts. This may all sound very clinical, but can be great fun and very informative.

Practical advice

Many travellers, unless on business and with considerable company resources behind them, do not have the time or money to go on courses that prevent or minimize culture shock. They have to leap in at the deep end and hope that they can swim. But there are some simple things they can do that may well prevent the shock and improve communications.

Before departure it is important to learn as much as possible about the society you are visiting. Areas of great importance include:

Language: Not only vocabulary but polite usage; when to use higher and lower forms; and particularly how to say "yes" and "no."

Non–verbal cues: Gestures, body contact, and eye gaze patterns differ significantly from one country to another and carry very important meanings. Cues of this sort for greeting, parting, and eating are most important, and are relatively easily learnt.

Social rules: Every society develops rules that regulate behaviour so that social goals can be attained and needs satisfied. Some of the most important rules concern gifts, buying and selling, eating and drinking, time keeping and bribery and nepotism.

Social relationships: Family relationships, classes and castes, and working relationships often differ from culture to culture. The different social roles of the two sexes is perhaps the most dramatic difference between societies, and travellers should pay special attention to this.

Motivation: Being assertive, extrovert and achievement–oriented may be desirable in America and Western Europe but this is not necessarily the case elsewhere. How to present oneself, maintain face, etc, is well worth knowing.

Once you have arrived, there are a few simple steps that you can take to help reduce perplexity and understand the natives:

Choose locals for friends: Avoid only mixing with compatriots or other foreigners. Get to know the natives who can introduce you to the subtleties and nuances of the culture.

Practical social activities: Don't be put off more complex social encounters but ask for information on appropriate etiquette. People are frequently happy to help and teach genuinely interested and courteous foreigners.

Avoid 'good'/'bad 'or 'us'/'them'–comparisons: Try to establish how and why people perceive and explain the same act differently, have different expectations, etc. Social behaviour has resulted from different historical and economic conditions and may be looked at from various perspectives.

Attempt mediation: Rather than reject your or their cultural tradition, attempt to select, combine and synthesize the appropriate features of different social systems whether it is in dress, food or behaviour.

When you return, the benefits of foreign travel and the prevention of the 'W–curve' may be helped by the following:

Become more self–observant: Returning home makes one realize the comparative and normative nature of one's own behaviour which was previously taken for granted. This in turn may alert one to which behaviour is culturally at odds (and, perhaps, why) —in itself helpful for all future travel.

Helping the foreigner: There is no better teaching aid than personal experience. That is why many foreign language schools send their teachers abroad not only to improve their language but to experience the difficulties their students have. Remembering this, we should perhaps be in a better position to help the hapless traveller who comes to our country.

Travel does broaden the mind (and frequently the behind), but requires some effort. Preparation, it is said, prevents a pretty poor performance and travelling in different social environments is no exception. But this preparation may require social, as well as geographic maps.

FOOD AND DRINK

by Dr Nick Beeching

Airline catering apart, one of the great pleasures of travel is the opportunity to sample new foods. Unfortunately the aphorism 'Travel broadens the mind and loosens the bowels' holds true for the majority of travellers. A huge variety of micro-organisms cause diarrhoeal illness with or without vomiting, and these are usually ingested with food or water. Food may carry other health hazards –unpasteurized milk and milk products transmit brucellosis in the Middle East and parts of Africa, and raw fish and crabs harbour a number of unpleasant worm and fluke infections. Even polar explorers face hazards —the liver of carnivores such as polar bears and huskies causes human illness due to Vitamin A poisoning.

Although it is impossible to avoid infection entirely, the risk can be reduced by following some simple rules. The apparent prestige and expense of a hotel are no guide to the degree of hygiene employed in its kitchens, and the following guidelines apply equally to luxury travellers and those travelling rough.

Assurances from the local population (including long–term expatriates) that food is safe, should not be taken too literally. They are likely to have developed immunity to organisms commonly present in their water supply. Sometimes it is impossible to refuse locally prepared food without causing severe offence, and invitations to village feasts will need to be dealt with diplomatically.

The major sources of external contamination of food are unclean water, dirty hands and flies. Pay scrupulous attention to personal hygiene, and only eat food with your fingers (including breads or fruit) if they have been thoroughly washed. Avoid food handled by others who you suspect may not have been so careful with their hands —and remember that in many countries toilet paper is not used.

Water

The mains water supply in many countries is contaminated with sewage, while streams, rivers, lakes and reservoirs are freely used as toilets, and for personal bathing and clothes washing. The same water may be used for washing food (especially salads and fruit) and may also be frozen to make ice cubes for drinks. Water should always be boiled or treated before drinking or use in the preparation of uncooked food (detailed advice is given in this chapter in the article on water purification).

Hot tea or coffee are usually safe, as are beer and wine. Bottled water and carbonated drinks or fruit juice are not always safe, although the risk of adulteration or contamination is reduced if you keep to internationally– recognized brands. Insist on seeing the bottle (or can) before it is opened, thus confirming that the seal is tight and the drink has not been tampered with.

If you have any doubts about the cleanliness of plates and cutlery, they can be rinsed in a sterile solution such as tea or coffee, or wiped with an injection swab. If this is not feasible, leave the bottom layer of food on the plate, especially if it is served on a bed of rice. If drinking utensils appear to be contaminated, it may be preferable to drink straight from the bottle.

Food

Food that has been freshly cooked is the safest, but must be served hot. Beware of food that has been pre–cooked and kept warm for several hours, or desserts (especially those containing cream) that have been inadequately refrigerated after cooking. This includes many hotel buffets. Unpasteurized milk or cheese should be avoided, as should ice cream. Food that has been visited by flies is certain to have been contaminated by excrement and should not be eaten.

Salads and peeled fruit prepared by others may have been washed with contaminated water. In some parts of the tropics, salads may be highly contaminated by human excrement used as fertilizer. Salads and fruits are best avoided unless you can soak them in water that you know is clean. Unpeeled fruit is safe provided that you peel it yourself without contaminating the contents. 'Wash it, peel it, boil it or forget it' seems to be the best advice.

Shellfish and prawns are particularly high risk foods because they act as filters, concentrating illness (they often thrive near sewage outfalls). They should only be eaten if thoroughly cooked and I recommend resisting the temptation altogether. Shellfish and prawns also concentrate biological toxins at certain times of the year, causing a different form of food poisoning. Raw fish, crustaceans and meat should always be avoided.

Hot spices and chillies do not sterilize foods, and chutneys and sauces that are left open on the table may have been visited by flies. Be cautious with chillies: they contain capsicin which is highly irritable to the bowel lining. Beware of trying to impress your hosts by matching their consumption of hot foods.

Alcohol

The temptation to over–indulge starts on the airplane, but in–flight alcohol should be taken sparingly as it increases the dehydration associated with air travel and worsens jet lag. Intoxicated airline passengers are a menace to everybody, and drinking impairs your ability to drive on arrival.

In hot countries, beware of rehydrating yourself with large volumes of alcoholic drink. Alcohol promotes the production of urine and can actually make you more dehydrated.

Excessive alcohol consumption promotes diarrhoea and prolonged abuse reduces the body's defences against infection. The deleterious social, domestic and professional hazards of prolonged alcohol abuse are well recognized problems for expatriates.

WATER PURIFICATION

by Julian McIntosh

Polluted water can at best lead to discomfort and mild illness, at worst to death, so the travelling layman needs to know not only what methods and products are available for water purification but also how to improvise a treatment system in an emergency.

Three points about advice on water treatment cause misunderstanding. Firstly, there is no need to kill or remove all the micro–organisms in water. Germs do not necessarily cause disease. Only those responsible for diseases transmitted by drinking water need be treated. And even some water–borne diseases are harmless when drunk. Legionnaires' disease, for example, is caught by breathing in droplets of water containing the bacteria, and not by drinking them.

Secondly, in theory, no normal treatment method will produce infinitely safe drinking water. There is always a chance, however small, that a germ might, by virtue of small size or resistance to chemicals or heat, survive and cause disease. But the more exacting your water treatment process, the smaller the risk —until such time as the risk is so tiny as to be discounted. The skill of the experts lies in assessing when water is, in practice, safe to drink. Unfortunately different experts set their standards at different levels.

Thirdly, beware the use of words like 'pure', 'disinfect' and 'protection,' common claims in many manufacturers' carefully written prose. Read the descriptions critically and you will find that most are not offering absolutely safe water but only a relative improvement.

Suspended solids

If you put dirty water in a glass the suspended solids are the tiny particles that do not readily sink to the bottom. The resolution of the human eye is about one–hundredth of a millimetre, a particle half that size (5 microns) is totally invisible to the naked eye and yet there can be over 10 million such particles in a litre of water without any visible trace. Suspended solids are usually materials such as decaying vegetable matter or mud and clay. Normally mud and clay contamination is harmless, but extremely fine rock particles including mica or asbestos occasionally remain in glacier water or water running through some types of clay.

Chemical contamination

Most people will have experienced the taste of chlorine, the metallic taste of water from jerricans or the stale taste from water out of plastic containers. These tastes, and many others including those from stagnant water, are caused by minute quantities of chemicals that make the water unpleasant or even undrinkable but can easily be removed by charcoal or carbon filtration.

Microbiological contamination

Eggs, worms, flukes, etc: Organisms, amongst others, that lead to infections of roundworm (*Ascaris*), canine roundworm (*Toxocara canis*), guinea worm (*Dracunculus*) and bilharzia (*Schistosomiasis*). They are relatively large, although still microscopic, and can be removed by even crude forms of filtration. The very tiny black things that you sometimes see wriggling in very still water are insect larvae, not germs, and are not harmful. Practically any form of pre–treatment will remove them.

Protozoa: In this group of small, single–celled animals are the organisms that cause Giardiasis (*Giardia lamblia*), an unpleasant form of chronic diarrhoea, and amoebic dysentery (*Entamoeba histolytica*). Both of these protozoa have a cyst stage in their life cycle, during which they are inert and resistant to some forms of chemical treatment. However, they quickly become active and develop when they encounter suitable conditions such as the human digestive tract. They are sufficiently large to be separable from the water by the careful use of some types of pre–filter.

Bacteria: Very small, single–celled organisms responsible for many illnesses from cholera, salmonella, typhoid and bacillary dysentery, to the many less serious forms of diarrhoea known to travellers as Montezuma's Revenge or Delhi Belly. A healthy person would need to drink thousands of a particular bacterium to catch the disease. Luckily, the harmful bacteria transmitted by drinking contaminated water are fairly 'soft' and succumb to chemical treatment —their minute size means only a very few filters can be relied upon to remove them all.

Viruses: These exceptionally small organisms live and multiply within host cells. Some viruses such as Hepatitis A and a variety of intestinal infections are transmitted through drinking water. Even the finest filters are too coarse to retain viruses. The polio and hepatitis viruses are about 50 times smaller than the pore size in even the finest ceramic filter.

Selection of a water supply

Whatever method of water treatment you use, it is essential to start with the best possible supply of water. Learning to assess the potential suitability of a water supply is one of the traveller's most useful skills.

Good points: Ground water, eg wells, boreholes, springs. Water away from or upstream of human habitation. Fast running water. Water above a sand or rock bed. Clear, colourless and odourless water.

Bad points: Water close to sources of industrial, human or animal contamination. Stagnant water. Water containing decaying vegetation. Water with odour or a scum on its surface. Discoloured or muddy water.

Wells and boreholes can be contaminated by debris and excreta falling or being washed in from the surface, so the top should be protected. A narrow wall will stop debris. A broad wall is not so effective as people will stand on it and dirt from their feet can fall in. Any wall is better than no wall at all. Fast running water is a hostile environment for the snails that support bilharzia.

Pre-treatment

If you are using water from a river, pool or lake, try to not to draw in extra dirt from the bottom or floating debris from the surface. If the source is surface water such as a lake or river, and very poor, some benefit may even be gained by digging a hole adjacent to the source. As the water seeps through, a form of pre-filtration will take place, leaving behind at least the coarsest contamination.

Pouring the water through finely woven fabrics will also remove some of the larger contamination. If you have fine, clean sand available, perhaps taken from a stream or lake bed, an improvised sand filter can be made using a tin can or similar container with a hole in the bottom. Even a (clean!) sock will do. Pour the water into the top, over the sand. Take care to disturb the surface of the sand as little as possible. Collect the water that has drained through the sand. The longer the filter used, the better the quality of the water so re-filter or discard the first water poured through. Discard the contaminated sand after use.

If you are able to store the water without disturbing it, you could also try sedimentation. Much of the dirt in water will settle out if left over a long enough period. Bilharzia flukes die after about 48 hours. The cleaner water can then be drawn off at the top. Very great care will be needed not to disturb the dirt at the bottom. Siphoning is the best method.

If the water you are using has an unpleasant taste or smell, an improvement can be achieved by using coarsely crushed wood charcoal wrapped in cloth. When the 'bag' of charcoal is placed in the water or the water is run through the charcoal (like a sand filter) the organic chemicals responsible for practically all the unpleasant tastes and smells will be removed. Some colour improvement may also be noticed. The water will still not be safe to drink without further treatment but you should notice some benefit.

Treatment of a water supply

Boiling: Boiling at 100°C kills all the harmful organisms found in water except a few such as slow viruses and spores which are not dangerous if drunk. However, as your altitude above sea level increases, the weight of the atmosphere above you decreases, the air pressure drops, as does the temperature at which water boils. A rule of thumb for calculating this is that water boils at 1°C less for every 300 metres of altitude. Thus if you are on the summit of Kilimanjaro, at 5895m, the water will boil at only 80°C.

At temperatures below 100°C, most organisms can still be killed but it takes longer. At temperatures below 70°C, some of the harmful organisms can survive indefinitely and as the temperature continues to drop, so they will flourish.

There is one more important consideration. When water is boiling vigorously there is a lot of turbulence and all the water is at the same temperature. While water is coming to the boil, even if bubbles are rising, there is not only a marked and important difference between the temperature of the water and the temperature at a full boil but there can also be a substantial difference in temperature between water in different parts of the pan, with the result that harmful organisms may still be surviving.

To make water safe for drinking you should bring water to a full boil for at least two minutes. Boil water for one minute extra for every 300 metres above sea level. Do not cool water down with untreated water.

Filtration: The key to understanding the usefulness of a filter is ensuring you know the size of the particles that the filter will reliably separate, and the dirt load the filter can tolerate before it clogs up. If the pores in the filter are too large harmful particles can pass through. If small enough to stop harmful particles, the pores can block up quickly, preventing any more water from being filtered.

To reduce this problem, manufacturers employ ingenious means to increase the filter area, and filter in at progressively smaller stages. But even in one apparently clean litre of water there can be a hundred thousand million particles the same size or larger than bacteria. And to stop a bacterium, the filter has to take out all the other particles as well. If the filter is small (of the drinking straw type for instance) or if the water is at all visibly dirty, the filter will block in next to no time.

There are three solutions: water can be filtered first through a coarse filter to remove most of the dirt, and then again through a fine filter to remove the harmful bacteria; a re–cleanable filter can be used; or finally, only apparently clean water could be used with the filter. The use of a coarser filter is called pre–filtration. Viruses are so small they cannot be filtered out of drinking water by normal means. However, because they are normally found with their host infected cells and these are large enough to be filtered, the finest filters are also able to reduce the risk of virus infection from drinking water.

A filter collects quite a lot of miscellaneous debris on its surface and in order to prevent this providing a breeding ground for bacteria, the filter needs to be sterilised from time to time. Some are self–sterilising and need no action but others should be boiled for 20 to 30 minutes at least once every two weeks.

Where filters are described as combining a chemical treatment, this is for self–sterilisation. The chemical is in such small concentrations and in contact with water passing through the filter for such a short period that its use in improving the quality of the filtered water is negligible.

Pre–filtration: Pre–filters should remove particles larger than 5 to 10 microns in size and be very simple to maintain. They will be more resistant to clogging since they take out only the larger particles. They will remove larger microbiological contamination including protozoal cysts, flukes and larger debris that might form a refuge for bacteria and viruses. Pre–filtration is normally adequate for washing. Further treatment is essential for safe drinking supplies.

Fine filtration: To remove all harmful bacteria from water a filter must remove all particles larger than 0.5 microns (some harmless bacteria are as small as 0.2 microns). Filters using a disposable cartridge are generally more compact and have high initial flow rates but are more expensive to operate. Alternatively there are ceramic filters that use porous ceramic 'candles.' These have low flow rates and are fairly heavy. Some need special care in transport to ensure they do not get cracked or chipped thus enabling untreated water to get through. Ceramic filters can be cleaned easily and are very economic in use.

Activated carbon/charcoal filters: Carbon filters remove a very wide range of chemicals from water including chlorine and iodine and can greatly improve the quality and palatability of water. But they do not kill or remove germs and may even provide an ideal breeding ground unless self–sterilising. Some filters combine carbon with other elements to make a filter that improves the taste as well as removing harmful organisms.

Chemical treatment

There are broadly three germicidal chemicals used for drinking water treatment. For ease of use, efficiency and storage life, the active chemical is usually made up as a tablet suitable for a fixed volume of water although the heavier the contamination, the larger the dose required.

Germs can also be embedded in other matter and protected from the effects of a chemical, so where water is visibly dirty you must pre–filter first. Chlorine and iodine have no lasting germicidal effect so on no account should untreated water be added to water already treated.

Silver: Completely harmless, taste free and very long lasting effect, protecting stored water for up to six months. The sterilisation process is quite slow and it is necessary to leave water for at least two hours before use. Silver compounds are not effective against cysts of Amoeba and Giardia, so use pre–filtration first if the water is of poor quality.

Chlorine: Completely harmless, fast acting and 100 per cent effective if used correctly. A minimum of 10 minutes is required before water can be used. The cysts of Amoeba and Giardia are about 10 times more resistant to chlorine than bacteria but both are killed if treatment time and dose are adequate. If in doubt, we recommend that the period before use be extended to at least 20 and preferably 30 minutes.

If heavy contamination is suspected, double the dosage. Alternatively, pre–filter. Some people find the taste of chlorine unpleasant particularly if larger doses are being used. The concentration of chlorine drops quickly over several hours and more so in warm temperatures so there is very little lasting effect. Excess chlorine may be removed by using Sodium Thiosulphate or a carbon filter.

Iodine: Fast acting and very effective, normally taking 10 minutes before water is safe to use. It has a quicker action against cysts than chlorine. Double dosage and extended treatment times or pre–filtration are still very strongly recommended if heavy contamination is suspected. Iodine is more volatile than chlorine and the lasting effect is negligible. Excess iodine may be removed by Sodium Thiosulphate or a carbon filter.

Note: Iodine can have serious, lasting physiological side effects and should not be used over an extended period. Groups particularly at risk are those with thyroid problems and the unborn foetuses of pregnant women. Thyroid problems may only become apparent when the gland is faced with excess iodine, so in the unlikely event of the use of iodine compounds being unavoidable, ask your doctor to arrange for a thyroid test beforehand —or use a good carbon filter to remove excess iodine from the water.

Rules

Order of treatment: If chemical treatment and filtration are being combined, filter first. Filtration removes organic matter which would absorb the chemical and make it less effective. If of a carbon type, the filter will also absorb the chemical leaving none for residual treatment.

In some cases, the filter may also be a source of contamination. If water is being stored prior to treatment then it is worthwhile treating chemically as soon as the water is collected and again after filtration. The first chemical dose prevents algae growing in the stored water.

Storage of water: Use separate containers for treated and untreated water, mark them accordingly and don't mix them up. If you are unable to use separate containers take particular care to sterilise the area round the filler and cap before treated water is stored or at the time treatment takes place. In any case, containers for untreated water should be sterilised every two to three weeks.

Treated water should never be contaminated with any untreated water. Treated water should never be stored in an open container. Treated water left uncovered and not used straight away should be regarded as suspect and re–treated.

SEX AND DRUGS

by Dr Nick Beeching

Casual sex is risky everywhere in the world. In many parts of the tropics, the classic venereal diseases such as syphilis, gonorrhoea and chancroid are extremely common, and resistance to antibiotics is widespread. Any sexual encounter with a new partner carries the risk of acquiring infection with these or more familiar infections such as lice, NSU (non specific urethritis), herpes and genital warts.

The commonest symptoms are pain when passing water, discharge from the penis or vagina, soreness or a swelling or ulcer in the genital area. However, symptoms may not be apparent, especially in women, and close inspection of a prospective partner is no guarantee of safety! Self–medication should not be attempted, and any sexual encounter with a new partner while travelling should be followed by a detailed check up on your return home.

HIV

The dangers of casual sex have been highlighted by the rapid spread of HIV throughout the world. HIV (the human immunodeficiency virus) eventually causes AIDS in the majority of people who have been infected. The interval between infection and the development of AIDS, however, may be more than 10 years. At present there is no vaccine against HIV infection and no treatment cures infection, although medical management of people with HIV infection is improving dramatically. The majority of 'HIV positive' individuals are unaware that they have been infected and cannot be distinguished from non–infected people.

The commonest route of infection with HIV worldwide is heterosexual intercourse, despite the emphasis in the western press on 'high risk' groups such as homosexual men and intravenous drug users. Transfusion with infected blood is also a major route of transmission of HIV in countries that do not screen donated blood. Unsterilized or inadequately sterilized needles and syringes also harbour infection. Infected mothers can pass the virus on to their unborn child.

HIV is not transmitted by casual sexual contact, hugging or social kissing, or using the same toilet seat, swimming pool or cup as an HIV infected person. There is no evidence that it is transmitted by mosquitoes or other insects.

For a number of reasons, the amount of HIV infection present in any country is consistently underestimated in official figures reported to the World Health Organization (WHO). *Claims that a country is free of HIV infection should be disregarded.* Even in countries where adequate diagnostic facilities exist, many people do not acknowledge that they might be at risk of having been exposed to HIV, or have personal or social reasons for not wishing to be tested. In some countries, only people suffering from AIDS are officially notified to WHO, rather than the larger number who are HIV positive but do not have any related illness. Official statistics may be deliberately suppressed for political and economic reasons, including the fear of deterring tourists.

In many parts of the tropics, medical facilities are inadequate for diagnosing HIV infection or collating figures for those already diagnosed. Striking examples of unreported infection have come to light recently with the acknowledgement of the rapid spread of HIV among prostitutes in Thailand and some Indian cities, and a realization of the extent of HIV infection among institutionalized children and other groups of patients in eastern Europe.

Hepatitis B

Hepatitis B is another virus infection that is widespread in the tropics and local people are usually infected before birth or in early childhood. A minority will continue to carry the virus but will have no obvious signs of infection. This minority is large —up to 20 per cent of young adults in the Far East and five to 15 per cent of young adults in Africa, the Middle East and South and Central America. Hepatitis B is spread by the same means as HIV but is 100 times more infectious than HIV and may also be transmitted by bed bugs. Blood transfusions are not routinely screened for hepatitis B in many parts of the tropics.

Drug users who share needles, syringes and other drug injecting paraphernalia, also share a large number of infections, including hepatitis B, HIV, malaria and some exotic infections such as Chaga's disease (found in South America). The risk of acquiring hepatitis or HIV is substantially increased if your partner is an injecting drug user and more than 50 per cent of drug users in some cities in Italy, Spain and the USA are HIV positive. HIV is rapidly spreading among drug abusers in countries bordering the Golden Triangle and nearby countries which have traditionally been centres for 'sex tourism.'

Are these risks exaggerated? The simple answer is no. Every year I treat men and women who have acquired hepatitis B from 'one–night stands' during brief package holidays in the Mediterranean region, and I have a number of HIV positive patients who have been infected by heterosexual affairs abroad.

Avoiding infection

Abstinence or strict monogamy is the best advice, but human nature is such that many are unable to keep to this dictum of perfection. Try to avoid instant affairs and do not visit prostitutes. A romantic moonlit evening on a tropical beach may not seem the best setting for quizzing your prospective partner about his or her sexual history over the past 10 years (and about the sexual and drug taking history of their previous partners). However, some attempt should be made to assess possible risks —both for you or your partner. Close inspection of your partner may not be logistically possible, but signs of ulcers or sores near the genital area should discourage further involvement. If in doubt, consider giving mutual pleasure other than vaginal, oral or anal sex.

If your resolve is still outweighed by your desire, use a condom which provides moderate protection against all sexually transmitted diseases and is easy to carry. Limited extra protection against HIV is provided by some contraceptive foams and creams containing Noronyl. Condoms may be difficult to obtain and are of substandard manufacture in many countries. I suggest that all adults who are (or might be) sexually active and who are not strictly monogamous should take a supply of reliable condoms in their travel bag. Even if you do not need them yourself, someone in your party may be grateful for their availability.

Intravenous drug users who are not deterred by the serious legal consequences of their habit, should not share 'works' or 'mixing spoons' under any circumstances. To share is to invite disaster.

If you are hospitalized, try to ensure that needles and syringes are disposable. Ask the attending doctors whether a blood transfusion is absolutely necessary to save life (in which case there is little choice). If transfusion is essential but can be deferred for a short period, members of your own party or local expatriates or donors who know their own HIV and hepatitis B status, may be able to donate blood for you. Avoid tattooers, acupuncturists and dentists who cannot demonstrate adequate sterilization of their instruments.

People planning to live abroad for more than six months or who may have new sexual encounters while travelling should consider having hepatitis B immunization which is highly effective. This advice applies to all drug abusers, although many will have already been infected at home.

HEALTH IN THE HEAT

by Dr Richard Dawood

Travel broadens the mind and brings untold benefits to the human spirit, but in doing so it often rains a multitude of physiological insults upon the human body. **Dehydration** is one of the most fundamental of these, but there have been some important recent developments in our understanding of its mechanisms and how to avoid it.

In a temperate climate, most people need a daily fluid intake of two litres of water to remain in balance. In a hot, humid climate, and with increased physical activity ten litres a day —one seventh of body weight —and sometimes more.

It takes about three weeks for people who normally live in a temperate climate to acclimatise to a hot one: for most trips by British holiday-makers, there is therefore no chance of acclimatising fully. During acclimatisation sweat glands develop the ability to produce more, to start more quickly, and to lose less salt; stomach and intestines become better able to absorb salt and water more efficiently. Without acclimatisation, newcomers to hot climates have difficulty conserving water and salt and are at a significant risk of developing heat-related illnesses. (Excessive physical exertion increases the risk; avoid this until acclimatisation is complete.)

Acclimatisation is usually much more difficult in hot and humid climates than hot and dry ones. In humid climates, sweat does not evaporate easily and temperature and humidity tend to remain high through the night. This is a continuous stress, whereas in dry climates they both tend to fall, allowing the sweating mechanism to rest.

Small, thin people tend to acclimatise most easily to the heat —because their body surface area is relatively higher in relation to their volume, giving a relatively greater area from which to sweat and lose heat. Unfit, overweight people acclimatise more slowly, and do badly in the heat. People with high blood pressure and heart disease may be at risk from complications.

To remain in balance under such conditions, the body needs a greatly increased intake of salt and water. The trouble is that thirst and taste give an extremely poor indication of exactly how much is required. Many people have a reduced appetite on first arrival in a warm climate, which may reduce salt intake even further.

Deficiency of salt, water, or both, is called **heat exhaustion**. Lethargy, fatigue and headache are typical features, eventually leading to coma and death. Many sufferers do not even feel thirsty, and may have no idea that they are suffering from this problem. They feel 'hung over'. In fact, most symptoms of a typical, bad hangover are the direct result of dehydration. They feel irritable, and simply want to be left alone.

Prevention is by far the best approach. Perhaps the best method is the British Army's pre-salted water regime. Salt is added to all fluids —tea, coffee, soup, fruit juices, water. Required amount is one quarter of a level teaspoon (approx 1 gram) per pint —and result in a solution that is just below the taste threshold. (Don't use salt tablets —they are poorly absorbed, irritate the stomach and may cause vomiting.) Plenty of pre-salted fluid should be the rule for anyone spending much time in the tropics.

The only reliable guide to how much you need to drink in a tropical climate, is the colour of your urine. Always drink enough to ensure that it is consistently pale in colour, and don't just wait until you fell thirsty before drinking.

Heat exhaustion should not be confused with heatstroke (formerly called sunstroke). Although dehydration is almost always a factor, the main problem is a failure of the body's heat control mechanisms. Sweating diminishes and the body temperature rises, headache and delirium also occur. Prompt treatment is essential. Once the body temperature begins to rise, death may occur within four hours. The priority is to lower body temperature. Remove clothing, and cover the victim with a wet bed-sheet, while arranging transfer to hospital. There are well-documented cases of British travellers who have been left in their hotel rooms to die, simply because their condition was mistaken for a drunken stupor.

Infectious diseases that cause a fever can sometimes be mistaken for heatstroke, again with potentially fatal results. Malaria and meningitis are especially important in this context because in both cases deterioration is rapid if treatment is not given.

Prickly heat is the most common heat-related skin disorder —a sweat rash occurring on the sweatier parts of the body and consisting of tiny blisters on sore, reddened, mildly inflamed skin. You can prevent it with frequent showers and by keeping the skin clean and dry. Treat with calamine lotion.

Brown without burning

The effects of the sun on skin include sunburn, thickening and —in the longer term —drying, loss of elasticity, wrinkling, loosening, discolouration, premature ageing and skin cancer. People with fair, blond or red hair are most at risk, even after they've turned grey. Acute sunburn is a miserable way to begin a holiday. It results in a blotchy uneven tan and is all the more miserable for children whose skin is easily damaged.

If you're not bothered about a tan, cover up and use a high protection factor sunscreen. But if vanity gets the better of you, tan *very* slowly. The protection factor numbers on skin preparations provide a rough measure of how much longer you can stay out in the sun without burning. If your skin normally burns in strong sunlight after 20 minutes' exposure, for example, a sunscreen with a protection factor of 4 will allow you to stay out for 4 times as long (80 minutes). After that you would have to cover up; you would have had your maximum dose of sunlight and more factor 4 would not protect you. If you wanted to stay out in the sun for 160 minutes, you would burn if you used anything less than a protection factor of 8.

Apart from cosmetic acceptability and protection factor, there is very little to choose between the different brands of sunscreen. Whichever brand you pick, you should re-apply it frequently, especially when swimming or sweating. Most of the leading manufacturers now produce waterproof sunscreens which are particularly useful for children.

Some parts of the body are especially vulnerable and need extra care —the face, particularly the nose and forehead, neck and ears; parts of the body that are normally covered; the tops of the collar bones, bald patches on the scalp; and feet. Avoid sunbathing in the hottest part of the day and be guided by the habits of those more accustomed to hot climates, who take a relaxing indoor siesta instead.

If you burn, calamine lotion will soothe affected areas and mild painkillers are often helpful. More extensive or severe burns should be treated with a mild antiseptic and kept clean and dry. Stay out of the sun or use a total block sunscreen until the skin has healed.

The eyes, too, can be affected by the sun. The conjunctiva and retina are sensitive to ultra-violet light and are easily damaged. Pain usually begins several hours after exposure, when the delicate cells of the conjunctiva swell and become painful and inflamed. In the long term, excessive exposure to the elements causes a 'pterygium' —an unsightly yellow patch on the white of the eye that may need to be removed. Good quality sunglasses provide effective protection.

Skin cancer and the sun

In the last few years the number of cases of skin cancer in the UK has risen. The number of people taking holidays abroad has also risen so the Royal College of Physicians in London commissioned a special study to determine whether or not there was a link. The results of this work have important implications for travellers: it found that the risks of skin cancer and skin damage from strong sunlight relate not just to long-term exposure, but also to the number of episodes of acute sunburn.

Skin cancers grow slowly and tend to destroy the area of skin in their immediate vicinity. Since they usually occur on exposed area —President Reagan's nose was one well-publicized site —they can inflict much cosmetic damage. Some types —melanomas especially —become able to spread through the body. The Royal College of Physicians advises examining every pigmented patch and mole on your skin as follows:

1. Does it itch, or sensation alter over it?
2. Is its diameter 1cm or more?
3. Is it increasing in size?
4. Is its border irregular in shape?

5. Does the density of black or brown colour within it vary?
6. Is the patch inflamed?
7. Is there bleeding or crusting?

If the answer is *'yes'* to three or more of these questions, you should seek medical advice for diagnosis and treatment. Treatment is simple if the cancer is detected at an early stage.

ALTITUDE SICKNESS

by Dr Richard Dawood

My first exposure to the effect of high altitude was in Nepal, several years ago. I was on a trek six days' journey from Kathmandu. It is a bizarre and unnerving feeling to discover that your exercise tolerance is suddenly no more than a few slow paces; that your pulse races with each step you take, and that you are obliged to stop to catch your breath every few feet, waiting for the palpitations to subside while local people of all ages —some carrying heavy loads — stop, stare, then overtake. I was a fit young medical student, but my body felt as though it belonged to the victim of some dreadful disease that I had just been studying —chronic bronchitis perhaps, emphysema or asbestosis.

I developed a hammering headache, and became more and more breathless, even at rest. I was lucky; although I didn't know it, these were important warning signs of acute mountain sickness (AMS). I decided to come down. In fact, the medical profession has a poor track record when it comes to heeding their own symptoms, and an especially poor record at high altitude. In a report on the seven deaths from mountain sickness on Himalayan treks, three of the seven who died were themselves doctors.

The tragic fact about deaths from mountain sickness is that they are preventable in every case. The purpose of this article is therefore threefold: to offer some practical information about AMS, its warning signs and prevention: to question the merit of drugs that are sometimes suggested for prevention: and to report on a new and revolutionary approach to emergency treatment.

Mountain sickness

The driving force for the absorption of oxygen through the lungs into the bloodstream is atmospheric pressure —the 'weight' of the column of air that extends for ten miles or so above our heads. As we ascend, atmospheric pressure is reduced. Complex mechanisms exist to compensate for the resulting oxygen lack: these include an increase in breathing rate and depth, and changes in the blood and tissues that increase their efficiency in carrying and using oxygen. However, the increased breathing results in reduced levels of carbon dioxide, causing the body to become more alkaline, and in turn causing numerous other physiological changes to occur, not all of which are clearly understood. The kidneys are able to compensate for changes in alkalinity and acidity, but the process of acclimatisation to high altitude can take several days —longer under conditions of low temperature and increased exercise.

AMS tends to occur within two days of exposure. It usually begins with loss of appetite, headache, nausea, vomiting and sleeplessness. This is the early, benign form. It may simply resolve, but may also progress to a more serious so-called 'malignant' form. It should be regarded as an important warning.

Malignant AMS may be fatal, and it may begin with little or no warning. Pulmonary oedema develops —a build–up of fluid in the lung tissues, that further interferes with absorption of oxygen, leading to breathlessness that persists even at rest. There is also a cough, with white, pink or frothy sputum, and the lips may turn blue. A build–up of tissue may also occur in the brain —cerebral oedema. This results in headache, drowsiness, impaired coordination, abnormal or drunken behaviour, confusion, impaired consciousness, and coma. Progression to coma may occur quite rapidly.

Benign AMS can be handled initially by remaining at the same altitude until symptoms resolve. If they do not improve, the best treatment is prompt descent. Victims of malignant AMS need to be brought down immediately, and most sufferers need to be carried down. Experts on AMS advise that descent should not be delayed while aid is summoned, and should start even at night if possible.

Mountain sickness is most often a problem at altitudes over nine or ten thousand feet, though in some people it may occur as low as seven or eight thousand, this means that a hazard exists at many popular travel destinations. Crucial factors in determining susceptibility to AMS are speed of ascent, and the altitude at which you sleep. If possible, begin by avoiding sleeping above ten thousand feet for the first few nights. "Climb high, Sleep low," is the rule to follow. Then increase your sleeping altitude by no more than one thousand feet per day — even this may be too fast for some people to adapt to.

High on drugs

Two drugs seem to be increasingly recommended to trekkers and climbers for prevention of AMS, but there is considerable controversy regarding their use. These drugs are dexamethasone and acetazolamide (Diamox). A third drug, nifedipine, has shown promising results in preliminary trials, but experience with it is still only limited.

Acetazolamide is a diuretic drug that increases excretion of bicarbonate by the kidney, tending to counteract the increase in alkalinity referred to above. Some experts consider that it speeds acclimatisation, while others believe that it merely masks early symptoms that are not a great nuisance in themselves, but that provide useful warning signs that severe AMS may be developing. There is no consensus. I have spoken to doctors who swear by acetazolamide, and to others who are greatly troubled by such side–effects as nausea, tiredness, poor sleep, and 'pins and needles' in the arms and legs. There are many cases on record of malignant AMS occurring despite the use of acetazolamide. The altitude-sickness expert I trust most is Dr John Dickinson, who has spent many years working in Nepal, and has a vast experience of looking after trekkers with AMS. I have been gradually persuaded to his view that acetazolamide is of limited value for prevention. Dexamethasone is a powerful 'steroid' drug that has many actions; the most beneficial of these, as far as high altitude is concerned, is a tendency to reduce oedema. It does not affect acclimatisation, but merely alleviates some of the symptoms. As Dr Dickinson has pointed out, it is perhaps surprising that the use of the drug is suggested quite widely for mountaineering, while it is banned in almost every other sport. It is safe for most people when taken for only short periods, but serious side-effects do occur, especially in people with diabetes.

The Gamow bag

The best treatment for a victim of the effects of reduced atmospheric pressure is, obviously, to increase the pressure. Bringing the victim down is usually the fastest and simplest way of doing this. However, a new approach also has its appeal. This is the use of a simple, portable compression chamber known as the Gamow bag. It looks like an oversized sleeping bag that can be inflated with a foot–pump. It has to be pumped continuously, to eliminate waste gases, and this can be tiring at altitude. Alternatively, a carbon dioxide extractor is also available for it. A larger model capable of accommodating two people is also available.

Achievable compression is roughly equivalent to a five–thousand–foot descent, depending on your altitude. This would certainly buy time in an emergency, though there is no substitute for descent for people who are seriously ill. It has already been used with great success by expeditions to remote places where rescue is difficult. Its cost makes it suitable for groups and expeditions rather than routine treks.

Gamow bags can be purchased or rented from Altitude Technologies Inc., 100 Araphoe Avenue, Suite 10, Boulder, Colorado 80302 USA Tel: (303) 444 8683 Fax: (303) 494 6994. The bag (one person) and accessories weigh 14.5lbs and cost approx $2200. A one-month rental costs $250.

Conclusion

The best approach to AMS is prevention, and the most important measure is gradual ascent. Problems are particularly common with people on a tight time schedule, who fly in to high altitude destinations, and try to cram in the maximum amount of sights and activity into the shortest time possible. One simply cannot expect to be able to fly in to places like La Paz, Cuzco or Leh and carrying on sightseeing without allowing ample time —perhaps several days —for rest and acclimatisation. Yet there are cases on record where unfit, elderly people have been booked on tours to Peru without any warning about the dangers of high altitude, and have died as a result.

Mountain sickness is a preventable illness, and all travellers to high altitude regions should make sure they are fully informed about it. Improved availability of the Gamow bag should do much to facilitate treatment and rescue of people who are seriously affected.

MALARIA

by Drs Emma Woolfenden and Nick Beeching

Malaria remains rife throughout much of the tropics, and is a huge burden in terms of illness and death for the indigenous population. It poses a significant and difficult problem for the traveller. The ever–changing pattern of drug resistance, results in confusion regarding the selection of anti-malarial drugs and other preventive measures. Awareness of the very real hazard of malaria and the importance of gaining accurate pre-travel information is vital for travellers to the tropics.

It is a parasitic infection transmitted by the bite of the female anopheline mosquito. There are four types of malaria: *Plasmodium falciparum*, *Plasmodium ovale*, *Plasmodium vivax* and *Plasmodium malariae*. *P. falciparum*, also known as malignant malaria, is the most serious: half to two million people living in endemic areas die as a result of it each year. In spite of persisting efforts, adequate control of malaria has not yet been achieved and there is a significant risk for travellers to most parts of the Indian Sub-continent and the Far East, Sub-Saharan Africa and parts of Central and South America. The risks in North Africa and countries in the east Mediterranean littoral and the Middle East is more variable.

The illness

The incubation period after a mosquito bite varies from a minimum of 8-10 days to several years. Most people who are infected by falciparum malaria develop symptoms within a couple of months, but the longest symptom–free period we have seen was over a year. The early symptoms of general aches and pains, headache and fever are often mistaken for influenza and it is essential that travellers have an immediate blood test for malaria if they develop fever while in a malarious area or within six months of their return. If left untreated, patients (especially expatriates who have not been exposed to malaria before) can rapidly develop high fevers or lapse into a coma and die. About a quarter of patients have pronounced vomiting and/or diarrhoea among earlier symptoms and mistake the illness for infective gastroenteritis. The number of malaria deaths in the UK has risen to about 12 a year, and many of these are due to delay in seeking medical advice.

The other three forms of malaria are rarely life-threatening but can have a more prolonged incubation period of up to two years. They cannot be distinguished from life-threatening falciparum malaria unless a blood film is examined. These three forms of malaria sometimes relapse after effective treatment of the first illness, so prolonged treatment is usually required to prevent relapse.

Prevention

Personal protection for the traveller focuses on two main aspects: the first is an effort to try to prevent being bitten by malaria carrying mosquitoes. The second relies on taking antimalarial drugs, which inhibit the malaria parasites from developing within the body.

There are several ways of protecting oneself against mosquito bites. The malaria carrying mosquitoes bite during the evening and after dark. Exposed skin should therefore be kept to a minimum by wearing long sleeved clothing, trousers, skirts etc. Where possible rooms should be screened and 'knock down' spray used to kill any mosquitoes which may have entered during the day. Good bed nets are a valuable protective asset, those impregnated with a repellent such as permethrin are the most effective and can be bought prior to travel. In areas where mosquito biting is a real problem, exposed skin can be covered in repellent —those containing diethyltoluamide (DEET) are the best. Clothing can also be soaked in repellent, 30 millilitres of repellent dissolved in two hundred and fifty millilitres of water is an effective mixture. For long term travellers the bed nets should be treated with permethrin —0.2 grams of permethrin per metre of material.

Anti-malarial drug therapy is an area fraught with difficulty. The changing pattern of drug resistance, together with possible side-effects of the drugs, have made it increasingly difficult to choose the correct regimens. With this in mind it is advisable for all travellers to obtain specialist advice prior to their trip.

In Britain there are currently four main anti-malarial drugs in use: chloroquine, proguanil (Paludrine), mefloquine and doxycycline. Chloroquine and proguanil are the oldest and most widely used. They are safe to take long-term and during pregnancy, and are associated with a low incidence of side effects. Unfortunately there is now widespread resistance to these drugs rendering them much less effective. Depending on the area to be visited, they are either taken alone or together. Travellers should start anti-malarials at least a week before travel, mainly to make sure they do not react to the medication, and for at least four weeks after leaving a malarious area. A typical regimen is chloroquine 2 tablets once a week together with proguanil 2 tablets daily. The main side effects of the chloroquine/proguanil combination (apart from an unpleasant taste) are nausea and mouth ulcers. Chloroquine should not be taken by people who suffer from psoriasis, a common skin disorder.

Mefloquine is a much newer drug and has the advantage that only one tablet needs to be taken on a weekly basis. It is recommended for areas where there is widespread chloroquine resistance such as sub-Saharan Africa. Mefloquine should not be taken by women who are pregnant or who might become pregnant within three months of taking the last tablet —this makes it an impractical choice for many young women. People with a history of epilepsy or a strong family history of epilepsy, and those who have psychiatric problems, should also avoid the drug. It should not be used by people who are taking certain kinds of blood pressure tablets (ß blockers) and it is not recommended for people whose jobs depend on a high degree of coordination, such as airline pilots. The main side-effects are nausea and, rarely, a feeling of strangeness or more severe behaviour disturbance. Despite this alarming list of potential problems, the drug is very effective and has been widely used for several years by French and German tourists, and it is now prescribed in the UK and USA. It is not suitable for young children.

The third alternative is an antibiotic called doxycycline (a form of tetracycline). This is particularly popular with Australian travellers but British authorities mainly recommend it for travellers to the borders areas of Thailand/Myanmar/Cambodia, where falciparum malaria is often resistant to both chloroquine and mefloquine. Doxycycline should not be taken by pregnant women or children under the age of seven. It should be taken with liberal quantities of fluid to prevent ulceration and discomfort in the oesophagus (gullet). The main side-effect is that some people become very sensitive to the sun and become sunburnt easily. Women taking regular doxycycline may be prone to recurrent vaginal thrush. Balancing these side effects, doxycycline does appear to reduce the incidence of travellers diarrhoea as well as providing anti-malarial protection.

Children require lower doses of anti-malarials, depending on their age and weight. They soon learn to dislike both chloroquine and proguanil. Although chloroquine syrup is available, it is difficult to administer. we have had to resort to grinding tablets up and hiding them in treats (jam sandwiches, sweets etc.) to persuade children to take them. Pregnant women should only travel to areas with a significant malaria risk —especially sub Saharan Africa —if it is essential, and must take malaria prophylaxis. It is wise to take folic acid (a vitamin) at the same time as proguanil.

Long-term expatriates are more difficult to advise. Many adopt a 'macho' attitude to malaria and discontinue any malaria prophylaxis in the mistaken belief that they have developed protective immunity. Due to rapid emergence of drug resistant malaria, we believe that this is an unwise option. We are seeing increasing numbers of expatriates flown back to the UK with life-threatening malaria as a result of this attitude.

Standby treatment

The more adventurous traveller going to places where rapid access to medical advice is not available may wish to carry a course of anti-malarial 'stand by' treatment. This should be taken if symptoms of possible malaria develop, but we still advise trying to reach a local clinic as soon as possible for a blood test and medical help. Two alternatives are recommended —three tablets of 'Fansidar' taken at the same time is the most convenient, but this is not suitable for people who are allergic to sulpha drugs. The alternative is mefloquine, two tablets taken together followed by 2 tablets 12 hours later. The main problem with this dose of mefloquine is severe nausea and vomiting. Until recently a third option 'Halofantrine' was very popular for self treatment, particularly in East Africa, but side-effects of this drug affecting the heart have now been identified and we recommend that it should not be used.

Summary

From the foregoing it will be appreciated that malaria is a severe and largely preventable risk for the traveller. It is essential that medical advice is sought before travelling, and that all possible measures do not entirely prevent one from catching malaria, and travellers must be prepared to consult doctors immediately about any symptoms, during or after travelling, and ensure that the doctor they see is aware that they have been to a malarious area within the preceding two years. If this advice is ignored, the diagnosis of malaria will not be considered until too late, and tragic and preventable deaths will continue to occur.

Key points

1. Prevent bites - repellents
                   bed nets
                   suitable clothing
2. Take appropriate anti-malarial drugs.
3. Even if the above rules are followed carefully, you may still catch malaria.
4. Consider carrying 'standby treatment'.
5. Seek medical attention quickly should you develop fever.

DIARRHOEAL ILLNESS

by Dr Nick Beeching

The worldwide distribution of traveller's diarrhoea is reflected in its many geographical synonyms —Delhi belly, the Aztec two–step, Turista, Malta dog, Rangoon runs, to name a few. Typically, the illness starts a few days after arrival at your destination and consists of diarrhoea without blood, nausea with some vomiting and perhaps a mild fever. The mainstay of treatment is adequate rehydration and rest, and the illness is usually self–limiting within a few days. Antibiotics to treat or prevent this common illness are not usually prescribed in anticipation of an infection. Exceptions to this rule are business travellers or others embarking on short trips (less than two to three weeks) for whom even a short period of illness would be disastrous, eg. athletes attending international meetings.

The most important aspect of treatment of diarrhoea is the replacement of fluids and salts that have been lost from the body. For most adults, non–carbonated, non–alcoholic drinks that do not contain large amounts of sugar are quite adequate. For adults with prolonged diarrhoea and for children, it is more important to use balanced weak salt solutions which contain a small amount of sugar that promotes absorption of the salts. These can be obtained in pre–packaged sachets of powder (eg *Dioralyte*, *Rehidrat*) that are convenient to carry and are dissolved in a fixed amount of sterile water. *Dioralyte* can also be bought in the UK as effervescent tablets.

If pre–packaged mixtures are not available, a simple rehydration solution can be prepared by adding eight level teaspoonfuls of sugar or honey and half a teaspoon of salt to one litre of water (with flavouring to tempt small children).

Nausea, which frequently accompanies diarrhoea, can usually be overcome by taking small amounts of fluid as often as possible. For small children it may be necessary to give spoonfuls of fluid every few minutes for prolonged periods. If you or your child have severe vomiting which prevents any fluids being taken, medical attention must be sought immediately.

Anti–diarrhoeal drugs are not usually recommended and should rarely be given to children. Kaopectate is safe for children aged over two years but not very effective (Kaolin and morphine should not be carried). For adults, codeine phosphate, loperamide (*IMODIUM* or *Arret*) or diphenoxylate (*Lomotil*) are sometimes useful. These drugs should never be given to children and should not be used for bloody or prolonged diarrhoea. They are best reserved for occasional use to prevent accidents while travelling —for example before a prolonged rural bus trip. Prolonged use of these medications may prevent your body from eliminating the diarrhoea —causing organisms and toxins which may lead to constipation.

Preparations containing clioquinol are still widely available outside the UK, where it was previously sold under the trade name *Enterovioform*. These preparations are useless and should not be taken (they have been linked with severe side effects in some parts of the world). Other than rehydration solutions or the medications discussed in this section, I do not recommend purchasing medicines for diarrhoea from pharmacies or chemists.

Prevention

Travellers who wish to prevent travellers diarrhoea should consult their medical adviser about preventative medication (a controversial issue within the profession) before travel. Liquid bismuth preparations (not an antibiotic) are effective but huge volumes need to be carried in luggage (very messy if broken), and bismuth tablets are difficult to obtain in the UK. Various groups of antibiotics may be used, including tetracyclines (eg doxycycline), sulphur containing antibiotics (eg. *Steptrotriad* or cotrimoxazole, *Septrin* or *Bactrim*) and quinolone agents (eg. ciprofloxacin, norfloxacin).

Prophylactic antibiotics are not recommended for the majority of travellers because of the limited duration of effectiveness and the possibility of drug side effects, including, paradoxically, diarrhoea.

Self–treatment

Self–treatment with antibiotics for established diarrhoeal illness is usually inappropriate unless qualified medical attention is impossible to obtain. Travellers to remote areas may wish to carry a course of antibiotics for this eventuality. Bloody diarrhoea with abdominal pain and fever may be due to bacillary dysentery (shigella organisms) or a variety of other organisms such as campylobacter or salmonella. The most appropriate antibiotic would be a quinolone such as ciprofloxacin, or a sulphur drug such as cotrimoxazole. Prolonged bloody diarrhoea with mucus (jelly), especially without much fever, may be due to amoebic dysentery which is treated with metronidazole (*Flagyl*) or tinidazole (*Fasigyn*).

Prolonged, explosive diarrhoea with pale creamy motions may be due to giardia, a common hazard for overlanders travelling through the Indian subcontinent. This responds to metronidazole or tinidazole. These two antibiotics should not be taken at the same time as alcohol because of severe reactions between them.

If you have to treat yourself, obtain qualified medical investigation and help at the earliest opportunity. This is essential if symptoms do not settle after medication. Travellers who anticipate the need for self–treatment should take Richard Dawood's book *Travellers Health: How to Stay Healthy Abroad*. Diarrhoea may be caused by other, more severe illnesses, including typhoid and malaria, and these will need specific treatment.

HEALTH PROBLEMS ABROAD

by Dr. Nick Beeching

Travellers should always seek qualified medical attention if any illness they are suffering gets worse despite their own remedies. Large hotels usually have access to doctors, typically a local family doctor or private clinic. In more remote areas, the nearest qualified help will be a rural dispensary or pharmacist, but seek advice from local expatriate groups, your consulate or embassy for details of local doctors. In large towns, university–affiliated hospitals should be used in preference to other hospitals. In remote areas, mission hospitals usually offer excellent care and often have English–speaking doctors. The International Association for Medical Assistance to Travellers (IAMAT) produces directories of English–speaking doctors and some addresses are listed in Section 11 of the Directory.

If you feel that your medical condition is deteriorating despite (or because of) local medical attention, consider travelling home or to a city or country with more advanced medical expertise —sooner rather than later.

Medication

Medicines sold in tropical pharmacies may be substandard. Always check the expiry date and check that medications that should have been refrigerated are not being sold on open shelves. There is a growing market in counterfeit drugs and locally–prepared substitutes are often of low potency. Stick to brand names manufactured by large international companies, even if these cost more. Insist on buying bottles that have unbroken seals and, wherever possible, purchase tablets or capsules that are individually sealed in foil or plastic wrappers. It is difficult to adulterate or substitute the contents of such packaging.

It is usually wise to avoid medications that include several active pharmacological ingredients, most of which will be ineffective and will push up the cost. Medication that is not clearly labelled with the pharmacological name as well as the brand name of ingredients is suspect (eg *Nivaquine* contains chloroquine).

Fevers

Fever may herald a number of exotic infections, especially when accompanied by a rash. Fever in a malarious area should be investigated by blood tests, even if you are taking antimalarials. A raised temperature is more commonly due to virus infections such as influenza, or localized bacterial infections that have obvious localizing features such as middle ear infections or sinusitis (local pain), urinary tract infections (pain or blood passing water), skin infections (obvious) or chest infections including pneumonia (cough, chest pain or shortness of breath).

If medical attention is not available, the best antibiotic for amateurs is cotrimoxazole (*Bactrim* or *Septrin*) which contains a sulphur drug and trimethaprim. This covers all the above bacterial infections as well as typhoid fever. Travellers who are allergic to sulphur drugs could use trimethoprim alone or coamoxyclav (*Augmentin*) which is a combined oral penicillin preparation.

Local Infections

Eyes: If the eyes are pink and feel gritty, wear dark glasses and put in chloromycetin ointment or drugs. Seek medical attention if relief is not rapid or if a foreign body is present in the eye.

Ears: Keep dry with a light plug of cotton wool but don't poke matches in. If there is discharge and pain, take an antibiotic.

Sinusitis: Gives a headache (feels worse on stooping), 'toothache' in the upper jaw, and often a thick, snotty discharge from the nose. Inhale steam or sniff a tea brew with a towel over your head to help drainage. Decongestant drops may clear the nose if it is mildly bunged up, but true sinusitis needs an antibiotic so seek advice.

Throat: Cold dry air irritates the throat and makes it sore. Gargle with a couple of Aspirins or table salt dissolved in warm water, or suck antiseptic lozenges.

Teeth: When it is difficult to brush your teeth, chew gum. If a filling comes out, a plug of cotton wool soaked in oil of cloves eases the pain; *gutta percha*, softened in boiling water, is easily plastered into the hole as a temporary filling. Hot salt mouth-washes encourage pus to discharge from a dental abscess but an antibiotic will be needed.

Feet: Feet take a hammering so boots must fit and be comfortable. Climbing boots are rarely necessary on the approach march to a mountain; gym shoes are useful. At the first sign of rubbing put on a plaster.

Blisters: Burst with a sterile blade or needle (boiled for three minutes or hold in a flame until red hot). Remove dead skin. Cover the raw area with zinc oxide plaster and leave in place for several days to allow new skin to form.

Athlete's Foot: Can become very florid in the tropics so treat this problem before departure. The newer antifungal creams eg. *Canesten*, are very effective and supersede antifungal dusting powders, but do not eliminate the need for sensible foot hygiene. In very moist conditions, eg. in rain forests, on cave explorations or in small boats, lacerated feet can become a real and incapacitating problem. A silicon–based barrier cream in adequate supply is essential under these conditions.

In muddy or wet conditions, most travellers will get some skin sepsis or small wounds. Without sensible hygiene these can be disabling, especially in jungle conditions. Cuts and grazes should be washed thoroughly with soap and water or an antiseptic solution.

Large abrasions should be covered with a vaseline gauze eg. *Jelonet* or *Sofratulle*, then a dry gauze, and kept covered until a dry scab forms, after which they can be left exposed. Anchor dressings are useful for awkward places eg. fingers or heels. If a cut is clean and gaping, bring the edges together with *Steristrips* in place of stitches.

Unconsciousness

The causes range from drowning to head injury, diabetes to epilepsy. Untrained laymen should merely attempt to place the victim in the coma position —lying on their side with the head lower than the chest to allow secretions, blood or vomit to drain away from the lungs. Hold the chin forward to prevent the tongue falling back and obstructing the airway. Don't try any fancy manoeuvres unless you are practised, as you may do more harm than good. *All unconscious patients from any cause, particularly after trauma, should be placed in the coma position until they recover. This takes priority over any other first aid manoeuvre.* Fainting: lay the unconscious person down and raise the legs to return extra blood to the brain.

Injury

Nature is a wonderful healer if given adequate encouragement.

Deep wounds: Firm pressure on a wound dressing will stop most bleeding. If blood seeps through, put more dressings on top, secured with absorbent crepe bandages and keep up the pressure. Elevate the part if possible.

On trips to remote spots at least one member of the party should learn to put in simple sutures. This is not difficult —a friendly doctor or casualty sister can teach the essentials in 10 minutes. People have practised on a piece of dog meat and on several occasions this has been put to good use. Pulling the wound edges together is all that is necessary, a neat cosmetic result is usually not important.

Burns: Superficial burns are simply skin wounds. Leave open to the air to form a dry crust under which healing goes on. If this is not possible, cover with *Melolin* dressings. Burn creams offer no magic. Deep burns must be kept scrupulously clean and treated urgently by a doctor. Give drinks freely to replace lost fluids.

Sprains: A sprained ankle ligament, usually on the outside of the joint, is a common and likely injury. With broad *Elastoplast* 'stirrup strapping', walking may still be possible. Put two or three long lengths from mid–calf on the non–injured side, attach along the calf on the injured side. Follow this with circular strapping from toes to mid–calf overlapping by half on each turn. First Aid treatment of sprains and bruises is immobilization (I), cold eg. cold compresses (C) and elevation (E); *remember ICE*. If painful movement and swelling persist, suspect a fracture.

Fractures: IMMOBILIZE the part by splinting to a rigid structure; the arm can be strapped to the chest, both legs can be tied together. Temporary splints can be made from a rolled newspaper, an ice–axe or a branch. Pain may be agonizing and is due to movement of broken bone ends on each other; full doses of strong pain killers are needed.

The aim of splinting fractures is to reduce pain and bleeding at the fracture site and thereby reduce shock. Comfort is the best criterion by which to judge the efficiency of a splint but remember that to immobilize a fracture when the victim is being carried, splints may need to be tighter than seems necessary for comfort when at rest, particularly over rough ground. Wounds at a fracture site or visible bones must be covered immediately with sterile or the cleanest material available, and if this happens, start antibiotic treatment at once. Pneumatic splints provide excellent support but may be inadequate when a victim with a broken leg has a difficult stretcher ride across rough ground. They are of no value for fractured femurs (thigh bones). If you decide to take them, get the Athletic Long Splint which fits over a climbing boot where the Standard Long Leg splint does not.

Swimming

Freshwater swimming is not advisable when crocodiles or hippopotamuses are in the vicinity. Beware of polluted water as it is almost impossible to avoid swallowing some. Never dive into water of unknown depth. Broken necks caused by careless diving are a far greater hazard to travellers than crocodiles.

Lakes, ponds, reservoirs, dams, slow streams and irrigation ditches may harbour bilharzia (schistosomiasis). This is a widespread infection in Africa, the Middle East and parts of the Far East and South America, and is a genuine hazard for swimmers. The mature human infection is a blood fluke, the eggs of which are passed out in human urine or faeces and which infect snails in the water. These in turn release minute larval forms (*cercariae*) which readily penetrate unbroken skin exposed to infected freshwater. Non–immune travellers often develop short–lived itching within a few hours of water contact, or may have no symptoms for some months when fever, bloody diarrhoea or blood in the urine may become evident. Treatment of bilharzia has improved in recent years and any traveller who has had contact with infected water should have a tropical check up in case they have undiagnosed infection.

Personal protection consists of avoiding bathing or wading in infected water whenever possible, however tempting it may appear. Local advice that the water is 'safe' should usually be disregarded. Contrary to common belief, it is not safe to swim from a boat in deeper water in the middle of an infected lake. If you have to wade through streams or ditches, do so upstream of areas of human habitation and try to cover skin that is exposed. Rubber boots and wetsuits offer some protection but should be thoroughly dried after use. Skin that has been in contact with water should be dried by vigorous rubbing as soon as possible.

Water that is chlorinated is safe to drink or swim in, but be wary of private swimming pools supplied by a local stream or that have been neglected allowing colonization by snails. Water for drinking should be filtered and allowed to stand for 48 hours if chlorine or other purification methods are not available.

Sea swimming has many hazards other than sharks. Scratches from coral easily become infected, and most waters harbour sea urchins and more venomous fish. Footwear is strongly recommended, especially when swimming on coral beaches. Avoid swimming in water that contains jellyfish, and shuffle through shallow water to warn stingrays and stonefish of your approach. Do not attempt to handle sea snakes or colourful tropical fish (particularly the 'lion fish' or 'zebra fish') and do not poke your hand in crevices in reefs.

The pain of most marine stings is relieved by immersion of the affected limb in hot water —as hot as the sufferer can stand. Obvious imbedded stings or spines should be removed intact, and medical attention may be needed to extract residual foreign material as this easily becomes infected. Jellyfish tentacles should be neutralized before removal by strong alcohol (eg. gin), vinegar or sand before being *lifted* off the person, rather than being dragged across the skin. Stonefish, jellyfish and conefish stings can all lead to rapid development of shock and mouth–to–mouth resuscitation and heart massage should be continued for prolonged periods until medical aid is summoned. A tight tourniquet around the thigh or upper arm will delay absorption of venom.

Scuba divers should be sure that local instruction and equipment is adequate and should always swim with a partner. Do not fly within three hours of diving, or within 24 hours of any dive requiring a decompression stop on the way back to the surface. Travellers who anticipate scuba diving in their travels are strongly advised to have proper training before setting out.

Mammalian bites

All mammalian bites (including human ones) are likely to become infected and medical advice should be obtained about appropriate antibiotics and tetanus immunization. First aid measures start with immediate washing of the wound in running water for at least five minutes, scrubbing with soap or detergent, and removal of any obvious imbedded foreign material. Wiping with topical iodine, an alcohol injection swab or neat alcohol (gin or whisky will do) helps to sterilize the area. Colourful topical agents such as mercurochrome are useless. At the hospital or dispensary the wound should be further cleaned and dressed as necessary, but do not allow the wound to be sutured.

Rabies is a serious hazard throughout most of the world, including continental Europe and the USA. Domestic or wild animal contact should be avoided at all times, particularly if a normally wild animal is unusually docile or vice versa. Rabies affects a wide variety of mammals, particularly carnivores and bats. Wild dogs are a common nuisance in the tropics and should be given a wide berth.

The rabies virus is carried in the saliva of affected animals and can be transmitted to man by *any* contact of saliva with broken skin, the cornea (eye) or the lining of the nose or mouth. Even minor scratches or grazes of the skin can allow the virus through human skin after it is licked by an infected dog. Deep or multiple bites carry more risk, especially if unprovoked. Rarely, cavers in a bat–infested cave may inhale the virus.

All potentially infected exposures should be taken seriously. First aid measures above may kill the virus in the wound, but specific medical attention should be obtained immediately. If it is not available locally, break your journey to get to suitably qualified doctors, returning home if necessary. Modern rabies vaccines (such as the human diploid cell vaccine made by Merieux) are not always available in the tropics but are safer, more effective and less unpleasant than older vaccines. Depending on the apparent severity of exposure or bites, you will need a prolonged course of vaccinations and may also need specific antiserum against rabies. As the incubation period may extend to weeks or months, late post–exposure vaccination is better than none. Once symptoms develop, an unpleasant death is inevitable.

If exposure involves a domestic animal, try to ascertain from the owner whether it has been vaccinated against rabies and whether it has been behaving abnormally. Record details of how to contact the owner one week later to see if the animal remains healthy (in which case rabies is much less likely). If it is safe to do so, other animals should be captured and placed under safe observation for signs of illness, or killed for specialist examination of the brain for signs of rabies.

Local folk remedies are useless against rabies and should not be used. British doctors may not be as aware of the risks of rabies abroad as they should be, and you should insist on obtaining specialist advice on the correct course of vaccinations after possible exposure. This can be obtained from units with an interest in tropical medicine (see the Directory) or from the Central Public Health Laboratory in London (tel: 081–200 4400).

Snakes

Snakes only attack humans if provoked and snakebite is a rare hazard for most travellers. Never handle a snake, even if it appears to be dead, and try not to corner or threaten live snakes. If you encounter a snake on the path, keep absolutely still until it moves away. Always look for snakes on paths ahead, using a torch at night. If hiking on overgrown paths, through undergrowth or sand, wear adequate boots, socks and long trousers. Snakes are often found in wood piles, crevices or under rocks and these should not be handled. Integral groundsheets and tightly closed tent flaps help to keep snakes out of tents, and make it less likely that you will roll over on a snake in your sleep (generally viewed as threatening behaviour by the snake).

Not all snakes are venomous and only a minority of bites by venomous species are accompanied by a successful injection of venom. The most important first aid for a victim is to keep calm and provide reassurance that envenomation is unlikely. Immobilize the bitten limb by splinting and rest the victim.

Do not offer alcohol. Even if venom has been injected, severe effects take several hours to develop and there should be adequate time to carry the patient to a dispensary or hospital for trained help. A tight tourniquet around the thigh or upper arm is only indicated for bites by cobras, kraits, coral snakes, sea snakes and most Australian snakes. Alternatives include a tight pressure dressing over the bite or crepe bandaging on the affected limb.

'Boys' Own' remedies such as incision of the wound to suck out the venom are harmful and should not be employed. Local sprays, cold packs, topical antiseptics and even electric shocks are equally useless.

If the snake has already been killed, place it in a bag or box and take it for identification by medical staff attending the victim. Amateur attempts to capture a snake that has been provoked may result in further bites and a good description of the snake by an unbitten comrade is preferable.

Depending on the type of snake, venom may reduce the clotting activity of the blood, causing bleeding, typically from the gums, or induce paralysis —first manifested by an inability to open the eyes properly, followed by breathing problems. Shock and kidney failure are possibilities and some venoms cause extensive damage to tissue around the bitten area. Immediate pain relief should never include Aspirin, which impairs the ability of blood to clot. All bites, with or without envenomation, carry a risk of infection.

Antivenom should never be used unless there are definite signs of envenomation, and then only with adequate medical support. Travellers should not routinely carry antivenom. Expatriates working in high–risk remote areas or expedition organizers may wish to carry a small stock of antivenom. British travellers who wish to carry antivenom should obtain specialist advice from the WHO Centre at the Liverpool School of Tropical Medicine several months before they intend to travel. Package inserts with multi–purpose antivenoms and even local advice are often incorrect.

Scorpions

Scorpion stings are far more likely to be a problem for travellers and are always very painful. Scorpions are widespread, particularly in hot dry areas. If travelling in such areas wear strong footwear and always shake out your clothes and shoes before putting them on. The pain of stings requires medical attention, which may include strong, injected pain–killers. Many species are capable of inflicting fatal stings, particularly in children, and antivenoms should be available in areas where these species are present.

Other beasts

A myriad of other stinging and biting beasts threaten the traveller. Some spider bites can cause rapid paralysis and should be treated with a local pressure dressing or tight tourniquet until medical help is obtained. Leeches can be encouraged to drop off by applying salt, alcohol or vinegar or a lighted cigarette end. Do not pull them off, as infection may follow if parts of the mouth remain in the wound. Leeches inject an anticoagulant into the wound and local pressure may be required to reduce bleeding. If travelling in damp jungle areas through water with leeches, inspect all exposed areas regularly for leeches.

FEAR OF FLYING

by Sheila Critchley

More people fly today than ever before, yet many experienced air travellers, as well as novices, suffer anguish and apprehension at the mere thought of flying. A survey by Boeing suggested that as many as one out of seven people experience anxiety when flying and that women outnumber men two to one in these feelings of uneasiness. The crews know them as 'the white–knuckle brigade.'

A certain amount of concern is perhaps inevitable. The sheer size of modern jet aircraft, which appear awkward and unwieldy on the ground, makes one wonder how they will manage to get into the air — and stay there. Most of these fears are irrational and are perhaps based on the certain knowledge that as passengers, once we are in the aircraft we are powerless to control our fate (this being entirely dependent on the skill and training of the crew). These nervous travellers find little comfort in the numerous statistical compilations which show that modern air transport is many times safer than transport by car or rail.

According to Lloyd's of London it is 25 times safer to travel by air than by car. A spokesman for Lloyd's Aviation Underwriting said that if you consider all the world's airlines, there are some 600 to 1000 people killed every year on average. This figure compares to an annual toll on the roads of some 55,000 in the United States, 12,000 in France and 5000 in the UK. One sardonic pilots used to announce on landing,"You've now completed the safest part of your journey. Drive carefully."

Anxiety

Most people's fear remains just that —anxiety which gives rise to signs of stress but remains on a manageable scale. For others, however, the anxiety can become an unimaginable fear, known as *aviophobia* or fear of flying. Symptoms include feelings of panic, sweating, palpitations, depression, sleeplessness, weeping spells, and sometimes temporary paralysis. Phobias are deep seated and often require therapy to search out the root cause. Psychologists studying aviophobia suggest that in serious cases, there may be an overlap with claustrophobia (fear of confined places) and aerophobia (fear of heights).

Professional help can be obtained from specialists in behavioural psychotherapy. However, unlike other phobias which may impair a person's ability to function in society, those suffering from aviophobia may simply adopt avoidance of air travel as a means of coping. Only those whose lifestyles necessitate a great deal of foreign travel are forced into finding a solution.

One source of many people's fear of flying is simply a lack of knowledge about how an aircraft works and about which sounds are usual and to be expected. Visiting airports and observing planes taking off and landing can help overcome this problem. Reading about flying can also help (though air disaster fiction can hardly be recommended).

What to do...

Talking to other people who fly regularly can also be reassuring. Frequent air travellers are familiar with the sequence of sounds which indicates everything is proceeding normally: the dull 'thonk' when the landing gear retracts on take–off; the seeming deceleration of the engines at certain speeds among other things. Since most people are familiar with the sounds in their cars and listen almost subconsciously to the changed 'tones' that indicate mechanical difficulties, those aircraft passengers who are unsure about flying often feel a certain disquiet when they can't identify 'normal' from 'abnormal' sounds in an aircraft.

Air turbulence can also be upsetting. Most modern aircraft fly above areas of severe winds (such as during thunderstorms) and pilots receive constant reports of upcoming weather conditions. Nonetheless, air currents up to 20,000 feet may buffet aircraft and the 'cobblestoning' effect can be frightening even to experienced air travellers. Flight crews are aware of this problem and usually make an announcement to allay undue worries.

If you are afraid to fly, tell the stewardess when you board so that the crew can keep an eye on you. Hyperventilation is a common symptom of anxiety; the cure is to breathe slowly and deeply into a paper bag. Remember that all aircraft crew are professionals; their training is far more rigorous than, say, that required to obtain a driving license.

Emergencies

It is probably worth mentioning that the cabin crew's main responsibility is not dispensing food and drink to passengers but rather the safety of everyone on board. There is usually a minimum of one flight attendant for every 50 passengers. The briefings on emergency procedures which are given at the beginning of every flight are not routine matters: they can mean the difference between life and death and should be taken seriously. Each type of aeroplane has different positions for emergency exits, oxygen supplies and different design and positioning of life jackets. The air crews' demonstrations of emergency procedures are for the benefit of everyone on board and should be watched and listened to attentively. In an emergency situation, reaction is vital within the first 15 seconds —there is no time to discover that you don't know where the emergency exits are situated. Learning about what to do in an emergency should reduce fear, not increase it.

Relaxation

One way of coping with fear of flying (at least in the short term) is to learn how to relax. In fact, in–flight alcohol (in sensible quantities), movies, reading material and taped music are all conducive to relaxation.

If these are not sufficient to distract you, some airlines conduct programmes for those they call 'fearful flyers.' These seminars consist of recorded tapes offering advice on relaxation techniques, statistical information on how safe it really is, group discussions where everyone is encouraged to discuss their fears and recorded simulations of the sounds to be expected in flight.

Familiarisation is the key concept behind all of these behaviourist therapy programmes; instruction in rhythmic deep breathing and sometimes even hypnosis can assist the person in learning to control his or her physical signs of anxiety. A graduate of one of these programmes confirmed its beneficial effects: "I enjoyed the course, especially sharing my misgivings with other people and discovering I wasn't alone with my fears. At the end of the course, we actually went up on a one–hour flight and I was able to apply all the techniques I had learned. In fact, I actually managed to enjoy the flight – something I would not have ever believed I could do."

A certain amount of anxiety about flying is to be expected. For most people, a long distance flight is not something one does every day. On the other hand, there is always a first time for everyone —even those who have chosen to make flying their career. The more you fly, the more likely you are to come to terms with your fears. Some anxiety is inevitable, but in the case of flying, the statistics are on your side.

Aviatours (Pinewoods, Eglington Road, Frensham, Surrey GU10 2DH, tel: 025 125 3250) run a one–day *Fear of Flying* course. The course is led by Dr. Maurice Yaffe, clinical psychologist and expert in the field, and includes a mass counselling session by Dr Yaffe and a 45–minute flight. Dr Yaffe's book *Taking the Fear Out of Flying* (David and Charles) is recommended for further reading.

FLYING IN COMFORT

by Richard Harrington

Flying is physically a lot more stressful than many people realize. And there's more to the problem than time zones. Modern jet aircraft are artificially pressurized at an altitude pressure of around 1500 to 2000m. That means that when you're flying at an altitude of, say, 12,000m in a Boeing 747, the cabin pressure inside is what it would be if you were outside at a height of 1500 to 2000m above sea level. Most people live a lot closer to sea level than this, and to be rocketed almost instantly to a height of 2000m (so far as their body is concerned) takes a considerable amount of adjustment. Fortunately, the human body is a remarkably adaptable organism, and for most individuals the experience is stressful, but not fatal.

Although it might seem more practical to pressurize the cabin to sea level pressure, this is currently impossible. A modern jet with sea level cabin pressure would have to have extremely strong (and therefore heavy) outside walls to prevent the difference between inside and outside walls causing the aircraft walls to rupture in mid–flight. At present, there is no economically viable lightweight material that is strong enough to do the job. Another problem is that if there were a rupture at, say, 14,000m with an interior pressure equal to that at sea level, there would be no chance for the oxygen masks to drop in the huge sucking process that would result from the air inside the cabin emptying through the hole in the aircraft. A 2000m equivalent pressure at least gives passengers and oxygen masks a chance if this occurs.

Inside the cabin, humidifiers and fragrance disguise all the odours of large numbers of people in a confined space. On a long flight you're breathing polluted air.

Surviving the onslaught

What can you do to help your body survive the onslaught? First you can loosen your clothing. The body swells in the thinner air of the cabin, so take off your shoes (wear loose shoes anyway, it can be agony putting tight ones back on at the end of the flight), undo your belt, tilt your seat right back, put a couple of pillows in the lumbar region of your back and one behind your neck, and whether you're trying to sleep or simply rest, cover your eyes with a pair of air travel blinkers (ask the stewardess for a pair if you haven't brought any with you).

Temperatures rise and fall notoriously inside an aircraft, so have a blanket ready over your knees in case you nod off and later find that you're freezing. When I look at all the space wasted over passengers' heads in a Boeing 747, and all those half–empty hand baggage lockers, I often wonder why aircraft manufacturers don't arrange things so that comfortable hammocks can be slung over our heads for those who want to sleep —or better still, small couchettes in tiers like those found in modern submarines. Personally, I'd prefer such comfort, whatever it might do to the tidiness of the cabin interior. Though if you don't mind paying, you can actually lie down in bed both on Philippine Airlines' First Class and now also on British Airways. BA will tuck you up in a 'comfort suit', with hot chocolate and biscuits to complete the experience.

On a long flight it is tempting to feel you're not getting your money's worth if you don't eat and drink everything that's going. Stop and resist the temptation —even if you're travelling in First Class and all that food and drink seems to be what most of the extra cost is about. Most people find it best to eat lightly before leaving home and little or nothing during the flights. Foods that are too rich or spicy and foods that you're unaccustomed to will do little to make you feel good in flight. Neither will alcohol. Some people claim that they travel better if they drink fizzy drinks in flight, although if inclined to indigestion, the gas can cause discomfort as it is affected by the lower pressure in the cabin. Tea and coffee are diuretics (increase urine output) and so have the undesirable effect of further dehydrating the drinker who is already in the very dry atmosphere of the cabin. Fruit juices and plain water are best.

Smoking raises the level of carbon monoxide in the blood (and, incidentally, in the atmosphere, so that non–smokers can also suffer the ill effects if seated close to smokers) and reduces the smoker's tolerance to altitude. A smoker is already effectively at 1500 to 2000m before leaving the ground, being more inclined to breathlessness and excessive dryness than the non–smoker.

Walk up and down as frequently as possible during a flight to keep your circulation in shape, and don't resist the urge to go to the loo (avoid the queues by going before meals). The time will pass more quickly, and you'll feel better for it, if you get well into an unputdownable novel before leaving home and try to finish it during the flight. This trick always works better than flicking half–heartedly through an in–flight magazine.

You may try to find out how full a 'plane is before you book, or choose to fly in the low season to increase your chance of getting empty seats to stretch out on for a good sleep. If you've got a choice of seats on a 'plane, remember there's usually more leg room by the emergency exit over the wings. On the other hand, stewardesses tend to gather at the tail end of the 'plane on most airlines, so they try not to give seats there away unless asked. That means you may have more chance of ending up with empty seats next to you if you go for the two back rows (also statistically the safest place in a crash). Seats in the middle compartment over the forward part of the wing are said to give the smoothest ride; the front area of the 'plane is, however, the quietest.

You might try travelling with your own pillow, which will be a useful supplement to the postage–stamp sized pillows supplied by most airlines.

Finally, if you plan to sleep during the flight, put a 'Do Not Disturb' notice by your seat and pass up the chance of another free drink or face towel every time your friendly neighbourhood stewardess comes round. You probably won't arrive at the other end raring to go, but if you've planned to arrive just before nightfall, and if you take a brisk walk before going to bed, you might just get lucky and go straight to sleep without waking up on home time two hours later.

BATTLES WITH JET LAG

by Dr Richard Dawood

The human body has in-built rhythms that organize the body function on roughly a 25–hour daily cycle. These rhythms can be influenced and adjusted to a large extent by environmental factors —the time on your wristwatch, whether it's light or dark, and changes in temperature. Rapid passage across time zones disrupts the natural rhythms, outstripping the ability of the body to readjust.

Few people who travel are unfamiliar with the resulting symptoms: general discomfort, fatigue, inability to sleep at the appropriate time, reduced concentration, impaired mental and physical performance, altered bowel habit and disrupted appetite and eating patterns —all typical features of jet lag.

Adaptation

The body adapts to time changes at a rate of roughly one hour per day so that after a journey across eight time zones, it may take up to eight days to adjust fully to the new local time. Westward travel is, for many people, slightly better tolerated than eastward travel: westward travel results in a longer day which benefits those whose natural body rhythm is longer than a 24–hour cycle. Clearly a flight that does not cross time zones —north/south travel, for example— will not cause jet lag.

Further problems may also be experienced by those on medication that has to be carefully timed (eg., insulin doses for diabetics require careful planning and women on low does contraceptive pills may lose contraceptive protection when doses are missed or much delayed).

Children are often less affected by jet lag than adults; the elderly may have great difficulty. Altogether, around 70 per cent of travellers are much disturbed by the symptoms. A wide variety of solutions has been proposed for those unfortunate enough to be badly affected.

Solutions

Melatonin

Melatonin is a naturally-occurring hormone that functions in the body as a powerful internal signal of the approach of night. Melatonin is secreted by the pineal gland in the brain, in a pattern that normally follow a strict daily cycle. Melatonin secretion is suppressed by the presence of bright light .

In a number of balcebo-controlled studies, small evening doses of melatonin have been shown to have a significant effect on speeding up recovery from jet lag —by about thirty per cent. Unfortunately, conducting trials on a large scale is a complicated process. The fact that melatonin is cheap and difficult to protect with patents means that pharmaceutical companies have had little commercial incentive to explore its potential in full —though they are working ion melatonin analogues —synthetic substances that might have similar properties, but that could be patented.

Melatonin capsules are available in the USA as a food supplement, and sold there in health food stores. It has not been approved by the FDA or by drug regulating bodies elsewhere, but it is widely in use by travellers who have found it helpful.

Light Exposure

Exposure to light suppresses melatonin secretion, and controlled exposure is known to alleviate jet lag. Various strategies have been proposed, some of which are difficult to understand and follow. At the simplest level, it is possible to use daylight simply as an environmental cure. More complex formulas claim to use precisely timed light and darkness to achieve dramatic jumps in 'clock setting'.

Researchers at Harvard have attempted to patent various regimens of light exposure, a controversial move that will be interesting to follow.

The Jet Lag Diet

Ehret and Scanlon's book, *Overcoming Jet lag* (1983), with its jet lag diet, was an instant best-seller —trading heavily on the claim that this was the strategy used by Ronald Reagan during his Presidency. In the diet, protein and carbohydrate intake is scheduled in an attempt to enhance the synthesis of certain neurotransmitters within the brain at appropriate times. It is suggested that protein-rich meals that are high in tyrosine, when taken at breakfast and at lunch-time, increase catecholamine levels during the day, while an evening meal high in carbohydrates provides tryptophan for serotonin (and therefore melatonin) synthesis at night.

In travel medicine circles, the diet has achieved a reputation for being almost impossible to follow —and so almost impossible to disprove.

It is true, however that meal timing is an important *zeitgeber* —a significant factor in influencing the body clock in it adaptation to a new time zone. So, if it is not your habit to eat heavy meals in the middle of the night, don't do so when served a meal during a flight, if you are offered food at a time that is inappropriate to the time at your intended destination.

Sleeping Medication

Carefully-timed sleeping medication can help reduce the fatigue of the journey —an issue quite separate from that of jet lag. The important points are to choose a drug that is short acting and has no hangover, and to avoid alcohol while taking it. It is important only to take sleeping medication during flights that are long enough to permit at least 6 hours' sleep.

Widespread use of the drug Halcion during the late Eighties, taken halfway across the Atlantic, often with alcohol, resulted in an epidemic of short-term travel amnesia: travellers would develop amnesia for everything they did during the first few hours following arrival.

Sleeping medication can also reduce fatigue during adjustment to a new time zone —it can help you get some sleep when you need to rest at what —for your body —is still an inappropriate time, and it can also help you sleep through the night when you might otherwise awake inappropriately. Zopoclone is believed to cause the least sleep disturbance; the best alternative is probably Temazepam; for any drug always use the lowest dose in the recommended range.

Melatonin also has a soporific effect, and some specialists have argued that this is the only explanation for its effect on jet lag.

Aromatherapy
One range of products appears to be extremely successful —in terms of sales, anyway. It is Danielle Ryman's *Awake* (said to smell like a walk through a pine forest) and *Asleep,* available from the aromatherapy shop at London's Park Lane Hotel. Aromatherapy products are offered to passengers on a routine basis by a small number of airlines.

Vitamins
E-mergen-C is a fizzy cocktail produced by the Alacer Corporation of California, intended to give a natural boost to sufferers from post-flight exhaustion; "Having sampled it, I would say a Diet Coke at breakfast to me might be more beneficial" was the verdict of one reviewer.

Homeopathy
A much used homeopathic remedy is Arnica 6c, every six hours during a flight and the following day —it is recommended by Abercrombie and Kent, for example.

The Tudor Hotel, New York, and the Rembrandt Hotel, London
Both of these have 'circadian rooms' —in which guests and their body functions can be left in peace, operating on whichever time zone meets their needs.

Concorde
Travelling supersonically cuts the transatlantic journey time down to about three hours, dramatically reducing the fatigue of the journey. It makes no difference to jet lag, however: the process of adjusting to a new time zone is still the same.

Experience
There is no doubt that over time, frequent travellers develop their own strategy, almost without thinking about it. That is one reason why formal evaluation of cures for jet lag can be so difficult —the task of unscrambling the influence of other factors is a major problem, and large numbers of travellers are necessary for scientific study.

Planning your own jet lag strategy
Whatever you approach to jet lag, here are some tips to bear in mind:

1. Flying westbound has the effect of lengthening your day. Avoid taking naps during the flight—this may prevent you from falling asleep later.

2. Avoid alcohol, tea or coffee, during and after your flight —all of them interfere with sleep.

3. During eastbound overnight flights —such as the transatlantic 'red eyes', eat only a light meal *before* taking off, and ask the cabin crew not to disturb you during the flight, so as to get the maximum amount of sleep possible. Consider taking a mild sleeping tablet.

4. If you can afford the luxury of time, take daytime flights where possible; although they do not necessarily help you adjust better to the time difference, these cause the least fatigue and loss of sleep, and allow you to arrive in best

shape.

5. Expose yourself to cues that belong to your new time zone, as soon as you can: reset your watch, eat meals and go to bed at appropriate times, and spend plenty of time outdoors.

6. Body temperature falls naturally during the night, and a common symptom of jet lag is to feel cold during the day: try a hot bath.

7. Accept that there is bound to be some loss of performance when you first arrive in a new time zone, and plan your trip to avoid important business meetings for the first 24 hours after arrival; if you have to schedule a meeting on arrival, choose a time of day when you would normally —on home time —be most alert.

On arrival

On arrival at your destination, it is best to stay awake until night time, without taking a nap. On the first night in the new time zone, a sleeping tablet is again useful to help initiate sleep at an unusual time (and to maintain it when one would otherwise be likely to wake up at an inappropriate time during the night).

The occasional use in this way of short–acting, mild sleeping tablets can be valuable and does no harm. Most doctors are willing to prescribe small quantities for this purpose. Possibly the best suited drug is zimovane (it has a slightly bitter taste) which is short acting and causes very little sleep disturbance. A drug called temazepam is less expensive and more widely used in the UK; American doctors tend to prescribe triaxolam (Halcion).

Clearly, sleeping tablets should only be used on flights that are long enough: it is not sensible to take a tablet that will make you drowsy for eight hours, two hours into a five–hour flight. A well established phenomenon in travellers who attempt this —especially if they have also taken alcohol— is 'travel amnesia,' complete amnesia for the first few hours after arrival. Use the lowest dose that will work, and avoid alcohol. And remember that alcohol, sleeping tablets, fatigue and jet lag do not mix well with driving: too many people stagger off aircraft after a long journey and attempt to drive when clearly in an unfit state to do so —with predictable consequences.

Whatever one's approach, however, it is important to recognize that one's performance is almost inevitably going to be reduced and it is sensible to avoid important commitments and business arrangements for at least the first 24 hours after arrival. ■

EQUIPPING FOR A TRIP
Chapter 12

LUGGAGE

by Hilary Bradt

The original meaning of 'luggage' is 'what has to be lugged about.' Lightweight materials have made lugging obsolete for sensible travellers these days, but there is a bewildering choice of containers for all your portable possessions.

What you buy in the way of luggage and what you put in it obviously depends on how and where you are travelling. If your journey is in one conveyance and you are staying put when you arrive, you can be as eccentric as the Durrell family who travelled to Corfu with "two trunks of books and a briefcase containing his clothes" (Lawrence) —and "four books on natural history, a butterfly net, and dog and a jam jar full of caterpillars all in imminent danger of turning into chrysalides" (Gerald, who described this vast logistical exercise in *My Family and Other Animals*).

If, however, you will be constantly on the move and will rarely spend more than one night in any place, your luggage must be easy to pack, transport and carry.

What to bring

There are two important considerations to bear in mind when choosing luggage. First, weight is less of a problem than bulk. Travel light if you can, but if you can't, travel small. Second, bring whatever you need to keep you happy. It's a help to know yourself. If you can travel, like Laurie Lee, with a tent, a change of clothes, a blanket and a violin, or like Rick Berg, author of *The Art and Adventure of Travelling Cheaply* who took only a small rucksack (day pack) for his six–year sojourn, you will indeed be free. Most people however are too dependent on their customary possessions and must pack accordingly.

Suitcase or backpack

Your choice of luggage is of the utmost importance and will probably involve making a purchase. Making do with Granny's old suitcase or Uncle John's scouting rucksack may spoil your trip.

Anyone who's had to stand in a crowded Third World bus or the London Underground wearing an external frame rucksack will know how unsuitable they can be for travelling. You take up three times more room than normal, and the possessions strapped to the outside of your pack may be out of your sight, but will certainly not be out of the minds of your fellow passengers, or out of their eyes, laps and air space. It is no wonder backpackers have a bad name. And because they do many Third World countries are prejudiced to the extent of banning them. On arriving at the Paraguayan border some years ago I was forced to wrap my pack in a sheet sleeping bag and carry it through.

That aluminium frame is fragile, as you will soon discover when someone stands on it, and since you carry the backpack behind you, you're particularly vulnerable to thieves. Or have you ever hitch-hiked in a Mini carrying your pack on your lap? Can you honestly say you were comfortable? Leave the frame packs to the genuine backpackers they were designed for. Hitchhikers and travellers should still carry a backpack, but one with an internal frame. This small variation in design makes all the difference —the pack can be carried comfortably on your lap, it need be no wider than your body, and everything can be fitted inside. It can be checked onto a 'plane with no trouble, and carried on a porter's head or mule's back.

For the average overland traveller, the ideal solution is the combination bag and backpack. This type of luggage has become justly popular in recent years. Basically it is a sturdy bag with padded shoulder straps that can be hidden in a special zip compartment when approaching a sensitive border or when travelling by plane.

If you are joining an organized group or do not expect to carry your own luggage, you will find a duffel bag the most practical solution. Or two duffel bags since you have two hands. These soft zipped bags are strong and light and can fit into awkward spaces that preclude rigid suitcases. They fit snugly into the bottom of a canoe or the back of a bus and are easily carried by porters or pack animals. When selecting a duffel bag, choose one made from a strong material with a stout zip that can be padlocked to the side, or otherwise secured against thieves. Avoid those khaki army sausage bags with the opening at one end. The article you need will invariably be at the bottom.

Suppose you are a regular air traveller, what will be the best type of suitcase for you? Probably the conventional suitcase, and in that case, you will be well advised —as with most travel purchases— to get the best you can afford, unless you want to replace your 'bargain' luggage after virtually every flight. Cheap materials do not stand up to the airline handling, which usually involves being thrown 20 feet onto a hard surface, standing on the tarmac in all weathers, and generally being flung about fairly violently. Now that some airlines have eliminated the weight allowance in favour of a limit of two pieces, neither of which must measure more than 67 inches (that's height by length by width), it's as well to buy luggage that conforms to that size. Suitcases with built-in wheels can be an advantage in the many airports which do not supply trolleys. But be careful, they can easily get snapped off or broken during the suitcase's passage, so recessed wheels are probably the best.

The traditional hard cases do tend to survive best of all, choose items made from a strong material eg. nylon. These can go up to 1000 denier. Leather items should be scrutinized around the expanded areas: the leather should be of a uniform thickness throughout the item. Check the zip, which should not only be strong but also unobtrusive so as not to catch on clothing etc, and the stitching, which should be even and secure with no gaps or loose threads. If you have the choice, get a bag with one handle only: porters tend to toss luggage around by one handle and this can play havoc with a bag designed to be carried by two. Conveyor belts have a nasty habit of smearing luggage: darker colours stand up to this treatment more happily. Before walking away with your purchase, remember to ask about its care, especially which cleaning materials you should use.

All unnecessary appendages (straps, hangers, clips, etc) should be removed before check–in, especially old destination labels, which can cause the case to be misdirected.

Luggage experts and even those in the airline business often recommend sticking to a carry–on bag if possible. If you can manage to cram everything in, it's preferable to submitting your case to the violence of the handling, the damage and even loss that may ensue. If not, use a carry–on bag for anything you can't do without for a few days, whether it's photos of your children, your own special sleeping tablets or the address of the friend you're going straight from the airport to visit. Not to mention 'uninsurables' such as sums of money or vital papers. To fit under an aeroplane seat, a carry–on bag must measure no more than 450 x 350 x 150mm (18 x 14 x 6 ins).

As well as a carry–on bag, you are allowed the following free items: a handbag (women only —as this is in addition to the carry–on luggage, better take as big a handbag as possible to make the most of your luck), an overcoat, an umbrella or walking stick, a small camera, a pair of binoculars, infant's food for the flight, a carrying basket, an invalid's fully collapsible wheelchair, a pair of crutches, reading material in reasonable quantities and any duty free goods you have acquired since checking–in.

Some thought should be given to accessory bags. Everyone ends up with more luggage than they started because of presents, local crafts, maps etc. collected on the way, and a light foldable bag is very useful. Canvas and straw have their followers. I'm devoted to plastic bags myself and carry a good supply, even though the bottoms usually fall out or the handles tear.

Security

Choose your luggage with security in mind. Your possessions are at risk in two ways: your bag may be opened and some items removed, or the whole bag may be stolen. Most travellers have been robbed at some time or other, the most frequent occurrence being that small items simply disappear from their luggage. Make sure that your luggage can be locked. With duffel bags, this is no problem —a small padlock will secure the zip to the ring at the base of the handle. Adapt the bag yourself if necessary. Combination locks are more effective than standard padlocks as they are rarely seen in the Third World and so thieves have not learned how to pick them. They also protect the clients of those manufacturers whose products are all fitted with the same key! It is harder to lock a backpack; use your ingenuity. One effective method is to make a strong pack cover with metal rings round the edges, through which can be passed a cable lock to secure the cover round the pack. Luggage may also be slashed, but this treatment is usually reserved for handbags. Apart from buying reinforced steel cases there is little you can do about it. A strong leather strap around a suitcase may help to keep your luggage safe and will be a life saver should the clasps break.

For easy identification, try coloured tape or some other personal markings on the outside. Stick–on labels are safer than the dangling kind, as they cannot be ripped off so easily.

During my travels, I've been robbed of five small bags. I finally learned never to carry something that is easily run off with unless it is firmly secured to my person. If you keep your most valuable possessions in the centre of a locked heavy pack or bag they're pretty safe. If you can barely carry your luggage, a thief will have the same problem.

Weight allowances for air travel

On international flights, the IATA Tourist and Economy Class allowance is normally 20kgs (44lbs), for First Class 30kgs (66lbs). For transatlantic flights and some others (eg. USA to South America), however, you can take far more luggage since the weight system has been cancelled and the only restriction is to two pieces of luggage no larger than 67 inches. Before you fly, always ask the airline about luggage allowances and ask if the same applies to the home journey. For instance, if you fly Ecuatoriana from Miami to Quito, you will fly down on the two piece system, but will be restricted to 20kgs for your return —a nasty shock for the present–laden tourist.

What to do if you have excess baggage? You could, of course, just pay the charges. If you know in advance, you could send the excess freight. Do not, under any circumstances, entrust luggage to anyone else, nor agree to carry someone's bags for them. Drugs or bombs could easily be secreted. If you are not much over the limit, don't worry. The airlines will usually give you some leeway. My record is five bags weighing a total of 70kgs transported from South America to Miami (weight limit 20kgs) and on to London (piece limit – two) without paying excess charges.

Packing

Joan Bakewell, in *The Complete Traveller*, suggests thinking of what to take under the following headings: toiletries and overnight, unders, overs, accessories, paperwork and extras. While it is true to say that everything can be classified under these headings, campers and others who must take with them the appurtenances of home will almost certainly find that the 'extras' section expands dramatically over the normal few extras required by, say, airline passengers.

The latter should be warned that aerosol and the ink in fountain pens tend to leak in the pressurized atmosphere of an aeroplane —such items should not be packed in your suitcases but may be safe enough in your hand luggage where you can keep an eye on them. Lighter fuel is not permitted on an aircraft. Knives, even pen knives, may be confiscated from your hand luggage. You are meant to get them back, but in practice this is rare.

When packing, put irregular–shaped and heavy items such as shoes at the bottom, remembering the case will be on its end while being carried topped by clothes in layers separated by sheets of plastic or tissue paper (and don't forget to fill up the shoes with soft or small items such as underwear or jewellery). Trousers, skirts and dresses, still on their hangers or folded with tissue paper between layers, go towards the top, but the topmost stratum in your case should be occupied by T–shirts, blouses and shirts, small items of clothing, and then some enveloping piece such as a dressing gown or shawl over everything. Some travellers like to keep their toilet items in different groups, which makes sense when you consider that you don't wash your hair with the same frequency as you wash your face or go out in strong sun.

Do not over pack: if you have to force the lid of your suitcase, you may bend the frame or break the hinges, with the obvious ensuing risk to the contents. Underpacking, especially in soft–sided luggage is also undesirable since the cases need to be padded out to resist tears to the outer covering.

TRAVEL CLOTHING

by Jan Glen, Tony Pearson and Melissa Shales

Your method of travel can be a big deciding factor in your choice of suitable clothing. The amount of storage space available is the ultimate restriction for backpackers, a major one for motor–cyclists but less so for motorists who can pack clothes for every climate and other eventuality. On a business trip, you will need suits, ties and all the other paraphernalia involved in making you look fresh, eager and keen. If you are going off into the bush, you need not see a suit for months. Initially, choosing which clothing to pack is often a matter of trial and error. Clothes that prove unnecessary can, of course, be posted home and additional clothing bought along the way if routes and climates change. However, prices and quality en route may not be to your liking. Good quality shoes and boots are often extremely difficult to find, so take these with you.

Climate has to enter into one's calculations. If several different climatic zones are to be crossed, then the problem is compounded. If, for example, one travels from Britain to the Sahara by road in mid–winter, warm winter clothing has to be packed for the European leg of this journey. However, at this time of year the Sahara is cold during the night only and some warm clothing could become redundant.

Travelling in deserts really causes few problems, provided all clothing is wrapped in plastic to protect it from the fine, penetrating dust. Cotton clothing is best for both men and women and a wide–brimmed hat is a good idea if you intend walking in the sun. Flip–flops or 'thonged' sandals suffice for footwear in most places, except in Sahel regions where scorpions and large lethal thorns are hazards.

Rain forest, with its tropical heat and clammy humidity, is a very different story. Humidity can be very exhausting and may make the actual temperature seem much higher than it really is. For walking, one must keep in mind the hazards of this environment. Muddy and slippery leech–infested tracks make sandals or flip–flops less suitable than closed–in leather or rubber shoes or boots. Cottons are again more comfortable than synthetics, and in both desert and rain forest environments, cotton underwear can minimize discomfort.

Custom and status

Social custom is also a very important consideration. The last thing one wants to do is offend. Yet this often happens unintentionally and local people are frequently too polite to complain. If you are able to swim where you are travelling, remember that local custom may find bikinis and men's brief trunks offensive. It is always safer to have modest wear: one–piece costumes for women and well–covering trunks or shorts for men. Careful observation of how local people dress when, and if, they swim can set your standard.

Because a Western woman's status is quite superior to that of her counterparts in other societies, she should be especially cautious in her dress. Some countries, Malawi for example, have been very concerned since the 1960's about the dress of their Western visitors. Dresses above the knee, shorts and trousers for women are actually illegal in that country. In the Saharan oasis town of Tamanrasset a Western girl wearing only a tight pair of shorts and a bikini top, and with bare feet, was physically thrown out of a bar. In Algeria, Morocco, Tunisia, Libya, Iran and many other Muslim countries, the sort of dress which would arouse least hostility towards a Western woman would include both a headscarf, a long, dark–coloured skirt, and a top that covers the shoulders. Iran, especially since the Revolution, is even stricter than some other Islamic states. In many Islamic countries, women are rarely seen, seldom heard, and when they are seen, they are covered from head to toe. Let the local standard be your guide even if allowances are made for Westerners.

Even Mediterranean countries can be a problem for women if the customs of modesty are not observed. Many are the stories of women being approached and having their bottoms pinched, or worse, in Greece and Italy. Bikinis and shorts in these places should be reserved strictly for resorts where they have become acceptable for foreigners. In Athens, a seemingly cosmopolitan city, I have been harassed when dressed in conservative jeans and accompanied constantly by my husband.

Papua New Guinea has long been a home for expatriates, chiefly Australians, who are renowned for casual dress and an 'anything goes' attitude. However, attitudes have been modified to conform to local custom. Bikinis and shorts are generally out and although a long skirt is not at all necessary in Port Moresby, it would be wise to be careful in outlying regions.

When visiting India, dress conservatively out of respect for that country's large Muslim population. Hindu women also wear long saris, are very modest and often have an inferior social status. If visiting a Sikh temple, it is also customary to wear a hat or some form of head covering.

Although anything theoretically goes in Western countries, female hitchhikers in very provocative shorts or bikinis are asking for trouble —sometimes violent trouble.

Further complications to your luggage occur when you are going to be mixing trips off the beaten track with city stops and the social and cultural occasions these entail. Try and have at least one dress or skirt that rolls up into a ball, comes out looking pristine and will do for a formal evening. You will often find expat communities, in particular, still dress for dinner, trips to the theatre etc.

Men's wear

A man's position is quite different when travelling in male–dominated societies. Because of the significant difference between formal and informal dress for men, travellers should carry both. In hot, isolated regions where you are unlikely to encounter local people, men can comfortably wear shorts and flip–flops and go about shirtless. In towns and at borders, however, the traveller's appearance should be much more formal. Long, straight–legged trousers, a clean, conservative shirt, shoes and tidy hair will give a look of affluence and respectability. Even a tie may be handy at times. The impression this dress creates will promote a more gracious attitude from shopkeepers and businessmen and could well moderate the zealousness of authoritarian border officials.

In Australia, New Zealand, and Southern Africa, shorts are the accepted daily dress —even for businessmen. However, even in cosmopolitan London they attract curious glances. Therefore, shorts are best reserved for the out of the way places.

Long hair and untidy beards on men are a bone of contention in many countries. Malawi forbids entry to men with long hair and flared trousers. Morocco's entry requirements empower border officials to refuse entry to men with long hair or 'hippy' appearance despite their having valid travel documents. And even where this disapproval is not specified by law, it often exists in practice. Officials may discriminate against travellers of 'unsuitable' appearance by considerably delaying their entry. Incidentally, men with greying hair are often well respected in less developed countries.

Blend in

Dress is far more important for the independent traveller than for the regular tourist travelling on the beaten track who has the protection of tour guides and the safety of numbers. Offending the local people can have unpleasant consequences for the individual alone and away from civilization. Adopting local dress because of a desire to 'go ethnic' is suitable when actually travelling and living as the locals do. One example of this would be as a member of a camel caravan, where it would not only be justified but sensible to adopt the *tagoulmoust* to protect your face from the dust and dryness. On a camel, you would also be more comfortable wearing a *sarouel* (baggy trousers) and loose shirt. The *jellabah*, the flowing Arab gown found all round the world, is an extremely useful garment, and one that I would consider taking anywhere: it can be used as everyday wear in most Muslim countries; it is cool in the sun, protecting you from the fierce mid–day heat, and warm at night; you can use it as a cover–up on the beach over a swimming costume; in place of pyjamas or even, if glamorous enough, as evening wear. On top of all this, it is modest enough not to offend local custom anywhere in the world.

However, in many circumstances, no matter how practical the local dress may be it is wise to wear it with discretion. Imagine how ridiculous a Western tourist would look on the streets of Port Moresby wearing nothing but 'arsegrass' strung around his waist. You surely don't wish to offend the local people, but neither do you want to become a laughing stock. A good rule of thumb is to aim to blend in. As a foreigner, you are at times already at a disadvantage but you can try to minimize this by, for example, avoiding pretentiousness. Wearing a 10 gallon hat, pith helmet or slouch hat tends to attract unwanted attention.

It is strictly illegal for tourists to wear military clothing in the Niger and, however cheap army surplus may be, it is best avoided in many other countries where it can have unwanted connotations. This is especially so in 'white mercenary' sensitive Africa. Obvious jewellery is also best avoided by travellers because its style will be unusual and it is regarded as a sign of wealth. Displaying it invites theft. Worn by men, moreover, (together with shorts) it has other meanings. An example is the attractive young man, shirtless, with shorts, silver bangles and neck chains, in a Saharan oasis hotel, who was most put out because he had been approached and propositioned by several local men. Homosexuality occurs internationally and advances are made to willing–looking men in the same way as they are made to women in the heterosexual sense. My husband, always a conservative dresser, did once forget this in Beirut and wore standard Australian businessmen's shorts and long socks. The resultant cat calls and wolf whistles from the young men sent him fleeing back to his hotel to change into long trousers.

A pair of overalls or very tatty old clothes are most useful for dirty work such as vehicle maintenance en route, allowing you to protect your other clothes from grease and dirt.

If you run out of small change or presents to reward local people who have been very helpful, especially in less developed countries, second–hand Western clothing is often prestigious and it can suit everybody if you give away some clothes as you travel. Jeans are a popular example.

We are not being prudish by urging conservative and demure dress in Third World countries. Rather, by dressing sensitively, one can travel unharassed in almost any area. In places still relatively untouched by Western influence, the impression one creates can ensure that travellers who follow are welcome visitors.

Cold weather clothing

The totally synthetic clothing system for general backpacking or trekking is almost upon us, with the exception of a small cotton content in one or two garments and woollen socks. Consider, for example, this layered clothing system which has become my own personal choice within the last few years.

It starts with polypropylene underwear, Lifa by Helly Hansen in warm weather, and heavier warmer top and long johns by Mountain Equipment in the winter. This layer is topped by an all–nylon, fibre–pile jacket, again Helly Hansen, and a pair of either polyester/cotton breeches (Rohan) or polyester/cotton trousers by Mountain Equipment. A polyester/cotton double jacket (Rohan) acts as a windproof and multi–pocketed storage system and the whole assembly is then covered (in really foul weather) by a Gore–Tex nylon suit. Add to this lot a pair of mitts (nylon outer, synthetic pile inner) and a Thermafleece synthetic balaclava and we're almost there. Socks are still basically wool, though with nylon added to increase their durability. Finally, my boots are currently leather, but their water resistance owes a great deal more to the skills of the chemist than to nature.

The advantages of this synthetic personal environment I create are largely connected with drying times, which are conveniently short, and weights, which are kept to a minimum. The disadvantages are the static build–up (which can be spectacular when undressing) and the much quicker rate at which the synthetic underwear becomes unsavoury. No doubt many people will leap to the defence of wool and cotton on reading this, but all tastes are subjective and my choice is based on experience of both natural and synthetic fabric clothing, and for me at least, technology wins hands down.

Look out in the shops for an absolute profusion of garments made from a fabric called fleece (the Americans call it bunting). This is destined to take over from fibre–pile as the number one fabric for what I call intermediate warmwear, ie the layers between underwear and windproofs. Fleece is all–synthetic and has a rather tighter weave than fibre–pile, making it marginally more wind resistant. But don't be misled by talk of 'windproofing qualities' as this is a gross exaggeration. It certainly has an attractive look and feel to it with its exceptionally soft texture, and it wears a little like wool, going "agreeably shaggy" in the words of Mountain Equipment. As to whether it is warmer than fibre–pile, the laboratories say it certainly is, my experience in the hills says that it isn't and so the argument will go on.

PHOTOGRAPHIC EQUIPMENT FOR TRAVELLERS

by Michael Busselle

No matter whether you are making an afternoon's excursion onto the Marlborough Downs or a month's safari into the Kalahari desert, to have a camera fail when a great picture is lined up in the view–finder can be very upsetting. Even when you are not off the beaten track, equipment problems can be time–wasting and frustrating, when you are in a far–flung location they can be disastrous.

If photography is to be anything more than a casual record of a trip then it is worth spending some time considering what to take and how best to be prepared for the journey. During the past decade there has been considerable resistance by many professionals and serious amateur photographers to the influx of electronically–controlled equipment, especially for travel photography in out–of–the–way places. The main argument has been that being battery–dependent makes such cameras vulnerable to replacement difficulties. However, cameras are also film–dependent and this drawback has usually been successfully overcome.

The truth is that as time progresses, the cameras which are fully mechanical become thinner on the ground and the point will soon be reached where the main source of such instruments will be ancient, second–hand examples. I've been using electronically controlled cameras for a decade or more and of the half–dozen occasions when I've suffered a failure most have been caused by mechanical components.

The solution to the battery problem is simply to take plenty of them and to ensure that they are fresh and of the long–life variety designed specifically for camera equipment —the manufacturer's recommendations will indicate the best type for a particular instrument.

The main drawback with batteries is that they lose efficiency when subjugated to temperature extremes. If you are travelling in desert or arctic conditions, it is advisable to follow the manufacturer's advice, many professional cameras have separate insulated battery packs which afford much more protection than when batteries are placed in the camera–body compartment.

The main criteria for the choice of camera to take on a trip is one which is ruggedly built with proven reliability, the leading manufacturers like Nikon, Olympus and Canon have models which are built to withstand hard professional use and a fair degree of ill–treatment.

I would be very reluctant to take a camera on an important assignment abroad unless I had been using it for an extended period beforehand. Sometimes I've been obliged to take a relatively new piece of equipment as a back–up but hope that I do not have to depend on it.

Never be tempted to take a new piece of equipment without trying it out quite thoroughly first. One advantage of using very familiar equipment is that if anything does go wrong with it you are much more likely to detect it promptly. If you are well accustomed to its normal function, even the sound of a camera firing or the feel of its winding mechanism can indicate if it has developed a fault. What is more, an accessory such as a new tripod or flash gun, can be found to have awkward or unsuitable features when put to hard use on location —very irritating and limiting if you are forced to use it every day for a month.

The question of camera types is largely a question of personal taste, budget and the specific needs of the photographer. Travel by any means other than one's own car means that weight and bulk are usually an important consideration.

There's no doubt that the 35mm format offers the best compromise between size, weight, cost and image quality and that the SLR variety provides the most flexible and adaptable system. Rangefinder cameras, like the Leica, can have advantages where discretion is required since they are quieter in operation, but they have a more limited range of lenses and cannot be used so readily for subjects like close–ups. The effects of filters are also much easier to control and judge when an SLR camera is used.

A point–and–shoot camera is often a useful addition to a more elaborate outfit since it encourages the taking of more casual 'fun' shots which may not be part of the brief, but which are, nonetheless, nice to have when you get back home. A good quality camera of this type can also be useful as a potential back–up. A fully automatic camera like the Olympus ISO 1000 which has a high quality zoom lens and an additional manual exposure facility can serve as both a casual snapper and an instrument for more serious work.

The larger roll–film format is, unarguably, heavier and bulkier to carry, more expensive to buy and feed with film and tends to be rather slower in use as well as being less suitable for candid or reportage photography. However, the larger image provides a significant advance in reproduction quality and can be an advantage when photographs are taken for stock or photo library use.

Whatever system you choose, if a trip is important to you in photographic terms then it is vital to carry at least two camera bodies. Apart from the consideration of possible breakdowns, additional bodies will allow you to be loaded with two or more film types —fast, slow, colour negative, transparency, tungsten, daylight, black and white, and so on. Adopting a belt and braces philosophy, it is also a good idea to carry a separate exposure meter in addition to those built into the cameras.

Choice of lenses depends partly upon the nature of the trip and your own particular interests and aims. For a 35mm camera the basic armoury is a wide–angle of either 28mm or 35mm, a standard 50mm lens and a long–focus of 135mm or 150mm. This can be achieved in a single zoom but I would not recommend it. For one thing, a zoom with this sort of range tends to be quite large and heavy, it will probably be rather prone to flare and have a more limited maximum aperture, making focusing in poor light less accurate.

There is also the danger of having all your eggs in one basket. On one trip to Africa my trusty 70mm–150mm zoom locked solid, unable to zoom or focus leaving me with a choice of 50mm or 200mm and nothing in between. I now carry a 70–210mm zoom as well as the replaced 70–150mm.

A zoom can be very useful but I would hesitate to choose a wider range than 1 to 3 and I would want to have at least three fixed focal–length lenses in my bag. In my experience with general travel photography, wider than 28mm or longer than 210mm are seldom used. I do, however, carry both 24mm and 20mm lenses, and if I am likely to have the opportunity for wildlife photography, I take my 400mm. However, even this can be limiting for serious safari photography and a 600mm will provide more opportunities.

I have a X 1.4 converter for my 210mm zoom but the transparencies lack the bite of a prime lens even when stopped down. I also have 35mm and 28mm shift lenses for my Nikon which I find invaluable for architectural photography, and often very useful for landscapes. For close–up shots, a macro–focusing lens is ideal —or a set of extension tubes.

Autofocus lenses are a matter of personal taste. Advanced designs have now made them extremely efficient but the added weight and bulk, together with the fairly delicate mechanism should be considered in relation to the nature of your trip.

A sea or beach–based trip would make a weather–proof or underwater camera like the Nikinos a very useful addition to an outfit. However, serious underwater photography calls for special lighting equipment as well.

A set of filters is vital, especially if you are shooting on transparency film. In my bag I always carry a polarising filter, neutral graduates in various strengths together with a set of 81A to 81EF. The square resin filters are ideal in that the same set of filters can be fitted, via adaptor rings, to a variety of lens mounts. They are, however, more vulnerable to scratches and are also quite brittle so it makes sense to carry a spare set.

A small flash gun takes up little space and you never know when it might be useful. However, if flash lighting is going to be an important aspect of a trip, a more powerful battery or mains–powered unit with two or more heads together with an umbrella or soft box will be necessary for more creative lighting. A camera with a Polaroid back is really essential in these circumstances to check the lighting balance and exposure.

Serious photography requires the use of a tripod. Some photographers claim they can take sharp hand–held pictures at exposures like 1/30 or 1/15 of a second. But, can they do it every time and just how sharp is sharp? Even in bright sunlight when using a slow, fine–grained film of ISO 50, a polarising filter and with the lens stopped down to f16 for maximum depth of field, exposures of 1/2 or 1 second are not unusual. There are not many people who can guarantee to hold a camera that steady!

In addition, many of the most interesting lighting effects occur when the light level is so low that exposures of several seconds are needed. I carry a small pocket torch so that I can see the camera settings in the gloom in which I take some of my shots and a tripod in these circumstances is vital.

The camera bag is also an important item of equipment. An awkwardly laid–out or uncomfortable bag can be a misery to use. The secret is not to over-fill it. It is easy to plan all the neat little compartments to take each camera, lens and accessory in what seems a convenient way in the comfort of your home or hotel room, but when you start shooting in earnest, with the bag on your shoulder, it can soon become a giant muddle with not nearly enough space.

If you are carrying your equipment with you at all times, the soft type of bag tends to be the most comfortable and convenient to use, especially when working from it while carried on the shoulder. However, the rigid metal compartment cases offer more protection if the equipment is to be placed in aircraft or bus luggage holds. They can also be locked securely, chained and padlocked to fixtures if they have to be left unattended, and hermetically sealed versions can be obtained to protect equipment from dust and humidity. Two bags are, in any case, useful to have on a trip since, on occasions, it can be desirable to leave some of your unneeded equipment behind in a safe place. For trips where walking or climbing is likely to be a feature, camera bags can be obtained with detachable rucksack–style straps, and belts with removable pouches.

Along with Swiss Army knives, jeweller's screwdrivers, a torch and so on, a mini–tape recorder is an invaluable accessory to keep in your camera bag. I use one to make caption notes, as soon as I've taken a shot I give a brief description and identify the location and any other information which might be needed. It's easy to imagine you will remember where all your shots were taken but if you are away for some time and shoot a large number of rolls, on returning, in the cold light of day, your processed films can often reveal some alarming blank spots in your memory. A picture which does not have adequate caption information can be of limited use for editorial or photo–library purposes.

Two favourite personal items are one of those stretchy ropes used for holding suitcases onto car roof–racks and a length of bendy wire with a large bulldog clip fixed to each end. The former is used to hold the camera really firm on the tripod when using long–focus lenses for landscapes and in windy conditions. I simply anchor one end to the base of the centre column, stretch it over the end of the lens barrel and anchor the other end in the same place. It takes all of the play from the camera and tripod top and holds everything quite firm, considerably reducing vibration even with a fairly lightweight tripod. One end of the bendy wire is clipped to the camera or tripod top and the other bulldog clip holds a piece of black card which can be finely adjusted to shade the lens when shooting into the light —much more efficient than a lens hood.

Since if something is going to go wrong it will invariably do so at the most inconvenient and damaging time, it is sensible to carry out frequent checks along with normal cleaning procedures. I once returned from a long trip through Eastern Europe and on receiving a preliminary batch of film from the processing lab was horrified to discover that one roll was so over–exposed that there was no discernible image. On checking my camera I found that the wide–angle lens for my Hasselblad had a detached iris blade which meant that it was not closing down. I had taken a large proportion of shots using this lens and it was not until all my rolls had been processed that I discovered, to my immense relief, that the fault had occurred on the very last roll.

Periodically throughout a trip I will open up my camera backs and fire a few frames at different speeds and apertures to ensure that the shutter is operating correctly, the mirror is flipping up fully and the iris mechanism is stopping down to the pre–set f number. I also cross–check my TTL meters and hand meter to ensure that none have developed a fault. It is also wise to use a magnifier to check the film gate, with the shutter held open on bulb, for any hairs which might be trapped in the film path. These will not be visible in the view–finder but can ruin a lot of film if not detected.

SPACE TO SPARE

by Jack Jackson

If you have a roomy vehicle, are not worried about weight and are not constantly on the move, you might as well plan to make yourselves as comfortable as possible. Do not stint on things that might seem frivolous before you leave, but can make an enormous difference to your morale. This is particularly true if camping.

Fragile items and paperwork, which must be kept away from dust and water, are best kept in Pelican or Underwater Kinetics cases, which have silicone gasket seals. These come in many sizes, with foam inserts that you can customize to fit fragile equipment. These cases are so effective, that even if you have descended a couple of thousand feet down an escarpment, you will have to release the purge button, before you can open the case.

Cases containing clothes can be sealed with strips of foam. Good strong cases are now available in polypropylene, but are usually awkward shapes. Fibre suitcases are available in squared-off shapes that pack better, but they loose their shape if they get wet. Lashing down cleats will keep baggage in place and cut down annoying rattles.

If you plan to sleep without a tent, you will need a mosquito net in some areas. There are several types on the market, but they are not usually big enough to tuck in properly to make sure there are not any gaps. Ex–military ones have the extra advantage of needing only one point of suspension. A camera tripod or ice axe will do for this if there is not a vehicle or tent nearby.

Malaria is an increasingly serious problem, so it is worth getting a net that is already impregnated with a safe insecticide. On a long journey, carry the correct insecticide to re-impregnate the net.

If you do sleep without a tent, make a note of where the sun should rise and position yourself to be in the shade, or the sun could wake you up earlier than you would like to.

A full-length roof rack covered in plywood not only makes a good sleeping platform, but acts as a double skin, to keep the vehicle cooler in sunny conditions.

Mattresses

In cold places, you should not sleep directly on the ground, so use some form of insulation. Air beds are very comfortable and are preferred by some to foam, but they do have disadvantages. They are generally too heavy to carry unless you have a vehicle and inflating them is hard work. Thorns and sunlight all work against them and you will certainly spend a lot of time patching holes in them.

If you decide to use one, be sure it is made of rubber and not of plastic, and only pump it up half full. If you inflate it any harder you will roll around and probably fall off. Perspiration condenses against the surface of air mattresses and on cold nights you will wake up in a puddle of cold water, unless you have put a blanket or woollen jumper between yourself and the mattress.

Camp beds tend to be narrow, collapse frequently, tear holes in the groundsheet and soon break up altogether. Even worse, cold air circulates underneath the bed, since your body weight compresses the bedding. Only several layers of blankets under you will give you the insulation you need.

Open cell foam mattresses are comfortable but often too thin, so it is best to have two thicknesses or else to put a closed cell foam mattress, such as a Karrimat, on the ground and an open cell foam mattress on top of it. Open cell mattresses wear quickly, but if you make a washable cotton cover that fully encloses them, they will last for several years. Foam mattresses, being bulky, are best wrapped in strong waterproof covers during transport. One advantage of foam mattresses is that the perspiration that collects in them evaporates very quickly when aired so they are easy to keep fresh and dry. Remember to give the foam an airing every second day.

The most popular mattresses these days are self-inflating ones. As with air beds, in really cold climates you will be warmer if you put a blanket or sweater between your sleeping bag and the mattress.

Closed cell foam mats, such as Karrimat come in a 3mm thickness, suitable for putting under a groundsheet for protection against sharp stones or on ice, where otherwise the tent groundsheet could stick to the ice and be torn when trying to get it free.

On a long overland trip, you can combat changing conditions with a combination of two sleeping bags. First get a medium quality nylon covered, down sleeping bag and if you are tall, make sure it is long enough for you. This bag will be the one you use most often for medium cold nights. Secondly, get a cheap all–synthetic bag, ie. one filled with artificial fibre. These cheap, easily washable bags are best for use alone on warmer nights and outside the down bag for very cold nights. Make sure the synthetic bag is big enough to go outside the down bag, without compressing the down bag when it is fully lofted up.

In polar and high mountain areas, the golden rule when travelling is never to be parted from your own sleeping bag, in case a blizzard or accident breaks up the party. This would hold true when travelling anywhere that is cold.

Furniture and utensils

The aluminium chairs on the market today are covered with light cotton. This rots quickly in intense sunlight. Look around for nylon or terylene covered chairs or replace the cotton covers with your own. Full–size ammunition boxes are good for protecting kitchenware and make good seats.

When buying utensils, go for dull–grey aluminium billies. Shiny–type aluminium billies tend to crack and split with repeated knocks and vibration. Billies, pots and pans, plates, mugs, cutlery, etc. should be firmly packed inside boxes, with cloth or thin foam separating metal utensils and cutlery, or they will rub against each other and become covered in a mass of metal filings.

A pressure cooker guarantees sterile food and can double as a large billy, so if you have room it is a good investment.

Kettles with lids are preferable to whistling kettles, which are difficult to fill from cans or streams. For melting snow and ice, it is best to use billies. Big, strong aluminium ones are best bought at the Army and Navy auctions or surplus stores. If you are flying out to the Third World, good alternatives will be readily available in local markets.

A wide range of non–breakable cups and plates are available, but you will find that soft plastic mugs leave a bad after–taste, so it is better to pay a little more and get melamine. Stick to large mugs with firm, wide bases, that will not tip over easily. Insulated mugs soon become smelly and unhygienic, because dirt and water get between the two layers and cannot be cleaned out.

Many people like metal mugs, but if you like your drinks hot you may find the handle too hot to touch, or burn your lips on the metal. Melamine mugs soon get stained with tea or coffee, but there are cleaners available, or Steradent tablets are a perfectly adequate and cheaper substitute. Heavyweight stainless steel cutlery is much more durable than aluminium for a long expedition.

Head torches, such as those by Petzl, are useful to keep both hand free when camping, or for vehicle maintenance

For carrying water, ex–military plastic jerry cans are best, as they are light-proof and therefore algae will not grow inside them —as it does with normal plastic containers.

Stoves and gas

The 2.7 kgs cartridge or the 4.5 gas cylinder, are the best sizes to carry. Gas is the easiest and cleanest fuel to use for cooking.

Liquid petroleum gas is usually called Calor Gas or butane gas in the UK and by various oil company names worldwide, such as Shellgas or Essogas. Though available worldwide, there are different fittings on the cylinders in different countries and these are not interchangeable. Where you use a pressure reduction valve on a low pressure appliance, there will always be a rubber tube connection. Make sure that you carry some spare lengths of the correct size rubber tubing.

Gas cylinders are heavy and re–filling can be difficult. Refillable Camping Gaz cylinders as supplied in Europe, are intended to be factory re–filled; but in some countries, eg. Algeria, Morocco and Yemen, they are available with an overfill release valve, so that you can fill them yourself from a larger domestic butane gas supply. In Asia enterprising campsite managers and gas suppliers have discovered ways of filling gas cylinders from their supply. Stand well clear while they do this, as the process involves pushing down the ball valve with a nail or stone, then over–filling from a supply of higher pressure. This can cause flare–up problems when the cylinder is first used with standard cooking equipment, so if you use such a source of supply, it is advisable to release some of the pressure by opening the valve for a couple of minutes (well away from any flame), before connecting up.

Lighting any stove is always a problem in cold climates or at altitude. Local matches never work, unless you strike three together, so take a good supply of the 300 match size, called Cooks' Household Matches. The best answer seems to be a butane cigarette lighter, kept in your trouser pocket, where it will be warm. Remember to carry plenty of refills.

There are many good camping gas stoves available, but when cooking for large groups outside, I prefer to use the large cast-iron gas rings used by builders to melt bitumen. These are wide, heavy and stable when very large billies are used and do not blow out in the wind.

In cold areas, try to get propane gas instead of butane gas,

If gas supplies are a problem, there are good twin burner stoves that use unleaded petrol or kerosene. There are also single burner, multi-fuel stoves, that will operate on diesel fuel.

Space blankets

Space blankets, very much advertised by their manufacturers, are, on the evidence, not much better than a polythene sheet or bag. Body perspiration tends to condense inside them, making the sleeping bag wet, so that the person inside gets cold. In hot or desert areas, however, used in reverse to reflect the sun, they are very good during the heat of the day to keep a tent or vehicle cool. If necessary, a plastic sheet or space blanket can be spread over a ring of boulders to make an effective bath; they are also ideal for making desert stills.

Buying

When buying equipment be especially wary of any shop that calls itself an expedition supplier, but does not stock the better brands of equipment. All the top-class equipment suppliers will give trade discounts to genuine expeditions, or group buyers such as clubs or educational establishments, and some, such as Field and Trek and Cotswold Camping, have special contract departments for this service.

Check–list

For a party of four with no worries about travelling light:

Good compass, maps and guidebooks
Selection of plastic bags for packing, waste disposal, etc
Clingfilm and aluminium foil for food and cooking

Large bowl for washing up and washing
4 x 20 litre water cans —strong ex–military type (polypropylene)
Fire extinguisher
Large supply of paper towels, toilet paper, scouring pads, dish cloths and tea towels
Large supply of good matches in waterproof box and/or disposable lighters
Washing up liquid for dishes (also good for mechanics' greasy hands)
Frying pan
Pressure cooker
Selection of strong saucepans or billies
Kettle with lid (not whistling type, which is difficult to fill from cans or streams)
Tin opener —good heavyweight or wall type
Stainless steel cutlery
Plastic screw top jars for sugar, salt, washing powder etc. (Nalgene are the best)
1 large sharp bread knife
2 small sharp vegetable knives
Kitchen scissors
1 large serving spoon and soup ladle
Plates and/or bowls for eating
Wide base mugs, which do not tip over easily
Good twin burner for your gas supply, otherwise petrol or kerosene twin burner cooker - multi fuel stoves are available, that will work with diesel fuel
Good sleeping bag or sleeping bag combination for the climate expected, plus mattress of your choice
Mosquito nets
Combined mosquito and insect repellent spray
Battery-powered fluorescent light
4 lightweight folding chairs
Short–handled hand axe, for wood fires
Thin nylon line to use as clothes line, plus clothes pegs
Washing powder for clothes 2 separate 6–metre lengths of plastic tubing, one to fill water tank or water cans; the other for fuel cans
2 tubes of universal glue/sealant eg Bostik
Chamois leather
Sponges
6 heavy rubber 'tie downs'
Water purification filters plus tablets or iodine as back–up
Phrase books/dictionaries
2 torches plus spare batteries
Ordinary scissors
Small plastic dustpan and brush
Soap, shampoo, toothpaste, towels
Medical first aid kit, plus multivitamins and rehydration salts
Elastic bands, sewing kit and safety pins
Cassette player and selection of cassettes
Selection of reading material including local book on local flora and fauna plus AA multilingual vehicle parts guide.
Hidden strong box and money belt

Passports, visas, traveller cheques, cash, vaccination certificates, car papers, insurance papers, UK and International driving licence, permissions to drive letter (if you do not own the vehicle), photocopies of travel and medical insurance policies and 6 spare passport photographs.

Many other things can be taken along, but most of these are personal belongings. They include: dental floss; waterproof watch; tissues (good for many other reasons than blowing your nose); clothing, including a tie for formal occasions that may crop up and dealing with embassies (store the tie rolled up in a jar with a lid), dress (for that same occasion), jackets, waterproofs, gloves, swimming costume, sweaters, parkas with hoods; moisturizing cream; toothbrushes; comb; Swiss army knife; camera; film; photographic accessories; anti–malaria tablets and salt tablets where required; sun barrier cream; sunglasses; medicines; spare prescription spectacles if worn; insurance papers; airmail writing paper; envelopes and pens.

FOOD ON THE MOVE

by Ingrid Cranfield

Living a regular life, in one place most of the time, people get to know what foods they like and dislike and base a balanced diet on this rather than on text book nutrition. The problem is, how do you ensure you'll have good food on the move? When travelling, you are constantly faced with new foods and it can be easy to lose track of how you are eating, simply because your rule of thumb menu–planning breaks down. This can lead to fatigue, a lack of energy and even poor health.

Essentially there are two ways of coping. You can either pick up local food as you travel, or you can take with you all your needs for the duration. Eating local food may give you a feeling of being closer to a country's way of life, but could also make you severely ill. Taking your own supplies is safe and very necessary if you are going into the wilds, but how do you stop your palate becoming jaded with endless supplies of dried food?

It is sensible to be able to recognize the constitution of all foods and to know what is necessary to keep you well fed. A balanced diet breaks down into six main areas: sugars, carbohydrates, fats, proteins, minerals/vitamins/salts and water —all are necessary, some in greater quantities than others.

Sugars: Technically called simple sugars, these are the simplest form of energy–stored–as–food. Because they are simple, the body finds them easy to absorb into the bloodstream —hence the term blood sugar. From here sugars are either turned directly to energy, or are stored as glycogen. The brain is very partial to using sugars for energy and if it is forced to run on other forms of food energy it complains by making you feel tired, headachy, and generally wobbly–kneed.

Though it is important to have some sugars in your diet, try not to depend on them too much. Weight for weight they give you fewer calories than other food types. Also if you take in lots of sugars at once, the body will react by over–producing insulin because your blood sugar is too high, so that in the end your blood sugar is taken down to a lower level than before. If you feel a desperate need for instant energy, try to take sugars with other food types to prevent this happening. While travelling, it is simple enough to recognize foods with lots of sugars —they're sweet. Simple enough, too, to avoid sugar excesses, whose pitfalls are well documented in the West. In less developed areas, sugar is still something of a luxury.

Carbohydrates: Basically, carbohydrates are complex structures of simple sugars. Plants generally store energy as carbohydrate while animals store food energy as fat or glycogen. Carbohydrates have to be broken down into simple sugars by the body before they can be used as energy, so it takes longer to benefit from them after eating. Weight for weight, however, you will get three or four times more calories from carbohydrates than from sugars.

Recognizing carbohydrates is simple. They are stodgy, starchy and very filling: breads in the Western world, mealies in Africa, rice in the East, etc. The majority of food energy comes from carbohydrates, so, when travelling, find the local equivalent and base a diet around it.

Fats: Next to carbohydrates, most of our energy comes from fats. Our bodies store energy as fat because it is the most efficient way to do so. Weight for weight, fats give you nearly three times the energy of carbohydrates, so they are an extremely efficient way of carrying food energy. The body can take quite a while to break down fat into a usable form —from minutes to half an hour.

Fats, of course, are fatty, oily, creamy and sometimes congeal. Foods high in fat include butter, dairy foods, etc, although there are other high fat foods that are less well known, such as egg yolk or nut kernels. Fats are necessary now and again because one reclusive vitamin is generated from a fat and, more obviously, because without these concentrated doses of energy it would take a lot longer to eat all the food you need, as with cows or elephants.

Proteins: One of the most misunderstood types of food in the West is protein. Traditionally thought of as something essential, and the more the better, the truth is that for adults very little is needed each day and bodies in the West work very hard to convert unnecessary protein into urea so that it can be flushed away.

Protein is used to build and repair bodies, so children need plenty of it, as do adults recovering from injury. Otherwise, the amount of protein needed each day is small —maybe a small egg's worth. Other than that, protein cannot be readily used for energy, and the body doesn't bother converting it unless it is heading for a state of starvation. Those people on a red meat diet are using very little of the protein it contains, relying on the fat content which can be up to 45 per cent. When you are wondering where protein appears in your food, bear in mind that protein is for growth, so young mammals have protein–packed milk, unhatched chicks have their own supply in the meat of an egg and to help trees off to a good start there is a healthy package of protein in nuts. Even the humble grain of wheat has a little, if it isn't processed away.

Minerals, Vitamins and Salts: All of these are essential for all–round health and fitness. Most of them can't be stored by the body and so they should be taken regularly, preferably daily. Ten days' shortage of Vitamin C, for instance, and you feel run–down, tired and lethargic —perhaps without knowing why.

In the normal diet, most of your minerals and vitamins come from fresh fruit and vegetables. If you feel that you may not get enough fresh food, take a course of multivitamin tablets with you for the duration of your travels. They don't weigh very much and can save you lots of trouble.

If you are getting your vitamins and minerals from fresh foods, remember that they are usually tucked away just under the skin, if not in the skin itself. Polished and refined foodstuffs have lost a lot, if not all, of their vitamins, minerals and dietary fibre.

As regards salts, there is little cause for concern. It is easier to take too much than too little, and if you do err on the low side your body often tells you by craving salty foods. So don't take salt tablets. You could upset your stomach lining.

How much

Nutritionists have a term for the amount of food energy needed to keep a body ticking over —the basal metabolic rate. Take a man and put him in a room at ideal temperature, humidity, etc., and make sure he does no work at all except stay alive and he will use about 600kCal in a day. This is his basal metabolic rate.

Those of us who do not lie stock still in a room all day need energy over and above that basic amount, to work and to keep warm. For living and working in average conditions, our daily energy requirement rises to about 2500kCal. If you are going to be physically active (backpacking, say) in a temperate climate, your energy use will go up to around 3500kCal per day. If we do the same hard work in an extremely cold climate, our energy rate could go up to 5000kCal. To need more than this we would need to do immense amount of work or have an incredibly fast metabolism. Sadly for women, they do not burn up nearly as much energy doing the same work as men.

A little experience will tell you whether you need a little more or a little less than the average. With this knowledge, you are ready to plan just how much food you need to take for the number of days you are travelling.

When you come to work out amounts of various foodstuffs that make up your calorie intake for the day, books for slimmers or the health conscious are invaluable. They list not only calories, but often protein and other nutritional breakdown. Sometimes, nutritional information is also given on the packet.

Eating local food

In developing countries, canned, powdered and dried foods are usually safe to eat, provided they are made up with purified water. Staples such as flour and cooking oils are nearly always safe.

Meat, poultry, fish and shellfish should look and smell fresh and be thoroughly cooked, though not over–cooked, as soon as possible after purchasing. They should be eaten while still hot or kept continuously refrigerated after preparation. Eggs are safe enough if reasonably fresh and thoroughly cooked.

Milk may harbour disease–producing organisms (tuberculosis, brucellosis). The 'pasteurized' label in underdeveloped countries should not be depended upon. For safety, if not ideal taste, boil the milk before drinking. (Canned or powdered milk may generally be used without boiling for drinking or in cooking).

Butter and margarine are safe unless obviously rancid. Margarine's keeping qualities are better than those of butter. Cheeses, especially hard and semi–hard varieties, are normally quite safe; soft cheeses are not so reliable.

Vegetables for cooking are safe if boiled for a short time. Do check, though, that on fruit or vegetables the skin or peel is intact. Wash them thoroughly and peel them yourself if you plan to eat them raw.

Moist or cream pastries should not be eaten unless they have been continuously refrigerated. Dry baked goods, such as bread and cakes, are usually safe even without refrigeration.

Always look for food that is as fresh as possible. If you can watch livestock being killed and cooked or any other food being prepared before you eat it, so much the better. Don't be deceived by plush surroundings and glib assurances. Often the large restaurant with its questionable standard of hygiene and practice of cooking food ahead of time is a less safe bet than the wayside vendor from whom you can take food cooked on an open fire, without giving flies or another person the chance to contaminate it. Before preparing bought food, always wash your hands in water that has been chlorinated or otherwise purified.

In restaurants, the same rules apply for which foods are safe to eat. Restaurants buy their food from shops just as you would. It is wise to avoid steak tartare and other forms of raw meat in the tropics as there is a risk of tapeworm. Fruit juice is safe if pressed in front of you. Protect freshly bought meat from flies and insects with a muslin cover.

Meat that is just 'on the turn' can sometimes be saved by washing it in strong salty water. If this removes the glistening appearance and sickly sweet smell, the meat is probably safe to eat. Cold or half–warmed foods may have been left standing and are therefore a risk. Boil such meats and poultry for at least 10 minutes to destroy bacteria before serving. Ice-cream is especially to be avoided in all developing countries.

Rice and other grains and pulses will probably have preservatives added to them. These will need to be removed by thorough washing as they are indigestible.

Eating in developed countries is not entirely hazard–free. You should remember that the Mediterranean countries and the former USSR host typhoid (against which vaccination is recommended), and that Delhi Belly is no respecter of language and is just as likely to strike in Spain as in India. The rules for avoiding tummy trouble are much as above: stick to foods that are simple and hygienically prepared, and as close as possible to those you know and love —at least until your digestive system slowly adapts to change.

Off the beaten track

There is no right menu for a camping trip, because we all have slightly different tastes in food and there is an almost endless number of menu possibilities. So, what should you pack? Here are a few points you'll want to consider when choosing the right foods: weight, bulk, cost per kg.

Obviously, water-weighted, tinned foods are out. So are most perishables — especially if you are going to be lugging your pantry on your back. You'll want only lightweight, long–lasting, compact food. Some of the lightest, of course, are the freeze drieds. You can buy complete freeze dried meals that are very easily prepared: just add boiling water and wait five minutes. They have their drawbacks, however. First, they're very expensive. Second, even if you do like these pre–packaged offerings, and many people don't, you can get tired of them very quickly.

A much more exciting and economical method is to buy dehydrated foods at the supermarket and combine them to create your own imaginative dinners. Dried beans, cereals, instant potato, meat bars, crackers, dry soup mixes, cocoa, pudding, gingerbread and instant cheesecake mixes are just a few of the possibilities. But don't forget to pack a few spices to make your creations possible.

Quantity and palatability

Most people tend to work up a big appetite outdoors. About 0.9kg to 1.2kg of food per person per day is average. How much of which foods will make up that weight is up to you. You can guess pretty accurately about how much macaroni or cheese or how many pudding mixes you are likely to need.

Last, but not least, what do you like? If you don't care for instant butterscotch pudding or freeze dried stew at home, you'll probably like it even less after two days on the trail. And if you've never tried something before, don't take the chance. Do your experimenting first. Don't shock your digestive system with a lot of strange or different new foods. Stick as closely as possible to what you're used to in order to avoid stomach upsets and indigestion. And make sure you pack a wide enough variety of foods to ensure you won't be subjected to five oatmeal breakfasts in a row or be locked into an inflexible plan.

Packaging your food

After purchasing your food, the next step is to re–package it. Except for freeze dried meals or other specially–sealed foods, it's a good idea to store supplies and spices in small freezer bags. Just pour in your pudding powder, salt or gingerbread mix, drop an identifying label in, to take all the guesswork (and fun) out of it, and tie a loose knot. Taking plastic into the wilderness may offend one's sensibilities but it works well. Out in the wilds you learn just how handy these lightweight, flexible, recyclable, moisture–proof bags really are.

Preparing great meals

Although cooking over an open fire is great fun, many areas don't allow and can't support campfires. So don't head off without a stove. When choosing a stove, remember that the further off the beaten track you go, the more important become size, weight and reliability. Aside from a stove, you'll also need a collapsible water container, means of water purification and a heavy bag in which to store your soot–bottomed pans. You'll also need individual eating utensils: spoon, cup and bowl will do. Also take a few recipes with you, or learn them before you leave. You can even have such luxuries as fresh baked bread if you are prepared to make the effort. Some tips about camp cooking learned the hard way:

1. Cook on a low heat to avoid scorching
2. Taste before salting (the bouillon cubes and powdered bases often added to camp casseroles are very salty: don't overdo it by adding more)
3. Add rice, pasta, etc, to boiling water to avoid sticky or slimy textures and add a knob of butter or margarine to stop the pan from boiling over
4. Add freeze dried or dehydrated foods early on in your recipes to allow time for rehydration
5. Add powdered milk and eggs, cheese and thickeners to recipes last when heating
6. When melting snow for water, don't let the bottom of the pan go dry or it will scorch (keep packing the snow down to the bottom
7. Add extra water at high altitudes when boiling (water evaporates more rapidly as you gain altitude) and allow longer cooking times —20 minutes at 1000m, for example, as against 10 minutes at sea level

Cleaning up

Soap residue can make you sick. Most seasoned campers, after one experience with 'soap sickness of the stomach,' recommend using only a scouring pad and water. Boiling water can be used to sterilize and, if you have ignored the above advice, is good for removing the remains of your glued–on pasta or cheese dinners. Soak and then scrub.

Use these recyclable plastic bags to store leftovers and to carry away any litter. Leave the wilderness kitchen clean —and ready for your next feat of mealtime magic!

LIGHTWEIGHT EQUIPMENT

by Martin Rosser

When I first came to lightweight backpacking, I knew very little and didn't bother to ask for advice. I learned from bitter experience and, interspersed with misery, very exciting it was too. The main drawback is expense. Based on trial and error, costs soon mounted to prohibitive proportions before I had what I wanted. The lesson: if you're beginning, a little advice is worth a lot. When you become more practised, then is the time for bitter experience to take over.

In this article, I intend only to cover the main purchases you will make, missing out on the way food, clothing, any more technical sporting equipment. This leaves (in descending order of what it will probably cost you) tent or shelter, sleeping gear, rucksack, boots and cooking and eating gear.

If you are going backpacking, there are a number of objectives you will have in mind. *Weight* is usually at the top of the list: you want everything as light as possible. *Performance*: you want it to be good enough for everything you are going to put it through. *Expense*: you have to be able to afford it. These three criteria form what could be termed the eternal triangle of backpacking.

As we go on, you will see compromises arising, but one aspect of weight can be covered now. Most lightweight gear comes marked with a weight, but manufacturers being manufacturers, these are not always as accurate as they might be. Furthermore, some sleeping bags come marked with the weight of the filling only. It is easy to become confused or misled. The easiest answer is to shop for your kit armed with a spring balance (anything measuring up to 15 lbs is sufficient if it can be read to the nearest ounce or two). If you want to know where to get a balance, ask a fisherman.

Tents and shelters

At one time, the ridge pole was the only tent you could get, short of a marquee. Then some bright spark designed an A–pole ridge so that the pole didn't come straight down the doorway. Today you can still get both these designs and the ridge pole (in the form of the Vango Force Ten) is still preferred by many as a heavy duty tent that can take a lot of punishment.

However, with the advent of flexible poles that could be shoved through sleeves, new designs became possible and new advantages arose. Such models give you plenty of headroom, something as important as ground space if you intend to live in your tent during bad weather. There are disadvantages of course. The tents are both more expensive and more fragile. To get a structurally strong flexible–pole tent, you have to go up–market to the geodesic designs, and that costs a lot of money.

After flexible poles, Gore–tex made its mark on the tent scene with single–skin tents. Reputably water tight, with built–in breathability, you get a condensation–free tent that weighs even less than regular flexible pole types. These tents also tend to employ flexible poles so the space inside is good. However, Gore–tex is a very expensive material, so as the weight goes down, the prices go up.

Single skin tents soon became available in one–man versions with only the barest skeleton of a frame. Because the material breathes, it doesn't matter if there is no circulation of air around it. With one hoop at the front, these tents resemble a tunnel that you have to crawl into feet first. Then the hoop was removed and the Gore–tex 'bivi–bag' was born —a waterproof and fully breathable covering for your sleeping bag. These are probably the ultimate luxury in bivouacking, but the cost is again high. However, weighing in at next to nothing, these bags are well worth considering.

Last, but not least comes the humble bivouac sheet or, to use the army parlance, the 'basha sheet.' This 6ft by 8ft piece of PU nylon has tags around the outside so that it can be pegged down. It is the most versatile, lightweight, inexpensive and durable of all shelters so far discussed. It is limited only by the ingenuity and expertise of the user —and therein lies its fault: you need to know how to use it. But if you don't have any money, or if you can put the occasional soaking down to experience, give it a go.

So which one do you choose? Narrow the field by asking yourself these questions: how many people do you want it to sleep? How high up are you going to camp? (The higher you camp, the harsher the conditions, so the sturdier the tent you need.) Is headroom important to you? (Perhaps you want a flexible hoop design.) Do you want it to last a long time? (If so you will have to go for a heavier duty model.)

It has to be said that even if you designed the tent yourself, compromises would have to be made, so be prepared to make them when buying. However, with care and proper scrutiny of the maker's specifications, you should get something suitable.

Whatever you end up with, try to get a tent with mosquito netting on every entrance, even the vents. Rare indeed are the countries with no flying biters. The tent you end up with will probably have a super thin ground–sheet to save weight, so you might want to get some 2mm foam to use as an underlay. It will keep you surprisingly warm and will cut down on wear and tear. However, this will add to the weight and bulk of your tent system. Bear this in mind before you reject the heavier tent with the stronger ground sheet.

Sleeping gear

Without a shadow of a doubt, the best you can sleep in is a down bag. It promotes fine dreams, is aesthetically pleasing, is lighter for any given warmth rating than any other fill and packs away smaller than any other bag, lofting up afterwards to coset you at night. Nothing else comes close to down, unless, of course, you are allergic to feathers.

Yet down has a terrible Achilles heel. If it gets wet, it is next to useless and very unpleasant to be next to. Furthermore, wet it a few times and it starts to feel very sorry for itself, losing efficiency rapidly.

If your bag is likely to get wet, steer clear of down. The alternative is a man–made fibre bag. These come in many guises but the principle is the same in all. A long, man–made fibre is hollow and thus traps air. As with down, it is the trapped air that keeps you warm. Call it Holofill, Superloft, Microsoft or whatever, the consensus of opinion is that the difference in performance is marginal. The fibres probably differ slightly to get around patents rather than to improve performance.

The advantages of artificial fibres are clear. The bags are cheaper than down, they are warmer underneath you (because they are harder to compress), they keep you warmer when wet, and they are easier to keep clean. Disadvantages? They are substantially heavier and bulkier than down, and won't last you anywhere near as long.

The compromise is clear. If you can stay out of the wet and can afford to pay more, invest in down which lasts longer, so costing the same in the long run. If you constantly get wet when camping, buy a man–made fibre bag and stick to feeling the down bags in the shops lovingly.

There is one more alternative, Buffalo Bags, made from fibre pile covered in pertex. These are unique and have their own special advantages, though the disadvantages can be stated easily: they are very heavy and bulky. Buffalo Bags are based on the layer system, making it handy to add layers for cold weather and subtract for hot. They are tough and very washable. Thanks to the pertex covering they aren't easily wetted, and if they do get wet, the pile wicks away moisture and the pertex cover dries it out rapidly. The same pertex covering makes the bag very windproof. The bag is very good for those who bivouac and can be used to effect with a good down inner bag. Handle, or better still, borrow one to try before you buy.

Try the bag on in the shop, however foolish you feel, and leave your clothes on while you do so. This minimizes embarrassment, and one day you might be cold enough out in the wilds to sleep fully clothed. Pull the hood of the bag tight around your face to cover the head. If you can't do this, the bag can't be used for any kind of cold weather. A large part of the body's heat loss is from the head. Shove your feet into the bottom of the bag and wriggle. If the bag constricts you it is too small. Any point where you press against the bag will turn into a miserable cold spot at night. If you are a restless sleeper, make sure the bag is wide enough around the middle to contain all your squirming. If you feel like a solitary pea rattling around in an empty pod, the bag is too large and you will waste heat warming up empty space.

General good points in a bag include a box or elephant–type foot; a draw–cord at the shoulder as well as the head; and the option of a right or left handed zip so that in an emergency you can share your warmth with an extra special friend. Zips should all be well baffled to prevent loss of heat. If the sack you choose is of man–made fibre, check to see if it comes with a compression stuff sack. If it doesn't and you want one, this will add a few pounds to the final price.

I have deliberately ignored baffle constructions as the subject is complicated and best covered with examples to hand. Seek advice on site. Similarly with the season rating of the bag: 'season' system is simple but should only be used as a rough guide. One season (summer) for very casual use in warm weather; two season (summer and spring) is a little better; three seasons should be good for winter use; and five seasons for use in severe conditions. However, simple systems like this leave room for manufacturers to fudge their claims. One man's three seasons is another man's four. Query the general reputation of the bag you fancy with as many experts as you can find. I find that 'lowest temperatures' to use the bags in are next to useless: they are inevitably rated for still air, and who camps in that? As well as ignoring the massive effect of wind chill, they can also ignore the fact that some people maintain a higher body temperature at night than others.

Last but not least with sleeping gear, you would be well advised to put something under your sleeping bag; namely a 'kip mat.' The most widely used is the closed cell foam type which is bulky but lightweight and durable. Ignore all advice that tells you that they are all made of the same stuff and that for expensive ones you simply pay for the name —it is patently untrue. A simple test is to inflict severe damage on various types —such damage as scoring, tearing, and compressing flat. Choose one that withstands these injuries best and it will probably be the one that feels warmest when pressed between the palms. It will probably cost more, but in my experience the cheap ones are simply not worth it.

Rucksacks

With rucksacks two things are important from the outset: size and waterproofness. You have available to you any size of 'sack you want and (whatever the manufacturer may say to the contrary) none of them are waterproof. The capacity of a 'sack is measured in litres. A small day pack weighs in at about 25 litres. From there you have various sizes up to a general all round 'sack sized at 75 litres. With one of these you will be able to manage anything up to mountaineering (at a push), but you pay a price for the facility. Having 75 litres to play with you feel a terrible urge to fill up all the space, even for summer camping in the lowlands.

To restrict yourself to what you need rather than what you have room for, takes discipline. Because of this, some people prefer a 65 or even a 50–litre sack. Going upwards from 75 litres, there is almost no end, but the higher you go the more specialized the use; expedition travel overseas perhaps or for humping all you need up to a base camp from which you intend making sorties with smaller loads.

When you look at the vast array of rucksacks available, you will find that fashion dictates two things at present. First is the anatomical, internal frame system. External frames are fuddy duddy now, though the internal frame is not the all-round answer to carrying loads. The second (and far less valid) fashion is adjustable harnesses. If you can (and it gets harder every season) avoid these. There are more fiddly bits that can go wrong, usually at an awkward moment (mine went halfway up the ascent to a glacier), and as your back shouldn't be due to change shape significantly for another 30 years at least you may as well save yourself some bother. Settle for a 'sack that is fixed at one size and just happens to fit you.

Something that has always been a very important asset to a rucksack is a hip belt. When walking, the hip belt transfers roughly 60 per cent of the pack weight to your legs, leaving only 40 per cent for your more delicate shoulders and back. Therefore any rucksack you buy should have a wide, sturdy, and very well padded hip belt. That thick padding should also appear at the shoulder straps. Thin bands will cut off the circulation, giving you the sensation of having two useless and heavy ropes dangling from your shoulders instead of arms.

After those important criteria, the rest more or less comes down to personal preference. If you are organized in the way you pack, a one–section rucksack is simpler and more effective. It is an advantage if your pockets can be detached, but having them fixed saves a bit of weight. Some harnesses leave more room for air to circulate between you and the 'sack. If you hate getting hot and sweaty as you walk, try for one of these.

When you buy your pack, enquire about the repair service. Well established manufacturers such as Karrimor and Berghaus give excellent service, often without charging. Some will even give a lifetime's guarantee, though I can never work out if this applies to the life of the 'sack or the life of its owner.

Boots

As far as boots are concerned, leather is still the most wonderful material going. Fabric boots have come and gone, and plastic shell boots have managed to retain only a very small part of the market. Meanwhile, leather goes from strength to strength. To spot a good leather boot is fairly simple. It is as far as possible made from one bit of leather. The stitching is double, sometimes triple.

The ankle is well padded to give comfortable support. The inside of the boot is lined with soft leather, and there are no rough seams around the heel. Feet tend to blister in disapproval of poor design.

Check the weight of several different pairs. It costs you energy to clump around with a heavy weight on each foot, and you may well decide that the terrain you usually walk on isn't demanding enough to require such solidness.

If you intend to use your boots with crampons, however, you will need a fairly rigid sole at the least. If you intend to go front pointing you will need a boot with a steel shank in the sole. For the common walker, though, these should be avoided. The boot becomes very heavy and uncomfortable to walk in over any great distance.

Traditionally, two pairs of socks are worn with boots, and some celebrated old timers even wear more, choosing oversize boots to compensate. However, modern thinking says that boots aren't as uncomfortable as they used to be and one pair of socks is quite enough. So unless you suffer terribly from cold feet, prepare to try on your boots with just one pair of thick socks. With the boots laced up, rap the heel on the floor and check to see if you can wiggle your toes freely. If you can, the boots are not too tight for you, the blood will still circulate and you should be free from the horrors of gangrene and cold toes.

Cooking and eating

For this pleasant pastime you will need a stove, something to cook in, something to eat out of, something to eat with and (very importantly) something to carry water in.

A water container should hold about a litre and can be of any shape or design that takes your fancy. The solid plastic army types are robust but heavy. The thin aluminium ones are lighter but more fragile. One rule goes with all water bottles, though. Put anything other than water in them and they will be tainted for life.

The essential part of the 'something to eat with' is a general purpose blade. This will cut up anything you want to eat into manageable portions as well as whittle sticks and slice your tongue open if you lick it once too often. Beyond this, you only need a spoon. Anything more is redundant. Save the weight by cutting down on the number of utensils you take rather than by using flimsy 'camping' ones which bend the first time you use them.

For those who are into time and motion, what you eat out of is also what you cook in. Those who find this idea displeasing will know best what they want. However, when you look for a cooking/eating billy make sure of two things. Firstly, it should have a good handle (preferably one that will not get too hot to hold whilst cooking is in progress). Secondly, it must have a close–fitting lid. This too must have a handle, so it can be lifted on or off, or be used as a frying pan by those terrible people who can suffer fried eggs and bacon for breakfast.

There are many styles of billy available to choose from. I use a two pint 'paint tin' type, because I like the shape and enjoy hanging it over wood fires. Others choose the rectangular army type that hold up to a litre. These fit nicely into the side pocket of a rucksack and can be filled with snack foods and brew kit.

On now to the more complex subject of stoves. The choice here is between solid fuel, liquid or gas. Solid fuel comes in blocks that resemble white cough candy. A packet fits neatly into the metal tray that you burn them in. The whole affair is little bigger than a pack of playing cards. The system is foolproof since you merely set a match to the blocks and add more for extra heat, take away for less heat. The fuel is resistant to water, though you may have trouble lighting it if it is damp. Its main drawback is that it doesn't produce an intense heat and so is slow to use. It also produces noxious fumes and so should not be used in an enclosed space.

Moving on to liquid stoves, your choice increases considerably. Most simple of all is the meths burner. Here you have a container into which you pour meths and then set fire to it. The more sophisticated (and expensive) sets have a windshield built round the container which also neatly holds the billy. Again the design is foolproof. Its advantages include a cleaning, burning flame, and quite a range of burners, from inexpensive to high–tech and costly. However, the fuel is relatively expensive and may be difficult to get hold of if you are off the beaten track. Furthermore, the rate of burn cannot be controlled. The choice is simply on or off.

Still in the liquid fuel range, there are the pressurized burners, running on either paraffin or petrol. The burner for paraffin is the well known primus stove. Though it is a relatively complicated device, compared with other stoves it can be readily mastered. Once burning, the flame is intense and efficient and can be adjusted to give various rates of heat. As a fuel, paraffin is cheap and almost universally available. The disadvantages of pressurized paraffin are that a small amount of a second fuel must be carried to prime the stove which needs some maintenance. However, primus stoves are known in most parts of the world, so spare parts should not be too much of a problem.

An alternative to pressurized paraffin is pressurized petrol. Again this type of stove is quite complicated and needs occasional maintenance. Furthermore it usually demands to be fed unleaded petrol, so buying fuel whilst travelling could present problems. Like paraffin, however, it burns hot and fast, heating quickly and efficiently. Petrol and paraffin also produce noxious fumes and both should be used in a well ventilated space.

Gas stoves are simple to use. They are relatively cheap to buy but are expensive to run. They burn cleanly and the flame can be controlled, but when pressure runs low the flame stays stubbornly and annoyingly feeble. You can usually find somewhere to buy replacement canisters, but in out of the way places the cost will be high. The little Camping Gaz canisters that are ubiquitous around Europe are difficult to find in the Third World and you are not allowed to take them on 'planes. Unlike paraffin, gas is not an everyday fuel in most places. Using gas stoves in low temperatures is inadvisable as their performance drops dramatically.

As with most areas of equipment, there is a stove to beat all stoves. It can run on any liquid fuel you care to feed it, including (apparently) vodka, should you be so inclined. It comes with an attachment that screws directly into a regular metal fuel bottle and away you go. Should you be interested in buying one, be prepared to spend a lot.

Once again, compromise is the final solution. You will generally find that pressurized paraffin is the tried and trusted stove for most formal expeditions, and is the general favourite of many. Solid fuel I find a useful last resort to have available when you are travelling light and having difficulty lighting wood fires. Gas fuel is simple to use in all but extreme conditions. You pays your money and you takes your choice.

With so much wonderful equipment around it is easy to get carried away and aim for the best in everything. A large rucksack to carry a five season down bag with a Gore–tex bivi–bag, a 'superstove' and a geodesic dome tent. Thankfully most people's pockets refuse to support such notions.

In reality, if you think carefully about the use to which your equipment will be put, you will often find that the best is not suitable for you and you are just as well off with something cheaper. Then, when your style of travelling or camping does demand the best, the expense becomes worthwhile and supportable. So don't end up being parboiled in a five season sleeping bag which you only ever use in summer. The money could be better spent elsewhere.

PERSONAL FREIGHT AND UNACCOMPANIED BAGGAGE
by Paul Melly

Few people bother to think about baggage. Until, that is, they become that annoying person at the front of the airport check–in queue, searching for a credit card to pay the extortionate bill for bringing home an extra suitcase on the same plane.

The alternative —shipping separately— is often disregarded, or looked upon as the sort of thing that people did in the days when Britain had an empire — shipping luggage seems to conjure up images of gigantic Victorian trunks or battered tea chests creaking home from the Far East in the hold of a mail steamer.

But it's actually worth investigating. With just a little planning, you can save a fair sum of money for relatively little delay by sending your surplus bags as freight.

The alternative is to pay the full whack for excess baggage while making a handsome contribution to airline profits. This is such a good earner it is given a separate entry in the multi–million dollar revenue graph of one Middle Eastern carrier's annual report.

Costly limits

The reason excess baggage charges are so high is the strict limit on how much weight an airliner can carry. There is a premium on the limited reserve space. So, if you significantly exceed your individual quota as a passenger and want to take that extra bag on the same flight, you must pay dearly for the privilege.

Of course, it then comes up on the luggage carousel with everything else at the end of your journey, which is more convenient but it is also very much more expensive than sending it unaccompanied by air, sea, road or rail. With advance planning, you can arrange for baggage to be waiting for you on arrival.

For those caught unawares, one UK operator, the London Baggage Company

(Gatwick London Air Terminal, Victoria Place, London SW1W 9SJ, tel: 071–828 2400) is conveniently located by Victoria Station, the London check–in terminal for several airlines flying out of Gatwick.

Your local Yellow Pages will give details of all the various specialist companies under 'Freight Forwarding and Shipping and Forwarding Agents. While the British International Freight Association (Redfern House, Browells Lane, Feltham, Middlesex TW13 7EP, tel: 081–844 2266) publishes the *Year Book*, listing all BIFA members and their freight speciality.

Of course freight services are not only useful for those who have too much travel baggage. If you're going to work abroad, take an extended holiday, embark on a specialist expedition or even a long business trip, you may well have equipment or samples to take. And if you have just finished or are about to start a course of academic or vocational study, there could be a hefty pile of books for which your normal baggage allowance is totally inadequate.

The more you send...

Although one, two, three or even half a dozen cases may seem a lot to you, for a specialist freight forwarder, airline or shipping company, handling hundreds of tonnes, it is peanuts. Generally, in the cargo business, the more you send the cheaper the price by weight —above a basic minimum which, unless you are sending small expensive items express, can be more than most private individuals want to send. Naturally you can send less than the minimum, but you still have to pay that standard bottom rate because most freight companies are in business to cater for the needs of industry, not individuals.

When industry does not come up with the traffic, however, they can be glad to get what private business is around. The depressed oil market in 1986, for example, led to an economic slowdown in the Gulf and a consequent slump in export cargo to the region, but airline freight bookings out of Bahrain, Abu Dhabi and Dubai were bolstered by expatriate workers sending home their goods and chattels after their contracts expired and not renewed.

However there are specialist outfits catering for the private individuals using their bulk buying power to get cheap rates which are then passed on to customers. They can also help with technical problems: how to pack, what you cannot send, insurance and so on.

Sending by sea

Seafreight is little–used these days except for shipments between Europe and Australia or New Zealand where the great distances involved make it a lot cheaper than air. The time difference between air and sea freight is from seven weeks (sea) and perhaps seven to 10 days (air). Air takes longer than one might expect because of red tape, the time needed for goods to clear Customs and the wait until the freight company has a bulk shipment going out.

The London Baggage Company reports that nearly all its seafreight bookings are for Australasia, with most of the remainder for New York or California. On these routes, there is enough business for freighting firms to arrange regular shipments of personal cargo but when it comes to the Third World, the traffic is more limited so the price is higher and it is often just as cheap —and more secure to use the air.

Seafreight is charged by volume rather than weight and is therefore particularly suitable for books or heavy household items, the goods can be held in the UK and then shipped out to coincide with your expected date of arrival in, for example Melbourne or Auckland.

If you want to send stuff straight away, you should remember it will wait an average of seven days before actually leaving —freight forwarders book a whole container and only send it when there is enough cargo to fill it. Shipping on some routes is regarded as high risk so insurance premiums increase —further reducing any price differential with airfreight.

Road and rail

Within Europe, rail is a useful option especially for Italy. There is only limited and relatively expensive airfreight capacity from London to Milan and Rome. A rail shipment to Naples from the UK may take just six to eight days. Rail has the added advantage that most stations are in the city centre so you can avoid the tiresome trek out to an airport cargo centre to collect your bags. Of course, it may well be cheaper to travel by train yourself and pay porters at each end to help you carry the cases, than to spend hundreds of pounds having items sent separately while you fly. There is normally no official limit on what baggage you are allowed to take free with you on a train.

Trucking is also an option for continental travellers. There is a huge range of haulage services and some carriers do take baggage. But prices are often comparable to airfreight and journey times are probably a day or two slower. European airfreight is a highly competitive business and can actually be cheaper than trucking if you measure size and weight carefully. There are direct routes to most destinations and delivery can normally be guaranteed the next day. However, the short distances involved mean that rail and road operators can often compete on timing as, although most flights last only a couple of hours (or less) many hours can be used up waiting for a consolidation —bulk air shipment— or, at the end of the trip, for Customs clearance.

Express services, operated by the airlines themselves or specialist companies, are growing rapidly but they are expensive and only worthwhile for high value items or those of commercial value such as scientific equipment, computer disks, spare parts or industrial samples. Normally these will offer a guarantee of least–guideline transit time.

Whatever your method of shipment, there are some practical problems to be wary of. For example, Spanish and Portuguese Customs can be finicky if items are sent by truck, and you may find yourself paying duty on some goods when they arrive even though you were first told that there would be no charge.

Into remoter regions

More surprising is the ease of getting stuff to quite remote, long–haul destinations. The key question is: how far is your final delivery point from the nearest international airport? Normally you, or someone representing you, will need to collect the bags at the place where they clear Customs and it is often impossible to arrange local onward shipment, at least under the umbrella of the baggage service in your home country. Delivery can sometimes be arranged within the city catchment area of the airport but that rarely extends to more than 20 or 30 kilometres away. If you are based in Europe, it is also often difficult to get detailed information about onward transport services in the Third World — whether by air, train, truck or even mule.

One option is to go to a specialist freight forwarder who has detailed knowledge of a particular region of the world and is competent to arrange for local distribution. However, as a personal customer providing a relatively small amount of business, you may not be able to get an attractive price and it could prove cheaper in the end to collect the bags from the airport yourself. There do not have to be direct flights from London, as long as your cargo can be routed to arrive in a country at the right city and pass Customs there.

You can take the bags into a country yourself across the land border but you may face more complications taking five suitcases alone through a small rural frontier post than if they arrive at the main airport under the aegis of an established freight company. Customs regulations are complex and it is vital that the status of research equipment or commercial samples is checked with Customs on arrival by the freight group's local agent.

There is no firm rule as to which places are most difficult to reach but perhaps the complications are greatest when you want to ship to a remote corner of a large Third World country, and you may well find the only reliable option is to collect the bags from the capital city yourself. Life is not even always easy in places which are regarded as 'developed.'

Shipping to small island destinations such as Fiji, Norfolk Island or the Maldives, can be fairly routine, but there are also good services to some places with particularly tough reputations.

Pricing

Pricing in general has two elements: a standard service charge which covers documentation, handling and administration by the shipping agent, and a freight charge per kilo which varies according to the airline, destination and particular bulk shipment deal the agent has been able to negotiate. Storage can be arranged as can collection within the company's catchment area —sometimes free of charge. Outside this radius you will probably have to use a domestic rail or road parcel service rather than asking the agent to arrange a special collection, although a few larger companies do have regional offices.

Do's and don't's

There are a number of important practical tips to bear in mind. A highly individual distinguishing mark on a case or carton will make it easier for you to pick out when you go to collect it from a busy warehouse or office. It is also important to mark it with your address and telephone number in the destination country so the receiving agent there can let you know when it has arrived.

If you must send really fragile items, pack them in the middle of the case and tell the freighting office. Many have full packaging facilities and will certainly let you know if they think a bag should be more securely wrapped: for some destinations they cover boxes with adhesive banding rape so that anyone can see if it has been tampered with. You should not overload a case and you should watch out for flimsy wheels or handles that could easily be broken off. The agent's packers can provide proper crates if needed.

Proper packing is vital — especially if you plan to ship the luggage by road. In many countries the wet season turns cart tracks into swamps. Expeditions or development aid teams will often have to ship into remote areas with poor roads.

If you are moving abroad, do try and differentiate between household items and personal effects such as clothing or toiletry. The latter are covered by a quite strict legal definition for regulations. You may find it best to send heavy household items separately by sea.

If you have something awkwardly shaped to send such as a bicycle, the agent is probably much more experienced in packing it safely than you will be. He also knows what the airline rules are: some carriers will not accept goods unless they are 'properly' packed and that can sometimes mean banding with sticky tape.

Insurance is essential. You may find you are covered by your own travel or company policy but the agents can also provide cover specially designed for unaccompanied personal freight. Without insurance, you are only protected against provable failure by the freighting company you booked the shipment with, and only in accordance with the strict limits of their trading terms and conditions.

As with normal airline baggage, there are certain items you cannot put in the hold of a plane. This is an extraordinary hotch–potch list, but here are some of the main banned items:

Matches
Magnetized material
Poison weedkiller
Flammable liquids
Camping gas cylinders
Most aerosols
Car batteries
Glue or paint stripper

For shipment by sea or land there are also strict restrictions on dangerous goods which have to be packed specially.

If you buy things in the UK for immediate shipment abroad, you are entitled to claim back the VAT (17.5%) paid on the purchase. Some freight forwarders offer a specialist service whereby you can send them the goods directly to be certified for export and thus reclaim the tax more quickly. Several other countries operate similar schemes which are worth investigating.

One key point to watch is payment. Special vouchers called Miscellaneous Charge Orders (MCOs), available from airlines, can be used at the traveller's convenience to pay for freight. But these are made out for that particular airline and can only be used on another if specially endorsed by the issuing airline. They can be used with some freight companies, but they could restrict the agent's ability to get you the best price if, for example, he had a cheap deal arranged on a carrier competing directly with the company which sold you the

MCO. Clearly the issuing airline would probably not be prepared to endorse the MCO so that you can ship with a rival.

You should particularly avoid MCOs which specify that they can only be used for 'excess baggage' because you may then be forced to pay the full excess rate rather than the lower unaccompanied freight price. And having bothered to make all the arrangements to ship your personal freight unaccompanied and more cheaply, that would be a pity! ■

COMMUNICATIONS
Chapter 13

LEARNING A LANGUAGE

by Dr Jay Kettle–Williams and Caroline Brandenburger

Whether for holiday purposes, for business reasons or simply for the sheer joy of its possibilities and new horizons, foreign–language learning is all the rage —in higher demand now than at any other time in recent years. The interest we see in foreign language acquisition across Europe owes much to the developments associated with 1992.

English and Empire

For reasons of historical accident —19th Century hegemony of the British Empire, technological advances under the banner of North American English— it is now the turn of English to be the world's *lingua franca*, the preferred medium of international communication. And those whose mother tongue is English are often lulled into a false sense of security.

But to ignore the forces of today's international developments, is to ignore the fact that we now live in a multilingual society, one for which we must all be prepared.

Improved communications over recent years have expanded our vision to encompass the entire globe —the whole world has become one theatre, but now with a variety of languages. Although the full force of recent developments has yet to be appreciated, one problem stands out sharply: shortfall in foreign language competence.

New materials

To match the increased demand for foreign languages, dozens of people these days seem to be joining the bandwagon in devising their own method or material to help people along the road to foreign language acquisition. There is a lot to choose from: Interactive Video Discs (IV) for self–paced, individual tuition which weighs in at a few thousand pounds for the hardware and about £1500 for software; accelerated–learning audio–lingual packages retailing from £10 to £100; Computer–Assisted Language Learning (CALL) packages —£15 to £100; the BBC Tutored Video Instruction (TVI) packages for the dedicated telly addict and CD–ROM command programmes at £100 plus which enhance the CALL option and offer voice cards. Alternatively you can opt for the 'executive toy' school of language learning with a pocket, computerised translator.

For the future, would–be linguists can look forward to the Computer Disc–Interactive (CD–I) which, once moving graphics become the norm, will offer a highly cost–effective programme through the TV screen.

How to learn

Private tuition: Private language schools and some LEAs have private classes. **The Institute of Linguists** (24a Highbury Grove, London N5 2EA, tel: 071–359 7445) can give details of private tutors or where to find out about them; also look under 'Tutoring' in the Yellow Pages or the small ads in, for example, the LEA guides to courses. Cost: from £12 per hour. Intensive courses can be very expensive. **Berlitz Language School** (9-13 Grosvenor Street, London W1A 3BZ, tel: 071–580 6482), offers short crash courses for beginners and a two–week *Total Immersion* course for people with some previous knowledge.

Prices of courses are dependent on the structure of the individual course. They also have branches in Birmingham, Leeds, Manchester and Edinburgh. Probably the most expensive programme is offered by **Stillitron** (72 New Bond Street, London W1, tel: 071–493 1177). It runs an intensive 10–day, non–consecutive language programme which is geared towards each person's interests and uses direct as well as audio visual methods. Languages included are French, German, Spanish, Portuguese, Italian and Arabic. The cost is £5,500.

Correspondence courses: Offered by some colleges and listed by the **Council for the Accreditation of Correspondence Colleges** (CACC), 27 Marylebone Road, London NW1 5JS, tel: 071–935 5391). Costs start from £100. Intensive or advanced courses can cost a lot more.

Teach yourself: Using books, cassette tapes, records, radio, video, computer, television. Books cost nothing if borrowed or you can spend up to several hundred pounds for a full programme of cassettes and learning books.

Language laboratories: Offered by LEAs (particularly in the larger polytechnics or technical colleges) and private language schools. They may be flexible, 'use–the–lab–when–you–want' schemes, fixed classes or supplementary to other courses (mainly group). The style varies from simple tape recordings with headphones to computer–controlled systems with individual booths connected to a master console. In some laboratories, students can work at their own pace, recording and then listening to their own voices. In others, pace is controlled by the teacher, so a student can't play back his own tapes. A lot depends on how much supervision the teacher is able to give, and the strength of the material. Repeated drills can quickly become boring.

Residential short courses: Details are available in the booklet *Time to Learn* (£4.25 inc. postage) published by the **National Institute of Adult Education**, 21 De Montfort Street, Leicester, tel: 0533 551451.

Full information about these methods can be obtained from the **Centre for Information on Language Teaching and Research** (CILT), 80 Bedfordbury, London WC2N 4LB, tel: 071–379 5101. Their publication *Language Courses for Adults* is a guide to part–time and intensive study opportunities for learning languages and is especially useful.

From 16 April 1995 all national and international codes change — see page 587 for details.

CILT's publications catalogue contains many other guides and books you might find helpful. Their library is very informative and includes directories and lists of course materials as well as advice on the type of course to suit you, and where you can find it. Write to them, giving as many details of yourself and your needs as you can.

Which to choose

People learn at different rates, often in different ways. Your training programme will further depend on the time you have available, your starting point, your dedication and discipline, your goals and your budget.

The old adages about horses for courses and paying for your choice hold good. Your next step should take into account the following points and considerations:

Training: Residential or non–residential; self–disciplined, partially or fully–tutored; tele–guided; individual or group study; time of the day/week?

Costs: Intensive one–to–one training costs start at about £1500 per week of residential training at home or abroad, from £1000 per non–residential week with an eight–hour day.

Intensity: Intensive (8 hours plus per day), extended or on–going? In general terms you should dedicate 80 hours to achieve a functional level or to progress from one level to another.

Design: Languages for specific purposes; ratio between the linguistic and para–linguistic (eg cultural/social awareness and cross–cultural briefing); initial and refresher courses; competences and grades.

Materials: Printed word/manuals; graphics; radio; audio cassettes; Tutored Video Instruction (TVI); passive video viewing; Interactive Video (IV); Compact Disc Interactive (CD–I); Computer Assisted Language Learning (CALL); CD ROM with or without voice cards.

Content: Active/reactive; encoding/decoding; one–to–one or group; role–play or contexts?

Accreditation: Professional progression; external or internal awards; identification of appropriate standards and awarding bodies?

BREAKING THE BARRIERS

by Jon Gardey

Barriers to communication off the beaten track exist just because of who you are —a visitor from another civilization. It is necessary to show the local people that underneath the surface impression of strange clothes and foreign manners exists a fellow human being.

The first step is to approach local inhabitants as if you are their guest. You are. It is their country, their village, their hut, their lifestyle. You are a welcome, or perhaps unwelcome, intruder into their familiar daily routine. Always be aware that they may see very few faces other than those of their family or the other families in the village. Their initial impression of you is likely to be one of unease and wariness. Be reassuring. Move slowly.

If possible learn a few words of local greeting and repeat them to everyone you meet in the village. It is very important to keep smiling, carry an open face, even if you feel exactly the opposite. Hold your body in a relaxed, non–aggressive manner.

In your first encounter, try to avoid anything that might anger them or make them shy with their initial approaches to you. If they offer a hand, take it firmly, even if it is encrusted with what you might consider filth. Don't hold back or be distant, either in attitude or voice. On the other hand, coming on strong in an effort to get something from a local person will only build unnecessary barriers to communication.

Words and pictures

Begin with words. If you are asking for directions, repeat the name of the place several times, but do *not* point in the direction you think it is, or suggest possible directions by voice. Usually the local person, in an effort to please his visitor, will nod helpfully in the direction in which you are pointing, or agree with you that, yes, Namdrung *is* that way, 'If you say so.' It may be in the opposite direction.

Merely say 'Namdrung' and throw up your hands in a gesture that indicates a total lack of knowledge. Most local people are delighted to help someone genuinely in need, and, after a conference with their friends, will come up with a solution to your problem. When *they* point, repeat the name of the place several times more (varying the pronunciation) to check if it is the same place you want to go. It is also a good idea to repeat this whole procedure with someone else in another part of the village (and frequently along the route) to check for consistency.

In most areas it is highly likely that none of the local people will speak any language you are familiar with. Communicating with them then becomes a problem in demonstration: you must *show* them what you want, or perform your message.

If you are asking for information that is more difficult to express than simple directions, use your hands to build a picture of what you need. Pictures, in the air, on the sand, on a piece of paper, are sometimes your only means of communication and, frequently, the clearest. Use these symbols when you receive blank stares in answer to your questions. Use sound or objects that you have in your possession that are similar, or of which you would like more.

Giving and getting

Not all of your contact with local people will be about getting something from them. Don't forget that you have a unique opportunity to bring them something from your own culture and try to make it something that will enrich theirs. Show them what it looks like with the help of postcards and magazines. Let them experience its tools. If you have a camera, let the local people, especially the children, look through the viewfinder. Put on a telephoto lens so they can get a new look at their own countryside. If you have a Polaroid camera, photograph them, and give them the print (a very popular offering but be careful, don't finish by photographing the whole village). And most important of all, become involved. Carry aspirin to cure headaches —real or imagined. If someone in the village seems to need help, say in lifting a log, offer a hand. Contribute yourself as an expression of your culture.

If you want to take photographs, be patient. Don't bring out your camera until you have established a sufficient rapport, and be as unobtrusive as possible. If anyone objects, stop. A bribe for a photograph or payment for information is justified only if the situation is unusual. A simple request for directions is no reason for a gift. If the local people do something out of the ordinary for you, reward them as you would a friend at home. The best gift you can give them is your friendship and openness. They are not performers doing an act, but ordinary people living out their lives in circumstances that seem strange to us.

I have found myself using gifts as a means of *avoiding* contact with remote people, especially children, as a way of pacifying them. I think it is better to enter and leave their lives with as much warmth as I can give, and now I leave the sweets at home. If you are camped near a village, invite some of the local people over to share your food, and try to have them sit among your party.

On some of the more travelled routes, such as Morocco, or the main trekking trails of Nepal, the local children, being used to being given sweets by passing trekkers, will swarm around for more. I suggest that you smile (always) and refuse them. Show them pictures or your favourite juggling act then give them something creative, such as pencils.

If a local event is in progress, stand back, try to get into a shadow, and watch from a distance. You will be seen and noticed, no matter what you do, but it helps to minimize your presence. If you want to get closer, edge forward slowly, observing the participants, especially the older people, for signs that you are not wanted. If they frown, retire. Respect their attempts to keep their culture and its customs as free as possible from outside influence.

The people in the remote places are still in an age before machines, and live their lives close to the earth in a comfortable routine. Where you and I come from is sophisticated, hard and alien to them. We must come into their lives as gently as possible, and when we go, leave no trace.

Officialdom

In less remote areas where the local people have had more experience of travellers, you must still observe the rule of patience, open–mindedness and respect for the lifestyle of others. But you will encounter people with more preconceived notions about foreigners —and most of those notions will be unfavourable.

In these circumstances —and indeed anywhere your safety or comfort may depend on your approach— avoid seeming to put any local person, especially a minor official, in the wrong. Appeal to his emotions, enlist his magnanimous aid, save his face at all costs. Your own calmness can calm others. If you are delayed or detained, try 'giving up,' reading a book, smiling. Should you be accused of some minor misdemeanour, such as 'jumping' a control point, far better to admit your 'mistake' than to be accused of spying —though even this is fairly standard practice in the Third World and shouldn't flap you unduly.

Wherever you go in the Third World, tones and pitches of voice will vary; 'personal distance' between people conversing may be less than you are used to; attitudes and priorities will differ from your own. Accept people as they are and you can hope that with time and a gentle approach, they will accept you also.

Language

When you have the opportunity of learning or using a smattering of the local language, try to make things easier for yourself by asking questions that limit responses to what you understand and prompt responses which will add helpfully and manageably to your vocabulary. Make it clear to your listeners that your command of the language is limited. Note down what you learn and try constantly to build on what you know.

Always familiarize yourself with the cultural limitations that may restrict topics of conversation or choice of conversation partner.

Keep your hands to yourself

Gestures can be a danger area. The British thumbs–up sign is an obscenity in some countries, such as Sardinia and parts of the Middle East, where it means roughly 'sit on this' or 'up yours.' In such places (and anywhere, if in doubt) hitch a ride by waving limply with a flattened hand.

The ring sign made with thumb and forefinger is also obscene in Turkey and elsewhere. And in France it can mean 'zero' ie worthless —the exact opposite of the meaning 'OK' or 'excellent' for which the British and Americans use it.

By contrast, our own obscene insult gesture, the two–finger sign, is used interchangeably in Italy with the Churchillian V–sign. Which way round you hold your fingers makes no difference —it's still understood as a friendly gesture meaning 'victory' or peace.

In Greece, as the anthropologist Desmond Morris tells us, there is another problem to do with the gesture called the *moutza*. In this, the hand is raised flat, "palm towards the victim and pushed towards him as if about to thrust an invisible custard pie in his faces". To us it means simply to 'go back', but to a Greek it is a hideous insult. It dates from Byzantine times, when chained prisoners were paraded through the streets and abused by having handfuls of filth from the gutter picked up by onlookers and thrust into their faces.

Though naturally the brutal practice has long since ceased, the evil meaning of *moutza* has not been forgotten.

HOW TO BE IN WITH ISLAM

by Peter Boxhall

Like any nation with an important history, the Arab people are proud of their past. Not only because of an empire which once stretched from the far reaches of China to the gates of France, or their many great philosophers, scientists, seafarers, soldiers and traders; but because they are one people, sharing a common language and culture, and following the same religion which has become an integral part of their lives and behaviour.

Language

Arabic is a difficult language for us to learn but it is a beautiful, expressive language which, in the early days of Islam, came to incorporate all the permissible culture, literature and poetry of Arab society. Small West African children sitting under *cola* trees write their Koranic lessons on wooden boards; infant Yemenis learn and chant in unison *Surahs* of the Holy Book; school competitions are held perennially in the Kingdom of Saudi Arabia and elsewhere to judge the students' memory and knowledge of their written religion.

So, as in any foreign environment, the traveller would do well to try and learn some Arabic. For without the greetings, the enquiries, the pleasantries of everyday conversation and the ability to purchase one's requirements, many of the benefits and pleasures of travel are foregone. Best, too, to learn classical (Koranic) Arabic which is understood throughout the Arabic-speaking world (although the farther one is away from the Arabian Peninsula in, for example, the Magribian countries of Morocco, Tunisia, and Algeria, the more difficult it is to comprehend the dialectal replies one receives).

Not long ago, before the advent of oil, when one travelled in the harsh environment of the Arabian Desert, the warlike, nomadic Bedu tribes would, if they saw you came in peace, greet you with *salaam alaikum* and afford you the hospitality of their tents. If 'bread and salt' were offered to you, you were 'on their face': inviolate, protected, a welcome guest for as long as you wished to stay. *Baiti Baitak* (my house is your house) was the sentiment expressed. This generous, hospitable principle still prevails throughout the Arab world.

Bureaucracy

Although they are subordinate to the overall sense of Arabness, each of the Arab kingdoms, emirates, sultanates and republics has its own national characteristics. In those far-off medieval days of the Arab Empire, there were no frontiers to cross, no need for passports, there was a common currency, a purer language. Today it is different. There is bureaucracy abroad in the Arab world —mostly, it can be said, a legacy of former colonial administrations. So be patient, tolerant and good-humoured about passports, visas, immunization, currency controls and customs. And remember that many of the Arab countries emerged only recently to their present independent status and it has taken us, in the West, some hundreds of years to evolve our systems of public administration and bureaucratic procedure.

One has to remember that generally the Arab does not have the same pressing (obsessional?) sense of urgency that we do. No discourtesy is meant. Does it really matter? Tomorrow is another day and the sun will rise again and set. Neither in his bureaucratic or even everyday dealings with you does the Arab take much notice of your status, official or induced.

When I was Personal Secretary to the Governor of Jeddah, important corporation chiefs and industrialists used to visit him in his *majlis* . They were received courteously and served the traditional *qahwa* . The Arab, however, is a great democrat and even these important people had, often to their annoyance, to wait their turn. Yet on one occasion, a comparatively poor *shaiba* came straight up to His Excellency, kissed him on the shoulder and extracting a scroll from the voluminous folds of his *thobe* (the uniform dress worn by all Saudis), proceeded to read its full, eulogistic length in a high–pitched quavering voice.

To the Arab, it is of little importance to know who or what you represent; he is more interested in who you are. If he likes you, you will soon be aware of it. The sense of touch is to the Arabs a means of communication. Westerners, from colder climates, should not therefore be too reticent, distant or aloof.

Watch and listen, for example, to how the Yemenis greet each other: the long repetitious enquiries as to each other's state of health; the handshake; the finger that will sometimes curl towards the mouth, to indicate they are merely on speaking terms, casual acquaintances; sometimes to the heart, to indicate that they are intimate friends. The embrace, the kiss on both cheeks, which are mainly customary in the Near East and Magribian countries… If you allow the Arab to take you as a friend in his way, he may even invite you to his house.

Social conventions

Baiti Baitak is the greatest courtesy. Do not, though, be critical, admiring or admonitory towards the furniture in the house. If you admire the material things, your hospitable host may feel impelled to give you the object of your admiration. Conversely, remember that if your taste in furnishing does not correspond with that of your host, the Arab is not much in the possession of beautiful material goods.

If it is an old–style house, you must always take your shoes off, and may be expected to sit on the floor supported by cushions. Then all manner of unfamiliar, exotic dishes may be served to you. If it is painful to plunge your fingers into a steaming mound of rice, and difficult to eat what are locally considered to be the choice pieces of meat, forget your inhibitions and thin skin, eat everything you are offered with your right hand and at least appear to enjoy it. Remember, your host is probably offering the best, sometimes the last remaining provisions in his house.

Once, in the Jordan desert, I was entertained by an important tribal sheikh in his black, goat–hair tent. An enormous platter, supported by four tribal retainers, was brought in and put in our midst. On the platter, surmounted by a mound of rice, was a whole baby camel, within that camel a sheep, within that sheep, pigeons. Bedu scarcely talk at all at a meal; it is too important, too infrequent an occasion. So we ate quickly, belching often from indigestion, with many an appreciative *Al Hamdulillah*, for it is natural to do so. When replete, rose–water was brought round for us to wash our hands and we men moved out to the cooling evening sands to drink coffee, converse and listen to stories of tribal life, while the tribal ladies, who had cooked the meal, entered the tent from the rear with the children, to complete the feast.

In some Arab countries, alcoholic drink is permitted. In others, it is definitely not. From my two years' experience in Saudi Arabia and three in Libya, I know it is actually possible to obtain whisky, for example, but it is at a price —perhaps as much as £70 a bottle which, for me at least, is too expensive an indulgence, even if it were not for the penalties for being caught.

Coffee and tea are the habitual refreshments: in Saudi Arabia, as was the custom in my municipal office, the small handle-less cups of *qushr* are poured from the straw–filled beak of a brass coffee pot. 'Arabian coffee' is also famous: almost half coffee powder, half sugar. One should only drink half or two thirds, however, and if you are served a glass of cold water with it, remember that an Arab will normally drink the water first (to quench his thirst) then the coffee — so the taste of this valued beverage may continue to linger in the mouth.

In North Africa, tea is a more customary drink. Tea *nuss wa nuss* with milk, in Sudan, for example; tea in small glasses with mint in the Magrib; tea even with nuts, in Libya. Whoever was it said that the English are the world's greatest tea drinkers? Visiting the Sanussi tribe in Libya, in Cyrenaica, I once had to drink 32 glasses of tea in the course of a morning. The tea maker, as with the Arabian coffee maker, is greatly respected for his art.

Dress

In most of the Arab world, normal European–type dress is appropriate, but it should be modest in appearance. Again, if, as we should do, we take notice of Arab custom, which is based in history on sound common sense, we might do well to remember that in hot, dusty conditions, the Bedu put on clothes to protect themselves against the elements, not take them off, as we Westerners do.

As to whether one should adopt the local dress in the particularly hot, arid countries of the Arab world is probably a matter of personal preference. The *thobe* is universally worn in Saudi Arabia, the *futah* in the Yemen and South Arabia. I personally used to wear the *futah*; in Saudi Arabia, however, the Governor suggested I should wear the *thobe* but I felt inhibited from doing so, as none of the other expatriates appeared to adopt it.

Religion

The final, and perhaps most important, piece of advice I can offer to the traveller is to repeat the need to respect Islam. The majority of Arabs are Muslim, and Islam represents their religion and their way of life, as well as their guidance for moral and social behaviour.

In the same sense that Muslims are exhorted (in the Koran) to be compassionate towards the non–believer (and to widows, orphans and the sick), so too should we respect the 'Faithful.' Sometimes one may meet religious fanatics, openly hostile, but it is rare to do so and I can only recall, in my many years in Arab countries, one such occasion. Some schoolboys in south Algeria enquired why, if I spoke Arabic, I was not a Muslim, and, on hearing my answer, responded: "*inta timshi fi'n nar*" ("You will walk in the fires of Hell").

In some countries, you can go into mosques when prayers are not in progress, in others entry is forbidden altogether. Always ask for permission to photograph mosques and (in the stricter countries) women, old men and children.

Respect, too, the various religious occasions and that all–important month–long fast of Ramadan. My Yemeni doctors and nurses all observed Ramadan, so one year I joined them, to see exactly what an ordeal it was for them. Thereafter, my admiration for them, and for others who keep the fast, was unbounded, and I certainly do not think we should exacerbate the situation in this difficult period by smoking, eating or drinking in public.

Ahlan wa sahlan: welcome! You will hear the expression often in the Arab world, and it will be sincerely meant.

TRAVELLING IN A BUDDHIST COUNTRY

by Gill Cairns

"**D**alai Lama Pic-a chur? You how much? How much you say?" Anyone who has travelled in Tibet, will have heard this constant refrain from children, accompanied by constant tugging on your shirt sleeve. A photograph of Tibet's spiritual leader, who has lived in exile since 1959, is a highly prized item in this part of the world, followed closely by "school pens, miss?" The photos of the Dalai Lama are scattered on the shrines in Buddhist temples, along with rice grains and *katha,* white offering scarves that are part of the rich panoply of offerings made by devotees who circumambulate the shrines, with strings of *mala* beads in their hands, counting the *mantras* they repeat with intense murmurings.

In Tibet, Buddhism has been entwined with the fabric of its culture as far back as the seventh century. Today there are still practising Buddhists, men and women, lay and monk, despite the desecration brought to their temples by the Chinese occupation in the Fifties and the Cultural Revolution in the Sixties and Seventies and intensifying sinofication of the area. Others who, with the invasion of Lhasa in 1959, fled along with the Dalai Lama into exile at Dharamsala, have set up communities on the Indian side of the Himalayas, in parts of Nepal and beyond.

Buddhism originates from the teaching of Siddharthur Gautama, who was born around 2,500 years ago, the son of Suddhodana of the Sakya clan, in Lumbini on the Nepal/Indian border. Having heard that there was life beyond the confines of his luxurious palace, he went forth to seek and eventually gain 'Enlightenment' and liberation from the cyclic existence of birth, death and rebirth. After his Enlightenment he was known as Buddha, which means Awakened One, and his subsequent teaching spread from India, south into Sri Lanka, then to Myanmar (Burma), Thailand, Cambodia and east into Tibet, China and Japan. While in India Buddhism was subsumed into Hinduism and then eroded by the Muslim Moguls, it has enjoyed a small but significant revival more recently, since Independence, with pockets of Buddhists, notably around Bombay and the South and in North-Eastern India near the borders with Tibet; Ladakh, which is know as Little Tibet, Sikkim, and the area around Dharamsala, where the Dalai Lama and his government in exile are based.

Today there are several schools of Buddhism. The Theravadins, who maintain traditional rules regarding discipline for monks and practitioners, based on the original letter of the teachings of Buddha, are found in parts of southern India, Sri Lanka, Myanmar (Burma), Thailand and Cambodia. The Mahayana, developed in northern India and Nepal among the lay as well as monastic population, emphasize not only on the historical teachings of Buddha but also the

Buddhas of the past and future and the altruistic ideal of seeking Enlightenment for the benefit of all beings (the Bodhisattva Ideal). In the 8th century Mahayana Buddhism was introduced into Tibet, where it developed a distinct flavour of its own with the beginning of Lamaism, in which highly spiritually developed religious teachers are revered as incarnations, or *tulkus*, of their predecessors. It is said that the current Dalai Lama, the fourteenth in the lineage, is the embodiment of the compassionate aspect of Enlightenment, which is archetypally represented in religious paintings by the Bodhisattva Avalokoteshvara, whose most common form has 11 heads and a thousand arms. A further development from the Mahayana in Tibet was the *Vajrayana* or *Tantra*, an even more devote version (not for the faint-hearted) which introduced the possibility of reaching Enlightenment in one lifetime.

Today Buddhism flourishes in pockets of Asia. In some countries, like Bhutan, it is the state religion, in others Buddhism is virtually outlawed. In some places tradition allows for people to be a Buddhist monk for a week, while in others you might not be part of a monastic order but you may very well be a sincere practitioner. All this may seem a little confusing to the Western traveller. Perhaps it is enough to say that the wearing of a robe is not the only indication that you may be travelling among Buddhists.

In Tibet, Ladakh, and the Himalayan regions, the outward expression of Buddhism is manifested not only in the richly decorated monasteries or *gompas* (places of meditation) which are often found wedged in impossibly inaccessible mountain tops, but also in the character of its people both lay and monk. It is as if all the positive emotion generated by Buddhist practice has infused its people with a remarkable cheerfulness, humour and lightness. The rugged monochrome landscape is sprinkled with intense colours that are characteristic of Buddhist devotion: brightly coloured prayer flags flutter from the golden roof tops of temples; boulders painted with Buddhist deities; the famous *mantra* of Avaolkiteshvara 'Om Mani Padme Hum' and *chortens*, stone structures containing relics built on a stack of geometrical shapes to represent the five elements of earth, fire, water, air, and ether.

Many of the *gompas*, are encircled by a pilgrim circuit, a narrow trail which devotees circumambulate, often prostrating themselves (raising their hands above their heads, and then flinging their bodies forward to the ground, the process is then repeated until the circuit is complete). The prostration practice is said to engage the body, speech and the mind fully in devoting one's life to the Buddha and the ideal of Enlightenment.

On approaching a *gompa* you may find, built into the perimeter walls, a row of prayer wheels, which are turned in a clockwise direction —inside these brass and wooden barrels are scrolls inscribed with hundreds of *mantras*, as they are turned the *Dharma* or Buddhist teachings and prayers are sent.

When you enter a *gompa* it is customary to remove footwear and ensure that you are modestly dressed. Monks take vows of celibacy and it is therefore respectful not to wear revealing clothing. At the entrance of larger temples, white offering scarves are on sale, these can be placed on the shrines, along with small amounts of change. The darkness of the interior of the *gompa* takes some adjusting to, so a torch is handy, for on close inspection, every inch of wall space is either painted with scenes from the life of the Buddha, Buddhist iconography, or adorned with Thangkas (wall hangings depicting particular deities, mounted on silk). It is disrespectful to touch any of the Buddhist statues (*rupas*) or these paintings. Butter lamps are lit as a prayer and often you can approach a *konyer* (chaplain) and give him money to light one for you. Buddhists make their way round the shrine room in a clockwise direction and to do otherwise is considered offensive. On leaving places of worship, Buddhists either back out, or bow gently to the shrine before turning to leave, it is courteous to do the same.

You may be lucky enough to witness a *Puja,* (devotional worship) which involves the chanting of *sutras* or scriptures, and *matras,* which are orchestrated by the occasional ringing of bells, and beating of drums, and the haunting call of strange horns fashioned from giant brilliant white conch shells. Sit quietly at the back of the gathering while the ritual is carried out. Monks at the *Puja* ceremonies sit on the ground, and care should be taken not to step over them, or pieces of text or books. During the course of the ceremony offerings are made to the shrines of the Buddhas and Bodhisattvas: incense, rice grains, yak butter lamps. At the end of the ceremony a bowl of salty butter tea may be put in front of you, this is definitely an acquired taste, however it is disrespectful to show dislike, so if you find it undrinkable, leave the bowl full without any fuss.

Regarding photography, as a general rule, taking photographs in temples is regarded as an intrusion, the dark interior would require a flash and this interrupts the concentration of devotees. In some *gompas,* however, monks will allow photography but normally for a fee.

Taking pictures of the Dalai Lamas into Tibet as gifts, should be viewed cautiously, whilst they might be very much appreciated, there is no doubt that this is a politically sensitive issue. According to the Tibet Information Network, several tourists have recently had problems with the Chinese authorities. It is therefore perhaps more prudent to show pictures of the Dalai Lama in your guide book, rather than making presents of them.

One recent abhorrent development that has affronted Tibetan sensitivities is the increasing number of tourists who have shown a morbid fascination in witnessing the sky burial ritual. A sky burial involves taking a corpse to a special site on a mountainside, where it is cut into pieces and left to be eaten by birds. Following the offensive behaviour of tourists not only photographing but also videoing this ritual, Westerners have now been banned from such ceremonies in Lhasa. Although in other parts of Tibet you may still be invited, it is strongly advised to turn down the offer, as a mark of respect to the dead and their relatives.

While travelling in a Buddhist country, especially Tibet, it is recommended to be perceptive to others' feelings. It is often difficult to discern when you might be crossing the boundaries of acceptability and unintentionally cause offence. Tibetan culture appears to be happy-go-lucky, and while that may largely be the case, it does not necessarily mean that anything goes. Politeness is a part of Tibetan culture, to the point that many are loathe to say no to requests from travellers. For example, if a woman in a short skirt asks the incumbent monk of a temple if she can go inside, he may mutter that it is rather cold inside, indicating he feels uneasy about it, but he would be unlikely to refuse her entry.

As always, the key to travelling is awareness and sensitivity —obviously we don't always get it right all the time, but an effort is always appreciated, and in a culture that is fast being eroded in the face of sinofication, the Tibetans need all the respect they can get.

Finally for those who want to learn more about Buddhism, there are a number of centres where travellers can not only learn about the religion and meditation, but go on a meditation retreat. The Friends of the Western Buddhist Order in Kathmandu runs meditation courses and retreats which are held in Pulchowk monastery in Patan (contact PO Box 5336 Thamel, Kathmandu, Nepal). The Mt Everest Centre for Buddhist Studies at the Kopan Monastery, GPO Box 817, Kathmandu can also be of help.

OVER THE AIRWAVES

By Steve Weinman

The magic of shortwave radio is that it can turn the homebound into travellers while keeping travellers in touch with home. Roaming the international wavebands from the comfort of an armchair is an agreeably painless —and cheap— way to travel. No visas, tickets or baggage are needed and often, because so many nations broadcast externally in English, there is no language barrier.

Some 140 stations broadcast internationally in English whether you tune in to Radio Moscow, Voice of America, Deutsche Welle or HCJB The Voice Of The Andes, you will find that the world is only too willing to come to you.

Once you venture abroad, of course, especially off the beaten track, short-wave can become a lifeline. Not only does it supply you with news from home but, if your home station is BBC World Service, it might well provide more reliable news and information about those parts of the world you are visiting than will be available from local services.

This reflects the fact that so much of the world's media is government–sponsored and controlled —the listener believes all he hears at his peril. New short-wave users are confused to find a number of stations broadcasting in English which sound superficially like the BBC: this is because they model their style and delivery on that of World Service with the aim of boosting their credibility as objective global reporters.

The BBC World Service broadcasts in English 24 hours a day, every day of the year, although it will not necessarily be audible all day in the places you intend to visit. It carries news on the hour backed up by current affairs and business affairs analysis and commentary, and in between offers a rich and varied diet of sport, music, features, science, drama and light entertainment. Close to home, it can be heard on mediumwave and at times longwave, but beyond northwestern Europe and out of reach of the morning papers you'll need a short-wave receiver to keep in touch.

Shortwave radio

So what is shortwave (also known as world band radio), and how can the trav-eller get the best out of it? Signals from the familiar longwave, mediumwave and FM stations on which you listen to domestic broadcasts, travel in a straight line from transmitter to receiver and so are limited not only by the strength of the signal but by the curvature of the Earth. In other words, if you venture more than about 300 miles from London, you will be over the horizon and probably unable to pick up *The Archers* on Radio 4 longwave.

Shortwave signals overcome such earthbound restrictions by proceeding from the transmitter in a series of giant hops between Earth and the ionosphere to the receiver —your radio set. The ionosphere is the Earth's natural satellite, a series of electrified layers of gas which extend hundreds of miles above the planet. As shortwave signals bounce around the world a certain amount of clarity can be lost in the process. Broadcasters compensate for this by enhancing the signal from strategically–placed relay stations.

The complication is that reception varies depending on where you are in the world, the time of year and even the time of day. In the late 20th century we have come to expect our news at the touch of a button. Shortwave listening can be like that, but often, when you are on the move, it is not. To get the most from it requires a little planning.

Because the ionosphere is created by the sun's rays, it is denser during the day than at night, and denser during the summer than in winter. Broadcasters use different shortwave frequencies depending on the time and the target area to take account of these effects, as well as interference from other stations, sunspot activity and so on.

The stations will be happy to provide you with frequency guides which set out which wavelengths to try, when and where. BBC World Service is unusual in offering a magazine, *BBC Worldwide,* which is able to reflect frequency changes from month to month. It also tells you when you can expect to pick up transmissions wherever you are, and provides full programme details. Most major broadcasters offer a six–monthly or yearly outline schedules of programmes and frequencies.

For the traveller there are likely to be three main considerations in choosing a radio: budget, compactness and efficiency. Shortwave receivers can cost anywhere between £30 and £3,000, but if your priority is good quality contact with your home station rather than shortwave hobbyism, the practical price range for a portable is between £75 and £300.

The traditional analogue set has manual tuning and either a single tuning scale or a number of separated shortwave bands (as well as a combination of mediumwave, longwave and FM bands). Separating the huge spectrum of shortwave frequencies into bands makes tuning simpler as the stations are less crowded on the scale: the more bands the better.

Using the frequency guide you can navigate around the airwaves on an analogue set and pick out the desired station by turning the knob or adjusting the slider. This is not particularly easy or precise process and now that analogue sets offer little price advantage, they are increasingly being displaced by the type of receiver which has a memory and digital display.

If you do decide to go for a low-priced analogue model you might find that, lower battery consumption apart, it proves a false economy once on the road. A digital set allows greater precision in tuning. Using preset frequencies you can cover all the possibilities in the part of the world you are visiting at the touch of a keypad.

Nowadays leading shortwave radio manufacturers like Sony and Grundig often preselect the frequencies of major shortwave stations on their sets before they leave the factory. This gets you off to a good start and you can later customise the selection as required.

Good digital sets start at around £180 and for that price you can buy one of the ultra-mini receivers which are so useful when travelling light is a consideration. These sets are no bigger than audio cassettes, so they will fit comfortably in a pocket and won't even pull it out of shape with a weight of 220g. An average compact set might weigh 600g and measure 20cm, while bigger portables weigh 1.75kg and measure 30cm. You wouldn't want to take that on a trek.

You will want at least ten memory presets; many sets carry 40-plus. Shortwave transmission can be susceptible to interference from other stations as well as an assortment of fades and spacey noises. Fortunately modern technology comes to the rescue in the shape of features like microprocessor-locked synthesised tuning, to ensure that the best possible signal is heard at all times, and automatic scanning of a selected waveband for the best signal.

Ideally the set you choose will allow close control of bandwidth (a narrow band cuts out interference, a wider one improves the audio quality and, like heads, two band-width are better than one) and sensitivity, which enables you to maximize the signal from a weak station without increasing any surrounding noise. International broadcasters usually schedule their programmes in Greenwich Mean Time and to help you follow the guides many sets have built in dual-time clocks which can be set to both GMT and local time.

It isn't always easy to try out shortwave radio in a shop, especially if it is part of a metal-framed building. If you can, take the set outside. Listen to find out whether it is 'lively' —that is, it picks up plenty of stations with a minimum of interference.

Once on the move you will probably not be listening in for more than an hour or two each day but bear in mind that batteries run down fast with heavy use. In some parts of the world batteries are hard to come by, so unless you want to carry a lot of spares or a charger, a worldwide mains adaptor might be a good investment.

Also worth the outlay is a portable booster aerial, because while built-in telescopic antennae are often adequate there are times when a booster can make an enormous difference to reception quality. For most purposes £220-£250 will cover the cost of a good quality compact set with adaptor and booster aerial.

A rough guide to tuning

The Hertz is the standard unit of frequency (the number of waves that pass a fixed point each second), the metre is the unit of wavelength (the distance between each wave). The tuning scales of modern sets are most often marked in kiloHertz (1 kHz = 1000Hz) or megaHertz (1 MHz = 1,000,000Hz).

Shortwave stations are generally spaced out at 5kHz intervals within each waveband. Your receiver should cover at least 6 to 17MHz (49 to 16 metres) shortwave. During the day, long-range reception is better on high frequencies (15 to 21MHz) while at night lower frequencies (6 to 7MHz) are recommended.

There is a transition period at dawn and dusk when 9 and 11MHz is probably best. During periods of sunspot activity higher frequencies are generally advisable.

Remember to keep any aerial, whether telescopic, booster or simply a length of insulated wire, clear of metallic obstructions and be prepared to experiment with its length and position within a room. Reception can often be improved by standing the set itself on a large metal object such as a radiator, kitchen appliance, water pipes or filing cabinet, or putting it near a window, particularly if you are in a steel–framed building.

The strongest shortwave signals arrive at a steep angle, so if the ground in front of the receiver slopes down in the direction of the transmitter the signal will be better than if the ground slopes upwards. This is worth bearing in mind if you are in a hilly area and find you are having any difficulties.

Shortwave listening does involve a certain level of commitment on the part of the listener but hundreds of millions of people around the world are clearly prepared to make that commitment. Don't be put off —when it comes down to it all you need is a shortwave radio, a frequency guide and some ideas about how to improve the weaker signals.

And remember that you will often find yourself in an area in which your preferred station is 'rebroadcast'. This means that a local station, perhaps broadcasting on FM, will arrange to pick up shortwave programmes from an international broadcaster and relay them on its own wavelength, in some cases 24 hours a day. By this means you can pick up BBC World Service as clearly in, say, New Zealand as you can in Belgium.

TELECOMMUNICATIONS AND THE TRAVELLER

by Stephen McClelland

Modern telecommunications empowers the traveller to go almost anywhere and still be in touch. However, telecommunications is a complex and confusing field, with an enormous range of products and services available both for voice and data applications. Making a decision about the best option is therefore very difficult. Moreover, these products and services are not necessarily identical in every country and getting international mixes to work together may prove impossible in spite of widespread international standardization. This article will attempt to simplify the range of international voice and data offerings now available for travellers.

Voice telephony

Telecommunications activities around the world are dominated by a group of (usually) government–owned organizations, the PTTs. The PTTs are responsible for the national and international provision of postal services. Whilst the PTTs are national organizations, a huge range of international agreements covering procedural and technical standardization has made it possible to make international communications possible.

In international telephone communication, for example, international direct dial (IDD) enabling effectively person to person calling, is available to almost all countries, except those which have little developed infrastructure in any terms. For these countries, there is little recourse to other than making an operator–connected call.

For most users, access and payment are the most important considerations. These vary very greatly from country to country. Access is a problem in many developing countries simply because of the sheer inadequacy of the public network (more accurately described as the Public Switched Telephone Network — PSTN) and the massive demand for telephone installations from domestic and business subscribers alike. It is not uncommon to wait many years for telephone connections to be made in Asia, Africa, Latin America and many parts of Mediterranean and Eastern Europe, even with sympathetic PTTs. This in turn has stimulated a massive interest in mobile communications. Where facilities are limited, the options for making a call —especially an international call— may be restricted to either using a hotel facility (for good quality facilities this usually means an internationally–recognized hotel) or calling personally at the PTT bureaus which maintain telephony and telegraphic facilities for members of the public.

Of the many enhancements and innovations in telephony, two are worth particular note for the traveller: collect calling and voice messaging. Collect calling or reverse charge calling is a well–established facility whereby the called party pays for the call. It is generally an operator–assisted call. Recently, however, this service is increasingly available for international use.

Among major PTTs, several services are being marketed under various names such as 'Home Direct' or similar schemes. Particular 'phone boxes are equipped with facilities so at the push of a single button you can be connected with an operator speaking your language in your home country. The call proceeds as a conventional collect call.

Another variant uses the charge card principle using a designated individual card acquired before departure. In making the call the card details are communicated to the operator who is able to validate the call, and arrange for billing. Pre–paid, card–based 'phones are another option now appearing which represent cheaper (or more controlled) billing —particularly in countries like Japan where it has traditionally been both difficult and expensive for the independent traveller to make international calls.

Voice messaging is the voice equivalent of electronic mail (see below). If the called party is unavailable, the operator system responds with a suitable message and invites the caller to leave the message in a voice mailbox; it is recorded by the network operator (usually the PTT). To listen to the message the called party can call up the messaging system —theoretically from anywhere in the world— and listen to it. Alternatively, an answering machine may be used, although the cost effectiveness may be different. Most advanced PSTNs have call redirection facilities too enable automatic transfer from one number to another; conference calling for multiple users sharing the same conversation simultaneously is yet another option.

Mobile telephony

The massive change in voice telephony from the user's point of view has undoubtedly been stimulated by the upsurge in the use of mobile telephones in the 1980s. Usually this has been due to so–called 'cellular' technology. This splits countries or areas up into 'cells' a few miles wide, and in doing so vastly increases the network radio capacity. The intelligence of the system is mainly due to the fact that it can detect when callers and those called are moving around from one cell to another and re–route the call approximately.

The cellular phone, unlike other radio systems, acts exactly the same as a conventional fixed phone and invariably links into the PSTN at some point; consequently anyone who could be called with a conventional phone can be called with a cellular one. 'Cordless' radio technology, fundamentally different to cellular technology, permits a very short range (up to 100 or 200 metres) of wireless extensions to conventional phones.

The international traveller, however, will probably be faced with a disfunctional phone if he or she decides to take it overseas. Currently, with very few exceptions, conventional (or analogue) cellular phones may only be used in the country of purchase because of major or, in some cases, minor technological differences. For example, a US cellphone cannot be used in Europe (not the converse), and most European cellphones will not function in other European countries. The only exception to this is the Nordic Mobile Telephone (NMT) system which can be used anywhere in the Scandinavian (and a few other) countries. In some countries (and some airport bureaux) it is possible to rent a cellular phone on a short term basis, although this is likely to prove expensive.

GSM

Help is hopefully at hand. During 1992, most developed European countries will begin to commercially offer a digital cellular phone service, called 'Groupe Special Mobile' (GSM). Not only should call quality and reliability be superior with the new technology to conventional analogue technology now being used, but pan–European operation using identical handsets should be possible in many Western European countries. This should greatly ease life for the international traveller —at a price.

Although details of international billing and subscriptions have yet to be fully worked out, it seems likely that these phones will usher in a new generation of smart cards which can be plugged in and which can store details of the subscriber and charges and country etc.

Paging

Paging is a well–established technique growing in popularity, and worth thinking about for the traveller. Wide–area paging systems have regional or national coverage (for larger countries this is usually broken down into regions), and local–area systems cover particular sites (like hospitals). Two kinds of pagers are basically available: tone, and alphanumeric which 'beep', and display short messages, respectively.

Paging systems provide extremely portable and lightweight facilities but suffer from two disadvantages: they are invariably one–way; and again few systems work internationally. The latter problem is likely to be solved by ERMES, a pan–European facility which promises pan–European paging operational in the same way that GSM promises for voice transmission.

Electronic mail

All developed countries have public data communications services and most have a publicly–accessible service which enables one computer (such as a personal computer or lap top) to communicate with another computer elsewhere in the country via a special messaging service known as electronic mail ('e–mail').

There are many e–mail systems now in use in the world. Amongst the best known are *Telecom Gold* and *Link 7500* in the UK, *MCI Mail*, *AT&T Mail* and the *Western Union Easylink* in the US. Each system differs in fine detail but all e–mail systems perform the same basic functions, allowing computer to computer communications.

Every registered e–mail possesses an 'electronic mailbox' in which messages may be stored or received or from which messages may be sent. The mailbox does not have a physical reality as such but is a unique numbered location on a large computer (called a 'host') usually owned by the PTT or network computer). The personal computer's communications software and a modem together convert the message into a form suitable for transmission down an ordinary phone line to the host, instructing it to transfer the message into the mailbox of the desired addressee. There the message will wait for retrieval at some time by the addressee. The addressee will be able to read his or her message by using his or her computer to contact the host in a similar way by 'reading' the mailbox contents.

The advantages of e–mail are that it is nearly instantaneous and probably cheaper on a per message basis than ordinary post, at least for inland use. Messages may also be sent to overseas subscribers to the system or to systems which connect with it (most of the major e–mail systems have a transfer arrangement between their networks). E–mail is suitable for messages of almost any length although cost varies with message size. In many cases different types of data can be transferred over the network including both text files produced by word processing and spreadsheet information.

The principal disadvantages that you need a computer system to both send and receive it, and also that the recipient is not automatically aware that he or she has a message waiting in the mailbox; regular ad hoc box interrogation is therefore necessary. In urgent cases, it may also be necessary to phone or fax or page the recipient.

Additional services

To encourage greater use of e–mail to generate more profitable traffic, the network operators in various countries have added other features to their basic e–mail systems. For example, the British Telecom (BT) *Telecom Gold* e–mail system offers the facility to deliver fax, telex and page BT pager users. Whilst telex messages can be two–way (that is, you may send and receive telex messages from your computer with the Telecom Gold system making the conversion to enable telex machines at the recipient end to understand them) fax messages can only be transmitted. Some systems also offer a telegram conversion and delivery facility. MCI Mail offers a variety of mixed e–mail, fax and telegram delivery and courier services tailored to various applications depending on cost and urgency.

Bulletin boards and on–line databases

Two data services which are closely related to e–mail should be noted. Bulletin boards are publicly and communally accessible stores of information in electronic format which may be supplied ('up–loaded') or extracted ('down–loaded') by callers. Frequently callers will want to add their own information and opinions, so the system contents are fluid and change over time, as a physical bulletin board would. They have proved very popular in the US where they now number many hundred but are relatively less widespread in Europe. They usually cater to special interest groups (hobbyist, environmental, educational, religious) and are generally free of charge.

On–line databases also provide for publicly accessible stores of data but it is usually of a specific, structured type; for example, national newspapers and magazines or specialist journals extending over many years. With simple procedures, such information can be 'searched' by means of key words for particular facts and details.

In these contexts, *CompuServe* should be mentioned. *CompuServe* is a US–based system (although also accessible in Europe) claiming the largest network of personal computers in the world with over 700,000 members. Users can access some 1400 files of database information, send and receive e–mail, access many bulletin boards, play games and even make their own airline and hotel reservations.

Accessing e–mail and other on–line systems

As a basic kit, you will need:

1. A data terminal device (the desktop, laptop or even notebook–sized computer)

2. Suitable word processing and communications software with which the message may be written and formatted in a form suitable for sending, respectively

3. A modem, which converts the streams of computer data into a form suitable for transmission through the national PSTN

4. E–mail registration for the country/service you are using

5. Access to a public telephone connection eg by socket or phone

6. Cables to connect the above (and power supplies)

Typically for systems like BT's *Telecom Gold* current charges include registration, with a monthly rental for the mailbox. For message creation and storage there are transmission and box storage charges; the mail charge is calculated on the number of characters and destination of message sent. For example, a 1000–character message to the US from the UK would cost less than 30p depending on the time of day it was transmitted in addition to the fixed costs above. The call to the host computer is charged as a standard telephone call; a good hint is to use any facilities the e–mail system has for local access (incurring local call charge only); these invariably use the national packet switching facility.

International access

E–mail provides a convenient and relatively low cost (for the occasional, low volume user) service for inland travellers in a particular country. It is also increasingly possible to send e–mail from one national system to another because of agreements between the various PTTs and system operators. However, the international traveller, who requires the ability to roam and still communicate, will find life rather more difficult.

In theory it should be possible to take a computer and modem overseas and use it on any developed telephone network in the world. Due to differences in technical characteristics it remains generally difficult (and in most cases illegal) to connect a device, specified for one country, to the PSTN of another. The differences can be quite minor but infuriating: 'phone jack sockets differ from one country to another, and even where physically similar, may be wired differently. The dialling system of the modem may not work or may connect incorrectly because of national technical and numbering differences.

Some computer–literate travellers determined to use the facilities abroad have been known to carry sets of clips and tools in luggage to temporarily wire up connections (particularly in hotel rooms) to get around this problem —with varying degrees of success. Clearly this becomes highly dubious in legal terms, and although prosecutions are reportedly extremely rare, both imprisonment and heavy fines are possible for offenders.

If connection is absolutely necessary, it is advisable either to fully register with the e–mail operator in the particular country and buy an approved modem (increasingly lap top computer makers are selling modems compatible for each country), or use an acoustic coupler (which fits into the telephone handset without any jack connection being needed). This replaces a conventional modem unit and should be used on a low data speed (ideally 300 bits per second or 1200 bits per second).

Where there is no e–mail registration in a particular country (this can take some time), it is possible to use this arrangement to contact a home e–mail box and send and receive messages from here. It will probably be necessary to dial the e–mail service manually using a separate phone keypad. The access call to the mailbox will be treated as a conventional (voice) international call at the appropriate charges, although if you are happy to work with the PTT, by application and arrangement it is possible to use cheaper packet switching facilities (similar to national access as outlined above).

By disk

If you have very large amounts of text or data to send or receive, this could well prove the simplest and cheapest method. You simply make a copy of the disk and send it through the post to the recipient and computer. This is very effective where the data is not required speedily (use express post or courier service requiring special customs documentation and labelling for magnetic —disk— media where you do) and very large amounts of data can be shipped in this way. Using a 1.2 M'byte disk for example you will be able to store some 50,000 words, equivalent to a good–sized novel. Floppy discs generally weigh under 20g so more than 20 could be packed into a half–kilo package, the first charge band for many international courier services. No e–mail registration or communications facility is required. Compared with more or less any other form of data transfer this shipment (equivalent to a capacity of 10 million individual bits) would represent very good value indeed, being some 10–100 times cheaper than the same volume of traffic sent on e–mail or even typed out sheets sent by fax.

Fax facilities

The explosion of fax machine sales over the past 10 years testifies to their popularity and ease of use. Unlike most other forms of data communication, fax machines use the voice network (PSTN) exclusively. International fax format standardization has progressed to the point where any so–called Group II/III machine in the world should be able to communicate with any other, and this alone probably makes fax an easier proposition to use internationally than for example e–mail. The principal drawback is that it is by definition a paper–based service; further manipulation of fax information means that it generally has to be re–keyed. Unlike telex messages, fax messages are not usually regarded as legally binding documents.

Whilst e–mail facilities usually incorporate a fax capability (see above), most fax transmission is by means of a dedicated machine, not a computer. Portable fax machines (battery driven) are now available. These can be set up and used almost anywhere where there is access to a telephone point. This may require you to have access to a variety of plugs and sockets (see e–mail). It is also possible to connect portable fax machines to cellular phone systems in some countries via an interface unit enabling a truly mobile office to be built around the phone, fax and even portable computer and e–mail facility.

Another option is the facility to turn personal computers into fax machines directly by the addition of a "fax–card" into the machine. Fax cards are basically high speed modems which enable the computer to look like a fax machine to the telephone network. This sort of facility saves carrying bulky fax machines around; unfortunately whilst fax messages can be sent from the computer directly, fax messages can only be printed out on receipt by the addition of a computer printer.

A potentially costly item will be the number of PSTN connections needed overall for equipment like faxes, computers, telephone/answering machines. Ideally, it should be one per item but since lines may take a long time to install and accrue both an installation charge and a rental charge in most countries, it may be necessary to economize. A particularly useful device now widely available is the 'fax–splitter' which is directly connected to the phone socket, and determines whether incoming calls are for the fax machine or the telephone, routing them appropriately. Outgoing calls are not affected. ∎

WHEN THINGS GO WRONG
Chapter 14

AVOIDABLE HASSLES

by Tony Bush and Richard Harrington

A traveller's best friend is experience and it can take dozens of trips to build this —and the hard way. Fortunately, there are some tips that can be passed on to help the unwary before they even step on a plane.

Most people have the good sense to work out their journey time to the airport and then add a 'little extra' for unforeseen delays. But is that little extra enough should something major go wrong —if the car breaks down, for instance, or there are traffic tailbacks due to roadworks or an accident.

Remember, too, to try and avoid travelling at peak periods such as Christmas, Easter and July and August when families are taking their holidays. This applies particularly to weekends, especially Saturdays.

Taxis and taxes

Most travellers would agree that the task of dealing with taxi drivers could just about be elevated to a science. In some parts of the world overcharging alone would be a blessing. What is really disconcerting is the driver who cannons through red lights or uses part of the pavement to overtake on the inside.

And what about the fare? Without a meter, the obvious foreigner will almost certainly be overcharged. But even the sight of a rank full of taxis with meters should not raise too much hope. Meters often 'break' just as you are getting in.

Two good tips for dealing with the drivers of unmetered taxis are:

1. Know a little of the local language —at least enough to be able so say "hello" "please take me to…" and "how much ?" and "thank you." This throws the driver a little. After all, the driver's aim is only to try and make an extra pound or two. He doesn't want to get involved in a major row at the risk of being reported to the authorities.
2. Try and have the correct amount ready to hand over. It prevents the driver pleading that he has not got sufficient change —a ruse that often succeeds, particularly when the fare is in a hurry. It also avoids 'misunderstandings.'

A typical misunderstanding might go like this: the traveller hands over a note worth, say, 100 blanks for a tip that he believed was going to cost him 20 blanks. However, the driver, with the note safely tucked into his pocket, tells him he was wrong, he misheard or was misinformed. In fact, the journey cost 30 blanks and 70 blanks is handed over. This leaves the passenger in an invidious position.

He cannot snatch his note back and is faced instead with the indignity of having to argue about a relatively small amount (very rarely would a driver attempt to cheat on too large scale).

In most cases, the traveller will shrug his shoulders, walk away and put his loss down to experience. And this is what the driver is relying on. That is the reason he is not greedy. He knows that even the most prosperous–looking passenger would baulk at too big a reduction in his change.

The traveller should find out before or during his trip whether he will be required to pay an airport tax on departure and, if so, how much. This is normally only a token sum, but it would be frustrating to have to change a £50 traveller's cheque in order to pay it. Departure taxes are almost always payable in local currency. Occasionally an equivalent sum in US dollars will be accepted. The ideal arrangement is to work out roughly how much transport to the airport will cost, add on the airport tax, if any, and then throw in a little extra for incidentals.

Tea oils the wheels

If you must spread around a little 'dash' to oil the palms that facilitate your progress, do so carefully after checking how to do it properly with someone who knows the ropes. You may be able, for instance, to avoid a few days in a Mexican jail for a mythical driving offence. On the other hand, you could end up in jail for trying to bribe an officer of the law —and then you might have to hand out a great deal more to get out rather than rot for a few months while waiting for a trial.

The $1 or $5 bill tucked in the passport is the safest approach if you do decide on bribery, as you can always claim that you keep your money there for safety. But it may only be an invitation to officials to search you more thoroughly — and since all officials ask for identity papers, you could go through a lot of dollars in this way. When you think a bribe is called for, there's no need for excessive discretion. Ask how much the 'fine' is or whether there is any way of obtaining faster service...

Bribes, by the way, go under an entertaining assortment of different names. 'Dash' is the term in West Africa, except in Liberia, where the euphemistic expression is 'cool water.' *Mattabiche*, which means 'tip', 'corruption' or 'graft', oils the wheels in Zaire. In East Africa, the Swahili word for tea, *chai*, serves the same function. *Baksheesh* is probably the best known name for the phenomenon and is widely used in the Middle East. It is a Persian word, found also in Turkish and Arabic, that originally meant a tip or gratuity, but took on the connotation of bribe when it was used of money paid by a new Sultan to his troops. *El soborno* is 'payoff' in Spanish–speaking countries, except Mexico, where the word for 'bite', *la mordida*, is used. In India you have the 'backhander'; in Japan *wairo* or, when referring more generally to corruption *kuori kiri*, which translates lyrically as 'black mist.' The French refer to the 'jug of wine' or *pot de vin*; the Italians use the term 'little envelope', a *bustarella*, and Germans have an honestly distasteful term for a distasteful thing: *Schmiergeld* which means 'lubricating money.' Even here, however, exporters gloss over the matter by simply using the abbreviation 'N.A.', *Nuzlich Abgabe*, which means 'useful contribution.'

Smiling strangers

Beware of the 'Smiling Strangers' when abroad. It is here that experience really counts as it is often extremely difficult to separate the con man from a genuinely friendly person. A favourite ploy is for him to offer his services as a guide. If he asks for cash, don't say "I would like to help, but all my money is tied up in traveller's cheques." The Smiling Stranger has heard that one before and will offer to accompany you to your hotel and wait while a cheque is cashed.

The warning about confidence tricksters also applies to some extent to street traders. Not the man who operates from a well set–up stand, but the fellow who wanders about with his arms full of bracelets or wooden carvings. He may give the souvenir hunter a good deal, but prices on the stands or in the shops should be checked first. Sometimes they will be cheaper in the latter, when, frankly, they should not even compare. After all, the wanderer does not have any overheads.

Local courtesies

One of the biggest minefields for the unsuspecting traveller is local courtesies and customs, and most of us have our pet stories about how we have unwittingly infringed them.

It is worth knowing that you should not insult a Brazilian by talking to him in Spanish. The Brazilians are proud of the fact that they are the only nation in South America to speak Portuguese.

It's also important to understand that the Chinese, Japanese and Koreans believe in formalities before friendship and that they all gobble up business cards. Everyone should certainly realise that they must not ask a Muslim for his Christian name. And it is of passing interest that Hungarians like to do a lot of handshaking.

It is easy to become neurotic about the importance of local customs, but many Third World people today, at least in the major towns, have some understanding of Western ways and, although they do not want to see their own traditions trampled on or insulted, they don't expect all travellers to look like Lawrence of Arabia or behave like a character from The Mikado! Civility, politeness, warmth and straight dealing transcend any language and cultural barriers.

The model visitor

Men should wear a dark suit, white shirt, and a dark tie. Women should make sure their skirts are well below the knees, their necklines demure and their arms, if not always their heads, covered. Sometimes dark glasses are not a good idea—take them off, so your eyes can be seen. In practice, this is not much fun when the temperature is 45°C in the shade, the humidity is 100 per cent and your luggage weighs 35kg. Nevertheless, try to keep your clothes clean. If not backpacking, use a suitcase instead of a rucksack and (if male) shave and get your hair cut as close to a crew–cut as possible without looking like an astronaut. A moustache is better than a beard, but avoid both if possible. Long hair, as long as it is suitably neat, is usually more acceptable for women, who thereby look suitably feminine.

Do not try smuggling anything through customs, especially drugs. Hash and grass may be common in the countries you visit, but be careful if you buy any. A local dealer may be a police informer. Prosecutions are becoming more common and penalties increasingly severe —from 10 years' hard labour to mandatory death for trafficking in 'hard' drugs —and in some countries, sentences are hardly more lenient for mere possession. There's no excuse for failing to research the countries you intend to visit. Talk to people who have lived in or visited them and find out what problems you are likely to encounter. If you go prepared and adopt a sympathetic, understanding frame of mind you should be able to manage without trouble.

THEFT

by Christopher Portway and Melissa Shales

Obviously one of the most important things to keep in mind while travelling is the safety of your possessions. Do your best to minimize the chances of theft and you will run far less of a risk of being left destitute in a foreign country. Try and separate your funds, both in your luggage and on your person, so as to frustrate thieves and reduce losses. And before you leave home, make arrangements with a reliable person whom you can contact for help in an emergency.

American Express probably issue the most reliable and easily negotiable traveller's cheques, have the most refund points in the world and possibly hold the record for the speediest reimbursements. If you don't have plenty of plastic to keep you going for the two to three weeks it can take to get replacement cheques or new funds via the bank, take these.

Play for sympathy

If you come face to face with your robbers then use all the skills in communication you have picked up on your travels. Try humour. At least try and get their sympathy, and always ask them to leave items which will be of no immediate value to them but are inconvenient for you to replace. They are usually after cash, and valuables which are easily converted into cash. Try to get the rest back and risk asking for enough money for a taxi fare if you feel the situation is not too tense. Acting mad can help, as can asking for help or advice. One man, when approached in Kenya, claimed to be a priest and put on such a convincing act that the robbers ended by giving him a donation!

Many thefts will be carried out (without your noticing) from your hotel room —or by pick–pockets in a crowded street. Never use a handbag that isn't zipped, and keep your hand covering the fastener at all times. They can still slit the fabric or leather, but the odds are lengthened as to their success. Never carry anything valuable in the back pocket of your trousers of the outside pocket of a jacket. Even the top inner pocket can be picked easily in a crowd. A money–belt is the most secure method of carrying valuables although even this isn't foolproof.

Never leave valuables in a hotel room, even out of sight. A good thief will know far more tricks than you and is probably likely to check under the mattress, or behind the drawers of the dressing table before searching more obvious places. As long as the hotel is fairly respectable and isn't likely to be in cahoots with local criminals, put valuables in the hotel safe, and make sure you get a proper receipt.

While on the move, never let your luggage out of your sight. Wrap the straps round your leg while sitting down (a good reason for a longer shoulder strap) so you can feel it if not see it. Lock or padlock everything. This will not deter the most hardened types, but should lessen the chance of casual pilfering. A slightly tatty case is far less inviting than brand new matching leather Gucci.

Violence

The crime of violence is usually committed with the aim of robbery. My advice in this unhappy eventuality is to offer no resistance. It is virtually certain that those who inflict their hostile attentions upon you know what they are doing and have taken into account any possible acts of self–defence on the part of their intended victim. It may hurt your pride but this way you live to tell the tale, and after all, if you're insured, the material losses will be made good by your insurance company following the submission of a police report of the incident.

In many poorer countries, it is advisable not to wear or hold anything that is too obviously expensive, especially at night. You should be particularly wary in Africa and South America. The most robbery–with–violence prone city I know is Bogota, Colombia, where in certain streets you can be 99 per cent certain of being attacked. Having had most of my worldly goods lifted off me —but not violently— in neighbouring Ecuador, I made sure I lost nothing else by walking Bogota's treacherous streets with a naked machete in my hand. This, however, is probably a little drastic and not generally advised. You could become a target for the macho element —and you could get arrested for carrying an offensive weapon.

The British exporter robbed three times —once at gunpoint— in as many days in Rio, spent his remaining week there avoiding *favelas* (shanty towns on the outskirts of the city where many thieves live) and making sure that he was in a taxi after nightfall (when local drivers start to shoot the lights for fear of being mugged if they stop). Sometimes rolled–up newspapers are thrust through quarter–lights and drivers find themselves looking at the end of a revolver or the tip of a sheath–knife.

One of the worst cities in Africa for theft is Dar Es Salaam where locals tell of Harlem–style stripping —a practice that is spreading across the continent anywhere cars or parts are in short supply. Drivers return to where they are parked to find that their wheels, and often anything else that can be removed down to the windscreen and doors, have been removed. An expert gang can pick a vehicle clean in under 10 minutes.

In 1977 I walked right through Peru not knowing that the region was infested with cattle rustlers reputed to kill without mercy if they thought they'd been seen. Occasionally, ignorance can be bliss. Since then, of course, the situation in Peru has worsened, the bandits being joined by guerrillas to make the mountains decidedly unsafe.

Within urban areas, the best advice is to stay in the city centre at night. If it is imperative to move away from the lights, go by taxi and try not to go alone. And don't forget to press down the door locks when you get in. There are some countries —Egypt is a prime example— where other people just jump in if the car has to stop for any reason. Naturally, they're normally just an extra fare, but you can never be certain.

If, by mischance, you do find yourself walking along a remote, unlit road at night, at least walk in the middle of it. This will lessen the chances of being surprised by someone concealed in the shadows. And when you have to move over for a passing car, use its headlights as your 'searchlight' over the next 10 or 20 metres.

Protecting yourself from attack by carrying a firearm is *not* recommended. Even in those countries that do permit it, the necessary papers are difficult to come by and in countries where the law is ticklish over the subject of mercenaries, a gun of any sort could brand you as one. One traveller was arrested in Zambia just for having a bullet on him! But that is not the point. The idea that a pistol under the car seat or one's belt is protection is usually nonsense. In many countries a gun is a prize itself to a violent thief who will make every effort to procure one.

What to do next

Consider what action you can take if you find yourself penniless in a foreign land. Report thefts to the police and obtain the necessary form for insurance purposes. You may have to insist on this and even sit down and write it out for them to sign. Whatever it takes, you musn't leave without it. It may be essential to you for onward travel.

Local custom may play a part in your success. In Lima, for instance, the police would only accept statements on paper with a special mark sold by one lady on the steps of an obscure church found with the help of a guide. They have a way of sharing in your misfortune —or sharing it out!

If there is an embassy or consulate, report to them for help. In a remote spot, you are more likely to get help from the latter. You may have to interrupt a few bridge parties, but insist it is your right to be helped. In cases of proven hardship, they will pay your fare home by (in their opinion) the most expedient route in exchange for your passport and the issue of travel papers. If your appearance suits they may also let you phone your family or bank for funds.

Have the money sent either to the embassy via the Foreign Office or to the bank's local representative with a covering letter or cable sent to you under separate cover. This will give you proof that the money has been sent when you turn up at the bank. I have met many starving people on the shiny steps of banks being denied money which is sitting there in the care of a lazy or corrupt clerk —or in the wrong file. Other countries do not always use our order of filing and letters could be filed under 'M' or 'J' for Mr John Smith. Have your communications addressed to your family name followed by initials (and titles if you feel the need).

Quite an effective, proven way of moving on to a more sophisticated place or getting home, is to 'phone your contact at home and ask him to telex or fax air tickets for a flight out. They pay at home and the airline is much more efficient than the bank. This has the additional advantage of circumventing the Mickey

Mouse currency regulations which various countries impose. Algeria is a perfect example. The country insists that airfares are paid in 'hard' currency, but the money transferred into the country is automatically changed into the Algerian currency as it arrives. One then has to apply to the central bank for permission to change it back (at a loss) in order to buy your air ticket. A telexed ticket can have you airborne in a couple of hours (I've done it).

Local generosity

In desperate situations, help can be obtained from people locally. These fall into two main groups. Expatriates, who live unusually well, are often not too keen on the image that young travellers seriously trying to meet the local scene create, but once you have pierced the inevitable armour they have put up from experience, they are able to help.

They often have fax facilities at their disposal, business connections within or out of the country and friends amongst the local officialdom. Their help and experience is usually well worth having.

Next, the missionaries. From experience I would suggest you try the Roman Catholics first as the priests often come from fairly poor backgrounds themselves and have a certain empathy with empty pockets. Other denominations tend to live better but put up more resistance to helping. (I came across an American/Norwegian group in the Cameroons suffering from a crisis because the last plane had left no maple syrup). Swallow your principles or keep quiet and repay the hospitality when you can. They often need their faith in human nature boosted from time to time.

You will receive kindness from other temples, mosques and chapels and can go there if you are starving. Again, do not abuse assistance and repay it when you can.

Real desperation may bring you to selling blood and branded clothes in which you have thoughtfully chosen to travel, in exchange for cheap local goods. But local religious communities are the best bet and usually turn up an intelligent person who can give advice.

In Third World countries, being poor and going without is no big deal —you may be in the same boat as some 90 per cent of the population. A camaraderie will exist, so you will probably be able to share what little is available. It would be wrong to abuse the customs of hospitality, but on the other hand, be very careful of your hygiene, so as not to give yourself even more problems through illness.

IN TROUBLE WITH THE LAW

by Bryan Hanson

Ignorance of the law is no more of an excuse abroad than it is at home. Consideration is usually given to the traveller but this is often in direct proportion to the funds available.

Always keep calm: to show anger is often regarded as a loss of face. Be humble and do not rant and rave unless it is the last resort and you are amongst your own kind who understand. Try to insist on seeing the highest official possible. Take the names of all others you come across on the way up —this tends to lead you to someone who is senior or intelligent enough to make a decision away from the book of rules. Also, in totalitarian regimes, having your name taken is positively threatening.

Pay the fine

If you are guilty and the offence is trivial, admit it. Do not get involved with lawyers unless you really have to. The fine will most probably be less painful on your funds than legal fees.

On the other hand, do not misinterpret the subtleties of the local system. In Nigeria, I pleaded guilty to a trivial offence without a lawyer and found myself facing the maximum sentence. If I had used one, an 'agreement' fee would have been shared with the magistrate and the case dismissed on a technicality. In other words, if we had paid the small bribe initially demanded by the police, we would not have gone to court!

More serious situations bring more difficulties and you should make every effort to contact your local national representative. The cover is thinning out — 'our man in Dakar', for instance, has to cover most of West Africa. A lawyer is next on the list to contact, probably followed by a priest.

It is a good idea to carry lists of government representatives in all the countries through which you intend to travel —especially if you are leaving the beaten track. Remember they work short office hours (I once had a long and very fruitless conversation with a Serbo–Croat cleaner because I expected someone to be there before 10 and after noon!). There should be a duty officer available at weekends.

Keep in contact

Regular messages home are a good practice. Even if they are only postcards saying 'Clapham Common was never like this,' they narrow down the area of search should one go missing. If doubtful of the area you are travelling in, also keep in regular contact with the embassy, and give them your proposed itinerary so that if you don't show up by a certain time, they know to start looking.

The tradition of bribery is a fact of life in many countries and often reaches much further down the ladder than it does in the Western world. I find the practice distasteful and have avoided it on many occasions, only to find myself paying eventually in other ways. In retrospect, I am not sure if 'interfering with these local customs' is wise. But how to go about it when all else has failed?

In detention

Once you've been locked up and all attempts to contact officials have been denied, a more subtle approach is needed. One can only depend on locals delivering messages to the outside world or, probably more reliable, a religious representative prepared to take the risk. Sometimes it is possible to use a local lad and send him cash on delivery to the nearest embassy or consulate (even if it's over the border) with a suitably written plea.

Third World detention premises are usually primitive and provide the minimum of filthy food. You may even have to pay to feed yourself. Time has little significance, so make your means spin out. Even though money talks the world over, try not to declare your resources or you may not get any satisfaction until the last penny has been shared out among the locals. If you get stuck Prisoners Abroad is a helpful organisation: Prisoners Abroad, 78-82 Rosebery Avenue, London EC1R 4RR, tel: 071-833 3467.

Humour and a willingness on your part to lose face can often defuse a tense and potentially awkward moment. Travelling gives you life skills in judging people and an instinctive knowledge of how to act. Use your experience to your advantage and don't let daunting lists of advice keep you quivering at home.

If you have the gall, it is often a good idea to learn the names of a few high–ranking officials and name drop blatantly. How far you carry this is up to you, but when I married off my cousin to the Minister of Justice in Turkey, he didn't mind a bit.

Additional Information

by Christopher Portway

Being something of an inquisitive journalist with a penchant for visiting those countries normal people don't, I have, over the years, developed a new hobby. Some of us collect stamps, cigarette cards, matchboxes. I collect interrogations. And the preliminary to interrogation is, of course, arrest and detention, which makes me, perhaps, a suitable person to dwell for a few moments on some of the activities that can land the innocent traveller in prison as well as the best way of handling matters arising thereof.

In some countries, there are no set rules governing what is and is not a crime. Different regimes have different ways of playing the game and it's not just cut–and–dried crimes like robbing a bank or even dealing on the black market that can put you behind bars. Perhaps a brief resumé of some of my own experiences will give you the idea and suggest means of extracting yourself from the clutches of a warped authority.

Espionage: a multitude of sins

It is that nasty word 'espionage' that becomes a stock accusation beloved by perverted authority. Spying covers a multitude of sins and is a most conveniently vague charge for laying against anyone who sees more than is good for him (or her). It is often in Communist countries where you have to be most careful, but some states in black Africa, Central America and the Middle East are picking up the idea fast. Spying, of a sort, can be directed against you too. In my time I have been followed by minions of the secret police in Prague and Vladivostok for hours on end. Personally, I quite enjoyed the experience and led a merry dance through a series of department stores in a vain effort to shake them off. If nothing else, I gave them blisters.

In World War II, to go back a bit, I escaped from my POW camp in Poland through the unwitting courtesy of the German State Railway. The journey came to an abrupt end at Gestapo HQ in Cracow. In post–war years, the then Orient Express carried me visa-less, into Stalin–controlled Communist

Czechoslovakia. That journey put me inside as a compulsory guest of the STB, the former Czech secret police. I have met minor inconveniences of a similar nature in countries like Russia, Albania, Yugoslavia and several in the Middle East but it was only in the '70s that I bumped into real trouble again —in Idi Amin's Uganda.

Interrogations à la James Bond

The venues of all my interrogations have been depressingly similar. That in Kampala, for instance, consisted of a bare, concrete–walled office containing a cheap desk, a hard–backed chair of two, a filing cabinet, a telephone and an askew photograph of Idi Amin. This consistency fitted Cracow, Prague and Kishinev, except that in Nazi days nobody would dream of an askew Fuhrer. Prague boasted an anglepoise lamp, but then Communist methods of extracting information always did border on the James Bond.

Methods of arrest or apprehension obviously vary with the circumstances. For the record, in World War II, I was handed over to the Gestapo in Cracow by a bunch of Bavarian squaddies who could find no excuse for my lobbing a brick through the window of a bakery after curfew. In Czechoslovakia I was caught crossing a railway bridge in a frontier zone and, with five burp–guns aligned to one's navel, heroics are hard to come by. In the Soviet Union it was simply a case of my being caught with my trousers down in a 'soft–class' toilet and with an out–of–date visa valid only for a place where I was not. And in Uganda there was no reason at all beyond an edict from Idi that stipulated a policy of 'let's–be–beastly–to–the–British!'

Keep your answers simple

But the latter's line of questioning was different. It wasn't so much why had I come, but why had I come for so brief a period? That and the young Ugandan law student arrested with me. Being in close confinement in a railway carriage for 24 hours, we had become travelling companions which, coupled with my suspiciously brief stay, spelt 'dirty work at the cross–roads' to the Ugandan authorities. And rummaging about in our wallets and pockets, they found bits of paper on which we had scribbled our exchanged addresses. It had been the student's idea and a pretty harmless one but, abruptly, I was made aware how small inconsistencies can be blown up into a balloon of deepest suspicion. All along I maintained I hardly knew the guy. Which reminds me that the Gestapo too had an irksome habit of looking for a scapegoat amongst the local populace.

Then we came to the next hurdle. "How is it your passport indicates you are a company director and this card shows you are a journalist?" To explain that I was once a company director and had retained the title in my passport in preference to the sometimes provocative 'journalist' would have only complicated matters. So I offered the white lie that I was still a company director and only a journalist in my spare time. It didn't help much.

And, you know, there comes a moment when you actually begin to believe that you are a spy or whatever it is they are trying to suggest you might be. It creeps up on some harmless answer to a question. In Kampala I felt the symptoms and resolved to keep my answers simple and remember them the second time round.

For instance: "What school did you attend?" I gave the one I was at the longest. There was no need to mention the other two.

My regimental association membership card came up for scrutiny. "What rank were you?" I was asked. "Corporal," I replied, giving the lowest rank I had held. Pride alone prevented me from saying "Private." "Which army?" came the further enquiry. I had to admit that it was British.

Every now and again I would get in a bleat about having a train to catch — more as a cornerstone of normality than a hope of catching it. And there comes a point in most interrogations when there is a lull in proceedings during which one can mount a counter–attack. The "Why–the–hell–am–I–here? What–crime–am–I–supposed–to–have–committed?" sort of thing which at least raises the morale if not the roof.

Of course, in Nazi Germany such outbursts helped little, for, in declared wartime, one's rights are minimal and the Gestapo had such disgusting methods of upholding theirs. But in the grey world of a cold war the borderline of bloody mindedness was ill–defined. At Kishinev the KGB had the impertinence to charge me a fiver a day for my incarceration in a filthy room in a frontier unit's barracks. I voiced my indignation loud and clear and eventually won a refund. In Czechoslovakia my outburst had a different effect. The interrogator was so bewildered that he raised his eyes to the ceiling long enough for me to pinch one of his pencils. And in the cell that became my home for months, a pencil was a real treasure. Now let it be said, in general, that the one demand you have the right to make is that you be put in touch with your own embassy or consulate. I once wasn't and it caused an international incident.

In another of Kampala's Police HQ interrogation rooms, all my proffered answers had to be repeated at dictation speed. It was partly a ruse, of course, to see if the second set matched the first and I was going to be damn sure it did.

I suppose one lesson I ought to have learnt from all this is to take no incriminating evidence like press cards, association membership cards, other travellers' addresses and the like. But a few red herrings do so add to the entertainment.

SURVIVING A HIJACK

by Mike Thexton

Hijacking comes and goes as a fashion among terrorists. It is probably something that most travellers will think about at some time —to some it may be a vague anxiety; to others, part of a Rambo–style daydream. Anyone who worries about it a great deal is likely to be too nervous to be a regular traveller.

The most important thing is *not* to worry about it. The whole point of terrorism is to create a fear completely out of proportion to the risk —to get the maximum effect for the minimum effort. Don't give them that victory. Think about the huge number of trouble–free flights every day. It's very unlikely to happen to you.

However, it sometimes does. It happened to me on 5th September 1986, when four Palestinian terrorists stormed a Pan Am 747 on the ground at Karachi airport, Pakistan. Any hijacking is likely to be different (the security forces try to bolt all the stable doors, so the successful terrorist will have to do something original) but there are some points which could be useful in any such situation. Armed men ran up the steps and took over the cabins as the last passengers were boarding. Accept it that you will not react very fast in this situation, nor should you. Civilians are usually stunned by violence, or the threat of it, because it is so shocking. If you do have an opportunity to escape at this time, make sure that it is a clear and safe one —the terrorists are also most hyped–up, and are most likely to shoot you. It may be better to wait a while.

You will need to get control of yourself. If fear takes over, you will not be able to do anything useful if an opportunity presents itself. Everyone will have to fight their own battle in their own head. I started by thinking that some people usually escape hijacks, and I saw no reason why I would not be included. I admit that I took comfort from the fact that there were Americans aboard. Since Ronald Reagan had ordered the bombing of Libya, they had to be more unpopular than the British —not much, but a bit more unpopular.

Make yourself inconspicuous. It is generally fatal to be memorable: if the terrorists single someone out, it is usually to shoot them. Don't volunteer for anything, even if you think you might ingratiate yourself with them. Keep your head down. Don't catch their eyes. I was wearing a red duvet jacket, which was a bad start, but I knocked my Panama hat off my head with my raised hands, and sank into the seat as far as possible.

Do what they say, within reason. I would not co–operate to the extent of joining them (as happened in a famous Stockholm siege), but if they say, "Hands up, no moving," do it. We all sat in silence with our hands above our heads, looking into our laps. There is a problem here. Two terrorists kept about 350 passengers completely quiet for the whole day. No one dared to look round. They could have gone away for a cup of tea and come back in half an hour, and we would still have been in our seats —no one would have looked round, for fear that a terrorist was standing right behind them. If you can, you want to get as much information as possible about the number of terrorists, weapons and position, but you are safer taking no risks.

The pilots escaped right at the beginning, so we were stuck on the ground – a great relief. We sat with our hands in the air for the first three hours of the siege. I was beginning to think it would really be all right when one of the flight attendants came around collecting passports. If you can avoid giving your papers in, do —they become a means of singling you out. Take any opportunity to dispose of anything which might be 'incriminating' in the mind of the terrorist. Of course, if you have a wholly 'terrorist–credible' nationality, it matters less, but I heard one of them venting his hatred for "all Westerners." He listed practically every nation, including the *Spanish*. I didn't think the Spanish had ever done anything to offend anyone. These people are indoctrinated.

The flight attendant knew that American passports were what the terrorists were after, so she dropped them all under the seats as she went. This was very brave and quite proper, but it promoted the British as second most unpopular nation. My passport was picked out, and I was summoned to the front of the plane. I didn't think that it would be possible to play hide–and–seek, so I went.

Controlling fear at this point is an entirely different exercise. I went from thinking, "Some people always get off," to "Someone always gets shot." Dealing with the expectation of imminent death must be very personal. I started with blind panic; I moved on to prayer, but felt very hypocritical ("Er, God, remember me? I haven't been good at keeping in touch, but could you..."); I made some promises to God in case he was listening, but only ones which I felt I could keep (and I did). What seemed to work best was to think of all my family and friends in turn, and to say goodbye to them. I thought about the mountaineering expedition I had just completed, and what a good time it had been. I settled in my mind any arguments I had with my friends so that the sun would not go down on my anger. I also determined that I was not going to die frightened —if they wanted to shoot me, I would stiffen my upper lip, shake them by the hand, and tell them to make a decent job of it. I doubt if I could have done it, but I felt better for the intention.

They kept me at the front of the plane for 12 hours or so, thinking about shooting me to emphasise some particular demand. I think it is important to retain your dignity —begging would not help, nor would offering bribes or assistance. You don't have anything they need. To them, you are simply a piece of breathing merchandise, to be traded or cashed in. If you can obtain their sympathy, or in some way turn yourself into a human being, try it —but don't speak unless spoken to, and don't irritate them. They may be trigger happy. I think that the sight of me praying, and my calm acceptance (after a while!) of my situation may have impressed them. As the day went on, it became harder for them to shoot me.

I thought about telling them that I was Irish, and a fervent supporter of the IRA, but I doubt if it would have helped. If they know enough for it to benefit you, they will also probably know enough to see through it. They asked me if I was a soldier, and I guessed that it was important to say 'No.' I gave 'teacher' as a neutral occupation —after all, no one *admits* to being a chartered accountant. When asked later if I liked 'Mogret Thotcher', I was able to give the required answer with conviction. It would be more difficult if they had asked me to say something I really disagreed with (perhaps in a statement to those outside) — it may seem safest to go along with them, and it may be extremely dangerous to do anything else. However, you may need to keep your self–respect to avoid mental collapse, and you may need to keep their respect as well. I am glad I did not have this test.

You must not raise your expectations of release. Set long horizons. Disappointment could be crushing. This was easy for me, as I was convinced I was not getting out anyway. You should ignore any information given to you by the terrorists. Remember that the authorities are the 'good guys', and they will be trying hard to get you out, but they *cannot* give in —if they do, there will be another plane–load of passengers in your situation the next week, and the week after. Hostages are sometimes convinced by their captors that the authorities are being uncooperative, that it is all the authorities' fault: hold on to reality. It isn't.

Make yourself as comfortable as possible. It might be a long stay. Massage your joints, if you are allowed to. Stretch whatever you can. Clench your fingers and toes to keep the blood moving. Any movement will stop you seizing up, and will give you something to do. It can be very boring! Any exercise for the mind is also useful —you do not want to dwell on the nastier possibilities of the position. Remembering favourite pieces of writing, picturing peaceful scenes, daydreaming— all help.

Back in economy, the passengers enjoyed a slightly more relaxed atmosphere for a while. Afterwards I met two who spent the afternoon playing cards. Anything which passes the time is useful. It also helps to exchange names, addresses and messages for next–of–kin.

Take advantage of any opportunity you get to do anything which may make yourself more comfortable or safe —get a more inconspicuous seat, go to the toilet, eat or drink. You don't know whether you will get another chance for days. However, you should probably *not* take advantage of an opportunity to make yourself a hero. You will probably get killed, and will also cause the deaths of a number of others.

Movies are unrealistic. A large man with a Kalashnikov is very hard to take on with your bare hands; a man holding a grenade in his hand with the pin between his teeth *cannot* be over-powered, unless you want a posthumous medal for bravery. In case you are unsure, you can't put the pin back in once he's dropped the grenade. It *will* explode.

The most important piece of advice is to be ready to get out, if the opportunity comes. Some experienced travellers think it's 'cool' to sleep through the safety announcements. It's more cool to know where the doors are, and to be sure how to open them. Think through the quickest way out, and have alternatives ready in case your exit is blocked. Think about how far down it is, and know about pulling the red handle if the chute does not come down. Remember that all this takes time, and that it will not be possible to get out of a door in the time that one of your captors has turned his back!

After 12 hours, they put me back with the rest of the passengers. The lights went out, because the generator had broken down. I could feel the tension increasing, and crouched as low as possible in my seat. For a reason which has never been established, they started shooting at random in the darkness, and throwing hand–grenades about. Some of the passengers decided that they had had enough, and opened the emergency doors. The man in the next seat told me to keep down, but I was not staying —the plane had been refuelled for an eight–hour flight. I pushed him in front of me towards one of the doors… I was out on the wing, looking for a way down… the chute had not come out automatically… I'm afraid of heights, but I jumped off the back of the wing without much hesitation (about two storeys up but still the lowest point) and ran away. Many people were hurt jumping off the wings because they had taken their shoes off to make themselves comfortable. Be ready, and move quickly.

It was a bloody event, with more than 20 dead and more than a hundred injured. I was very lucky to escape with a scratched elbow. But I was very unlucky to be hijacked in the first place —it *won't* happen to you!

THE EXECUTIVE TARGET

by Roy Carter

All over the world, in such diverse areas as Central America, or the Middle East, the level of politically–motivated violence increases almost daily. The victim's nationality —or supposed nationality— is often the sole reason for him or her being attacked. Gone forever are the days when kidnap and murder threatened only the wealthy and influential. Instead, political and religious fanatics often regard ordinary citizens as legitimate targets, and this view will become more prevalent as prominent people take ever more effective steps to protect themselves. The average traveller is much more vulnerable, but still worthy of publicity —which is generally the motive behind all terrorist action.

Measuring the threat

Measuring the threat is difficult, if only because of conflicting definitions of what constitutes terrorist activity. Incidents involving civil aviation, however, afford a generally uncontentious barometer. In the decade to mid–1983, a fearsome total of 748 people were murdered worldwide in terrorist attacks against aircraft or airports. A similar number suffered serious injury, and the problem is by no means confined to the traditionally volatile areas of the world. Of 144 significant terrorist acts recorded against civil aviation in 1983, no less than 55 took place in Europe. Almost all the victims were innocent travellers. And it is self–evident that this single aspect of the problem represents only the tip of a much larger iceberg.

No one travelling to certain parts of the world can sensibly afford to ignore the danger. If the risk exists everywhere it naturally increases dramatically in known trouble spots. Nor is it wise to rely on the law of averages for protection. Terrorism and crime thrive on complacency and a fatalistic attitude can actually create danger. Awareness is vital, and it is surprisingly easy for any intelligent person to do the sort of homework that can pay life–saving dividends.

The first step is to understand something of the anatomy of political crime. Terrorist violence is rarely, if ever, carried out quite as randomly as it sometimes appears. Particularly in the case of kidnapping, the victim will first be observed —often for a period of days— for evidence of vulnerability.

Simple precautions

Translating an awareness of the threat into a few simple precautions means offering a difficult target to people who want an easy one. Invariably they will look elsewhere. It is impossible to say how many lives have been saved in this way, because the threat, by its very nature, is covert, but the number is undoubtedly high. The huge majority of terrorist abductions are facilitated by the victim developing a regular pattern of behaviour, or by being ignorant of the dangers in a strange country. No experienced traveller would forego vital inoculations or fail to enquire about the drinking water. Testing the political climate should be regarded as a natural extension of the same safeguards. After all, the object is the same, and the price of failure at least as high.

Of course, the most straightforward response to ominous events is simply to cancel or postpone the visit. In extremes this option should not be disregarded, but there will be occasions, especially for the business traveller, when such a drastic answer is difficult or impossible. An intelligent interest in the press and television news is a fundamental requirement in making the final decision. And sensible analysis of media reports will answer many questions about known trouble spots and help predict others. If nothing else, it will highlight areas for further study. Equally important, but easily overlooked, sound research can help put less serious situations into perspective. Unnecessary worry based on sensationalism or rumour can be a problem in itself.

Official attitude

It is crucial to get a balanced idea of the official attitude in the country to be visited. The host government's status and its relationship with the visitor's country are always critical factors. A basically hostile or unstable government will always increase the danger to individual travellers, either directly, or by such indirect means as ineffective policing. A recent example of the former risk was seen very clearly in the imprisonment of British businessmen in both Libya and Nigeria, following diplomatic rows. The latter risk is exemplified on a regular basis in the Lebanon, Mozambique and Angola.

Finding the truth will usually involve delving below the headlines. In Britain, an approach to the Foreign Office can produce surprisingly frank answers. Next, and more obviously, an analysis of recent terrorist activity should aim to answer three essential questions: when and where it happens, what form it takes and most important, whom is it directed against? The first two answers will help establish precautionary measures. The third may indicate the degree of risk by revealing common factors. A series of identical abductions from motor vehicles in a particular part of the city, involving the same nationalities or professions for example, should be augury enough for even the most sceptical observer.

Local feeling

It is also as well to know as much as possible about feelings among the local populace, which are by no means guaranteed to be the same as those of the government. National identity, and even religion, are often viewed quite differently 'on the streets', although the bias is just as likely to be favourable as not. One need not even step outside the UK to demonstrate the validity of this advice, as an Englishman on the streets of West Belfast could quickly discover. And in a country with a large Western expatriate community, for instance, any Caucasian will generally be regarded as belonging to the predominant race. Depending on the local situation, this type of mistaken identity can be dangerous or advantageous. At least one case, the March 1985 abduction of three British visitors to Beirut by anti–American Muslim extremists, resulted from a mistake in the victims' nationality.

These attacks, and others involving French and US citizens, took place outside the victims' homes, highlighting perfectly standard terrorist methods. Known reference points such as home or places of work, are always by far the most dangerous. The much–publicized kidnap and subsequent murder of former Italian premier, Aldo Moro, by the so–called Red Brigade was a notable example of this fact.

Soft targets

Importantly, but often forgotten, this demonstrates more than a need for extra care at home and in the office. It shows equally the terrorist's need for soft targets and their reluctance to proceed beyond basic research to find them. Terrorist resources and abilities are limited and to regard them as omnipotent is both mistaken and dangerous. Sensible precautions, like varying times of arrival and departure, parking in different places —facing in different directions, watching for and reporting suspicious activity before leaving home, and entering and leaving by different doors, sound almost too simple, but they really do work. Only the most specific kind of motivation would justify continued surveillance of a clearly unpredictable and cautious target.

Company image

In addition to this kind of general precaution, the business traveller will usually need to examine more particular issues. He will need to know how his company is perceived by various local factions. Previous threats or attacks on company employees should be studied with great care, as should incidents involving similar organizations. Where applicable, the local knowledge of expatriate colleagues will be useful, but watch for bias or over–familiarity. In the absence of any actual events, examine the company's standing in the community, especially where a conflict of interest exists between government and opposition groups. Never forget that a company will often be judged solely on the basis of its clients and associates. Always consider the status of the people you intend to visit. In these days of trade sanctions and mutually antagonistic markets, the chances are high that any association will offend someone.

Practical action

But analysis is only a partial answer. The results must be translated into coherent action. In extreme cases, the business traveller might need special training in such areas as defensive driving, emergency communication and surveillance recognition. Many of the larger companies will provide special briefings but their failure to do so should never be taken as a sign that no danger exists. It could equally indicate a lack of awareness of a misguided decision not to cause alarm. There is nothing at all wrong with alarm if it is justified. It may even be a necessity.

Regardless of whether special training is given or not, all travellers to high–risk areas should follow certain basic rules as a matter of course. Keep friends and colleagues informed of your whereabouts and stay in company as much as possible. Use inconspicuous transport but avoid public transport in favour of taxis. If in doubt, wait for the second cab in the rank. Never take a taxi if the driver is not alone. Dress down and leave expensive accessories at home. Don't book hotels in the company's name. In all, practise being nondescript in public.

Try not to think of these rules as an inconvenience, but as a natural consequence of your stay in a strange country, like remembering to use a foreign language. Relaxing one rule might be tempting but it could be the mistake that negates all the rest. Better to extend precautions than limit them. For example, travelling regularly by the same route can undo all the good work on the home front. The kidnap and murder of German industrialist Hans–Martin Schleyer was carried out because his attackers were able to predict confidently both his route and timing. The murder in India of British diplomat Percy Norris by Middle Eastern terrorists likewise occurred along his regular route to work. Mr Norris was shot to death in the back seat of his chauffeur–driven car when it halted at traffic lights.

On the move

Make a habit of changing places in the car if you have a driver or use a taxi now and then instead. The chances of being attacked on the move are extremely remote. It follows that road junctions, traffic signals etc are always more dangerous than, say, stretches of dual carriageway. A prospective attacker will study his victim's route carefully and identify vulnerable spots. If he can do so, so can you. Be aware of these danger areas and stay on the alert when negotiating them. If driving yourself, keep the car in gear and ready for a quick getaway at temporary halts. Keep sufficient space between yourself and any leading vehicles to avoid being boxed in. Routinely lock all doors and keep the windows wound up.

Last of all, remember that you stand more chance of being an accident casualty than a terrorist victim. Far from being dangerous, a little knowledge can stack the odds even higher in your favour. You'll probably never know if it passes the acid test —but you'll be in no doubt at all if it doesn't.

SAFETY AND SURVIVAL AT SEA

by Robin Knox–Johnston

A very sensible list of safety equipment to be carried on board a boat is published by the Offshore Racing Council (ORC) in their 1994/5 Special Regulations Governing Offshore Racing. The list is extensive, but because it is comprehensive, it is given below:

2 Fire extinguishers; accessible and in different places
2 Manually operated bilge pumps
2 Buckets; strong construction, fitted with lanyards
2 Anchors and cables (chain for cruising is sensible)
2 Flashlights; water resistant and capable of being used for signalling, with spare bulbs and batteries
1 Foghorn
1 Radar reflector
1 Set of International Code Flags and a code book
1 Set of emergency navigation lights
1 Storm trysail
1 Storm jib
1 Emergency tiller
1 Tool kit

1 Marine radio transmitter and receiver
1 Radio, capable of receiving weather forecasts
Life–jackets: sufficient for the whole crew
1 Buoyant heaving line at least 50 feet (16m) long
2 Life buoys or rings
1 Set of distress signals
12 Red parachute flares
4 Red hand flares
4 White hand flares
2 Orange smoke day signals
1 Life–raft of a capacity to take the whole crew, which has: a valid annual test
certificate; two separate buoyancy compartments; a canopy to cover the occupants; a sea anchor and drogue; bellows or pump to maintain pressure; a signalling light; 3 hand flares; a baler repair kit; 2 paddles; a knife; emergency
water and rations; a first–aid kit and manual.
In addition, it is worth carrying a portable, waterproof VHF radio and an emergency distress transmitter (E.P.I.R.B.)

Medical

The health of the crew is the Skipper's responsibility and he or she should see
that the food is nourishing and sufficient, that the boat is kept clean and that the
crew practise basic hygiene. A good medical kit must be carried.

There is an excellent book (published by HMSO for the British Merchant
Navy) called *The Ship Captain's Medical Guide*. It is written for a ship that does
not carry a doctor and includes a recommended list of medical supplies. Most
doctors will supply prescriptions for antibiotics when the purpose has been
explained. Two other books to recommend are *The International Medical for
Ships*, published by the World Health Organization and *First Aid at Sea*, by
Douglas Justins and Colin Berry (Adlard Coles Nautical, London)

Safety on deck

Prevention is always better than the cure. Everyone on board should know their
way about the deck, and know what everything is for. A good way of training is
to take the boat out night sailing so that the crew get to know instinctively where
everything is and what to avoid. Train the crew to squat whenever the boat
lurches —it lowers the centre of gravity and makes toppling overside less likely.

In rough weather, make sure that all the crew wear their life–jackets and safety harnesses when on deck, and that they clip their harness to a strong point. If
the crew have to go out from the cockpit, they should clip the harness to a wire
which runs down the middle (the length of the boat) for this purpose.

Man overboard

If someone falls overside, immediately summon the whole crew on deck and
throw a lifebuoy to the person in the water. The problem is to get back and pick
them up as quickly as possible, so post a look–out to keep an eye on the casualty,
and the rest of the crew should assist with turning the boat around. It is worthwhile putting the boat straight in the wind, as this stops you close to the casualty,

then start the engine and motor back. On one occasion in the Southern Ocean, we lost a man overside, and we ran on more than half a mile before we could get the spinnaker down. The only way we could see him when we turned round was by the sea–birds that were circling him. We got him back, after about 20 minutes, by which time he was unable to assist himself because of the cold.

In the upper latitudes, there is a real danger from hypothermia and it is vital to warm the person as quickly as possible. Strip off their wet clothing and towel them dry, then put them in a warm sleeping bag. The heat is retained better if the sleeping bag can be put into a plastic bag. If the person is very cold, it may be necessary for someone else to strip and climb into the bag with the casualty and warm them with their own body.

If the casualty is conscious, feed them hot soup or tea. Remember that it can be a nerve–shattering experience and that they may need time to get over the shock.

Abandoning the boat

When, as a last resort, it becomes necessary to leave the boat, inflate the life–raft and pull it alongside. Put one or two of the crew on board, and, if there is time, pass over as much food, water and clothing as possible, plus the Distress Beacon. If the boat's dinghy is available, tie it to the life–raft, as it will give extra space and also help create a larger target. Only leave the boat if there is absolutely no alternative. Life–rafts are small and not particularly robust, and it is always preferable to keep the boat afloat if humanly possible.

The usual reason for abandoning a boat is that it has been holed. One method of improving its survivability is to fit it with watertight bulkheads so that its volume is roughly divided into three. This is now a rule for the BOC Challenge Around Alone Race, and means that if the boat is holed, the chances are that it will lose only one third of its buoyancy and there will still be dry, safe shelter for the crew. From the comparative safety of one of the 'safe' parts of the boat, a plan can probably be made to fix the leak.

When it is necessary to abandon the boat, having got as much food and useful equipment aboard as possible, cut the painter and get clear. Then take stock of what you have, and post a look–out. Activate the Distress Beacon to alert aircraft and ships to the fact that someone is in distress.

Ration supplies from the start. The best way to do this is to avoid food for the first day, as the stomach shrinks and the body's demand for food falls. Ration water to about half a pint (quarter of a litre) a day and issue it in sips. On no account should sea water be drunk, but it can be used for washing and cooling in hot weather. Humans can last for amazingly long times without food, but they do need water. Any rain should be trapped and saved. The canopy of the life–raft can be used for this purpose, as could the dinghy if it has been taken along. Unless there is a plentiful water supply, do not eat raw fish as they are very rich in protein and ruin the liver unless the surplus can be washed out of the system. As a general rule, one volume of protein will require two volumes of water. Where water is plentiful, fish should be hunted. Most pelagic fish are edible, and quite often they will swim around a boat or dinghy out of curiosity. Inedible fish are found close to land or on reefs.

Keep movement to a minimum to conserve energy, and in cold weather, hold onto urine as long as possible to retain its heat. In hot, sunny weather, try to keep everyone in the shade. Find some mental stimulus in order to maintain morale, and remember that the crew will be looking to the skipper to set an example, so remain positive. Humans have survived for well over three months on a life–raft, but only because they had a strong will to live and were able to improvise. My book *Seamanship* (Hodder and Stoughton) may prove useful further reading.

SURVIVAL IN THE DESERT

by Jack Jackson

The most important thing about desert survival is to avoid the need for it in the first place! Know your vehicle's capabilities and do not overload it. Know how to maintain and repair it. Carry adequate spares and tools. Be fit yourselves and get sufficient sleep. Start your journey with 25 per cent more fuel and water than was calculated as necessary to cover extra problems such as bad terrain, leaking containers and extra time spent over repairs or sitting out a bad sandstorm.

Know accurately where your next supplies of fuel and water are. Carry plastic sheet to make desert stills; carry space blankets. Carry more than one compass and know how to navigate properly. Use magnetic compasses well away from vehicles and cameras. Do not rely exclusively on electronic Global Positioning Systems, or the batteries that power them and do not leave the piste unless you really do know what you are doing. Travel only in the local winter months. Know how correct your odometer is for the wheels and tyres fitted to the vehicle. Make notes of distances, compass bearings and obvious landmarks as you go along, so you can retrace your route easily if you have to.

Observe correct check–in and out procedures with local authorities. Preferably convoy with other vehicles. When lost, do not continue. Stop, think and, if necessary, retrace your route.

Back–up plans

If you are a large party, you should arrange a search and rescue plan before you start out. This would include the use and recognition of radio beacons or flares for aircraft search. Many countries do not allow you to use radio communication; but if you can use them, carry modern portable satellite communications.

For most people, an air search is highly unlikely and high–flying commercial passenger aircraft overhead are unlikely to notice you whatever you do. A search, if it does come, will be along the piste or markers. Most often this will just be other vehicles travelling through being asked by the local authorities to look out for you because you have failed to check in.

Local drivers will not understand or appreciate coloured flares, so your best signal for outside help is fire. If you hear a vehicle at night, cardboard boxes or wood are quickly and easily lit, but during the day you need lots of thick black smoke. The best fuel for this is a tyre. Bury most of a tyre in the sand to control the speed at which it burns (keep it well away from and down wind of the vehicles or fuel) and start the exposed part burning with a rag soaked in either petrol or diesel fuel. As the exposed part of the tyre burns away, you can uncover more from the sand to keep it going, or cover all of it with sand if you wish to put out the fire. Avoid inhaling the sulphurous fumes.

Headlights switched on and off at night can be used while the battery still has charge.

If you are found by aircraft, the International Ground/Air Code, for wanting to be picked up, is to stand up with your arms held aloft, in an obvious 'V' shape.

A need to survive

Once you are in a 'need to survive' situation, the important things are morale and water. Concentrate on getting your vehicles moving again. This will keep you occupied and help to keep up morale. To minimize water loss, do not do manual work during the day, work at night or in the early morning. Build shade and stay under it as much as possible, keeping well covered with loose cotton clothing. 'Space blankets,' with the reflective side facing out make the coolest shade. Keep warm and out of the wind at night. In really hot climates, replacing lost potassium with Slow K can make a big difference to your general alertness.

Unless you are well off the piste with no chance of a search, you should stay with your vehicle. If someone must walk out, pick one or two of the strongest and most determined persons to go. They must have a compass, torch, salt, anti–diarrhoea medicine, loose, all–enveloping clothes, good footwear, good sunglasses and as much water as they can sensibly carry. In soft sand, a jerry can of water can easily be hauled along on a rope from the waist. On mixed ground, tie the jerry can to a sand ladder, one end of which is padded and tied to the waist.

Those who walk out should follow the desert nomad pattern of walking in the evening till about 2300 hours, sleep until 0400 hours, walk again till 1000 hours, then dig a shallow hollow in the sand and lie in it under a space blanket, reflective side out, until the sun has lost its heat. If they have a full moon they can walk all night. In this way, fit men would make 60 to 70 kilometres on 10 litres of water — less in soft sand.

Water

In a 'sit it out and survive' situation, with all manual labour kept to a minimum, food is unimportant and dehydration staves off hunger, but water is *vital*. The average consumption of water in a hot, dry climate should be eight litres a day. This can be lowered to four litres a day in a real emergency. Diarrhoea increases dehydration, so should be controlled by medicine where necessary. Salt intake should be kept up. Licking your bare arms will replace some lost salt.

Water supply should be improved by making as many desert stills as possible. To make one, dig a hole about one third of a metre deep and one metre in circumference, place a clean saucepan or billy in the centre of the hole with a two metre square plastic sheet weighted down with stones, jerry cans or tools, at the edges. Put one stone or similar object in the centre to weigh it down directly over the billy. Overnight, water vapour from the sand will evaporate and then condense on the underside of the plastic sheet. In the morning, running a finger down from the edge to the centre of the sheet will cause the condensation to run down and drip into the pan. All urine should be conserved and put into shallow containers around the central billy can. The water so collected should be boiled or sterilized before drinking.

If you have anti–freeze in your radiator, *don't* try to drink it as it is *highly poisonous*. Even if you have not put anti–freeze in the radiator yourselves, there is still likely to be some left in it from previous use, or from the factory when the vehicle was first manufactured. Radiator water should be put into the desert still in the same way as the urine and the resulting condensate should be boiled or sterilized before drinking. Water from bad or brackish wells can be made drinkable in the same way. Note, however, that solar stills can take a lot of energy to create and will yield little water in return. Until the situation is really desperate, they are probably not worth considering as a viable means of collecting water.

The minimum daily water required to maintain the body's water balance at rest, in the shade, is as follows: If the mean daily temperature is 35°C, then you will need 5.3litres per 24 hours. If 30°C, then 2.4 litres, if 25°C then 1.2 litres, if 20°C and below then 1.0 litres. It must be stressed that this is for survival. There will be a gradual kidney malfunction and possibly urinary tract infection, with women more at risk than men.

The will to live is essential. Once you give up, you will be finished. If you find people in such a situation and do not have a doctor to handle them, feed them water (to which has been added one level teaspoon of salt and two tablespoons of sugar per litre of water), a teaspoonful at a time, every few minutes for a couple of hours. It is essential to try to stabilize them in this way before trying to take them on a long tough drive to hospital. Sachets of salts for rehydration are available for your medical kit.

SURVIVAL IN THE JUNGLE

by Robin Hanbury-Tenison

The key to survival in the tropics is comfort. If your boots fit, your clothes don't itch, your wounds don't fester, you have enough to eat and you have the comforting presence of a local who is at home in the environment, then you are not likely to go far wrong.

Of course, jungle warfare is something else. The British, Americans and, for all I know, several other armies, have produced detailed manuals on how to survive under the most arduous conditions imaginable and with the minimum of resources. But most of us are extremely unlikely ever to find ourselves in such a situation. Even if you are unlucky enough to be caught in a guerrilla war or survive an air crash in the jungle, I believe that the following advice will be as useful as trying to remember sophisticated techniques which probably require equipment you do not have to hand anyway.

A positive will to survive is essential. The knowledge that others have travelled long distances and lived for days and even months without help or special knowledge gives confidence, while a calm appraisal of the circumstances can make them seem far less intimidating. The jungle need not be an uncomfortable place, although unfamiliarity may make it seem so. Morale is as important as ever, and comfort, both physical and mental, a vital ingredient.

Clothing and footwear

To start with, it is usually warm, but when you are wet, especially at night, you can become very cold very quickly. It is therefore important to be prepared and always try to keep a sleeping bag and a change of clothes dry. Excellent strong, lightweight plastic bags are now available in which these items should always be packed with the top folded over and tied. These can then be placed inside your rucksack or bag so that if dropped in a river or soaked by a sudden tropical downpour —and the effect is much the same— they, at least, will be dry. I usually have three such bags, one with dry clothes, one with camera equipment, notebooks, etc., and one with food. Wet clothes should be worn. This is unpleasant for the first 10 minutes in the morning, but they will soon be soaking wet with sweat and dripping in any case, and wearing them means you need carry only one change for the evening and sleeping in. It is well worth taking the time to rinse them out whenever you are in sunshine by a river so that you can dry them on hot rocks in half an hour or so. They can also be hung over the fire at night which makes them more pleasant to put on in the morning, but also tends to make them stink of wood smoke.

Always wear loose clothes in the tropics. They may not be very becoming but constant wetting and drying will tend to shrink them and rubbing makes itches and scratches far worse. Cotton is excellent but should be of good quality so that the clothes do not rot and tear too easily.

For footwear, baseball boots or plimsolls are usually adequate but for long distances good leather boots will protect your feet much better from bruising and blisters. In leech country, a shapeless cotton stocking worn between sock and shoe tied with a drawstring below the knee, outside long trousers gives virtually complete protection. As far as I know, no one manufactures these yet, so they have to be made up specially, but they are well worth it.

Upsets and dangers

Hygiene is important in the tropics. Small cuts can turn nasty very quickly and sometimes will not heal for a long time. The best protection is to make an effort to wash all over at least once a day if possible, at the same time looking out for any sore places, cleaning and treating them at once. On the other hand, where food and drink are concerned, it is usually not practical or polite to attempt to maintain perfectionist standards. Almost no traveller in the tropics can avoid receiving hospitality and few would wish to do so. It is often best therefore to accept that a mild stomach upset is likely —and be prepared

In real life and death conditions, there are only two essentials for survival, a knife or machete and a compass (provided you are not injured, when if possible the best thing to do is to crawl to water and wait for help). Other important items I would put in order of priority as follows:

1. A map
2. A waterproof cover, cape or large bag
3. Means of making fire, lifeboat matches or a lighter with spare flints, gas or petrol
4. A billy can
5. Tea or coffee, sugar and dried milk.

There are few tropical terrains which cannot be crossed with these, given time and determination. Man can survive a long time without food, so try to keep your food supplies simple, basic and light. Water is less of a problem in the jungle, except in limestone mountains, but a metal water container should be carried and filled whenever possible. Rivers, streams and even puddles are unlikely to be dangerously contaminated, while *rattans* and *lianas* often contain water as do some other plants whose leaves may form catchments, such as pitcher plants. It is easy to drink from these, though best to filter the liquid through cloth and avoid the 'gunge' at the bottom.

Hunting and trapping are unlikely to be worth the effort to the inexperienced, although it is surprising how much can be found in streams and caught with hands. Prawns, turtles, frogs and even fish can be captured with patience and almost all are edible —and even tasty if you're hungry enough. Fruits, even ripe and being eaten by other animals are less safe while some edible–looking plants and fungi can be very poisonous and should be avoided. Don't try for the honey of wild bees unless you know what you are doing as stings can be dangerous and those of hornets even fatal.

As regards shelter, there is a clear distinction between South America and the rest of the tropical world. In the South American interior, almost everyone uses a hammock. Excellent waterproof hammocks are supplied to the Brazilian and US armies and may be obtainable commercially. Otherwise, a waterproof sheet may be stretched across a line tied between the same two trees from which the hammock is slung. Elsewhere, however, hammocks are rarely used and will tend to be a nuisance under normal conditions. Lightweight canvas stretchers through which poles may be inserted before being tied apart on a raised platform make excellent beds and once again a waterproof sheet provides shelter. Plenty of nylon cord is always useful.

Fight it or like it

The jungle can be a frightening place at first. Loud noises, quantities of unfamiliar creepy crawlies, flying biting things and the sometimes oppressive heat can all conspire to get you down. But it can also be a very pleasant place if you decide to like it rather than fight it —and it is very seldom dangerous. Snakebite, for example is extremely rare. During the 15 months of the Royal Geographical Society's Mulu Expedition, in Borneo, no one was bitten, although we saw and avoided or caught and photographed many snakes and even ate some! Most things, such as thorns, ants and sandflies are more irritating than painful (taking care to treat rather than scratch usually prevents trouble).

Above all, the jungle is a fascinating place —the richest environment on earth. The best help for morale is to be interested in what is going on around you and the best guide is usually a local resident who is as at home there as most of us are in cities. Fortunately, in most parts of the world where jungles survive, there are still such people. By accepting their advice, recognizing their expertise and asking them to travel with you, you may help to reinforce their self–respect in the face of often overwhelming forces which try to make them adopt a so–called 'modern' way of life. At the same time, you will appreciate the jungle far more yourself —and have a far better chance of surviving in it.

SURVIVAL IN THE COLD

by Dr Mike Stroud

"The wind was blowing briskly as I stepped out of the tent, but the sun was shining and it didn't feel too bad. When I had been out earlier, briefly, answering nature's call, the air had been still, and despite it being minus 40°C it had seemed quite warm in the sunshine. I had decided to wear only a cotton windproof over underwear and fleece salopettes. It was amazing how little one needed to keep warm as long as you kept on working hard.

Ran and I took down the tent and packed up our sledges. The South Pole was only 30 kms away and with luck we would reach it within two days. It helped to have it so close. We had been going twelve hours a day for more than two months, and the effort has taken a terrible toll. It had been both mental and physical hell. It was not long after we set off that I realised my mistake. As well as only putting on a single jacket, I was wearing only thin contact gloves inside outer mitts and after an hour with the wind rising even more my hands were suffering badly and not warming up despite moving. They became so bad that Ran had to help me put on the extra mittens from my sledge, my fingers were too useless to get them on. When we set off again, I was getting generally chilled. After the long stop fighting with the gloves, I found that I could barely pull the sledge with my cold muscles. I was in trouble, and I realised I would have to stop and put my fleece jacket on as well, but to do this meant removing my outer jacket completely and once again my fingers were useless and I was unable to do up the zips. Ran was there to help again, but I had entered a vicious circle. My thinking was beginning to fade, and although I kept walking for another half-hour or so, I was never with it. It was only through Ran's description, that I know what happened next.

I had apparently begun to move very slowly and to wander from side to side. When Ran asked if I was okay, I had been unintelligible, and he had realised immediately that I must be hypothermic. He then tried to get me to help with the ten, but I just stood around doing nothing. So he put it up alone and pushed me inside. Eventually he got me in my sleeping bag and forced me to take some hot drinks. After an hour or so I recovered, but it had been another close call. Obviously we were getting vulnerable and we discussed pulling out at the Pole ...."

The above is an exert from my book '*Shadows on the Wasteland*' about my crossing of Antarctica with Sir Ranulph Fiennes. Under the circumstances, it was perhaps not surprising that I became hypothermic, for cold easily creates casualties and can even kill. Yet, with the correct preparation, man can operate successfully even in the harshest of climates. The secret is to match the body's heat production —chiefly dictated by activity —with its heat losses —chiefly governed by clothing and shelter. You should aim to neither overheat nor cool down. Both can have unwelcome consequences.

An inactive adult produces about a light bulb's worth of heat (100 Watts), which is not really much to keep the whole body warm in the face of the cold, wind and rain. It is therefore generally wise to keep moving for the most of the time in cold conditions until you have either reached or created proper shelter. However, many reasons, such as getting lost or injured, may force you to halt or lie up under adverse circumstances and you are then going to need to reduce your heat losses to less than the 100 watts that you will be producing. This may be an impossibility if ill-equipped or conditions are really harsh. If you can't reduce heat losses enough, your body will cool and you will start to shiver. This can increase your resting heat production to as much as 500 watts, but even this may be inadequate and the shivering itself is uncomfortable and tiring for the muscles. If cooling still continues, you will become hypothermic and can be in great danger. It is definitely best to carry enough protection to deal with getting stuck out in the worst possible conditions you may meet.

When you are active, things are quite different. Working hard leads the body to produce as much as a good room heater —2000 watts or even more. It is therefore more common to get too hot rather than too cold, even in the worst conditions. Initially, getting too hot may not be important, but it does lead to sweating which can ruin the insulation of your clothing by wetting it from the inside and later, when you have decreased your activity or the conditions have worsened, this wet clothing will have lost its ability to protect you properly. Sweating may also lead to dehydration which in turn will make you vulnerable to fatigue, and it is with the onset of tiredness and then slowing up, that heat production will start to fall and you will cool rapidly to become at risk from the 'exhaustion/hypothermia' syndrome. Even the most experienced of people have become victims under such circumstances.

In order to match heat losses to heat production, clothing must have the flexibility to be both cool and warm. It must also be able to provide windproofing and waterproofing. Such flexibility can only be achieved by the use of layers which must be easy to put on and take off and comfortable to wear together. In all but the very coldest regions —where rain or melting snow won't occur —I would favour the use of modern synthetics in the insulation layers which tend not to degrade very much when wetted by sweat or the environment, and which also dry spectacularly quickly. If affordable, waterproofs/windproofs should be moisture vapour permeable (MVP) since these will limit the accumulation of sweat and condensation in inner garments and will allow the evaporation of some sweat which will help to keep you cool if overheating. However, it needs to be remembered that even MVP garments are only partially vapour permeable (especially in the cold when water vapour will condense or even freeze on the inner surface of the garment and will then be trapped by its waterproof qualities) and so it is always better to remove the waterproof if it is not actually raining and activity is making you too hot.

Additional flexibility when trying to maintain a comfortable body temperature can be granted by changing your head covering. In the cold, when wearing good clothing, as much as ninety percent of your heat losses can come from your head, so by putting on or taking off a warm hat or balaclava and by adjusting a windproof hood, you can make enormous changes to your heat losses much more easily than by adjusting other garments. It is often said that if you get cold hands you should put on a hat.

Eating is also an important factor in keeping warm. Even at rest a meal will rev up your metabolism and make that 100 watt bulb glow brighter, while during exercise it will considerably increase your heat output for any given level of activity. More importantly, food also helps to sustain the supply of fuels to the muscles and this will allow you to continue working, or for that matter shivering, for longer. In addition, it will make it much less likely that you will develop a low blood sugar —a factor now thought to be important in the onset of some cases of exposure/exhaustion. Almost any food will help, but it is probably best for it to contain a fair amount of carbohydrate. Grain-based snack bars are as good as anything, but snacks based on chocolate are also excellent, even if there is a greater fat content.

When hypothermia does begin to occur in an individual, a number of changes are seen which make the diagnosis pretty easy as long as the possibility is carefully considered. Unfortunately, the person suffering from the cold is often unable to consider things properly, since he or she may not realise what is happening and often, after feeling cold, shivery and miserable initially, they may feel quite happy and even warm. It therefore goes without saying that a problem may only become evident when things have already become quite bad, and that if a victim is alone or everybody in a party becomes hypothermic simultaneously, things are very serious. The signs to watch out for are quite similar to those seen with becoming increasingly drunk. At first the victim may slur speech and begin to be unnaturally happy with the situation. This normally corresponds to a core temperature of around 35°C compared to the normal 37°C, although the actual temperature varies from individual to individual and some people feel quite unwell at 36°C. Then, as cooling continues, the victim may begin to stumble or stagger and may go on to become aggressive or confused. This often correlates with a core temperature of around 33-34°C. Eventually, at a core temperature of around 32°C, they will collapse and become unconscious, and they can go on cooling to stop breathing at around 27°C. However, their heart may not stop until core temperature is as low as 22°C and so it is vital to remember that however bad things seem, attempting rewarming and resuscitation may still work.

When someone first starts getting cold, act quickly by increasing clothing insulation, increasing activity or by seeking shelter. However, if choosing to shelter, remember that it may entail lying up in bad conditions and the loss of activity will cut heat production right down. This may have devastating results, and so the decision to go on or to seek emergency protection requires great judgement. Generally, I would recommend that if the victim is only just beginning to cool, push on if proper warm conditions are likely to be reached reasonably quickly. Hot drinks and food are also of great value and will only be helpful while the victim is conscious and cooperative. Once again, however, remember that sitting around preparing them may have adverse effects.

If the victim is worse and is actually showing signs of staggering or confusion, the situation is becoming dangerous. Obviously additional clothing, hot drinks, or seeking a course out of the wind remain of paramount importance, but the question of carrying on becomes more difficult since now it is probably better to stop if reasonable shelter is available. When going out in cold environments, you should always plan to carry some sort of windproof and waterproof bivouac protection —noting that, although tempting weight-wise, lightweight silvered survival blankets have been shown to be no more effective than a plastic sheet and definitely worse than a plastic or more rugged waterproof bag. You may of course be planning on camping anyway, in which case you need only ensure that your tent is adequate and that you have practised pitching it when the wind is up. It's no good finding out that it can't be done with your model when you need it in emergency. Ideally, you should also be carrying a sleeping bag even if you had no plans to get trapped outside, for there is no doubt that putting a victim in a good bag, and if necessary getting in it with them, is the best course of action if you are forced to stop.

Obviously, shelter can be sought as well as carried. In an emergency it is a nice warm building that's best, but this is not normally an option. The priority then becomes getting out of the wind and wet, and any natural feature that you can get under or into the lee of is of great value. Also remember that effective shelter may often be found close in on the windward side of an object, particularly if it has a vertical side which will generate back pressure and a 'dead spot' immediately in front of it. Much to many people's surprise, the shelter there may even be better than to leeward since swirling vortices of snow don't come curling round and drifting over you. In conditions with decent snow cover, compacted snow or ice can be used to create a whole range of possible shelters ranging from simple snowholes to multiple roomed camps, but really you need to have been taught how to make them and be carrying a suitable snow shovel. Reading about building such shelters cannot replace experience and before going out in really severe conditions one should have practised in safe conditions. Ideally you should have attended a proper course on winter survival such as those run by the British Mountaineering Council in Scotland or North Wales.

If a victim has cooled so much that they are unconscious, they need medical attention urgently. However, while this is sought or awaited, every measure mentioned above should be made to protect them from further cooling. As a general rule, never give up trying to protect and warm them, even if they appear to be dead. People have been successfully resuscitated many hours after they have apparently stopped breathing and you cannot rely upon being able to feel a pulse or hear their heart. It is said the hypothermia victims are 'not dead until they are warm and dead', and so generally it is impossible to be sure while you are still out in the field.

I would reiterate that with the correct preparation you can operate safely and relatively comfortably in terrible conditions but doing so is an art. That art needs to be learned and it is a mixture of education, preparation and forethought. Remember that hypothermia could happen to you or one or your party even in a temperate climate and indeed, it is more likely to happen in milder wetter conditions than in the truly cold regions of the Earth.

I will finish with an anecdote that illustrates just how easy it is to be caught out, and how simple it is to remedy the situation.

"As he approached, I wondered what was wrong. He was moving slowly and seemed to be fiddling with his clothing, trying to undo the zip on the front of his sodden jacket. He was smiling and certainly looked happier than he had done fifteen minutes back but I noticed that he stumbled a couple of times despite it being pretty flat. He drew up beside me where I stood with my back to the gale.

"Jusht a moment" he said, and then after quite a pause, "I've jusht got to get thish jacket off."

His voice was slurred and I looked at him more closely. Although he smiled, there was a strange, wild expression on his face and his eyes were slightly glazed. He wasn't shivering any more but his skin was as white as marble and I noticed that he had taken his gloves off and they were nowhere to be seen. He was also swaying as he began to almost rip at his clothing, frustrated by his fruitless attempts to pull down the zip with cold fingers.

"Are you OK?" I asked, but I got no reply, only an inane black grin as he continued with his attempts to undress. The truth began to dawn on me.

"Come on," I said, grasping him by the arm and pulling him towards the edge of the ridge. "We'll go down here and drop out of the wind."

The effect was quite spectacular. As we entered the lee of the Cwm the noise and buffeting that we had endured all day ceased and the world became an almost silent place. It seemed so much warmer that as I hurried downward, I began to sweat, but for my companion who I almost dragged along beside me, the move into shelter brought a different experience. Although he too began to warm, it only brought him back towards the normal and with it he began to shiver and feel miserably cold.

I could scarcely believe what I had just witnessed. It was only September on Snowdon, yet my father had been to the edge of disaster ..."

Remember, always treat the cold with respect and never underestimate what even the UK weather can produce.

Additional information

by Dr Richard Dawood

Colonel Jim Adam, the military physiologist until recently responsible for maintaining 'combat-effectiveness' of British troops under all conditions, advises observing the following steps:

1. Stop all activity.
2. Protect those at risk by rigging a make-shift shelter from the wind, rain and snow; lay the victim on the ground, on a ground sheet or space blanket.
3. Remove wet clothing, and insulate the victim in a sleeping bag.
4. Re-warm the victim with hot drinks, followed by hot food or high-energy snacks; unconscious victims need to be rewarmed by the body warmth of a companion.
5. Observe the victim for the cessation of breathing or pulse, and start mouth-to-mouth resuscitation or cardiac massage if necessary.
6. Send for help.
7. Insist on treating the victim as a stretcher case.

Acute hypothermia

This is a medical emergency, and is almost always the result of falling into water colder than 5°C: the victim shivers violently, inhales water, panics, may have respiratory or cardiac arrest, and is dead from drowning in about five to fifteen minutes. Survival is more likely if the victim is wearing a life-jacket that keeps the face out of the water, and is able to keep perfectly still.

Careful first-aid is essential. Following rescue from the water, do not allow the victim to move or make any physical effort. Keep the victim horizontal or slightly head-down; protect against further heat loss, and arrange transportation immediately to a hospital so that rapid re-warming may begin. The most effective way of re-warming is a bath —at 42°C or as hot as the bare elbow can tolerate. Until normal body temperature is restored, the victim is at high risk from sudden death, partly because re-warming may actually trigger an initial further drop in body temperature: many victims of accidents at sea die after they have been removed from the water —sometimes even in hospital.

Frostbite

Localised injuries from the cold can affect the limbs of exposed skin even when core body temperature is entirely normal, when insulation is not adequate or on account of other factors such as a restricted blood supply due to clothing that is too tight. Injuries of this kind range from frostbite following freezing of the tissues of the nose, checks, chin, ears, fingers and feet, to more common problems like frost nips and chapping of the skin, especially of the lips, nose and hands, and often compounded by sunburn.

The best way to deal with frostbite is to take careful steps to prevent it. Ensure, particularly, that gloves, socks and footwear are suitable for the conditions and the task in hand and don't choose extreme conditions to wear any of these items for the first time. Carry a face-mask to protect from high wind and driving snow. Also carry chemical handwarmers that can be used when needed.

Impending frostbite is usually signalled by intense pain in the part at risk: this should not be ignored, and prompt re-warming is necessary. For example, hands and fingers should be slipped under the clothes and warmed in the opposite armpit. If the pain is ignored it eventually disappears: the part becomes numb, white and hard to touch —it is frozen.

Established frostbite is a serious problem that may need lengthy hospital treatment: once thawing has taken place, tissue is liable to much more extensive damage from even slight chilling. During evacuation, keep the affected part clean and dry and give pain killers and antibiotics (if available) to prevent infection. Never rub frostbite with snow or anything else, because the tissues are extremely fragile and will suffer more damage.

Some do's and don'ts

1. Don't drink: alcohol causes peripheral vasoldilation —it increases blood flow through the skin —which can dramatically increase heat loss in extreme temperatures.
2. Don't smoke: nicotine can cause vasi-constriction —reduction in blood flow to hands, fingers and toes —increasing the likelihood of frostbite.

3. Carry high-energy carbohydrate snacks —such as glucose sweets or Mars bars.

4. Carry extra layers of clothing.

5. Carry chemical hand-warming sachets to put inside gloves and shoes in extreme conditions.

6. If you are on an expedition, or are looking after a large group, carry a special low-reading thermometer to measure body temperature: normal clinical thermometers are not adequate for detecting hypothermia. You may also be well advised to carry instruments for measuring high wind speed and estimating wind chill.

7. Anything that reduces activity such as being stranded on a chair lift, or being injured, can result in a rapid fall in body temperature; if this happens to you, try to maintain some muscular activity to generate warmth.

8. Children are at special risk. In particular, they are likely to need extra head protection (mechanical as well as against heat loss), and frost nip and frostbite can affect later growth.

9. In cold conditions it is easy to under-estimate the need to protect skin and eyes against excessive sunlight. Take extra care.

SURVIVING A SKIING ACCIDENT

by Arnie Wilson

Skiing injuries can and do happen when you least expect them, let alone when you are taking risks: there are documented cases of skiers breaking a leg as they climb down the aircraft steps before even setting foot in a ski resort.

Some years ago a producer working on a TV commercial —in which a hero clutching a box of chocolates had to out-ski an avalanche —fell over and broke her leg when she was just standing on a mountainside watching.

Last spring a ski holiday rep damaged his cruciate ligament while skiing without even falling over —he just hit a bump awkwardly and tore it. Ligaments, cartileges and tendons are the things that get hurt these days. Thanks to modern equipment, including more and more sophisticated bindings, broken legs are much rarer than they used to be. But something's got to give, and if it's not your leg, it's likely to be your cruciate.

Although advanced skiers travel at speed and are vulnerable to spinal and head injuries, surprisingly often it is the beginners who are most at risk. They tend to ski slowly, and more often than not it is the slow, sickening, twisting fall that causes the damage —not the high speed fall which catapults the skier out of his bindings. Unless of course the fall projects him or her into a rock. Which leads us to head injuries and protective helmets. Are they necessary?

A lot of people believe that by the end of the century or earlier, skiers should be required to wear them. Yet statistics show that remarkably few skiing accident cause head injuries. What they also show is that a frightening number of accidents on the slopes are drink-related.

Drink is freely available —and its consumption encouraged —in a host of mountain restaurants. Marco Grass, a member of the Saas Ski School in

Klosters, Switzerland says: "Drinking when you are skiing is just as dangerous as when you are driving a car. You think you are in control but in reality your reactions are slow and ill-judged.

"The latest statistics relating to injuries in this major ski area of Klosters/Davos show that more and more are drink–related. And we have no reason to think this trend is only happening here".

In North America, people skiing recklessly can have their lift ticket taken away and even be arrested. In practise —unless they actually injure another skier —they often get away with it. Having monitored American skiing in almost 100 resorts right across the continent, the closest I have come to seeing an errant skier being punished was in Snowshoe, Virginia, this year when a member of the ski patrol leapt onto a chair to catch the culprit but lost him on the mountain.

Colin Allum, whose Fogg (as in Philleas) Travel Insurance Services specialises in skiing insurance, says: "Skiing is a high risk sport. About one person in 50 who goes skiing is liable to receive some form of medical treatment during the course of a normal winter-sports holiday. This can range from a twisted ankle or bruised shoulder to the extreme cases of serious back or head injury, or in those fortunately very remote cases, the skier is killed."

If you happen to be the first on the scene after an accident, it is important to cross two skis in the snow about 10 metres up the slope from the injured skier. This will protect the injured skier from other skiers and also help attract the attention of the ski patrol who will organise a blood wagon —or even a helicopter if necessary —to get the victim down the mountain for medical treatment.

Don't try to move the victim, and if it is a leg injury, don't try to remove the boot: it can act as a splint. Keep the injured skier warm, but do not give him or her any alcohol. Knees are the most prone to injury, but almost no part of the human body is immune from one sort of skiing injury or another. A broken leg or a damaged cruciate ligament are among the worst things than can happen to your legs: but it's not always the big injuries that can cause pain and curtail skiing. Some skiers —myself included —can endure endless agonies over boots. Like many other skiers, I have the wrong fundamental foot shape for most boots. (They were described as "shaped like bricks" by one expert boot fitter in Aspen.)

Even my Koflach RC837s —chosen specifically to give my broad feet as comfortable a fit as possible —have had to be "blown-out" (enlarged by heating the crucial area).

I remember cracking or at least bruising a rib or two when I was learning to ski in Verbier, Switzerland, and a friend of mine is always damaging hers. You can't do much with cracked ribs except perhaps strap them up, but she always continues to ski regardless.

Like many skiing injuries, it is often less painful to carry on skiing than walk around or even lie down in bed. That goes for shoulders too.

Skiing with an injured shoulder is not always a problem (except the worry of falling on it again) but it can be agony in every day life. Usually an anti-inflammatory cream and resting it will do wonders. Wearing a sling can help. Shoulders are always a problem. They have such a sophisticated collection of moving parts that any one of them could be damaged in an accident without the others being affected. You may find you can ski yourself silly without so much as a twinge, but looking at your watch almost kills you!

Says Allum: "The advent of quick-release bindings has dramatically reduced the number of fractures —but dramatically increased the number of ligaments. In the days when bindings simply did not release, it was almost inevitable that a leg would be broken. Nowadays 50% of what may be regarded as 'serious' injuries —those which in due course will require some operative treatment — are knee ligaments injuries.

"Many accidents are caused by people skiing across the tops of protruding rocks which are seen too late. This type of accident tends to produce head injuries, because the skier is released from the bindings and propelled forward, rather on the lines of a swimmer in a start in the 100 metres Olympic swimming trials!

"Skis themselves can cause accidents if they are the wrong ski for the skier concerned, It is always important that skiers ski within their limitations, and ski a length of ski to which they are suited rather than one decided by bravado. It is much more sensible to have a happy and successful holiday skiing a 195 centimetre ski than finish up in hospital skiing a 210."

So much for the skis. But what about the skier? "There are those of us who may readily admit to being beginners even after 20 years of skiing. And there are others who will only admit to being advanced after 20 minutes," says Allum.

One good way to try to prevent injury on the slopes is to get fit before you go. Enter the Cybex machine. It sounds like something out of Dr Who, but what it actually does is check the strength of your hamstrings, quads abductors and adductors and then target any of these for strengthening with a customised programme of weight training and exercises.

Among Alan Watson's clients at the BiMAL Clinic in Hammersmith, West London is Will Carling. Says Watson: "Cybex will pinpoint any weakness in strength or symmetry."

Weather and altitude can all play their part in making a skier's life a pain. Some people can get serious altitude sickness in America, where skiing in the Rockies can mean altitudes of 11,000 or 12,000 feet or more. At such height it is not unusual to feel some effects, including headaches, nausea, breathlessness etc. These should wear off after two or three days (a good reason not to go skiing in the USA just for the week, or your holiday might be half over before you're ready to face it) but if they persist you should see a doctor. Drinking plenty of water —much more than you think you need —helps alleviate the problem. But serious altitude sickness can only be dealt with by getting the patient to a lower altitude as quickly as possible. Your doctor can prescribe tablets to lessen the impact of altitude.

As for weather: watch out for frostbite! The trouble is you never know you've been affected unless someone tell you (it's a bit like the old B.O. adverts!) As a damage limitation exercise, it is important to cover any frostbitten extremity and keep it warm. Experts argue over whether it is better just to cover it or knead it slightly to get the blood back in. Those against kneading say it could damage the cells while they are frozen. The consensus is just keep it warm: if you need it again, don't knead it!

Strong sunlight can be a major problem too. Always wear good protective creams even when it may seem that the sun is not coming out today. As the saying goes, you may not be able to see the sun, but the sun can see you! Even a couple of hours skiing in high altitude without protection, especially during the later months of March, April and May can cause serious sunburn and even sunstroke, because of the strong ultra-violet rays.

Skiing off piste is often considered much more dangerous than using groomed resort slopes because of the danger of being caught up in avalanches and even falling into a crevasse.

However skiing in a resort on a marked run is arguably just as dangerous. In fact when you compare the numbers of people on piste with those who ski off them, the chances of a collision in a resort must be just as high as falling foul of nature outside a resort. Almost 10% of skiers who end up in Davos hospital have been involved in collisions. And collisions nearly always cause injuries, sometimes serious ones.

Even skiing off-piste with a guide, however, is no guarantee that no harm will come to you. Or the guide for that matter. There is a cynical saying that all the avalanche experts are dead. Tragically, there is some truth in this.

According to the rescue service SOS which operates in the Parsenn area of Davos —one of the most extensive ski areas in Europe, which also prides itself on its avalanche research centre —"Avalanches are a natural phenomenon and therefore no absolute safety from them can be guaranteed. We must emphasise that even after the most experienced judgement and safety measures have been taken, an avalanche can still break loose and run over an open and marked piste."

Always obey avalanche warning signs and stay out of high–risk areas unless a qualified high mountain guide is skiing with you. He may have specialist knowledge and will certainly not take you off–piste if there is a serious risk.

Just as experts argue over the best way of dealing with frostbite, they also have different views about how to try to survive an avalanche. There is no way of guaranteeing that you will not die, If an avalanche has your name on it, there is nothing you can do about it. There are all sorts of avalanche patterns, from powder avalanches which drown you to slab avalanches which can break every bone on your body or at least batter you senseless. You might start it yourself, or you might be engulfed in one started by another skier. Most likely it will start spontaneously and trap you in its path.

Avalanches can move frighteningly fast. You may only have a second or two to react. One possible reaction is to ski diagonally out of the avalanche's path. Another is to take your skis off and try to 'swim' on the surface of the snow. If you are sucked under the surface, try to keep a pocket of air in front of you by cupping your mouth and nose with your hand. When skiing off-piste wear an avalanche transceiver, never ski alone and if possible always take a guide.

On a more optimistic note, the latest figures for skiing in the Davos/Klosters area are encouraging: in the winter of 1973/74, out of 5.5 million skiers there, there were 628 accidents. Almost two decades later, in the winter of 1992/93, the number of skiers had risen to 7.5 million, yet the number of injuries fell to 428 —a reduction of almost 32%.

Ueli Frei, President of the Mountain Guides Association in Grindelwald, who specialises in helicopter skiing and regularly rescues climbers stranded on the North face of the Eiger, one of Europe's most feared peaks, says: "You have to respect the mountain. But for me there is more risk in crossing a busy street in London." Yet he admits that two of his most experienced colleagues have died in avalanches this season.

Incidentally, 3% of injured skiers each year are those with broken thumbs. But that can happen even before you go skiing. Many people who practice on dry ski slopes sprain or break thumbs when they fall on the unforgiving plastic surface and sandwich a thumb between the slope and their body. But don't let that encourage you to give skiing the thumbs down. It's far too much fun. Just take it easy!

FILL THE BATH —IT LOOKS LIKE CIVIL WAR

by Anne Sharpley

Don't take it too personally when the shooting starts. They're almost certainly not shooting at you – and if they are, it's even safer since the level of marksmanship is so low, at least in all street–shooting I've been caught up in, that you're almost invulnerable. Hollywood never comes to your aid at such moments. You'd have thought that the rigorous early training we all get at the movies in both armed and unarmed fighting would have got into our reflexes. But it's all so much more muddled when it happens. Far from knowing when and where to duck, I could never make out where the fighting was coming from or which side of the wall or handy car to duck behind.

As for hand–to–hand fighting, far from the balletic, clearly defined movements of cinematic bouts, everyone gets puffed, or sick, or falls over in a shambles of misunderstood intentions. Nor is there that crack on the jaw to let you know who's being hit when. So it's even poor for spectator interest.

As a reporter, it is usually my actual work to be there and see what's happening. This means I can't follow my own best advice, which is to get out.

Sticking around is the easy bit. It is the next stage of events, which sets in during and after the street blocks, cordons, summary arrests and general paralysis as order is imposed on a troubled area that presents the visitor with new problems.

Communications with the outside world cease, public utilities go wrong and airports close. It is this sort of scene you can guarantee will take over. So forget the bullet–proof vest you wish you'd thought of and get on with the practicalities. The first and best rule is worth observing before you leave home —never pack more than you can run with. Always include a smaller, lighter bag such as an airline bag because if things get really nasty you need something handy with a shoulder strap to pick up and clear out in a hurry.

Essentials

If you're in a situation in which something is likely to happen, it is worth keeping this bag packed with essentials. Don't run about with suitcases, it can't be done for long.

Always bring in your duty free allowances if you know things are likely to get tough. Even if you're a non–smoking, tee–totaller who hates scent, they're the stuff of which bribes and rewards for favours are made. And as banks close or the money exchange goes berserk, they may end up as your only bargaining resource. And remember that drink is a useful stimulant, as well as solace. If I have to stay up all night, I do it on regular small nips of whisky.

The next bit of advice will seem absurd at first, but you'll regret having laughed if you ever get into one of those long–standing, semi–siege situations that sometimes happen when you're stuck in a hotel that either can't or won't provide for you. Take one of those little aluminium pans with a solid fuel burner —so small it will slip into your pocket. You can boil water at the rate of quarter of a pint to one solid fuel stick, which is about the size of a cigarette. You can get the whole thing from camping shops for relatively little.

If you take a few tea bags or a small jar of instant coffee, this will not only help if you're an addict of these things, but again wins friends and allies in an hour of need. Serve it up in a tooth mug, but don't forget to put in a spoon before you pour in boiling water or you'll crack the glass.

As the water either goes off completely, or turns a threatening colour, it is just as well to have a means of making water sterile. And at the very least it provides a shave.

If things look ugly, it is a good idea to fill the bath. You can keep filling it if supplies continue, but you can't get water at all if they really stop. Not only have you a means of keeping the toilet in a less revolting state, but you can wash yourself and keep away thirst (boil the water first, of course). I always like to carry a small box of biscuits, although this isn't anything more than a psychological trick to reinforce a feeling of self–sufficiency.

If things get really hectic, nobody in a hotel wants to know about you but they get rather interested in your property. It's a great time for getting everything stolen. I came back from Prague in 1968 with scarcely a thing left. What's yours suddenly becomes theirs. So remember that overnight bag and carry it with you everywhere.

Whether you should try to look less conspicuously foreign is a moot point. War correspondents usually get themselves kitted out in a sort of quasi–military set of clothes and where there are women soldiers, as in Israel, I have too. If nothing else, it meant I could fill my taxi with girl soldiers and let them get me past the road blocks with their papers. But when I found myself in action before I had time to change, I was told later by a captured sniper that it had only been my pretty pink blouse that had saved me. He'd had me on his sights and liked the colour so he couldn't bring himself to shoot me!

However, you're much more likely to be holed up in your hotel. If things are exploding, it's as well to get whatever glass is removable down on the floor, draw curtains and blinds against window glass and drape mirrors you can't take down with blankets and towels. Glass is the biggest danger you face. Locate the fire escape and if it's remote, get yourself somewhere else to stay either in the same hotel or elsewhere.

Identity in a crisis

It's always worth trying to pretend you're from a country they're not having a row with, although local knowledge of nationalities is always limited, so don't try Finnish or Papuan. This is for occasional use when they're running around looking for someone to duff up. Hit the right nationality and you're so popular they won't put you down. Crowds are very emotional and the least thing sends them one way or the other. In Algeria, I found I had a winning ticket by saying I was British —or English, to be more precise. I became the object of gallant attention from a group of youths who decided to accompany me as a sort of bodyguard. All very honourable and very sweet.

Women are still quite often chivalrously treated in the Middle East. I found that to get through road blocks in Algeria I could simply say I was an 'English Miss' without having to hand over my passport with the damning word 'journalist' in it. What echoes it evoked, why they were so responsive, I never quite found out but I liked to think that I modestly linked up with those amazingly bossy English women, from Hester Stanhope onwards, who'd been in the Middle East.

Certainly I found that Muslim sentries were unable to challenge me. I always walked straight through, looking determined. Another useful tip for visiting women in tricky situations in Muslim countries is to apply to visit the chief wife of whoever is in power. There's always a go–between who will arrange it for a sum, escort you there and help generally. As women in harems are bored out of their minds, they're usually delighted to see another woman from the outside world. If they like you, which you must make sure of (that's where the duty free scent or your best blouse or scarf come in), they'll do a great deal to help. They always have more power than is generally believed.

Keep calling

While ordinary communications often stop altogether, it is a good idea to tell your family or company to keep on telephoning you from the outside. So often, I've found it impossible to get calls out while incoming calls made it.

You can always try the journalist's old trick of getting out to the airport and picking a friendly face about to board whatever aircraft is leaving and get them to take a message.

One belief I've always had, which may not necessarily work, but always has for me, is that befriending a taxi driver can be extremely useful. They're a much maligned lot. What you do is to practice your basic physiognomy —a derided skill, but it's all you've got— and pick a driver you think you could trust. Then use him all the time, paying him over the odds, of course. Take an interest in him and his family, and you will find a friend.

A taxi driver not only knows where everything is and what's going on, but can also act as interpreter and spare hand. Explain what you're trying to do and they soon enter into the spirit of things. There was one taxi driver in Cyprus who virtually did my job for me. He was not only fearless, he was accurate too! ■

TRAVEL WRITING AND PHOTOGRAPHY
Chapter 15

THROUGH THE LENS

by *Michael Busselle*

It's hard to imagine a world without electricity, the combustion engine or air travel and yet most of the discoveries and inventions made during the past two centuries have been completely absorbed into our way of life and are seldom given much thought.

Photography is like that and yet it too has had a profound effect on our society. It began 150 years ago, largely as an absorbing pastime for gentlefolk who might otherwise have been occupied with poetry or watercolours. Photography has now become the kingpin of the entertainment world as well as information and education processes, and many things we take for granted would simply not be possible without it.

And yet, in spite of this, photography as a profession still has a slightly doubtful standing. The father of a young friend of mine who entered the profession asks him periodically: "When are you are going to get a proper job?" After more than 30 years of professional photography I must confess to having similar thoughts about myself.

The trouble is it simply doesn't seem like a serious profession. The 1960s film *Blow Up* has a lot to answer for and it doesn't help when friends and colleagues are told, "He's away for two weeks in the Maldives taking photographs." Earning a living doing what the majority regard as a rather expensive hobby tends to reduce your credibility as a worker.

Another reason is that most people think that they could do the job just as well if only they had the right camera and lenses. The truth is they probably could but not necessarily for those reasons. At the beginning of this century when the first Kodak Brownie was produced, it became possible for anyone with the will to create images with the minimum of fuss.

In comparison with sculpture and painting, it was also a medium which required minimal craft skills. Now few families in our society do not possess a camera.

There's a paradox in a way because taking a photograph is easy but producing a really powerful image can be very difficult. The difference is not, as most people believe, in the quality of the camera and a grasp of complex technical know–how, but simply in the way things are seen. The problem is that because actually taking the photograph is so easy it encourages a belief that all you have to do is point the camera and press the button.

A good photograph depends largely upon a good eye and a careful and thoughtful approach to aiming the camera. Travel and landscape photography in particular can also require an element of luck —being in the right place at the right time. Even luck, however, tends to depend a great deal upon photographic skills —the more you practise the luckier you get!

A good eye is perhaps the most difficult element to define. What one person regards as a fine photograph another might consider contrived or banal. There will always be different styles and fashions in a medium such as photography, a necessary part of development and progress. The common factor is always, however, that a 'good' photograph invites opinion and comment and makes people stop and look, no matter whether they are critical or complimentary.

We've all suffered the process of looking through other people's holiday pictures, a mindless flicker of similar successive images. Even the most casual snapper will sometimes produce an eye–stopping image among the dross. The art of photography, if it is an art, is in understanding why that one picture was so good and knowing how to take it again.

For this reason a good eye also needs to be coupled with a questioning mind. When you see a subject which makes you want to take out your camera, you need to think why. If it's a view, for instance, what particular quality or point of interest does it have which makes you want to take a photograph? Once you have determined this you may find that the picture needs to be taken from a different position, closer or perhaps from one side. The place from where you first see a potential picture is seldom the best place from which to shoot.

Choosing the most telling viewpoint is one of the crucial photographic skills. It is this choice which allows you to control the composition and structure of your image and often a change of a foot or so can make an enormous difference to the effect of a picture. As much as 90 per cent of the time and effort I put into taking a photograph is spent on choosing the best viewpoint.

There is usually an optimum time at which to take a photograph, which the great photographer Henri Cartier Bresson has succinctly described as 'The decisive moment.' This doesn't have to be a dramatic event. It can be something like a fleeting expression on the face of someone you are photographing, the moment at which clouds have moved into a pleasing arrangement in a landscape, or waiting until a distracting figure has moved from the background of a picture.

The key to these decisions is the camera view–finder. Inexperienced photographers tend to use it like a gunsight, aiming the camera by lining up the subject in its centre. In fact it should be treated like a frame so that you are aware of every detail and colour within its borders before you even consider pressing the button.

By varying the viewpoint and angling the camera, selecting a lens and choosing the moment to take the picture, you can have an enormous amount of control over the content of your frame. Not perhaps as much as a painter with a blank canvas but you should, nevertheless, think of the view finder in exactly the same way.

An observant eye and a thoughtful approach to the way the image is composed are the true skills of photography. Of course it's important that you give the right exposure and that the image is sharp but, with modern cameras, these are relatively simple factors to control. A few basic filters can also improve and enhance the quality of photographs in certain circumstances but this too is a simple matter to understand and easy to apply.

It only takes a fraction of a second to take a photograph but it is the time and thought you apply before you press the button which really count.

PHOTOGRAPHING NATURE

by Robert Holmes

Few subjects facing the camera produce such dismal failures as wildlife. I never again want to have to search for a bird lost in over–abundant foliage or watch the back end of an elephant disappearing into the bush.

The problem is that wildlife photography needs more than just technical expertise. An intimate knowledge of animal behaviour is equally as important, although fortunately you can improve your photographs without studying for an advanced degree in zoology.

Filling the frame

The most common problem is failing to fill the frame with the subject. This, of course, is easier said than done as most wild animals are so afraid of humans that a close approach is often impossible. The traditional method of setting up a hide and sitting there waiting, for hours on end, is out of the question for most travellers, so we have to resort to other methods. But whatever method we choose, this is not an area of photography that can be hurried.

Most animals and birds are less afraid of vehicles than they are of people and particularly in areas such as East Africa, you can drive right up to the wildlife without scaring it away. The vehicle will serve as a perfect mobile hide, but make sure the engine is switched off before you shoot or your camera will pick up the vibration. To steady long telephoto lenses, support the lens with a bean bag in the window opening. This will be much faster and more flexible than using a tripod.

If you approach the animal on foot, keep a low profile in the literal sense. Crouch down and crawl towards the subject. Wear colours that blend with the surroundings and try to avoid jerky movements.

Half the battle is being in the right place at the right time, and this is where a knowledge of animal behaviour comes in. A basic field guide to the animals and birds of the country you are visiting can go a long way towards helping with this problem. Also remember that most animals are active around water-holes and feeding places at dawn and dusk. It is unlikely that you will see much activity in the middle of the day. Many animals will come out into the open at night and if you have a powerful flash you can get some remarkable results.

Talk to locals and ask where you can see wildlife. Children are usually a mine of information in this respect and they will often be delighted to take you along to the good viewing points. Within the reserves, the rangers are often keen photographers themselves and are very sympathetic and knowledgeable.

Zoos

Many good 'wildlife' photographs are taken in zoos. These are the only places where you will be able to get close enough to many animals. You can get natural–looking photographs if you take care with your framing, select a natural–looking background and keep bars and wire netting out of the picture. You can do this by using a telephoto lens (100mm or more focal length) at maximum aperture. This will give you minimum depth of field and throw out of focus everything but the subject you are focused on. This technique will also let you shoot through cages without seeing them, if you are close enough to the cage to throw it out of focus. To shoot through glass, remove reflections by using a polarising filter and angling the camera at 30° to the surface.

Equipment

A good long lens is essential if you want to photograph birds, and it will be useful for most mammals too. I use a 400mm apochromatic lens —that is a lens that has special glass elements to ensure the highest colour fidelity. You can use it on maximum aperture and still get top quality results. Of course, specialist equipment like this comes with a high price tag and there are much more economical ways to solve the problem. I ordered my 400mm lens to take on a long trip to Alaska to photograph the wildlife in both Denali National Park and on the remote Pribilof Islands just off the coast of Siberia. The lens arrived two days after I had set off on this five–week journey. The longest lens that I owned was a 200mm, which, with a maximum aperture of f2.8 was pretty fast. I also had a 'doubler' which was made by the same manufacturer, Minolta, and fixed it onto the lens. A doubler, or 2x convertor, is an optical accessory that fits between the camera and the lens and doubles the focal length of the lens. A 135mm becomes a 270mm and my 200mm became a 400mm. The disadvantage is that you lose two stops, an f2.8 becomes an f5.6.

When doublers were first introduced, their optical quality left much to be desired. The bottom of a milk bottle would have produced better results. Fortunately, technology has improved dramatically and the new generation of doublers that are matched to specific lenses produce excellent results. Not only do they provide great versatility but they also take up very little space. I was forced to use this combination in Alaska and it enabled me to take photographs that have sold to one of the most technically demanding markets in the United States. This doubler has now become part of my standard travelling equipment and, with my newly acquired 400mm, I now have up to 800mm at my disposal without having to carry a huge chunk of glass around.

The other lens I find invaluable for wildlife is a 100mm macro. This will focus all the way from infinity to a few centimetres. Most macro lenses are in the 50mm range, but the 100mm lets you get the same degree of magnification at a greater distance —and as I have always had an aversion to creepy crawlies, the 100mm focal length is ideal. It also allows you to take close–ups of subjects in inaccessible locations.

The choice of a camera is always a very personal one and my only advice is to get one that can take interchangeable lenses. The semi–wide angle lenses on compact automatic cameras will rarely produce satisfactory wildlife shots.

Although I usually advocate using cameras in their manual mode, wildlife photography is one exception where the automatic camera comes into its own. Many lens and camera manufacturers now supply autofocus lenses up to 1000mm in focal length with fast aperture lenses up to 300mm. Sigma, for example, make a 300mm f2.8 Apo lens to fit Nikon, Minolta, Pentax, and Canon camera bodies as well as an 800mm f 2.8 1000mm. Generally, a camera with a black finish is less likely to distract the wildlife than a bright, shiny, chrome–finished model, but a black finish is more susceptible to excessive heating in hot climates. If you are planning to take a range of shots, and not just wildlife, I would suggest that you err towards the chrome finish.

The majority of current 35mm SLR and compact cameras are now made with an integral autowinder and some advanced cameras,like the Nikon F4, have a built-in high speed motor drive. In operation, the difference is that motordrives have a faster film advance rate —and they often incorporate a motorised film rewind.

Both offer single frame mode (you have to press the release for each exposure) and continuous mode (the shutter fires and the film advances continuously as long as the release is depressed). But how often do you need to shoot at five frames a second? In the last couple of years I have shot over 2000 rolls of film and not once have I ever used a motordrive in the continuous mode. Not only are motordrives more expensive than autowinders but they are also bigger and heavier. I would be lost without a winder because it helps me to concentrate completely on the subject, but its noise can be disturbing to some wildlife.

Plants

Rainforests contain some of the most beautiful plants and flowers imaginable —but what a nightmare for the photographer! Water drips continually from the trees and there is barely enough light to see by, let alone for taking photographs.

In the realm of plant photography, a rainforest is about as difficult a location as you will ever encounter. The light can be extremely contrasty, suggesting the use of a slow colour slide film (ISO 25 to 100) to handle the extremes of light and shade, but the overall darkness under the canopy of the forest cries out for a fast film (ISO 400 or more) which will be incapable of handling both highlights and shadowed detail. You can use the slow film with a tripod and long exposures, but plants are often moving, if only slightly, and none of the resulting photos will be really sharp.

My solution has been to use a fill flash. I use a small flash gun to illuminate the shadowed areas and thus reduce the overall contrast of the scene. With the new automatic flashguns, this technique is very simple. Measure the light falling on a highlight —a sun–splashed leaf, for example. If the reading for an ISO 64 film is 1/60 second at f16, all you need to do is set the auto setting on the flash gun for an aperture of F16. Make sure you never set the shutter at a speed too high to synchronise with the flash. Most 35mm SLR will now synchronised at 1/125 of a second and many at much faster speeds. If you use a shorter exposure, the illumination will be uneven. An additional advantage to using a flash fill is that the duration of a burst of light from a flash gun is extremely short and will freeze motion.

Plants and flowers in general present many interesting photographic problems. Lighting in the rainforests can be awkward but a wild flower in a more open landscape can be equally difficult to shoot well. I always carry a small sheet of baking foil that folds down to nothing and yet becomes an excellent reflector that can push light into dark corners and bring life to a bloom that would otherwise be dull and colourless.

Many interesting flowers are so small that you will need a macro, or close–up lens to get an acceptable photo of them. At the short distances involved, the lens will have to be stopped down to a small aperture, maybe as little as f22, to obtain as much depth of field as possible and ensure that all of the flower is in sharp focus. A small aperture means a long shutter speed and a long shutter speed means an inability to freeze movement. A portable wind break may help, or get a friend to provide shelter. Alternatively, resort again to lighting the flower with flash. Even a small gun will let you use an aperture of f16 or smaller if it is used at close range.

There are certain flowers that are impossible to photograph in their natural colour. These reflect an unusually high percentage of the infra–red and ultraviolet portions of the spectrum. Colour film is sensitive to these although our eyes are not and the resulting colour on the film appears to be a gross distortion of the truth. Blue flowers are particularly susceptible and frequently produce a pinkish hue. Careful use of filter can sometimes help but the problem is almost impossible to eliminate.

Filters

A photographer doesn't have full control over how the image will turn out but can go a long way towards avoiding problems with light. If you shoot portraits outdoors, there is no problem if the sky is overcast, but if the sun is shining disaster can strike in the form of ugly black shadows. To avoid these, move the subject into open shade. But now you are faced with another problem if you are using colour film. All colour film is balanced for a specific type of light, or should I say, colour temperature. Most of us use daylight film which will reproduce the true colours of any subject illuminated by light that has a colour temperature of 5500 Kelvin, that of normal sunlight. If the colour temperature of the light source is higher, then the subject will come out looking too blue. If it is lower, then it will be too yellow.

Once your portrait subject has moved from direct sunlight into open shadow, the illumination will be from the blue sky which may have a colour temperature of as much as 10,000 Kelvin —which is why portraits taken in the open shade always look too blue. To overcome this problem you can use a small flash gun (all electronic flashes are balanced for 5500K, the colour will then look correct).

Another way is to use warming filters which warm up the light and bring down the colour temperature. Their technical descriptions are series 81 and 85 filters, each of which comes in a variety of different strengths.Many professionals use a very expensive instrument called a colour temperature meter which will indicate precisely which filter is needed. But for practical purposes in the field, I would use an 81B as a general purpose warming filter. Another technique that I have used very successfully in harsh sunlight, is photographing the subject in reflected light. Look for a light wall or even use a white sheet or towel to bounce light from the sun into the subject's face. Be careful not to place the subject near surfaces with a strong colour or this will be reflected in the skin tones. People standing too close to foliage can look very sea–sick if you are not careful.

My favourite light for portraits is the Vermeer–like north light which gives an almost three–dimensional quality to the photograph. The important thing is to use your eyes and look to see how the light is playing on the subject matter.

Landscapes

This is equally true for landscapes. A landscape that looks dramatic to our eye may not be equally dramatic on film. Again, light is usually the problem. Good weather often provides the worst conditions for dramatic landscapes. I prefer to work on days when there are clouds blowing across the skies creating a modulation of light with interesting shadows and highlights —not to mention the beauty of the clouds themselves. Shafts of sunlight on a stormy day will transform any landscape.

Remember that it is the interplay of light and shade that creates the illusion of depth in photographs and provides graphic interest. The higher the sun is in the sky, the shorter the shadows will be. At home in California, I find that the best light is just before dawn until about two hours after and the last two hours before sunset. At these times the sun is still low in the sky, creating long shadows and emphasising the texture of the land. The closer you get to the Equator, the briefer this period becomes until you have only a few minutes when the light is at its optimum. In Europe, there is a much longer period to play with, particularly in winter, but I still think it is difficult to beat dawn light. And for someone who enjoys a nice warm bed as much as I do, that's saying a lot!

I am frequently accused of using special filters to create dramatic effects although in reality I use few. I rely on the light and my knowledge of how film will react to it. The few filters I do use, however, are certainly worth having. I have already mentioned the 81B warming filter, and along with this I also carry a polarising filter and a graduated grey. Graduated filters are what their name suggests. They fade from a strong colour to clear so when used over the lens, a wash of colour affects only part of the photograph.

The coloured grads, as they are called, which create such dramatic effects as brown or green skies are too artificial for my taste. The grey that I use does not affect the colour of the photograph, but brings the tones within the range of the film. For example, if the sky is very bright, it may not be possible to contain foreground detail and sky detail in the same photograph. If the exposure is correct for the foreground, the sky will be washed out. The graduated grey will tone down the sky and help you make a much more dramatic landscape that still has an air of reality.

Polarizers

Of all the filters used by colour photographers, none can surpass the polarizer. Not only is it extremely effective but also very simple to use.

Polarised light is everywhere. It bounces off non–metallic surfaces at an angle of 30° —off water, leaves and even from the sky. Its effect is to de–saturate colours. Most of the shine on a green leaf is polarised light; remove that light and you can see the pure, intense green of the leaf. A polarising filter will do this for you, and you can actually see what is happening through the viewfinder. All polarising filters are supplied in revolving mounts. You screw them onto the front of the lens in the normal way but are still able to rotate the filter through 360°. Look through the viewfinder while you turn the filter and you will see the reflections disappear from surfaces and the sky deepen to a glorious blue. It will not always work. The maximum amount of polarised light in the sky is from the area of the sky at 90° to the sun. Look directly away from the sun (or into it) and the polarising filter will not have any effect. It is also most dramatic when the sun is low in the sky. If you do a lot of tide pool photography, this filter can completely eliminate surface reflections from the water so that you can see everything below the surface. Again you can see this happening through your viewfinder.

I have seen photographers leaving this filter on their lenses permanently, which I feel is a mistake. The disadvantage is that it cuts down the amount of light reaching the film, thus necessitating longer exposures. If it has no effect, then take it off. And remember, no amount of equipment will improve your photographs unless you learn to use your eyes.

PHOTOGRAPHY BENEATH THE WAVES

by Dave Saunders

Anyone who has put on a mask and snorkel and floated over a coral garden or sunken boat will have had a glimpse of the fascinating world beneath the surface of the ocean. But we are not built to exist for long underwater and nor are most cameras. It is an alien environment with a new set of rules for the photographer.

The nice thing about underwater photography is that you can approach it at any level. It is possible to take satisfactory pictures with an ordinary land camera through the 'window' of a glass–bottomed boat, or even in rock pools using a bucket or water–tight box with a glass base. If the sun is shining on the subject, the pictures will be bright and clear.

But be careful when you are near water, especially salt water. Ordinary land cameras are like cats —they just don't want to get involved with water. So if you want to take a camera underwater, you will need either a purpose–built underwater camera or a water–tight housing.

The 110 format underwater cameras are no longer made as this film size has pretty well died out. Minolta make a Weathermatic DL for use with 35mm film down to 5 meters. It has both a 38mm and 50mm lens with a close-up attachment used underwater to overcome diffraction. It is fully automatic and has a built-in flash.

For deeper diving, Sea & Sea produce two models of 35mm underwater camera, the Explorer and the more expensive Motormarine 2, for use down to 40 meters, both have the option of interchangeable lenses and flash.

The Nikonos is probably the underwater camera most used by the scuba divers. It is no larger than an ordinary 35mm camera, it is easy to operate and can give good results. Based on the French Calypso design, it is continually being improved. The Nikonos V has a fully–automatic exposure system, optional motordrive and automatic flash gun. There is no rangefinder for focusing, so you have to estimate focusing distances. Being a non–reflex camera, with a direct vision viewfinder, you may have problems with parallax when close to the subject. An external sportsfinder frame can be fixed to the top of the camera making viewing easier. The Nikonos V has a choice of auto or manual exposure. A bright LCD display in the viewfinder tells you the shutter speed, warns of over or under exposure and has a 'flash ready' signal.

There is also the Nikonos RS, an autofocus SLR with interchangeable lenses and optional flash equipment.

The standard lens is the W–Nikkor 35mm f2.5. Also available are 15mm, 28mm and 80mm lenses. For detailed shots of coral and tame fish there are special close–up lenses or extension tubes.

Underwater housings

Rather than investing in a whole new camera system, an alternative approach is to use an underwater housing around your land camera. In shallow water of less than 10m, flexible plastic housings provide a relatively cheap method of protecting your camera. Controls are operated through a rubber glove which is set into the case.

In deeper water, the flexible design is inappropriate as pressure increases with depth and the housing would collapse. Ikelite housings are made for 110, 35mm reflex and non–reflex and roll film cameras. These are rigid and some models can safely be taken to a depth of 100m.

The housing has controls which link into the focusing and aperture rings, as well as shutter release and film advance mechanisms. Rubber 'O' ring seals produce a water–tight chamber which keeps the camera dry. To avoid flooding, the rings must be cleaned and lightly greased with silicone each time a film is changed. Metal housings are very strong and durable, but are heavy to carry and need careful attention to prevent corrosion. Plexiglass housings are much lighter and cheaper, and are available for a wider range of cameras. However, the plastic type ages more quickly and will eventually leak.

How light behaves

Light is refracted or bent more in water than in air. Objects underwater appear to be larger and nearer than they really are. Your eye sees the same distortion as the lens, so, with a reflex camera, you simply focus through the lens and the subsequent picture will then be in focus. The subject may be 1.5m away, but will appear closer to the eye and to the lens. However, if you then look at the focusing ring, it will set at about 1m.

Because of the way light refracts through water, the effective focal length of the lens is increased, making it more telephoto when a flat underwater porthole is used. So, in effect, a 35mm lens underwater is approximately equivalent to a 45mm lens on land. Likewise a 15mm lens is equivalent to a 20mm.

A dome–shaped porthole, on the other hand, enables light from all directions to pass through it at right angles. This eliminates the problem of refraction and the angle of view of the fitted lens is unchanged.

Lenses

Wide angle lenses are generally more useful underwater. Visibility is seldom as good above water, especially if there are numerous suspended particles. For a clear image it is important to move in close so as to reduce the amount of water between the camera and the subject. To include a whole diver in the frame when using a 35mm lens on a Nikonos, you need to be about 2m away. A wider lens, say 15mm, means you can move in much closer to the subject and thus minimise the amount of obstructing material between the camera and the subject.

Generally camera–to–subject distance should not exceed a quarter of the visibility. If the visibility is only 1.5m (as it often is in temperate seas or inland lakes), you should restrict yourself to only taking subjects up to 0.3m from the lens.

Flash

With high speed emulsions such as Ektachrome 400 (transparencies) and Kodacolour 400 (prints) it is often possible to get away without using flash, especially near the surface where it is brighter. When the sun is shining through the surface layers of water, you can obtain good results down to about 2m without flash. However, the deeper you go below the surface layers of water, the more the light is filtered out by the water. At 10m below the surface, all the red has been filtered out of the ambient light, and flash is needed to restore the absorbed colour.

In tropical waters, the guide number of the flash gun (which indicates its power) is usually reduced to about a third of the 'in air' number. It is much safer to bracket your exposures, as the expense of film is nothing compared to the trouble and expense of getting into the water.

Underwater flashguns are either custom–made, or normal land units in plastic housing. Custom–made guns generally have a good wide angle performance, whereas units in housings generally have a narrow angle.

Instead of using a flash gun mounted close to the camera, place it at arm's length away, or even further, to give a better modelling light to the subject. Having two flash guns is even better and will give much greater control over lighting. With the flashgun further from the camera, fewer particles between the camera and the subject will be illuminated. If the flashgun is near the camera, the particles will be illuminated and detract from the subject.

Aiming the flash can be tricky. Although your eye and the camera lens 'see' the subject to be, say, 2m away, it is actually further. As the flash must strike the subject directly in order to light it up, the unit must be aimed *behind* the apparent position of the subject.

Diving problems

Test your equipment in the swimming pool before you take it into the sea. Plan the shots before hand. It is always better to have a good idea of what you want *before* you go into the water so you can have the right lens on the camera to do the job.

Keeping yourself stable while trying to take a picture can be a problem. Underwater you should be neutrally buoyant, such that you can hang suspended in the water without moving up and down. By breathing in you should rise slowly, and by breathing out you should sink. Wearing an adjustable buoyancy life jacket will allow you to increase or decrease your buoyancy by letting air into or out of the jacket.

Sometimes you may need to grab onto a piece of coral to steady yourself. A wetsuit will help protect you against stings and scratches. And as you will be moving around slowly when taking pictures, you will feel the cold earlier than if you were swimming energetically, and you will appreciate the warmth the suit gives you.

Near the sandy sea bed it is easy to churn up the water and disturb the sand, making the water cloudy. The secret is to keep as still as possible, and remove your fins. Restricting rapid movements also avoids scaring the more timid fish away. Taking a plastic bag of bread down with you usually guarantees plenty of potential subjects for your photography.

Good subjects

Even with very simple equipment it is possible to record interesting effects simply by looking at what is naturally around you underwater. Rays of light burst through the water in a spectacular way and are especially photogenic when they surround a silhouette. And you can get impressive effects by catching reflections on the surface when you look up at the sky through the water.

The best pictures are usually simple and clear. Select something to photograph, such as an attractive piece of coral, then position yourself to show it off to best advantage without too many distractions in the picture.

With a little thought and planning before hand, achieving good results underwater is quite straightforward although you should not be deterred by a high failure rate at first.

THE TROUBLE WITH PHOTOGRAPHY

by David Hodgson

I have only been in jail three times in my life and, in each case, the stay was mercifully short! This was just as well since the jails were all in Africa and not amongst the healthiest places to spend a holiday. The cause, I hasten to add, was photographic rather than anything more sinister. A question of pointing a lens in the wrong direction at the wrong time. As a magazine photojournalist with an editor and offices to please, I was probably less discreet with my photography than the average traveller would ever need to be. All the same, great difficulties can be created quite unintentionally and with the most innocent of motives.

First of all, find out exactly what the restrictions are, and then stick to them. In many areas of the world, frontier security problems can turn an innocent border post picture into an excursion into espionage. At best you are likely to find your camera and film confiscated and the worst can be a whole lot worse. Many places now insist on you having a photographic permit. Make sure you get one. It is no guarantee against trouble but may help if you wave it under enough noses. Avoid photographing military installations, troop movements, airfields etc, unless you have a compelling reason for doing so. And I mean one which is worth doing time for! Some countries have a ban on photographing examples of civil engineering, scenes that make the country look primitive —ie. all the most photogenic places— and industrial plants. In Yugoslavia, some years ago, I was arrested for taking shots inside a chemical plant —and this after being given permission to do so. One traveller in Pakistan (which is full of absurd photographic restrictions) was nearly arrested for taking a picture of a river which just happened to have a bridge in the background. Train and aeroplane spotters beware: certain Eastern European and Third World countries regard the photographic or written record as an offence. A bribe sometimes secures a bending of the rules.

Watch out for religious or cultural prohibitions. These can result in mob violence against you, especially in the remoter parts of the world. If you want to take pictures in places where the natives are far from friendly, then be careful. Respect their dignity and right of privacy. In some countries such as Kenya, reluctant subjects have been persuaded to pose with hefty payments. If you start shooting without their permission and without paying the going rate, the mood can turn ugly remarkably fast. So take plenty of change and be prepared to negotiate. When in doubt, use a telephoto from a healthy distance. I should also add that a quite different problem can arise when you are *too* popular as a camera operator. Everybody in the neighbourhood seems to want to get in on the act. This happens mainly when a camera is a rare sight and you are looked on as a piece of street theatre. My advice here is to go through the pretence of taking pictures. If necessary (and you have sufficient film stock) waste a few frames or even a whole roll. You never know, some of the pictures may be worthwhile and you will satisfy the crowd's curiosity. When all the fuss has died down you can carry on with picture–taking without arousing much interest. If you are staying in an area for some time and want really candid shots, then let everybody get completely used to seeing you with your camera. Reckon on spending several days simply being seen around. Your novelty value will disappear very quickly.

One good way of persuading reluctant subjects to pose (and rewarding them if they do) is to carry a Polaroid camera. Take one shot and let them have it. Then shoot your main pictures. But a word of warning: you can get through a lot of expensive Polaroid film unless you save this tactic for an emergency.

CAMERA CARE AND PROTECTION

by Dave Saunders and Robert Holmes

You have spent as much as you can afford on good camera gear for your trip abroad. Naturally, you don't *expect* it to fail, but you are realistic enough to include an extra camera body —just in case. Camera repair shops tend to be in short supply in remote regions of the world and you don't want your pictures to turn into the fish that got away.

Even if the journey is short and conditions far from severe, equipment can easily let you down by getting lost, breaking when dropped or simply expiring after long, devoted service.

Minimising the frustrations of such technical hitches calls for attention to detail. Caring for your camera goes beyond dusting it with a brush from time to time. It begins long before you set out and ends with a final check and brush–up when you return home.

Check–list

It is worthwhile following a routine check–list to avoid on–the–spot panics. First decide exactly what equipment you are going to take. This will, of course, be controlled by what you can afford. It will inevitably be a compromise between the full range of camera bodies, lenses and accessories you might use and the amount of weight you can allocate for photographic gear.

Choose only those items you will need for the specific type of photographs you plan to bring, taking into account any harsh conditions such as sand, salt water or humidity you are likely to meet. Coping with travelling can be taxing enough without the additional burden of unnecessary accessories.

You may find two camera bodies, three lenses and a small flash gun are sufficient. A miniature camera in your pocket at all times and a Polaroid camera can also be very handy.

If you need to buy extra bits and pieces, check everything well before you leave. Run at least one test roll of film through the camera, using various shutter speeds and aperture settings. Change lenses, try out the shutter release cable, the self–timer and the motordrive. Make sure everything is clean and working smoothly. Then study the results for anomalies.

Protection

If your travels are going to take you very near salt water, mud, sand or snow, it may be worth investing in a Nikonos underwater camera or a waterproof housing, rather than risk destroying your land camera. A camera is generally pretty sturdy, but water will harm it. If you drop the camera in the sea, you have signed its death warrant and may as well give it to the kids to play with and claim a new one on insurance.

You can defend land cameras against salt spray by wiping with lint cloth lightly soaked in WD40 or a similar light oil. If you need to use a land camera in a sand storm, carefully apply 'O' ring grease to joints, mounts, and hinges, using a cotton bud. Tape over parts not in use, such as the sync socket and motordrive terminal.

Take spare plastic bags to help protect gear under adverse conditions. Also include spare 'O' rings for the Nikonos, 'O' ring grease, cotton buds, chamois leather, brush, Dust–Off spray and a small watchmaker's screw–driver for on–the–spot maintenance.

A skylight or ultraviolet filter cuts down haze, but is more important as a lens protector. A filter should remain on each lens all the time to protect the coated front element. Scratched filters are much cheaper to replace than lenses. A lens hood can also shield the lens as well as cut down flare on *contrejour* shots.

Bags

Now, where do you put all of this? I prefer to use a large, soft camera bag for most of my photographic gear. It can be taken as hand luggage on a plane and stowed under the seat. Purpose–made bags and pouches by Camera Care Systems, and Lowe Pro are excellent for adventurous photographers who are likely to find themselves hanging off a cliff face or swinging from the crow's nest. Expensive–looking cases are obvious targets for light–fingered locals. Don't rely on locks to keep out the thieves. If necessary, use a steel cable and padlock. Give the case distinguishing marks such as bright paint or coloured tape. You will then be able to identify it quickly and thieves will tend to avoid anything too conspicuous.

A watertight aluminium case will be useful for photography by the sea or in a desert as it will keep out the damp and dust. The sun is reflected by the silver, so the camera and films don't get too hot and you can use the case to stand or sit on. However, they are more awkward to work from when you are constantly 'dipping in' for something.

If you are carrying the minimum of photographic equipment, you may be able to 'wear' your camera bag in the form of a loose–fitting jacket with plenty of pockets —even in the sleeves. This protects your gear and enables you to be more agile —an important consideration if a camera bag is likely to be a hindrance.

Once you know what you are taking, insure it for its replacement value. Some household insurance policies do not cover photographic gear abroad and should be extended. Alternatively, shop around several insurance companies for the best deal, but watch out for small–print exemption clauses which may exclude travelling in private aircraft, scuba diving or mountaineering. Although it is only valid in common market countries, it can be worthwhile completing an EC carnet, obtainable from a VAT office at no charge. This itemises all your equipment, complete with serial numbers, and is stamped by British Customs when you leave. It can help if you have any difficulties with foreign Customs, and also backs up any insurance claim as well as eliminating the possibility of any potential problems when bringing your equipment back into Britain.

Keep a separate record of model and serial numbers, as this will help the police when items are lost or stolen. Reporting the loss will help when your claim is being processed.

By the time you actually set off, the bulk of the work will be done, though a special environment will call for special attention.

Extreme conditions

Cameras should not be left in direct sunlight when temperatures are high, as the glue holding the lens elements in place may melt and be knocked out of place.

When changing lenses or films, find a sheltered area. If it is sandy or dusty, keep the whole camera in a plastic bag. Cut a hole for the lens and secure the bag around the mount with a stiff elastic band. This can make composing and framing the picture a little difficult but may save the camera.

Extremely cold conditions will give as many problems as the heat. Batteries are affected by cold and lose power. Many modern cameras depend on batteries for through–the–lens (TTL) metering, or shutter and aperture adjustments.

On the more exposed ridges and summits, keep your camera inside your anorak (possibly inside a plastic bag) until you are ready to take a picture. Once you have decided what to photograph, act quickly; I have had cameras seize up on me after two or three shots taken on windswept ridges. But 10 to 15 minutes under my anorak and all was well again.

Where possible, try to keep cameras and film at a constant temperature. When changing films or lenses, find a sheltered spot and avoid getting snow inside the camera, or even breathing into it. Using a zoom lens reduces the need for continual lens changes.

If you are likely to experience really severe conditions, with temperatures below minus 32°C (minus 25°F) then you should take extra precautions. Older cameras should be winterised. This involves an oil change, using a lighter oil which is less viscous at low temperatures. But new cameras using modern lubricants should operate as smoothly in arctic as in temperate climates.

Tape over parts not in use, such as the flash sync socket and motordrive terminal. Store everything in hermetically–sealed metal cases and take plenty of gaffer tape to seal all hinges, cracks and joints against fine snow. Put cameras in airtight plastic bags with silica gel packets *before* coming indoors. Coming into the warm can be a traumatic time for your camera! Water vapour on cold metal and glass surfaces will condense rapidly and mist up with tiny water droplets. When you go out again, this water will freeze.

At the end of the day, wipe off all the moisture, and don't open the camera back or change the lens until the camera has warmed up because condensation inside the camera can give you even more problems.

Besides looking after your camera, don't forget to look after yourself! Keep warm so that *you* don't freeze up, and avoid touching frozen metal parts of the camera with bare skin —it will stick and can be extremely painful! Tape over exposed metal on the back of the camera and fit a large rubber eye-cup to the viewfinder.

Cleaning

Cleaning materials are essential for both the camera body and lenses. Lenses should be cleaned daily to prevent a build–up of dirt which will cause soft, muddy photographs as a result of flare and loss of definition. If you are using a UV filter, the same cleaning rules will apply to the filter as to the lens.

First remove the dust and loose dirt with a pocket 'Dust–Off' which emits a strong jet of inert gas. Be careful to hold the Dust–Off upright otherwise you will get vapour coming out which will leave a deposit on the lens or filter. Next, carefully remove any stubborn dirt with a small blower brush and finally use 'Dust–Off' once more. Don't forget to check the rear element of your lens too. If you get a fingerprint on the lens carefully wipe it off with lens tissue. Only buy tissues from a camera store. Lens tissues from opticians often contain silicones which can damage the coating on the lens. Breathing on the lens first can help, but be careful. In sub–zero temperatures, the resulting ice will be far worse than any fingerprints!

Lens tissues moistened with alcohol and packed in sealed sachets are very useful for removing any stubborn greasy smears. The new range of micro–fibre optical polishing cloths supplied by lens manufacturers like Pentax are an improvement on selvyt cloths.

It's not just the lens that should be cleaned regularly, so should the camera body —inside and out. Clean the outside with a stiff typewriter brush which removes even the most stubborn dirt and gets into all the nooks and crannies. Clean out any dirt that does escape into the camera with a blower brush, carefully avoiding the shutter which can be easily damaged. Using Dust–Off for the interior can do more harm than good by blasting dust into the camera mechanism. Look out for the tiny pieces of film which occasionally break off and get into the film, ruining whole rolls with deep scratches. I learnt my lesson in Nepal: a single hair from my brush got stuck in the film path and although I couldn't see it through the viewfinder, it appeared in varying degrees of focus in 10 rolls of film before it finally dislodged itself. That will not happen again!

FILM AND FILM CARE

by Dave Saunders

Film emulsion is sensitive material. Mistreat it, and it will complain by fogging or assuming a strange colour cast. All film deteriorates with time, and you will accelerate this process with careless handling.

Different films have different properties and some will complain more vehemently than others when subjected to adverse conditions. In general, 'amateur' film is more tolerant than 'professional' film, which is manufactured to more exacting standards. Amateur film is more stable and will last longer before processing. It is therefore the better choice for long trips, especially in hot climates where the deterioration process is speeded up.

Colour film

So how do you choose from the bewildering array of film types on the market? For our purposes, there are three broad categories of colour film:

1. Daylight reversal (transparency) films can be used with electronic flash, blue flashbulbs and, of course, in daylight
2. Tungsten reversal (transparency) for tungsten/artificial light
3. Colour negative (for prints) used for all lighting conditions and corrected during printing

Tungsten films can be corrected for daylight, and vice verse, by using filters. If you are hoping to sell any of your photographs, be warned that magazines, books and brochures prefer to reproduce from transparencies and many will not even consider colour prints. If necessary you can always have prints made from transparencies but you will lose definition with this process.

Kodachrome is usually first choice, and some publications and photo libraries insist on it. Kodachrome 25 is the sharpest and least grainy ordinary slide film available, but because it is slow (ISO 25) you forfeit flexibility. In anything other than bright conditions you may find you have to shoot at full aperture, which gives very little depth of field and/or a slow shutter speed, with the danger of camera shake. I start to feel nervous when using f/1.8 at 1/30th or 1/15th of a second.

Kodachrome 64 has similar sharpness and grain to Kodachrome 25, though it is a little more contrasty. The extra one and a half stops provided by the faster film (ISO 64) allows greater flexibility. To warm up skin tones and increase overall colour saturation, use 81 series filters with Kodachrome film. The density and strength of colour (saturation) will also increase if you slightly underexpose reversal film. Kodak now offers Kodachrome 200 Professional Film (ISO 200) which allows even more flexibility.

Ektachrome 64 has a more saturated colour than Kodachrome and is sharp with little grain. However, all Ektachrome films should be processed soon after exposure and are therefore not suitable for long journeys in remote areas. Kodachrome is more stable and should survive up to six months between being exposed and processed. Black and white film is even hardier and should last for a year.

Ektachrome 200 High Speed film is good for general use and allows the use of faster shutter speeds and/or smaller apertures. This enables you to use a longer focal length lens without the need for a tripod, a greater depth of field and to shoot in dull lighting conditions. The film can also be uprated by one or two stops, giving even greater versatility. Similarly, Ektachrome 400 can be pushed two stops, making it in effect ISO 1600, but this gives coarse grained results. The new Ektachrome P800/1600 Professional Film has speeds of ISO 800 or ISO 1600, depending on the way it is processed. Considering its speed, this film is impressively fine–grained with good image sharpness and colour reproduction.

Fuji film has improved markedly in recent years and **Fujichrome** 50, Fujichrome 100 and Fujichrome 400 are now serious competitors to Kodachrome. In fact, Fujichrome Velvia represents one of the most significant developments in colour transparency film. With a speed of ISO 50, a grain structure and definition comparable to Kodachrome 25, richly saturated colours and the major advantage of rapid E6 processing, it has become a widely used replacement for Kodachrome.

The new range of **Agfa** transparency and colour negative films show marked improvement in their grain quality and definition as well as displaying excellent neutrality and skin tones. Agfa 50 RS is particularly interesting. **3M's** Scotch Chrome 800/3200 which can be rated between these ISO numbers with adjusting processing times, is grainy, but impressively sharp considering its fast speed. Slow films are generally impractical for travel photography unless you can guarantee bright conditions and/or long exposure. When buying film, check if processing is included in the price. Kodachrome, for example, is process–paid only in certain countries. Also check the expiry date of the film, it should be stamped on the packet. If you have no choice but to buy an old film, you may get away with it. The expiry date has a built–in safety margin and out of date films are usually all right for some months after the date indicated.

It is best to take much more film than you anticipate using. You can always bring home unexposed film and use it later. When you are confronted by magnificent scenery or an interesting incident in the street, you don't want to have to scrimp. The chance may never come again. Running out of film abroad may, at best, be inconvenient. Prices may be highly inflated or your preferred film type may not be available. Kodachrome, Ektachrome, Fujichrome, and Agfachrome are fairly universal and usually available in places where film is on sale (but it is still unobtainable in far too many countries).

Black and white

If possible, take black and white film as well as colour. Some colour converts into mono satisfactorily if there is enough contrast, but there is inevitably a loss of quality, and to get the best quality can cost more per shot than a whole role of black and white film. Certain magazines stipulate that black and white prints must be derived from black and white originals.

Kodak T–Max 125 and Kodak T–Max 400 have finer grain and better control of contrast than Plus X and Tri X which they have replaced. Ilford's equivalent films —FP4 (ISO 125) and HP5 (ISO 400)— are also for general use and dull light conditions respectively. In each case, the faster films are grainier, though Ilford's new XP–1 400 is a finer grain fast film using C41 colour processing chemistry. Ilford's Pan F is a fine grain slow film (ISO 50). New Ilford black and white films include an improved version of their chromogenic black and white emulsion, now called XP2, and designed with the C41 process in mind. Delta 400, is a fast, fine–grained film which compares with Kodak's T Max 400. There is also a new, improved version of FP4 called FP4 plus.

Protection

It is a good idea to include the film on your insurance policy for camera equipment. But this normally only covers you for the price of replacement film. If you want them covered for the potential selling price of the pictures, premiums are exorbitant.

X–rays and fluorescent equipment can be a danger to unprocessed film. Some people are happy to pack spare film in the centre of their suitcase. Others will let the camera bag go through the X–ray machine at the airport. I always insist (pleasantly) on a hand search. I do this even if the machine claims to be safe for films because the bag is likely to pass through several airports and several X–ray machines. This can have a cumulative effect on the emulsion and fog the film. The faster the film (higher ISO rating) the more sensitive it will be to X–rays. A hand search may take a little longer, but I haven't missed a 'plane yet.

Lead–lined bags are available, but the protection they offer is nullified if the power of the X–ray machine is turned up so that the security people can see what's inside.

Some Eastern bloc countries will not let you take a camera as hand luggage, but they should not complain about film. In some countries you may be asked to pay import duty on unexposed film. It might be worth removing them from their packages so they appear to be exposed (for which no duty is payable).

Heat and humidity cause film to lose speed and contrast and colour film may show a magenta or green cast. If fungus grows on the film, there is very little you can do about it. But there are certain precautions you can take:

1. Leave film in its plastic container or foil wrapping until you need it as this improves protection. Colour film, in particular, should be carefully stored away from heat, humidity and extremes of cold or dryness.

2. Try to keep film at a constant temperature. In hot climates store it at or below 13°C (56°F) if possible. When you want to use the film, return it to room temperature slowly to avoid condensation inside the cassette. If you have access to a 'fridge, store the film there and take it out two hours before loading it.

Without a 'fridge, an airtight ice chest with freezer sachets may provide a possible solution. Packets of silica gel in an airtight container absorb moisture in humid climates. And insulated chamois bags are available to protect film from extremes of temperature. Exceptionally cold film becomes brittle and can crack or snap. Wind the film on gently to avoid tearing it, and take similar care when winding it back into the cassette. A motordrive will increase the risk of breaking the film. Wind off all exposed film so there is no danger of mistaking it for unexposed film and reusing it.

3. As a final note, unless you are abroad for several months, it is safer and cheaper to keep exposed film with you and have it developed when you return home. If you do opt to send film by post, mark the package 'Film Only: do not X-ray' and send it first class airmail. Some airmail post is x-rayed as a security measure, and it has been known for films to go missing, only to be sold later as unused film!

USEFUL EXTRAS IN THE CAMERA BAG

by Robert Holmes

A photographer's camera bag is not unlike some women's handbags. To the owner, an invaluable collection of essential paraphernalia; to everyone else, a miscellaneous hoard of junk.

I am always fascinated by what other photographers carry around with them and you may find it enlightening for me to share the secrets of my 'bag of junk.' The list is long, but has evolved over several years of hard travel and there is nothing that I could comfortably leave out.

Aside from photographic equipment and cleaning materials, I always carry a basic tool kit for simple repairs and equipment maintenance. It includes a set of **jeweller's screwdrivers** including a small **Phillips screwdriver** to tighten any screws that come loose. Periodically check the screws in both the camera body and lenses because the continual vibration you get from any method of transport can loosen screws surprisingly quickly. I once had a lens literally fall apart in a very remote part of Turkey because I failed to notice the first two screws fall out. A small pair of **jeweller's pliers** will help straighten out bent metal parts or tighten loose nuts.

Essential

Two universal accessories which no photographer should ever be without are a

Swiss army knife and a roll of **gaffer tape**. The Swiss army knife can be used for all the purposes it was made for plus a multitude of photographic applications which are limited only by your imagination. Gaffer tape is a two inch wide, tough, cloth–backed tape that can be used for anything from repairing torn trousers to holding a damaged camera together. A whole roll is pretty bulky, so I wind off as much as I think I will need around the **spanner that** I carry to tighten the legs of my tripod.

A **black felt–tip pen** that will write on any surface from film leaders to plastic bags and a **red felt-tip pen** to write processing instructions on blue and yellow Ektachrome cassettes supplement my ever–present **notebook**. However good you think your memory is, take notes. It's always surprising how people and places are forgotten or confused after a few weeks.

Within the last few years more and more **batteries** have found their way into my baggage. I never feel happy unless I have plenty of spares for cameras, motordrives, exposure meters and flash guns. What a headache modern technology is! I used to carry a couple of spare sets for my flash gun and that was that, but now I almost need a portable generator. When you buy batteries, get them from a shop with a fast turnover. They must be fresh. Date them as soon as you buy them and use them in date order. Lithium cells have a long shelf life and work in a wide range of temperatures but they may not have enough power output to cope with some of today's all–singing, all–dancing picture machines. If in doubt, ask your dealer.

Delving deeper

Down in the bottom of my bag are a few objects that apparently have no place in a photographer's armoury but are nevertheless irreplaceable when needed. A **small flash light** has saved my bacon on several occasions —particularly when there is not quite enough light left to read by and you still have to set your camera settings. It can also be useful to provide a source of light to focus on when the light is fading.

A tripod, light enough to travel, is prone to vibration so I carry a **string bag** that I can fill with rocks and hang under the tripod to steady it. It will also prevent vibration in long tele–photo lenses if I loop the handles of the bag over the lens (close to the camera body) to weigh it down on the tripod.

Weather rarely does what you want it to and on a cloudy, sunless day a **compass** will help you find out which direction the sun should be shining from. It will also tell you where to expect sunrise and sunset, the most photogenic times of day.

I often shoot architectural subjects with extreme wide–angle lenses and without a small **spirit level** I would not be able to keep my verticals vertical. It also keeps my horizons horizontal.

The **metal mirror** in my bag is not there because of any narcissistic tendencies. I occasionally use a camera on a tripod at its maximum height, and, although I can see through the view–finder, I cannot see to set the shutter and aperture. I can hold the mirror above the camera and check all the settings without leaving the ground. It also comes in handy for directing sunlight onto small objects and flowers in the shade.

I always used to worry about leaving equipment cases in hotel rooms so now I carry a **bicycle lock** with me. The long, thick cable type with a combination lock is the best and you can secure your camera cases to radiators or pipes or even the bed. It may not deter the determined thief but it will prevent any casual thefts.

So there it is. My innermost secrets revealed. Some of these things could help you be a better photographer but all of them will help you to be a more reliable one. By the way, there are two more important additions to the bag. However well you think you know your own equipment, when something goes wrong in the field, if you have your **camera manual** with you, at least you can check everything before writing the camera off. If you do have to write it off, keep the **international list of service agents** handy.

SELLING TRAVEL PHOTOGRAPHS

by John Douglas

A two–man canoe expedition up the Amazon... a one–man trek through Afghanistan... a full–scale assault on Everest involving a party of sixty... a student group studying the fauna and flora of a remote Pacific island.

Question: *What two features do these travellers have in common?*
Answer: *They will all be short of money and they'll all be taking at least one camera.*

The object of this article is to draw attention to the fact that these two features are not unrelated. Too few expeditions or independent travellers —whether they be on the grand scale or simply a student venture— are aware that the camera can make a substantial contribution to much–needed funds. When it is pointed out that a single picture may realise as much as £100, the hard–pressed traveller begins to see that he may be neglecting a very substantial source of revenue. While it is true that income from photography may not be received until some considerable time after arriving home, it can be used to pay off debts —or perhaps to finance the next excursion.

If photography is to pay, then advance planning is essential. Too often planning is no more than quick decisions regarding types of camera and the amount of film to be taken. Of course, these *are* essential questions and something might first be said about their relevance to potential markets.

Unless sponsorship and technical assistance are received, a movie camera is not worth taking. The production of a worthwhile expedition film or travelogue is such an expensive, specialised and time–consuming matter that it is best forgotten. In order to satisfy television and other markets, a film must approach near professional standards with all that implies in editing, cutting, dubbing, titling and so on, to say nothing of filming techniques. Of course, if a film unit from, for example, a regional TV network can be persuaded to send along a crew, then some of the profit, as well as a fine record of the traveller's achievements may accrue. But for the average trip this is unlikely, to say the least. By all means take along a good 8mm movie camera or video but don't think of it as a source of income.

Format and colour

With still photography, the position is quite different. It *is* worthwhile investing in a good range of equipment (or having on loan). It will probably be advisable to take perhaps as many as three cameras; two 35mm SLR's and a large format camera with an interchangeable back. If the latter is not available, then contrary to advice sometimes given, 35mm format is quite satisfactory for most markets (except some calendar, postcard and advertising outlets).

A common planning argument is the old 'black and white versus colour' controversy. It is *not* true that mono reproduction from colour is unacceptable. Expertly produced, a large proportion of colour shots will reproduce satisfactorily in black and white. However, conversion is more expensive and difficult than starting in the right medium, and there are far more markets for mono than for colour. Although prices paid for black and white will only be some 50 to 60 per cent of those for colour, it is the larger market that makes it essential to take both sorts of film. A good plan is to take one-third fast black and white film and two-thirds colour reversal film. For formats larger than 35mm, take colour only. The reason for this imbalance is that it is easier to improve a sub–standard black and white during processing. To all intents and purposes, the quality of a colour picture is fixed once the shutter closes.

It is advisable to keep to one type of film with which you are familiar. Different colour films may reproduce with contrasting colour quality and spoil the effect of an article illustrated with a sequence of colour pictures. Colour prints *will not* sell.

Outlets

Before leaving, the travel photographer should contact possible outlets for his work. Magazines generally pay well for illustrations, especially if accompanied by an article. You can approach UK markets such as *Traveller*, *Geographical* magazine, the colour supplements of the Sunday newspapers or *Amateur Photographer*. Although they may not be able to give a firm 'yes', their advice can be helpful. Specialist journals, assuming they are illustrated, may be approached if the trip is relevant, but it should be remembered that the smaller circulation of such journals yields a lower rate of payment. It can be worth advertising the journey in the hope of obtaining lucrative photographic commissions, but beware of copyright snags if the film is provided free.

Overseas magazines such as the American *National Geographic*, often pay exceptionally high rates but the market is tight. Much nearer home, local and national newspapers may take some pictures while the traveller is still abroad. If the picture editor is approached, he may accept some black and white pictures if they can be sent back through a UK agent. If the expedition is regionally based, local papers will usually be quite enthusiastic, but it is important to agree a reasonable fee beforehand, otherwise the payment may not cover the costs involved. Local papers may also agree to take an illustrated story on the return home, but again it is important to ensure that adequate payment will be made for the pictures published.

It is not the purpose of this article to discuss techniques of photography but before he or she leaves home, the photographer working with an expedition is well advised to seek guidance from others who have worked in the area. There can be problems with climate, customs and the like of which it is as well to be aware before starting out.

Finally, one potentially contentious point *must* be settled before the first picture is taken. This is the matter of copyright ownership and the income received from the sale of photographs. In law, copyright is vested in the owner of the film and *not* in the photographer. This can cause headaches if the traveller has had film given to him by a third party.

Universal appeal

Once the trip has started, the travel photographer should look for two sorts of photograph. Firstly, of course, there will be those which illustrate their travels, the changing scene, human and physical. But secondly, and so easily neglected, are those pictures which have a universal appeal irrespective of their location. Such shots as sunsets, children at play, brilliant displays of flowers and so on always have a market. It is important, too, not to miss opportunities that are offered en route to the main location in which the travel photographer is to operate. Don't pack away your film while travelling to your destination. Have the camera ready on the journey.

Not unnaturally, the question "What sells?" will be asked. There is no simple answer except to say that at some time or other almost any technically good photograph may have a market. (It is, however, assumed that the photographer is able to produce high quality pictures: there is never a market for the out–of–focus, under–exposed disaster.) Statements like, "The photograph that sells best is the one that no one else has" may not seem very helpful, yet this is the truth. It is no use building a collection which simply adds to an already saturated market. For example, a traveller passing through Agra will certainly visit the Taj Mahal —and photograph that splendid building. Yet the chances of selling such a photograph on the open market are dismal. It's all been done before, from every angle in every light and mood. Perhaps a picture of the monument illuminated by a thunderstorm might be unusual enough to find a buyer but the best that can reasonably be hoped for is that the photographer will hit on a new angle or perhaps a human interest picture with the Taj as background. On the other hand, a picture of village craftsmen at work might sell well, as will anything around which a story can be woven. Landscapes have a limited market but, given exceptional conditions of light, then a good scenic picture might reap high rewards in the calendar or advertising markets. The golden rule is to know the markets well enough to foresee needs. Sometimes the least obvious subjects are suddenly in demand.

Such was the case, for example, in 1976 during the raid on Entebbe Airport by Israeli forces. My own agency, Geoslides, was able to supply television with photographs of the old section of the airport and of the Kampala hospital just when they were needed. Yet who would expect a market for such subjects? Perhaps this is just another reason for carrying plenty of film. My own experience on my travels is that I am constantly looking around for subjects. Certainly it is no use sitting back waiting for something to appear in the viewfinder. It is wise not to ignore the obvious, everyday scenes —while I was preparing this article, Geoslides were asked for a photograph of a hailstorm in our Natal collection. Bad weather photographs sell well, so you should not always wait for brilliant sunshine.

Record keeping and processing

One most important but easily over–looked point is the matter of record keeping. In the conditions experienced by many travellers, this will not be easy, yet it cannot be emphasized too strongly that meticulous care must be taken to ensure that every picture is fully documented. It is true that certain photographs may be identified at a later date (macro-photography of plants, for example) but no shot should be taken without some recording of at least its subject and location. It is usually best to number the films in advance and to have an identification tag on the camera which will indicate the film being exposed. A notebook can also be prepared before the traveller leaves.

With the advertising market in mind, it is helpful to make sure that good photographs are taken which include the traveller's equipment. Less obviously, there is a market for photographs of proprietary brands of food, magazines, newspapers, items of clothing and equipment and so on in exotic and unusual settings.

If the traveller is to be away for a long time, it can be important to get some of the exposed film back home. There are dangers in this procedure because of the uncertainty of postal services, but provided some care is taken —perhaps with arrangements made through embassies— then there are advantages. Apart from the obvious problem of keeping exposed film in sub–optimum conditions, some preparatory work can be carried out by the traveller's agent. Of course, if the film is sent home, it is essential that labelling and recording are foolproof.

Serious selling

Once the travel photographer has returned home, the serious business of selling begins. Topicality is a selling point, so there is no excuse for taking even a few days off, no matter how exhausted you may feel. Processing the film is clearly the first task, followed by cataloguing and the reduction of sample black and white enlargements. No one is going to buy if the goods are badly presented, so it is worth making sure that a portfolio of high quality mono enlargements and colour transparencies is prepared with a really professional appearance. Put together a stock-list of all your photos (what countries and subjects, colour and black and white, and how many you have in each area) and circulate it around all the magazines and papers you can think of. As long as it is kept up to date, you should be able to sell one–offs for some way into the future.

The first market to tackle will be the local newspapers. Following up the advances made before you set out is very important, no matter how lukewarm the original response. It often *looks* more professional if there are both a writer and a photographer to produce a magazine article, but it should be made clear to editors that a separate fee is expected for text and illustrations. This is invariably better than a lump sum or space–payment.

A direct source of income from photography can be slide shows for which the audience is charged. These are relatively easy to organise but must be prepared with slides of maps and accompanying tape or live commentary. Incidentally, do not mix vertical and horizontal frames. It gives an untidy appearance to the show —even when the screen actually accommodates the verticals. The bigger the screen the better. If these shows are to have a wide audience, it may be necessary to put the organisation in the hands of an agent.

A photographic exhibition can provide helpful publicity but it will probably raise little or no income itself. Branch librarians are usually helpful in accommodating exhibitions and if these showings precede some other event like a lecture or slide show, they can be indirect money spinners. For an exhibition, great care should be taken in making the display as professional as possible. Again, the bigger the enlargements, the better. As far as photography is concerned, 'big is beautiful,' and it is worth investing in a few really giant enlargements.

Depending on the standing of the photographer, it can be a good plan to show some prints to the publicity department of the camera company or franchise agent whose equipment has been used, especially if you have made exclusive use of one company's products. The same may apply to the makers of the film that has been used.

If the traveller has not been too far off the beaten track, then travel firms may take photographs with which to illustrate brochures and posters. However, as with the calendar and postcard market, it must be pointed out that this is a specialist field, requiring not only particular sorts of photographs but pictures of a very high technical quality. This also applies to photographs used for advertising, although suggestions made earlier regarding pictures of proprietary brands leaves this door slightly wider than usual.

Whenever an original transparency or negative is sent to or left with a publisher or agent, a signature must be obtained for it, a value placed on it should it be lost or damaged (as much as £500 per original) and a record kept of its location.

Using an agency

Lastly, when the catalogue is complete, the travel photographer will wish to put the whole of his saleable photograph collection on the market. Now a decision must be reached on the thorny issue of whether or not to use an agency. Of course, direct sales would mean an almost 100 per cent profit, while the agency sales will probably net only 50 per cent of the reproduction rights fee. But, as so often happens, it is the enlargement of the market, the professional expertise and marketing facilities of the agency which are attractive. It is worth making enquiries of a number of agencies (see the *Writers' and Artists' Year Book*) and finding a company which offers the sort of terms and assistance that satisfy the travel photographer's requirements. It is usually preferable to deal with a company which does not expect to hold the collection but simply calls for pictures when needed. This allows much greater freedom to the copyright owner as well as being a check on what is happening in the market. Some agencies offer additional services to associate photographers in the way of help with the placing of literary as well as photographic material, and in the organization of lecture services.

It may even be better to contact an agency before leaving. For a small consultancy fee, a good agency may be able to advise on the sort of pictures which sell well and on the level of reproduction fees which should be charged. There is nothing more annoying than selling rights for £50 and then finding that the market would have stood £100. Many amateurs sell their pictures for too low a fee and others assume that there is a set price irrespective of the use to which the photographic material is put. In fact, the market for photographic reproduction is something of a jungle and it may be better to gain professional advice rather than get lost. The same applies to locating markets. It is almost impossible for the inexperienced amateur to identify likely markets for his work. There are thousands of possible outlets and a small fortune could be lost in trying to locate a buyer for a particular picture, no matter how high in quality.

An ambitious and skilled travel photographer should expect to make a substantial profit from his photography, providing an effort is made along the lines indicated. In the case of a specialised and well–publicised trip, it is not unknown for the whole of the cost of mounting the venture to be recouped from the sale of pictures. There are some simple points to remember: don't treat the camera as a toy; don't give the job of photographer to a non–specialist; don't put all those transparencies and negatives in the back of a drawer when you get home. As a money–spinner, the camera may be the most important piece of equipment the traveller carries.

THE TRAVELLING PAINTER

by Paul Millichip

"The ground reddish green–grey and apt to purple, the sea quite blue under the sun a warm vapour, from the sun blue relieving the shadow of the olive trees dark", the words of an observant traveller; the words, in fact, of the painter J M W Turner, writing a note in his sketch book during his first visit to Italy in 1819.

Like many travellers, painters make their journeys to experience a change of scene, perhaps to enjoy a warmer climate, to explore and to be strangers in a foreign land. However, unlike many travellers, painters go prepared and equipped to record their voyages, and the exotic and unexpected scenes they may encounter. Some will go armed with the materials to make finished paintings during their travels, others will take minimal equipment but make frequent and copious drawn and written notes, leading, perhaps, to paintings made when they return home —this was Turner's approach and that of many of his contemporaries.

Of course, not all travellers have the opportunity to acquire the skills of the professional painter but anyone with the inclination and the will can certainly enjoy the added dimension which drawing and painting can give to any voyage or visit. For many years s a painter and teacher, I have been introducing people to the pleasures of drawing and painting abroad, and I know that careful observation and persistence are the main needs of the travelling painter. The sure rewards are a heightened awareness and enjoyment of the traveller's surroundings —with the added bonus of a truly personal souvenir of the place visited.

There is no need for elaborate equipment. For a start, take a sketch book. A5 is large enough and will fit conveniently into a bag or pocket. Add two or three soft pencils, say 2B and 3B, a pencil sharpener, and perhaps a lightweight folding stool. I prefer an inflatable cushion which allows me to use any handy wall or rock as a seat. If it's a long time since you last did any drawing (10 or 20 years ago when you were at school) then start with a subject near to where you are sitting and draw just a part of it: the prow of a boat rather than the whole fishing fleet, the corner of that door rather than the entire street. Such fragments can be just as evocative of a place as can a whole panorama.

As you look at your chosen subject, check where the main source of light is shining from. Sunlight shining from behind and above you will flatten your subject and render it more difficult to draw, light coming from one side or another will show its form more clearly and there should be some interesting shadows. Shade these in, it will all add to the atmosphere.

Remember those notes of Turner's, and add some written reminders about colour. Add written notes on any other aspects of the scene which you can't draw: sounds, smells, encounters with people or animals. If you should decide to make a painting from your drawing when you get home, you may be glad of any information which helps you to evoke your feelings as you sat and drew. As I look through my sketch books and read my notes, I am reminded vividly of how it felt to be sitting and drawing in that village in Greece, that street in a Moroccan town or that coconut grove in India —how much more rewarding and exciting than a heap of mere holiday snaps!

Any traveller with a sketch book will find a constant source of interest —even on the most tedious journey. The long wait for the ferry, the delay spent in the airport departure lounges —these can become positive aspects of the journey, an opportunity to bring out the sketch book and record your travelling companions and their environment. Look at a row of people sitting and waiting for that flight, notice their variety of shapes, posture, costume. Try drawing a silhouette of the line of backs and heads and shoulders in the row of passengers seated just in front of you, noting that individual character depends not just on facial features but on the set of heads on shoulders, and on individual head shapes. Appreciate how your eye is gradually becoming 'tuned' as you persist and are increasingly aware of the look of the world around you.

As you become more confident of your ability to use a sketch book, through practice, trial and error, you may care to try using some colour in your book. I often carry a bundle of about eight coloured crayons in my painting–cum– voyage bag. By shading one colour over another I can produce quite a wide range of mixtures which help to give me extra information about the nature of colour and light in a particular location. Another possibility is to carry a tiny pocket watercolour box. Some of these have a built–in container for water and a little telescopic brush —hardly the thing for a grand broad statement in watercolour but certainly useful on the note–taking level.

Sooner or later, if you persist with your sketch book, you will begin to feel the need to work on a more ambitious scale. You are about to join that company of travellers who paint and for whom painting becomes a prime reason for travel. Easily spotted at airports and other departure points accompanied by various encumbrances such as easels, portfolios and folding stools and usually other painters, these are the voyagers who really enjoy their travel since they are always hopeful of returning bearing valued trophies: paintings which have captured something of the essence of their chosen venue. The sharp sunlight which threw that defined shadow on the wall, the reflection of a dinghy in harbour waters, the twist in the trunk of an olive tree, these are amongst the visual experiences distilled by the heightened perceptions of these fortunate travellers —on an auspicious day these experiences can be captured like some rare prey and perpetuated in paint.

Should you decide to take painting materials abroad with you, the golden rule to apply is to keep them simple. There is a vast and tempting range of papers, paints, brushes, palettes, crayons, etc, on the market. Be stringent in making your choice and remember that you have to pack and carry your choice. Whether you choose to work in watercolours, oil paints or pastels, you will need to have relative mobility once you have reached your destination. This is where simple lightweight equipment scores: six or seven well–chosen colours rather than a box–full, two or three brushes of various sizes including a large one, a palette or mixing plate, some painting boards for oil paints, some sheets of watercolour paper and a board to tape them to (rather than a book or block of paper), all of a size to fit easily into your case. In these days of plastic bottles, there is no need to bring heavy water containers for water–colourists. Oil painters should not bring turpentine since this is potentially inflammable en route.

Simplicity and lightness are the keys and your paintings should be all the better for it. As with drawings, the evocative glimpse rather than the grand view is likely to prove a good starting point when you look for a subject, remember though that your painting will probably keep you in one spot for longer than a drawing, so make a quick sketch book note so that you have some reference for the position of sun and shadows before these move round. This being the age of the motor car, it is worthwhile stationing yourself to paint away from the main streets since there is an unshakable law which says that the largest vehicle around will certainly park between you and your subject!

By now you may well have changed from a traveller who paints into a travelling painter; one for whom horizons and possibilities are limitless —whose best paintings are certainly the ones they haven't painted yet! If you wish for more information about this select company, you may care to read about it in my book *The Travelling Painter* (B T Batsford).

MOVIES ON THE MOVE

by Dominic Boland

Simple movie making is, like simple stills photography, is actually very straightforward, and once you have mastered the basic skills the potential is huge. Your resulting movies will soon start to look quite professional. Before looking at the essential techniques though, let's have a quick glance at the equipment hardware so that a decision can be made between the two movie-making formats —video or cine.

Video equipment

Using a video camera —a camcorder —is similar to using a 35 mm SLR camera, inasmuch that 'you see what you get' through the view finder. (There have been some direct vision camcorders but it's best to avoid these). You'll also find that most controls are pretty familiar. An autofocus zoom lens with manual override, plus auto exposure with some degree of manual control, are all pretty standard and of course there will be controls for the tape, which are essentially the same as for an audio tape recorder, Perhaps the biggest difference between video and stills, though, is that with video you can be up and taking pictures, and *viewing* them through the built-in monitor, within minutes of your first tentative steps. Getting the hang of using a camcorder is really simple, and as you are shooting on tape there are no processing costs and you can use the tape over and again.

When looking at camcorders, seek out one with a reasonably good zoom range, from wide angle to telephoto, but don't be to over-optimistic. A zoom range of 8mm to 64mm (equivalent to roughly 40-300mm on a 35mm SLR) will prove more than adequate for most purposes. Remember that ultra-long lenses will record every little jerk your body makes —even the thumping of your heart —making the picture jumpy. In any case, there are dozens of accessory lenses available top give extra wide or telephoto coverage, if needed at a later date.

Choice of video format these days is invariable 8mm. The tiny 8mm cassettes seem little different in appearance and size from an audio cassette but their dimensions belie their extraordinary performance, especially with the top quality Hi8 format. Small cassettes mean small camcorders ('palmcorders' for the really tiny models) which can often be no larger than the book you're holding.

Of course, there are other formats to choose from. There are camcorders that take the full format VHS cassette (the same as used in the video cassette recorder under a television), or its more diminutive cousin the VHS-C (compact) cassette. And there are the professional U-matic and S-Beta formats. But pro-formats are extremely expensive, VHS-C format appears to be losing out, by and large, to the alternative 8mm.

Whichever format you fancy, you'll be confronted by further choices, such as hi-fi stereo sound or the top quality Hi-band, Hi8, or S-VHS sub-formats, and there will be dozens of options such as 'shutter speeds' for slow–motion effects. More confusingly, there will be talk of digital results, from image stabilisation and zoom to character generation and effects. Sadly, video jargon has gone the way of hi-fi jargon and becomes quickly impenetrable, so when you reach this stage, talk to a knowledgeable friend or read up about the subject through the various camcorder magazines and books.

Just remember that video is extremely easy to use and, of course, simple to view. The built-in viewfinder allows you to immediately see what you have just recorded, or you can plug the camcorder straight into a TV set for full-colour, big screen replay —the camcorder itself acts as the replay machine. Some TV systems abroad may only play back a mono image, or a silent one, in which case simply rely on the built-in monitor.

The major drawback to video is the initial cost of the camcorder but if you aim for a fairly basic machine you can save up to half the cost of the latest models.

And remember too that hiring is a viable alternative to buying if you are looking at shooting only the occasional movie. Because the camcorder market is really booming there is also a lot of secondhand equipment available, but camcorders are electronic and electronics can go wrong, so you need to cover yourself. Until you really know what you're doing, only deal with reputable retailers if buying used equipment.

Cine is dead?

With video seeming so good why bother with cine? The traditional reasons are: superior image quality, higher reliability and specifications, and ease of editing. But times change and whilst film can still produce better quality than video tape, most people's movies are now viewed on television, not projection screens. (There's a huge growth of industry in converting cine to video for ease of viewing). Secondly, cine cameras, being still largely mechanical, can be more robust but camcorder manufacturers have realised the needs of travellers and produced models that are more rugged. Finally it used to be the case that if you wanted automatic fading, frame-by-frame exposure, ultra close-ups, time-lapse, sound-on-video and other such features, cine was the only real choice. Not any longer, as video can match it, and with video editing now so simple there is very little attraction to cine, especially when you add the inconvenience of actually viewing cine film.

Perhaps the final nails in the cine coffin, as far as most people are concerned, are the running costs. A cine film cartridge gives you roughly three minutes of single-use film which has to be reasonably carefully exposed and which can't be viewed until after processing. For the same price you can buy 30 minutes of top quality video tape that can be viewed straight after recording and which can be used over and over again.

However, cine is still top of the list for major documentaries and the professional 16mm form at is still alive and kicking —albeit horrendously expensive. The alternative, and the most popular format for the average traveller, has been Super-8mm film which comes in pre-loaded, drop-in cassettes. There is a small but active Super-8 following, but cine cameras are becoming increasingly few and far between, the best–known makes being imported from the USA.

Film and tape

Many video tapes, like audio tapes, are sourced from the same manufacturer. Avoid cheap extra–long play tapes. Simply keep to the best named, highest specification brand you can afford. Even so, tapes do wear out with use, particularly if you use freeze–frame when replaying. Tape wear varies with quality. A cheap tape will stretch, snap or show magnetic drop–out on the screen (white lines, dots, etc.) after 10 or so showings. Top quality tape will last for over 100 showings.

Video tapes play on one side only and can be extremely susceptible to damage. Keep them as you would film; heat, moisture and dust are the main enemies, but add to this magnetic fields created by loudspeakers and electric motors. Also, take care of the cassettes themselves. Believe it of not, they contain very advanced and delicate engineering and should be stored upright in their protective sleeves.

Super 8mm film is made in both sound and silent versions. Buy film in bulk for discount and make sure it's balanced for day light and not tungsten light. There's little choice in film sensitivities, ISO 40 being the most common, with ISO 160 also available.

Just like any 35mm transparency film, cine film exhibits the same variety of characteristics from make to make, the most popular brands being Kodak and Agfa. With the exception of Kodachrome, all other types of film incur processing charges. Processing quality varies too, so when you find a good lab stick with it.

Accessories and protection

Safety and precaution instructions come with your equipment. So read them before you use the gear. Video cameras in particular don't like extremes of heat (never point one at the sun) or cold, whilst direct contact with moisture usually results in complete failure. They can't cope with physical drops either and any sharp bang can ruin the 'tracking' of the camera sufficiently to turn it into a write–off. For this reason adequate insurance cover is a must. The key to using video? Be gentle! Field repairs aren't going to be easy as both cine and video equipment rely heavily on electronic components. Don't open up a video camera. Some delicate parts can be ruined even by moisture from your fingers. But a first aid kit comprising of a set of jeweller's screwdrivers, a "puffer brush", proper camera cleaning tissues (not cloths) and a roll of gaffer tape will see you through most emergencies.

As for accessories, the Boy Scout approach of 'essential, useful and luxurious' comes in here. Essential are spare batteries (at least two *spare* video battery packs —one to be recharging, one to have in the pocket when shooting), plenty of film or tape, and an intimate knowledge of the instruction book. It is also essential to check carefully the import controls of the countries you intend to visit well in advance. Video equipment, particularly, is often 'confiscated'. Several copies of receipts, equipment descriptions and serial numbers, to be stamped when entering and leaving countries, will be invaluable.

Useful would be a selection of ordinary photographic filters for special effects, a shoulder stock to help hold the camera steady against the body, and a customised bag to carry everything. As video batteries only last about 30 minutes between charges, another very useful accessory is a special vehicle battery adaptor cable. Many overland vehicles deliver higher than normal voltages, so you might need to have the lead regulated accordingly. Solar-powered recharges are also beginning to appear.

Sheer luxury would be a tripod, supplementary lighting, a separate audio tape recorder —and a sherpa.

Shooting skills

Whether you're intending eventually to use cine or video camera, your first step should be to borrow or hire a video camera so that you can begin learning the techniques without spending a fortune on film.

Golden rule number one is to read the instructions thoroughly. Also, plug into a television when you can. The larger screen is an enormous help.

Golden rule number two is to practice before you head off into the wilderness. This will teach you what works and what doesn't when it comes to using all those wonderful controls at your fingertips.

A good initial training run is to watch television with the sound turned down. See how the director chops and changes not only the scenes, but the angles and viewpoint. Even a 20 second commercial demonstrates the huge variety of techniques available. Don't try to pack it all in like this yourself or your audience will start suffering eye strain, but do experiment with the following ideas.

Calling the shots

You don't have a film crew with two or three cameras, so don't attempt the type of shoot they could. You're more like the documentary or news reporter. Remember that most of the time you won't have any control over the events you're capturing, so 'storyboarding,' where each shot is visualised as an illustration before the camera ever hits the action, won't be too useful. You'll learn far more from simply going and doing.

Where you do have control is over the type of shot you use and, especially with video, you should use 'in camera' editing. This just means thinking ahead and trying to put the shots in some logical sequence and not a random, haphazard series of takes that will need days of later editing.

There are four main types of shot you'll find useful. The *very long shot* (or vista shot) is used to give a sense of place. It will show the setting but isn't trying to capture action.

Next is the *long shot* which will move in tighter to show a specific point of interest. It could be a group of people, a row of houses, or a general view of an activity. A *medium shot* moves in closer still. Whereas the previous shot would include head and feet, the medium shot would only show the head and shoulders of an individual. It is commonly used during dialogue.

Finally, the *close-up* excludes most extra detail; a tightly cropped head shot, an isolated detail of architecture. Practice using these shots to relate a story. Start off with straightforward sequences, then be more adventurous. For instance, cutting from a long shot of a dangerous waterfall to a medium shot of a small boat drifting down a river, and then back to the waterfall again, implies that the boat is heading toward an accident —and all without a word being said.

Camera movements

The zoom action of the cine or video lens is a convenient way to change the focal length for each shot. You can of course zoom from one end of the lens range to the other whilst filming, but use this sparingly and gently. Constant zooming in and out of a scene ('tromboning') is very tiring for your audience.

Another very good technique to use is 'panning'. Start off with a couple of seconds of still scene, then slowly rotate your body at the hips keeping the camera perfectly horizontal. End the shot with another couple of seconds still shooting. A more interesting variation is to follow action whilst panning, ending on a descriptive shot. For instance, film a cyclist working his way down a busy street, past your position. Then let him ride out of shot (you stop panning) leaving the camera focused on a street sign that describes where you're filming.

'Tilting' is the same as panning but moving the camera vertically instead. Again the start and stop sequences allow the eye a resting place at either end of the shoot. Amateur films tend to include too much panning and tilting, known as 'hosepiping', so as with all techniques use them only when they're applicable.

The transition from one scene to another can be accomplished in a number of ways, the simplest being the 'cut'. Shoot a scene, stop the film or tape movement until you reach your new location, then shoot the next take. Sounds simple, and so it is. As often, the simplest things can be the most useful. Shooting a market scene with long and medium shots, you can add plenty of close–up cuts of hands, faces and other details to add activity and excitement. You can cut into a scene like this or cut out. Medium shots of camel drivers resting and eating can cut out to atmospheric vista shots of the desert with a shimmering heat haze.

If the cut technique is too short and sharp, another transitional device is the fade. Not all cameras allow this, but the idea is to slowly darken (or indeed lighten) the scene until only a blank screen is left. The tape or film is then paused until the opening sequence of the next shot when the new scene re–emerges from a fade. Why not mix cutting and fading? Try fading out from a tranquil vista shot then cut dramatically into a noisy, bustling close–up.

As you can see, there's enormous control available to you. Add to these basics other techniques such as using filters, creative exposure control, 'tracking' shots where the camera keeps alongside the subject as it moves, mixing still and moving pictures, and the exciting possibilities of video and cine seem endless. Do exercise care and caution though. Good camera technique shouldn't really be noticed —unless you have an audience of cameramen you're trying to impress!

Editing

The final act before you reveal your masterpiece to the world lies in editing, and it's arguably the most important single part of the movie–making process.

Although expensive, it is the film itself that in the past has been the major advantage that cine has had over video. Film can be easily edited using an inexpensive cutting tool and some tape or cement to splice it back together again in the chosen sequence. It is quite common to have a duplicate copy of the original made, and this is then edited first, with the final edit then being applied to the original. That way the original doesn't run the risk of becoming scratched, no matter how many times the edited pieces are reshuffled. Another advantage of film is that the whole lengths can be scanned very quickly to find a particular frame, not so convenient to do with video which often had to be copied in 'real time'.

A few years ago editing amateur video was fraught with problems. For a start, the tape itself couldn't be cut and pasted like cine because the electronic signal was laid down on the tape in a diagonal pattern, with the picture and sound signals often being physically apart. The best method, copying the original signal using an editing suite, was very expensive commercially and few parts of the country had editing facilities for the public to use. Instead, video makers resorted to the time consuming approach of having to physically wind and rewind the images between two tape machines, laying down out-of-sequence sections of the original onto a new tape. Fuzzy electronics 'joins' were common.

Today, thanks to the advances in electronics, home editing suites which can lift the signal from the original tape, store it and place it back accurately onto a copy with almost no loss of quality are not only available but also comparatively cheap. And the massive boom in interest with video means that there are clubs and societies which allow very sophisticated equipment to be shared amongst members. Video editing is one of the growth areas so prices will eventually fall whilst specifications, like the new true digital systems, will continue to arrive.

Whether its video or cine that you are editing you will find that a stopwatch and note pad are going to be used a great deal. Don't be too ambitious at the beginning, stick to a plan of action and be methodical. Just try to get your movies into a reasonable, understandable sequence that tell some sort of story. You will quickly realise that editing is made much simpler when you have developed a good shooting technique. If you start off with the highest quality images then the finished results will be that much better, so make sure that your cine or video camera is kept clean, that you use the best film and tapes that you can afford and pay special attention to focusing

You will quickly learn how even short sequences can be used to great effect when editing, even when relating fairly complicated storylines. You'll also learn how sound can be edited just as much as the picture, either in-camera when you are shooting or later when assembling the finals sequences.

No matter which medium you decide to use, shooting moving pictures is a fascinating, highly enjoyable and ultimately addictive way of recording the world through which you travel. Don't be put off by the apparent technical nature of shooting movies. The end result will always spark off the memories, and your journeys will never be forgotten.

TRAVEL WRITING FOR BEGINNERS

by Sarah Gorman

The profession of travel writer seems to excite the imagination of hordes of would-be authors, judging by the quantity of unsolicited manuscripts which land heavy —and largely unwelcome— on travel editors' desks. Is it because it combines the perceived glamour of travel and journalism, or is it (for those who haven't quite got the stomach for live ammunition) simply the next best thing to being a foreign correspondent?

Whatever the motivation, there's no reason for anyone not to try their hand at a spot of travel writing. After all, most of us born in the western world within the past 50 years are reasonably experienced travellers, and all of us, in some degree or other, have been inspired/educated/horrified/delighted by our encounters overseas —there's certainly no shortage of experiences to share. You may choose to keep a diary of your trip, and you may write a piece for your Parish magazine or a copy–starved features page on the local paper. But with all due respect to these more parochial publications, the journey between this level of 'journalism' and seeing yourself in print in one of the Sunday nationals is as long and as arduous as any of your own recent voyages of discovery, and the chances are that most of you reading this article will not have what it takes to finish the journey.

Sadly, travel editors do not often have the time or the heart to tell would–be contributors that they'd be "better off taking up gardening" (as one manuscript–weary editor confided). An unbroken stream of impersonal rejection letters is usually enough to discourage most embryonic Bruce Chatwins, but there are those who persevere —either through a justified belief in their their own talent or a staggering oblivion to their lack of it.

If you are one of the former (the latter, please seek help or an honest editor with time on his hands) you will need to develop a very thick skin, assuming that you have not done so already. As one freelance travel writer of many years' standing puts it: "If you are a good writer and if despite all the discouraging replies, you still persist, then you are probably the right person." If you have given up the proverbial day job in order to devote all your time to travelling and getting established within the field, you will invariably need a sympathetic bank manager —and possibly a degree in marketing. Selling yourself and your talent is an integral feature of life in the freelance lane, and as the freelancer quoted above points out "You do have to be very pushy. I hate selling pieces and I haven't yet met anyone who enjoys it."

So not only will you find travel writing a difficult field to break into, you may also discover that the lifestyle involves financial and personal sacrifices which are equally difficult —however great your talent. Yes, there are those romantic tales of amateur writers making their first submission to the *Daily Telegraph* and being welcomed with open arms. It does happen (occasionally) but not only is this the delighted amateur's *first* submission, it will more than likely be his only successful submission. Leaving aside the Colin Thubrons and Jan Morrises of the travel writing world, there are probably just a handful of travel writers who appear regularly in the travel pages of the national papers. In fact the current recession has seen a trend towards newspapers insisting that staff writers take up offers of press trips so saving the paper its contributors' costs.

The right stuff

Now that we've established that it is largely the talented (surprisingly, there are veteran exceptions) and the persistent who succeed, perhaps it wouldn't be too dangerous to try and define what makes a 'talented' travel writer. It is safe to say that what it is not is someone who belongs to the "what I did on my holidays" school of writing —a travel writer who boasts more 'I's than a hospital cornea unit. A rambling, unstructured piece is equally unwelcome, as is a fondness for superlatives (those with an affection for 'wonderful', 'magnificent' , 'superb', etc., should join Adjectivals Anonymous before making another submission). The other side of this unbankable coin is the rather dry, flat piece which leaves the reader yawning after the first few paragraphs. An experienced editor can usually get an idea of whether an article is 'possible' or 'impossible' from the first sentence, so bear this in mind when you are constructing your opening paragraph —it may be the only paragraph that is read. Articles that have clearly been 'cribbed' from guidebooks and which offer no fresh insight into a destination or event, also pass too frequently through a travel editor's in–tray, while material that displays no sign of research, historical or otherwise, will be very quickly rejected.

Originality of observation and expression are all. Michael Thompson–Noel, Travel Editor of the *Financial Times*, puts it succinctly: "Whether the destination is humdrum or exotic, it is the quality of the observation which counts." Such qualities are difficult to stage manage —either you've got the 'eye' for fresh observation or you haven't. Good journalistic training (that well worn path through provincial newspapers) will help disguise this lack to a point, but an ability to avoid cliché and to invoke a more than interesting picture of your chosen destination will depend largely on your command of vocabulary and, ultimately, your personality.

Preparing for the market

All the major national newspapers in the UK run regular travel pages (usually in the weekend supplements) while the vast majority of consumer magazines offer travel news and advice, or some kind of destination report. However, the number of specialist travel titles is limited. *Traveller* (first published by WEXAS in 1970) is probably the only surviving specialist UK title which features pure 'travel' as opposed to 'holiday' features. *Geographical* and *World* magazines offer some scope for travel pieces with an environmental 'angle', while the north American and Far Eastern markets boast a number of specialist travel titles (see Directory for listing).

One thing all these publications have in common is an excess of unused travel articles. Some of them will be excellent pieces which have been 'shelved' as emergency fillers or as 'unsuitable in the current political climate' (you may have noticed a distinct lack of feature material on the Middle East during the Gulf crisis). Other articles will be borderline cases which an editor will hang on to until something better comes along (it generally does). And then of course there will be the untried writers' material, freshly packed in large brown envelopes, full of expectation and eager to jump the queue.

If you are lucky, some publications may offer advice on how to get to the head of this apparently endless line, and *Traveller*, rather unusually, produces written 'guidelines' for contributors. However, your best preparation is simply to study the style and idiosyncrasies of the title you are targeting. And as a lady on *The Independent* features desk rather frostily put it, offering general guidelines to would–be contributors "is not our job." It is a buyer's market and the last thing a travel editor has time to do is wet–nurse you through stylistic and procedural requirements. Equally, he or she will be totally unsympathetic, and probably rather angry about wasting time on submitted material which is inappropriate — so do your homework first or you may spoil your chances for any future submissions. Another habit of greenhorn contributors which alternately amuses and invokes contempt is the phrase 'First British Serial Rights' written rather pompously on the title page of a submission. Unless you are Colin Thubron and plan to syndicate your material worldwide, 'FBSR' is something of a moot point.

Making a submission

It is highly unlikely that an editor will commission you to write a piece unless you have already been published —not quite Catch–22, but almost. Therefore your first unsolicited submission is all–important (if an editor has rejected you once because he didn't like your style, he will probably look upon a second submission with some scepticism —you couldn't come up with the goods first time around so why should your next piece be any different?) Leaving aside all issues of style and ability, double–spaced, cleanly typed/word processed copy is vital. Handwritten copy is *unacceptable* (although surprisingly the odd manuscript does still slip through), and if you want to ensure your material is returned, enclose a self–addressed, stamped envelope.

The length of the piece will depend entirely on the requirements of your chosen market but as a rule of thumb, anything more than 2000 words is too long, and under 300 in danger of being terminally brief. If you are not sure, a quick call to the editor might get you an informative response. You may also like to check in advance whether or not your planned destination will be welcome or if 'yet another feature' on Agra and the Taj Mahal has really had its day —at least for the next six months. Bear in mind that destinations can go through phases of being 'done to death' on the travel pages (usually for reasons of fashion) and that some publications will have a policy of not repeating coverage of destinations within a certain period. You may also find that some regions are out of bounds. *Traveller*, for example, rarely features material on western Europe so a piece on the delights of the Cornish coastline, however original, will get short shrift.

The quickest way to find out if a travel editor is interested in your proposed destination is a 'phone call. Don't waffle on about what a wonderful trip you had, and don't treat the call like a travel writer's help line. Remember the golden rule, it is a buyer's market and anything in your behaviour which will anger, irritate or simply waste the travel editor's time will do you no favours whatsoever.

A letter detailing proposals for a selection of features is an alternative, but you will probably have to wait longer for a reply (if you get any reply at all). Make sure your letter is correctly addressed to the travel editor, and avoid over familiar forms of address (most editors will not be impressed by letters addressed using either their first name, or that of their predecessor). A response of "yes, I would be interested to see something on hill walking in Tanzania" is not a signed and sealed contract to print whatever you submit. All the editor is telling you is that if your writing is up to scratch, and there happens to be an appropriate slot sometime in the future, yes, he may think about using your piece. This is the extent of his commitment so don't, as some rather naive contributors have been wont to do, assume that this is a definite commission. As already mentioned, editors only commission established writers whose material they know and like, and if you are reading this, it is unlikely to be you —yet!

Your next best move, once you have submitted the piece, is to forget about it. Don't badger the editor with 'phone calls or expect him to have read your article within a week or even four weeks of having received it. Travel editors, as has already been tirelessly pointed out, are inundated with manuscripts and don't need to be reminded that they haven't had a chance to read them all. If you would like an acknowledgement that your material has arrived safely, enclose a self–addressed, stamped postcard which can then be sent to you with little effort on the part of the editor or his staff. If you have had no reply within a period of three months, a letter requesting some kind of decision or response is reasonable, and, perhaps at a later date (deliberately indeterminate because a lot depends on the circumstances of your submission), a 'phone call to find out what's happening. It is at this stage that you must play a delicate balancing act between being firm about expecting a reply, and not pushing the editor so far that he says to hell with it and sends your piece to the post room as soon as he has put the phone down to an irate call from you. One thing you can be reasonably happy about, if the editor still has your piece after six months (yes, it can take that long for a decision) at least he hasn't yet said no!

You might like to submit your article to several publications but be careful about playing one off against the other, and if your material has come from a press trip, make sure that your fellow travelling journalists aren't selling a similar story to a competing publication. Two publications coming out with the similar story by different (or heaven forbid the same) journalist(s) does not a happy travel editor make.

Practical tips on the job

Although research is important, don't read too many guidebooks or you may find yourself, subconsciously (or otherwise) regurgitating the insight of others. Make a trip your own voyage of discovery. Talk to native inhabitants wherever possible (useful background and often the source of enlightening anecdote) and use your powers of observation to the fullest. If you can accompany your piece with a selection of photographs (colour transparencies for magazines and black and white for newspapers) so much the better, and you may find that using a camera will give you a fresh insight into your destination —alternatively don't spend your trip thinking like a travel photographer or you will miss other essential ingredients for a good travel piece.

Most professional travel writers make notes during their travels, and unless you have a photographic memory, a reporter's notebook is an important accessory. If you need to carry out a little research while you are away, contact the British Council or British Embassy/Consulate (if you are in a big city) for advice on libraries, sources of information, and so on. If you are travelling for a long period of time and want to submit material on the hoof, many branches of international hotel chains now offer business centres with secretarial and international communications facilities. Some destinations may have been the subject of international media coverage in recent years in which case you may like to check recent newspaper cuttings at the Colindale library (via the British library, tel: 081–200 5515).

If you have a particular theme in mind, or plan to tackle regional issues in a travel piece, you might try sending out a few letters of introduction to suitable contacts or interviewees before you go. The embassy or consulate of your intended destination may be able to help and *NewsGuides* (World Division Australia, I Vision Drive, Burwood East 3151, Victoria, Australia, tel: (613) 287 2233) who publish a series of country guides with journalists in mind, are an excellent source for contacts.

You can of course contact the editor before you go, warning him about your intended submissions. This may help him remember you when your piece on Timbuktu arrives along with all the other hopeful articles on a grey Monday morning, but previous contact is no guarantee that he will be more interested in your work than anyone else's.

Making a career of it

If you become so enamoured with travel writing that you plan to make it a permanent career, bear in mind the need for a *very* understanding bank manager. Unless you are of independent means, or have been organized enough to have saved for the possibility of lasting for at least six months without earning a penny, you will have to consider all your submissions as potential investments —even if they are accepted they are unlikely to pay dividends for many moons (getting money out of some newspapers and magazines is notoriously difficult). The most successful freelance journalists tend to be those who have been employed within their particular field of specialization and who have already established a career's worth of contacts willing to buy work from them. This is less likely in the travel writing business since most travel editors operate a one man show and are less likely to give up the combined advantages of a salaried position and travel perks. Consequently most travel writers are, and always will be freelance.

Contacts, nevertheless, are very important. If you can build up a relationship with any editors who like your work and trust you to deliver the copy when you say you will, you are in a strong position for laying the foundations of a freelance career. A regular outlet in a favoured publication is ideal but don't expect to rely on this to pay the electricity bills. You may need to diversify and above all, you must learn to get as many angles out of one trip as is humanly possible —without affecting the quality of your work. You may turn your nose up at trade journals and anything that is not pure 'travel' but this could be your only means of funding the time to do more personal, idiosyncratic pieces. "People come into the profession with this illusion that they are going to write delightful prose about interesting, exotic places," says one freelancer, "but in practice they are expected to produce more technical or 'holiday' stuff." If your idea of travel writing does not include a tour of the Manila Hilton's penthouse suite or a dawn visit to Jakarta's newest international conference centre, then strike all ideas of ever taking a press trip. If you become established on the circuit and you are invited on a press junket, you will probably discover that you and your hosts have very different ideas about what does and doesn't make for an interesting tour. You will also have to learn to find your own saleable angles on a trip where seven or eight other journalists are eagerly taking notes beside you. Also beware travel companies, tourist boards, etc., who will only offer you a trip in return for restrictions on what, when and where you publish material gleaned from a press trip, and consider that some publications including *The Independent* and The *New York Times* will not accept articles resulting from press trips or any other kind of 'freebie'.

Specializing in a particular continent or region may help ensure you regular work as an acknowledged expert, and if you are very familiar with a particular destination, guide book writing is a reliable, if occasionally tedious, means of plugging the commission gaps. Travel narratives are another possibility but they usually involve tales of travellers who have spent a good deal of time overseas, and unless you plan to uproot are not much use. The British Guild of Travel Writers, an association for established freelance travel writers could prove a useful source of advice and information, and will probably get you on the mailing list for just about every travel public relations company in the UK. Wading through sackfuls of press releases is probably not the sort of thing you had in mind when dreaming about purple prose among the hill tribes of Chaing Mai. ■

AND FINALLY...
Chapter 16

WHITHER THE BRITISH TRAVEL INDUSTRY?

by Roger Bray

A BRIEF encounter in Berlin vividly illustrated one of the fundamental dilemmas of tourism.

Andris Berkis is a young journalist working on Latvia's first travel trade newspaper. I had first met him a month or so earlier, in the run-down but beautiful Latvian capital of Riga. We had walked through the old city in search of a bar noisy with local drinkers.

The temperature was well below freezing, yet a man with a trumpet was busking on the snow–ridged pavement outside the Russian Theatre. It was so cold you wondered how his fingers could find the valves.

We found a bar but it was expensive and empty. It was barely 10pm, but at those prices the only people who can afford to paint the town are the few new rich and the criminal classes. Outside our hotel police were searching cars, perhaps in pursuit of stolen goods, more likely for guns to be used in robberies.

Now Andris had come to the vast International Tourism Exchange at Berlin's sprawling exhibition centre. Anyone still in doubt about the importance of travel among the world's biggest industries should spend a day there. From the familiar such as Majorca, to the obscure, such as Burkina Faso, it is hard to find a destination which is not represented here. Iraq remains one of the few absentees.

Miami had wheeled out its big guns to counter the damaging impact of violent crime against tourists which has seen bookings to Florida from Britain slump by some 20 per cent. At the end of their European mission they would jet home in comfort, to be met at the airport by limousines.

How was Andris getting back, I wondered? By coach, he said. And how long would that take? Maybe one day, maybe one and half days. It all depended on how long they were held up at the borders.

The dilemma it underlined is this: there is still plenty of room for tourism to expand but too many of the countries with space lack the resources to exploit. Although the Baltic states will probably never rank with the world's major holiday destinations, tourism there has the potential to become a nice little earner. There are good beaches. There is uncluttered countryside with excellent cross country skiing. Yet it will be years before the industry earns even a significant fraction of the revenue which Florida has lost through muggings and murder.

Some Western governments have already grasped the point that it is in their own interests to hasten the process. The European Union has funds to aid tourism development in non member countries. For example, Latvia itself has received help from the Irish Tourist Board to set up a bed and breakfast chain. But the argument needs to be hammered home again and again until this wisdom becomes conventional.

It is already conventional wisdom that international tourism is beginning to eat its own babies. In other words that excess of it is destroying the very things people travel to see and experience. More and more high–rise hotels cast long shadows over once deserted beaches. Cathedrals which were once places of tranquil contemplation are jammed with sightseers. Two minutes with a Velazquez is all you get. Move along please. There are more shuffling feet behind.

The authorities in Prague have seen such a massive invasion of visitors since the velvet revolution that they have considered charging people to enter the old heart of the city.

The Austrian resort of Lech will turn skiers away if more cars than it can handle come pouring over the Flexen Pass.

Many airports are close to saturation. BAA is ready to spend close to £1 billion on a fifth passengers' terminal at London's Heathrow. American Airlines chairman Robert Crandall says take-off and landing slots there are so precious he is prepared to pay some £5 million apiece for them.

Aviation authorities are spending enormous sums to expand the capability of air traffic control. The Civil Aviation Authority alone is investing £750 million to effectively increase airspace capacity in south-east England by one third.

Recognising that in densely populated countries it will be difficult, not to say impossible, to build new runways, major aircraft manufacturers are discussing with the airlines means of getting more out of existing ones —by developing a new generation of ultra-large aircraft which will carry more travellers in one go —perhaps as many as 1,000 passengers in later versions.

The impression is of imminent Apocalypse. If not now then very shortly. It was fuelled recently by an Economist Intelligence Unit report which predicted that, by the turn of the century, total tourism to the Mediterranean area would have roughly doubled in a decade, from 115 million to 200 million. Picture, in your mind's eye, a package beach on the Costa del Sol in July. Where on earth to put them all?

The Apocalyptic vision has not been dimmed by a perception that independent travel is increasing rapidly at the expense of package holidays, with the result that a new breed of tourist is reaching corners previously known only to the environmentally correct.

The logical extension of all this is enormous pressure on land and infrastructure —and consequently on prices. The palmy days of cheap travel will vanish unless there is a concerted international effort to tackle the problem.

It is vital that they should not vanish. I have always believed that tourism is more powerful as a force for education and peace than for reinforced prejudice and ignorance. Countries sending each other tourists are less likely to fight each other. There are always exceptions. Not even tourism was able to prevent the crumbling cement that bound the former Balkan states together as Yugoslavia.

But consider North Korea. If Kim Il Sung's fastness had not remained so isolated, would the world have faced such a crisis over its suspected nuclear capability? I doubt it.

The perception that the world is being overrun by tourists, that the day of the cut-price flight is done, is however, greatly exaggerated. There is plenty of world left. There are even beaches where you can still be alone.

It came home to me most forcibly on a recent visit to West Australia. We had parked our campervan for the night at Pardoo Station, a cattle spread off the highway from Port Hedland to the remote pearl fishing port turned sunshine holiday resort of Broome. In the morning we walked across the scrub to the ocean. Kangaroos leaped away from us as we crossed the dunes. We were roughly at the southern end of a stretch of shoreline known as Eighty Mile Beach. It seemed you could walk that far and never encounter another human.

Not long afterwards we were sitting by a camp fire at the entrance to Windjana Gorge in the Kimberely, the last frontier of the same world, as they like to call it, a rough expanse of country which was, until recently, inaccessible to most travellers. We had put up nylon tents in blazing heat with little shade, plagued by the flies that crawl into your eyes for moisture and cluster on your back like ripe blackberries. We had cooked over the flames, cracked beer and were feeling pretty hard bitten.

This is nothing, snorted a fellow camper at the fireside. this is not real wilderness. Now in Zambia .... Some people are never satisfied. And yet, unwittingly, she had struck a point. Everyone's tolerance of other tourists is different.

Most people would agree that parts of Kenya's Masai Mara game park have been turned into something uncomfortably close to a safari park by convoys of camera-happy tourists in open-topped Land Rovers.

For the biggest sector of the holiday market, however, even the Mara would seem a place of awesome emptiness.

The conventional sun, sea and sand holiday remains by far the most popular, representing around half those taken by the British, for example. Independent travel *has* grown at the expense of the package, but the change is happening much more slowly than many would have you believe.

It is true that small tour operators have prized open niches which might not have afforded them a living even ten years ago, successfully marketing anything from holiday homes in Asturias to cycling in Cuba. It is also true that more people have become confident about eating out, which is one reason why self-catering holidays have increased in popularity while hotel packages have declined.

But many of those switching to independent holidays have simply de-packaged the package. They are going to the same resorts but organising their own flights and car hire. Throw in the fact that the biggest destination for independent holidaymakers is France (around 36 per cent), which attracts a very particular market, and that the fastest growing in the US, where there is no real language barrier, and the premise that the British are suddenly striking out in numbers for the unknown looks somewhat shaky.

There is still time then, for countries not yet on the tourist milk run to ensure that they take due account of past mistakes their development is sensitively planned.

India could prove an early test bed. Though it is still haunted by extreme poverty it also has a burgeoning middle class and is experiencing a boom in investment. Tourism, whose value as a job creator is well documented, will inevitably by the target for a significant slice of that investment. Airlines and railways have been opened to private participation. Plans to launch eight new tourist trains in the grand manner of the existing Palace on Wheels are just one symptom of this change.

Government and developers must take care not to damage India's fundamental attraction, however. It is a profoundly seductive place whose allure depends on diversity, the mystery and some would say impenetrability, of its cultures. Harm them and you diminish the reason for going.

What right have we, the rich nations, to preach to the needy how they should earn their hard currency?

Happily for the future of diplomacy there is probably little need to lecture. There is encouraging evidence that governments with emerging tourist industries have already identified the pitfalls.

This is partly due to the belated efforts of established companies in developed countries which have also taken serious account of the threat to their continued success. British Airways Tourism for Tomorrow Awards, for example, have helped stimulate worldwide interest. They have rewarded initiatives as diverse as the deployment of a fleet of small electric buses to combat pollution from carbon emissions in the Alps to a drive by South Africa's Londolozi game park to ensure that tourism involves and benefits local villagers.

Beside bellyaching to governments that travel should not be regarded as a soft target for the continual imposition of new taxes, the World Travel and Tourism Council. A forum for some of the industry's most powerful and influential figures, has also launched a major environmental study.

On the other side Albania, for example, which is now attempting to shake off the years of introspection and has considerable potential as a beach holiday destination, has sought the advice of outside environmentalists in its efforts to develop a thriving tourist business.

The temptations will remain. The industry's history is littered with pious intentions. The world's coastlines are scarred with the results of broken promises.

But there is hope. There is at last general awareness, for instance, the march of the all-inclusive resort across the Caribbean has isolated holidaymakers in hermetically sealed enclaves, blindfolded them to the life of the islands and stunted development of small, tourist-related businesses such as restaurants and craft shops.

And there is time. The greying of Europe will lift some of the urgency from coastal development. Older travellers have gentler, less intrusive demands.

I have argued that tourism can be a force of peace between nations but sadly, as recent incident in Turkey and Egypt have again shown, it will remain a target for terrorism. The best hope is that through sympathetic development inspiring involvement rather than envy, it will weaken the economic justification for such violence.

CUSTOMS IN THE 1990s

by John Rose and David Shenkin

Contrary to popular belief, customs officers do accept that most travellers are ordinary citizens going about their legitimate business and are *not* smugglers. So why is it that most travellers claim to feel nervous whenever they approach Customs, and actually feel guilty when negotiating a Green Channel?

It may be the uncertainty about the extent of allowances and precisely what is and is not permissible. The lists in the Directory should help. It may also be apprehension about the possibility of being singled out for checking —having bags emptied and even being personally searched. The modern Customs service recognizes these pressures and considerable effort is made to make checks highly selective and well targeted at areas of highest risk so that the vast majority of travellers are not inconvenienced.

In the 1990s, Customs face a dramatically changing scenario, as trade barriers are dismantled, fiscal and physical frontiers are removed, journey times are reduced and ever–increasing traffic flows demand fast and efficient customs clearance.

A balance must be struck between the often conflicting demands of the free movement of travellers while at the same time protecting society. But from what? Serious threats are posed by the considerable number of prohibited and restricted items that may be either unwittingly carried by the uninformed traveller, or smuggled by and on behalf of the unscrupulous. Customs, Consulates and Ministries can give advice, often in the form of leaflets, about what can and cannot be imported. Examples which may be encountered by any traveller include the following:

Plant and animal health risks: Commercial importations are carefully controlled to prevent the spread of pests and disease, but the thoughtless importation could quickly introduce an epidemic. Rabies is the most publicized threat but there are many more, including bugs and grubs which could devastate crops in a new environment. A health certificate, licence and/or quarantine is necessary for many plants and animals, and all live birds.

Endangered species: Few people bring home a wild animal from their travels. But many buy articles made from them (a skin handbag and shoes, an ivory ornament) without knowing that the species is in danger of extinction. Even trade in tourist souvenirs can threaten the most endangered species. In many countries it is illegal to cut or pick wild plants and flowers for the same reasons. They may be freely available and on sale in the country you are visiting but if you do not get a permit before you import them they are likely to be seized.

Obscene and indecent material: Changing social and cultural attitudes make this a sensitive area so check first and you will not be embarrassed.

Firearms, weapons, explosives, gas canisters: Travellers face stringent security checks before the start of their journey in an effort to separate them from even the most legitimate of these such as the sporting gun or the fisherman's knife. But on arrival at the destination their importation is likely to require a licence, and may be prohibited. Check first, or be sure to tell Customs on arrival.

Drugs: Personally–prescribed drugs and medicaments are best carried in properly labelled containers and, if they are for regular use, carry a letter from your doctor. Illicit drugs are a major and increasing concern for all Customs services and are often the principal reason for checks on travellers. Whilst the possession of very small quantities may be permissible in a few countries, their carriage across frontiers is invariably prohibited. Penalties are severe, usually carry the risk of imprisonment.

Countries with long land frontiers may choose to exercise some controls inland but travellers through ports and airports provide a concentrated flow which enables an efficient screening and checking by Customs. Particularly in the prevention of drug trafficking, the search at the frontier enables Customs to identify and seize large commercial shipments, before they are distributed inland for sale in small, usable quantities. In addition, Customs and Police will often cooperate to monitor the delivery of a consignment to its inland destination in order to identify principals in smuggling organizations.

Many people think that drugs are found from tip–offs, and that routine checks are not necessary. That is not so. Valuable intelligence does come from co–operation between Customs and Police services around the world. But detections made in the day–to–day work of ports and airports depend on the Customs Officer's initiative and experience in assessing risks and choosing the right passenger. The overall Customs effort against drug trafficking is a mix of intelligence, information, judgement and intuition. Officers are carefully trained to observe, select, question and examine. 'Profiles' are built up from instances where patterns have emerged, but they are but one tool in a large bag, and need to be constantly up–dated and refined as methods and types of courier change. Spot checks may need to be done to test out Customs' perception of risk, and that is where the innocent traveller may come under examination. Co–operation will help allay suspicion of the innocent, and full searches — including a body search— are only undertaken under strict supervision and where there are strong grounds for suspecting an offence.

Checking travellers

An officer who stops a passenger needs information before making a decision (whether or not a full examination is needed) and so questions must be asked. The officer is looking for tell–tale signs that something is not right. The smuggler cannot be completely honest about himself and must tell lies to stand any chance of success. It is that deceit that a Customs officer is trying to see through. Travel documents, passports, questions about the purpose of the journey —all give a picture which the officer can test for credibility against what he sees and what he hears and, ultimately, what he feels. He may not get it right every time, but intelligent, intuitive assessments do result in the discovery of people attempting to smuggle.

The traveller who objects to the way they are dealt with at Customs should complain to a Senior Customs official at the time of the incident. In that way most complaints can be dealt with to everyone's satisfaction, and while events are fresh in everyone's mind. By all means follow up with a letter if you feel you have not got satisfaction. But a written complaint made for the first time several days after an incident is difficult to investigate and rarely produces a satisfactory outcome for the complainant.

In addition to their role in protecting society, the Customs service has a duty to collect import taxes (which can still be substantial on luxury goods, despite moves to harmonize more tax rates and remove barriers to trade). The expensive watch, silk carpet, video camera or item of jewellery can still result in a hefty tax bill on arrival home. Goods in excess of allowances must be declared to Customs, or you risk having them confiscated, and criminal proceedings taken for smuggling. Many offences of this nature are settled between Customs and the traveller by the payment of a fine and few cases go to Court. However, if you also have to buy your confiscated goods back the overall penalty can amount to a large sum. In addition, the amount of time and effort spent by Customs dealing with such irregularities increases the opportunity for the drugs courier to get through undetected.

The business traveller can usually be relied on to know what personal allowances can be carried into each country, but a misunderstanding can occur when business goods are carried.

Lap–top computers, replacement parts for equipment, parts for repair, sample prototypes can all find their way into a business traveller's baggage. Sometimes he will act only as a 'courier' for another part of his company. Such items are invariably liable to some form of control as frontiers are crossed and a declaration to Customs on each occasion is the safest way —unless you have personally checked with a reliable authority and you are confident you know what you are doing.

As a general rule, don't carry packages for anyone if you don't know what it contains. Whether it is personal or business, your freedom or even your life could be at stake if something goes wrong.

On 1 January 1993, the Single European Act heralded the free movement of goods and people within the European Community (EC). For visitors, controls on goods and the collection of taxes generally take place at the first point of entry into the Community, and subsequent travel involves only checks for prohibited and restricted goods. For travellers within the Community, personal allowances for tax paid goods have increased substantially. However, the very large differences in the price of alcoholic drink and tobacco goods within the European Community still result in some restrictions on the quantities permitted to be carried, for both health and fiscal reasons.

Since the advent of the single market, Customs' controls on EC passengers at airports and ferry ports have been improved to provide a faster and more efficient service which targets the high risk traveller, but permits the majority to move unimpeded through customs.

Make sure you are properly informed when you travel. A confident traveller will project their innocence and help Customs to concentrate on their own priorities, for all our good.

SHOPPING AND DUTY FREE

by Caroline Brandenburger

Shopping should perhaps carry a government health warning. Taken to excess, it can have damaging effects —and not only on your purse. Travelling, particularly in less developed countries where prices seem so much lower, can lead to a fatal shopping addiction —that one friend who lived in Hong Kong called 'shopping sickness.' Dazzled by items for sale that are so very different from what is available at home, by the staggering workmanship of arts and crafts, or simply the cheap pastiche of the familiar, shopping can become wholly obsessive and indiscriminate!

Nevertheless, it is possible to buy memorable souvenirs —the kind which will give you lasting pleasure, and not be discarded at the back of a cupboard soon after you arrive home.

Knowing where to go is half the battle. There are numerous shopping guides to different parts of the world but I invariably find their materialistic tone nauseating — as if the world were simply a bran tub for the sated Westerner to dip into. Recommendations are probably your best source of advice but keep your eyes peeled while you travel.

Clearly, the range of available goods will depend on where you are, as will the way in which you buy them. Bartering will be perfectly appropriate in some places —a street market in India or a stall in Mexico— while wholly inappropriate in a smart European boutique. Still, even in smart shops you may be able to negotiate on price according to whether you pay by cash or credit card.

Hardened bartering experts recommend starting at a quarter of the starting price. To most Western minds this seems cruelly low, but the argument runs that there is an instant mark–up on the price as soon as your tourist face appears on the horizon. Having said that, it is quite likely that the original price is still less than you would pay for a similar item back home (if you could get it), so half that price still represents quite a bargain. Don't get obsessional about driving a really hard bargain. Obviously you don't want to be ripped off, but equally, you don't want to screw the vendor into the ground, however much of a rascal you might think him.

If you simply can't arrive at a mutually agreed price, retire gracefully. Sometimes that's not always easy if you've been plied with mint tea or cold drinks and generally made to feel a sense of obligation. But don't get brow–beaten into buying something you don't want. My parents found themselves in an oriental antique shop in San Francisco, looking at a box for $2000. After half an hour of unusually intense and heavy selling technique on the part of the shopkeeper, they made moves to leave —without buying. At which point the shopkeeper flung himself into the corner of the shop and burst violently into tears. My parents looked on aghast as, through the tears, he explained that his business was about to go bust and he desperately needed $3000 to keep afloat. They tried to calm him, feeling quite distressed themselves, and only just emerged financially unscathed.

When you're contemplating buying something, do remember that you've got to get it home. It may be portable, in which case you can carry it yourself. Or you can pack it up and send it, parcel post, through the local post office —a process which may take as long as six or eight weeks. (See Chapter 12 for information about freight forwarding.)

If it's large and unwieldy, you'll have to investigate other ways of getting it back. Some shops may have a perfectly efficient system of sending goods to your home, whether by air or by sea, packing items free and charging only for the postage or freight. A major shop will probably use a good shipper who charges a reasonable amount, packs well, and is reliable. If you do choose to let the shop ship your goods for you, make sure you have a confirming receipt, emphasize careful packing, and check it's insured against loss or breakage. But do be careful: in some less reputable shops, the cost could be enormous, completely cancelling any discount you've just managed to negotiate.

Equally, there are horror stories of the happy shopper paying for his bolt of silk or lacquered pot, arranging for the dealer to send it home, and never seeing it again. But this can happen even if you arrange the passage yourself —things do unaccountably disappear and whether stolen or lost, you'll probably never know. On the whole, though, goods will arrive.

If you arrange the packing and shipping yourself, it may well be cheaper. But it can be a complicated process, involving working out local rules and regulations about permits, packing, materials, sizes and weights. Nevertheless, it could be worthwhile if you have several large items to send. Find out a reliable local shipper by asking in a good hotel.

Duty free

Perhaps one of the first things to be aware of is the distinction between 'duty free' and 'tax free.' Duty free is defined as a product free of duties and taxes, and applies to liquor and tobacco products only. It is really a historical hangover from the 17th Century when excise duty was introduced on alcohol to deter people from getting drunk.

While tax free is defined as products free of taxes (ie VAT), which covers perfumes, cosmetics, fashion accessories, watches, jewellery, electrical and electronic goods, photographic equipment, china, crystal and other gift items.

The shops in airports are administered by airport operators, and the in–flight or on–deck outlets by the relevant airline or shipping company. The British Airports Authority (BAA), the main airport operator in Britain, apparently establishes its prices conducting regular high street surveys.

Duty free discounts vary, but tax free discounts tend to be 20 per cent. Although the price will be lower than the high street, it will still be higher than the original price of the product from the manufacturer. As a spokesman for BAA explained, "We have a policy which splits the benefit between the passenger/purchaser and the company. It provides the passenger with a good bargain at high street prices, and also a significant source of revenue for the airport, which keeps down the price of landing charges, and therefore the fare prices. It also means we can provide new facilities. Duty free benefits all passengers, not just the one's that buy."

Nevertheless, the booming business of duty and tax free goods (earning BAA more than £150m annually) has taken a staggering blow. '1992' and the deregulation within the European Community, *in theory* has marked the end of duty free shopping since a single market inevitably means no duty free zones. BAA held the belief that the logistical problems of introducing harmonization of prices within the EC may well mean that the existing system continues. Bringing prices in line in all the different countries, they surmised, would lead to drastic reductions in some and increases in others —potentially the source of major political conflict. For instance in Denmark, a packet of 20 cigarettes is 1.96 European Currency Units (ECUs) while in Greece it is 0.28 ECU. Any attempt by the Greek government to raise cigarette prices in a nation of heavy–smokers would do little for their ratings in the polls. As ever, the solution is compromise. Duty-free is to be phased out during the 1990's, and clearly the loss of revenue means that BAA will be concentrating heavily on its ordinary retail activities to make up the shortfall.

Tips for travelling shoppers

1. Duty free items are more of a bargain than tax free, because you save on excise duty as well as VAT

2. Most airports in the UK have fairly similar duty free prices, but there are greater differences between the ferries.

3. If you want to buy perfume, it is probably best to buy it at the airport shop where it will be up to 20 per cent less than high street prices. If you buy it on the plane, there is usually only a limited range sold in small bottles.

4. Cameras also tend to be cheaper in UK airport duty free stores than in the High Street (10 per cent on average), but this is not a hard and fast rule. Also bear in mind that if you are passing through some of the Middle Eastern airports, or travelling to the Far East or New York, you will probably be able to find photographic equipment at even cheaper prices.

5. Duty free spirits are about 40 per cent cheaper than High Street prices for standard products, but in some European countries such as Spain you will find spirits are even cheaper.

6. When comparing prices of spirits, note different bottle sizes and alcohol strengths.

7. It is often possible to phone ahead to check what is in stock and the prices available, the airlines (with a little persuasion) should also be able to forward you a price list of in–flight duty free goods.

8. *Business Traveller* magazine carries a monthly feature on worldwide duty free news and information as well as a spot price comparison between major world airports on up to four items.

9. Don't forget that your best source of information is the personal experiences of recent and regular travellers. Don't be afraid to ask for their advice: shopping is usually a major feature of most traveller's journeys and many will be happy to wax lyrical about their 'bargains'.

GUIDE OR PORTER?

by Richard Snailham

There is something timeless about the problems of travel with guides and porters. Stories in Henry Morton Stanley's late–Victorian best sellers find their echoes today, and it was instructive to learn that a recent Cambridge University Expedition to Sangay in Ecuador had the same problems that I had had on an ill–fated expedition to Sangay 10 years before: the local Indians had either refused to take their mules to the agreed objective or simply defected.

Nevertheless, a local guide is often useful, sometimes indispensable. Small boys hover outside the souk in Marrakesh and we once spurned them only to become comprehensively lost in the myriad covered alleyways. Rather less useful is the young boy who tags along on the streets of a Third World city with which you might be quite well acquainted. He will get into a conversation with you and then offer to show you the principal sights. Before your tour is finished you may find you are sponsoring him through school.

Sometimes a guide is obligatory, as at a French chateau —and generally good value. Where they are not, a judgement has to be made. In wild, sparsely populated, ill–mapped country I would say a guide was essential, especially where you do not speak the prevailing language and the local people do not speak yours. In Samburu country recently, with a map that was far too large–scale, I needed our camel–handlers to steer us to the objective.

How to get the best

Fix your price. If a journey is involved and you require any form of transport or any great length of time, it is best to find out the cost in advance —if only to minimize the shock of the often inordinate sum asked. Guides have no meters and rarely are they governed by any regulations. A price agreed at the outset, especially if there are other guides in the offing (and thus a choice), is often substantially less than that demanded at the end. Even in Nairobi I recently fell into the trap of failing to establish the price before taking a taxi to the outer suburbs (and was still mightily stung, even after an unedifying argument at the journey's end). Before you clinch the deal, bargaining is generally possible and is often expected.

Pick the right man. Your selection of the right guide is very important. Unfortunately this often involves a snap judgement based on appearances. Women often seem to have better intuitive judgement than men, I find, and a few quick questions on the spot before departure are valuable in ensuring you have a good man. For how things can go wrong, read Geoffrey Moorhouse's *The Fearful Void*. Some unscrupulous guides lead their charges into remote regions and then refuse to conduct them back without a big bonus. Never entirely trust a guide's navigational ability. He will not usually admit to being lost, but can often become so. Try to keep a check on distance covered, note all prominent landmarks and take their bearings from identifiable points on your route and the time that you took them. Avoid questions like "Is it far?" or "Will we get there tonight?" Guides often have more inclination to please their employers than to tell the sometimes painful truth, and the answers to these two questions will invariably be "no" and "yes."

Problems with porters

The days of mammoth expeditions with armies of porters are probably over. I was once manager and paymaster of a constantly changing team of about 130 porters in Nepal, but smaller, faster–moving assaults are now the order of the day and they normally require less manpower. The problems are otherwise the same, however, and most have been hinted at in the above section on guides. Here are a few further suggestions:

1. Be totally familiar with the local currency and its exchange rate before you embark on any negotiation.
2. Try and secure the services of a local 'minder' to help firm up the local *bundobust* (useful Hindi word meaning 'the logistical arrangements'). On a recent camel safari I took a young NCO from the Kenya General Service Unit who was excellent in his dealings with porters and headmen. Policemen, soldiers, students have all served me well in this role.
3. Remember that guides and porters have to have food and shelter. Who is providing this, you or they? You may have to offer advance payment and provide for their journeys home.
4. This goes for their animals too (if any). Camels often have to carry their own forage across deserts and yaks carry theirs up the last stages of the climb to the Everest base camp. Remember they always travel home faster than they travel out!
5. A head porter or *sirdar* is often a good idea if you have a large number in your party. He will be worth his extra pay.
6. Only pay a portion of the agreed fee at the outset. Keep the balance in your money belt until you get there.
7. Guides should, of course, lead but porters should take up position in the middle of your party. This prevents 'disappearances' and enables you to react if a porter becomes ill or tired.

The brighter side

Finally, if in doubt take a guide or porter rather than try to struggle on without them. They add colour to the whole enterprise, are generally honest and good–hearted and could well end up firm friends. It is worth while taking a few presents with you as a mark of gratitude. Some of your own kit will be much appreciated. Otherwise, penknives, folding scissors and cigarettes go down well. British Commemorative coins, postcards of HM the Queen, empty screw–top tobacco tins —even my old shirts— have proved acceptable gifts.

SPONSORSHIP

by Myfanwy Vickers

The quest for sponsorship for your trip is not a bad test of qualities that will stand you in good stead as a happy and successful traveller: grit, tenacity, enthusiasm and unflagging energy. It is also the aspect of travel most reminiscent of the job you thought you were getting away from: raising money is hard work. It generates bureaucracy and admin., photocopying and 'phone calls —all of which absorb your well–saved money.

But it can also be rewarding in more ways than the purely financial; indeed, the contact you will have with people during the preparations prior to the trip can be every bit as heart–warming as that which you will experience once you are launched in far–flung places. But if you are to persuade people to give you funds, you are embarking on a campaign as well as an expedition. Securing the sponsorship is not the end of the matter, either, as you will have to execute the follow up, contacting donors and sponsors once again, keeping your side of the bargain, delivering the goods and saying thank you. Be realistic, and bear this in mind before you start. It is not easy; what *is* easy is to be caught up in the next stage of your own life once you're back home, having enjoyed all the backing. Don't promise more than you can deliver. You burn your boats for next time, and make it doubly difficult for everybody else who is seeking the same thing.

You can seek sponsorship from business and industry, the media, grant–giving organizations, clubs and local groups, friends and the public. The vast bulk will come from business and industry (in kind rather than cash) and in return for publicity. Some firms will offer their services, eg free printing, and many will offer you goods at reduced or cost price.

Remember how many appeals land on the desk of people you are targeting (Kodak receive 300 a week): they will be quick to dismiss a shoddy, ill–considered, greedy or otherwise unseductive approach. Capture their attention and command their interest from the word go. Make the package professional. Invent your own logo; do not use that of other organizations without their permission —for all your good intentions, you could end up with a court case on your hands. Each letter should be typed, addressed personally, and tailored to the individual or his company ('phone beforehand, if necessary, to get the right name). Don't duplicate round robins; canvassing indiscriminately is rarely worth the paper it is zeroxed on.

Where appropriate, an eminent patron can give an expedition authority and gravitas. A copy of a supportive letter from the patron will lend credibility to the venture, and tempt people to put their faith where others have already shown confidence.

Provide a clear outline of what you plan to do and why, enclose a route map, and a breakdown of costs. Indicate how much of the budget you are covering out of your own pocket, and stipulate what you would like, rather than issuing a general plea for anything and everything. Provide a concise profile of the team members, with any relevant experience or achievements to date. Show in your letter that you have already done considerable planning, research and preparation (which you have, of course!), and that departure is not wholly dependent on backing; sponsors are much more willing to help those with evidently serious intent who are already helping themselves. Once you have done all this, feel pleased with yourself if you get a 10% response rate!

Think local when appealing to businesses, companies, equipment stockists and so on. Smaller businesses receive fewer requests and they may like to be involved. Often you will simply find greater goodwill and a more personal approach than in a rule–bound conglomerate or multinational. Can you find a connection between the business and its interests, your trip and the destination?

The greater logic you can give to any potential generosity, the better.

The main, if not the only thing that most people can offer sponsors is publicity, and securing this is not always easy. Be realistic about what you are offering, clear that you know just what the company is asking for, and certain you are able to provide the goods. Are you offering to sport a shirt with the sponsor's logo on it, and if so, is anyone going to see it except the lost ape men of Sumatra? If it is photographs you are providing, give evidence of your ability with a camera; very few people take really good shots that can be used in a national campaign. They do not happen by themselves, either —you will have to set them up, and the best ones always present themselves when you are at your most exhausted. Can you get media coverage? Only pre–paid commissions will impress firms who know how unlikely you are to make headline news otherwise. So try to sell articles to papers, magazines and colour supplements before departure, finding out what particular angles interest the editor. Any contract with film or TV will assure you immediate and abundant offers of sponsorship as there is no more powerful publicity for any product. Is there a promising audio angle? If so you could sell to radio.

If publicity en route is to be part of the deal, start setting up contacts in the country concerned: ask the embassy for advice, arm yourself with the names of the appropriate people in the media, and find ways to overcome man's innate reluctance to give some sponsor a plug at his expense! Obviously, if you can give evidence of successful marketing in the past, and ways in which other companies have benefited from your efforts, you are at an advantage.

Having said all this, many companies and suppliers have a margin for those who will not, in their opinion, achieve much publicity but who they like, quite simply, as individuals. Some also invest in what they call 'good citizenship', although almost without exception this applies to field projects or research–based expeditions where a commercial company can be seen to be putting something back into the host country at the same time as raising its profile in the minds of potential new recruits. The "We're going to Tibet and we want to do some science so as to help raise funds" approach tends not to wash, and a sponsor such as Shell or the RGS looks for a prior degree of competence within, and commitment to, the field.

Most grant–giving organizations only provide money for specific 'scientific' or investigative projects, but sift discriminatingly through libraries and specialist directories and target the few that you think likely. It may seem unpromising, but the money has to go to someone.

Finally, you can raise money by arranging your own special events —anything from a sponsored parachute jump to selling cakes at the local jumble sale. If your project has a charitable goal, give lectures to schools, colleges, clubs etc. This, however, can be time consuming, with lots of unsuspected, hidden costs and a disproportionately small amount of money raised.

It is, naturally, easier to persuade people to give money away if you in turn are helping someone or something else, consequently many travellers decide to raise money for charity. But what it boils down is that: you personally are never going to make much out of it, and, let's face it, neither should you. A percentage of the money raised, say 10%, may go to defray your costs, but any more than this is likely to lose you sympathy. You *must* contact the charity concerned for their authority before you start; a letter from them will show that you are bona fide. And open a special bank account in the name of the cause, so as to keep careful track of the money.

Contacts are not essential in this game, but anybody can unearth them and even create them. Do not be timid about approaching people, however elevated they may seem, for their potential interest and support. More often than not you will be pleasantly surprised at the response and the extent to which people will put themselves out on behalf of a project they take to. Liaise with organizations that are happy to advise, such as the extremely helpful enthusiasts at the Royal Geographical Society.

Beware, however, of danger of having the 'freebie' tag attached to your efforts. Although pleasure is as valid a reason for travel as any other, people can, understandably, be quick to resent the idea that they should help finance what they see as 'a jolly' on your behalf. Bring your tact and your conviction to bear with such an attitude, but don't bang your head against a brick wall: if the reaction is resentful, try elsewhere.

Perhaps the best bit of advice is: start early, like the proverbial worm catching the bird. Plan ahead! It may seem unlikely, but some firms like as much as a year's notice; in this way the project can be incorporated into their plans for the following financial year's budget. Everything takes much longer than you think, and many appeals are disappointed because the departure date is just too imminent.

Sponsorship is one of the few gentleman's contracts that still exists. When you get back, stick to your word. Do not be disappointed if, after all this, they don't make full use of the material —but give them every opportunity to do so. Most companies say that they never hear from travellers again. A thank you, a copy of a published article —all will be appreciated, and will stand you in good stead for the next time.

Throughout the whole thing, be organized and efficient; keep a record of all correspondence. Don't take rejections personally; pursue those who show interest like a limpet. Be lively and polite. They don't *have* to give you anything. But don't bury your individuality in business–like formalities; at the end of the day, it is yourself rather than a journey you are selling. Apply your own flair, and enjoy it!

THE TICKET OUT

by Ingrid Cranfield

Many countries require travellers to show a ticket out of the country before they are issued with a visa or allowed over the border. This onward ticket is normally expected to be a 'plane ticket, though sufficient evidence of the traveller's respectability and solvency can ensure that ticket for some other means of transport will be accepted. The other alternative to an airline ticket is the purchase of traveller's cheques. Normally 600 of photocopied traveller's cheques is sufficient to demonstrate solvency. There is the option to cash in the cheques after the visa has been obtained.

Onward tickets are no problem for travellers who wish to use them, but many people, especially overlanders, want to enter a country, but have no intention of flying out. For them, it will be desirable to try and get a refund.

Some countries require that the onward ticket be shown on application for a visa, but not thereafter. The purchaser can get a visa and then cash in his ticket before actually leaving home. If you do this, it is best to buy the ticket on credit, so that no cash need change hands either on purchase or on refund.

However, countries with this pre–condition for a visa will nearly always want to see the onward ticket at the point of immigration. If the buyer does not intend to use it, he will have to obtain a refund either in the country or after leaving. For many reasons it is best, therefore, to buy direct from a large carrier with many offices in convenient places and not through a travel agency, and to pay in cash or traveller's cheques. In effect, a full fare ticket should be purchased to ensure a full refund.

Buying outside the region for travel to the Third World, you should use a hard currency which will be foreign to your destination. In many countries you will not be allowed to purchase in any but a hard currency. If you buy in one soft currency, you cannot expect to be refunded in another, and this could prove inconvenient. Some Third World authorities are anxious to prevent export of their currency and will prefer refunds to be given in hard currency. Elsewhere, they will be desperate to get their hands on your hard currency and refunds will be given in the local currency, which will generally be a soft one. If your original purchase was in hard currency, you are, at least, in a stronger position when requesting the same in exchange.

Buying in the region is usually cheaper, especially if the black market rate is favourable, except where taxes are very high. To avoid paying such taxes, buy elsewhere, or get a friend to buy you a ticket in another country and post it to you (suitably disguised). The rules on refunding tickets vary from one place and one carrier, sometimes even one office, to another. Tickets are sometimes stamped 'non–refundable' (and the ink is sometimes even eradicated by unscrupulous travellers), but such tickets are, in any case, usually transferable. Refunds in the form of MCOs (Miscellaneous Charges Orders) should be accepted, as these can be used to buy an airline ticket or service. An MCO can even serve as an altered ticket and, like a ticket, can be cashed in separately.

Finally, make a note of the ticket number in case of loss; buy yourself a return or onward ticket to avoid being stranded if you're visiting a really remote destination; and do, for the airline's sake, cancel any reservation you don't intend to use.

COMING HOME
by John Blashford-Snell

Until Rula Lenska joined us on a quest in Nepal I had no idea that actors and expeditioners suffer from the same problem at the end of the show. Both tend to get 'post project depression' (PPD) or 'after expedition blues'.

When a play ends or the filming of a series finishes, Rula explained, the cast is suddenly split up, left to find new jobs or return home for a well-earned rest. The friendships and working relationships break up, the team disappears and a different life style starts overnight. So it is with expeditioners and I imagine ocean voyagers.

Dr John Davies, one of Britain's leading exploration medics, once started a lecture at the Scientific Exploration Society with the statement, "Expeditions may endanger your health." He went on to point out that for the novice, the experience can be an introduction to negative aspects of one's personality easily suppressed in normal daily life. However, with appropriate counselling and support, this can be a journey of self-discovery leading to increased confidence and a more enlightened attitude to others.

Seasoned adventurers, like experienced actors, recognise post expedition blues, the symptoms of which are similar to bereavement. This is triggered by the loss of one's new found 'family' of expedition friends in a widely different culture and suddenly being cut off from the excitement on return home.

"I just can't face going back to 9 to 5 in the Tax office," groaned an Inland Revenue Officer who had spent three months in the Gobi. Routine and mundane life style aggravate the condition and for many it is cured only by involvement in another challenge. Returning explorers also face isolation from family and colleagues, who have no concept of their recent intense experience. They are often perplexed by the indifferent response to their stories and may end up silent and withdrawn. The envy and resentment of the uninitiated, who imagine that one has been on a jolly picnic or at best some self-inflicted masochism, is also common.

"Don't know what you've done to my mother," complained a son after his mum had returned from one of the Discovery Expeditions in South America, "She's awfully quiet". But meeting the lady in question at a reunion a few months later, I found her in great spirits, reliving the experience with her old pals.

John Davies, with whom I have been on many trips, advises 'returnees', especially the older ones, to spend several days enquiring about the day to day problems that have occurred in their absence, before slowly beginning to recount their experiences. So, on being met by my wife as I stepped off a comfortable British Airways flight from Delhi recently, I asked, "How are those new trees in the garden coming on?" "Have you gone mad?" replied Judith, well used to a dozen tales of high adventure before we reached the car park. But perhaps I'm beyond hope!

However, there may be medical problems, as I discovered a year after a Sandhurst expedition in Ethiopia when my right leg started shaking uncontrollably whilst I was lecturing. "How strange," I thought, trying not to notice the offending limb. Two weeks later, lying racked with a fever in hospital, it was found that I had malaria, by which time I also had blurred vision and had lost 20 pounds in weight. But once diagnosed, malaria is usually fairly easily cured and the doctors knew I'd been to the tropics.

Sadly not all ailments are so quickly dealt with, as I realised after 12 months of visits to the St. Pancras Hospital for Tropical Diseases. Strange hot flushes, violent stabbing pains in my stomach, aches and itches in awkward places were making life extremely uncomfortable. "There's nothing wrong with you," boomed one of the world's leading specialists in tropical diseases, after exhaustive tests proved negative. "You young fellows imagine you've caught everything under the sun if you spend six weeks in the jungle. When I was in Burma ..." he droned on . My morale was rock bottom and it took great courage to return to the hospital a few weeks later, after the symptoms had become almost unbearable.

As luck would have it a charming and much more sympathetic Asian doctor was on duty and in no time he had me face down on a trolley with a flexible viewing device inserted up my rear end and my shirt over my head. "Keep him still," he beseeched as two strapping Fijian nurses pinned me down. "Oh! my goodness," exclaimed the physician. "What a fine example." "Excuse me, sir, but you have a splendid parasite. It is quite unusual to see one so well developed. Would you mind if we allowed a class of medical students to see it?" Before I could even protest, I was wheeled in to a theatre full of students, many of them, I noted looking between my legs, were extremely attractive young women. One by one they came forward, without even a titter, to peer intently up my bottom. At last I was taken away and the awful tube removed. "What now?" I asked. "Oh —just swallow these pills and you'll be as right as rain," smiled the doctor.

So it is my advice that if you feel ill after an overseas visit, go straight to your GP and say where you have been. Mark you, they might diagnose jet lag which can affect one more than most care to admit.

This handbook contains useful tips on surviving the onslaught and reducing its effects to the minimum so I'll not dwell on it. Suffice to say that when I get home I keep going until nightfall, doing simple uncomplicated things like unpacking or weeding, then I take a very mild sleeping pill and totter off to bed. With luck I can usually sleep for six hours. The important thing is to avoid stressful situations and don't make any important decisions until after your body has readjusted. In my case this is usually 24 hours. Indeed, even weeding may not be a good idea. Having stepped off a long flight from Mongolia, I pulled up all my wife's carefully planted ground cover instead of the weeds.

If I am still feeling low, I concentrate on writing my thank-you letters (if not done on the 'plane!) and amending my packing list, whilst memory of all the things I forgot to take and all unnecessary items that went with me is still fresh. Then it's down to sorting out photos, slides, videos and writing reports and articles. Next comes repairs to kit, getting cameras serviced and preparing lectures.

If you start to feel sorry for yourself, you are not really bringing the benefits of you experiences to your life at home. Indeed I expect you will find that you have changed but the world has not.

The whole point is to keep active and look forward to the next challenge and if you can't afford another trip, why not use your vigour and energy to help others in your area, sick children, old people or anyone who could use some voluntary assistance.

For the adventurous there are some opportunities supporting organisations like the Duke of Edinburgh's Award or Riding for the Disabled and there are dozens of environmental groups needing help.

The great cry is, if you want to avoid PPD, keep busy. ■

Directory

Directory

NATIONAL AND INTERNATIONAL CODE CHANGES

ON 16 APRIL 1995 ALL UK NATIONAL CODES WILL CHANGE

In most cases, the changes will mean simply adding a '1' after the first '0' to the dialling code. **071** becomes **(0171)**, **0734** becomes **(01734)** and so on.

Individual numbers in five cities are being increased from six digits to seven, the existing number will be prefixed by a '2' or a '9' and their area code will change completely.

Leeds	0532 xxxxxx	becomes	**(0113) 2**xx xxxx
Sheffield	0742 xxxxxx	becomes	**(0114) 2**xx xxxx
Nottingham	0602 xxxxxx	becomes	**(0115) 9**xx xxxx
Leicester	0533 xxxxxx	becomes	**(0116) 2**xx xxxx
Bristol	0272 xxxxxx	becomes	**(0117) 9**xx xxxx

The changes on the 16 April 1995 will not affect:
Freefone or reduced rate services —eg. 0800 or 0345 or 0500 numbers
Information lines —eg. 0891 or 0898 numbers
Local Call lines —eg. 0645 numbers.

ON 16 APRIL 1995 THE INTERNATIONAL ACCESS CODE WILL CHANGE

The single international access code will change from **010** to **00**, bringing the UK in line with the rest of Europe.

For further information call British Telecom on **0800 01 01 01** before 16 April 1995.

If you dial an old code number between the 16 April 1995 and April 1996 , there will be a recorded message with the correct code, you will not be charged for this service.

WHERE AND WHEN
Section 1

GEOGRAPHICAL

Notes

Please note that all the information in this section is subject to change. The world has changed rapidly within the last few years, and will probably continue to do so. New countries have emerged, such as Eritrea, and the former Yugoslavia has split into individual republics, governments will change, and countries, such as Yemen, can become dangerous for the tourist within a matter of weeks. Therefore it is advisable to contact the Foreign Office on the latest up to date information. Please treat this section as a guideline only.

The Visas included in this section are applicable to Australians, Americans, British, Canadians and New Zealanders. Entry requirements can also change, especially in the CIS, therefore it is always advisable to contact the relevant embassy/consulate and check.

Inoculations also change, with new outbreaks of diseases, for example Diphtheria in various provinces of the Russian Federation, while other diseases disappear, please therefore check with an immunisation centre or your doctor several months before travelling . We have also included Cholera, which is still a serious risk in many parts of the world. However the World Health Organisation stated that the immunisation against Cholera was not effective. We have not included Tetanus, because it is felt that this is an injection worth having constantly up to date. Many other injections may be needed, for example, Japanese B Encephalitis, Meningococcal Meningitis, Rabies, so please check. Where inoculations have an asterisk*, this means that the vaccine is a requirement as opposed to a recommendation.

Airlines and the average length of flights are based from London.

Countries are listed by continent alphabetically.

Africa

Algeria
Capital Algiers (El Djezair) *Lang* Arabic and French *Currency* Dinar = 100 centimes *Govt.* Multi-party Republic *Rel* Islam (Sunni Moslem) *Size* 2,381,741 sq km - 919,595 sq miles *Pop* 25,324,000 *GMT* + 1 *When* North of the Sahara September to May South of the Sahara October to April *Visas* Required by all (No Israeli stamps in passports) *Validity* 30 days from date of issue *Time to Get:* 2-3 days *Safety* Precautions should be taken, travel to the southern areas is at present dangerous and should be avoided especially south of Tamanrasset *Inoc* Yellow Fever* if you have come from an infected area, Hepatitis A, Typhoid, Polio, Malaria *Airlines* Air Algerie, Iberia, Swiss Air *Average length of flight* 2.5 hours *Food* Meaty similar to Moroccan and Tunisian

Angola
Capital Luanda *Lang* Officially Portuguese and Bantu languages *Currency* New Kwanza = 100 lwei *Govt* Under the constitution of the Second Republic of Angola - unstable *Rel* Mostly Tribal *Size* 1,246,700 sq km - 481,354 sq miles *Pop* 10,020,000 *GMT* +1 *When* May to October - presently no travel allowed though *Visas* Required by all but no tourist visas issued at the moment *Safety* Extremely dangerous, check with Foreign Office *Inoc* Yellow Fever*, Hepatitis A, Cholera, Typhoid, Polio, Malaria *Airlines* Air France, Sabena *Average length of flight* 19.5 hours including stopovers *Food* Simple, Portuguese influence

Benin
Capital Porto Novo *Lang* French *Currency* CFA Franc = 100 centimes *Govt* Relatively stable democracy *Rel* Mainly Tribal *Size* 112,622 sq km - 43,484 sq miles *Pop* 4,736,000 *GMT* +1 *When* January to April *Visas* Required by all *Validity* 15 days within 3 months of issue *Time to get* 1 day or 30 days if

information has to come from Benin *Safety* Poorly lit roads make night travel hazardous. Armed robbery and muggings are on the increase *Inoc* Yellow Fever* Cholera Hepatitis A, Typhoid, Polio, Malaria *Airlines* Air France, Sabena *Average length of flight* 10 hours *Food* African seafood with French influence

Bophuthatswana

Capital Mmabatho *Lang* Setswana *Currency* South African Rand = 100 cents *Govt* Independent homeland of South Africa. Regional authorities elected by tribal chiefs-unstable *Rel* Christian *Size* 44 sq km - 17 sq miles *Pop* 1,800,000 *GMT* +2 *When* All year *Visas* Required by all except UK nationals *Safety* At time of writing unstable, cautious travel is advised *Inoc* Yellow Fever* if arriving from an infected area, Cholera, Typhoid, Polio, Malaria, Hepatitis A. *Airlines* Via Jan Smuts Johannesburg *Food* Local food is meal based - international cuisine available.

Botswana

Capital Gaborone *Lang* English and Setswana *Currency* Pula = 100 thebes *Govt* Botswana Democratic Party is currently in power, but elections in 1994 *Rel* Tribal *Size* 582,000 sq km - 224,711 sq miles *Pop* 1,325,291 *GMT* +2 (+1 in summer) *When to go* May to September *Visas* Not required *Inoc* Hepatitis A, Malaria, Typhoid, Polio, Cholera *Airlines* British Airways, Air France *Average length of flight* 15 hours *Food* Meat, maize and potato based. Western food also available

Burkina Faso

Capital Ouagadougou *Lang* French *Currency* CFA Franc *Govt* Presidential dictatorship *Rel* Animist *Size* 274,200 sq km - 105,870 sq miles *Pop* 9,001,000 *GMT*: GMT *When* December to March *Visas* Required by all *Validity* 3 months *Time to get* Immediately *Safety* Towns can be violent after dark, avoid unnecessary travel in rural areas *Inoc* Yellow Fever*, Hepatitis A, Cholera, Typhoid, Polio, Malaria *Airlines* Air France *Average length of flight* 8.5 hours *Food* Rice, maize and millet based

Burundi

Capital Bujumbura *Lang* French and Kirundi *Currency* Burundi Franc = 100 centimes *Govt* Front for Democracy is currently the elected Govt led by Ndadaye, a Hutu, initiating liberal reforms *Rel* Mainly Roman Catholic *Size* 27,834 sq km - 10,747 sq miles *Pop* 5,620,000 *GMT* +2 *When* June to September *Visas* Required by all *Validity* 30 days *Safety* Unsafe due to tribal tension *Inoc* Yellow Fever* if you have come from an infected area. Hepatitis A, Cholera, Typhoid, Polio, Malaria *Airlines*

Sabena, Air France, Ethiopian Airlines *Average length of flight* 10 hours *Food* Basic and limited

Cameroon

Capital Yaounde *Lang* French and English *Currency* CFA Franc = 100 centimes *Govt* Biya has been President since 1982, however there is now strong opposition to him and rumours abound of fraud *Rel* Animist, Christian and Muslim *Size* 475,442 sq km - 183,569 sq miles *Pop* 11,540,000 *GMT* +1 *When* November - February *Visas* Required by all *Validity* Up to 3 months use with 3 months of issue *Time to get* 2 days by person, longer by post *Safety* Douala can be dangerous after dark *Inoc* Yellow Fever*, Cholera, Hepatitis A, Malaria, Polio, Typhoid *Airlines* Swissair *Average length of flight* 7 hours *Food* Abundance of fruit and vegetables, French and Lebanese influences

Central African Republic

Capital Bangui *Lang* French and Sango *Currency* CFA Franc = 100 centimes *Govt* Although called a republic, Kolingba voids elections if he does not win *Rel* Animist *Size* 622,984 sq km - 240,535 sq miles *Pop* 2,688,426 *GMT* +1 *When* November to April, but always tropical heat *Visas* Required by all *Time to get* Normally 2 days *Safety* Armed robbery remains a problem in Bangui. Avoid travelling outside towns after dark *Inoc*. Yellow Fever*, Cholera, Hepatitis A, Typhoid, Polio, Malaria *Airlines* Air France *Average length of flight* 9.5 hours *Food* Simple

Chad

Capital Ndjamena *Lang* French *Currency* CFA Franc = 100 centimes *Govt* Unstable single-party state, although changing and national elections are set for 1994 *Rel* Muslim or Animist *Size* 1,284,000 sq km - 495,800 sq miles *Pop* 5,428,000 *GMT* +1 *When* November to March *Visas* Required by all *Validity* Varies *Safety* Dangerous *Inoc* Yellow Fever* Hepatitis A, Malaria, Cholera, Polio, Typhoid *Airlines* Flights via Paris Air France *Average length of flight* 7 hours *Food* Scarce

Congo

Capital Brazzaville *Lang* French *Currency* CFA Franc = 100 centimes *Govt* Although a multi-party democracy (since 1992) it has been a Socialist one-party state *Rel* Animist *Size* 342,000 sq km - 132,047 sq miles *Pop* 1,843,421 *GMT* +1 *When* May to September *Visas* Required by all except by French + German nationals *Validity* 15 days *Time to get* At least three weeks *Safety* UK nationals are advised not to transit or visit at the time of writing *Inoc* Yellow Fever*, Hepatitis A, Malaria, Polio, Cholera, Typhoid *Airlines* Air France, British Airways, Air Afrique *Average length of flight* 11 hours including stopover in Paris *Food* French influence with excellent seafood on the coast

Cote d'Ivoire (Ivory Coast)

Capital Yamoussoukro *Lang* French *Currency* CFA Franc = 100 centimes *Govt* Elected President, although other parties were allowed to stand at the last election it is really a one-party state *Rel* Tribal *Size* 322,462 sq km - 124,503 sq miles *Pop* 12,600,000 *GMT* GMT *When* Mid December to mid March *Visas* Not required by UK or US nationals *Validity* 3 months *Time to get* 2 days *Safety* Generally safe but has its full share of street crime after dark *Inoc* Yellow Fever*, Hepatitis A, Cholera, Malaria, Polio, Typhoid *Airlines* Sabena, Air France *Average length of flight* 6 hours *Food* Spicy and bananas are often used in cooking

Djibouti

Capital Djibouti *Lang* Arabic and French *Currency* Djibouti Franc = 100 centimes *Govt* Multi-party elections since 1992 *Rel* Muslim and Roman Catholic *Size* 23,200 sq km - 8,959 sq miles *Pop* 519,900 *GMT* +3 *When* October - April *Visas* Required by all *Validity* 1-3 months *Time to get* 2 days *Safety* Areas in the country remain closed. Casual visitors are advised to avoid this country at the time of writing *Inoc* Yellow Fever* if arriving from an infected area, Hepatitis A, Malaria, Polio, Typhoid *Airlines* Air France *Average length of flight* 11 hours *Food* shortages

Egypt

Capital Cairo *Lang* Arabic *Currency* Egyptian Pound = 100 piastres *Govt* Democracy *Rel* Islamic *Size* 997,739 sq km - 385,229 sq miles *Pop* 53,153,000 *GMT* +2 *When* All year *Visas* Required by all *Validity* Varies *Time to get* Up to a month *Safety* An increase of attacks on tourist by religious extremists *Inoc* Yellow Fever* if arriving from an infected area. Hepatitis A, Cholera, Malaria, Polio, Typhoid *Airlines* British Airways, Egyptair *Average length of flight* 4 hours 45 minutes *Food* Middle eastern cooking

Equatorial Guinea

Capital Malbabo *Lang* Spanish *Currency* CFA Franc = 100 centimes *Govt* Dictatorship, followed by a single party-state, reforms in place for multi-party elections with the next 2 years (hopefully) *Rel* Roman Catholic *Size* 28,051 sq km - 10,830 sq miles *Pop* 348,000 *GMT* +1 *When* November to March *Visas* Required by all *Time to get* At least two months

Safety Take special care of personal belongings. Don't travel after dark. There is no British Consular presence. If in difficulties seek assistance from the French or Spanish *Inoc* Yellow Fever* if arriving from an infected area. Cholera, Hepatitis A, Malaria, Polio, Typhoid, *Airlines* Iberia via Madrid *Average length of flight* 11 hours excluding stopover *Food* Good seafood, but few restaurants

Eritrea

Capital Asmara *Lang* Arabic and Tigrinya *Currency* No currency of their own Ethiopian Birr and Sudanese Pound are used *Govt* Since independence from Ethiopia in 1993 it is under the control of the Eritrean People's Liberation Front and new constitution has yet to be introduced *Rel* Orthodox and Muslim *Size* 124,000 sq km- 48,000 sq miles *Pop* 3,500,000 *GMT* +3 *When* May June, Sept, Oct *Visas* Required by all *Validity* 4 weeks from date of issue *Time to get* 1 day *Safety* Avoid Sudan border. Don't travel after dark. Register with the Consulate in Asmara if travelling outside the capital *Inoc* Yellow Fever* if arriving from an infected area, Cholera, Typhoid, Polio, Hepatitis A, Malaria *Airlines* Ethiopian Airlines *Average length of flight* 11.5 hours *Food* Spicy

Ethiopia

Capital Addis Ababa *Lang* Amharic *Currency* Ethiopian Birr = 100 cents *Govt* Democratic constitution *Rel* Christian *Size* 1,251,282 sq km - 483,123 sq miles *Pop* 50,383,000 *GMT* +3 *When* May, June, Sept, Oct *Visas* Required by all *Validity* 2 months *Commencing Time to get* 2 days *Safety* Sudan and Somalia borders areas should be avoided. Don't travel after dark and register with an Embassy if travelling outside the capital by road *Inoc* Yellow Fever* if coming from an infected area, Cholera, Malaria, Polio, Hepatitis A, Typhoid *Airlines* Ethiopian Airlines, Lufthansa *Average length of flight* 10.5 hours *Food* Spicy

Gabon

Capital Liberville *Lang* French *Currency* CFA Franc = 100 centimes *Govt* A multi-party constitution with rumours of fraud, previously a one-party state *Rel* Mainly Christian *Size* 267,667 sq km - 103,347 sq miles *Pop* 1,206,000 *GMT* +1 *When* May to September *Visas* Required by all *Validity* 3 months *Time to get* 2-4 weeks *Safety* The British embassy closed in July 1991 *Inoc* Yellow Fever*, Hepatitis A, Malaria, Polio, Cholera, Typhoid *Airlines* Air France, Sabena, Swissair *Average length of flight* 10.5 hours *Food* Distinctive flavourings

The Gambia

Capital Banjul *Lang* English *Currency* Gambian Dalasi = 100 bututs *Govt* Partly elected govt, currently held by People's Progressive Party *Rel* Muslim *Size* 11,295 sq km - 4,361 sq miles *Pop* 800,000 *GMT* GMT *When* Mid November - mid May *Visas* Required but not by British tourists, Australians and Canadians *Validity* 90 days *Time to get* 48 hours in person, longer by post *Safety* Ensure hotel rooms are secure and avoid isolated places and beaches. At time of going to press, a military coup *Inoc* Yellow Fever* if arriving from an infected area, Hepatitis A, Malaria, Polio, Cholera, Typhoid *Airlines* Air Gambia, Sabena *Average length of flight* 5.5 hours *Food* Spiced

Ghana

Capital Accra *Lang* English *Currency* Cedi = 100 pesewas *Govt* Although an elected Govt, Ghana is partly under the control of the armed forces *Rel* Christian *Size* 238,537 sq km - 92,100 sq miles *Pop* 15,028 *GMT* GMT *When* August - January *Visas* Required by all *Validity* 3 months from date of issue *Time to get* 2 days *Safety* Relatively safe *Inoc* Yellow Fever*, Hepatitis A, Cholera, Malaria, Polio, Typhoid *Airlines* Ghana Airways, British Airways *Average length of flight* 6.5 hours *Food* Plantains used in cooking - guinea fowl and grasscutters (rodent)

Guinea Republic

Capital Conakry *Lang* French *Currency* Guinea franc = 100 centimes *Govt* Having been a socialist regime, since 1990 it is changing to democracy, multi-party elections due in 1995 *Rel* Muslim *Size* 245,857 sq km - 94,926 sq miles *Pop* 5,718,000 *GMT* GMT *When* November to April *Visas* Required *Time to get* 5 weeks *Inoc* Yellow Fever* if arriving from an infected area, Hepatitis A, Malaria, Polio, Typhoid, Yellow Fever *Airlines* Air France, Sabena, Aeroflot *Average length of flight* 9 hours *Food* Very fond of hot maize soup (spicy)

Guinea-Bissau

Capital Bissau *Lang* Portuguese *Currency* Guinea-Bissau Peso = 100 centavos *Govt* Socialist, multi-party elections due in 1994 *Rel* Animist and Muslim *Size* 36,125 sq km - 13,948 sq miles *Pop* 943,000 *GMT* GMT *When* December to April *Visas* Required by all *Inoc* Yellow Fever* if arriving from an infected area, Hepatitis A, Malaria, Polio, Typhoid, Yellow Fever *Airlines* TAP, Aeroflot *Average length of flight* 10 hours *Food* Rice, chicken and fish dishes

Kenya

Capital Nairobi *Lang* Swahili and English *Currency* Kenyan Shilling = 100 cents *Govt* Lead by Moi, becoming more liberal having been a one-party state *Rel* Tribal and Christian *Size* 580,356 sq km - 224,081 sq miles *Pop* 25,905,000 *GMT* +3 *When* June to September *Visas* Not required by British and Canadian citizens *Validity* Up to 3 months *Time to get* normally 24 hours *Safety* Generally safe in tourist areas, but should be careful *Inoc* Yellow Fever* if arriving from an infected area, Malaria, Polio, Cholera, Typhoid, Hepatitis A *Airlines* British Airways, Kenyan Airways *Average length of flight* 8 hours *Food* Local food is maize based, international food available in all tourist areas

Lesotho

Capital Maseru *Lang* Sesotho and English *Currency* Loti = 100 lisente *Govt* Democracy, elections held in 1993, all seats won by the Basotho Congress Party *Rel* Christian mainly Catholic *Size* 30,355 sq km - 11,720 sq miles *Pop* 1,700,000 *GMT* +2 *When* May to September *Visas* Not required by UK *Validity* 3 or 6 months *Time to get* 1 day *Safety* Due to political uncertainty travel, at the time of writing, should be avoided *Inoc* Yellow Fever* if arriving from an infected area, Hepatitis A, Polio, Cholera, Typhoid *Airlines* British Airways, Air Lesotho *Average length of flight* 14 hours including stopover *Food* Lots of fresh water fish - other foods imported from South Africa

Liberia

Capital Monrovia *Lang* English *Currency* Liberian Dollar = 100 cents *Govt* Elected Govt, elections due 1994 *Rel* Officially Christian *Size* 97,754 sq km - 37,743 *Pop* 2,520,000 *GMT* GMT *When* November to March *Visas* Required by all *Validity* 60 days from date of issue *Time to get* 1 day *Safety* The British Embassy in Liberia was closed in 1991. The Foreign Office do not advise travel. *Inoc* Yellow Fever*, Hepatitis A, Malaria, Polio, Cholera, Typhoid *Airlines* No direct flights at the time of writing *Average length of flight* 9 hours 40 minutes *Food* Rice based, local dishes include toasted termites and frog soup

Libya

Capital Tripoli *Lang* Arabic *Currency* Libyan Dinar = 1000 dirhams *Govt* Muammar al-Qathafi is the Leader of the Revolution (socialist) and holds supreme power *Rel* Sunni Muslim *Size* 1,775,500 sq km - 685,524 sq miles *Pop* 3,773,000 *GMT* +1 *When* November to February *Visas* Required by all, extremely difficult to get, apply in Paris *Safety* Avoid internal air flights. Incidence of mugging increasing. Unwise to use of carry cameras. Harsh penalties are imposed for the possession or use of alcohol or drugs and for criticizing the country, its leadership or religion. Register with the British Interests Section of the Italian Embassy on arrival *Inoc* Yellow Fever* if arriving from an infected area, Typhoid, Cholera, Polio, Hepatitis A *Airlines* No flights, UN embargo *Average length of flight* 6 hours *Food* Arabic food with an Italian influence

Madagascar

Capital Antananarivo *Lang* Malagasy and French *Currency* Malagasy Franc = 100 centimes *Govt* Elected government, with Albert Zafy as President *Rel* Animist and Christian *Size* 587,041 sq km - 226,658 sq miles *Pop* 12,660,000 *GMT* + 3 *When* April to October *Visas* Required by all *Validity* 30 or 90 days, valid for 6 months from date of issue *Time to get* 1 day in person, 1 week by post *Safety* Be aware of mugging danger. Register presence at the Embassy *Inoc* Yellow Fever* if arriving from an infected area, Cholera, Hepatitis A, Typhoid, Polio, Malaria *Airlines* Air France, Air Madagascar, Aeroflot *Average length of flight* 14 hours including connection in Paris *Food* Rice based and can be very hot

Malawi

Capital Lilongwe *Lang* English *Currency* Kwacha = 100 tambala *Govt* A one-party state led by Banda, however multi-party elections have been promised for 1994, to satisfy foreign governments who have withheld aid until the regime improves its human rights record *Rel* Animist mainly *Size* 118,484 sq km - 45,747 sq miles *Pop* 8,556,000 *GMT* +2 *When* April to October *Visas* Not required *Safety* Avoid travelling after dark, especially of of the main towns *Inoc* Yellow Fever* if arriving from an infected area, Hepatitis A, Malaria, Polio, Typhoid *Airlines* British Airways direct, Air Zimbabwe, Kenya Airways, Air Malawi, South African Airways, Air France, Ethiopian Airlines *Average length of flight* 12 hours *Food* Delicious fish from Lake Malawi

Mali

Capital Bamako *Lang* French *Currency* CFA Franc = 100 centimes *Govt* Having been a military dictatorship, multi-party elections were held in 1992, however, the existing govt is unstable due to economic unrest *Rel* Majority Muslim *Size* 1,240,192 sq km - 478,841 sq miles *Pop* 8,461,000 *GMT* GMT *When* October - February *Visas* Required by all *Validity* 1 month from date of entry *Time to get* 5 days *Safety* Many areas north of Bamako are

unsafe due to clashes between Tuareg and army. *Inoc* Yellow Fever, Cholera, Hepatitis A, Malaria, Polio, Typhoid *Airlines* Air France, Sabena *Average length of flight* 11 hours *Food* Rice or millet based

Mauritania

Capital Nouakchott *Lang* Arabic and French *Currency* Mauritanian Ougiya = 5 khoums *Govt Rel* Islamic *Size* 1,030,700 sq km - 397,950 sq miles *Pop* 2,036,000 *GMT* GMT *When* November to March *Visas* Required by all *Validity* 1 month *Time to get* 3 Days *Safety* Disputes with Senegal, take advice *Inoc* Yellow Fever, Hepatitis A, Malaria, Polio, Typhoid *Airlines* Air France, Air Afrique *Average length of flight* 7 hours *Food* Shortages, there is very little local food on offer and very few restaurants. Saudi Arabian food aid being supplied

Morocco

Capital Rabat *Lang* Arabic *Currency* Moroccan Dirham = 100 centimes *Govt* Elected govt with King Hussan retaining executive power *Rel* Muslim *Size* 710,850 sq km - 274,461 sq miles *Pop* 25,208,000 *GMT* GMT *When* Apr - Oct *Visas* Not required *Safety* Safe for tourists, beware of drugs being offered though *Inoc* Hepatitis A, Polio, Typhoid *Airlines* Air France, Royal Air Maroc *Average length of flight* 3 hours *Food* Meat based - not suitable for vegetarians. Delicious couscous

Mozambique

Capital Maputo *Lang* Portuguese *Currency* Mozambique Metical = centavos *Govt* President holds all power. The country has been at civil war for 16 years, although there has been a recent peace agreement there is still unrest *Rel* Christian *Size* 799,380 sq km - 308,641 sq miles *Pop* 15,730,900 *GMT* +2 *When* April - September *Visas* Required by all *Validity* 1 month *Time to get* Well in advance (several months) *Safety* Not recommended for the tourist, great care should be taken at all times. *Inoc* Yellow Fever*, Cholera* Hepatitis A, Malaria, Polio, Typhoid *Airlines* Air Zimbabwe, South African Airways *Average length of flight* 14 hours including stopover in Johannesburg *Food* Portuguese and Far Eastern influences

Namibia

Capital Windhoek *Lang* English *Currency* South African rand = 100 cents *Govt* Elected President and National Assembly *Rel* Christian majority *Size* 823,144 sq km - 317,816 sq miles *Pop* 1,401,711 *GMT* +2 *When* September to May *Visas* Required by Australians and New Zealanders *Validity* 3 months *Time to get* 2 days *Safety* Relatively safe *Inoc* Yellow Fever* if arriving from an infected area, Hepatitis A, Polio, Malaria, Typhoid. *Airlines* Namib Air, Air France, Lufthansa, South African Airways, Air Zimbabwe, *Average length of flight* 18 hours *Food* German influence - meat based

Niger

Capital Niamey *Lang* French *Currency* CFA Franc = 100 centimes *Govt* Elected, 6-party coalition *Rel* Muslim *Size* 1,267,000 sq km - 489,191 sq miles *Pop* 7,984,000 *GMT* +1 *When* Oct - May *Visas* Required but not by UK citizens *Validity* Varies *Time to get* 24 hours *Safety* There has been a series of clashes between security forces and guerrillas belonging to the Tuareg *Inoc* Yellow Fever*, Cholera*, Hepatitis A, Malaria, Polio, Typhoid *Airlines* Air France *Average length of flight* 6 hours *Food* Rice based, couscous, can be shortages in remote areas

Nigeria

Capital Abuja (Lagos) *Lang* English *Currency* Naira = 100 Kobo *Govt* Unstable democracy *Rel* Islamic *Size* 923,768 sq km = 569,669 sq miles *Pop* 88,514,501 *GMT* +1 *When* Nov - April *Visas* Required by all *Time to get* 2 days *Safety* Political situation is uncertain. High incidence of street crime. Travelling outside cities after dark is unsafe *Inoc* Cholera*, Yellow Fever*, Hepatitis A, Malaria, Polio, Typhoid *Airlines* British Airways, Nigerian Airways *Average length of flight* 7 hours 40 minutes *Food* Yams, sweet potatoes, and plantains, typically West African

Rwanda

Capital Kigali *Lang* Kinyarwanda and French. Kiswahili *Currency* Rwandese FRANC = 100 Centimes *Govt* Extremely unstable *Rel* Christian *Size* 26,338 sq km - 10,169 sq miles *Pop* 7,148,496 *GMT*+2 *When* June to December *Visas* Required by all *Validity* 3 months *Time to get* Weeks - nearest Visa office to London is Brussels *Safety* Extremely dangerous with Tutsi and Hutu fighting *Inoc* Yellow Fever*, Cholera*, Hepatitis A, Malaria, Polio, Typhoid *Airlines* Sabena, Air France, Ethiopian Airways *Average length of flight* 13 hours *Food* French and Belgian influences

Sao Tome e Principe

Capital Sao Tome *Lang* Portuguese *Currency* Dobra = 100 centimos *Govt* Democracy *Rel* Roman Catholic *Size* 964 sq km - 372 sq miles *Pop* 116,000 *GMT* GMT *When* June through September *Visas* Required by all *Validity* varies *Inoc* Yellow Fever* if arriving from an infected area, Cholera, Hepatitis A, Malaria,

Polio, Typhoid *Airlines* Via Libreville in Gabon *Average length of flight* 10 hours *Food* Seafood

Senegal

Capital Dakar *Lang* French and Wolof *Currency* CFA Franc = 100 centimes *Govt* Elected president holds executive power, with a National Assembly responsible for legislation. The socialists have been in power since independence (1960) *Rel* Muslim *Size* 196,722 sq km - 75,955 sq miles *Pop* 6,881,919 *GMT* GMT *When* December through to May *Visas* Required by Australia and New Zealand nationals *Validity* 3 months from date of issue *Time to get* 1 day in person *Safety* Some unrest, take local advice *Inoc* Yellow Fever*, Antimarsh Fever (July and August) Cholera* Hepatitis A, Malaria, Polio, Typhoid *Airlines* Swissair, Sabena, Iberia, Air France *Average length of flight* 6 hours and 15 minutes *Food* Regarded as one of the best in Africa, can be spicy normally chicken or fish based

Sierra Leone

Capital Freetown *Lang* English *Currency* Leone = 100 cents *Govt* Unstable one-party state, led by 28-year old Captain Valentine Strasser, who overthrew the corrupt regime in 1992 *Rel* Animist *Size* 71,740 sq km - 27,699 sq miles *Pop* 4,260,000 *GMT* GMT *When* November to April *Visas* Required *Validity* 1 week (extendible) commencing on arrival *Time to get* 3 days normally *Safety* Dangerous, especially in the east, contact the Foreign Office before departing *Inoc* Yellow Fever* if arriving from an infected area, Cholera*, Hepatitis A, Malaria, Polio, Typhoid *Airlines* Air France, KLM, Aeroflot, Air Gambia *Average length of flight* 6.5 hours *Food* Excellent fish, lobster and prawns

Somalia

Capital Mogadishu *Lang* Somali and Arabic *Currency* Somali Shilling = 100 cents *Govt* As the country is in a state of civil war, there is no effective central government. The Military commander, General Aideed controls the capital *Rel* Muslim *Size* 637,657 sq km - 246,201 sq miles *Pop* 7,691,000 *GMT* +3 *When* Don't *Visas* Required by all *Validity* varies *Time to get* 1 month *Safety* All embassies are currently closed, fierce fighting at time of writing is still going on in the capital *Inoc* Yellow Fever* if arriving from an infected area, Cholera*, Typhoid, Polio, Malaria *Airlines* Daallo Airlines, Somali Airlines *Average length of flight* 11.5 hours *Food* Pork and seafood, often spiced

South Africa

Capital Pretoria *Lang* Afrikaans and English Currency Rand = 100 cents *Govt* Finally a fully democratic govt, giving all adults the vote regardless of colour *Rel* Mainly Christian *Size* 1,221,037 sq km - 471,445 sq miles including the 4 homelands (Transkei, Bophuthatswana, Ciskei and Venda) *Pop* 33,849,000 (including the homelands) *GMT* +2 *When* All year *Visas* Not required *Safety* Variable, depends on area, take advice *Inoc* Yellow Fever* if arriving from an infected area, Cholera, Malaria, Polio, Typhoid *Airlines* British Airways, South African Airways *Average length of flight* 12 hours 50 minutes *Food* Meat based - Braais (barbecues) and stews

Sudan
Capital Khartoum *Lang* Arabic *Currency* Sudanese pound = 100 piastres *Govt* Military government - unstable *Rel* Muslim in the north, Christian and Animist in the South *Size* 2,505,813 sq km - 967,500 sq miles *Pop* 23,797,000 *GMT* +2 *When* November to March *Visas* Required *Validity* 30 days within 3 months of issue *Time to get* 1-3 weeks *Safety* Not advised to travel anywhere in the South contact the Foreign Office *Inoc* Yellow Fever* if arriving from an infected area, but recommended anyway, Hepatitis A, Malaria, Polio, Typhoid *Airlines* Sudan Airways, Lufthansa, Air France, KLM *Average length of flight* 8 hours *Food* Fool (bean) and dura (millet or maize) is the staple diet

Swaziland
Capital Mbabane *Lang* English and Siswati *Currency* Lilangeni *Govt* Power rests with the monarch who appoints a Prime Minister and a Cabinet, with the exception of 10 elected senators *Rel* Mainly Christian *Size* 17,363 sq km - 6,704 sq miles *Pop* 768,000 *GMT* +2 *When* April to September *Visas* Not required *Inoc* Yellow Fever* if arriving from an infected area, Cholera, Hepatitis A, Malaria, Polio, Typhoid *Airlines* Air Zimbabwe, *Average length of flight* 16 hours *Food* Mealie Mealie and meat stew

Tanzania
Capital Dodoma *Lang* Swahili and English *Currency* Tanzanian Shilling = 100 cents *Govt* one-party state *Rel* Mixed - Muslim, Christian and traditional *Size* 945,087 sq km - 364,900 sq miles *Pop* 25,635,000 *GMT* +3 *When* June to November *Visas* Required, UK nationals require a Visitors Pass *Time to get* 5 days *Safety* At time of writing it was recommended to register with the High Commission/Embassy on arrival. Be aware of refugee problems from neighbouring Rwanda *Inoc* Yellow Fever, Cholera, Hepatitis A, Malaria, Polio, Typhoid

Airlines British Airways, Gulf Air, Aeroflot, Swissair, Egyptair, Sabena, KLM, Air France, Lufthansa *Average length of flight* 12 hours 45 minutes *Food* Maize based

Togo
Capital Lome *Lang* French *Currency* CFA Franc = 100 centimes *Govt* One-party military state *Rel* Mainly animist *Size* 56,785 sq km - 21,925 sq miles *Pop* 3,643,000 *GMT* GMT *When* mid July - mid September *Visas* Not required by UK, Canadian and US Citizens *Validity* 30 days *Time to Get* 2 days *Safety* Quiet at the moment, but potentially unstable, be vigilant *Inoc* Yellow Fever*, Cholera, Hepatitis A, Malaria, Polio, Typhoid *Airlines* Sabena, Air France, KLM *Average length of flight* 7 hours *Food* Spicy

Tunisia
Capital Tunis *Lang* Arabic *Currency* Tunisian Dinar = 1000 millimes *Govt* Multi-party state, although only certain parties are recognised *Rel* Islam *Size* 154,000 sq km - 59,460 sq miles *Pop* 8,200,000 *GMT* +1 *When* Spring and Autumn *Visas* Not Required by Canada, UK and US citizens *Validity* Up to 4 months *Safety* Relatively safe *Inoc* Yellow Fever* if arriving from an infected area, Cholera, Hepatitis A, Polio, Typhoid *Airlines* GB Airways, Tunis Air *Average length of flight* 2.5 hours *Food* Cooked with olive oil and delicately spiced

Uganda
Capital Kampala *Lang* English *Currency* Uganda Shilling = 100 cents *Govt* One-party state, with a president (Museveni) is Head of State and holds executive authority *Rel* Mainly Christian *Size* 241,139 sq km - 93,104 sq miles *Pop* 16,582,674 *GMT* +3 *When* June to October and December to March *Visas* Not Required *Validity* 3 months from date of issue *Time to get* 5 days *Safety* Armed robbery and road ambushes throughout Uganda. Do not travel at night *Inoc* Yellow Fever* if arriving from an infected area, Hepatitis A, Malaria, Polio, Typhoid, Yellow Fever *Airlines* Kenyan Airways, British Airways *Average length of flight* 8 hours *Food* Lots of bananas, millet bread and stews

Western Sahara (Disputed territory)

Zaire
Capital Kinshasa *Lang* Officially French many African languages used *Currency* Zaire = 100 makuta *Govt* Unstable *Rel* Christian mainly Roman Catholic *Size* 2,344,885 sq km - 905,365 sq miles *Pop* 36,672,000 *GMT* +1 and +2 depending on region *When* December to March in the North and May to October in the

south *Visas* Required by all *Validity* 1,2 or 3 months *Time to get* 2 days minimum *Safety* Check with Foreign Office, as country is unstable and therefore not safe for tourists, also be aware of the problems in neighbouring Rwanda *Inoc* Yellow Fever*, Hepatitis A, Cholera, Malaria, Polio, Typhoid, *Airlines* Sabena and Swissair *Average length of flight* 8 hours *Food* National dish is Moambe made with meat usually chicken in a peanut and palm oil spicy sauce. Very good pink bananas and pineapples

Zambia

Capital Lusaka *Lang* English *Currency* Kwacha = 100 ngwee *Govt* Having been a one-party state, the country is now led by the Movement for Multi-party Democracy Party and the constitution is changing *Rel* Christian *Size* 752,614 sq km - 290,586 sq miles *Pop* 8,023,000 *GMT* +2 *When* May to November *Visas* Required by US citizens *Validity* 3 months from date of issue *Time to get* At least 3 days *Safety* Travellers should be vigilant *Inoc* Yellow Fever* if arriving from an infected area, Cholera, Hepatitis A, Malaria, Polio, Typhoid *Airlines* British Airways, Zambia Airways *Average length of flight* 10 hours *Food* Very good fresh fish from Kariba

Zimbabwe

Capital Harare *Lang* English *Currency* Zimbabwe Dollar = 100 cents *Govt* Democracy *Rel* Christian *Size* 390,759 sq km - 150,873 sq miles *Pop* 10,401,767 *GMT* +2 *When* April, May, August and September *Visas* Not required *Safety* Safe *Inoc* Yellow Fever* if arriving from an infected area, Cholera, Hepatitis A, Malaria, Polio, Typhoid *Airlines* Air Zimbabwe , British Airways *Average length of flight* 9 hours *Food* Maize and beef varies from disgusting to delicious

North America

Canada

Capital Ottawa *Lang* French and English *Currency* Canadian Dollar = 100 cents *Govt* Liberal Party *Rel* Christian majority Roman Catholic *Size* 9,970,610 sq km - 3,849,674 sq miles *Pop* 27,408,900 *GMT* from -3.5 to -8 *When* All year *Visas* Not required *Safety* Safe *Airlines* Air Canada, British Airways amongst many many others *Average length of flight* Ottawa 7 hours *Food* Varied, French influences

United States of America

Capital Washington DC *Lang* English *Currency* US Dollar = 100 cents *Govt* A federal republic of states, with a stable democracy *Rel*

Christian *Size* 9,372,614 sq km - 3,618,770 sq miles *Pop* 255,082,000 *GMT* -5 to -10 *When* all year *Visas* Required by Australian and New Zealanders *Validity* Varies *Time to get* Can be up to 3 weeks by post *Safety* Depends on the area, take local advice, especially in Florida *Inoc* Polio for Hawaii *Airlines* United Airlines, Continental Airlines, British Airway fly direct to Washington - many other airlines operate to other cities in the USA *Average length of flight* 8 hours *Food* Home to the fast food chains, hamburgers, french fries. Pancakes for breakfast

Central America

Anguilla (UK)

Capital The Valley *Lang* English *Currency* Eastern Caribbean Dollar (EC$) = 100 cents *Govt* Separate dependency under the British Government *Rel* Christian *Size* 91 km sq - 35 sq miles *Pop* 8,960 *GMT* - 4 *When* Mid December to mid April *Visas* Not required *Safety* Safe *Airlines* LIAT, British Airways *Average length of flight* 12 hours including stopover in Antigua *Food* Caribbean a variety of seafood including lobster and whelk

Antigua and Barbuda

Capital St John's *Lang* English *Currency* Eastern Caribbean Dollar (EC$) = 100 cents *Govt* Elected Parliament (Antiguan Labour Party) with British Sovereignty *Rel* Christian *Size* 440 km sq - 170 sq miles *Pop* 66,000 *GMT* -4 *When* Mid December to Mid April *Visas* Not required *Safety* Safe *Inoc* Hepatitis A, Polio, Typhoid *Airlines* British Airways, BWIA, Lufthansa *Average length of flight* 8 hours *Food* Barbecues and roasts are a speciality, along with red snapper and lobster

Aruba (The Netherlands)

Capital Oranjestad *Lang* Dutch but English and Spanish are also spoken *Currency* Aruba Florin/Guilder = 100 cents *Govt* Part of the Kingdom of the Netherlands but own Governor *Rel* Roman Catholic *Size* 193 sq km - 74.5 sq miles *Pop* 72,000 *GMT* -4 *When* All year but showers in Oct, Nov and Dec *Visas* Not required *Safety* Safe *Inoc* Yellow Fever* if having come from an infected area, Polio, Typhoid *Airlines* KLM, VIASA, British Airways *Average length of flight* 11.5 hours *Food* Not a large variety of local food -meat or fish based. International cuisine also available

Bahamas

Capital Nassau *Lang* English *Currency* Bahamian Dollar = 100 cents *Govt* Governed by the Free National Movement party *Rel*

Christian *Size* 13,939 sq km - 5,382 sq miles *Pop* 254,646 *GMT* -5 (-4 in summer) *When* Mid December to Mid April *Visa* Not required *Safety* Safe *Inoc* Yellow Fever* if having come from an infected area, Polio, Typhoid *Airlines* American Airlines, Bahamasair, British Airways *Average length of flight* 9 hours *Food* Fresh fish and exotic fruit

Barbados
Capital Bridgetown *Lang* English *Currency* Barbados Dollar = 100 cents *Govt* Democratic Labour Party *Rel* Christian *Size* 430 sq km - 166 sq miles *Pop* 257,082 *GMT* -4 (-5 in summer) *When* Mid December to mid May *Visas* Not required for stays up to 90 days *Safety* Don't carry any valuables, mugging on the increase *Inoc* Yellow Fever* if having come from an infected area, Hepatitis A, Polio, Typhoid *Airlines* British Airways, BWIA *Average length of flight* 7.5 hours *Food* Mainly fish including the delicacy flying fish

Belize
Capital Belmopan *Lang* English *Currency* Belizean Dollar = 100 cents *Govt* A democracy led by the United Democratic Party *Rel* Christian - Mainly Roman Catholic *Size* 22,965 sq km - 8,867 sq miles *Pop* 190,792 *GMT* -6 *When* October to May *Visas* Not required *Safety* Be aware of pickpockets, but not as bad as South America *Inoc* Yellow Fever* if having come from an infected area, Typhoid, Polio, Hepatitis A, Malaria *Airlines* American Airlines *Average length of flight* 11 hours *Food* International but also Latin American and Creole

Bonaire (Netherland Antilles)
Capital Kralendjik *Lang* Dutch *Currency* Netherland Antilles Guilder or Florin = 100 cents *Govt* Part of The Netherland Antilles therefore part of the Dutch Govt, elected local council *Rel* Roman Catholic *Size* 288 sq km - 111 sq miles *Pop* 11,139 *GMT* -4 *When* Feb to June *Visas* Not required. UK nationals issued with Certificate of Admission on arrival *Inoc* Typhoid, Polio, Hepatitis A *Airlines* KLM *Average length of flight* 11 hours *Food* Creole

Cayman Islands (UK)
Capital George Town *Lang* English *Currency* Cayman Island Dollar = 100 cents *Govt* A British Dependent Territory with a Governor *Rel* Christian *Size* 259 sq km - 100 sq miles *Pop* 29,700 *GMT* -5 *When* October to May *Visas* Not required *Safety* Safe *Inoc* Polio, Typhoid *Airlines* British Airways, Cayman Airways *Average length of flight* 9 hours *Food* Seafood

Costa Rica

Capital San Jose *Lang* Spanish *Currency* Costa Rican Colon = 100 centimos *Govt* A democracy although one of the more stable govts in Central America, it's suffering from some civil unrest. *Rel* Roman Catholic *Size* 51,060 sq km - 19,720 sq miles *Pop* 2,993,676 *GMT* -7 *When* Dec to Apr *Visa* Not required *Safety* Beware of tides while swimming *Inoc* Hepatitis A, Malaria, Polio, Typhoid, *Airlines* KLM, Iberia, Viasa, American Airlines *Average length of flight* 12 hours *Food* Rice, beans, beef, yuca, corn, nampi and chayote

Cuba
Capital Havana *Lang* Spanish *Currency* Cuban Peso = 100 centavos *Govt* Communist *Rel* Roman Catholic *Size* 110,860 sq km - 42,803 sq miles *Pop* 10,736,000 *GMT* -4 *When* Nov to April *Visas* Required by all *Validity* 6 months *Time to get* 2-3 days *Safety* Take advice from the Foreign Office *Inoc* Hepatitis A, Polio, Typhoid *Airlines* Cubana, Iberia, Viasa, Aeroflot *Average length of flight* 19 hours including stopovers *Food* Continental and Cuban - fish and exotic fruit

Curaçao (Netherlands Antilles)
Capital Willemstad *Lang* Dutch *Currency* Netherlands Antilles Guilder or Florin = 100 cents *Govt* Self governing, part of the Netherlands *Rel* Christian *Size* 444 sq km - 171 sq miles *Pop* 143,816 *GMT* -4 *When* Mid December - mid April *Visas* Not required for visits up to 14 days *Inoc* Yellow Fever* if arriving from an infected area, Polio, Typhoid *Airlines* KLM *Average length of flight* 11 hours *Food* Dutch and spicy Creole

Dominica
Capital Roseau *Lang* English *Currency* East Caribbean Dollar = 100 cents *Govt* Democracy, held by the Dominican Freedom Party *Rel* Roman Catholic *Size* 750 sq km - 290 sq miles *Pop* 71,183 *GMT* -4 *When* January - May *Visas* Not required *Safety* Safe *Inoc* Yellow Fever* if arriving from an infected area. Polio, Typhoid, Hepatitis A *Airlines* British Airways, LIAT *Average length of flight* 10 hours *Food* Creole

Dominican Republic
Capital Santo Domingo *Lang* Spanish *Currency* Dominican Republic Peso = 100 centavos *Govt* Democracy elections to be held in 1994 *Rel* Roman Catholic *Size* 48,422 sq km - 18,696 sq miles *Pop* 7,313,000 *GMT* -4 *When* December - April *Visas* Not required for up to 60 days by US, Canada, Australia, UK nationals *Inoc* Hepatitis A, Polio, Malaria, Typhoid, *Airlines* Air France, Iberia, American Airlines *Average length of flight* 11 hours including stopover *Food* Spanish influences,

pork, goat and seafood are the staple diet

El Salvador

Capital San Salvador *Lang* Spanish *Currency* Colon (Peso) = 100 centavos *Govt* Unstable republic *Rel* Roman Catholic *Size* 21,721 sq km - 8,124 sq miles *Pop* 5,251,678 *GMT* -6 *When* Don't *Visas* Not required by UK or New Zealand nationals *Validity* Up to 90 days *Time to get* 10 days *Safety* El Salvador is dangerous due to political unrest, it is not recommended at all as a tourist destination, for advice contact the Foreign Office *Inoc* Yellow Fever* if arriving from an infected area, Hepatitis A, Malaria, Polio, Typhoid *Airlines* British Airways then AVIATECA *Average length of flight* 10.5 hours excluding stopover in Miami *Food* Like Mexican

Grenada

Capital St Georges *Lang* English *Currency* Eastern Caribbean Dollar = 100 cents *Govt* Democracy, currently ruled by the National Democratic Congress, elections due in 1995 *Rel* Christian *Size* 334.5 sq km - 133 sq miles *Pop* 95,343 *GMT* -4 *When* January to May *Visas* Not required if staying less than 14 days *Inoc* Yellow Fever* if arriving from an infected area, Polio, Typhoid *Airlines* British Airways *Average length of flight* 9 hours *Food* Seafood and vegetables

Guadeloupe

Capital Basse-Terre(admin) Pointe-a-Pitre (comm) *Lang* French *Currency* French Franc = 100 centimes *Govt* Four representatives in the French Govt *Rel* Roman Catholic *Size* 1,780 sq km - 687 sq miles *Pop* 387,034 *GMT* -4 *When* January - May *Visas* Required by Australians *Validity* Up to 3 months *Time to Get* Same day *Inoc* Yellow Fever* if arriving from an infected area, Hepatitis A, Polio, Typhoid *Airlines* Air France via Paris *Average length of flight* 12 hours 40 minutes *Food* Spicy Creole

Guatemala

Capital Guatemala City *Lang* Spanish *Currency* Quetzal = 100 centavos *Govt* Democracy *Rel* Roman Catholic *Size* 108,429 sq km - 42,042 sq miles *Pop* 9,453,953 *GMT* -6 *When* October - May *Visas* Not required by UK, Canada USA nationals if arriving by air *Validity* 30 days from date of entry *Time to get* 1 day in person *Safety* Beware of fighting between Guerrillas and Government soldiers *Inoc* Cholera, Yellow Fever* if arriving from an infected area, Hepatitis A, Malaria, Polio, Typhoid *Airlines* KLM, Iberia, American Airlines *Average length of flight* 8 hours *Food* Like but not as good as, Mexican food

Haiti

Capital Port-au-Prince *Lang* French and Creole *Currency* Gourde = 100 centimes *Govt* Following a strict regime it is now extremely unstable *Rel* Roman Catholic - Voodooism is also still practised *Size* 27,750 sq km - 10,714 sq miles *Pop* 6,625,000 *GMT* -5 *When* November to March *Visas* Not required by UK US and Canada but check *Validity* 90 days from date of issue *Safety* Due to political unrest it is strongly advised not to travel to Haiti *Inoc* Yellow Fever* if arriving from an infected area, Hepatitis A, Polio, Malaria, Typhoid *Airlines* Air France *Average length of flight* 8 hours *Food* Creole

Honduras

Capital Tegucigalpa *Lang* Spanish *Currency* Lempira = 100 centavos *Govt* Democratic *Rel* Roman Catholic *Size* 111,888 sq km - 43,277 sq miles *Pop* 4,915,900 *GMT* -6 *When* November to April *Visas* Not required *Validity* Up to 1 month *Safety* Violence has increased, do not wear jewellery or carry large amounts of cash *Inoc* Yellow Fever* if arriving from an infected country, Malaria, Hepatitis A, Polio, Cholera, Typhoid *Airlines* Via Houston and Miami, SAHSA or American Airlines *Average length of flight* 12.5 hours *Food* Seafood and tropical fruits

Jamaica

Capital Kingston *Lang* English *Currency* Jamaican Dollar = 100 cents *Govt* Elected Labour govt *Rel* Protestant *Size* 10,991 sq km - 4,244 sq miles *Pop* 2,374,193 *GMT* -5 *When* December to April *Visas* Required by NZ *Safety* Generally safe for tourists but be vigilant, do not walk at night or use public transport *Inoc* Yellow Fever* if arriving from an infected area, Hepatitis A, Polio, Typhoid. *Airlines* British Airways direct or American Airlines via Miami *Average length of flight* 10 hours *Food* Fire and spice

Martinique (France)

Capital Fort-de-France *Lang* French *Currency* French franc = 100 centimes *Govt* Overseas Department of the Republic of France sending 4 representatives to the French National Assembly *Rel* Roman Catholic *Size* 1,100 sq km - 425 sq miles *Pop* 359,572 *GMT* -4 *When* December to June *Visas* Not required *Inoc* Yellow Fever* if arriving from an infected area, Cholera, Hepatitis A, Polio, Typhoid *Airlines* British Airways, Air France *Average length of flight* 12 hours including stopover in Paris *Food* Creole and French cooking, delicious seafood

Mexico

Capital Mexico City *Lang* Spanish *Currency* Peso = 100 centavos *Govt* Federal republic, elected national congress, unstable due to guerrilla activity *Rel* Roman Catholic *Size* 1,958,201 sq km - 756,066 sq miles *Pop* 85,000,000 *GMT* -6 to -8 *When* October to May *Visas* Not required *Safety* Central Chaipas remains tense, seek local advice *Inoc* Cholera*, Yellow Fever* if arriving from an infected area, Hepatitis A, Malaria, Polio, Typhoid. *Airlines* British Airways (direct), KLM, Air France, Lufthansa, United Airlines, Iberia, Virgin Atlantic, Mexicana. *Average length of flight* 12 hours 20 minutes *Food* Tortillas, tacos, enchiladas, chilli and guacamole

Montserrat (UK)

Capital Plymouth *Lang* English *Currency* East Caribbean Dollar = 100 cents *Govt* Led by the National Progressive party *Rel* Christian *Size* 102 sq km - 40 sq miles *Pop* 11,900 *GMT* -4 *When* January - June *Visas* Not required *Inoc* Yellow Fever* if arriving from an infected area, Cholera*, Hepatitis A, Polio, Typhoid *Airlines* British Airways, LIAT *Average length of flight* 8.5 hours *Food* A delicacy is mountain chicken (frogs' legs) - barbecues are very popular

Nicaragua

Capital Managua *Lang* Spanish *Currency* Nicaraguan Gold Cordoba = 100 centavos *Govt* Elected National Assembly - unstable *Rel* Roman Catholic *Size* 120,254 sq km - 46,430 sq miles *Pop* 4,264,845 *GMT* -6 *When* Dec - May *Visas* Not required by UK and US Nationals *Validity* 1 month *Time to get* 48 hours *Safety* No longer at civil war, but political stability and safety can not be guaranteed, contact the Foreign Office for advice *Inoc* Yellow Fever* if arriving from an infected area, Hepatitis A, Malaria, Polio, Typhoid *Airlines* Iberia, Aeroflot *Average length of flight* 20 hours 30 minutes *Food* Little variety mainly eggs or meat, beans and rice.

Panama

Capital Panama City *Lang* Spanish *Currency* Balboa = 100 centesimos *Govt* Democracy, although unsteady due to economic difficulties *Rel* Roman Catholic *Size* 75,517 sq km - 29,157 sq miles *Pop* 2,514,586 *GMT* -5 *When* January through April *Visas* Not required by most nationalities if travelling as a tourist - check with Embassy *Validity* 30 days from date of entry *Time to get* 24 hours *Safety* Do not visit the Colombian border. Muggings have increased in tourist areas *Inoc* Yellow Fever*, Hepatitis A, Malaria, Typhoid *Airlines* KLM, American Airlines *Average length of flight* 14

hours *Food* Hot and spicy

Puerto Rico (USA)

Capital San Juan *Lang* Spanish *Currency* US Dollar = 100 cents *Govt* A Commonwealth State of the US, with an elected governor *Rel* Roman Catholic *Size* 8,959 sq km - 3,459 sq miles *Pop* 3,551,000 *GMT* -4 *When* Hot and tropical all year *Visas* The same as the USA *Safety* Beware of pickpockets *Inoc* Hepatitis A, Polio, Typhoid *Airlines* British Airways, American Airlines *Average length of flight* 8 hours *Food* Spanish based with rice and beans as the staple diet

Saba (Netherlands Antilles)

Capital The Bottom *Lang* English and Dutch *Currency* Netherlands Antilles Guilder or Florin = 100 cents *Govt* Part of the Kingdom of the Netherlands, but own Governor *Rel* Roman Catholic *Size* 13 sq km - 5 sq miles *Pop* 1,116s *GMT* -4 *When* Dec - July *Visas* Tourists allowed 14 days without visas *Inoc* Yellow Fever* if arriving from an infected area, Typhoid, Polio *Airlines who fly there* Via St Kitts *Average length of flight* 11 hours *Food* Exotic fruit and spicy meat

St Eustatius

Capital Oranjestad *Lang* English *Currency* Netherlands Antilles Guilder *Govt* Part of the Kingdom of the Netherlands, but own Governor *Rel* Protestant *Size* 21 sq km - 8 sq miles *Pop* 1,781 *GMT* -4 *When* January to June *Visas* Tourists allowed 14 days without a visa *Inoc* Yellow Fever* if arriving from an infected area, Polio, Typhoid *Airlines* Via Antigua and St Kitts *Average length of flight* 12 hours *Food* Creole - International

St Kitts and Nevis

Capital Basseterre *Lang* English *Currency* Eastern Caribbean Dollar = 100 cents *Govt* An independent state within the British Commonwealth, present government a coalition *Rel* Anglican *Size* 168.4 sq km - 65.1 sq miles *Pop* 44,000 *GMT* -4 *When* January to April *Visas* Not required *Safety Inoc* Yellow Fever* if arriving from an infected area, Typhoid, Polio *Airlines* British Airways to Antigua, then LIAT *Average length of flight* 10 hours *Food* Seafood and exotic fruits, St Kitts has a reputation for good food

St Lucia

Capital Castries *Lang* English *Currency* Eastern Caribbean Dollar = 100 cents *Govt* Elected govt, presently The United Workers Party are in power *Rel* Roman Catholic *Size* 616 sq km - 238 sq miles *Pop* 136,041 *GMT* -4

When Jan - April *Visas* Not required *Safety* Safe *Inoc* Yellow Fever* if arriving from an infected area, Hepatitis A, Polio, Typhoid *Airlines* British Airways, BWIA *Average length of flight* 8.5 hours *Food* Creole - very good local fish

St Maarten

Capital Philipsburg *Lang* English *Currency* Netherlands Antilles Guilder or Florin = 100 cents *Govt* French and Dutch dual sovereignty *Rel* Mainly Protestant *Size* 41 sq km - 16 sq miles *Pop* 36,408 *GMT* -4 *When* January to May *Visas* Not required by tourists if staying less than 14 days *Inoc* Yellow Fever* if arriving from an infected area, Hepatitis A, Polio, Typhoid *Airline* American Airlines, Lufthansa, British Airways, LIAT *Average length of flight* 12 hours *Food* Dutch, French, English and Creole

St Vincent and Grenadines

Capital Kingstown *Lang* English *Currency* Eastern Caribbean Dollar = 100 cents *Govt* Elected Govt, with the New Democratic Party winning every single seat in the last election *Rel* Christian *Size* 344 sq km - 133 sq miles *Pop* 106,499 *GMT* -4 *When* Jan - May *Visas* Not required *Safety* Safe *Inoc* Yellow Fever* if arriving from an infected area, Hepatitis A, Polio, Typhoid *Airlines* British Airways, LAIT *Average length of flight* 9 hours *Food* Delicious seafood

Trinidad and Tobago

Capital Port of Spain *Lang* English *Currency* Trinidad and Tobago Dollar = 100 cents *Govt* democracy *Rel* Christian *Size* 5,128 sq km - 1,980 sq miles *Pop* 1,253,000 *GMT* -4 *When* December to May *Visas* Required by Australia and New Zealand *Validity* 3 months *Time to get* 2 days *Inoc* Yellow Fever* if arriving from an infected area, Hepatitis A, Polio Typhoid *Airlines* BWIA, British Airways *Average length of flight* 10.5 hours *Food* Creole, very good seafood

Turks and Caicos (UK)

Capital Cockburn Town *Lang* English *Currency* US Dollar = 100 cents *Govt* British Monarch is Head of State with an elected parliament *Rel* Roman Catholic *Size* 430 sq km - 166 sq miles *Pop* 12,350 *GMT* -5 *When* January to August *Visas* Not required *Inoc* Polio, Typhoid *Airlines* Via Nassau or Miami *Average length of flight* 13.5 hours *Food* Seafood based

Virgin Islands (UK)

Capital Road Town *Lang* English *Currency*: US Dollar = 100 cents *Govt* Internal self-govt

lead by Stoutt leader of the Virgin Islands' Party, defence and foreign affairs controlled by London *Rel* Christian *Size* 153 sq km - 59 sq miles *Pop* 16,644 *GMT* -4 *When* All year *Visas* Not required *Safety* Safe *Inoc* Hepatitis A, Polio, Typhoid *Airlines* British Airways, LIAT *Average length of flight* 10 hours *Food* Bounteous seafood

Virgin Island (US)

Capital Charlotte Amalie *Lang* English *Currency* US Dollar = 100 cents *Govt* A US colony, the executive authority is vested in the elected Governor *Rel* Christian *Size* 354.8 sq km - 137 sq miles *Pop* 101,809 *GMT* -4 *When* All year *Visas* Required but not by UK, US and Canadian citizens *Safety* Safe *Inoc* Hepatitis A, Polio, Typhoid *Airlines* American Airlines *Average length of flight* 14 hours *Food* Some of the best in the Caribbean

South America

Argentina

Capital Buenos Aires *Lang* Spanish *Currency* Neuvo Peso = 100 centavos *Govt* Menem (a Peronist) is the elected President *Rel* Roman Catholic *Size* 2,766,889 sq km - 1,068,302 sq miles *Pop* 32,370,298 *GMT* -3 *When* All year round *Visas* Only required for Business visits, not tourists except by Australians *Validity* *Safety* Reasonably but as in any South American country beware of pick-pockets *Inoc* Hepatitis A, Malaria, Typhoid, Polio *Airlines* British Airways, Aerolineas Argentinas *Average length of flight* 18 hours *Food* Famous for their beef, the local cuisine has Basque, Spanish and Italian influences

Bolivia

Capital La Paz *Lang* Spanish *Currency* Boliviano = 100 centavos *Govt* Elected Govt, current President is Gonzalo Sanchez de Lozado *Rel* Roman Catholic *Size* 1,084,391 sq km - 424,164 sq miles *Pop* 7,612,000 *GMT* -4 *When* April - November *Visas* Required by Australians and Canadians and for business *Validity* 30 days from date of entry *Time to get* 1 day *Safety* Care should be taken, theft can be rife. The cocaine growing areas should be avoided *Inoc* Yellow Fever* if coming from an infected area or going to Beni or Santa Cruz, Hepatitis A, Malaria, Polio, *Airlines* American Airlines, Lufthansa *Average length of flight* 17 hours *Food* Hot chilli sauces - meat based

Brazil

Capital Brasilia *Lang* Portuguese *Currency* Cruzeiro = 100 centavos *Govt* Conservative - Itamar Franco as President *Rel* Roman Catholic

Size 8,511,996 sq km - 3,286,500 sq miles *Pop* 153,322,000 *GMT* from -3 to -5 *When* The Carnival in February and any other time as the country has four different climatic regions *Visas* Required by Australians, Canadians and Americans *Validity* 90 days *Time to get* 2 days *Safety* As with all countries in South America beware of pickpockets *Inoc* Yellow Fever* if arriving from an infected area, vaccines recommended for some rural areas, Polio, Hepatitis A, Malaria, Typhoid *Airlines* Varig, British Airways and many more *Average length of flight* 11 hours *Food* Varied, renowned for their beef

Chile

Capital Santiago *Lang* Spanish *Currency* Peso = 100 centavos *Govt* Democracy following Pinochet's dictatorship *Rel* Roman Catholic *Size* 756,626 sq km - 292,135 sq miles *Pop* 13,599,441 *GMT* -6 *When* October to April *Visas* Not required *Safety* Safe *Inoc* Hepatitis A, Polio, Typhoid *Airlines* American Airlines, British Airways, Viasa *Average length of flight* 18 hours 45 minutes *Food* Typically South American, except Conger Eel is their national dish.

Colombia

Capital Sante Fe de Bogota *Lang* Spanish *Currency* Peso *Govt* Elections scheduled in 1994 *Rel* Roman Catholic *Size* 1,141,748 sq km - 440,831 sq miles *Pop* 32,841,126 *GMT*-5 *When* December - March *Visas* Not required if staying less than 90 days - check with Embassy *Safety* Always be on the look out and look after your belongings. The South American Handbook recommends not to accept food, sweets or drinks from strangers, they can be drugged. *Inoc* Cholera, Hepatitis A, Malaria, Polio, Typhoid, Yellow Fever *Airlines* British Airways *Average length of flight* 13.5 hours *Food* Corn pancakes, chicken, seafood and rice, delicious avocados and exotic fruits

Ecuador

Capital Quito *Lang* Spanish *Currency* Sucre = 100 centavos *Govt* Democracy - far right *Rel* Roman Catholic *Size* 272,045 sq km - 104,506 sq miles *Pop* 11,078,400 *GMT* -5 (Galapagos Islands -6) *When* June to October *Visas* Not required *Safety* Ecuador is one of the safest countries in South America but still be on your guard *Inoc* Yellow Fever* if arriving from an infected area, Cholera, Hepatitis A, Malaria, Polio, Typhoid *Airlines* Lufthansa, American Airlines, Air France, Iberia, KLM *Average length of flight* 17 hours *Food* National delicacy - Guinea Pig

French Guiana (France)

Capital Cayenne *Lang* French *Currency* French franc = 100 centimes *Govt Rel* Roman Catholic *Size* 91,000 sq km - 35,135 sq miles *Pop* 114,808 *GMT* -3 *When* July to mid November *Visas* Required by Australians *Validity* varies *Time to get* 1 day *Inoc* Yellow Fever* if arriving from an infected area, Hepatitis A, Malaria, Polio, Typhoid *Airlines* Air France via Paris *Average length of flight* 11 hours *Food* Seafood - anything else is expensive

Guyana

Capital Georgetown *Lang* English *Currency* Guyana Dollar = 100 cents *Govt* Democracy *Rel* Mainly Christian - some Hindu *Size* 214,969 sq km - 83,000 sq miles *Pop* 739,553 *GMT* -3 *When* February to March and August to October *Visas* Not required *Safety* Violent crime common in Georgetown *Inoc* Yellow Fever* if arriving from an infected area, Hepatitis A, Malaria, Polio,Typhoid, Yellow Fever *Airlines* British Airways, BWIA *Average length of flight* 10 hours *Food* Indian, African and Portuguese influences

Paraguay

Capital Asuncion *Lang* Spanish and Guarani *Currency* Guarani *Govt* Having been a military regime until 1992, it is now a multi-party democracy *Rel* Roman Catholic *Size* 406,752 sq km - 157,048 sq miles *Pop* 4,397,306 *GMT* - 4 *When* June - Sept *Visas* Not required by US, Canada and UK nationals travelling as tourists for less than 90 days *Inoc* Hepatitis A, Malaria, Polio, Typhoid *Airlines* British Airways, American Airlines, Iberia *Average length of flight* 15 hours *Food* Maize based - soup very popular

Peru

Capital Lima *Lang* Spanish and Quechua *Currency* Nuevo sol = 100 centimos *Govt* Having been extremely unstable, Fujimori who was elected in 1990, then in 1992 with the backing of the security forces, ruled by decree, stability is returning with the imprisonment of Senedro (leader of the Shining Path) and democratic elections are due in 1995 *Rel* Roman Catholic *Size* 1,280,000 sq km - 496,225 sq miles *Pop* 22,453,861 *GMT* -5 *When* December through April *Visas* Not required by tourists from UK, US and Canada up to 90 days *Safety* Extremely dangerous in places, especially the central highlands. Tourists in the past have been attacked by the Shining Path (the terrorist organization) *Inoc* Cholera, Yellow Fever* if arriving from an infected area, Hepatitis A, Malaria, Typhoid, *Airlines* KLM, Lufthansa, Viasa, American Airlines, Iberia, Air France *Average length of* *flight* 14 hours *Food* Lots of vegetables and potatoes. In Lima ceviche (raw fish marinated in lemon juice and hot peppers) is popular

Suriname

Capital Paramaribo *Lang* Dutch *Currency* Suriname Guilder = 100 cents *Govt* Having been through various regimes and coups since independence in 1975, there now is an elected govt *Rel* Majority Christian *Size* 163,265 sq km - 63,037 sq miles *Pop* 404,310 *GMT* -3 *When* December to April *Visas* Required but not by UK nationals *Validity* Varies *Time to get* 1-6 weeks *Inoc* Yellow Fever* if arriving from an infected area, Cholera, Hepatitis A, Malaria, Typhoid, Yellow Fever *Airlines* KLM *Average length of flight* 10 hours *Food* Creole - Indonesian influences

Uruguay

Capital Montevideo *Lang* Spanish *Currency* Uruguayan Peso = 100 centesimos *Govt* Stable democracy *Rel* Roman Catholic *Size* 176,215 sq km - 68,037 sq miles *Pop* 3,112,000 *GMT* -3 *When* December to March *Visas* Not required by UK and US citizens *Time to get* 4 days *Inoc* Hepatitis A, Typhoid *Airlines* Iberia, Air France, Aerolineas Argentinas *Average length of flight* 15 hours *Food* Lots of meat, mainly beef

Venezuela

Capital Caracas *Lang* Spanish *Currency* Bolivar = 100 centimos *Govt* Now a more stable democracy *Rel* Roman Catholic *Size* 912,050 sq km - 352,144 sq km *Pop* 20,226,227 *GMT* -4 *When* January to April *Visas* Not required but issued with a Tourist Card on 'plane *Safety* Violent crime increasing in cities, be careful *Inoc* Yellow Fever, Hepatitis A, Malaria, Polio, Typhoid *Airlines* Viasa, British Airways *Average length of flight* 12 hours *Food* Good beef, maize bread, most food delicately spiced

Asia

Afghanistan

Capital Kabul *Lang* Pashtu and Dari, some English spoken *Currency* Afgani (Af) = 100 puls *Govt* At present a coalition but very unstable and only really applicable to Kabul *Rel* Islamic *Size* 652,225 sq km - 251,773 sq miles *Pop* 18,614,000 *GMT* + 4.5 *When* Summer and early Autumn - Winter can be very cold indeed in the mountains *Visas* Required by everyone but at present not being issued *Safety* Dangerous at present, strict Muslim majority therefore women should not travel alone and should be totally covered, outside Kabul in

tribal areas very little protection. At present politically unstable - check with Foreign Office British and US embassies are closed in Kabul *Inoc* Yellow Fever* if arriving from an infected area, Cholera, Typhoid, Polio, Malaria, Hepatitis A, *Airlines* Ariana Afghan Airlines *Average length of flight* 11 hours including stopovers *Food* Indian style (spicy)- lots of meat especially goat kebabs

Armenia (C.I.S.)

Capital Yerevan *Lang* Armenian and Russian *Currency* Newly introduced Dram notes are the official currency, the Russian rouble is still legal tender 200 roubles = 1 Dram *Govt* Levon Petrosyan is the elected President, Leader of the Armenian Pan-National Movement *Rel* Christian *Size* 29,88 sq km- 11,500 sq miles *Pop* 3,354,000 *GMT* +3 *When* June to September *Visas* Required by all *Validity* 21 days or 1 year *Time to get* Not less than 10 days before departure *Safety* Due to the political and religious unrest with Azerbaijan tourists are strongly advised not to go to any of the Trans-Causican republics *Airlines* Via Paris, State Airlines Company of Armenia (SACA) *Food* Lamb is favoured highly, sadly though unless you eat in a private house, the food tends to be heavy and greasy, an influence of the Soviet era.

Azerbaijan (C.I.S)

Capital Baku *Lang* Azerbaijani *Currency* Manat = 100 gyapik Russian Rouble is also legal tender *Govt* Elected President and Parliament. Aliyev is currently President, a communist he was a member of the Politburo *Rel* Muslim - mainly Shia *Size* 86,600 sq km - 33,400 sq miles *Pop* 7,174,000 *GMT* + 4 *When* June to September *Visas* Required by all *Time to get* Not less than 14 days before departure *Safety* Due to the political and religious unrest with Azberbaijan tourists are strongly advised not to go to any of the Trans-Causican republics. Baku is stable, but Nagomy karabkh still has fighting *Inoc* Malaria *Airlines* Azerbaijan Airlines *Food* Turkish, Georgian, and central Asia influences. Plov is the most common dish consisting of rice, mutton and spices

Bahrain

Capital Manama *Lang* Arabic and English *Currency* Dinar = 1000 fils *Govt* Ruled by an Arab monarchy (no elections) *Rel* Muslim *Size* 693 sq km - 267 sq miles *Pop* 503,022 *GMT* +3 *When* December to March rest of year very hot *Visas* Not required by UK, required by US, Australians and Canadians (no Israeli stamps in passports) *Time to get* 1 day *Safety* Safe *Inoc* Yellow Fever* if arriving from an infected area,

Polio, Cholera, Typhoid *Airlines* British Airways, Gulf Air, amongst others *Average length of flight* 6 hours *Food* Spicy and strongly flavoured - meat mainly lamb

Bangladesh

Capital Dhaka *Lang* Bengali and English *Currency* Bangladeshi Taka = 100 Poishas *Govt* Ruled by the Bangladesh National party *Rel* Muslim *Size* 147,570 sq km - 56,977 sq miles *Pop* 111,400,00 *GMT* +6 *When* November to March *Visas* Required by all-except Canadians and US nationals if staying less than 15 days *Validity* 3 months *Time to get* 1-5 working days *Safety* Safe if sensible, women should be covered *Inoc* Yellow Fever* if arriving from an infected area, Cholera Hepatitis A, Malaria, Polio, Typhoid *Airlines* Bangladesh Airlines, British Airways *Average length of flight* 10.5 hours *Food* Spicy seafood, chicken and lamb, limited Western food

Bhutan

Capital Thimphu *Lang* Dzongkha *Currency* 1 Ngultrum = 100 chetrums *Govt* Ruled by the monarch Jigme Singye Wangchuck *Rel* Buddhist *Size* 46,500 sq km - 17,954 sq miles *Pop* 1,375,400 *GMT* +6 *When* October, November and April to mid-June *Visas* Required by all. Can be difficult to obtain *Validity* Visas issued on arrival however application must be sent 3 months before departure *Safety* Extremely safe *Inoc* Yellow Fever* if arriving from an infected area, Cholera, Hepatitis A, Typhoid, Polio Malaria, *Airlines* Druk Air from India, Nepal or Thailand *Food* Like Nepalese food quite spicy with Chinese influence - mainly vegetarian

Brunei

Capital Bandar Seri Begawan *Lang* Malay (English also spoken) *Currency* Brunei Dollar = 100 sen *Govt* Sultan - His Majesty Paduka Seri Baginda Sultan Haji Hassanal Bolkiah Mu'izzaddin Waddaulah (Supreme) *Rel* Mainly Sunni Muslim *Size* 5,765 sq km - 2,226 sq miles *Pop* 256,500 *GMT* +8 *When* April - September *Visas* Required by Australians (US and Canadians if more than 14 days) *Validity* 3 months *Time to get* 2 - 3 days *Inoc* Yellow Fever* if arriving from an infected area, Cholera, Hepatitis A, Polio, Typhoid *Airlines* Royal Brunei Airlines *Average length of flight* 17 hours *Food* Abundance of fresh fish and rice - spicy Malay influence

Cambodia

Capital Phnom Penh *Lang* Khmer - Chinese and Vietnamese also spoken *Currency* Riel = 100 sen *Govt* An elected Govt with Prince Sihanouk as President still faces the threat from the Khmer Rouge, which controls large parts of the country *Rel* Buddhist *Size* 181,035 sq km - 69,898 sq miles *Pop* 8,246,000 *GMT* +7 *When* December - April *Visas* Required by all *Validity* 1 month *Time to get* Anything from 3 days to 2 weeks *Safety* Extremely unsafe, Khmer Rouge, the plague and unexploded mines *Inoc* Yellow Fever* if arriving from an infected area, Cholera, Hepatitis A, Malaria, Polio, Typhoid *Airlines* Thai Airways via Bangkok *Average length of flight* 11 hours *Food* Rice based, popular dishes include salted fish

China

Capital Beijing *Lang* Mandarin Chinese *Currency* 1 Yaun = 100 fen or 10 chiao *Govt* Communist, very strong since the Tiananmen Massacre *Rel* Buddhist *Size* 9,571,300 sq km - 3,695,500 sq miles *Pop* 1,158,230,000 *GMT* +8 *When* Any time as China is so vast there is a diversity of climate *Visas* Required *Validity* Dependent on length of stay *Time to get* Allow as much time as possible *Safety* Safe if sensible *Inoc* Yellow Fever* if arriving from an infected area, Hepatitis A, Cholera, Malaria, Polio, Typhoid *Airlines* British Airways, Air China *Average length of flight* 14 hours *Food* As expected, Chinese. Very good in cities, basic in outlying provinces

Georgia (CIS)

Capital Tbilisi *Lang* Georgian, Russian *Currency* Still using the Russian rouble, but are introducing their own currency the Lary *Govt* Elected President Eduard Schevardnadze *Rel* Christian majority *Size* 70,000 sq km - 27,000 sq miles *Pop* 5,471,000 *GMT* +4 *When* May to September *Visas* Required through the Russian embassy *Time to get* Allow 14 days *Safety* Travel is not advised contact the Foreign Office *Airlines* Via Moscow *Food* Best food found anywhere in the former Soviet Union

Hong Kong (UK)

Capital Hong Kong *Lang* Chinese and English *Currency* Hong Kong Dollar = 100 cents *Govt* Currently administered by the British Governor-General Chris Patten, this British Colony will revert to the People's Republic of China in June 1997 *Rel* Buddhists, Christians, Confucian, Taoists and Muslims *Size* 1,076 sq km - 415 sq miles *Pop* 5,757,900 *GMT* +8 *When* October to May *Visas* Not required *Safety* Safe *Inoc* Polio, Typhoid *Airlines* Cathay Pacific, British Airways, Virgin Atlantic *Average length of flight* 13.5 hours *Food* Better Chinese food than available in China - International

India

Capital New Delhi *Lang* English *Currency* Rupee = 100 paise *Govt* Federal republic currently ruled by the Congress Party *Rel* Majority Hindu *Size* 3,287,262 sq km - 1,269,218 sq miles *Pop* 846,302,688 *GMT* +5.5 *When* All year but if June - August go to far north (Ladakh) *Visas* Required by all *Validity* 1 or 6 months from date of issue *Time to get* 2 days in person, 4-5 weeks by post *Safety* Safe if sensible. Certain areas eg. Punjab and Kashmir, in state of unrest and should be avoided *Inoc* Yellow Fever* if having arrived from an infected country, Cholera, Hepatitis A, Malaria, Polio, Typhoid *Airlines* Air Canada, Air India, Thai International, British Airways *Average length of flight* 9 hours *Food* Delicious curries, suitable for vegetarians

Indonesia

Capital Jakarta *Lang* Bahasa Indonesian *Currency* Rupiah = 100 sen *Govt* Basically a military regime with Suharto as President, although there is an elected Govt *Rel* Muslim majority *Size* 1,904,569 sq km - 735,358 sq miles *Pop* 182,000,000 *GMT* +7 - +9 *When* June to September *Visas* Not required if a tourist *Safety* Safe *Inoc* Yellow Fever* if having arrived from an infected area, Hepatitis A, Malaria, Polio, Typhoid *Airlines* Garuda Indonesia, British Airways, other airlines fly there using transfer connections *Average length of flight* 20 hours 20 minutes *Food* Highly spiced

Iran

Capital Tehran *Lang* Persian(Farsi) *Currency* Iranian Rial = 100 dinars *Govt* Elected President (Rafsanjani) although all other candidates are hand-picked to loose *Rel* Islamic *Size* 1,648,000 sq km - 636,296 sq miles *Pop* 57,727,000 *GMT* +3.5 *When* November to March *Visas* Required by all *Validity* Up to 3 months from date of issue *Time to get* 4 weeks *Safety* Take sensible precautions, there is a total ban on video cameras *Inoc* Yellow Fever* if arriving from an infected area, Hepatitis A, Malaria, Polio, Typhoid *Airlines* British Airways, Iran air *Average length of flight* 8 hours *Food* Staple diet is rice and meat, mainly mutton

Iraq

Capital Baghdad *Lang* Arabic *Currency* Iraqi Dinar = 20 dirhams = 1000 fils *Govt* Dictatorship - Saddam Hussein, elections are meant to be held every 4 years, no elections since Saddam came to power in 1979 *Rel* Muslim both Sunni and Shi'ite *Size* 438,317 sq km - 169,235 sq miles *Pop* 17,250,000 *GMT* +3 *When* Nov - March *Visas* Required by all *Time to get* Extremely difficult for tourists, so apply months in advance *Safety* The Foreign Office do not recommend any visits to Iraq - extremely dangerous *Inoc* Yellow Fever* if arriving from an infected area, Hepatitis A, Malaria, Polio, Cholera, Typhoid. *Airlines* At present no aircraft allowed to land at Baghdad *Average length of flight* 6 hours *Food* Minced meat, spices and rice

Israel

Capital Jerusalem *Lang* Hebrew and Arabic *Currency* New Israel Shekel = 100 new Agorot *Govt* Elected (Labour - Rabin) *Rel* Jewish *Size* 21,946 sq km - 8,473 sq miles *Pop* 5,168,200 *GMT* +2 *When* All year (Red Sea) *Visas* Stamp issued on arrival *Safety* Mainly safe, but unrest in certain areas, take local advice *Inoc* Hepatitis A, Polio, Typhoid *Airlines* British Airways, El Al Israel Airlines *Average length of flight* 5 hours *Food* A combination of Oriental and European cuisine

Japan

Capital Tokyo *Lang* Japanese *Currency* Japanese Yen *Govt* Elected coalition *Rel* Shintoist and Buddhist *Size* 377,815 sq km - 145,875 sq miles *Pop* 123,587,297 *GMT* +9 *When* All year *Visas* Required by Australia *Time to get* 7 days *Safety* Safe *Inoc* Polio, Typhoid *Airlines* Aeroflot, British Airways, Virgin Atlantic, All Nippon Airway, Japan Airlines *Average length of flight* 11 hours 30 minutes *Food* Crisp vegetables and raw fish - Sake, hot rice wine

Jordan

Capital Amman *Lang* Arabic *Currency* Dinar = 1000 fils *Govt* Constitutional monarch with an elected House of Representatives *Rel* Sunni Muslim *Size* 97,740 sq km - 37,738 sq miles *Pop* 4,145,000 *GMT* +2 *When* All year - very hot in summer though *Visas* Required by all - passport must not have Israeli visas *Validity* Normally 3 months *Time to get* 2 days if applying in person *Safety* Safe *Inoc* Yellow Fever* if arriving from an infected area, Hepatitis A, Polio, Typhoid, Cholera *Airlines* Royal Jordanian Airlines, British Airways *Average length of flight* 5.5 hours *Food* Arabic and European dishes

Kazakhstan (C.I.S.)

Capital Almaty *Lang* Kazakh *Currency* 1 Tenge = 100 tiyin *Govt* Elected socialist Republic *Rel* Mainly Sunni Muslim *Size* 2,717,300 sq km - 1,049,150 sq miles *Pop* 16,900,000 *GMT* +5 (+6 in summer) *When* May - Sept *Visas* Required by all (liable to change) *Validity* Varies *Time to get* Allow weeks *Safety* Increase in attacks on trains and in larger cities, travel in groups *Inoc* Typhoid,

Polio *Airlines* Uzbekistan Airways, Aeroflot *Average length of flight* 8 hours via Moscow *Food* Mutton and horse-meat, Almaty is renowned for its apples

Korea (North)

Capital Pyongyang *Lang* Korean *Currency* Won = 100 jon *Govt* Communist, ruled with an iron rod by Kim Il Sung (The Great Leader), now deceased to be succeeded by his son *Rel* No official religion but some Buddhists *Size* 120,538 sq km - 46,540 sq miles *Pop* 22,193,000 *GMT* +9 *When* Spring and Autumn *Visas* Required by all and difficult to get *Inoc* Hepatitis A, Polio, Cholera, Typhoid *Airlines* Aeroflot *Average length of flight* 16 hours *Food* Rice and noodles based - fond of pickles

Korea (South)

Capital Seoul *Lang* Korean *Currency* Won *Govt* Elected Govt (Democratic Liberal Party) *Rel* Buddhist *Size* 99,299 sq km - 38,340 sq miles *Pop* 43,663,405 *GMT* +9 *When* Spring and Autumn *Visas* Not required if staying less than 15 days and have onward ticket *Safety* Safe *Inoc* If staying more than three months AIDS certificate is required. Hepatitis A, Polio, Typhoid *Airlines* Korean Air, British Airways *Average length of flight* 12 hours *Food* Like North Korean - as many as 20 side dishes to one main course

Kuwait

Capital Kuwait City *Lang* Arabic and English *Currency* Kuwait Dinar = 1000 fils *Govt* Executive power held by the Emir, a member of the Royal Al-Sabah family, elections held in 1992 for the consultative assembly. Political parties are banned *Rel* Muslim *Size* 17,818 sq km - 6,880 sq miles *Pop* 1,350,000 *GMT* +3 *When* October to May *Visas* Required by all *Validity* 1 month from date of entry *Time to get* 24 hours *Safety* Safe *Inoc* Hepatitis A, Polio, Cholera, Typhoid *Airlines* British Airways, Kuwait Airways *Average length of flight* 6 hours *Food* International and Arab cuisine

Kyrgyzstan (C.I.S.)

Capital Bishkek *Lang* Kyrgyz *Currency* 1 som = 100 tyn *Govt* Elected President, new constitution and elections set for 1997 *Rel* Sunni Muslim *Size* 198,500 sq km - 76,640 sq miles *Pop* 4,421,000 *GMT* +5 *When* May - Sept *Visas* Required by all - liable to change *Validity* Varies *Airlines* Kyrgyz Air via Moscow *Average length of flight* 8 hours excluding stopover *Food* Mutton and horse-meat

Laos

Capital Vientiane *Lang* Laotian *Currency*

Laotian New Kip = 100 cents *Govt* Communist regime *Rel* Hinayana (form of Buddhism), Confucianism and Animism and some Christian *Size* 236,800 sq km - 91,400 sq miles *Pop* 4,170,000 *GMT* +7 *When* Nov - April *Visas* Required by all *Validity* 7 days transit, tourist visas also available if tour booked through Laos agency *Time to get* As far in advance as possible *Inoc* Yellow Fever* if arriving from an infected area, Hepatitis A, Malaria, Polio, Cholera, Typhoid *Airlines* Thai Airways, British Airways, Loa Aviation *Average length of flight* 19 hours *Food* Similar to Thai - local dishes include rice and fermented fish

Lebanon

Capital Beirut *Lang* Arabic *Currency* Lebanese Pound = 100 piastres *Govt* Democracy elections held every 4 years *Rel* Majority Muslim but Christians also *Size* 10,452 sq km - 4,036 sq miles *Pop* 2,745,000 *GMT* +2 *When* Mid March to November *Visas* Required by all (no Israeli stamps in passport) *Validity* 2 weeks - 3 months *Time to get* 6-8 weeks *Safety* Unstable, check with Foreign Office *Inoc* Yellow Fever* if arriving from an infected area, Hepatitis A, Polio, Cholera, Typhoid *Airlines* Middle East Airlines, British Airways, Air France, Olympic Airways, Malev, Tarom, KLM *Average length of flight* 5 hours *Food* Staple diet of vegetables, rice and mutton

Macau

Capital Macau *Lang* Portuguese and Chinese *Currency* Pataca = 100 avos *Govt* A Special Territory of Portugal, headed by the Governor, however in 1999, like Hong Kong, Macau will be handed over to the Chinese *Rel* Diverse from Roman Catholic to Buddhism, Daoism and Confucianism. *Size* 18 sq km - 6.95 sq miles *Pop* 335,693 *GMT* +8 *When* October to March *Visas* Not required *Safety* Safe *Inoc* Hepatitis A, Polio, Typhoid *Airlines* There is no airport although one is being planned. For the moment most travel is via Hong Kong *Average length of flight* To Hong Kong 18 hours *Food* Spicy and combination of Chinese and Portuguese cooking

Malaysia

Capital Kuala Lumpur *Lang* Bahasa Malaysia *Currency* Ringgit = 100 sen *Govt* Elected Govt, presently the National Front Party, however some power still remains with the nine hereditary sultans who elect the Head of State *Rel* Mainly Muslim some Buddhist *Size* 329,758 sq km - 127,320 sq miles *Pop* 18,178,000 *GMT* +8 *When* The climate varies in different regions, generally though January - March *Visas* Not required, but a Visit Pass is issued on arrival *Safety* Safe *Inoc* Yellow Fever* if having arrived from an infected area, Hepatitis A, Cholera, Polio, Malaria, Typhoid *Airlines* Malaysia Airlines, British Airways *Average length of flight* 12 hours *Food* Subtly spicy

Mongolia

Capital Ulan Bator *Lang* Mongolian Khalkha *Currency* Tugrik = 100 mongos *Govt* Having been a one-party communist state, in 1992 it became a democratic parliamentary state *Rel* Buddhist Lamaism *Size* 1,565,000 sq km - 604,250 sq miles *Pop* 2,200,000 *GMT* +8 *When* May to September *Visas* Required by all *Validity* Varies *Time to get* 7 days *Safety* There is some street-crime in Ulan Bator *Inoc* Medical insurance certificate required, Hepatitis A, Polio, Typhoid *Airlines* Aeroflot *Average length of flight* 14 hours including stopovers *Food* Meat-based diet - not suitable for vegetarians. Lots of yak butter tea - an acquired taste

Myanmar (Burma)

Capital Yangon (Rangoon) *Lang* Burmese *Currency* Kyat = 100 Pyas *Govt* State Law and Order Restoration Council - dictatorship *Rel* Theravasa Buddhist *Size* 676,552 sq km - 261,218 sq miles *Pop* 41,550,000 *GMT* +6.5 *When* November to April *Visas* Required by all *Validity* 14 days within 3 months from date of issue *Time to get* 2 days *Safety* Unstable, check with Foreign Office *Inoc* Yellow Fever* if arriving from an infected area, Hepatitis A, Cholera, Malaria, Polio, Typhoid *Airlines* Thai Airlines, Singapore Airlines, Silk Air *Average length of flight* 23 hours including stopovers in Singapore or Bangkok *Food* Rice and rice noodle based, lightly spiced curries

Nepal

Capital Kathmandu *Lang* Nepali *Currency* Nepalese Rupee = 100 paisa *Govt* Constitutional monarchy *Rel* Buddhist and Hindu *Size* 147,181 sq km - 56,827 sq miles *Pop* 18,462,081 *GMT* + 5.45 *When* October to May *Visas* Required by all *Validity* 30 days within 6 months from date of issue *Time to get* 1 day or 10 minutes at the airport on arrival *Safety* Safe *Inoc* Yellow Fever* if arriving from an infected area, Cholera, Hepatitis A, Malaria, Paratyphoid, Polio, Typhoid. *Airlines* Royal Nepal Airlines, Aeroflot, PIA, Lufthansa. *Average length of flight* 10 hours *Food* Rice based, mild curries

Oman

Capital Muscat *Lang* Arabic and English *Currency* Omani Rial = 1000 baiza *Govt* Ruled by Sultan Qaboos whose family have held

power since the 18th century *Rel* Ibadi Muslim *Size* 300,000 sq km - 120,000 sq miles *Pop* 1,599,000 *GMT* +4 *When* August to May (still very hot though) *Visas* Required by all - will be denied if Israeli visa stamp in passport *Validity* 2 weeks within one month of issue *Time to get* 7 days *Safety* Safe *Inoc* Yellow Fever* if arriving from an infected area, Cholera, Hepatitis A, Malaria, Polio, Typhoid *Airlines* British Airways, Gulf Air *Average length of flight* 8 hours 10 minutes *Food* International

Pakistan

Capital Islamabad *Lang* Urdu and English *Currency* Pakistani Rupee = 100 paisa *Govt* Elected National Assembly *Rel* Muslim *Size* 796,095 sq km - 307,374 sq miles *Pop* 115,520,000 *GMT* +5 *When* November and March - South May, June, September, and October - North *Visas* Required by all *Validity* 3 months must be used within six months of issue *Safety* Safe if sensible in northern areas, however central and south Pakistan are unsafe and advice should be taken *Inoc* Yellow Fever* if arriving from an infected area within six days, Cholera* Hepatitis A, Malaria, Polio, Typhoid *Airlines* British Airways, PIA - more options if flying to Karachi *Average length of flight* 8 hours *Food* Masala Curry - not as hot as India. In the North Afghan influences such as goat kebab. Lots of chapatis

Philippines

Capital Manila *Lang* Filipino *Currency* Philippine Peso = 100 centavos *Govt* The new constitution introduced in 1987 is a directly elected government *Rel* Mainly Roman Catholic *Size* 300,00 sq km - 115,831 sq miles *Pop* 65,000,000 *GMT* +8 *When* November to June *Visas* Not required by EC tourists up to 21 days *Validity* 59 days from date of entry *Time to get* 1 day *Safety* Some areas unstable, take local advice *Inoc* Yellow Fever* if arriving from an infected area, Cholera, Hepatitis A, Malaria, Polio, Typhoid *Airlines* British Airways, Philippine Airlines *Average length of flight* 18 hours *Food* A mixture of Spanish, Malay and Chinese cooking - rice is the staple food

Qatar

Capital Doha *Lang* Arabic *Currency* Qatar Riyal = 100 dirhams *Govt* Ruled by the Al-Thani family *Rel* Muslim *Size* 11,437 sq km - 4,416 sq miles *Pop* 486,000 *GMT* +3 *When* October to May *Visas* Not required by UK nationals *Inoc* Yellow Fever* if arriving within 6 days from an infected area, Polio, Typhoid. If staying longer than 30 days a medical test is required *Airlines* Gulf Air, Air France *Average length of flight* 7 hours 15 minutes *Food* International

Russian Federation

Capital Moscow *Lang* Russian *Currency* Rouble = 100 kopeks *Govt* Having been part of the communist Soviet bloc is now a democracy with teething problems *Rel* Russian Orthodox *Size* 17,075,400 sq km - 6,592,850 sq miles *Pop* 148,485,000 *GMT* +3 to +12 *When* May- Sept *Visas* Required by all *Validity* Varies from date of entry *Time to get* 2 weeks *Safety* Moscow and St Petersburg both have a high crime rate, take local advice *Inoc* Typhoid *Airlines* SAS, Aeroflot *Average length of flight* 3 hours 45 minutes *Food* Salmon, caviar, borsch, on the whole however food in restaurants is not as good, and there can be shortages

Saudi Arabia

Capital Riyadh *Lang* Arabic *Currency* Saudi Arabian Riyal = 100 halalah *Govt* King Fahd is an absolute monarchy, with no political parties *Rel* Sunni Muslim *Size* 2,240,000 sq km - 864,869 sq miles *Pop* 14,870,000 *GMT* +3 *When* October - April *Visas* Required *Validity* Varies *Safety* Safe *Inoc* Yellow Fever* if arriving from an infected area, Cerbero-spinal meningitis if arriving from an infected area or during the month of August, Hepatitis A, Malaria, Polio, Typhoid *Airlines* British Airways, Saudi *Average length of flight* 6.5 hours *Food* Strongly flavoured and spicy, meat is normally lamb or chicken.

Singapore

Capital Singapore *Lang* Chinese *Currency* Singapore Dollar = 100 cents *Govt* Power lies with the elected Prime Minister, the current govt is the Peoples Action Party, who have held power since 1972 *Rel* Mixed - Confucian, Taoist, Buddhist, Christian Hindu and Muslim *Size* 626.4 sq km - 242 sq miles *Pop* 2,818,200 *GMT* +8 *When* February to October *Visas* Not required. Social Visit Pass issued on arrival *Safety* Safe *Inoc* Yellow Fever* if arriving from an infected area, Cholera, Polio, Typhoid *Airlines* Royal Brunei Airlines, Singapore Airlines, British Airways, Qantas *Average length of flight* 13 hours *Food* A gourmet's paradise - Chinese, Malay, every sort of dish

Sri Lanka

Capital Colombo *Lang* Sinhala, Tamil and English *Currency* Sri Lankan rupee *Govt* directly elected President and Assembly *Rel* Mainly Buddhist *Size* 64,454 sq km - 24,886 sq miles *Pop* 17,240,000 *GMT* +5.5 *When* July through Sept and Jan through March *Visas* Not required by tourists *Safety* Mainly safe, take local advice *Inoc* Yellow Fever* if arriving from an infected area, Cholera, Hepatitis A,

Malaria, Polio, Typhoid *Airlines* Air Lanka *Average length of flight* 13 hours 45 minutes *Food* Spicy

Syria

Capital Damascus *Lang* Arabic, French and English *Currency* Syrian Pound = 100 piastres *Govt* Democracy *Rel* Sunni Muslim *Size* 185,180 sq km - 71,498 sq miles *Pop* 12,529,000 *GMT* +2 *When* Spring and Autumn *Visas* Required by all *Validity* 3 months *Time to get* 3-4 days *Inoc* Yellow Fever* if arriving from an infected area, Cholera, Hepatitis A *Airlines* Syrian Arab Airlines, Air France, Lufthansa, Cyprus Airways, Malev, Tarom, Austrian Airlines and Turkish Airlines *Average length of flight* 7.5 hours *Food* Lots of minced meat

Taiwan

Capital Taipei *Lang* Mandarin Chinese and English *Currency* New Taiwan Dollar = 100 cents *Govt* Elected National Assembly, constitutional changes scheduled for 1995 *Rel* Buddhist *Size* 36,000 sq km - 13,900 sq miles *Pop* 20,556,842 *GMT* +8 *When* November to May *Visas* Required by all *Validity* 60 days within 3 months from date of issue *Time to get* depending on visa - 48 hours *Safety* Safe *Inoc* Cholera, Yellow Fever* if arriving from an infected area, Hepatitis A, Polio, Typhoid *Airlines* EVA Airways, British Airways *Average length of flight* 20 hours *Food* Delicious Chinese seafood

Tajikistan

Capital Dushanbe *Lang* Tajik *Currency* Russian rouble *Govt* Changes to the constitution are being introduced in 1994/5, with a President as head of state, and an elected parliament *Rel* Sunni Muslim *Size* 143,100 sq km - 55,250 sq miles *Pop* 5,556,000 *GMT* +5 *When* May- Sept *Visas* Required by all *Validity* Varies *Time to get* 10 days or longer through the Russian Embassies *Safety* Civil war at time of writing *Inoc* Cholera, Malaria *Airlines* Tajik Air *Average length of flight* 6 hours *Food* Sweet food as a starter, followed by meat dishes. Excellent fruits

Thailand

Capital Bangkok *Lang* Thai *Currency* Baht = 100 satang *Govt* Constitutional monarchy, with an elected House of Representative, large military influence and the Kind is regarded as a demi-god *Rel* Buddhist *Size* 513,115 sq km - 198,115 sq miles *Pop* 56,532,000 *GMT* +7 *When* November to February *Visas* Not required if a tourist and staying less than 15 days *Safety* Safe apart from border with Myanmar *Inoc* Yellow Fever* if arriving from

608

an infected area, Cholera, Hepatitis A, Polio, Malaria, Typhoid, *Airlines* Thai Airways, Philippine Airlines, Qantas, Eva Airlines, Garuda (Indonesia), British Airways *Average length of flight* 13 hours 40 minutes *Food* Hot and spicy

Turkey

Capital Ankara *Lang* Turkish *Currency* Turkish Lira *Govt* Democratic but increasing rise of fundamentalism *Rel* Muslim *Size* 779,452 sq km - 300,948 sq miles *Pop* 57,326,000 *GMT* +2 *When* April to October *Visas* Required by UK citizens obtainable at the airport on arrival *Safety* Dangerous in the east and southern east provinces, contact the Foreign Office for advice *Inoc* Hepatitis A, Malaria, Polio, Cholera, Typhoid *Airlines* Turkish Airlines, British Airways *Average length of flight* 3 hours 45 minutes *Food* Meat based normally lamb

Turkmenistan

Capital Ashgabat *Lang* Turkmen *Currency* 1 Manat=100 tenge *Govt* Elected govt *Rel* Sunni Muslim *Size* 488,100 sq km - 188,456 sq miles *Pop* 4,254,000 *GMT* +5 *When* Spring and Autumn *Visas* Required by all, liable to change *Validity* Varies normally 10 days if issued at the airport *Time to get* 5 days *Inoc* Malaria *Airlines* Turkish Airlines *Average length of flight* 6 hours excluding stopover in Turkey *Food* Typically Central Asian mutton and rice

United Arab Emirates

Capital Abu Dhabi *Lang* Arabic *Currency* UAE Dirham - 100 fils *Govt* The seven Emirates are each governed by the ruling family, each family is part of the Supreme Council which is the federal authority for UAE, the council appoints the President. There are no political parties *Rel* Sunni Muslim *Size* 77,700 sq km - 30,000 sq miles *Pop* 1,909,000 *GMT* +4 *When* October to May *Visas* Required but not by UK citizens *Validity* 30 days *Time to get* *Safety* Safe *Inoc* Malaria, Polio, Cholera, Typhoid *Airlines* British Airways, Gulf Air and Emirates *Average length of flight* 6 hours 35 minutes *Food* Salads, sheep's brains and delicious seafood

Uzbekistan

Capital Tashkent *Lang* Uzbek *Currency* Som Coupon with the Som being introduced in 1994 *Govt* One-party state, with Karimov as elected President *Rel* Mainly Sunni Muslim *Size* 447,400 sq km - 172,740 sq miles *Pop* 21,207,000 *GMT* +5 *When* Spring and Autumn *Visas* Required by all *Validity* Varies *Time to get* 20 days *Safety* Unsafe *Inoc* Cholera, Typhoid, Polio, Malaria, Hepatitis A *Airlines*

Uzbekistan Airways *Average length of flight* 7 hours *Food* Typically Central Asian - mutton and rice

Vietnam

Capital Hanoi *Lang* Vietnamese *Currency* New Dong = 10 hao = 100 xu *Govt* Communist *Rel* Buddhist *Size* 330,341 sq km - 127,545 sq miles *Pop* 66,200,000 *GMT* +7 *When* November to April *Visas* Required by all *Validity* 1 month *Time to get* 10 working days *Safety* Travel in some areas is dangerous, seek local advice *Inoc* Yellow Fever* if arriving from an infected area, Cholera, Typhoid, Polio, Malaria, Hepatitis A *Airlines* Aeroflot, Cathay Pacific, Thai Airways, Air France *Average length of flight* 17 hours *Food* A mixture of Thai and Chinese

Yemen

Capital Sana'a *Lang* Arabic *Currency* Yemeni Dinar = 1000 fils *Govt* Changing constitution *Rel* Sunni Muslim *Size* 527,969 sq km - 203,850 sq miles *Pop* 12,500,000 *GMT* +3 *When* October to April *Visas* Required by all *Validity* 1 month *Commencing* Within 3 months *Safety* Dangerous - civil war at time of writing *Inoc* Yellow Fever* if arriving from an infected area, Cholera, Hepatitis A, Malaria, Polio, Typhoid *Airlines* British Airways, Yemen Airways *Average length of flight* 10 hours *Food* Not highly recommended

Europe

Albania

Capital Tirana *Lang* Albanian but Greek is also spoken *Currency* Leks *Govt* Was communist until elections in 1991, but now ruled by the Democratic Party who continue to introduce economic reforms. *Rel* Previously forced atheism, now allowed to worship openly (70% Muslim) *Size* 28,748 sq km - 11,100 sq miles *Pop* 3,300,000 *GMT* + 1 (+2 in summer) *When* May/June and mid September to mid October *Visas* Not required by UK, US and Canadian citizens - required by Australians *Validity* Depending on length of stay *Time to get* 4 weeks *Safety* Crime rate has risen recently, women should not travel alone - generally cautious travel is advised *Inoc* Cholera present, Typhoid, Polio, Hepatitis A *Airlines* MALEV, Alitalia, Tatra Air Albanian Airlines, Swiss Air *Average length of flight* 4 to 5 hours *Food* Turkish influences

Andorra

Capital Andorra La Vella *Lang* Officially Catalan, but French and Spanish also used *Currency* French Francs and Spanish Pesetas

Govt No formal constitution - co-principality with France and the Spanish Bishop of Urgel *Rel* Roman Catholic *Size* 468 sq km - 181 sq miles *Pop* 54,507 *GMT* +1 (+2 in summer) *When* All year round (winter for skiing) *Visas* Not required for Andorra but Australians need visas for Spain and France *Safety* Safe *Airlines* Nearest airport Barcelona (Spain) *Food* Catalan

Austria

Capital Vienna *Lang* German *Currency* Austrian Schilling = 100 Groschen *Govt* Socialist *Rel* Roman Catholic *Size* 83,859 sq km - 32,378 sq miles *Pop* 7,812,100 *GMT* +1 *When* All year *Visas* Not required *Safety* Safe *Airlines* Austria Airlines, British Airways, Air France and many more *Average length of flight* 2 hours *Food* Influenced by southeast European cuisine- various types of cured and smoked meat.

Belarus (C.I.S.)

Capital Minsk *Lang* Belarussian *Currency* Belarussian Rubel = 10 Rub Russian roubles are also in use *Govt* Communist *Rel* Christian *Size* 207,595 sq km - 80,153 sq miles *Pop* 10,300,000 *GMT* +2 *When* May to September *Visas* Required by all *Validity* 30 days - 1 year *Time to get* 5 working days *Safety* Seek local advice *Airlines* Austrian Airlines *Average length of flight* 5 hours including stopover *Food* Vegetable based, most famous is Borsch - beetroot soup

Belgium

Capital Brussels *Lang* Flemish and French *Currency* Belgian Franc = 100 centimes *Govt* Coalition Government with a constitutional monarch - King Albert *Rel* Roman Catholic *Size* 30,519 sq km - 11,783 sq miles *Pop* 9,978,681 *GMT* +1 *When* All year *Visas* Not required *Safety* Safe *Airlines* Sabena, British Airways, British Midland, Air UK, Singapore Airlines *Average length of flight* 55 minutes *Food* Similar to French

Bosnia-Hercegovina

Capital Sarajevo *Lang* Serb-Croat and Croat-Serb *Currency* Yugoslav Dinar = 100 paras Croatian Dinar = 100 paras *Govt* Extremely unstable *Rel* Muslim, Orthodox and Roman Catholic *Size* 51,129 sq km - 19,736 sq miles *Pop* 4,364,574 *GMT* +1 *When* Don't *Visas* Not available *Safety* Extremely dangerous - in the middle of a bloody civil war *Airlines* None presently *Food* Shortages

Bulgaria

Capital Sofia *Lang* Bulgarian *Currency* Lev = 100 stotinki *Govt* Elected Govt currently the Union of Democratic Forces although under economic pressure *Rel* Eastern Orthodox Church *Size* 110,994 sq km - 42,855 sq miles *Pop* 8,989,165 *GMT* +2 *When* April - September *Visas* Required by all unless holiday booked through Balkan Tourist or a US citizen *Validity* 3 months *Time to get* 7 days *Safety* Beware of their driving habits *Airlines* Balkan Airlines *Average length of flight* 3 hours *Food* Spicy and filling

Croatia

Capital Zagreb *Lang* Croat-Serb and Serb-Croat *Currency* Croatian Dinar = 100 paras *Govt* Croatian Democratic Union is fighting to keep their lands within the former Yugoslav Republic *Rel* Roman Catholic *Size* 56,538 sq km - 21,829 sq miles *Pop* 4,800,000 *GMT* +1 *When* Don't (All year) *Visas* Not required for UK nationals *Safety* Extremely dangerous at time of writing, consult Foreign Office *Airlines* Croatian Airlines, Swiss Air and Lufthansa *Average length of flight* 2 hours *Food* The coast is noted for its seafood

Cyprus
(Southern part of the island)

Capital Nicosia *Lang* Greek *Currency* Cyprus Pound = 100 cents *Govt* Democratic *Rel* Greek Orthodox *Size* 9,251 sq km - 3,572 sq miles *Pop* 706,900 *GMT* +2 *When* All year *Visas* Not required *Airlines* Cyprus Airways, British Airways *Average length of flight* 4.5 hours *Food* Charcoal grills, kebabs, typical Greek food

Czech Republic

Capital Prague *Lang* Czech *Currency* Koruna or Crown = 100 haleru *Govt* Democratic state *Rel* Christian *Size* 78,864 sq km - 30,450 sq miles *Pop* 10,302,215 *GMT* +1 *When* May - September *Visas* Required but not by UK Nationals *Validity* 30 days within 6 months of date of issue *Time to get* Same day *Airlines* CSA, British Airways *Average length of flight* 1 hours 45 minutes *Food* Austro-Hungarian dishes - lots of pork

Denmark

Capital Copenhagen *Lang* Danish *Currency* Danish Krone =100 ore *Govt* Democracy currently held by the Social Democrats *Rel* Evangelical Lutheran *Size* 43,093 sq km - 16,638 sq miles *Pop* 5,162,126 *GMT* +1(+2 in summer) *When* All year *Visas* Not required by EC Nationals *Safety* Safe *Airlines* British Airways, Scandinavian Airlines, Maersk Air amongst others. *Average length of flight* 1 hour 50 minutes *Food* Rye bread, open sandwiches with seafood, meat or cheese - lots of pickled herrings and of course Schnapps

Estonia

Capital Tallinn *Lang* Estonian *Currency* 1 Kroon = 100 cents *Govt* Unstable coalition Govt *Rel* Protestant *Size* 45,226 sq km - 17,462 sq miles *Pop* 1,565,662 *GMT* +2 (+3 in summer) *When* April - October *Visas* Not required *Safety* Safe *Airlines* SAS *Average length of flight* 5 hours *Food* Fish especially trout and herring

Finland

Capital Helsinki *Lang* Finnish *Currency* Markka = 100 pennia *Govt* Coalition democracy *Rel* Lutheran *Size* 338,145 sq km - 130,559 sq miles *Pop* 5,029,002 *GMT* +2 *When* all year *Visas* not required *Safety* Safe *Airlines* Finnair, British Airways *Average length of flight* 2 hours 55 minutes *Food* Excellent, fish - French and Russian influences

France

Capital Paris *Lang* French *Currency* Franc = 100 centimes *Govt* Republic with Socialist Mitterand as President *Rel* Roman Catholic *Size* 543,965 sq km - 210026 sq miles *Pop* 57,049,000 *GMT* +1 *When* All year *Visas* Required by Australians *Validity* Up to 3 months *Time to get* 24 hours *Safety* Safe *Airlines* British Airways, Air France, British Midland, Air UK, Singapore Airlines, Cathay Pacific *Average length of flight* 1 hour 5 minutes *Food* Garlicky and rich, good cheese

Germany

Capital Berlin *Lang* German *Currency* Deutsche Mark = 100 Pfennigs *Govt* Democracy *Rel* Christian *Size* 356,854 sq km - 137,817 sq miles *Pop* 79,753,227 *GMT* +1 *When* All year *Visas* Not required *Safety* Safe *Airlines* British Airways, Lufthansa, Contiflug, United Airlines *Average length of flight* 1 hour and 40 minutes *Food* Heavy lunches and of course sausages (frankfurters)

Gibraltar

Capital Gibraltar *Lang* English and Spanish *Currency* Pound sterling = 100 new pence *Govt* Self-governing British Crown Colony *Rel* Mainly Roman Catholic *Size* 6.5 sq km - 2.5 sq miles *Pop* 28,074 *GMT* +1 *When* All year *Visas* Not required *Safety* Safe *Airlines* GB Airways *Average length of flight* 2 hours 45 minutes *Food* Offers British, French, Spanish and Moroccan food

Greece

Capital Athens *Lang* Greek *Currency* Drachma *Govt* Democracy *Rel* Greek Orthodox *Size* 131,957 sq km - 50,949 sq miles *Pop* 10,269,074 *GMT* +2 *When* April to October *Visas* Not required *Safety* Safe *Airlines* Olympic Airways, British Airways, Virgin Atlantic *Average length of flight* 3 hours 15 minutes *Food* Olive oil used in cooking, delicious fish and charcoal grilled meats

Greenland

Capital Nuuk *Lang* Greenlandic (like Inuit) *Currency* Danish Krone = 100 ore *Govt* Domestic Affairs dealt by the elected Landsstyre, foreign affairs controlled by the Danish Govt *Rel* Church of Greenland (Protestant) *Size* 2,175,600 sq km - 840.000 sq miles *Pop* 55,385 *GMT* -4 *When* May to September *Visas* Not required *Safety* Safe, beware of freezing temperatures *Airlines* Via Denmark, Greenlandair, SAS *Average length of flight* 5.5 hours *Food* Whale meat used locally, but thankfully not in every restaurant, also Reindeer, Musk Ox, and seafood

Guernsey

Capital St Peter Port *Lang* English *Currency* Pound Sterling = 100 pence *Govt* Internal self-Govt. British Govt responsible for external affairs *Rel* Church of England *Size* 65 sq km - 25 sq miles *Pop* 58,000 *GMT* GMT *When* All year *Visas* Not required *Safety* Safe *Airlines* British Airways, Air UK, Jersey European Airways, Air UK *Average length of flight* 45 minutes *Food* French and English cooking

Hungary

Capital Budapest *Lang* Hungarian *Currency* Forint = 100 filler *Govt* Formerly a soviet-style socialist state, it has since 1990 been governed by an elected coalition *Rel* Roman Catholic *Size* 93,033 sq km - 35,920 sq miles *Pop* 10,337,000 *GMT* +1 *When* Any time - winter can be very cold though *Visas* Required by Australia and NZ *Validity* 30 days within 6 months *Time to get* 2 days *Safety* Safe *Airlines* British Airways, Malev *Average length of flight* 2 hours 40 minutes *Food* Soups and stuffed vegetables

Iceland

Capital Reykjavik *Lang* Icelandic *Currency* Iceland Krona = 100 aurar *Govt* Elected coalition *Rel* Lutheran *Size* 103,000 sq km - 39,769 sq miles *Pop* 262,204 *GMT* GMT *When* All year but especially June for the summer solstice *Visas* Not required *Safety* Safe *Airlines* Icelandair *Average length of flight* 2 hours 50 minutes *Food* Fish and lamb based

Ireland (Eire)

Capital Dublin *Lang* English and Gaelic *Currency* Irish Punt = 100 pence *Govt* Elected coalition *Rel* Roman Catholic *Size* 70,283 sq km - 27,136 sq miles *Pop* 3,523,401 *GMT* GMT *When* All year *Visas* Not required *Safety*

Safe *Airlines* Aer Lingus, British Midland, British Airways, Ryanair. *Average length of flights* 50 minutes *Food* Irish Stew, Connemara lamb, Dublin Bay prawns, soda bread and the famous Guinness

Italy

Capital Rome *Lang* Italian *Currency* Italian Lira *Govt* Democracy *Rel* Roman Catholic *Size* 301,227 sq km - 116,324 sq miles *Pop* 2,791,354 *GMT* +1 *When* All year round *Visas* Not required *Safety* Safe *Airlines* Alitalia, British Airways, Ethiopian Airways, Philippine Airlines, Kenya Airways, Air Seychelles *Average length of flight* 2.5 hours *Food* Pasta, pizza, pepperoni, prosciutto, pesto, and swilled down with Peroni, and Prosecco

Jersey

Capital St Helier *Lang* English *Currency* Pound Sterling = 100 pence *Govt* British dependency (not part of UK) *Rel* Christian *Size* 116 sq km - 45 sq miles *Pop* 84,082 *GMT* GMT *When* All year *Visas* Not required *Safety* Safe *Airlines* British Airways, Jersey European Airways, Air UK *Average length of flight* 40 minutes *Food* English and French influences

Latvia

Capital Riga *Lang* Latvian *Currency* 1 Latvian Lat = 100 santimi *Govt* New constitution being drafted since independence *Rel* Lutheran *Size* 64,589 sq km - 24,938 sq miles *Pop* 2,606,176 *GMT* +2 *When* Apr - Oct *Visas* Not required by UK citizens *Validity* 3 months *Time to get* 1 day *Safety* Safe *Inoc* Hepatitis A *Airlines* Baltic International Airlines, SAS, Lufthansa *Average length of flight* 5.5 hours *Food* Rye bread and fish and thick soups

Liechtenstein

Capital Vaduz *Lang* German *Currency* Swiss Franc = 100 centimes *Govt* Elected coalition with the Monarch being head of state *Rel* Christian - mostly Roman Catholic *Size* 160 sq km - 62 sq miles *Pop* 29,386 *GMT* +1 *When* All year *Visas* Same as Switzerland *Safety* Safe *Airlines* There is no airport in Liechtenstein, most convenient is Zurich and then a 75-mile drive. Flights to Zurich include British Airways, Swissair, Cathay Pacific Kenya Airways, Crossair *Average length of flight* To Zurich 1.5 hours *Food* Swiss and Austrian influences

Lithuania

Capital Vilnius *Lang* Lithuanian *Currency* The Litas = 100 centu *Govt* Elected Govt currently held by the ex-communist Lithuanian Democratic Labour Party *Rel* Mainly Roman Catholic *Size* 65,300 sq km - 25,212 sq miles

Pop 3,761,400 *GMT* +2 *When* April to October *Visas* Not required by citizens of the UK *Validity* 90 days *Time to get* 5 days *Safety* Safe *Airlines* Lithuanian Airlines direct or SAS, Lufthansa, Austrian Airlines *Average length of flight* 4 hours *Food* Lots of pork and cabbage

Luxembourg

Capital Luxembourg-ville *Lang* German *Currency* Luxembourg franc = 100 centimes *Govt* Constitutional monarch and elected govt currently a coalition *Rel* Roman Catholic *Size* 2,586 sq km - 999 sq miles *Pop* 389,800 *GMT* +1 *When* All year *Visas* Not required *Safety* Safe *Airlines* Luxair, British Airways *Average length of flight* 1 hour *Food* French, Belgian and German influences

Macedonia (Former Yugoslav Republic of Macedonia)

Capital Skopje *Lang* Macedonian *Currency* Macedonian Denar = 100 deni - a new currency in the form of coupons *Govt* Elected assembly *Rel* Eastern Orthodox Macedonians *Size* 25,713 sq km - 9,928 sq miles *Pop* 2,033,964 *GMT* + 1 *When* Apr - Sept *Visas* Not required by UK and US nationals *Validity* 3 or 6 months *Time to Get* Australian and Canadian nationals can obtain visas on entry *Safety* Seek advice from the Foreign Office *Airlines* via Berlin, Copenhagen and Vienna *Food* Turkish and Greek influences

Malta

Capital Valletta *Lang* Maltese *Currency* Maltese Lira = 100 cents = 1000 mils *Govt* Elected centre-right government *Rel* Roman Catholic *Size* 316 sq km - 122 sq miles *Pop* 359,543 *GMT* +1 *When* Apr - Sept *Visas* Not required *Safety* Safe *Inoc* Yellow Fever* if arriving from an infected area *Airlines* Air Malta, Austrian Airlines, Swissair *Average length of flight* 3 hours *Food* Good simple cooking, thick vegetable soup and rabbit is the national dish

Moldova (C.I.S.)

Capital Chisinau *Lang* Romanian *Currency* Leu =100 bani *Govt* A member of the CIS, with an elected president, currently the constitution is under reform *Rel* Mostly Eastern Orthodox *Size* 33,700 sq km - 13,000 sq miles *Pop* 4,394,000 *GMT* +2 *When* May - Sept *Visas* Required by all *Validity* Varies can be obtained at the airport *Time to get* Immediately *Safety* Seek advice from the Foreign Office before travelling *Airlines* Aeroflot, Air Moldova *Average length of flight* 6 hours *Food* Romanian influenced

Monaco
Capital Monaco-ville *Lang* French *Currency* French franc *Govt* Elected govt presently the National and Democratic Union although supreme authority rests with Prince Rainier *Rel* Roman Catholic *Size* 1.95 sq km - 0.75 sq miles *Pop* 29,876 *GMT* +1 *When* All year *Visas* Not required *Safety* Safe *Airlines* There is no airport, a helicopter links the Principality to Nice Airport *Food* French

The Netherlands
Capital Amsterdam *Lang* Dutch *Currency* Guilder = 100 cents *Govt* Constitutional monarchy *Rel* Christian *Size* 33,938 sq km - 13,104 sq miles *Pop* 15,200,000 *GMT* +1 *When* All year *Visas* Not required *Safety* Safe *Airlines* KLM, British Airways, British Midland, Air UK, Transavia Airlines, *Average length of flight* 1 hour 5 minutes *Food* Prepared meats, sausages and cheese is a typical meal

Norway
Capital Oslo *Lang* Norwegian *Currency* Norwegian Krone = 100 ore *Govt* A constitutional monarch, with an elected parliament *Rel* Lutheran *Size* 323,877 sq km - 125,050 sq miles *Pop* 4,274,030 *GMT* +1 *When* May to September *Visas* Not required *Safety* Safe *Airlines* British Airways, SAS *Average length of flight* 1 hour 45 minutes *Food* Fish, cold meats and cheese. Open sandwiches are a favourite at lunchtime

Poland
Capital Warsaw *Lang* Polish *Currency* Zloty = 100 groszy *Govt* Elected parliament with Walesa as President *Rel* Roman Catholic *Size* 312,685 sq km - 120,728 sq miles *Pop* 38,417,000 *GMT* +1 *When* All year *Visas* Not required if tourists from UK and US *Validity* 6 months *Time to get* 7 days *Safety* Safe *Airlines* British Airways, LOT-Polish Airlines *Average length of flight* 2.5 hours *Food* Soups and sour cream - meat can be scarce at times - lots of cabbage and onions

Portugal
Capital Lisbon *Lang* Portuguese *Currency* Escudo = 100 centavos *Govt* Elected government- Social Democrats *Rel* Roman Catholic *Size* 92,389 sq km - 35,672 sq miles *Pop* 9,858,600 *GMT* GMT *When* March to October *Visas* Not required for tourists up to 2 months *Safety* Safe *Airlines* TAP, British Airways *Average length of flight* 2.5 hours *Food* Fish based

Romania
Capital Bucharest *Lang* Romanian *Currency* Leu = 100 bani *Govt* Having been a communist regime, now an elected govt - Democratic National Salvation Front *Rel* Romanian Orthodox and Roman Catholic *Size* 237,500 sq km - 91,699 sq miles *Pop* 22,760,449 *GMT* +2 *When* May to October *Visas* Required *Validity* 3 months from date of issue *Time to get* 7 or more days can pay extra for urgent visas *Safety* Safe *Inoc* Hepatitis A, Typhoid, Polio *Airlines* Tarom, British World Airlines and Austrian Airlines, Lufthansa, Delta Airlines, Swissair, Malev *Average length of time* 3 hours *Food* Not the highlight of the country

San Marino
Capital San Marino *Lang* Italian *Currency* Italian Lira *Govt* Elected govt (Great and General Council) currently a coalition of The Christian Democrats and the Socialists *Rel* Roman Catholic *Size* 60.5 sq km - 23.4 sq miles *Pop* 23,719 *GMT* +1 *When* All year *Visas* Not required *Safety* Safe *Airlines* Nearest airport Bologna - Alitalia and British Airways *Average length of flight* 2.5 hours *Food* Italian

Slovak Republic
Capital Bratislava *Lang* Slovak *Currency* Koruna or Slovak Crown = 100 haleru *Govt* Democratic state, having split from the Czech Republic in Jan 1993 *Rel* Roman Catholic *Size* 49,035 sq km - 18,932 sq miles *Pop* 5,289,608 *GMT* +1 *When* May to September *Visas* Not required by UK and USA nationals *Validity* 30 days within 6 months of issue *Time to get* 1-2 day have to apply in person *Safety* Relatively safe *Airlines* Czechoslovak Airlines *Average length of flight* 1 hour 45 minutes *Food* Hungarian influences but still uninspiring- mainly pork

Slovenia
Capital Ljubljana *Lang* Slovene *Currency* Slovene Tolar = 100 stotins *Govt* Multi-party democracy *Rel* Roman Catholic *Size* 20,254 sq km - 7,820 sq miles *Pop* 1,965,986 *GMT* +1 *When* May to September *Visas* Not required except by New Zealanders *Validity* 1 week - 3 months *Safety* Safe *Airlines* Adria Airways *Average length of flight* 2 hours *Food* Austrian influence

Spain
Capital Madrid *Lang* Spanish *Currency* Peseta *Govt* Democracy - socialist *Rel* Roman Catholic *Size* 504,782 sq km - 194,897 sq miles *Pop* 38,872,268 *GMT* +1 *When* All year *Visas* required by Australians *Validity* 30 days *Time to get* 1 day *Safety* Spain *Airlines* Iberia, British Airways, Viva Air *Average length of flight* 2 hours *Food* Tapas, seafood

Sweden

Capital Stockholm *Lang* Swedish *Currency* Swedish Krona = 100 ore *Govt* Democracy, currently a four-party centre-right coalition *Rel* Evangelical Lutheran *Size* 440,945 sq km - 170,250 sq miles *Pop* 8,692,013 *GMT* +1 *When* May to September *Visas* Not required *Safety* Safe *Airlines* SAS, British Airways, Transwede Airways, *Average length of flight* 2 hours 30 minutes *Food* Fish based - pickled herrings etc.

Switzerland

Capital Bern *Lang* German *Currency* Swiss Franc *Govt* Democracy *Rel* Roman catholic and Protestant *Size* 41,293 sq km - 15,943 sq miles *Pop* 6,833,750 *GMT* +1 *When* All year *Visas* Not required *Safety* Safe *Airlines* Air France, Swiss Air, British Airways *Average* 1.5 hours *Food* Delicious cheese especially the fondues

Ukraine

Capital Kiev *Lang* Ukrainian *Currency* Karbovanets *Govt* Elected Parliament with executive power being held by the elected President (Yuri Meshkov) *Rel* Ukrainian Orthodox *Size* 603,700 sq km - 241,200 sq miles *Pop* 52,057,000 *GMT* +2 *When* May - Sept *Visas* Required by all *Validity* 90 days from date of issue *Time to get* 3-10 days depending on type of visa *Safety* Safe *Inoc* Diphtheria *Airlines* Air Ukraine International *Average length of flight* 3.5 hours *Food* Soups - beetroot, cabbage, mainly

United Kingdom

Capital London *Lang* English *Currency* Pound = 100 pence *Govt* Stable democracy *Rel* Church of England *Size* 242,429 sq km - 93,602 sq miles *Pop* 57,649,200 *GMT* GMT *When* Spring to Autumn *Visas* Not required *Safety* Safe *Food* Roast beef and Yorkshire pudding - steam pudding and crumbles - fish and chips

Vatican City

Capital Vatican City *Lang* Italian *Currency* Vatican Lira *Govt* Ruled by the Pope who is elected for life, by the College of Cardinals *Rel* Roman Catholic *Size* 0.44 sq km - 0.17 sq miles *Pop* 752 *GMT* +1 *When* All year *Visas* Not required *Safety* Extremely safe *Airlines* Alitalia, British Airways *Average length of flight* 2.5 hours *Food* Italian

Yugoslavia (Montenegro and Serbia)

Capital Belgrade *Lang* Serbo-Croat *Currency* New Yugoslav dinar = 100 paras *Govt* A Federal Republic controlled by Milosevic's Serbian Socialist Party and Bulatovic's League of Communists of Montenegro *Rel* Eastern Orthodox Serb *Size* 102,173 sq km - 39,447 sq miles *Pop* 10,406,742 *GMT* +1 *When* May to September *Visas* Required by all *Validity* 6 months from date of issue *Time to get* 3 days by post, immediate by person *Safety* Extremely dangerous due to extreme political instability in the former Yugoslavia *Airlines* No foreign airline is allowed to land at Belgrade and JAT Yugoslav Airlines is grounded in Belgrade *Food* Heavy

Islands of the Atlantic and Indian Oceans

Bermuda

Capital Hamilton *Lang* English *Currency* Bermuda Dollar = 100 cents *Govt* A British colony with its own Government currently ruled by the United Bermuda Party *Rel* Christian *Size* 53 sq km - 20.6 sq miles *Pop* 58,433 *GMT* -4 *When* May to November *Visas* Not required *Safety* Safe *Airlines* British Airways *Average length of flight* 7 hours *Food* International and seafood in abundance

Cape Verde

Capital Cidade de Praia *Lang* Portuguese *Currency* Cape Verde Escudo = 100 centavos *Govt* Ruled by the Movimento Para Democracia who won the multi-party elections in 1991 *Rel* Roman Catholic *Size* 4,033 sq km - 1,557 sq miles *Pop* 347,000 *GMT* -1 *When* November to June *Visas* Required by all *Time to get* Can be immediate, but allow as much time as possible *Inoc* Yellow Fever* if from an infected area, Polio, Cholera, Malaria Typhoid *Airlines* Transportes Aeros de Cabo Verde, American Airlines, TAP *Average length of flight* 7 hours *Food* Wholesome, bumper crops of exotic fruits

Comoros

Capital Moroni *Lang* French and Arabic *Currency* Comoros Franc = 100 centimes *Govt* Union of Democrats for Democracy *Rel* Muslim *Size* 1,862 sq km - 719 sq miles *Pop* 475,000 *GMT* +3 *When* May to November *Visas* Required by all *Validity* Various 45 and 90 days *Inoc* Hepatitis A, Malaria, Polio, Typhoid *Airlines* Air France *Average length of flight* 18 hours including stopover in Paris *Food* Spicy

Falkland Islands (UK)

Capital Stanley *Lang* English *Currency* Falkland Island Pound = 100 pence *Govt* British Crown Colony *Rel* Christian *Size* 12,173 sq km - 4,700 sq miles *Pop* 2,121 *GMT* -4(-3 in winter) *When* October - May *Visas* Not required *Safety* Safe, except there are marked unexploded mines left over from the war, seek local advice. *Inoc* Yellow Fever in case of diversion of RAF aircraft to endemic zone *Airlines* RAF from Brize Norton *Average length of flight* 18 hours *Food* Essentially British - good island lamb and beef and lots of fish

Maldives

Capital Male *Lang* Dhivehi *Currency* Maldivian Rufiya = 100 laris *Govt* Elected President and 40 out of 48 members of the Majli are also elected *Rel* Sunni Muslim *Size* 298 sq km - 115 sq miles *Pop* 223,000 *GMT* +5 *When* November to April *Visas* Issued on arrival at the airport *Validity* 30 days on arrival *Safety* Safe *Inoc* Yellow Fever* if having arrived from an infected area, Cholera, Hepatitis A, Polio, Typhoid *Airlines* Air Lanka, Emirates, PIA *Average length of flight* 11 hours *Food* Spicy fish - international food also available

Mauritius

Capital Port Louis *Lang* English *Currency* Mauritian Rupee = 100 cents *Govt* A republic since 1992 *Rel* Hindu majority *Size* 2,040 sq km - 788 sq miles *Pop* 1,058,775 *GMT* +4 *When* June - November *Visas* Not required *Safety* Safe *Inoc* Yellow Fever* if arriving from an infected area, Hepatitis A *Airlines* Air Mauritius, British Airways *Average length of flight* 11.5 hours *Food* Creole and international

Reunion (France)

Capital Saint-Denis *Lang* French *Currency* French Franc = 100 centimes *Govt* An Overseas Department of the Republic of France, right-wing General Council *Rel* Roman Catholic *Size* 2,512 sq km - 970 sq miles *Pop* 597,828 *GMT* +4 *When* May to October *Visas* Not required except by Australians *Validity* 15 days *Time to get* 1 day *Safety* Safe *Inoc* Yellow Fever* if arriving from an infected area, Typhoid, Polio. *Airlines* Air France *Average length of flight* 14 hours 40 minutes *Food* Creole cuisine

Seychelles

Capital Victoria (Mahe) *Lang* Creole *Currency* Seychelles Rupee = 100 cents *Govt* A one-party state from 1977 (the coup) to 1992, it is now multi-party with the People's Progressive Party in power with Rene who has been president since 1977 *Rel* Roman Catholic *Size* 454 sq km - 175 sq miles *Pop* 68,000 *GMT* +4 *When* June to September *Visas* Not required *Safety* Safe *Inoc* Yellow Fever* if arriving from an infected area in Africa, Hepatitis A, Polio, Typhoid *Airlines* Somali, British Airways, Air France, Aeroflot *Average length of flight* 11.5 hours *Food* Creole - fish based can be spicy - exotic fruits

Oceania

American Samoa (US)

Capital Pago Pago *Lang* Samoan and English *Currency* US Dollar *Govt* Self-Government with elected Governor *Rel* Christian *Size* 194.8 sq km - 76.1 sq miles *Pop* 46,800 *GMT* - 11 *When* Winter (theirs) May to September *Visas* Not needed if staying for less than 30 days *Safety* Safe *Inoc* Yellow Fever* if arriving form an infected area Typhoid, Polio *Airlines* Polynesian Airlines, Hawaiian Airlines *Average length of flight* 25 hours with stopovers *Food* Polynesian and American - exotic fruits

Australia

Capital Canberra *Lang* English *Currency* Australian Dollar = 100 cents *Govt* Labour Government led by Paul Keating *Rel* Christian *Size* 7,682,300 sq km - 2,966,151 sq miles *Pop* 17,292,000 *GMT* +8-+10 *When* All year round *Visas* Required *Validity* 3 months to be used within 4 years *Time to get* 1-5 day if by person or 4 weeks by post *Safety* Relatively safe *Airlines* British Airways, Qantas and many more *Average length of flight* 22 hours *Food* Beef is the most popular meat followed closely by lamb

Cook Islands (New Zealand)

Capital Avarua on the island Rarotonga *Lang* Maori, English also spoken *Currency* New Zealand Dollar = 100 cents *Govt* Self Government as a New Zealand dependency *Rel* Christian *Size* 237 sq km - 91 sq miles *Pop* 18,547 *GMT* -10 *When* May to October *Visas* Not required *Safety* Safe *Inoc* Polio, Typhoid *Airlines* Air New Zealand via Los Angeles *Average length of flight* 24 hours *Food* Copious exotic fruits and fish

Fiji

Capital Suva *Lang* Fijian and Hindi *Currency* Fijian Dollar = 100 cents *Govt* Following a period of unrest and military coups, elections were held in 1994 *Rel* Christian and Hindu *Size* 18,333 sq km - 7,078 sq miles *Pop* 746,326 *GMT* +12 *When* May to October *Visas* Not required *Safety* Safe *Inoc* Yellow Fever* if arriving from an infected area, Polio, Typhoid *Airlines* Canadian Airlines, Air New Zealand *Average length of flight* 27 hours 45 minutes *Food* Marinated steamed fish, coconuts and Indian cuisine

French Polynesia (France)

Capital Papeete (Tahiti) *Lang* Tahitian and French *Currency* French Pacific Franc = 100 centimes *Govt* Internally self-governing, with the exception of the French High

Commissioner who controls not only foreign policy but also the judicial system *Rel* Christian mainly Protestant *Size* 4,167 sq km - 1,609 sq miles *Pop* 199,031 *GMT* -9 or -10 *When* March to November *Visas* Required by Australians *Time to get* 1 day *Safety* Safe *Inoc* Yellow Fever* if having arrived from an infected area, Polio, Typhoid *Airlines* Air France, Air New Zealand *Average length of flight* 20 hours *Food* Fruit and fish - French influences

Guam (US)
Capital Agana *Lang* English and Chamorro *Currency* US Dollar = 100 cents *Govt* Internal self-govt *Rel* Christian *Size* 549 sq km - 212 sq miles *Pop* 133,152 *GMT* +10 *When* January, February and March *Visas* Same as USA *Safety* Safe *Inoc* Typhoid, Polio *Average length of flight* 14.5 hours *Food* Like Spanish food

Kiribati
Capital Tarawa *Lang* I-Kiribati and English *Currency* Australian Dollar - 100 cents *Govt* Directly elected President who is head of state and Govt, 36 elected govt members *Rel* Christian *Size* 861 sq km - 332 sq miles *Pop* 72,298 *GMT* +12 *When* August to November *Visas* Not required by UK (except N Ireland) New Zealand and Canadian citizens *Validity* Varies *Safety* Safe *Inoc* Yellow Fever* if arriving from an infected area, Polio, Typhoid *Airlines* Air Nauru via Sydney *Average length of flight* 30 hours excluding stopovers *Food* Lots of coconuts - canned food regarded as a luxury

Marshall Islands (US)
Capital Majuro *Lang* Marshallese *Currency* US Dollar = 100 cents *Govt* Self-governing state, with the US guidelines for foreign policy *Rel* Christian *Size* 494 sq km - 191 sq miles *Pop* 43,355 *GMT* +12 *When* December to April *Visas* Required by all except US *Validity* 90 days *Time to get* 1 week by post *Safety* *Inoc* Paratyphoid, Typhoid *Food* Fish, rice and breadfruit

Micronesia (US) (607 islands)
Capital Pohnpei *Lang* English and Micronesian Japanese *Currency* US Dollar = 100 cents (Local residents on Yap still use giant stone money - some coins weigh up to 4.5 tons and are 12ft in diameter) *Govt* Democracy *Rel* Roman Catholic *Size* 270 sq miles *Pop* 100,000 *GMT* +9 or +10 depending on island *When* January to March (less rain but still very wet) *Visas* Not required if staying less than 30 days *Safety* Safe *Inoc* Paratyphoid, Typhoid *Airlines* Air Micronesia *Average length of flight* 23 hours *Food* Fish

Naura
Capital Yaren *Lang* Nauran and English *Currency* Australian Dollar = 100 cents *Govt* Elected parliament, which in turn elects the president *Rel* Christian *Size* 21.3 sq km - 8.2 sq miles *Pop* 9,350 *GMT* + 12 *When to go* Apr-June and Sept - Nov *Visas* Required by all *Validity* Up to 4 months *Time to get* As much time as possible (months) *Inoc* Yellow Fever* if arriving from an infected area, Polio, Typhoid *Airlines* Via Hong Kong, Manila, Koror and Guam *Average length of flight* 31 hours *Food* International - all imported - mostly canned. Some fresh fish can be found

New Caledonia (France)
Capital Noumena *Lang* French *Currency* French Pacific Franc = 100 centimes *Govt* French Overseas Territory Governed by an interim constitution, with a referendum on full independence set to take place in 1998 *Rel* Christian - Roman Catholic *Size* 19,203 sq km - 7,376 sq miles *Pop* 164,173 *GMT* +11 *When* All year round *Visas* Not required if staying less than one month *Safety* Safe *Inoc* Cholera* and Yellow Fever* if arriving from an infect area, Polio, Typhoid *Airlines* Air France *Average length of flight* 26 hours *Food* French influenced

New Zealand
Capital Wellington *Lang* English *Currency* New Zealand Dollar = 100 cents *Govt* Elected Parliament, currently the National Party, the British monarch is Head of State *Rel* Christian *Size* 2270,534 sq km - 104,454 sq miles *Pop* 3,454,900 *GMT* +12 *When* All year *Visas* Not required *Safety* Safe *Airlines* British Airways, Air New Zealand, Canadian Airlines, United Airlines amongst others *Average length of flight* 30 hours *Food* Meat based - very good lamb

Niue (New Zealand)
Capital Alofi *Lang* English *Currency* New Zealand Dollar *Govt* Elected govt, with New Zealand looking after foreign affairs *Rel* Christian *Size* 260 sq km - 100 sq miles *Pop* 2239 *GMT* -11 *When* All year *Visas* Not required by tourists *Safety* Safe *Inoc* Typhoid, Polio *Airlines* Niue Airlines, Air Naura *Average length of flight* 32 hours *Food* Roots, coconuts and tropical fruits

Northern Mariana Islands (US)
Capital Saipan *Lang* English *Currency* US Dollar = 100 cents *Govt* US Commonwealth Territory, domestically self-governing *Rel* Roman Catholic *Size* 457 sq km - 177 sq miles *Pop* 31,563 *GMT* +10 *When* January to June *Visas* Not required for visits of less than thirty

days *Inoc* Paratyphoid, Typhoid *Airlines* Air Micronesia *Average length of flight* 23 hours *Food* Fish, coconuts and chicken

Republic of Palau (formerly part of the Caroline Islands)

Capital Koror *Lang* English and Palauan *Currency* US Dollar = 100 cents *Govt* Elected president - unstable *Rel* Roman Catholic *Size* 508 sq km - 196 sq miles *Pop* 15,105 *GMT* +10 *When* Hot and humid all year *Visas* Not required if staying less than 30 days *Inoc* Paratyphoid, Typhoid *Airlines* Air Micronesia *Average length of flight* 24 hours *Food* Fresh fish and fruit delicious langusta (like a lobster)

Papua New Guinea

Capital Port Moresby *Lang* English and Pidgin English *Currency* Kina = 100 toea *Govt* Democracy *Rel* Christian *Size* 462,840 sq km - 178,840 sq miles *Pop* 3,772,000 *GMT* +10 *When* May to November *Visas* Required by all *Validity* 2 months *Time to get* At least 2 days *Safety* Take local advice, Port Moresby has gangland violence *Inoc* Yellow Fever* if arriving from an infected area, Hepatitis A, Malaria, Polio, Typhoid *Airlines* No direct flights - Philippine Airlines, Air Nuigini or Cathay Pacific/British Airways and Air Nuigini *Average length of flight* 30 hours *Food* Lots of fruit, locals tend to eat mostly root crops. Pigs are cooked in the earth on special feast days

Samoa (Western)

Capital Apia *Lang* Samoan *Currency* Western Samoan Dollar or Tala = 100 cents *Govt* Stable democracy *Rel* Christian *Size* 2,831 sq km - 1,093 sq miles *Pop* 159,862 *GMT* -11 *When* May to October *Visas* Not required for visits up to 30 days *Safety* Safe *Inoc* Yellow Fever* if arriving from an infected area, Hepatitis A, Polio, Typhoid *Airlines* Air New Zealand (lots of stopovers) *Average length of flight* 26 hours 30 minutes *Food* Fish, pork or chicken based

Solomon Islands

Capital Honiara *Lang* English *Currency* Solomon Island Dollar = 100 cents *Govt* Multi-party democracy *Rel* Christian *Size* 27,566 sq km - 10,639 sq miles *Pop* 318,707 *GMT* +11 *When* May through September *Visas* Not required *Safety* Safe *Inoc* Yellow Fever* if arriving from an infected area, Hepatitis A, Malaria, Polio, Typhoid *Airlines* Via Brisbane Qantas and Solomon Airlines *Average length of flight* 29 hours 45 minutes *Food* Fish based

Tonga

Capital Nuku'alofa *Lang* Tongan and English *Currency* Pa'anga = 100 seniti *Govt* The King is head of state and Government, the govt is elected *Rel* Roman Catholic *Size* 748 sq km - 289 sq miles *Pop* 94,485 *GMT* +13 *When* May to November *Visas* Not required *Safety* Safe *Inoc* Yellow Fever* if arriving from an infected area, Polio, Typhoid *Airlines* Via Australia or New Zealand *Average length of flight* 20 hours *Food* Fish, tropical fruits and salads

Tuvalu

Capital Funafuti *Lang* Tuvaluan and English *Currency* Australian Dollars and Tuvaluan Dollars = 100 cents *Govt* The British Monarch is Head of State, with an elected parliament *Rel* Protestant *Size* 26 sq km - 10 sq miles *Pop* 9,500 *GMT* + 12 *When* March to October *Visas* Required by citizens of the USA *Safety* Safe *Inoc* Yellow Fever* if arriving from an infected area, Polio, Typhoid *Airlines* Via Fiji *Average length of flight* 30 hours *Food* Fresh fish and tropical fruits

Vanuatu

Capital Port Vila *Lang* Bislama *Currency* Vatu = 100 centimes *Govt* democracy *Rel* Christian *Size* 12,190 sq km - 4,707 sq miles *Pop* 147,000 *GMT* +12 *When* May to October *Visas* Not required *Safety* Safe *Inoc* Hepatitis A, Malaria, Polio, Typhoid *Airlines* Via Australia or New Zealand *Average length of flight* 30 hours *Food* Very good with Chinese and French influences

WORLDWIDE WEATHER GUIDE

The information given below details temperature and humidity at major cities throughout the world:

Temperature: Average daily maximum and minimum temperatures are shade temperatures. Maximum temperatures usually occur in early afternoon, and minimum temperatures just before sunrise.

Humidity: Measured as a daily figure at one or more fixed hours daily. It is normally lowest in the early afternoon and highest just before sunrise. High humidity combined with high temperatures increases discomfort.

Precipitation: Includes all forms of moisture falling on the earth, mainly rain and snow. Average monthly.

		J	F	M	A	M	J	J	A	S	O	N	D
Accra, Ghana													
Temperature °F	Max	87	88	88	88	87	84	81	80	81	85	87	88
	Min	73	75	76	76	75	74	73	71	73	74	75	75
Temperature °C	Max	31	31	31	31	31	29	27	27	27	29	31	31
	Min	23	24	24	24	24	23	23	22	23	23	24	24
Humidity %	am	95	96	95	96	96	97	97	97	96	97	97	97
	pm	61	61	63	65	68	74	76	77	72	71	66	64
Precipitation	mm	15	33	56	81	142	178	46	15	36	64	36	23
Amsterdam, Netherlands													
Temperature °F	Max	40	42	49	56	64	70	72	71	67	57	48	42
	Min	31	31	34	40	46	51	55	55	50	44	38	33
Temperature °C	Max	4	5	10	13	18	21	22	22	19	14	9	5
	Min	-1	-1	1	4	8	11	13	13	10	7	3	1
Humidity %	am	90	90	86	79	75	75	79	82	86	90	92	91
	pm	82	76	65	61	59	59	64	65	67	72	81	85
Precipitation	mm	68	53	44	49	52	58	77	87	72	72	70	64
Athens, Greece													
Temperature °F	Max	55	57	60	68	77	86	92	92	84	75	66	58
	Min	44	44	46	52	61	68	73	73	67	60	53	47
Temperature °C	Max	13	14	16	20	25	30	33	33	29	24	19	15
	Min	6	7	8	11	16	20	23	23	19	15	12	8
Humidity %	am	77	74	71	65	60	50	47	48	58	70	78	78
	pm	62	57	54	48	47	39	34	34	42	52	61	63
Precipitation	mm	62	37	37	23	23	14	6	7	15	51	56	71
Auckland, New Zealand													
Temperature °F	Max	73	73	71	67	62	58	56	58	60	63	66	70
	Min	60	60	59	56	51	48	46	46	49	52	54	57
Temperature °C	Max	23	23	22	19	17	14	13	14	16	17	19	21
	Min	16	16	15	13	11	9	8	8	9	11	12	14
Humidity %	am	71	72	74	78	80	83	84	80	76	74	71	70
	pm	62	61	65	69	70	73	74	70	68	66	64	64
Precipitation	mm	79	94	81	97	127	137	145	117	102	102	89	79
Bahrain													
Temperature °F	Max	68	70	75	84	92	96	99	100	96	90	82	71
	Min	57	59	63	70	78	82	85	85	81	75	69	60
Temperature °C	Max	20	21	24	29	33	36	37	38	36	32	28	22
	Min	14	15	17	21	26	28	29	29	27	24	21	16
Humidity %	am	85	83	80	75	71	69	69	74	75	80	80	85
	pm	71	70	70	66	63	64	67	65	64	66	70	77
Precipitation	mm	8	18	13	8	0	0	0	0	0	0	18	18

		J	F	M	A	M	J	J	A	S	O	N	D
Bangkok, Thailand													
Temperature °F	Max	89	91	93	95	93	91	90	90	89	88	87	87
	Min	68	72	75	77	77	76	76	76	76	75	72	68
Temperature °C	Max	32	33	34	35	34	33	32	32	32	31	31	31
	Min	20	22	24	25	25	24	24	24	24	24	22	20
Humidity %	am	91	92	92	90	91	90	91	92	94	93	92	91
	pm	53	55	56	58	64	67	66	66	70	70	65	56
Precipitation	mm	8	20	36	58	198	160	160	175	305	206	66	5
Beirut, Lebanon													
Temperature °F	Max	62	63	66	72	78	83	87	89	86	81	73	65
	Min	51	51	54	58	64	69	73	74	73	69	61	55
Temperature °C	Max	17	17	19	22	26	28	31	32	30	27	23	18
	Min	11	11	12	14	18	21	23	23	23	21	16	13
Humidity %	am	72	72	72	72	69	67	66	65	64	65	67	70
	pm	70	70	69	67	64	61	58	57	57	62	61	69
Precipitation	mm	191	158	94	56	18	3	0	0	5	51	132	185
Berlin, Germany													
Temperature °F	Max	35	37	46	56	66	72	75	74	68	56	45	38
	Min	26	26	31	39	47	53	57	56	50	42	36	29
Temperature °C	Max	2	3	8	13	19	22	24	23	20	13	7	3
	Min	-3	-3	0	4	8	12	14	13	10	6	2	-1
Humidity %	am	89	89	88	84	80	80	84	88	92	93	92	91
	pm	82	78	67	60	57	58	61	61	65	73	83	86
Precipitation	mm	46	40	33	42	49	65	73	69	48	49	46	43
Bombay, India													
Temperature °F	Max	83	83	86	89	91	89	85	85	85	89	89	87
	Min	67	67	72	76	80	79	77	76	76	76	73	69
Temperature °C	Max	28	28	30	32	33	32	29	29	29	32	32	31
	Min	12	12	17	20	23	21	22	22	22	21	18	13
Humidity %	am	70	71	73	75	74	79	83	83	85	81	73	70
	pm	61	62	65	67	68	77	83	81	78	71	64	62
Precipitation	mm	2.5	2.5	2.5	0	18	485	617	340	264	64	13	2.5
Brussels, Belgium													
Temperature °F	Max	40	44	51	58	65	72	73	72	69	60	48	42
	Min	30	32	36	41	46	52	54	54	51	45	38	32
Temperature °C	Max	4	7	10	14	18	22	23	22	21	15	9	6
	Min	-1	0	2	5	8	11	12	12	11	7	3	0
Humidity %	am	92	92	91	91	90	87	91	93	94	93	93	92
	pm	86	81	74	71	65	65	68	69	69	77	85	86
Precipitation	mm	66	61	53	60	55	76	95	80	63	83	75	88
Buenos Aires, Argentina													
Temperature °F	Max	85	83	79	72	64	57	57	60	64	69	76	82
	Min	63	63	60	53	47	41	42	43	46	50	56	61
Temperature °C	Max	29	28	26	22	18	14	14	16	18	21	24	28
	Min	17	17	16	12	8	5	6	6	8	10	13	16
Humidity %	am	81	83	87	88	90	91	92	90	86	83	79	79
	pm	61	63	69	71	74	78	79	74	68	65	60	62
Precipitation	mm	79	71	109	89	76	61	56	61	79	86	84	99
Cairo, Egypt													
Temperature °F	Max	65	69	75	83	91	95	96	95	90	86	78	68
	Min	47	48	52	57	63	68	70	71	68	65	58	50
Temperature °C	Max	18	21	24	28	33	35	36	35	32	30	26	20

		J	F	M	A	M	J	J	A	S	O	N	D
Cairo continued...													
	Min	8	9	11	14	17	20	21	22	20	18	14	10
Humidity %	am	69	64	63	55	50	55	65	69	68	67	68	70
	pm	40	33	27	21	18	20	24	28	31	31	38	41
Precipitation	mm	5	5	5	3	3	0	0	0	0	0	3	5

Calcutta, India

		J	F	M	A	M	J	J	A	S	O	N	D
Temperature °F	Max	80	84	93	97	96	92	89	89	90	89	84	79
	Min	55	59	69	75	77	79	79	78	78	74	64	55
Temperature °C	Max	27	29	34	36	36	33	32	32	32	32	29	26
	Min	13	15	21	24	25	26	26	26	26	24	18	13
Humidity %	am	85	82	79	76	77	82	86	88	86	85	79	80
	pm	52	45	46	56	62	75	80	82	81	72	63	55
Precipitation	mm	10	31	36	43	140	297	325	328	252	114	20	5

Christchurch, New Zealand

		J	F	M	A	M	J	J	A	S	O	N	D
Temperature °F	Max	70	69	66	62	56	51	50	52	57	62	66	69
	Min	53	53	50	45	40	36	35	36	40	44	47	51
Temperature °C	Max	21	21	19	17	13	11	10	11	14	17	19	21
	Min	12	12	10	7	4	2	2	2	4	7	8	11
Humidity %	am	65	71	75	82	85	87	87	81	72	63	64	67
	pm	59	60	69	71	69	72	76	66	69	60	64	60
Precipitation	mm	56	43	48	48	66	66	69	48	46	43	48	56

Colombo, Sri Lanka

		J	F	M	A	M	J	J	A	S	O	N	D
Temperature °F	Max	86	87	88	88	87	85	85	85	85	85	85	85
	Min	72	72	74	76	78	77	77	77	77	75	73	72
Temperature °C	Max	30	31	31	31	31	29	29	29	29	29	29	29
	Min	22	22	23	24	26	25	25	25	25	24	23	22
Humidity %	am	73	71	71	74	78	80	79	78	76	77	77	74
	pm	67	66	66	70	76	78	77	76	75	76	75	69
Precipitation	mm	89	69	147	231	371	224	135	109	160	348	315	147

Copenhagen, Denmark

		J	F	M	A	M	J	J	A	S	O	N	D
Temperature °F	Max	36	36	41	51	61	67	71	70	64	54	45	40
	Min	28	28	31	38	46	52	57	56	51	44	38	34
Temperature °C	Max	2	2	5	10	16	19	22	21	18	12	7	4
	Min	-2	-3	-1	3	8	11	14	14	11	7	3	1
Humidity	am	88	86	85	79	70	70	74	78	83	86	88	89
	pm	85	83	78	68	59	60	62	64	69	76	83	87
Precipitation	mm	49	39	32	38	43	47	71	66	62	59	48	49

Delhi, India

		J	F	M	A	M	J	J	A	S	O	N	D
Temperature °F	Max	70	75	87	97	105	102	96	93	93	93	84	73
	Min	44	49	58	68	79	83	81	79	75	65	52	46
Temperature °C	Max	21	24	31	36	41	39	36	34	34	34	29	23
	Min	7	9	14	20	26	28	27	26	24	18	11	8
Humidity %	am	72	67	49	35	35	53	75	80	72	56	51	69
	pm	41	35	23	19	20	36	59	64	51	32	31	42
Precipitation	mm	23	18	13	8	13	74	180	173	117	10	3	10

Frankfurt, Germany

		J	F	M	A	M	J	J	A	S	O	N	D
Temperature °F	Max	38	41	51	60	69	74	77	76	69	58	47	39
	Min	29	30	35	42	49	55	58	57	52	44	38	32
Temperature °C	Max	3	5	11	16	20	23	25	24	21	14	8	4
	Min	-2	-1	2	6	9	13	15	14	11	7	3	0
Humidity %	am	86	86	84	79	78	78	81	85	89	91	89	88

		J	F	M	A	M	J	J	A	S	O	N	D

Frankfurt continued…

		J	F	M	A	M	J	J	A	S	O	N	D
	pm	77	70	57	51	50	52	53	54	60	68	77	81
Precipitation	mm	58	44	38	44	55	73	70	76	57	52	55	54

Hamilton, Bermuda

		J	F	M	A	M	J	J	A	S	O	N	D
Temperature °F	Max	68	68	68	71	76	81	85	86	84	79	74	70
	Min	58	57	57	59	64	69	73	74	72	69	63	60
Temperature °C	Max	20	20	20	22	24	27	29	30	29	26	23	21
	Min	14	14	14	15	18	21	23	23	22	21	17	16
Humidity %	am	78	76	77	78	81	82	81	79	81	79	76	77
	pm	70	69	69	70	75	74	73	69	73	72	70	70
Precipitation	mm	112	119	122	104	117	112	114	137	132	147	127	119

Harare, Zimbabwe

		J	F	M	A	M	J	J	A	S	O	N	D
Temperature °F	Max	78	78	78	78	74	70	70	74	79	83	81	79
	Min	60	60	58	55	49	44	44	47	53	58	60	60
Temperature °C	Max	26	26	26	26	23	21	21	23	26	28	27	26
	Min	16	16	14	13	9	7	7	8	12	14	16	16
Humidity %	am	74	77	75	68	60	58	56	50	43	43	56	67
	pm	57	53	52	44	37	36	33	28	26	26	43	57
Precipitation	mm	196	178	117	28	13	3	0	3	5	28	97	163

Hong Kong

		J	F	M	A	M	J	J	A	S	O	N	D
Temperature °F	Max	64	63	67	75	82	85	87	87	85	81	74	68
	Min	56	55	60	67	74	78	78	78	77	73	65	59
Temperature °C	Max	18	17	19	24	28	29	31	31	29	27	23	20
	Min	13	13	16	19	23	26	26	26	25	23	18	15
Humidity %	am	77	82	84	87	87	86	87	87	83	75	73	74
	pm	66	73	74	77	78	77	77	77	72	63	60	63
Precipitation	mm	33	46	74	137	292	394	381	367	257	114	43	31

Istanbul, Turkey

		J	F	M	A	M	J	J	A	S	O	N	D
Temperature °F	Max	46	47	51	60	69	77	82	82	76	68	59	51
	Min	37	36	38	45	53	60	65	66	61	55	48	41
Temperature °C	Max	8	9	11	16	21	25	28	28	24	20	15	11
	Min	3	2	3	7	12	16	18	19	16	13	9	5
Humidity %	am	82	82	81	81	82	79	79	79	81	83	82	82
	pm	75	72	67	62	61	58	56	55	59	64	71	74
Precipitation	mm	109	92	72	46	38	34	34	30	58	81	103	119

Jakarta, Indonesia

		J	F	M	A	M	J	J	A	S	O	N	D
Temperature °F	Max	84	84	86	87	87	87	87	87	88	87	86	85
	Min	74	74	74	75	75	74	73	73	74	74	74	74
Temperature °C	Max	29	29	30	31	31	31	31	31	31	31	30	29
	Min	23	23	23	24	24	23	23	23	23	23	23	23
Humidity %	am	95	95	94	94	94	93	92	90	90	90	92	92
	pm	75	75	73	71	69	67	64	61	62	64	68	71
Precipitation	mm	300	300	211	147	114	97	64	43	66	112	142	203

Jeddah, Saudi Arabia

		J	F	M	A	M	J	J	A	S	O	N	D
Temperature °F	Max	84	84	85	91	95	97	99	99	96	95	91	86
	Min	66	65	67	70	74	75	79	80	77	73	71	67
Temperature °C	Max	29	29	29	33	35	36	37	37	36	35	33	30
	Min	19	18	19	21	23	24	26	27	25	23	22	19
Humidity %	am	58	52	52	52	51	56	55	59	65	60	55	55
	pm	54	52	52	56	55	55	50	51	61	61	59	54
Precipitation	mm	5	0	0	0	0	0	0	0	0	0	25	31

		J	F	M	A	M	J	J	A	S	O	N	D
Jerusalem, Israel													
Temperature °F	Max	55	56	65	73	81	85	87	87	85	81	70	59
	Min	41	42	46	50	57	60	63	64	62	59	53	45
Temperature °C	Max	13	13	18	23	27	29	31	31	29	27	21	15
	Min	5	6	8	10	14	16	17	18	17	15	12	7
Humidity %	am	77	74	61	56	47	48	52	58	61	60	65	73
	pm	66	58	57	42	33	32	35	36	36	36	50	60
Precipitation	mm	132	132	64	28	3	0	0	0	0	13	71	86
Johannesburg, South Africa													
Temperature °F	Max	78	77	75	72	66	62	63	68	73	77	77	78
	Min	58	58	55	50	43	39	39	43	48	53	55	57
Temperature °C	Max	26	25	24	22	19	17	17	20	23	25	25	26
	Min	14	14	13	10	6	4	4	6	9	12	13	14
Humidity %	am	75	78	79	74	70	70	69	64	59	64	67	70
	pm	50	53	50	44	36	33	32	29	30	37	45	47
Precipitation	mm	114	109	89	38	25	8	8	8	23	56	107	125
Kathmandu, Nepal													
Temperature °F	Max	65	67	77	83	86	85	84	83	83	80	74	67
	Min	35	39	45	53	61	67	68	68	66	56	45	37
Temperature °C	Max	18	19	25	28	30	29	29	28	28	27	23	19
	Min	2	4	7	12	16	19	20	20	19	13	7	3
Humidity %	am	89	90	73	68	72	79	86	87	86	88	90	89
	pm	70	68	53	54	61	72	82	84	83	81	78	73
Precipitation	mm	15	41	23	58	122	246	373	345	155	38	8	3
Kuala Lumpur, Malaysia													
Temperature °F	Max	90	92	92	91	91	91	90	90	90	89	89	89
	Min	72	72	73	74	73	72	73	73	73	73	73	72
Temperature °C	Max	32	33	33	33	33	33	32	32	32	32	32	32
	Min	22	22	23	23	23	22	23	23	23	23	23	22
Humidity %	am	97	97	97	97	97	96	95	96	96	96	97	97
	pm	60	60	58	63	66	63	63	62	64	65	66	61
Precipitation	mm	158	201	259	292	224	130	99	163	218	249	259	191
Lagos, Nigeria													
Temperature °F	Max	88	89	89	89	87	85	83	82	83	85	88	88
	Min	74	77	78	77	76	74	74	73	74	74	75	75
Temperature °C	Max	31	32	32	32	31	29	28	28	28	29	31	31
	Min	23	25	26	25	24	23	23	23	23	23	24	24
Humidity %	am	84	83	82	81	83	87	87	85	86	86	85	86
	pm	65	69	72	72	76	80	80	76	77	76	72	68
Precipitation	mm	28	46	102	150	269	460	279	64	140	206	69	25
Lima, Peru													
Temperature °F	Max	82	83	83	80	74	68	67	66	68	71	74	78
	Min	66	67	66	63	60	58	57	56	57	58	60	62
Temperature °C	Max	28	28	28	27	23	20	19	19	20	22	23	26
	Min	19	19	19	17	16	14	14	13	14	14	16	17
Humidity %	am	93	92	92	93	95	95	94	95	94	94	93	93
	pm	69	66	64	66	76	80	77	78	76	72	71	70
Precipitation	mm	3	0	0	0	5	5	8	8	8	3	3	0
Lisbon, Portugal													
Temperature °F	Max	57	59	63	67	71	77	81	82	79	72	63	58
	Min	46	47	50	53	55	60	63	63	62	58	52	47
Temperature °C	Max	14	15	17	20	21	25	27	28	26	22	17	15

		J	F	M	A	M	J	J	A	S	O	N	D

Lisbon continued…

		J	F	M	A	M	J	J	A	S	O	N	D
	Min	8	8	10	12	13	15	17	17	17	14	11	9
Humidity %	am	85	80	78	69	68	65	62	64	70	75	81	84
	pm	71	64	64	56	57	54	48	49	54	59	68	72
Precipitation	mm	111	76	109	54	44	16	3	4	33	62	93	103

London, UK

		J	F	M	A	M	J	J	A	S	O	N	D
Temperature °F	Max	43	44	50	56	62	69	71	71	65	58	50	45
	Min	36	36	38	42	47	53	56	56	52	46	42	38
Temperature °C	Max	6	7	10	13	17	20	22	21	19	14	10	7
	Min	2	2	3	6	8	12	14	13	11	8	5	4
Humidity %	am	86	85	81	71	70	70	71	76	80	85	85	87
	pm	77	72	64	56	57	58	59	62	65	70	78	81
Precipitation	mm	54	40	37	37	46	45	57	59	49	57	64	48

Madrid, Spain

		J	F	M	A	M	J	J	A	S	O	N	D
Temperature °F	Max	47	52	59	65	70	80	87	85	77	65	55	48
	Min	35	36	41	45	50	58	63	63	57	49	42	36
Temperature °C	Max	9	11	15	18	21	27	31	30	25	19	13	9
	Min	2	2	5	7	10	15	17	17	14	10	5	2
Humidity %	am	86	83	80	74	72	66	58	62	72	81	84	86
	pm	71	62	56	49	49	41	33	35	46	58	65	70
Precipitation	mm	39	34	43	48	47	27	11	15	32	53	47	48

Manila, Philippines

		J	F	M	A	M	J	J	A	S	O	N	D
Temperature °F	Max	86	88	91	93	93	91	88	87	88	88	87	86
	Min	69	69	71	73	75	75	75	75	75	74	73	70
Temperature °C	Max	30	31	33	34	34	33	31	31	31	31	31	30
	Min	21	21	22	23	24	24	24	24	24	23	22	21
Humidity %	am	89	88	85	85	88	91	91	92	93	92	91	90
	pm	63	59	55	55	61	68	74	73	73	71	69	67
Precipitation	mm	23	13	18	33	130	254	432	422	356	193	145	66

Melbourne, Australia

		J	F	M	A	M	J	J	A	S	O	N	D
Temperature °F	Max	78	78	75	68	62	57	56	59	63	67	71	75
	Min	57	57	55	51	47	44	42	43	46	48	51	54
Temperature °C	Max	26	26	24	20	17	14	13	15	17	19	22	24
	Min	14	14	13	11	8	7	6	6	8	9	11	12
Humidity %	am	58	62	64	72	79	83	82	76	68	61	60	59
	pm	48	50	51	56	62	67	65	60	55	52	52	51
Precipitation	mm	48	46	56	58	53	53	48	48	58	66	58	58

Mexico City

		J	F	M	A	M	J	J	A	S	O	N	D
Temperature °F	Max	66	69	75	77	78	76	73	73	74	70	68	66
	Min	42	43	47	51	54	55	53	54	53	50	46	43
Temperature °C	Max	19	21	24	25	26	24	23	23	23	21	20	19
	Min	6	6	8	11	12	13	12	12	12	10	8	6
Humidity %	am	79	72	68	66	69	82	84	85	86	83	82	81
	pm	34	28	26	29	29	48	50	50	54	47	41	37
Precipitation	mm	13	5	10	20	53	119	170	152	130	51	18	8

Miami, USA

		J	F	M	A	M	J	J	A	S	O	N	D
Temperature °F	Max	74	75	78	80	84	86	88	88	87	83	78	76
	Min	61	61	64	67	71	74	76	76	75	72	66	62
Temperature °C	Max	23	24	26	27	29	30	31	31	31	28	26	24
	Min	16	16	18	19	22	23	24	24	24	22	19	17
Humidity %	am	81	82	77	73	75	75	75	76	79	80	77	82

		J	F	M	A	M	J	J	A	S	O	N	D
Miami continued...													
	pm	66	63	62	64	67	69	68	68	70	69	64	65
Precipitation	mm	71	53	64	81	173	178	155	160	203	234	71	51
Moscow, Russia													
Temperature °F	Max	15	22	32	50	66	70	73	72	61	48	35	24
	Min	3	8	18	34	46	51	55	53	45	37	26	15
Temperature °C	Max	-9	-6	0	10	19	21	23	22	16	9	2	-5
	Min	-16	-14	-8	1	8	11	13	12	7	3	-3	-10
Humidity %	am	82	82	82	73	58	62	68	74	78	81	87	85
	pm	77	66	64	54	43	47	54	55	59	67	79	83
Precipitation	mm	39	38	36	37	53	58	88	71	58	45	47	54
Nairobi, Kenya													
Temperature °F	Max	77	79	77	75	72	70	69	70	75	76	74	74
	Min	54	55	57	58	56	53	51	52	52	55	56	55
Temperature °C	Max	25	26	25	24	22	21	21	21	24	24	23	23
	Min	12	13	14	14	13	12	11	11	11	13	13	13
Humidity %	am	74	74	81	88	88	89	86	86	82	82	86	81
	pm	44	40	45	56	62	60	58	56	45	43	53	53
Precipitation	mm	38	64	125	211	158	46	15	23	31	53	109	86
Nassau, Bahamas													
Temperature °F	Max	77	77	79	81	84	87	88	89	88	85	81	79
	Min	65	64	66	69	71	74	75	76	75	73	70	67
Temperature °C	Max	25	25	26	27	29	31	31	32	31	29	27	26
	Min	18	18	19	21	22	23	24	24	24	23	21	19
Humidity %	am	84	82	81	79	79	81	80	82	84	83	83	84
	pm	64	62	64	65	65	68	69	70	73	71	68	66
Precipitation	mm	36	38	36	64	117	163	147	135	175	165	71	33
New York, USA													
Temperature °F	Max	37	38	45	57	68	77	82	80	79	69	51	41
	Min	24	24	30	42	53	60	66	66	60	49	37	29
Temperature °C	Max	3	3	7	14	20	25	28	27	26	21	11	5
	Min	-4	-4	-1	6	12	16	19	19	16	9	3	-2
Humidity %	am	72	70	70	68	70	74	77	79	79	76	75	73
	pm	60	58	55	53	54	58	58	60	61	57	60	61
Precipitation	mm	94	97	91	81	81	84	107	109	86	89	76	91
Oslo, Norway													
Temperature °F	Max	28	30	39	50	61	68	72	70	60	48	38	32
	Min	19	19	25	34	43	50	55	53	46	38	31	25
Temperature °C	Max	-2	-1	4	10	16	20	22	21	16	9	3	0
	Min	-7	-7	-4	1	6	10	13	12	8	3	-1	-4
Humidity %	am	86	84	80	75	68	69	74	79	85	88	88	87
	pm	82	74	64	57	52	55	59	61	66	72	83	85
Precipitation	mm	49	35	26	43	44	70	82	95	81	74	68	63
Ottawa, Canada													
Temperature °F	Max	21	22	33	51	66	76	81	77	68	54	39	24
	Min	3	3	16	31	44	54	58	55	48	37	26	9
Temperature °C	Max	-6	-6	1	11	19	24	27	25	20	12	4	-4
	Min	-16	-16	-9	-1	7	12	14	13	9	3	-3	-13
Humidity %	am	83	88	84	76	77	80	80	84	90	86	84	83
	pm	76	73	66	58	55	56	53	54	59	63	68	75
Precipitation	mm	74	56	71	69	64	89	86	66	81	74	76	66

		J	F	M	A	M	J	J	A	S	O	N	D

Papeete, Tahiti, French Polynesia

		J	F	M	A	M	J	J	A	S	O	N	D
Temperature °F	Max	89	89	89	89	87	86	86	86	86	87	88	88
	Min	72	72	72	72	70	69	68	68	69	70	71	72
Temperature °C	Max	32	32	32	32	31	30	30	30	30	31	31	31
	Min	22	22	22	22	21	21	20	20	21	21	22	22
Humidity %	am	82	82	84	85	84	85	83	83	81	79	80	81
	pm	77	77	78	78	78	79	77	78	76	76	77	78
Precipitation	mm	252	244	429	142	102	76	53	43	53	89	150	249

Paris, France

		J	F	M	A	M	J	J	A	S	O	N	D
Temperature °F	Max	43	45	54	60	68	73	76	75	70	60	50	44
	Min	34	34	39	43	49	55	58	58	53	46	40	36
Temperature °C	Max	6	7	12	16	20	23	25	24	21	16	10	7
	Min	1	1	4	6	10	13	15	14	12	8	5	2
Humidity %	am	88	87	85	82	83	83	83	87	90	91	91	90
	pm	80	73	63	54	55	58	57	61	65	71	79	82
Precipitation	mm	56	46	35	42	57	54	59	64	55	50	51	50

Port-of-Spain, Trinidad

		J	F	M	A	M	J	J	A	S	O	N	D
Temperature °F	Max	87	88	89	90	90	89	88	88	89	89	89	88
	Min	69	68	68	69	71	71	71	71	71	71	71	69
Temperature °C	Max	31	31	32	32	32	32	31	31	32	32	32	31
	Min	21	20	20	21	22	22	22	22	22	22	22	21
Humidity %	am	89	87	85	83	84	87	88	87	87	87	89	89
	pm	68	65	63	61	63	69	71	73	73	74	76	71
Precipitation	mm	69	41	46	53	94	193	218	246	193	170	183	125

Prague, Czech Republic

		J	F	M	A	M	J	J	A	S	O	N	D
Temperature °F	Max	31	34	44	54	64	70	73	72	65	53	42	34
	Min	23	24	30	38	46	52	55	55	49	41	33	27
Temperature °C	Max	0	1	7	12	18	21	23	22	18	12	5	1
	Min	-5	-4	-1	3	8	11	13	13	9	5	1	-3
Humidity %	am	84	83	82	77	75	74	77	81	84	87	87	87
	pm	73	67	55	47	45	46	49	48	51	60	73	78
Precipitation	mm	18	18	18	27	48	54	68	55	31	33	20	21

Rio de Janeiro, Brazil

		J	F	M	A	M	J	J	A	S	O	N	D
Temperature °F	Max	84	85	83	80	77	76	75	76	75	77	79	82
	Min	73	73	72	69	66	64	63	64	65	66	68	71
Temperature °C	Max	29	29	28	27	25	24	24	24	24	25	26	28
	Min	23	23	22	21	19	18	17	18	18	19	20	22
Humidity %	am	82	84	87	87	87	87	86	84	84	83	82	82
	pm	70	71	74	73	70	69	68	66	72	72	72	72
Precipitation	mm	125	122	130	107	79	53	41	43	66	79	104	137

Rome, Italy

		J	F	M	A	M	J	J	A	S	O	N	D
Temperature °F	Max	52	55	59	66	74	82	87	86	79	71	61	55
	Min	40	42	45	50	56	63	67	67	62	55	49	44
Temperature °C	Max	11	13	15	19	23	28	30	30	26	22	16	13
	Min	5	5	7	10	13	17	20	20	17	13	9	6
Humidity %	am	85	86	83	83	77	74	70	73	83	86	87	85
	pm	68	64	56	54	54	48	42	43	50	59	66	70
Precipitation	mm	71	62	57	51	46	37	15	21	63	99	129	93

San Francisco, USA

		J	F	M	A	M	J	J	A	S	O	N	D
Temperature °F	Max	55	59	61	62	63	66	65	65	69	68	63	57
	Min	45	47	48	49	51	52	53	53	55	54	51	47
Temperature °C	Max	13	15	16	17	17	19	18	18	21	20	17	14

		J	F	M	A	M	J	J	A	S	O	N	D

San Francisco continued...

		J	F	M	A	M	J	J	A	S	O	N	D
	Min	7	8	9	9	11	11	12	12	13	12	11	8
Humidity %	am	85	84	83	83	85	88	91	92	88	85	83	83
	pm	69	66	61	61	62	64	69	70	63	58	60	68
Precipitation	mm	119	97	79	38	18	3	0	0	8	25	64	112

Singapore

		J	F	M	A	M	J	J	A	S	O	N	D
Temperature °F	Max	86	88	88	88	89	88	88	87	87	87	87	87
	Min	73	73	75	75	75	75	75	75	75	74	74	74
Temperature °C	Max	30	31	31	31	32	31	31	31	31	31	31	31
	Min	23	23	24	24	24	24	24	24	24	23	23	23
Humidity %	am	82	77	76	77	79	79	79	78	79	78	79	82
	pm	78	71	70	74	73	73	72	72	72	72	75	78
Precipitation	mm	252	173	193	188	173	173	170	196	178	208	254	257

Stockholm, Sweden

		J	F	M	A	M	J	J	A	S	O	N	D
Temperature °F	Max	30	30	37	47	58	67	71	68	60	49	40	35
	Min	23	22	26	34	43	51	57	56	49	41	34	29
Temperature °C	Max	-1	-1	3	8	14	19	22	20	15	9	5	2
	Min	-5	-5	-4	1	6	11	14	13	9	5	1	-2
Humidity %	am	85	83	82	76	66	68	74	81	87	88	89	88
	pm	83	77	68	60	53	55	59	64	69	76	85	86
Precipitation	mm	43	30	25	31	34	45	61	76	60	48	53	48

Sydney, Australia

		J	F	M	A	M	J	J	A	S	O	N	D
Temperature °F	Max	78	78	76	71	66	61	60	63	67	71	74	77
	Min	65	65	63	58	52	48	46	48	51	56	60	63
Temperature °C	Max	26	26	24	22	19	16	16	17	19	22	23	25
	Min	18	18	17	14	11	9	8	9	11	13	16	17
Humidity %	am	68	71	73	76	77	77	76	72	67	65	65	66
	pm	64	65	65	64	63	62	60	56	55	57	60	62
Precipitation	mm	89	102	127	135	127	117	117	76	74	71	74	74

Tehran, Iran

		J	F	M	A	M	J	J	A	S	O	N	D
Temperature °F	Max	45	50	59	71	82	93	99	97	90	76	63	51
	Min	27	32	39	49	58	66	72	71	64	53	43	33
Temperature °C	Max	7	10	15	22	28	34	37	36	32	24	17	11
	Min	-3	0	4	9	14	19	22	22	18	12	6	1
Humidity %	am	77	73	61	54	55	50	51	47	49	53	63	76
	pm	75	59	39	40	47	49	41	46	49	54	66	75
Precipitation	mm	46	38	46	36	13	3	3	3	3	8	20	31

Tokyo, Japan

		J	F	M	A	M	J	J	A	S	O	N	D
Temperature °F	Max	47	48	54	63	71	76	83	86	79	69	60	52
	Min	29	31	36	46	54	63	70	72	66	55	43	33
Temperature °C	Max	8	9	12	17	22	24	28	30	26	21	16	11
	Min	-2	-1	2	8	12	17	21	22	19	13	6	1
Humidity %	am	73	71	75	81	85	89	91	92	91	88	83	77
	pm	48	48	53	59	62	68	69	66	68	64	58	51
Precipitation	mm	48	74	107	135	147	165	142	152	234	208	97	56

Vancouver, Canada

		J	F	M	A	M	J	J	A	S	O	N	D
Temperature °F	Max	41	44	50	58	64	69	74	73	65	57	48	43
	Min	32	34	37	40	46	52	54	54	49	44	39	35
Temperature °C	Max	5	7	10	14	18	21	23	23	18	14	9	6
	Min	0	1	3	4	8	11	12	12	9	7	4	2

		J	F	M	A	M	J	J	A	S	O	N	D

Vancouver continued...

Humidity %	am	93	91	91	89	88	87	89	90	92	92	91	91
	pm	85	78	70	67	63	65	62	62	72	80	84	88
Precipitation	mm	218	147	127	84	71	64	31	43	91	147	211	224

Vienna, Austria

Temperature °F	Max	34	38	47	58	67	73	76	75	68	56	45	37
	Min	25	28	30	42	50	56	60	59	53	44	37	30
Temperature °C	Max	1	3	8	15	19	23	25	24	20	14	7	3
	Min	-4	-3	-1	6	10	14	15	15	11	7	3	-1
Humidity %	am	81	80	78	72	74	74	74	78	83	86	84	84
	pm	72	66	57	49	52	55	54	54	56	64	74	76
Precipitation	mm	39	44	44	45	70	67	84	72	42	56	52	45

Warsaw, Poland

Temperature °F	Max	32	32	42	53	67	73	75	73	66	55	42	35
	Min	22	21	28	37	48	54	58	56	49	41	33	28
Temperature °C	Max	0	0	6	12	20	23	24	23	19	13	6	2
	Min	-6	-6	-2	3	9	12	15	14	10	5	1	-3
Humidity %	am	90	89	90	85	80	82	86	90	92	93	93	92
	pm	84	80	70	61	56	59	63	63	64	73	83	87
Precipitation	mm	27	32	27	37	46	69	96	65	43	38	31	44

Yangon, Myanmar

Temperature °F	Max	89	92	96	97	92	86	85	85	86	88	88	88
	Min	65	67	71	76	77	76	76	76	76	76	73	67
Temperature °C	Max	32	33	36	36	33	30	29	29	30	31	31	31
	Min	18	19	22	24	25	24	24	24	24	24	23	19
Humidity %	am	71	72	74	71	80	87	89	89	87	83	79	75
	pm	52	52	54	64	76	85	88	88	86	77	72	61
Precipitation	mm	3	5	8	51	307	480	582	528	394	180	69	10

Zurich, Switzerland

Temperature °F	Max	36	41	51	59	67	73	76	75	69	57	45	37
	Min	26	28	34	40	47	53	56	56	51	43	35	29
Temperature °C	Max	2	5	10	15	19	23	25	24	20	14	7	3
	Min	-3	-2	1	4	8	12	14	13	11	6	2	-2
Humidity %	am	88	88	86	81	80	80	81	85	90	92	90	89
	pm	74	65	55	51	52	52	52	53	57	64	73	76
Precipitation	mm	74	69	64	76	101	129	136	124	102	77	73	64

Weather Information

London Weather Centre
Penderel House
284-286 High Holborn
London
WC1V 7HX
Public Enquiries : tel: 071-836 4311
Climatological Enquiries: tel: 071-430 5709
General Enquiries: tel: 071-430 5511
Will answer all regional weather enquiries

Meteorological Office (Overseas Enquiry
Bureau)
Tel: 0344 420242 *and ask for appropriate
country*

Weather call *(Major cities)* 0891 500 +
Northern Europe 969;
Central Europe 970;
Southern Europe 971;
USA 972;
Far East 973

Holiday Weatherline 0891 500 +
Eastern Mediterranean 974;
Spain/Portugal 975;
France 976;
Italy/Malta 977;
North Africa 978;
USA 979

GUIDE TO RAINY SEASONS

Within each region, the destinations listed are arranged in order of decreasing latitude north of the equator, increasing latitude south of the equator. This is a reminder that at any given time of the year, opposite seasons are to be found north and south of the equator. December to February, for example, bring winter to the northern hemisphere, summer to the southern hemisphere. In the belt stretching about up to 10° north and south of the equator, the equatorial climate tends to prevail: the seasons are almost indistinguishable from each other and rain, broadly speaking, is more evenly spread throughout the year than elsewhere. But a lot depends on altitude and other features of geographical location —proximity to the seas or to mountains, and the nature of prevailing winds and currents.

The places listed are not necessarily typical of other places within the same region or country. And they represent only a minute sample globally. Total annual rainfall should always be taken into account, since the rainy season in one place may well be less wet than the dry season in another. At best, this table is a rough guide only.

Δ represents a month having more than $1/12$ of the annual total rainfall

∞ represents a month having less than $1/12$ of the annual total rainfall

• indicates the month(s) with the highest average rainfall of the year

Asia

	Total annual rainfall (cm)	J	F	M	A	M	J	J	A	S	O	N	D	Latitude
Istanbul, Turkey	80.5	Δ	Δ	Δ	∞	∞	∞	∞	∞	∞	Δ	Δ	•	41°00'N
Beijing, China	134.1	∞	∞	∞	∞	∞	∞	Δ	•	•	Δ	∞	∞	39°50'N
Seoul, Korea.	125.0	∞	∞	∞	∞	∞	Δ	•	•	Δ	∞	∞	∞	37°31'N
Tokyo, Japan	156.5	∞	∞	Δ	Δ	Δ	Δ	Δ	Δ	•	Δ	∞	∞	35°45'N
Tehran, Iran	24.6	•	Δ	•	Δ	∞	∞	∞	∞	∞	∞	∞	Δ	35°44'N
Osaka, Japan	133.6	∞	∞	∞	Δ	Δ	•	Δ	Δ	Δ	Δ	∞	∞	34°40'N
Kabul, Afghanistan	34.0	•	Δ	•	•	∞	∞	∞	∞	∞	∞	∞	Δ	34°28'N
Beirut, Lebanon	89.7	•	Δ	Δ	∞	∞	∞	∞	∞	∞	∞	Δ	•	33°53'N
Damascus, Syria	22.4	•	•∞	∞	∞	∞	∞	∞	∞	∞	∞	Δ	Δ	33°30'N
Baghdad, Iraq	15.0	Δ	Δ	•	Δ	∞	∞	∞	∞	∞	∞	Δ	Δ	33°20'N
Nagasaki, Japan	191.8	∞	∞	Δ	Δ	Δ	•	Δ	Δ	Δ	∞	∞	∞	32°47'N
Amman, Jordan	27.9	•	•	Δ	∞	∞	∞	∞	∞	∞	∞	Δ	Δ	32°00'N
Jerusalem, Israel	53.3	•	•	Δ	∞	∞	∞	∞	∞	∞	∞	Δ	Δ	31°47'N
Shanghai, China	113.5	∞	∞	∞	∞	∞	•	Δ	Δ	Δ	∞	∞	∞	31°15'N
Wuhan, China	125.7	∞	∞	∞	Δ	Δ	•	Δ	∞	∞	∞	∞	∞	30°32'N
Kuwait City, Kuwait	12.7	Δ	Δ	•	∞	∞	∞	∞	∞	∞	∞	Δ	•	29°30'N
Delhi, India	64.0	∞	∞	∞	∞	∞	Δ	•	•	Δ	∞	∞	∞	28°38'N
Kathmandu, Nepal	142.7	∞	∞	∞	∞	Δ	Δ	•	•	Δ	∞	∞	∞	27°45'N
Agra, India	68.1	∞	∞	∞	∞	∞	Δ	•	•	Δ	∞	∞	∞	27°17'N
Cherrapunji, India	1,079.8	∞	∞	∞	∞	Δ	•	•	•	Δ	∞	∞	∞	25°17'N
Taipei, Taiwan	212.9	∞	∞	Δ	∞	Δ	Δ	Δ	•	Δ	∞	∞	∞	25°20'N
Karachi, Pakistan	18.3	∞	∞	∞	∞	∞	∞	•	Δ	∞	∞	∞	∞	24°53'N
Riyadh, Saudi Arabia	9.1	∞	Δ	Δ	•	Δ	∞	∞	∞	∞	∞	∞	∞	24°41'N
Guangzhou, China	164.3	∞	∞	∞	Δ	Δ	•	Δ	Δ	∞	∞	∞	∞	23°10'N
Calcutta, India	160.0	∞	∞	∞	∞	Δ	Δ	•	•	Δ	∞	∞	∞	22°36'N
Hong Kong	216.1	∞	∞	∞	∞	Δ	•	•	•	Δ	∞	∞	∞	22°11'N
Mandalay, Myanmar	82.8	∞	∞	∞	∞	•	•	Δ	Δ	Δ	Δ	∞	∞	22°00'N
Jeddah, Saudi Arabia	8.1	∞	∞	∞	∞	∞	∞	∞	∞	∞	∞	•	•	21°29'N
Hanoi, Vietnam	168.1	∞	∞	∞	∞	Δ	Δ	Δ	•	Δ	∞	∞	∞	21°50'N
Bombay, India	181.4	∞	∞	∞	∞	∞	•	•	Δ	Δ	∞	∞	∞	18°55'N
Hyderabad, India	75.2	∞	∞	∞	∞	∞	Δ	Δ	Δ	•	Δ	∞	∞	17°10'N
Yangon, Myanmar	261.6	∞	∞	∞	∞	Δ	Δ	•	Δ	Δ	∞	∞	∞	16°45'N

	Total annual rainfall (cm)	J	F	M	A	M	J	J	A	S	O	N	D	Latitude
Manila, Philippines	208.5	∞	∞	∞	∞	∞	Δ	•	•	Δ	Δ	∞	∞	14°40'N
Bangkok, Thailand	139.7	∞	∞	∞	∞	Δ	Δ	Δ	Δ	•	Δ	∞	∞	13°45'N
Madras, India	127.0	∞	∞	∞	∞	∞	∞	∞	Δ	Δ	•	•	Δ	13°80'N
Bangalore, India	329.2	∞	∞	∞	∞	∞	•	•	•	Δ	∞	∞	∞	12°55'N
Aden, Yemen	4.8	Δ	∞	Δ	∞	∞	∞	∞	Δ	•	∞	∞	∞	12°50'N
Colombo, Sri Lanka	236.5	∞	∞	∞	Δ	•	Δ	∞	∞	∞	•	•	∞	6°56'N
Sandakan, Malaysia	314.2	•	Δ	∞	∞	∞	∞	∞	∞	∞	∞	Δ	Δ	5°53'N
Kuala Lumpur, Malaysia	244.1	∞	∞	Δ	•	Δ	∞	∞	∞	Δ	Δ	Δ	∞	3°90'N
Singapore	241.3	•	∞	∞	∞	∞	∞	∞	∞	∞	Δ	•	•	1°17'N
Jakarta, Indonesia	179.8	•	•	Δ	∞	∞	∞	∞	∞	∞	∞	∞	•	6°90'S

Africa

	Total annual rainfall (cm)	J	F	M	A	M	J	J	A	S	O	N	D	Latitude
Algiers, Algeria	76.5	Δ	Δ	Δ	∞	∞	∞	∞	∞	∞	Δ	•	•	36°42'N
Tangier, Morocco	90.2	Δ	Δ	Δ	Δ	∞	∞	∞	∞	∞	Δ	•	•	35°50'N
Tripoli, Libya	38.9	Δ	Δ	Δ	∞	∞	∞	∞	∞	∞	∞	Δ	Δ	32°49'N
Marrakesh, Morocco	23.9	Δ	Δ	•	Δ	∞	∞	∞	∞	∞	Δ	Δ	Δ	31°40'N
Cairo, Egypt	3.6	Δ	Δ	Δ	∞	∞	∞	∞	∞	∞	∞	∞	Δ	30°10'N
Timbuctou, Mali	24.4	∞	∞	∞	∞	∞	∞	Δ	•	Δ	∞	∞	∞	16°50'N
Khartoum, Sudan	17.0	∞	∞	∞	∞	∞	∞	Δ	•	Δ	∞	∞	∞	15°31'N
Dakar, Senegal	155.4	∞	∞	∞	∞	∞	∞	Δ	•	Δ	∞	∞	∞	14°34'N
Zungeru, Nigeria	115.3	∞	∞	∞	Δ	Δ	Δ	Δ	•	∞	∞	∞	∞	9°45'N
Harar, Ethiopia	89.7	∞	∞	Δ	Δ	Δ	Δ	•	Δ	∞	∞	∞	∞	9°20'N
Addis Ababa, Ethiopia	123.7	∞	∞	∞	∞	Δ	•	•	Δ	∞	∞	∞	∞	9°20'N
Freetown, Sierra Leone	343.4	∞	∞	∞	∞	Δ	•	•	Δ	∞	∞	Δ		8°30'N
Lagos, Nigeria	183.6	∞	∞	∞	Δ	•	Δ	∞	∞	∞	∞	∞		6°25'N
Cotonou, Benin	132.6	∞	Δ	Δ	•	•	∞	∞	∞	Δ	∞	∞		6°20'N
Monrovia, Liberia	513.8	∞	∞	∞	Δ	•	•	•	Δ	∞	∞	•		6°18'N
Accra, Ghana	72.4	∞	∞	Δ	Δ	Δ	•	∞	∞	∞	Δ	•		5°35'N
Mongalla, Sudan	94.5	∞	∞	Δ	Δ	Δ	•	Δ	Δ	∞	∞			5°80'N
Libreville, Gabon	251.0	Δ	Δ	Δ	Δ	Δ	∞	∞	∞	Δ	•	Δ		0°25'N
Entebbe, Uganda	150.6	∞	Δ	•	Δ	∞	∞	∞	∞	∞	Δ	∞		0°30'N
Nairobi, Kenya	95.8	∞	∞	Δ	•	Δ	∞	∞	∞	∞	Δ	Δ		1°20'S
Mombasa, Kenya	120.1	∞	∞	∞	Δ	•	Δ	∞	∞	∞	∞	∞		4°00'S
Kinshasa, Zaire	135.4	Δ	Δ	Δ	Δ	Δ	∞	∞	∞	∞	•	Δ		4°20'S
Kananga, Zaire	158.2	Δ	Δ	Δ	∞	∞	∞	∞	∞	Δ	•	•		5°55'S
Lilongwe, Malawi	78.7	•	•	Δ	∞	∞	∞	∞	∞	∞	∞	Δ		14°00'S
Lusaka, Zambia	83.3	•	Δ	Δ	∞	∞	∞	∞	∞	∞	Δ	Δ		15°25'S
Harare, Zimbabwe	82.8	•	Δ	Δ	∞	∞	∞	∞	∞	∞	Δ	Δ		17°50'S
Tamatave, Madagascar	325.6	Δ	Δ	•	Δ	∞	Δ	∞	∞	∞	∞	∞		18°20'S
Beira, Mozambique	152.2	•	Δ	Δ	∞	∞	∞	∞	∞	∞	Δ	•		19°50'S
Johannesburg, SA	70.9	Δ	Δ	Δ	∞	∞	∞	∞	∞	∞	∞	•		26°10'S
Maputo, Mozambique	75.9	•	Δ	Δ	∞	∞	∞	∞	∞	∞	∞	Δ	Δ	26°35'S
Cape Town, South Africa	50.8	∞	∞	∞	(Δ)	Δ	Δ	•	Δ	Δ	∞	∞	∞	35°55'S

Sub–Arctic

	Total annual rainfall (cm)	J	F	M	A	M	J	J	A	S	O	N	D	Latitude
Reykjavik, Iceland	77.2	Δ	∞	∞	∞	∞	∞	∞	∞	Δ	•	Δ	Δ	64°10'N

Australasia and the Pacific

	Total annual rainfall (cm)	J	F	M	A	M	J	J	A	S	O	N	D	Latitude
Honolulu, HI, USA	64.3	Δ	Δ	Δ	∞	∞	∞	∞	∞	∞	∞	Δ	•	21°25'N
Tulagi, Solomon Is.	313.4	Δ	•	Δ	Δ	∞	∞	∞	∞	∞	∞	∞	∞	9°24'S
Port Moresby, PNG	101.1	Δ	•	Δ	Δ	∞	∞	∞	∞	∞	∞	∞	Δ	9°24'S
Manihiki, Cook Is.	248.2	•	Δ	∞	∞	∞	∞	∞	∞	Δ	Δ	Δ	Δ	10°24'S
Thursday Is., Australia	171.5	Δ	Δ	Δ	∞	∞	∞	∞	∞	∞	∞	Δ	Δ	10°30'S
Darwin, Australia	149.1	•	Δ	Δ	∞	∞	∞	∞	∞	∞	∞	Δ	Δ	12°20'S
Apia, Western Samoa	285.2	•	Δ	Δ	Δ	∞	∞	∞	∞	∞	∞	Δ	Δ	13°50'S

	Total annual rainfall(cm)	J	F	M	A	M	J	J	A	S	O	N	D	Latitude
Cairns, Australia	225.3	Δ	Δ	•	Δ	∞	∞	∞	∞	∞	∞	∞	Δ	16°55'S
Tahiti, French Polynesia	162.8	•	•	Δ	Δ	∞	∞	∞	∞	∞	∞	Δ	•	17°45'S
Suva, Fiji	297.4	Δ	Δ	•	∞	∞	∞	∞	∞	∞	∞	∞	Δ	18°00'S
Perth, Australia	90.7	∞	∞	∞	∞	Δ	•	•	Δ	Δ	Δ	∞	∞	31°57'S
Sydney, Australia	118.1	∞	Δ	Δ	•	Δ	Δ	Δ	∞	∞	∞	∞	∞	33°53'S
Auckland, NZ	124.7	∞	∞	∞	∞	Δ	Δ	•	Δ	∞	∞	∞	∞	36°52'S
Melbourne, Australia	65.3	∞	Δ	Δ	Δ	∞	∞	∞	∞	Δ	•	Δ	Δ	41°19'S
Wellington, NZ	120.4	∞	∞	∞	∞	Δ	Δ	•	Δ	∞	Δ	∞	∞	41°19'S
Christchurch, NZ	63.8	Δ	∞	∞	∞	Δ	Δ	•	∞	∞	∞	∞	Δ	43°33'S

Central America

		J	F	M	A	M	J	J	A	S	O	N	D	
Monterey, Mexico	58.2	∞	∞	∞	∞	∞	Δ	Δ	Δ	•	Δ	∞	∞	25°40'N
Mazatlan, Mexico	84.8	∞	∞	∞	∞	∞	∞	Δ	Δ	•	∞	∞	∞	23°10'N
Havana, Cuba	122.4	∞	∞	∞	∞	Δ	Δ	Δ	Δ	Δ	•	∞	∞	23°80'N
Merida, Mexico	92.7	∞	∞	∞	∞	Δ	•	Δ	Δ	Δ	Δ	∞	∞	20°50'N
Mexico City, Mexico	74.9	∞	∞	∞	∞	∞	Δ	•	Δ	Δ	∞	∞	∞	19°20'N
Port–au–Prince, Haiti	135.4	∞	∞	∞	Δ	•	∞	∞	Δ	Δ	∞	∞	∞	18°40'N
Santo Domingo, Dom. Rep.	141.7	∞	∞	∞	∞	Δ	Δ	Δ	Δ	•	Δ	Δ	∞	18°30'N
Kingston, Jamaica	80.0	∞	∞	∞	∞	Δ	Δ	∞	Δ	Δ	•	Δ	∞	18°00'N
Acapulco, Mexico	154.2	∞	∞	∞	∞	∞	•	Δ	Δ	Δ	Δ	∞	∞	16°51'N
Salina Cruz, Mexico	102.6	∞	∞	∞	∞	∞	∞	Δ	Δ	•	∞	∞	∞	16°10'N
Dominica, Leeward Island	197.9	∞	∞	∞	∞	∞	Δ	•	Δ	Δ	Δ	Δ	∞	15°20'N
Guatemala City, Guatemala	131.6	∞	∞	∞	∞	Δ	•	Δ	Δ	Δ	Δ	∞	∞	14°40'N
Tegucigalpa, Honduras	162.1	∞	∞	∞	∞	∞	•	Δ	∞	Δ	Δ	∞	∞	14°10'N
San Jose, Costa Rica	179.8	∞	∞	∞	∞	Δ	Δ	Δ	Δ	•	•	∞	∞	10°00'N
Balboa Heights, Panama	177.0	∞	∞	∞	∞	Δ	Δ	Δ	Δ	Δ	•	•	∞	9°00'N

South America

		J	F	M	A	M	J	J	A	S	O	N	D	
Caracas, Venezuela	83.3	∞	∞	∞	∞	Δ	•	•	•	•	•	Δ	∞	10°30'N
Ciudad Bolivar, Venezuela	101.6	∞	∞	∞	∞	Δ	Δ	•	Δ	Δ	∞	Δ	∞	8°50'N
Georgetown, Guyana	225.3	Δ	∞	∞	∞	Δ	Δ	•	Δ	∞	∞	∞	Δ	6°50'N
Bogota, Colombia	105.9	∞	∞	Δ	Δ	Δ	∞	∞	∞	∞	•	Δ	∞	4°34'N
Quito, Ecuador	112.3	Δ	Δ	Δ	•	Δ	∞	∞	∞	∞	∞	∞	∞	0°15'S
Belem, Brazil	243.8	Δ	•	•	Δ	Δ	∞	∞	∞	∞	∞	∞	∞	1°20'S
Guayaquil, Ecuador	97.3	•	•	•	Δ	∞	∞	∞	∞	∞	∞	∞	∞	2°15'S
Manaus, Brazil	181.1	Δ	Δ	•	∞	∞	∞	∞	∞	∞	∞	Δ	Δ	3°00'S
Recife, Brazil	161.0	∞	Δ	Δ	Δ	Δ	•	Δ	Δ	∞	∞	∞	∞	8°00'S
Lima, Peru	4.8	∞	∞	∞	∞	Δ	Δ	Δ	•	•	∞	∞	∞	12°00'S
Salvador (Bahia), Brazil	190.0	∞	∞	∞	•	•	Δ	Δ	∞	∞	∞	∞	∞	13°00'S
Cuiaba, Brazil	139.5	Δ	Δ	•	∞	∞	∞	∞	∞	∞	Δ	Δ	Δ	15°30'S
Concepcion, Bolivia	114.3	•	Δ	Δ	∞	∞	∞	∞	∞	∞	∞	•	Δ	15°50'S
La Paz, Bolivia	57.4	•	Δ	Δ	∞	∞	∞	∞	∞	∞	∞	Δ	Δ	16°20'S
Rio de Janeiro, Brazil	108.2	Δ	Δ	Δ	∞	∞	∞	∞	∞	∞	∞	Δ	•	23°00'S
Sao Paolo, Brazil	142.8	Δ	Δ	Δ	Δ	∞	∞	∞	∞	∞	∞	Δ	•	23°40'S
Asuncion, Paraguay	131.6	Δ	Δ	∞	Δ	Δ	∞	∞	∞	∞	Δ	Δ	•	25°21'S
Tucuman, Argentina	97.0	•	Δ	Δ	∞	∞	∞	∞	∞	∞	∞	Δ	Δ	26°50'S
Santiago, Chile	36.1	∞	∞	∞	∞	Δ	•	Δ	Δ	∞	∞	∞	∞	33°24'S
Buenos Aires, Argentina	95.0	∞	∞	Δ	Δ	∞	∞	∞	∞	∞	Δ	Δ	∞	34°30'S
Montevideo, Uruguay	95.0	∞	∞	•	•	Δ	Δ	∞	∞	∞	∞	∞	∞	34°50'S
Valdivia, Chile	260.1	∞	∞	∞	Δ	Δ	•	Δ	Δ	∞	∞	∞	∞	39°50'S

SELECTED SEA TEMPERATURES (°C)

	J	F	M	A	M	J	J	A	S	O	N	D
Acapulco Mexico	24	24	24	25	26	27	28	28	28	27	26	25
Agadir Morocco	17	17	18	18	19	19	22	22	22	22	21	18
Algiers Algeria	15	14	15	15	17	20	23	24	23	21	18	16
Athens Greece	14	14	14	15	18	22	24	24	23	21	19	16
Bangkok Thailand	26	27	27	28	28	28	28	28	28	27	27	27
Barcelona Spain	13	12	13	14	16	19	22	24	22	21	16	14
Cairo Egypt	15	15	18	21	24	26	27	27	26	24	21	17
Copenhagen Denmark	3	2	3	5	9	14	16	16	14	12	8	5
Corfu Greece	14	14	14	16	18	21	23	24	23	21	18	16
Dubrovnik Croatia	13	13	13	15	17	22	23	24	22	19	16	14
Faro Portugal	15	15	15	16	17	18	19	20	20	19	17	16
Hong Kong	18	18	21	24	25	27	28	28	27	26	24	21
Honolulu Hawaii, USA	24	24	24	25	26	26	27	27	27	27	26	25
Istanbul Turkey	8	8	8	11	15	20	22	23	21	19	15	11
Kingston Jamaica	26	26	26	27	27	28	29	29	28	28	27	27
Las Palmas Canary Islands	19	18	18	18	19	20	21	22	23	23	21	20
Lisbon Portugal	14	14	14	15	16	17	18	19	19	18	17	15
Los Angeles USA	14	14	15	15	16	18	19	20	19	18	17	15
Malaga Spain	15	14	14	15	17	18	21	22	21	19	17	16
Malta	15	14	15	15	18	21	24	25	24	22	19	17
Miami USA	22	23	24	25	28	30	31	32	30	28	25	23
Mombasa Kenya	27	28	28	28	28	27	25	25	27	27	27	27
Naples Italy	14	13	14	15	18	21	24	25	23	21	18	16
Nassau Bahamas	23	23	23	24	25	27	28	28	28	27	26	24
New Orleans USA	13	14	14	15	18	21	24	25	23	21	18	16
Nice France	13	12	13	14	16	20	22	23	21	19	16	14
Palma Majorca	14	13	14	15	17	21	24	25	24	21	18	15
Rio de Janeiro Brazil	25	25	26	25	24	23	22	22	22	22	23	24

Rome Italy	14	13	13	14	17	21	23	24	23	20	18	15
San Francisco USA	11	11	12	12	13	14	15	15	16	15	13	11
Stockholm Sweden	3	1	1	2	5	10	15	15	13	10	7	4
Sydney Australia	23	24	23	20	18	18	16	17	18	19	19	21
Tahiti French Polynesia	27	27	27	28	28	27	26	26	26	26	27	27
Tel Aviv Israel	16	16	17	18	21	24	25	27	27	24	21	18
Tenerife Canary Islands	19	18	18	18	19	20	21	22	23	23	21	20
Tunis Tunisia	15	14	14	15	17	20	21	22	23	23	21	20
Vancouver Canada	8	7	8	9	11	13	14	14	13	12	11	10
Venice Italy	9	8	10	13	17	21	23	24	21	18	14	11
Wellington New Zealand	17	18	18	17	14	14	13	13	12	14	14	17

SELECTED CITY ALTITUDES (M)

Amsterdam, Netherlands	5	Karachi, Pakistan	15
Asuncion, Paraguay	77	Kingston, Jamaica	8
Athens, Greece	0	La Paz, Bolivia	3720
Auckland, New Zealand	0	Lima, Peru	153
Bangkok, Thailand	12	Lisbon, Portugal	87
Beirut, Lebanon	8	Madrid, Spain	55
Bogota, Colombia	2590	Manila, Philippines	8
Bridgetown, Barbados	0	Mexico City, Mexico	2240
Brussels, Belgium	58	Montevideo, Uruguay	9
Buenos Aires, Argentina	14	Moscow, Russia	191
Calcutta, India	26	Oslo, Norway	12
Cape Town, South Africa	8	Panama City, Panama	12
Caracas, Venezuela	964	Port-au-Prince, Haiti	8
Casablanca, Morocco	49	Port-of-Spain, Trinidad	8
Cayenne, French Guiana	8	Quito, Ecuador	2819
Copenhagen, Denmark	8	Rabat, Morocco	0
Curaçao, Netherlands Antilles	0	Rio de Janeiro, Brazil	9
Damascus, Syria	213	Rome, Italy	14
Dublin, Ireland	9	St George's, Grenada	0
Frankfurt, Germany	91	St John's, Antigua	0
Geneva, Switzerland	377	Santiago, Chile	550
Glasgow, Scotland	59	Singapore	8
Guatemala City, Guatemala	1478	Stockholm, Sweden	11
Havana, Cuba	9	Suva, Fiji	0
Helsinki, Finland	8	Sydney, Australia	8
Hong Kong	8	Tegucigalpa, Honduras	975
Istanbul, Turkey	9	Tehran, Iran	1220
Jerusalem, Israel	762	Tokyo, Japan	9
Juneau, Alaska	0	Vienna, Austria	168
Kabul, Afghanistan	2219	Yangon, Myanmar	17

PUBLIC HOLIDAYS

The following is a list of selected public holidays worldwide and dates of some Religious Holidays may change from one year to another according to Lunar Calendar.

Afghanistan Ramadan; Mar 21, New Year's Day, Iranian calendar; Apr 28, Islamic Revolution Day; May 1, Workers Day; Aug 19, Independence Day; Plus all Muslim festivals, dates vary from year to year.

Albania Jan 1; Jan 11, Proclamation of the Republic; Easter;May 1; Nov 28, Independence Day; Nov 29, Liberation Day; Christmas.

Algeria Jan1; Ramadan; Jun 10, Islamic New Year; Jun 19; July 5; Aug 19, Prophet's Birthday; Nov 1; Plus all Muslim festival dates very year to year

Andorra Jan 1; Easter; Sept 8, National Holiday of Meritxell; Christmas.

Angola Jan 1; Feb 4; Mar 27, Victory Day; Apr 14, Youth Day; May 1, Workers Day; Aug 1, Armed Forces' Day; Sep 17, National Heroes' Day; Nov 11, Independence Day; Dec 1, Pioneers' Day; Dec 10; Dec 25, Family Day.

Anguilla Jan 1; Easter; Whitsun; May 30, Anguilla Day; Jun 10, Queen's Birthday; Mon and Thu of first week in Aug; Aug 5; Dec 19; Christmas.

Antigua and Barbuda Jan 1; Easter; May 1; Whitsun; Jul 4, Caricom Day; Aug 1-2 , Carnival; Nov 1; Christmas.

Argentina Jan 1; Easter; May 1,Labour Day; May 25, Revolution Day; Jun 10, Malvinas Day; Jun 20, Flag Day; Jul 9, Independence Day; Aug 17, San Martin's Day; Oct 12, Colombus Day; Dec 8, Immaculate Conception; Christmas.

Armenia Jan 1; Jan 6, Armenian Christmas; Easter; Apr 25, Commemoration of 1915 Genocide; May 28, Anniversary of First Armenian Republic; Sep 21 Independence Day; Dec 7, Commemoration of 1988 Earthquake.

Australia Jan 1; Australia Day (last monday in Jan); Easter; Apr 25, Anzac Day; Jun 13, Queen's Birthday; Christmas.

Austria Jan 1; Jan 6; Easter Monday; May 1, Labour Day; May 12, Ascension Day; Whit Monday; Jun 2, Corpus Christi; Aug 15; Assumption Day; Oct 26, National Day; Nov 1, All Saints Day; Dec 8, Immaculate Conception; Christmas.

Azerbaijan Jan 1; Mar 8, International Women's Day; Mar 21-27, National Culture Week; May 28, Republic Day; Oct 9, Day of Armed Forces; Oct 18, Independence Day; Nov 17 National Renaissance Day; Dec 31 Azeri World Solidarity Day.

Bahamas Jan 1; Easter; Whitsun; Jun 3, Labour Day Whit Monday; July 11 Independence Day; Aug 4, Emancipation Day; Oct 12, Discovery Day; Christmas.

Bahrain Jan 1; Ramadan; Jun 10, Islamic New Year; Jun 19, Ahoura; Aug 19, Prophet's Birthday; Dec 16, National Day; Plus all other Muslim Holidays which vary year to year.

Bangladesh Jan 1; Feb 21, National Mourning Day; Ramadan; Mar 26, Independence Day; Easter; May 1; Jun 10, Islamic New Year; Aug 19, Prophet's Birthday;

Nov 7, National Revolution Day; Dec 16, Victory Day; Christmas; plus all Muslim Holidays which vary year to year.

Barbados   Jan 1; Jan 21, Errol Barrow Day; Easter; Whitsun; Aug 1 Kadooment Day; Oct 7, United Nations Day; Nov 30, Independence Day; Christmas.

Belarus   Jan 1; Jan 7, Russian Orthodox Christmas; Mar 8, International Women's Day; Apr 27, Belarus Popular Republic Day; May 1, Labour Day; May 9, Victory in Europe Day; Jun 27, Independence Day; Christmas.

Belgium   Jan 1; Easter; May 1, Labour Day; Ascencion Day; Whitsun; July 21, National Holiday; Aug 15. Assumption Day; All Saints Day; Nov 11, Armistice Day; Nov 15, King's Birthday (only for administrative and public offices, schools etc); Christmas.

Belize   Jan 1; Mar 9, Baron Bliss Day; Easter; May 1, Labour Day; May 24, Commonwealth Day; Sept 10, St George's Cay Day; Sept 21, Independence Day; Oct 12, Pan American Day; Nov 19, Garifuna Settlement Day; Christmas.

Benin   Jan 1; Jan 16, Martyr's Day; Ramadan; Apr 1, Youth Day; Easter; May 1, Worker's Day; Ascension Day; Whitsun; Oct 26, Armed Forces Day; Nov 30, National Day; Christmas; Dec 31, Harvest Day; plus all Muslim Holidays which vary year to year.

Bermuda   Jan 1; Easter; May 24, Bermuda Day; Jun 20, Queen's Birthday; Jul 28, Cup Match Day; Jul 29, Somer's Day; Sep 5, Labour Day; Nov 11, Remembrance Day; Christmas.

Bhutan   Nov 11, King's Birthday; Dec 17, National Day; plus all Buddhist festivals which vary year to year.

Bolivia   Jan 1; Feb, Carnival Week (preceding Lent); Holy Week (3 days preceding Easter; May 1, Labour Day; Jun 10, Corpus Christi; Aug 6, Independence Day; Nov 1, All Saints Day; Christmas.

Botswana   Jan 1; Jan 2; Easter; May 12, Ascension Day; July 16, President's Day; Sep 30, Botswana Day; Christmas.

Brazil   Jan 1; Carnival (3 days preceding Lent); Easter; Apr 21, Discovery of Brazil; May 1, Labour Day; Sept 7, Independence Day; Oct 12, Our Lady Aparecida; Nov 2, All Souls' Day; Nov 15, Proclamation of the Republic; Christmas.

British Virgin Islands   Jan 1; Mar 6, Commonwealth Day; Easter; Whitsun; Jun 6, Queen's Official Birthday; Jul 1, Territory Day; 1st Mon, Tue, Wed in Aug; Oct 21, St Ursula's Day; Nov 14, Prince of Wales' Birthday; Christmas.

Brunei   Jan 1; Chinese New Year; Ramadan; Jun 1, Royal Brunei Armed Forces Day; Jun 10, Islamic New Year; Jul 15, Sultan's Birthday; Aug 19, Prophet's Birthday; Christmas; plus all Muslim holidays which vary year to year.

Bulgaria   Jan 1; Mar 3, National Day; Easter; May 1, Labour Day; May 24, Education Day; Christmas.

Burkina Faso   Jan 1; Jan 3, Anniversary of the 1966 *coup d'etat*; Ramadan; Easter; May 1, Labour Day; May 12, Ascension Day Whitsun; Aug 4, National Day; Aug 15, Assumption; Aug 19, Prophet's Birthday; Nov 1, All Saints Day; Christmas; plus all Muslim festivals that vary year to year.

Burundi Jan 1; Easter; May 1, Labour Day; May 12, Ascension Day; Jul 1, Independence Day; Aug 15, Assumption; Sep 3, Anniversary of the Third Republic; Sep 18, Victory of UPRONA Party; Nov 1, All Saints; Christmas.

Cambodia Jan 1; Apr, Camodian New Year; May 1; Sep, Feast of the Ancestors; Nov, Full Moon Water Festival.

Cameroon Jan 1; Feb 11, Youth Day; Ramadan; Easter; May 1, Labour Day; May 12, Ascension Day; May 20, National Day; May 21, Festival of Sheep; Aug 15, Assumption; Dec 10, Reunification Day; Christmas.

Canada Jan 1; Easter; May 23, Victoria Day; July 1, Canada Day; Sep 5, Labour Day; Oct Thanksgiving; Nov 11, Remembrance Day; Christmas.

Cape Verde Jan 1; Mar 8, Women's Day; May 1, Labour Day; Jul 5, Independence Day; Aug 15, Assumption; Nov 1, All Saints; Christmas.

Cayman Islands Jan 1, Easter;May 2, Labour Day; May 16, Discovery Day; Whitsun; Jun 13, Queen's Official Birthday;Jul 4, Constitution Day; Nov 14, Remembrance Day; Christmas.

Central African Republic Jan 1; Mar 29, Anniversary of the Death of Barthelemy Boganda; Easter; May 1, May Day; May 12, Ascension; Whitsun; Jun 30, National Day of Prayer; Aug 13, Independence Day; Aug 15, Assumption; Nov 1, All Saints; Dec 1, National Day; Christmas.

Chad Jan 1; Ramadan; Easter; May 1, Labour Day; Whitsun; May 25, OUA Foundation Day; Aug 11, Independence Day; Aug 15, Assumption; Aug 19, Prophet's Birthday; Nov 1, All Saints; Nov 28, Proclamation of the Republic; Christmas; plus all Muslim festivals which vary year to year.

Chile Jan 1; Easter; May 1, Labour Day; May 21, Battle of Iquique Navy Day; May 30, Corpus Christi; Jun 29, St Peter and St Paul; Aug 15, Assumption; Sep 18, Independence Day; Sep 19, Army Day; Oct 12, Columbus Day; Nov 1, All Saints; Dec, Immaculate Conception; Christmas.

China Jan/Feb, Chinese New Year; Mar 8, International Women's Day; May 1, Labour Day; May 4, Chinese Youth Day; Jun 1, International Children's Day; Jul 1, Founding of the Communist Party of China; Aug 1, Army Day; Sep 9, Teacher's Day; Oct 1-2, National Days.

Colombia Jan1; Jan 6, Epiphany; Mar 19 St Joseph's Day; Easter; May 1, Labour Day; May 12, Ascension Day; Jun 2, Corpus Christi; June 29, Sts Peter and Paul; July 20, Independence Day; Aug 7, Battle of Boyaca; Aug 15, Assumption; Oct 12, Discovery of America; Nov 1, All Saints Day; Nov 11, Independence of Cartagena; Dec 8, Immaculate Conception; Christmas.

Congo Jan 1; Easter; May 1, Labour Day; Aug 15, Independence Day; Christmas.

Costa Rica Jan 1; Mar 19, St. Joseph's Day; Easter; Apr 11, Anniversary of the Battle of Rivas; May 1, Labour Day; Jun 2, Corpus Christi; June 29, Sts Peter & Paul; July 25, Anniversary of the Annexation of Guanacaste Province; Aug 2, Our Lady of Angels; Aug 15, Assumption; Sept 15, Independence Day; Oct 12, Columbus Day; Dec 8, Immaculate Conception; Christmas - New Year, Holy Week.

Cote d'Ivoire Jan 1; Ramadan; Easter; May 1, Labour Day; May 12, Ascension Day; Whit Monday; Aug 15, Assumption; Nov 1, All Saints Day; Dec 7, Independence Day; Christmas; plus all Muslim holidays which vary year to year.

Cuba	Jan 1, Liberation Day; May 1, Labour Day; Jul25-27 Anniversary of the 1953 Revolution; Oct 10, Wars of Independence Day.
Cyprus	Jan 1; Epiphany; Mar 6, Green Monday; Mar 25, Greek National Day; Apr 1,Greek-Cypriot National Day; Easter; Jun 20, Festival of the Flood; Aug 15, Assumption; Oct 1, Independence Day; Oct 28, Greek National Day; Christmas.
Czech Republic	Jan 1; Easter; May 1, Labour Day; Jul 5, Day of the Apostles St Cyril and St Methodius; Jul 6, Anniversary of the Martyrdom of Jan Hus; Oct 28, Independence Day; Christmas.
Denmark	Jan 1; Easter; Apr 29 General Prayer Day; May 12, Ascension Day; Whit Monday; June 5, Constitution Day; Christmas.
Djibouti	Jan 1; Ramadan; May 1, Workers Day; Jun 10, Islamic New Year; Jun 27, Independence Day; Aug 19, Prophet's Birthday; Christmas; plus all Muslim holidays which vary year to year..
Dominica	Jan 1; Feb, Carnival; Easter; May 1, May Day; 1st Monday in Aug; Nov 3, National Day; Nov 4, Community Service Day; Christmas.
Dominican Republic	Jan 1; Jan 6, Epiphany; Jan 21, Our Lady of Altagracia; Jan 26, Duarte; Feb 27, Independence Day; Easter; May 1, Labour Day; Jun 2, Corpus Christi; Aug 16, Restoration Day; Sept 24, Our Lady of Las Mercedes; Oct 12, Columbus Day; Nov 1, All Saints; Christmas.
Ecuador	Jan 1; Feb, Carnival; Easter; May 1, Labour Day; May 24, Battle of Pichincha; Jul 24, Birthday of Simon Bolivar; Aug 10, Independence of Quito; Oct 9, Anniversary of the Independence of Guayaquil; Oct 12, Discovery of America; Nov 1, All Saints; Nov 2, All Soul's Day; Nov 3, Independence of Cuenca; Dec 6, Foundation of Quito; Christmas.
Egypt	Jan ; Ramadan; Jun 10, Islamic New Year; Jun 18, Evacuation Day; Jun 23, Revolution Day; Aug 19, Prophet's Birthday; Oct 6, Armed Forces Day; Oct 24, Popular Resistance Day; Dec 23, Victory Day; Dec 30, Ascension of the Prophet; plus all Muslim festival which vary year to year.
El Salvador	Jan 1; Easter; May 1, Labour Day; Jun 2, Corpus Christi; Aug 1-6approx, San Salvador Festival; Sept 15, Independence Day; Oct 12, Discovery of America; Nov 2, All Souls' Day; Nov 5, First Call for Independence; Christmas.
Equatorial Guinea	Jan 1; Mar 5, Independence Day; Easter; May 1, Labour Day; May 25, OAU Day; Dec 10, Human Rights Day; Christmas.
Eritrea	Jan 1; Jan, Timket; Ramadan; May 24, Liberation Day; Jun 20, Martyrs Day; Aug 19, Prophet's Birthday; Sep 1, Start of the Armed Struggle; plus all Muslim Holidays that vary year to year.
Estonia	Jan 1; Feb 24, Independence Day; Easter; May 1, Labour Day; Jun 23, Victory Day; Jun 24, Midsummer Day; Christmas.
Ethiopia	Ethiopia still uses the Julian Calendar; Jan 7, Christmas; Jan 19, Epiphany; Ramadan; Mar 2, Battle of Adowa Day;Apr 6, Victory Day; Easter; Aug 19, Prophet's Birthday; Sep, New Years Day; Sep 27, Feast of the True Cross; plus all Muslim festivals that very year to year.
Falkland Islands	Jan 1; Easter; Apr 21, HM Queen's Birthday; Jun 14, Liberation Day; Aug 14, Falkland Day; Oct 5; Dec 8, Anniversary of the Battle of the Falkland Islands; Christmas.

Fiji	Jan 1; Easter; May 30, Ratu Sir Lala Sukuna Day; Jun 13, Queen's official Birthday; Oct 9, Independence Day; Nov 3, Diwali; Christmas; plus Hindu and Muslim festivals which vary year to year.
Finland	Jan 1; Jan 6, Epiphany; Easter; May 1; May 12, Ascension; Whitsun; June 24, Midsummer's Day; Nov5, All Saint's Day 3; Dec 6, Independence Day; Christmas.
France	Jan 1; Easter; May 1, Labour Day; May 8, Liberation Day; May 12, Ascension Day; Whitsun; July 14,National day, Fall of the Bastille; Aug 15, Assumption; Nov 1, All Saints' Day; Nov 11, Remembrance Day; Christmas.
Gabon	Jan 1; Ramadan; Mar 12, Renovation Day; Easter; May 1, Labour Day; Whit Monday; Aug 17, Anniversary of Independence; Aug 19, Prophet's Birthday; Nov 1, All Saints' Day; Christmas; plus all Muslim holidays which vary year to year.
Gambia	Jan 1; Ramadan; Feb 18, Independence Day; Easter; May 1,Labour Day; Aug 15, Assumption; Aug 19, Prophet's Birthday; Christmas; plus all Muslim festival which vary year to year.
Georgia	Jan 1; Jan 7, Orthodox Christmas; Easter; May 26, Independence Day; Aug 28, St Marian's Day; Oct 14, Khetkhob; Nov 23, St George's Day.
Germany	Jan 1; Jan 6, Epiphany; Easter; May 1, Labour Day; May 12, Ascension Day; Whit Monday; Jun 2, Corpus Christi; Aug 15, Assumption; Oct 3, Day of Unity; Oct 31, Reformation Day; Nov 1, All Saint's Day; Nov 16, Day of Prayer and Repentance; Christmas.
Ghana	Jan 1; Jan 7, Fourth Republic Anniversary; Mar 6, Independence Day; Easter; May 1, Labour Day; Jul 1, Republic Day; Christmas.
Gibraltar	Jan 1; Mar 14, Commonwealth Day; Easter; May 1, Nay Day; last Mon in May; Jun 13,Queen's Birthday; last Mon in Aug; Sep 12, Referendum Day; Christmas.
Greece	Jan 1; Jan 6, Epiphany; Shrove Monday; Mar 25, Independence Day; Easter; May 1, Labour Day; June 20, Day of the Holy Spirit; Aug 15, Assumption; Oct 28, Ochi Day; Christmas.
Greenland	Jan 1; Easter; Apr 29, General Prayer Day; May 12, Ascension; Whit Monday; Jun 5, Constitution Day; Jun 2, National Day; Christmas.
Grenada	Jan 1; Feb 7, Independence Day; Easter; May 1, Labour Day; Whit Monday; Jun 2, Corpus Christi; Aug 1-2, Emancipation Day; Aug Carnival; Oct 25, Thanksgiving; Christmas.
Guatemala	Jan 1; Jan 6, Epiphany; Easter; May 1, Labour Day; Jun 30, Anniversary of the Revolution; Aug 15, Assumption; Sep 15, Independence Day; Oct 12, Columbus Day; Oct 20, Revolution Day; Nov 1, All Saints' Day; Christmas.
Guernsey	Jan 1; Easter; May 1, May Day; May 9, Liberation Day; last Mon in May; last Mon in Aug; Christmas.
Guinea Republic	Jan 1; Ramadan; Easter; May 1, Labour Day; Aug 19, Prophet's Birthday; Aug 27, Anniversary of the Women's Revolt; Sep 28, Referendum Day; Oct 2, Republic Day; Nov 1, All Saints' Day; Nov 22, Day of the 1970 Invasion; Christmas; plus all Muslim festivals which vary year to year.

Guinea-Bissau   Jan 1; Jan 20, Death of Amilcar Cabral; Mar 2, Korite; May 1, Labour Day; May 21, Tabaski; Aug 3, Anniversary of the Killing of Pidjiguiti; Sep 24, National Day; Nov 14, Anniversary of the Movement of Readjustment; Christmas; plus all Muslim festivals that vary year to year.

Guyana   Jan 1; Feb 23, Republic Anniversary; Ramadan; Easter; May 1, Labour Day; May 5, Indian Heritage Day; Jun 27, Carribean Day; Aug 1, Freedom Day; Christmas; plus all Muslim festivals that vary year to year.

Honduras   Jan 1; Easter; Apr 14, Pan-American Day; May 1, Labour Day; Sep 15, Independence Day; Oct 3, Birth of General Morazan; Oct 12, Discovery of America Day; Oct 21, Armed Forces Day; Christmas.

Hong Kong   The first weekday in Jan; Lunar New Year; Easter; Apr 5, Ching Ming Festival; Jun 13, the Queen's Birthday; Jun 14, Dragon Boat Festival; Aug 29, Liberation Day; Day following the Chinese Mid-Autumn Festival; Chung Yeung Festival; Christmas.

Hungary   Jan 1; Mar 15, Anniversary of 1848 uprising against Austrian rule; Easter; May 1, May Day; Aug 20, Constitution Day; Oct 23, Day of Proclamation of the Republic; Christmas.

Iceland   Jan 1; Easter; Apr 20, first Day of Summer; May 12, Ascension Day; Whit Monday; June 17, National Day; Christmas.

India   Jan 1; Jan 26, Republic Day; Aug 15, Independence Day; Oct 2 Mahatma Gandhi's Birthday; Dec 25. Also 32 other religious (Hindu, Christian and Muslim) or special occasions which are observed either with national or regional holidays.

Indonesia   Jan 1; Ramadan; Easter; May 12, Ascension Day; Jun 10, Islamic New Year Aug 17,Indonesian National Day; Aug 19 Prophet's Birthday; Christmas; plus all Muslim festival which vary year to year.

Iran   Feb 11, National Day (Fall of the Shah); Ramadan; Mar 20, Oil Nationalisation Day; Mar 21, Iranian New Year; Apr 1, Islamic Republic day; Apr 2, Revolution Day; Jun 4, Passing away of Imam Khomeini, Jun 19, Ashoura; Jul 14, Martyrdom of Iman Ali; Aug 19 Prophet's Birthday; Dec 30, Ascension of the Prophet; plus all Muslim festivals which vary year to year.

Iraq   Jan 1; Jan 6, Army Day; Ramadan; May 21, Feast of the Sacrifice; Jun 10, Islamic New Year; Jun 19, Ashoura; Jul 14, Republic Day; Aug 19 Prophet's Birthday; July 17;.Dec 30, Ascension of the Prophet; plus all Muslim festivals which vary year to year.

Ireland   Jan 1; Mar 17, St Patrick's Day; Easter; May 1, May Day; Jun 6, Bank Holiday; First Mon in Aug; Oct 21; Christmas.

Israel   (All business activity ceases on Saturdays and religious holidays, the dates of which vary from one year to another. Passover, first day; Passover, last day; Apr 14, Israel Independence Day; Shavout (Feast of Weeks); Pentecost; Rosh Hashana (New Year); Yom Kippur (Day of Atonement); First Day of Tabernacles; Last Day of Tabernacles; Hanukkah.

Italy   Jan 1; Jan 6, Epiphany; Easter; Apr 25, Liberation Day; May 1, Labour Day; Aug 15, Assumption; Nov 1, All Saints' Day; Nov 5, National Unity Day; Dec 8, Immaculate Conception; Christmas.

Jamaica   Jan 1; Ash Wednesday; Easter; May 23, Labour Day; Aug 1, Independence

Day; Oct 17, National Heroes' Day; Christmas.

Japan	Jan 1; Jan 16, Coming of Age Day; Feb 11, National Foundation Day; Vernal Equinox Day (variable date); Apr 29, Greenery Day; May 3, Constitution Memorial Day; May 5, Children's Day; Sept 15, Respect of the Aged Day; Autumnal Equinox Day (variable date); Oct 10, Physical Culture Day; Nov 3, Culture Day; Nov 23, Labour Thanksgiving Day; Dec 23, Birthday of the Emperor;
Jersey	Jan 1; Easter; May 1, May Day; May 9, Liberation Day; last Mon in May; last Mon in Aug; Christmas.
Jordan	Jan 15, Arbour Day; Ramadan; Mar 22, Arab League Day; May 25, Independence Day; Jun 10, Islamic New Year; Aug 11, King Hussein's Accession; Aug 19, Prophet's Birthday; Nov 14, King Hussein's Birthday; Plus all Muslim holidays which vary year to year.
Kazakhstan	Jan 1; Jan 27, Constitution Day; Mar 8, International Women's Day; May Labour Day; May 9, Victory Day; Dec 16, Republic Day; plus some Muslim holidays which vary year to year.
Kenya	Jan 1; Ramadan; Easter; May 1, Labour Day; Jun 1, Madraka Day; Oct 10, Moi Day; Oct 20;, Kenyatta Day; Dec 12, Jamhuri Day; Christmas; plus some Muslim festivals which vary year to year.
Korea (South)	Jan 1; Lunar New Year; Mar 1, Independence Day; Apr 5, Arbor Day; May 5, Children's Day; May 18, Buddha's birthday; Jun 6, Memorial Day; Jul 17, Constitution Day; Aug 15, Liberation Day; Thanksgiving Day; Oct 3, National Foundation Day; Christmas.
Kuwait	Religious holidays vary from one year to another. The only fixed holidays in Kuwait are New Year's Day and Kuwait National Day (Feb 25).
Kyrgyzstan	Jan 1; Jan 7, Russian Orthodox Christmas; Lunar New Year; Mar 8, International Women's Day; May 1, Labour Day; May 5, Constitution Day; May 9, Victory Day; Jun 13, Day of Remembrance; Aug 31, Independence Day; plus some Muslim holidays which vary year to year.
Laos	Jan 1; Apr, Lao New Year; May 1, Labour Day; Dec 2, National Day;
Latvia	Jan 1; Easter; May 1, Labour Day; Jun 23, Ligo Festival; Jun 24, Midsummer Festival; Nov 18, National Day; Christmas.
Lebanon	Jan 1; Feb 9, Feast of St Marron; Ramadan; Mar 22, Arab League Anniversary; Easter; Ascension Day; Jun 10, Islamic New Year; jun 19, Ashora; Aug 15, Assumption; Aug 19 Prophet's Birthday; Nov 1, All Saints Day; Nov 22, Independence Day; Christmas; Dec 31, Evacuation Day. plus all Muslim festival which vary year to year.
Liberia	Jan 1; Mar 12 Decoration Day; Mar 15, J.J. Robert's birthday; April 12, National Redemption Day; May 14, National Unification Day; Jul 26, Independence Day; Aug 24, National Flag Day; Thanksgiving Day; Nov 12, National Memorial Day; Nov 29, President Trubman's Birthday; Christmas.
Liechtenstein	Jan 1; Jan 6, Epiphany; Shrove Tuesday; Mar 19, St Joseph's Day; Easter; May 1, Labour Day; Ascension; Whit Monday; Jun 2; Corpus christi; Aug 15, Assumption; Sep 8, Nativity of the Virgin Mary; Nov 1, All Saints; Dec 8, Immaculate Conception; Christmas.

Lithuania   Jan 1; Feb 16, Independence Day; Mar 11, Day of Restoration of the Lithuanian State; Easter; May 1, Mother's Day; Jun 14, Day of Mourning and Hope; Jul 6, Day of Statehood; Nov 1, All Saints' Day; Christmas.

Luxembourg   Jan 1; Easter; May 1, Labour Day; Ascension Day; Whit Monday; June 23, National Day; Aug 15, Assumption Day; Nov 1, All Saints' Day; Christmas.

Macau   Jan 1; Feb, Chinese New Year; Apr 5, Ching Ming Festival; Apr 25, Anniversary of Portuguese Revolution; Easter; May 1, Labour Day; Jun 10, Camoens Day and Portuguese Communities; Jun 13, Dragon Boat Festival; Jun 24, Feast of St.John the Baptist; Sept, Mid-Autumn Festival; Oct 1, National Day of the People's Republic of China; Oct 5, Republic Day; Oct 13 Festival of Ancestors; Nov 2, All Souls' Day; Dec 1, Restoration of Independence; Dec 8, Feast of Immaculate Conception; Dec 22, Winter Solstice; Christmas.

Madagascar   Jan 1; Mar 29, Commemoration of the 1947 Rebellion; Easter; May 1, Labour Day; May 12, Ascension; June 26, Independence Day; Nov 1, All Saint's Day; Christmas; Dec 30, Anniversary of the Republic.

Malawi   Jan 1; Mar 3, Martyr's Day; Easter; May 14, Kamuzu Day, President Banada's Birthday; Jul 6, Republic Day; Oct 17, Mother's Day; Dec 21, National Tree Planting Day; Christmas.

Malaysia   Chinese New Year; Ramadan; May 1, Labour Day; May, Vesak Day; Jun 3, King's Birthday; Aug 18, Prophet's Birthday; Aug 31, Independence Day; Christmas; plus all Muslim festivals which vary year to year.

Maldives   Jan 2, Martyr's Day; Ramadan; Jun 10, Islamic New Year; Jul 26, Independence Day; Aug 18, Prophet's Birthday; Nov 3, Victory Day; Nov 11, Republic Day; plus all Muslim festivals which vary year to year.

Mali   Jan 1; Jan 20, Armed Forces Day; Ramadan; Easter; May 1, Labour Day; May 25, Africa Day; Aug 18, Prophet's Birthday; Aug 29, Assumption; Nov 1, All Saint's; Nov 3, Batism of the Prophet; Nov 19, Anniversary of the 1968 Coup; Christmas. Plus all Muslim festivals which vary year to year.

Malta   Jan 1; Feb 10, St Paul's Shipwreck; Mar 19, St Joseph's Day; Mar 31, Freedom Day; Easter; May 1, Worker's Day; Jun 7, Commemoration of 1919 Riot; Jun 29, Feast of St Peter and St Paul; Aug 15, Assumption;Sep 8, Feast of our Lady of Victories; Sep 21, Independence Day; Dec 8, Immaculate Conception; Dec 13, Republic Day; Christmas.

Mauritius   Jan 1; Jan 2; Feb 10, Chinese Spring Festival; Ramadan; Mar 12, Independence Day; May 1, Labour Day; Nov 1, All Saints; Christmas; plus all Muslim festivals which vary year to year.

Mexico   Jan 1; Feb 5, Constitution Day; Mar 21, Birth of Benito Jaurez; Easter; May 1, Labour Day; May 5, Anniversary of the Battle of Puebla; Sep 1, President's Annual Message; Sep 16, Independence Day; Oct 12, Discovery of America; Nov 20, Anniversary of the Mexican Revolution; Christmas.

Monaco   Jan 1; Jan 27, St Devote's Day; Easter; May 1, Labour Day; Ascension; Whit Monday; Corpus Christi; Aug 15, Assumption; Nov 1, All Saint's Day; Nov 19, Monaco National Day; Dec 8, Immaculate Conception; Christmas.

Mongolia   Jan 1; Tsagaan Sar (Lunar New Year); Mar 8, International Women's Day; Jul 11-13, National Days; Nov 26, Republic Day;

Monserrat   Jan 1; Mar 17, St Patrick's Day; Easter; May 1, Labour Day; Whit Monday; Jun 13, Queen's Official Birthday; First Mon in Aug; Nov 23, Liberation Day; Christmas

Morocco   Jan 1; Ramadan; Mar 3, Festival of the Throne; May 1, Labour Day; Jun 10, Islamic New Year; Jun 19, Ashora; Aug 19, Prophet's Birthday; Nov 6, Anniversary of the Green March; Nov 18, Independence Day; plus all Muslim festivals which vary year to year.

Myanmar   Jan 4, Independence Day; Feb 12, Union Day; Mar 2, Peasants' Day; Mar 27, Armed Forces Day; mid-Apr Thingyan Water Festival ;May 1, Worker's Day; early May, Tazaundaing Festival of Lights; Dec 1, National Day; Christmas.

Namibia   Jan 1, Mar 21, Independence Day; Easter; May 1, Worker's Day; May 4, Casinga Day; Ascension; May 25, Africa Day; Aug 26, Heroes' Day; Dec 10, Human rights Day; Christmas.

Nepal   Jan 11, National Unity Day; Jan 30, Martyr's Day; Feb 18, King's Birthday; Mar 8, Nepalese Women's Day; Apr 10, Teacher's Day; Apr 14, New Year; Nov 7, Queen's Birthday; Nov 9, Constitution Day; Dec 17, Mahendra Jayanti; Dec 28, King's Birthday; many other religious, holidays which change every year according to Lunar and other calendars. Biggest festival Dassain (Sept/Oct) when everything closes for a week.

Netherlands   Jan 1; Easter; Apr 30 Queen's Day; May 5, National Liberation Day; May 12, Ascension Day; Whit Monday; Christmas.

New Zealand   Jan 1; Easter; Apr 25, ANZAC Day; Jun 1, the Queen's Birthday; Oct 26, Labour Day; Christmas; each province has its own particular holiday.

Nicaragua   Jan 1; Easter; May 1, Labour Day; Jul 19, Liberation Day; Sep 14, Battle of San Jacinto; Sep 15, Independence Day; Christmas.

Niger   Jan 1; Ramadan; Easter; Apr 15, Anniversary of the 1974 coup; Jun 10, Islamic New Year; Aug 3, Independence Day; Aug 19, Prophet's Birthday; Dec 18, Republic Day; Christmas; plus all Muslim festivals which vary year to year.

Nigeria   Jan 1; Ramadan; Easter; May 1, May Day; Oct 1, National Day; Christmas; plus all Muslim festivals which vary year to year.

Norway   Jan 1; Easter; May 1, May Day; Ascension; May 17, National Independence day; Christmas.

Oman   Ramadan; Jun 10, Muslim New Year; Aug 18, Prophet's Birthday; Nov 18, Sultan's Birthday; plus all Muslim festivals which vary year to year.

Pakistan   Ramadan; Mar 23, Pakistan Day; Easter; May 1, Labour Day; Jun 10, Islamic New Year; Jun 19, Ashora; Aug 14, Independence Day; Sep 6, Defence of Pakistan Day; Sep 11, Anniversary of the death of Quaid-i-Azam; Nov 9, Iqbal day; Dec 25, Quaid-i-Azam's Birthday, Christmas; plus all Muslim festivals which vary year to year.

Panama   Jan 1; Jan 9, National Martyr's Day; Shrove Tuesday; Easter; May 1, Labour Day; Aug 15, Foundation of Panama City; Oct 11, Revolution Day; Nov 1, National Anthem Day; Nov 2, All Soul's Day; Nov 3, Independence from Colombia Day; Nov 4, Flag Day; Nov 5, Independence Day; Nov 10, First Call for Independence; Nov 28, Independence from Spain; Dec 8, Mother's Day; Christmas.

Papua New Guinea	Jan 1; Easter; Jun 6, Queen's Official Birthday; Jul 23, Remembrance Day; Sep 16, Independence Day; Christmas; plus various regional festivals.
Paraguay	Jan 1; Feb 3, San Blas Patron Saint; Mar 1, Hero's Day; Easter; May 1, Labour Day; May 14 and 15, Independence Day; June 12, Chaco Peace; Corpus Christi; Aug 15, Founding of Asuncion; Aug 25, Constitution Day; Sep 29, Battle of Boqueron (Chaco War); Oct 12, Colombus Day, Nov 1, All Saints Day; Dec 8, Immaculate Conception; Christmas.
Peru	Jan 1; Easter; May 1, Labour Day; June 24, Day of the Peasant; June 29, St Peter and St. Paul; July 28/29, Independence Days; Aug 30, St. Rose of Lima; Oct 8, Battle of Angamos; Nov 1, All Saints' Day; Dec 8, Immaculate Conception; Christmas.
Philippines	Jan 1; Easter; May 1, Labour Day; May 6, Day of Valour; Jun 12, Independence Day;Nov 1, All Saints' Day; Nov 30, Bonifacio Day; Dec 25; Dec 30, Rizal Day.
Poland	Jan 1; Easter; May 1, Labour Day; May 3, Polish National Day; May 9, Victory Day; Corpus Christi; Nov 1, All Saints' Day; Nov 11, Independence Day; Christmas.
Portugal	Jan 1, Carnival; Easter; Apr 25, National Day; May 1, Labour Day; Corpus Christi; Jun 10, Portugal Day; Aug 15, Assumption; Oct 5, Republic Day; Nov 1, All Saint's Day; Dec 1, Independence Day; Dec 8, immaculate Conception; Dec 25. Carnival is also an important event in Portugal and takes place during the four days preceding Lent.
Qatar	Ramadan; Sep 3, Independence Day. Plus all Muslim festivals which vary year to year.
Romania	Jan 1; Orthodox easter; May1-2, International Labour Day; Dec 1, National Day; Christmas.
Russian Federation	Jan 1; Jan 7, Orthodox Christmas; Mar 8, International Women's Day; May 1-2, International Solidarity Day; May 9, Victory in Europe Day; Jun 12, Russian Independence Day: Nov 7, October Revolution.
Rwanda	Jan 1; Jan 28, Democracy Day; Easter; May 1, Labour Day; Whit Monday; Jul 1, Anniversary of Independence; Jul 5, National Peace and Unity Day; Aug 15, Assumption; Sep 25, Kamarampaka Day; Oct 26 Armed Forces Day; Nov 1, All Saints' Day; Christmas.
St Kitts & Nevis	Jan 1; Easter; May 4, Labour Day; Whit Monday; Jun 11, Queen's Official Birthday; first Mon in Aug; Sep 19, Independence day; Nov 14, Prince of Wales' Birthday; Christmas.
St Lucia	Jan 1; feb, Carnival; Easter; May 1, Labour Day; Whit Monday; Jun 11, Queen's Official Birthday; f~st Mon in Aug; Oct 3, Thanksgiving Day; Dec 13, St Lucia Day; Christmas.
St Vincent	Jan 1; Jan 22, St Vincent & The Grenadines Day; Easter; May 1, Labour Day; Whit Monday; Jul 11, Caricom Day; Carnival, first Mon in Aug; Oct 27, Independence day; Christmas.
San Marino	Jan 1, Jan 6, Epiphany; Feb 5, Liberation and St Agatha's Day; Mar 25, Anniversary of the Arengo; Apr 1, Captain-Regent Investiture; Easter; May 1, Labour Day; Corpus Christi; Jul 28, Anniversary of the fall of Fascism; Aug 15, Assumption; Sep3, Republic Day; Nov 1, All Saints' Day; Nov 2, Commemoration of the Dead; Dec 8, Immaculate Conception; Christmas.

Saudi Arabia   Ramadan; plus all Muslim festivals which vary year to year.

Seychelles   Jan 1; Easter; May 1, Labour Day; June 5, Liberation Day; June 29, Independence Day; Corpus Christi; Aug 15, Assumption of Mary; Nov 1, All Saints' Day; Dec 8, Immaculate Conception; Christmas.

Sierra Leone   Jan 1; Ramadan; Easter; Apr 27, Independence Day; 25 Dec; plus all Muslim festivals which vary year to year.

Singapore   Jan 1; Chinese New Year; May 1, Labour Day; Vesak Day; Aug 9, National Day; Oct 29, Dec 25; plus all Muslim festivals which vary year to year.

Slovak Republic   Jan 1; Jan 6, Epiphany; Easter; May 1, Labour Day; Jul 5, Day of the Apostles St Cyril and St Methodius; Aug 29, Anniversary of the Slovak National Uprising; Sep 1, Day of Constitution of the Slovak Republic; Sep 15, Our Lady of the Seven Sorrows; Nov 1, All Saints' Day; Christmas.

Slovenia   Jan 1; Feb 8, Culture Day; Easter; Apr 27, Resistance Day; May 1, Labour Day; Jun 25, Statehood Day; Aug 15, Assumption; Oct 31, Reformation Day; Nov 1, Remembrance Day; Dec 25; Dec 26, Independence Day.

South Africa   Jan 1; Apr 4, Family Day; Apr 6, Founder's Day; Easter; May 1, Worker's Day; Ascension Day; May 31, Republic Day; Oct 10, Kruger Day; Dec 16, Day of the Vow; Dec 25; Dec 26, Day of Goodwill.

Spain   Jan 1; Jan 6; Easter; May 1, St Joseph the Workman; June 24, King Jaun Carlos' Day; July 25, St James of Compostela; Aug 15, Assumption; Oct 12, National Day; Nov 1, All Saint's; Dec 8, Immaculate Conception; Dec 25.

Sri Lanka   Jan 1; Feb 4, Independence Day; Ramadan; Easter; May 1, May Day; May 22, National Heroes' Day; Jun 30; Dec 25; plus all Muslim festivals which vary year to year.

Sudan   Jan 1, Independence Day; Ramadan; Mar 3, Unity Day; Apr 6, Uprising Day; Jun 10, Islamic New Year; Jul 1, Decentralisation Day; Aug 19, Prophet's Birthday; Dec 25, Christmas; plus all Muslim festivals which vary year to year.

Suriname   Jan 1; Ramadan; Easter; May 1, Labour Day; Jul 1, National Union Day; Nov 25, Independence Day; Dec 25, Christmas; plus all Muslim and Hindu holidays which vary year to year.

Sweden   Jan 1; Jan 6, Epiphany; Easter; May 1, Labour Day; Ascension Day; Whit Monday; Midsummer's Day; All Saints' Day; Dec 25; Dec 26.

Switzerland   Jan 1; Easter; Ascension Day; Whit Monday; Aug 1, National Day; Dec 25; Dec 26.

Syria   Jan 1; Ramadan; Mar 8, Revolution Day; Easter; Jun 10, Islamic New Year; Aug 19, Prophet's Birthday; Oct 6, Beginning of October War; Nov 16, National Day; Dec 25, Christmas; plus all Muslim holidays which vary year to year.

Taiwan   Jan 1, New Year and Founding Day; End of Jan, Chinese New Year; Mar 29, Youth Day; Apr 5, Women and Children's Day, Tomb Sweeping Day and Death of President Chiang Kai-shek; May 1, Labour Day; Jun 13, Dragon Boat Festival; Sep 28, Teacher's Day; Oct 10, Double Tenth National Day; Oct 25, Retrocession Day; Oct 31, Birthday of Chiang Kai-shek (Veteran's Day) Nov 12, Dr Sun Yat Sen's Birthday; Dec 25, Constitution Day.

Tajikistan	Jan 1; Ramadan; Mar 21, Navrus; Sep 9, Independence Day.
Tanzania	Jan 12, Zanzibar Revolution Day; Feb 5, Chama Cha Mapinduzi Day; Ramadan; Easter; Apr 26, Union Day; May 1, International Labour Day; Jul 7, Saba Saba (Peasants's Day); Aug 19, Prophet's Birthday; Dec 9, Independence Day; Dec 25, Christmas; plus all Muslim holidays which vary year to year.
Thailand	Jan 1; Apr 12, the Songkran Festival (Buddhist New Year); May 5, Coronation Day; May 11, Royal Ploughing Ceremony; May, Visakhja Pua (Buddhist Festival); June/July, Buddhist Lent Begins; Aug 12, Queen's Birthday; Oct 23, Chulalongkorn Day; Dec 5, King's Birthday; Dec 31.
Tonga	Jan 1; Easter; Apr 25, ANZAC Day; May 4, Birthday of Crown Prince Tupouto'a; Jun 4, Independence Day; Jul 4, King's Birthday; Nov 4, Constitution Day; Dec 4, King Tupou I Day; Dec 25, Dec 26.
Trinidad and Tobago	Jan 1, Carnival; Easter, Whit Monday; Corpus Christi; Labour Day; first Monday in Aug, Discovery Day; Aug 31, Independence Day; Sept 24, Republic Day; Eid-Ul-Fitr (Muslim Festival), Divali (Hindu Festival); Dec 25; Dec 26.
Tunisia	Jan 1; Ramadan; Mar 20, Independence Day; Mar 21, Youth Day; Apr 19, Martyr's Day; May 1, Labour Day; Jun 25, Republic Day; Aug 13, Women's Day; Oct 15, Evacuation of Bizerta; Nov 7, Accession of President Ben Ali; plus all Muslim festivals which vary year to year.
Turkey	Jan 1; Apr 23, National Independence Children's Day; May 19, Youth and Sports Day; Aug 30, Victory Day (Anniversary of the Declaration of the Turkish Republic). plus all Muslim holidays which vary year to year.
Turkmenistan	Jan 1; Jan 12, Remembrance Day; Feb 19, Birthday of Turkmen President Sapurmurat Turkmenbashi; May 9, Victory Day; May 18, Day of Revival and Unity; Oct 27, Independence Day; plus all Muslim holidays which vary year to year.
Turks & Caicos	Jan 1; Mar 8, Commonwealth Day; Easter; May 30, National Hero's Day; Jun 11 HM the Queen's Birthday; Aug 1, Emancipation Day; Sep 30, National Youth Day; Oct 10, Columbus Day; Oct 24, International Human Rights Day; Dec 25; Dec 26.
Uganda	Jan 1; Easter; May 1, labour Day; Jun 3, Martyr's Day; Jun 9, hero's Day; Oct 9, Independence Day; Christmas.
Ukraine	Jan 1; Jan 7, Orthodox Christmas; Mar 8, International Women's Day; May 1, Labour Day; May 9, Victory Day; Aug 24, Independence Day.
United Arab Emirates	Jan 1; Ramadan Jun 6, Islamic New Year; Aug 6, Accession Day of HH Sheikh Zayed, President; Aug 18, Prophet's Birthday; Dec 2, National Day; plus all Muslim holidays which vary year to year.
United Kingdom	Jan 1; Easter; first and last Mon of May; last Mon in Aug; Christmas.
USA	Jan 1; Jan 17, Martin Luther King Day; Feb 21, President's Day; May 30, Memorial Day; Jul 4, Independence Day; Sep 5, Labor Day; Oct 10, Columbus Day; Nov 11, Veteran's Day; Thanksgiving; Christmas.
Uruguay	Jan 1; Jan 6; Carnival; Apr 19, Landing of the 33 Patriots; May 1, Labour Day; May 18, Battle of Las Piedras; June 19, Birth of Artigas; July 18, Constitution Day; Aug 25, Independence Day; Oct 12, Colombus Day; Nov

2, All Souls' Day; Dec 8, Blessing of the Waters; Dec 25.

Uzbekistan   Jan 1; Ramadan; Mar 8, International Women's Day; Sep 1, Independence Day; Dec 8, Constitution Day; plus all Muslim holidays which vary year to year.

Vanuatu   Jan 1; Easter; May 1, Labour Day; May 12, Ascension Day; Jul 30, Independence Day; Aug 15, Assumption; Oct 5, Constitution Day, Nov 29, Unity Day; Christmas.

Venezuela   Jan 1; Carnival; Easter; Apr 19, Declaration of Independence; May 1, Labour Day; Jun 24, Battle Of Carabobo; Jul 5, Independence Day; Jul 24, Birth of Simon Bolivar and Battle of Lago de Maracaibo; Sep 4, Civil Servant's day; Oct 12, Columbus Day; Christmas.

Virgin Islands (US)   Jan 1; Jan 6, Three Kings Day; Jan 17, Martin Luther King's Birthday; Feb 21, President's Day; Mar 31, Transfer Day; Easter; Apr, Carnival; May 30, Memorial Day; Jun 20, Organic Act Day; Jul 3, Emancipation Day; Jul 4, Independence Day; Sep 5, Labor Day; Oct 10, Columbus Day; Oct 17, Virgin Island's Thanksgiving Day; Nov 1, Liberty Day; Nov 11, Veteran's Day; Christmas.

Yemen   Jan 1; Ramadan; Mar 8, International Women's Day; May 1, labour Day; Jun 10, Islamic New Year; Jun 13, Corrective Movement Anniversary; Jun 19, Ashoura; Aug 19, Prophet's Birthday; Oct 14, national Day; plus all Muslim holidays which vary year to year.

Yugoslavia   (Serbia and Montenegro) Jan 1; Jan 2; May 1-2, Labour Days; Jul 4, Fighter's Day; Jul 7, Serbian National Day; Jul 13, Montenegrin National Day; Nov 29-30, Republic Days.

Zaire   Jan 1; Jan 4, Day of the Martyr's of Independence; May 1, Labour Day; May 20, Anniversary of the Movement Populaire de la Revolution; Jun 24, Day of the Fisherman; Jun 30, Independence Day; Aug 1, Parent's Day; Oct 14, Youth Day; Oct 27, Anniversary of the name Zaire; Nov 17, Army Day; Nov 24, Anniversary of the Second Republic; Dec 25.

Zambia   Jan 1; Mar 11, Youth Day; Easter; May 1, Labour Day; May 24, African Freedom Day; Jul 5, Hero's Day; Jul 8, Unity Day; Aug 5, Farmer's Day; Oct 24, Independence Day; Dec 25; Dec 26.

Zimbabwe   Jan 1; Easter; Apr 18, Independence Day; May 1, Worker's Day; May 25, African Day; Aug 11, Hero's Day; Aug 12, Armed Forces Day; Christmas.

BUSINESS HOURS WORLDWIDE

Afghanistan	08.00-12.00, 13.00-16.30 Sat-Wed; 08.30-13.30 Thurs.
Albania	07.00-14.00 Mon-Sat, 17.00-20.00 Mon-Tue, Apr-Sept; 07.00-14.30 Mon-Sat, 16.00-19.00 Mon-Tue, Oct-Mar.
Algeria	08.00-12.00, 14.00-17.30 Sat-Wed.
Andorra	09.00-13.00, 15.00-18.45 Mon-Fri.
Angola	07.30-12.00, 14.30-18.00 Mon-Thu; 07.30-12.03, 14.30-17.30 Fri.
Anguilla	08.00-12.00, 13.00-16.00 Mon-Fri.
Antigua and Barbuda	08.00-12.00, 13.00-16.00 Mon-Fri.
Argentina	09.00-19.00 Mon-Fri.
Aruba	08.00-17.00 Mon-Fri.
Australia	09.00-17.30 Mon-Fri.
Austria	08.00-16.00 Mon-Fri.

Bahamas	09.00-17.00 Mon-Fri.
Bahrain	07.30-12.00, 14.30-1800 Sat-Thurs.
Bangladesh	09.00-16.00 Sun-Thurs.
Barbados	08.00/08.30-16.00/16.30 Mon-Fri.
Belarus	09.00-18.00 Mon-Fri.
Belgium	08.30-17.30 Mon-Fri.
Belize	08.00-12.00, 13.00-17.00 Mon-Thurs; 08.30-12.00, 13.00 -16.45 Fri.
Benin	08.30-12.30, 15.00-18.30 Mon-Fri.
Bermuda	09.00-17.00 Mon-Fri.
Bolivia	08.00-12.00, 14.00-18.00 Mon-Fri.
Bonaire	08.00-12.00, 14.00-18.30 Mon-Fri.
Botswana	08.00-17.00 Mon-Fri, Apr-Oct; 07.30-16.30 Mon-Fri, Oct-Apr.
Brazil	09.00-18.00 Mon-Fri.
British Virgin Is	08.30-17.00 Mon-Fri.
Brunei	08.00-12.00, 13.00-17.00 Mon-Thurs; 08.00- 12.00 Sat.
Bulgaria	08.00-18.00 Mon-Sat.
Burkina Faso	08.00-12.30, 15.00-17.30 Mon-Fri.
Cambodia	07.30-12.00, 14.30-17.00 Mon-Fri.
Cameroon	08.00-12.00, 14.30-17.30 Mon-Fri.
Canada	09.00-17.00 Mon-Fri
Cayman Islands	08.30-17.00 Mon-Fri.
Central African Rep	06.30-13.30 Mon-Fri; 07.00-12.00 Sat.
Chad	07.30-14.00 Mon-Sat; 07.00-12.00 Fri
Chile	09.30-18.00 Mon-Fri; 09.00-13.00 Sat.
China	08.00-12.00, 14.00-18.00 Mon-Sat.
Colombia	08.00-12.00, 14.00-17.30 Mon-Fri.
Comoro Islands	07.30-17.30 Mon-Thurs; 07.30-11.00 Fri.
Congo	08.00-12.00, 15.00-18.00 Mon-Fri; 07.00-12.00 Sat.
Cook Islands	08.00-16.00 Mon-Fri.
Costa Rica	08.00-11.30, 13.30-17.30 Mon-Fri.
Cote d'Ivoire	07.30-12.00, 14.30-17.30 Mon-Fri; 08.00-12.00 Sat.
Croatia	08.00-16.00 Mon-Fri.
Cuba	08.30-12.30, 13.30-17.30 Mon-Fri.
Curaçao	08.00-12.00, 13.30-16.30 Mon-Fri.
Cyprus	08.00-13.00, 16.00-19.00 Mon-Fri; half-day Wed.
Czech Republic	08.00-16.00 Mon-Fri.
Denmark	09.00-17.00 Mon-Fri.
Djibouti	06.30-13.00 Sat-Thurs.
Dominica	08.00-13.00, 14.00-16.00 Mon-Fri.
Dominican Rep.	08.30-12.00, 14.00-18.00 Mon-Fri.
Ecuador	09.00-13.00, 15.00-19.00 Mon-Fri; 08.30-12.30 Sat.
Egypt	09.00- 14.00 Sat-Thurs.
El Salvador	08.00-12.30, 14.30-17.30 Mon-Fri.
Equatorial Guinea	08.00-17.00 Mon-Fri.
Eritrea	08.00-12.00, 14.00-17.00 Mon-Fri; 08.00-14.00 Sat.
Estonia	08.30-18.30 Mon-Fri.
Ethiopia	08.00-12.00, 13.00-16.00 Mon-Fri;.08.00-12.00 Sat.
Fiji	08.00-16.30 Mon-Fri.
Finland	08.00-16.15 Mon-Fri.
France	09.00-12.00, 14.00-18.00 Mon-Fri.
French Guiana	08.00-13.00, 15.00-18.00 Mon-Fri.
French Polynesia	07.30-17.00 Mon-Fri.
Gabon	07.30-12.00, 14.30-18.00 Mon-Fri.
Gambia	09.00-16.00 Mon-Thurs; 08.00-12.00 Fri, Sat.
Germany	08.00-16.00 Mon-Fri.
Ghana	08.00-12.00, 14.00-17.00 Mon-Fri.
Gibraltar	09.00-13.00, 15.00-18.00 Mon-Fri.
Greece	09.00-18.00 Mon-Fri.
Greenland	09.00-15.00 Mon-Fri.
Grenada	08.00-12.00, 13.00-16.00 Mon-Fri.

Guadeloupe	08.00-17.00 Mon-Fri; 08.00-12.00 Sat.
Guatemala	08.00-18.00 Mon-Fri; 08.00-12.00 Sat.
Guernsey	09.00-17.00 Mon-Fri.
Guinea	08.00-16.30 Mon-Thurs; 08.00-13.00 Fri.
Guinea-Bissau	08.00-16.30 Mon-Thurs; 08.00-13.00 Fri.
Guyana	08.00-12.00, 13.00-16.30 Mon-Fri.
Haiti	07.00-16.00 Mon-Fri.
Honduras	08.00-12.00, 14.00-17.00 Mon-Fri; 08.00-11.00 Sat.
Hong Kong	09.00-13.00, 14.00-17.00 Mon-Fri; 09.00-12.30 Sat.
Hungary	08.30-17.00 Mon-Fri.
Iceland	09.00-17.00 Mon-Fri.
India	09.30-17.30 Mon-Fri; 09.30-13.00 Sat.
Indonesia	07.00/09.00-15.00/17.00 Mon-Fri.
Iran	08.00-14.00 Sat-Wed; 08.00-13.00 Thurs.
Iraq	08.00-14.00 Sat-Wed; 08.00-13.00 Thurs.
Ireland	09.00-17.30 Mon-Fri.
Israel	08.00-13.00, 15.00 18.00 Sun-Thurs.
Italy	09.00-13.00, 14.00-18.00 Mon-Fri.
Jamaica	08.30-16.30/17.00 Mon-Sat.
Japan	09.00-17.00 Mon-Fri.
Jersey	09.00/09.30-17.00/17.30 Mon-Fri.
Jordan	08.00-13.00, 15.30-18.00 Sat-Thurs
Kenya	08.00-13.00, 14.00-17.00 Mon-Fri; 08.30-12.00 Sat.
Kiribati	08.00-12.30, 13.30-16.15 Mon-Fri.
Korea (South)	08.30-18.00 Mon-Fri; 09.00-13.00 Sat.
Kuwait	08.00-13.00, 16.00-20.00 Sat-Thurs, winter; 08.00-13.00, 15.00-19.00 Sat-Wed, summer.
Kyrgyzstan	09.00-17.30 Mon-Fri.
Laos	08.00-12.00, 14.00-17.00 Mon-Fri; 08.00-12.00 Sat.
Latvia	08.30-17.30 Mon-Fri.
Lebanon	08.00-13.00 Mon-Sat, summer; 08.30-12.30, 15.00-18.00 Mon-Fri, 08.30-12.30 Sat, winter.
Lesotho	08.00-13.00, 14.00-16.30 Mon-Fri; 08.00-13.00 Sat.
Liberia	08.00-12.00, 14.00-16.00 Mon-Fri.
Libya	07.00-14.00 Sat-Thurs.
Liechtenstein	08.00-12.00, 14.00-18.00 Mon-Fri.
Lithuania	09.00-13.00, 14.00-18.00 Mon-Fri
Luxembourg	08.30-17.30 Mon-Fri.
Macau	09.00-17.00 Mon-Fri; 09.00-13.00 Sat.
Macedonia	07.00/08.00-15.00/16.00 Mon-Fri.
Madagascar	07.30-17.00 Mon-Fri; 07.30-11.30 Sat.
Malawi	07.30-17.00 Mon-Fri.
Malaysia	08.30-16.30 Mon-Fri; 08.30-12.30 Sat.
Maldives	07.30-13.30 Sat-Thurs.
Mali	07.30-12.30, 13.00-16.00 Mon-Thur; 07.30-12.30, 14.30-17.30 Fri.
Malta	08.30-12.45, 14.30-17.30 Mon-Fri; 08.30-12.00 Sat.
Martinique	08.00-17.00 Mon-Fri; 08.00-12.00 Sat.
Mauritania	08.00-15.00 Sat-Wed; 08.00-13.00 Thurs.
Mauritius	09.00-16.00 Mon-Fri; 09.00-12.00 Sat.
Mexico	08.00-15.00 Mon-Fri.
Monaco	09.00-12.00, 14.00-17.00 Mon-Fri.
Mongolia	09.00-18.00 Mon-Fri; 09.00-15.00 Sat.
Montserrat	08.00-12.00, 13.00-16.00 Mon-Fri.
Morocco	08.30-18.30 Mon-Fri.
Mozambique	08.00-12.00, 14.00-17.00 Mon-Fri; 08.00-12.00 Sat.
Myanmar	09.30-16.30 Mon-Fri.
Namibia	07.30-16.30/17.00 Mon-Fri.
Nepal	10.00-17.00 Sun-Fri, summer; 10.00-16.00 Sun-Fri, winter.
Netherlands	08.30-17.00 Mon-Fri.
New Caledonia	07.30-11.30, 13.30-17.30 Mon-Fri; 07.30-11.30 Sat.

New Zealand	09.00-17.00 Mon-Fri.
Nicaragua	08.00-12.00, 14.30-17.30 Mon-Fri; 08.00-13.00 Sat.
Niger	07.30-12.30, 15.30-18.30 Mon-Sat; 07.30-12.30 Sat.
Nigeria	07.30-15.30 Mon-Fri.
Niue	07.30-15.00 Mon-Thurs; 07.30-16.00 Fri.
Norway	08.00-16.00 Mon-Fri.
Oman	08.30-13.00, 16.00-19.00 Sat-Wed; 08.00-13.00 Thur.
Pakistan	09.00-16.00 Sat-Thur.
Panama	08.00-12.00, 14.00-17.00 Mon-Fri.
Papua New Guinea	08.00-17.00 Mon-Fri.
Paraguay	08.00-12.00, 15.00-17.30/19.00 Mon-Fri; 08.00-12.00 Sat.
Peru	09.00-17.00 Mon-Fri.
Philippines	08.00-12.00, 13.00-17.00 Mon-Fri.
Poland	07.00-16.00 Mon-Fri.
Portugal	09.00-13.00, 15.00-19.00 Mon-Fri.
Puerto Rico	08.30-16.30 Mon-Fri.
Qatar	07.30-12.00, 15.00-18.00 Sat-Thurs
Reunion	08.00-12.00, 14.00-18.00 Mon-Fri.
Romania	07.00-15.30 Mon-Fri; 07.00-12.30 Sat.
Russian Federation	09.00-18.00/19.00 Mon-Fri.
Rwanda	08.00-16.00 Mon-Fri; 08.00-12.00 Sat.
Saba	08.00-12.00, 13.30-16.30 Mon-Fri.
St Eustatius	08.00-12.00, 13.30-16.30 Mon-Fri.
St Kitts & Nevis	08.00-12.00, 13.00-16.00 Mon-Sat.
St Lucia	08.00-16.00 Mon-Fri.
St Maarten	08.00-12.00, 13.30-16.30 Mon-Fri.
St Vincent &	
The Grenadines	08.00-12.00, 13.00-16.00 Mon-Fri; 08.00-12.00 Sat.
Saudi Arabia	09.00-13.00, 16.30-20.00 Sat-Thurs.
Senegal	08.00-12.00, 14.30-18.00 Mon-Fri; 08.00-12.00 Sat.
Seychelles	08.00-12.00, 13.00-16.00 Mon-Fri.
Sierra Leone	08.00-12.00, 14.00-16.45 Mon-Fri.
Singapore	09.00-17.00 Mon-Fri; 09.00-13.00 Sat.
Slovak Republic	08.00-16.00 Mon-Fri.
Slovenia	07.00-15.00 Mon-Fri.
Solomon Islands	08.00-12.00, 13.00-16.30 Mon-Fri; 07.30-12.00 Sat.
Somalia	08.00-12.30, 16.30-19.00 Sat-Thurs.
South Africa	08.30-16.30 Mon-Fri.
Spain	09.00-18.45 Mon-Fri winter; 09.00-14.00, 16.00-19.00 Mon-Fri, summer.
Sri Lanka	08.30/09.00-16.30/17.00 Mon-Fri.
Sudan	07.30-14.30 Sat-Thurs.
Suriname	07.00-15.00 Mon-Fri; 07.00-14.30 Sat.
Swaziland	08.00-13.00, 14.00-17.00 Mon-Fri; 08.00-13.00 Sat.
Sweden	09.00-17.00 Mon-Fri.
Switzerland	08.00-12.00, 14.00-17.00 Mon-Fri.
Syria	08.00-14.30 Sat-Thurs.
Taiwan	08.30-17.30 Mon-Fri; 08.30-12.30 Sat.
Tajikistan	09.00-17.00/18.00 Sat-Thurs.
Tanzania	07.30-14.30 Mon-Fri; 07.30-12.00 Sat.
Thailand	08.30-16.30 Mon-Fri.
Togo	07.30-12.00, 14.30-17.30 Mon-Fri.
Tonga	08.30-16.30 Mon-Fri; 08.00-12.00 Sat.
Trinidad & Tobago	08.00-16.00 Mon-Fri.
Tunisia	08.00-12.30, 14.30-18.00 Mon-Fri; 08.00-12.00 Sat, winter; 07.00-13.00 Mon-Sat, summer.
Turkey	08.30-12.00-13.00-17.30 Mon-Fri.
Turks& Caicos Islands	08.00-13.00, 14.00-16.30 Mon-Fri; 08.00-12.00 Sat.
Uganda	08.00-12.30, 14.00-16.30 Mon-Fri.
Ukraine	09.00-13.00, 14.30-17.00/18.00 Mon-Fri.
United Arab Emirates	08.00-13.00, 16.00-19.00 Sat-Wed; 07.00-12.00 Thurs.

United Kingdom	09.00/09.30-17.00/17.30 Mon-Fri.
United States	09.00-17.30 Mon-Fri.
Uruguay	08.30-12.00, 14.30-18.30/19.00 Mon-Fri.
Uzbekistan	09.00-17.00 Sat-Thurs.
Vanuatu	07.30-11.30, 1330-16.30 Mon-Fri.
Venezuela	08.00-18.00 Mon-Fri (long lunch).
Vietnam	07.30-12.00, 13.00-16.30 Mon-Fri; 08.00-12.30 Sat.
Western Samoa	08.00-12.00, 13.00-16.30 Mon-Fri.
Yemen	08.00-12.30, 16.00-19.00 Mon-Wed; 08.00-11.00 Thurs.
Yugoslavia (Serbia and Montenegro)	07.00-14.30 Mon-Fri.
Zaire	07.30-17.00 Mon-Fri; 07.30-12.00 Sat.
Zambia	08.00-13.00, 14.00-17.00 Mon-Fri.
Zimbabwe	08.00-16.30 Mon-Fri.

Note: These are only the official hours, and generally apply to the capital. There will be considerable variation according to area and the size of the business. Banking hours tend to be shorter. ■

FINDING OUT MORE
Section 2

BOOK AND MAP RETAILERS

Austicks Map Shop
64 The Headrow
Leeds LS1 8EH
Tel: **0532 452326**
*Best travel bookshop in Yorkshire. A large map
selection including large-scale Ordnance
Survey maps.*

B.H. Blackwell Ltd
50 Broad Street
Oxford OX1 3BQ
Tel: **0865 792792**

The Booksellers' Association
Minster House
272-4 Vauxhall Bridge Road
London SW1W 1BA
Tel: **071-834 5477**
*Publishes an annual Directory of members
detailing information on bookshops nation-
wide.*

The British Cartographic Society
Hon Membership Secretary
JK Atherton
12 Elworthy Drive
Wellington
Somerset TA21 9AT
Tel: **0823-663 965**

Compendium Bookshop
234 Camden High Street
London NW1 8QS
Tel: **071-485 8944**
*A useful source of books which are difficult to
obtain elsewhere.*

Daunt Books
83 Marylebone High Street
London W1M 4DE

Tel: **071-224 2295**
*Large and comprehensive travel bookshop
which stocks all the usual guide series as well
as backlisted titles, second-hand, out of print
novels, political histories and biographies.
Mail order service available.*

Foyles
Travel Department
Ground Floor
113-119 Charing Cross Road
London WC2H 0EB
Tel: **071-437 5660**
Mail order or in person only.

Geographia
58 Ludgate Hill
London EC4M 7HX
Tel: **071-248 3554**

The Good Book Guide
24 Seward Street
London EC1V 3PB
Tel: **071-580 8466**
*Worldwide mail order service based on selec-
tion featured in the Good Book Guide catalogue.*

W. Hartley Seed
152-160 West Street
Sheffield
Yorks S1 3ST
Tel: **0742 738906**

Heffers
20 Trinity Street
Cambridge CB2 3NG
Tel: **0223 358351**
Very good selection of travel guides and books.

Heffers Map Shop
19 Sidney Street
Cambridge CB2 3HL
Tel: **0223 358241**
Leading map sellers for the region.

The National Map Centre
22-24 Caxton Street
London SW1H 0QU
Tel: **071-222 2466**
*Main agent for Ordnance Survey maps, and
retailers for all major publishers. Also the retail
outlet for cartographic printing company,
Cook, Hammond & Kell Ltd.*

Map Marketing
92–104 Carnwath Road
London SW6 3HW
Tel: **071-736 0297**
*Offer a range of over 400 laminated maps,
framed or unframed. The range includes world
maps, individual country maps and over 300
section maps of the UK.*

The Map Shop
15 High Street
Upton-upon-Severn
Worcestershire WR8 OHJ
Tel: **0684 593146**
*Agents for Ordnance Survey, large-scale maps
and guides for Europe and other areas worldwide –in stock or to order. Send for free catalogue stating area of interest.*

McCarta Ltd
122 King's Road
London WC1X 9DS
Tel: **071-359 6063**
*Book and map publishers as well as distributors
and retailers. Agents for various foreign map
publishers and offer an extensive list of guide
books and maps (particularly Europe) as well
as scientific publications related to geography
and geology.*

Nomad
781 Fulham Road
London SW6 5HD
Tel: **071-736 4000**
*Basement devoted to travel guides, literature
and history.*

Dick Phillips
Whitehall House
Nenthead
Alston
Cumbria CA9 3PS
Tel: **0434 381440**
*Specializes in books and maps of Iceland and
Faroe.*

Nigel Press Associates Ltd
1 Fircroft Way
Edenbridge
Kent TN8 6HS
Tel: **0732 865023**
*Offers a free service to bona fide expeditions for
the supply of map-like, satellite images, of
which they have a large archive covering most
parts of the world.*

Rallymaps of West Wellow
PO Box 11
Romsey
Hampshire S051 8XX
Tel: **0794 515444**
Mail order specialists for Ordnance Survey.

Stanfords
12-14 Long Acre
London WC2 9LP
Tel: **071-836 1321**
and…
c/o British Airways
156 Regent Street
London W1
Tel: **071-434 4744**
*The largest map seller in the world carrying a
wide range of maps, globes, charts and atlases,
including Ordnance Survey and Directorate of
Overseas Surveys. The Long Acre branch stocks
the full range of guide books and offers a mail
and telephone order service. For anyone within
reach of London and planning to buy a specific
map, Stanfords should be the first port of call.*

John Smith & Son Ltd
57 St Vincent Street
Glasgow G2 5TB
Tel: **041-221 7472**
*Ordnance Survey agents for western Scotland.
Foreign and Michelin maps.*

Trailfinders Travel Centre
42-48 Earls Court Road
London W8 6EJ
Tel: **071-938 3366**
*Stocks a wide range of guides and maps as well
as travel equipment.*

The Travel Bookshop
13 Blenheim Crescent
London W11 2EE
Tel: **071-229 5260**
*London's first bookshop specializing in travel
literature, opened in 1980 to provide a 'complete package' for the traveller, including
regional guides, histories, cookery books, relevant fiction and so on. They produce a general
and some regional catalogues of stock and will
produce a computer print out for stock on a particular destination. They also stock old and new
maps and topographical prints.*

From 16 April 1995 all national and international codes change — see page 587 for details.

The Travellers' Bookshop
25 Cecil Court
London WC2N 4EZ
Tel: 071-836 9132
One of the newest specialist travel bookshops, it boasts a wide range of antiquarian travel guides as well as the current crop of guide series. The shop will buy your old travel books from you and invites comments about guides and any other aspects of travel for the shop bulletin board.

Waterstones
17 St Anne's Square
Manchester M2 7DP
Tel: 061-834 7055
Leading map and guide retailers.

Whitemans Bookshop
7 Orange Grove
Bath BA1 1LP
Tel: 0225 464029
An extensive range of guide books and maps, atlases, walking guides, natural history guides and so on. Will undertake to order any obtainable map or book (at no extra charge) and operate a worldwide mail order service.

YHA Bookshops
14 Southampton Street
London WC2E 7HY
Tel: 071-836 8541
Books, maps and guides for backpackers, hostellers, adventure sportsmen and budget travellers.

Further reading:
Sheppards Book Dealers in the British Isles
–A Directory of Antique and Second Hand Book Dealers (Richard Joseph, £24)
This very useful reference work includes a section on topography and travel and will be very helpful for anyone looking for rare or out of print travel books, etc.
Also publishes guides to North America; Europe; Australia and New Zealand; India and the Orient; Japan; International Printed Mapsellers.

World Tourism Directory
K. G. Saur Verlag
Ortlertsrasse 8
81373 Munchen
Germany

BOOK AND MAP PUBLISHERS AND DISTRIBUTORS

AA Publications
Automobile Association
Fanum House
Basingstoke Hants
RG21 2EA
Tel: 0256 491513
Guide and map publishers and distributors including the Baedeker guides.

John Bartholomew/Times
78-85 Fulham Palace Road
London W6 8JB
Tel: 081-741 7070
Publish tourist, road, topographic/general maps and atlases and guides. Free catalogue from Marketing Dept.

B.T.Batsford Ltd
4 Fitzhardinge Street
London W1H 0AH
Tel: 071-486 8484
Guides and topographical publications, large backlist.

BBC Books
80 Wood Lane
London W12 0TT
Tel: 081-576 2000
Publishes books related to television and radio series, and more. Also publishes language learning books and materials.

A & C Black
35 Bedford Row
London WC1R 4JH
Tel: 071-242 0946
Publishes the Blue Guide series.

Bookpeople
2929 Fifth Street
Berkeley
CA 94710
USA

Bradt Publications
41 Nortoft Road
Chalfont St Peter
Bucks SL9 0LA
Tel: 02407 3478
Publish a comprehensive range of travel guides aimed at the more adventurous or backpacking traveller.

Cadogan
Letts House
Parkgate Road
London SW11 4NQ
Tel: **071-738 1961**
Publishes the Cadogan travel guide series.

Century
Random Century House
20 Vauxhall Bridge Road
London SW1V 2SA
Tel: **071-973 9670**
Publishes a regular flow of travel narratives.

Chatto & Windus Ltd
Random Century House
20 Vauxhall Bridge Road
London SW1V 2SA
Tel: **071-973 9740**
Publishes a range of titles including archaeology and travel.

Cicerone Press
2 Police Square
Milnthorpe
Cumbria LA7 7PY
Tel: **05395 62069**
Publishers of books on outdoor activities including climbing and walking.

The Crowood Press
The Stable Block
Crowood Lane
Ramsbury
Marlborough
Wilts SN8 2HR
Tel: **0672 20320**
Lists include mountaineering and climbing books.

Department of Defense and Mapping Agency
Hydrographic/Topographic Center
Washington DC 20315
USA
Publish charts of oceans and coasts of all areas of the world and pilot charts. Supply maps or photocopies of maps on request provided that the exact area is specified.

Geocenter
The Viables Centre
Harrow Way
Basingstoke
Hampshire RG22 4BJ
Tel: **055 817987**
Publishers of the Insight Guides series.

Michael Haag
PO Box 369
London NW3 4DP
Tel: **071-794 2647**
Publishers of the Discovery Guide series.

Hippocrene Books
171 Madison Avenue
New York
NY 10016
USA
Tel: **718 454 2366**
Publishers of travel guides, international literature and dictionaries with an extensive backlist.

Hodder Headline
338 Euston Road
London NW1 3BH
Tel: **071-873 6000**
Publish numerous mountaineering and climbing narratives as well as the Which? travel guides.

Hydrographic Department
MOD (Navy)
Taunton
Somerset TA1 2DN
Tel: **0823 337900**
Publishes world series of Admiralty Charts and hydrographic publications. Available from appointed Admiralty Chart Agencies.

Institut Géographique National
170 Rue la Boétie
75008 Paris
France
Tel: **4 225 8790**
Mail Order Sales for Individuals. Publish and sell maps of France and very many of the former French possessions.

Kummerly und Frey Ltd
Hallerstrasse 6-10
CH-3001 Bern
Switzerland
Publish charts and political, topographic, road and other maps.

Roger Lascelles
47 York Road
Brentford
Middlesex TW8 0QP
Tel: **081-847 0935**
Guide and map publisher and distributor. Catalogue published twice a year, extensive selection.

Lonely Planet Publications
PO Box 617
Hawthorn
Victoria 3122
Australia
One of the world's largest guide book publishers. Extensive selection of off-beat destinations.

Rand McNally & Co
c/o distributor :
Springfield Books
(see below)
*Large American publisher of maps, atlases,
guides and globes.*

Michelin Guides
Edward Hyde Building
38 Clarendon Road
Watford WD1 1SX
Tel: **0923-415000**
*Publish excellent maps and the famous Red and
Green Guides.*

John Murray
50 Albermarle Street
London W1X 4BD
Tel: **071-493 4361**
Publishes the Literary Companion series.

Moon Publications
722 Wall Street
Chico
CA 95928-9960
USA
Tel: **916-345 5473**
Publishers of the Moon Handbook series.

Moorland Publishing
Moor Farm Road West
Ashbourne
Derbyshire DE6 1HD
Tel: **0335 44486**
Prolific guide book publisher.

National Geographic Society
17th and Main Street, NW
Washington DC 20036
USA
Tel: **202-857 7000**
*Publish mainly topographical maps to accompany National Geographic magazine. Also sell
wall, relief and archaeological maps, atlases
and globes. Also magazines and books.*

NOAA Distribution Branch
N/CG33
National Ocean Service
Riverdale
Maryland 20737
USA
*The National Ocean Service (NOS) publishes
and distributes aeronautical charts of the US.
Charts of foreign areas are published by the
Defense Mapping Agency Aerospace Center
(DMAAC) and are sold by the NOS.*

Ordnance Survey
Romsey Road
Maybush
Southampton SO16 4GU
Tel: **0703 775555**
*The official mapping agency for the UK. The
Overseas Surveys Directorate at the same
address publishes maps of former and current
British possessions.*

Passport Publications
20 N Wacker Drive
Chicago IL 60606
USA

George Philip & Son Ltd
Michelin House
81 Fulham Road
London SW3 6RB
Tel: **071-581 9393**
*Publish a wide range of topographical and thematic maps, globes, atlases and charts, and
some guides.*

RAC Publishing
RAC House
PO Box 100
South Croydon
Surrey CR2 6XW
Tel: **081-686 0088**
*Publishers of guides, handbooks and maps for
motorists and travellers in the UK and on the
continent.*

Reed Travel Group
Church Street
Dunstable
Beds LU5 4HB
Tel: **0582 600111**
*Publishes a comprehensive range of guides
geared towards the professional travel planner.*

Regenbogen-Verlag
Schmidgasse 3
CH-8001
Postfach 240
CH-8025 Zurich
*Switzerland and c/o Los Amigos del Libro
Casilla Postal 450 Cochabamba Bolivia.
Publish books for the independent traveller.*

Rough Guides
1 Mercer Street
London WC2H 9QJ
Tel: **071-379 3329**
Publishers of the Rough Guide series.

Royal Geographical Society
Publications Dept.
1 Kensington Gore
London SW7 2AR
Tel: **071-589 5466**
Sells maps originally published in the Geographical Journal and maps published separately by the Society. Expedition pamphlets, G.J. reprints, and other papers on geography, expeditions and related subjects are also available.

Springfield Books Ltd
Norman Road Denby Dale
Huddersfield
W Yorks HD8 8TH
Tel: **0484 864955**
Publishers and distributors of maps and guides, including the Freytag & Berndt maps.

Thames and Hudson
30-40 Bloomsbury Street
London WC1B 3QP
Tel: **071-636 5488**
Publishers of numerous illustrated, large format books on travel ranging from the academic to the exotic.

Trade and Travel Publications
6 Riverside Court
Riverside Road
Lower Bristol Road
Bath BA2 3DZ
Tel: **0225-469141**
Publishers and distributors of numerous continental travel guides including the famous South American Handbook.

US Department of the Interior
Geological Survey
National Cartographic Information Center
(NCIC)
516 National Center
Reston
VA 22092
USA
Information about maps and related data for US areas.

Vacation Work Publications
9 Park End Street
Oxford OX1 1HJ
Tel: **0865 241 978**
Publishers of books for budget travellers and for anyone wanting to work or study abroad.

Wilderness Press
2440 Bancroft Way
Berkeley

CA 94704
USA
Tel: **415 843 8080**
Natural history, adventure travel guides and maps of North America. All mail order, including from abroad, to be paid in US dollars.

PERIODICALS

Adventure Road
360 Madison Avenue
New York
NY 10017
USA
Tel: **212 880 2170**
Bi-annual travel magazine.

African Affairs
Dept of Politics
University of Reading (Peter Woodward)
Tel: **0734 875123**
Quarterly journal, featuring learned articles on contemporary African issues.

Australian Gourmet Traveller
Australian Consolidated Press
PO Box 4088
54 Park Street
Sydney
NSW 2000
Tel: **2-282 8000**
Consumer publication for travellers who enjoy their food.

BBC Holidays
101 Bayham Street
London NW1 OAG
Tel: **071-331 3939**
Monthly holidays magazine

BBC Wildlife Magazine
Broadcasting House
Whiteladies Road
Bristol BS8 2LR
Tel: **0272 732211**
Monthly wildlife and conservation issues worldwide.

BBC Worldwide
BBC World Service
Bush House
Strand
London WC2B 4PH
Tel: **071-257 2875**
Monthly magazine with world outlook and full radio and television guide.

The Bookseller
12 Dyott Street
London WC1A 1DF
Tel: 071-836 8911
Monthly trade journal for the book retailers and publishers, lists all new publications by category.

Bulletin Voyages
Case Postale 85, Succ. 'E'
Montreal PQ H2T 3A5
Canada
Tel: 514-287 9773

Business Traveller
Compass House
22 Redan Street
London W2 4SZ
Tel: 071-229 7799
A monthly magazine aimed at the business traveller and featuring airfare cost-cutting information that will show quickly and clearly how to save your air travel costs.

Canadian Geographic
39 McArthur Avenue
Vanier ON K1L 8L7
Canada
Tel: 613-745 4629

Camping and Caravanning
Greenfields House
Westwood Way
Coventry CV4 8JH
Tel: 0203 694995
Monthly journal for enthusiasts

Camping Magazine
Link House
Dingwall Avenue
Croydon CR9 2TA
Tel: 081-686 2559
Monthly magazine focusing on walking and camping for the family.

Condé Nast Traveller
360 Madison Avenue
New York
NY 10017
USA
Glossy, monthly consumer publication featuring travel news, information etc.

Reports Travel Letter
301 Junipero Serra Blvd
Suite 200
San Francisco
CA 94127
USA
Comprehensive examination of major travel

questions, with company-by-company, dollars and cents comparisons of competitive travel services based on own 'original, independent, professional' research. Feature length articles on places, issues.

Destinations
444 Front St West
Toronto ON M5V 2S9
Canada
Tel: 416-585 5411

Discover North America
Phoenix Publishing
18-20 Scrutton Street
London EC2 4RJ
Tel: 071-247 4518
Quarterly travel information magazine covering North America.

Executive Travel
6 Chesterfield Gardens
London W1Y 8DN
Tel: 071-355 1600
Monthly consumer travel publication aimed at the business traveller.

The Expatriate
56A Rochester Row
London SW1P 1JU
Tel: 071-834 9192
Monthly title dealing with such issues as investment, pensions information, selection of job advertisements, health, tax, etc, for the British expatriate.

Explore
Suite 400
301-14 St N.W.
Calgary
Alberta
Canada T2N 2A1
Tel: 403-270 8890
Quarterly colour magazine devoted to adventure travel worldwide.

Expedition World
333 Ludlow Street
Stanford
CT 06912
USA
Tel: 203-967 2900

The Explorers Journal
4 The Explorers' Club
46 East 70th St
New York
NY 10021
USA
Official quarterly of The Explorers Club.

Established 1904. Articles on scientific discoveries, expeditions, personalities and many other branches of exploration. Reviews.

Expressions
101 Bayham Street
London NW1 OAG
Tel: 071-331 3939
Glossy title for American Express card holders featuring travel, food, wine and general consumer issues.

Flight International
2-6 Homesdale Road
Bromley
Kent BR2 9WL
Tel: 081-402 8491
Highly respected weekly journal covering everything to do with the aviation industry – both commercial and military.

Freighter Travel News
Freighter Travel Club of America
1745 Scotch Ave, SE
PO Box 12693
Salem
OR 79309
USA
News and letters, reports on freighter cruises.

Geographical
Centurion Publications
52 George Street
London W1H 5RF
Tel: 071-487 1082
The monthly magazine of the Royal Geographical Society.

Globe
The Globetrotters Club
BCM/Roving
London WC1N 3XX
Newsletter for the Globetrotters Club. Travel information. Articles on individual experiences, news of 'members on the move', tips, mutual-aid column for members.

Great Expeditions
PO Box 64699
Station G
Vancouver
BC V6R 4GT
Canada
Tel: 604 734 3938
For people who want to travel and explore, offers trips, a free classified ads service, discounts on books, an information exchange, articles and travel notes.

The Great Outdoors
The Plaza Tower
East Kilbride
Glasgow G74 1LW
Tel: 03552 46444
Monthly publication featuring walking, backpacking and countryside matters.

Holiday Which?
2 Marylebone Road
London NW1 4DX
Tel: 071-486 5544
Quarterly publication published by the Consumers' Association, featuring destinations worldwide and reporting on all travel-related news and issues.

Islands
3886 State Street
Santa Barbara
CA 93105
USA
Tel: 805-682 7177
Glossy colour title devoted to the world's islands, large and small.

International Travel News
Martin Publications Inc
2120 28th Street
Sacramento
CA 95818
USA
News source for the business and/or pleasure traveller who often goes abroad. Contributions mostly from readers. Free sample copy on request.

The Lady
39-40 Bedford Street
Strand
London WC2E 9ER
Tel: 071-379 4717
Classified ads in this weekly publication can be a useful source for self-catering accommodation and some overseas jobs.

London Calling
(Now part of BBC Worldwide)
PO Box 7677
Bush House
Strand
London WC2B 4PH
Monthly magazine for listeners to the BBC's World Service, listing programme times and frequencies.

Lonely Planet Newsletter
Lonely Planet Publications
PO Box 617

Hawthorn
Victoria 3122
Australia
Quarterly newsletter giving updates on all the LP guidebooks and lots of useful tips from other travellers.

Mountainbiking UK
Beaufort Court
30 Monmouth St
Bath BA1 2AP
Tel: **0225 442244**
Monthly publication for mountainbiking enthusiasts.

National Geographic
National Geographic Society
17th and Main St, NW
Washington DC 20036
Tel: **202-857 7000**
USA
Something of an institution, this monthly publication will be familiar to many. The photography is proverbially excellent and the destination features long and comprehensive.

National Geographic Traveller
PO Box 37054
Washington DC 20036
USA
Quarterly consumer title from the National Geographic stable devoted to travel and destination reports.

Nomad
BCM-Nomad
London WC1V 6XX
Newsletter aimed at people on the move and written by peripatetic publisher, with many readers' reports.

Official Airlines Guide (OAG)
World Timetable Centre
Church Street
Dunstable
Bedfordshire
LU5 4HB
Tel: **0582-600111**
Monthly airline timetable in pocket format, aimed at the consumer.

The Outrigger
c/o Pacific Islands Society
Tom Hughes
Alpines
Franklands Village
Haywards Heath
Sussex RH16 3RL

Outside Magazine
1165 N Clark St
Chicago
IL 60610
USA
Tel: **312 -664 5397**
Aimed at the active adult, it is a contemporary lifestyle magazine that features sports, fitness, photography, adventure travel and portraits of men and women adventurers.

The Railway Magazine
King's Reach Tower
Stamford Street
London SE1 (LS
Tel: **071-261 5533**
Monthly title established in 1897.

Resident Abroad
Greystoke Place
Fetter Lane
London EC4A 1ND
Tel: **071-405 6969**
Monthly publication for British expatriates.

The South American Explorer
South American Explorers Club
Casilla 3714
Lima 100
Peru
Subscriptions:
PO Box 18327
Denver
CO 80218
USA
Official journal of the South American Explorers Club. Accounts of scientific studies, adventure, and sports activities in South America. Also, sections on news, Club activities, book reviews, letters, tips and notes.

South East Asia Traveller
Compass Publishing
336 Smith Street
04-303 New Bridge Centre
Chinatown
Singapore 0105
Tel: **221 1111**
Glossy title geared at frequent and business travellers to the region.

Thrifty Traveler Newsletter
Traveling Free Publications Inc.
P.O. Box 8168
Clearwater
Florida 34618
USA
Tel: **813-791 1945**
8-page monthly newsletter for the thrifty traveller.

Time Off
Time Off Publications
60 Berwick Street
Fortitude Valley
QLD 4006
Australia
Tel: 7-252 9761

Travel and Leisure
1120 Avenue of the Americas
New York
NY 10019
USA
Tel: 212-350 4173

Travel News
6 Chesterfield Gardens
London W1Y 8DN
Tel: 071-355 1600
Weekly trade newspaper in competition with the TTG.

Travel Trade Gazette
Morgan Grampian Plc
30 Calderwood St
London SE18 6QH
Tel: 081-855 7777
Oldest weekly newspaper for the UK travel industry.

Traveller
WEXAS International
45-49 Brompton Road
Knightsbridge
London SW3 1DE
Tel: 071-581 4130
Quarterly publication established in 1970 as Expedition . Photo-features on travel outside western Europe. Letters, news, book reviews, travel photography and medical advice.

Travel Smart
40 Beechdale Road
Dobbs Ferry
NY 10522
USA
Travel Smart newsletter for sophisticated travellers who expect honest value for their money. Also discount-cruises, super-charters, hotel, car rentals, etc, for members.

Travel Tips
PO Box 188
Flushing
NY 11358
USA
First person accounts of freighter and passenger ship travel to all parts of the world. Cruise guide, budget travel news, tips on trips.

Der Trotter
Deutsche Zentrale für Globetrotter e.v.
Birkenweg 19
D-2359
Henstedt-Ulzburg
Germany
German language newsletter featuring articles and news on destinations largely outside Europe. Tips, readers' reports and advice for club members.

RECOMMENDED READING

compiled by Tim Ellerby

The following list is arranged geographically, each section beginning with a selection of the most popular guide books followed by recommended samples of travel writing.

The catalogue of guide books is inevitably incomplete, and you would be well advised to visit a specialist travel book shop to find the full range of choices for your destination. Most of the guides listed here are part of a standard series, whose distinguishing features are more fully described in the article *A Guide to Guides*, Chapter 2. Each entry gives only the title and publisher of the book, as prices and edition dates will vary.

Fine travel writing can be a rewarding supplement to your own trip, and although the selections below are few, the chosen books are justly renowned. The entries give only the title and author of the book, as the publisher may vary from edition to edition.

World Travel

Work your way around the World (Vacation Work)
Summer Jobs Abroad (Vacation Work)
Women Travel (Rough Guide)
Hostelling International - Africa, America, Asia and Oceania (International Youth Hostel Association.)
Nothing Ventured - Disabled People Travel the World (Rough Guide)
Travel with Children (Lonely Planet)
Airports Guide - Europe (Thomas Cook)
Overseas Timetable - Railway, Road and Shipping (Thomas Cook)
Family Travel Handbook (Bloomsbury)
The Vegetarian Traveller (Grafton)
Traveller's Health - How to Stay Healthy Abroad (OUP)
The Traveller's Health Guide (Lascelles)

An Explorer's Handbook (Hodder & Stoughton)
The SAS Survival Handbook (Collins)
The World Weather Guide (Hutchinson)

World travel writing

A Book of Travellers' Tales (Eric Newby)
The Oxford Book of Exploration (Robin Hanbury-Tenison)
Travelling the World (Paul Theroux)
The Best of Granta Travel (Ed. Bill Buford)
Blessings of a Good Thick Skirt (Mary Russell)

Africa

General

Africa on a Shoestring (Lonely Planet)
A Field guide to the Mammals of Africa (Collins)
A Field guide to the Larger Mammals of Africa (Collins)
Africa's Top Wildlife Countries (Global Travel Publishers)
Spectrum Guide to African Wildlife Safaris (MPC)

North Africa

North Africa Handbook (Trade & Travel)
Sahara Handbook (Lascelles)
Morocco, Algeria & Tunisia - A Travel Survival Kit (Lonely Planet)
Morocco (Rough Guide)
Morocco (Cadogan guide)
Morocco (Insight guide)
Morocco (Blue guide)
Morocco (Berlitz)
Morocco (Everyman Guide)
The Atlas Mountains - A Walker's Guide (Cicerone Press)
Algeria (Berlitz)
Tunisia (Rough Guide)
Tunisia (Insight guide)
Tunisia (Berlitz)
Tunisia (Cadogan Guide)
Egypt & the Sudan - A Travel Survival Kit (Lonely Planet)
Egypt Handbook (Moon)
Egypt (Fodor's Guide)
Egypt (Blue Guide)
Egypt (Cadogan Guide)
Introduction to Egypt (Odyssey Guide)
Discovery Guide to Cairo (M. Haag)

West Africa

West Africa (Rough Guide)
West Africa - Travel Survival Kit (Lonely Planet)
A Field Guide to the Birds of West Africa (Collins)

Backpacker's Africa - West and Central (Bradt)
The Gambia and Senegal (Insight Guide)

East Africa

East Africa Handbook (Trade & Travel)
East African Wildlife (Insight Guide)
Kenya, Tanzania, Seychelles (Fodor's Guide)
Kenya (Rough Guide)
Kenya (Lonely Planet)
Camping Guide to Kenya (Bradt)
Kenya (Insight Guide)
Kenya (Berlitz)
Spectrum Guide to Kenya (MPC)
Swahili for Travellers (Berlitz)
Swahili Phrasebook (Lonely Planet)

Central & Southern Africa

Central Africa - A Travel Survival Kit (Lonely Planet)
Backpacker's Africa - East and Southern (Bradt)
Zimbabwe and Botswana (Rough Guide)
Zimbabwe, Botswana and Namibia (Lonely Planet)
Guide to Zimbabwe and Botswana (Bradt)
South Africa, Lesotho and Swaziland (Lonely Planet)
South Africa (Insight Guide)
South Africa Travel Guide (Hildebrand)
South Africa (Berlitz)
A Guide to South Africa (Bradt)
Namibia (Insight Guide)
Guide to Madagascar (Bradt)
Madagascar and Comores - A Travel Survival Kit (Lonely Planet)
Spectrum Guide to Seychelles (MPC)
Mauritius, Reunion and Seychelles (Lonely Planet)
Guide to Mauritius (Bradt)

Travel writing

A Cure for Serpents (The Duke of Pirajno)
A Year in Marrakesh (Peter Mayle)
Lords of the Atlas (Gavin Maxwell)
The Lost World of the Kalaharia (Laurens Van Der Post)
A Walk with a White Bushman (Laurens Van Der Post)
Impossible Journey (Michael Asher)
A Good Man in Africa (William Boyd)
Travels with Pegasus (Christina Dodwell)
Jungle Lovers (Paul Theroux)
Journey Without Maps (Graham Greene)
Out of Africa (Karen Blixen/Isaak Dinesen)
White Mischief (James Fox)
The Flame Trees of Thikka (Elspeth Huxley)
West with the Night (Beryl Markham)
Our Grandmothers' Drums (Mark Hudson)
The Innocent Anthropologist (Nigel Barley)
The Tree Where Man Was Born (Peter Matthiessen)

Cameroon with Egbert (Dervla Murphy)
White Boy Running (Christopher Hope)
Muddling Through Madagascar
(Dervla Murphy)

America, Central and South

Mexico & Central America Handbook (Trade &
Travel)
Travellers' Survival Kit Central America
(Vacation Work)
Central America (Fodor's Guide)
Latin-American Spanish for Travellers (Berlitz)
Mexico (Insight Guide)
Mexico - A Travel Survival Kit (Lonely Planet)
Mexico (Rough Guide)
Mexico (Fodor's Guide)
Mexico (Cadogan Guide)
Budget Guide to Mexico (Let's Go)
Mexico Green Guide (Michelin)
Mexico Pocket Guide (American Express)
Mexico City (Berlitz)
Cancun (Fodor's Guide)
Belize Handbook (Moon)
Costa Rica, Guatemala & Belize
(Frommer's Guide)
Guatemala & Belize (Rough Guide)
Costa Rica (Passport Press)
Costa Rica Handbook (Moon)
Belize Guide (Passport Press)
Guatemala Guide (Passport Press)
La Ruta Maya (Lonely Planet)
The Maya Road (Bradt)
South American Handbook (Trade & Travel)
South America on a Shoestring (Lonely Planet)
South America (Fodor's Guide)
South America (Insight Guide)
Ecuador (Cadogan Guide)
Ecuador & the Galapagos Islands - A Travel
Survival Kit (Lonely Planet)
A Field Guide to the Birds of Galapagos
(Collins)
Colombia - A Travel Survival Kit (Lonely
Planet)
Peru - A Travel Survival Kit (Lonely Planet)
Peru (Rough Guide)
Peru (Insight Guide)
Backpacking & Trekking in Peru & Bolivia
(Bradt)
Exploring Cuzco (Nueves Imagenes)
Bolivia - A Travel Survival Kit (Lonely Planet)
Brazil - A Travel Survival Kit (Lonely Planet)
Brazil (Rough Guide)
Brazil (Fodor's Guide)
Rio (Insight Guide)
Rio de Janeiro (Berlitz)
Rio (Frommer's Guide)
Argentina, Uruguay and Paraguay (Lonely
Planet)
Argentina (Insight Guide)
Buenos Aires (Insight Guide)

Backpacking in Chile & Argentina (Bradt)
Chile & Easter Island - A Travel Survival Kit
(Lonely Planet)
Chile (Insight Guide)
Trekking in the Patagonia Andes (Lonely
Planet)

Travel writing
The Lawless Roads (Graham Greene)
Mornings in Mexico (DH Lawrence)
So Far from God (Patrick Marnham)
Travels in a Thin Country (Sara Wheeler)
Three Letters from the Andes (Patrick Leigh-
Fermor)
Time Among the Maya (Ronald Wright)
The Jaguar Smile - A Nicaraguan Journey
(Salman Rushdie)
A Visit to Don Otavio (Sybille Bedford)
Ninety-Two Days (Evelyn Waugh)
The Mosquito Coast (Paul Theroux)
Eight Feet in the Andes (Dervla Murphy)
Brazilian Adventure (Peter Fleming)
Far Away & Long Ago (W.H Handson)
The Old Patagonian Express (Paul Theroux)
In Patagonia (Bruce Chatwin)

America, North

General
Moneywise Guide to North America (Bunac)
Bed & Breakfast Guide to North America
(Fodor's)
Travellers' Survival Kit USA & Canada
(Vacation Work)
Crossing America (Insight Guide)
Native America (Insight Guide)
Field Guide to the Birds of North America
(National Geographic Society)

Canada
Canada Green Guide (Michelin)
Canada (Fodor's Guide)
Canada - A Travel Survival Kit (Lonely Planet)
Canada (Insight Guide)
Outdoor Traveller's Guide to Canada (Stewart,
Tabori, Chang)
Western Canada, & Alaska (Let's Go)
Toronto, Montreal & Quebec City Pocket
Guide (American Express)
Toronto (Berlitz)
Montreal & Quebec City (Fodor's Guide)
Montreal (Berlitz)
British Columbia Handbook (Moon)

USA
Budget Guide to USA (Let's Go)
USA (Fodor's Guide)
Where to Stay USA (Frommer's Guide)
How to Live & Work in America (Northcote
House)
National Parks of the USA

(National Geographic Society)
Mobil Travel Guides of the USA – 8 Regions
(Simon & Schuster)
Smithsonian Guides to North America
(Stewart, Tabori, & Chang)
Alaska (Fodor's Guide)
Alaska (Insight Guide)
Budget Guide to the Pacific Northwest,
Western Canada, & Alaska (Let's Go)
The Pacific Northwest (Insight Guide)
Washington Handbook (Moon)
Oregon Handbook (Moon)
Seattle & Portland (Frommer's Guide)
California (Fodor's Guide)
California (Rough Guide)
California (Insight Guide)
Essential California (AA)
California (Berlitz)
Budget Guide to California and Hawaii (Let's
Go)
Northern California (Insight Guides)
Northern California Handbook (Moon)
San Francisco (American Express)
San Francisco (Everyman Guide)
San Francisco (Virago Women's Travel Guide)
San Francisco (Rough Guide)
San Francisco (Fodor's Guide)
San Francisco (Insight Guide)
The Unofficial Guide to Disneyland (Prentice
Hall Press)
Southern California (Insight Guide)
Los Angeles (Fodor's Guide)
Los Angeles (Insight Guide)
Los Angeles (Frommer's Guide)
Los Angeles (Access Guide)
Los Angeles & San Diego (American Express)
Nevada Handbook (Moon)
Las Vegas (Fodor's Guide)
The Rockies (Insight Guide)
Colorado (Fodor's Guide)
Colorado Guide (Fulcrum)
Colorado Handbook (Moon)
Dollarwise Southwest (Frommer's Guide)
Arizona (Fodor's Guide)
Arizona Traveller's Handbook (Moon)
New Mexico (Frommer's Guide)
Texas (Insight Guide)
Texas Handbook (Moon)
New England Green Guide (Michelin)
New England (Fodor's Guide)
New England (Insight Guide)
Boston (Insight Guide)
Cape Cod (Fodor's Guide)
Chicago (Fodor's Guide)
Chicago (Access Guide)
New York State (Insight Guide)
New York City (Fodor's Guide)
New York City (Insight Guide)
Pocket New York City (Fodor's Guide)
New York (Cadogan Guide)

New York (Blue Guide)
New York (AA Baedeker)
New York (Berlitz)
New York (Collins Traveller)
New York Pocket Guide (American Express)
New York (Eyewitness Guide)
New York (Virago Women's Travel Guide)
New York (Michelin Green Guide)
Budget Guide to New York (Let's Go)
Philadelphia (Fodor's Guide)
Philadelphia (Frommer's Guide)
Washington DC (Fodor's Guide)
Washington DC Pocket Guide (American
Express)
Washington DC (Berlitz)
Washington DC (Access Guide)
Virginia & Maryland (Fodor's Guide)
The South (Fodor's Guide)
Atlanta (Frommer's Guide)
New Orleans (Fodor's Guide)
Florida (Insight Guide)
Florida (Fodor's Guide)
Florida (Berlitz)
Florida (Nelles Guide)
Miami (Insight Guide)
Greater Miami (Berlitz)
Miami & the Keys (Fodor's Guide)
Orlando (Frommer's Guide)
Disney World & the Orlando Area (Fodor's
Guide)
The Unofficial Guide to Walt Disney World &
Epcot (Prentice Hall Press)

Travel writing
Hunting Mr. Heartbreak (Jonathan Raban)
Old Glory (Jonathan Raban)
A Turn in the South (V.S. Naipaul)
The Lost Continent (Bill Bryson)

Asia

West Asia
Travellers' Survival Kit to the East - From
Istanbul to Indonesia (Vacation Work)
Middle East (Lonely Planet)
Israel (Insight Guide)
Israel - A Travel Survival Kit (Lonely Planet)
The Budget Guide to Israel & Egypt (Let's Go)
Israel (Fodor's Guide)
Jerusalem (Blue Guide)
Jerusalem (Insight Guide)
Jordan (Insight Guide)
Jordan & Syria - A Travel Survival Kit (Lonely
Planet)
Iran (Lonely Planet)
Yemen (Insight Guide)
Yemen - A Travel Survival Kit (Lonely Planet)
Arab Gulf States (Lonely Planet)
Saudi Arabia (Berlitz)
Arabia for Travellers (Berlitz)

Indian Subcontinent
Central Asia (Cadogan Guide)
India - A Travel Survival Kit (Lonely Planet)
India Handbook (Trade & Travel)
Introduction to India (Odyssey Guide)
India (Cadogan Guide)
India in Luxury (Century Hutchinson)
India (Fodor's Guide)
India File - Inside the Subcontinent (John Murray)
India (Insight Guide)
India Wildlife (Insight Guides)
Southern India (Nelles Guide)
South India (Insight Guide)
Delhi, Jaipur, Agra (Insight Guide)
Calcutta (Insight Guide)
Kathmandu (Insight Guide)
Nepal - A Travel Survival Kit (Lonely Planet)
Nepal (Rough Guide)
Nepal Handbook (Moon)
Trekking in Nepal, West Tibet & Bhutan (Hodder & Stoughton)
Pakistan - A Travel Survival Kit (Lonely Planet)
Pakistan Handbook (John Murray)
Pakistan (Insight Guide)
Pakistan Trekking Guide (Odyssey)
Trekking in Pakistan and India (Hodder & Stoughton)
Sri Lanka (Insight Guide)
Sri Lanka - A Travel Survival Kit (Lonely Planet)
Bangladesh - A Travel Survival Kit (Lonely Planet)
Maldives & Islands of the East Indian Ocean (Lonely Planet)

South East Asia
South East Asia, The Traveller's Guide (Springfield Books)
South East Asia Handbook (Moon)
South East Asia on a Shoestring (Lonely Planet)
The Insider's Guide to Thailand (Moorland)
Thailand - A Travel Survival Kit (Lonely Planet)
Thailand (Insight Guide)
Budget Guide to Thailand (Let's Go)
Bangkok (Insight Guide)
Introduction to Thailand (Odyssey Guides)
Thailand and Burma Handbook (Trade & Travel)
Guide to Burma (Bradt)
Burma - A Travel Survival Kit (Lonely Planet)
Vietnam (Lonely Planet)
Cambodia (Lonely Planet)
Laos (Lonely Planet)
Vietnam, Laos and Cambodia Handbook (Trade & Travel)
Malaysia (Insight Guide)
Malaysia, Singapore, Brunei - A Travel Survival Kit (Lonely Planet)

Singapore (Insight Guide)
Indonesia (Insight Guide)
Indonesia Handbook (Moon)
Indonesia, Malaysia and Singapore Handbook (Trade & Travel)
Indonesia - A Travel Survival Kit (Lonely Planet)
Bali Handbook (Moon)
Bali & Lambok - A Travel Survival Kit (Lonely Planet)
Philippines - A Travel Survival Kit (Lonely Planet)
Philippines (Insight Guide)
Philippino Phrasebook (Lonely Planet)
Thai Phrasebook (Lonely Planet)
Indonesian Phrasebook (Lonely Planet)
Burmese Phrasebook (Lonely Planet)
Malay Gem Dictionary (Collins)

Far East
North East Asia on a Shoestring (Lonely Planet)
East Asia (Insight Guide)
China (Blue Guide)
China (Fodor's Guide)
China (Insight Guide)
China - A Travel Survival Kit (Lonely Planet)
Shanghai Rediscovered (Lascelles)
Xian (Odyssey)
Beijing (Odyssey)
Shanghai (Odyssey)
Beijing (Insight Guide)
Mongolia (Lonely Planet)
Tibet - A Travel Survival Kit (Lonely Planet)
Trekking in Tibet (Cordee)
Taiwan - A Travel Survival Kit (Lonely Planet)
Introduction to Hong Kong (Odyssey Guide)
Hong Kong (Insight Guide)
Hong Kong (Rough Guide)
Hong Kong - In Depth (Odyssey)
Hong Kong & Taiwan (American Express)
Hong Kong, Macau, Canton - A Travel Survival Kit (Lonely Planet)
Korea - A Travel Survival Kit (Lonely Planet)
Korea (Fodor's Guide)
South Korea Handbook (Moon)
Japan (Fodor's Guide)
Japan - A Travel Survival Kit (Lonely Planet)
Tokyo Pocket Guide (American Express)
Tokyo (Insight Guide)
Tokyo (Fodor's Guide)
Japanese Cassette & Phrasebook (BBC Books)
Japanese Phrasebook (Lonely Planet)
Tibet Phrasebook (Lonely Planet)
Chinese Phrasebook (Lonely Planet)
Korean Phrasebook (Lonely Planet)
Japanese Phrasebook (Harrap)
Colloquial Chinese (Routledge)

Travel writing
The Great Railway Bazaar (Paul Theroux)
All the Wrong Places (James Fenton)
God's Dust - A Modern Asian Journey
(Burma)
Arabia (Jonathan Raban)
The Arabs (Mansfield)
Arabian Sands (Wilfred Thesiger)
The Marsh Arabs (Wilfred Thesiger)
The Snow Leopard (Peter Matthiessen)
Dreams of the Peaceful Dragon (Katie Hickman)
In Xanadu (William Dalrymple)
To the Frontier (Geoffrey Moorhouse)
City of Djinns (William Dalrymple)
Calcutta (Geoffrey Moorhouse)
Midnight's Children (Salman Rushdie)
The Road to Oxiana (Robert Byron)
Breaking the Curfew (Emma Duncan)
A Reed Shaken by the Wind (Gavin Maxwell)
Plain Tales from the Hills (Rudyard Kipling)
Om - An Indian Pilgrimage (Geoffrey Moorhouse)
Travels on my Elephant (Mark Shand)
Traveller in China (Christina Dodwell)
A Shaggy Yak Story (Peter Somerville-Large)
Slowly Down the Ganges (Eric Newby)
Chasing the Monsoon (Alexander Fraser
India - A Million Mutinies (V.S. Naipaul)
A Goddess in the Stones (Norman Lewis)
One Indian Summer (James Cameron)
Borderlines (Charles Nicholl)
Under the Mountain Wall (Peter Matthiessen)
Golden Earth (Norman Lewis)
Into the Heart of Borneo (Eric Hansen)
Hong Kong (Jan Morris)
Slow Boats to China (Gavin Young)
Wild Swans (June Chang)
A Dragon Apparent (Norman Lewis)
The Roads to Sutu (Alan Booth)
Riding the Iron Rooster (Paul Theroux)
Behind the Wall (Colin Thubron)

Australasia and the Pacific

Australasia
Australia (Fodor's Guide)
Australia - A Travel Survival Kit (Lonely Planet)
Australia (Insight Guide)
Bushwalking in Australia (Lonely Planet)
Australia Great Barrier Reef (Insight Guide)
Sydney (Insight Guide)
Melbourne (Insight Guide)
Australia & New Zealand Travellers' Survival Kit (Vacation Work)
New Zealand - A Travel Survival Kit (Lonely Planet)
New Zealand Handbook (Moon)
New Zealand (Insight Guide)

Tramping in New Zealand (Lonely Planet)

The Pacific
South Pacific Handbook (Moon)
Rarotonga & Cook Islands (Lonely Planet)
Solomon Islands (Lonely Planet)
Vanuatu (Lonely Planet)
New Caledonia (Lonely Planet)
Micronesia (Lonely Planet)
Tonga (Lonely Planet)
Fiji (Lonely Planet)
Fiji (Moon)
Tahiti (Lonely Planet)
Tahiti (Moon)
Samoa (Lonely Planet)

Travel writing
The Songlines (Bruce Chatwin)
Tracks (Robyn Davidson)
A Secret Country (John Pilger)
The Fatal Shore (Robert Hughes)

Caribbean

Caribbean Islands Handbook (Trade & Travel)
Caribbean (Frommer's Guide)
Caribbean (Fodor's Guide)
Caribbean - The Lesser Antilles (Insight Guide)
The Caribbean (Cadogan Guides)
Birds of the West Indies (Collins)
Highlights of the Caribbean (Berlitz)
Bermuda (Fodor's Guide)
Bermuda (Insight Guide)
Bermuda (Berlitz)
Bermuda (Collins Traveller)
Jamaica Handbook (Moon)
Jamaica (Berlitz)
Jamaica (Fodor's Guide)
Jamaica (Insight Guide)
Cuba - Official Guide (Macmillan)
Cuba - Traveller's Survival Kit (Vacation Work)
Puerto Rico (Insight Guide)
Puerto Rico (Berlitz)
Pocket Guide to Puerto Rico (Fodor's Guide)
French West Indies (Berlitz)
Barbados (Insight Guide)
Barbados - A Traveller's Guide (Lascelles)
Barbados (Fodor's Guide)
Southern Caribbean (Berlitz)
Trinidad & Tobago (Insight Guides)

Travel writing
The Traveller's Tree (Patrick Leigh Fermor)
Tap-Taps to Trinidad (Zenga Longmore)
Driving Through Cuba (Carlo Gebler)

Europe

General
Europe (Rough Guide)

Traveller's Survival Kit Europe (Vacation Work)
Continental Europe (Insight Guide)
Western Europe (Lonely Planet)
Mediterranean Europe (Lonely Planet)
Touring Europe (Fodor's Guide)
Which Weekend Breaks in Europe (Hodder & Stoughton)
Europe '94 (Fodor's Guide)
Budget Guide to Europe (Let's Go)
Main Cities Europe, Hotel Guide (Michelin)
Europe by Train (Fontana)
On the Rails Around Europe (Thomas Cook)
Europe on 50 Dollars a Day (Frommer's Guide)
Hitch Hiker's Guide to Europe (Harper Collins)
Which Self-Catering Holidays Abroad (Which Books)
Hostelling International - Europe and the Mediterranean (International Youth Hostel Association)
Camping & Caravanning in Europe (AA)
Cheap Eats Guide to Europe (Harper Collins)
Cheap Sleep Guide to Europe (Harper Collins)
Thomas Cook European Timetable (Thomas Cook) - published monthly

Travel writing
A Grand Tour (Morritt)
The European Tribe (Caryl Philips)
A Time of Gifts (Patrick Leigh Fermor)
Between the Woods & the Water (Patrick Leigh Fermor)
Neither Here nor There (Bill Bryson)

Great Britain & Ireland

General
Great Britain (Fodor's Guide)
Great Britain & Ireland (Michelin Red Guide)
Great Britain & Ireland (Let's Go)
Places to Visit in Britain (AA)
Great Britain (Insight Guide)
England (Blue Guide)
Literary Britain (Blue Guide)
Gardens of England (Blue Guide)
Which? Hotel Guide (Which Books)
Which? Good Bed and Breakfast Guide (Which Books)
Egon Ronay's Guide Hotels & Restaurants (MacMillan)
Charming Small Hotels Britain (AA)
Staying off the Beaten Track (Arrow)
Bed & Breakfast in Britain (AA)
Good Food Guide (Which Books)
YHA Accommodation Guide (YHA)
Camping & Caravanning in Britain (AA)
Holiday Which Guide to Weekend Breaks (Which Books)
Self-Catering Holiday Homes (E.T.B.)
Good Walks Guide (Which Books)
Walks & Tours in Britain (AA)

Village Walks in Britain (AA)
Summer Jobs Britain (Vacation Work)

Space does not permit listing guides to individual regions of Britain, of which there are innumerable, many published locally. There are several useful series of guides, however, that cover tourist regions of Britain:

Ordnance Survey Leisure Guides (AA)
Visitor's Guides (MPC)
National Trail Guides (O.S./Aurum)
Wainwright's Walking Guides (Michael Joseph/Westmoreland Gazette)
Walk the... series (Bartholomews)

Regional
Scotland (Fodor's Guide)
Scotland (Insight Guide)
Scotland (Cadogan Guide)
Scotland (Michelin Green Guide)
Scotland (Berlitz)
Scotland (Blue Guide)
Scotland (Rough Guide)
Which Guide to Scotland (Which Books)
Edinburgh (Insight Guide)
Edinburgh City Guide (AA)
Glasgow (Insight Guide)
Glasgow (Collins Traveller)
Companion Guide to the Western Highlands (Collins)
Wales (Insight Guide)
Wales (Blue Guide)
Visitor's Guide North Wales Snowdonia (MPC)
Ireland (Blue Guide)
Budget Guide to Ireland (Let's Go)
Ireland (Insight Guide)
Ireland (Cadogan Guide)
Ireland (Rough Guide)
Ireland (Fodor's Guide)
Ireland (Berlitz)
Dublin (Insight Guide)
Dublin (Collins Traveller)
Dublin (American Express)
New Irish Walks Guides (Gill & MacMillan)
London (Blue Guide)
London (Everyman Guide)
London (Virago Women's Travel Guide)
London (Eyewitness Guide)
London (Michelin Green Guide)
London Pocket Guide (American Express)
London (Berlitz)
London (Let's Go Guide)
London (Fodor's Guide)
Time Out Guide to London (Penguin)

Travel writing
The Kingdom by the Sea (Paul Theroux)
A Tour through the Whole Island of Great Britain (Daniel Defoe)

France

General
France (Blue Guide)
France (Insight Guide)
France (Rough Guide)
France (Fodor's Guide)
France (Lonely Planet)
France (Berlitz)
France (AA Baedeker)
France Red Guide (Michelin)
France Green Guide (Michelin)
Which Guide to France (Which Books)
France on Backroads (Duncan Petersen)
French Country Welcome - Bed & Breakfast
(Gites de France)
Charming Small Hotels of France (AA)
The Gites Guide (FHG)
Logis de France (Federation National des Logis
de France)
Camping Caravanning France (Michelin)
The Wine Roads of France (Grafton)
Living in France (Hale)
French for Travellers (Berlitz)
French Phrasebook & Dictionary (Collins
Traveller)
French Gem Dictionary (Collins)
Michelin Green Guides to the Regions of
France - 14 titles (Michelin)
Walking in France - Guides to the Long
Distance Footpaths (Robertson McCarta)

Regional
Paris (Blue Guide)
Paris (Rough Guide)
Paris Pocket Guide (American Express)
Paris (Berlitz)
Paris Essential Guide (AA)
Paris (Fodor's Guide)
Paris (Insight Guide)
Paris Walks (Robson)
Paris Step by Step (Pan)
Paris Guide (Time Out/Penguin)
Paris (Eyewitness Guide)
Paris (Virago Women's Travel Guide)
Paris (Cadogan Guide)
Paris (Christopher Helm)
Budget Guide to Paris Let's Go
Pauper's Paris (Pan)
Cheap Eats in Paris (Chronicle Books)
Cheap Sleeps in Paris (Chronicle Books)
Gault Millau Paris (Gault Millau, in French)
The Country Round Paris (Collins Companion
Guide)
Normandy (Rough Guide)
Normandy (Insight Guide)
Which Guide to Normandy and Brittany
(Which Books)
Brittany (Insight Guide)
Brittany & Normandy (Rough Guide)
Brittany (Christopher Helm)

Brittany (Berlitz)
The Loire Valley (Christopher Helm)
Loire Valley (Insight Guide)
The Dordogne (Philip's Travel Guide)
The Dordogne (Crowood Travel Guide)
A Guide to the Dordogne (Penguin)
The Visitor's Guide to the Dordogne (MPC)
South-West France - Independent Traveller's
Guide (Collins)
Languedoc & Roussillon (Christopher Helm)
Languedoc (Philip's Travel Guide)
The Pyrenees (Rough Guide)
Walks & Climbs in the Pyrenees (Cicerone
Press)
Alsace - The Complete Guide (Simon &
Schuster)
Alsace (Insight Guide)
The Visitor's Guide to Massif Central (MPC)
Auvergne & the Massif Central (Christopher
Helm)
The Visitor's Guide to Alps & Jura (MPC)
Chamonix/Mont Blanc - A Walking Guide
(Cicerone Press)
The Rhone Valley & Savoy (Christopher
Helm)
French Riviera Essential Guide (AA)
French Riviera (Berlitz)
The Visitor's Guide to Provence & Cote d'Azur
(MPC)
Provence & the Cote d'Azur (Rough Guide)
Provence & the Cote d'Azur (American
Express)
Provence & the Cote d'Azur (Christopher
Helm)
Provence (Philip's Travel Guide)
A Guide to Provence (Penguin)
Corsica (Rough Guide)
Corsica (Blue Guide)
Landscapes of Corsica (Sunflower Guide)

Travel writing
Three Rivers of France (Frieda White)
Aspects of Provence (Hennessy)
A Year in Provence (Peter Mayle)
Travels with a Donkey (Robert Louis
Stevenson)
A Little Tour in France (Henry James)

Italy

General
Italy (Lonely Planet)
Italy (AA/Baedeker)
Charming Small Hotel Guides: Italy (AA)
Italy (Insight Guide)
Italy (Fodor's Guide)
Italy (Frommer's Guide)
Italy (Let's Go)
Italy (Rough Guide)
Italy (Michelin Green Guide)
Italy (Michelin Red Guide)

Northern Italy (Blue Guide)
Italian Lakes (Moorland)
North-West Italy (Cadogan)
Italian Riviera (Berlitz)
Italian Adriatic (Berlitz)
The Dolomites of Italy (A & C Black)

Regional
Venice (Everyman Guide)
Venice (Berlitz)
Venice (Collins Companion Guide)
Venice for Pleasure (Bodley Head)
Venice (Collins Traveller)
Venice (Rough Guide)
Venice (Cadogan)
Venice (American Express/Mitchell Beazley)
Venice (Blue Guide)
Venice (Insight Guide)
Venice (AA/Essential)
Florence & Tuscany (Eyewitness Guide)
Florence & Tuscany Pocket Guide
(American Express/Mitchell Beazley)
Tuscany (Insight Guide)
Tuscany (Blue Guide)
Florence (Everyman Guide)
Florence (Collins Traveller)
Florence (Berlitz)
Florence (Blue Guide)
Florence (Insight Guide)
Tuscany & Umbria (Rough Guide)
Tuscany & Umbria & the Marches (Cadogan)
Rome (Fodor's Guide)
Rome (Eyewitness Guide)
Rome Guide (Time Out/Penguin)
Rome (Collins Companion Guide)
Rome (Cadogan)
Rome (Insight Guide)
Rome (Blue Guide)
Rome (Michelin Green Guide)
Budget Guide to Rome (Let's Go)
Rome (Virago Women's Travel Guide)
Rome (Frommer's)
Rome (AA/Baedeker)
Rome (Berlitz)
Rome Pocket Guide
(American Express/Mitchell Beazley)
Rome (Collins Traveller)
South Italy (Cadogan)
Italian Islands (Cadogan)
Sicily (Blue Guide)
Sicily (Rough Guide)
Sicily (Berlitz)
Italian for Travellers (Berlitz)
Italian Dictionary (Collins Gem)
Italian Travel Pack (BBC)
Italian Phrase Book & Dictionary (Collins Traveller)
Malta (Berlitz)
Malta (Insight Guide)
Malta (Collins Traveller)
Landscapes of Malta (Sunflower)

Malta & Gozo (Blue Guide)
Malta and Gozo (Cadogan Guide)
Malta (Windrush Islands Guide)
Sardinia (Insight Guide)
Sardinia (Windrush Islands Guide)

Travel writing
Venice (Jan Morris)
Voices of the Old Sea (Norman Lewis)
DH Lawrence and Italy (Lawrence)
Love & War in the Appenines (Eric Newby)
Venice: a travellers' companion (Ed John Julius Norwich)

Greece & Turkey

Greece
Greece (Fodor's Guide)
Greece (Blue Guide)
Greece (Let's Go)
Greece on $45 a Day (Frommer's)
Greece (Rough Guide)
Greece (Insight Guide)
Greece (Michelin Green Guide)
Mainland Greece (Collins Companion Guide)
Salonica & Northern Greece (Berlitz)
Peloponnese (Berlitz)
Athens (Insight Guide)
Athens (Frommer's)
Athens (Collins Traveller)
Greek Islands (Collins Companion Guide)
Greek Islands (Berlitz)
Greek Islands (Insight Guide)
Greek Islands (Cadogan Guide)
Which Guide to the Greek Island (Which Books)
Corfu (Windrush Islands Guide)
Corfu (AA/Essential)
Corfu (Collins Traveller)
Corfu (Berlitz)
Rhodes (Collins Traveller)
Rhodes (Insight Pocket Guide)
Landscapes of Rhodes (Sunflower)
Landscapes of Paxos (Sunflower)
Landscapes of Samos (Sunflower)
Crete (Rough Guide)
Crete (Moorland)
Crete (Berlitz)
Crete (Collins Traveller)
Crete (AA/Essential)
Crete (Blue Guide)
Crete (Insight Guide)
Landscapes of Eastern Crete (Sunflower)
Landscapes of Western Crete (Sunflower)
Trekking In Greece (Lonely Planet)
Greece on Foot (Cordee)
The Mountains of Greece - A Walkers Guide (Cicerone Press)
Greek Phrase Book (Harrap)
Greek Phrase Book (Penguin)
Greek Phrase Book (Berlitz)

Greek Phrase Book & Dictionary (Collins)
Greek Dictionary (Collins Gem)

Turkey
Turkey A Companion Guide (Collins)
Introduction to Turkey (Odyssey)
Turkey (Fodor's Guide)
Turkey (Nelles Guide)
Turkey (Rough Guide)
Turkey - A Travel Survival Kit (Lonely Planet)
Turkey (Cadogan Guide)
Trekking in Turkey (Lonely Planet)
Turkey (Insight Guide)
Landscapes of Turkey and Antalya (Sunflower)
Istanbul (Everyman Guide)
Istanbul (Insight Guide)
Istanbul (Blue Guide)
Istanbul (Berlitz)
Turkish Phrasebook (Lonely Planet)
Turkish (Harrap)

Cyprus
Cyprus (Blue Guide)
Cyprus (Windrush Islands Guide)
Guide to North Cyprus (Bradt)
Cyprus (Rough Guide)
Landscapes of Cyprus (Sunflower Books)

Travel writing
Journals of a Landscape Painter in Greece & Albania (Edward Lear)
Eleni (Nicholas Gage)
Mani (Patrick Leigh Fermor)
Istanbul - a traveller's companion (Ed Laurence Kelly)
Greece- a traveller's companion (Ed Martin Garrett)
Roumeli (Patrick Leigh Fermor)

Spain & Portugal

Spain
Spain & Portugal (Michelin Red Guide)
Spain (Michelin Green Guide)
Spain (Blue Guide)
Spain (Rough Guide)
Spain (Insight Guide)
Spain (Fodor's Guide)
Spain (Cadogan Guide)
Budget Guide to Spain, Portugal & Morocco (Let's Go)
Charming Small Hotel Guide Spain (AA)
Living in Spain (Hale)
Which Guide to Spain (Which Books)
Trekking in Spain (Lonely Planet)

Regional
Madrid (Insight Guide)
Madrid (Berlitz Guide)
Madrid & Barcelona (Fodor's Guide)
Barcelona (Insight Guide)

Barcelona (Berlitz)
Barcelona and Beyond (Lascelles)
Barcelona (Collins Traveller)
Barcelona (Blue Guide)
Barcelona (American Express)
Paupers Barcelona (Pan)
Catalonia (Insight Guide)
The Pyrenees (Rough Guide)
Walks & Climbs in the Pyrenees (Cicerone Press)
Walks and Climbs in the Picos de Europa (Cicerone)
Visitor's Guide: Costa Brava to Costa Blanca (MPC)
Costa Brava (Berlitz)
Costa Brava (Collins Traveller)
Southern Spain (Cadogan Guide)
Southern Spain (Insight Guide)
Seville (Berlitz)
The Visitor's Guide to Southern Spain & Costa del Sol (MPC)
Costa del Sol (Collins Traveller)
Mallorca & Ibiza (Insight Guide)
Mallorca, Ibiza, Menorca Essential Guide (AA)
Mallorca & Minorca (Berlitz)
Mallorca (Collins Traveller)
Landscapes of Mallorca (Sunflower Guide)
Walking in Mallorca (Cicerone Press)
Menorca (Windrush Islands Guide)
Landscapes of Menorca (Sunflower Guide)
Canary Islands (Berlitz)
Canary Islands Essential Guide (AA)
Tenerife & the Western Canary Islands (Insight Guide)
Tenerife (Collins Traveller)
Tenerife (Lascelles)
Landscapes of Southern Tenerife & La Gomera (Sunflower Guide)
Lanzarote (Windrush Islands Guide)
Landscapes of Lanzarote (Sunflower Guide)
Landscapes of Ibiza & Formentera (Sunflower Guide)
Ibiza & Formentera (Berlitz)
Gran Canaria, Lanzarote, Fuerteventura (Insight Guide)
Landscapes of Gran Canaria (Sunflower Guide)
Spanish for Travellers (Berlitz)
Spanish Phrasebook & Dictionary (Collins Traveller)
Spanish Gem Dictionary (Collins)

Portugal
Portugal (Fodor's)
Portugal (Michelin Green Guide)
Portugal (Cadogan)
Portugal (Collins Independent Traveller's Guide)
Portugal (Rough Guide)
Portugal (Blue Guide)
Portugal (Insight Guide)
Lisbon, Madrid & Costa del Sol (Frommer's)

Lisbon (Berlitz)
Algarve (Berlitz)
Algarve (Collins Travellers)
Algarve (Insight Pocket Guide)
Landscapes of Madeira (Sunflower)
Landscapes of Portugal: Estoril Coast & Costa
Verde (Sunflower)
Madeira (Insight Guide)
Madeira (Windrush Islands Guide)
Madeira (Berlitz)
Landscapes of Lanzarote & Fuerteventura
(Sunflower)
Landscapes of the Azores: Sao Miguel
(Sunflower)
Portuguese for Travellers (Berlitz)
Portuguese Phrase Book & Dictionary (Collins
Traveller)
Portuguese Dictionary (Collins Gem)

Travel writing
The Spaniards (Harper)
The Face of Spain (Gerald Brenan)
Spain (Jan Morris)
Travels on Horseback (Christina Dodwell)
As I Walked Out One Mid-Summer Morning
(Laurie Lee)
They Went to Portugal (Rose Macauley)
Spanish Pilgrimage (Robin Hanbury-Tenison)
Madrid- a traveller's companion (Ed Hugh
Thomas)
Spain: A Literary Companion (Ed Jimmy
Burns)

Germany and Austria

Germany (Cadogan Guide)
The New Germany (Insight Guide)
Germany (Fodor's)
Germany - Gault Millau (RAC)
Germany Red Guide (Michelin)
Germany Green Guide (Michelin)
Germany (Frommer's)
Germany (Rough Guide)
Charming Small Hotels of Germany (AA)
Budget Guide to Germany (Let's Go)
Berlin City Guide (Collins Travellers)
Berlin (Rough Guide)
Berlin (Cadogan Guide)
Berlin, Postdam & Dresden (American
Express)
Rhine Valley (Berlitz)
The Rhine (Insight Guide)
Visitor's Guide to Bavaria (Moorland)
Visitor's Guide to Black Forest (Moorland)
Dusseldorf (Insight Guide)
Frankfurt (Insight Guide)
Dresden (insight Guide)
Hamburg (Insight Guide)
Munich (Berlitz)
Munich (Insight Guide)
German Dictionary (Collins Gem)

German Phrase Book (Harrap)
German Phrase Book & Dictionary (Collins)
Austria Austria Green Guide (Michelin)
Austria (Fodor's)
Austria Blue Guide (A & C Black)
Exploring Rural Austria (Helm)
Austria (Frommer's Guide)
Budget Guide to Austria (Lets Go)
Vienna (Everyman Guide)
Vienna (American Express)
Vienna (AA Baedeker)
Vienna (Insight Guide)
Mountain Walking in Austria (Cicerone Press)

Switzerland

Switzerland (Michelin Green Guide)
Off the Beaten Track Switzerland (Moorland)
Switzerland (Blue Guide)
Switzerland (AA Baedeker)
Switzerland (Lonely Planet)
Switzerland (Michelin Red Guide)
Switzerland (Insight Guide)
Charming Small Hotels of Switzerland (AA)
A Walkers Guide to Central Switzerland
(Cicerone Press)
Walks in the Engadine (Cicerone Press)

Benelux

Belgium
Holland Belgium and Luxembourg (Rough
Guide)
Belgium (Insight Guide)
Netherlands, Belgium and Luxembourg
(Fodor's Guide)
Benelux Red Guide (Michelin)
Belgium/Luxembourg Green Guide (Michelin)
Belgium (Blue Guide)
Brussels (Berlitz)

Holland
Holland (Blue Guide)
Visitors' Guide to Holland (Moorland)
Netherlands (Insight Guide)
Netherlands (Fodor's Guide)
Netherlands (AA Baedeker)
Amsterdam (Everyman Guide)
Amsterdam (Cadogan Guide)
Amsterdam (Virago Women's Travel Guide)
Amsterdam (Berlitz)
Amsterdam (Rough Guide)
Amsterdam (Time Out)
Amsterdam (American Express)
Dutch - Berlitz (Cassette & Phrase Book)

Scandinavia

Scandinavia (Fodor's Guide)
Scandinavia (Lonely Planet)
Scandinavia (Rough Guide)

Sweden (Fodor's Guide)
Sweden (Insight Guide)
Sweden Visitors' Guide (Moorland)
Stockholm (Berlitz)
Driving around Norway (Grafton)
Visitors' Guide to Norway (Moorland)
Norway (Insight Guide)
Norwegian Cassette and Phrasebook (Berlitz)
Visitors' Guide to Finland (Moorland)
Norway (Insight Guide)
Norwegian Cassette and Phrasebook (Berlitz)
Visitors' Guide to Finland (Moorland)
Finland (Insight Guide)
Finnish Cities (Oleander)
Helsinki (Berlitz)
Finnish for Travellers (Berlitz)
Denmark (Blue Guide)
Denmark (Insight Guide)
Drive around Denmark (Trafton)
Copenhagen (Berlitz)
Danish Cassette Pack (Berlitz)
Scandinavian Phrase Book (Lonely Planet)
Iceland (Insight Guide)
Iceland, Greenland & the Faroe Islands (Lonely Planet)
Guide to Spitsbergen (Bradt)
Teach Yourself Icelandic (Hodder & Stoughton)

Eastern Europe

General
Eastern Europe - A Travel Survival Kit (Lonely Planet)
Eastern Europe (Insight Guide)
Eastern Europe (Fodor's Guide)
Traveller's Survival Kit Eastern Europe (Vacation Work)
Eastern European Phrase Book (Lonely Planet)

Czech and Slovak Republics
Guide to Czechoslovakia (Bradt)
Czechoslovakia (Blue Guide)
Czech and Slovak Republics (Rough Guides)
Czech and Slovak Republics (Fodor's Guide)
Czech and Slovak Republics (Insight Guide)
Prague (Eyewitness)
Prague (Rough Guide)
Prague City Guide (Cadogan)
Prague (Berlitz)

Hungary
Hungary (Rough Guide)
Hungary (lonely Planet)
Hungary (Blue Guide)
Hungary (Frommer's Guide)
Hungary (Insight Guide)
Budapest (Insight Guide)

Albania
Albania (Bradt)

Albania (Blue Guide)
Albania (Philip Ward)

Romania
Romania (AA Essential Guide)
Hiking in Romania (Bradt)
Teach Yourself Romanian (Hodder & Stoughton)

Bulgaria
Bulgaria (Rough Guide)

Poland
Poland (Rough Guide)

The Former Yugoslavia
Yugoslavia Mountain Walks (Bradt)
Serbo-Croat for Travellers (Berlitz)
Istria & Dalmatian Coast (Berlitz)
Dubrovnik (Berlitz)

Travel writing
Between the Woods and the Water (Patrick Leigh Fermor)
The Uses of Adversity (Timothy Garton Ash)
Queen of Romania (Pakula)
Danube (C. Magrio)

Former Soviet Bloc States (CIS)

Russia (Insight Guide)
Russia and Baltic States (Fodor's Guide)
Moscow (Insight Guide)
Moscow (Blue Guide)
Moscow & St Petersburg Handbook (Moon)
Moscow & Leningrad (Berlitz)
Introduction to Moscow (Odyssey Guide)
Moscow & St. Petersburg (Lascelles)
Moscow (AA Baedeker)
St Petersburg (Rough Guide)
St Petersburg (Insight Guide)
St Petersburg (AA Baedeker)
Introduction to Leningrad (Odyssey Guide)
Georgian Republic (Odyssey)
Baltic States (Insight Guide)
Trekking in the Caucasus (Cicerone Press)
Russian Gem Dictionary (Collins)
Russia for Travellers (Berlitz)

Travel writing
Among the Russians (Colin Thubron)
Journey into Russia (Laurens Van der Post)
On Sledge and Horseback to Outcast Siberia
Beyond Siberia (Christina Dodwell)
Lepers (Kate Marsden)
Between the Hammer and the Sickle (Simon Vickers)
Big Red Train Ride (Eric Newby)

FOREIGN TOURIST BOARDS IN THE UK

Please note some Tourist Offices have 0891 telephone numbers, there is a charge incurred when ringing them.
Please also note that if there is no Tourist Office listed the Embassy or Consulate may be able to provide tourist information.

Andorra
63 Westover Road
London SW1 8RF
Tel: 081-874 4806

Anguilla
3 Epirus Road
London SW6 7UJ
Tel: 071-937 7725

Antigua & Barbuda
Antigua House
15 Thayer Street
London W1M 5LD
Tel: 071-486 7073

Argentina
Fifth Floor
Trevor House
100 Brompton Road
London SW3 1ER
Tel: 071-589 3104

Australia
Gemini House
10/18 Putney Hill
London SW15 6AA
Tel: 081-780 2227

Austria
30 St George Street
London W1R 0AL
Tel: 071-629 0461

Bahamas
10 Chesterfield Street
London W1X 8AH
Tel: 071-629 5238

Barbados
263 Tottenham Court Road
London
W1P 9AA
Tel: 071-636 9448

Belgium
29 Princes Street
London W1R 7RG
Tel: 071-629 0230

Bermuda
1 Battersea Church Road
London SW11 3LY
Tel: 071-734 8813

Brazil
32 Green Street
London W1Y 4AT
Tel: 071 499 0877

British Virgin Islands
110 St Martin's Lane
London WC2N 4DY
Tel: 071 240 4259

Bulgaria
18 Princes Street
London W1R 7RE
Tel: 071-499 6988

Canada
Canada House
Trafalgar Square
London SW1Y 5BJ
Tel: 071-258 6346

Caribbean Tourism
Vigilant House
120 Wilton Road
London SW1V 1JZ
Tel: 071-233 8382

Cayman Islands
Trevor House
100 Brompton Road
London SW3 1EX
Tel: 071-581 9960

China
4 Glentworth Street
London NW1 5PG
Tel: 0891 200 273

C.I.S see Russian Federation

Cyprus
213 Regent Street
London W1R 8DA
Tel: 071-734 9822

Czech Republic
Cedok
49 Southwark Street
London SE1 1RU
Tel: 071-378 6009

Denmark
55 Sloane Street
London SW1X 9SR
Tel: 071-259 5959

Dominica
1 Collingham Gardens
London SW5 0HW
Tel: **071-835 1937**

Egypt
170 Piccadilly
London W1V 9DD
Tel: **071-493 5282**

Falkland Islands
Falkland House
14 Broadway
London SW1
Tel: **071-222 2542**

Finland
66 Haymarket
London SW1Y 4RF
Tel: **071-839 4048**

France
178 Piccadilly
London W1V 0AL
Tel: **0891 244 123**

Gambia
57 Kensington Court
London W8 5DG
Tel: **071-376 0093**

Germany
Nightingale House
65 Curzon St
London W1Y 7PE
Tel: **0891 600 100**

Ghana
102 Park Street
London W1Y 3RT
Tel: **071-493 4901**

Gibraltar
179 The Strand
London WC2R 1EH
Tel: **071-836 0777**

Greece
4 Conduit Street
London W1R 0DJ
Tel: **071 734 5997**

Grenada
1 Collingham Gardens
London SW5 0HW
Tel: **071-370 5164**

Hong Kong
125 Pall Mall
London SW1Y 5EA
Tel: **071-930 4775**

Iceland
172 Tottenham Court Road
London W1P 9LG
Tel: **071-388 5346**

India
7 Cork Street
London W1X 1PB
Tel: **071-437 3677**

Ireland
150/151 New Bond Street
London W1Y 0AQ
Tel: **071-493 3201**

Israel
18 Great Marlborough Street
London W1V 1AF
Tel: **071-434 3651**

Italy
1 Princes Street
London W1R 8AY
Tel: **071-408 1254**

Jamaica
1-2 Prince Consort Road
London SW7 2BZ
Tel: **071-224 0505**

Japan
167 Regent Street
London W1R 7FD
Tel: **071-734 9638**

Jersey
38 Dover Street
London W1X 3RB
Tel: **071-493 5278**

Jordan
211 Regent Street
London W1R 7DD
Tel: **071-437 9465**

Kenya
25 Brook's Mews
London W1Y 1LG
Tel: **071-355 3144**

Korea (South)
20 St George Street
London W1R 9RE
Tel: **071-409 2100**

Luxembourg
122 Regent Street
London W1R 5FE
Tel: **071-434 2800**

Macau
6 Sherlock Mews
Off Paddington Street
London W1M 3RH
Tel: **071-224 3390**

Malawi
33 Grosvenor Street
London W1X 0DE
Tel: **071-491 4172**

Malaysia
Malaysia House
57 Trafalgar Square
London
WC2N 5DU
Tel: **071-930 7932**

Maldives
c/o Maldives Travel Ltd
3 Ester House
11 Edith Terrace
London SW10 0TH
Tel: **071-352 2246**

Malta
Mappin House
Suite 300
4 Winsley Street
London W1N 7AR
Tel: **071-323 0506**

Mauritius
32/33 Elvaston Place
London SW7 5NW
Tel: **071-581 0294**

Mexico
60/61 Trafalgar Square
London
WC2N 5DS
Tel: **071-734 1058**

Monaco
3/18 Chelsea Garden Market
Chelsea Harbour
London
SW10 0XE
Tel: **071-352 9962**

Monserrat
3 Epirus Road
London SW6 7UJ
Tel: **071-730 7144**

Morocco
205 Regent Street
London W1R 7DE
Tel: **071-437 0073**

Netherlands
P.O. Box 253
London SW1E 6NT
Tel: **0891 200 277**

New Zealand
New Zealand House
Haymarket
London SW1Y 4TQ
Tel: **071-973 0360**

Norway
Charles House
5-11 Lower Regent Street
London SW1Y 4LR
Tel: **071-839 2650**

Peru
10 Grosvenor Gardens
London SW1W 0BD
Tel: **071-824 8693**

Philippines
17 Albermarle Street
London W1X 7HA
Tel: **071-499 5443**

Poland
82 Mortimer Street
London W1N 7DE
Tel: **071-580 8028**

Portugal
22/25a Sackville Street
London W1X 1DE
Tel: **071-494 1441**

Puerto Rico
67/69 Whitfield Street
London W1P 5RL
Tel: **071-636 6558**

Romania
83 Marylebone High Street
London W1M 3DE
Tel: **071-224 3692**

Russian Federation
Intourist
219 Marsh Wall
Isle of Dogs
London E14 9FG
Tel: **071-538 8600**

Saudi Arabia
Cavendish House
18 Cavendish Square
London W1M 0AQ
Tel: **071-629 8803**

Seychelles
Eros House
111 Baker Street
London W1M 1FE
Tel: **071-224 1670**

Sierra Leone
375 Upper Richmond Road West
London SW14 7NX
Tel: **081 392 9188**

Singapore
Carrington House
126/130 Regent Street
London W1R 5FE
Tel: **071-437 0033**

Slovak Republic
Cedok
49 Southwark Street
London SE1 1RU
Tel: **071-378 6009**

Slovenia
Moghul House
57 Grosvenor Street
London W1X 9DA
Tel: **071 494 4688**

South Africa
5/6 Alt Grove
Off St George's Road
Wimbledon
London SW19 4DZ
Tel: **081-944 8080**

Spain
57-58 St. James's Street
London SW1A 1LD
Tel: **071-499 0901**

Sri Lanka
13 Hyde Park Gardens
London W2 2LU
Tel: **071-262 5009**

St. Kitts & Nevis
10 Kensington Court
London W8 5DL
Tel: **071-376 0881**

St. Lucia
421a Finchley Road
London NW3 6HT
Tel: **071-431 3675**

St. Vincent & The Grenadines
10 Kensington Court
London W8 5DL
Tel: **071-937 6570**

Sweden
72-73 Welbeck Street

London W1M 8AN
Tel: **071-0891 200 280**

Switzerland
Swiss Court
New Coventry Street
London W1V 8EE
Tel: **071-734 1921**

Tanzania
78/80 Borough High Street
London SE1 1LL
Tel: **071-407 0566**

Thailand
49 Albermarle Street
London W1X 3FE
Tel: **071-499 7679**

Trinidad & Tobago
8a Hammersmith Broadway
London W6 7AL
Tel: **081-741 4466**

Tunisia
77A Wigmore Street
London W1H 9LJ
Tel: **071-224-5561**

Turkey
170-173 Piccadilly (1st Floor)
London W1V 9DD
Tel: **071-734 8681**

Turks & Caicos
47 Chase Side
Enfield
Middlesex EN2 6HB
Tel: **081-364 5188**

USA
P.O. Box 1EN
London W1A 1EN
Tel: **071-495 4466**

US Virgin Islands
2 Cinnamon Row
Plantation Wharf
London SW11 3TW
Tel: **071-978 5262**

Zambia
2 Palace Gate
London W8 5NG
Tel: **071-589 6343**

Zimbabwe
429 The Strand
London WC2R 0QE
Tel: **071-836 7755** ■

WHAT TYPE OF TRAVEL?
Section 3

ASSOCIATIONS AND TOUR OPERATORS

Environmental

Action d'Urgence Internationale
10 Rue Felix-Aiem
75018 Paris
France
Tel: **264 74 19**
Runs training courses for people interested in helping rescue operations in times of natural disasters. Branches in France, UK, Morocco, India, Dominican Republic and Guadeloupe.

Arcturus Expeditions
Po Box 850
Gartochan
Dunbartonshire G83 8RL
Tel: **0389-83204**
Observing and monitoring wildlife in Greenland

Bellerive Foundation
Alp Action
PO Box 6
CH-1211
Geneva 3
Switzerland
Tel: **22-468866**
New organisation devoted to protecting the Alps from pollution and thoughtless tourism.

Centre for the Advancement of Responsive Travel (CART)
Dr Roger Milman
70 Dry Hill Park Road
Tunbridge
Kent TN10 3BX
Dr Milman runs a consultancy at the centre and CART produces guidelines for 'caring travellers' and a publication The Responsive Traveller's Handbook – a guide to Ethical Tourism Worldwide (£5).

Charioteer Travel Tours
PO Box 10400
10 Agias Sofias St
Thessaloniki
Greece GR 541 10
Tel: **31 229 230**
Tailor-made birdwatching and natural history tours of Greece, 10 per cent of profits towards conservation.

Convention of International Trade in Endangered Species of Wild Flora and Fauna (CITES)
Conservation Monitoring Centre (CMC)
219C Huntingdon Road
Cambridge CB3 0DL
Tel: **0223 277314**
Charity devoted to end the trade in rare flora and fauna.

Coral Cay Conservation Expeditions
The Ivy Works
154 Clapham Park Road
London SW4 7OE
Tel: **071-498 6248**
Recruits qualified divers over 18 to help establish a marine park in Belize.

Discover the World Ltd
The Flatt Lodge
Bewcastle
Nr Carlise
Cumbria CA6 6PH
Tel: **06977 48356**
Organises tours on behalf of the WWF and for the Whale and Dolphin Conservation Society

Earthwatch
Belsyre Court
57 Woodstock Road
Oxford OX2 6HU

Tel: **0865 311600**
Environmental charity which matches paying volunteers to scientific research projects worldwide.

Ecumenical Coalition on Third World Tourism (ECTWT)
PO Box 24
Chorakhebua
Bangkok 10230
Thailand
Tel: **662 510 7287**
Church organization concerned with monitoring tourism development and preventing exploitation.

Elefriends
162 Boundaries Road
London SW12 8HG
Tel: **081-682 1818**
Campaign for the protection of the elephant.

Europa Nostra
Lange Voorhut 35
2514 EC
The Hague
Holland
Tel: **317-035 17865**
Devoted to preserving Europe's national and cultural heritage, improving the environment and encouraging high standards of town and country planning.

Europe Conservation
Via Fusetti, 14
20143 Milano
Italy
Tel: **2-5810 3135**
Charity which runs ecological and archaeological holiday and research programmes in Europe's parks and nature reserves.

Field Studies Council
Central Services
Preston
Montford Hall
Montford Bridge
Shrewsbury
SY4 1DX
Tel: **0742-850674**
Devoted to promoting environmental awareness, the council runs courses and expeditions in the UK and overseas.

Field Studies Council Overseas
Mrs Anne Stephens, Overseas
Expeditions Co-ordinator
Montford Bridge
Shrewsbury SY4 1HW
Tel: **0743 850164**
Runs environmental study courses of one to three weeks' duration in countries ranging from the Orkneys to the Galapagos Islands.

Friends of the Earth
26 Underwood Street
London N1 7JT
Tel: **071-490 1555**
Campaigning organization promoting policies which protect the natural environment.

Green Flag International
PO Box 396
Linton
Cambridgeshire CB1 6UL
Environmental consultancy for the tourism industry and the general travelling public.

Greenpeace
30-31 Islington Green
London N1 8XE
Tel: **071-354 5100**
International environmental pressure group.

Interface – North-South Travel
Moulsham Mill Centre
Parkway
Chelmsford
Essex CM2 7PX
Tel: **0245 492882**
A travel agency which ploughs back its profits into development projects in the Third World.

International Union for the Conservation of Natural Resources (IUCN)
World Conservation Centre
Avenue de Mont Blanc
CH-1196 Gland
Switzerland
International organization co-ordinating the work of various charities working in the field of conservation.

Marine Conservation Society
9 Gloucester Road
Ross-on-Wye
Herefordshire HR9 5BU
Tel: **09895 66017**

Mediterranean Action Plan (MAP)
48 Vassileos Konstnatinou Avenue
11635 Athens
Greece
Tel: **301-7244536**
Conservation body which carries out research into the protection of the Mediterranean coastal and marine environment.

National Trust Discovery Holidays
Oliver York Travel
1 Starnes Court
Union Street
Maidstone ME14 1EB
Tel: **0622 691042**
A variety of art, architectural and garden tours, a percentage of holiday costs goes towards National Trust special appeals.

National Trust for Scotland
5 Charlotte Square
Edinburgh EH2 5DU
Tel: **031-226 5922**
A variety of cruises around the world, the profits of which go to the Islands Fund

Naturetrek
40 The Dean
Arlesford SO24 9AZ
Tel: **0962 733051**
Birdwatching, natural history and botanical tours worldwide, donate a percentage of profits to environmental charities.

English Nature
Northmister House
Peterborough PE1 1UA
Tel: **0733 40345**
Aims to raise public awareness of conservation issues and will act as a consultancy on environmental matters.

Reef and Rainforest Tours
205 North End Road
London W14 9NP
Tel: **071-381 2204**
Small outfit running wildlife and diving tours to Peru, Belize, Ecuador and Costa Rica.

Royal Society for the Protection of Birds (RSPB)
The Lodge
Sandy
Bedfordshire SG19 2DL
Tel: **0767 80551**

Save the Rhino International
4th Floor
105 Park Street
London W1Y 3FB
Tel: **071-409 7981**
Offer unique safaris to Namibia to see desert rhinos, and then the proceeds of the safari go directly to protecting them.

Survival International
310 Edgware Road
London W2 1DY
Tel: **071-723 5535**
Charity devoted to protecting the human rights of the world's tribal peoples.

Tourism Concern
Froebel College
Roehampton Lane
London SW15 5PU
Tel: **081-994 0464**
Founded in the late 1980s, the organization runs regular seminars and meetings dealing with tourism development, and aims to link interested parties concerned with tourism development – especially in the Third World.

Tourism with Insight
Hadorfer Strasse 9
D-8130 Starnberg
Germany
A consortium of concerned organizations (including Tourism concern) promoting 'green' tourism

University Research Expeditions Program
University of California
Berkeley
CA 94720
Tel: **510-642 6586**
Organizes a range of expeditions from Environmental studies to Art and Culture.

Vacations for Wildlife
2 Elizabeth Cottage
Mead Lane
Bognor Regis PO22 8AB
Tel: **0243 866287**
Small groups stay in native accommodation for birdwatching and natural history holidays in destinations including the Gambia and British Columbia. Raising funds for tree planting and environmental education in the Gambia.

Whale and Dolphin Conservation Society
Alexander House
James Street West
Bath
Avon BA1 2BT
Tel: **0225 334511**

World Wide Fund for Nature (WWF)
Weyside Park
Catteshall Lane
Godalming
Surrey GU7 1XR
Tel: **0483 426444**
Major international nature conservancy body which concerns itself with all aspects of the environment including the problems associated with tourism development.

Adventure and sporting

Access Tours
5th Floor 58 Pitt St
Sydney
NSW 2070
Australia
Tel: **2-241 1128**
Activity holidays in the former Soviet Union and Southeast Asia.

Adirondack Mountain Club
174 Glen St
Glens Falls
NY 12801
USA
Tel: **518-793 7737**
Founded in 1922, the ADK is a non-profit

membership organization. Works to retain the wilderness and magic of New York's Adirondack and Catskill parks. Assists in construction and maintenance of trails and campsites, shelters and permanent facilities on private land acquired for that purpose. Hiking, skiing, snow-shoeing, canoeing and mountaineering. Winter mountaineering schools, canoe and wilderness skills workshops, rock climbing schools and other programmes. Publish a series of guidebooks for Adirondack and Catskill Mountains of New York and other books on the Adirondacks. Several types of membership available. For details write to above address.

Airtrack Services Ltd
16-17 Windsor Street
Uxbridge
Middlesex
UB8 1AB
Tel: **0895 810 810**
Organizes sporting holidays around the world, from bungy jumping in Switzerland to tickets for the IndyCar championships in the US

Alternative Travel Group
1-3 George St
Oxford OX1 2AZ
Tel: **0865 251196**
Walking and trekking holidays for groups and individuals in Europe

Andrews Safaris
PO Box 31993
Lusaka
Zambia
Foot safaris in the Luangwa.

Appalachian Trail Conference
Box 807
Harpers Ferry
WV 25425
USA

The American Hiking Society
1701 18th St NW
Washington DC 20009
USA

Arctic Experience
29 Nork Way
Banstead SM7 1PB
Tel: **0737 362321**
Specialists in tours to the Arctic and Sub Arctic. Most holidays custom-made.

Aventura
52 Gatwick Road
Worthing BN11 4BH
Tel: **0903 201784**
Trail riding holidays in Spain's Sierra Nevada.

The Backpackers club
PO Box 381
Reading RG3 4RL

Bike Events
4 Edgar Building
George Street
Bath BA2 2EE
Tel: **0225 480130**

British Activity Holiday Association (BAHA)
Rock Park
Llandrindod Wells
Powys
Wales LD1 6AE
Tel: **0597 3902**
Provides information on activity holidays in the UK.

The British Association of Parachute Clubs (BAPC)
18 Talbot Lane
Leicester LE1 4LR
Tel: **0533 530318**

British Balloon and Airship Club
PO Box 1006
Birmingham B5 5RT
Tel: **021-643 3224**
Information and advice on all aspects of ballooning.

British Canoe Union (BCU)
Adbolton Lane
West Bridgeford
Nottinghamshire NT2 5AS
Tel: **0602 821100**
Advice and information on courses, clubs, etc.

British Gliding Association
Kimberley House
47 Vaughan Way
Leicester LE1 4SE
Tel: **0533 531051**

British Hang Gliding Association
Cranfield Airfield
Cranfield
Beds MK43 0YR
Tel: **0234 751688**

British Mountaineering Council (BMC)
Crawford House
Precinct Centre
Booth St East
Manchester M13 9RZ
Tel: **061-273 5835**
Reference books and information on all aspects of mountaineering.

British Orienteering Federation
Riverdale
Dale Road North

Darley Dale
Matlock
Derbyshire DE4 2HX
Tel: **0629 734042**

British Parachute Association
Kimberley House
47 Vaughan Way
Leicester LE1 4SG
Tel: **0533 519778**

British Sub-Aqua Club
16 Upper Woburn Place
London WC1H 0QW
Tel: **071-387 9302**
Diving instruction through regional branches and a diving holidays information service.

Canadian Wilderness Trips
187 College St
Toronto
Ontario M5T 1P7
Canada
Tel: **416-977 3703**
Whitewater rafting and canoeing in Northern Ontario.

Continental Divide Trail Society
PO Box 30002
Bethesda
MD 20814
USA

Destination USA
Clipstone House
Hospital Road
Hounslow TW3 3HT
Tel: **081-577 1786**
Golfing holidays in the USA.

Encounter Overland
267 Old Brompton Road
London SW5 9JA
Tel: **071-370 6845**
Worldwide adventure travel, with tours lasting as long as 29 weeks.

Erna Low Consultants
9 Reece Mews
London SW7 3HE
Tel: **071-584 2841**
Golfing and spa holidays in Europe.

Eurogolf
156 Hatfield Road
St Albans AL1 4JD
Tel: **0727 42256**
Golfing holidays worldwide

Exodus Expeditions
9 Weir Road
London SW12 0LT
Tel: **081-673 0779**

Varied itineraries for offbeat, adventurous holidays.

Expeditions Inc
Route 4
Box 755
Flagstaff
Arizona 86001
USA
Tel: **602-774 8176**
Kyaking and rafting tours in the Grand Canyon.

Explore
1 Frederick Street
Aldershot
GU11 1LQ
Tel: **0252 333031**
Adventure tours around the world and walking holidays.

Flamingo Tours Ltd
PO Box 44899
Nairobi
Kenya
Camel safaris in the Samburu.

Four Corners School of Outdoor Education
East Route
Monicello
Utah 84535
USA
Tel: **801-587 2859**
Adventure activities in the Colorado Plateau from 14 years old upwards including backpacking and rafting.

Globepost Travel Services
324 Kennington Park Road
London SE11 4PD
Tel: **071-735 1879**
Motorcycling in north-eastern China.

Go Fishing
Swan Centre
Fishers Lane
London W4 1RX
Tel: **081-742 3700**
Organizes fishing trips to the Falklands Islands, Canada, and the USA

Golf en France
Model Farm
Rattlesden
Bury St Edmunds
Suffolk
IP30 0SY
Tel: **0449 737664**

Guerba Expeditions
101 Eden Vale Road
Westbury BA13 3QX
Tel: **0373 826611**
Camping tours to Africa.

International Adventure
Melbourn St
Royston
Herts SG8 7BP
Tel: **0763 242867**
Winter sports holidays above the Arctic Circle.

The International Long River Canoeist Club
c/o Peter Salisbury
238 Birmingham Road, Redditch
Worcs B97 6EL
*The International Long River Canoeist Club is
the only United Kingdom association that can
offer details of thousands of rivers around the
World, from the As in France to the Zambezi in
Zambia, from the Alesk in Canada/Alaska to the
Zure in Zuire. Members in 26 countries ready to
offer help and advice.*

Journey Latin America
14-16 Devonshire Road
Chiswick
London W4 2HD
Tel: **081-747 3108**
*Large selection of South American tours to suit
all pockets.*

The London Underwater Centre
13 Glendower Road
London SW14 8NY
Tel: **081-876 0735**
*Scuba diving holidays worldwide for reason-
ably experienced divers.*

Motor Safari
Pinfold Lane
Buckley
Clwyd CH7 3NS
Tel: **0244 548849**
*Jeep mountain safaris, squad biking and
amphibious vehicles in Wales and Cyprus.*

Outward Bound Trust
Chestnut Field
Regent Place
Rugby CV21 2PJ
Tel: **0788 560423**
Adventure holidays in off-beat regions of UK.

Pacific Crest Club
PO Box 1907
Santa Ana
CA 92702
USA

The Ramblers Association
1-5 Wandsworth Road
London SW8 2XX

Ramblers Holidays
PO Box 43
Welwyn Garden City AL8 6PQ
Tel: **0707 331133**

*Walking holidays throughout Europe from an
offshoot of the Ramblers' Association.*

Safari Drive Ltd
104 Warriner Gardens,
London SW11 4DU
Tel: 071-622 3891
*Organises self-drive safaris in Africa, also
white water rafting and microlighting.*

Sheerwater
PO Box 125
Victoria Falls
Zimbabwe
Canoe trips along the Zambezi.

The Sierra Club
730 Polk St
San Francisco
CA 94109
Tel: **415-776 2211**
Every sort of adventure holiday.

Ski Challenge
16-17 Windsor Street
Uxbridge
Middlesex UB8 1AB
Tel: **0895 810810**
Snowboarding in the Alps

Ski Club of Great Britain
118 Eaton Square
London SW1W 9AF
Tel: **071-245 1033**
*Offers members: unbiased advice on resorts,
travel and equipment; snow reports; club flights
and special discounts; reps in the Alps and UK;
British Ski Tests; unique skiing parties for all
standards and ages; artificial slope courses for
intermediate and advanced skiers; insurance;
Ski Survey magazine and a busy programme of
lectures, film-shows and parties at the Club
House in central London. Ski Club Winter
Arrangements Ltd runs annual holidays.*

Ski Alpine
Alpine Adventure Club
1 West Bank
Richmond Road
Bowden
Altrincham
Cheshire WA14 2TY
Tel: **061-928 2737**
*Summer skiing holidays combined with
mountaineering, canoeing, windsurfing etc.*

Sobeck Expeditions Inc
Box 1089
Angels Camp
California 95222
USA
Tel: **800-777 7939**

Sporting International
13201 Northwest Freeway
Suite 800
Houston
TX 77040
USA
Tel: **713-744 5260**
They control Ker, Downey and Selby who have vast concessions for safaris in the Okavango, notably Pom Pom, Shinid Island and Mahcaba.

The Survival Club
The Square
Moorland
Cumbria CA10 3AZ
Offers a range of courses, adventure trips and expeditions to members, including litter-clearance projects, and survival training.

Tana Delta Ltd
PO Box 24988
Nairobi
Kenya
River journeys along the Tana Delta aboard the African Queen.

Travel Alternative
27 Park End Street
Oxford OX1 1HU
Tel: **0865 791636**
Trekking, riding and abseiling worldwide.

Voluntary

Action Health 2000
International Voluntary Health Association
The Director
The Bath House
Gwydir St
Cambridge CB1 2LW
Tel: **0223 460853**
Charitable organization which places medical school, nursing and physiotherapy students in voluntary health programmes in developing countries.

British Executive Service Overseas
164 Vauxhall Bridge Road
London SW1 2RB
Tel: **071-630 0644**
Consider retired applicants with lots of experience to advise projects overseas using technical and managerial skills. Short-term placements on an expenses only basis.

British Trust for Conservation Volunteers
36 St Mary's Street
Wallingford
Oxon OX10 0EU
Tel: **0491 39766**
Practical conservation work and training courses for all age groups throughout England,

Wales, Northern Ireland and overseas (18+ for overseas placements), including leadership courses.

Bureau for Overseas Medical Service
Africa Centre
38 King Street
London WC2 8JT
Tel: **071-836 5833**
Provides details of job vacancies and training for health workers in developing countries.

Catholic Institute for International Relations
22 Coleman Fields
London WC2E 8JT
Tel: **071 354 0883**
Recruits skilled, qualified people for minimum of two year's work experience overseas.

Christians Abroad
1 Stockwell Green
London SW9 9HP
Tel: **071-222 9011**
Places qualified workers, mainly teachers, abroad for two year minimum placements, committed Christians preferred.

Christian Outreach
1 New Street
Leamington Spa
Warwickshire CV31 1HP
Tel: **0926 315301**
Welcomes well-qualified applicants for one year minimum for overseas placements, but must have Christian commitment.

Christian Service Centre
Unit 2
Holloway St West
Lower Gornal
West Midlands
DY3 2DZ
Short and long term voluntary opportunities for work overseas ranging from missionary work to engineering and farming.

CIT
7b Broad Street
Nottingham NG1 3AJ
Tel: **0606 470906**
Skilled people wanting short-term 3-6 month placements. Pay own fares and expenses. Africa and Nicaragua.

Concordia (Youth Service Volunteers)
8 Brunswick Place
Hove
Sussex BN3 1ET
Tel: **0273 772086**
International voluntary work camps, should be over 17. Accommodation provided but not expenses.

Community Service Volunteers
237 Pentonville Road
London N1 9NJ
Tel: **071-278 6601**
*Provides volunteering opportunities for people
aged 16-35, helping people in need for period of
4-12 months, in the UK. Volunteers work with
people with physical disabilities and learning
difficulties in the community.*

Council Of Churches for Britain and Ireland
Youth Matters,
35-41 Lower Marsh
London SE1 7RL
Tel: **071-620 4444**
*Part of international interdominational youth
service of the Ecumenical Youth Council in
Europe. Groups of young people to carry out
four-week projects.*

East European Partnership (EEP)
317 Putney Bridge Road
Putney
London SW15
Tel: **081-780 2841**
*Part of VSO. English teachers needed in East
European countries. Special education teachers
and others required for Albania.*

Gap Activity Projects
Gap House
44 Queens Road
Reading
Berkshire RG1 4BB
Tel: **0734 594914**
*Offers school leavers 17+ employment abroad
before going to university. Apply 1st term of
final year at school.*

Health Projects Abroad
HMS President
Victoria Embankment
London EC4 OHJ
Tel: **071-583 5727**
*Volunteers, 18-28, needed with a willingness to
work hard in a team for four month in Tanzania.
Must raise over £2,450 for travel and project.*

Health Unlimited
3 Stamford Street
London SE1 9NT
Tel: **071-928 8105**
*Recruits volunteers for one year or more in
primary health care, including health educators
and nutritionists.*

H.E.L.P. (Scotland)
60 The Pleasance
Edinburgh EH8 9TJ
Tel: **031-556 9497**
*Work camps run by a committee of Scottish
students. Expansion planned into long term*

*projects and to other Scottish Universities,
working in E. Europe and the Third World.*

**International Cooperation For Development
(ICD)**
Unit 3
Canonbury Yard
190a New North Road
London N1 7BJ
Tel: **071-354 0883**
*Qualified, experienced argriculturalists,
technical and health people for two years in
Nicaragua, Peru, Honduras, Ecuador, El
salvador, Dominican Rep, Yemen, Zimbabwe
and Namibia.*

International Voluntary Service (IVS)
Old Hall
East Bergholt
Colchester
Essex CO7 6TQ
*Arranges short term placements in Work
camps, welfare and manual projects for mixed
nationality teams in the UK, Europe and USA.*

International Voluntary Service (IVS)
162 Upper New Walk
Leicester LE1 7QA
Tel: **0533 549430**

Involvement Volunteers
PO Box 218
Port Melbourne
Victoria 3207
Australia
*Opportunities for voluntary conservation
projects.*

Kibbutz Representatives
1a Accommodation Road
London NW11
Tel: **081-458 9235**
*Working Holidays on Kibbutzim in Israel. Must
be 18-32 years. Applicants pay air fare and
insurance. Free board and small allowance.*

Project 67
10 Hatton Garden
London EC1N 8AH
Tel: **071-831 7626**
Kibbutz and Moshav voluntary work in Israel.

Project Trust
The Hebridean Centre
Bally Hough
Isle of Coll
PA78 6TE
Tel: **0879 3444**
*Opportunities for young people 17 to 19 years
to serve in developing countries, 3-12 month
projects. Must be in full time education at time
of application. Volunteer must raise part of the
costs.*

Quaker International Social Projects
Friends House
173-177 Euston Road
London NW1 2BJ
Tel: **071-387 3601**

Raleigh International
27 Parsons Green Lane
London SW6 4HS
Tel: **071-371 8585**
Organises challenging expeditions worldwide, based around community conservation, for young people aged 17-25, also skilled people over 25 years.

Skillshare Africa
3 Belvoir Street
Leicester LE1 6SL
Tel: **0533 541862**
Offers qualified and experienced people opportunities for working in southern Africa for a minimum of two years.

Teaching Abroad
10 Drew Street
Brixham
Devon TQ5 9JU
Tel: **0803 855 565**
Opportunities to teach conversational English in Moldavia, Romania and Ukraine, for graduates, undergraduates and those delaying entry in to university. All year from one month to one year. Volunteers pay for accommodation and travel.

Tear Fund Gap Programme
100 Church Road
Teddington Middlesex
TW11 8QE
Tel: **081-977 9144**
Christian organisation with strong development programmes, needing qualified volunteers prepared to serve two to four years.

Third World First
232 Cowley Road
Oxford OX4 1HU
Tel: **865 245678**
Organises student groups in the UK, can help with useful addresses.

Unias
Suite 3a
Hunter House
57 Goodramgate
York YO1 2LS
Tel: **0904 647799**
Agricultural, health and engineering professionals needed for two years in Brazil, Bolivia, Burkina Faso, Mali, West Bank and Gaza.

United Nations Volunteers (UNV)
Palais des Nations
1211 Geneva 10
Switzerland
Tel: **010 4122 798 5850**
Qualified volunteers from all members of the UN needed with relevant experience. Normally two years but shorter humanitarian relief work also. British Passport holders enquire through VSO London.

Universities' Educational Fund for Palestinian Refugees (UNIPAL)
Volunteer Programme Organiser
12 Helen Road
Oxford OX2 0DE
Voluntary English teachers for education and caring programme in the occupied West Bank and in the Gaza Strip.

University of California Research Expeditions Programme (UREP)
Desk L University of California
Berkeley
CA 94270 USA
Tel: **415-642 6586**
Will take inexperienced volunteers on UREP expeditions world-wide. Wide variety of areas and subjects.

US Peace Corp
Washington DC 20526
USA
Places volunteers in 62 developing countries. Volunteers with all kinds of backgrounds are accepted, though naturally those with specific skills, being more in demand, are easier to place.

Vacation Work International
9 Park End Street
Oxford OX1 1HJ
Tel: **0865 241978**
Produces useful, regularly updated, publications on work, travel and study abroad.

Volunteers for Peace
43 Tiffany Road
Belmont
Vermont 05730
USA
Tel: **802-259 2759**
Publishes an International Work Camp Directory, featuring voluntary opportunities in work camps worldwide.

Voluntary Service Overseas
317 Putney Bridge Road
London SW15 2PN
Tel: **071-780 2266**
Volunteers are selected from people with skills and qualifications eg. teaching, nursing,

agriculturalists, social workers, carpenters to work in the Third World. Volunteers must be aged between 20 and 65 and prepared to work for 2 years minimum. VSO pay the volunteer's airfare and a small wage and living accommodation are provided by the host country.

VSO Canada
Lynn Sim
35 Centennial Boulevard
Ottawa
KIY 2H8
Recruiting Canadian experienced, qualifies, teachers and foresters for VSO.

World Council of Churches
Ecumenical Youth Action
150 Route de Ferney
PO Box 2100
1211 Genera 2
Switzerland
Tel: **791 6111**
Opportunities for young volunteers aged 18 to 30 to work in international work camps contributing to local and national development in developing countries.

For further information there are many useful books available including: "International Directory of Voluntary Work" and "Directory of Work and Study in Developing Countries" published by Vacation Work, 9 Park End Street, Oxford OX1 1HJ and "Volunteer Work" published by the Central Bureau for Educational Visits and Exchange, Seymour Mews, London W1H 9PE, Tel: 071-486 5101.

Expeditionary

Alpine Club
118 Eaton Square
London SW1 9AF
Tel: **071-259 5591**
Has an important reference collection of mountaineering literature, guidebooks and map. View by appointment only.

Archaeology Abroad
31-34 Gordon Square
London WC1 0PY
Tel: **071-387 7050**
Archaeology Abroad provides information about opportunities for archaeological field work and excavations outside Britain. Archaeologists, students of archaeology and specialists who wish to be considered for archaeological work abroad are enrolled and information is provided on request to organizers of excavations who wish to recruit personnel. Others interested in archaeology,

and preferably with some experience of excavation, are also eligible.

Brathay Exploration Group
Brathay Hall
Ambleside
Cumbria LA22 0HP
Tel: **05394 33942**
Provides expedition and training opportunities for young people – 40 years of experience. Write to the Expeditions Coordinator for details.

British Schools Exploring Society
1 Kensington Gore
London SW7 2AR
Tel: **071-584 0710**
Organises major adventurous and scientific expeditions each year for 17 to 20 year olds.

Earthquest
54 Sunderland Terrace
Ulverston
Cumbria LA12
Tel: **0229 57885**
Runs worldwide research and development expeditions, volunteer leaders and support staff required.

Earthwatch
Belsyre Court
57 Woodstock Road
Oxford OX2 6HU
Tel: **0865 311600**
Environmental charity which matches paying volunteers to scientific research projects worldwide.

Erskine Expeditions
16 Braid Farm Road
Edinburgh EH10 6LF
Tel: **031-447 7218**
Organizes adventure tours in Arctic regions including dog-sledging, mountaineering and cross-country skiing.

Expedition Advisory Centre
Royal Geographical Society
1 Kensington Gore
London SW7 2AR
Tel: **071-581 2057**
The Expedition Advisory Centre provides an information and training service for those planning expeditions. It was founded by the Royal Geographical Society and the Young Explorer's Trust. In addition to organizing a variety of seminars and publications including The Expedition Planners' Handbook and Directory, the Advisory Centre maintains a database for expedition planners. This includes a register of planned expeditions, lists of

expedition consultants and suppliers, information on individual countries and a register of personnel who have offered their services to expeditions. Write with s.a.e. to the Information Officer for further details.

Exploration Logistics
Rank Xerox Business Park
Mitcheldean
Gloucestershire GL17 0DD
Tel: **0594-544733**
Tailor-made support service for expeditions, with consultancy, design and purchase of equipment, survival courses and field support.

The Explorers Club
46 East 70th St
New York
NY 10021 USA
Tel: **212- 628 83 83**
Founded in 1904 and dedicated to the search for new knowledge of the earth and outer space. It serves as a focal point and catalyst in the identification and stimulation of institutional exploration, independent investigators and students.

The club has over 3000 members who continue to contribute actively to the constructive role of the explorer. The classes of membership are Member, Fellow, Student, Corporate, each class being divided into Resident (living within 50 miles of the Headquarters) and Non-Resident. The Club has financed over 140 expeditions and awarded its flag to over 300 expeditions.

The James B Ford Memorial Library contains over 25,000 items, including maps, charts, archives and photographs, and is probably the largest private collection in North America wholly devoted to exploration.

Foundation for Field Research
PO Box 2010
Alpine
California 92001
USA
Sponsors research expeditions and finds volunteers to staff projects.

Iceland Information Centre
PO Box 434
Harrow
Middlesex HA1 3HY
Specializes in expeditions to Iceland and publishes useful Iceland: the Traveller's Guide.

National Geographical Society
17th and M Streets, NW
Washington DC 20036
USA
The Society's aim is to pursue and promulgate

geographical knowledge and to promote research and exploration. The Society often sponsors significant expeditions.

Mountain and Wildlife Adventures
Brow Foot
High Wray
near Ambleside
Cumbria LA22 0JE
Tel: **05394-33285**
Specializes in travel and expedition advice for Scandinavia.

Operation Raleigh
The Power House
Alpha Place
Flood Street
London SW3 5SZ
Tel: **071-351 7541**
Runs a series of international expeditions for young people aged 17-25, with one Executive Expedition each year where there is no upper age limit. Tasks include conservation and community projects.

Dick Phillips
Whitehall House
Nenthead Alston
Cumbria CA9 3PS
Long-established specialist in travel in those parts of Iceland beyond the interests of the mainstream travel trade.

Quest Ltd
Cow Pasture Farm
Louth Road
Hainton
Lincoln LN3 6LX
Directors Ken and Julie Slavin are expedition and aid consultants offering complete support services to individual and commercial clients on projects throughout the world. They are advisers to Land Rover Ltd in the expeditionary field and have a special franchise for the direct export of expedition-equipped Land Rovers and Range Rovers.

Royal Geographical Society
1 Kensington Gore London
SW7 2AR
Tel: **071-589 5466**
A focal point for geographers and explorers. It directly organizes and finances its own scientific expeditions and gives financial support, approval and advice to numerous expeditions each year. The Society honour outstanding geographers and explorers with a series of annual medals and awards.

The RGS maintains the largest private map collection in Europe and has a large library with books and periodicals on geography, travel and exploration. There is also an archive of historical records and expedition reports. There are regular lectures, children's lectures, discussions, symposia and academic meetings in the society's 760-seat lecture hall. Most of the leading names in exploration, mountaineering and geography have addressed the Society.

Anyone with a geographical interest can apply for a Fellowship of the RGS. An applicant must be proposed and seconded by existing Fellows.

Royal Scottish Geographical Society
10 Randolph Crescent
Off Queensbury St
Edinburgh EG3 7TU
Tel: 031-225 3330
Also has centres in Aberdeen, Dundee, Dunfermline and Glasgow. It offers the following classes of Membership: Ordinary, Life, Student Associate, Junior, School Corporate, Country Areas, and Overseas. The society houses a library, a map collection and over 200 periodicals. It arranges tours, excursions and lectures, and sells map reproductions and publications.

Scientific Exploration Society
Honorary Secretary, Phyllis Angliss
Waterpark
Frogmore
Kingsbridge
Devon TQ7 2NR
Tel: 0548-531450
Was formed in 1969 by a group of explorers, many of whom had been together on expeditions, with the aim of making their association more permanent so that personnel and useful equipment would not be dispersed but instead kept together for future undertakings. The society exists to organise expeditions and help others (universities, schools, services and individuals) organise their own. It maintains close links with commerce, industry, educational establishments, the services and other kindred scientific and exploration organisations. The society has 500 members, many of them expert explorers.

All are eligible to take part in expeditions. Fully sponsored expeditions generally appoint their Leader, Secretary and Treasurer and many of their personnel from among the Society's membership. Other expeditions can be given the approval and support of the SES by the council and may then borrow equipment, receive advice and use the SES name in their publicity.

Though the Society 'approves and supports' expeditions it rarely gives cash to any project.

Members have to be proposed and seconded by existing members, and then elected by the Council.

Scott Polar Research Institute
Lensfield Road
Cambridge CB2 1ER
Tel: 0223-336540
Has a specialist library concerned with all aspects of polar expeditions and research.

South American Explorers Club
Lima Clubhouse
Casilla 3714
Lima 100
Peru
Exists to promote travel and sporting aspects of exploration; and to record, co-ordinate and publicise academic research on a wide variety of natural and social sciences. Membership is open to all. It publishes a magazine, The South American Explorer.

The Club House, with reading rooms, maps and guidebooks is open most days and people are welcome to visit. The address is: Avenida Portugal 146, Brena District, Lima, Peru, near the US Embassy.

Trekforce
58 Battersea Park Road
London SW11 4JP
Tel: 071-498 0855
Mounts several expeditions each year to study the tropical forests of Indonesia.

University Research Expeditions Program
University of California
Berkeley
CA 94720
Tel: 510-642 6586
Organizes a range of expeditions from Environmental studies to Art and Culture.

Vander-Molen Foundation
The Model Farm House
Church End
Hendon
London NW4 4JS
Tel: 081-203 2344/1214
Helps to organise expeditions especially for the handicapped.

World Challenge Expeditions
Walham House
Walham Grove
London SW6 1QP
Tel: 071-386 9828
Month-long, fee-paying projects in a variety of locations with the emphasis on personal development for the 16-20 year old age group.

Young Explorers Trust (The Association of British Youth Exploration Societies)
The Royal Geographical Society
1 Kensington Gore
London SW7 2AR
Exists to promote youth exploration and to provide a forum within which societies and individuals can exchange information and act together for their mutual benefit. It does not organise its own expeditions or make travel bookings. The Trust is a registered charity.

Membership is open to groups or societies wishing to take part in the Trust's activities and to contribute to the Trust's aims. Present members include all major national and regional bodies active in the field of youth expeditions as well as school and university groups.

The Trust has a team of volunteer regional co-ordinators to assist with the flow of information and to provide a local focus for members as well as being the 'first link' for the 'unattached' youngster, enabling them to join in adventurous activities.

Awards and Grants

BP Conservation Expedition Award
32 Cambridge Road
Girton Cambridge CB3 0DL
Tel: **0223-277318**
Is jointly administered by the International Council for Bird Preservation and the Fauna and Flora Preservation Society. Each year a total of 20,000 is given in grant funding in the following categories: Tropical Rainforests, Wetlands, Oceanic Islands, and Globally Threatened Environments. Detailed guide-lines for conditions of entry are available on request. Closing dates for applications 31st December.

Mount Everest Foundation
Hon Secretary: W H (Bill)
Ruthven Gowrie
Cardwell Close
Warton
Preston PR4 1SH
Tel: **0772-635346**
Sponsors British and New Zealand expeditions only, proposing new routes or research in high mountain regions. For grant application forms write to above address. Closing dates August 31 and December 31 for the following year. Give 40-50 grants a year from 300 to 1000.

The Rolex Awards for Enterprise
The Secretariat
PO Box 178
1211 Geneva 26
Switzerland
The Rolex Awards provide financial assistance for persons who have manifested the spirit of enterprise in order to bring to fruition projects which are off the beaten track and come within three broad fields of human endeavour: Applied Sciences and Invention, Exploration and Discovery, the Environment. The Rolex Awards enjoy world renown. To enter: send for official application form from the 'Rolex Awards for Enterprise Secretariat' at the above address. Project description must be in English.

Royal Geographical Society
1 Kensington Gore
London SW7 2AR
Tel: **071-589 5466**
Administer not only their own awards and grants but those of many other sponsors. Details and applications from the Administrative Secretary at the above address. Applications to be submitted by January 31st each year. (See article on expeditionary travel, Chapter 3.)

WEXAS International
Awards administered by The Royal Geographical Society. Write for details to: The Information Officer, The Royal Geographical Society, 1, Kensington Gore, London SW7 2AR.

Winston Churchill Memorial Trust
15 Queens Gate Terrace
London SW7 5PR
The Winston Churchill Memorial Trust awards about 100 travelling Fellowships annually to enable UK citizens, irrespective of their age or educational achievements, to carry out study projects overseas in approximately 10 categories of interest or occupation which are varied annually. Grants are not normally given for formal or academic studies.

Young Explorers Trust
Royal Geographical Society
1 Kensington Gore
London SW7 2AR
Gives grants to school expeditions.

Further reading:
The International Directory of Voluntary Work (Vacation Work)
Volunteer Work (Central Bureau)
Expedition Planners' Handbook (Expedition Advisory Centre)

Educational and Exchange

ACE Study Tours
Babraham
Cambridge CB2 4AP
Tel: **0223 835055**
Established in 1958, the Association of Cultural Exchange runs worldwide study tours.

Anglo French Walks
8 Westward Avenue
Rishton
Blackburn BB1 4BZ
Tel: **0254 885738**
Language learning combined with walking in France.

Council of Churches of Britain and Ireland
Youth Unit
Inter-Church House
38-41 Lower Marsh
London SE1 7RL
Tel: **071-620 4444**
Promotes international exchanges between young Christians.

Central Bureau for Education Visits and Exchanges
Seymour Mews House
London W1H 9PE
Tel: **071-486 5101**
and...
3 Bruntsfield Crescent
Edinburgh EH10 4HD
Tel: **031-447 8024**
and...
16 Malone Road
Belfast BT9 5BN
Tel: **0232-664418/9**
The national organisation responsible for the provision of information and advice on all forms of educational visits and exchanges. The font of all knowledge and wisdom on the subject and publisher of a number of useful booklets and books including: Working Holidays, Volunteer Work, Study Holidays, and Home from Home: a comprehensive guide to international homestays.

Commonwealth Youth Exchange Programme
7 Lion Yard
Tremadoc Road
Clapham
London SW4 7NF
Tel: **071-498 6151**
Promotes two-way exchange visits by young people between 16 and 25 in Britain and developing countries of the Commonwealth.

Council on International Education Exchange (CIEE)
205 East 42nd Street
New York
NY10017
USA
Tel: **212-661 1414**

Cultural and Educational Services Abroad
Western House
Malpas
Truro TR1 1SQ
Tel: **0273 683304**
Language learning courses in Europe, Russia and Japan.

En Famille Overseas
The Old Stables
60b Maltravers Street
Arundel
W Sussex BN18 9BG
Tel: **0903-883266**
Stay as a paying guest with a French family and language courses in Paris also available.

European Community Young Worker Exchange Programme
Central Bureau for Educational Visits and Exchanges
Vocational and Education Department
Seymour Mews
London W1H 9PE
Tel: **071-486 5101**
EC nationals aged 18 to 25 with vocational experience can apply for placements lasting between three and 16 months.

Gap Activity Projects
44 Queens Road
Reading
Berkshire RG1 4BB
Tel: **0734 594914**
Provides school leavers with work experience opportunities overseas including the Soviet Union, Poland and China.

Goodwill Holidays
Manor Chamber
The Green
School Lane
Welwyn AL6 9EB
Tel: **0438-71 6421**
Holidays in the CIS that provide an opportunity to gain insight into the culture, society and politics.

Headwater Holidays
146 London Road
Northwich
Cheshire
CW9 5HH
Tel: **0606-48699**
Runs holidays called Accents, in France, which

offers language sessions in the morning and local guided tours in the afternoon.

Inscape Fine Art Tours
Austins Farm
High Street
Stonesfield
Whitney
Oxon OX9 8PU
Tel: **0933 891726**
Fine-art study tours to Europe.

International Educational Opportunities
28 Canterbury Road
Lydden
Dover
Kent CT15 7ER
Tel: **0304 823631**
An educational agency arranging language courses, homestays and term stays abroad.

International Farm Experience Programme
YFC Centre
National Agricultural Centre
Kenilworth
Warwickshire CV8 2LG
Offers opportunities for young agriculturist and horticulturists to further their knowledge through international exchanges.

International Association for the Exchange of Students for Technical Experience (IAESTE-UK)
Seymour Mews House
Seymour Mews
London W1H 9PE
Tel: **071-486 5101**
Worldwide opportunities for undergraduates to gain industrial, technical or commercial experience.

Le Touron
St Mayme de Pareyrol
24380 Vergt
France
Tel: **53-54 7907**
Offers dinner party cookery courses and wine safari weeks in France.

LSG Theme Holidays
201 Main Street
Thornton
Leicestershire
Tel: **0509-231713**
Conversational French in all areas of France.

Painting School of Montmiral
Rue de la Port Neuve
81140 Castelnau de Montmiral
Tel: **010 33 63 33 1311**
Painting courses with individual tuition.

Study Tour Service
39 Burgess Road
Bassett
Southampton S01 7AP
Special interest study holidays for the over 50s.

Youth for Understanding
International Exchange
3501 Newark St, NW
Washington DC 20016
USA
Tel: **202-966 6800**
Devoted to promoting world peace through high school student exchange programmes worldwide. Large and established organization.

Special interest

Amathus
51 Tottenham Court Road
London W1P 0HS
Tel: **071-636 9873**
Archaeological tours to Greece.

Animal Watch
Manama House
Hollybush Lane
Sevenoaks
Kent TN13 3TL
Tel: **0732-741612**
Wildlife tours around the world.

Arblaster and Clarke
104 Church Road
Steep
Petersfield GU32 2DD
Tel: **0730 66883**
European wine tours.

Art of Travel Ltd
268 Lavender Hill
London SW11 1Jl
Tel: **071-738 2038**
Tailor-made safaris.

Birdwatching Breaks
26 School Lane
Herne Bay
Kent CT6 7AL
Tel: **0227 740799**
Birdwatching holidays in Europe, Britain and North America.

Blair Travel
117 Regent's Park Road
London NW1 8UR
Tel: **071-483 2290**
Music holidays with either of two subsidiaries Travel for the Arts and Travel with the Friends (Friends of Covent Garden).

The British Institute
Palazzo Lanfredini
Lungarno Guicciardini, 9
Florence 50125
Italy
Tel: **55-284031**
Drawing and art history holidays in Florence.

British Museum Tours
46 Bloomsbury Street
London WC1B 3QQ
Tel: **071-323 3395**
Worldwide tours .

Butterfield's Tours
Burton Fleming,
Driffield
Yorkshire YO25 0PQ
Tel: **0262-470230**
Indian railway tours.

Camera Carriers
49 Bare Avenue
Morecambe LA4 6BD
Tel: **0524 411436**
Group photography holidays worldwide.

Cara Spencer Safaris
75 Weydon Hill Road
Farnham
Surrey GU9 8NY
Tel: **0252-424513**

Cricketer Holidays
4 The White House
Beacon Road
Crowborough
Kent TN6 1AB
Tel: **0892 664242**
Painting and drawing holidays.

Cygnus Wildlife Holidays
57 Fore St
Kingsbrige
Devon TQ7 1P6
Tel: **0548 856178**
Birdwatching and wildlife holidays.

David Sayers
Andrew Brock Travel Ltd
10 Barley Mow Passage
London W4 4PH
Tel: **081-995 3642**
or
54 High Street East
Uppingham
Rutland LE15 9PZ
Tel: **0572-821330**
Specialist in Botanical and Garden Travel

Eustudio al Raso
102 Fairfoot Road
Bow

London E3 4EH
Tel: **071-515 773**
Painting holidays in Sierra Nevada.

Explorers Tours
223 Coppermill Road
Wraysbury TW19 5NN
Tel: **0753 681999**
Astronomical tours.

Festival Tours International
BCM Festival Tours
London WC1N 3XX
Tel: **071-431 3086**
Music festival tours worldwide.

Francophiles Discover France
66 Great Brockeridge
Bristol BS9 3UA
Tel: **0272-621975**
Art and architecture tours and literature holidays to France.

Galina International Battlefield Tours
711 Beverley High Road
Hull HU6 7JN
Tel: **0482 804409**
Tours of Famous European battlefields.

Hosking Tours
Pages Green House
Wetheringsett
Stowmarket
Suffolk IP14 5QA
Tel: **0728-861113**
Wildlife photographic holidays.

James Keogh Tours
138 Hanworth Road
Hounslow
TW3 1UG
Tel: **081-570 4228**
Archaeology, art and architecture tours.

Jasmine Tours
23 High St
Chalfont St Peter
Bucks SL9 9QE
Tel: **0628 531121**
Long-haul archaeological tours.

Ker & Downey
13201 Northwest Freeway
Suite 850
Houston
Texas 77040-6096
Tel: **713-744 5260**
or
18 Albemarle Street
London W1X 3HA
Tel: **071-629 2044**
Tailor-made safaris in Africa and trekking in Nepal.

Limosa Holidays
Suffield House
Northrepps
Norfolk NR27 OLZ
Tel: **026378 8143**
Birdwatching.

Major and Mrs Holt's Battlefield Tours
The Golden Key Building
15 Market Street
Sandwich
Kent CT13 9DA
Tel: **0304-612248**
Battlefield tours.

Major R N Spafford
29 Queen's Road
Weston-Super-Mare
Avon BS23 2LH
Tel: **0934 622025**
Organises tours to the Falkland Islands for philatelists.

Martin Randall
Andrew Brock Travel Ltd
10 Barley Mow Passage
London W4 4PH
Tel: **081-995 3642**
or
54 High Street East
Uppingham
Rutland LE15 9PZ
Tel: **0572-821330**
Specialist in art history and architectural tours.

Middlebrook's Battlefield Tours
48 Linden Way
Boston PE21 9DS
Tel: **0205 364555**
Guided battlefield tours.

Naturetrek
Chautara
Bighton
Arlesford
Hants. SO24 9RB
Tel: **0962 733051**
Birdwatching and natural history.

Ornitholidays
1-3 Victoria Drive
Bognor Regis PO21 2PW
Tel: **0243 821230**
Established operator offering a large variety of birdwatching holidays worldwide.

Page and Moy
136-140 London Road
Leicester LE2 1EN
Tel: **0533 552521**
Established specialist operator offering motor racing holidays to Grand Prix events

worldwide, as well as golfing, music and archaeological tours.

Papyrus Tours
9 Rose Hill Court
Bessacarr
Doncaster DN4 5LY
Tel: **0302-530778**
Wildlife tours in East Africa.

Peregrine Holidays
41 South Parade
Oxford OX2 7JP
Tel: **0865-511642**
Birdwatching.

Photo Travellers
PO Box 58
Godalming
Surrey GU7 5BT
Tel: **0483 425448**
Escorted worldwide tours designed for photographers.

Prospect Music and Art
454-458 Chiswick High Road
London W4 5TT
Tel: **081-995 2151**
Worldwide music and art history tours.

Railroad Enthusiast Tours
PO Box 1997
Portoloa
California 96122
Tel: **916-836 1745**
Trains unlimited tours.

Reef and Rainforest Tours
205 North End Road
London W14 9NP
Tel: **071-381 2204**
Diving and natural history.

Snail's Pace
25 Thorpe Lane
Almondbury
Huddersfield HD5 8TA
Tel: **0484 426259**
Gentle, natural history tours.

Special Tours Ltd
81a Elizabeth Street
London SW1W 9PG
Tel: **071-730 2297**
Organises art history tours in behalf of the National Art Collections Fund

Steamond International
278 Battersea Park Road
London SW11 3BS
Tel: **071-978 5500**
Tailor made birdwatching, natural history and archaeology tours.

Swan Hellenic
77 New Oxford St
London WC1A 1PP
Tel: 071-831 1515
*Expertly guided archaeological and art history
cruises to Greece, Turkey, Egypt, Cyprus, Italy,
France, Spain, Portugal, Ireland, Scotland,
Morocco, Bulgaria, Tunisia, Syria, Jordan and
Israel.*

Twickers World
22 Church St
Twickenham TW1 3NW
Tel: 081-892 7606
*Established company offering birdwatching
and natural history tours around the world.
Also diving in the Red Sea.*

Vacations for Wildlife
29 Hedge End
Barnham
Bognor regis
PO22 OJP
Tel: 0243 552630
Birdwatching

World Wine Tours
69-71 Banbury Road
Oxford OX2 6PE
Tel: 0865 310344
Wine tours.

Luxury

Abercrombie and Kent
Sloane Square House
Holbein Place
London SW1
Tel: 071-730 9600
and...
1420 Kensington Road
Suite 111
Oakbrook IL
60521
USA
Tel: 312-954 2944
*One of the most extensive tour company
programmes, emphasis on luxury.*

Caribbean Connections
Concorde House
Forest Street
Chester CH1 1QR
Tel: 0244-329556

Continental Villas
52 Station Road
Petersfield
Hampshire GU32 3ES
Tel: 01730 233988
*Villas in France, West Indies, Spain, Portugal,
Italy, Greece, Cyprus.*

Cox and Kings Travel Ltd
St. James Court Hotel
Buckingham Gate Road
London SW1E 6AF
Tel: 071-931 9106

Cruise Advisory Service
30 Blue Boar Row
Salisbury
Wiltshire SP1 1DA
Tel: 0722-335505

Cunard Line Ltd
South Western House
Canute Road
Southampton SO9 1ZA
Tel:0703 229933
30a Pall Mall
London SW1Y 5LS
Tel: 071-491 3930
*QE2: World cruise, Caribbean, Mediterranean,
South Pacific, Far East, America, Africa,
Atlantic Isles, Norwegian Fjords, Bermuda,
North America. Sea Goddess: Mediterranean,
Greek Islands and the Holy Land, Aegena Sea,
Black Sea, Western Europe, North Africa,
Baltic, Fjords.*

CV Travel
43 Cadogan Street
London SW3 2PR
Tel: 071-581 0851

Elegant Resorts
24 Nicholas Street
Chester CH1 2ER
Tel: 0244 350408
Top of the range resorts in the Caribbean.

Venice Simplon Orient Express Ltd
Suite 200 Hudson's Place
Victoria Station
London SW1V 1JL
Tel: 071-928 6000

WEXAS International
45-49 Brompton Road
London SW3 1DE
Tel: 071-589 3315
Can organise all possibilities of luxury travel.

World Apart
PO Box 44209
Nairobi
Kenya
Tel: 228961
and c/o...
Flamingo Tours of East Africa
Tel: 081-995 3505
Luxury, traditional tented safaris.

TRAVEL ASSOCIATIONS

Alliance of Canadian Travel Associations
(ACTA)
75 Albert Street
Suite 1106
Ottawa KIP 5E7
Canada
Tel: **613-238 1361**

Alliance of Independent Travel Agents
(ARTAC)
Hurlington
Orton Malborne
Peterborough
Cambridgeshire PE25 5PR
Tel: **0733 390900**

American Society of Travel Agents (ASTA)
PO Box 23992
Washington DC 20026
USA
Tel: **703-739 2782**

Association of British Travel Agents (ABTA)
55-57 Newman Street
London W1P 4AH
Tel: **071-637 2444**

Association of Independent Tour Operators
(AITO)
133a St Margarets Road
Twickenham
Middlesex TW1 1RG
Tel: **081-744 9280**

Association of National Tourist Office Representatives (ANTOR)
42D Compayne Gardens
London NW6 3RY
Tel: **071-624 5817**

Australian Federation of Travel Agents
309 Pitt Street
Sydney
NSW 2000
Australia
Tel: **2-264 3299**

British Incoming Tour Operators Association
(BITOA)
Vigilant House
120 Wilton Road
London SW1V 1JZ
Tel: **071-931 0601**

British Tourist Authority (BTA)
Thames Tower
Black's Road
Hammersmith
London W6 9EL
Tel: **081-846 9000**

British Vehicle Rental and Leasing Association
13 St John's Street
Chichester
West Sussex PO19 1UU
Tel: **0243 786782**

Bus and Coach Council
Sardinia House
52 Lincoln's Inn Fields
London WC2A 3LZ
Tel: **071-831 7546**

Department of Transport
2 Marsham Street
London SW1P 3EB
Tel: **071-276 3000**

Federation of International Youth Travel Organizations (FIYTO)
Bredgade 25H
DK-1260 Copenhagen K
Denmark
Tel: **45-33 339 600**

Guild of Business Travel Agents (GBTA)
Suite 3
Premier House
10 Greycoat Place
London SW1P 1SB
Tel: **071-222 2744**

Guild of Guide Lecturers
Professional Association of Registered Guides
in Great Britain
The Guild House
52D Borough High Street
London SE1 1XN
Tel: **071-403 1115**

Institute of Travel and Tourism
113 Victoria Street
St Albans
Herts AL1 3TJ
Tel: **0727 854395**

International Association of Tour Managers
397 Walworth Road
London SE17 2AW
Tel: **071-703 9154**

International Bureau for Youth and Tourism
(BITEJ)
PO Box 147
1389 Budapest
Hungary
Tel: **1154095**

Irish Travel Agents Association (ITAA)
31-32 South William Street
Dublin 2
Eire
Tel: **6794179**

National Association of Independent Travel Agents (NAITA)
46 Oxford Street
London W1N 9FJ
Tel: **071-323 3408**

Pacific Asia Travel Association (PATA)
PO Box 2DQ
London W1A 2DQ
Tel: **071-224 2194**

Retail Travel Agents Association
13 Paxton St
Piccadilly
Manchester M1 2AX
Tel: **061-236 1717**

SA Travel Organisers Association (SATOA)
c/o Hartley's Safaris
12 Queensbury Mews West
London SW7 2DU
Tel: **071-584 5005**

School and Group Travel Association (SAGTA)
Honeycroft House
Pangbourne Road
Upper Basildon
Berkshire RG8 8LR
Tel: **0491-671631**

School Journey Association of London
48 Cavendish Road
London SW12 0DG
Tel: **081-673 4849**

Syndicat National des Agents de Voyages
6 rue Villaret de Joyeuse
75017 Paris
France

The Travel Agents Association of New Zealand
PO Box 1888
1st Floor
NCR House
186 Vivian Street
Wellington
New Zealand
Tel: **64-43 842 063**

Tour Operators Study Group (TOSG)
66 High St
Lewes
East Sussex BN7 1XG
Tel: **0273 477722**

World Association of Travel Agencies
37 quai Wilson
CH-1201 Geneva
Switzerland
Tel: **22-731 4760**

World Tourism Organisation (WTO)
Capitan Haya 42
Madrid 28020
Spain
Tel: **34-1 5710628**

RECOMMENDED TRAVEL AGENTS

National Agency Chains

The following major companies offer national coverage and a broad range of travel service including discounts on package holidays, plus flight bookings, currency and traveller's cheques.

American Express
6 Haymarket
London SW1Y 4BS
Tel: **071-930 4411**

Going Places
7 Haymarket
London SW1Y 4BT
Tel: **071-930 2411**
Owned by Airtours Plc

Lunn Poly
16 High Holborn
London WC1V 6RD
Tel: **071-831 2991**
Part of Thomson Travel Group

A T Mays
Moffat House
Nineyard Street
Saltcoats
KA21 5EF
Tel: **0294 62199**

Thomas Cook
45 Berkeley Street
London W1A 1EB
Tel: **071-408 4525**

Local Independent Agents

Most towns have their 'local' travel agent who will offer a broader range of specialist tour operators brochures and a more personalised service, based on experience to compensate for the lack of buying power to offer big discounts on big package holiday company brochures. These local agents, too numerous to list individuall,y should be ABTA members but are also more likely to offer a range of AITO brochures (Association of Independent Tour Operators).

Tailor-made Travel

National newspapers offer a good source of specialist agencies, often concentrating on a specific destination such as America or Australia. To ensure full financial protection, ensure that they offer ABTA, IATA and ATOL cover.

Respected names include:

Blair Travel & Leisure Ltd
117 Regent's Park Road
London NW1 8UR
Tel: **071-483 2297**
Including art tours

Bridge the World
1/3 Ferdinand Street
London NW1 8ES
Tel: **071-485 5868**
Long haul

STA
Priory House
6 Wrights Lane
London W8 6TA
Tel: **071-938 4711**
Student travel

Trailfinders
42/50 Earls Court Road
London W8 6EJ
Tel: **071-938 3366**
Australasia and worldwide

Travelbag
12 High Street
Alton
Hampshire GU34 1BN
Tel: **0420-541441**
Australia.

WEXAS International
45-49 Brompton Road
London SW3 1DE
Tel: **071-589 3315**
Australasia, Far East, America and worldwide

Business Travel

Many travel agencies offer leisure and business travel services but GBTA members (Guild of Business Travel Agents, tel 071-222 2744) specialize in Business Travel Management. Leading members include:

Ayscough Travel
41-45 Fish Street Hill
London EC3R 6BT
Tel: **071-623 1611**

Britannic Travel
124 Central Road

Worcester Park
KT4 8HT
Tel: **081-330 2701**

Carlson Travel Networks
Moffat House
Nineyard Street
Saltcoats KA21 5HS
Tel: **0294 621995848**

Gray Dawes Travel
Dugard House
Peartree Road
Stanway
Colchester
Essex CO3 5UL
Tel: **0206-762241**

Hogg Robinson Travel
Abbey House
282 Farnborough Road
Farnborough
Hampshire GU 14 7NJ
Surrey GU21 5XD
Tel: **0252-3722000**

The Travel Company
Marble Arch House
66/68 Seymour Street
London W1H 5AF
Tel: **071-262 5040**

Portman Travel Ltd
15 Berners Street
London W1P 3DE
Tel: **071-753 8127**

Ian Allan Travel Ltd
Terminal House
Shepperton
Middlesex TW17 8AS
Tel: **0932-228950**

WEXAS International
45-49 Brompton Road
London SW3 1DE
Tel: **071-589 3315**
Offers business travel services to its Gold Card members ■

GETTING THERE BY AIR
Section 4

AIR TRANSPORT ASSOCIATIONS

Air Accidents Investigation Branch
Department of Transport
Royal Aerospace Establishment
Farnborough
Hants GU14 6TD
Tel: **0252 510300**

Air Transport Operators Association (ATOA)
Clembro House
Weydown Road
Haslemere
Surrey GU27 2QE
Tel: **0428 4804**

Aircharter Brokers (ABA)
22 St Andrews St
London EC4A 3AN
Tel: **071-353 5691**

Airport Association Co-Ordination Council (AACC)
PO Box 125
CH-1215 Geneva 15-Airport
Geneva
Switzerland
Tel: **798 4141**

Association of European Airlines
Avenue Louise 350
Bte 4
1050 Brussels
Belgium
Tel: **322-648 4017**

Aviation Training Association
125 London Road
High Wycombe
Bucks HP11 1BT
Tel: **0494 445262**

British Air Line Pilots Association (BALPA)
81 New Road
Harlington
Hayes
Middlesex UB3 5BG
Tel: **081-759 7957**

British Airports Authority (BAA)
Public Affairs Department
D'Albiac House
Heathrow Airport
Hounslow TW6 1JH
Tel: **081-759 4321**
and...
Public Affairs Department
Gatwick Airport Ltd
PO Box 93
Gatwick
West Sussex RH6 0NH
Tel: **0293 505000**

British Air Transport Association (BATA)
c/o The Royal Aeronautical Society
4 Hamilton Place
London W1V 0BQ
Tel: **071-499 3515**

British Helicopter Advisory Board (BHAB)
Building C2
West Entrance
Fairoaks Airport
Chobham
Surrey GU24 8HX
Tel: **0276 856126**

Business Aircraft Users Association (BAUA)
PO Box 29
Wallingford
Oxon OX10 0AG
Tel: **0491 37903**

Civil Aviation Authority
CAA House
45-49 Kingsway
London WC2B 6TE
Tel: **071-379 7411**

**Commonwealth Air Transport Council
(CATC)**
Room S5/05A
2 Marsham St
London SW1P 3EB
Tel: **071-276 5436**

**European Civil Aviation Conference
(ECAC)**
3 bis Villa Emile Bergerat
92522-Neuilly sur Seine
France
Tel: **46-379645**

**European Regional Airlines Organisation
(ERA)**
The Baker Suite
Fairoaks Airport
Chobham
Surrey GU24 8HX
Tel: **0276 857038**

Federation Aeronautique International
6 Rue Galilee
75782
Paris 16
France
Tel: **72 09185**

Flight Safety Committee
Aviation House
South Area
Gatwick Airport
West Sussex RH6 0YR
Tel: **0737 60664**

Foreign Airlines Association
4 Summerhays
Cobham
Surrey KT11 2HQ
Tel: **0932 63639**

**Guild of Air Pilots and Air Navigators
(GAPAN)**
Cobham House
291 Grays Inn Road
London WC1X 8QF
Tel: **071-837 3323**

**International Federation of Airline Pilots
Associations (IFALPA)**
Interpilot House
116 High St
Egham
Surrey TW20 9HQ
Tel: **0784 437361**

Institute of Air Transport (ITA)
103 rue La Boetie
75008
Paris
France
Tel: **43 593868**

**International Air Carrier Association
(IACA)**
Abelag Building
PO Box 36
Brussels National Airport
B-1930 Zaventum 2
Belgium
Tel: **720 5880**

International Air Transport Association
POB 672
CH-1215 Geneva 15 Airport
Geneva
Switzerland
Tel: **022-799 2525**

International Airline Passengers Association
Carolyn House
Dingwall Road
Croydon
Surrey CRO 9XF
Tel: **081-681 6555**

**International Civil Airports Association
(ICAA)**
Building 266
Orly Sud 103
F-94396 Cedex
Orly Aerogare
France
Tel: **49-754470**

**International Civil Aviation Organisation
(ICAO)**
3 bis Villa Emile Bergerat
Neuilly sur Seine
Cedex
France

Royal Aeronautical Society
4 Hamilton Place
London W1V 0BQ
Tel: **071-499 3515**

AIRLINE HEAD OFFICES WORLDWIDE

Adria Airways
6100 Ljublijana
Republic of Slovenia
Tel: **61 313 366**
Fax: 38 61 323 356
Telex: 31268 ADAIR YU

Aer Lingus
Dublin Airport
Dublin
Republic of Ireland
Tel: **370011**
Fax: 420801
Telex: 25101

Aeroflot-Russian International Airlines
Leningradski Prospekt 37
Moscow 125167
Russian Federation
Tel: **155 54 94**
Telex: 411969

Aerolinas Argentinas
Paseo Colon 185
1063 Buenos Aires
Argentina
Tel: **308 551**
Fax: 331 0356
Telex: 18182

Aeromexico
Paseo de la Reforma 445
Mexico City 06500
Mexico
Tel: **286 4422**
Telex: 1772765

Aeroperu
Av. Jose Pardo 601
Miraflores
Lima 18
Peru
Tel: **478900**

Air Afrique
PO Box 3927
Abidjan 01
Cote d'Ivoire
Tel: **20 30 00**
Fax: 20 30 08

Air Algerie
1 Place Maurice Audin
Algiers
Algeria
Tel: **642428**

Air Botswana
PO Box 92
Gaborone
Botswana
Tel: **52812**
Fax: 374802
Telex: 2413BD

Air Burkina
BP 1459
Ougadougou
Burkina Faso
Tel: **306143**
Fax: 31 02 69

Air Canada
Place Air Canada
Montreal
Quebec H2Z 1X5
Canada
Tel: **422 5000**
Fax: 879 7990
Telex: 06 217537

Air China
Capital International Airport
Beijing 100621
P.R. China
Tel: **601 6667/513 8833**
Telex: 229722 AIRCN CN

Air France
1 Square Max Hymans
Paris 15e
France
Tel: **43 23 81 81**
Fax: 43 37 35 15
Telex: 200666

Air Gabon
B.P 2206
Libreville
Gabon
Tel: **73 21 97**
Telex: 5218 GO

Air Gambia
7/9 Cameron Street
P.O. Box 432
Banjul
Gambia
Tel: **27824**
Fax: 29354
Telex: 2255 LENNAP

Air India
216 Backbay Reclamation
Nariman Point
Bombay 400 021
India
Tel: **202 4142**
Fax: 202 1210
Telex: 0112 427

Air Jamaica
72-76 Harbour St
Kingston
Jamaica
West Indies
Tel: **922-3460**
Fax: 922-0107
Telex: 2389 AIRJCA

Air Lanka
37 York St
Colombo 1
Sri Lanka
Tel: **421291**
Fax: 449841
Telex: 21401 LANKAIR CE

Air Madagascar
BP 437
31 Avenue de l'Independence
Antananarivo
Madagascar
Tel: **22222**
Fax: 33760
Telex: 22232 MG

Air Malawi
PO Box 84
Robins Road
Blantyre
Malawi
Tel: **620811**
Fax: 620042
Telex: 44245

Air Malta
Luqa Airport
Malta
Tel: **824330**
Fax: 673241
Telex: MW1389

Air Mauritanie
BP41
Nouakchott
Islamic Republic of Mauritania
Tel: **22 11 2681**
Telex: 573

Air Mauritius
PO Box 60
Port Louis
Mauritius
Tel: **08 7700**
Fax: 08 8331
Telex: 4415

Air Namibia
Eros Airport
Windhoek 9000
Namibia
Tel: **61 298 2057**

Fax: 61 298 2078
Telex: 56 657 SA

Air New Zealand
Air New Zealand House
1 Queen St
Auckland 1
New Zealand
Tel: **797515**
Fax: 3663759
Telex: NZ 2541

Air Pacific
Private Mail Bag
Raiwaga
Fiji
Tel: **386444**
Fax: 300976
Telex: 2131FJ

Air Rwanda
PO Box 808
Kigali
Rwanda
Tel: **4493**
Telex: 554

Air Seychelles
PO Box 386
Victoria
Mahe
Seychelles
Tel: **25300**
Fax: 25159
Telex: 2314 AIRSEY SZ

Air Tahiti
BP 314
Quai Bir Hakiem
Papeete
Tahiti
French Polynesia
Tel: **864000**
Fax: 864069

Air Tanzania
PO Box 543
Dar-es-Salaam
Tanzania
Tel: **42111**
Telex: 41253

Air UK
Stansted House
Stansted Airport
Essex CM24 1QT
Tel: **0279 680146**
Fax: 0279 680012
Telex: 877060

Air Zaire
BP 8552
4 Avenue du Port

Kinshasa
Zaire
Tel: **24 986**
Telex: 21313

Air Zimbabwe
PO Box API
Harare Airport
Zimbabwe
Tel: **737011**
Fax: 731444
Telex: 4548 ZW

Alaska Airlines
19300 Pacific Highway South
P.O. Box 68900
Seattle
WA 98168
USA
Tel: **433 3100**
Fax: 248 7676
Telex: 32 303

Albanian Airlines
Pruga Kongresi 1 Permetit 202
Tirana
Albania
Fax: 512 2222 625

Alitalia
Vial E Alessendro Marchetti 111
Roma
Italy 1-00148
Tel: **65621**
Fax: 592 0089
Telex: 626211

All Nippon Airways
Kasumigaseki Building
3-2-5 Kasumigaseki
Chiyoda-ku
Tokyo 100
Japan
Tel: **592 3248**
Fax: 592 3389
Telex: J33670

Aloha Airlines
371 Aokea St
PO Box 30028
Honolulu International Airport
Hawaii 96820
USA
Tel: **936 4125**

Alymeda – Democratic Yemen Airlines
PO Box 6006
Khormaksar Civil Airport
Aden
Yemen
Tel: **52267**

American Airlines Inc
PO Box 619616
Dallas/Fort Worth Airport
Texas 75261-9616
USA
Tel: **963 1234**
Telex: 4630158

Ansett Australia
501 Swanston St
Melbourne
Victoria 3000
Australia
Tel: **623 3333**
Fax: 623 2029
Telex: AA30085

Ansett New Zealand
PO Box 4168
Auckland 1000
New Zealand
Tel:**309 6235**
Fax: 307 9218

Ariana Afghan Airlines
Ansari Watt
P.O. Box 76
Kabul
Afghanistan
Tel: **25541 65/60361**
Telex: 28 AFGAIRCO

Austrian Airlines
PO Box 50
Fontanastrasse 1
A-1107 Vienna
Austria
Tel: **68 35 11**
Fax: 68 55 05
Telex: 131811

AVIANCA
Av Eldorado No 93-30
Bogota
Columbia
Tel: **63 96 28**
Telex: 44427

AVIATECA S.A.
Avenida Hincapie
Aeropuerto La Aurora
Guatemala City
Guatemala
Tel: **63227**
Telex: 4160

Bahamas Air
Po Box N-4881
Nassau
Bahamas
Tel: **327-8451**
Fax: 327 7409
Telex: 20 239

Balkan-Bulgarian Airlines
Sofia Airport
1540 Sofia
Bulgaria
Tel: **2 796189**
Fax: 2 732708
Telex: 22342

Biman Bangladesh Airlines
Biman Bangladesh Building
100 Mitijheel
Dhaka
Bangladesh
Tel: **255901**
Telex: 642649

Braathens Safe Air Transport
Oksenoy veien 3
PO Box 55
1330 Oslo
Lufthavn
Norway
Tel: **47 2 59 70 00**
Fax: 47 2 59 13 09
Telex: 71595 BUOSLN

Britannia
Luton International Airport
Luton
Bedfordshire LU2 9ND
Tel: **424155**
Fax: 458594
Telex: 82239

British Airways
P.O. Box 10
Heathrow Airport
Hounslow
Middlesex
TW6 2JA
Tel: **081-759 5511**
Fax: 081-562 9930
Telex: 881-3983 BAWYSC

British Midland
Donington Hall
Castle Donington
Derby DE7 2SB
Tel: **0332 810741**
Fax: 0332 852238
Telex: 37172 BMAOBD

BWIA International Trinidad & Tobago Airways
E and M Hangar Compound
Piarco
Trinidad
Tel: **664 4871**
Telex: 2942 5523

Cameroon Airlines
BP 4092

3 Avenue General de Gaulle
Douala
Republic of Cameroon
Tel: **42 25 25**
Telex: 5345

Canadian Airlines International
Suite 2800
700 2nd St SW
Calgary
Alberta T2P 2W2
Canada
Tel: **294 2000**
Fax: 294 6160
Telex: 043 55587

Cathay Pacific Airways
Swire House
9 Connaught Road
Central
Hong Kong
Tel: **5 8425000**
Fax: 5 8452039
Telex: 82345 CXAIR HX

Cayman Airways
PO Box
1101 George Town
Grand Cayman
British West Indies
Tel: **94 92673**
Fax: 97607
Telex: 4272

China Airlines
131 Nanking East Road
Section 3
Taipei 104
Taiwan
Tel: **7152626**
Fax: 7174641
Telex: 11346

Compania de Avacion Faucett
Aeropoerto Jorge Chavez
PO Box 1429
Lima
Peru
Tel: **643 424**
Telex: 25225 PE

Continental Airlines
2929 Allen Parkway
Houston
Texas 77019
USA
Tel: **713 630 5000**
Telex: 06 74402

Croatian Airlines
Savska Cesta 41
41000 Zagreb

Republic of Croatia
Tel: 38 41613111
Fax: 38 41530475

Crossair AG
P.O. Box CH-4030
Basel-Mullhouse
Switzerland
Tel: **061 572658**
Telex: 965822

Cyprus Airways
PO Box 1903
21 Ali..ou St
Nicosia
Cyprus
Tel: **443054**
Fax: 443167
Telex: 2225 CYPRUSAIR

Czechoslovak Airlines
Revolucni 1
11000 Praha 1
Czech Republic
Tel: **236 2146**
Fax: 236 3352
Telex: 121068

Delta Airlines
Hartsfield International Airport
Atlanta
Georgia 30320-6001
USA
Tel: **404 715 2600**
Telex: 542316

Dragonair
22nd Floor
Devon House
Tailkoo Place
979 Kings Road
Quarry Bay
Hong Kong
Tel: **590 1328**
Fax: 590 1333
Telex: 45936

Druk Air Corporation
P.O. Box 209
Thimpu
Kingdom of Bhutan
Tel: **22215/22825**
Fax: 22775
Telex: 219

Eastwest Airlines
P.O. Box 727F
GPO Melbourne 3001
Victoria
Australia
Tel: **623 3333**
Fax: 623 2029

Egyptair
6 Adly Street
Cairo
Egypt
Tel: **3902444**
Fax: 3904459

El Al – Israel Airlines
PO Box 41
Ben-Gurion Airport
Tel Aviv 70100
Israel
Tel: **9716111**
Fax: 9711442
Telex: 371107

Emirates
PO Box 686
Dubai
United Arab Emirates
Tel: **228151**
Fax: 214560
Telex: 45728

Ethiopian Airlines
PO Box 1755
Bole Airport
Addis Ababa
Ethiopia
Tel: **18 22 22**
Fax: 18 84 74
Telex: 21012

Finnair
Mannerheimintie 102
00250 Helsinki
Finland
Tel: **81881**
Fax: 818 8736
Telex: 124404

Gambia Airways
68/69 Wellington Street
Banjul
The Gambia
Tel: **220 27778**
Fax: 220 29339

Garuda Indonesia
Jalan Merdeka Selatan No 13
Jakarta10110
Indonesia
Tel: **3801901/380059**
Fax: 363595/363370
Telex: 49113

GB Airways
Ian Stewart Centre
Beehive Ringroad
Gatwick Airport
West Sussex
RH6 OPB
Tel: **0293 664228**
Fax: 0293 664218

Ghana Airways
PO Box 1636
Ghana Airways House
White Avenue
Accra
Ghana
Tel: **773321**
Fax: 777675

Gulf Air
PO Box 138
Manama
Bahrain
Tel: **322200**
Fax: 530082
Telex: 8255 GULF HQ BAH BN

Guyana Airways
32 Main Str
PO Box 102
Georgetown
Guyana
Tel: **59490**
Telex: 2242

Hawaiian Airlines
1164 Bishop St
Suite 800
Honolulu
Hawaii 96813
USA
Tel: **537 5100**
Fax: 525 6719

Iberia
130 Calle Velazquez
28006 Madrid
Spain
Tel: **587 8787**
Fax: 587 7193
Telex: 27775

Icelandair
Reykjavik Airport
IS-101 Reykjavik
Iceland
Tel: **690100**
Fax: 690391
Telex: 2021 ICEAIR IS

Indian Airlines
Airlines House
113 Gurdwara Rakabganj Road
Parliament St
New Delhi 110001
India
Tel: **388951**
Fax: 381730
Telex: 031-66110

Iran Air
Iran Air Building
Mehrabad Airport

Tehran
Iran
Tel: **9111**
Fax: 903248
Telex: 212795 IRAN IR

Iraqi Airways
Kiss Sundas al-Junabi
Baghdad
Iraq
Tel: **551 8888**
Telex: 212297

Istanbul Airlines
Incirli Cad
50/4,
34740 Barkikroy
Istanbul
Turkey
Tel: **583 1641**
Fax 572 0690
Telex: 26333

Japan Airlines – JAL
Tokyo Building
7-3 Marumouchi
2-Chome Chiyoda-ku
Tokyo 100 Japan
Tel: **284 2831**
Fax: 284 2719
Telex: 24827

Jersey European Airways
Exeter Airport
Exeter
Devon
England
Tel: **0392 078400**
Fax: 0392 66151
Telex: 42761

Kenya Airlines
Jomo Kenyatta International Airport
PO Box 19002
Nairobi
Kenya
Tel: **822171**
Telex: 22771

KLM Royal Dutch Airlines
PO Box 7700
1117 ZL Schiphol
The Netherlands
Tel: **6499123**
Fax: 6412872
Telex: 11252 NL

Korean Air
41-3 Seosomun-Dong
Jung-Gu
Seoul
Korea
Tel: **7517 114**

Fax: 751 7522
Telex: 27526

Kuwait Airways
Kuwait International Airport
Kuwait
Tel: **434 5555**
Fax: 431 9912
Telex: 23036

LAN-Chile SA
Huerfanos 757
Piso 8
Santiago
Chile
Tel: **394411**
Fax: 383884
Telex: 441061 LASCL CZ

Lao Aviation
BP Box 119
2 Rue Pan Kham
Vientiane
Lao People's Democratic Republic
Tel: **2094**
Telex: 310 LAO AVON LS

LAP (Lineas Aereas Paraguayas)
Oliva 455
Asuncion
Paraguay
Tel: **91040**
Telex: 5230

Latvian Airlines
54 Brivibas Street
LV 1050 Riga
Latvia
Fax: 223 297

Lauda Air
P.O. Box 56
A-1300 Vienna Airport
Vienna
Austria
Tel: **7 1110 2081**
Fax: 7 1110 3157
Telex: 133850

LIAT
PO Box 819
VC Bird International Airport
Antigua
West Indies
Tel: **46 2 0700**
Fax: 46 2 2682
Telex: 2124 AK

Lina Congo
PO Box
2203 Brazzaville

Republic of the Congo
Tel: **813 065**
Telex: 5243 LINCONGO KG

Lithuanian Airlines
8 Radunes
Vilnius Airport
Vilnius
Lithuania
Tel: **63 78 17**
Telex: 26116

LOT - Polish Airlines
65/79 Jerozolmskie Av
00-697 Warsaw
Poland
Tel: **628 75 80**
Fax: 630 55 03
Telex: 814327

Lufthansa – German Airlines
Von-Gablenz-Strasse 2-6
D-5000 Koln 21
Germany
Tel: **221 8261**
Fax: 696 3002
Telex: 8873531

Luxair
Aeroport de Luxembourg
L-2987 Luxembourg
Tel: **4798 2311**
Fax: 43 24 82
Telex: 2372

Maersk Air
Copenhagen Airport South
Dk-2791
Dragoer
Denmark
Tel: **32 45 44 44**
Telex: 31125

Malaysia Airlines
33rd Floor
Bangunan MAS
Jalan Sultan Ismail 50250
Kuala Lumpur
Malaysia
Tel: **261 0555**
Fax:746 2581
Telex: MA 37614

Malev – Hungarian Airlines
Roosevelt Ter 2
Budapest
Hungary
Tel: **266 9033**
Fax: 266 2685
Telex: 22-4954

From 16 April 1995 all national and international codes change — see page 587 for details.

Manx Airlines
Isle of Man Airport
Ballasalla
Isle of Man
Tel: 0624 824111
Fax: 0624 824041
Telex: 629683

MEA (Middle East Airlines)
P.O. Box 206
Beirut
Lebanon
Tel: 316316
Fax: 8711754104
Telex: 20820LE

Mexican
Xola No 535
Piso 13
Col del Valle
Mexico City 03100
Mexico
Tel: 543 9240
Fax: 523 3692
Telex: 71247 CMARME

Monarch Airlines
Luton International Airport
Luton
Bedfordshire LU2 9NU
Tel: 424211
Fax: 416168

Mount Cook Airlines
PO Box 4644
Christchurch
New Zealand
Tel: 348 2099
Fax: 633-611
Telex: NZ4297

Nigeria Airways
Airways House
Murtala Muhammed International Airport
Ikeja
Lagos
Nigeria
Tel: 900476
Telex: 22646

Northwest Airlines Inc
Minneapolis/St Paul International Airport
St Paul
Minnesota 55111
USA
Tel: 726 2111

Olympic Airways
96 Syngrou Avenue
Athens 11741
Greece
Tel: 929 2111
Fax:926 7156

PIA- Pakistan International Airlines
PIA Building
Quaid-e-Azam International Airport
Karachi
Pakistan
Tel: 412011
Fax: 727727
Telex: KAR 2832

Philippine Airlines
111 Building
1 Legazpi St
Legazpi Village
Makati
Metro Manila
Philippines
Tel: 818 0111
Fax: 818 3298

Polynesian Airlines
Air Centre
PO Box 599
Beech Road
Apia
Western Samoa
Tel: 21 261
Fax: 20 023
Telex: 249 PALAPW SX

Qantas Airways
Qantas Centre
203 Coward Street
Mascot
New South Wales 2020
Australia
Tel: 691 3636

Royal Air Maroc
Anfa Airport
Casablanca
Morocco
Tel: 36 16 20
Fax: 36 05 20
Telex: 21880

Royal Brunei Airlines
PO Box 737
Bandar Seri Begawan
Brunei Darussalam 2085
Tel: 240500
Telex: BU2737

Royal Jordanian Airlines
Housing Bank Commercial Centre
Queen Noor Street
P.O. Box 302
Amman
Jordan
Tel: 672 872
Fax: 672 527
Telex: 21501

Royal Nepal Airlines
RNAC Building
Kanti Path
Kathmandu
Nepal
Tel: **214511**
Telex: 2212 NP

Ryanair
Dublin Airport
Dublin
Republic of Ireland
Tel: **844 4400**
Fax: 844 4402
Telex: 91608 RYAN EI

Sabena Belgian World Airlines
35 Rue Cardinal Mercier
B-1000 Brussels
Belgium
Tel: **723 31 11**
Telex: 21322

SAS – Scandinavian Airlines
Frosundavik Allee 1
S-161 87 Stockholm
Sweden
Tel: **797 000**
Fax: 885 8287
Telex: 22263

Saudi
P.O. Box 620
Jeddah
Saudi Arabia
Tel: **686 000**
Fax: 686 4589

Singapore Airlines
Airline House
25 Airline Road
Singapore 1781
Tel: **542 3333**
Fax: 545 5749
Telex: RS21241

SAA – South African Airways
Airways Towers
PO Box 7778
Johannesburg 2000
Transvaal
South Africa
Tel: **773 9433**
Fax: 773 8988
Telex: 424210

Sudan Airways
PO Box 253
Khartoum
Sudan
Tel: **41766**

Fax: 47987
Telex: 24212 SATCO SD

Suriname Airways
Coppenamelaan 136
Pararibo
Republic of Suriname
Tel: **65700**
Fax: 99495
Telex: SURAIR SN292

Swissair
Zurich Airport
Zurich
Switzerland 825601
Tel: **812 1212**
Fax: 810 5633
Telex: 825601

Syrian Arab Airlines
PO Box 417
Social Insurance Building
5th Floor
Jabri St
Damascus
Syrian Arab Republic
Tel: **22343**
Telex: 119192

Taca International Airlines
Edificio Caribe
2 Piso
San Salvador
El Salvador
Tel: **232244**
Fax: 233757
Telex: 20456 TACAIR SAL

Tajik Air
Dushanbe Airport
Dushanbe
Republic of Tajikistan
Tel: **22 32 83**

TAP Air Portugal
Edificio 25
Aeroporto (Apartado 5194)
Lisboa 5
Portugal
Tel: **841 5000**
Telex: 12331

TAROM (Romanian Air Transport)
Otopeni Airport
Bucharest
Romania
Tel: **333137**
Telex: 11181 AIRBUH R

Thai Airways International
89 Vibhavadi Rangsit Road
Bangkok 9
Thailand
Tel: **513 0121**
Fax: 513 3341
Telex: 82359 THANTER TH

Transavia Airlines
P.O. Box 7777
1118 ZM Amsterdam Schiphol Airport
Netherlands
Tel: **6046318**
Fax: 484637
Telex: 13067

Transbrasil–Linhas Aeras
Aeroporto de Congohas Hangar
Sao Paulo
Brazil
Tel: **740 7411**
Telex: 021471

TWA – Trans World Airlines
100 South Bedford Road
Mount Kisco
New York
10549
USA
Tel: **242 3000**
Telex: 217711

Tunis Air
Boulevard du 7 Novembre 1987
Tunis Carthage 2035
Tunisia
Tel: **700 100**
Fax: 700 008
Telex: 15283

Turkish Airlines
Ataturk Hava Limani
Yesilkoy
Istanbul
Turkey
Tel: **547 7300**
Fax: 574 7444
Telex: 28871

Uganda Airlines
PO Box 5740
Kimathi Road
Kampala
Uganda
Tel: **32990**
Telex: 61239

Ukraine International Airlines
Prospekt Pobedy 14,
135 Kiev
Ukraine
Tel: **216 6758**
Fax: 216 7994

United Airlines
PO Box 66100
O'Hare International Airport
Chicago
Illinois 60666
USA
Tel: **952 4000**
Fax: 952-4081
Telex: 287419

VARIG – Brazilian Airlines
365 Avenida Almirante
Sylvio de Noronha
Edificio Varig
Rio de Janeiro
20000
Brasil
Tel: **292 6600**
Fax: 240 6859
Telex: 31373

VIASA – Venezolana Internacional de Aviación
Torre Viasa
Avenida Sur 25
Plaza Morelos
Caracas 105
Venezuela
Tel: **572 9522**
Telex: 21125 VIASA VC

Virgin Atlantic Airways
Sussex House
High Street
Crawley
West Sussex RH10 1DQ
Tel: **0293 562345**
Fax: 0293 561721
Telex: 877077

Windward Island Airways International
PO Box 288
Philipsburgh
St Maarten
Netherlands Antilles
Tel: **5 425 68**
Fax: 5 44229

Yemenia – Yemen Airways
PO Box 1183
Airport Road
Sana'a
Republic of Yemen
Tel: **2 232389**
Fax: 252991
Telex: 2204 YEMAIR YE

Zambia Airways
Ndeke House
Haile Selassie Avenue
PO Box 30272

Lusaka
Zambia
Tel: **228274**
Fax: 254281
Telex: 43850 NDEKE ZA

AIRLINE OFFICES IN
THE UK

Aer Lingus
223 Regent Street
London W1R 0AJ
Tel: **081-569 4646**
Fax: 081-569 4410

Aeroflot
70 Piccadilly
London W1V 9HH
Tel: **071-355 2233**
Fax: 071-335 2323

Aerolineas Argentinas
54 Conduit Street
London W1R 9FD
Tel: **071-494 1001**
Fax: 071-494 1002

Air Afrique c/o Air France

Air Algerie
10 Baker Street
London W1M 1DA
Tel: **071-487 5709**
Fax: 071-935 1715
Telex: 24606 ALGAIR

Air Botswana
177/178 Tottenham Court Road
London W1P 9LF
Tel: **071-757 2737**
Fax: 071-757 2063

Air Burundi c/o Air France

Air Canada
7/8 Conduit Street
London W1R 9TG
Tel: **081-465 0900**
Fax: 081-759 4126

Air China
41 Grosvenor Gardens
London SW1W 0BP
Tel: **071-630 0919**
Fax: 071-630 7792

Air France
177 Piccadilly
London W1 0LX
Tel: **071-499 9667**
Fax: 071-499 6737

Air Gabon c/o Air France

Air India
17-18 New Bond Street
London W1Y 0BD
Tel: **071-493 4050**

Air Inter c/o Air France

Air Lanka
22 Regent Street
London SW1Y 0QD
Tel: **071-930 2099**
Telex: 269171 LANKA

Air Malawi c/o British Airways

Air Malta
314/316 Upper Richmond Road
Putney
London SW15 6TV
Tel: **081- 785 3199**
Fax: 081-785 7468
Telex: 923213

Air Mauritius
49 Conduit Street
London W1R 9FB
Tel: **071-434 4375**
Fax: 071-439 4101
Telex: 24469 AIR MK

Air Namibia
1 Approach Road
Raynes Park
London SW20 8BA
Tel: **081-543 2122**
Fax: 081-543 3398
Telex: 913069

Air New Zealand
Elsinore House
77 Fulham Palace Road
Hammersmith
London W6 8JA
Tel: **081-846 9595**
Fax: 081-741 4645
Telex: 265206 AIRNZ

Air Seychelles
Suite 6
Kelvin House
Kelvin Way
Crawley
West Sussex RH10 2SE
Tel: **0293 542101**
Fax: 0293 562353
Telex: 877033

Air UK
Stansted House
Stansted Airport
Stansted
Essex CM24 8QT
Tel: **0345 666777**
Fax: 0279 680012
Telex: 817312

Air Zaire
29-30 Old Burlington Street
London W1X 1LB
Tel: **071-434-1151/2**
Fax: 071-734 1699
Telex: 298947 QCZAIR

Air Zimbabwe
Colette House
52-55 Piccadilly
London W1V 9AA
Tel: **071-491 0009**
Fax: 071-355 3326
Telex: 25251 AIRZIM

Alitalia
205 Holland Park Avenue
London W11 4XB
Tel: **071-602 7111**
Fax: 071-602 5584
Telex: 27572 ALIT

All Nippon Airways
ANA House
6/8 Old Bond Street
London W1X 3TA
Tel: **071-355 1155**
Fax: 071-915 3365

American Airlines
23/59 Staines Road
Hounslow
Middlesex TW3 3HE
Tel: **081-572 5555**
Fax: 081-572 8646
Telex: 23939 AMMAIR

Ansett Australia
20 Savile Row
London W1X 2AN
Tel: **071-494 2141**
Fax: 071-734 4333

Arian Afghan Airlines
169 Piccadilly
London W1V 9DD
Tel: **071-493 1411**
Fax: 071-629 1611
Telex: 22668

Austrian Airlines
5th Floor

10 Wardour Street
London W1V 4BQ
Tel: **071-434 7350**
Fax: 071-434 7363

Avianca
Linen Hall
162-8 Regent Street
London W1R 5TA
Tel: **071-437 3664**
Fax: 071-494 3786
Telex: 22896

AVIATECA
Ocean House
Hazelwick Avenue
Three Bridges
Crawley
Surrey RH10 1NP
Tel: **0293 553330**
Fax: 0293 553321
Telex: 878317

BWIA International Trinidad & Tobago
48 Leicester Square
London WC2H 7LT
Tel:**071-839 9333**
Fax: 071-839 5396
Telex: 918746

Bahamasair
79 Dean Street
London W1V 5AB
Tel: **071-437 8766**
Fax: 071-734 6460

Balkan Bulgarian
322 Regent Street
London W1R 5AB
Tel: **071-637 7637**
Fax: 071-637 2481
Telex: 296547 BALKAN

Biman Bangladesh
17 Conduit Street
London W1R 9DD
Tel: **071-629 0252**
Fax: 071-629 0736
Telex: 28766 BIMAN

British Airways
PO Box 10
London-Heathrow Airport
Hounslow
Middlesex TW6 2JA
Tel: **081-897 4000**
and...
156 Regent Street
London W1R 5TA
Tel: **071-434 4700**
Fax: 071-434 4636

British Midland
Donington Hall
Castle Donington
Derby DE7 2SB
Tel: **0332 854000**
Fax: 0332 852662
Telex: 37172

Cameroon Airlines c/o Air France

Canadian Airlines
1st Floor Rothschild House
Whitgift Centre
Croydon
Surrey CR9 3HN
Tel: **081-667 0666**
Fax: 081-688 2997
Telex: 22625

Cathay Pacific
7 Apple Tree Yard
Duke of York Street
London SW1Y 6LD
Tel: **071-747 7000**
Fax: 071-839 4597
Telex: 918120 CATHEX

Cayman Airways
Trevor House
100 Brompton Road
London SW3 1EX
Tel: **071-581 9960**
Fax: 071-584 4463

China Airlines
5th Floor
Nuffield House
41-46 Piccadilly
London W1V 9AJ
Tel: **071-434 0707**
Fax: 071-439 4888
Telex: 265400 LONCI

Conti-Flug
612 Kingston Road
London SW20 8DN
Tel: **0293 568885**
Fax: 0293 512229

Continental Airlines
Beulah Court
Albert Road
Horley
Surrey RH6 7HZ
Tel: **0293 776464**
Fax: 0293 773726
Telex: 877008 CALLGW

Croatian Airlines
Ina House
210 Shepherds Bush Road
London W6 7NL

Tel: **071-371 1122**
Fax: 071-371 1119

Cubana c/o British Airways

Cyprus Airways
29-31 Hampstead Road
Euston Centre
London NW1 3JA
Tel: **071-388 5411**
Fax: 071-383 0126
Telex: 23881 CYPAIR

Cyprus Turkish Airlines
41 Pall Mall
London SW1Y 5JG
Tel: **071-930 4851**
Fax: 071-930 1046
Telex: 885614

Czechoslovak Airlines
72 Margaret Street
London W1N 7HA
Tel: **071-255 1898**
Fax: 071-323 1633
Telex: 265776

Delta Airlines
Ground Floor
Oakfield Court
Consort Way
Horley
Surrey RH6 7AF
Tel: **0800 414767**
Fax: 0293 821374
Telex: 87534

Dragonair c/o Cathay Pacific

Egyptair
296 Regent Street
London W1R 6PH
Tel: **071-580 5477**
Fax: 071-637 4328

El Al Israel Airlines
185 Regent Street
London W1R 8EU
Tel: **071-437 9255**
Fax: 071-439 2920
Telex: 22198

Emirates
125 Pall Mall
London W1V 9DE
Tel: 071-930 3711
Fax: 071-930 9647
Telex: 298909

Ethiopian Airlines
Foxglove House
166 Piccadilly
London W1V 9DE

Tel: **071-491 9119**
Fax: 071-491 1892
Telex: 917855 ETHAIR

Faucett-The First Airline of Peru
Suite 163
27 Cockspur Street
London SW1Y 5BN
Tel: **071-930 1136**
Fax: 071-839 5379
Telex: 893369

Finnair
14 Clifford Street
London W1X 1RD
Tel: **071-408 1222**
Fax: 071-629 7289
Telex: 918783 FNNAIR

GB Airways
Ian Stewart Centre
Beehive Ring Road South
Gatwick Airport
Surrey RH6 0PB
Tel: **0293 664239**
Fax: 0293 664218

Gambia Airways
Unit 3b
Gatwick Metro Centre
Balcombe Road
Horley
Surrey RH6 9GA
Tel: **0293 774141**
Fax:0293 774080
Telex:87337

Garuda Indonesia
35 Duke Street
London W1M 5DF
Tel: **071-486 3011**
Fax: 071-224 3971
Telex: 295896 GRUDA

Ghana Airways
3 Princes Street
London W1R 7RA
Tel: **071-499 0201**
Fax: 071-491 1504
Telex: 21415 GHNAIR

Gulf Air
10 Albermarle Street
London W1X 3HE
Tel: **071-408 1717**
Fax: 071-629 3989
Telex: 28591 GFRES

Iberia Airlines
Venture House
29 Glasshouse Street

London W1R 5RG
Tel: **071-413 1201**
Fax: 071-413 0024

Icelandair
172 Tottenham Court Road
London W1P 9LG
Tel: **071-388 5599**
Fax: 071-387 5711
Telex: 23689 ICEAIR

Iran Air
73 Piccadilly
London W1V 0QX
Tel: **071-409 0971**
Fax: 071-408 1360
Telex: 27285 IRHOMA

Japan Airlines
5 Hanover Court
Hanover Square
London W1R 0DR
Tel: **071-408 1000**
Fax: 071-499 1071
Telex: 23692 JALLON

JAT – Yugoslav
37 Maddox Street
London W1R 1AQ
Tel: **071-629 2007**
Fax:071- 493 8092
Telex: 261826 JATLON

Jersey European Airways
Exeter Airport
Exeter EX5 2BD
Tel:**0345 676676**
Fax: 0392 366151
Telex: 42761

Kenya Airways
16 Conduit Street
London W1R 9TD
Tel: **071-409 0277**
Fax: 071-4992973
Telex: 263793 KENAIR

KLM
8 Hanover Street
London W1R 9HF
Tel: **081-750 9000**
Fax: 081-750 9990

Korean Airlines
66-68 Piccadilly
London SW1Y 4RF
Tel: **071-495 0077**
Fax: 071-495 1616
Telex: 919954 KALLDN

Kuwait Airlines
16-20 Baker Street
London W1M 2AD
Tel: **071-412 0006**
Fax: 071-412 0008
Telex: 262518 KWIAIR

LAB (Lloyd Aereo Boliviano)
Suite 051
4th Floor
27 Cockspur Street
London SW1Y 5BN
Tel: **071-930 1442**
Fax: 071-930 1878
Telex: 893369

LAN Chile
150 Buckingham Palace Road
London SW1W 9TR
Tel: **071-730 2128**
Fax: 071-730 1180
Telex: 911455

LIAT c/o British Airways

LOT – Polish
313 Regent Street
London W1R 7PE
Tel: **071-580 5037**
Fax: 071-323 0774
Telex: 27860 LOTLON

Lufthansa
Lufthansa House
10 Old Bond Street
London W1X 4EN
Tel: **081-730 3500**
Fax: 081-750 3460
Telex: 22751

Luxair
Room 2003
Terminal 2
London-Heathrow Airport
Hounslow
Middlesex TW6 1HL
Tel: **081-745 4254**
Fax: 081-759 7974
Telex: 935580 LUXAIR

Malaysia Airlines
191a Askew Road
London W12 9AX
Tel: **081-759 2595**
Fax: 081-862 0117
Telex: 25396 LAYANG

Malev Hungarian
10 Vigo Street
London W1X 1AJ
Tel: **071-439 0577**
Fax: 071-734 8116
Telex: 24841 MALEVL

Mexican
61 High Street
Barnet
Herts EN5 5UR
Tel: **081-441 4084**
Fax: 081-449 5504
Telex: 893313 MEXIIC

Middle East Airlines
45 Albemarle Street
London W1X 3FE
Tel: **071-493 6321**
Fax: 071-629 4163
Telex: 24406 MEAAIR

Nigeria Airways
11-12 Conduit Street
London W1R 0NX
Tel: **071-493 9726**
Fax: 071-491 9644
Telex: 23474

Northwest Airlines
Northwest House
Tinsley Lane North
Crawley
West Sussex RH10 2TP
Tel: **0293-565454**
Fax: 0293-574537
Telex: 266658 NWAIR

Olympic Airways
11 Conduit Street
London W1R 0LP
Tel: **071-409 2400**
Fax: 071-493 0563
Telex: 23135

PIA
1-5 King Street
Hammersmith
London W6 9HR
Tel: **071-734 5544**
Fax: 081-741 9376
Telex: 262503 PIALON

Philippine Airlines
Euro Head Office
Centrepoint
19th Floor
103 New Oxford Street
London WC1 1QD
Tel: **071-836 5508**
Fax: 071-379 6656
Telex: 266479 FILAIR

Qantas
QF House
395/403 King Street
London W6 9NJ
Tel: **081-846 0466**
Fax: 081-748 8551
and...

182 Strand
London WC2
Tel: **0800-477767**

Royal Air Maroc
205 Regent Street
London W1R 7DE
Tel: **071-439 4361**
Telex: 263163 RAMLON

Royal Brunei Airlines
49 Cromwell Road
London W1R 7DD
Tel: **071-584 6660**
Fax: 071-581 9279

Royal Jordanian
211 Regent Street
London W1R 7DD
Tel: **071-734 2557**
Fax: 071-494 0433
Telex: 24330 ALIARJ

Royal Nepal
c/o Dabin Travel Ltd
Butler House
177/178 Tottenham Court Road
London W1P 0HL
Tel: **071-757 2757**
Fax: 071-757 2277
Telex: 265241 DABIN

Ryanair
235-7 Finchley Road
London NW3 6LS
Tel: **071-435 7101**
Fax: 071-794 3373
Telex: 264507

SAA
251-259 Regent Street
London W1R 7AD
Tel: **071-734 9841**
Fax: 071-734 2218
Telex: 25215 SAALON

SAS
52 Conduit Street
London W1R 0AY
Tel: **071-734 4020**
Fax: 071-465 0125
Telex: 8811707 SASLON

Sabena
177 Piccadilly
London W1V 0BU
Tel: **071-495 7272**
Fax: 071-495 0774

Saudia
508-510 Chiswick High Road
London W4 5RG
Tel: **081-995 7777**
Fax: 081-995 8444

Telex: 937957 SAUDIA

Singapore Airlines
580-586 Chiswick High Road
London W4 5RB
Tel: **081-747 0007**
Telex: 935458 SIACHW

Sudan Airways
12 Grosvenor Street
London W1X 9FB
Tel: **071-499 8101**
Fax: 071-499 0976
Telex: 261850 SDLON

Swissair
Swiss Centre
10 Wardour Street
London W1V 4BJ
Tel: **071-439 4144**
Fax: 071-439 7375
Telex: 27784

TAP – Air Portugal
Gillingham House
38-44 Gillingham Street
London SW1V 1JW
Tel: **071-828 0262**
Fax: 071-828 1742
Telex: 261239 TAPLON

Tarom
17 Nottingham Street
London W1M 3RD
Tel: **071-224 3693**
Fax: 071-487 2913
Telex: 262107

Thai International Airways
41 Albermarle Street
London W1X 3FE
Tel: **071-499 9113**
Telex: 21491 THAINT

TWA
200 Piccadilly
London W1V 0DH
Tel: **071-439 2233**
Fax: 071-494 3497
Telex: 22343 TWARES

Turkish Airlines
11/12 Hanover Street
London W1R 9HF
Tel: **071-499 9249**
Fax: 071-495 2441
Telex: 262039

Uganda Airlines
Uganda House
58/59 Trafalgar Square

London WC2N 5DS
Tel: **071-925 0593**
Fax: 071-930 9482
Telex: 8813909

United Airlines
United House
Southern Perimeter Road
London Heathrow Airport
Hounslow TW6 3LP
Tel: **081-990 9988**
Fax: 081-750 9429

Varig Brazilian
16-17 Hanover Street
London W1R 0HG
Tel: **071-629 5824**
Fax: 071-495 6135
Telex: 24686 VRGLON

VIASA
c/o Iberia Airlines

Virgin Atlantic
Ashdown House
High Street
Crawley
West Sussex RH1 1DQ
Tel: **0293-38222**
Fax: 0293 561721
Telex: 877077 VIRAIR

Yemenia
52 Stratton Street
London W1X 5FF
Tel: **071-491 7186**
Telex: 269292 YEMAIR
Fax: 071-355 3062

Zambia Airways
163 Piccadilly
London W1V 9DE
Tel: **071-491 0658**
Fax: 071-491 2795
Telex: 27127 ZAMAIR

AIRLINE TWO–LETTER CODES

The codes listed below are often used in
timetables, brochures and tickets to identify
airlines.

A

AA	American Airlines
AC	Air Canada
AE	Mandarin Airlines
AF	Air France
AH	Air Algerie

AI	Air India
AJ	Air Belgium
AM	AERO MEXICO
AN	Ansett Australia
AO	AVIACO
AQ	Aloha Airlines
AR	Aerolineas Argentinas
AS	Alaska Airlines
AT	Royal Air Maroc
AV	AVIANCA
AY	Finnair
AZ	Alitalia

B

BA	British Airways
BD	British Midland
BG	Biman Bangladesh Airlines
BI	Royal Brunei Airlines
BL	Pacific Airlines
BO	Bouraq Indonesia Airlines
BP	Air Botswana
BR	EVA Airways
BU	Braathens SAFE
BV	Bop Air
BW	BWIA International Trinidad & Tobago Airways
BY	Britannia Airways

C

CA	Air China
CF	Compania de Aviacion Faucett
CI	China Airlines
CK	Gambian Airways
CM	COPA Compania Panamena
CO	Continental Airlines
CP	Canadian Airlines
CU	CUBANA
CW	Air Marshall Islands
CX	Cathay Pacific
CY	Cyprus Airways
CZ	China Southern Airlines

D

DD	Conti-Flug
DL	Delta Airlines
DM	Maersk Air
DO	Dominicana
DS	Air Senegal
DT	TAAG-Angolan Airlines
DY	Alyemda-Democratic Yemen Airlines

E

EF	Far Eastern Air Transport
EG	Japan Asia Airways
EH	SAETA
EI	Aer Lingus
EL	Air Nippon
EM	Empire Airlines

ET	Ethiopian Airlines		KM	Air Malta
EU	ECUATORIANA		KQ	Kenya Airways
EW	Eastwest Airlines		KU	Kuwait Airways
			KV	Transkei Airways
			KX	Cayman Airways

F

FG	Ariana Afghan Airlines
FI	Icelandair
FJ	Air Pacific
FQ	Air Aruba
FR	Ryanair

L

LA	LAN Chile
LB	Lloyd Aereo Boliviano
LC	Loganair
LG	Luxair
LH	Lufthansa
LI	LIAT
LO	LOT Polish Airlines
LR	LACSA
LY	El Al Israel Airlines
LX	Crossair
LZ	Balkan

G

GA	Garuda Indonesia
GE	Trans Asia Airways
GF	Gulf Air
GH	Ghana Airways
GJ	Equatorial International Airlines of Sao Tomé
GN	Air Gabon
GT	GB Airways
GU	AVIATECA
GV	Riga Airlines
GY	Guyana Airways

M

MA	MALEV
MD	Air Madagascar
ME	Middle East Airlines
MK	Air Mauritius
MO	Calm Air International
MR	Air Mauritanie
MS	Egyptair
MW	Maya Airways
MX	Mexicana

H

HA	Hawaiian Airlines
HM	Air Seychelles
HO	Airways International
HP	America West Airlines
HV	Transavia Airlines
HY	Uzbekistan Airlines

N

NF	Air Vanuatu
NG	Lauda Air
NH	All Nippon Airways
NN	Air Martinique
NW	Northwest Airlines
NZ	Air New Zealand

I

IB	IBERIA
IC	Indian Airlines
IE	Solomon Airlines
IJ	TAT European Airlines
IL	Istanbul Airlines
IP	Airlines of Tasmania
IR	Iran Air
IV	Air Gambia
IY	Yemen Airways
IZ	Arkia Israeli Airlines

O

OA	Olympic Airways
OG	Air Guadeloupe
OK	Czechoslovak Airlines
ON	Air Nauru
OS	Austrian Airlines
OU	Croatian Airlines
OV	Estonian Air

J

JE	Manx Airlines
JL	Japan Airlines
JM	Air Jamaica
JP	Adria Airways
JR	Aero California
JY	Jersey European Airways

P

PB	Air Burundi
PC	Fiji Air
PF	Vayudoot
PG	Bangkok Airways
PH	Polynesian Airlines
PK	Pakistan International Airlines
PL	AeroPeru
PR	Philippine Airlines
PS	Ukraine International Airways
PV	Latvian Airlines

K

KA	Dragonair
KB	Druk-Air
KE	Korean Air
KI	Air Atlantique
KL	KLM

PX	Air Niugini
PY	Surinam Airways
PZ	Lineas Aereas Paraguayas

Q

QC	Air Zaire
QF	Qantas Airways
QL	Air Lesotho
QM	Air Malawi
QU	Uganda Airlines
QV	Lao Aviation
QW	Turks and Caicos National Airline
QZ	Zambia Airways

R

RA	Royal Nepal Airline
RB	Syrian Arab Airlines
RG	VARIG
RJ	Royal Jordanian
RK	Air Afrique
RO	TAROM
RR	Royal Air Force
RY	Air Rwanda

S

SA	South African Airways
SD	Sudan Airways
SF	Shanghai Airlines
SH	SAHSA - Servicio Aereo de Honduras
SK	SAS
SN	Sabena
SO	Austrian Air Services
SQ	Singapore Airlines
SR	Swissair
SU	Aeroflot
SV	Saudia
SW	Namib Air
SZ	China Southwest

T

TA	Taca International Airlines
TC	Air Tanzania
TE	Lithuanian Airlines
TG	Thai Airways International
TK	Turkish Airlines
TM	Linhas Aereas de Mocambique
TN	Australian Airlines
TP	TAP Air Portugal
TQ	Transwede
TR	Transbrasil Linhas Aereas
TS	Samoa Aviation
TT	Airline Lithuania
TU	Tunis Air
TW	TWA - Trans World Airlines

U

UA	United Airlines

UB	Myanmar Airways
UK	Air UK
UL	Air Lanka
UM	Air Zimbabwe
UP	Bahamasair
UY	Cameroon Airlines

V

VA	VIASA
VE	AVENSA
VH	Air Burkina
VJ	Kampuchea Airlines
VN	Vietnam Airlines
VO	Tyrolean Airways
VP	VASP
VR	Transportes Aereos de Cabo Verde
VS	Virgin Atlantic
VT	Air Tahiti
VU	Air Ivoire

W

WM	Windward Islands Airways International
WN	Southwest Airlines
WT	Nigeria Airways
WY	Oman Aviation Services

X

XY	Ryan Air (Alaska)

Y

YK	Cyprus Turkish Airlines
YT	Skywest

Z

ZB	Monarch Airlines
ZQ	Ansett New Zealand

AIRPORT/CITY CODES

A

AAK	Aranuka, Kiribati
ABJ	Abidjan, Ivory Coast
ABT	Al-Baha, Saudi Arabia
ABZ	Aberdeen, UK
ACA	Acapulco, Mexico
ACC	Accra, Ghana
ACE	Lanzarote, Canary Islands
ACY	Atlantic City International, USA
ADA	Adana, Turkey
ADD	Addis Ababa, Ethiopia
ADE	Aden, South Yemen
ADL	Adelaide, Australia
AEP	Buenos Aires Airport, Argentina
AGA	Agadir, Morocco
AGP	Malaga, Spain

AGR	Agra, India
AIY	Atlantic City, NJ, USA
AJA	Ajaccio, Corsica
AKL	Auckland, New Zealand
AKS	Auki, Solomon Islands
ALA	Almaty, Kazakhstan
ALB	Albany, NY USA
ALC	Alicante, Spain
ALG	Algiers Algeria
ALP	Aleppo, Syria
ALY	Alexandria, Egypt
AMM	Amman, Jordan
AMS	Amsterdam, Netherlands
ANC	Anchorage, Alaska, USA
ANK	Ankara, Turkey
ANR	Antwerp, Belgium
ANU	Antigua, Leeward Islands
APW	Apia, Samoa
AQJ	Aqaba, Jordan
ARN	Stockholm Arlanda Apt, Sweden
ASB	Ashkhabad, Turkmenistan
ASM	Asmara, Eritrea
ASP	Alice Springs, NT, Australia
ASU	Asuncion, Paraguay
ASW	Aswan, Egypt
ATH	Athens, Greece
ATL	Atlanta, GA, USA
AUA	Aruba, Neth. Antilles
AUH	Abu Dhabi, UAE
AVN	Avignon, France
AXA	Anguilla, Leeward Islands
AYT	Antalya, Turkey

B

BAH	Bahrain
BAK	Baku, Azerbijan
BBQ	Barbuda, Leeward Islands
BBR	Basse-Terre, Guadeloupe
BBU	Bucharest Banfasa Apt, Romania
BCN	Barcelona, Spain
BDA	Bermuda Kindley Field, Bermuda
BEL	Belem, PA Brazil
BER	Berlin West, Germany
BEY	Beirut, Lebanon
BFN	Bloemfontein, South Africa
BFS	Belfast, UK
BGF	Bangui, Central African Rep.
BGI	Barbados
BGO	Bergen, Norway
BGW	Baghdad, Iraq
BHX	Birmingham, UK
BIM	Bimini, Bahamas
BIO	Bilbao, Spain
BJL	Banjul, Gambia
BJM	Bujumbua, Burundi
BJS	Beijing, P R China
BKK	Bangkok, Thailand
BKO	Bamako, Mali
BLQ	Bologna, Itlay
BLZ	Blantyre, Malawi

BNA	Nashville, TN, USA
BNE	Brisbane, QL Australia
BNJ	Bonn, Germany
BOB	Bora Bora, Society Islands
BOD	Bordeaux, France
BOG	Bogota, Colombia
BOM	Bombay, India
BON	Bonaire, Netherland Antilles
BOS	Boston, MA USA
BRE	Bremen, Germany
BRN	Berne, Switzerland
BRU	Brussels, Belgium
BSB	Brasilia, Brazil
BSL	Basle, Switzerland
BTH	Batu Besar, Indonesia
BTS	Bratislava, Slovakia
BUD	Budapest, Hungary
BUE	Buenos Aires, Argentina
BUH	Bucharest, Romania
BUQ	Bulawayo, Zimbabwe
BWI	Baltimore, MD, USA
BWN	Bandar Seri Begawan, Brunei
BXO	Bissau, Guinea-Bissau
BZE	Belize City
BZV	Brazzaville, Congo

C

CAI	Cairo, Egypt
CAP	Cap Haitien, Haiti
CAS	Casablanca, Morocco
CAY	Cayenne, French Guiana
CBR	Canberra, ACT, Australia
CCS	Caracas, Venzuela
CCU	Calcutta, India
CDG	Paris Charles de Gaulle, France
CEB	Cebu, Phillipines
CFU	Corfu, Greece
CGH	Sao Paulo Congonhas Apt, Brazil
CGK	Jakarta Airport, Indonesia
CGN	Cologne, Germany
CGP	Chittagong, Bangladesh
CHC	Christchurch, New Zealand
CHI	Chicago, IL USA
CIA	Rome Ciampino Apt, Italy
CJU	Chetu, Republic of Korea
CKY	Conakry, Guinea
CLE	Cleveland, OH, USA
CLT	Charlotte, NC, USA
CMB	Colombo, Sri Lanka
CNS	Cairns, QL, Australia
COO	Cotonou, Benin
COS	Colorado Springs, CO, USA
CPH	Copenhagen, Denmark
CPT	Cape Town, South Africa
CUE	Cuenca, Ecuador
CUN	Cancun, Mexico
CUR	Curacao, Neth. Antilles
CVG	Cincinnati, OH, USA
CYB	Cayman Brac, Cayman Islands

D

DAC	Dhaka, Bangladesh
DAD	Da Nang, Vietnam
DAL	Dallas, Fort Worth, TX , USA
DAM	Damascus, Syria
DAR	Dar es Salaam, Tanzania
DBV	Dubrovnik, Croatia
DCF	Dominica Airport
DEL	Delhi, India
DEN	Denver, CO, USA
DFW	Dallas/Fort Worth, TX USA
DHA	Dharan, Saudi Arabia
DKR	Dakar, Senegal
DLA	Douala, Cameroon
DME	Moscow Domodedovo Apt., Russia
DOH	Doha, Qatar
DOM	Dominica
DRS	Dresden, Germany
DRW	Darwin, NT, Australia
DTT	Detroit, MI, USA
DUB	Dublin, Ireland
DUR	Durban, South Africa
DUS	Dusseldorf, German
DXB	Dubai, UAE
DYB	Dushanbe, Tajikistan

E

EBB	Entebbe, Kampala, Uganda
EDI	Edinburgh, UK
EIS	Beef Island, British Virgin Islands
EMA	East Midlands Airport, UK
ERS	Windhoek Eros A/port, Namibia
ESB	Ankara International Apt, Turkey
ETH	Eilat, Israel
EWR	New York Newark Apt, NJ, USA
EZE	Ministro Pistarini, Buenos Aires Apt, Brazil

F

FAE	Faroe Islands, Denmark
FAI	Fairbanks, AK, USA
FAO	Faro, Portugal
FBU	Oslo Int A/port, Norway
FCO	Rome, Leonardo da Vinci Apt, Italy
FDF	Fort de France A/port, French West Indies
FEZ	Fez, Morocco
FIH	Kinshasa, Zaire
FKI	Kisangani, Zaire
FLL	Fort Lauderdale, FL, USA
FLR	Florence, Italy
FMY	Fort Myers, Florida, USA
FNA	Freetown, Sierra Leone
FNC	Funchal, Madeira
FNJ	Pyongyang, North Korea
FPO	Freeport, Bahamas
FRA	Frankfurt Int Apt, Germany
FUK	Fukuoka, Japan

G

GBE	Gaborone, Botswana
GCI	Guernsey, UK
GCM	Grand Cayman, Cayman Islands
GDN	Gdansk, Poland
GDT	Grand Turk, Turks and Caicos
GEN	Oslo Gardermoen Apt, Norway
GEO	Georgetown, Guyana
GGT	George Town, Bahamas
GIB	Gibraltar
GIG	Rio de Janeiro Int Apt, Brazil
GLA	Glasgow, UK
GND	Grenada, Windward Islands
GOT	Gottenburg, Sweden
GUA	Guatemala City, Guatemala
GUM	Guam
GVA	Geneva, Switzerland
GYE	Guayaquil, Ecuador

H

HAJ	Hanover, Germany
HAK	Haikou, PR China
HAM	Hamburg, Germany
HAN	Hanoi, Vietnam
HAV	Havana, Cuba
HEL	Helsinki, Finland
HIR	Honiara, Solomon Islands
HKG	Hong Kong Int Apt, Hong Kong
HKP	Phuket, Thailand
HLP	Jakarta Airport, Indonesia
HND	Tokyo Haneda Apt, Japan
HNL	Honolulu Int Apt, HI USA
HOU	Houston, TX USA
HRE	Harare, Zimbabwe

I

IAD	Washington Dulles Int Apt, DC
IAH	Houston Int Apt, TX USA
IBZ	Ibiza, Spain
IEV	Kiev, Ukraine
IHO	Ihosy, Madagascar
IND	Indianapolis, IN, USA
INN	Innsbruck, Austria
INU	Nauru
IOM	Isle of Man, UK
ISB	Islamabad, Pakistan
IST	Istanbul, Turkey
IUE	Niue

J

JAX	Jacksonville, FL, USA
JED	Jeddah, Saudi Arabia
JER	Jersey, UK
JFK	New York John F. Kennedy Apt, NY USA
JIB	Djibouti
JKT	Jakarta, Indonesia
JNB	Johannesburg, South Africa
JOG	Yogyakarta, Indonesia

JRS	Jerusalem, Israel

K

KAN	Kano, Nigeria
KBL	Kabul, Afghanistan
KEF	Reykjavik Keflavik Apt, Iceland
KGL	Kigali, Rwanda
KHH	Kaohsiung, Taiwan
KHI	Karachi, Pakistan
KIN	Kingston, Jamaica
KMS	Kumasa, Ghana
KRT	Khartoum, Sudan
KTM	Kathmandu, Nepal
KUL	Kuala Lumpur, Malaysia
KWI	Kuwait

L

LAD	Luanda, Angola
LAS	Las Vegas, NY USA
LAX	Los Angeles, CA USA
LBV	Libreville, Gabon
LCA	Larnaca, Cyprus
LCY	London City Airport, UK
LED	St Petersburg, Russia
LFW	Lome, Togo
LGA	New York La Guardia Apt, NY
LGW	London, Gatwick Apt UK
LHE	Lahore, Pakistan
LHR	London, UK - Heathrow Apt
LIM	Lima, Peru
LIN	Milan Int A/port, Itlay
LIS	Lisbon, Portugal
LJU	Ljubljana, Slovenia
LLG	Lilongwe, Malawi
LON	London, UK
LOS	Lagos, Nigeria
LPB	La Paz, Bolivia
LTN	London, UK - Luton Int.
LUN	Lusaka, Zambia
LUX	Luxembourg
LXA	Lhasa, Tibet, China
LXR	Luxor, Egypt
LYS	Lyon, France

M

MAA	Madras, India
MAD	Madrid, Spain
MAH	Menorca, Spain
MAN	Manchester
MAO	Manaus, Brazil
MAR	Maracaibo, Venezuela
MBA	Mombasa, Kenya
MBJ	Montego Bay, Jamaica
MCM	Monte Carlo, Monaco
MCT	Muscat, Oman
MDL	Mandalay, Myanmar
MED	Medina, Saudi Arabia
MEL	Melbourne, Australia
MEM	Memphis, TN, USA

MEX	Mexico City, Mexico
MGA	Managua, Nicaragua
MGQ	Mogadishu, Somalia
MIA	Miami, FL USA
MIL	Milan, Italy
MKC	Kansas City, MO, USA
MKE	Milwaukee, WI, USA
MLA	Malta
MLE	Male, Maldives
MLW	Monrovia, Liberia
MNI	Montserrat, Leeward Islands
MNL	Manila, Philippines
MOW	Moscow, Russia
MPM	Maputo, Mozambique
MQS	Mustique
MRS	Marseille, France
MRU	Mauritius
MSP	Minneapolis, MN, USA
MSQ	Minsk, Belarus
MST	Maastricht, Netherlands
MSU	Maseru, Lesotho
MUC	Munich, Germany
MVD	Montevideo, Uruguay

N

NAN	Nadi International Airport, Fiji
NAP	Naples, Itlay
NAS	Nassau, Bahamas
NBO	Nairobi, Kenya
NCE	Nice, France
NCL	Newcastle, UK
NGU	Nagoya, Japan
NIM	Niamey, Niger
NKC	Nouakchott, Mauritania
NOU	Noumea, New Caledonia
NRT	Tokyo Narita Apt, Japan
NSN	Nelson, New Zealand
NUE	Nuremberg, Germany
NYC	New York, NY USA

O

OKA	Okinawa, Naha Airport, Japan
OKA	Oklahoma, OK, USA
OOL	Gold Coast, QL, Australia
OPO	Porto, Portugal
ORD	Chicago O'Hare Int Apt, IL USA
ORG	Paramaribo Zorg En Hoop Apt, Suriname
ORL	Orlando, FL, USA
ORY	Paris Orly Apt, France
OSA	Osaka, Japan
OSL	Oslo, Norway
OTP	Bucharest Int A/Port, Romania
OUA	Ouagadougou, Burkina Faso

P

PAC	Panama City Paitilla Apt, Panama
PAP	Port au Prince, Haiti
PAR	Paris, France

PBM	Paramaribo, Suriname
PCC	Puerto Rico, Colombia
PDX	Portland, OR, USA
PEK	Beijing Capital Apt, China
PEN	Penang Int Apt, Malaysia
PER	Perth, WA, Australia
PHL	Philadelphia, PA, USA
PHX	Pheonix, AZ, USA
PIT	Pittsburg, PA, USA
PLZ	Port Elizabeth, South Africa
PMI	Palma de Mallorca, Spain
PNH	Phnom-Penh, Cambodia
PNI	Pohnpei Int, Micronesia
POM	Port Moresby, Papua New Guinea
POS	Port of Spain, Trinidad and Tobago
PPG	Pago Pago, American Samoa
PPT	Papeete, Tahiti
PRG	Prague, Czech Republic
PTP	Pointe-a-Pitre, Guadeloupe
PTY	Panama City, Panama

R

RAI	Praia, Cape Verde
RAK	Marrakesh, Morocco
ARA	Rarotonga, Cook Islands
RBA	Rabat, Morocco
REK	Reyjavik, Iceland
RGN	Yangon, Myanmar
RIO	Rio de Janeiro, Brazil
RIX	Riga, Latvia
ROC	Rochester, NY, USA
ROM	Rome, Italy
RTM	Rotterdam, Netherlands
RUH	Riyadh, Saudi Arabia
RUN	St Denis, Reunion

S

SAH	Sanaa, Republic of Yemen
SAL	San Salvador, El Salvador
SAN	San Diego, CA, USA
SAO	Sao Paulo, Brazil
SAT	San Antonio, TX, USA
SCL	Santiago, Chile
SDA	Baghdad Saddam Int Apt, Iraq
SDQ	Santo Domingo, Dominican Rep.
SDV	Tel Aviv Sde - Dov Int Apt, Israel
SEA	Seattle, WA, USA
SEL	Seoul, Korea
SEZ	Mahe Island, Seychelles
SFO	San Francisco, CA USA
SGN	Ho Chi Minh City, Vietnam
SHA	Shanghai, China
SHJ	Dubai, Int, A/Port
SID	Sal Amilcar Int A/port, Cape Verde
SIN	Singapore
SJO	San Jose, Costa Rica
SJU	San Juan, Puerto Rico
SKB	St. Kitts, Leeward Islands
SKP	Skopje, Macedonia
SLC	Salt Lake City, UT, USA

SLU	St Lucia
SNN	Shannon, Ireland
SOF	Sofia, Bulgaria
SRZ	Santa Cruz, Bolivia
STL	St Louis, MO USA
STN	London Stansted Apt, UK
STO	Stockholm, Sweden
STR	Stuttgart, Germany
SVO	Moscow Sheretyevo Apt, Russia
SXB	Strasbourg, France
SXF	Berlin A/Port, Germany
SXM	Saint Maarten, Netherland Antilles
SXR	Srinagar, India
SYD	Sydney, Australia
SZG	Salzburg, Austria

T

TAB	Tobago, Trinidad & Tobago
TAS	Tashkent, Uzbekistan
TCI	Tenerife, Canary Islands
THF	Berlin Tempelhof Apt, Germany
THR	Tehran, Iran
TIP	Tripoli, Libya
TLL	Tallinn, Estonia
TLS	Toulouse, France
TLV	Tel Aviv Israel
TNG	Tangier, Morocco
TNR	Antananarivo, Madagascar
TPE	Taipei, Taiwan
TRN	Turin, Itlay
TSR	Timisoara, Romania
TUN	Tunis, Tunisia
TXL	Tegel Berlin Aport, Germany
TYO	Tokyo, Japan
TZA	Belize City Municipal Apt, Belize

U

UIO	Quito, Ecuador
UVF	Saint Lucia, Int A/port

V

VCE	Venice, Itlay
VIE	Vienna, Austria
VNO	Vilnius, Lithuania
VTE	Vientiane, Laos

W

WAS	Washington, DC USA
WAW	Warsaw, Poland
WDH	Windhoek, Namibia
WLG	Wellington, New Zealand

X

XCH	Christmas Island

Y

YAP	Yap, Caroline Islands
YAO	Yaounde, Cameroon

YEA	Edmonton, AL, Canada
YEG	Edmonton Int A/Port, AL, Canada
YHZ	Halifax, NS, Canada
YMQ	Montreal, Quebec, Canada
YMX	Montreal Int A/port, Canada
YOW	Ottawa Ontario, Canada
YQB	Quebec City, QU, Canada
YTO	Toronto, OT, Canada
YTZ	Toronto Island A/Port, Canada
YUL	Montreal Dorval Int A/port Canada
YVR	Vancouver, BC, Canada
YWG	Winnipeg, MN, Canada
YYC	Calgary, AL, Canada
YYJ	Victoria, BC, Canada
YYZ	Toronto Int A/Port, OT, Canada

Z

| ZAG | Zagreb, Croatia |
| ZRH | Zurich, Switzerland |

MAJOR AIRPORTS WORLDWIDE

Country	City	Airport Name	Distance from town Miles	kms	Telephone No
Argentina	Buenos Aires	Ministro Pistarini	31.5	50	54-620 0011
Australia	Adelaide	Adelaide	3.7	6	61 8-352 9211
	Brisbane	International	7	11	61 7-860 8600
	Cairns	International	3	5	61 70-523 877
	Canberra	Canberra	4	6	61 6-243 5911
	Darwin	International	10	16	61 89-201811
	Melbourne	Melbourne	13	21	61 3-339 1805
	Perth	Perth	6	10	61 9-478 8888
	Sydney	Kingsford Smith	6	10	61 2-667 9978
Austria	Innsbruck	Flughafen	3.5	5.5	43 512 22525
	Salzburg	Salzburg	2.5	4	43 662 8555
	Vienna	Vienna	11	18	43 171110
Bahamas	Nassau	International	10	16	809-32 77281
Bahrain	Manama	International	4	6.5	973-321 000
Bangladesh	Dhaka	Zia International	11	20	880 289 4375
Barbados	Bridgetown	Grantley Adams	6.8	11	1 809 428 7101
Belgium	Antwerp	Deurne	2	3	32 3-218 1211
	Brussels	National	8	13	32 2-722 3211
Belize	Belize City	PSW Goldson Int.	10	16	501-25 2045
Bermuda	Hamilton	Civil Air	10	16	1 809-293 1640
Bolivia	La Paz	El Alto	9	14.5	591-2 812064
Botswana	Gaborone	Sir Seretse Khama	9	15	26 735 1191
Brazil	Rio de Janeiro	International	13	21	55 213984597
	Sao Paulo	Guarulhos Int.	16	25	55 11-945 2200
Bulgaria	Sofia	International	6	10	359-2 72291
Canada	Calgary	International	5	8	1 403-292 8400
	Edmonton	International	17	28	1 403-890 8324
	Montreal	Dorval Int.	15	25	1 514-633 3105
		Mirabel	33	53	1 514-476 3010
	Ottawa	International	11	17.5	1 613-998 3151
	Toronto	Lester B Pearson Int.	17	27	1 905-247 7678
	Vancouver	International	9	15	1 604-276 7780
	Winnipeg	International	6	10	1 204-983 8400
Chile	Santiago	Comodoro Arturo Merino Benitez	13	21	56 2-601 9001
China	Beijing	Capital	16	26	86 1-456 4201
	Shanghai	Hongqiao	8	13	86 21-253 6530
Colombia	Bogotá	Eldorado	7.5	12	57 1-266 9200
Croatia	Zagreb	Zagreb	10	16	385 41 462222
Cuba	Havana	José Marti Int.	11	18	53-707701
Cyprus	Larnaca	Larnaca	5	8	357-4654 389
Czech Republic	Prague	Ruzyné	11	17	42 2334 3113
Denmark	Copenhagen	International	5	8	45-32 509333
Ecuador	Quito	Mariscal Sucre	5	8	59 34546333
Egypt	Cairo	International	14	22	20 2-2914 4255
Finland	Helsinki	Vantaa	12	19	35 8-08771
France	Bordeaux	Merignac	7	12	33-56 345000
	Lyons	Satolas	15	24	33-72 227221
	Marseille	Provence	15	24	33-42 782100
	Nice	Côte d'Azur	4	6	33-93 213030
	Paris	Charles de Gaulle	14	23	33-1 4862 1212
		Orly	9	14	33-1 4975 1515
	Strasbourg	International	7	12	33-88 646767

From 16 April 1995 all national and international codes change — see page 587 for details.

Country	City	Airport Name	Distance from town Miles	kms	Telephone No
Germany	Berlin	Schonefeld	12	19	49-306 6091
		Tegel	5	8	49-304 1011
	Cologne	Cologne-Bonn	9	14	49-2203 400
	Düsseldorf	International	5	8	49-211 421
	Frankfurt	International	6	10	49-69 6901
	Hamburg	Fuhlsbüttel	5	9	49-40 5075
	Munich	Flughafen	18	28	49-89 97500
Greece	Athens	Athinai	9	14	30-1 96991
Hong Kong	Hong Kong	International	2.8	4.5	852-769 8488
Hungary	Budapest	Ferihegy	10	16	36-1 157 7906
Iceland	Reykjavik	Keflavik	32	51	354-2 50600
India	Bombay	International	18	29	91-22 612 3135
	Calcutta	International	8	13	91-33 569977
	Delhi	Indira Gandhi Int.	14	20	91-11 391351
Indonesia	Jakarta	Soekarno-Hatta	14	20	62-21 5505001
Iran	Tehran	Mehrabad	3	5	98 21 91021
Iraq	Baghdad	Saddam International	11.25	18	964-1 549 8000
Ireland	Dublin	Dublin	5	8	353 1 8444900
Israel	Tel Aviv	Ben Gurion	12	19	972-3 97 10111
Italy	Milan	Linate	6	10	39-2 28106306
	Naples	Capodichino	4	6	39-81 789 661
	Rome	Leonardo da Vinci	22	35	39-6 60121
	Venice	Marco Polo	8	13	39-41 2606111
Jamaica	Kingston	Norman Manley	11	17	809-924 8452
Japan	Osaka	International	10	16	81-684 31121
	Tokyo	Narita	40	65	81-476 322802
Jordan	Amman	Queen Alia	20	32	962-8 5 2000
Kenya	Mombasa	Moi International	8.1	13	254-11 433211
Korea	Seoul	Kimpo International	10	17	82- 2 660 2234
Kuwait	Kuwait	International	10	16	965-335599
Lebanon	Beirut	International	10	16	961-220 500
Luxembourg	Luxembourg	Findel	3	5	352-4798 2008
Malaysia	Kuala Lumpur	Subang International	14	22	60-3 746 1833
Malta	Valletta	International	3	5	35 624 9400
Mexico	Acapulco	Juan N Alvarez	16	26	52-748 44741
	Mexico City	Benito Juarez	8	13	52 5 571 3600
Morocco	Casablanca	Mohammed V	19	30	212-33 9040
Netherlands	Amsterdam	Schiphol Int.	9	14	31-20 517 9111
New Zealand	Auckland	International	14	22	64-9 275 0789
	Christchurch	International	6	10	64-3 585 029
	Wellington	International	5	8	64-43 888500
Nigeria	Lagos	Murtala Muhammed	14	22	234 1 901707
Norway	Oslo	Fornebu	5	8	47-2 675 93340
Pakistan	Karachi	International	10	15	92-21 45914444
	Islamabad	International	5	8	92-51 590256
Peru	Lima	Jorge Chavez Int.	10	16	51-14 529570
Philippines	Manila	Ninoy Aquino Int.	7	12	63-2 832 1961
Portugal	Lisbon	Lisbon	4.5	7	351-1 881 101
Qatar	Doha	Doha	5	8	974-321 550
Romania	Bucharest	Otopeni	10	16	4016333137
Russia	Moscow	Sheremetyevo	18	29	7-095 578 7742
	St Petersburg	Pulkovo	10.5	17	7-812 1043456
Saudi Arabia	Dhahran	International	8	13	966-386 40817
	Jeddah	King Abdulaziz	11	18	966-216854212
	Riyadh	King Khaled	22	35	966-1 2211000
Singapore	Singapore	Changi	12	20	65-542 1122

From 16 April 1995 all national and international codes change — see page 587 for details.

Country	City	Airport Name	Distance from town Miles	kms	Telephone No
South Africa	Johannesburg	Jan Smuts	15	24	27-11 2169111
Spain	Barcelona	Barcelona	6	10	34-3 478 5032
	Madrid	Madrid	10	16	34-1 3056112
Sri Lanka	Colombo	Katunayake	20	32	944 52861
Sweden	Stockholm	Arlanda	25	40	46-8 797 6000
Switzerland	Basle	Basle	4	7	41-61 325 3111
	Berne	Belp	5.5	9	41-31 9613411
	Geneva	Geneva	3	5	41-22 7177111
	Zurich	Zurich	7	11	41-1 816 2211
Syria	Damascus	International	18	29	963-11 430405
Taiwan	Taipei	Chaing Kai Shek Int.	25	40	886-3 398 2001
Tanzania	Dar Es Salaam	International	9	15	255 51 44211
Thailand	Bangkok	International	13	22	66-2 5351515
Turkey	Ankara	Esenboga	22	35	90-4 3980329
	Istanbul	Atatürk	15	24	90-1 573 2920
UAE	Abu Dhabi	International	21	35	971-2 757611
	Dubai	International	3	5	971-4 245777
UK	Aberdeen	Dyce	7	11	0224 722331
	Belfast	International	13	21	08494 22888
	Birmingham	International	8	13	021-767 5511
	Bristol	Bristol	7	11	0275 474444
	Cardiff	Cardiff-Wales	12	19	0446 711111
	Derby	East Midlands Int	12	19	0332 810621
	Edinburgh	Edinburgh	7	11	031-333 1000
	Glasgow	Glasgow	9	14	041-887 1111
	Liverpool	Liverpool	7	11	051-486 8877
	London	London City	6	10	071-474 5555
		Gatwick	28	46	0293 535353
		Heathrow	15	24	081-759 4321
		Stansted	34	50	0279 680 500
	Luton	Luton Int.	3.1	5	0582 405100
	Manchester	Manchester	10	16	061-489 3495
	Newcastle	International	5	8	091-286 0966
	Norwich	Norwich	4	6.4	0603 411923
	Darlington	Teeside Int.	6	10	0325 332811
USA	Atlanta	Hartsfield	10	16	1 404 530 6834
	Baltimore	International	10	16	1 410 859 7111
	Boston	Logan International	4	6	1 617-5671 1800
	Chicago	O'Hare International	17	27	1 312-686 8069
	Cincinnati	Northern Kentucky	12	20	1 606 283 3151
	Cleveland	Hopkins International	12	19	1 216 265 6000
	Dallas	Fort Worth	15	24	1 214-574 3197
	Denver	Stapleton International	6	10	1 303 270 1250
	Detroit	Metropolitan	20	32	1 313 942 3550
	Honolulu	International	6	10	1 808 838 8709
	Houston	Intercontinental	20	32	1 713 443 1714
	Kansas City	International	20	32	1 816 243 5237
	Las Vegas	McCarran Int.	9	14	1 702-261 5211
	Los Angeles	International	15	27	1 213-646 5252
	Miami	International	7	11	1 305-876 7017
	Minneapolis	International	10	16	1 612 726 5555
	New Orleans	International	10	16	1 504 464 0831
	New York	JFK	14	22	1 718-656 4520
		La Guardia	8	13	1 718-533 3400
	Newark	International	2	3	1 201-9616000
	Orlando	International	10	16	1 407-825 2055

From 16 April 1995 all national and international codes change — see page 587 for details.

Country	City	Airport Name	Distance from town		Telephone No
			Miles	kms	
	Philadelphia	International	8	13	1 215 937 1930
	Pheonix	Sky Harbour	4	6	1 602 273 3321
	Pittsburg	Greater Pittsburg	16	26	1 412 778 2500
	Portland	International	9	14.5	1 503 335 1121
	St Louis	Lambert International	13	21	1 314 426 8000
	San Diego	International	2	3	1 619 231 5221
	San Francisco	International	15	25	1 415-876 2217
	Seattle	Tacoma International	14	22	1 206 433 4645
	Washington DC	Dulles Int.	26	43	1 703-661 2700
		National	4	7	1 703 419 9800
Zambia	Lusaka	Lusaka	16	26	260 1 271044
Zimbabwe	Harare	Harare	7.5	12	0-50422

Further reading:
The International Air Travel Handbook (ABC)
BAA Flight Guide (BAA)
ABC Air Travel Atlas (ABC)
ABC World Airways Guide – Part 1 & 2 (ABC)

AIRPORT/DEPARTURE TAXES

Please note taxes can and do change, and although the information below was correct at the time of going to press it is advisable to check with your travel agent.

Afghanistan	Af2000
Albania	1000 Leks
Algeria	*None*
American Samoa	*None*
Angola	*None*
Anguilla	XCD 13
Antigua & Barbuda	US$ 8 for nationals
	US$10 for others
Argentina	US$3 (domestic)
	US$10 (international)
Aruba	US$10
Australia	A$25
Austria	*None*
Bahamas	BSD13
Bahrain	BHD3
Bangladesh	BDT300
Barbados	BBD 25
Belgium	BFr250 (Antwerp)
	BFr350 (Brussels)
Belize	Bz$22.50
Benin	CFAFr2500
Bermuda	B$15
Bolivia	BOD 8 (domestic)
	US$15(international)
Botswana	*None*
Brazil	BRR 360 (domestic)
	US$17 (international)
British Virgin Islands	US$5
Brunei	BN$5 to Malaysia and
	Singapore
	BN$12 to all other
	destinations
Bulgaria	*None*
Burkina Faso	*None*
Burundi	BIF2420 or US$20
Cambodia	US$8
Cameroon	*None*
Canada	Included in ticket
	except from Vancouver
	CA$5 for destinations
	within British
	Colombia, CA$ 10 for
	other N American
	destinations, otherwise
	CA$15.
Cape Verde	*None*
Cayman Islands	CI$8 or US$9.40
Central African Rep.	CFA2000
Chad	CFA2500
Chile	US$12.50
China	CNY25 (domestic)
	CNY90 (international)
Colombia	US$17
Comoro Islands	CFA Fr 100-500
Congo	CFA500
Cook Islands	NZ$20;
	NZ$10 (Children)
Costa Rica	US$31
Cote d'Ivoire	XOF 3 (Africa)
	XOF 5 (elsewhere)
Croatia	US$4 (domestic)
	US$8 (international)
Cuba	*None*
Curacao	NAG18 (US$10)
Cyprus	*None*
Czech Republic	*None*
Denmark	*None*
Djibouti	DJF2000 (except Air
	France passengers)
Dominica	*None*
Dominican Republic	US$10
Ecuador	US$25
Egypt	EG£21
El Salvador	ESc 148 or USD14
Equatorial Guinea	CFA Fr 4000 (can vary)
Eritrea	Br50 international +
	Br3 for security charge
Estonia	*None*
Ethiopia	US$10
Falkland Islands	*None*
Fiji	FJD10
Finland	*None*
France	*None*
French Guiana	*None*
French Polynesia	*None*
Gabon	*None*
Gambia	Di35 for residents
	Di112 for non-residents
Georgia	*None*
Germany	*None*
Ghana	US$10
Gibraltar	*None*
Greece	*None*
Grenada	XCD35
Guatemala	GTQ 50
Guinea	GNF4800 (Africa)
	GNF9000 (elsewhere)
Guinea-Bissau	US$8 (local)
	US$12 (long-haul)
Guyana	GYD1500
Haiti	US$15
Honduras	L95 or US$10
Hong Kong	HKD150
	+20 security tax
Hungary	*None*
Iceland	£13
India	INR150 (sub continent)
	INR300 (long-haul)
Indonesia	IDR3500-4000 (dom)
	INR17000 (Intern.)
Iran	IRR1500
Iraq	ID10
Ireland	*None*

Israel	None
Italy	None
Jamaica	JMD400
Japan	JPY2000
Jordan	JOD10
Kenya	US$20 (international)
	KE$50 (domestic)
Kiribati	AUD 5
Korea (south)	KRW7200
Kuwait	KD2
Lebanon	None
Lesotho	LSL10
Liberia	US$20
Laos	US$5
Latvia	None
Lithuania	None
Luxembourg	None
Macau	None
Madagascar	MGF33000
Malawi	US$20
Malaysia	MYR3 (domestic)
	MYR20 (international)
Maldives	US$10
Mali	CFA Fr2500 (Africa)
	CFA FR (elsewhere)
Malta	None
Martinque	Ffr15
Mauritania	MRO 220 (Africa)
	MRO 560 (outside Africa)
Mauritius	MUR100
Mexico	US$9.40 (domestic)
	US$11.50 (intern.)
Micronesia	US$6
Mongolia	None
Montserrat	US$8
Morocco	None
Mozambique	US$20 (international)
	US$10 (domestic)
Myanmar	US$6
Namibia	None
Nauru	AUD10
Nepal	NPR6 (subcontinent)
	NPR7 (elsewhere)
Netherlands	None
New Caledonia	None
New Zealand	NZD20
Nicaragua	US$10
Niger	CFA3500
Nigeria	US$20
Niue	NZ$20
Norway	None
Oman	OR3
Pakistan	PKR20 (domestic)
	PKR200-400 (Intern.)
Panama	US$20
Papua New Guinea	PGK15
Paraguay	US$15
Peru	US$15
Philippines	PHP24 (domestic)
	PHP500(international)

Poland	None
Portugal	None
Puerto Rico	None
Qatar	None
Reunion	None
Romania	None
Russian Federation	None
Rwanda	RWF300 (domestic)
	RWF1500(intern.)
Saba	US$5 to St Kitts
	US$2 other Windward Islands
St Eustatius	US$10
St. Kitts & Nevis	XCD20 or US£8
St. Lucia	EC$20(Caribbean)
	EC$27 (other)
St Maarten	US$5 Caribbean
	US$10 International
St. Vincent & the Grenadines	ECD20
Samoa (American)	None
Sao Tomé e Principe	US$ 20 or local equivalent
Saudi Arabia	None
Senegal	CFA2000 (domestic)
	CFA4000 (Africa)
	CFA5000 (Ex Africa)
Seychelles	None
Sierra Leone	Le 5000
Singapore	SGD15
Slovak Republic	US$5.98
Slovenia	DM22
Solomon Islands	SBD30
Somalia	US$20
South Africa	None
Spain	None
Sri Lanka	SLr 500
Sudan	SDP500
Suriname	None
Swaziland	SZL10
Sweden	None
Switzerland	None
Syria	SYP200
Tawain	TWD300
Tanzania	US$20
Thailand	Bt200
Togo	None
Tonga	T$15
Trinidad & Tobago	TTD75
Tunisia	TD 4.50
Turkey	None
Turks & Caicos	US$15
Tuvalu	A$10
Uganda	US$23 or local equivalent
United Arab Emirates	None
UK	£5 domestic and EU Destinations
	£10 others
United States	None
Uruguay	US$11

Vanuatu	VUV200 (domestic)
	VUV1500 (intern.)
Venezuela	VEB505
	Also VEB530 for exit
	form and stamp
Vietnam	US$5
Western Samoa	S$20
Yemen	US$10
Zaire	US$8 (domestic)
	US$20 (international)
Zambia	US$20 (international)
	ZMK200 (domestic)
Zimbabwe	US$20

Transit passengers, children and diplomats are often exempted or charged a reduced rate.

AIRPASSES

Airpasses are an increasingly popular option for air travellers seeking flexibility and a wider range of destinations for an all-inclusive price. The variety and number will change regularly as will the price. The information quoted below was correct at the time of going to press.

Africa

Air Zimbabwe
No longer issue Air Passes, however the domestic fares within Zimbabwe are cheap.

Royal Air Maroc
Discover Morocco Fare US$119-149
Any 4 or 6 domestic sectors (one month)

South African Airlines
Do not issue Air Passes as such, although they do have competitive add-on fares when flying long haul.

Europe

British Midland
The Diamond Europass £799
Valid for 5 return flights from Heathrow to key cities in Europe. Regional departures and a wider range of destinations are available for £999. Both passes are valid for 3 months.

Finnair
Holiday Ticket US$400
Up to 10 flights within Finland valid for 30 days.

SAS
The Visit Scandinavia Pass from £55
Covers domestic flights within Denmark, Norway and Sweden plus international flights between all 3 countries. Prices start at £55 for 1 coupon, 2 coupons £110. Additional coupons, up to a maximum of 6 are £55 each and are valid for the same duration as the international ticket to Scandinavia

Sabena
Skypass £599 plus £50 tax
Offers 30 days unlimited travel in Economy Class on all Sabena services from London Heathrow and City airports to Brussels and Antwerp. A Business Skypass offers unlimited Business Class travel for the same duration and destinations for £799 plus £50 tax.

Latin America

Aerolineas Argentinas:
Visit Argentina Pass from US$450
Allows a minimum of 4 coupons for US$450 to a maximum of 8 with additional coupons costing US$120 each. One stopover allowed per city. Valid for 30 days. International flights must be be with Aerolineas Argentinas.

Mercosur Pass
Links 36 Argentine cities with those of Brazil, Uruguay and Paraguay, valid on the services of Aerolineas Argentinas and eight other carriers. Fares based on the number of kilometres travelled, with a maximum of 2 stops per country, valid for 30 days.

Avianca
Visit Colombia from US$220
Prices vary with the amount of stops made. The minimum 5 in low season costs $220 and the maximum 8 is $340 in low season if the international flight is booked with Avianca. The pass is still available to those who use alternative airlines, however it is more expensive. The pass is valid for 21 days

Avianca/Varig/LAB/Faucett
Condor Pass from £1087
Covers Colombia, Argentina, Venezuela, Peru, Bolivia, Uruguay, Brazil, Chile and Ecuador

Faucett
30-day Pass from US$99
The price depends on the amount of sectors, 2 coupons $99; 3 coupons $139; 4 coupons $169 and 5 coupons $199. These can be issued by most international carriers who fly to Peru.

90-day Passes from £159
These passes are unlimited in the amount of sectors flown, however you can only fly to each Faucett destination once. If the international flight to Peru is with Faucett the cost is £159, for other airlines £194.

Iberia:
Visit Peru Fare US$250
Valid for a maximum of 7 flights within Peru within 45 days.

Lloyd Aereo Boliviano (LAB):
VIBOLPASS £108
Allows unlimited flight within Bolivia to the following destinations La Paz, Cochabamba, Trinidad, Tarija, Santa Cruz, Sucre. The pass is only available if international flights to Bolivia is with LAB. The pass is valid for 28 days.

LAN Chile
Visit Chile Pass from US$300
Certain set routings in Chile (max. 21 days)

Mexicana
MexiPass from US$140
Prices vary depending on amount of sectors flown and in which zones. Zone A is $70 a sector: Zone B is $Certain routes (21 days)

Varig
Brazil Air Pass US$440
Available if international flight to Brazil is with Varig. The air pass costs from US$ 440 for up to 5 sectors to a maximum of 9 from US$840. One stopover per city is allowed and it is valid for 21 days.

North and America and the Carribean

Air Canada
Transatlantic Visit North America Pass
Valid on all Air Canada and Continental Airlines domestic routes within the USA and Canada with a maximum of 2 stopovers per city. A minimum of 3 coupons from £240 to a maximum of 8 from £450. Validity 60 days. Prices increase if transatlantic flight is not with Air Canada or Continental Airlines

Visit North Eastern America Pass
Covers the north east regions of USA and Canada from £170 for 3 coupons to a maximum of 8 from £420. Valid for 60 days and has to be used in conjunction with a transatlantic flight with Air Canada.

American Airlines
Visit USA Pass from £229
A minimum of 3 coupons from £229, 4 from £289 and 5 from £339 to a maximum of 10 from £629. Maximum 2 stopovers at any one city and valid for 60 days. Transatlantic flights must be with American Airlines; or BA or Virgin if flying the American Airlines routings. If flying a non-American airline transatlantic the pass is still available but is more expensive.

America West Airlines:
Nationwide Pass from £230
A Minimum of 4 coupons from £230 to a maximum of 12 from £ 501. Only one transcontinental flight permitted and valid for 180 days.

Coast to Coast Pass £175
Two coupons for £175, Can only fly in one direction across the States and also valid for 180 days.

Tristate Pass from £108
Travel between points in California, Arizona and Nevada, 2 coupons £108 to a maximum of 12 for £453 and valid for 180 days.

Bahamasair
Bahamasair Pass from US$125
Travel from Miami via Nassau from US$125 for 2 coupons to a maximum of 8 coupons from $320 including three Bahamian Islands or from Orlando from US$185 for 2 coupons to a maximum of 8 from $380. Both are valid only in conjunction with fares from the UK and Europe and are valid from 3 to 21 days.

BWIA
Inter-Carribean Air Pass from US$356
Unlimited travel for up to 30 days on BWIA flights within the Carribean. Travel must be in a general circular direction and only one stopover is permitted at each point $356. A First Class 30 day pass is US$565 with the same booking conditions.

Canadian Airlines International
Go Canadian Travel Pass from C$436
Has a minimum of 3 coupons from C$436 to a maximum of 8 from C$686. Valid on all routes within Canada and mainland USA, except Hawaii. Minimum stay 7 days, with a maximum of 2 stopovers per city and 60 days' validity.

Delta Airlines:
Discover America from US$349
Has a minimum of 3 coupons from US$349 up to a maximum of 8 from $649. It covers mainland USA and Delta Services between USA and Canada with add-ons to Hawaii, Mexico and the Carribean available. Valid for 60 days from first flight.

Standby Air Pass from US$549
Available in conjunction with a Delta Airline transatlantic schedule fare. For 30 days' unlimited mainland flights on a standby basis for US$549 or US$899 for 60 days.

Northwest Airlines:
Air Pass from US$359
Minimum purchase of 3 coupons from US$359 with 4 from US$459 to a maximum of 8 from

US$649, the pass is only available in conjunction with a transatlantic flight with Northwest Airlines or KLM.

Standby Pass US$549
Also only available if flying with KLM or Northwest , offers unlimited air travel on a standby basis for 30 days within continental USA (not Alaska of Hawaii)

TWA
TWA Air Pass from £261
Valid across the network of 48 mainland US states. Minimum of three coupons from £261 to a maximum of 8. Valid up to 60 days and in conjunction with the internation flight on this airline.

United Airlines
US Airpass from £229
Minimum 3 coupons from £229 available in conjunction with the international sector on United Airlines. Further coupons are available to a maximum of 10 from £629. Valid on all routes in mainland US and some Canadian destinations for 60 days.

Pacific/Asia

Air New Zealand
Explore New Zealand Air pass from £164
A minimum of 3 coupons at £164 to a maximum of 8 at £420, valid up to one year and with any schedule airline on international flights.

Ansett Airlines
G'Day Pass from £140
Available with any international airline to Australia and New Zealand. Fares from £140 to £200 for 2 coupons with additional coupons from £70 to £100 each up to a maximum of 8 per visit to Australia or New Zealand.

Garuda Indonesia
Visit Indonesia Airpass from US$300
Covers domestic routes with one stopover permitted per city. Minimum purchase of 3 coupons for $300 with additional coupons at US$100 to a maximum of 10. The period of validity increases with the number of coupons booked - from 5 to 60 days. International flights must be with Garuda

Hawaiian Airlines
Visit Hawaiian Island Pass from US$169
A flexible multi-island pass, valid from 5 - 14 days. 5 days is $169, 7 days $189, 10 days $229 and 14 days $269. Valid with any international carrier to Hawaii and can not be extended beyond the maximum 14 days.

Indian Airlines
Regional Airpasses
Regional airpasses available (Northern, Southern, Western and Eastern) using specified routings.

Discover India Pass US$400
Valid on Indian Airlines network in India with one stopover at each point. 21 days validity.

Malaysia Airlines:
Visit Malaysia Pass US$194
5 sectors within the Malaysian Peninsula , Sabah and Sarawak (i.e. between all 3) valid for 21 days. At least one international flight either to or from Malaysia must be with Malaysia Airlines (excluding Singapore and Brunei).

Visit Malaysia Pass US$99
5 sectors within the Malaysian Peninsula, or within Sabah or within Sarawak (i.e. within one of the regions) valid for 21 days. At least one international flight either to or from Malaysia must be with Malaysia Airlines (excluding Singapore and Brunei).

Qantas
Australia Explorer Pass from £150
For travellers to Australia on any airline, offers 2 coupons from £150-200 with additional coupons to a maximum of 8 from £75 to 100 each.

Thai Airways
Discover Thailand from US$239
Valid for 60 days on domestic network, the minimum 4 coupons is $239 with addition coupons to a maximum of 8 at $50 each. ∎

GETTING THERE BY ROAD
Section 5

MOTORING ORGANIZATIONS WORLDWIDE

Algeria

Touring Club d'Algerie
30 Rue Hassen Benamane
BP 18
Les Vergers Birkhadem
Alger
Tel: 213-2 541 313

Andorra

Automobil Club d'Andorra
4 rue Babot Camp
Andorra La Vella
Tel: 33-628 20890

Argentina

Automovil Club Argentino
1850 Avenida del Liberator
Buenos Aires 1425
Tel: 54 1-802 6061

Touring Club Argentino
Esmeralda 605
3er piso
CP1007 Buenos Aires
Tel: 322 7994/392 8170

Australia

Australian Automobile Association
212 Northbourne Avenue
Canberra ACT 2601
Tel: 61-6 247 7311

National Roads & Motorists Association
NRMA House
151 Clarence St
Sydney NSW 2000
Tel: 02 260 92 22

RAC of Australia
89 Macquarie St
Sydney NSW 2000
Tel: 02 233 2355

Austria

**Osterreichischer Automobil-Motorad-und
Touring Club**
Postfach 252
Schubertring 1-3
1015 Vienna
Tel: 43-1 711 99-0

Bahamas

Bahamas Automobile Club
West Avenue
Centreville
Nassau
Tel: 500-809 325 0514

Bangladesh

Automobile Association of Bangladesh
3/B Outer Circular Road
Dacca 17
Tel: 880-2 23 07 82

Belarus

Orsha Tourist Club
PO Box 14
11030 Orsha
Tel: 880-2-230 782

Belgium

Royal Auto-club de Belgique
53 Rue d'Arlon
B-1040 Brussels
Tel: 02 230 08 10

Touring Club Royal de Belgique
Rue de la Loi 44
1040 Brussels
Tel: 32-2 233 2211

Bolivia

Automovil Club Boliviano
Avenida 6 de Agosto
2993 San Jorge
Castilla 602
La Paz
Tel: 591-2 351 667

Brazil

Automovel Club do Brasil
Rua do Passeio 90 Lapa
20021 Rio de Janeiro
Tel: 021 297 4455

Bulgaria

Union des Automobilistes Bulgares
BP 257
Sofia 1000
Tel: 359-2 86151

Canada

Canadian Automobile Association
1775 Courtwood Crescent
Ottawa K2C 3J2
Ontario
Tel: 1-613 226 7631

Chile

Automovil Club de Chile
PO Box 142
Santiago 30
Tel: 56-2 212 57 02

China

**China Touring Automobile and Ship
Association**
10 Yue Tan North Street
Beijing 100 045
Tel: 861-867 084

Colombia

Touring y Automovil Club de Colombia
Av Caracas No 46-72 D
Santafe de Bogota DC
Tel: 57-1 228 1900

Costa Rica

Automobile-Touring Club de Costa Rica
Apartado 46-46
San Jose
Tel: 200443

Cote D'Ivoire

**Federation Ivorienne du Sport Automobile
et des Engines Assimilees (FISA)**
BP 3883
Abidjan 01
Tel: 32 29 78

Croatia

Hrvatski Auto-klub
PO Box 0218
41000 Zagreb
Tel: 38 41 454 433

Cyprus

Cyprus Automobile Association
12 Chrysanthou Mylonas St
Nicosia 141
Tel: 357-2 31 32 33

Czech Republic

Ustredni Automotoklub
na Rybnicku 16
120 76 Prague 2
Tel: 42-2 2491 1830

Denmark

Forenede Danske Motorejere
Firskovvej 32
2100 Copenhagen
Tel: 45 45 93 0800

Ecuador

Touring y Automovil Club del Ecuador
PO Box 17-21 0087
Quito
Tel: 593-2 237 779
PO Box 17-21-087

Egypt

Automobile et Touring Club d'Egypte
10 rue Kasr el Nil
Cairo
Tel: 20-2 574 3176

Estonia

Estonian Auto-Moto Union
Pikk 41
200 001 Talinn
Tel: 70142-601215

El Salvador

Automovil Club de El Salvador
la Calle Poniente 930
Entre 15 y 17 Av. Notre
San Salvador
Tel: 228950

Finland

Autoliitto Automobile and Touring Club of Finland
PO Box 35
00551 Helsinki
Tel: **358-0 7747 6400**

France

Automobile Club National
5 Rue Auber
75009 Paris
Tel: **33-1 44 51 53 99**

Automobile Club de France
6-8 Place de la Concorde
75008
Paris
Tel: **1 42 65 34 70**

Germany

Allgemeiner Deutscher Automobil-Club E.V.
Am Westpark 8
81373 Munich 70
Tel: **49-89 76 760**

Automobilclub von Deutschland
Lyoner Strasse 16
6000 Frankfurt
Tel: **069 66060**

Deutscher Touring Automobil Club
Amalienburgstrasse 23
8000 Munchen
Tel: **49-89 811 1048**

Ghana

The Automobile Association of Ghana
Fanum House
1 Valley View
Labadi Road
Christriansborg
Accra
Tel: **233 77 42 29**

Greece

Automobile et Touring Club de Grece
2 Messogion St
103 Athens
Tel: **30-1 779 1615/19**

Touring Club Hellenique
12 Polytechniou St
11527 Athens
Tel: **30-1 524 08 72**

Holy See

Conseil Pontifical pour la Pastorale des Migrants et des Personnes en Deplacement
Palace Saint-Calixle
Vatican City
Tel: **39-6 698 87131**

Hong Kong

Hong Kong Automobile Association
405 Houston Centre
63 Mody Road
Tsim Sha Tsui East
Kowloon
Hong Kong
Tel: **852 739 52 73**

Hungary

Magyar Autoklub
Romer Floris u 4/a
1024 Budapest
Tel: **36-1 212 2938**

Iceland

Felag Islenzkra Bifreidaeigenda
Borgartun 33
105 Reykjavik
Tel: **35-41 62 99 99**

India

Federation of Indian Automobile Associations
76 Veer Nariman Road
Bombay 400 020
Tel: **91-22 204 1085**

Indonesia

Ikatan Motor Indonesia
Tennis Stadium
Right Wing Senayan
Jakarta 10270
Tel: **62-21 571 2032**

Iran

Touring and Automobile Club of the Islamic Republic of Iran
Ave Martyr Dr Fayazbakhsh No 37
11146 Tehran
Tel: **98-21 679 146**

Iraq

Iraq Automobile and Touring Association
Al-Mansour
Baghdad
Tel: **964-1 537 5862**

Ireland

The Automobile Association Ireland Ltd
23 Rock Hill
Blackrock
Co Dublin
Tel: **353-1 283 3555**

Israel

Automobile and Touring Club of Israel
19 Derech Petah Tikva
66183 Tel Aviv
Tel: **972-3 564 1122**

Italy

Automobile Club d'Italia
Via Marsala 8
00815 Rome
Tel: **39-6 49 9821**

Touring Club Italiano
10 Corso Italia
20122 Milan
Tel: **32- 85 261**

Jamaica

The Jamaica Automobile Association
41 Half Way Tree Road
Kingston 5
Tel: **500-809 929 1200**

Jamaica Motoring Club
PO Box 49
Kingston 10

Japan

Japan Automobile Federation
3-5-8 Shibakoen
Minato-Ku
Tokyo 105
Tel: **81-3 3436 2811**

Jordan

Royal Automobile Club of Jordan
Wadi Seer Cross Roads
8th Circle
Amman
Tel: **962-6 81 52 61**

Kazakhstan

**Automotorsport Federation of the Rep.
Kazakhstan**
BP 253
463022 Aktubinsk
Tel: **31-322 22202**

Kenya

Automobile Association of Kenya
AA Nyaku House
Hurlingham
Nairobi
Tel: **254-2 72 03 82**

Korea

Korea Automobile Association 1
592-4 Shinsa-dong
Kangnam-gu
Seoul
Tel: **515 2131**

Kuwait

**The Automobile Association of Kuwait and
the Gulf**
Airport Road
Khaldiyah 72300
Tel: **483 24 06**

**Kuwait International Touring and
Automobile Club**
Address as before

Latvia

Auto-moto Society of Latvia
16b Raunas
1039 Riga
Tel: **3712-568 339**

Lebanon

Automobile et Touring Club du Liban
Immeuble Fattal
Avenue Sami Solh - Imm Kalot
Beirut
Tel: **961-9 932 020**

Libya

Automobile and Touring Club of Libya
PO Box 3566
Tripoli
Tel: **33310**

Liechtenstein

**Automobile Club des Furstentums
Liechtenstein**
Schwefelstr 33
9490 Vaduz
Tel: **075 2 60 66**

Luxembourg

**Automobile Club du Grand-Duche de
Luxembourg**
Route de Longwy 54
8007 Bertrange
Tel: **352 45 0045**

Macedonia

Auto Moto Sojuz na Makedonija
PO Box 180
91000 Skoipje
Tel: **3891-226825**

Malaysia

The Automobile Association of Malaysia
No 25 Jalan Yap Kwan Seng
50450 Kuala Lumpur
Tel: **60-3 242 5777**

Malta

Touring Club Malta
Philcyn House
Ursuline Sisters St
G'Mangia
Tel: **256-453 230**

Mexico

Asociacion Mexicana Automovilistica
PO Box 24-486
06700 Mexico D F
Tel: **52-5 208 8329**

Morocco

Royal Automobile Club Marocain
3 Rue Lemercier
Casablanca
Tel: **212 25 00 30**

Touring Club du Maroc
3 Avenue F. A. R.
Casablanca
Tel: **212 20 30 64**

Namibia

Automobile Association of Namibia
Carl List House
15 Independence Avenue
Peter Muller St
9000 Windhoek
Tel: **264-61 22 42 01**

Nepal

Automobile Association of Nepal
Traffic Police
Ramshah Path, Opp. Sinhdwar
Kathmandu
Tel: **977 11093**

Netherlands

Koninklijke Nederlandse Toeristenbond ANWB
Wassenaarseweg 220
2596 The Hague
Tel: **31-70 314 7147**

New Zealand

The New Zealand Automobile Association
PO Box 5
Auckland
Tel: **64 9 377 4660**

Nigeria

Automobile Club of Nigeria
48 Adegbola Street
Anifowoshe
Lagos
Tel: **960514**

Norway

Norges Automobil-Forbund
PO Box 494 Sentrum
0105 Oslo 1
Tel: **47-22 34 14 00**

Kongelig Norsk Automobilklub
Drammensveien 20-C
0255 Oslo 2
Tel: **02 56 10 00**

Oman

Oman Automobile Association
PO Box 7776
Muttrah
Tel: **510 239**

Pakistan

The Automobile Association of Pakistan
62 Shadman Market
Lahore
Tel: **92-42 758 8854**

Papua New Guinea

Automobile Association of Papua New Guinea
GPO Box 5999
Boroko
Tel: **675 25 63 25**

Paraguay

Touring y Automovil Club Paraguayo
Casila de Correo 1204
Asuncion
Tel: **59521 210549**

Peru

Touring y Automovil Club del Peru
PO Box 2219
Lima 100
Tel: **51-14403 270**

Philippines

Philippine Motor Association
683 Aurora Boulevard
Quezon City
Manila
Tel: **63-2 721 5761**

Poland

Polski Zwiazek Motorway
ul Kazimierzowska 66
02-518 Warsaw
Tel: **48-22 499 361**

Portugal

Automovel Club de Portugal
Rua Rosa Araujo 24
1200 Lisbon
Tel: **351-1 356 39 31**

Qatar

Qatar Automobile and Touring Club
PO Box 18
Doha
Tel: **974 41 32 65**

Romania

Automobil Clubul Roman
Str. Tache Ionescu 27
70154 Bucarest 22
Tel: **40-1 615 5510**

Russian Federation

Intourist
13 Mokhoraya Street
103009 Moscow
Tel: **7095-292 2260**

Saudi Arabia

Saudi Automobile and Touring Association
PO Box 51880
Riyadh 11553
Tel: **966-1 464 5214**

Senegal

Automobile Club du Senegal
Immeuble Chambre de Commerce
Place de l'Independence BP 295
Dakar
Tel: **226-04**

Touring Club du Senegal
12 Bd Pinet Laprade -
1er Etage
Dakar
Tel: **221 231025**

Singapore

The Automobile Association of Singapore
AA Centre
336 River Valley Road
0923 Singapore
Tel: **65 737 2444**

Slovenia

Auto-moto zve za Slovenije
PO Box 75
61113 Ljubljana
Tel: **386-61 168 1111**

Slovak Republic

Ustredni Automotoklub
Slovenskej Republiky
Volkrova 4
851 01 Bratislava
Tel: **42-7 850 910**

South Africa

AA House
66 De Korte St
Braamfontein
Johannesburg 2001
Tel: **27-11 407 1000**
PO Box 596
Johannesburg 2000

Spain

Real Automovil Club de Espana
Jose Abascal 10
28003 Madrid
Tel: **34-1 447 3200**

Sri Lanka

Automobile Association of Ceylon
40 Sir M M M Mawatha
Colombo 3
Tel: **941 42 15 28**

Sweden

Motormannens Riksforbund
Sturegatan 32
Stockholm 10248
Tel: **46-8 782 38 00**

Switzerland

Automobile Club de Suisse
Wasserkgasse 39
3000 Berne 13
Tel: **22 47 22**

Touring Club Suisse
9 Rue Pierre Fatio
1211 Geneva 3
Tel: **41-22 737 12 12**

Syria

Automobile et Touring Club de Syrie
Rue Baron Imm Jesuites
Aleppo
Tel: **963-21 21 22 30**

Automobile Club of Syria
Rue du 29 Mai
Damascus
Tel: **963 11 427 079**
PO Box 3364
Damascus

Tanzania

The Automobile Association of Tanzania
PO Box 3004
Dar Es Salaam
Tel: **255-51 21965**

Thailand

Royal Automobile Association of Thailand
151 Rachadapisek Road
Bang Khen
Bangkok 10900
Tel: **662-511 2230**

Trinidad & Tobago

Trinidad & Tobago Automobile Association
41 Woodford St
Newtown
Port-of-Spain
Tel: **500-809 622 7194**

Tunisia

National Automobile Club de Tunisie
29 Avenue Habib Bourguiba
1000 Tunis
Tel: **241 176**

Touring Club de Tunisie
15 rue d'Allemagne
Tunis
Tel: **216-1 243 182**

Turkey

Turkiye Turing Ve Otomobil Kurumu
Halskargazi Cad 364
80222 Sisli-Istanbul
Tel: **90-212 231 46 31**

United Arab Emirates

Automobile and Touring Club for United Arab Emirates
Al Nasr St
PO Box 27487
Abu Dhabi
Tel: **971-2 21 21 75**

UK

The Automobile Association
Fanum House
Basingstoke
Hampshire RG21 2EA
Tel: **0256 20123**

The Royal Automobile Club
PO Box 100
RAC House
7 Brighton Road
South Croydon CR2 6XW
Tel: **081-686 0088**

The Royal Scottish Automobile Club
11 Blythswood Square
Glasgow G2 4AG
Tel: **041-221 38 50**

USA

American Automobile Association
1000 AAA Drive
Heathrow
Florida 32746-5063
Tel: **1-407 444 7000**

American Automobile Touring Alliance
188 The Embarcadero
San Francisco
CA 94105
Tel: **415-777 40 000**

Uruguay

Centro Automovilistica del Uruguay
Boulevard Artigas 1773, esq Dante
Montevideo
Tel: **589-2 4486 131**

Venezuela

Touring y Automovil Club de Venezuela
Aptdo 68102
Attamira 1062-A
Caracas
Tel: **58-2 915 571**

Yemen

Yemen Club for Touring and Automobile
PO Box 10473
San'a
Tel: **976-1 275 032**

Zaire

Federation Automobile du Zaire
Av. des Inflammables 25
Kingabwa
Kinshasa

Zimbabwe

Automobile Association of Zimbabwe
57 Samora Michel Avenue
C1 Harare
Tel: **263-4 707 021**

MAJOR CAR RENTAL COMPANIES

Australia

Avis Rent-a-Car
327 Pacific Highway
North Sydney
NSW 2060
Tel: **02-439 3733**
and...
46 Hill St
Perth
WA 6000
Tel: **325 7677**

Budget Rent-a-Car
21 Bedford Street
North Melbourne
Victoria 3051
Tel: **61-3320 6222**

Hertz Rent-a-Car
39 Milligan St
Perth
WA 6000
Tel: **093-217 7777**

Canada

Avis Rent-a-Car
624 Princess Street
(Princess + Nelson Street)
Kingston
Ontario
Tel: **613-549 2847**

Budget Rent-a-Car
185 The West Mall
Suite 900
Etobicoke
Ontario M9C 5L5
Tel: **1-416-622 3366**

Hertz Rent-a-Car
1073 Drummond Street
Montreal
Quebec
Tel: **514 938 1717**

France

Europcar International
65 Avenue Edouard Vaillant
92100 Boulogne
Billancourt
Paris
Tel: **010-33-1-4910 5454**

UK

Alamo Rent A Car
Alamo House
Stockley Close
Stockley Road
West Drayton
Middlesex UB7 9BA
Tel: **0800-272 200** (toll free)

Avis Rent-a-Car
Avis House
Park Road
Bracknell Berks
RG12 2EW
Tel: **0344 426644**

Budget Rent-a-Car International Inc
41 Marlowes
Hemel Hempstead
Herts HP1 1LD
Tel: **0442 232 555**
One of the top three car and van rental companies in the world.

Europcar International
Europcar Intervent House
Aldenham Road
Watford WD2 2LX
Tel: **0923-811000**

Hertz Rent-a-Car
Radnor House
1272 London Road
Norbury
London SW16 4XW
Tel: **081-679 1777**
The world's largest vehicle rental and leasing company.

Euro-Dollar Rent-a-Car
James House 55
Welford Road
Leicester LE2 7AR
Tel: **0533 545020**

USA

Avis Rent-a-Car
217 East 43rd Street
(between 2nd + 3rd Avenue)
New York City
Tel: **212-593 8378**

From 16 April 1995 all national and international codes change — see page 587 for details.

Budget Rent-a-Car
200 North Michigan Avenue
Chicago
Ill 60601
Tel: **1-312-580 5000**

Dollar Rent-a-Car Systems Inc
World Headquarters
6141 W. Century Blvd
PO Box 45048
Los Angeles
CA 900045
Tel: **213-776 8100**

Hertz Rent-a-Car Headquarters
10401 North Pennysylvania Avenue
Oklahoma City
Tel: **1-405 721 6640**

INTERNATIONAL VEHICLE LICENCE PLATES

A	*Austria*
AL	*Albania*
AND	*Andorra*
AUS	*Australia*
B	*Belgium*
BDS	*Barbados*
BG	*Bulgaria*
BH	*Belize*
BR	*Brazil*
BRN	*Bahrain*
BRU	*Brunei*
BS	*Bahamas*
C	*Cuba*
CDN	*Canada*
CH	*Switzerland*
CI	*Cote d'Ivoire*
CL	*Sri Lanka*
CO	*Colombia*
CR	*Costa Rica*
CZ	*Czech Republic*
CY	*Cyprus*
D	*Germany*
DK	*Denmark*
DOM	*Dominican Republic*
DY	*Benin*
DZ	*Algeria*
E	*Spain*
EAK	*Kenya*
EAT	*Tanzania*
EAU	*Uganda*
EAZ	*Zanzibar*
EC	*Ecuador*
EIR	*Ireland*
ET	*Egypt*
F	*France*
FJI	*Fiji*
FK	*Slovak Republic*
FL	*Liechtenstein*
FLO	*Slovenia*
G	*Gabon*
GB	*United Kingdom*
GBA	*Alderney*
GBG	*Guernsey*
GBJ	*Jersey*
GBM	*Isle of Man*
GBZ	*Gibraltar*
GH	*Ghana*
GLA	*Guatemala*
GR	*Greece*
GUY	*Guyana*
H	*Hungary*
HK	*Hong Kong*
HKJ	*Jordan*
HR	*Croatia*
I	*Italy*
IL	*Israel*
IND	*India*
IR	*Iran*
IRQ	*Iraq*
IS	*Iceland*
J	*Japan*
JA	*Jamaica*
K	*Cambodia*
K	*Myanmar*
L	*Luxembourg*
LAO	*Laos*
LAR	*Libya*
LB	*Liberia*
LS	*Lesotho*
M	*Malta*
MA	*Morocco*
MAL	*Malaysia*
MC	*Monaco*
MEX	*Mexico*
MS	*Mauritius*
MW	*Malawi*
N	*Norway*
NA	*Netherlands Antilles*
NIC	*Nicaragua*
NIG	*Niger*
NL	*Netherlands*
NZ	*New Zealand*
P	*Portugal*
PA	*Panama*
PAK	*Pakistan*
PE	*Peru*
PI	*Philippines*
PL	*Poland*
PY	*Paraguay*
R	*Romania*
RA	*Argentina*
RB	*Botswana*
RC	*Taiwan*
RCA	*Central African Republic*
RCB	*Congo*
RCH	*Chile*

From 16 April 1995 all national and international codes change — see page 587 for details.

RH	Haiti
RI	Indonesia
RIM	Mauritania
RL	Lebanon
RM	Madagascar
RMM	Mali
RNR	Zambia
ROK	Korea
RSM	San Marino
RSR	Zimbabwe
RU	Burundi
RUS	Russian Federation
RWA	Rwanda
S	Sweden
SD	Swaziland
SDV	Vatican City
SF	Finland
SGP	Singapore
SME	Suriname
SN	Senegal
SY	Seychelles
SYR	Syria
T	Thailand
TG	Togo
TN	Tunisia
TR	Turkey
TT	Trinidad & Tobago
U	Uruguay
UA	Ukraine
USA	USA
VN	Vietnam
WAG	Gambia
WAL	Sierra Leone
WAN	Nigeria
WD	Dominica
WG	Grenada
WL	St. Lucia
WS	Western Samoa
WV	St. Vincent
YU	Yugoslavia
YV	Venezuela
Z	Zambia
ZA	South Africa
ZR	Zaire
ZRE	Yemen

VEHICLE SHIPMENT

Car ferry operators from the UK

B&I Line
PO Box 19
12 North Wall Dublin 1
Ireland
Tel: **788266**
and...
Reliance House
Water Street
Liverpool L2 8TP

Tel : **051-734 4681**

Belgian Maritime Transport Authority
Premier House
10 Greycoat Place
London SW1P 1SB
Tel: **071-233 0365**

British Channel Island Ferries
Corbiere House
Newquay Road
Poole
Dorset BH15 4DY
Tel: **0202 681155**

Brittany Ferries
The Brittany Centre
Wharf Road
Portsmouth Hants PO2 8RU
Tel: **0705 827701**

Caledonia MacBrayne
The Ferry Terminal
Gourock PA19 1QP
Tel: **0475-34531**

DFDS Seaways
Scandinavia House
Parkeston Quay
Harwich
Essex CO12 4QG
Tel: **0255 243456**
and...
Tyne Commission Quay
North Shield
Tyne & Wear NE29 6EE
Tel: **091-296 0101**

DFDS Travel Centre
15 Hanover St
London W1
Tel: **071-409 6060**

Fred Olsen Lines
Whitehouse Road
Ipswich
Suffolk IP1 5LL
Tel: **0473 292200**
and
65 Vincent Square
London SW1P 2RX
Tel: **071-931 8888**

Hoverspeed Ltd
Maybrook House
Queens Gardens
Dover Kent CT17 9UQ
Tel: **0304 240241**

Irish Ferries
2/4 Merrion Row
Dublin
Ireland

Tel: **1-610511**

Isles of Scilly Steamship Co.
Quay Street
Penzance
Cornwall TR18 4QX
Tel: **0736 62009**

Jahreline
c/o Colorline
Tyne Commission Quay
North Shields
Tyne & Wear
NE29 6EA
Tel: **091-296 1313**

Norfolk Line
Norfolk House
The Dock
Felixstowe
Suffolk IP11 8UY
Tel: **0394-673676**

North Sea Ferries
King George Dock
Hedon Road
Hull HU9 5QA
Tel: 0482 795141

Orkney Island Shipping Co.
4 Ayre Road
Kirkwall
Orkney KW15 1QX
Tel: **0856 872044**

P&O European Ferries
Channel House
Channel View Road
Dover Kent CT17 9TJ
Tel: **0304 203388**

P&O Ferries (Orkney & Shetland Services)
PO Box 5
Jamiesons Quay
Aberdeen AB9 8DL
Tel: **0224 572615**

Sally Line
Argyle Centre
York Street
Ramsgate
Kent CT11 9DS
Tel: **0800 63645**

Scandinavian Seaways
15 Hanover Street
London W1Y 9HG
Tel: **071-493 6696**

Sealink Stena Line
Charter House
Park Street

Ashford
Kent TN24 8EZ
Tel: **0233 647047**

Shannon Ferries
Killimer
Kilrush
Co Clare
Ireland
Tel: **65-53124**

Viking Line
c/o Finman Travel
87-89 Church Street
Leigh
Greater Manchester WN7 1AZ
Tel: **0942-262662**

Western Ferries
Hunters Quay
Dunoon
Argyll
Tel: **0369 4452**

Other helpful organizations

Michael Gibbons Freight
Powell Duffryn House
Tilbury Docks
Tilbury Essex RM18 7JT
Tel: **0375 843461**
One of the biggest shipment companies, with offices worldwide. Both the AA and the RAC refer their members to this company.

Verband Der Automobilindustrie e.V (VDA)
Westendstrasse 61
6000 Frankfurt am Main 1
Germany
Tel: **69 75 70-0**

Motor Vehicle Manufacturers' Association of the United States
7430 Second Avenue
Suite 300
Detroit
Michigan 48202
USA Tel: **313-872 4311**

Federal Chamber of Automotive Industries
10 Rudd St
Canberra City ACT
2601 Canberra
Australia
Tel: **6-247 3811**

Further reading:
ABC Passenger Shipping Guide (Reed Travel Group)

DRIVING REQUIREMENTS WORLDWIDE

For further information, contact the appropriate embassy, consulate or motoring organization. For insurance details see Chapter 9. International Driving Permit = IDP, CPD = *Carnet de Passages en Douanes*.

Country	Vehicle Import Requirements	Driving Permits	Fuel Availability
Afghanistan	Prior authorization from Ministry of Commerce in Kabul	IDP	Unclear
Albania	Borders closed to tourist traffic	IDP	Expensive and scarce
Algeria	CPD maybe required Customs document issued on entry — valid for three months	IDP	Good. Spares are difficult to find
Andorra	None	Yes, all licences	Good
Antigua	None	Driver's permit obtained at police station by showing national licence	Good
Argentina	Written undertaking to export or CPD	IDP	Good
Australia	CPD	All accepted but IDP preferred	Good
Bahamas	For under 6 months, redeemable bond must be paid	IDP British licence	Spares rare
Bahrain	—	IDP	Good
Bangladesh	CPD	IDP or national licence	Unclear
Barbados	—	Licences recognized if presented to police and BD$10 fee paid	Good
Belgium	None	National licences	Good
Belize	—	Licences recognized for 3 months	Good
Benin	—	IDP	OK
Bermuda	—	Visitors not permitted to drive a motor vehicle	Good
Bolivia	—	IDP	Unclear
Botswana	CPD.	Local licence after 6 months All licences recognized	Good
Brazil	—	IDP required National licence valid for 6 months if certified	No fuel sold on Saturday, Sunday or after 8pm every day
British Virgin Islands	—	BVI temporary licence issued on presentation of foreign licence	

Country	Vehicle Import Requirements	Driving Permits	Fuel Availability
Brunei	—	Local licence required on presentation of foreign licence	Good
Bulgaria	None	Foreign licences recognized for short periods, otherwise IDP	Good
Burkina Faso	Acquit-a-caution	Certain licences recognized, otherwise IDP	Unclear
Cameroon	Written undertaking	IDP	Scarce
Canada	Free entry but deposit may be required	IDP accepted, national licence valid for 3 months	Good
Cayman Islands	—	IDP	Good
Central African Rep	CPD	IDP	Scarce
Chad	CPD	IDP	Expensive
Chile	CPD	IDP	Diesel only on Pan Am Highway
China	No foreign vehicles allowed except trade vehicle		Unclear
CIS		IDP or national licence with authorised translation	Scarce
Colombia	CPD	National licence accepted, accompanied by local licence	Good
Congo	CPD	IDP	Good
Costa Rica	Written undertaking to re-export	National licences accepted	Good
Cote d'Ivoire	CPD	IDP	OK
Croatia		National licence or IDP	
Cuba	—	National licences accepted for 6 months	Good
Cyprus	Written undertaking to export vehicle	National licence accepted for 1 year	Good
Czech Republic	Must be entered on passport	National licence accepted	Filling stations often closed in evening
Denmark	None	National licence accepted	Good
Dominican Republic	—	National licence accepted	Good
Ecuador	CPD	IDP	Good
Egypt	CPD through Alexandria only	IDP National licence accepted	Good
El Salvador	Written undertaking to export	National licence of IDP	
Ethiopia	Deposit of customs duty	Temporary Ethiopian licence should be obtained on arrival	Unclear
Fiji	—	National licence accepted	Good
Finland	None	National licence accepted	Good
France	None	National licence accepted	Good

Country	Vehicle Import Requirements	Driving Permits	Fuel Availability
Gabon	CPD	National licence	Unclear
Gambia	Advance permission from Controller of Customs and Excise	National licence accepted for short visit	Good
Germany	None	Certain licences accepted, otherwise IDP required	Good
Ghana	CPD	Commonwealth country licence accepted for 90 days. IDP recommended	Unclear
Gibraltar	None	National licence accepted	Good
Greece	Non-EEC visitors issued with vehicle-free entry card	Certain licences recognized otherwise IDP	Good
Grenada	—	National licence accepted and local licence	Good
Guinea	Visas not issued for tourist purposes	IDP	OK
Guyana	Deposit of duty	Certain licences recognized, otherwise IDP	OK
Haiti	—	IDP	OK
Honduras	—	National licence	OK
Hong Kong	Import declaration required	National licence –after 12 months must apply for HK driving licence	Good
Hungary	None. Registration number entered on documents at border	IDP	Good
Iceland	None. Diesel vehicles must pay weight tax for each week in Iceland	Certain licences accepted otherwise licence/IDP presented to police for temporary licence	Good
India	CPD. Duty is around 300%. Virtually impossible to get Carnet Indemnity Insurance	To get a local licence, 5yr licence costs RS20/ you must do an oral test. Certain licences recognized, otherwise IDP	Good
Indonesia	Border closed to tourist vehicles	IDP	Good
Iran	CPD. You usually have to be escorted and pay for it	IDP	OK
Iraq	CPD (validity 3 months)	IDP	Unclear
Ireland	None	National licence	Good
Israel	None	National licence recognized but IDP preferred	Good
Italy	None	Certain licences accepted or accompanied by translation or ID	Good. Concessionary petrol coupons available

Country	Vehicle Import Requirements	Driving Permits	Fuel Availability
Jamaica	CPD or deposit of duty	Certain licences accepted otherwise IDP	Good
Japan	CPD. Tax has to be paid–customs clearance. And will need modifying to conform to standard. NB Not advised to take car	IDP. Local will be given after sight and co-ordination tests.	Good
Jordan	CPD	IDP Visitor not allowed to drive vehicles with normal Jordanian reg. plates	Good
Kenya	CPD	National licence. IDP required to drive for up to 90 days Kenyan registered vehicle	OK
Korea (South)	—	IDP	Good
Kuwait	CPD	IDP. National licence accepted if accompanied by local temporary licence	Unclear
Laos	Borders closed	National licence accepted but IDP preferred	OK
Lebanon	CPD	National licence must be validated	Unclear
Leeward Islands	—	All licences accepted if presented to police on arrival for temporary three month licence	OK
Lesotho	CPD	National licence if in English/translated	Unclear
Liberia	Deposit of duty	National licence accepted if presented to police on arrival for temporary 30-day licence	Unclear
Libya	CPD	National licence good for three months	Good
Luxembourg	None	National licence accepted	Good
Macau	Cannot bring cars in	IDP (except UK drivers)	Good
Madagascar	Advance permission and local guarantee	National licence accepted	Unclear
Malawi	Written undertaking	Certain licences recognized otherwise IDP	Good
Malaysia	CPD	Certain licences accepted otherwise IDP	Good
Malta	Temporary import permit issued on entry. Valid for 3 months	National licence	Petrol stations closed on Sundays
Mauritania	CPD	National licence accepted for limited period or IDP	Unclear
Mauritius	CPD	National licence accepted if endorsed by police	Good
Mexico	Temporary importation of vehicle noted on Tourist Card or Visa	National licences or IDP	Good

Country	Vehicle Import Requirements	Driving Permits	Fuel Availability
Mongolia	Borders closed	IDP	OK
Morocco	Temporary importation form is issued at border	National licence is accepted for 3 months. IDP required to hire car	Good
Myanmar	No entry overland allowed	IDP presented to police for issue of visitor's driving licence	OK
Nepal	CPD	IDP accepted for 15 days then local licence required. Certain licences recognized, otherwise IDP	Good
Netherlands		National licence	Good
New Zealand		Certain national licences otherwise IDP	Good
Nicaragua	Written undertaking to export vehicle	National licence/IDP valid 1 month for vehicle registered abroad then local licence	OK
Niger	CPD	IDP	OK
Nigeria	Temporary importation document issued at border	IDP	Good
Norway	None	National licence or IDP	Good
Oman	No	National licence valid seven days then local licence issued, valid 3 months	Good
Pakistan	CPD	IDP	OK
Panama	Proof of ownership	National licence accepted	Good
Papua New Guinea	—	National licence accepted	Unclear
Paraguay	CPD	National licence or IDP	Good
Peru	CPD	IDP	OK
Philippines	CPD	IDP with national licence	Good
Poland	None	Certain licences recognized otherwise IDP	Good
Portugal	None	National licence or IDP	Good
Qatar	CPD	National licence accepted if accompanied by local temp. driving licence from police for 90days	Good
Romania	None	National licence or IDP	Unclear
Rwanda	—	IDP	Unclear
Saudi Arabia	Carnets are not valid	Women are not permitted to drive. Local licence essential for longer stays	Good
Senegal	CPD	IDP	Good
Seychelles	—	National licence accepted	Good
Sierra Leone	CPD	IDP	Unclear
Singapore	CPD	IDP	Good
Solomon Islands	—	National licence accepted	Good
Slovak Republic		National licence	
Slovenia	None	National licence	
South Africa	CPD	IDP	Good

Country	Vehicle Import Requirements	Driving Permits	Fuel Availability
Spain	None	IDP or translating of national licence	Good
Sri Lanka	CPD	National licence accepted if accompanied by temporary driving licence available on arrival	Good
Sudan	CPD	International licence OK for six months. National licence accepted if presented to police	Unclear
Swaziland	CPD	English-text licences accepted or IDP	Good
Sweden	None	National licence accepted	Good
Switzerland	None	National licence accepted	Good
Syria	CPD	IDP	Good
Tahiti	—	National licence accepted	Good
Tanzania	CPD	Temporary licence on presentation of national licence to police or IDP which must be endorsed	Unclear
Thailand	Deposit of duty	IDP	Good
Togo	Entry by land: written undertaking. Entry by sea: bank guarantee and advance authorization	IDP	Unclear
Tonga	—	Local licence required, issued by police dept, need an international or national licence and T$8	Good
Trinidad & Tobago	CPD. Left-hand drive cars restricted	Most national licences accepted if accompanied by an English translation where necessary for 90 days	Good
Tunisia	Written undertaking	National licence	Good
Turkey	None – vehicle details entered on passport	National licences in English or French, accepted for temporarily imported vehicles, otherwise IDP	Good
Turks & Caicos	—	Local licence required	Good
Uganda	Deposit of duty	National licence accepted for 90 days or IDP	OK
United Kingdom		National licence accepted	Good
United Arab Emirates	CPD recommended	National licences must be presented to Traffic Dept. with letters from sponsor	Good
US Virgin Islands	No	National licence	Good
USA	None	National licence or IDP	Good
Uruguay	CPD	National licence accepted if presented to authorities	Good
Vanuatu	—	National licence accepted	Good
Venezuela	CPD	IDP	Good

Country	Vehicle Import Requirements	Driving Permits	Fuel Availability
Vietnam	Borders closed	IDP	OK
Yemen	—	IDP	OK
Zaire	CPD	IDP	—
Zambia	None –guaranteed written undertaking	IDP	OK
Zimbabwe	None –guaranteed written undertaking or CPD	IDP	Good

Note:
1. *The requirements given here are the minimum accepted by each country. In some countries, visitors are recommended to carry an IDP in addition to a national licence.*
2. *Many countries will let you take in a car for a brief tourist visit without a carnet and without paying duty, but this should not be relied upon.*
3. *Generally, a motor vehicle may be temporarily imported into a European country from between 6 and 12 months, without formality.*
Information supplied by the RAC

METRIC CONVERSIONS

Tyre pressures

lbs per sq in	kg per sq cm	Atmosphere	Kilo Pascals (kPa)
14	0.98	0.95	96.6
16	1.12	1.08	110.4
18	1.26	1.22	124.2
20	1.40	1.36	138.0
22	1.54	1.49	151.8
24	1.68	1.63	165.6
26	1.83	1.76	179.4
28	1.96	1.90	193.2
30	2.10	2.04	207.0
32	2.24	2.16	220.8
36	2.52	2.44	248.4
40	2.80	2.72	276.0
50	3.50	3.40	345.0
55	3.85	3.74	379.5
60	4.20	4.08	414.0
65	4.55	4.42	448.5

Litre to gallon conversion

To convert:	Multiply by
Gallons to Litres	4.546
Litres to Gallons	0.22

Measures of capacity

2 pints =	1 quart =	1.136 Litres
4 quarts =	1 gallon =	4.546 Litres
	5 gallons =	22.73 Litres

Distances

1 yard=	0.91 metres
100 yards=	91 metres
1 mile=	1.6 kilometres

To convert:
Miles to kilometres divide by 5 then multiply by 8
Kilometres to miles divide by 8 then multiply by 5

VEHICLES: PURCHASE, HIRE & CONVERSION

Allied Self-Drive Rental
117 Crawford St
London W1H 1AG
Tel: **071-224 2257**
Specialists in Audi and Volkswagen rentals.

Brownchurch (Land Rovers) Ltd
Hare Row off Cambridge Heath Road
London E2 9BY
Tel: **071-729 3606**
Specialist safari preparation for Land Rovers, Range Rovers and Discovery: roof racks, light guards, bush bars, jerry can holders, suspension and over-drive modifications, winches, sand ladders, high-lift jacks, oil cooler kits etc. Cover all Land Rover needs for trips anywhere, including the fitting of jerry cans and holders, sand ladders, sump and light guards, crash bars, winches, water purifying plants, roof-racks (custom-made if necessary), overdrive units. They also supply new vehicles and offer a maintenance and spares service for Land, Range Rovers and Discovery.

Cross Country Vehicles Ltd
Hailey
Witney
Oxon OX8 5UF
Tel: **0993-776622**
Sell and convert vehicles, prepare them for safari use. Range Rover and Land Rover specialists - new and used vehicles and any other 4WD vehicle too. They offer service, special preparation, conversion parts (new and reconditioned). Parts and preparation quotes by return.

Dunsfold Land Rovers Ltd
Alfold Road
Dunsfold
Surrey GU8 4NP
Tel: **0483 200567**
Offers free travel advice to those contemplating overland travel: comprehensive stores, rebuilding to owner's specifications.

Goodwinch: The Off-Road Specialist
East Foldhay
Zeal Monachorum
Crediton
Devon EX17 6DH
Tel: **0734-82666**
Vehicle modifications, accessories and 4x4 driver training.

Harvey Hudson
50-56 High Road
South Woodford
London E18 1AS
Tel: **081-989 6644**
Isuzu and Subaru specialists, suppliers of new and used vehicles to expeditions.

Land Rover Ltd
Direct Sales Department
Lode Lane Solihull
West Midlands B92 8NW
Tel: **021-722 2424**
Manufacturers of Land Rovers and Range Rovers. Purchase must be through authorized dealers.

Overlander
Tel: **0734-84402**
Hire, supply, equip and prepare vehicles especially Land Rovers and Pinzagauers, and provides help with planning and preparation.

RAC Enterprises
RAC House
PO Box 100
South Croydon
Surrey CR2 6XW
Tel: **081-686 0088**
Produce a range of maps, atlases, guides and touring accessories.

Sanderson Ford
Oxford Road
Manchester M13 0JD
Tel: **061-272 6000**
Deal in Mevaride 4WD vehicles

MOTORIST'S CHECK–LIST
by Jack Jackson

If you are an experienced off-road motorist and vehicle camper, you are, without doubt, the best person to decide exactly what you need to do and take for your trip. Even so, extensive experience doesn't guarantee perfect recall and everyone might find it useful to jog their memories by consulting other people's lists.

These lists do assume some experience — without some mechanical expertise, for example, an immaculately stocked tool-box is of limited use. It is also assumed that the motorist in question will spend at least some time driving off–road, most probably in a four-wheel drive vehicle.

Vehicle spares and tools

Petrol Engines
3 fan belts (plus power steering pump belts and air conditioning pump belts if fitted)
1 complete set of gaskets

4 oil filters (change every 5000 km)
2 tubes of Silicone RTV gasket compound
1 complete set of radiator hoses
2 metres of spare heater hose
2 metres of spare fuel pipe hose
0.5 metres of spare distributor vacuum pipe
hose
2 exhaust valves
1 inlet valve
1 complete valve spring
Fine and coarse valve grinding paste and valve
grinding tool
1 valve spring compressor
1 fuel pump repair kit (if electric type, take a
complete spare pump)
1 water pump repair kit
1 carburettor overhaul kit
2 sets of sparking plugs
1 timing light or 12 volt bulb and holder with
leads
3 sets of contact breaker points (preferably with
hard fibre cam follower, because plastic types
wear down quickly and close up the gap in the
heat)
2 distributor rotor arms
1 distributor condenser
1 distributor cap
1 sparking plug spanner
1 set of high tension leads (older, wire type)
1 ignition coil
Slip ring and brushes for alternator or a
complete spare alternator.
2 cans of spray type ignition sealant, for dusty
and wet conditions
2 spare air intake filters, if you do not have the
oil–bath type

Extras for diesel engines

Delete sparking plugs, contact breaker points,
distributor, vacuum pipe hose, rotor arms,
distributor cap and condenser, high tension
leads, coil, and carburettor overhaul from the
above list and substitute:
1 spare set of injectors, plus cleaning kit
1 complete set of high pressure injector pipes
1 set injector copper sealing washers plus steel
sealing washers where these are used
1 set injector return pipe washers
1 metre of plastic fuel pipe, plus spare nuts and
ferrules
A second in–line fuel filter
4 fuel filter elements
3 spare heater plugs, if fitted

Brakes and clutch

2 wheel cylinder kits (one right and one left)
1 flexible brake hose
1 brake bleeding kit
1 brake, master cylinder seals kit
1 clutch, master cylinder seals kit

1 clutch, slave cylinder kit (or a complete unit
for Land Rover series III or 110). (It is
important to keep all these kits away from heat)
1 clutch centre plate
If you have an automatic gearbox, make sure
you have plenty of the special fluid for this, a
spare starter motor and a spare battery, kept
charged.
If you have power steering, carry the correct
fluid and spare hoses.
Some Land Rovers have automatic gearbox
fluid in a manual gearbox.

General spares

2 warning triangles (compulsory in most
countries)
1 good workshop manual (not the car
handbook)
1 good torch and a fluorescent light with leads
to work it from vehicle battery, plus spare bulbs
and tubes
1 extra tyre in addition to that on the spare
wheel. (Only the spare wheel and tyre will be
necessary if two identical vehicles are travelling
together.)
3 extra inner tubes (6 in areas of Acacia thorns)
1 large inner tube repair kit
1 set of tyre levers and 1 kg sledge hammer for
tyres
5 spare inner tube valve cores and 2 valve core
tools
4 inner tube valve dust caps (metal type)
1 Schrader tyre pump, which fits into sparking
plug socket threads. Or a 12 volt electric
compressor, which is the only system available
if you have a diesel engine
Plenty of good quality engine oil
2 litres of distilled water or 1 bottle of water
de–ionizing crystals
12-volt soldering iron and solder
Hand drill and drills
16 metres of nylon or terylene rope, strong
enough to upright an overturned vehicle
1 good jack and wheel brace (if hydraulic, carry
spare fluid)
1 (at least) metal fuel can, eg. a jerry can
1 grease gun and a tin of multi–purpose grease
5 litres of correct differential and gearbox oil
1 large fire extinguisher suitable for petrol and
electrical fires
1 reel of self–vulcanizing rubber tape, for
leaking hoses
1 pair heavy-duty electric jump leads at least 3
metres long
10 push fit electrical connectors (of type to suit
vehicle)
2 universal joints for prop shafts
0.5 litre can of brake and clutch fluid
1 small can of general light oil for hinges, etc
1 large can WD40
1 starting handle, if available

2 complete sets of keys, kept in different places
1 small Isopon or fibre glass kit for repairing fuel tank and body holes
2 kits of general adhesive eg. Bostik or Araldite Rapid
1 tin of hand cleaner (washing up liquid will do in an emergency)
Spare fuses and bulbs for all lights, including those on the dash panel, the red charging light bulb is often part of the charging circuit
1 radiator cap
Antifreeze —if route passes through cold areas
Spare windscreen wipers for use on return journey (keep away from heat)
Inner and outer-wheel bearings

A good tool kit containing:

Wire brush to clean dirty threads
Socket set
Torque wrench
Ring and open-ended spanners
Hacksaw and spare blades
Large and small flat and round files
Selection of spare nuts, bolts and washers, of type and thread/s to fit vehicle 30cm Stillson pipe wrench
1 box spanner for large wheel-bearing lock nuts
Hammer
Large and small cold chisels, for large and stubborn nuts
Self–grip wrench, eg. Mole type
Broad and thin nosed pliers
Circlip pliers
Insulating tape
3 metres electrical wire (vehicle type, not mains)
1 set of feeler gauges
Small adjustable wrench
Tube of gasket cement, eg. Red Hermetite
Tube Loctite thread sealant
Large and small slot head and Phillips head screwdrivers
Accurate tyre pressure gauge
Hardwood or steel plate, to support the jack on soft ground

Extras for off–road use

2 sand ladders per vehicle (4 if vehicle travels alone)
3 wheel bearing hub oil seals
1 rear gearbox oil seal
1 rear differential oil seal
1 rear spring main leaf, complete with bushes
1 front spring main leaf, complete with bushes
4 spare spring bushes
4 spring centre bolts
1 set (=4) of spring shackle plates
1 set (=4) of spring shackle pins
2 rear axle 'U' bolts
1 front axle 'U' bolt.

If instead of leaf springs you have coil springs, carry one spare plus 2 mountings and 4 bushes
1 set of shock absorber mounting rubbers
2 spare engine mounting rubbers
1 spare gearbox mounting rubber
2 door hinge pins
1 screw jack (to use it on its side when changing springs and/or bushes)
2 metres of strong chain plus bolts to fix it, for splinting broken chassis axle or spring parts
Snow chains if you expect a lot of mud or snow
5cm paint brush, to dust off the engine, so that you can work on it
Large groundsheet for lying on when working under the vehicle or repairing tyres, so as to prevent sand from getting between the inner tube and the tyre
1 high lift jack
2 long-handled shovels for digging out
2 steering ball joints
2 spare padlocks
Radiator stop leak, compound (dry porridge or raw egg will do in an emergency)

Specific to Series IIA Land Rovers

1 set rear axle half shafts (heavy duty)

Specific to Series III Land Rovers

1 complete gear change lever, if you have welded bush type (or replace with groove and rubber ring type)
4 nylon bonnet hinge inserts (or 2 home–made aluminium ones)
2 windscreen outer hinge bolts (No 346984)
2 windscreen inner tie bolts
2 rear differential drain plugs
1 set big end nuts
1 rear axle drive plate (Salisbury)

Specific to Land Rover Turbo Diesel and Tdi Engines

2 spare glass fibre main timing belts, stored flat and in a cool place
3 pushrods
3 brass cam followers
2 air filter paper elements

Maintenance check before departure

1. Change oil and renew all oil and fuel filters
2. Clean air filter and change oil bath or air filter element
3. Lubricate drive shafts, winch, speedometer cable
4. Lubricate all locks with dry graphite
5. Adjust and lubricate all door hinges
6. Inspect undercarriage for fluid leaks, loose bolts etc.
7. Rotate all tyres, inspecting for cuts and wear
8. Check and adjust brakes

9. Check adjustment of carburettor or injection pump
10. Check fan belts and accessory belts
11. Check sparking plugs. Clean and re–gap if necessary (replace as necessary). If diesel, clean or replace injectors.
12. Check ignition timing
13. Check and top up: front and rear differentials, swivel–pin housings, transmission, transfer case, overdrive, power steering pump, and air conditioning pump (if applicable), steering box, battery, brake and clutch fluid, cooling system
14. Check that there are no rattles
15. Inspect radiator and heater hoses
16. Check breather vents on both axles, gearbox and fuel filler cap
17. Check all lights and direction indicators
18. Check wheel balance and steering alignment (always do this with new wheels and/or tyres)
19. Check battery clamps and all electrical wiring for faulty insulation ■

GETTING THERE BY OTHER MEANS
Section 6

CYCLING ASSOCIATIONS AND HOLIDAY OPERATORS

Apex Cycles
40-42 Clapham High Street
London SW4 7UR
Tel: **071-622 1334**
Large retailer of bikes and equipment with a number of branches nationwide.

Backround Bicycle Touring
1516 5th Street
Suite M23
Berkeley
California 94710
Tel: **245-3874**

Bents Bicycle Tours
The Priory
High Street
Redbourne
Hertfordshire AL3 7LZ
Tel: **0582 793249**
Worldwide cycling tours from China to Bavaria.

Bicycle Africa
4887 Columbia Drive S
Seattle
Washington 98108-1919
USA
Tel: **202-682 9314**
Cycle tours through Africa lasting two to four weeks.

Bicycle Australia
PO Box K499
Haymarket
NSW 2000
Australia
Tel: **46-272 186**

Bicycle Association of New Zealand
PO Box 2454
Wellington
New Zealand
Tel: *Wellington* **843989**
Auckland **489233**
Christchurch **265514**

Bicycle Federation of Australia
399 Pitt Street
Sydney 2000
New South Wales
Australia
Tel: **02-264 8001**
Federation of Australian cycling organizations.

Bike Events Ltd
PO Box 75
Bath Avon BA1 1BX
Tel: **0225 310859**
Organizes a range of activities from day events to touring holidays in Britain and worldwide. Also produces a magazine, Be Magazine.

British Cycling Federation
36 Rockingham Road
Kettering
Northants NN16 8HG
Tel: **0536 412211**
The national association of cycle-racing clubs, offering an information service for members.

British Mountainbike Federation
36 Rockingham Road
Kettering Northants
NN16 8HG
Tel: **0536 412211**
The national governing body for sport and recreational mountainbiking, whose services

include insurance, racing licences, newsletter, information leaflets. The BMBF also works towards greater access to the countryside.

Canadian Cycling Association
1600 James Naismith Drive
Gloucester
Ontario K1B 5N4
Canada
Tel: **416-781 4717**

Cyclists' Touring Club (CTC)
Cotterell House
69 Meadrow
Godalming
Surrey GU7 3HS
Tel: **0483 417217**
Britain's oldest and largest national association for all types of cyclists, with a touring information service available to members. The CTC also offers insurance, a magazine, organised cycling holidays worldwide, as well as campaigning for cyclists' rights.

Freewheel
2 Nottingham Court
Covent Garden
London WC2H 9AY
Tel: **071-836 1752**

League of American Wheelmen
190 West Ostend Street
Suite 120
Baltimore
MD 21230
USA Tel: **301 944 3399**

London to Paris Bike Ride
Sports Pro International Ltd
26A The Terrace
Riverside
Barnes
London SW13
Fax: **081-392 1539**
Fax the organizers, Sports Pro, by mid-April for an application form.

Susie Madron's Cycling for Softies
2-4 Birch Polygon
Rusholme
Manchester M14 5HX
Tel: **061-248 8282**
Tours of rural France, equipment provided, accommodation in two and three star hotels.

United States Cycling Federation
1750 East Boulder St
Colorado Springs
CO 80909
Tel: **719-578 4581**

HITCH-HIKING ASSOCIATIONS

Allostop
The collective name for the associations Allauto, Provoya and Stop-Voyages. Allostop puts you in contact with drivers with a view to sharing petrol costs.Enrol sufficiently in advance. A small sum of between £15 and £20 (which constitutes an annual subscription fee and which cannot be refunded) allows you to an unlimited number of journeys in a year starting from the date of enrolment. If you wish to make only one journey, the subscription is less.

The main offices are:

Alsace Allostop-Provoya
5 Rue de Général Zimmer
6700 Strasbourg
Tel: 88-37 13 13
Open from 15.00 hrs to 18.30 hrs from Monday to Friday and from 10.00 hrs to 12.00 hrs on Saturday.

Bretagne Allostop-Provoya
Au C.I.J. Bretagne
Maison du Champs de Mars
35043 Rennes
Tel: **99-30 98 87**
Open from 15.00 hrs to 18.00 hrs on Monday to Friday and from 9.00 hrs to 12.00hrs on Saturday.

Languedoc Allostop-Provoya
9 Rue du Plan de l'Olivia
3400 Montpelier
Tel: **67-66 02 29**
Open from 15.00 hrs to 18.00 hrs on Monday to Friday and 10.00hrs to 12.30 hrs on Saturday.

Midi-Pyrénées Allostop-Provoya
au C.R.I.J.
2 Rue Malbec
31000 Toulouse
Tel: **61-22 68 13**
Open from 15.30 hrs to 18.30 hrs from Tuesday to Friday and 10.30 hrs to 12.30 hrs on Saturday.

Nord-Pas-de-Calais Allostop-Provoya
l'Office du Tourism
Palais Rihour
59800 Lille
Tel: **20-57 96 69**
Open from 15.00 hrs to 18.00 hrs on Monday to Friday and 10.30 hrs to 12.30 hrs on Saturday.

Pays de la Loire Allostop-Provoya au C.R.I.J.
10 Rue Lafayette
44000 Nantes
Tel: **40-89 04 85**
Open from 15.30 hrs to 18.30 hrs from Tuesday to Friday and from 10.00 hrs to 12.00 hrs on Saturday.

Provence-Alpes de Sud-Cote d'Azur Allostop-Provoya
3 Rue du Petit St-Jean
13100 Aix-en-Provence
Tel: **42-38 37 51**
Open from 15.00 hrs to 18.30 hrs on Monday, Tuesday, Thursday and Friday. From 9.30 hrs to 11.00 hrs and 17.00 hrs to 19.00 hrs on Wednesday and 10.00 hrs to 13.00 hrs on Saturday.

Allostop-Provoya M.J.X. Picaud
23 Avenue Raymond Picaud
06400 Cannes
Tel: **93-38 60 88**
Open from 14.00 hrs to 18.00 hrs on Tuesday to Friday and 10.00 hrs to 12.00 hrs on Saturday.

Paris Allostop-Provoya
84 Passage Brady
75010 Paris
Tel: **1-246 00 66**
Open from 9.00 hrs to 19.30 hrs on Monday to Friday and from 9.00 hrs to 13.00 hrs and 14.00 hrs to 18.00 hrs on Saturday.

Rhone-Alpes Allostop-Provoya
8 Rue de la Bombarde (quartier Saint-Jean)
69005 Lyon
Tel: **78 42 38 29**
Open from 14.00 hrs to 18.00 hrs on Monday to Friday and from 10.00 hrs to 12.00 hrs on Saturday.

Voyage au Fil (au Crit)
28 Rue du Calvaire
Nantes
Tel: **40-89 04 85**
Agent for Allostop, Billets BIGE (discount on ferry services) and the YHA. Belgium.

The Backpackers Club
PO Box 381
Reading RG3 4RL

Mitfahrzentrale
Lammerstrasse 4,
8 Munich 2
Tel: **594561**
Autostop agency in Germany, offices in Hamburg, Frankfurt, Berlin. £7 fee will put you in touch with drivers going your way on expenses basis.

Taxi-stop
The Allostop card can be used for Taxi-stop in Belgium. Taxi-stop offices are:

Infor-Jeunes
27 Rue du Marche-aux-Herbes
100 Brussels
Tel: **02-511 69 30**

Taxi-stop
24 Rue de France
Charleroi
Tel: **071-31 63 42**

Taxi-stop
34 Rue des Dominicains
Liége
Tel: **041-32 38 70**

Taxi-stop
31 Rue de Bruxelles
1300 Wavre
Tel: **010-22 75 75**

Travelmates
496 Newcastle St
West Perth
Western Australia 6005
Tel: **09-328 66 85**
Share a Car Service - A unique service operated from their office arranges for people to share cars on Interstate Trips departing Perth. They introduce the owner/drivers to intending passengers who are about to embark to the Northern Territory or to the Eastern States. Usual arrangement is to share part of the petrol cost and assist with driving. No bookings ... simply standby operation; it is only suited to backpackers.

Polorbis
Department of Tourism
Ul. Marszalkowska 142
PL-00-061- Warsaw
Poland
Tel: **22-273673**
Poland has an official hitchhiking scheme run by Polorbis. Drivers get points for helping you. Ask before going.

PASSENGER CRUISE LINES AND PASSENGER/CARGO FREIGHTER TRAVEL

UK

Blue Star Line
34-35 Leadenhall St
London EC3A 1AR
Cargo/Passenger services from Great Britain to Canada (West Coast) and the USA.

Carnival Cruise Lines (also Star Lauro Lines)
Equity Tours (UK) Ltd
77-79 Great Eastern St
London EC2A 3HU
Tel: **071-235 1656**
Cargo/Passenger services - Mediterranean to the Caribbean, Central America and back. Also South America.

Costa Line Cruises
6-10 Frederick Close
Stanhope Place
London W2 2HD
Tel: **071-724 9911**

CTC Lines
1 Regent St
London SW1Y 4NN
Tel: **071-930 5833**

Cunard Line Ltd
South Western House
Canute Road
Southampton SO9 1ZA
Tel: **0703-229933**
and...
30a Pall Mall
London SW1Y 5LS
Tel: **071-491 3930**
Cruises.

Gdynia America Shipping Lines Ltd
238 City Road
London EC1V 2QL
Tel: **071-251 3389**

Geest Line
The Windward Terminal
Herbert Walker Avenue
Southampton
SO1 0XP
Tel: **0703-334414**
Cargo/Passenger service from Britain to the West Indies.

Ocean Cruise Lines
6-10 Frederick Close
Stanhope Place
London W2 2HD
Tel: **071-723 5557**
Cruises.

St. Helena Shipping Co. Ltd
Curnow Shipping Ltd
The Shipyard
Porthleven
Helston
Cornwall TR13 9JA
Tel: **03265 63434**
From Great Britain to the Canary Islands, St. Helena, Ascension Island, South Africa.

USA

Carnival Cruises Lines, Inc
Carnival Place 3655 NW 87 Avenue
Miami
Florida

Commodore Cruise Line Ltd
800 Douglas Road
Suite 700
Coral Gables
Florida 33134

Cunard Line Ltd
55 Fifth Avenue
New York
NY 10017
Tel: **212-880 7500**

Holland America Line
300 Elliott Avenue
West Seattle
WA 98119
Tel: **206-281 3535**
Cruises.

Windjammer Barefoot Cruises
PO Box 120
Miami Beach
FL 33119
Cruises.

Advice

The Strand Cruise Centre
Charing Cross Shopping Concourse
The Strand
London WC2N 4HZ
Tel: **071-836 6363**
For advice on voyages on passenger-carrying cargo ships around the world.

The Cruise Advisory Travel
35 Blue Boar Row
Salisbury

Wiltshire SP1 1DA
Tel: **0722-335505**
General advice on cruising holidays world-wide.

TRAVEL BY RAIL

Foreign railway reps in the UK

Amtrack (American)
2 Cinnamon Row
Plantation Wharf
York Place
London SW11 3TW
Tel: **071-978 5222**
Fax: 071-924 3171

Australia
c/o Longhaul Leisure Rail
PO Box 113
Peterborough PE1 8HY
Tel: **0733 335599**

Austrian Federal Railways
30 St George St
London W1R 0AL
Tel: **071-629 0461**
Fax: 071-499 6038

Belgian National Railways
Premier House
10 Greycoat Place
London SW1
Tel: **071-233 0360**

Rail Canada
c/o Longhaul Leisure Rail
PO Box 113
Peterborough PE1 8HY
Tel: **0733 335599**
Fax: 071-233 0360

Danish State Railways
c/o Scandinavian Seaways
Scandinavia House
Parkeston Quay
Harwich
Essex CO12 4QG
Tel: **0255 241234**

Finnish State Railways
Finlandia Travel Agency
227 Regent Street
London W1R 7DP
Tel: **071-409 7334**
Fax: 071-409 7733

French Railways (SNCF)
179 Piccadilly
London W1V 0BA

Tel: **071 493 9731**
Fax: 071-409 1652

German Rail
Suite 4
The Sanctuary
23 Oakhill Grove
Surbiton
Surrey KY6 6DU
Tel: **081-399 3661**
Fax: 081-399 4700

India Rail
c/o S D Enterprises Ltd
103 Wembley Park Drive
Wembley
HA9 8HG
Tel: **081-903 3411**
Fax: 081-903 0392

Ireland - Coras Iompair Eirann
185 London Road
Croydon
Surrey CR0 2RJ
Tel: **081-667 0011**
Fax: 081-686 1218

Italian State Railways
3/5 Lansdowne Road
Croydon
Surrey CR9 1LL
Tel: **081-686 0677**
Fax: 081-686 0328

Japan Railways Group
167 Regent Street
London W1R 7FD
Tel: **071-734 9638**

Luxembourg National Railways
122 Regent Street
London W1R 5FE
Tel: **071-434 2800**
Fax: 071-734 1205

Netherlands Railways
25 Buckingham Gate
London SW1E 6LD
Tel: **071-630 1735**
Fax: 071-233 5832

New Zealand Railways Corporation
c/o Longhaul Leisure Rail
PO Box 113
Peterborough PE1 8HY
Tel: **0733 335599**

Norwegian State Railways
21 Cockspur Street
London SW1Y 5DA
Tel: **071-930 6666**
Fax: 071-321 0624

Polish Sate Railways
Polorbis Travel Ltd
82 Mortimer Street
London W1N 7DE
Tel: **071-637 4971**
Fax: 071-436 6558

Portuguese Railways
c/o Portuguese National Tourist Office
New Bond Street House
1 New Bond Street
London W1Y 0NP
Tel: **071-493 3873**

South Africa (Sartravel)
266 Regent Street
London W1R 5DA
Tel: **071-287 1133**

Spanish National Railways
c/o Spanish National Tourist Office
57-8 St James' Street
London SW1Y 5DA
Tel: **071-499 0901**

Swedish State Railways
c/o Norwegian State Railways
21-24 Cockspur St
London SW1Y 5DA
Tel: **071-930 6666**
Fax: 071-321 0624

Swiss Federal Railways
Swiss Centre
Swiss Court
London W1V 8EE
Tel: **071-734 4577**

USA - see Amtrak

Specialist rail tour operators

Abercrombie & Kent
Sloane Square House
Holbein Place
London SW1W 8NS
Tel: **071-730 9600**
Rail tours France, Germany, Spain and Switzerland.

Butterfield's Tours
Burton Fleming
Driffield YO25 0PQ
Tel: **026-287230**
Established operator running a variety of railway tours in India.

Cox & Kings Travel
St James Court
45 Buckingham Gate
London SW1E 6AF
Tel: **071-931 9106**
Palace on Wheels tour through Rajasthan.

International Rail Centre
Victoria Centre
London SW1V 1JY
Tel: **071-928 5151**
Fax: 071-922 9874

Intourist Moscow
Intourist House
219 Marsh Wall
London E14 9FJ
Tel: **071-538 5902**
Trans-Siberian Express.

Longhaul Leisure Rail
PO Box 113
Peterborough PE1 8HY
Tel: **0733 335599**

TEFS Travel
77 Frederick St
Loughborough LE11 3TL
Tel: **0509 262745**
Specialist rail holidays.

Trains Unlimited
PO Box 1997
Portola
California 96122
USA
Tel: **916-836 1745**

Venice Simplon Orient-Express
Sea Containers House
20 Upper Group
London SE1 9FF
Tel: **071 620 0003**

Further reading:
International Timetable (Thomas Cook)
Overseas Timetable (Thomas Cook)
ABC Rail Guide (Reed Travel Group), UK and Europe.

LOW COST TRAVEL PASSES WORLDWIDE

Below is listed a selection of the numerous travel passes available on bus and rail networks worldwide. The passes listed are valid for the whole national system unless otherwise stated.

Europe

BIJ - Billet International pour Jeune
Reduced fares for under 26 valid up to 2 months

Eurail
A pass for 1st class travel with no age restrictions for travel in 17 European countries, valid for 15 or 21 days or 1,2 or 3 months.

Eurail Saver Pass
For 2-5 people travelling and is valid for 15 or 21 days in 1 month in First Class.

Eurail Youth Flexipass
For 3 people under 26 travelling together in 2nd Class

Eurail Flexi Pass
Same as the Eurail Pass except it is valid for a period of 5, 10 or 15 days with 2 months.

Eurail Drive Pass
First Class pass with a Hertz Rental car with unlimited tickets

Euro Domino and Freedom Pass
Flexible pass, giving unlimited travel up to one month in 19 countries

Inter Rail
For the under-26, Inter Rail pass allows one month travel of unlimited distance in Western Europe, and also Czech Republic, Hungary, Morocco, Romania and Turkey.

Inter Rail + Boat
Adds free travel on many Mediterranean, Scandinavian and Irish Sea ships - for 10 days, or one month.

The Rail Europ Senior Card
Valid for one year, for purchasers over 60. Gives reductions up to 50 per cent (normally 30 per cent) in more than 20 European countries.

Rail Europ Family
One adult member of the family pays full fare for tickets, and up to two other adults travel for half price. Children aged 4 to 12 pay half-fare and one child under 4 travels free.

Please note as well as general passes to Europe, passes to individual countries are also available, please see under country heading.

Argentina

Argenpass
Valid for 30 days; 60 days; 90 days. Under-26 receive 20 per cent reduction.

Australia

Aussie Pass
7-10 days in each month or 15 days in 2 months

Austrailpass
Valid for 14 - 60 days, must be bought outside Australia and can only be used by non-Australian passport holders

Kangaroo Road 'n' Rail Pass
Combines Trains and buses, must be used within 6 months of purchase

Down-Under Coach Pass
Valid for 9 days' travel on Greyhounds in Australia and Mount Cook Lines in New Zealand.

Ansett Pioneer Aussiepass
Up to 60 days' travel on Ansett Lines.

Austria

Puzzle-Ticket and Puzzle-Ticket Junior (under 26)
Valid on any 4 days within a 10-day period in one of the countries 4 zones (West, South, North, East)

National Rail Pass
Available for one month and valid on all Austrian railways

Environmental Ticket
Purchase a half-fare pass and pay half fares for all train travel for one year. Also available are Environmental Tickets for pensioners

Belgium

Roundabout Tickets
Validity varies, but offers unlimited mileage.

Benelux 5 Day Tour Rail
Pass for Belgium, Luxembourg and The Netherlands

Canada

Canrailpass
For state-owned VIA rail system and associated buses only. 15-30 days. 20 per cent discount for under-24s. Also 8-day Eastern, Western and Marine regional passes. Must be purchased outside Canada

Canada Travel Pass
7, 15 or 30 days unlimited travel on all scheduled Greyhound routes between British Colombia and Ontario. Must be bought before arriving in Canada

Canada Travel Pass
15 or 30 days, includes coach routes to maritime Provinces. Must be bought before arriving in Canada

Denmark

Scanrail
Valid for 21 days in Scandinavian countries

France

Rail 'n' Drive
Available in the US only

French Rail Pass
For travel for 4 days within 15 days or 9 days within 1 month

Germany

Bodensee Pass
Valid for a month for under 23's and students under 26.

Greece

Touring cards available

India

Indrail Pass
Seven days; 15 days; 21 days; 30 days. Passes also available for longer period but must be used within 1 year..

Ireland

Rambler Pass (Republic Only)

Overlander (all Ireland)

Italy

Travel at Will
Gives unlimited travel

Israel

Egged Round About Bus Tickets
Seven days; 14 days; 21 days; 30 days.

Japan

Japan Rail Pass
Valid for 7 days; 14 days; 21 days, must be purchased before arrival in Japan Can be used on Rail, Buses and ferries..

Luxembourg

Benelux 5 Day Tour Rail
Pass for Belgium, Luxembourg and The Netherlands

Malaysia

Malayan Railpass
Valid for 10 days; 30 days.giving unlimited travel

Morocco

Carte d'Abonnement
Valid for 1 month.

The Netherlands

Benelux 5 Day Tour Rail
Pass for Belgium, Luxembourg and The Netherlands

New Zealand

New Zealand Travelpass
Also covers inter-island ferries and some coaches. 8 days; 15 days; 22 days. Down-Under Coach Pass - see Australia.

Norway

Scanrail
Valid for 21 days in Scandinavian countries.

Pakistan

Offers concessions up to 25% discount to tourists

Poland

Polerail Pass
Available for 7,14 and 21 days.

Singapore

The Malaysian-Singapore Rail Pass
Covers Singapore, Malaysia and Thailand and lasts for 10 days.

Sweden

Scanrail
Valid for 21 days in Scandinavian countries.

Switzerland

The Swiss Pass
Also includes some lake steamers and the extensive network of postal buses.

UK

Young Persons Coach Card
If a full-time student in UK, or under 23, gives 30% of standard fares.

Britexpress Card
Overseas visitors can buy this which gives 30% off over 30 consecutive days

Tourist Trail Pass
Unlimited travel for periods from 5-30 days

USA

Amtrak National Rail Pass
Valid for 45 days. Regional passes available.

Greyhound Ameripass
Thirty days' use of Greyhound bus network. Must be bought before arriving in the US. Contact: Longhaul Leisure Rail, tel: 0733-51780

Trailways USA Pass
Valid for 5 days' minimum travel on the Trailways network throughout the States.

EQUESTRIAN ASSOCIATIONS AND TOUR OPERATORS

The American Horseshows Association Inc
220 East 42nd Street
Suite 409
New York
NY10017
Tel: **212-972 2472**

Arctic Experience
29 Nork Way
Banstead SM7 1PB
Tel: **0737 362321**
Riding in Iceland.

**Association Nationale de Tourisme Equestre
Hippotour**
Rue du Moulin 12
B-1331 Rosieres
Belgium
Tel: **2653 24 87**
Organises riding holidays in Belgium. Also Morocco, Mali and Senegal.

Aventura Ltd
42 Greenlands Road
Staines
Middlesex TW18 4LR
Tel: **0784 459018**
Riding holidays in Southern Spain.

The British Horse Society
The British Equestrian Centre
Stoneleigh
Kenilworth
Warwickshire CV8 2LR
Tel: **0203 696697**

Boojum Expeditions
2625 Garnet Avenue
San Diego
California 92109
USA
Tel: **619-581 3301**
Riding tours of China, Tibet and Inner Mongolia.

Canadian Equestrian Federation
1600 James Naismith Drive
Gloucester
Ontario K1B 5N4
Tel: **613 748 5632**

The New Zealand Equestrian Federation
PO Box 47
Hastings
Hawks Bay
Tel: **6470 850 85**

Equitour/ Peregrine Holidays
40/41 South Parade
Summertown
Oxford OX2 7JP
Tel: **0865-511642**
Holidays in France, Austria, Spain, Portugal, Hungary and Italy. Also Tanzania and Botswana, Argentina, Belize, Egypt amongst others.

The Equestrian Federation of Australia Inc
52 Kensington Road
Rose Park
South Australia 5067
Tel: **618 311 8411**

Explore Worldwide Ltd
1 Frederick St
Aldershot
Hants GU11 1LQ
Tel: **0252 344161**
Pony trekking in Kashmir.

Inntravel
Horingham
York YO6 4JZ
Tel: **0653-628862**
Holidays in France and Spain.

International Horse Travel Association
12 Rue du Moulin
1331 Rosieres
Belgium
Tel:**32-2652 1010**
Equestrian holidays worldwide.

Living Planet Travel Ltd
PO Box 922
London N10 3UZ
Tel: **0582 429365**
Guided treks in South America.

Pyrenee Trail Rides
Cas Martina
Farrera Del Pallars
Llavorsi
Lerida
Spain
Tel: **34-73 630029**

Sobek Expeditions Inc
Box 1089
Angels Camp
California 95222
USA
Tel: **800-777 7939**
Riding tours in the Canadian Rockies.

Steamond International
278 Battersea Park Road
London SW11 3BS
Tel: **071 978 5500**
Riding tours in Argentina, also polo playing.

SAILING ASSOCIATIONS AND HOLIDAY OPERATORS

Australian Yachting Federation
Locked Bag 806
Post Office
Milsons Point
New South Wales 2060
Australia
Tel: **9224 333**

British Marine Industries Federation
Mead Lake Place
Thorpe Lea Road
Egham
Surrey TW20 8HE
Tel: **0784 473377**
Body representing sailing holiday companies, offers Boatline, a holiday information service.

Canadian Yachting Association
1600 James Naismith Drive
Gloucester
Ontario K1B 5N4
Canada
Tel: **613 748 5687**

Centro Velico Capera
Corso Italia 10
Milana 20122
Italy
Tel: **2-86452191**
Sailing courses and cruising near Sardinia, minimum age 17.

Chichester Sailing Centre
Chichester Marina
Sussex PO20 7EL
Tel: **0243 512557**
Holidays for beginners and experienced sailors, with facilities for the physically, visually and mentally handicapped.

Crestar Yachts Ltd
Colette Court
125-126 Sloane St
London SW1X 9AU
Tel: **071-730 9962**
Luxury charters in Europe, the South Pacific and the Caribbean, complete with crew.

National Federation of Sea Schools
Fetchwood Lane
Totton
Southampton SO4 2D2
Tel: **0703 869956**
Full details of sail training nationwide and affiliated to the International Sailing Schools Association.

Ocean Youth Club
South St
Gosport
Hampshire PO12 1EP
Tel: **0705 528421**
Adventure sailing holidays for young people.

New Zealand Yachting Federation
PO Box 90900
Mail Centre
Auckland 1
New Zealand
Tel: **649-303 2360**

Royal Yachting Association (RYA)
Royal Yachting Association House
Romsey Road
Eastleigh
Hants SO5 4YA
Tel: **0703 629962**

United States Yachting Racing Union
PO Box 209
Newport
Rhode Island 02840
USA
Tel: **401 849 5200**

Wave Yacht Charters
1 Hazel Drive
Dundee DD2 1QQ
Tel: **0382 68501**
Sailing on the west coast of Scotland.

Yacht Charter Association
c/o D. R. Howard
60 Silverdale
New Milton
Hants BH25 7DE
Listing of approved members available.

Further reading:
Adventure Holidays (Vacation Work)

WALKING ASSOCIATIONS

Long Distance Walkers Association
117 Higher Lane
Rainford
St Helens
Merseyside
Tel: **0744 822 638**

Ramblers Association
1-5 Wandsworth Road
London SW8 2XX
Tel: **071-582 6878**

For tour operators, please see Adventure and Sporting in Section 3, page 677

MICROLIGHTING ASSOCIATIONS

British Microlight Aircraft Association
Bullring
Deddington
Oxford
Tel: **0869-734042**

MOUNTAINEERING

Alpine Club
55 Charlotte Road
London EC2A 3QT
Tel: **071-613 0755**

British Association of Parascending Clubs
18 Talbot Lane
Leicester LE1 4LR
Tel: **0533-530318**

British Mountaineering Council
Crawford House
Precinct Centre
Booth Street East
Manchester
M13 9RZ
Tel: **061-273 5835**

Mount Everest Foundation
Gowrie
Cardwell Close
Preston
Lancashire PR4 1SH
Tel: **0772-635346**

Mountain Medicine Data Centre
Department of Neurological Sciences
St Bartholomew's Hospital
38 Little Britain
London EC1A 7BE
Tel: **071-600 9000**

Mountaineering Council of Ireland
Wilmont Cottage
99 Dunmurray Lane
Belfast
BT17 4JU ■

GREAT JOURNEYS OVERLAND
Section 7

OVERLAND OPERATORS AND ASSOCIATED CLUBS

AAT Kings Tours
2nd Floor William House
14 Worple Road
Wimbledon SW19 4DD
Tel: **081-944 5855**
Four wheel drive safaris in the Australian Outback.

Acacia Expeditions Ltd
5 Walm Lane
London NW2 5SJ
Tel: **081-451 3877**
Camping safaris in Africa.

The Adventure Travel Centre
131-135 Earls Court Road
London SW5 9RH
Tel: **071-370 4555**
Agency for all the most overland companies.

Adventure Center
1311 63rd Street
Duite 200
Emmeryville
California 94608
Tel: **510-654 1879**

The Africa Travel Centre
4 Medway Court
Leigh St
London WC1H 9QX
Tel: **071-387 1211**
Offer a consultancy service to overland travellers.

American Adventures Inc
6762a Centinela Avenue
Colver City
California 90230
Tel: **310-390 7495**
Tel: **800 864 0335** (Toll Free)

American Adventures Inc
45 High Street
Tunbridge Wells
Kent TN1 1XL
Tel: **0892 511894**
Tours in the USA, Canada and Mexico.

American Pioneers
PO Box 229
Westlea
Swindon
Wiltshire SN5 7HJ
Tel: **0793 881882**
Camping tours in Venezuela, Mexico, Canada and the US.

Bridge the World
1 Ferdinand Street
London NW1 8ES
Tel: **071-284 0040**
Travel agency stocking most of the overland companies brochures.

Dragoman Adventure Travel
Camp Green
Debenham
Suffolk IP14 6LA
Tel: **0728 861133**
Overland trips in Asia, South Africa and South America.

Encounter Overland
267 Old Brompton Road
London SW5 9JA
Tel: **071-370 6845**
Founded over 30 years ago, they now operate 45 different expeditions ranging from 10 days to 32 weeks throughout Asia, Africa, Central and South America.

From 16 April all national and international codes change — see page 587 for details.

Exodus Expeditions
9 Weir Road
Balham
London SW12 OLT
Tel: 081-675 5550
Transcontinental expeditions lasting between two and 26 weeks.

Explore Worldwide Ltd
1 Frederick St
Aldershot GU11 1LQ
Tel: 0252 344161
Wide variety of tours (4-wheel drive, camel, riverboat) overland in 50 countries worldwide.

The Globetrotters Club
BCM/Roving
London WC1N 3XX
An informal association of travellers from all over the world, linked by an interest in low cost travel and the desire to study the cultures of other lands. Members share their experiences and knowledge. The club concentrates on attracting 'non-tourist' members with a genuine empathy for the people in other lands.

Guerba Expeditions
101 Eden Vale Road
Westbury BA13 3QX
Tel: 0373 826611
Camping safaris tours from one to 27 weeks in Africa.

Journey Latin America Ltd
16 Devonshire Road
Chiswick
London W4 2HD
Tel: 081-747 8315
Experts in South American travel, guided tours using local transport.

Mountain Travel, Inc
6420 Fairmount Avenue
El Cerrito
CA 94530
USA
Tel: 415-527 8100
Overland through Patagonia.

Sundowners Travel Centre
151 Dorcas Street
South Melbourne
Victoria 3205
Australia
Tel: 03-690 2499

Sun Travel Ltd
407 Great South Road
Penrose
Auckland
New Zealand
Tel: 09-525 3074

Top Deck Travel
131-135 Earls Court Road
London SW5 9RH
Tel: 071-244 8641
London to Kathmandu via Africa, and a variety of escorted tours in Southeast Asia.

Trailfinders
194 Kensington High Street
London W8 7RG
Tel: 071-938 3939
Travel agency which can organise some trips with some overlanding companies.

Trek America
Trek House
The Bullring
Deddington
Oxon OX5 4TT
Tel: 0869 38777
North American adventure camping and trekking tours.

WEXAS International
45-49 Brompton Road
London SW3 1DE
Tel: 071-589 3315
A travel club, which can offer advice and book overlanding trips for its members. ■

YOUR SPECIAL NEEDS
Section 8

AGENCIES FOR SINGLES AND COMPANIONS

Great Company
31 Amwell Street
London EC1R 1UN
Tel: **071-278 0328**
Worldwide destinations and single room accommodation without the usual supplement.

Single Parent Travel Club
37 Sunningdale Park
Queen Victoria Road
New Tupton
Chesterfield
Derbyshire S42 6DZ
Tel: **0246-865069**

Solo's Holidays
41 Watford Way
Hendon
London NW4 3JH
Tel: **081-202 0855**
Holidays for singles over 30 (no married travellers allowed) in Europe, the Far East, Australasia and East Africa.

SPLASH
19 North Street
Plymouth PL4 9AH
Tel: **0752 674067**
Holidays for single-parents and their families as well as for unaccompanied children.

Travelmate
15 Cavendish Road
Bournemouth BH7 7AD
Tel: **0202 558314**
Introduction service for travellers.

Travel Companions
110 High Mount
Station Road
London NW4 3ST
Tel: **081-202 8478**
Introduction service for travellers.

WOMEN'S TRAVEL ASSOCIATIONS

Adventure Trekking
26 Paisley Crescent
Edinburgh EH8 7JP
Tel: **031-661 1959**
Company specializing in women's group adventures in Nepal, which include trekking, river rafting and safari. Also tailor-made walking tours in Scotland.

Silvermoon Women's Bookshop
68 Charing Cross Road
London WC2H 0BB
Tel: **071-836 7906**

Women's Corona Society
Commonwealth House
18 Northumberland Avenue
London WC2N 5BJ
Tel: **071-839 7908**
Primarily a support and advice group for expatriate women, offering courses and advice. to those about to move abroad and services in the UK such as shepherding children from plane to school and back.

Women's Sailing Holidays
51 Salisbury Road
Edinburgh EH16 5AA
Tel: **031-667 8299**
Sailing holidays in small groups for beginners or experienced sailors.

Women's Travel Advisory Bureau
Lansdowne
High Street
Blockley
Gloucestershire GL56 9HF
Tel: **0386-701 082**
Supplies information packs tailored to individuals travel plans.

Women Welcome Women
8a Chestnut Avenue
High Wycombe Bucks.
HP11 1DJ
Tel: **0494-439481**
Organization to promote international friendship by helping female travellers to stay with other members and their families.

ASSOCIATIONS FOR THE ELDERLY

Age Concern England
1268 London Road
London SW16 4EJ
Tel: **081-679 8000**
Provides excellent holiday fact sheets and books.

Help the Aged
16-18 St James's Walk
London EC1R 0BE
Tel: **071-253 0253**

Holiday Helpers
2 Old Bank Chambers
Station Road
Horley
Surrey RH6 9HW
Tel: **0293-775137**
Matchmaking service for helpers and elderly travellers.

Pre-Retirement Association
Holiday Courses
78 Capel Road East
Barnet
Herts EN4 8JF
Tel: **081-449 4506**
Organizes retirement-planning holidays in conjunction with Pontins.

Saga Holidays
The Saga Building
Middelburg Square
Folkestone CT20 1AZ
Tel: **0303-857000**
Extensive range of holidays worldwide for the over 60's (companions can be over 50).

Tripscope
The Courtyard
Evelyn Road
London W4 5JL
Tel: **081-994 9294**
Transport information service for disabled or elderly people.

Wallace Arnold Tours
62 George Street
Croydon
Surrey CR9 1DN
Tel: **081-688 7255**
Coach holidays on the continent.

Further reading:
Life in the Sun
– A guide to Long-stay Holidays and Living Abroad in Retirement (Age Concern)

CONTACTS FOR DIABETIC TRAVELLERS

The British Diabetic Association
10 Queen Anne St
London W1M 0BD
Tel: **071-323 1531**

British Airways Medical Services For Travellers Abroad
Tel: **071-831 5333**

Health Care Abroad
DHSS Overseas Branch
Newcastle upon Tyne NE98 1YX

Worldwide Diabetes Assocation
Diabetes Care Department
British Diabetic Association
10 Queen Anne St
London W1M 0BD
Tel: **071-323 1531**

Identification

Medic Alert Foundation
Tel: **071-833 3034**

Golden Key Company
Tel: **0795- 663403**

SOS Talisman Co Ltd
Tel: **081-554 5579**

Travel Insurance

Diabetes Care Department
British Diabetic Association
10 Queen Anne St
London W1M 0BD
Tel: **071-323 1531**

Vaccinations

Thomas Cook Vaccination Centre
45 Berkeley St
London W1A 1EB
Tel: 071-499 4000

Diabetes supplies

Novo Nordisk Pharmaceuticals Ltd
Broadfield Park
Brighton Road
Pease Pottage
Crawley
West Sussex RH11 9RT
Tel: 0293 613555

ELI Lilly & Co Ltd
Dextra Court
Chapel Hill
Basingstoke
Hampshire
Tel: 0256 473241

Becton-Dickinson UK Ltd
Between Towns Road
Cowley
Oxford OX4 3LY
Tel: 0865 777722

Ames Division
Evans House
Hamilton Close
Basingstoke
Hampshire
Tel: 0256 29181

Boeringer Manheim UK
Bell Lane
Lewes
East Sussex BN7 1LG
Tel: 0273 480444

CONTACTS FOR VEGETARIAN TRAVELLERS

The Australian Vegetarian Society
PO Box 65
2021 Paddington
Tel: 2-349 4485

Canadian Natural Health Society Inc
6250 Mountain Sights
H3W 2Z3 Montreal

The European Vegetarian Union
Larensweg 26
NL 1221 CM Hilversum

Brussels
Belgium
Tel: **31-35 834 796**
Based at the offices of the Dutch Vegetarian Society, it aims to encourage better communications between the European vegetarian groups, and has a regular newsletter.

The International Vegetarian Union (IVU)
Mr Maxwell Lee
Honorary General Secretary
King's Drive
Marple
Stockport
Cheshire SK6 6NQ
Tel: **061-427 5850**

Honorary Regional Secretaries -

Africa
Mr Jan Beeldman
82 Darrenwood Village
First St
Darrenwood 2194
Randburg
South Africa

Australasia
PO Box
Paddington 20120

Middle East
Mr Mark Weintraub
8 Balfour Street
Jerusalem 92101
Israel

India and the East
Sri Jashu Shah
114a Mittal Court
Narriman Point
400 021 India

USA
Dr Kay Sheehan
7617 E Mineral Drive
Englewood
Colorado 80112
USA

Europe
Mr Rob Snijders
Vondelstraat 9A2
1054 GB Amsterdam
The Netherlands

New Zealand Vegetarian Society Inc
Box 77-034
Auckland 3
New Zealand

North American Vegetarian Society (NAVS)
PO Box 72
Dolgeville
13329
USA

Vegetarian Awareness Network (VEGANET)
PO Box 76390
USA 20013
Tel: 202-347 8343

The Vegetarian Society of the United Kingdom
Parkdale
Dunham Road
Altrincham
Cheshire WA14 4QG
Tel: 061-928 0793

The Vegetarian Society of Russia
Moscow 109462
Volsky Bulwar
39-3-23 T-Pavlova
Russia

VegiVentures
Castle Cottage
Castle Square
Castle Acre
Norfolk PE23 2AG
Tel: 0621 784285
Specialist company which organises European group holidays for vegetarians.

Further reading:
The Vegetarian Travel Guide (The Vegetarian Society), *a worldwide guide to vegetarian restaurants, societies and vegetarian meals in transit.*
The Vegetarian Traveller (Grafton), *Andrew Sanger's excellent guide to worldwide travel for vegetarians.*

CONTACTS FOR THE DISABLED TRAVELLER

Access to the Skies
c/o RADAR
25 Mortimer St
London W1N 8AB
Tel: 071-637 5400
Information on airline facilities and services for the disabled.

ACROD
(The Australian Council for the Rehabilitation of the Disabled)
PO Box 60
Curtin

ACT 2605
Canberra
Tel: 010 61 62 82 4333
Australia's national organisation for disability, offers information for disabled travellers.

The Across Trust
70-72 Bridge Road
East Molesey
Surrey KT8 9HF
Tel: 081-783 1355
Operates large luxury fully-equipped ambulances called 'Jumbulances' which take severely disabled people on organized group pilgrimages and holidays across Europe.

Assist Travel
P.O. Box 83
Lara
Victoria 3212
Australia
Tel: 010 61 52 84 1284
Specialist tour operator

Association of British Insurers
Aldermary House
10-15 Queen St
London EC4N 1TT
Tel: 071-248 4477
For information on travel insurance for the disabled.

Barrier-Free Travel
36 Wheatley Street
North Bellingen
New South Wales 2454
Australia
Tel: 010 61 66 552733
Offers a consultancy service for disabled travel, commercial-based operation.

BREAK
20 Hooks Hill Road
Sheringham
Norfolk NR26 8NL
Tel: 0263 823170
Holidays in Norfolk for the physically and mentally handicapped.

British Railways Board
Liaison Manager (Disabled Passengers)
Euston House
24 Eversholt St
PO Box 100
London NW1 1DZ
Tel: 071-928 5151

British Red Cross
9 Grosvenor Crescent
London SW1 7ET
Tel: 071-235 5454
Can provide companions for disabled travellers.

British Ski Club for the Disabled
Mr H.M. Sturgess
Spring Mount
Berwick St John
Shaftesbury
Dorset SP7 OFQ
Tel: 0747 88515

British Sports Association for the Disabled
34 Osnaburgh St
London NW1 3ND
Tel: 071-388 7277

Camping for the Disabled
20 Burton Close
Dawley
Telford
Shropshire TF4 2BX
Tel: 0743 75889
Advice and information on camping in the UK and overseas.

Canadian Rehabilitation Council for the Disabled
45 Sheppard Avenue E
Toronto
Ontario M2N 5W9
Tel: 010 1 52 84 1284
Gives advice and publishes 'Handi-Travel', a book of tips for the disabled traveller.

Carefree Holidays
64 Florence Road
Northampton
NN1 4NA
Tel: 0604 34301

CPA
(Canadian Paraplegic Association)
1550 Don Mills Road
Suite 201
Don Mills
Ontario M3B 3K4
Tel: 010 0 416 391 0203

Department of Transport Disability Unit
Room S10/21
2 Marsham St
London SW1P 3EB
Tel: 071-276 5256

DIAL UK
Park Lodge St Catherine's Hospital
Tickhill Road
Balby
Doncaster DN4 8QN
Tel: 0302 310123

Disabled Drivers Association
Ashwellthorpe Hall
Norwich
NR16 1EX
Tel: 0508 41449

Disabled Drivers' Motor Club
Cottingham Way
Thrapston
Northants
NN14 4PL
Tel: 0801 24724

Disabled Kiwi Tours (NZ) Ltd
East Coast Highway
P.O. Box 55
Opotiki
New Zealand
Tel: 010 64 7 315 7867
Personalised tours of NZ for the disabled.

Disabled Living Foundation
380-384 Harrow Road
London W9 2HU
Tel: 071-289 6111

Disabled Motorists Federation
Unit 2a
Atcham Estate
Upton Magna
Shrewsbury
Sy4 4UG
Tel: 0743 761889

Disabled Persons Assembly
P.O. Box 10-138
The Terrace
Wellington
New Zealand
Tel: 010 64 4 472 2626
National organisation for the disabled.

Disaway Trust
2 Charles Road
Merton Park
London SW19 3BD
Tel: 081-543 3431
Holidays for groups overseas and in the UK.

Going Down
46 Hill Drive
Hove
Sussex
BN3 6QL
Tel: 0273 566616
Arranges diving expeditions for people with disabilities.

Health Services Information Centre
Jewish Rehabilitation Hospital
3205 Place Alton Goldbloom
Chomedey
Laval
Quebec H7V 1R2
Canada
Tel: 010 1 514 688 9550
Has over 800 access guides and extensive information on travel within Canada.

Help the Handicapped Holiday Fund
147a Camden Road
Tunbridge Wells
Kent TN1 2RA
Tel: **0892 547474**
Free holidays for the physically disabled.

Holiday Care Service
2 Old Bank Chambers
Station Road
Horley
Surrey RH6 9HW
Tel: **0923 774535**
Travel advice and information. Also has a service called 'Holiday Helpers' which matches volunteer helpers with elderly or disabled travellers.

Holidays for the Disabled
c/o Mr J A Stacey
12 Ryle Road
Farnham
Surrey GU9 8PRW
Tel: **0252 721390**
Organises one annual holiday abroad for disabled people aged 30-60.

John Grooms Association for Disabled People
10 Gloucester Drive
London N4 2LP
Tel: **081-800 8695**
This charity has launched Grooms Holidays, which specialises in holidays for the disabled.

Joint Committee on Mobility for Disabled People
Tim Shapley OBE
9 Moss Close
Pinner
Middlesex HA5 3AY

Journey of a Lifetime Trust
Mrs D.K. Dalton
Vincent House
32 Maxwell Road
Northwood
Middlesex HA6 2YF
Tel: **09274 25453**

Jubilee Sailing Trust
Test Road
Eastern Docks
Southampton
SO1 1GG
Tel: **0703 631395**
Offers the opportunity of working as a crew member on the tall ship, the 'Lord Nelson'.

The Les Evans Holiday Fund
Unit 6
Monometer Business Park

Woodrolfe Road
Tollesbury
Essex CM9 8SJ
Tel: **0206 47120**
Holidays arranged for children who are sick or severely disabled. Caters for children aged 8-15 who are accompanied by fully qualified medical staff. Destinations - Florida's Disneyworld & California's Disneyland.

London Regional Transport
Unit for Disabled Passengers
55 Broadway
London SW1H OBD
Tel: **071-918 3312**

Mobility International USA
P.O. Box 3551
Eugene
Oregon 97403
USA
Tel: **010 1 503 343 1284**
International club offering travel and educational exchanges for the disabled, annual membership $35.

Mobility International
228 Borough High St
London SE1 1JX
Tel: **071-403 5688**
Exists to encourage the integration of handicapped people with the non-handicapped, by arranging international projects with a wide appeal, varying from youth festivals to more professional conferences and seminars. Handicap is not the common denominator; rather people attend because of their interest in the topic or emphasis of the particular project. Mobility International News is published three times a year.

New Zealand CCS
P.O. Box 6349
Te Aro
Wellington
New Zealand
Tel: **010 64 4 384 5677**
Agency providing services to help disabled travellers

Physically Handicapped and Able Bodied (PHAB)
12-14 London Road
Croydon CRO 2TA
Tel: **081-667 9443**
Holidays for all ages and abilities.

Project Phoenix Trust
68 Rochfords
Coffee Hall
Milton Keynes MK6 5DJ
Tel: **0908 678038**

A non-profit organization the Trustees of which organize and run visits overseas. Mixed ability groups of adults include those who (a) would like a holiday which has a focal point, such as art, history, etc, (b) would need some physical help in order to make such a visit possible, (c) would be prepared to provide physical help to others to make the visit viable and may need some financial assistance in order to take part. These tours involve a lot of activity and are probably best suited to energetic and strong disabled people.

RADAR Royal Association for Disability and Rehabilitation
25 Mortimer St
London W1N 8AB
Tel: **071-637 5400**
A registered charity devoted to helping and promoting the rights of the disabled. RADAR finds suitable accommodation and facilities for holidays for the disabled. Publishes two guides entitled Holidays for Disabled People and Holidays and Travel Abroad which are updated each year and a monthly Bulletin and a quarterly journal called Contact . They also publish excellent comprehensive lists of publications and useful addresses for the disabled holidaymaker.

Rehabilitation Inter USA
1123 Broadway
New York
NY 10010
USA
Disability society with information on disabled travel in North America .

Society for the Advancement of Travel for the Handicapped (SATH)
347 Fifth Avenue
Suite 610
New York NY 10016
USA
Tel: **010 1 212 447 7284**
Is a 'non-profit educational forum for the exchange of knowledge and the gaining of new skills in how to facilitate travel for the handicapped, the elderly and the retired'. SATH publishes 'The United States Welcomes Handicapped Visitors'. For further info please send a s.a.e. Affiliated member of the World Tourism Organisation (UN) and represented on the US Congress Tourism Advisory Board. Membership is open to all who share SATH's concerns.

Threshold Travel
80 Newry Street
Banbridge
Co Down BT3 3HA
Tel: **08206 62954**

ABTA travel agent which specialises in disabled travel.

TRIPSCOPE
The Courtyard
Evelyn Road
London W4 5JL
Tel: **081-994 9294**
or:
Tripscope-South West
Pamwell House
160 Pennywell Road
Bristol
BS5 0TX
Tel: **0272 414094**
A registered charity, they provide reliable transport advice and information for local or international journeys.

The United States Travel and Tourism Administration
P.O. Box 1EN
London W1A 1EN
Tel: 071-439 7433
Provides information for people planning to visit the USA.

Uphill Ski Club of Great Britain
12 Park Crescent
London W1N 4EQ
Tel: **071-636 1989**
Organises wintersports for disabled people.

The Wheel Resort
39-51 Broken Head Road
Byron Bay
NSW 2481
Australia
Tel: **010 61 66 85 6139**
Luxury cabins designed for disabled travellers and owned by wheelchair users.

Winged Fellowship Trust
Angel House
20-32 Pentonville Road
London N1 9XD
Tel: **071-733 3388**
UK and overseas holidays for severely disabled adults.

Young Disabled on Holiday
c/o Miss R Girdlestone
33 Longfield Avenue
Heald Green
Cheadele
Cheshire
SK8 3NN
Organises holidays for 18-35 year old, in Britain and overseas with the emphasis on activities and entertainment.

776

Further reading:
Nothing Ventured (Harrap Columbus), distributed in Canada by Penguin Books and in US by Viking Penguin and called *Able to Travel*) *personal accounts of journeys worldwide by disabled travellers, plus advice, and detailed listings of useful contacts for every aspect of travel for the disabled.* ∎

PAPERWORK AND MONEY
Section 9

VISA AGENCIES

Alliance Visa and Consular Services
Room 21, Building 8
Manchester Airport
Manchester M22 5PJ
Tel: **061-489 3201**

Intercontinental Visa Service
Los Angeles World Trade Center
350 South Figueroa Street
Los Angeles
CA 90071
USA
Tel: **(213) 625 7175**

Port Reps
PO Box 290
Slough SL1 7LF
Tel: **06286-4714**

PVS (UK) Ltd
(Passport and Visa Services)
10b Parlaunt Road
Langley
Slough
Berks SL3 8BB
Tel: **0753 683160**

Rapid Visa Service
Adventure Travel Centre
131-135 Earls Court Road
London SW5 9RH
Tel: **071-373 3026**

Ross Consular Services
6 The Grove
Slough
Berks SL1 1QP
Tel: **(0753) 820881**

Thames Consular Services
363 Chiswick High Road
London W4 4HS
Tel: **081-995 2492**

The Visa Service
2 Northdown Street
London N1 9BG
Tel: **071-833 2709**

Thomas Cook Passport and Visa Service
45 Berkeley Street
London W1A 1EB
Tel: **071-408 4141**

Visas International
3169 Barbara Ct Ste F
Los Angeles
California 90068
USA
Tel: **(213) 850 1191**

Worldwide Visas Ltd
9 Adelaide Street
Charing Cross
London WC2
Tel: **071-379 0419/0376**

For Visas Requirements, please see under the Geographical Section at the beginning of this Directory, where visas are listed under the country.

The next section can seem confusing with endless addresses.
The first part is the Government Representatives Worldwide ie. all Australian representatives in every country, Argentina, Austria etc. followed by all Canadian representatives across the world, then the New Zealand representatives followed by the UK and USA.
The second part lists all the addresses of Foreign representatives, first of all in Australia, for example the Algerian representative in Canberra etc., followed by all foreign representatives in Canada, then New Zealand, followed by those represented in the UK and lastly in the USA.

GOVERNMENT REPRESENTATIVES WORLDWIDE

Australia

ARGENTINA
Avenida Santa Fe 846
Piso 8
Swiss Air Building
Buenos Aires
Tel: **312 6841/8**
Telex: 21946
Fax: 311 1219

AUSTRIA
Matiellistrasse 2-4
A-1040
Vienna
Tel: **512 8580**
Telex: 114313
Fax: 513 2908

BANGLADESH
184 Gulshan Avenue
Gulshan
Dhaka
Tel: **60 0091/5**
Telex: 642317

BELGIUM
Guimard Centre
Rue Guimard 6-8
1040 Brussels
Tel: **231 0500**
Telex: 21834
Fax: 230 6802

BRAZIL
SHIS QI-9
Conjunto 16
Casa 1
Brasilia DF
Tel: **248 5569**
Telex: 611025

BRUNEI
PO Box 2990
Bandar Seri Begawan 2085
Negara
Brunei
Tel: **2 9435/6**
Telex: 2582
Fax: 2 1652

CANADA
Suite 710
50 O'Connor Street
Ottawa
Ontario K1P 6L2
Tel: (613) **236 0841**
Telex: 533391
Fax: (613) 236 4376

CHILE
420 Gertrudis Echenique
Las Condes
Santiago de Chile
Tel: **(2) 228 5065**
Telex: 240855
Fax: (2) 48 1707

CHINA
15 Donzhimenwai Street
San Li Tun
Beijing
Tel: (1) **532 2331/7**
Telex: 22263
Fax: (1) 532 4065

DENMARK
Kristianagade 21
DK-2100
Copenhagen
Tel: **(31) 26 2244**
Telex: 22308
Fax: (31) 43 2218

EGYPT
5th Floor
Cairo Plaza South
Corniche El-Nil Boulac
Cairo
Tel: **(2) 77 7900**
Telex: 92257
Fax: (2) 76 8220

FIJI
7th and 8th Floors
Dominion House
Thomson Street
Suva
Tel: **(679) 31 2844**
Telex: 2126
Fax: 679-300 900

FRANCE
4 Rue Jean Rey
F-75724 Paris
Cedex 15
Tel: **4059 3300**
Telex: 216803,202313
Fax: 4059 3310

GERMANY
Godesberger Allee 105-107
DW 5300 Bonn 2
Tel: **8 1030**
Telex: 885466
Fax: 37 6268

GREECE
37 Dimitriou Soutsou Street
Ambelokipi
Athens 11521
Tel: **644 7303**
Telex: 215815
Fax: 644 3633

From 16 April 1995 all national and international change — see page 587 for details.

HONG KONG
25 Harbour Road
Wanchai
Hong Kong
Tel: **873 1881**
Telex: 73685
Fax: 838 4145

HUNGARY
Delibab Utca 30
1062
Budapest
(PO Box 231)
Tel: **153 4233/4577/4687**
Telex: 227708
Fax: 513 2908

INDIA
No.1/50-G
Shantipath Chanakyapuri
New Delhi 110021
Tel: **60 1336/7**
Telex: 31-82001
Fax: 688 5199

INDONESIA
Bank Niaga Building
6th Floor G
Jalan M.H. Thamrin 55
Jakarta 10350
Tel: **32 3109**
Telex: 46214
Fax: 32 2406

IRAN
123 Shalid Khalid Al-Islambuli Avenue
Abassabad
Tehran
Tel: **62 6202**
Telex: 212459
Fax: 62 6415

IRELAND
Fitzwilton House
Wilton Terrace
Dublin 2
Tel: **76 1517/8/9**
Fax: 68 5266

ITALY
Via Alessandra 215
Rome 1- 00198
Tel: **83 2721**
Telex: 610165
Fax: 8327 2300

JAPAN
2-1-14 Mita
Minato-Ku
Tokyo 180
Tel: **(3) 523 24111**
Telex: 22298
Fax: (3) 523 24149

KOREA
11th Floor
Kyobo Building
1 Chongro
Chong-ro-ku
Seoul 110-714
Tel: **730 6491/5**
Telex: 23663
Fax: 734 5085

MALAYSIA
6 Jalan Yap Kwan Seng
Kuala Lumpur 50450
Tel: **242 3122**
Telex: 30260
Fax: 241 5773

MALTA
6th Floor
Airways House
Gaiety Lane
Sliema
Tel: **33 8201**
Telex: 1269

MEXICO
Plaza Polanco Torre B-Piso
Jaime Balmes 11
COL Los Morales 11510
Mexico DF
Tel: **395 9988/7870**
Telex: 1773920
Fax: 395 7153

MICRONESIA
PO Box 5
Kolonia
Pohnpei State 96941
Tel: **320 5448**
Fax: 320 5449

MYANMAR
88 Strand Road
Yangon
Tel: **80965**
Telex: 21301
Fax: 71434

NAURU
Civic Centre
Nauru
Tel: **5230/1, 3356**
Telex: 33084
Fax: 674 3027

NEPAL
Bhat Bhateni
Kathmandu
PO Box 879
Tel: **41 1578/1579/1304**
Telex: 2395

NETHERLANDS
Koninginnegracht 23-24
2514AB The Hague
Tel: **3108200, 3630983, 3647908**

Telex: 32008
Fax: 310 7863

NEW CALEDONIA
8th Floor
18 Rue du Marechal Foch
Noumea
(Boite Postale 22)
Tel: **27 2414**
Telex: 3087
Fax: 27 8270

NEW ZEALAND
72-78 Hobson Street
Thorndon
Wellington
Tel: **473 6411/2**
Telex: 3375
Fax 473 6420

PAPUA NEW GUINEA
PO Box 9129
Hohola
Tel: **25 9333**
Telex: 22109
Fax: 25 9183

PHILIPPINES
Bank of the Philippine Islands Building
Ayala Avenue
cnr Paseo de Roxas
Makati
Metro Manila
(PO Box 1274, Makati, Manila)
Tel: **817 7911**
Telex: 63744
Fax: 817 3603

RUSSIA
Kropotkinsky Pereulok 13
Moscow 119034
Tel: **246 5012/6**
Telex: 413474
Fax: 230 2606

SAUDI ARABIA
Diplomatic Quarter
Riyadh
(PO Box 94400, Riyadh 11693)
Tel: **488 7788**
Telex: 405944
Fax: 488 7458

SINGAPORE
25 Napier Road
Singapore 1025
Tel: **737 9311**
Telex: 21238
Fax: 733 7134

SOLOMON ISLANDS
PO Box 589
Honiara
Tel: **2 1561**
Telex: 66325
Fax: 2 3691

SOUTH AFRICA
4th Floor
Mutual and Federal Building
220 Vermeulen Street
Pretoria 0001
Tel: **325 4315**
Telex: 322012
Fax: 323 0557

SPAIN
Paseo de la Castellano 143
E-28046 Madrid
Tel: **279 8504/5700253**
Telex: 27817
Fax: 570 9026

SRI LANKA
PO Box 742
30 Cambridge Place
Colombo 7
Tel: **59 8767/8/9, 59 6468/7479/7589**
Telex: 21157

SWEDEN
PO Box 7003
Sergels Torg 12
S-103 86 Stockholm
Tel: **613 2900**
Telex: 10382
Fax: 24 7414

SWITZERLAND
29 Alpenstrasse
CH-3006 Berne
Tel: **43 0143**
Telex: 911992
Fax: 44 1234

THAILAND
37 South Sathorn Road
Bangkok 12
Tel: **287 2680**
Telex: 82149
Fax: 287 2589

TONGA
Salote Road
Nuku'alofa
Tel: **2 1244/5**
Telex: 66238
Fax: 2 3243

TURKEY
83 Nenehatun Caddesi
Gazi Osman Pasa
Ankara
Tel: **436240/1/2/3**
Telex: 42213
Fax: 4361246

UNITED ARAB EMIRATES
PO Box 9303
Dubai
Tel: **378444**
Telex: 49393
Fax: 372812

From 16 April 1995 all national and international change — see page 587 for details.

UNITED KINGDOM
Australia House
The Strand
London WC2B 4LA
Tel: **379 4334**
Telex: 27565
Fax: 240 5333

UNITED STATES
1601 Massachusetts Avenue
Washington DC 20036
Tel: **797 3000**
Telex: 892621
Fax: 797 3300

VANUATU
PO Box 111
Port Vila
Tel: **22777**
Telex: 1030
Fax: 3948

VIETNAM
66 Ly Thuong Kiet
Hanoi
Tel: **252763, 254468**
Telex: 4410

WESTERN SAMOA
PO Box 704
Apia
Tel: **2 3411/2**
Telex: 242
Fax: 2 3159

**THE FORMER YUGOSLAVIA
(SERBIA AND MONTENEGRO)**
13 Cjika Ljubina
11000 Belgrade 6
Tel: **62 4655, 63 2261**
Telex: 11206
Fax: 62 4029

ZIMBABWE
4th Floor
Karigamombe Centre
Samora Machel Avenue
Harare
(PO Box 4541)
Tel: **79 4591**
Telex: 4159
Fax: 70 4615

Canada

AUSTRALIA
Commonwealth Avenue
Canberra
ACT 2600
Tel: 2733844
Telex: 62017
Fax: 2733285

AUSTRIA
Dr Karl Leuger Ring 10
a-1010 Vienna
Tel: **5333691**
Telex: 115320
Fax: 5354473

BAHAMAS
PO Box SS-6371
Nassau
Tel: 3932123
Fax: 3931305

BELGIUM
2 Avenue de Tervuren
B-1040 Brussels
Tel: **7356040**
Telex: 21613
Fax: 7353383

BRAZIL
Avenida das Nacoes Lote 16
Brasilia 70410
Tel: **2237515**
Telex: 61-1296
Fax: 2255233

CHILE
Ahumada 11, Piso 10
Casilla 427
Santiago de Chile
Tel: **6962256/7/8/9**
Telex: 240341
Fax: 6960738

CHINA
10 San Li Yun Road
Chao Yang District
Beijing
Tel: **5323536**
Telex: 22717
Fax: 5321684

COSTA RICA
Apartado 10303
San Jose
Tel: **553522**
Fax: 232395

CROATIA
Mihanoviceva 1
41000 Zagreb
Tel: **435666, 435111, 428783**
Fax: 428781

DENMARK
Kr Bernikowsgade 1
DK-1105 Copenhagen
Tel: **122299**
Fax: 140585

EGYPT
6 Mohamed Fahmi El Sayed Street
Garden City
Cairo
Tel: **3543110**

Telex: 92677
Fax: 3557276

ESTONIA
Toomkooli 13/11
Tallinn
Tel: **449056**

FRANCE
35/37 Avenue Montaigne
F-75008 Paris
Tel: **47230101**
Telex: 280806
Fax: 47235628

GERMANY
Friedric-Wilhelm-Str 18
DW-53000 Bonn 1
Tel: **231061**
Telex: 886421
Fax: 230857

GREECE
4 Ioannou Ghennadiou Street
GR-11521 Athens
Tel: **723 9511**
Telex: 215584
Fax: 7247123

GREENLAND
PO Box 800
3900 Nuuk
Tel: **299-26666**
Telex: 90683
Fax: 299-20244

HONG KONG
GPO Box 11142
Hong Kong
Tel: **9104321**
Telex: 73391
Fax: 8106736

HUNGARY
Budakeszi ut 32
H-1121 Budapest
Tel: **1766312, 1767512, 1767711**
Telex: 224588
Fax: 1767689

INDIA
7/8 Shantipath
Chanakapuri
New Delhi 110021
Tel: **6876500**
Telex: 31-72363
Fax: 687 6500 ext 401

IRELAND
66 St Stephens Green
Dublin 2
Tel: **781988**
Telex: 938 03
Fax: 781285

ISRAEL
PO Box 6410
Tel Aviv 61063
Tel: **527 2929**
Telex: 341293
Fax: 527 2333

ITALY
Via G de Rossi 27
1-00161 Rome
Tel: **841-5341**
Telex: 610056
Fax: 884 8752

JAPAN
3-38 Akasaka
7-chome
Minato-ku
Tokyo 107
Tel: **34082101**
Telex: 22218
Fax: 34795320

KENYA
PO Box 30481
Nairobi
Tel: **334033**
Telex: 22198
Fax: 334090

KOREA
10th Floor
Kolon Building
45 Mugyo-Dong
Chung-Ku
Seoul
Tel: **753 2605**
Fax: 755 0686

LATVIA
Elizabetes 45/47
Riga
Tel: **333355**
Fax: 225189

MEXICO
Calle Schiller No 529
Colonia Polanco Rincon del Bosque
11560 Mexico DF
Tel: **254 3288**
Telex: 1771191
Fax: 254 3103

THE NETHERLANDS
Sophialaan 7
NL-2500 GV The Hague
Tel: **361 4111**
Telex: 31270
Fax: 356 1111

NEW ZEALAND
ICI House
Milesworth Street
Wellington
Tel: **473 9577**
Fax: 471 2082

PANAMA
Apartado 3658
Balboa
Panama
Tel: **647014**
Fax: 233508

PERU
Libertad
Miraflores
Lima
Tel: **14-444015**
Fax: 14-444347

PORTUGAL
Avenida da Liberdade 144/56
Piso 4
P-1200 Lisbon
Tel: **347 4892**
Fax: 347 6466

PUERTO RICO
Scotiabank Plaza
Piso 6
Avenida Ponce de Leon 273
Hato Rey 00917
Tel: **809-250 0367**

RUSSIA
23 Starokonyushenny Per.
Moscow
Tel: **241 9155, 241 5070**
Telex: 413401
Fax: 241 4400, 241 9155 Ext 227

SAUDI ARABIA
PO Box 94321
Riyadh 11693
Tel: **488 2288**
Telex: 404893
Fax: 488 0137

SINGAPORE
IBM Towers
14th & 15th Floors
80 Anson Road
Singapore 0207
Tel: **225 63663**
Fax: 225 2450

SOUTH AFRICA
PO Box 26006
Arcadia 0007
Tel: **324 3970**
Telex: 322112
Fax: 232 1534

SPAIN
Calle Nunez de Balboa 35
Edificio Goya
E-28001 Madrid
Tel: **431 4300**
Telex: 27347
Fax: 431 2367

SWEDEN
Tegelbacken 4/VII
PO Box 16129
S-10323 Stockholm 16
Tel: **237920**
Telex: 10687
Fax: 242491

SWITZERLAND
Kirchenfeldstr 88
CH-3005 Bern
Tel: **31-446381**
Telex: 911308
Fax: 31-447315

TAIWAN
Suite 707
Bank Tower
205 Tunhua N Road
Taipei
Tel: **2-713 268**
Telex: 29484
Fax 2-712 7244

UKRAINE
Hotel Zhovtnevy
5 Roza Luxembourg Street
Kiev
Tel: **291 8858**

UNITED KINGDOM
MacDonald House
1 Grosvenor Square
London W1X0AB
Tel: **071-629 9492**
Telex: 261592
Fax: 071-491 3968

UNITED STATES
866 UN Plaza
Suite 250
New York
NY 10017
Tel: **212-715 5600**
Telex: 126269
Fax: 212-486 1295

New Zealand

AUSTRALIA
Commonwealth Avenue
Canberra
ACT 2600
Tel: **(6) 273-3611**
Telex: 62019
Fax: (6) 273-3194

BELGIUM
Boulevard du Regent 47-48
1000 Brussels
Tel: **(2) 512 1040**
Telex: 46-22025
Fax: (2) 513 48 56

BRAZIL
Rua Hungria, 888-6
CEP 01455
Sao Paolo
Tel: **(11) 212-2288**
Telex: 81017
Fax: (11) 212-7728

CANADA
Suite 727
99 Bank Street
Ottawa
ON K1P 6G3
Tel: **(613) 238-5991**
Telex: 210-534282
Fax: (613) 238-5707

CHILE
Avenida Isidora Goyenechea 3516
Las Condes
Santiago
Tel: **(2) 231-4204**
Telex: 40066
Fax: (2) 231-9040

CHINA
Ritan Dongerjie No. 1
Chao Yang District
Beijing
Tel: **(1) 532-2731/2/3/4**
Telex: 22124
Fax: (1) 532-4317

FIJI
PO Box 1378
Suva
Tel: **311-422**
Telex: 701-2161
Fax: 300-422

FRANCE
7 Rue Leonard de Vinci
75116 Paris
Tel: **(1) 4500 2411**
Telex: 611929
Fax: (1) 4501 26 39

GERMANY
Bonn Centre HI 902
Bundeskanzlerplatz 2-10
5300 Bonn 1
Tel: **(228) 22 80 70**
Telex: 886322
Fax: (228) 22 16 87

GREECE
An. Tsoha 15-17
Ambelokopi
115 21 Athens
Tel: **(1) 641-0311/2/3/4/5**
Telex: 216630
Fax: (1) 641-0735

HONG KONG
GPO Box 2790
3414 Jardine House

Connaught Road
Hong Kong
Tel: **525 5044**
Telex: 73932
Fax: 845 2915

INDIA
25 Golf Links
110003
New Delhi
Tel: **(11) 697-318/697592**
Telex: 031-65100
Fax: (11) 693-615

INDONESIA
PO Box 2439 JKT
41 Jalan Diponegoro
Menteng
Jakarta
Tel: **(21) 330-680, 333-696**
Telex: 46109
Fax: (21) 310-4866

ITALY
Via Zara 28
Rome 1-00198
Tel: **(6) 440-2928/30/81**
Telex: 626615
Fax: (6) 440-2984

JAPAN
20-40 Kamiyama-Cho
Shibuya-ku
Tokyo 150
Tel: **(3) 467-2271/5**
Telex: 22462
Fax: (3) 467-2285

KIRIBATI
PO Box 53
Tarawa
Tel: **21-400**
Fax: 21-402

KOREA
CPO Box 1059
Kyobo Building
Rooms 1802-1805
1 Chongno 1-GA
Chongno-Gu
Seoul
Tel: **(2) 730-7794/95, (2) 735-3707**
Telex: 27367
Fax: (2) 737-4861

MALAYSIA
PO Box 12-003 (KL 50764)
193 Jalan Tun Razak
Kuala Lumpur 50400
Tel: **(3) 2486-422/560**
Fax: (3) 241 3094

MEXICO
Homero 229
Piso 8
11570 Mexico City D.F.

Tel: **(5) 254 4253, 254 4264**
Telex: 1763154
Fax: (5) 255 4142

NETHERLANDS
Mauritskade 25
2514 HD
The Hague
Tel: **(70) 346 93 24**
Telex: 431557
Fax: 363 29 83

NEW CALEDONIA
4 Boulevard Vauban
BP 2219
Noumea
Tel: **27 25 43**
Fax: 27 17 40

PAPUA NEW GUINEA
PO Box 1144,
Boroko
Port Moresby
Tel: **259444**
Telex: 22191
Fax: 217158

PERU
Apartado 3553
Miguel Seminario 320
San Isidro
Lima 27
Tel: **(14) 416709**
Telex: 2111
Fax: (14) 426603

THE PHILIPPINES
Cammon Centre
3rd Floor
126 Alfaro Street
Salcedo Village
Makati
Metro Manila
Tel: **(2) 818 0916**
Telex: 63509
Fax: (14) 426603

RUSSIA
44 Ulitsa Voroskovo
Moscow 121069
Tel: **(095) 290 5704, 290 1277**
Telex: 64-413187
Fax: (095) 290 46 66

SAUDI ARABIA
PO Box 94 397
Riyadh 11693
Tel: **(1) 476 2789, 476 7686**
Telex: 405878
Fax: (1) 4887620

SINGAPORE
13 Nassim Road
Singapore 1025
Tel: **2359-966**

Telex: 21244
Fax: 235 2550

SOLOMON ISLANDS
Soltel House
PO Box 697
Mendana Avenue
Honiara
Tel: **21-502/503**
Telex: 66322
Fax: 22377

SWEDEN
Arsenalsgatan 8C
(Box 16174, S-10324)
Stockholm
Tel: **(8) 23 37 90**
Fax: (8) 11 63 48
Telex: 17990

SWITZERLAND
28A Chemin du Petit-Saconnex
CH-1209 Geneva
Tel: **(22) 734 95 30**
Telex: 412969
Fax: (22) 734 30 62

TAHITI
BP 73
Papeete
Tel: **430170**
Telex: 702-340
Fax: 424544

THAILAND
PO Box 2719
93 Wireless Road
Bangkok 10500
Tel: **(2) 251-8165**
Telex: 86-81165
Fax: (2) 253-9045

TONGA
PO Box 830
Nuku'alofa
Tel: **23122**
Fax: 23487

UNITED KINGDOM
New Zealand House
80 Haymarket
London SW1Y 4TQ
Tel: **071-930 8422**
Telex: 24368
Fax: 071-839 4580

UNITED STATES
37 Observatory Circle NW
Washington DC 20008-3686
Tel: **(202) 328-4848, 328-4800**
Telex: 230-89526, 230-64272
Fax: (202) 667-5227

VANUATU
PO Box 161
Prouds Building

From 16 April 1995 all national and international change — see page 587 for details.

Kumul Highway
Port Vila
Tel: **22933, 23467**
Telex: 771 121
Fax: 22518

WESTERN SAMOA
PO Box 1876
Beach Road
Apia
Tel: **21711, 21714**
Telex: 779 222
Fax: 20086

UK

ALGERIA
Residence Cassiopee
Batiment B
7 Chemin des Glycines
Algiers
Tel: **605601/605411/605038**
Telex: 66151
Fax: 604410

ANTIGUA AND BARBUDA
Box 483
11 Old Parnham Road
St. Johns
Antigua
Tel: **4620008/9**
Telex: 2113
Fax: 462 2806

ARGENTINA
Dr. Luis Agote 2412/52
Casilla de Correo
1425 Buenos Aires
Tel: **8037070/71**
Fax: 803 1731

AUSTRALIA
Commonwealth Avenue
Yarralumla
Canberra ACT 2600
Tel: **270 6666, 273 0422**
Telex: 62222
Fax: 270 6653

AUSTRIA
Jauresgasse 12
A-1030 Vienna
Tel: **713 1575**
Telex: 132810
Fax: 715 7824

BAHAMAS
PO Box N 7516
Nassau
Tel: **325 7471/2/3/4**
Telex: 20112
Fax: 323 3871

BAHRAIN
21 Government Avenue
Manama
306 Bahrain
Tel: **534404**
Fax: 531273

BANGLADESH
Abu Bakr House
Plot 7
Road 84
Gulshan
Dhaka
Tel: **600133/7**
Telex: 671006
Fax: 883437

BARBADOS
Lower Collymore Rock
PO Box 676
Bridgetown
Tel: **4366694**
Telex 2219
Fax: 436 5398

BELGIUM
Britannia House
28 Rue Joseph II 28
1040 Brussels
Tel: **217 9000, 217 7041**
Telex: 22703
Fax 217 6763

BELIZE
PO Box 91
Belmopan
Tel: **2146/7**
Telex: 284
Fax: 2761

BOTSWANA
Private Bag 0023
Gabarone
Tel: **52841/2/3**
Telex:2370
Fax: 56105

BRAZIL
Setor de Embaixadas Sul
Quadra 801
Conjunto K
70.408 Brasilia
Tel: **2252710**
Telex:61 1360
Fax: 225 1777

BULGARIA
Boulevard Marshal Tolbukhin 65-67
Sofia 1000
Tel: **885361/2**
Telex:22363
Fax 656022

CAMEROON
Avenue Winston Churchill
BP 547 Yaounde

Tel: **220545, 200796**
Telex: 8200
Fax: 223347

CANADA
80 Elgin Street
Ottawa KIP 5K7
Tel: **2371530**
Telex: 533318
Fax: 237 7980

CHINA
11 Guang Hua Lu
Jian Guo Men Wai
Peking
Tel: **5321961/5**
Telex: 22191

CROATIA
Illica 21/1
41000 Zagreb
Tel: **424888, 426200**
Fax: 420100

CYPRUS
PO Box 1978
Alexander Pallis Street
Nicosia
Tel: **473131/7**
Telex: 2208
Fax: 367198

CZECH REPUBLIC
Thunovska 14
CS-11800 Prague 1
Tel: **533347/8/9**
Telex: 121011
Fax: 250986

DENMARK
36/38/40 Kastelsvej
DK-2100 Copenhagen
Tel: **31264600**
Telex: 19903
Fax: 381 012

EGYPT
Ahmed Ragheb Street
Garden City
Cairo
Tel: **354 0850/2/8**
Telex: 94188
Fax: 354 0859

ESTONIA
Kentmanni 20. ll floor
0001 Tallinn
Tel: **455328, 455329**
Telex: 173974
Fax: 298107

FIJI
Victoria House
47 Gladstone Road
Suva
Tel: **311033**

Telex: 2129
Fax: 301406

FINLAND
Uudenmaankatu 16-20
SF-00120 Helsinki 12
Tel: **647922**
Telex: 121122
Fax: 611747

FRANCE
35 Rue du Faubourg St Honore
75383 Paris
Cedex 08
Tel: **4266 9142**
Telex: 650264
Fax: 426 69590

GAMBIA
48 Atlantic Road
Fajara
Banjul
Tel: **95133/4**
Telex: 2211
Fax: 96134

GERMANY
Friedrich Elert Allee 77
5300 Bonn 1
Tel: **234061**
Telex: 886887
Fax: 234070

GHANA
PO Box 296
Osu Link
Off Gamel Abdul Nasser Avenue
Accra
Tel: **221665**
Telex: 2323

GREECE
1 Ploutarchou Street
106 75 Athens
Tel: **7236211**
Telex: 216440
Fax: 724 1872

GRENADA
14 Church Street
St George's
Grenada
Tel: **440 3222, 440 3536**
Telex: 3419
Fax: 440 4939

GUYANA
44 Main Street
Georgetown
Tel: **65881**
Telex: 2221
Fax: 53555

HONG KONG
9th Floor
Bank of America Tower

12 Harcourt Road
Hong Kong
Tel: **5230176**
Telex: 73031
Fax: 854 2870

HUNGARY
Harmincad Utca 6
H-1051 Budapest
Tel: **1182888**
Telex: 224527
Fax: 118 0907

ICELAND
Laufasvegur 49
IS-121 Reykjavik
Tel: **15883/4**
Telex: 2037
Fax: 27940

INDIA
Shanti Path
Chanakyapuri
New Delhi 110021
Tel: **690371**
Telex: 31-65125
Fax: 6872882

INDONESIA
Jalan M H Thamrin 75
Jakarta 10310
Tel: **330904**
Telex: 61166
Fax: 321824

IRAN
PO Box 11365-4474
143 Ferdowsi Avenue
Tehran 11344
Tel: **675011**
Telex: 212493

IRAQ
House 12
Street 218
Hai Al Khelood
Baghdad
Tel: **537 2121**
Telex: 2134141

IRELAND
33 Merrion Road
Dublin 4
Tel: **269 5111**
Telex: 25296
Fax: 283 8423

ISRAEL
192 Rechov Hayarkon
Tel Aviv 63405
Tel: **524 9171**
Telex: 33559
Fax: 291699

ITALY
Via XX Settembre 80A
1-00187 Rome
Tel: **4825441**
Telex: 626119
Fax: 487 3324

JAMAICA
Trafalgar Road
Kingston 10
Tel: **9269050**
Telex: 2110
Fax: 929 7869

JAPAN
No 1 Ichiban-cho
Chiyoda-ku
Tokyo 102
Tel: **32655511**
Telex: 22755
Fax: 32655580

JORDAN
PO Box 87
Abdoun
Amman
Tel: **823100**
Telex: 22209
Fax: 813759

KAZAKHSTAN
Hotel Kazakhstan
Alma Ata

KENYA
PO Box 30465
Bruce House
Standard Street
Nairobi
Tel: **335944**
Telex: 22219
Fax: 333196

KOREA
4 Chung-dong
Chung-ku
Seoul 100
Tel: **735 7341**
Telex: 27320
Fax: 733 8368

KUWAIT
Arabian Gulf Street
PO Box 2
13001 Safat
Tel: **243046**
Fax: 240 7395

LATVIA
Elizabetes 2
Riga
Tel: **320737**

LESOTHO
PO Box 521
Maseru 100

Tel: **313961**
Telex: 4343
Fax: 310210

LIBERIA
PO Box 10-0120
Monrovia 10
Tel: **221055, 221107, 221491**
Telex: 44287

LIBYA
PO Box 4206
Tripoli
Tel: **31191**
Telex: 20296

MALAWI
PO Box 30042
Lingadzi House
Lilongwe
Tel: **731544**
Telex: 44727

MALAYSIA
185 Jalan Ampang
PO Box 11030
50732
Kuala Lumpur
Tel: **2482122**
Telex: 35225
Fax: 248 0880

MALTA
PO Box 506
7 St Anne Street
Floriana
Tel: **233134/8**
Telex: 1249
Fax: 622001

MAURITIUS
King George V Avenue
Floreal
Mauritius
Tel: **20865795/6/7/8/9**
Telex: 4266
Fax: 208 65792

MEXICO
Lerma 71
Col Cuauhtemoc
06500 Mexico City
Tel: **2072089**
Telex: 1773093
Fax: 2077672

MOROCCO
17 Boulevard de la Tour Hassan
Rabat
Tel: **720905/6**
Telex: 31022

MYANMAR
PO Box 638
80 Strand Road
Yangon

Tel: **81700/2/3/8**
Telex: 21216
Fax: 89566

NAMIBIA
116A Leutwein Street
Windhoek 9000
Tel: **223022**
Fax: 228895

NEPAL
PO Box 106
Lainchaur
Kathmandu
Tel: **410583, 411789, 414588**
Telex: 2343
Fax: 411789

NETHERLANDS
Lange Voorhout 10
2514 ED
The Hague
Tel: **3645800**
Telex: 31600
Fax: 360 3839

NEW ZEALAND
Reserve Bank of New Zealand Building
9th Floor
2 The Terrace
Wellington 1
Tel: **4726049**
Telex: 3325
Fax: 4711973

NIGERIA
Private Mail Bag 12136
11 Eleke Crescent
Victoria Island
Lagos
Tel: **619531/7**
Telex: 21247
Fax: 666909

NORWAY
Thomas Heftyesgate 8
0244 Oslo 2
Tel: **552400, 563890**
Telex: 71575
Fax: 551041

OMAN
PO Box 300
Muscat
Tel: **738501**
Telex: 5216
Fax: 706467

PAKISTAN
PO Box 1122
Diplomatic Enclave
Ramna 5
Islamabad
Tel: **822131**
Telex: 54122
Fax: 823439

790

PANAMA
Apartado 889
Calle 53
Marbella
Panama City
Tel: **690866**
Fax: 230730

PAPUA NEW GUINEA
PO Box 4778
Boroko
National Capital District
Port Moresby
Tel: **251677**
Telex: 22142
Fax: 253547

PERU
Edificio El Pacifico Washington (Piso 12)
Plaza Washington
Avenida Arequipa
Lima 100
Tel: **334783/9**
Telex: 25230
Fax: 334735

PHILIPPINES
LV Locsin Building
6752 Ayala Avenue cor Makati Avenue
Makati
Metro,
Manila 3116
Tel: **8167116**
Telex: 63282
Fax: 8197206

POLAND
Aleja Roz No 1
PL 00-556
Warsaw
Tel: **6281001**
Telex: 813964
Fax: 217161

PORTUGAL
35-37 Rua de Sao Domingos a Lapa 37
1200 Lisbon
Tel: **3961191**
Telex: 12278
Fax: 626678

ROMANIA
24 Strada Jule Michelet
70154 Bucharest
Tel: **111634**
Telex: 11295
Fax: 595090

RUSSIA
Naberezhnaya Moriza Toreza 14
Moscow 72
Tel: **231 8511**
Telex: 413341
Fax: 249 4636

SAINT LUCIA
24 Micoud Street
PO Box 227
Castries
Tel: **452 2484**
Telex: 6314
Fax: 453 1543

SAINT VINCENT
PO Box 132
Kingstown
Tel: **457 1701**
Telex: 7516
Fax: 456 2750

SAUDI ARABIA
PO Box 94351
Riyadh 11693
Tel: **4880077**
Telex: 406488
Fax: 4882373

SENEGAL
BP 6025
20 Rue du Docteur Guillet
Dakar
Tel: **237392**
Telex: 21690
Fax: 232766

SEYCHELLES
Victoria House
3rd Floor
161 Mahe
Tel: **25225**
Telex: 2269
Fax: 25127

SIERRA LEONE
Standard Bank of Sierra Leone Building
Lightfoot Boston Street
Freetown
Tel: **223961**
Telex: 3235

SINGAPORE
Tanglin Road
Singapore 1024
Tel: **4739333**
Telex: 21218
Fax: 475 9700

SOUTH AFRICA
91 Parliament Street
Cape Town 8001
Tel: **4617220**
Fax: 461 0017

SPAIN
Calle de Fernando el Santo 16
28004 Madrid
Tel: **3190200**
Telex: 27656
Fax: 3190423

SRI LANKA
Galle Road
Kollupitiya
Colombo 3
Tel: **437336, 437340**
Telex: 21101
Fax: 437344

SUDAN
PO Box 801
Off Sharia Al Baladiya
Khartoum East
Tel: **70760**
Telex: 22189

SWAZILAND
Allister Miller Street
Mbabane
Tel: **42581**
Telex: 2079
Fax: 42585

SWEDEN
Skarpogatan 6-8
115 27 Stockholm
Tel: **6670140**
Telex: 19340
Fax: 6629989

SWITZERLAND
Thunstrasse 50
3005 Berne 15
Tel: **445021/6**
Telex: 911929
Fax: 440583

TANZANIA
Hifadhi House
Samora Avenue
Dar es Salaam
Tel: **29601**
Telex: 41004
Fax: 30365

THAILAND
Wireless Road
Bangkok
Tel: **2530191/9**
Telex: 82263
Fax: 255 8619

TONGA
PO Box 56
Nuku'alofa
Tel: **21020, 21021**
Telex: 66226
Fax: 24109

TRINIDAD AND TOBAGO
3rd and 4th Floor
Furness House
90 Independence Square
Port of Spain
Tel: **6252861/6**
Telex: 22224
Fax: 623 0621

TUNISIA
5 Place de la Victoire
Tunis
Tel: **245100**
Telex: 14007
Fax: 354877

TURKEY
Sehit Ersan Caddesi 46/A
Cankaya
Ankara
Tel: **4724310**
Telex: 942329
Fax: 468 3214

UGANDA
10/12 Parliament Avenue
PO Box 7070
Kampala
Tel: **257054/9**
Telex: 61202
Fax: 257304

UKRAINE
Hotel Zhovtevy
5 Roza Luxembourg Street
Kiev
Tel: **291 8907, 291 8974, 291 8850**
Fax: 291 5468

UNITED ARAB EMIRATES
PO Box 248
Abu Dhabi
Tel: **326600**
Telex: 22243
Fax: 341774

UNITED STATES
3100 Massachusetts Avenue
NW Washington DC 20008
Tel: **4621340**
Telex: 440015
Fax: 898 4255

VENEZUELA
Apartado 1246
Caracas 1010-A
Tel: **7511022**
Telex: 234268
Fax: 923292

VIETNAM
16 Pho Ly Thuong Kiet
Hanoi
Tel: **52349**
Telex: 411405

YEMEN
PO Box 1287
129 Haddah Road
Sana'a
Tel: **215630**
Telex: 2251
Fax: 263059

**THE FORMER REPUBLIC OF
YUGOSLAVIA (SERBIA & MONTENE-
GRO)**
Generala Zdanova 46
11000 Belgrade
Tel: **645055**
Telex: 11468
Fax: 659651

ZAMBIA
PO Box 50050
Lusaka
Tel: **228955**
Telex: 41150
Fax: 253421

ZIMBABWE
6th Floor
Stanley House
Jason Moyo Avenue
Harare
Tel: **793781**
Fax: 728380

USA

ALBANIA
Rruga Labinoti 103
Tirana
Tel: **32875, 33520**
Fax: 32222

ALGERIA
4 Chemin Cheikh El Ibrahimi
(BP Box 549 (Alger-Gare) 16000
Tel: **601425, 601255**
Telex: 66047
Fax: 601863

ANGOLA
BPA Building
11th Floor
Caixa Postal 648=4
Luanda
Tel: **390242**
Fax: 390515

ARGENTINA
4300 Colombia
1425 Buenos Aires
Tel: **7747 7611, 774 8811**
Telex: 18156

AUSTRALIA
Moonah Place
Canberra ACT 2600
Tel: **270 5000**
Telex: 62104
Fax: 270 5970

AUSTRIA
Boltzmanngasse 16
A-1091
Vienna
Tel: **31-55-11**

Telex: 114634
Fax: 310 0682

AZERBAIJAN
Intourist Hotel
Baku
Tel: **917965**

BAHAMAS
Mosmar Building
Queen Street
Nassau
(PO Box N-8197)
Tel: **322-1181/328-2206**
Telex: 20-138
Fax: 328-7838

BAHRAIN
Building No. 979
Road No. 3119
Block/Area 331 ZINJ
Manama
(PO Box 26431)
Tel: **273300**
Telex: 9398
Fax: 272594

BARBADOS
Canadian Imperial Bank of Commerce Building
Broad Street
Bridgetown
(PO Box 302 Bridgetown)
Tel: **436-4950**
Telex: 2259
Fax: 429-5246

BELGIUM
27 Boulevard du Regent
B-1000 Brussels
Tel: **513-3830**
Telex: 846-21336
Fax: 511-2725

BELIZE
Gabourel Lane and Hutson Street
Belize City
(PO Box 286)
Tel: **77161**
Fax: 30802

BELARUS
Storovilinskaya 6
Minsk
Tel: **690802**

BERMUDA
PO Box HM 325
Hamilton
Tel: **295-1342**
Fax: 295-1592

BOLIVIA
Banco Popular del Peru Building
Corner of Calles Mercado and Colon
La Paz
Tel: **350251, 350120**

Telex: 3268
Fax: 350875

BOTSWANA
PO Box 90
Gaborone
Tel: **353-982**
Telex: 2554
Fax: 356-947

BRAZIL
Avenida das Nacoes
Lote 3
Brasilia
Tel: **321-7272**
Telex: 061-1091
Fax: 225-9136

BULGARIA
1 A. Stamboliski Boulevard
Sofi
Tel: **88-48-01**
Telex: 22690 BG
Fax: 801977

BURKINA FASO
BP 01-35
Ougadougou
Tel: **30-67-23/4/5**
Telex: 5290 BF
Fax: 312368

CAMBODIA
27 EO Street 240
Phnom Phen
Tel: **26436/8**
Fax: 26437

CAMEROON
Rue Nachtigal
Yaounde
(BP 817)
Tel: **234014**
Telex: 8223KN
Fax: 230753

CANADA
100 Wellington Street
Ottawa ON K1P 5TI
Tel: **238 5335**
Telex: 533582
Fax: 238 5720

CHILE
Codina Building
1343 Agustinas
Santiago
Tel: **671 0133**
Telex: 240062
Fax: 697 2051

CHINA
Xiu Shui Bei Jie 3
Beijing
Tel: **532-3831**

COLOMBIA
Calle 38
No.8-61
Bogota
Tel: **285-1300/1688**
Telex: 44843
Fax: 288-5687

COSTA RICA
Pavas
San Jose
Tel: **203939**
Fax: 202305

COTE D'IVOIRE
5 Rue Jesse Owens
Abidjan
Tel: **210979**
Telex: 23660
Fax: 223259

CROATIA
Andrije Herbranga 2
41000 Zagreb
Tel: **444800**
Telex: 21180
Fax; 440235

CZECH REPUBLIC
Trziste 15-12548
Prague CS 12548
Tel: **53 6641/6**
Telex: 21196
Fax: 532547

DENMARK
Dag Hammarskjolds Alle 24
Copenhagen
Tel: **423144**
Telex: 22216
Fax: 427273

DOMINICAN REPUBLIC
Corner of Calle Cesar Nicholas Penson & Calle
Leopoldo Navarro
Santo Domingo
Tel: **5412171**
Telex: 3460013
Fax: 686 7437

ECUADOR
Avenida 12 de Octobre y Avenida Patria
Quito
PO Box 538
Tel: **548000, 562890**
Telex: 22329
Fax: 502-052

EGYPT
Lazougi Street
Garden City
Cairo
Tel: **355-7371**

Telex: 93773
Fax: 355-7375

EL SALVADOR
25 Avenida Norte No 1230
San Salvador
Tel: **267100**
Telex: 20657
Fax: 265839

ESTONIA
Kentmanni 20
Tallinn
Tel: **455005, 455313**
Fax: 306817

ETHIOPIA
Entoto Street
Addis Ababa
(PO Box 1014)
Tel: **550666**
Telex: 21282
Fax: 551-166

FIJI
PO Box 218
31 Loftus Street
Suva
Tel: **314-466 314069**
Telex: 2255
Fax: 300081

FINLAND
Itainen Puistotie 14A
SF-00140
Helsinki
Tel: **171931**
Telex: 121644 USEMB SF
Fax: 174681

FRANCE
2 Avenue Gabriel
75008 Paris Cedex 08
Tel: **42-96-12-02**
Telex: 650221 AMEMB
Fax: 42-66-97-83

GABON
Boulevard de la Mer
Libreville
(BP 4000)
Tel: **762003/4**
Telex: 5250 GO
Fax: 745507

GEORGIA
Metechi Palace Hotel
Tblissi
Tel: **744623**

GERMANY
Deichmanns Aue
5300 Bonn 2
Tel: **3391**
Telex: 885-452
Fax: 339 2663

GHANA
Ring Road East
(PO Box 194)
Tel: **775348**
Telex: 2579

GREECE
91 Vasilissis Sophias Blvd
10160 Athens
Tel: **721-2951/8401**
Telex: 21-5548
Fax: 646-3450

GRENADA
PO Box 54
St. George's
Tel: **444-1173/8**
Fax: 444-4820

GUATEMALA
7-01 Avenida de la Reforma
Zone 10
Tel: **31-15-41/4**
Fax: 318885

GUYANA
99-100 Young Duke Street
Kingston
Georgetown
Tel: **54900-9**
Telex: 213
Fax: 58497

HAITI
Harry Truman Boulevard
PO Box 1761
Port-au-Prince
Tel: **220354**
Fax: 239007

HONDURAS
Avenido La Paz
Tegucigalpa
Tel: **32-3120**
Fax: 32-0027

HONG KONG
26 Garden Road
Hong Kong
Tel: **523 9011**
Telex: 63141
Fax: 845 1598

HUNGARY
V. Szabadsag Ter 12
Budapest
Tel: **112-6450**
Telex: 224-222
Fax: 132-8934

ICELAND
Laufasvegur 21
Reykjavik
Tel: **29100**
Telex: USEMB IS3044
Fax: 29139

INDIA
Shanti Path
Chanakyapuri 110021
New Delhi
Tel: **600651**
Telex: 31-82065
Fax: 6872028

INDONESIA
5 Medan Merdeka Selatan 5
Jakarta
Tel: **21 360-360**
Telex: 44218
Fax: 360644

IRELAND
42 Elgin Road
Ballsbridge
Dublin
Tel: **268 8777**
Telex: 93684
Fax: 268 9946

ISRAEL
71 Hayarkon Street
Tel Aviv
Tel: **654338**
Telex: 3376
Fax: 663449

ITALY
Via Veneto 119/A
100187 Rome
Tel: **46741**
Telex: 622322
Fax: 4674-2356

JAMAICA
Jamaica Mutual Life Center
2 Oxford Road
3rd Floor
Kingston
Tel: **929-4850**
Fax: 926-6743

JAPAN
10-5 Akasaka 1-chome
Minato-ku
Tokyo 107
Tel: **322 45700**
Telex: 22115
Fax: 3505 1862

JORDAN
Jabel Amman
(PO Box 354)
Tel: **644371**
Fax: 646301

KAZAKHSTAN
Hotel Kazakhstan
Alma Ata
Tel: **619056**

KENYA
Moi/Haile Selassie Avenue
Nairobi
(PO Box 30137)
Tel: **334141**
Telex: 22964
Fax: 340838

KOREA
82 Sejong-Ro
Seoul
Tel: **732-2601/8**
Fax: 738-8845

KUWAIT
PO Box 77 SAFAT
13001 SAFAT
Kuwait City
Tel: **242-4151**
Telex: 2039
Fax: 240-7368

KYRGYZSTAN
Derhinsky Prospeckt 66
Bishkek
Tel: **222270**

LATVIA
Raima Bulv 7
226050 Riga
Tel: **227045, 211572, 21005**
Fax: 220502

LEBANON
PO Box 70-840
Beruit
Tel: **41774, 415802, 402200**
Fax: 407112

LESOTHO
PO Box 333
Maseru 100
Tel: **312666**
Telex: 4506
Fax: 310116

LIBERIA
PO Box 98
111 United Nations Drive
Monrovia
Tel: **222991**
Fax: 223710

MADAGASCAR
14 and 16 Rue Rainitovo
Antsahvola
Antananarivo
(BP 620)
Tel: **212-57**
Telex: 22202
Fax: 34539

MALAWI
PO Box 30016
Lilongwe
Tel: **730-166**

Telex: 44627
Fax: 732-282

MALAYSIA
376 Jalan Tun Razak
50400 Kuala Lumpur
Tel: **248-9011**
Telex: 32956
Fax: 243-5207

MARSHALL ISLANDS
PO Box 1379
Majuro 96960
Tel: **692 4011**
Fax: 692 4012

MEXICO
Paseo de la Reforma 305
06500 Mexico DF
Tel: **211-0042**
Telex: 1773091
Fax: 511-9980

MOLDOVA
103 Strada Alexi Mateevich
Chisinau
Tel: **232894**

MOROCCO
2 Ave. de Marrakech
Rabat
Tel: **762265**
Telex: 31005
Fax: 765661

MOZAMBIQUE
Avenida Kenneth Kaunda 193
Maputo
Tel: **49-27-97**
Telex: 6-143
Fax: 49-01-14

MYANMAR
581 Merchant Street
Yangon
(GPO Box 521)
Tel: **82055, 82181**
Telex: 21230
Fax: 490114

NAMIBIA
Ausplan Building
14 Lossen Street
Windhoek 9000
Tel: **221601, 222675**
Fax: 229792

NEPAL
Pani Pokhari
Kathmandu
Tel: **411179**
Telex: 2381
Fax: 419963

NETHERLANDS
Lange Voorhout 102
The Hague

Tel: **3109209**
Fax: 361-4688

NEW ZEALAND
29 Fitzherbert Terrace
Thorndon
Wellington
(PO Box 1190)
Tel: **4722068**
Fax: 4723537

NICARAGUA
Km. 4-1/2 Carretera Sur.
Managua
Tel: **666010**
Fax: 666046

NIGERIA
2 Eleke Crescent
Lagos
(PO Box 554)
Tel: **610097**
Telex: 23616
Fax: 610257

NORWAY
Drammensveien 18
0244 Oslo 2
Tel: **44-85-50**
Fax: 43-07-77

OMAN
PO Box 50202 Madinat Qaboos
Muscat
Tel: **698-989**
Telex: 3785
Fax: 604316

PAKISTAN
Diplomatic Enclave
Ramna 5
Islamabad
(PO Box 1048)
Tel: **826161**
Telex: 5864
Fax: 822004

PANAMA
Apartado 6959
Panama 5
Rep. de Panama
Tel: **27-1777**
Fax: 03-9470

PAPUA NEW GUINEA
Armit Street
Port Moresby
(PO Box 1492)
Tel: **211-455**
Telex: 22189 USAEM
Fax: 213-423

PARAGUAY
1776 Mariscal Lopez Avenue
Asuncion
(Casilla Postal 402)

Tel: **213-715**
Fax: 213-728

PERU
Corner Avenidas Inca Garcilaso de la Vega &
Espana
Lima
(PO Box 1995, Lima 100)
Tel: **338-000**
Telex: 25212 PE
Fax: 316682

PHILIPPINES
1201 Roxas Blvd
Manila
Tel: **521-7116**
Telex: 722-27366
Fax: 5224361

POLAND
Aleje Ujazdowskie 29/31
Warsaw
Tel: **6283041**
Telex: 813304
Fax: 628 9326

PORTUGAL
Avenida das Forcas Armadas
1600 Lisbon
Tel: **726-6600**
Telex: 12528 AMEMB
Fax: 726-9109

ROMANIA
Strada Tudor Arghezi 7-9
Bucharest
Tel: **10-40-40**
Telex: 11416
Fax: 118447

RUSSIA
Ulitsa Chaykovskogo 19/21/23
Moscow
Tel: **252-2541**
Telex: 413160
Fax: 255 9965

SAUDI ARABIA
Collector Road M
Riyadh Diplomatic Quarter
(PO Box 94309 Riyadh 11413)
Tel: **488-3800**
Telex: 406866
Fax: 488 3278

SENEGAL
BP 49
Avenue Jean XXII
Dakar
Tel: **23-42-96**
Telex: 21793 AMEMB SG
Fax: 22-29-91

SINGAPORE
30 Hill Street
Singapore

Tel: **338-0251**
Telex: RS 42289
Fax: 338 4550

SOUTH AFRICA
Thibault House
225 Pretorius Street
Pretoria 0001
Tel: **28-4266**
Telex: 322143
Fax: 219278

SPAIN
Serrano 75
28006
Madrid
Tel: **577-4000**
Telex: 27763
Fax: 577-5735

SRI LANKA
210 Galle Road
Colombo 3
(PO Box 106)
Tel: **448007**
Telex: 21305
Fax: 427345

SUDAN
Sharia Ali Abdul Latif
Khartoum
(PO Box 699)
Tel: **74700**
Telex: 22619 AMEM SD

SURINAME
Dr. Sophie Redmondstraat 129
Paramaribo
PO Box 1821
Tel: **472900**
Telex: 373
Fax: 475051

SWAZILAND
Central Bank Building
Warner Street
Mbabane
(PO Box 199)
Tel: **46441**
Telex: 2016
Fax: 45959

SWEDEN
Strandvagen 101
11589 Stockholm
Tel: **783-5300**
Telex: 12060
Fax: 661-1964

SWITZERLAND
Jubilaeumstrasse 93
3005 Bern
Tel: **437-011**
Telex: 912603
Fax: 437-344

TAIWAN
7 Lane
134 Hsin Yi Road
Sec 3
Taipei
Tel: **7092000**
Telex: 23890
Fax: 702675

TAJIKISTAN
Oktyabrskaya Hotel
39 Ainii Street
Dushanbe
Tel: **248223**

TANZANIA
36 Laibon Road (off Bagamoyo Road)
Dar Es Salaam
(PO Box 9123)
Tel: **37501-4**
Telex: 41250
Fax: 37408

THAILAND
95 Wireless Road
Bangkok
Tel: **66010/3**
Telex: 20966
Fax: 66701

TOGO
Rue Pelletier Caventou & Rue Vauban
Lome (BP 852)
Tel: **21-77-17**
Fax: 217952

TRINIDAD & TOBAGO
15 Queen's Park West
Port-of-Spain
(PO Box 752)
Tel: **622-6372**
Fax: 628 5462

TUNISIA
144 Avenue de la Liberte
1002 Tunis-Belvedere
Tel: **782-566**
Telex: 13379
Fax: 789-719

TURKEY
110 Ataturk Buluvari
Ankara
Tel: **426 5470**
Fax: 467 0057

TURKMENISTAN
Yuvelinaya Hotel
Ashkabhad
Tel: **244908**

UGANDA
Parliament Avenue
Kampala
(PO Box 7007)
Tel: **259792**

UNITED ARAB EMIRATES
Al-Sudan Street
Abu Dhabi
(PO Box 4009)
Tel: **336691**
Telex: 23513
Fax: 318411

UNITED KINGDOM
24/31 Grosvenor Square
London W1 1AE
Tel: **071-499-9000**
Telex: 266777
Fax: 071-409-1637

URUGUAY
Lauro Muller 1776
Montevideo
Tel: **23-60-61**
Fax: 488611

VENEZUELA
Avenida Francisco de Miranda and Avenida
Principal de la Floresta
(PO Box 62291, Caracas 1060-A)
Tel: **285-3111/2222**
Telex: 25501
Fax: 285-0336

YEMEN
PO Box 22347
Sanaa
Tel: **238842**
Telex: 2697 EMBSAN YE
Fax: 251-563

**THE FORMER REPUBLIC OF
YUGOSLAVIA (SERBIA & MONTENE-
GRO)**
Kneza Milosa 50
11000 Belgrade
Tel: **645-655**
Telex: 11529
Fax: 645-221

ZAIRE
310 Avenue des Aviateurs
Tel: **21532**
Telex: 21405
Fax: 21232

ZAMBIA
PO Box 31617
Lusaka
Tel: **228-595/601**
Telex: 41970
Fax: 251578

ZIMBABWE
172 Herbert Chitapo Avenue
Harare
(PO Box 3340)
Tel: **794-521**
Telex: 24591 USFCS ZW
Fax: 796488

FOREIGN GOVERNMENT REPRESENTATIVES OVERSEAS

Australia

ARGENTINA
1st Floor
MLC Tower
Woden
Canberra ACT 2606
Tel: **2824555**

AUSTRIA
12 Talbot Street
Forrest
Canberra
Tel: **2951533**

BANGLADESH
11 Milneaux Place
Farrer
Canberra
Tel: **2861200**

BELGIUM
19 Arkana Street
Yarralumla
Canberra ACT 2600
Tel: **2732502**

BRAZIL
19 Forster Crescent
Yarralumla
Canberra
Tel: **2732372**

BRUNEI
16 Bulwarra Close
O'Malley
Canberra
Tel: **2904801**

CANADA
Commonwealth Avenue
Canberra ACT 2600
Tel: **2733844**

CHILE
10 Culgoa Circuit
O'Malley
 anberra
Tel: **2864027/2862430**

CHINA
14 Federal Highway
Watson
Canberra ACT 2602
Tel: **2412446**

CYPRUS
37 Endeavour Street
Red Hill

Canberra
Tel: **2953713/2952120**

CZECH REPUBLIC
47 Culgoa Circuit
O'Malley
Canberra
Tel: **2901516**

DENMARK
15 Hunter Street
Yarralumla
Canberra
Tel: **2732195/6**

EGYPT
1 Darwin Avenue
Yarrlumla
Canberra
Tel: **2734437**

FIJI
9 Beagle Street
Red Hill
Canberra ACT 2600
Tel: **2959148/2958774**

FINLAND
10 Darwin Avenue
Yarralumla
Canberra ACT 2600
Tel: **2733800**

FRANCE
6 Perth Avenue
Yarralumla
Canberra
Tel: **2705111**

GERMANY
119 Empire Circuit
Yarralumla
Canberra ACT 2600
Tel: **2701911**

GREECE
9 Turrana Street
Yarralumla
Canberra
Tel: **2733011**

HUNGARY
79 Hopetown Circuit
Yarralumla
Canberra ACT 2600
Tel: **2823226/9**

INDIA
3-5 Moonah Place
Yarralumla
Canberra ACT 2600
Tel: **2733999/2733774**

INDONESIA
8 Darwin Avenue
Yarralumla
Canberra
Tel: **2733222**

IRAN
14 Torres Street
Red Hill
Canberra
Tel: **2952544**

IRAQ
48 Culgoa Circuit
O'Malley
Canberra ACT 2606
Tel: **2861333**

IRELAND
20 Arkana Street
Yarralumla
Canberra ACT 2606
Tel: **2733022**

ISRAEL
6 Turrana Street
Yarralumla
Canberra ACT 2600
Tel: **2731309**

ITALY
12 Grey Street
Deakin
Canberra ACT 2600
Tel: **2733333**

JAPAN
112 Empire Circuit
Yarralumla
Canberra ACT 2000
Tel: **2733244**

JORDAN
20 Roebuck Street
Red Hill
Canberra
Tel: **2959951**

KENYA
33-35
Ainslie Avenue
Canberra City
Tel: **2474688**

KOREA
113 Empire Circuit
Yarralumla
Canberra ACT 2600
Tel: **2733044**

LAOS
1 Dalman Crescent
O'Malley
Canberra
Tel: **2844595**

LEBANON
27 Endeavour Street
Red Hill
Canberra
Tel: **2957478**

MALAYSIA
7 Perth Avenue
Yarralumla
Canberra
Tel: **2731543**

MALTA
261 La Perouse Street
Red Hill
Canberra ACT 2603
Tel: **2951586**

MAURITIUS
43 Hampton Circuit
Yarralumla
Canberra
Tel: **2811203**

MEXICO
14 Perth Avenue
Yarralumla
Canberra ACT 2600
Tel: **2733905**

NETHERLANDS
120 Empire Circuit
Yarralumla
Canberra ACT 2600
Tel: **2733111**

NEW ZEALAND
Commonwealth Avenue
Canberra ACT 2600
Tel: **2733611**

NIGERIA
7 Terrigal Crescent
O'Malley
Canberra
Tel: **2861322**

NORWAY
17 Hunter Street
Yarralumla
Canberra
Tel: **2733444**

PAKISTAN
59 Franklin Street
Forrest
Canberra ACT 2603
Tel: **2950021/2**

PAPUA NEW GUINEA
Forster Crescent
Yarralumla
Canberra ACT 2600
Tel: **2733322**

PERU
9th Floor
197 London Circuit
Canberra ACT 2604
Tel: **2572953**

PHILIPPINES
1 Moonah Place
Yarralumla

Canberra ACT 2600
Tel: 2722535

POLAND
7 Turrana Street
Yarralumla
Canberra ACT 2600
Tel: 2731211

PORTUGAL
1st Floor
6 Campion Street
Deakin
Canberra
Tel: 2852084

RUSSIA
78 Canberra Avenue
Griffith
Canberra ACT 2603
Tel: 2959033/ 2959474

SAUDI ARABIA
12 Culgoa Circuit
O'Malley
Canberra
Tel: 2862099

SINGAPORE
17 Forster Crescent
Yarralumla
Canberra
Tel: 2733944

SOUTH AFRICA
Cnr State Circle and Rhodes Place
Yarralumla
Canberra
Tel: 2732424

SPAIN
15 Arkana Street
Yarralumla
Canberra
Tel: 2733555

SRI LANKA
35 Empire Circuit
Forrest
Canberra ACT 2603
Tel: 2953521

SWEDEN
5 Turrana Street
Yarralumla
Canberra ACT 2600
Tel: 2733033

SWITZERLAND
7 Melbourne Avenue
Forrest
Canberra ACT 2603
Tel: 2733977

THAILAND
111 Empire Circuit
Yarralumla

Canberra ACT 2600
Tel: 2731149/2732937

TURKEY
60 Mugga Way
Red Hill
Canberra
Tel: 2950227

UNITED KINGDOM
Commonwealth Avenue
Canberra
Tel: 2706666

UNITED STATES
State Circle
Yarralumla
Canberra ACT 2603
Tel: 2705000

URUGUAY
Suite 5
Bonner House
Woden
Canberra
Tel: 2824418

VENEZUELA
1st Floor
M.L.C. Tower
Woden
Canberra
Tel: 2824828

VIETNAM
6 Timbarra Crescent
O'Malley
Canberra
Tel: 2866059

THE FORMER REPUBLIC OF YUGOSLAVIA
11 Nuyts St
Red Hill
Canberra ACT 2603
Tel: 2951458

ZAMBIA
26 Guilfoyle Street
Yarralumla
Canberra
Tel: 2810111

ZIMBABWE
11 Culgoa Circuit
O'Malley
Canberra
Tel: 2862700

Canada

ANTIGUA
60 St. Clair Avenue East
Toronto
ON M4T 1N5
Tel: 416- 961 3143

ARGENTINA
90 Sparks Street
Suite 620
Ottawa
ON K1P 5B4
Tel: **613- 236-2351/4**

AUSTRALIA
50 O'Connor Street
Ottawa
ON K1P 6L2
Tel: **613- 236-0841**

AUSTRIA
445 Wilbrod Street
Ottawa
ON K1N 6M7
Tel: **613- 563-1444**

BANGLADESH
85 Range Road
Suite 402
Ottawa
ON K1N 8J6
Tel: **613- 236-0138/9**

BARBADOS
151 Slater Street
Suite 210
Ottawa
ON K1P 5H3
Tel: **613- 236-9517/8**

BELGIUM
85 Range Road
Ottawa
ON K1N 8J6
Tel: **613- 236-7267**

BENIN
58 Glebe Avenue
Ottawa
ON K1S 5L6
Tel: **613- 233-4429**

BOLIVIA
77 Metcalfe Street
Suite 608
Ottawa
ON K1P 5L6
Tel: **613- 236-8237**

BRAZIL
255 Albert Street
Suite 900
Ottawa
ON K1P 6A9
Tel: **613- 237-1090**

BULGARIA
325 Stewart Street
Ottawa
ON K1N 6K5
Tel: **613- 232-3215**

BURKINA FASO
48 Range Road
Ottawa
ON K1N 8J4
Tel: **613- 238-4796**

BURUNDI
151 Slater Street
Suite 800
Ottawa
ON K1P 5H3
Tel: **613- 236-8483**

CAMEROON
170 Clemow Avenue
Ottawa
ON K1S 2B4
Tel: **613- 236-1522**

CHILE
151 Slater Street
Suite 605
Ottawa
ON K1P 5H3
Tel: **613- 246-9940**

COLOMBIA
150 Kent Street
Suite 404
Ottawa
ON K1P 5P4
Tel: **613- 230-3760**

COSTA RICA
150 Argyle Avenue
Suite 115
Ottawa
ON K2P 1B7
Tel: **613- 234-5762**

COTE D'IVOIRE
9 Marlborough Avenue
Ottawa
ON K1N 8E6
Tel: **613- 236-9919**

CUBA
388 Main Street
Ottawa
ON K1S 1E3
Tel: **613- 563-0141**

CZECH REPUBLIC
50 Rideau Terrace
Ottawa
ON K1M 2A1
Tel: **613- 749-4442**

DENMARK
85 Range Road
Suite 702
Ottawa
ON K1N 8J6
Tel: **613- 234-0704**

From 16 April 1995 all national and international change — see page 587 for details.

DOMINICAN REPUBLIC
1464 Rue Crescent
Montreal
PQ H3G 2B6
Tel: **514- 843-6525**

ECUADOR
150 Kent Street
Suite 302
Ottawa
ON K1P 5P4
Tel: **613- 238-2939**

EGYPT
454 Laurier Avenue East
Ottawa
ON K1N 6R3
Tel: **613- 234-4931**

EL SALVADOR
150 Kent Street
Suite 302
Ottawa
ON K1P 5P4
Tel: **613- 238-2939**

FINLAND
55 Metcalfe Street
Ottawa
ON K1P 6L5
Tel: **613- 236-2389**

FRANCE
42 Sussex Drive
Ottawa
ON K1M 2C9
Tel: **613- 232-1795**

GAMBIA
363 St. Francois Xavier Street
#300
Montreal
PQ H2Y 3P9
Tel: **514- 849-2889**

GERMANY
1 Waverley Street
Ottawa
ON K2P 0T8
Tel: **613- 232-1101**

GHANA
1 Clemow Avenue
Ottawa
ON K1S 2A9
Tel: **613- 236-0871**

GREECE
76-80 MacLaren Street
Ottawa ON K2P 0K6
Tel: **613- 238-6271**

GUINEA
483 Wilbrod Street
Ottawa
ON K1N 6N1
Tel: **613- 232-1133**

GUYANA
151 Slater Street
#309
Ottawa
ON K1P 5H3
Tel: **613- 235-7249**

HAITI
112 Rue Kent Street
#1308
Place de Ville
Tour B
Ottawa
ON K1P 5P2
Tel: **613- 236-1628**

HONDURAS
151 Slater Street
#300-A
Ottawa
ON H1P 5H3
Tel: **613- 233-8900**

HUNGARY
7 Delaware Avenue
Ottawa
ON K2P 0Z2
Tel: **613- 232-1711**

ICELAND
6100 Deacon Road
#2C
Montreal
PQ H3S 2V6
Tel: **514- 342-6451**

INDIA
10 Springfield Road
Ottawa
ON K2P 0L9
Tel: **613- 236-7403**

INDONESIA
287 McLaren Street
Ottawa
ON K2P 0L9
Tel: **613- 236-7403**

IRAN
411 Roosevelt Avenue
Ottawa
ON K2A 3X9
Tel: **613- 729-0902**

IRAQ
215 McLeod Street
Ottawa
ON K2P 0Z8
Tel: **613- 236-9177**

IRELAND
170 Metcalfe Street
Ottawa
ON K1P 6L2
Tel: **613- 233-6381**

ISRAEL
50 O'Connor Street
#1005
Ottawa
ON K1P 6L2
Tel: **613- 237-6450**

ITALY
275 Slater Street
Ottawa
ON K1P 5H9
Tel: **613- 232-2401**

JAMAICA
275 Slater Street
#402
Ottawa
ON K1P 5H9
Tel: **613- 233-9311**

JAPAN
255 Sussex Drive
Ottawa
ON K1N 9E6
Tel: **613- 236-8541**

JORDAN
100 Bronson Avenue
Suite 701
Ottawa
ON K1R 6G8
Tel: **613- 238-8090**

KENYA
415 Laurier Avenue East
#600
Ottawa
ON K1N 6R4
Tel: **613- 563-1773**

LEBANON
640 Lyon Street
Ottawa
ON K1S 3Z5
Tel: **613- 236-5825**

LESOTHO
202 Clemow Avenue
Ottawa ON K1S 2B4
Tel: **613- 236-9449**

MADAGASCAR
451 Rue St. Sulpice
Montreal
PQ H2Y 2V9
Tel: **514- 849-9649**

MALAWI
7 Clemow Avenue
Ottawa
ON K1S 2A9
Tel: **613- 236-8931**

MALAYSIA
60 Bolteler Street
Ottawa

ON K1N 8Y7
Tel: **613- 237-5182**

MALI
50 Goulburn Avenue
Ottawa
ON K1N 8C8
Tel: **613- 232-1501**

MEXICO
130 Albert Street
#1800
Ottawa
ON K1P 5G4
Tel: **613- 233-8988**

MOROCCO
38 Range Road
Ottawa
ON K1N 8J4
Tel: **613- 236-7391**

NETHERLANDS
275 Slater Street
Ottawa
ON K1P 5H9
Tel: **613- 237-5030**

NEW ZEALAND
99 Bank Street
Suite 727
Ottawa
ON K1P 6G3
Tel: **613- 238-5991**

NICARAGUA
170 Laurier Avenue West
Suite 908
Ottawa
ON K1P 5V5
Tel: **613- 234-9361**

NIGER
38 Avenue Blackburn
Ottawa
ON K1N 8A2
Tel: **613- 232-4291**

NIGERIA
295 Metcalfe Street
Ottawa
ON K2P 1R9
Tel: **613- 236-0521**

NORWAY
90 Sparks Street
Suite 534
Ottawa
ON K1P 1R9
Tel: **613- 238-6571**

PAKISTAN
151 Slater Street
Suite 608
Ottawa
ON K1P 5H3
Tel: **613- 238-7881**

PERU
170 Laurier Avenue West
Suite 1007
Ottawa ON K1P 5V5
Tel: **613- 238-1777**

PHILIPPINES
130 Albert Street
Suite 606
Ottawa
ON K1P 5G4
Tel: **613- 233-1121**

POLAND
443 Daly Avenue
Ottawa
ON K1N 6H3
Tel: **613- 236-0468**

PORTUGAL
645 Island Park Drive
Ottawa
ON K1Y 0B8
Tel: **613- 729-0883**

RUSSIA
285 Charlotte Street
Ottawa
ON K1N 8L5
Tel: **613- 235-4341**

RWANDA
121 Sherwood Drive
Ottawa
ON K1Y 3V1
Tel: **613- 722-5835**

SAUDI ARABIA
99 Bank Street
Suite 901
Ottawa
ON K1P 6B9
Tel: **613- 237-4100**

SENEGAL
57 Marlborough Avenue
Ottawa
ON K1N 8E8
Tel: **613- 238-6392**

SOMALIA
130 Slater Street
#1000
Ottawa
ON K1P 6E2
Tel: **613- 563-4541**

SOUTH AFRICA
15 Sussex Drive
Ottawa
ON K1M 6E2
Tel: **613- 744-0330**

SPAIN
350 Sparks Street
Suite 802
Ottawa

ON K1R 7S8
Tel: **613- 237-2193**

SRI LANKA
85 Range Road
The Sandringham
Suites 102-104
Ottawa
ON K1N 8J6
Tel: **613-233-8440**

SWEDEN
441 MacLaren Street
Ottawa
ON K2P 2H3
Tel: **613- 236-8553**

SWITZERLAND
5 Marlborough Avenue
Ottawa
ON K1N 8E6
Tel: **613- 235-1837**

TANZANIA
50 Range Road
Ottawa
ON K1N 8J4
Tel: **613- 232-1509**

THAILAND
180 Island Park Drive
Ottawa
ON K1Y 0A2
Tel: **613- 722-4444**

TRINIDAD & TOBAGO
75 Albert Street
Suite 508
Ottawa
ON K1P 5E7
Tel: **613- 232-2418**

TUNISIA
515 Oscannor Street
Ottawa
ON K1S 3P8
Tel: **613- 237-0330**

TURKEY
197 Wurtemburg Street
Ottawa
ON K1N 8LN
Tel: **613- 232-1577**

UNITED STATES
100 Wellington Street
Ottawa
ON K1P 5T1
Tel: **613- 238-5335**

URUGUAY
130 Albert Street
#1905
Ottawa
ON K1P 5G4
Tel: **613- 234-2727**

From 16 April 1995 all national and international change — see page 587 for details.

VENEZUELA
32 Range Road
Ottawa
ON K1N 8J4
Tel: 613- 235-5151

**THE FORMER REPUBLIC OF
YUGOSLAVIA (SERBIA & MONTENE-
GRO)**
17 Blackburn Avenue
Ottawa
ON K1N 8A2
Tel: 613- 233-6289

ZAIRE
18 Range Road
Ottawa
ON K1N 8J3
Tel: 613- 236-7103

ZAMBIA
130 Albert Street
#1610
Ottawa
ON K1P 5G4
Tel: 613- 563-0712

ZIMBABWE
322 Somerset Street West
Ottawa
ON K2P 0J9
Tel: 613- 237-4388

New Zealand

ARGENTINA
Harbour View Building
52 Quay Street
(PO Box 2320)
Auckland
Tel: 391 757

AUSTRALIA
72-28 Hobson Street
Thorndon
(PO Box 4036)
Wellington
Tel: 736 411

AUSTRIA
Security Express House
2nd Floor
22 Garrett Street
(PO Box 6016)
Wellington
Tel: 801 9709

BELGIUM
Robert Jones House
1-3 Willeston Street
(PO Box 3841)
Wellington
Tel: 729 558/9

BRAZIL
135 Tamaki Drive
Mission Bay
(PO Box 4356, Auckland)
Auckland 5
Tel: 528 6681

CANADA
61 Molesworth Street
(PO Box 12049)
Wellington
Tel: 739 577

CHILE
Robert Jones House
1-3 Willeston Street
(PO Box 3861)
Wellington
Tel: 725 180/1

CHINA
2-6 Glenmore Street
Wellington
Tel: 721 382

COSTA RICA
50 Lunn Avenue
Mount Wellington
(PO Box 686)
Auckland
Tel: 527 1523

CZECH REPUBLIC
12 Anne Street
Wadestown
(PO Box 2843)
Wellington
Tel: 723 142

DENMARK
c/o Morrison Morpeth
MARAC House
105-109 The Terrace
(PO Box 10035)
Wellington
Tel: 720 020

ECUADOR
Wool House
2nd Floor
10 Brandon Street
(PO Box 2987)
Wellington
Tel: 722 633

EL SALVADOR
24 Seccombes Road
Epsom
Auckland
Tel: 524 9376

FIJI
13th level
Plimmer City Centre
Cnr Boulcott Street and Gilmer Terrace
(PO Box 3940)

Wellington
Tel: **735 401/2**

FINLAND
NZI House
25-33 Victoria Street
(PO Box 1201)
Wellington
Tel: **724 924**

FRANCE
Robert Jones
1-3 Willeston House
Wellington
Tel: **720 200/201**

GERMANY
90-92 Hobson Street
Thorndon
(PO Box 1687)
Wellington
Tel: **736 063/4**

GREECE
8th Floor
Cumberland House
237 Willis Street
(PO Box) 27-157
Wellington
Tel: **847 556**

ICELAND
88 Oriental Parade
(PO Box 702)
Wellington
Tel: **857 934**

IRELAND
2nd Floor
Dingwall Building
87 Queen Street
(PO Box 279)
Auckland
Tel: **302 2867**

INDIA
10th Floor
Princess Tower
180 Molesworth Street
(PO Box 4045)
Wellington
Tel: **736 390/1**

INDONESIA
70 Glen Road
Kelburn
(PO Box 3543)
Wellington
Tel: **758 697/8/9**

IRAN
PO Box 10 249
The Terrace
Wellington
Tel: **862 976/983**

ISRAEL
Plimmer City Centre
Plimmer Steps
(PO Box 2171)
Wellington
Tel: **722 362/8**

ITALY
34 Grant Road
Thorndon
(PO Box 463)
Wellington
Tel: **735 339, 728 302**

JAPAN
Norwich Insurance House
3-11 Hunter Street
(PO Box 6340)
Wellington
Tel: **731 540**

KOREA
Level 6
Elders House
86-96 Victoria Street
(PO Box 11 143)
Wellington
Tel: **739 073**

MALAYSIA
10 Washington Avenue
Brooklyn
(PO Box 9422)
Wellington
Tel: **852 439/019**

MALTA
18 Barlow Place
Birkenhead
Auckland
Tel: **799 860**

MAURITIUS
33 Great South Road
Otahuhu
Auckland
Tel: **276 3789**

MEXICO
Eagle Technology House
150-154 Willis Street
(PO Box 3029)
Wellington
Tel: **852 145**

NETHERLANDS
Investment Centre
Corner Ballance and Featherston Streets
(PO Box 840)
Wellington
Tel: **738 652**

NORWAY
55-67 Molesworth Street
(PO Box 1990)

From 16 April 1995 all national and international change — see page 587 for details.

Wellington
Tel: **712 503**

PAKISTAN
PO Box 3830
Auckland 1
Tel: **528 3526**

PAPUA NEW GUINEA
FAI House
180 Molesworth Street
(PO Box 197)
Wellington
Tel: **731 560/1/2**

PERU
199-209 Great North Road
Grey Lynn
(PO Box 28-083)
Auckland
Tel: **780 366**

PHILIPPINES
50 Hobson Street
Thorndon
(PO Box 12042)
Wellington
Tel: **729 848/921**

POLAND
Apt D
196 The Terrace
(PO Box 10211)
Wellington
Tel: **712 456**

PORTUGAL
Deloitte Ross Tohmatsu
Southpac House
1 Victoria Street
(PO Box 1990)
Wellington
Tel: **721 677**

RUSSIA
57 Messines Road
Karori
Wellington
Tel: **766 113**

SINGAPORE
17 Kabul Street
Khandallah
(PO Box 29023)
Wellington
Tel: **792 076/7**

SPAIN
PO Box 71
Papakura
Auckland
Tel: **298 5176**

SWEDEN
Greenock House
39 The Terrace
(PO Box 5350)

Wellington
Tel: **720 909/10**

SWITZERLAND
Panama House
22-24 Panama Street
Wellington
Tel: **721 593/594**

THAILAND
2 Cook Street
Karori
(PO Box 17226)
Wellington
Tel: **768 618/9**

TURKEY
404 Khyber Pass Road
Newmarket
Auckland 1
Tel: **522 2281/524 4198**

UNITED KINGDOM
Reserve Bank Building
2 The Terrace
(PO Box 1812)
Wellington
Tel: **726 049**

UNITED STATES
29 Fitzherbert Terrace
(PO Box 1190)
Wellington
Tel: **722 068**

URUGUAY
178 Cashel Street
(PO Box 167)
Christchurch
Tel: **650 000, 798 606**

WESTERN SAMOA
1A Wesley Road
Kelburn
(PO Box 1430)
Wellington
Tel: **720 953/4**

**THE FORMER REPUBLIC OF
YUGOSLAVIA (SERBIA &
MONTENEGRO)**
24 Hatton Street
Karori
Wellington
Tel: **764 200**

UK

Consulates are closed on English Public Holidays and on the national holidays observed in their own countries. Where there is no embassy in the UK, the nearest available has been listed.

AFGHANISTAN
31 Prince's Gate
London SW7 1QQ
Tel: **071-589 8891**

ALBANIA
131 Rue de la Pompe
75016 Paris
France
Tel: **(1) 45 53 51 32**

ALGERIA
54 Holland Park
London W11 3RS
Tel: **071-221 7800**

ANGOLA
87 Jermyn Street
London W1
Tel: **071-839 5743**

ANTIGUA
15 Thayer Street
London W1M 5LD
Tel: **071-486 7073**

ARGENTINA
53 Hans Place
London SW1
Tel: **071-589 3104**

AUSTRALIA
Australia House
The Strand
London WC2B 4LA
Tel: **071-379 4334**

AUSTRIA
18 Belgrave Mews West
London SW1X 8HU
Tel: **071-235 3731**

BAHAMAS
10 Chesterfield Street
London W1X 8AH
Tel: **071-499 0587**

BAHRAIN
98 Gloucester Road
London SW7
Tel: **071-370 5132**

BANGLADESH
28 Queen's Gate
London SW7 5JA
Tel: **071-584 0081**

BARBADOS
1 Great Russell Street
London WC1B 3NH
Tel: **071-631 4975**

BELGIUM
103 Eaton Square
London SW1W 9AB
Tel: **071-235 5422**

BELIZE
200 Sutherland Avenue
London W9 1RX
Tel: **071-266 3485**

BENIN
87 Avenue Victor-Hugo
75116 Paris
France
Tel: **(1) 45 00 98 40**

BOLIVIA
106 Eaton Square
London SW1W 9AD
Tel: **071-235 2257**

BOTSWANA
6 Stratford Place
London W1N 9AE
Tel: **071-499 0031**

BRAZIL
32 Green Street
London W1Y 3FD
Tel: **071-499 0877**

BRUNEI
49 Cromwell Road
London SW7 2ED
Tel: **071-581 0521**

BULGARIA
186-8 Queen's Gate
London SW7 3HL
Tel: **071-584 9400**

BURKINA FASO
150 Buckingham Palace Road
London SW1W 9SA
Tel: **071-730 8141**

BURUNDI
46 Square Marie Louise
1040 Brussels
Belgium
Tel: **(2) 230 4535**

CAMEROON
84 Holland Park
London W11 3SB
Tel: **071-727 0771**

CANADA
MacDonald House
1 Grosvenor Square
London W1X 0AB
Tel: **071-629 9492**

CENTRAL AFRICAN REPUBLIC
29 Boulevard de Montmorency
75016 Paris
France
Tel: **(1) 42 24 42 56**

CHAD
65 Rue des Belles-Feuilles
75116 Paris
Tel: **(1) 45 53 36 75**

CHILE
12 Devonshire Street
London W1N 2DS
Tel: **071-580 6392**

CHINA
31 Portland Road
London W1N 3AG
Tel: **071-636 5726**

COLOMBIA
3 Hans Crescent
London SW1 0LR
Tel: **071-589 9177**

CONGO
37 bis
rue Paul Valery
75016 Paris
Tel: **(1) 45 00 60 57**

COSTA RICA
93 Star Street
London W2
Tel: **071-723 1772**

CUBA
167 High Holborn
London WC1
Tel: **071-240 2488**

CYPRUS
93 Park Street
London W1Y 4ET
Tel: **071-499 8272**

CZECH REPUBLIC
25 Kensington Palace Gardens
London W8 4QX
Tel: **071-229 1255**

DENMARK
55 Sloane Street
London SW1X 9SR
Tel: **071-235 1255**

DJIBOUTI
26 Rue Emile-Menier
75116 Paris
France
Tel: **(1) 47 27 49 22**

DOMINICA
1 Collingham Gardens
London SW5 0HW
Tel: **071-370 5194**

DOMINICAN REPUBLIC
5 Braemar Mansions
Cornwall Gardens
London SW7 4AG
Tel: **071-937 1921**

ECUADOR
3 Hans Crescent
London SW1X 0LS
Tel: **071-584 1367**

EGYPT
26 South Street
London W1Y 8EL
Tel: **071-499 2401**

EL SALVADOR
62 Welbeck Street
London W1M 7HB
Tel: **071-486 8182**

ETHIOPIA
17 Prince's Gate
London SW7 1PZ
Tel: **071-589 7212**

FIJI
32-34 Hyde Park Gate
London SW7 5BN
Tel: **071-584 3661**

FINLAND
38 Chesham Place
London SW1X 8HW
Tel: **071-235 9531**

FRANCE
58 Knightsbridge
SW1X 7JT
Tel: **071-235 8080**

GABON
48 Kensington Court
London W8
Tel: **071-937 5285**

GAMBIA
57 Kensington Court
London W8 5DG
Tel: **71-937 6316**

GERMANY
23 Belgrave Square
London SW1X 8PZ
Tel: **071-235 5033**

GHANA
13 Belgrave Square
London SW1X 8PR
Tel: **071-235 4142**

GREECE
1A Holland Park
London W11 3TP
Tel: **071-727 8040**

GRENADA
1 Collingham Gardens
London SW5 0HW
Tel: **071-373 7800**

GUATEMALA
73 Rue de Courcelles
75008 Paris
France
Tel: **(1) 47 63 90 83**

GUINEA-BISSAU
8 Palace Gate
London W8 4RP
Tel: **071-589 5253**

GUINEA
24 Rue Emile-Meunier
75016 Paris
France
Tel: **(1) 45 56 72 25**

GUYANA
3 Palace Court
London W2 4LP
Tel: **071-229 7684**

HAITI
33 Abbots House
St Mary Abbots Terrace
London W14 8NU
Tel: **071-602 3194**

HONDURAS
115 Gloucester Place
London W1H 3PJ
Tel: **071-486 4880**

HONG KONG
125 Pall Mall
5th Floor
London SW1Y 5EA
Tel: **071-930 4775**

HUNGARY
35 Eaton Place
London SW1
Tel: **071-235 4048**

ICELAND
1 Eaton Terrace
London SW1W 8EY
Tel: **071-730 5131**

INDIA
India House
Aldwych
London WC2B 4NA
Tel: **071-836 8484**

INDONESIA
38 Grosvenor Square
London W1X 9AD
Tel: **071-499 7661**

IRAN
4 Avenue d'Iena
75116 Paris
France
Tel: **(1) 47 23 61 22**

IRAQ
22 Queen's Gate
London SW7 5JG
Tel: **071-584 7141**

IRELAND
17 Grosvenor Place
London SW1X 7HR
Tel: **071-235 2171**

ISRAEL
2 Palace Green
London W8 4QB
Tel: **071-937 8050**

ITALY
14 Three Kings Yard
London W1Y 2EH
Tel: **071-629 8200**

JAMAICA
50 St. James's Street
London SW1
Tel: **071-499 8600**

JAPAN
46 Grosvenor Street
London W1X 0BA
Tel: **071-493 6030**

JORDAN
6 Upper Phillimore Gardens
London W8
Tel: **071-937 3685**

KENYA
45 Portland Place
London W1N 4AS
Tel: **071-636 2371**

SOUTH KOREA
4 Palace Gate
London W8 5NF
Tel: **071-581 0247**

KUWAIT
45-6 Queen's Gate
London SW7
Tel: **071-589 4533**

LAOS
74 Avenue Raymond-Poincare
75116 Paris
France
Tel: **(1) 45 53 02 98**

LEBANON
21 Kensington Palace Gardens
London W8 4QM
Tel: **071-229 7265**

LESOTHO
10 Collingham Road
London SW5 0NR
Tel: **071-373 8581**

LIBERIA
2 Pembridge Place
London W2
Tel: **071-221 1036**

From 16 April 1995 all national and international change — see page 587 for details.

LUXEMBOURG
27 Wilton Crescent
London SW1X 8SD
Tel: **071-235 6961**

MACAU
22 Devonshire Street
Suite 0101
London W1N 1RL
Tel: **071-224 3390**

MADAGASCAR
69-70 Mark Lane
London EC3R 7JA
Tel: **071-481 3899**

MALAWI
33 Grosvenor Street
London W1X 0DE
Tel: **071-491 4172**

MALAYSIA
45 Belgrave Square
London SW1X 8QT
Tel: **071-235 8033**

MALI
89 Rue du Cherche-Midi
75016 Paris
France
Tel: **(1) 45 48 58 43**

MALTA
16 Kensington Square
London W8 5HH
Tel: **071-938 1712**

MAURITANIA
89 Rue du Cherche-Midi
75016 Paris
France
Tel: **(1) 45 48 23 88**

MAURITIUS
32-3 Elvaston Place
London SW7
Tel: **071-581 0294**

MEXICO
8 Halkin Street
London SW1
Tel: **071-235 6393**

MONACO
4 Audley Square
London W1Y 5DR
Tel: **071-629 0734**

MONGOLIA
7 Kensington Court
London W8 5DL
Tel: **071-937 0150**

MOROCCO
49 Queen's Gate Gardens
London SW7 5NE
Tel: **071-581 5001**

MOZAMBIQUE
21 Fitzroy Square
London W1P 5HJ
Tel: **071-283 3800**

MYANMAR
19A Charles Street
London W1X 8ER
Tel: **071-629 6966**

NEPAL
12A Kensington Palace Gardens
London W8 4QU
Tel: **071-229 1594**

NETHERLANDS
38 Hyde Park Gate
London SW7 5DP
Tel: **071-584 5040**

NEW ZEALAND
New Zealand House
London SW1Y 4TQ
Tel: **071-930 8422**

NICARAGUA
8 Gloucester Road
London SW7 4PP
Tel: **071-584 4365**

NIGER
154 Rue de Longchamp
75116 Paris
France
Tel: **(1) 45 04 80 60**

NIGERIA
9 Northumberland Avenue
London WC2
Tel: **071-839 1244**

NORWAY
25 Belgrave Square
London SW1X 8QD
Tel: **071-235 7151**

OMAN
44A/B Montpelier Square
London SW7 1JJ
Tel: **071-584 6782**

PAKISTAN
35-6 Lowndes Square
London SW1X 9JN
Tel: **071-235 2044**

PANAMA
109 Jermyn Street
London SW1
Tel: **071-930 1591**

PAPUA NEW GUINEA
14 Waterloo Place
London SW1R 4AR
Tel: **071-930 0922**

PARAGUAY
Braemar Lodge
Cornwall Gardens

London SW7 4AQ
Tel: **071-937 1253**

PERU
52 Sloane Street
London SW1X 9SP
Tel: **071-235 1917**

PHILIPPINES
199 Piccadilly
London W1V 9LE
Tel: **071-493 3481**

POLAND
47 Portland Place
London W1N 3AG
Tel: **071-580 4324**

PORTUGAL
62 Brompton Road
London SW3 1BJ
Tel: **071-581 8722**

QATAR
27 Chesham Place
London SW1X 8HG
Tel: **071-235 0851**

ROMANIA
4 Palace Green
London W8 4QD
Tel: **071-937 9666**

RUSSIA
13 Kensington Palace Gardens
London W8 4QX
Tel: **071-229 3628**

RWANDA
70 Boulevard de Coucelles
75017 Paris
France
Tel: **(1) 42 27 36 31**

SAUDI ARABIA
30 Belgrave Square
London SW1X 8QB
Tel: **071-235 0831**

SENEGAL
11 Phillimore Gardens
London W8 7QG
Tel: **071-937 0925**

SEYCHELLES
50 Conduit Street
London W1A 4PE
Tel: **071-439 0405**

SIERRA LEONE
33 Portland Place
London W1N 3AG
Tel: **071-636 6483**

SINGAPORE
2 Wilton Crescent
London SW1X 8RW
Tel: **071-235 8315**

SOMALIA
60 Portland Place
London W1N 3DG
Tel: **071-580 7140**

SOUTH AFRICA
Trafalgar Square
London WC2N 5DP
Tel: **071-930 4488**

SPAIN
24 Belgrave Square
London SW1X 8QA
Tel: **071-235 5555**

SRI LANKA
13 Hyde Park Gardens
London W2 2LU
Tel: **071-262 1841**

SUDAN
3 Cleveland Row
London SW1A 1DD
Tel: **071-839 8080**

SWAZILAND
58 Pont Street
London SW1X 0AE
Tel: **071-581 4976**

SWEDEN
11 Montagu Place
London W1H 2AL
Tel: **071-724 2101**

SWITZERLAND
16-18 Montagu Place
London W1H 2BQ
Tel: **071-723 0701**

SYRIA
8 Belgrave Square
London SW1X 8PH
Tel: **071-245 9012**

TAIWAN
432-6 Grand Buildings
Trafalgar Square
London WC2 5HG
Tel: **071-839 5901**

TANZANIA
43 Hertford Street
London W1Y 7TF
Tel: **071-499 8951**

THAILAND
29-30 Queen's Gate
London SW7 5JB
Tel: **071-589 2944**

TOGO
30 Sloane Street
London SW1
Tel: **071-235 0147**

TONGA
New Zealand House
Haymarket

From 16 April 1995 all national and international change — see page 587 for details.

London SW1Y 4TQ
Tel: **071-839 3287**

TRINIDAD & TOBAGO
42 Belgrave Square
London SW1X 8NT
Tel: **071-245 9351**

TUNISIA
29 Prince's Gate
London SW7 1QG
Tel: **071-584 8117**

TURKEY
43 Belgrave Square
London SW1X 8AP
Tel: **071-235 5252**

TURKS & CAICOS
3 Epirus Road
London SW6
Tel: **071-376 2981**

UGANDA
58-9 Trafalgar Square
London WC2N 5DX
Tel: **071-839 5783**

UNITED ARAB EMIRATES
30 Prince's Gate
London SW7
Tel: **071-581 1281**

UNITED STATES
24-32 Grosvenor Square
London W1A 1AE
Tel: **071-499 9000**

URUGUAY
48 Lennox Gardens
London SW1X 0DL
Tel: **071-589 8835**

VENEZUELA
1 Cromwell Road
London SW7
Tel: **071-584 4206**

VIETNAM
12-14 Victoria Road
London W8 5RD
Tel: **071-937 1912**

YEMEN
57 Cromwell Road
London SW7 2ED
Tel: **071-584 6607**

**THE FORMER REPUBLIC OF
YUGOSLAVIA (SERBIA & MONTENE-
GRO)**
5 Lexham Gardens
London W8 5JJ
Tel: **071-370 6105**

ZAIRE
26 Chesham Place
London SW1X 8HH
Tel: **071-235 6137**

ZAMBIA
2 Palace Gate
London W8 5NG
Tel: **071-589 6343**

ZIMBABWE
429 Strand
London WC2R 0SA
Tel: **071-836 7755**

USA

AFGHANISTAN
2341 Wyoming Avenue
NW, Washington DC 20008-1683
Tel: **(202) 234-3770**

ALGERIA
2137 Wyoming Avenue
NW, Washington DC 20008-3905
Tel: **(202) 750-1960**

ARGENTINA
1600 New Hampshire Avenue
NW, Washington DC 20009
Tel: **(202) 939-6400**

AUSTRALIA
1601 Massachusetts Avenue
NW, Washington DC 20036-2273
Tel: **(202) 797-3000**

AUSTRIA
2343 Massachusetts Avenue
NW, Washington
DC 20008-2803
Tel: **(202) 483-4474**

BAHAMAS
600 New Hampshire Avenue
NW, #865
Washington DC 20037-2403
Tel: **(202) 338-3940**

BAHRAIN
3502 International Drive
NW, Washington DC 20008-3035
Tel: **(202) 342-0741**

BANGLADESH
2201 Wisconsin Avenue
NW, #300, Washington DC 20007
Tel: **(202) 342-8372**

BARBADOS
2144 Wyoming Avenue
NW, Washington DC 20008
Tel: **(202) 333-6900**

BELGIUM
3330 Garfield Street
NW, Washington DC 20008
Tel: **(202) 333-6900**

BENIN
2737 Cathedral Avenue
Washington DC 20008
Tel: **(202) 232-6656**

BOLIVIA
3014 Massachusetts Avenue
NW, Washington DC 20008
Tel: **(202) 483-4410**

BOTSWANA
Van Ness Center
#404
4301 Connecticut Avenue
NW, Washington DC 20008
Tel: **(202) 244-4990**

BRAZIL
3006 Massachusetts Avenue
NW, Washington DC 20008-3699
Tel: **(202) 745-2700**

BURKINA FASO
2340 Massachusetts Avenue
NW, Washington DC 20008
Tel: **(202) 332-5577**

BULGARIA
1621 22nd Street
NW, Washington
DC 20008-1921
Tel: **(202) 387-7969**

BURUNDI
2233 Wisconsin Avenue
NW, Suite 212
Washington DC 20007-4104
Tel: **(202) 342-2574**

CAMEROON
2349 Massachusetts Avenue
NW, Washington DC 20008
Tel: **(202) 265-8790**

CANADA
501 Pennsylvania Avenue
Washington DC 20001
Tel: **(202) 682-1740**

CAPE VERDE
3415 Massachusetts Avenue
NW, Washington DC 20007
Tel: **(202) 965-6820**

CENTRAL AFRICAN REPUBLIC
1618 22nd Street
NW, Washington DC 20008-1920
Tel: **(202) 483-7800**

CHAD
2002 R. Street
NW Washington DC 20009
Tel: **(202) 462-4009**

CHILE
1732 Massachusetts Avenue
NW, Washington DC 20036
Tel: **(202) 785-1746**

CHINA
2300 Connecticut Avenue
NW, Washington DC 20008
Tel: **(202) 328-2500**

COLOMBIA
2118 Leroy Place
NW, Washington DC 20008-1895
Tel: **(202) 387-8338**

CONGO
4891 Colorado Avenue
NW, Washington
DC 20011-3731
Tel: **(202) 725-5500**

COSTA RICA
1825 Connecticut Avenue
NW, #211, Washington DC 20009
Tel: **(202) 234-2945**

CUBAN INTERESTS
2630 & 2639 16th Street
NW, Washington DC 20009
Tel: **(202) 797-8518**

CYPRUS
2211 R Street
NW, Washington DC 20008-4017
Tel: **(202) 462-5772**

CZECH REPUBLIC
3900 Linnean Avenue
NW, Washington DC 20008-3897
Tel: **(202) 363-6315**

DENMARK
3200 White Haven Street
NW, Washington DC 20008
Tel: **(202) 234-4300**

DOMINICAN REPUBLIC
1715 22nd Street
NW, Washington DC 20008
Tel: **(202) 332-6280**

ECUADOR
2535 15th Street
NW, Washington DC 20009
Tel: **(202) 234-7200**

EGYPT
2300 Decatur Plaza
NW, Washington DC 20008
Tel: **(202) 232-5400**

EL SALVADOR
2308 California Street
NW, Washington DC 20008
Tel: **(202) 265-3480**

EQUATORIAL GUINEA
801 Second Avenue
Room 1403
New York
NY 10017
Tel: **(212) 599-1523**

ETHIOPIA
2134 Kalorama Road
NW, Washington DC 20008
Tel: **(202) 234-2281**

FIJI
2233 Wisconsin Avenue
NW, #240
Washington DC 20007
Tel: **(202) 337-8320**

FINLAND
3216 New Mexico Avenue
NW, Washington DC 20016-2782
Tel: **(202) 363-2430**

FRANCE
4101 Reservoir Road
NW, Washington DC 20007
Tel: **(202) 944-6000**

GABON
2034 20th Street
NW, Washington DC 20009
Tel: **(202) 797-1000**

GAMBIA
1030 15th Street
NW, #720
Washington DC 20005
Tel: **(202) 842-1356**

GERMANY
4645 Reservoir Road
NW, Washington DC 20007-1918
Tel: **(202) 298-4000**

GHANA
3512 International Drive
NW, Washington DC 20008
Tel: **(202) 686-4500**

GREECE
2221 Massachusetts Avenue
NW, Washington DC 20008-2873
Tel: **(202) 667-3168**

GRENADA
1701 New Hampshire Avenue
NW, Washington DC 20008
Tel: **(202) 265-2561**

GUATEMALA
2490 Tracy Place
NW, Washington DC 20008
Tel: **(202) 265-6900**

GUINEA
2112 Leroy Place
NW, Washington DC 20008
Tel: **(202) 483-9420**

GUINEA-BISSAU
211 East 43rd Street
Suite 604
New York
NY 10017
Tel: **(212) 661-3977**

GUYANA
2490 Tracy Place
NW, Washington DC 20008
Tel: **(202) 265-6900**

HAITI
2311 Massachusetts Avenue
NW, Washington DC 20008
Tel: **(202) 322-4090**

HONDURAS
3007 Tilden Street
Pod.4M
Washington DC 20008
Tel: **(202) 966-7702**

HUNGARY
3910 Shoemaker Street
NW, Washington DC 2008-3811
Tel: **(202) 362-6730**

ICELAND
2022 Connecticut Avenue
NW, Washington DC 20008-6194
Tel: **(202) 265-6653**

INDIA
2107 Massachusetts Avenue
NW, Washington DC 20008-2811
Tel: **(202) 939-7000**

INDONESIA
2020 Massachusetts Avenue
NW, Washington DC 20036
Tel: **(202) 775-5200**

IRAQ
1801 P Street
NW, Washington DC 20036
Tel: **(202) 483-7500**

IRELAND
2234 Massachusetts Avenue
NW, Washington DC 20008
Tel: **(202) 462-3939**

ISRAEL
3514 International Drive
NW, Washington DC 20008-3099
Tel: **(202) 364-5500**

ITALY
1601 Fuller Street
NW, Washington DC 20009
Tel: **(202) 328-5500**

COTE D'IVOIRE
2424 Massachusetts Avenue
NW, Washington DC 20008
Tel: **(202) 483-2400**

JAMAICA
1850 K Street
NW, #355
International Square Building
Washington DC 20006
Tel: **(202) 452-0660**

From 16 April 1995 all national and international change — see page 587 for details.

JAPAN
2520 Massachusettes Avenue
NW, Washington DC 20008
Tel: **(202) 234-2266**

JORDAN
3504 International Drive
NW, Washington DC 20008
Tel: **(202) 966-2664**

KENYA
2249 R Street
NW, Washington DC 20008
Tel: **(202) 387-6101**

KOREA (SOUTH)
2370 Massachusetts Avenue
NW, Washington DC 20008
Tel: **(202) 939-5600**

KUWAIT
2940 Tilden Street
NW, Washington DC 20008
Tel: **(202) 966-0702**

LAOS
2222 S Street
Washington DC 20008-4014
Tel: **(202) 332-6416**

LEBANON
2560 28th Street
NW, Washington DC 20008-2744
Tel: **(202) 939-6300**

LESOTHO
2511 Massachusetts Avenue
NW, Washington DC 20008-2823
Tel: **(202) 797-5533**

LIBERIA
5201 16th Street
Washington DC 20011
Tel: **(202) 723-0437**

LIBYA
309 East 48th Street
New York
NY 10017-1746
Tel: **(212) 752-5775**

LUXEMBOURG
220 Massachusetts Avenue
NW, Washington DC 20008
Tel: **(202) 265-4171**

MADAGASCAR
2373 Massachusetts Avenue
NW, Washington DC 20008
Tel: **(202) 265-5525**

MALAWI
2408 Massachusetts Avenue
NW, Washington DC 20008
Tel: **(202) 797-1007**

MALAYSIA
2401 Massachusetts Avenue
NW, Washington DC 20008
Tel: **(202) 328-2700**

MALI
2130 R Street
NW, Washington DC 20008-1907
Tel: **(202) 332-2249**

MAURITANIA
2129 Leroy Place
NW, Washington DC 20008-1848
Tel: **(202) 232-5700**

MAURITIUS
#134
Van Ness Centre
4301 Connecticut Avenue
NW, Washington DC 20008-2381
Tel: **(202) 244-1491**

MEXICO
2829 16th Street
NW, Washington
DC 20009
Tel: **(202) 234-6000**

MOROCCO
1601 21st Street
NW, Washington DC 20009
Tel: **(202) 462-3611**

NEPAL
2131 Leroy Place
NW, Washington DC 20008
Tel: **(202) 667-4550**

NETHERLANDS
4200 Linnean Avenue
NW, Washington DC 20008-1848
Tel: **(202) 244-5304**

NEW ZEALAND
37 Observatory Circle
NW, Washington DC 20008-3686
Tel: **(202) 328-4800**

NICARAGUA
1627 New Hampshire Avenue
NW, Washington DC 20009
Tel: **(202) 387-4371**

NIGER
2204 R Street
NW, Washington DC 20008-8001
Tel: **(202) 483-4224**

NIGERIA
2201 M Street
NW, Washington DC 20037
Tel: **(202) 822-1500**

NORWAY
2820 34th Street
NW, Washington DC 20008-2799
Tel: **(202) 333-6000**

From 16 April 1995 all national and international change — see page 587 for details.

OMAN
2342 Massachusetts Avenue
NW, Washington DC 20008
Tel: **(202) 387-1980**

PAKISTAN
2315 Massachusetts Avenue
NW, Washington DC 20008
Tel: **(202) 939-6200**

PANAMA
2862 McGill Terrace
NW, Washington DC 20008
Tel: **(202) 483-1407**

PARAGUAY
2400 Massachusetts Avenue
NW, Washington DC 20008
Tel: **(202) 483-6960**

PERU
1700 Massachusetts Avenue
NW, Washington DC 20036-1903
Tel: **(202) 833-9860**

PHILIPPINES
1617 Massachusetts Avenue
NW, Washington DC 20036
Tel: **(202) 483-1414**

POLAND
2640 16th Street
NW, Washington DC 20009-4202
Tel: **(202) 234-3800**

PORTUGAL
2125 Kalorama Road
NW, Washington DC 20008-1619
Tel: **(202) 328-8610**

QATAR
600 New Hampshire Avenue
NW, #1180
Washington DC 20037
Tel: **(202) 338-0111**

ROMANIA
1607 23rd Street
NW, Washington DC 20008-2809
Tel: **(202) 232-4747**

RUSSIA
1125 16th Street
NW, Washington 20036-4801
Tel: **(202) 628-7551**

RWANDA
1714 New Hampshire Avenue
NW, Washington DC 20009
Tel: **(202) 232-2882**

SAINT LUCIA
2100 M Street
NW, #309
Washington DC 20037
Tel: **(202) 463-7378**

WESTERN SAMOA
820 Second Street
#800
New York
NY 10017
Tel: **(212) 599-6196**

SAUDI ARABIA
601 New Hampshire Avenue
NW, Washington DC 20037
Tel: **(202) 342-3800**

SENEGAL
2112 Wyoming Avenue
NW, Washington DC 20008-3906
Tel: **(202) 234-0540**

SEYCHELLES
820 2nd Avenue
#900F
New York
NY 10017-4504
Tel: **(212) 687-9766**

SIERRA LEONE
1701 19th Street
NW, Washington DC 20009
Tel: **(202) 939-9261**

SINGAPORE
1824 R Street
NW, Washington DC 20009-1691
Tel: **(202) 265-7915**

SOMALIA
600 New Hampshire Avenue
NW, #710
Washington DC 20037
Tel: **(202) 342-1575**

SOUTH AFRICA
3051 Massachusetts Avenue
NW, Washington DC 20008-3693
Tel: **(202) 232-4400**

SPAIN
270 15th Street
NW, Washington DC 20009
Tel: **(202) 265-0190**

SRI LANKA
2148 Wyoming Avenue
NW, Washington DC 20008
Tel: **(202) 483-4025**

SUDAN
2210 Massachusetts Avenue
NW, Washington DC 20009-2812
Tel: **(202) 338-8565**

SWAZILAND
#441 Van Ness Centre
4301 Connecticut Avenue
NW, Washington DC 20008
Tel: **(202) 362-6683**

SWEDEN
600 New Hampshire Avenue
NW, #1200
Washington DC 20037-2462
Tel: **(202) 944-5600**

SWITZERLAND
2900 Cathedral Avenue
NW, Washington DC 20008-3405
Tel: **(202) 745-7900**

SURINAME
4301 Connecticut Avenue
NW, Suite 108
Washington DC 20008
Tel: **(202) 244-7488**

SYRIA
2215 Wyoming Avenue
NW, Washington DC 20008
Tel: **(202) 232-6313**

TANZANIA
2139 R Street
NW, Washington DC 20008
Tel: **(202) 939-6125**

THAILAND
2300 Kalorama Road
NW, Washington DC 20008
Tel: **(202) 483-7200**

TOGO
2208 Massachusetts Avenue
NW, Washington DC 20008
Tel: **(202) 234-4212**

TRINIDAD & TOBAGO
1708 Massachusetts Avenue
NW, Washington DC 20036
Tel: **(202) 467-6490**

TUNISIA
1515 Massachusetts Avenue
NW, Washington DC 20005
Tel: **(202) 234-6644**

TURKEY
1606 23rd Street
NW, Washington DC 20008
Tel: **(202) 387-3200**

UGANDA
5909 16th Street
NW, Washington DC 20011-2816
Tel: **(202) 726 7100**

UNITED ARAB EMIRATES
600 New Hampshire Avenue
NW, #740
Washington DC 20037
Tel: **(202) 338-6500**

UNITED KINGDOM
3100 Massachusetts Avenue
NW, Washington DC 20008
Tel: **(202) 462-1340**

URUGUAY
1918 F Avenue
NW, Washington DC 20006
Tel: **(202) 331-1313**

VENEZUELA
2445 Massachusetts Avenue
NW, Washington DC 20008-2805
Tel: **(202) 797-3800**

YEMEN
600 New Hampshire Avenue
NW, #840
Washington DC 20037
Tel: **(202) 965-4760**

THE FORMER REPUBLIC OF YUGOSLAVIA
2410 California Street
NW, Washington DC 20008-1697
Tel: **(202) 462-6566**

ZAIRE
1800 New Hampshire Avenue
NW, Washington DC 20009-1697
Tel: **(202) 234-7690**

ZAMBIA
2419 Massachusetts Avenue
NW, Washington DC 20008-2805
Tel: **(202) 265-9717**

PASSPORT OFFICES IN THE UK

Clive House
70-78 Petty France
London SW1H 9HD
Tel: **071-279 3434**

5th Floor
India Buildings
Water Street
Liverpool L2 0QZ
Tel: **051-237 3010**

Olympia House
Upper Dock Street
Newport
Gwent NP9 1XA
Tel: **0633-244500**

Aragon Court
Northminster Road
Peterborough
Cambs PE1 1QG
Tel: **0733-894445**

3 Northgate
96 Milton Street
Cowcaddams
Glasgow G4 0BT
Tel: **041-332 0271**

TRAVEL INSURANCE SPECIALISTS

Automobile Association
Fanum House
Leicester Square
London W1
Tel: **0345 500600** (General enquiries)
*Has a reasonably priced scheme to cover over-
land travel abroad. Will also provide carnets
and Green Cards.*

Assist-Card
745 Fifth Avenue
New York
NY 10022
Tel: **(212) 752 2788**
Outside New York **1-800-221-4564**
*An organization to help with travel crises such
as loss of passport, illness, theft. legal trouble.
Cardholders may telephone the office (collect)
from 28 European countries and both North and
South American countries. A multilingual staff
is on call 24 hours a day.*

Hanover Insurance Brokers
80-86 Westow St
Upper Norwood SE19 3AF
Tel: **081-771 8844**
*Can arrange insurance on motor vehicles of most
types in the UK throughout the whole of Europe
including the C.I.S.. Other countries in Near
Middle and Far East as well as Africa are available by special arrangement for which a full
itinerary should be sent. They can obtain cover
for sea transit of vehicles to countries other than
those mentioned and for goods and equipment to
all ports of the world. They also offer personal
accident, sickness and baggage insurance.*

Campbell Irvine Ltd
48 Earls Court Road
Kensington
London W8 6EJ
Tel: **071-937 6981**
*Specialize in unusual insurance and can offer
travellers insurance against medical expenses,
repatriation, personal accident, cancellation and
curtailment and personal liability, also baggage
and money cover subject to certain restrictions.
Vehicle insurance can be arranged and usually
takes the form of Third Party insurance (for countries where British insurers have adequate representation), accidental damage, fire and theft
insurance (worldwide, including sea transit risks)
Carnet Indemnity insurance is available in order
that travellers can obtain carnet de passages documents from the Automobile Association. Will
also do quotations for expeditions.*

**Centre de Documentation et d'Information
de l'Assurance**
2 Rue de la Chassee d'Antin
75009 Paris, France
Tel: **4247 9000**
*Will give advice to travellers on insurance
problems.*

R.L. Davison & Co Ltd
Lloyd's Insurance Brokers
5 Stone House
London EC3A 7AX
Tel: **071-377 9876**
Offer Carnet Indemnity insurance.

Kemper Group
Long Grove
IL 60049, USA
*Offer a 12-month travel accident policy which
gives the same cover and at the same premium
as the insurance offered at airport terminals for
only 21 days' cover. The policy, which must be
ordered a week in advance, covers approved
charter flights.*

**Medisure Frizzell Insurance and Financial
Services Ltd**
Frizzell House
County Gates
Poole BH13 6BH
Tel: **(0202) 292 333**
*Medisure is a medical insurance scheme which
pays for National Health Service emergency
hospital treatment for overseas visitors not covered by reciprocal agreements. Premium payment can be made at any Post Office in the
United Kingdom and application forms are
available from Post Offices at Heathrow,
Birmingham, Wolverhampton and Leicester
and from Frizzell's in Poole. Advice is obtainable 24 hours a day on an emergency telephone
line.*

Pinon Assureur
8 Rue de Liège
75009 Paris, France
Tel: **4878 0298/9530**
*Is one of the rare insurance companies that will
insure cameras and photographic equipment.
Premiums amount to about 3 per cent of the
value of the items insured and the firm will
insure for a minimum premium of 650 Francs.*

WEXAS International
45-49 Brompton Road
London SW3 1DE
Tel: **01-589 3315**
*Offers members a comprehensive range of trav-
el insurance packages at extremely competitive
prices, Including a year-round policy allowing
any number of journeys lasting no more than
three months.*

CURRENCY RESTRICTIONS

Many countries impose restrictions on the import or export of local and foreign currency. Often these take the form of ceilings, normally reasonably generous, so that the traveller should rarely be aware of their existence. However, it is worth checking every country you intend to visit.

The following is a list applicable at the time of going to press, of currency regulations which may impinge on the traveller. The list is not comprehensive, as those countries with no restrictions, or restrictions relating only to residents are not included.

KEY TO COLUMNS
(1) Import of local currency prohibited.
(2) Export of local currency prohibited.
(3) Foreign currency may be imported but must be declared.
(4) Foreign currency may be exported by non-residents up to the amount imported and declared.
(5) Other.

Country	(1)	(2)	(3)	(4)	(5)
Afghanistan	yes	yes	yes	yes	Import of local currency is restricted to Af2000 and export to Af500
Albania	yes	yes	yes	yes	
Algeria	yes		yes		Non-residents must change a min. of DZD1000 on arrival. May re-export amounts above this only
Angola	yes	yes	yes		Local currency import limit of AKZ15,000. Export of local currency prohibited; up to AKZ5000 equivalent of foreign currency may be exported by those leaving on a return ticket purchased in Angola
Anguilla					Free import and export of local and foreign currency
Antigua & Barb.					Free import and export of local and foreign currency
Aruba					Free import and export of local and foreign currency
Australia					Export restricted to A$5000 unless specially authorised
Austria					No limit on exporting foreign currency, or Austrian currency, but advance permission is needed to take out more than Sch 100,000
Bahamas		no			Prior permission of the Central Bank of Bahamas required for the export of local currency in excess of Ba$70
Bangladesh	no	no	yes	yes	Only Tk100 may be imported or exported in local currency. On departure, up to Tk500 may be reconverted
Barbados					Free import of local currency, subject to declaration
Belize		no	yes	yes	Up to Bze$100 may be exported or imported in local without permission
Benin	no	no	yes	no	Export limited to CFAFr25,000
Bermuda	no	yes	yes	yes	Up to B$250 can be exported in local currency without permission

British Virgin Islands			yes	yes	
Brunei	no	no	yes	yes	Can take in or out up to B$1000 in banknotes of local or Singaporean currency. Indonesian and Indian banknotes prohibited
Bulgaria	yes	yes	yes	yes	
Burundi			yes	yes	Import and export of local currency limited to BuFr2000
Cameroon		no			Up to CFAFr20,000 can be exported
Cape Verde	yes	yes	yes	yes	Maximum allowable export of foreign currency is the equivalent of CVE20,000 or the amount declared, whichever is the larger
Cayman Islands					No restriction on the import or export of local or foreign currency
Central African Republic	no	no	yes	yes	Can export up to CFAFr25,000
Chad	no	no	yes	yes	Up to CFAFr10,000 can be exported in local currency
Chile					No restrictions on the import or export of local or foreign currency
China	yes	yes	yes	yes	
Colombia	no	no	yes	yes	Import and export of local currency limited to Col$7000 approx.
Congo	no	no	yes	yes	Up to CFAFr10,000 can be exported in local currency
Costa Rica					No restrictions
Cote d'Ivoire			yes		Import of foreign and local currencies is unlimited, but if other than the French Franc or CFA Franc, must be declared
Cuba	yes	yes	yes	no	Maximum of Cub$10 may be re-converted when exporting foreign currency
Cyprus	no	no	no	no	Can import and export up to C$50. Foreign currency, except Sterling, must be declared on entry
Czech Republic	yes	yes			
Denmark	no	no	yes	yes	Export of Danish currency is limited to the amount declared on import
Dominica		yes	yes	yes	Export of foreign currency up to US$50
Dominican Rep.	yes	yes	yes	yes	
Egypt	no	no	yes	yes	Import and export of local currency is limited to E£20
Equatorial Guinea	no	yes	no	no	Export of local currency is limited to CFA Fr20,000
Ethiopia	no	no			Up to ETB10 may be imported in local currency

Finland	no	no			Local currency of up to FIM10,000 may be exported
France	no	yes	no	no	There is a limit of FFr12,000 unless you have declared a higher amount on arrival
Gabon	no	yes	no	yes	Up to CFAFr25,000 may be taken out in local currency
Gambia					Will not accept currencies of Algeria, Ghana, Guinea Rep., Morocco, Nigeria, Sierra Leone and Tunisia
Germany					No restrictions
Ghana	no	no	yes	yes	Local currency import or export limited to C40. Unused currencies may be re-exchanged on presentation of a form to show that they were obtained from an authorized dealer while in Ghana
Gibraltar					No restrictions
Greece	no	no	no	yes	Up to DRA100,000 may be imported in local currency. Export limit is Dr20,000
Guinea Rep.	no	no	yes	yes	Import or export of Guinea currency is limited to FG5000
Guinea-Bissau	yes	yes	yes	yes	
Guyana	no	no			Up to G$40 may be imported or exported in local currency
Honduras					No restrictions on import but US$ must be declared. All visitors required to import minimum of US $100
Hungary	no	no	yes	yes	Import and export of local currency limited to FOR100
Iceland	no	no	yes	yes	Up to IKr8000 may be imported or exported in local currency
India	yes	yes	yes	yes	Must declare any currency above a value of US$1000
Indonesia	no	no	no	no	Up to Rp50,000 allowed in or out in local currency
Iran	no	no	yes	yes	May bring in or take out up to RL20,000 in local currency. Export of local currency limit is RL5000
Iraq	no	no	yes	yes	Import of local currency limited to ID5, export to ID100
Ireland	no	no	yes	yes	Max. of IRL100 in local currency may be taken out. May only export up to IRL500 in foreign currency if not declared on entry
Israel	no	no	yes	yes	A maximum of NIS500 in local currency may be exported. Up to US$3000 may be reconverted on provision of exchange receipts
Italy					No limit to amount of local currency allowed in and out of the country. Re-export of more than L5,000,000 requires V2 form, obtained on arrival
Jamaica	no	no	yes	yes	Import and export of local currency is limited to J$20

Japan	no	no	no	no	A max. of 5 million yen may be exported in local currency
Jordan	no	no	yes	yes	May export up to JD300 in local currency
Kenya	yes	yes	yes	yes	Each visitor is required to carry equivalent of £250 sterling for maintenance
North Korea	yes	yes	yes	yes	
South Korea	no	no	yes	yes	Import or export limit for local currency 500,000won. Any currency over US$10,000 in value must be declared on arrival
Libya	yes	yes	yes	yes	Tourists are expected to spend a minimum of US$50 equivalent
Madagascar	no	no	yes	yes	Can take in or out up to FMG5000 in local currency
Malawi	no	no	yes	yes	May import or export up to MWK20 in local currency
Mali	no	no	yes	yes	Export of local currency limited to CFA Fr50,000
Malta	no	no	yes	yes	Movement of local currency is limited to Lm50 coming in and Lm25 leaving per person
Mauritania	yes	yes	yes	yes	
Mauritius	no	no	yes	yes	Allowed to bring in MR700 and take out MR350 in local currency
Mexico					No restrictions
Mongolia	yes	yes	yes	yes	
Montserrat	no	no	yes	yes	
Morocco	yes	yes	yes	yes	Foreign currency over the value of Dh15,000 must be declared
Mozambique	yes	yes	yes	yes	Visitors must exchange minimum equivalent to US$30
Myanmar	yes	yes	yes	yes	A minimum equivalent to US$100 must be exchanged on entry. Only a quarter of the foreign currency converted to Kyats during stay in Myanmar can be re-converted on exit
Nepal	yes	yes	yes	yes	Indian currency also prohibited. May only reconvert 15% of amount converted
Netherland Antilles			no	no	A max. of NAf200 may be imported or exported in local currency
New Caledonia			yes	yes	
New Zealand					No restrictions
Niger	no	no	yes	yes	A max. of CFA Fr25,000 may be exported in local currency, and CFA Fr175,000 in foreign currency
Nigeria	no	no	yes	yes	May import or export up to NGN20 in local notes. The equivalent of US$100

Niue		no	yes	yes	Can export up to NZ$100 in local currency. Must get authorisation from a bank for export of foreign exchange
Norway	no	no	yes	yes	A maximum of Kr5000 local currency may be taken out of the country
Pakistan	no	no	yes	yes	May take up to PR100 in or out in local currency
Papua New Guinea	no	yes	yes	yes	
Philippines	no	no	yes	yes	May take out up to PP500 in local currency. Import of over US$3000 must be declared
Poland					No restrictions
Portugal	no	no	yes	yes	You can export up to ESP100,000 cash, or equivalent of Esc500,000 in foreign currency. Or more if can show that a greater amount was imported
Romania	yes	yes			
Russian Fed.	yes	yes	yes	yes	
Rwanda	no	no	yes	yes	Up to FRW5000 may be imported or exported in local currency
St Christopher & Nevis					No restrictions. Free import of local currency, subject to declaration; export limited to amount declared
St Vincent & the Grenadines					No restrictions. Free import of local currency subject to declaration
Sao Tomé & Principe	yes	yes	yes	yes	Export of foreign currency limited to STD30,000 or equivalent, unless declared on arrival
Senegal	no	no	yes	yes	May export up to CFA Fr20,000 local currency, CFA50,000 without declaration on entry
Sierra Leone	no	no	yes	yes	May import or export Le20 in local currency
Solomon Islands	no	no	yes	yes	Export of local currency limited to SBD250
Somalia	no	no	yes	yes	May take in or out SOS 200 in local currency
South Africa	no	no	yes	yes	Up to R500 may be taken in or out in local banknotes
Spain					No formal limits on import, but if taking in more than PTS100,000 in local currency and PTS500,000 in foreign currency you should declare it. Can export up to PTS100,000 in local currency
Sri Lanka	no	no	yes	yes	The import and export of local currency is limited to RS250. The import of Indian and Pakistani currency is also prohibited
Sudan	yes	yes	no	no	
Suriname	no	no	yes	yes	Up to SF100 may be imported or exported in local currency

Sweden				No restrictions
Syria	no	no	yes	yes	Must change US$100 or equivalent on arrival. Local currency export limit of S£100
Taiwan	no	no	yes	yes	Export limit of NT$8000 in local currency, US$5000 or equivalent foreign currency for passengers leaving within 6 months
Tanzania	yes	yes	yes	yes	Export of local currency limited to TS100
Thailand	no	no	yes	yes	You may take in up to BHT2000 per person or BHT4000 per family and take out up to BHT500 per person in local currency. You may take in or out up to US$10,000 in foreign currency without declaring it
Togo	no	no	yes	yes	
Trinidad and Tobago	no	no	yes	yes	Import and export of local currency is limited to TT$200
Tunisia	yes	yes	no	no	Import of over £500 must be declared. May re-exchange 30% of local into foreign currency up to a max. of TUD100
Turkey	no	no	yes	yes	Can export up to equivalent of US$5000 in local currency
Uganda	yes	yes	yes	yes	Visitors must cash US$150 into Ugandan shillings on arrival. On departure, must show have cashed a minimum of $30/day
USA	no	no	yes	yes	Must declare anything over US$10,000 or equivalent
Vietnam	yes	yes	yes	yes	
Yemen	no	no	yes	yes	May import or export up to YEM5000 or equivalent in local currency
The Former Rep. of Yugoslavia	no	no			May import or export up to YD1200 in local currency
Zaire	yes	yes	yes	yes	
Zambia	no	no	yes	yes	A maximum of K20 can be taken in or out in local currency
Zimbabwe	no	no	yes	yes	A maximum of Z$40 can be taken in or out in local currency

WORKING RESTRICTIONS WORLDWIDE

Afghanistan	No work visas at present
Algeria	Only possible if with a company that has a govt. contract. Need a work permit if staying more than 3 months and must produce diplomas.
Andorra	There is an annual allocation of work permits that must be applied for personally in Andorra - after the applicant has secured a position.
Antigua & Barbuda	Work permits required. You can only work if locals cannot perform the function. Must arrange the permit in advance.
Argentina	Need a work permit.
Australia	Must have a work permit - not easy to get hold of.
Austria	Work permits are required for all types of employment, but are never issued for part-time employment.
Bahamas	Need a work permit, but no expatriate may be offered employment in a post for which a suitably qualified Bahamian is available. You may not apply once in the country. Rigidly enforced.
Bahrain	Employer must get permit in Bahrain and send it to the employee to be stamped by the embassy in his or her own country. Difficult to get renewed.
Barbados	Must have sponsorship from a local employer. Permits only given to people with specialist skills needed by the country.
Bangladesh	Can work for up to three months without a permit.
Barbados	Work permits are issued to employers not employees - you must apply for a job before hand.
Belgium	The Belgian employer must apply for the permit.
Belize	Work permit required. Must have job offer for which there are no suitable nationals. Apply to Ministry of Labour, Belmopan.
Bhutan	Can work by government invitation only.
Bermuda	Must have a job and work permit before entering.
Benin	Need to have a contract with a company of the Benin Government before applying.
Bolivia	Only residents in Bolivia are allowed employment.
Botswana	Need work permit. No rigid restrictions and there are usually jobs available.
Brazil	Working visas are only issued on the presentation of a work contract, duly certified by the Brazilian Ministry of Labour.
British Virgin Islands	Work permit required.
Brunei	Work permit required in all cases. Must be proposed by a registered Brunei company and have trade qualifications and experience above those available locally.
Bulgaria	It is not possible to get a work permit.
Cameroon	You need a work permit, which can be obtained in the Cameroon.
Canada	Work permit required. Must apply from outside the country. Will not be granted if there is a permanent resident or qualified Canadian for the job.
Cayman Islands	You must satisfy the Cayman Protection Board that no local can do the job to get a work permit. Contact the Dept. of Immigration. Permits for 1-5 years usually granted to professionals.
Chile	Must have a contract with a company before applying.
China	No work unless either a teacher or technician when one works under contract.
Cocos (Keeling Islands)	All non-locals work for the Australian Govt. No casual work available.

Colombia	Work visa needed. Normally for 2 years at a time. Renewable. Only granted for work no national can do.
Cook Islands	Apply to New Zealand High Commission for temporary residence permit. Not normally given unless you have special skills not available locally.
Costa Rica	Need a signed contract with employer and 'resident' status to be able to work.
Cote d'Ivorie	You are not allowed to work here unless sent by a private company which will arrange your permit for you.
Cuba	It is not possible to work here.
Cyprus	Work permit needed - must be obtained by employer. Usually granted for one year but can be renewed. Can be prosecuted and deported for working without one.
Czech Republic	Permission to work involves a complicated procedure - enquire at embassy before you go.
Denmark	Nationals of EC countries do not need permits. Others do, but they are not being issued at present.
Djibouti	Not much work available.
Dominica	Need work permit obtained from country of origin.
Dominican Republic	Work permit required.
Eastern Caribbean	Work permit offered only if a national cannot do the job.
Ecuador	Work permit required. Available only if being brought in by an Ecuadorean company for professional reasons (ie. training, or for your specialist skills). Must register permit on arrival.
El Salvador	Work permit can be obtained for technical or specialized work. Employer must apply.
Ethiopia	Employer must apply on your behalf to Ministry of Labour and Social Affairs. Casual work forbidden.
Falkland Islands	Employer must apply for work permit.
Fiji	Need a work permit before entering Fiji. Rarely given.
Finland	Work permit required.
France	Nationals of EC countries do not need work permits. Others do.
Gabon	Work permit required.
Gambia	Work permit required.
Germany	Nationals of EC countries do not need permits. Others do, but they are only issued once work has been found.
Ghana	Work permit required.
Gibraltar	All foreign nationals except the British need work permits.
Greece	Need a permit issued by the Greek Ministry of Labour. Yearly, renewable. Employer should also apply.
Grenada	Work permit needed.
Guadeloupe	EC nationals don't need work permits; others do.
Guyana	Work permit needed.
Haiti	First need to get a Permit de Sejour, then your employers must apply for a work permit for you.
Hong Kong	You need a work permit if working in the private sector but not if working for the Hong Kong Government or a UK citizen.
Hungary	Work permit needed. Only granted if you are immigrating permanently. Apply to Foreign Nationals Office, Budapest Police HQ.
Iceland	Need a work permit prior to arrival - prospective employer should apply and prove no suitable Icelander is available. Permits renewable yearly.

India	No permit is needed, but you cannot take the money earned out.
Indonesia	Apply for the work permit through Foreign Affairs Dept. and the Dept. of Manpower. Getting more difficult and impossible for casual work. Must have a skill not available locally.
Ireland	Not required by EC citizens, but needed by all others.
Iran	Work permit required.
Iraq	Work permit may be arranged by foreign companies working in Iraq. Otherwise it is impossible.
Israel	Apply to the embassy in your home country with letter from your potential employer.
Italy	Nationals of EC countries may work without permits. All others need them.
Jamaica	Work permit required.
Japan	Long-term commercial business visa is needed if working for your own company in Japan. Others require work permits. Can do part-time casual work on a study visa.
Jordan	You can only get work through a local company or a foreign company's local offices.
Kenya	Prospective employer in Kenya must obtain a permit for you before you arrive. Heavy fines/deportation for working without a permit.
South Korea	Need a work permit from the Korean embassy in your normal country of residence.
Kuwait	Need a contract from Kuwait before the permit will be issued. No casual work. Can get 2 year contracts for specialist jobs.
Lesotho	Employer must apply and prove no local is suitable. Permits for 2 years but renewable.
Liberia	Work permit required. Must go to Ministry of Labour and Immigration and Labour. Permits valid for one year but can be renewed.
Liechtenstein	Very rare to be granted a permit.
Luxembourg	EC citizens may work without a permit. All other nationals require one.
Macao	Work permit
Madagascar	Not required if working for a cultural institution such as the American School. Most expats working for the govt. More difficult for individuals.
Malawi	Work permit required
Malaysia	Work permit required. You need a sponsor in Malaysia who agrees to assure your maintenance and repatriation.
Malta	Permits only issued for specialized skills not found on the island.
Mauritius	Work permit required. Must provide good reasons and only available if no local can do the job. Permits usually for one or two years, renewable. Fee payable.
Mexico	No work allowed unless you are specifically requested by a Mexican company.
Morocco	Work permit required. Employer must apply. Permit included with residence certificate.
Myanmar	Government approval required.
Nepal	Work permits required. Complex process - usually only possible for aid/embassy staff, govt. projects and airlines.
Netherlands	EC citizens do not need work permits. All other nationalities do.
New Zealand	All nationalities except Australian need a work permit.

Nigeria	Work permit compulsory for all foreigners. Employers are given a yearly quota. Two years, renewable. Some expat wives can get part-time `unofficial' work.
Norway	Work permit required.
Oman	Work permit required. Need a sponsor - either an Omani company or Omani national. Two years' renewable permits for specific employment. Casual labour not allowed.
Panama	Permit required. Apply in Panama.
Papua New Guinea	Permit required - usually for a 3 year contract - obtained before arrival. Must be sponsored by an employer. Casual work not allowed.
Paraguay	No permit needed.
Peru	Arrange everything in Peru
Philippines	Permit required. Only if you already have a job. Employer should apply.
Poland	Foreigners cannot work in Poland.
Portugal	Work permit required.
Qatar	Must have sponsorship and resident's status. Work permit must be obtained by employer.
American Samoa	Severe restrictions. Immigration approval is necessary first, and this is only granted for special needs and skills that cannot be satisfied locally.
Saudi Arabia	Must obtain job and residence permit before arrival. Formalities horribly complicated, so leave it to your employer.
Senegal	Work permits can be obtained in Dakar with great difficulty for working with international or private organizations. Impossible for semi-private or official companies.
Seychelles	Apply for a Gainful Occupation Permit. Permit granted only if the job cannot be filled locally and for the duration of the contract. Difficult and expensive to get without political connections.
Sierra Leone	Required even for casual labour. Apply to Principal Immigration Officer, who is secretary of the Business Immigration Quota Committee.
Singapore	All non-residents require work permit. Apply to Ministry of Labour and Dept. of Immigration.
South Africa	Not allowed to accept employment without special permission from the Director General, Internal Affairs.
Spain	Permit needed to work legally.
Sri Lanka	Cannot work without Government approval which is rarely given. 1 year permits occasionally granted for specific projects.
St. Christopher & Nevis	Permits required but will only be granted when no national is available. Apply to Ministry of Home Affairs
Sudan	Permits required. Available for aid workers etc. but more difficult for others.
Swaziland	Work permit required
Sweden	Work permit required
Switzerland	Work permit required. Employer must apply. Permit renewable annually.
Syria	Work permits required, but whether you'll get one depends on who you'd be working for.
Tahiti	Work permit difficult to obtain. Employer must apply and ensure the employee's return to his country of origin.
Tanzania	Work permit required. Employer must apply on your behalf. If you haven't got a job, write to the ministry concerned with your field to offer your services.

Tibet	Generally no foreigners allowed to work, but a few teachers are being given one year contracts for Lhasa.
Togo	Work permit required.
Tonga	Work permit required. Length of permit depends on individual circumstances.
Trinidad & Tobago	Work permit required. Employer must apply.
Tunisia	Work permit required. Need a job contract before applying to the Ministry of Social Affairs. Only for those skills unobtainable in the country.
Turkey	Working visa required. Minimal restrictions but must apply through prospective employer
Turks and Caicos	Work permit required.
Uganda	Work permits required - restricted and difficult to obtain. Normally granted for a max. of 3 years for those with skills lacking in Uganda.
United Arab Emirates	Work permit needed. No casual work and permit must be obtained before arrival. Permit normally for 2/3 years dependent on job/nationality. Must be sponsored by a UAE-based company or individual.
United Kingdom	Commonwealth nationals aged 17 to 27 can work for two years on a holiday visa. All others (apart from EC) need a work permit.
US Virgin Islands	Work permit required.
United States	Work permit (Green Card) required for permanent jobs. Difficult to obtain. Some types of work allowed under exchange or temporary workers' visas.
Uruguay	Work permit needed.
Vanuatu	Work permit required. Given to people in positions which locals can't fill for 1 year.
Zambia	Work permit must be arranged by your employer before you enter. Will only be given for skills not obtainable locally.
Zimbabwe	Apply for a work permit through your prospective employer. Max. stay as an expat usually 3 years. ■

A PLACE TO STAY
Section 10

CAMPING ASSOCIATIONS

Camp and Cabin Association
4A Kanawa Street
Waikanae
New Zealand

Camping and Caravanning Club
Green Fields House
Westwood Way
Coventry CV4 8SH
Tel: **0203 694995**

Camping and Caravanverband der DDR
Helmut Koch Lichtenberger Str.27
DDR-1020
Berlin
Germany

Canadian Camping Association
1806 Avenue Road,
#2 Toronto ON M5M 3Z1
Canada
Tel: **416-781 4717**

The Caravan Club
East Grinstead House
East Grinstead
West Sussex RH19 1UA
Tel: **0342-326 944**

Federation Francaise de Camping et de Caravaning
78 rue de Rivoli
F-75004 Paris
France
Tel: **42-728408**

Federacion Internacional de Campings
Edificion Espana
Grupo 4 Pl.11
E-28013 Madrid
Spain
Tel: **1-242 1089**

Federazione Italiana del Campeggio e del Caravannia
PO Box 23
Via V Emanuelle 11
1-50041 Florence
Italy
Tel: **55-882391**

Campgrounds of America
PO Box 30558
Billings MT 59114
USA
Tel: **406-248 7444**

Motor Camping America
PO Box 127
8189 Valleyview Road
Custer
WA 98240
USA

National Campground Owners Association
11706 Bowman Green
Reston
VA 22090
USA
Tel: **703-471 0143**

Netherlands Camping Reservation Service
Het Kolkije 4
NL-7606 CA Almelo
Netherlands
Tel: **5490-18767**

Outdoor Recreation Information Centre
Art Centre
Worcester Street
Christchurch
New Zealand
Tel: **3-799395**

From 16 April 1995 all national and international codes change — see page 587 for details.

SELF-CATERING HOLIDAYS

Alpine Homes
The Red House
Garstons Close
Titchfield
Fareham PO14 4EW
Tel: **0329 844405**
Alpine village homes.

American Dream Holidays
Station Parade
High St North
London E6 1JD
Tel: **081-470 1181**
Villas and apartments in Hawaii and Florida

Austravel
44 Colcton Street
Bristol BS1 5AX
Tel: **0272 277425**
Apartments in Australia and New Zealand.

Brittany Ferries
Millbay Docks
Plymouth
Devon PL1 3EW
Tel: **0705-751708**
Brittany, the Dordogne.

English Tourist Board
Thames Tower
Black's Road
Hammersmith
London W6 9EL
Tel: **081-846 9000**

Interhomes
383 Richmond Road
Twickenham
Middlesex TW1 2EF
Tel: **081-891 1294**
Apartments, chalets, villas all over Europe.

Landmark Trust
Shotterbroke
Maidenhead
Berkshire SL6 3SW
Tel: **062 882 5925**

The Meridian Travel Co
28b High Street
Hampstead
London NW3 1QA
Tel: **071-431 5393**
Traditional Scandinavian summer houses.

Meon Travel
Meon House
College Street

Petersfield
Hampshire GU32 3JN
Tel: **0730 261926**
Villas in Corfu.

National Trust Holiday Cottages
36 Queen Anne's Gate
London SW1
Tel: **071-222 9251**

P & O European Ferries
Channel House
Channel View Road
Dover
Kent CT17 9TJ
Tel: **0304-214422**

Sealink Holidays
Charter House
Park Street
Ashford
Kent TN24 8EX
Tel: **0233-647033**
Cote d'Azur, Brittany, the Dordogne, the Loire, Costa Brava.

Simply Caribbean
3 Victoria Avenue
Harrogate HG1 1EQ
Tel: **0423 526887**
Apartments in Bermuda.

Villas Italia
13 Hillgate Street
London W8 7SP
Tel: **071-221 4432**
Villas in Italy.

MAIN HOTEL CHAIN RESERVATION NUMBERS

Apart Hotels International
UK **081-446 0126**

Best Western
Australia **2-212 6444** Fax: 2-281 2395
New Zealand **9-5205 418** Fax: 9-5205 413
USA **602-957 4200** Fax: 602-780 6099
UK **081-541 0050** Fax: 081-546 1638

Choice Hotels International
USA **0800 544 4444** Fax: 301-681 7478
UK **071-928 3333** Tlx: 295004

Ciga Hotels
USA **212-935 9540** Fax 2-29003595
UK **071-930 4147** Fax: 071-839 1566
Canada **800 955 2442**

Concorde Hotels
UK 071-630 1704 Fax: 071-630 0391
USA 800-888 4747 Fax: 212-752 8916

Forte Hotels Inc.
UK 0345-404040
USA 2212-686 4081 Fax: 212-686 5054
Australia 2-267 2144

Four Seasons Hotels
UK 0800 526648
Australia 2-247 13131
Canada 416-449 1750 Fax: 416-441 4374

Golden Tulip International
UK 0800-951000
USA 800-344 1212

Hilton International
Australia 2-266 0610
UK 071-602 0022 Fax: 0923-817319
USA 212-973 2200

Holiday Inns International
UK 0800-897121
USA 404-604 2000 Fax: 404-604 2782
Australia 2-261 4922 Fax: 2-264 3733

Hyatt
Australia 008-222 188 Fax: 2-237 3619
UK 071-580 8197 Fax: 081-785 4572
USA 800-233 1234 Fax: 3-490 31 09

Inter-Continental
Australia 008-22 1335
USA 800-327 0200
UK 081-847 2277

Inter-Europe Hotels
UK 081-446 1306
USA 800-221 6509

Leading Hotels of the World
UK 0800 181 123 Fax: 071-353 1904
USA 800-223 6800 Fax: 212-758 7367
Australia 2-233 8422 Fax: 2-223 5372

Loews Representation International
UK 081-941 7400 Fax: 081-941 5168
USA 212-545 2000 Fax: 212-545 2468
Australia 2-233 7351 Fax: 2-212 1750

Mandarin Oriental
UK 0800-526 6566
USA 212-7529710
Australia 2-957 5529

Marriott Hotels and Resorts
Australia 008-251259 Fax: 2-299 5895
UK 071-434 2299 Fax: 071-287 2979
USA 301-380 9000 Fax: 301-897 5045

Meridien Hotels
UK 071-439 1244
USA 800-543 4300
Australia 2-235 1311

New Otani Co
UK 071-731 1002 Fax: 071-437 1004
USA 212-308 7491 Fax: 212-980 1932

Nikko Hotels International
UK 0800 282502
USA 800-645 5687

Oberoi Hotels International
UK 081-788 2070 Fax: 081-789 5369
USA 212-682 7655 Fax: 212-983 5692
Australia 2-274 6061 Fax: 2-247 8850

Preferred Hotels and Resorts Worldwide
UK 0800 893391
Australia 2-247 6537

Ramada Hotels International
UK 0800-18173 Fax: 0293-823923
USA 800-854 7854 Fax: 310-339 8925
Australia 008-222 431 Fax 2-251 8491

Regent International Hotels
UK 071-371 7999 Fax: 071-371 7692
USA 212-980 0101 Fax: 212-980 8270
Australia 2-251 3755 Fax: 2-251 2406

SRS Hotels Steigenberger Reservation Service
UK 071-323 0127 Fax: 071-323 0129
USA 212-956 0200 Fax: 212-956 2555
Australia 2-241 3377 Fax: 2-241 3584

ITT Sheraton Group
UK 0800 353 535
USA 617-367 3600 Fax: 617-367 5676

Southern Pacific Hotel Corporation
UK 0345-404040 Fax: 071-494 1709
USA 310-557 2292 Fax: 310-557 0870
Australia 2-267 2144 Fax: 2-290 2265

Supernational Hotels
UK 071-937 8033 Fax: 071-938 3658
USA 800-843 3311

Utell
Australia 008-22 1176 Fax:2-419 6533
UK 071-413 8881 Fax: 071-413 8883
USA 402-398 3200 Fax: 402-398 5484

Further reading:
Official Hotel Guide (3 volumes) - Published annually by Reed Travel Group

HOSTELLING ASSOCIATIONS

Listed below are a selection of Hostelling Associations. Virtually every single country in the world has an Hostel Association or at least an Associate Organization. For further contact addresses the International Youth Hostel Federation annually publishes the Hostelling international Book (2 Volumes).

Algeria

Federation Algerienne des Auberges de Jeunesse
213 Rue Hassiba Ben Bouali
BP 15
El-Annasser 16015
Algeria
Tel: **2-670321**

America

American Youth Hostels
National Offices
PO Box 37613
Washington DC 20013-7613
USA
Tel: **202-783 6161**

Austria

Osterreichischer Jegendherbergsverband
1010 Wien
Schottenring 28
Austria
Tel: **43-1-533 5353**

Australia

Australian Youth Hostels Association Inc
Level 3
10 Mallett Street
Camperdown
New South Wales 2050
Tel: **565 1699**

Belgium

Centrale Wallonne des Auberges de la Jeuness
rue Van Oost 52
B-1030
Bruxelles
Belgium
Tel: **322-215 3100**

Canada

Canadian Hostelling Association
1600 James Naismith Drive
Suite 608
Gloucester
Ontario K1B 5NG
Tel: **613-748 5638**

Cyprus

Cyprus Youth Hostel Association
34th Theodotou St
PO Box 1328
Nicosia
Cyprus
Tel: **442027**

Czech and Slovak Republic

KMC Club of Young Travellers
Zaroliny Svetle 30
Prague 1
Czech Republic
Tel: **4 22 235 6388**

Denmark

Landsforeningen Danmarks Vanderhjem
Vesterbrogade 39
DK-1620
Kobenhavn V
Tel **31-313612**

Ireland

An Oige
Irish Youth Hostel Association
61 Mountjoy Street
Dublin 7
Republic of Ireland
Tel: **35-31 304555**

Israel

Israel Youth Hostel Association
PO Box 1075
3 Dorot Rishonim St
Jerusalem 91009
Israel
Tel: **97 22 252706**

New Zealand

Youth Hostelling Association of New Zealand
PO Box 436
Christchurch 1
Tel: **379-9970**

Philippines

Youth & Student Hostel Foundation of the Philippines (YSHFP)
4227 Tomas Claudio St
Paranaque
Metro Manila
Philippines
Tel: **832 0680**

Poland

Polish Association of Youth Hostels
00-791 Waszawa
Ul.
Chocimska 28
Poland
Tel: **48 248 8354**

South America

Youth Hostel Association (South America)
Talcahuano 214 2'6'
1013 Capital Federal
Buenos Aires
Argentina
Tel: **54-1476 1001**

UK

Scottish Youth Hostel Association
7 Glebe Crescent
Stirling FK8 2JA
Tel: **0786-451181**

Youth Hostel Association
Trevelyan House
8 St Stephens Hill
St Albans
Herts AL1 2DY
Tel: **07278 55215**

Youth Hostel Association of Northern Ireland
56 Bradbury Place
Belfast BT7 1RU
Tel: **0232 324733**

USA

American Youth Hostels Inc
National Offices
PO Box 37613
Washington DC 20013-7613
USA
Tel: **202-783 6161**

TIMESHARE AND HOME EXCHANGE ORGANIZATIONS

The Timeshare Council
23 Buckingham Gate
London SW1E 6LB
Tel: **071-821 8845**
Gives free advice to members, and makes a small charge for affiliation where owners belong to non-member resorts.

Homelink International
Linfield House
Gorse Hill Road
Virginia Water
Surrey GU25 4AS
Tel: **0344 842642**

International Home Exchange
DAT/TRAVEL
Level 2
17 Sydney Road
Manly NSW 2095
Australia
Tel: **8-232 2022**

International Home Exchange
PO Box 38615
11 Peach Parade
Ellerslie
New Zealand
Tel: **9-522 2933**

Intervac
6 Siddals Lane
Allestree
Derby DE3 2DY
Tel: **0225 892208**

Vacation Exchange Club
PO Box 820
Haleiwa, HI 96712
USA
Tel: **800 638 3841**
The longest-established home exchange agency in the United States, publishes two directories each year.

West World Holiday Exchange
1707 Platt Crescent
North Vancouver
BC VJ7 1X9
Canada
Tel: **604-987 3262**

Worldwide Home Exchange Club
45 Hans Place
London SW1X 0JZ
Tel: **071-589 6055** ∎

A BASIC GUIDE TO HEALTH
Section 11

VACCINATION CENTRES AND INFORMATION

In the UK, most vaccinations can be given by the traveller's own doctor. Yellow fever vaccine can be given by some general practitioners or this and unusual vaccinations can be obtained from clinics run by the Public Health Department in most large towns or cities and from the centres listed below, unless otherwise indicated. Most vaccines for travel will have to be paid for by the traveller. Consult your own doctor before ringing any of the hospital-based clinics (unless they have an 0839 or 0891 number, however you will be charged for making these calls).

Vaccination requirements are listed under each country in the Geographical Section in Section 1 of the Directory. Please note these are only guidelines as inoculations can change with new outbreaks of diseases, so please check with your own doctor or with a travel clinic as far in advance as you can.

British Airways Travel Clinics
Tel: **071-831 5333** *for your nearest travel clinic, 25 clinics nationwide.*

British Airways Immunization Centre
156 Regent Street
London W1
Tel: **071-439 9584**
Open Monday-Friday 9am-4.30pm and Saturday 10.00am - 4.00pm. No appointment necessary.

British Airways' Victoria Clinic
Victoria Plaza
Victoria Station
London SW1
Tel: **071-233 6661**
Open 8.15am-11.30am; 12.30pm-3.45pm Also at: North Terminal, Gatwick Airport. Open all day, evenings and weekends for emergencies.

Centers for Disease Control Traveler's Health section
Tel: **404-332 4559**
Based in Atlanta, they run a 24-hour automated system giving advice by region and on special problems such as malaria, food, water precautions and advice for pregnant travellers.

Central Public Health Laboratory
61 Colindale Avenue
Colindale
London NW9 5HT
Tel: **081-200 4400**
Provides advice and supplies of rabies vaccines and supplies of gammaglobulin to general practitioners for immunization against hepatitis A.

Convenience Care Centers
Suite 100
10301 East Darvey
Armani
CA 91733
USA
Undertakes all necessary vaccinations

Department of Health
Public Enquires Office
Richmond House
79 Whitehall
London SW1A 2NS
Tel: **071-210 4850**
Fax: 071-210 5523

Department of Infections and Tropical Medicine
Birmingham Heartlands Hospital
Bordesley Green East
Birmingham B9 5ST
Tel: **021 766 6611**
Pre-travel telephone advice and expertise in investigation and treatment of tropical illness. Does not offer pre-travel immunization or sup-

plies or routine post-travel medicals.

Department of Infectious Diseases & Tropical Medicine
North Manchester General Hospital
Delaunays Road
Manchester M8 6RB
Tel: **061-795 4567**

Department of Infection and Tropical Medicine
Ruchill Hospital
Glasgow G20 9NB
Tel: **041-946 7120**
Fax: 041-946 4359
Together with Communicable Disease (Scotland) Unit, provides telephone advice for general practitioners and other doctors and maintains 'Travax', a computerized database on travel medicine that may be accessed remotely by modem. Pre- and post-travel clinics and limited travel health supplies. Enquiries and referrals to clinics are best initiated by your general practitioner.

Health Control Unit
Terminal 3 Arrivals
Heathrow Airport
Hounslow
Middlesex TW6 1NB
Tel: **081-745 7209**
Can give at any time up-to-date information on compulsory and recommended immunizations for different countries.

Hospital for Tropical Diseases
4 St. Pancras Way
London NW1 0PE
Tel: **071-637 6099** (Travel clinic)
Fax: 071-383 0041
Pre-recorded healthline: **0898 337 733**
Comprehensive range of pre–travel immunizations and advice, and post–travel check-ups in travel clinic and large travel shop. Pre-recorded healthline gives country-specific health hazards — you will be asked to dial the international dialling code of the relevant country, so have it ready. Centre for investigation and treatment of tropical illness.

Intermedic
777 Third Avenue
New York
NY 10017
A list of recommended English-speaking doctors in many countries is available to members (subscription US$6)

International Association for Medical Assistance to Travelers
417 Center Street

Lewiston
NY 14092
A non-profit organisation dedicated to the gathering and dissemination of health and sanitary information worldwide

International Association for Medical Assistance to Travellers
Gottardstrasse 17
CH-63000 Zug
Switzerland
Membership is free, but voluntary contributions welcome. The association issues a directory of English-speaking doctors and leaflets on climate, acclimatisation, immunisation etc.

Liverpool School of Tropical Medicine
Pembroke Place
Liverpool L3 5QA
Tel: **051-708 9393** (pre-recorded pre-travel advice and medical queries) or **051-709 2298** (travel clinic)
Fax: 051-708 8733
Regular immunization and post-travel clinics and limited range of travellers' health supplies. International centre of expertise and research on venoms and snake bites, and investigation and management of tropical diseases.

Malaria Reference Laboratory
Tel: **071-636 7921/8636**
Advice on malaria prophylaxis and prevention.

MASTA
London School of Hygiene and Tropical Medicine
Keppel Street
London WC1E 7BR
Tel: **071-631 4408**
Health Brief: **0891 224 100**
Markets a wide range of products. For detailed advice on all health requirements for your intended destination(s), ring the Health Brief line; calls typically take 3-4 minutes and following this your health brief arrives by first class post (covered by the cost of the call).

Manchester Airport Medical Unit
Manchester M22 5PA
Tel: **061-489 3344**
Fax: 061-489 3813
Immunizations and travel advice

Ross Institute Malaria Advisory Service
London School of Hygiene & Tropical Medicine
Keppel Street
London WC1E 7HT
Tel: **071-636 7921**
24-hour taped advice.

Thomas Cook Vaccination Centre
45 Berkeley Street
London W1A 1EB
Tel: **071-408 4157**
*Vaccinations and certificates given on the spot,
also all vaccination information.
Open 8.30am-5.30pm Mon-Fri; 9am-12pm Sat
(by appointment only on Saturdays).*

Travellers Healthline
Tel: **0891-224 100**
*This is a regularly updated advice line (with
inter-active technology) for travellers seeking
information about vaccinations etc.*

**UDS Department of Health and Human
Services**
Public Health Service
Centers for Disease Control,
Center for Prevention Service
Division of Quarantine
Atlanta
GA 303333
Tel: **404-331 2316**

**West London Designated Vaccination
Centre**
53 Great Cumberland Place
London W1H 7HL
Tel: **071-262 6456**
*Open 8.45am-5pm Mon-Fri, no appointment
necessary.*

Additional helpful medical organizations

Department of Social Security
Overseas Branch
Newcastle upon Tyne NE98 1YX
or
Department of Health and Social Services
Overseas Branch
8-14 Callender Street
Belfast BT1 5DP
For residents of Northern Ireland
Freefone **0800 555 777**
For supplies of leaflets only
Prestel Page 50063

*For advice on eligibility for health care abroad,
and supplies of leaflets giving general and specific details (Freefone). The selected vaccination
requirements for all countries are updated on
Prestel. Does not provide immunizations etc.*

National AIDS Helpline
Tel: **0800 567 123**
*24-hour free helpline providing advice on all
aspects of HIV infection.*

Terence Higgins Trust
Tel: **071-242 1010**
Hours: 12.00-22.00 daily
*Confidential phoneline for detailed information
about travel restrictions, insurance etc for HIV
positive individuals.*

EMERGENCY MEDICAL TRAVEL KIT SUPPLIERS

Homeway Promotions Ltd
The White House
Littleton
Winchester
Hampshire SO22 6OS
Tel: **0962-881526**
*Provides a Travel with Care package and also
sells sterile medical packs.*

Dr Jones and Partners
Charlotte Keel Health Centre
Seymour Road
Easton
Bristol BS5 0UA
Tel: **0272 512244**
Travel medical kits.

**Medical Advisory Services for Travellers
(Masta)**
London School of Hygiene & Tropical
Medicine
Keppel Street
London WC1
Tel: **071-631 4408**
*MASTA has helped to design the 'Travel-Well'
personal water purifiers. It removes particulate
matter, bacteria, protozoa and viruses from
contaminated water. The Trekker Travel Well
costs £24.95 and the Pocket Travel Well £9.95.
They also sell Sterile Medical Equipment Packs
and Emergency Dental Packs.*

Nomad
3-4 Turnpike Lane
London N8 0PX
Tel: **081-889 7014**
or
4 Potters Rad
New Barnet
Hertfordshire
EN5 5HW
Tel: **081-441 7208**
*Full medical centre, immunisation and pharma-
cy. Wide range of not only medical equipment,
but also clothing and mosquito nets. Mail order
service available.*

Oasis
High Street
Stoke Ferry
King's Lynn
Norfolk
PE33 9SP
Tel: 0366-500466
Not only sells mosquito nets, but will also send a free malaria advice sheet, also can provide sterile medical kits.

Safety and First Aid (SAFA)
59 Hill Street
Liverpool L8 5SA
Tel: 051-708 0397
As well as general medical kits also provide Aids and Hepatitis B prevention kits. ■

EQUIPPING FOR A TRIP
Section 12

EQUIPMENT SUPPLIERS

Alpine Sports
205 Kensington High Street
London W8 6PD
Tel: 071-938 1911
Travel and mountaineering equipment.

Berghaus
34 Dean Street
Newcastle Upon Tyne NE1 1PG
Tel: 091-232 3561
*Britain's leading suppliers of specialist packs
and clothing for hiking and climbing. Suppliers
to many expeditions.*

Blacks Camping and Leisure Ltd
38-40 Marsh Street
Hanley
Stoke-on-Trent ST1 1JD
Tel: 0782-212870
*Have lightweight, mountain and touring tents;
camp furniture, kitchen kits, stoves and lamps;
clothing and accessories and convertible
specialist and summer-weight sleeping bags.*

Clothtec
92 Par Green
Par, Cornwall PL24 2AG
Tel: 0726 813602
*Manufacturers of special products that have
been supplied to expeditions all over the world.
Specialists in jungle sleeping units, mosquito
nets. Also repairs equipment. Will give advice
over the telephone to first time expeditioners.*

Cotswold Camping
42-44 Uxbridge Road
London W12 8ND
Tel: 081 743 2976
*Supply a wide store of outdoor equipment and
have a comprehensive range of water filtering
and purification equipment.*

Darr Expeditions Service
Theresienstrasse 66
D-8000 Munchen
Germany
Tel: 089-282032

Derby Mountain Centre Ltd
85/89 King Street
Derby DE1 3EE
Tel: 0332-365650
*Specialist lightweight outdoor equipment and
clothing. Also ski and mountaineering
equipment.*

Field and Trek (Equipment) Ltd
Mail Order:
3 Wates Way
Brentwood
Essex CM15 9TB
Tel: 0277-233122
Retail:
3 Palace Street
Canterbury Kent CT1 2DU
Tel: 0227-470023
*Illustrated catalogue with products at
discounted prices on most leading makes of
expedition equipment – tents, rucksacks, boots,
waterproof clothing, sleeping bags and
mountaineering gear.*

Laurence Corner
62/64 Hampstead Road
London NW1 2NU
Tel: 071-813 1010

Nomad
4 Potters Road
New Barnett
Hertfordshire EN5 5HW
Tel: 081-441 7208
*Equipment, clothing and information for the
independent traveller including travel*

pharmacy and travel reference from their shop.
Can also supply medical kits and vaccinations
at 3–4 Wellington Terrace, Turnpike Lane,
London N8 0PX Tel: 081-889 7014

Penrith Survival Equipment
Morland
Penrith
Cumbria CA10 3AZ
Tel: 09314-444
Mail order retail outfit for Survival Aids

Rohan
30 Maryland Road
Tongwell
Milton Keynes MK14 8HN
Tel: 0908 618888
Design practical clothes for everyday wear,
with particular attention to the needs of the
serious traveller and outdoor enthusiast.

**Tent and Tarpaulin Manufacturing
Company**
101-103 Brixton Hill
London SW2 1AA
Tel: 081-674 0121

Travelling Light
Morland House
Morland
Penrith
Cumbria
CA10 3AZ
Tel: 0931-44 488
Mail Order

YHA Adventure Shop
14 Southampton Street
London WC2E 7HY
Tel: 071-836 8541

USA

Advanced Filtration Technology
2424 Bates Avenue
Concord
CA 94520
Portable water filter and Super Straw

Austin House Inc
P.O. Box 117
Sta 'B', Buffalo
NY 14207
Tel: 1 800-268-5157
Specialize in travel accessories such as money
belts, miniature packs, locks, hangers,
converters, adaptor plugs, transformers, etc.

Banana Republic
Box 7737
San Francisco
CA 94120

Tel: 800- 527 5200
Mail order travel clothing and books.

Basic Designs, Inc
5815 Bennett Valley Rd
Santa Rosa
CA 95404
Tel: 707- 575 1220
Telex: 9103806641
Make the H20 Sun Shower, a solar-heater
portable shower consisting of a heavy duty vinyl
bag which holds 11½ litres of water and heats
the water to between 32 and 49 C depending on
exposure and the heat of the day. The pack
measures 10 by 33cms and weighs only 340g.

L.L. Bean Inc
Freeport
ME 04033
Tel: 207- 865 3111
Operates a mail order service and has a
salesroom which is open 24 hours a day, 365
days a year. Firm sells outdoor garments and
accessories, boots and other footwear, canoes,
compasses, axes, knives, binoculars,
thermometers, stoves, tents, sleeping bags,
packs and frames, skis and snowshoes,
campware, travel bags, lamps, blankets.

The Complete Traveller
199 Madison Avenue
New York, NY 10016
Tel: 212- 679 4339
Annual catalogue US$1.

Early Winters Ltd
110 Prefontaine Pl.
Seattle, WA 98104
Makers of backpacking and outdoor gear,
including the Thousand Mile socks which are
guaranteed not to wear out before 1 year or
1,000 miles/1,600 km of walking whichever
comes last- and manufacturers of a full line of
gore-tex tents and rain-gear. Free colour
catalogue.

Franzus Company, Inc
352 Park Avenue South
New York
NY 10010
Tel: 212- 889 5850
Makes travel irons, blow dryers, garment
steamers, beverage makers, converters,
converter sets and adapter plug kits. Travel
care appliances for worldwide use.

Katadyn USA, Inc
Warehouse + Service-Center
3020 North Scottsdale Road
Scottsdale
AZ 85251
Tel: 602- 990 3131

North by Northeast
181 Conant Street
Pawtucket
RI 02862

Parks Products
3611 Cahuenga
Hollywood
CA 90068
Tel: **212-876 5454**
*Make voltage converters and adaptor plugs to
fit electronic/portable appliances anywhere in
the world.*

John Posey Co
PO Box 337
Jenks
OK 74037
*Makes protective skin creams to protect against
cold, wind, sun, insects and poisonous plants.
All for use outdoors.*

Sierra West
6 East Yanonali Street
Santa Barbara
CA 93101
Tel: **805-963 87 27**
*Sierra West is a manufacturer of high quality
rainwear, outer-wear, tents and backpacking
accessories. For further information, please
write and request a free colour catalogue.*

Survival Cards
PO Box 1805
Bloomington, IN 47402
*Supplies Survival Cards measuring 7.5 by 12.5
cms and made from plastic, which are crammed
with information, including edible plant
classification, emergency shelter construction,
first aid, Morse Code, climbing techniques and
knot tying.*

Thinsulate
6 Thermal Insulation 3M
3M Centre
Building 220-7W
St Paul
MN 55114
Tel: **0800 328 1689** toll free.

Traveler's Checklist
Cornwall Bridge Road
Sharon
CT 06069
Tel: **203-364 0144**
*International mail order company sells hard-to-
find travel accessories, including electrical
devices, security, health and grooming aids,
money convertors and other travel items.*

Wilderness Way International
PO Box 334
Northridge
CA 91324
*Make the collapsible two gallon/nine litre
Water Sack which weighs 3oz/100gm and
consists of two bags, the inner being the larger
so that it can never expand to its full size and is
therefore less subject to stress.*

SPECIALIST EQUIPMENT SUPPLIERS

Medical

BCB Ltd
Moorland Road
Cardiff CF2 2YL
Tel: **(0222) 464464**
*First Aid and medical kits to any specification.
Catalogues available.*

John Bell and Croyden
50 Wigmore Street
London W1
Tel: **01-935 5555**
*Chemists in London who specialize in making
up travel and expedition supplies.*

MASTA
c/o London School of Hygiene and Tropical
Medicine
Keppel Street (Gower Street)
London WC1E 7HT
Tel: **071-631 4408**
*Medical advisory service. Will also provide
sterile kits of syringes, needles etc. for those
going into areas with a high incidence of AIDS
or Hepatitis B.*

Rhone-Poulenc Rorer Ltd
Dagenham
Essex RM10 7XS
Tel: **081-592 3060**
*May & Baker are one of the largest
pharmaceutical manufacturers in the UK. They
have several remedies for the minor everyday
accidents that occur at home or abroad.*

Tender Corp
After Bite
Box 42
Littleton
NH 03561
USA
*America's leading treatment for the relief of
pain and irritation due to insect bites or stings.*

From 16 April 1995 all national and international codes change — see page 587 for details.

Wyeth Laboratories
PO Box 8299
Philadelphia
PA 19101
USA
Manufacturer of anti-venoms against poisonous snakes of the United States. The serum is sold in a freeze-dried condition, making it ideally suited for expeditions (no need for refrigeration), and in small quantities.

Optical

Heron Optical Co
23-25 Kings Road
Brentwood
Essex CM14 4ER
Tel: (0277) 222 230
Mail Order: 3 Wates Way Brentwood Essex CM15 9TB Tel: (0277) 233 122 Stock all leading makes of binoculars, telescopes. Associate company of Field and Trek (Equipment) Ltd.

Viking Optical Ltd
Blythe Road Industrial Estate
Halesworth
Suffolk IT19 8EN
Tel: 0986 875315
Supplies Sunto compasses and binoculars, and other precisions instruments.

Olympus Optical Co (UK) Ltd
2-8 Honduras St
London EC1Y 0TX
Tel: 071-253 2772

Photographic

Agfa UK
27 Great West Road
Brentford
Middlesex TW8 9AX
Tel: 081-560 2131

British Photographic Enterprise Group
1 West Ruislip Station
Ruislip
Middlesex HA4 7DW
Tel:0895 634515
Association of British manufacturers of photographic, cine and audio-visual equipment.

Camera Care Systems
Vale Lane
Bedminster
Bristol BS3 5RU
Tel: (0272) 635263
Manufacture protective casings for and distribute fine photographic equipment.

Canon UK Ltd
Brent Trading Centre
North Circular Road
Neasden
London NW10 0JF
Tel: 081-459 1266

Ilford UK Ltd
14 Tottenham Street
London W1
Tel: 071-636 7890

Jessop Photo Centre
67 New Oxford Street
London WC1A 1DG
Tel: 071-240 6077
Low price film, other branches around Britain.

KJP
93 Drummond St
London NW1 2HJ
Tel: 071-380 1144
Major suppliers for all photographic equipment and accessories, including a selection of second-hand goods.

Kodak Ltd
Kodak House
PO Box 66
Station Road
Hemel Hempstead
Herts HP1 1JU
Tel: (0442) 61122

Minolta UK Ltd
Rooksley Park
Precedent Drive
Rooksley
Milton Keynes MK13 8HF
Tel: (0908) 200400

Nikon UK
Nikon House
380 Richmond Road
Kingston Upon Thames
Surrey KT2 5PR
Tel: 081-541 4440

Olympus Optical Co (UK) Ltd
2-8 Honduras St
London EC1
Tel: 071-253 2772

Pentax UK Ltd
Pentax House
Heron Drive
Langley
Slough SL3 8PNHA2 OLT
Tel: 0753 792792

Photo Paste (Odeon Photo)
110 Blvd St Germain
75006

Paris, France
Tel: **329 4050**
*Is a photographic developing and printing
service that will process photos of films sent
from anywhere in the world, and send the results
on anywhere. They will undertake a variety of
processes; will give advice on film handling and
photographic technique; will retain negatives
safely until your journey is over; and charge
reasonable prices for these services.*

TAMRAC
6709 Independence Ave
Canoga Park
CA 91303
USA
*Make the TeleZoom Pak (Model 517), Photo
Backpack (Model 757) and a full line of instant
access foam padded weatherproof cases for
35mm systems.*

FREIGHT FORWARDERS

Abco Shipping Ltd.
1 Fenning Street
Off St. Thomas Street
London SE1 3QR
Tel: **071-407-2220**

Action Shipping Ltd.
Action House
Unit 3B
Tideway Industrial Estate
87 Kirtling Street
London SW8 5BP
Tel: **071-627 0282**

Atlasair Ltd.
UPS House
Forest Road
Feltham
Middlesex TW13 7DY
Tel: **081-844 1122**

Claydon NCOY Ltd
Ensign House
42/44 Thomas Road
London E14 7BJ
Tel: **071-987 8211**

Evan Cook Ltd
134 Queen's Road
London SE15 2HR
Tel: **071-635 0224**

Hogg Robinson (GFA) Ltd
City House
190-196 City Road

London EC1V 2QH
Tel: **071-251 5150**

Jeppesen Heaton Ltd
94A Whitechapel High Street
London E1 7QY
Tel: **071-377 9080**

Sealandair Transport Company
101 Stephenson Street
Canning Town
London
E16 4SA
Tel: **071-511 2288**

Tasit Transport & Forwarding Ltd
27 Montpelier Street
London SW7 1HF
Tel: **071-584 9700**

Further information:
**British International Freight Association
(BIFA)**
Redfern House
Browells Lane
Feltham
Middlesex TW13 7EP
Tel: **081-844 2266**
BIFA publishes a directory of members. ■

COMMUNICATIONS
Section 13

COUNTRY-BY-COUNTRY
GUIDE TO CONTACTING THE UK

Afghanistan
Air mail post to UK: About 7 days.
Telegrams: May be sent from Central Post Office, Kabul (closes 21.00 hours.)
Telex: Public terminal at PTT Office, Jad Ibn Sina (next to Kabul Hotel).
Telephoning the UK: International operator service, reasonably efficient; shortage of lines may cause delay.

Albania
Air mail post to UK: Up to 2 months.
Telegrams: Not available.
Telex: Only available in emergencies through Government Offices.
Telephoning the UK: The only public phones are in the Main Post Office.

Algeria
Air mail post to UK: 3-4 days.
Telegrams: May be sent from any post office (8.00-19.00). Main post office in Algiers at 5 Blvd Mohamed Khemisti offers 24 hour service.
Telex: At main post office, Algiers; also public facilities at Aurassi and Aletti Hotels.
Telephoning the UK: IDD to UK, also international operator service 24 hours, but subject to delays.

American Samoa
Air mail post to UK: Up to 2 weeks.
Telegrams: Available in main towns and hotels.
Telex: Available in main towns and hotels.
Telephoning the UK: IDD available.

Andorra
Air mail post to UK: 4-5 days.
Telegrams: Services available throughout.
Telex: Services available throughout.
Telephoning the UK: Normal code dial system.

Angola
Air mail post to UK: 5-10 days.
Telegrams: In Post Offices, fairly reliable.
Telex: In good hotels.
Telephoning the UK: IDD from Luanda, elsewhere calls have to be booked 6 hours in advance through the operator.

Anguilla
Air mail post to UK: Up to 2 weeks.
Telegrams: May be sent from Cable & Wireless, Booth, The Valley.
Telex: May be sent from Cable & Wireless, as above.
Telephoning the UK: Full IDD available.

Antigua
Air mail post to UK: 3-4 days.
Telegrams: May be sent from Cable & Wireless, High Street, St. Johns or from your hotel.
Telex: From Cable & Wireless, St. Johns.
Telephoning the UK: IDD or through hotel operator, or via Cable & Wireless.

Argentina
Air mail post to UK: About 7 days.
Telegrams: May be sent from General Post Office (Correo Central), corner of Samrieto and L N Alem.
Telex: ENTEL (state-owned telephone and telegraph company) has two booths in Buenos Aires; also from General Post Office.
Fax: Available in most hotels.
Telephoning the UK: IDD; also 24 hour international operator service. (Expensive).

Armenia
Air mail post to UK: Erratic - months or never
Telegrams and Telex: Not available
Telephoning the UK: All international calls

made through operator, long delays.

Aruba
Air mail post to UK: 7-10 days.
Telegrams and Telex: Available at the Telegraph and Radio Office in the Post Office Building, Oranjestad and in good hotels.
Telephoning the UK: IDD available.

Australia
Air mail post to UK: About 7 days.
Telegrams: May be sent from local Post Offices and by telephone.
Telex: Telecom operates Public Telex Bureaux at all capital city Chief Telegraph Offices and at the following Telecom country offices: Canberra, Newcastle, Dubbo, Wollongong, Ballarat, Townsville, Rickhampton, Mt Gambier, Darwin, Alice Springs, Launceston.
Fax: Available at OTC offices (Overseas Telecommunications Commission).
Telephoning the UK: IDD; also operator-connected calls.

Austria
Air mail post to UK: 3-5 days.
Telegrams: From Post Offices Mon-Fri 0800-1200, 1400-1800. Sat 0800-1000 in selected offices.) Main and station post offices in larger cities open round the clock including Saturdays, Sundays and public holidays).
Telex: From Post Offices and hotels.
Telephoning the UK: IDD, from Post Offices or international call boxes.

Azerbaijan
Air mail post to UK: Long delays, perhaps months.
Telegrams and Telex: Not available.
Telephoning the UK: Through the operator and extremely difficult.

Bahamas
Air mail post to K: 3-5 days.
Telegrams and Telex: May be sent through BatelCo offices in Nassau and Freeport.
Fax: From the Centralised Telephone Office, East Street, Nassau.
Telephoning the UK: IDD and International operator service.

Bahrain
Air mail post to UK: 3-4 days.
Telegrams: Ordinary, letter telegrams may be sent 24 hours a day from Cable & Wireless, Mercury House, Al-Khalifa Road, Manama.
Telex: Public call offices at Cable & Wireless open 24 hours.
Fax: From Bahrain Telecom, Sh Mubarak Building on Government Avenue.
Telephoning the UK: IDD.

Bangladesh
Air mail Post to UK: 3-4 days.
Telegrams: From telegraph and post offices; major hotels.
Telex: Links with almost every country in the world. Hotel Intercontinental in Dacca has a public telex service. Telex facilities also available from Chittagong, Khulna.
Telephoning the UK: Limited IDD.

Barbados
Air mail post to UK: 4-7 days.
Telegrams: via Cable & Wireless (WI) Ltd, Wildey, St. Michael.
Telex: via Cable & Wireless.
Fax: Available at large hotels.
Telephoning the UK: IDD.

Belarus
Air mail post to UK: At least 10 days
Telegrams: From major hotels
Telex: From major hotels, eg. the Yubileynaya and the Planeta in Minsk
Fax: Public fax office at ul. Opanskogo 5, Minsk and at ul. Chkalova 1, Minsk, normal office hours.
Telephoning the UK: IDD available in major cities.

Belgium
Air mail post to UK: 3-4 days.
Telegrams: In main towns, telegraph offices (usually found in the stations or close at hand) are open day and night.
Telex: Extensive facilities available throughout.
Fax: Extensive facilities.
Telephoning the UK: IDD.

Belize
Air mail post to UK: Up to 5 days.
Telegrams: Available at BTL - Belize Telecommunications LTD, public booths in Belize City and Belmopan.
Telex: As telegrams but also major hotels.
Fax: Available from BTL public booths
Telephoning the UK: IDD.

Benin
Air mail post to UK: 3-5 days
Telegram: Not available
Telex: Available in major hotels and post offices in Cotonou.
Telephoning the UK: IDD available in major towns.

Bermuda
Air mail post to UK: 5-7 days.
Telegrams: From all post offices.
Telex: Via Cable & Wireless.
Fax: Available at hotels.
Telephoning the UK: IDD.

Bhutan
Air mail post to the UK: Up to 2 weeks.
Telegrams: Not available
Telex: Available in main centres, but disruptions frequent
Telephoning the UK: Only in main centres, through the operator.

Bolivia
Air mail post to UK: About 4 days.
Telegrams: From West Coast of America Telegraph Co Ltd, main office at Edificio Electra, Calle Mercado 1150, La Paz and Sheraton Libertador, Crillon, El Dorado, Gloria. Ordinary, urgent and letter telegrams.
Telex: Public telex facilities also available at West Coast of America Telegraph offices.
Fax: Services available.
Telephoning the UK: IDD and international operator service.

Bonaire
Air mail post to UK: 4-6 days.
Telegrams and Telex: Main post office in Kralendijk.
Telephoning the UK: IDD available.

Bophuthatswana
Air mail post to UK: Up to 10 days.
Telegrams and Telex: All post offices.
Fax: Available at major hotels and conferences centres.
Telephoning the UK: IDD available.

Bosnia-Hercegovina
Air mail to the UK: Postal service badly disrupted.
Telegrams and Telex: Intermittent and uncertain.
Telephoning the UK: Extremely difficult.

Botswana
Air mail post to UK: 1-3 weeks.
Telegrams: May be sent via post office.
Telex: Via post offices.
Fax: Available in major centres.
Telephoning the UK: IDD and international operator service.

Brazil
Air mail post to UK: 4-6 days.
Telegrams: From EMBRATEL (Empresa Brasileira de Telecomunicacoes SA) offices in Rio de Janeiro and Sao Paulo.
Telex: International Telex facilities available at EMBRATEL offices.
Fax: From main post offices and major hotels.
Telephoning the UK: IDD.

British Virgin Islands
Air mail post to UK: Up to 1 week.
Telegrams and Telex: Available through Cable

& Wireless offices
Fax: Available through Cable & Wireless
Telephoning the UK: IDD

Brunei
Air mail post to the UK: 2-5 days.
Telegrams: Available at the Government Telecommunication Office in Bandor Seri, Begawan.
Telex: No public telex, available in some hotels.
Telephoning the UK: IDD available.

Bulgaria
Air mail post to UK: 4 days.
Telegrams: From General Post Office, 4 Gurko Street, Sofia.
Telex: Public telex available at post offices.
Fax: Available at Bulgarian Telegraph Agency.
Telephoning the UK: IDD in main cities.

Burkina Faso
Air mail post to UK: Up to 2 weeks.
Telegrams: Limited facilities.
Telex: Major hotels in Ougadougou.
Telephoning the UK: IDD available in Ougadougou.

Burundi
Air mail post to UK: 1 week.
Telegrams and Telex: From Direction des Tele-communications in Bujumbura.
Telephoning the UK: Mainly through operator, although IDD available.

Cambodia
Air mail post to UK: 4-5 days.
Telegrams and telex: Few facilities available.
Fax: Few facilities available
Telephoning the UK: IDD has now been restored.

Cameroon
Air mail post to UK: 7 days.
Telegrams: Telegraph office does not operate at night, and messages are apt to be delayed.
Telex: Facilities are available from the main intelcom office in Yaounde and also larger hotels in Yaounde and Douala.
Fax: At intelcom offices.
Telephoning the UK: IDD and international operator service.

Canada
Air mail post to UK: 4-8 days.
Telegrams: Cannot be sent through the post offices in Canada. Telegrams or 'Telepost' messages should be phoned or delivered to CN/CP Telecommunications – address and telephone number can be found in the local telephone directory. In Newfoundland and Labrador telegrams are sent through Terra Nova Tel.

Telex: Telex facilities easily located in all major Canadian cities.
Fax: Most hotels.
Telephoning the UK: IDD

Cape Verde
Air mail post to UK: 1-2 weeks.
Telegrams: Not available.
Telex: Available in some hotels.
Telephoning the UK: IDD in main towns.

Cayman Islands
Air mail post to UK: About 5 days.
Telegrams: Public Telegraph operates daily from 07.30-18.00 hours Cayman time. Telecommunications are provided by Cable and Wireless (West Indies) Ltd.
Telex: Available at Cable & Wireless office; many hotels and apartments have their own telex.
Telephoning the UK: IDD.

Central African Republic
Air mail post to UK: 1-3 weeks.
Telegrams: Available in major post offices.
Telex: The main post office in Bangui and some major hotels.
Telephoning the UK: IDD available.

Chad
Air mail post to UK: 1 week.
Telegrams and Telex: Few facilities available
Telephoning the UK: Through the operator.

Chile
Air mail post to UK: 3-4 days.
Telegrams: From Transradio Chilena at Bandera 168, Santiago, and at Esmerelda 932, Valparaiso; ordinary and letter telegrams.
Telex: Facilities at Transradio Chilena, Bandera 168, and at ITT Communicaciones Mundiales SA, Agustinas 1054, Santiago.
Telephoning the UK: IDD.

China
Air mail post to UK: 1 week.
Telegrams: From Administration of Telecommunications at 11 Sichanganjian Street, Beijing, and at Nanking Road East 30, Shanghai, or any telegraph office. Ordinary, urgent or letter telegrams.
Telex: Telex facilities available at Administration of Telecommunications offices and major hotels.
Fax: At major hotels.
Telephoning the UK: IDD.

Colombia
Air mail post to UK: 5-7 days.
Telegrams: From any chief telegraph office in main towns. Ordinary and urgent telegrams.
Telex: International telex facilities available

at hotels Tequendama and Hilton, Bogota, at Telecom (Empresa Nacional de Telecommunicaciones) offices and chief telegraph offices in main towns.
Fax: Major hotels in Bogota.
Telephoning the UK: IDD and operator service.

Comoro Islands
Air mail post to UK: 1-2 weeks.
Telegrams and Telex: Few facilities available.
Telephoning the UK: Through international operator.

Congo
Air mail post to UK: Unreliable 1-2 weeks.
Telegrams and Telex: Main post offices in the cities.
Telephoning the UK: IDD.

Cook Islands
Air mail post to UK: 1-2 weeks.
Telegrams and Telex: From the telecom office in Rarotonga.
Telephoning the UK: IDD available

Costa Rica
Air mail post to UK: 6-10 days.
Telegrams: Facilities available at all main post offices, but not to the UK.
Telex: From Radiografica, Costariricense SA on the corner of Calle 1 and Avenida 5 in San Jose.
Telephoning the UK: IDD.

Côte d'Ivoire
Air mail post to UK: About 10 days.
Telegrams: May be sent from the post offices.
Telex: Facilities in the post offices and major hotels.
Telephoning the UK: IDD and international operator service.

Croatia
Air mail post to UK: Limited service, can take months
Telegrams and Telex: Badly disrupted
Fax: Limited service.
Telephoning the UK: IDD available.

Cuba
Air mail post to UK: Up to 1 month
Telegrams: Can be sent from post office in Havana and RCA offices.
Telex: Not available.
Telephoning the UK: IDD from Havana only

Curaçao
Air mail post to UK: 4-6 days.
Telegrams and telex: Available in large hotels and main post office in Willemstad
Telephoning the UK: IDD service.

Cyprus

Air mail post to UK: 3 days.
Telegrams: From any telegraphic office, including Electra House, Museum Street, Nicosia. 24 hour service. Ordinary and urgent telegrams.
Telex: No public telex offices, but larger hotels have telex facilities.
Fax: Available at the District Post Office.
Telephoning the UK: IDD.

Czech Republic

Air mail post to UK: About 7 days.
Telegrams: Facilities available at all main post offices.
Telex: Telex for tourists not available.
Telephoning the UK: IDD.

Denmark

Air mail post to UK: About 3 days.
Telegrams: May be sent from main post offices.
Telex: Facilities available from your hotel or main post offices in major towns.
Fax: Available at most post offices.
Telephoning the UK: IDD.

Djibouti

Air mail post to UK: About 7 days.
Telegrams: May be sent from main post offices.
Telex: Available from any post office.
Telephoning the UK: IDD. International telephone calls (by satellite) are possible 24 hrs a day.

Dominica

Air mail post to UK: About 7 days.
Telegrams: Available from All America Cables and Radio ITT, Julio Verne 21, Santo Domingo; RCA Global Communications, El Conde 203, Santo Domingo.
Telex: Facilities available from All America Cables and Radio ITT and RCA Global Communications.
Telephoning the UK: IDD and international operator service.

Ecuador

Air mail post to UK: 6-7 days.
Telegrams: From chief telegraphic office in main towns. In Quito, 24 hour service. Also from Hotel Quito and Hotel Coloìn up to 20.00 hours. Ordinary and urgent telegrams.
Telex: Public booths at Hotels Quito, Coloìn and Humboldt, Quito; Hotel Humboldt, Continental, Grand Hotel, Palace, Guayaquil; also at IETEL (Instituto Ecuatoriano de Telecommunicaciones) offices.
Telephoning the UK: IDD and international operator service; sometimes long delays in securing connection.

Egypt

Air mail post to UK: Minimum 2 days.
Telegrams: From telegraph offices. Ordinary telegrams.
Telex: Public telex facilities at major hotels for guests only; other telex services in Cairo at: 19 El Alfi Street (24 hours); 26 July Street, Zamalek; 85 Abdel Khalek Sarwat Street, Attaba; El Tazaran Street, Nasr City; Transit Hall, Cairo Airport.
Telephoning the UK: IDD. International operator calls should be booked in advance.

El Salvador

Air mail post to UK: 7-10 days.
Telex: From ANTEL
Telephoning the UK: IDD.

Equatorial Guinea

Air mail post to UK: 2 weeks
Telegrams and Telex: Not available
Telephoning the UK: IDD available, however more likely to get through via the operator.

Eritrea

Air mail post to UK: Long delays likely
Telegrams: Not available.
Telex: From the telex office in Asmara
Telephoning the UK: IDD but only from Asmara, Massawa and Assab.

Estonia

Air mail post to UK: 6 days.
Telegrams and Telex: Not available.
Telephoning the UK: IDD available.

Ethiopia

Air mail post to UK: 4 days.
Telegrams: From Telecommunications Authority, Adoua Square, Addis Ababa, and telegraphic offices. Ordinary, urgent and letter telegrams.
Telex: Facilities available at Telecommunications Board, Churchill Road, Addis Ababa.
Fax: In major hotels.
Telephoning the UK: IDD. Link available from Addis 15.00-20.00 East African Time.

Falkland Islands

Air mail post to UK: 4-7 days.
Telex: By satellite from Cable & Wireless
Fax: New system installed - available.
Telephoning the UK: IDD.

Fiji

Air mail post to UK: 10 days.
Telegrams: Overseas telegrams accepted at all telegraph offices. Ordinary and deferred (LT) telegrams.
Telex: International telex facilities available at Fiji International Telecommunications Ltd

(FINTEL), Victoria Parade, Suva, or at major hotels.
Fax: Major hotels and the FINTEL office.
Telephoning the UK: IDD and international operator service.

Finland
Air mail post to UK: About 3 days.
Telegrams: Can be left with the nearest post office or hotel desk.
Telex: Facilities available at Post Offices. The Central Post Office, Mannerheimintie 11, Helsinki.
Fax: Major hotels and businesses.
Telephoning the UK: IDD.

France
Air mail post to UK: 2 days.
Telegrams: Facilities available throughout.
Telex: Extensive facilities available, in post offices.
Fax: Widely available.
Telephoning the UK: IDD.

French Guiana
Air mail post to UK: 2 weeks.
Telex: Facilities in Cayenne.
Fax: Widely available.
Telephoning the UK: IDD available.

French Polynesia
Air mail post to UK: 2 weeks.
Telegrams: Limited services available.
Telex: Available at the Post Office, Boulevard Pomare, Papeete, Tahiti.
Fax: At some post offices and major hotels.
Telephoning the UK: IDD available.

Gabon
Air mail post to UK: 1-2 weeks.
Telegrams and Telex: Main post office in Libreville and major hotels.
Telephoning the UK: IDD available.

Gambia
Air mail post to UK: 3 days.
Telegrams: From GAMTEL, Cameron Street, Banjul. Ordinary telegrams.
Telex: Public telex booth at Russell Street, Banjul.
Fax: At the 9 GAMTEL offices in Banjul.
Telephoning the UK: IDD and 24-hour international operator service.

Georgia
Air mail post to UK: months.
Telegrams and Telex: Not available.
Telephoning the UK: IDD in theory available, in practice almost impossible.

Germany
Air mail post to UK: 3 days.
Telegrams: May be sent from post offices.

Telex: From main post offices and hotels.
Fax: Available throughout.
Telephoning the UK: IDD.

Ghana
Air mail post to UK: Up to 2 weeks.
Telegrams: From External Tele-communications Service of Posts and Telecommunications Corporation, Extelcom House, High St, Accra, and Stewart Avenue, Kumasi. Ordinary, urgent and letter telegrams.
Telex: Public call facilities at External Telecommunication Service offices.
Telephoning the UK: IDD. Operator connected calls may be made 08.15-18.15 hours, weekdays only. Often difficult and delays sometimes of 2-3 days.

Gibraltar
Air mail post to UK: 2-6 days.
Telegrams and Telex: From Gibtel, 60 Main Street or Mount Pleasant, 25 South Barracks Road.
Fax: Available in some hotels..
Telephoning the UK: IDD

Greece
Air mail post to UK: 4-5 days.
Telegrams: May be sent from OYE (Telecommunications Centre).
Telex: Facilities available from OTE.
Telephoning the UK: IDD.

Greenland
Air mail post to UK: 4-5 days.
Telegrams: All towns have a telegraph station.
Telephoning the UK: IDD available.

Grenada
Air mail post to UK: 10 days
Telegrams and Telex: Available from International Cable & Wireless (West Indies) Ltd
Fax: Cable & Wireless in St Georges.
Telephoning the UK: IDD

Guadeloupe
Air mail post to UK: 1 week.
Telex: Available in Point-a-Pitre
Telephoning the UK: IDD

Guam
Air mail post to UK: Up to 2 weeks
Fax: In major hotels
Telephoning the UK: Only in Agana

Guatemala
Air mail post to UK: 6-12 days
Telegrams: only available locally
Telex: Available in Guatemala City
Fax: In some major hotels in the city.
Telephoning the UK: IDD available.

Guinea Republic
Air mail post to UK: Up to 2 weeks
Telex: Available at the Hotel de
L'Indépépéndence and Grand Hotel de L'Unité
Telephoning the UK: IDD.

Guinea-Bissau
Air mail post to UK: Up to 2 weeks.
Telex: Available at the main post office in
Bissau
Telephoning the UK: IDD available.

Guyana
Air mail post to UK: 7-10 days.
Telegrams: Can be sent 24 hours a day from
Bank of Guyana Bldg, Avenue of the Republic
and Church Street, Georgetown. Ordinary and
night letter telegrams.
Telex: Public call offices at the Bank of Guyana
Building.
Fax: As Telegrams
Telephoning the UK: IDD and international
operator service at all times.

Haiti
Air mail post to UK: 1 week.
Telex: At main hotels and office of TELECO
Telephoning the UK: IDD

Honduras
Air mail post to UK: Up to 1 week.
Telegrams and Telex: Available at
HONDUTEL.
Fax: At HONDUTEL.
Telephoning the UK: IDD

Hong Kong
Air mail post to UK: 3-5 days.
Telegrams: From telegraphic offices. Ordinary,
letter and social telegrams.
Telex: Public telex facilities available at
Mercury House, 3 Connaught Road, Central,
Hong Kong Island, and at Ocean Terminal,
Kowloon and from Kai Tak Airport.
Fax: From BureauFax.
Telephoning the UK: IDD and 24-hour
international operator service.

Hungary
Air mail post to UK: About 4 days.
Telegrams: May be sent from hotel desks.
Telex: At major hotels and main post office in
Budapest.
Telephoning the UK: IDD.

Iceland
Air mail post to UK: All items automatically
sent by air - 7-10 days.
Telegrams: From Chief Telegraphic Office,
Reykjavik.
Telex: From post offices.
Fax: At the telephone headquarters in

Austurvoil Square and hotels.
Telephoning the UK: IDD and international
operator services 24 hours a day.

India
Air mail post to UK: 6-7 days.
Telegrams: From any telegraphic office.
Express, letter and urgent.
Telex: International telex facilities available
24 hours a day at large hotels, and at
telegraph/telex offices in major cities.
Fax: At Overseas Communications Service in
major cities.
Telephoning the UK: IDD and international
operator service.

Indonesia
Air mail post to UK: 7-10 days.
Telegrams: From any telegraphic office. In
Jakarta, facilities available 24 hours a day.
Telex: Public telex facilities operated from
Directorate General for Posts and
Communications, Medan Merdeka Selatan 12
(24 hours); also in some major hotels; and at the
chief telegraphic offices in Semarang;
Jogjakarta, Surabaya and Denpasar.
Telephoning the UK: IDD and international
operator service 24 hours, seven days a week.

Iran
Air mail post to UK: 2-3 weeks.
Telegrams: Must be dispatched from Chief
Telegraph Office, Meidane Sepah, Tehran,
which is open all night. Ordinary, letter and
urgent telegrams.
Telex: Public facilities at Chief Telegraph
Office and some some hotels.
Telephoning the UK: IDD and international
operator service.

Iraq
Air mail post to UK: 5-10 days.
Telegrams: Telegraph office attached to central
post office in Rashid Street, Baghdad, also at
Basrah, Kerkuk and Musul.
Telex: Facilities available at the PTT in Rashid
Street, Baghdad, and at a number of hotels.
Telephoning the UK: IDD

Ireland
Air mail post to UK: 2-3 days.
Telex: Main post offices and hotels.
Fax: Many hotels.
Telephoning the UK: IDD

Israel
Air mail post to UK: 4-7 days.
Telegrams: From telegraphic offices. Ordinary.
Telex: Facilities available to guests in most de
luxe hotels in Jerusalem and Tel Aviv. Public
telex booths at 23 Rehov Yafo, Jerusalem; 7
Rehov Mikve Yisrael, Tel Aviv.

Fax: 4 and 5 star hotels.
Telephoning the UK: IDD 19.00-07.00
weekdays; 15.00-07.00 Sunday at cheaper rate.

Italy
Air mail post to UK: 1 week.
Telegrams: Italcable available over the phone.
Telex: Main Post Offices.
Fax: Some hotels.
Telephoning the UK: IDD.

Jamaica
Air mail post to UK: About 10-14 days.
Telegrams: Telegram service available from
any post office (inland).
Telex: Telex service available from Jamaica
International Telecommunication Ltd, Jamintel
Centre, 15 North Street, Kingston.
Fax: As Telex.
Telephoning the UK: IDD

Japan
Air mail post to UK: 4-6 days.
Telegrams: May be sent from the main hotels,
from offices of Kokusai Denshin Denwa Co Ltd
and from Nippon Denshin Denwa Kosha and
from larger post offices in major cities.
Ordinary, letter and express telegrams.
Telex: Telex booths are available at main post
offices and main offices of Kokusai Denshin
Denwa Co Ltd and Nippon Denshin Denwa
Kosha.
Fax: Major hotels and KDD offices.
Telephoning the UK: IDD

Jordan
Air mail post to UK: About 5 days.
Telegrams: Overseas service reasonably good.
May be sent from the Central Telegraph Office;
Post Office, 1st Circle, Jebel Amman; or any
post office.
Telex: Public telex facilities are available at the
Central Telegraph Office and in a number of
hotels.
Fax: Most hotels.
Telephoning the UK: IDD.

Kazakhstan
Air mail post to UK: 2-3 weeks.
Telex: At main hotels.
Telephoning the UK: Telephone offices are next
to the post offices or at the Hotel Otar.

Kenya
Air mail post to UK: 3-4 days.
Telegrams: Overseas telegrams can be sent
from all post and telegraphic offices. Nairobi
GPO open 24 hrs. Ordinary, letter and urgent
telegrams.
Telex: Facilities available at Nairobi GPO. New
Stanley and Hilton Hotels have facilities for
their guests, otherwise no public call booths.

Fax: Main Post Office in Nairobi and The
Kenyatta International Conference Centre.
Telephoning the UK: IDD and operator service.

Kiribati
Air mail post to UK: Up to 2 weeks
Telegrams: Possible but delays.
Telex: Available at Telecom offices.
Fax: At Telecom offices.
Telephoning the UK: IDD in Tarawa or through
operator.

Korea
Air mail post to UK: 7-10 days.
Telegrams: May be sent by dialling 115 and
delivering message in English or by visiting a
telegraph office of the Korea International
Telecommunications Office (KIT) near Capitol
Building and delivering message in written
English.
Telex: Telex facilities available in main hotels;
also from the Post Office in Seoul and office of
Korea International Telecommunications
Services.
Fax: At major hotels
Telephoning the UK: IDD.

Kuwait
Air mail post to UK: 5 days.
Telegrams: Telegrams sent from Chief
Telegraph Office 6 hours after being handed in
at the Post Office.
Telex: Facilities available at main hotels or from
main Post Office (24 hours).
Fax: Several hotels.
Telephoning the UK: IDD.

Kyrgyzstan
Air mail post to UK: 2 weeks - 2 months
Telegrams: Post offices in large towns.
Telex: In main hotels for residents only.
Telephoning the UK: Through the operator, can
have delays.

Laos
Air mail post to UK: Months
Telephoning the UK: Limited, - links to
Bangkok, where messages can be passed on.

Latvia
Air mail post to UK: 6 days.
Telegrams: From public phones
Telex: Main post office in Riga, Brivibas
Bulvaris 21.
Fax: Same as telex.
Telephoning the UK: IDD

Lebanon
Air mail post to UK: 4-6 days.
Telex: Contact the Embassy in emergency.
Telephoning the UK: IDD.

Lesotho
Air mail post to UK: 1 week.
Telegrams and Telex: Limited, in the main post office only.
Telephoning the UK: IDD available in Maseru

Liberia
Air mail post to UK: 7-10 days.
Telegrams: Facilities provided by the Liberian Telecommunications Corporation and French Cables, Monrovia.
Telex: Services provided by the Liberian Telecommunications Corporation.
Telephoning the UK: IDD

Libya
Air mail post to UK: 2 weeks but can be subject to censorship.
Telex: At the larger hotels.
Telephoning the UK: IDD.

Lithuania
Air mail post to UK: 6 days.
Fax: Services in Vilnius, at the Telegraph Centre, Universteto 14 and at the Hotel Lietuva, Ukmerges 20 and at the Comilet Office, Architeku 146.
Telephoning the UK: IDD.

Luxembourg
Air mail post to UK: About 3 days.
Telegrams: Telegram facilities available at the Main Post Office in Luxembourg City; Bureau de Postes, 8a Avenue Monterey (open 07.00 20.45 Mon Sat); Luxembourg Railways Station Main Post Office, 9 Place de la Gare (open 24 hours, 7 days a week).
Telex: Facilities available from post offices named above. Also Luxembourg Airports Post Office, inside main airport terminal, 1st floor.
Fax: At the main post office.
Telephoning the UK: IDD

Macau
Air mail post to UK: About 3 days.
Telegrams: May be sent from hotels and from General Post Office in Leal Senado Square.
Telex: Facilities from the General Post Office.
Fax: Several hotels
Telephoning the UK: Most hotels have direct dial telephones but otherwise through operators or from the General Post Office.

Macedonia
Air mail post to UK: 10 days
Telegrams and Telex: At the main post office in Skopje.
Telephoning the UK: IDD available.

Madagascar
Air mail post to UK: 7-10 days.

Telegrams: PTT in Antananarivo.
Telex: At PTT and Colbert and Hilton Hotels
Telephoning the UK: IDD in major towns.

Malawi
Air mail post to UK: 10 days.
Telegrams: Main post office
Telex: Bureaux in Blantyre and Zomba
Fax: Same as telex
Telephoning the UK: IDD available.

Malaysia
Air mail post to UK: 4-7 days.
Telegrams: May be sent by 'phone 24 hours a day by dialling 104, or at any Telegraph office and most post offices. Ordinary, urgent letter and greetings telegrams.
Telex: Public facilities available 24 hours at Telegraph Office, Djalan Raja Chulan, Kuala Lumpur, and most hotels.
Fax: Main post offices.
Telephoning the UK: IDD

Maldives
Air mail post to UK: Up to 1 week.
Telegrams: Telecommunications service in Malé.
Telex: Available at Dhiraagu and other resorts.
Fax: Services in Malé.
Telephoning the UK: IDD available.

Mali
Air mail post to UK: 2 weeks.
Telex: Central telex office in Bamako and main hotels.
Telephoning the UK: Limited IDD service.

Malta
Air mail post to UK: 3 days.
Telegrams: From Telemalta offices and most hotels.
Telex: Facilities from Telemalta and most hotels.
Fax: Through Telemalta
Telephoning the UK: IDD.

Martinique
Air mail post to UK: 1 week.
Telex: Available in some hotels.
Telephoning the UK: IDD available.

Mauritania
Air mail post to UK: 2 weeks at least.
Telex: Available in Nouakchott and Nouadhibou
Telephoning the UK: Limited IDD available.

Mauritius
Air mail post to UK: 5-7 days.
Telegrams and Telex: From the Mauritius.Telecommunications Service at Cassis and Port Louis. Also available at the Overseas Telecoms Services Ltd, Rogers

House, President John F Kennedy Street, Port Louis.
Fax: Most hotels.
Telephoning the UK: IDD is available.

Mexico
Air mail post to UK: About 7 days.
Telegrams: Telegraphic system maintained by Telegrafos Nacionales, and telegrams to be handed in to their offices. In Mexico City the main office for international telegrams is at Balderas y Coloìn, Mexico 1 DF.
Telex: International telex facilities available at a number of locations in Mexico City; hotels reluctant to despatch messages for guests but willing to receive them.
Fax: Major hotels.
Telephoning the UK: IDD.

Moldova
Air mail post to UK: 6-8 weeks.
Telephoning the UK: IDD in major towns.

Monaco
Air mail post to UK: 2-3 days.
Telegrams and Telex: Available at hotels and post offices.
Fax: Some major hotels.
Telephoning the UK: IDD.

Mongolia
Air mail post to UK: Up to 2 weeks.
Telex: Limited facilities in Ulan Bator.
Telephoning the UK: Must be booked through the operator.

Montserrat
Air mail post to UK: 1 week.
Telegrams and Telex: Cable & Wireless in Plymouth.
Telephoning the UK: IDD.

Morocco
Air mail post to UK: At least 5 days.
Telegrams: From all telegraph offices. Ordinary and urgent telegrams.
Telex: International telex facilities available at Hotels Hilton and Tour Hassan, Rabat; Hotels El Manour and Marhaba, Casablanca.
Fax: Major 4 and 5 star hotels.
Telephoning the UK: IDD. Calls may be made at any time, but delays might be experienced. also from major hotels.
Telephoning the UK: IDD.

Mozambique
Air mail post to UK: 7-10 days.
Telex: Services in Maputo and Beira
Telephoning the UK: IDD in main towns

Myanmar
Air mail post to UK: 1-2 weeks.
Telegrams: From Central Office on Maha

Bandoola Street, and also Post Office and Telecommunications Corporation in Yangon
Telex: At some main hotels form businessmen.
Telephoning the UK: IDD in main cities.

Namibia
Air mail post to UK: 4-7 days
Telegrams and Telex: Good facilities in every town.
Telex: Good facilities available in every town.
Fax: Available in some hotels.
Telephoning the UK: IDD available.

Naura
Air mail post to UK: 1 week.
Telegrams and Telex: Available through the Naura Government Communications Office.
Telephoning the UK: Through operator.

Nepal
Air mail post to UK: 4-10 days.
Telegrams: Telecommunication Office, Tripureshwar, Kathmandu.
Telex: International telex facilities available at large hotels and Telecommunication Office, Kathmandu.
Fax: Available through some travel agents and 4 and 5 star hotels.
Telephoning the UK: IDD from Kathmandu. International operator service in other towns.

The Netherlands
Air mail post to UK: 4-5 days.
Telegrams: At all post offices.
Telex: Main hotels and conference centres.
Fax: Widely available.
Telephoning the UK: Full IDD service available.

Netherland Antilles
Air mail post to UK: 1 week.
Telegrams and Telex: Through Lands Radio Dienst and All American Cables.
Telephoning the UK: IDD, through the operator is very expensive.

New Caledonia
Air mail post to UK: 1 week.
Telegrams and Telex: Through the Central Office at rue Eugène Porcheron, Nouméa.
Telephoning the UK: IDD.

New Zealand
Air mail post to UK: About 7 days.
Telegrams: From all post offices 09.00 17.00 hours, and telephoned through at any time. Ordinary, letter and urgent telegrams.
Telex: All major hotels, banks, Government offices and some commercial practices have telex facilities.
Fax: Many hotels.
Telephoning the UK: IDD.

Nicaragua
Air mail post to UK: 1 week.
Telegrams and Telex: Facilities in Managua
Telephoning the UK: IDD.

Niger
Air mail post to UK: Up to 2 weeks.
Telegrams: From Chief Telegraph Office,
Niamey, and at all other telegraph offices.
Ordinary, urgent, and letter telegrams.
Telex: Public facilities available at Chief
Telegraph Office, Niamey.
Telephoning the UK: IDD. Good quality, direct
telephone line to Paris from Niamey, which
links with UK. Service available 08.30, 12.30,
15.30 and 18.00 hours daily in Niamey. Calls
should be made by asking exchange for L'Inter
Radio.

Nigeria
Air mail post to UK: Unreliable - up to 3 weeks.
Telegrams and Telex: Through the Nigerian
Telecommunications Ltd (NITEL) in all major
cities.
Telephoning the UK: IDD.

Niue
Air mail post to UK: Up to 2 weeks.
Telegrams and Telex:: Available at the
Telecommunications Department, Central
Reservations Building, Alofi, which is open 24
hours a day.
Telephoning the UK: IDD.

Norway
Air mail post to UK: 2-4 days
Telegrams: Via the telephone.
Telex: Televerket's, Teledirektoratet,
Universitetgt 2, Oslo.
Fax: Major hotels.
Telephoning the UK: IDD.

Oman
Air mail post to UK: 1 week - 10 days
Telegrams: May be sent from post offices.
Telex: Facilities available from post offices.
Fax: At the GTO (Post Office).
Telephoning the UK: IDD.

Pakistan
Air mail post to UK: 5-10 days.
Telegrams: Post offices, telegraph offices and
hotels. The Central Telegraph Office, 1.1
Chundrigar Road, Karachi, provides 24 hours
service.
Telex: The Central Telegraph Office provides
telex facilities 24 hrs.
Telephoning the UK: IDD. International
operator service.

Panama
Air mail post to UK: 5-10 days.

Telegrams: In main post office in the main
towns.
Telex: In Panama City and major hotels.
Fax: Main post offices and major hotels.
Telephoning the UK: IDD.

Papua New Guinea
Air mail post to UK: 7-10 days.
Telegrams: In the main centres.
Telex: Some hotels have telex machines.
Fax: Through companies and government
offices.
Telephoning the UK: IDD.

Paraguay
Air mail post to UK: 5-7 days.
Telegrams: May be sent from post offices,
banks, and hotels, through Antelco
(Administración Nacional de
Telecommicaciones.
Telex: Facilities available from post offices,
banks and hotels.
Telephoning the UK: IDD or via operator.

Peru
Air mail post to UK: About 10 days.
Telegrams: From ENTEL PERU telegraph
offices. Ordinary and night telegrams.
Telex: Telex machines with international
connections installed at Hotels Bolivar, Crillon
and Sheraton in Lima.
Fax: Some hotels.
Telephoning the UK: IDD or international
operator service at all times.

Philippines
Air mail post to UK: 10 days, often more.
Telegrams: From Eastern Telecommunications
Philippines Inc. offices. Ordinary and urgent
telegrams.
Telex: Public telex booths operated by Eastern
Telecommunications Philippines Inc, Globe
Mackay Cable and Radio Corporation, and
RCA Communications Inc.
Fax: 3 to 5 star hotels.
Telephoning the UK: IDD or international
operator service 24 hrs a day.

Poland
Air mail post to UK: 4 days.
Telegrams: Most post offices and by 'phone.
Telex: At Foreign Trade Enterprises and Urzad
Pocztowy, Warsaw and Orbis hotels.
Telephoning the UK: IDD.

Portugal
Air mail post to UK: About 3 days.
Telegrams: Facilities available from all post
offices.
Telex: From post offices and the Public Telex
Office, Praca D Luis 30-1, Lisbon which is open
09.00-18.00 Monday to Friday.

Fax: Fax Bureaux is main towns.
Telephoning the UK: IDD.

Puerto Rico
Air mail post to UK: Up to a week.
Telex: In main hotels in the capital.
Telephoning the UK: IDD.

Qatar
Air mail post to UK: Up to a week.
Telegrams: For telegraph service dial 130.
Telex: Facilities available from Qatar National Telephone Service (QNTS) and the Cable & Wireless office in Doha.
Fax: Major hotels.
Telephoning the UK: IDD.

Réunion
Air mail post to UK: 2-3 weeks.
Telegrams and Telex: Available only in St Denis.
Telephoning the UK: IDD.

Romania
Air mail post to UK: Up to 2 weeks.
Telegrams: At post offices and night telegrams can be sent in Bucharest.
Telex: Large hotels.
Fax: In large hotels.
Telephoning the UK: Through the operator.

Russian Federation
Air mail post to UK: 10 days.
Telegrams: From hotels.
Telex: In an emergency through the Commercial Department at the British Embassy, Kutuzovsky Prospekt 7/4, 12148 Moscow.
Telephoning the UK: IDD from Moscow, St Petersburg and Novgorod, elsewhere through the operator.

Rwanda
Air mail post to UK: 2-3 weeks.
Telegrams and Telex: In Kigali and main hotels
Telephoning the UK: Through the operator.

St Kitts and Nevis
Air mail post to UK: 5-7 days
Telegrams: Through SKANTEL, Canyon Street, Basseterre and Main Street, Charlestown.
Fax: Available at SKANTEL.
Telephoning the UK: IDD.

St Lucia
Air mail post to UK: 1 week.
Telegrams: Through Cable & Wireless, Casteries.
Telex: Public telex booth at Cable & Wireless.
Fax: Cable and Wireless.
Telephoning the UK: IDD.

St Vincent and The Grenadines
Air mail post to UK: Up to 2 weeks.
Telex: Limited to main hotels.
Fax: From most hotels .
Telephoning the UK: IDD.

Sâo Tomé e Principe
Air mail post to UK: 2-3 weeks.
Telex: Main hotel in Sâo Tomé.
Telephoning the UK: Limited IDD - Through operator.

Saudi Arabia
Air mail post to UK: Up to 1 week.
Telegrams: From all post offices.
Telex: From major hotels.
Fax: Major hotels.
Telephoning the UK: IDD.

Senegal
Air mail post to UK: 7-10 days.
Telegrams and Telex: Available at most major post offices.
Fax: SONATEL has a fax machine.
Telephoning the UK: IDD.

Seychelles
Air mail post to UK: Up to 1 week.
Telegrams and Telex: SEYTELS?Cable & Wireless Ltd, Francis Rachel Street, Victoria, Mahé
Fax: Same as telegrams
Telephoning the UK: Through the operator.

Sierra Leone
Air mail post to UK: 5 days.
Telegrams: From Mercury House, 7 Wallace Johnson Street, Freetown. Ordinary, urgent and letter telegrams.
Telex: Facilities available at Mercury House.
Telephoning the UK: IDD or international operator calls between 11.00 and midnight local time any day of the week.

Singapore
Air mail post to UK: Usually 5 days, but can take 10-14.
Telegrams: From telegraph offices. Ordinary, urgent, letter and social telegrams.
Telex: Public telex facilities available at Central Telegraph Office, 35 Robinson Road and the Comcentre near Orchard Road.
Telephoning the UK: IDD; operator service 24 hours.

Slovak Republic
Air mail post to UK: 4-6 days.
Telegrams and Telex: Main hotels and Kollárkska 12, Bratislava.
Telephoning the UK: Special Kiosks for International calls - IDD.

Slovenia
Air mail post to UK: 10-14 days.
Telegrams and Telex: Limited
Fax: Available
Telephoning the UK: IDD.

Solomon Islands
Air mail post to UK: 7 days
Telegrams and Telex: At Solomon Telekom
Fax: At the Solomon Telekom office in
Honiara.
Telephoning the UK: IDD.

Somalia
Air mail post to UK: Up to 2 weeks, long at the
time of writing due to the civil war.
Telex: Main post office in Mogadishu and Hotel
Juba.
Telephoning the UK: IDD.

South Africa
Air mail post to UK: 3-7 days.
Telegrams: Telegraph service available in
every town, however small.
Telex: Public call facilities available in Cape
Town, Durban, Johannesburg and Pretoria post
offices. Most hotels and offices have telex.
Fax: Main hotels.
Telephoning the UK: IDD available from all centres.

Spain
Air mail post to UK: 4-5 days.
Telegrams: May be sent from main post offices.
Telex: Facilities from main post offices.
Fax: Most 4 and 5 star hotels.
Telephoning the UK: IDD.

Sri Lanka
Air mail post to UK: 4-7 days.
Telegrams: From all post offices. Ordinary,
letter and urgent telegrams.
Telex: Public telex booth at OTS Building,
Duke Street, Colombo.
Fax: General post office in Colombo.
Telephoning the UK: IDD and international
operator service 24 hours.

Sudan
Air mail post to UK: Up to a week.
Telegrams: The central Telegraph Office,
Gamma Avenue, Khartoum.
Telex: Main post offices.
Telephoning the UK: Through the operator.

Suriname
Air mail post to UK: At least a month.
Telegrams and Telex: At the Government
Telegrapgh Office, Gravenstraat 33,
Paramaribo.
Telephoning the UK: IDD.

Swaziland
Air mail post to UK: About 10 days.

Telegrams: May be sent from most post offices.
Telex: Facilities from most post offices.
Fax: Some hotels.
Telephoning the UK: IDD

Sweden
Air mail post to UK: 3-4 days.
Telegrams: Telephone the telegrams in by
dialling 0021 or send by post.
Telex: Public Telexes not available.
Telephoning the UK: IDD.

Switzerland
Air mail post to UK: 2-4 days.
Telegrams: May be sent from post offices and
hotels.
Telex: Some hotels have telex facilities.
Fax: At telegraph offices, post offices and
major hotels.
Telephoning the UK: IDD.

Syrian Republic
Air mail post to UK: Up to a week.
Telegrams: Telegraph office in Damascus.
Telex: From main hotels.
Telephoning the UK: IDD.

Taiwan
Air mail post to UK: Up to 10 days.
Telegrams: ITA offices, 28 Hangchow South
Road, Section 1, Taipei.
Telex: Major hotels and ITA.
Fax: ITA.
Telephoning the UK: IDD.

Tahiti
Telegrams: Facilities can be found at the Office
des Postes et Telecommunications, Boulevard
Pomare, Papeete.
Telex: Services from the Office des Postes et
Telecommunications.
Telephoning the UK: IDD or dial 19 for
international operator service.

Tajikistan
Air mail post to UK: 2-4 weeks.
Telegrams: Limited facilities.
Telex: Major hotels in Dushanbe.
Telephoning the UK: From International
telephone offices only, usually adjoining the
main post office in a town.

Tanzania
Air mail post to UK: About 7 days.
Telegrams: From post office. Ordinary, urgent,
letter and greetings telegrams.
Telex: Public telex at post office in Mkwepu
Street, Dar Es Salaam,and in some hotels.
Telephoning the UK: IDD or international
operator service 24 hours.

Thailand
Air mail post to UK: 5 days.

Telegrams: From GPO Building, New Road, Bangkok, or any telegraph office. Ordinary, urgent, letter telegrams.
Telex: Public call office facilities at the GPO, New Road, Bangkok.
Fax: Facilities widely available.
Telephoning the UK: IDD or international operator service, by contacting Long Distance Telephone Office behind GPO in New Road (tel: 32054 or 37056).

Togo
Air mail post to UK: Up to 2 weeks.
Telegrams: Main post offices.
Telephoning the UK: IDD

Tonga
Air Mail post to UK: 10 days.
Telegrams: Via Cable & Wireless, Salote Rd. Tel: 21 499.
Telex: Via Cable & Wireless. Private booths available.
Telephoning the UK: IDD or dial 913 for International Operator.

Trinidad and Tobago
Air mail post to UK: About 10 days.
Telegrams: Via Trinidad and Tobago External Telecommunications Company Ltd (Textel) located at 1 Edward Street, Port of Spain, Trinidad.
Telex: Textel provide a telex agency service for the receipt of telex messages on behalf of customers who do not have their own installations.
Telephoning the UK: IDD.

Tunisia
Air mail post to UK: About 5 days.
Telegrams: From Central Post Office in Rue Charles de Gaulle, Tunis (24 hrs), and other telegraph offices.
Telex: At the Telecommunications Centre, 29 Jamal Abdelnassel, Tunis.
Telephoning the UK: IDD and international operator service 24 hours a day.

Turkey
Air mail post to UK: 3 days.
Telegrams: From telegraph and post offices. Ordinary and urgent telegrams.
Telex: Public call office at main post office, Ulus, Ankara and at main post office, Telegraf Gisesi, Sirkeci, Istanbul (24 hrs).
Fax: At some hotels.
Telephoning the UK: IDD or international operator service.

Turkmenistan
Air mail post to UK: 2-4 weeks.
Telegrams: At some post offices
Telex: Major hotels.

Telephoning the UK: Booked through the international operator.

Turks and Caicos Islands
Air mail to UK: 5-10 days.
Telegrams: Via Cable & Wireless.
Telex: Via Cable & Wireless.
Fax: Available.
Telephoning the UK: IDD or through operator.

Tuvalu
Air mail post to UK: 5-10 days.
Telegrams: Via the post office in Funafuti.
Telex: Telecommunications centre in Funafuti.
Fax: Same as telex.
Telephoning the UK: IDD.

Uganda
Air mail post to UK: 2 weeks.
Telex: Postal and Telecommunications Office in Kampala.
Telephoning the UK: Through the operator.

Ukraine
Air mail post to UK: 2-3 weeks.
Telegrams and Telex: From central post offices in main towns.
Fax: Some offices and hotels.
Telephoning the UK: Limited IDD.

United Arab Emirates
Air mail post to UK: 5 days.
Telegrams: Phone and send telegrams from ETISALAT offices in each town.
Fax: ETISALAT offices.
Telephoning the UK: IDD.

USA
Air mail post to UK: 5-6 days but varies. More from West Coast.
Telegrams: From all post and telegraph offices. Full and night letter telegrams.
Telex: Western Union international telex facilities throughout the USA.
Fax: Widely available.
Telephoning the UK: IDD.

Uruguay
Air mail post to UK: About 7 days.
Telegrams: Public booths in main banking and commercial offices.
Telex: Facilities in main banking and commercial offices.
Telephoning the UK: IDD or via the operator.

Uzbekistan
Air mail post to UK: 4 weeks.
Telegrams: Limited.
Telex: Main hotels.
Fax: Major hotels for residents only.
Telephoning the UK: Through operator as IDD is limited.

Vanuatu
Air mail post to UK: 7 days.
Telegrams and Telex: Central post office in Port Vila.
Fax: Some hotels.
Telephoning the UK: Through operator.

Venezuela
Air mail post to UK: 4-7 days.
Telegrams: Usual telegram services from public telegraph offices, ordinary, and night letter telegrams.
Telex: Public telex facilities provided by CANTV.
Fax: Large hotels.
Telephoning the UK: IDD.

Virgin Islands
Air mail post to UK: 5-10 days.
Telegrams: Via Cable & Wireless.
Telex: Via Cable & Wireless.
Telephoning the UK: IDD or through operator.

Western Samoa
Air mail post to UK: 3 weeks.
Telegrams: Telegraph desk at the post office.
Telephoning the UK: Through the operator.

Yemen
Air mail post to UK: 4-5 days.
Telegrams: From any telegraph office. Ordinary, urgent and letter telegrams.
Telex: Telex booths at Cable & Wireless offices in Sana'a, Hodeida and Taiz.
Telephoning the UK: IDD or operator service. Telephone link available 08.00 20.30 local time.

Yugoslavia (Serbia and Montenegro)
Air mail post to UK: Disrupted, normally 4-5 days.
Telegrams: Facilities at post offices.
Telex: Via post offices.
Telephoning the UK: IDD.

Zaire
Air mail post to UK: 4-10 days.
Telegrams: From Chief Telegraph Offices. Ordinary and urgent telegrams.
Telex: Facilities only available at Kinshasa and Lubumbashi Chief Telegraph Offices; also at Intercontinental Hotel.
Telephoning the UK: IDD or international operator service.

Zambia
Air mail post to UK: 5-7 days.
Telegrams: From telegraph offices. Urgent will be accepted at Lusaka Central Telegraph Offices up to 21.00 hrs Mon Sat.
Telex: Public telex facilities at Lusaka GPO; also main hotels.

Telephoning the UK: IDD or international operator service.

Zimbabwe
Air mail post to UK: About 5-7 days.
Telegrams: Facilities found in all major cities and tourist centres.
Telex: From all major cities and tourist centres.
Telephoning the UK: IDD or operator service.

Note: Although most countries now have some form of IDD connection, this is often only operative in major centres and even this can involve lengthy delays in some cases. Be warned.

INTERNATIONAL DIRECT DIALLING

Countries in alphabetical order to which international-direct dialling is available. Country codes are the same from anywhere in the world. Please see notes at the end for changes to international dialling on 16th April 1995.

Country	Country Code	Time Difference (based on GMT)
Afghanistan	93	(+4½)
Albania	355	(+1)
Algeria	213	(+1)
Andorra	33 628	(+1)
Angola	244	(+1)
Anguilla	1 809	(-4)
Antigua	1 809	(-4)
Antilles	559	(_4)
Argentina	54	(-3)
Aruba	2 978	(-4)
Ascension	247	GMT
Australia	61	(+8-10)
Austria	43	(+1)
Azores	351	(-1)
Bahamas	1 809	(-5)
Bahrain	973	(+3)
Bangladesh	880	(+6)
Barbados	1 809	(-4)
Belgium	32	(+1)
Belize	501	(-6)

Benin	229	(+1)	*Ethiopia*	251	(+3)
Bermuda	1 809	(-4)	*Falkland Islands*	500	(-4)
Bhutan	975	(+6)	*Faroe Islands*	298	GMT
Bolivia	591	(-4)	*Fiji*	679	(+12)
Bosnia-Hercegovina	38	(+1)	*Finland*	358	(+2)
Botswana	267	(+2)	*France*	33	(+1)
Brazil	55	(-2-5)	*French Guiana*	594	(-4)
Brunei	673	(+8)	*French Polynesia*	689	(-10)
Bulgaria	359	(+2)	*Gabon*	241	(+1)
Burkina Faso	226	(GMT)	*Gambia*	220	GMT
Burundi	257	(+2)	*Germany*	49	(+1)
Cambodia	855	(+7)	*Ghana*	233	GMT
Cameroon	237	(+1)	*Gibraltar*	350	(+1)
Canada	1	(-3½-9)	*Greece*	30	(+2)
Canary Islands	34	GMT	*Greenland*	299	(-3)
Cape Verde Islands	238	(-1)	*Grenada*	1 809	(-4)
Cayman Islands	1 809	(-5)	*Guadeloupe*	590	(-4)
Central African Republic	236	(+1)	*Guam*	671	(+10)
Chad	235	(+1)	*Guatemala*	502	(-6)
Chile	56	(-4)	*Guinea*	224	GMT
China	86	(+8)	*Guinea-Bissau*	245	GMT
Christmas Island	6724	(+7)	*Guyana*	592	(-3)
Cocos Island	6722	(+6½)	*Haiti*	509	(-5)
Colombia	57	(-5)	*Honduras*	504	(-6)
CIS	7	(+3-+10)	*Hong Kong*	852	(+8)
Comoros	269	(+3)	*Hungary*	36	(+1)
Congo	242	(+1)	*Iceland*	354	GMT
Cook Islands	682	(-10½)	*India*	91	(+5½)
Costa Rica	506	(-6)	*Indonesia*	62	(+7-9)
Côte d'Ivoire	225	GMT	*Iran*	98	(+3½)
Cuba	53	(-5)	*Iraq*	964	(+3)
Cyprus	357	(+2)	*Ireland*	353	GMT
Czech Republic	42	(+1)	*Israel*	972	(+2)
Denmark	45	(+1)	*Italy*	39	(+1)
Djibouti	253	(+3)	*Jamaica*	1 809	(-5)
Dominica	1 809	(-4)	*Japan*	81	(+9)
Dominican Rep	1 809	(-5)	*Jordan*	962	(+2)
Ecuador	593	(-5)	*Kenya*	254	(+3)
Egypt	20	(+2)	*Kiribati*	686	GMT
El Salvador	503	(-6)	*Korea (North)*	850	(+9)
Equatorial Guinea	240	(+1)	*Korea (South)*	82	(+9)
Eritrea	291	(+3)	*Kuwait*	965	(+3)
Estonia	7	(+3)	*Laos*	856	(+7)
			Latvia	7	(+3)

From 16 April 1995 all national and international codes change — see page 587 for details.

Lebanon	961	(+2)		*Palau*	6 809	(+9)
Lesotho	266	(+2)		*Panama*	507	(-5)
Liberia	231	GMT		*Papua New Guinea*	675	(+10)
Libya	218	(+1)		*Paraguay*	595	(-3)
Liechtenstein	41 75	(+1)		*Peru*	51	(-5)
Lithuania	7	(+3)		*Philippines*	63	(+8)
Luxembourg	352	(+1)		*Poland*	48	(+1)
Macau	853	(+8)		*Portugal*	351	GMT
Madagascar	261	(+3)		*Puerto Rico*	1 809	(-4)
Madeira	351 91	GMT		*Qatar*	974	(+3)
Malawi	265	(+2)		*Reunion*	262	(+4)
Malaysia	60	(+8)		*Romania*	40	(+2)
Maldives	960	(+5)		*Russian Federation*	7	(+3-+12)
Malta	356	(+1)		*Rwanda*	250	(+2)
Mali	233	GMT		*St Kitts & Nevis*	1 809	(-4)
Marshall Islands	692	(+12)		*St Lucia*	1 809	(-4)
Martinique	596	(-4)		*St Pierre*	508	(-3)
Mauritania	222	GMT		*& Miquelon*		
Mauritius	230	(+4)		*St Vincent*	1 809	(-4)
Mayotte	269	(+3)		*& Grenadines*		
Mexico	52	(-6-8)		*American Samoa*	684	(-11)
Micronesia	691	(+10-+11)		*Western Samoa*	685	(-11)
Monaco	33 93	(+1)		*San Marino*	39 541	(+1)
Mongolia	976	(+8)		*Sâo Tomé e Principe*	239 12	GMT
Montserrat	1 809	(-4)		*Saudi Arabia*	966	(+3)
Morocco	212	GMT		*Senegal*	221	GMT
Mozambique	258	(+2)		*Seychelles*	248	(+4)
Myanmar	95	(+6½)		*Sierra Leone*	232	GMT
Namibia	264	(+2)		*Singapore*	65	(+8)
Nauru	674	(+13)		*Slovak Republic*	42	(+1)
Nepal	977	(+5½)		*Slovenia*	38	(+1)
Netherlands	31	(+1)		*Solomon Islands*	677	(-11)
Neth. Antilles	599	(-4)		*Somalia*	252	(+3)
New Caledonia	687	(+11)		*South Africa*	27	(+2)
New Zealand	64	(+12)		*Spain*	34	(+1)
Nicaragua	505	(-6)		*Sri Lanka*	94	(+5½)
Niger	227	(+1)		*Sudan*	249	(+2)
Nigeria	234	(+1)		*Suriname*	597	(-3)
Niue	683	(-11)		*Swaziland*	268	(+2)
Norfolk Island	672 3	(+11½)		*Sweden*	46	(+1)
Northern Marianas	670	(+10)		*Switzerland*	41	(+1)
Norway	47	(+1)		*Syria*	963	(+2)
Oman	968	(+4)		*Taiwan*	886	(+8)
Pakistan	92	(+5)		*Tanzania*	255	(+3)
				Thailand	66	(+7)

From 16 April 1995 all national and international codes change — see page 587 for details.

Togo	228	GMT
Tonga	676	(+13)
Trinidad & Tobago	1 809	(-4)
Tunisia	216	(+1)
Turkey	90	(+2)
Turks and Caicos	1 809	(-5)
Tuvalu	688	(+12)
Uganda	256	(+3)
UAE	971	(+4)
Uruguay	598	(-3)
USA	1	(-5-11)
Vanuatu	678	(+11)
Venezuela	58	(-5)
Vietnam	84	(+7)
Virgin Islands	1 809	(-4)
Yemen	967	(+3)
Yugoslavia	38	(+1)
(Serbia + Montenegro)		
Zaire	243	(+1/2)
Zambia	260	(+2)
Zimbabwe	263	(+2)

Charge bands, standard and cheap rates

These vary worldwide due to time differences. For further information on charge bands dialling from UK, please see the front of any telephone directory. IDD cheap rate, available to most countries from the UK, is from 8pm to 8am Monday to Friday, all day Saturday and Sunday. For charge bands and standard rates elsewhere contact the local operator.

Note: New countries are constantly being added to the international network. If you would prefer to dial direct and the number is not listed here, ask the operator for an update.

International Codes Changes on Phone Day

On 16 April 1995 all national codes will change. International calls will also be affected. from 16th April 1995 the code to dial abroad from the UK will change from 010 to 00. This is part of a move to provide a single code for all European countries to access the international network.

TRAVEL SERVICES

There are numerous American Express and Thomas Cook travel service offices worldwide and travellers can use them as *post restante* addresses (letters and telegrams only, no parcels). You may also cash and purchase your American Express and Thomas cook traveller's cheques or buy foreign currency.

American Express

Australia

Melbourne
American Express Travel Service
105 Elizabeth St
Tel: **3-608 0333**

Cairns
Northern Australia Travel Agency
91 Grafton St
Tel: **70-516472**

Darwin
Travellers World Pty Ltd
18 Knuckley St
Tel: **89-814699**

Perth
American Express Travel Service
78 William St
Tel: **9-426 3777**

Sydney
American Express Travel Service
American Express Tower
345 George St
Tel: **2-262 3666**

Canada

Calgary
American Express Travel Service
421 - 7th Ave S.W.
Tel: **403-261 5982**

Edmonton
American Express Travel Service
Principal Plaza
10305 Jasper Avenue
Tel: **403-421 0608**

Halifax
American Express Travel Service
City Center Atlantic
5523 Spring Garden Road
B3J 1G8
Tel: **902- 423 3900**

Montreal
American Express Travel Service
The Bay

Place Versailles
7525 Sherbrooke ESt
Tel: **514-354 8442**

Ottawa
American Express Travel Service
The Bay
Bayshore Mall
100 Bayshore Mall Drive
Tel: **613-563 1161**

Quebec City
American Express Travel Service
The Bay
5401 Boulevard des Galeries
G2K 1N4
Tel: **418-627 2580**

Toronto
American Express Travel Service
The Bay 44 Bloor St E
5th Floor
Tel: **416 963 6060**

Vancouver
American Express Travel Service
The Bay
674 Granville St
V6C 1Z6
Tel: **604-687 7686**

New Zealand

Auckland
American Express Travel Service
101 Queen St
PO Box 2412
Tel: **9-379 8243**

Christchurch
Guthreys Travel Centre
126 Cashel St
The Guthrey Centre
PO Box 343
Tel: **3-379 3560**

Queenstown
Mount Cook travel Line Centre
Rees Street
PO Box 359
Tel: **3-442 7650**

Rotorua
Blackmore's Galazy Travel
411 Tutanekai St
PO Box 2149
Tel: **7-347 9444**

Wellington
Century 21 Travel
203 Lambton Quay
Tel: **4-473 1221**

UK

Aberdeen
American Express Travel Service
2nd Floor
4-5 Union Terrace
Tel: **0224 642961**

Birmingham
American Express Travel Service
New Terminal Building
Birmingham Int Airport
Tel: **021-782 0616**

Bristol
American Express Travel Service
74 Queens Road
Clifton BS8 1QU
Tel: **0272 750750**

Edinburgh
American Express Travel Service
139 Prince St
Tel: **031-225 7881**

Glasgow
American Express Travel Service
115 Hope St
Tel: **041-221 4366**

London
American Express Travel Service
4-12 Lower Regent St
Tel: **071-839 2682**

Oxford
Keith Bailey Travel
99 St Aldates
Tel: **0865 790099**

USA

Arizona
American Express Travel Service
2508 E Camelback Road
Biltmore Fashion Park
Phoenix
Tel: **602-468 1199**

California
American Express Travel Service
The Hilton Center
901 West 7th St
Los Angeles
Tel: **213-627 4800**

American Express Travel Service
295 California St
San Francisco
Tel: **415-788 4367**

Colorado
Aspen Club Express Inc
730 East Durant
Aspen
Tel: **303-920 2000**

Florida
American Express Travel Service
Suite 100
330 Biscayne Boulevard
Miami
Tel: **305-358 7350**

Georgia
American Express Travel Service
Colony Square
1175 Peachtree St NE
Atlanta
Tel: **404-892 8175**

Illinois
Chicago
American Express Travel Service
34 N Clark St
Chicago
Tel: **312-263 6617**

Massachussetts
American Express Travel Service
One Court St
Boston
Tel: **617-705 3171**

New York
American Express Travel Service
Bloomingdale's
59th St & Lexington
New York City
Tel: **212-687 3700**

Further information
*American Express Guide to Travel Service
Offices* (A worldwide listing available from all
major American Express Travel Service Offices
published annually).

Thomas Cook

Australia

ACT
Shop 51
Ground Floor
Canberra Centre
Bunda Street
Canberra 2601
Tel: 6-257 2222

New South Wales
3rd Floor
95-99 York Street
PO Box Q384 QVB
Sydney 2000
Tel: **2- 224 6400**

Northern Territory
Suite 5
Second Floor
13 Cavenagh Street
Darwin
Tel: **89-816182**

Queensland
Shop 56
The Myer Centre
Corner of Elizabeth & Albert Street
Brisbane
Tel: **7-221 9749**

South Australia
State Bank of South Australia
97-105 King William Street
Adelaide 5000
Tel: **8-212 3777**

Victoria
Ground Floor
257 Collins Street
Melbourne 3000
Tel: **3-654 7305**

Western Australia
Suite 6
25 Barrack Street
GPO Box X2246
Perth 60000
Tel: **9-221 5432**

Canada

Alberta
1250-605 5th Avenue
SW Calgary
Tel: **403-263 0031**

Edmonton Eaton Centre
10250
102 Avenue NW
Edmonton
Tel: **403-448 9867**

British Colombia
1016 West Georgia Street
Vancouver V6E 2Y3
Tel: 604-687 6111

Manitoba
One Canada Centre
220-447 Portage Avenue
Winnipeg
Tel: **204-958 7800**

Ontario
222-234 Laurier Avenue West
Ottawa
Tel: **613-237 5434**

16th Floor
100 Yonge Street
Toronto

Ontario M5C 2W1
Tel: **416-360 7867**

Quebec
677 Ouest Rue Ste-Catherine
Montreal
Tel: **514-284 7388**

Washington
928 Third Avenue
Seattle
Tel: 206-621 8650

Further information:
Thomas Cook Worldwide Network Guide
(Thomas Cook Publishing)

New Zealand

125 Kitchener Street
Po Box 33-1231
Milford
Auckland
Tel: **9- 489 8743**

472 Papanui Road
Papanui
Christchurch
Tel: **3-352 4504**

United Kingdom

45 Berkeley Street
London W1A 1EB
Tel: **071-499 4000**

PO Box 36
Thorpe Wood
Peterborough PE3 6SB
Tel: **0733 63200**

United States

100 Cambridge Park Drive
PO Box 9104
Cambridge
MA 02140
Tel: **617- 868 9800**

California
Hilton Hotel Center
900 Wilshire Boulevard
Los Angelos 90017
Tel: **213 624 4221**

Columbia
1800 K Street N W
Washington
Tel: **202-623 8888**

Massachusetts
222 Berkeley Street
Boston
Tel: **617-236 1331**

New York
779 Broadway
Ground Floor
New York 10036
Tel: **212-387 7800**

WORLD SERVICE FREQUENCIES

Frequencies are given in kiloHertz and a choice is given as they vary depending on the time of day

Afghanistan	17790; 15575; 15310; 11955; 9740; 9580; 5975; 5965; 1413
Albania	17640; 15070; 12095; 9410; 6180
Algeria	17705; 15070; 12095; 9410; 7325; 6195
Angola	21660; 17790; 15400; 9600; 6005;
Argentina	17790; 15260; 15190; 11750; 9915; 7325
Australia	17830; 11955; 11695; 9740; 9640; 7110; 6110
Austria	15575; 15070; 12095; 9410; 6195
Azores	17705; 15400; 15070; 12095; 9410
Bangladesh	17790; 15310; 11955; 11750; 9740; 7160; 5975; 5965; 792
Belgium	15575; 12095; 9410; 6195; 648; 198
Bolivia	17840; 15260; 15220; 9915; 9640; 9590; 7325
Borneo	17830; 15360; 11955; 9740; 6195; 3915
Bosnia-Herzegovina	15070; 12095; 9410; 6195
Botswana	21660; 21470; 17885; 17880; 15420; 15400; 11940; 6190; 3255
Brazil	17790; 15260; 15190; 11750; 9915; 7325
Brunei	17830; 15360; 11955; 9740; 6195; 3915
Bulgaria	17640; 15070; 12095; 9410; 6180
Burundi	21470; 17885; 15575; 15420; 9630; 6135; 6005
Cambodia	17830; 17790; 15360; 11955; 11750; 9740; 9570; 6195; 3915
Cameroon	21660; 17880; 17790; 15400; 9600; 6005
Canada	17840; 15260; 15220; 11820; 9740; 9640; 9590; 9515; 7325; 6175; 5975
Canary Islands	17705; 15400; 15070; 12095; 9410
Caribbean	17840; 15220; 9915; 7325; 6195; 5975; 930
Cent. America	17840; 15220; 9915; 9640; 9590; 7325; 5975
Central African Rep	21660; 17880; 17790; 15400; 9600; 6005
Chad	21660; 17880; 17790; 15400; 9600; 6005
Chile	17790; 15260; 15190; 11750; 9915; 7325
China	21715; 17830; 17790; 15360; 15280; 9740; 9570; 7180; 6195
CIS	17640; 15070; 12095; 9410; 6195
Colombia	17840; 15260; 15220; 9915; 9640; 9590; 7325
Congo	21660; 17880; 17790; 15400; 9600; 6005
Czech Republic	15575; 15070; 12095; 9410; 6195; 1296
Denmark	12095; 9410; 6195; 198
Djibouti	21470; 17885; 15420; 11730; 9630; 6135; 6005
Ecuador	17840; 15260; 15220; 9915; 9640; 9590; 7325
Egypt	17640; 15575; 15070; 12095; 9410; 7325; 1323; 639
Eritrea	21470; 17885; 15420; 11730; 9630; 6135; 6005
Estonia	15070; 12095; 9410; 6195
Ethiopia	21470; 17885; 15420; 11730; 9630; 6135; 6005
Falkland Islands	17790; 15260; 15190; 11750; 9915; 7325
France	15070; 12095; 9410; 7325; 6195; 648; 198
Gabon	21660; 17880; 17790; 15400; 9600; 6005
Germany (NE)	15575; 15070; 12095; 9410; 6195; 1296
Germany (NW)	15575; 12095; 9410; 6195; 648; 198
Germany (S)	15575; 15070; 12095; 9410; 6195
Gibraltar	17705; 15070; 12095; 9410; 7325; 6195
Greece	17640; 15070; 12095; 9410; 6180; 1323
India (W)	17790; 15575; 156310; 11955; 11750; 9580; 7160; 5965; 1413
India (E)	17790; 15310; 11955; 11750; 9740; 7160; 5975; 5965; 792
Indonesia	17830; 15360; 11955; 9740; 6195; 3915

Iran	15575; 15070; 12095; 11955; 11760; 9740; 7235; 7160; 1413
Ireland	15575; 12095; 9410; 6195; 648; 198
Israel	1323; 639
Italy	17640; 15575; 15070; 12095; 9410; 6195
Japan	21715; 17830; 15280; 11955; 11820; 9740; 7180
Jordan	1323; 639
Kenya	21470; 17885; 15575; 15420; 9630; 6135; 6005
Korea	21715; 17830; 15280; 11955; 11820; 9740; 7180
Laos	17830; 17790; 15360; 11955; 11750; 9740; 9570; 6195; 3915
Latvia	17640; 15070; 12095; 9410; 6195
Lebanon	1323; 720
Lesotho	21660; 21470; 17885; 17880; 15420; 15400; 11940; 6190; 3255
Libya	17640; 15575; 15070; 12095; 9410; 7325
Lithuania	17640; 15070; 12095; 9410; 6195
Luxembourg	15575; 12095; 9410; 6195; 648; 198
Macedonia	17640; 15070; 12095; 9410; 6180
Madagascar	21470; 17885; 15575; 15420; 9630; 6135; 6005
Malawi	21660; 21470; 17885; 17880; 15420; 15400; 11940; 6190; 3225
Malaysia	17830; 15360; 11955; 9740; 6195; 3915
Maldives	17790; 15310; 11955; 11750; 9740; 7160; 5975; 5965; 792
Malta	17640; 15575; 15070; 12095; 9410
Mauritius	21470; 17885; 15575; 15420; 9630; 6135; 6005
Mexico	17840; 15220; 9915; 9640; 9590; 7325; 5975
Middle East	15575; 15070; 12095; 11760; 9410; 7160; 1413
Mongolia	21715; 17830; 17790; 15360; 15280; 9740; 9570; 7180; 6195
Morocco	17705; 15070; 12095; 9410; 7325; 6195
Mozambique	21660; 21470; 17885; 17880; 15420; 15400; 11940; 6190; 3225
Myanmar	17830; 17790; 15360; 11955; 11750; 9740; 9570; 6195; 3915
Namibia	21660; 17790; 15400; 9600; 6005; 1197
Nepal	17790; 15310; 11955; 11750; 9740; 7160; 5975; 5965; 792
Netherlands	15575; 12095; 9410; 6195; 648; 198
Norway	12095; 9410; 6195; 198
Pacific Islands	17830; 11955; 11695; 9740; 9640; 7110; 6110
Pakistan	17790; 15575; 15310; 11955; 9740; 9580; 5975; 5965; 1413
Papua New Guinea	17830; 11955; 11695; 9740; 7110; 6110
Paraguay	17790; 15260; 15190; 11750; 9915; 7325
Peru	17840; 15260; 15220; 9915; 9640; 9590; 7325
Philippines	21715; 17830; 15360; 11955; 9740; 6195
Poland	15575; 15070; 12095; 9410; 6195; 1296
Portugal	17705; 15070; 12095; 9410; 7325; 6195
Romania	17640; 15070; 12095; 9410; 6180
Rwanda	21470; 17885; 15575; 15420; 9630; 6135; 6005
Serbia	17640; 15070; 12095; 9410; 6180
Slovak Republic	15575; 15070; 12095; 9410; 6195; 1296
Somalia	21470; 17885; 15420; 11730; 9630; 6135; 6005
South Africa	21660; 21470; 17885; 17880; 15420; 15400; 11940; 6190; 3255; 1197
Spain	17705; 15070; 12095; 9410; 7325; 6195
Sri Lanka	17790; 15310; 11955; 11750; 9740; 7160; 5975; 5965; 792
Sudan	17640; 15575; 15070; 12095; 9410; 7325
Swaziland	21660; 21470; 17885; 17880; 15420; 15400; 11940; 6190; 3255
Switzerland	15575; 15070; 12095; 9410; 6195
Syria	1323; 720
Tanzania	21470; 17885; 15575; 15420; 9630; 6135; 6005
Thailand	17830; 17790; 15360; 11955; 11750; 9740; 9570; 6195; 3915

Tunisia	17705; 15070; 12095; 9410; 7325; 6195
Turkey	17640; 15070; 12095; 9410; 6180
Uganda	21470; 17885; 15575; 15420; 9630; 6135; 6005
UK	15575; 12095; 9410; 6195; 648; 198
Uruguay	17790; 15260; 15190; 11750; 9915; 7325
USA	17840; 15260; 15220; 11820; 9740 9640; 9590; 9515; 7325; 6175; 5975
Vietnam	17830; 17790; 15360; 11955; 11750; 9740; 9570; 6195; 3915
West Africa	17790; 17705; 15400; 15105; 15070; 9600; 9410; 6005
Zaire (E)	21470; 17885; 15575; 15420; 9630; 9135; 6005
Zaire (W)	21660; 17880; 17790; 15400; 9600; 6005
Zambia	21660; 21470; 17885; 17880; 15420; 15400; 11940; 6190; 3255
Zimbabwe	21660; 21470; 17885; 17880; 15420; 15400; 11940; 6190; 3255

For further information the BBC publish a monthly magazine called BBC Worldwide which lists not only frequencies, but also the World Service Radio and Television listings, and is available in some shops and airports or by subscription. Contact Rosemarie Reid on 071-257 2211 (Answerphone) Current subscription 94/95 £30 ($48) per year.

ENGLISH LANGUAGE NEWSPAPERS

This is a selection of newspapers found in a selection of countries.

Afghanistan
The Kabul Times - daily

Argentina
Buenos Aires Herald - weekly
The Review of the River Plate (on financial matters)

Armenia
Yerevan News - weekly

Antigua
Nation's Voice - twice a month
Worker's Voice - once a week
Standard - once a week
Outlet - once a week

Bahamas
Nassau Guardian - daily
Nassau Tribune - daily
Freeport News- daily

Bahrain
Gulf Daily News - daily

Bangladesh
Bangladesh Observer - daily
Bangladesh Times - daily
News Nation - daily
Holiday - weekly
Bangladesh Today - weekly
Tide - weekly

Barbados
The Advocate - daily
The Nation - Mon-Fri
Junior Nation - Mon-Fri

Belgium
The Bulletin

Belize
The Belize Times - weekly
Reporter - weekly
Amandala - weekly
Government Gazette - weekly
The Labour Beacon - weekly
The People's Pulse - weekly

Bermuda
Royal Gazette - daily
Mid Ocean News - Fri
Bermuda Sun - Fri

Botswana
Botswana Daily News - Free
Botswana Guardian - Fri

Brazil
The Brazil Herald - only in Rio

British Virgin Islands
The BVI Beacon - Weekly

Bulgaria
Sofia News - Weekly

Cambodia
The Phnom Penh Post - Daily
Cambodia Times
Cambodian Daily

Cameroon
Cameroon Tribune - Daily
Cameroon Post
The Herald

Cayman Islands
Cayman Compass - Mon - Fri
The New Caymanian - weekly
Tourist Weekly - Free
Looking - Free, monthly

China
China Daily
The People's Daily
The Guangming Daily
Beijing Review - weekly

Cook Islands
Cook Islands News - daily

Costa Rica
Tico Times - weekly

Cuba
Gramma - weekly

Curaçao
The Guardian - daily

Cyprus
Cyprus Mail - daily
Cyprus Weekly - weekly

Domincan Republic
Santo Domingo News - weekly
Dominican News - monthly

Egypt
Egyptian Gazette - daily
The Middle East Observer - weekly

El Salvador
The El Salavador News Gazette - daily

Estonia
The Baltic Independent - weekly

Ethiopia
The Ethiopian Herald - daily

Falkland Islands
Penguin News - fortnightly

Fiji
Fiji Times - daily
Fiji Sun - daily

Gambia
The Gambia Weekly
The Gambia Times
Gambia News Bulletin - twice a week
The Senegambia Sun - daily

Georgian Times
Georgian Times - weekly

Ghana
The Ghanian Times - daily
The People's Daily Graphic - daily
The Pioneer

Greece
Athens News - daily
Greece Today - daily

Grenada
The Grenadian Voice - weekly

Guam
The Pacific Daily News

Guyana
Guyana Chronical - daily

Honduras
Honduras This Week - weekly

Hong Kong
South China Morning Post - daily & Sunday
Asian Wall Street Journal - daily
Hong Kong Standard - daily & Sunday

Hungary
Daily News
Hungarian Week

Iceland
News from Iceland - monthly

India
The Times of India - daily
The Hindustan Times - daily
Indian Express - daily
The Statesman - daily

Indonesia
The Indonesian Times - daily
Indonesian Observer - daily
The Jakarta Post - daily

Iran
Tehran Times - daily

Iraq
Baghdad Observer - daily

Israel
Jerusalem Post - daily
Jerusalem Report - weekly

Italy
Daily American - daily

Jamaica
The Daily Gleaner - daily
The Jamaica Herald - daily
The Star - daily

Japan
The Asahai Evening News - daily
The Daily Yomiuri - daily
The Japan Times - daily

Jordan
Jordan Times - daily
Jerusalem Star - weekly

Kenya
The Standard - daily
Nation - daily
Kenya Times - daily
The Weekly Review

Korea (south)
Korea Herald - daily excl. Mon
Korea Times - daily excl. Mon
Korea News Review - weekly

Kuwait
The Arab Times - daily
Kuwait Times - daily

Kyrgyzstan
Kyrgyzstan Chronicle - weekly

Latvia
The Baltic Observer - weekly

Lesotho
Lesotho Today - daily

Liberia
The Daily Observer -daily
The New Liberian - daily
The Express - daily
The Mirror - daily

Lithuania
The Baltic Independent - weekly
Lithuanian Weekly - weekly
The Baltic News - weekly
The Baltic Observer - weekly

Macau
The South China Morning Post - daily
The Standard - daily

Madagascar
Madagscar Tribune - daily

Malawi
The Daily Times
The Malawi News - weekly

Malaysia
Business Times - daily
New Straits Times - daily
Malay Mail - daily
Sunday Mail - weekly
The Star - daily
The National Echo
Sarawak Tribune
Sarawak Vanguard
Malaysia Focus
Sabah Times
Daily Express
Sarawak Herald

Malta
The Times of Malta - daily
The Independent - daily

Mexico
The News - daily

Myanmar
The Working People's Daily
The Guardian Daily

Namibia
The Windhoek Advertiser - daily
The Namibian - daily

Nepal
The Rising Nepal - daily
The Commoner - daily

Nigeria
The Chronicle - daily
Nigerian Herald - daily
Nigerian Tribune - daily
The Observer - daily

Oman
Oman Daily Observer - daily
Times of Oman - weekly
Akhbar Oman - weekly

Pakistan
The Frontier Post - daily

Papua New Guinea
Papua New Guinea Post Courier - daily

Peru
Lima Times

Philippines
Manila Times - daily
Manila Standard - daily
Philippine Daily Inquirer - daily
Philippine Star - daily

Portugal
Anglo-Portuguese News - weekly

Puerto Rico
The San Juan Star - daily

Qatar
Daily Gulf Times
Weekly Gulf Times

Russian Federation
Moscow Times - daily
Moscow News - weekly

Saudi Arabia
Arab News - daily
Saudi Gazette - daily
Saudi Review - daily

Seychelles
The Seychelles Nation - daily
Seychelles Weekend Nation - weekly

Sierra Leone
The Daily Mail - daily

Singapore
The Business Times - daily
The New Paper - daily
Straits Times - 7 days

Sri Lanka
Daily News - daily
Observer - daily

Swaziland
Times of Swaziland - daily
Swazi Observer - daily

Taiwan
China News - daily
China Post - daily
Free China Journal - daily

Thailand
Bangkok Post - daily
The Nation - daily

Tonga
The Times of Tonga - weekly
Tonga Chronicle - weekly

Trinidad and Tobago
Trinidad and Tobago Express - daily
The Sun - daily
Trinidad Guardian - daily

Tunisia
Tunisia News - weekly

Turkey
Daily News
Middle East Review - monthly
Outlook - weekly

Uganda
The People - daily
The Monitor - daily
The Star - daily
New Vision - daily

United Arab Emirates
Gulf News - daily
Khaleej Times - daily
Emirate News - daily
Gulf Mirror - daily
Gulf Commercial Magazine - weekly
Recorder - weekly

Venezuela
The Dial Journal - daily

Vietnam
Saigon Times - daily

Zambia
The Times of Zambia - daily
The Zambia Daily Mail - daily

Zimbabwe
The Herald - daily
The Chronicle - daily

LEARNING A LANGUAGE

CILT
20 Bedfordbury
London WC2 4LD
Tel: **071-379 5101**
The Centre for Information on Language Teaching and Research, which is sponsored by the Department of Education and Science (DES), offers information and guidance on language learning/teaching. The Centre produces information sheets, bulletins and other publications. It also has its own library open to members of the public.

The Institute of Linguists
24a Highbury Grove
London N5 2EA
Tel: **071-359 7445**
The Institute of Linguists is a professional association for all linguists (translators, interpreters, language teachers and people in industry who work with languages) It is also an examining body and will set examinations in any language at any level. The Linguist is the Institute's bi-monthly journal, and a Directory and List of Members is produced every two years containing Registers of translators, interpreters and tutors which is invaluable to anyone seeking the services of a linguist. The Institute's library is situated at Regent's College.

Training Access Points (TAPS):
Government interest in promoting training and vocational skills has prompted the establishment of TAPS across the country. As the name suggests, TAPS identify where training - including but not exclusively language training - is available from providers in the public and private sectors. Any local Civic Library or Chamber of Commerce should be able to put you in contact with the local office/reference point. Alternatively your local TAPS office should be in Yellow Pages (see Training Agency/Training Enterprise: TEAD)

Yellow Pages: For a variety of providers in the maintained (public) or private sector, your local Yellow Pages should offer a wealth of information. Search through colleges, language/linguist service, translators, interpreters, Chambers of Commerce, Training Agency (now TEAD), TAPS.

Services:

Accelerated Learning Systems Ltd
50 Aylesbury Road
Aston
Clinton
Aylesbury
Buckinghamshire HP22 5AH
Tel: **0296 631177**
They offer a variety of self-disciplined open learning language training packages using audio cassettes and suggestopaedia. Retailing at £100+/- these packages offer a new and innovative technique in general language acquisition.

The Berlitz Schools of Language Ltd
Wells House
79 Wells Street
London W1A 3BZ

Tel: **071-580 6482**
*Berlitz offers a range of language learning
materials and courses ranging from low budget,
pocket books.*

BBC Enterprises
Woodlands
80 Wood Lane
London W12 0TT
*The BBC offers a range of language learning
materials and courses including videos, audio
cassettes and books. Prices range from the GET
BY series (eg. GET BY in Spanish) from £10 to
the more expensive video language courses.*

Linguaphone
St Giles House
50 Poland Street
London W1V 4Ax
Tel: **071 734 0574**
*This company, although most noteworthy for
language training courses, offers a range of
support and services for the language learner*

Richard Lewis Communications plc
Robins
Woodlane
Bramdean
Hampshire SO24 0JN
Tel: **0962 868888**
*RLC specialises in tailor-made course,
including the residential, for the corporate
market administered from centres at home and
abroad. RLC's sister company, Riversdown
Services publishes Cross Culture, a magazine
dealing with international cross-cultural issues.*

The French Institute
17 Queensbury Place
London SW7 2DT
Tel: **071-589 6211**

The Goethe Institute
50 Prince's Gate
Exhibition Road
London SW7 2PH
Tel: **071-411 3451**

The Spanish Institute
102 Eaton Square
London SW1W 9AN
Tel: **071 235 1484** ■

WHEN THINGS GO WRONG
Section 14

LEGAL REPRESENTATION WORLDWIDE

Anguilla

Anguillan Bar Association
c/o The Valley
Anguilla
Tel: **497-23200**
Fax: 497-3177

Antigua and Barbuda

The Antigua Bar Association
2B Corn Alley
PO Box 551
St. John's
Antigua
Tel: **462-1351**
Fax: 462-1354

Australia

Law Council of Australia
1st Floor
Beauchamp House
Edinburgh Avenue
Canberra ACT 2600
Tel: **(062) 473788**
Fax: 062-48 0639

Australian Bar Association
7?F Selbourne Chambers
174 Philip Street
Sydney
New South Wales
Tel: **061-2 232 7754**
Fax: 061-2 221 5386

Austria

Österreichischer Rechtsanwaltskammertag
Postfach 612
Rotenturmstrasse 13
A-1010 Vienna 1
Tel: **43-1533 27180**
Fax: 43-1 533 271844

Bahamas

The Bahamas Bar Association
PO Box N 4632
Nassau 8
Tel: **809-323 3630**

Bangladesh

The Bangladesh Bar Council
Bangladesh Bar Council Building
Ramna
Dhaka 1000
Tel: **880-257 759**
Fax: 880-863 409

National Bar Association of Bangladesh
57/2 Central Road
Dhanmondi
Dhaka 1205
Tel: **880-502448**

Barbados

The Barbados Bar Association
Reece Chambers
Mottley House
Coplergidge Street
Bridgetown
Tel: **809-436 6725**
Fax: 809-429 3769

Belgium

Ordre National des Avocate de Belgique
Maison de l'Advocat
Avenue de la Toison d'Or 65
1060 Brussels
Tel: **32-2 511 75 66**
Fax: 32-2 539 39 20

Belize

The Bar Association
PO Box 675
Belize City

Bermuda

The Bermuda Bar Association
PO Box 125
Hamilton 5
Tel: **809-295 9393**

Botswana

The Law Society of Botswana
Attorney-General's Chambers
Private Bag 009
Gaborone
Tel: **267-55 333**

British Virgin Islands

British Virgin Islands Bar Association
c/o JS Archibald QC
PO Box 191
Main Street
Road Town
Tortola
Tel: **809-494 2457/4927**
Fax: 809-494 2458

Brunei

The Hon. Attorney General
Secretariat Building
Bandar Seri Begawan
Brunei Darussalam
Tel: **673-2 22416**
Fax: 673-2 23100

Canada

Canadian Bar Association
Suite 902
50 O'Connor Street
Ottawa K1P 6L2
Tel: **(613) 237 2925**
Fax: 613-237 0185

Federation of Law Societies of Canada
Bureau 480
445 Boulevard St-Laurent
Montreal
Quebec
Tel: **514-875 6350**
Fax: 514 875 6115

Cayman Islands

Cayman Islands Law Society
PO Box 309
George Town
Grand Cayman
Tel: **809-94 9 0100**
Fax: 809-94 9 7886

Cook Islands

The Hon. Attorney-General
Crown Law Office
PO Box 494
Government of the Cook Islands
Rarotonga
Tel: **682-29 337/228**

Cyprus

The Cyprus Bar Association
23 Loukis Akritas Avenue
PO Box 1446
Nicosia
Tel: **357-2 466 156**
Fax: 357-2 462 135

Czech Republic

Ceska Advokaini Komora
V Praze 1
Narodni trida 16
CS-110 00 Praha 1
Tel: **422-20 55 56-8**

Denmark

Det Danske Advokatsamfund
Advokaternes Hus
Kronprinsessegade 28
DK 1306 Copenhagen
Tel: **45-33 93 4950**
Fax: 45-33 32 1831

Dominica

The Dominican Bar Association
66 Queen Mary Street
Roseau
Tel: **809 448 3149**
Fax: 809-448 3813

Estonia

Eesti Advokaatide Kolleegiumi
Viru Street 19
Tallinn 200 001
Tel: **7-014 419 180**
Fax: 7-014 440 298

Falkland Islands

Attorney General
Attorney-General's Chambers
PO Box 143
Stanley
Falkland Islands
Tel: **(500) 17173/4**
Fax: 500-27276

Finland

Suomen Asianajajaliitto
Simonkatu 12 B 10
SF-00100 Helsinki
Tel: **3580-694 3744**
Fax: 3580-694 4891

France

La Conférence des Bâtonniers de France et d'Outre Mer
12 Place Douphine
75001 Paris
Tel: **33-1 43 29 89 24**
Fax: 33-1 43 25 12 69

Gambia

The Gambia Bar Association
No 2 Allen Street
PO Box 19
Banjul

Germany

Lawyers Union
Adenaueralle 106
D-5300 Bonn 1
Tel: **49-228 26 07 0**
Fax: 49-228 26 07 46

Ghana

The Ghana Bar Association
National Secretariat
PO Box 4150
Accra
Tel: **233-21 228748**
Fax: 233 21 772295

Gibraltar

General Council of the Bar
PO Box 919
Gibraltar
Tel: **350-74469**

Greece

Co-ordinating Committee of Greek Bars
60 Akadimias Street
GR 10679 Athens
Tel: **30-1 361 42 89**

Grenada

The Grenada Law Society
Church Street
St. George's
Grenada
West Indies
Tel: **809-440 2207**

Guyana

The Guyana Bar Association
1 Crowl Street
Stadbroek
Georgetown
Tel: **0592-2 64871**

Hong Kong

Hong Kong Bar Association
LG3 Supreme Court Buildings
38 Queensway
Tel: **852-869 0210**
Fax: 852-869 0189

Hungary

Orszagos Ugyuedi Tanacs
Szemere Utca 8
1054 Budapest
Tel: **36-1 111 9800**

Iceland

Logmannafelag Island
Alftamyri 9
108 Reykjavik
Tel: **354-1 685 620**
Fax: 354-1 687 057

India

The Bar Council of India
AB/21 Lal Bahdur Shastri Marg
Facing Supreme Court Building
New Delhi 110001
Tel: **91-11 386845**

The Bar Association of India
93 Lawyers' Chambers
Supreme Court of India
New Delhi 110001
Tel: **91-11 385902**

Ireland

General Council of the Bar of Ireland
The Law Library
PO Box 2424
Four Courts
Dublin 78
Tel: **353-16 73 56 89**
Fax: 353-16 71 07 04

Israel

Lishkat Orcheir Hadin B'Israel
1 Chopin Street
Jerusalem
Tel: **972-2 660271**
Fax: 972-2 788 738

Italy

Consiglio Nazionale Forense
Ministero di Grazie e Giustizia
Via Arenula 71
1 00186 Rome
Tel: **39-6 360 1622**

Jamaica

The Jamaican Bar Association
78 Harbour Street
PO Box 1093
Kingston
Tel: **1-809 922 3728/2319**

Kenya

The Law Society of Kenya
The Professional Centre
St. John's Gate
Parliament Road
PO Box 72219
Nairobi
Tel: **254-25558/29915**

Kiribati

The Attorney-General
PO Box 62
Bairiki
Tarawa Island
Tel: **686-21242**
Fax: 686-21025

Latvia

Latvijas Advokatu Kolegijas Prezidijs
Brivibas Bulv 34
Riga 226165
Tel: **7-0132 282 277/283 358**

Lesotho

The Law Society of Lesotho
PO Box 1176
Kingsway
Maseru 100
Tel: **266-322643**

Liechtenstein

Liechtensteinischer Rechtsanwaltsverband
Aeulestrasse 38
Postfach 822
Fl-9490 Vaduz

Tel: **41-75 58100**

Lithuania

Lietuvos Respulikos Advokaturos Prezidiumas
Jogailos g Nr 11
132600 Vilnius
Tel: **7-012 624 546/616 216**

Luxembourg

Ordre des Avocats à la Cour Supérieure de Justice
BP15
Palais de Justice
2010 Luxembourg
Tel: **352-44 70 21**
Fax: 352-46 02 61

Malawi

The Malawi Law Society
PO Box 1712
Blantyre

Malaysia

The Bar Council of Malaysia
No 5 Jalan Tun Perak
50050 Kuala Lumpur
Peti Surate 12478
Tel: **60-3 291 1366/7**
Fax: 60-3 291 2439

Maldives

The Hon. Attorney General
Attorney-General's Office
Male
Republic of Maldives

Malta

The Malta Chamber of Advocates
(Camera degli Avocati)
Superior Court
Kingsway
Valletta

Mauritius

The Mauritius Bar Association
c/o Crown Law Office
11 Hennessy Street
Port Louis
Tel: **220-22177**

Montserrat

Attorney-General
Attorney-General's Chambers
Plymouth
Tel: **1-808-491 2444/2383**
Fax: 1-809-491 2367

Nauru

The Nauru Law Society
PO Box 54
Nauru

Netherlands

Nederlandse Orde van Advocaten
Houtweg 60
Postbus 30851
2514 BN the Hague
Tel: **31-70 328 8328**
Fax: 31-70 328 2787

New Zealand

The New Zealand Law Society
Law Society Building
26 Waring Taylor Street
PO Box 5041
Wellington 1
Tel: **64-4 727 837**
Fax: 64-4 727 909

Nigeria

The Nigerian Bar Association
Ozumba Mbadiwe Street
Victoria Island
PMB 12610
Lagos 21083
Tel: **234-1 610 778/617 083**
Fax: 234-1 664 449

Norway

Den Norske Advokatforening
Kritian Augustsgate 9
N-0164 Oslo 1
Tel: **47-2 11 68 68**
Fax: 47-2 11 53 25

Pakistan

Pakistan Bar Council
Supreme Court Building
Peshawar Road
Rawalpindi
Tel: **92-51 562539/563789**

Papua New Guinea

Papua New Guinea Law Society Inc.
PO Box 1994
Boroko
Tel: **675-258485**
Fax: 675-256609

Portugal

Conselho Geral Ordem dos Advogados
Largo de S Domingos 14-1
P1194 Lisboa
Tel: **351-1 86 21 92/93**
Fax: 351-1 28 47 053

St Helena

Attorney-General
Legal and Lands Department
Government of St. Helena
Tel: **290-2270**
Fax: 290-2598

St Kitts & Nevis

St. Kitts/Nevis Bar Association
PO Box 180
Chambers
Basseterre

St Lucia

The St Lucia Law Society Chambers
PO Box 462
Castries

The St. Lucia Bar Association
7 High Street
PO Box 629
Castries
Tel: **1-809-45 3058/2801**

St Vincent and the Grenadines

The St Vincent Law Society
Hillsborough Street
PO Box 726
Kingstown

Bar Association of St Vincent & the Grenadines
Post Box 380
Halifax Street
Kingstown

Seychelles

Bar Association of Seychelles
PO Box 297
State House Avenue
Victoria
Mahe
Tel: **248-22608**
Fax: 248-25176

Sierra Leone

The Sierra Leone Bar Association
The Secretariat
14 East Street
Freetown

Singapore

The Law Society of Singapore
#08-29/301
Colombo Court
Singapore 0617
Tel: **65-338 3165**
Fax: 65-339 7358

Solomon Islands

Attorney-General
Attorney-General's Chambers
PO Box 111
Honiara
Guadlcanal
Tel: **667-22263/21616/21617**
Fax: 677-21608

Spain

Consejo General de la Abogacia Espanola
Calle de Serrano 9
Madrid 28001
Tel: **34-1 522 77 11**
Fax: 34-1 431 93 65

Sri Lanka

The Bar Association of Sri Lanka
129 Hulftsdorp Street
Colombo 12
Tel: **94-547134**

Swaziland

The Law Society of Swaziland
Swazi Plaza
PO Box A 93
Mbabane

Sweden

Sveriges Advokatsamfund
Laboratoriegatan 4
Box 27321
10254 Stockholm
Tel: **468-24 58 70**
Fax: 468-660 07 79

Switzerland

Fédération Suisse des Avocats
Lavaterstrasse 83
CH-8027 Zurich
Tel: **41-1 202 5650**
Fax: 41-1 202 3328

Tanzania

The Law Society of Tanzania
PO Box 2148
Dar es Salaam
Tel: **255-21907**

Thailand

Thai Bar
Na Hub Puey Road
Bangkok 10200

Tonga

The Law Society of Tonga
c/o PO Box 11
Nuka'alofa

Trinidad & Tobago

Bar Association of Trinidad & Tobago
PO Box 75
Port of Spain
Tel: **1-809-623 2124/5**
Fax: 1-809-623 0805

Turkey

Turkiye Barola Birligi
Karanfil Sokak 5
62 Kizilay
Ankara
Tel: **90-4 418 1346**
Fax: 90-4 418 7857

Turks and Caicos Islands

Turks and Caicos Islands Bar Association
PMB 10
Hibiscus Square
Pond Street
Grand Turk
Tel: **1-809 946 2080/2139/2140**
Fax: 1-809 946 2888

Tuvalu

Attorney-General
Office of the Attorney-General
Government Offices
Funafuti
Tel: **688-823**
Fax: 688-800

Uganda

The Uganda Law Society
PO Box 200028
Kampala
Tel: **256-41 42878**

United Kingdom

General Council of the Bar
3 Bedford Row
Gray's Inn
London WC1R 5EL
Tel: **071-242 1124**
Fax: 071-405 9217

The Law Society
The Law Society's Hall
113 Chancery Lane
London WC2A 1PL
Tel: **071-242 0082**
Fax: 071-831 0057

USA

Bar Association of San Francisco
Suite 700
645 Markett Street
San Francisco
California 94105-4212
Tel: **415-392 3960**

Bar Association of the District of Columbia
12th Floor
1819 H Street NW
Washington DC 20007
Tel: **202-223 6600**
Fax: 202-293 3383

The Association of the Bar of the City of New York
42 West 44th Street
New Yorl NY 10036
Tel: **518-463 3200**
Fax: 212-398 6634

State Bar of Texas
1414 Colorado
PO Box 12487
Austin
Texas 78700
Tel: **512-463 1463**

Washington State Bar Association
500 Westin Building
2001 Seattle
Washington 98121-2599
Tel: **206-448 0441**

American Bar Association
750 North Lake Shore Drive
Chicago
Illinois 60611
Tel: 312-988 5245
Fax: **312-988 4665**

Vanuatu

The Attorney General
Attorney General's Chambers
PO Box 996
Port Vila
Tel: **678-2362**

Zambia

The Law Association of Zambia
PO Box 71729
Ndola
Tel: **260-2 615 824**
Fax: 260-2 615 824

Zimbabwe

The Law Society of Zimbabwe
5th Floor
Throgmorton House
51 Samora Machel Avenue
Harare
Tel: **263-4 726 041**
Fax: 263-4 728 489

Bar Council of Zimbabwe
Advocates' Chambers, Bude House
Third Street/Baker Avenue
PO Box 3920
Harare
Tel: **263-4 727 053**

RED CROSS AND RED CRESCENT SOCIETIES

Afghanistan

Puli Harlan
Kabul
Tel: **32357/32211**

Albania

Rue Qumil Guranjaku No.2
Tirana
Tel: **25855**

Algeria

15bis
Boulevard Mohammed V
Algiers
Tel: **3645727/2645728/2610741**

Andorra

Prat de la Creu 30
Andorra La Vella
Tel: **25225**

Angola

Av. Hoji Ya Henda 107 2 andar
Luanda
Tel: **341189/344690**

Antigua & Barbuda

Red Cross House
Old Parham road
St John's
Tel: **4620800**

Argentina

H. Yrigoyen 2068
1089 Buenos Aires
Tel: **9511391/9511854/9512389**

Armenia

Antarain str. 188
Yerevan 375019
or
c/o International Federation Delegate
Dom Jurnalista
3a ulitsa Pushkinskaya
Yerevan 10
Tel: **8852-583630**

Australia

206 Clarendon Street
East Melbourne
Victoria 3002
Tel: **4197533**

Austria

Wiedner Hauptstrasse 32
Wien 4
Tel: **58900-0**

Azerbaijan

Prospekt Azerbaijan 19
Baku
Tel: **8922-931212/938481**

Bahamas

PO Box N.8331
Nassau
Tel: **32-373-70/71/72/73**

Bahrain

PO Box 882
Manama
Tel: **973-293171**

Bangladesh

684-686 Bara Magh Bazar
Dhaka 1217
GPO Box 579
Tel: **407908/406902/400188/400189/402540**

Barbados

Red Cross House
Jemmotts Lane
Bridgetown
Tel; **426-2052**

Belgium

Ch. de Vleurgat 98
1050 Bruxelles
Tel: **6454411**

Belize

PO Box 413
Belize City
Tel: **73319**

Benin

BP No.1
Porto Novo
Tel: **212886**

Bolivia

Avenida Simon Bolivar 1515
Casilla No 741
La Paz
Tel: **340948/326568/376874**

Botswana

135 Independence Avenue
PO Box 485
Gaborone
Tel: **352465/312352/53**

Brazil

Praça Cruz Vermelha 10/12
20.230 Rio de Janeiro
Tel: **232 3223**

Bulgaria

61 Dondukov Boulevard
1527 Sofia
Tel: **441443/441444/441445**

Burkina Faso

PO Box 340
Ougadougou
Tel: **300877**

Burundi

PO Box 324
Bujumbura
Tel: **223159**

Cameroon

Rue Henri-Dunant
POB 631
Yaounde
Tel: **224177**

Canada

1800 Alla Vista Drive
Ottawa
Ontario K1G 4J5
Tel: **739-3000**

Cape Verde

Rua Andrada Corvo
PO Box 119
Praia
Tel: **238-611701/614169/611621**

Central African Republic

BP 1428 Bangui
Tel: **236-612223**

Chad

BP 449
N'Djamena
Tel: **235-513434/515217**

Chile

Avenida Santa Maria No. 0150
Correo 21
Casilla 246-V
Santiago de Chile
Tel: **7771448**

China

53 Oanmien Huong
Beijing 100010
Tel: **51 24 447**

Colombia

Avenida 68
No.66-31 Apartado
Aereo 11-10
Bogota D.E.
Tel: **250 6611**

Congo

Place de la Paix
BP 4145
Brazzaville
Tel: **82 88 25**

Costa Rica

Calle 14
Avenida 8
Apartado 1025
San Jose
Tel: **506-337033/337121/337333/337625**

Cote d'Ivoire

BP 1244
Abidjan
Tel: **225-321335**

Croatia

Ulica Crvenog kriza 14
41 000 Zagreb
Tel: **385-415 458/467**

Cuba

Calle Calzada 51 Vedado
Cuidad Habana
Habana 4
Tel: **324664**

Cyprus

'Z' Compound
Off Prodromos Street
Nicosia
Tel: **446956/7**

Czech Republic

Thunovska 18
11804 Prague 1
Tel: **24510347**

Denmark

Postboks 2600
2100 Kopenhavn
Tel: **38 14 44**

Djibouti

B P 8
Djibouti
Tel: **35 24 51/35 35 52**

Dominica

National Headquarter
Federation Drive
Goodwill
Tel: **809-4488280/4483105**

Dominican Republic

Apartado Postal 1293
Santo Domingo
Tel: **809-6823793**

Ecuador

Av. Colombia y Elizalde Esq
Casilla 17-01-2119
Quito
Tel: **582-485**

From 16 April 1995 all national and international codes change — see page 587 for details.

Egypt

29 El Galaa Street
Cairo
Tel: **750558/750397**

El Salvador

17C Pte y Av. Henri Dunam
San Salvador
Apartado Postal 2672
Tel: **22-7749/22-7743/71-4152**

Equatorial Guinea

Alcalde Albilio Balboa 92
Apartado postal 460
Malabo
Tel: **2398**

Estonia

Lai Street 17
200001 Tallinn
Tel: **448876**

Ethiopia

Ras Desta Damtew Avenue
PO Box 195
Tel: **449364/159074**

Fiji

22 Gorrie Street
PO Box 569
Suva
Tel: **314133/314138**

Finland

Tehnankatu 1 A.
Box 168
00141 Helsinki 14115
Tel: **12931**

France

1 Place Henri Dunam
75384 Paris
Cedex 08
Tel: **44431100**

Gambia

PO Box 472
Banjul
Tel: **392405/393179**

Georgia

15 ulitsa Krilova
Tbilisi
Tel: **8832-953826/954282**

Germany

Friedrich-Erbert-Allee 71
5300
Bonn 1
Postfach 1460
Tel: **228-5411**

Ghana

National Headquarters
Ministries Annex A3
PO Box 835
Accra
Tel: **662298**

Greece

Rue Lycavittou 1
Athens 10672
Tel: **3646005/3628648**

Grenada

PO Box 551
St. George's
Tel: **440-1483**

Guatemala

3 Calle 8-40
Zona 1
Ciudad de Guatemala
Tel: **532026**

Guinea

PO Box 376
Conakry
Tel: **443825**

Guinea-Bissau

Avenida Unidade Africana 12
Bissau
Tel: **245-212405**

Guyana

PO Box 10524
Eve Leary
Georgetown
Tel: **65174**

Haiti

Places des Nations Unies (Bicentenaire)
BP 1337
Port-au Prince
Tel: **22-1033/34/35/54**

Honduras

7a Calle
entre la. y. 2a Avenidas
Comayaguela D C
Tel: 228876/224628

Hungary

V. Arany Janos utca 31
Budapest 1367
Tel: 1313950

Iceland

Raudararstigur 18
125 Reykjavik
Tel: 626722

India

1 Red Cross Road
New Delhi 110001
Tel: 3716441

Indonesia

J1 Jend Gatot Subroto Kar 96
Jakarta Selatan 12790
PO Box 2009
Tel: 7992322

Iran

Avenue Ostad Nejatollahi
Tehran
Tel: 8827788/8820432

Iraq

Mu'ari Street
Mansour
Baghdad
Tel: 5433799/534922

Ireland

16 Merrion Square
Dublin 2
Tel: 6765135/6765136

Italy

12 Via Toscana
00187 Rome
Tel: 47591

Jamaica

76 Arnold Road
Kingston 5
Tel: 9847860

Japan

1-3 Shiba-Daimon
1-Chome
Minato-Ku
Tokyo 105
Tel: 34381311

Jordan

PO Box 10001
Madaba Street
Amman
Tel: 77 31 41

Kazakhstan

86 Ulitsa Karla Marxa
480100 Almaty
Tel: 616291/610058

Kenya

PO Box 40712
Nairobi
Tel: 50 3781

Kiribati

PO Box 213
Bikenibeu
Tarawa
Tel: 686-28128

Korea (North)

Ryonhwa 1
Central District
Pyongyang
Tel: 35822

Korea (South)

32-3KA Nam San Dong
Choong-Ku
Seoul 100-043
Tel: 7559301

Kuwait

PO Box 1359
Safat
Tel: 4188084

Kyrgyzstan

10 ulitsa Dzerdjinskogo
720000 Bishkek
Tel: 222414

From 16 April 1995 all national and international codes change — see page 587 for details.

Laos

BP 650 et 2948
Vientiane
Tel: **216610/214504/212036**

Latvia

28 Soklas Street
LV-1350 Riga
Tel: **275635**

Lebanon

Rue Spears
Beirut
Tel: **368086**

Lesotho

PO Box 366
Maseru 100
Tel: **313911**

Liberia

National Headquarters
107 Lynch Street
1000 Monrovia 20
Tel: **225172**

Libya

PO Box 541
Benghazi
Tel: **95827/99420**

Liechtenstein

Heiligkreuz 25
FL-9490 Vaduz
Tel: **2322294**

Lithuania

Gedimino Ave 3a
2600 Vilnius
Tel: **619923**

Luxembourg

Parc de la Ville BP 404
Luxembourg 2
Tel: **4502021**

Macedonia

No 13 Bul. Koco Racin
91000 Skopje
Tel: **114355**

Madagascar

1 Rue Patrice Lumumba
Antananarivo
Tel: **22111**

Malawi

PO Box 983
Lilongwe
Tel: **744566**

Malaysia

JKR 32 Jalan Nipah
off Jalan Ampang
Kuala Lumpur 55000
Tel: **4578122/4578236**

Mali

BP 280
Bamako
Tel: **224569**

Malta

104 St Ursola Street
Valetta 15400
Tel: **222645**

Mauritania

BP 344
Avenue Gamal Abdel Nasser
Nomakchott
Tel: **52670**

Mauritius

Ste Therese Street
Curepipe
Tel: **6763604**

Mexico

Calle Luis Vives 200
Col. Polanco
Mexico 10
ZP 11510
Tel: **5575711**

Monaco

27 Boul. de Suisse
Monte Carlo
Tel: **506701**

Mongolia

Central Post Office
Post Box 537
Ulan Bator
Tel: **20635**

Morocco

BP 189
Rabat
Tel: **50898**

Mozambique

Caixa Postal 2986
Mapato
Tel: **430045**

Myanmar

Red Cross Building
42 Strand Road
Yangon
Tel: **95232**

Namibia

Red Cross House
100 Leutwein Street
Windhoek
Tel: **35226**

Nepal

Tahchal Kalimali
PB 217 Kathmandu
Tel: **270761**

Netherlands

POB 28120
2502 KC The Hague
Tel: **384 6868**

New Zealand

Red Cross House
14 Hill Street
Wellington 1
Tel: **472 3750**

Nicaragua

Apartado 3279
Mangua DN
Tel: **51 592/406**

Niger

BP 11386
Niamey
Tel: **733037**

Nigeria

11 Eko Akete Close
off St. Gregory's Road
PO Box 764
Lagos
Tel: **683701**

Norway

PO Box 6875
St. Olavspl. N-0130 Oslo 1
Tel: **943030**

Pakistan

National Headquarters
Sector H-8
Islamabad
Tel: **854885/855292**

Panama

Apartado Postal 668
Panama 1
Tel: **28 3014/2786**

Papua New Guinea

PO Box 6546
Boraku
Tel: **258577**

Paraguay

Brasil 216 esq.
Jose Berges
Asuncion
Tel: **22797**

Peru

Av. Camino del Inca y Nazarenas
Urb. Las Gardenias - Surco-Apartado 1534
Lima
Tel: **489431**

Philippines

Bonifacio Drive
Port Area
PO Box 280
Manila 2803
Tel: **481680**

Poland

Mokotowska 14
00-950 Warsaw
Tel: **6285201**

Portugal

Jardim 9 Abril
1 a 5
1293 Lisbon
Tel: 605571/605650

Qatar

PO Box 5449
Ebassy Road
Doha
Tel: 435111

Romania

Strada Biserica Amzei
29 Bucarest
Tel: 6593385

Russia

Tcheremushkinski Proezd 5
117036 Moscow
Tel: 1266770

Rwanda

BP 425
Kigali
Tel: 73302/74402

St Kitts & Nevis

Red Cross House
Horsford Road
Basseterre
St Kitts
Tel: 2584

St Lucia

PO Box 271
Castries St. Lucia W.1
Tel: 452 5582

St Vincent and the Grenadines

PO Box 431
Kingstown
Tel: 45-71816

San Marino

Via Scialoja
Cailungo
47031
Tel: 994360

Sao Tomé e Principe

CP 96
Sao Tomé
Tel: 22305

Saudi Arabia

Riyadh 11129
Tel: 4054175

Senegal

Bd. Franklin-Roosevelt
POB 299
Dakar
Tel: 236532

Sierra Leone

6 Liverpool Street
POB 427
Freetown
Tel: 222384

Singapore

Red Cross House
15 Penang Lane
Singapore 0923
Tel: 3373587

Slovakia

Grosslingova 24
814 46 Bratislava
Tel: 53305

Slovenia

Mirje 19
SLO 61000 Ljubljana
Tel: 126 1200

Solomon Islands

PO Box 187
Honiara
Tel: 677-22682

Somalia

PO Box 937
Mogadishu
Tel: 1312646

South Africa

25 Erlswold Way
Saxonwold
PO Box 2829
Parklands 2121
Johannesburg
Tel: 4861313

Spain

Rafael Villas
28023 El Plantio
Madrid
Tel: **3354444**

Sri Lanka

106 Dharmapala Mawatha
Colombo 7
Tel: **691095**

Sudan

PO Box 235
Khartoum
Tel: **72011**

Suriname

Gravenberchstrast 2
Postbus 2919
Paramaribo
Tel: **498410**

Swaziland

PO Box 377
Mbabane
Tel: **42532**

Sweden

Box 27316
102-54 Stockholm
Tel: **6655600**

Switzerland

Rainmattstrasse 10
BP 2699
3001 Berne
Tel: **3877111**

Syria

Bd. Mahdi Ben Barake
Damascus
Tel: **331441/339261**

Tanzania

Upanga Road
POB 1133
Dar Es Salaam
Tel: **46855/24563**

Thailand

Paribatra Building
Central Bureau
Rama IV Road
Bangkok 10330
Tel: **2564037/2564038**

Togo

51 rue Boko Soga
PO Box 655
Lome
Tel: **212110**

Tonga

PO Box 456
Nuku'Alofa
South West Pacific
Tel: **21360/21670**

Trinidad & Tobago

PO Box 357
Port of Spain
Trinidad
West Indies
Tel: **6278215/6278128**

Tunisia

19 rue d'Angleterre
Tunis 1000
Tel: **240630/245572**

Turkey

Genel Baskanligi
Karanfil Sokak 7
06650 Kizilay-nkara
Tel: **4317680**

Uganda

Plot 97
Buganda Road
PO Box 494 Kampala
Tel: **258701**

Ukraine

30 Ulitsa Pushkinskaya
252004 Kiev
Tel: **2250157**

United Arab Emirates

PO Box 3324
Abu Dhabi
Tel: **434300**

From 16 April 1995 all national and international codes change — see page 587 for details.

United Kingdom

9 Grosvenor Crescent
London SW1X 7EJ
Tel: **071-235 5454**

United States

17th and D. Streets NW
Washington DC 20006
Tel: **639-3320**

Uruguay

Avenida 8 de Octubre 2990
Montevideo
Tel: **800714**

Uzbekistan

33 ulitsa Suleimanova
700017 Tashkent
Tel: **327260**

Vanuatu

PO Box 618
Port Vila
Tel: **22599**

Venezuela

Avenida Andres Bello 4
Apartado 3185
Caracas 1010
Tel: **571 4380**

Vietnam

68 Rue Ba-Trieu
Hanoi
Tel: **262315**

Western Samoa

PO Box 1616
Apia
Tel: **22 676**

Yemen

PO Box 1257
Sana'a
Tel: **283131/283132**

Former Yugoslavia (Serbia & Montenegro)

Simina 19
11000 Belgrade
Tel: **623564**

Zaire

41 av. de la Justice
Zone de la Gombe BP 1712
Kinshasa
Tel: **31096**

Zambia

PO Box 50 001
2837 Saddam Hussein Boulevard
Longacres
Lusaka
Tel: **250607**

Zimbabwe

PO Box 1406
Harare
Tel: **724653** ■

TRAVEL WRITING AND PHOTOGRAPHY
Section 15

TRAVEL/FEATURES EDITORS

National Newspapers

Daily Express
Ludgate House
245 Blackfriars Road
London SE1 9UX
Tel: **071-928 8000**
Jeremy Gates

Daily Mail
Northcliffe House
2 Derry St
London W8 5TT
Tel: **071-938 6000**
Cathy Wood

Daily Mirror
1 Canada Square
Canary Wharf
London E14 5AP
Tel: **071-510 3000**
Sue Carroll

Daily Record
Anderston Quay
Glasgow
G3 8DA
Tel: **041-248 7000**
Rob Bruce

Daily Sport
19 Great Ancoats Street
Manchester
M60 4BT
Tel: **061-236 4466**
Rob Skellon

Daily Star
Ludgate House
245 Blackfriars Road
London SE1 9UX
Tel: **071-928 8000**
Brian O'Hanlon

Daily/Sunday Telegraph
1 Canada Square
Canary Wharf
London E14 5AP
Tel: **071-538 5000**
Gill Charlton

The European
Orbit House
5 New Fetter Lane
London EC4A 1AP
Tel: **071-418 7777**
Henry Sutton

Financial Times
1 Southwark Bridge
London SE1 9HL
Tel: **071-873 3000**
Michael Skapinker

The Guardian
119 Farringdon Road
London EC1R 3ER
Tel: **071-278 2332**
Alex Hamilton

The Herald (Glasgow)
195 Albion Street
Glasgow
G1 1QP
Tel: **041-552 6255**
Raymond Gardner

The Independent
(Independent on Sunday)
40 City Road
London EC1Y 2DB
Tel: **071-253 1222**
Simon Calder

From 16 April 1995 all national and international codes change — see page 587 for details.

Mail on Sunday
Northcliffe House
2 Derry St
London W8 5TT
Tel: **071-938 6000**
Frank Barrett

The Observer
Chelsea Bridge House
Queenstown Road
London SW8 4NN
Tel: **071-278 2332**
Desmond Balmer

The Scotsman
20 North Bridge
Edinburgh
EH1 1YT
Tel: **031-225 2468**
David Robertson

The Sun
1 Virginia Street
London E1 9XP
Tel: **071-782 4000**
Annette Brown

Sunday Express
Ludgate House
245 Blackfriars Road
London SE1 9UX
Tel: **071-928 8000**
Jill Crawshaw

The Sunday Times
1 Pennington St
London E1 9XN
Tel: **071-782 5000**
Christine Walker

The Times
1 Pennington Street
London E1 9XN
Tel: **071-782 5000**
Graham Patterson

Today
1 Virginia St
London E1 9BS
Tel: **782 4600**
John Jackson

Magazines

Business Traveller
Compass House
22 Redan Place
London W2 4SZ
Tel: **071-229 7799**
Alex McWhirter

Camping and Caravanning
Greenfields Hose
Westwood Way
Coventry
CV4 8JH
Tel: **0203-694995**
Peter Frost

Camping Magazine
Link House
Dingwall Avenue
Croydon
Tel: **081-686 2599**
John Lloyd

Climber and Hill Walker
The Plaza Tower
East Kilbride
Glasgow G74 1LW
Tel: **03552-46444**
Tom Prentice

Cosmopolitan
National Magazine Co Ltd
72 Broadwick St
London W1V 2BP
Tel: **071-439 7144**
Elaine Robertson

Country Living
National Magazine House
72 Broadwick St
London W1V 2BP
Tel: **439 5000**
Anne Boston

Elle
20 Orange Street
London WC2H 7ED
Tel: **071-957 8383**
Susan Ward-Davies

Executive Travel
6 Chesterfield Gardens
London W1Y 8DN
Tel: **071-355 1600**
Mike Toynbee

The Great Outdoors
The Plaza Tower
East Kilbride
Glasgow G74 1LW
Tel: **03552-46444**
Cameron McNeish

Harpers and Queen
National Magazine House
72 Broadwick St
London W1V 2BP
Tel: **071-439 5000**
John Hatt

House and Garden
Vogue House
1 Hanover Square
London W1R 0AD
Tel: **071-499 9080**
Carol Wright

The Lady
39-40 Bedford St
The Strand
London WC2E 9ER
Tel: **071-379 4717**
Arline Usden

Marie Claire
2 Hatfields
London SE1 9PG
Tel: **071-261 5240**
David Wickers

Practical Photography
Apex House
Oundle Road
Peterborough
Cambs PE2 9NP
Tel: **0733 898100**
Roger Payne

Saga Magazine
The Saga Building
Middelburg Square
Folkestone
Kent CT20 1AZ
Tel: **0303 857523**
Paul Bach

The Tatler
Vogue House
1 Hanover Square
London W1R 0AD
Tel: **071-499 9080**
Features Editor

Traveller
WEXAS International
45-49 Brompton Road
Knightsbridge SW3 1DE
Tel: **071-589 3315**
Caroline Brandenburger

Vogue
Vogue House
Hanover Square
London W1R 0AD
Tel: **071-499 9080**
Rebecca Willis

Further reading:
The Writer's Handbook (Macmillan/PEN)
Writers' & Artists' Yearbook (Black)
Pimms United Kingdom Media Directory
(PIMS)

ASSOCIATIONS FOR WRITERS AND PHOTOGRAPHERS

The Association of Authors' Agents
c/o 2nd 507 The Chambers
Chelsea Harbour
Lots Road
London SW10
Tel: **071-344 1000**

Association of Photographic Laboratories
Peel Place
50 Carver Street
Hockley
Birmingham B1 3AS
Tel: **021-212 0299**

Book Trust
Book House
45 East Hill
Wandsworth
London SW18 2QZ
Tel: **081-870 9055**

British Amateur Press Association
Michaelmas
Cimarron Close
South Woodham Ferrers
Essex CM3 5PB
Tel: **0245-324059**

British Association of Picture Libraries and Agencies (BAPLA)
13 Woodberry Crescent
London N10 1PJ
Tel: **081-883 2531**

The British Council
10 Spring Gardens
London SW1A 2BN
Tel: **071-930 8466**

British Guild of Travel Writers
Bolts Cross Cottage
Peppard
Henley-on-Thames
Oxon RG9 5LG
Tel: **04917-411**

British Institute of Professional Photography
Fox Talbot House
Amwell End
Ware
Herts SG12 9HN
Tel: **0920 464011**

Bureau of Freelance Photographers (BFP)
Focus House
497 Green Lanes
London N13 4BP
Tel: **081-882 3315**

From 16 April 1995 all national and international codes change — see page 587 for details.

Foreign Press Association in London
11 Carlton House Terrace
London SW1Y 5AJ
Tel: **071-930 0445**

The Institute of Journalists
Unit 2
Dock Offices
Surrey Quays Road
London SE16 2XL
Tel: **071-252 1187**

Master Photographers Association
Halmark
2 Beaumont Street
Darlington
Co Durham DL1 55D
Tel: **0325-356555**

National Union of Journalists
314 Gray's Inn Road
London WC1X 8DP
Tel: **071-278 7916**

Press Council
1 Salisbury Square
London EC4Y 8AE
Tel: **071-353 1248**

The Royal Photographic Society
The Octagon Milsom St
Bath BA1 1DN
Tel: **0225 462841**

The Society of Authors
84 Drayton Gardens
London SW10 9SB
Tel: **071-373 6642**

Society of Women Writers and Journalists
110 Whitehall Road
London E4 6DW
Tel: **081-529 0856**

The Writers' Guild of Great Britain
430 Edgware Road
London W2 1EH
Tel: **071-723 8074** ■

AND FINALLY...
Section 16

CUSTOMS REGULATIONS

Australia

Each passenger over the age of 18 is entitled to the following duty free admissions:

200 cigarettes

or

250 grams cigars

or

250 grams tobacco

plus

1 litre of alcoholic liquor (including wine and beer).

General Items:

Gifts, souvenirs, household articles unused or less than 12 months old are duty free to a value of A$200. Goods to the value of a further A$160 are duty-payable at 20 per cent.

You may also take in: Items of the type normally carried on your person or in your personal baggage including jewellery or toilet requisites, but not electrical items.

Binoculars

Portable typewriters

Exposed film

Photographic cameras

Personal sporting requisites

Bicycles and motorcycles

Clothing (excepting fur apparel, unless it is valued at A$150 or less or you have owned and worn it for 12 months or more).

In order to qualify for duty-free status, goods should be for your personal use, and not have been bought on behalf of someone else, and should have travelled with you.

Prohibited Articles:

Drugs of dependence. Firearms and weapons.

Wildlife - there is a strict control of all wildlife and wildlife products in and out of Australia. Travellers should be warned that articles of apparel, accessories, ornaments, trophies, etc., made from endangered species of fauna will be seized if imported into Australia. This includes animals such as alligators and crocodiles, elephants, rhinoceros, snakes, lizards, turtles, zebra, and the large cats.

Domestic pets - you cannot bring in cats or dogs, except from the United Kingdom and Ireland, Papua New Guinea, Fiji, New Zealand, Hawaii and Norfolk Island. The animals must have been resident in one of these approved countries for at least six months. A permit is required in all cases.

Other goods - most meat and meat products, dairy produce, plants and plant produce.

Canada

Visitors may bring in duty free all items of personal baggage including clothing, jewellery, etc. Sporting equipment, radios, television sets, musical instruments, typewriters, cameras, are all included in this category.

Alcoholic Beverages:

The age limit is 18 in some provinces, and 19 in others, and should be checked before travelling.

1.1 litres (40 oz) of liquor or wine

or

24 x 336ml (12oz cans or bottles) of beer, or its equivalent of 8.2 litres (28fl oz).

A further 9 litres (two gallons) of alcoholic beverages may be imported (except to Prince Edward Island and the Northwest Territories) on payment of duty.

Tobacco:

Persons over 16 years of age may bring in:

50 cigars

200 cigarettes
0.9kg (2lb) of manufactured tobacco.

Gifts:

Gifts may be imported duty free to a value of $40.

Prohibited and Restricted Goods

Animals - any pet or bird requires a Canadian import permit and a veterinary certificate of health from its country of origin. Domestic dogs and cats may be imported only from rabies-free countries without quarantine or vaccination if: they are shipped directly from the country, and they are accompanied by a vet's certificate, and that the country has been rabies-free for the six months prior to the animal's departure.

Endangered species - restrictions on the movement of endangered species stretch also to products made from them. A permit is required for many skins, trophies, etc, as well as live animals.

Foods - meat and meat products are only allowed in if canned and sterile; or commercially cooked and prepared; and the total weight accompanying the traveller does not exceed 10kg per person.

Processed cheese and cooked eggs are the only permissible dairy products.

Food, in general, can be imported duty free provided the amount is only sufficient for two days' personal use by the importer.

Plants - it is forbidden to import plants or plant produce without permission under the Plant Quarantine Act.

Firearms - hand guns are not allowed entry to Canada. Firearms are restricted to those with a legitimate sporting or recreational use. A permit is not required for long guns.

All explosives, ammunitions, pyrotechnic devices, etc, except the following, are forbidden entry to Canada: sporting and competitive ammunition for personal use, distress and life-saving devices such as flares.

New Zealand

Personal effects will be allowed to enter duty free, provided they are your own property, are intended for your own use, and are not imported for commercial purposes. Items such as clothing, footwear, articles of adornment, watches, brushes and toilet requisites can be included here. Jewellery can be included, but not unmounted precious or semi-precious stones, and fur apparel purchased overseas can only be included if you have owned and worn it for more than 12 months.

Tobacco:

Passengers over 17 years of age are allowed the following:
200 cigarettes
or
250 grams of tobacco
or
50 cigars
or
A mixture of all three, weighing not more than 250 grams.

Alcohol:

Passengers over 17 years of age are allowed the following:4.5 litres of wine (this is the equivalent to six 750ml bottles)
and
One bottle containing not more than 1125ml of spirits or liqueur.

All passengers are given a general concession on goods up to a combined value of NZ$250. Persons travelling together may not combine their allowances. Children may claim their allowances provided the goods are their own property and of a type a child would reasonably expect to own.

Visitors to New Zealand are also permitted to bring in such items as a camera, a pair of binoculars, a portable radio and camping equipment, on condition that the goods leave the country with them.

Prohibited or Restricted Items

Drugs - the import of drugs is strictly forbidden and incurs heavy penalties. Should they be necessary for your health, carry a letter of authorization and carry the medication in its original, clearly marked bottle.

Firearms - the importation of any weapon is strictly controlled and requires a Police permit. Flick knives, sword sticks, knuckle dusters, and other such weapons are prohibited.

Flora and Fauna - the entry of domestic dogs and cats is governed by the Agricultural Quarantine Service to whom you should apply for further details. The following goods must be declared:-
Food of any kind
Plants or parts of plants (dead or alive).
Animals (dead or alive) and animal products.
Equipment used with animals.
Equipment such as camping gear, golf clubs and used bicycles.

United Kingdom

The following are legal limits, per adult, for goods brought into the UK duty and tax free, having been obtained duty and tax free outside the UK:

Tobacco:
200 cigarettes
or
100 cigarillos
or
50 cigars
or
250 grammes of tobacco.
Alcoholic Drinks:
1 litre of alcoholic drinks over 22% vol
or
2 litres of fortified or sparkling wine or other liqueurs.
plus
2 litres of still table wine.
Perfume: 60 cc of perfume
250 cc of toilet water
Other Goods:
£136 worth (if obtained outside the EC)
or
£71 worth (if obtained within the EC.

GOODS OBTAINED IN THE EC

Countries of the EC: Belgium, Greece, The Netherlands, Denmark, Italy, Portugal, France, The Irish Republic, Spain (not the Canary Islands), Germany, Luxembourg, The UK (not the Channel Islands). At the time of going to press Sweden, Finland and Austria were about to join.

Duty Free
Duty-free shops can sell you goods for each journey only up to the levels listed above. Eg. if flying from London to Paris for the weekend you can buy 200 cigarettes on the outward bound flight and 200 on your return.

Duty and Tax paid
Provided they are for your personal use there is no further tax to be paid on goods you have obtained duty and tax paid in the European Community.
Personal use includes gifts, but if you are receiving any payment in return for buying alcohol and tobacco (such as help with travelling expenses) the transaction will be dutiable and you should contact HM Customs and Excise to arrange to pay the duty due.
European Community law sets-out guide levels and if you bring more than the amounts in the guide levels you must be able to show that the goods are for your personal use.
The guide levels are:
Tobacco:
800 cigarettes
400 cigarillos
200 cigars
1 kg of smoking tobacco.
Alcoholic Drinks:
10 litres of spirits

20 litres intermediate products (such as port and sherry)
90 litres of wine (of which not more than 60 litres sparkling)
110 litres of beer.
There are special schemes for private purchases of motor vehicles, boats and planes contact HM Customs and Excise for details

Notes:
1. Persons under 17 are not entitled to tobacco and drinks allowances.
2. If you are visiting the UK for less than six months, you are also entitled to bring in all personal effects (except those mentioned above) which you intend to take with you when you leave (except for prohibited or restricted goods).

The following goods are restricted or prohibited if travelling to the UK directly from another EC country:

Drugs
Firearms
Certain weapons, eg flick knives
Explosives
Obscene material
Indecent and obscene material featuring children
Unlicensed mammals susceptible to rabies, eg cats, dogs and mice.
Please note this is not a complete list, but covers the main restrictions.

If you are travelling to the UK from a country outside the EC:
All of the above, plus amongst others:
Horror and pornographic literature, films, videos, etc.
Radio transmitters (eg CB) capable of operating on certain frequencies.
Counterfeit and fake goods eg. watches, garments, CDs and other audio equipment, and goods with false origin markings.
Improperly cooked meat and poultry.
Plants, parts thereof and plant produce.
Most animals and birds - alive or dead; certain articles derived from animals including ivory, fur skins, reptile leather goods.
Any live mammal - unless a British import licence (rabies) has previously been issued.
Goods over 50 years old, including photographs valued at £2,000 or more, clothing, footwear, textiles and portraits of British Heritage Personages valued at £6,000 or more, firearms, arms and armour valued at £20,000 or more, oil and tempera paintings valued at £119,000 or more and all other goods valued at £39,600 or more, require an export licence issued by the Department of National Heritage before they can be exported.

United States

Print:
Everyone entering the United States will be asked to fill in a Customs declaration listing everything except clothes, jewellery, toilet articles, etc, owned by you and intended for your own use. The exceptions are duty free. If jewellery worth $300 or more is sold within three years, duty must then be paid or the article will become subject to seizure.

Alcoholic Drinks:
Adult non-residents can bring in not more than 1 US quart of any form of alcohol for personal use. The amount varies from state to state, and in the more restrictive states, only the legal quantities will be released to you.
If you are only in transit, you are permitted up to 4 litres of alcohol, as long as it accompanies you out of the country. Liquor-filled candy and absinthe are prohibited goods.

Tobacco:
Your personal exemption may include 200 cigarettes (one carton), 100 cigars, and a reasonable quantity of tobacco.

Perfume:
Reasonable quantity.

Gift Exemption:
A non-resident may take in goods valued at up to $100 for use as gifts, provided he/she is to remain in the country for at least 72 hours. This allowance may only be claimed once every 6 months.

Notes:
Antiques are free of duty if produced 100 years prior to the date of entry.
A person emigrating may bring in professional equipment duty free.
If in transit, you may take dutiable goods worth up to $200 through the United States without payment.

Prohibited Items:
Lottery tickets, narcotics and dangerous drugs, obscene publications, seditious and treasonable materials, hazardous articles (e.g. fireworks, dangerous toys, toxic or poisonous substances), products made by convicts or forced labour, switchblade knives, pirate copies of copyright books. Leather items from Haiti.
Firearms and ammunition intended for lawful hunting or sporting purposes are admissible, provided you take the firearms and unfired ammunition with you out of the country.
Cultural objects, such as ethnic artwork, will be allowed in only if accompanied by a valid export certificate from their country of origin.

Bakery items, all cured cheeses, professionally canned foods are permitted. Most plants, or plant products are prohibited or require an import permit. The importation of meat or meat products is dependent on the animal disease condition in the country of origin.
A traveller requiring medicines containing habit-forming drugs or narcotics should always carry a doctor's letter or prescription; make sure that all medicines are properly identified; and do not carry more than might normally be used by one person.
Cats and dogs must be free of diseases communicable to man. Vaccination against rabies is not required for dogs and cats arriving from rabies-free countries. There are controls and prohibitions on all livestock, and anyone wishing to import any should apply to the US Customs for further information.

Vehicles:
All countries will let you bring in a vehicle, whether car, camper van or yacht, without paying duty, either on presentation of a carnet de passages or on an assurance that you will not sell the vehicle for a certain length of time.
You may have to have the vehicle steam-cleaned to help prevent the spread of diseases in the soil.

CUSTOMS OFFICES

Australia

The Collector of Customs
Sydney
NSW 2000
Tel: 02- 20521

The Collector of Customs
Melbourne
Victoria 3000
Tel: 03- 630461

The Collector of Customs
Brisbane
Queensland 4000
Tel: 08- 310361

The Collector of Customs
Perth
WA 6000
Tel: 09- 321 9761

The Collector of Customs
Hobart
Tasmania 7000
Tel: 002- 301201

The Collector of Customs
Darwin
NT 5790
Tel: 089- 814444

The Secretary
Department of Business and Consumer Affairs
Canberra
ACT 2600
Tel: **062- 730414**

The Australian Customs Representative
Canberra House
Maltravers St
off Arundel St
The Strand
London WC2R 3EF
Tel: **01-438 8000**

The Australian Customs Representative
636 Fifth Avenue
New York
NY 10020
USA
Tel: **212- 245 4078**

Officer of the Counsellor (Customs)
Australian Embassy
7th Floor
Sankaido Building
9-13 Akasaka
1-Chome
Minato-Ku
Tokyo
Japan

The Australian Customs Representative
c/o Australian Commission
Connaught Centre
Connaught Road
Hong Kong

The Australian Customs Representative
c/o Australian Trade Commissioner
Lorne Towers 9th Floor
12 Lorne Street
PO Box 3601
Auckland
New Zealand

Canada

Revenue Canada
Customs and Excise
Public Relations Branch
Ottawa
Ontario
Canada K1A 015
Tel: **613- 593 6220**

Canada Customs
2 St André St
Quebec
Quebec G1K 7P6
Tel: **418- 694 4445**

400 Carre Youville
Montreal
Quebec H2Y 3N4
Tel: **514- 283 2953**

360 Coventry Road
Ottawa
Ontario K1K 2C6
Tel: **613- 993 0534** 8.00am to 4.30pm
   613- 998 3326 after 4.30pm and weekends

Manulife Centre, 10th Floor
55 Bloor St
West Toronto
Ontario M5W 1A3
Tel: **416- 966 8022** 8.00am to 4.30pm
   416- 676 3643 evenings and weekends

Federal Building
269 Main St
Winnipeg
Manitoba R3C 1B3
Tel: **204- 949 6004**

204 Towne Square
1919 Rose St
Regina
Saskatchewan S3P 3P1
Tel: **306-359 6212**

220 4th Avenue SE, Ste 720
PO Box 2970
Calgary Alberta T2P 2M7
Tel: **403-231 4610**

1001 West Pender Street
Vancouver
British Columbia
V6E 2M8
Tel: **604- 666 1545/6**

New Zealand

PO Box 29
Auckland
Tel: **(09) 773-520**

PO Box 73003
Auckland Int. Airport
Tel: **(09) 275-9059**

PO Box 2098
Christchurch
Tel: **(03) 796-660**

Private Bag
Dunedin
Tel: **(03) 4779-251**

PO Box 840
Invercargill
Tel: **(03) 2187-329**

PO Box 440
Napier
Tel: **(06) 8355-799**

PO Box 66
Nelson
(054) 81-484

From 16 April 1995 UK national dialling codes change. Please see page 587 for details.

PO Box 136
New Plymouth
(067) 85-721

PO Box 5014
Mt Maunganui
Tauranga
Tel: **(075) 759-699**

PO Box 64
Timaru
Tel: **(03) 6889-317**

PO Box 11746
Wellington
Tel: **(04) 736-099**

PO Box 873
Whangarei
Tel: **(089) 482-400**

United Kingdom

For notices and forms contact any Customs and Excise Office. Addresses are shown in local telephone directories or write to:
H.M. Customs and Excise
New King's Beam House
22 Upper Ground
London SE1 9PJ
Tel: **071-620 1313**

Live Animals:
Ministry of Agriculture, Fisheries & Food
Animal Health Division
Hook Rise South
Tolworth
Surrey KT6 7WF
Tel: **081-330 4411**

Endangered Species:
Department of the Environment
Endangered Species Branch
Tollgate House
Houlton St
Bristol BS2 9DJ
Tel: **0272 218202**

Plant Health:
Ministry of Agriculture, Fisheries & Food
Plant Health Division
Room 211
Whitehall Place (East Block)
London SW1A 2HH
Tel: **071-270 8863**

Meat and Poultry:
Ministry of Agriculture, Fisheries & Food
Meat Hygiene Department
Tolworth Tower
Surbiton
Surrey KT6 7DX
Tel: **081-330 4411**

USA

US Customs Service
PO Box 7118
Washington DC
20044 USA
For detailed information and suggestions write to above address. **Customs Hints for Visitors, and Importing a Car,** *available on request.*

United States Embassy
Grosvenor Square
London W1A 2JB
For complaints and suggestions write to above address. On request:
Customs Hints for Returning US Residents - Know Before You Go.

Further information:
The Customs Co-operation Council
Rue L'Industrie 26-38
B1040 Brussels
Belgium
Tel: **322-514 3372**

Shopping Hours Worldwide

Afghanistan	08.00 18.00 Sat Thurs. Closed Thurs afternoon and all day Fri.
Andorra	08.00 20.00. Varied midday closing.
Antigua & Barbuda	08.30 16.00 Mon Fri; 09.00 12.00 Sat.
Argentina	Generally 09.00 19.00 Mon Fri.
Australia	Generally 09.00 17.30 Mon Fri; 09.00 12.00 Sat. Corner stores open later, but all shops close on Sunday. Late night shopping on Thurs or Fri.
Austria	08.00 18.00 with one or two hour breaks at midday Mon Fri; Sat 08.00 12.00 noon.
Bahamas	09.00 17.00 Mon Sat.
Bahrain	08.00 12.00, 15.30 18.30 Sat Thurs. Closed Fri.
Bangladesh	10.00 20.00, Mon Fri; 09.00 14.00 Sat.
Barbados	08.00 16.00 Mon Fri; 08.00 12.00 Sat.
Belgium	09.00 18.00 daily.
Belize	08.00 12.00, 13.00 16.00 Mon Fri; 08.00 12.30 Sat.
Benin	08.00 11.30, 14.30 15.30 Mon Fri.
Bermuda	Generally 09.00 17.00 Mon Sat.
Bolivia	08.00 12.00, 13.00 18.30 Mon Sat.
Botswana	08.00 1300, 14.15 17.30 Mon Fri; 08.00 13.00 Sat.
Brazil	09.00 19.30 Mon Fri, 08.00 13.00 Sat.
British Virgin Is.	09.00 17.00 Mon Fri.
Burkina Faso	07.30 12.30, 15.00 17.30 Mon Fri.
Burundi	07.00 12.00, 14.00 17.00 Mon Fri.
Canada	Open until 17.30/18.00; Thurs and Fri open till 21.00. Small neighbourhood stores open late.
Cayman Islands	09.00 17.00 Mon Sat.
Central African Rep.	08.00 12.00, 16.00 19.00 Mon Sat.
Chad	07.00/8.00 18.30/19.00, Tues Sat with long lunch closing.
Chile	09.00 18.00 every day.
China	08.00 12.00, 14.00 18.00 daily.
Colombia	09.00 16.30 Mon Sat, 2 hour lunch closing.
Congo	08.00 18.30 Tues Sun, 2 hour lunch closing.
Costa Rica	09.00 18.00 Mon Sat.
Cote d'Ivoire	08.00 12.00, 14.30 16.30 Mon Fri. Close 17.30 Sat.
Cuba	12.30 19.30 Mon Sat.
Cyprus	Usually 08.00/09.00 12.00, 15.00 18.00/19.00 Mon Sat.
Czech Republic	09.00 12.00, 14.00 18.00 or 09.00 18.00. Some major shops open still 20.00 on Thurs; Sat till noon.
Denmark	09.00 17.30 Mon Thurs; 09.00 19.00/20.00 Fri; 09.00 12.00/13.00/14.00 Sat.
Djibouti	08.00/09.00 12.00, 15.00 20.00 Mon. Sat.
Dominica	09.00 12.30, 14.00 15.00 Mon Fri.
Dominican Rep.	08.30 12.00, 14.00 18.00 Mon Sat.
Eastern Caribbean	08.30 12.00, 13.00 16.00 Mon Sat. Half day Thurs.
Ecuador	08.30 18.30 Mon Fri, 2 hour lunch closing.
Egypt	Usually 09.00 20.00 in summer, and 10.00 19.00 in winter.

El Salvador	09.00 12.00, 14.00 1800 Mon Fri; 08.00 12.00 Sat.
Ethiopia	08.00 20.00 Mon Fri, 2 or 3 hour lunch closing.
Fiji	08.00 17.00 Mon Fri; late night Fri.
Finland	08.00 20.00 Mon-Fri; 08.00 18.00 Sat.
France Food shops:	07.00 18.30/19.30 Mon Sat. Others: 09.00 18.30/19.30. Many close for all or half day Monday. Some food shops are open on Sunday morning.In small towns many shops close between 12.00 and 14.00 for lunch.
French West Indies	08.00 12.00, 15.00 18.00 Mon Sat.
Gabon	08.00 18.30 Tues Sat. Long lunch closing. Closed Mon.
Gambia	08.00 18.00 Mon Fri, 2 or 3 hour lunch closing; 08.00 12.00 Sat.
Eastern Germany	09.00 17.00 Mon Fri; 09.00 13.00 Sat.
Western Germany	09.00 18.00 Mon. Fri; 08.00 13.00 Sat.
Ghana	09.00 15.30 Mon Thurs; 09.00 15.30, 17.00 18.00 Fri, closed Sat.
Greece	08.00 14.30 Mon, Wed, Sat; 08.00 13.30, 17.00 20.00 Tues, Thurs, Fri.
Guinea	07.30 16.30, 2 hour lunch closing.
Guyana	08.00 16.00 Mon Fri. Lunchtime closing. Open Sat morning.
Honduras	08.00 18.00 Mon Fri. Lunchtime closing. Open Sat morning.
Hong Kong Central District	10.00 18.00. Elsewhere 10.00 21.00. Most shops remain open on Sunday.
Hungary	10.00 18.00 Mon Fri; open till 20.00 on Thurs; 09.00 12.00 Sat.
Iceland	09.00 18.00 Mon Thurs; 09.00 22.00 Fri. Open Sat morning.
India	09.00 18.00 Mon Sat.
Indonesia	08.00 18.30 Sat Wed.; long lunch.
Iraq	09.00 13.00, 16.00 20.00 Sat Thurs. Everything closes on Friday.
Israel	08.00 13.00, 16.00 19.00 Sunday Fri (NB Arab shops are closed on Fri and Christian ones on Sunday.)
Italy	08.30/09.00 12.30/13.00, 15.30/16.00 19.30/20.00 Mon Sat. In Northern Italy the lunch-break is shorter and shops close earlier.
Jamaica	08.30 16.30, half day closing Wed in Kingston.
Japan	09.00 17.00 or 10.00 18.00 Mon Fri; 09.00 12.00 Sat. Closed Sun. Some stores also close one other day in the week.
Jordan	08.00 13.00, 16.00 18.00 Sat Thurs.
Kenya	08.00 18.00 Mon Sat. A few shops open Sun. 08.00 13.00
Korea Dept. Stores:	10.30 19.30. Small shops: 08.00 22.00 Mon Fri with half day on Sat.
Kuwait	08.30 12.30, 16.30 21.00. Some close Thurs evening. Closed Fri.
Lebanon	Hours vary. Open late in winter.
Leeward Islands	08.00 16.00 Mon Sat. Closed Thurs afternoon.
Liberia	08.00 18.00 Mon Sat. Closed for lunch.
Libya	Closed Fri.
Luxembourg	08.00 12.00, 14.00 18.00 Tues Sat. Closed Mon morning. Only the largest supermarkets remain open at lunchtime.
Macao	09.00 22.00 Mon Sat (Some stores close earlier depending on the location).
Madagascar	08.00 12.00, 14.00 18.00 Mon Fri.
Malawi	08.00 16.00 Mon Fri. Malaysia 09.30 19.00 Daily. Supermarkets and Dept. Stores open from 10.00 22.00.
Mali	09.00 12.00, 15.00 18.00 Mon Fri. Open Sat morning.

Malta	08.30 12.00, 16.00 19.00 Mon Sat.
Mauritius	08.00 19.00 Mon Sat.
Mexico	09.00 19.00 generally Mon, Tue, Thurs and Fri.
Morocco	08.30 12.00, 14.00 18.30 Mon Sat.
Myanmar	09.30 16.30 Mon Fri
Nepal	10.00 20.00 Sun Fri. Closed Sat.
Netherlands Antilles	08.00 12.00, 14.00 18.00 Mon Sat.
New Zealand	Normally 09.00 17.00 Mon Fri. One late night per week usually Fri in each town. Food and ice cream shops known as dairies generally open 09.00 19.00 Sat and Sun sometimes too.
Nicaragua	09.00 12.00, 14.00 16.00 Mon Sat.
Niger	08.00 12.00, 15.00 18.30 Mon Fri, 08.00 12.00 Sat.
Nigeria	08.30 12.30, 14.00 17.00 Mon Fri. Usually closed Sat and Sun.
Norway	09.00 17.00 Mon Sat.
Oman	08.00 13.00 Sat Thurs.
Pakistan	09.30 13.00 Mon Thurs; 9.00 10.30 Sat in rural areas; 9.00 11.30 in main cities.
Panama	08.00 18.00 Mon Sat, long lunch closing.
Paraguay	07.00 11.30, 15.00 18.30 Mon Fri; 7.00 11.30 Sat.
Peru	10.00/10.45 19.00/19.50 Mon Fri.
Philippines	09.00 12.00, 14.00 19.30 Mon Sat. Department stores and supermarkets open Sun.
Poland	07.00 19.00 Food Stores; 11.00 19.00 other shops.
Portugal	09.00 13.00, 15.00 19.00 Mon Fri; 09.00 13.00 Sat.
Qatar	07.30 12.30, 14.30/15.30 18.00 Sun Thurs.
Reunion	08.00 12.00, 14.00 18.00.
Russia (Food stores:)	11.00 20.00. Some big dept stores: 08.00 21.00. Only food stores open on Sundays - till 19.00.
American Samoa	08.30 16.30 Mon Fri; 8.30 12.00 Sat.
Saudi Arabia	09.00 13.00, 16.00 20.00 Sat. Thurs.
Senegal	08.00 12.00, 14.30 18.00 Dec May. Longer lunch and open later June Nov.
Seychelles	08.00 12.00, 13.00 16.00/17.00 Mon Fri.
Singapore (Shops in the city)	10.00 18.00; Dept Stores: 10.00 22.00. Most shops are open 7 days a week.
Slovakia	09.00 12.00, 14.00 18.00 or 09.00 18.00. Some major shops open till 20.00 on Thurs; Sat till noon.
South Africa	08.30 17.00 Mon Fri. 08.30 12.45/13.00 Sat. Most shops are closed on Sun.
Spain	09.00/10.00 12.00/13.30, 15.00 15.30 19.30/20.00. There are general stores in most towns that are open all day from 10.00 20.00.
Sri Lanka	08.30 04.30 Mon Fri; 8.30 13.00 Sat.
Sudan	08.00 13.00, 17.00 20.00 Sat Thurs.
Suriname	07.00 13.00, 16.00 18.00 Mon Sat.
Swaziland	08.00 17.00 Mon Fri; 08.30 14.00 Sat.
Sweden	09.30 17.30 Mon Fri; 09.30 14.00 Sat.
Switzerland	08.00 12.00, 14.00 18.00. Close at 16.00 on Sat. Often closed all day Mon.
Syria	08.00 13.30, 16.30 21.00 Sat Thurs.

Tahiti	07.30 11.30, 13.30 17.30 Mon Fri; 07.30 11.30 Sat.
Tanzania	08.00 12.00, 14.00 17.00 Mon Sat.
Thailand	Usually open until 19.00 or 20.00. No standard hours.
Togo	08.00 18.00 Mon Fri, 2 hour lunch closing. Open Sat morning.
Tonga	08.30 12.30, 13.30 16.40 Mon Fri; 8.30 12.00 Sat. Closed Sun.
Trinidad & Tobago	08.00 16.00 Mon Fri and Sat morning. Supermarkets closed Thurs afternoon.
Tunisia	08.30 13.00, 15.00 17.00 Mon Fri; Sat 09.00 14.00.
Turkey	09.00 13.00, 14.00 19.00 Mon Sat. Small shops may stay open late and not close for the lunch hour.
US Virgin Islands	09.00 17.00 Mon Sat.
United Arab Emirates	08.00 12.00, 16.00 19.00. Closed Fri.
United Kingdom	09.30 17.30 Mon Sat; late night Thurs or Fri; half day on Wed or Thurs in small towns.
Uruguay	09.00 12.00, 14.00 19.00 Mon Fri. Many stores stay open at lunchtime.09.00 12.30 Sat.
Venezuela	09.00 13.00, 14.00 16.30 Mon Fri.
Windward Islands	Usually 08.00 12.00 and 12.00 13.00 or 13.30 16.00. Some closing Wed or Thurs afternoon.
Zimbabwe	08.00 17.00 often with an hour for lunch. Closed Sat afternoon and Sunday. Selected pharmacies have day and night services in all main centres.

DUTY FREE ALLOWANCES WORLDWIDE

Afghanistan	Reasonable quantities of tobacco products, alcoholic beverages for personal use.
Albania	Reasonable quantity of tobacco products, alcoholic beverages and perfume for personal use.
Algeria	200 cigarettes or 50 cigars or 250gr. tobacco. 1 bottle spirits (opened)
Andorra	No restrictions.
Angola	A reasonable quantity of tobacco products, perfume in opened bottles. No alcohol.
Anguilla	200 cigarettes or 50 cigars or 1/2lb tobacco and 1 quart of wine or spirits.
Antigua and Barbuda	200 cigarettes or 100 cigarillos or 50 cigars or 250 grammes of tobacco.1 litre of wine or spirits and 6oz. perfume.
Argentina	400 cigarettes and 50 cigars. 2 litres alcoholic beverages, 5kgs foodstuffs.
Aruba	200 cigarettes or 50 cigars or 250gr. tobacco. 2 lit. of alcoholic beverages, 1/4 lit. perfume. Gifts to a value of AWG100.
Austria	200 cigarettes or 50 cigars or 250gr. tobacco. 1 litre spirits and 2.1 litres of sparkling wine or 0.25 litres of wine.(see note on custom regulations UK/EC earlier in this chapter)
Bahamas	200 cigarettes or 100 cigars or 1lb tobacco or 200 cigarillos. 1 litre of spirits, 50gr. perfume.
Bahrain	200 cigarettes or 50 cigars or 1/2lb tobacco for personal use. 2 bottles alcoholic beverages (non-Muslim passengers only). Reasonable amount of perfume for personal use.
Bangladesh	200 cigarettes or 50 cigars or 1/2lb tobacco. 2 opened bottles of alcoholic beverages, except Bangladeshi passport holders.
Barbados	200 cigarettes in one carton or 1/2lb tobacco products. 1 bottle (26 fl. oz.) alcoholic beverages. 150gr. perfume. Gifts up to value of BBD100.

Belgium	Travellers from EC countries see notes earlier in this chapter on Custom Regulations UK/EC. Travellers from non-EC countries (goods bought or acquired outside EC); 2 lit. still wine and 1 lit. spirits or 2 lit. liqueur wine, 50gr. perfume and 1/4lit. lotion.
Belize	200 cigarettes or 1/2lb tobacco products. 20 fl. oz. alcoholic products. 1 bottle perfume for personal use.
Benin	200 cigarettes or 100 cigarillos or 25 cigars or 250gr. tobacco. 1 bottle wine and spirits. 1/2 lit. of toilet water and 1/4 lit. of perfume.
Bermuda	200 cigarettes and 50 cigars and 1lb tobacco. 1.137 lit. liquor and wine.
Bhutan	As for India.
Bolivia	200 cigarettes, 1lb tobacco or 50 cigars. 1 opened bottle of spirits, a reasonable amount of perfume.
Botswana	200 cigarettes and 50 cigars and 250gr. tobacco. 2 lit. wine and 1 lit. alcoholic beverages. 50ml. perfume and 250ml. toilet water.
Brazil	(a) 400 cigarettes and 250gr. tobacco and 25 cigars. (b) Bought before arriving in Brazil: 2 bottles of any liquor (c) Articles bought for passengers personal use at duty-free shop on arrival, with a total value not exceeding US$300, however alcoholic beverages are restricted to 3 wine, 2 champagne, 2 spirits per person.
Brunei	200 cigarettes or 1/2lb tobacco or tobacco products. 1 bottle of spirits or 1 bottle of wine. A reasonable amount of perfume.
Bulgaria	250gr. tobacco products, 1 lit. spirits and 2 lit. wine. 100gr. perfume. Gifts up to value of BGL 100.
Burkina Faso	200 cigarettes or 25 cigars or 100 cigarillos or 250gr. tobacco. 1 bottle wine and 1 bottle spirits. 1/2 lit. eau de cologne and a small bottle of perfume.
Burundi	1000 cigarettes or 1kg. tobacco. 1 lit. of alcoholic beverages. Reasonable amount of perfume.
Cameroon	400 cigarettes or 125 cigars or 500gr. tobacco. 1 lit. of spirits and 3 lit. wine. A reasonable amount of perfume.
Cape Verde	No free import of tobacco products or alcohol. A reasonable quantity of lotion, perfume or eau de cologne allowed in opened bottles.
Cayman Islands	200 cigarettes or 50 cigars or 1/2lb tobacco. 1 quart of spirits (incl. wines).
Central African Rep.	1000 cigarettes or 250 cigars or 2kg of tobacco products. (Ladies: cigarettes only). A reasonable quantity of alcoholic beverages and perfume.
Chad	400 cigarettes or cigarillos or 125 cigars or 500gr. tobacco (ladies: cigarettes only). 3 bottles of wine and 1 bottle of spirits.
Chile	400 cigarettes and 500gr. of pipe tobacco and 50 large cigars or 50 small cigars (Tiparillos). A reasonable quantity of perfume for personal use. 2.5 lits. alcoholic beverages.
China	400 cigarettes (for stay of up to 6 months), 600 cigarettes (for stay of over 6 months) or equivalent in tobacco products. 2 lits. alcoholic beverage, a reasonable quantity of perfume for personal use.
Colombia	200 cigarettes and 50 cigars and 500gr. tobacco. 2 bottles alcoholic beverage. Reasonable amount of perfume or toilet water for personal use.
Comoro Islands	400 cigarettes or 100 cigars or 500gr. tobacco. 1 lit. alcoholic beverage. 75cl perfume.
Congo	200 cigarettes or 1 box of cigars or tobacco (ladies, cigarettes only). 1 bottle of alcoholic beverage. A reasonable amount of opened perfume.
Cook Islands	200 cigarettes or 50 cigars or 1/2lb tobacco. 1 lit. spirits, wine or liqueurs or 4.5 lits. beer.
Costa Rica	450gr. tobacco products, 3 lit. alcoholic beverages, a reasonable amount of perfume for personal use.

Cote d'Ivoire	200 cigarettes or 25 cigars or 250gr. tobacco products. 1 bottle spirits and 1 bottle wine. Reasonable amount of perfume.
Cuba	200 cigarettes or 25 cigars or 220gr. tobacco. 2 bottles alcoholic beverages, and reasonable amount of perfume.
Cyprus	200 cigarettes or 250gr. tobacco or cigars. 0.75 lit. wine and 1 lit. spirits. 0.3 lit. perfume and toilet waters. Articles of any other category (excluding jewellery) up to a total value of CYP50.
Czech Republic	250 cigarettes or equivalent in tobacco. 1 lit. spirits, 2 lits. wine, 1/2 lit. perfume, gifts imported up to CSK500.
Denmark	For residents of the EC see notes on Custom Regulations UK/EC earlier in this chapter. For non-EC residents, 200 cigarettes or 50 cigars or 250gr. tobacco. 1lit. spirits or 2 lit. alcoholic beverage and 2 lit. table wine.same as above, other goods to value of DKK3100.
Djibouti	As for France.(Not EC regulations though)
Dominica	200 cigarettes or 2 packets tobacco or 24 cigars. 52 oz. alcoholic beverage.
Dominican Republic	200 cigarettes or tobacco products to value of US$5. 1 bottle alcoholic beverage, opened (not to exceed local value of US$5). Reasonable quantity of perfume (opened). Gifts up to value of US$100.
Ecuador	300 cigarettes or 50 cigars or 200gr. tobacco. 1 lit. alcoholic beverages. Reasonable quantity of perfume and gifts up to US$200.
Egypt	200 cigarettes or 25 cigars or 200gr. tobacco. 2 lit. alcoholic beverage. A reasonable amount of perfume. Gifts up to the value of EGP500.
El Salvador	1 kg. tobacco products or 100 cigars or 480 cigarettes. 2 bottles alcoholic beverages. A reasonable amount of perfume. Other articles up to a value of US$100.
Equatorial Guinea	200 cigarettes or 50 cigars or 250gr. tobacco. 1 lit. wine and 1 lit. alcoholic beverages. Reasonable amount of perfume.
Falkland Islands	A reasonable quantity of tobacco products and a reasonable amount of alcoholic beverage for personal use.
Fiji	200 cigarettes or equivalent in tobacco or cigars. 1 lit. of spirits or 2 lit. wine or 2 lit. of beer. No perfume restrictions. Goods to value of FJD150.
Finland	For EC residents see note on Custom Regulations earlier in this chapter (UK/EC). For non-EC travellers: 200 cigarettes or 250gr. tobacco products. 2 lit. beer and 1 lit. mild alcoholic beverages and 1 lit. other alcoholic beverages.
France	For EC residents see note on Custom Regulations earlier in this chapter (UK/EC). For non-EC travellers: 200 cigarettes or 50 cigars or 100 cigarillos or 250gr. tobacco. 1 lit. spirits of more than 22% proof or 2 lit. spirits up to 22% proof and 2 lit. wine. 50g perfume and 1/4 lit. toilet water. Other goods to value of FRF300.
French Guiana	As for France (not EC regulations).
French Polynesia	200 cigarettes or 50 cigars or 100 cigarillos or 250gr. tobacco. 1 lit. spirits and 2 lit. wine. 50gr. tobacco and 1/4lit. toilet water. Other goods to value of XPF5000.
French West Indies	As for France (not EC regulations).
Gabon	200 cigarettes or 50 cigars or 250gr. tobacco. 2 lit. alcoholic beverages. 50gr. perfume. Gifts up to CFA5000.
Gambia	200 cigarettes or 50 cigars/cigarettes or mixed pro rata. 1 lit. spirits plus 1 litre wine plus article of any other description to value of GMD1000.

Germany	For EC residents see note on Custom Regulations earlier in this chapter (UK/EC). For non-EC travellers: 200 cigarettes or 50 cigars or 250gr. tobacco. 1 lit. spirits of more than 22% proof or 2 lit. spirits up to 22% proof or 2 litres sparkling wine or liqueur wine and 2 lits. wine. 50gr. perfume. Other goods to value of DEM115.
Ghana	400 cigarettes or 100 cigars or 1lb tobacco. 1 bottle wine and 1 bottle spirits. 8oz. perfume.
Gibraltar	200 cigarettes or 100 cigarillos or 50 cigars or 250gr. tobacco. 1 lit or 2 lit. of fortified or sparkling wine or 2 lit. table wine. Perfume 50gr. and 0.25 lit. toilet water.
Greece	For EC residents see note on Custom Regulations earlier in this chapter (UK/EC). For non-EC travellers: 200 cigarettes or 100 cigarillos or 50 cigars or 250gr. pipe tobacco. 1 lit. alcoholic beverage or 2 lits. wine. 50gr. perfume and 0.25lit. toilet water. Gifts up to total value of GRD7000.
Grenada	200 cigarettes or 1/2lb tobacco or 50 cigars. 1 quart wine or spirits. Reasonable amount of perfume.
Guatemala	80 cigarettes or 3.5oz. tobacco. 2 bottles of liquor (opened). 2 bottles of perfume (opened).
Guinea-Bissau	Reasonable quantity of tobacco products. Reasonable quantity of perfume (opened bottles). Alcohol banned.
Guinea Republic	1000 cigarettes or 250 cigars or 1kg tobacco. 1 bottle alcoholic beverage (opened). A reasonable amount of perfume. All foreign newspapers banned.
Guyana	200 cigarettes or 50 cigars or 225gr. tobacco. 0.57 lit. spirits and 0.57 lit. wine. A reasonable amount of perfume.
Haiti	200 cigarettes or 50 cigars or 250gr. tobacco. 1 lit. spirits. A small quantity of perfume for personal use.
Honduras	200 cigarettes or 100 cigars or 1lb tobacco. 2 bottles alcoholic beverages. A reasonable quantity of perfume for personal use. Gifts up to a total value of US$50.
Hong Kong	200 cigarettes or 50 cigars or 250gr. tobacco. 1 lit. alcoholic beverage, 60ml. perfume, 250ml. toilet water.
Hungary	250 cigarettes or 50 cigars or 250gr. tobacco. 2 lit. wine and 1 lit. spirits. 250gr. perfume. Souvenirs to value of HUF5000.
Iceland	200 cigarettes or 250gr. tobacco. 1 lit. alcoholic beverages and 1lit. wine less than 21% alcoholic content by volume or 6 lit. beer (8 lits. Icelandic beer).
India	200 cigarettes or 50 cigars or 250gr. tobacco. Alcoholic liquor up to 0.95 lits. 0.25lit. toilet water.
Indonesia	(a) For one-week stay: 200 cigarettes or 50 cigars or 100gr. tobacco. For two-week stay: 400 cigarettes or 100 cigars or 200gr. tobacco. More than two-week stay: 600 cigarettes or 150 cigars or 300gr. tobacco. (b) Less than 2 lit. alcohol (opened). (c) a reasonable amount of perfume. (d) Gifts up to value of US$100.
Iran	200 cigarettes or equivalent in tobacco products. A reasonable amount of perfume for personal use. Gifts of which the applicable import duty/tax does not exceed IRIR11,150. Alcohol banned.
Iraq	200 cigarettes or 50 cigars or 250gr. tobacco. 1 lit. wine or spirits.1/2lit. perfume. Total value may not exceed IQD100,000.
Ireland	For EC residents see note on Custom Regulations earlier in this chapter (UK/EC). For non-EC travellers: P 200 cigarettes or 100 cigarillos or 50 cigars or 250gr. tobacco. 1 lit. alcoholic beverage of more than 22% vol. or a total of 2 lit. alcoholic beverage of not more than 22% vol. or sparkling or fortified wine plus 2 lit. other wine. 50gr. perfume and 1/4lit. toilet water. Other goods to a value of IEP34 per person.

Israel	250 cigarettes or 250gr. tobacco products. 2 lit. wine and 1 lit. spirits. 0.25 lit. eau de cologne or perfume. Gifts totalling not more than US$125 in value.
Italy	For EC residents see note on Custom Regulations earlier in this chapter (UK/EC). For non-EC travellers: 400 cigarettes or 100 cigars or 200 cigarillos or 500gr. tobacco. 0.75 lit. spirits of more than 22% proof or 2 lit. beverage of a max. of 22% proof. 50gr. perfume and 0.25lit. toilet water. Other goods to the value of ITL 67,000. 500gr. coffee or 200gr. coffee extract. 100gr. tea or 40gr. tea extract.
Jamaica	200 cigarettes or 50 cigars or 1/2lb tobacco. 1 lit. spirit and 2 lit.wine. 12fl.oz. toilet water and 6oz. perfume spirits.
Japan	400 cigarettes or 100 cigars or 500gr. tobacco. 3 bottles alcoholic beverages. 2 oz. perfume. Other goods including watches to the value of JPY 200,000.
Jordan	200 cigarettes or 25 cigars or 200gr. tobacco. 2 bottles wine or 1 bottle spirits. A reasonable amount of perfume for personal use.
Kenya	200 cigarettes or 1/2lb tobacco. 1 bottle wine or 1 bottle spirits. 1 pint perfume.
Kiribati	200 cigarettes or 50 cigars or 225gr. tobacco. 1 lit. wine and 1 lit. spirit. A reasonable amount of perfume.
Korea (South)	A reasonable amount of tobacco products and alcoholic beverages.
Korea, Republic of	400 cigarettes, 50 cigars, 200gr, pipe tobacco and 100gr. other tobacco (total not to exceed 500gr.) 2 bottles alcoholic beverages (not to exceed 1520cc), 2oz. perfume. Gifts up to value of KRW300,000.
Kuwait	500 cigarettes or 2lb tobacco. Alcohol banned.
Laos	500 cigarettes or 100 cigars or 500gr. tobacco. 1 bottle alcoholic beverage and 2 bottles wine. Perfume for personal use.
Lebanon	200 cigarettes or 200gr. cigars or 200gr. tobacco (500 cigarettes or 500gr. tobacco over summer period). 1 lit. wines and spirits, 60gr. perfume.
Lesotho	400 cigarettes and 50 cigars and 250gr. tobacco. 1 lit. alcoholic beverage (no liquor if national of South Africa), 300ml. perfume.
Liberia	200 cigarettes or 25 cigars or 250gr. tobacco products. 1 lit. alcoholic beverage. 100gr. perfume. Other goods to value of US$125.
Libya	200 cigarettes or 25 cigars. A reasonable amount of perfume. Alcohol banned. Any goods of Israeli origin, or of firms trading with Israel.
Luxembourg	For EC residents see note on Custom Regulations earlier in this chapter (UK/EC). For non-EC travellers: 200 cigarettes or 50 cigars or 100 cigarillos or 250gr. tobacco. 1 lit. spirits over 22% proof or 2 lit. spirits under 22% proof or 2 lit. sparkling wine and 2 lit. other wine. 50gr. perfume and 0.25 lit. toilet water. Other goods to value of LUF2000.
Macau	A reasonable amount of tobacco, liquor and perfume for personal use.
Madagascar	500 cigarettes or 25 cigars or 500gr. tobacco. 1 bottle alcoholic beverage.
Malawi	200 cigarettes or 250gr. tobacco. 1 lit. spirits, 1 lit. beer or wine.1/4 lit. toilet water and 50gr. perfume.
Malaysia	200 cigarettes or 50 cigars or 250gr. tobacco, 100 matchsticks. 1 lit.wine or 1 lit. spirits or 1 lit. malt liquor. Perfumes in bottles up to the value of MYR 200 (opened). Gifts and souvenirs not exceeding a total value of MYR200.
Maldives	No restrictions on tobacco or perfume. Alcohol banned.
Mali	1000 cigarettes or 250 cigars or 2kg of tobacco. Reasonable quantity of alcoholic beverages and perfume in opened bottles and for personal use.
Malta	200 cigarettes or 250gr. tobacco. 1 bottle spirits, 1 bottle wine. A reasonable amount of perfume/toilet water but not to exceed MTL2 in value.
Mauritania	200 cigarettes or 25 cigars or 450gr. tobacco for adults (ladies: cigarettes only). 50gr. perfume.

Mauritius	250 cigarettes or 50 cigars or 250gr. tobacco. 2 bottles wine, ale or beer, and 1 lit. spirits. 0.5 lit. toilet water and small quantity of perfume for personal use.
Mexico	400 cigarettes or 2 boxes of cigars or a reasonable quantity of pipe tobacco. 3 bottles of wine or liquor. A reasonable quantity of perfume, eau de cologne and lotions for personal use. Various objects with a value up to US$300. One camera and 12 rolls of film.
Micronesia	400 cigarettes or 1lb cigars or pipe tobacco. 3 bottles of alcoholic beverage.
Mongolia	A reasonable amount of tobacco products and of alcoholic beverages.
Montserrat	200 cigarettes or 50 cigars. 40oz. of alcoholic beverages, 6oz. perfume, gifts up to a value of XCD250.
Morocco	200 cigarettes or 50 cigars or 400gr. tobacco. 1 lit. spirits, 1 lit. wine, 50gr. perfume.
Mozambique	200 cigarettes or 250gr. tobacco. 1/2lit. liquor. A reasonable quantity of perfume.
Myanmar	400 cigarettes or 100 cigars or 250gr. tobacco. Quart of alcoholic beverages. 0.5 lit. perfume/eau de cologne. All jewellery should be declared on arrival.
Namibia	400 cigarettes or 50 cigars or 250gr. tobacco. 1 lit. wine and 1 lit. spirits. 50ml. perfume and 250ml. toilet water. Gifts up to value of ZAR1000.
Nauru	400 cigarettes or 50 cigars or 450gr. tobacco. 3 bottles of alcoholic beverage. A reasonable amount of perfume.
Nepal	A reasonable quantity of tobacco, alcoholic beverages and perfume for personal use.
Netherlands	For EC residents see note on Custom Regulations earlier in this chapter (UK/EC). For non-EC European travellers: 200 cigarettes or 50 cigars or 100 cigarillos or 250gr. tobacco. 1 lit. spirits of more than 22% proof or 2 lit. spirits up to 22% proof or 2 lit. liqueur wine and 2 lit. wine. 8 lit. non-sparkling Luxembourg wine. 50gr. perfume. Other goods to value of NLG125. From an EC country: 300 cigarettes or 75 cigars or 150 cigarillos or 400gr. tobacco. 1.5 lit. spirits more than 22% proof or 3 lit. spirits below 22% proof or 5 lit. non-sparkling wine and 8 lits. Luxembourg wine. 75gr. perfume and 3.8lit. toilet water. Other goods to the value of NLG910. From outside Europe: 400 cigarettes or 100 cigars or 500gr. tobacco. Wines, spirits and perfume as for countries outside EC. Other goods to the value of NLG125.
Netherland Antilles	400 cigarettes or 50 cigars or 250gr. tobacco. 2 lit. alcoholic beverages, 0.25lit. perfume, gifts up to a value of ANG100.
New Caledonia	400 cigarettes or 100 cigars or 500gr. tobacco. 2 bottle of alcoholic beverage. A reasonable amount of perfume for personal use.
Nicaragua	500gr. tobacco products. 3 lit. spirits. 1 bottle perfume.
Niger	200 cigarettes or 100 cigarillos or 25 cigars or 250gr. tobacco, 1lit. alcoholic beverage.
Nigeria	200 cigarettes or 50 cigars or 200gr. tobacco. 1 lit. spirits. Small amount of perfume. No sparkling wines.
Niue	200 cigarettes or 50 cigars or 227gr. tobacco or a combination of each to a maximum weight of 227gr. 1 bottle of wine and 1 bottle of spirits.
Norway	From Europe: 200 cigarettes or 250gr. cigars or tobacco and 200 leaves of cigarette papers. 1 lit. spirits not exceeding 60% alcohol by volume and 1 lit. wine not exceeding 23% alcohol by volume or 2 lit. wine not exceeding 23% alcohol by volume and 2 lit. beer. Other goods to the value of NOK1200. From non-European countries: 400 cigarettes or 500gr. cigars or tobacco and 200 leaves of cigarettes papers. 1 lit. spirits not exceeding 60% alcohol by volume and 1 lit. of wine not exceeding 23% alcohol by volume or 2 lit. wine not exceeding 23% by volume and 2 lit. beer. Other goods to value of N200.
Oman	A reasonable quantity of tobacco products, 8 oz. perfume. 1 bottle alcoholic beverage if passenger is non-Omani and non-Muslim.

Pakistan	200 cigarettes or 50 cigars or 1/2kg of tobacco. 0.25lit. toilet water/perfume (opened).
Panama	500 cigarettes or 50 cigars or 500gr. tobacco. 3 bottles alcoholic beverage for personal use. Reasonable amount of perfume.
Papua New Guinea	200 cigarettes or 250gr. tobacco, 1 lit. alcoholic beverages, a reasonable amount of perfume, and new goods to value of PGK200.
Paraguay	Reasonable quantities of tobacco, alcoholic beverages and perfume for personal use.
Peru	400 cigarettes or 50 cigars or 0.5kg tobacco. 2 lit. spirits or 2 lit.wine. Reasonable amount of perfume for personal use.
Philippines	400 cigarettes or 50 cigars or 250gr. tobacco. 2 lit. alcoholic beverages. Small quantity of perfume.
Poland	250 cigarettes or 50 cigars or 250gr. tobacco. 1 lit. wine and 1 lit. other alcoholic beverages.
Portugal	For EC residents see note on Custom Regulations earlier in this chapter (UK/EC). For non-EC travellers: 200 cigarettes or 100 cigarillos or 50 cigars or 250gr. tobacco products. 1 bottle spirits over 22% or 2 lits. of other alcoholic beverages of max. 22% and up to 2 lits. wine. 50gr. perfume and 0.25lit. toilet water. Gifts up to PTE7500.
Puerto Rico and US Virgin Islands.	As for USA
Qatar	1lb tobacco. No wine or spirits unless a licence is held. Perfume up to the value of QAR20.
Reunion	As for France (not EC regulations).
Romania	200 cigarettes or 300gr. tobacco. 2 lit. alcoholic beverages, 4 lit.wine or beer. Presents up to the value of ROL2000.
Russia	250 cigarettes or 250gr. of other tobacco products. 1 lit. spirits and not more than 2 lit. wine. A reasonable amount of perfume for personal use. Gifts up to value of SUR30.
Rwanda	200 cigarettes or 50 cigars or 1lb tobacco.
St. Kitts & Nevis	200 cigarettes or 50 cigars or 1/2lb tobacco. 1 quart of wine or spirits. 6oz. perfume.
St. Lucia	200 cigarettes or 250gr. tobacco products. 1 quart alcoholic beverage.
St. Vincent & the Grenadines	200 cigarettes or 1/2lb tobacco products or 50 cigars. 1 quart alcoholic beverage.
Samoa (American)	200 cigarettes or 50 cigars. 2 bottles liquor (fifths). Reasonable amount of perfume.
Samoa (Western)	200 cigarettes or 50 cigars or 1.5lb tobacco. 1 bottle liquor.
Sao Tomé e Principe	A reasonable amount of tobacco products. A reasonable amount of perfume (opened) and alcoholic beverages (opened).
Saudi Arabia	600 cigarettes or 100 cigars or 500gr. tobacco. A reasonable amount of perfume. No alcohol.
Senegal	200 cigarettes or 50 cigars or 250gr. tobacco. A reasonable quantity of perfume. No free import of alcohol.
Seychelles	200 cigarettes or 50 cigars or 250gr. tobacco. 1 lit. spirits and 1lit. wine. 125cc. of perfume and 25cl. toilet water. Other dutiable goods to a total value of SCR400.
Sierra Leone	200 cigarettes or 1/2lb tobacco. 1 quart wine or 1 quart spirit. 1 quart perfume.
Singapore	200 cigarettes or 50 cigars or 250gr. tobacco. 1 lit. wine and beer and 1 litre spirits. A reasonable quantity of perfume (allowances not applicable when arriving from Malaysia).

Slovakia	250 cigarettes or equivalent in tobacco. 1 lit. spirits, 2 lits. wine, 1/2 lit. perfume, gifts imported up to CSK500.
Solomon Islands	200 cigarettes or 250gr. of cigars or 1/2lb tobacco. 2 lit. bottles of wine/spirits. Other dutiable goods not exceeding SBD40 in value.
Somalia	400 cigarettes or 400gr. tobacco. 1 bottle wine or spirits. A reasonable amount of perfume for personal use.
South Africa	400 cigarettes and 50 cigars and 250gr. tobacco. 2 lit. wine and 1lit. spirits. 50ml. perfume and 250 ml. toilet water. Gift articles to value of ZAR500.
Spain	For EC residents see note on Custom Regulations earlier in this chapter (UK/EC). For non-EC travellers from Europe and Mediterranean countries of Africa and Asia: 200 cigarettes or 50 cigars or 100 cigarillos or 250gr. tobacco. Double for all other passengers. 1 lit. alcoholic beverage of over 22% proof or 2 lit. alcoholic beverage under 22% proof and 2 lit. other wines. 1/4lit. eau de cologne and 50gr. perfume. Gifts to value of ESP5000. (ESP8000 if arriving from Canary Islands. No other restrictions from Canary Islands).
Sri Lanka	200 cigarettes or 50 cigars or 12oz. tobacco. 2 bottles wine and 1.5lit. spirits. Perfume for personal use and 1/4lit. toilet water.
Sudan	200 cigarettes or 50 cigars or 1/2lb tobacco. A reasonable quantity of toilet requisites (incl. perfume) for personal use. No alcohol.
Suriname	400 cigarettes or 100 cigars or 200 cigarillos or 500gr. tobacco. 2lits. spirits and 4 lits. wine. 50gr. perfume, 1 lit. eau de cologne. 8 rolls of unexposed film, 60 metres unexposed cine-film (8 or 16mm)and 100 metres unrecorded tape.
Swaziland	As for South Africa.
Sweden	For EC residents see note on Custom Regulations earlier in this chapter (UK/EC). Residents of Europe: 200 cigarettes or 100 cigarillos or 50 cigars or 250gr. tobacco. 1 lit. spirits, 1 lit. wine and 2 lit. beer. A reasonable amount of perfume. Gifts up to the value of SEK1000. Residents of non-European countries: 400 cigarettes or 200 cigarillos or 100 cigars or 500gr. tobacco. 1 lit. spirits and 1 lit. wine. or 2lit. beer. Reasonable amount of perfume. Gifts up to value of SEK1000.
Switzerland	Residents of European countries: 200 cigarettes or 50 cigars or 250gr. tobacco. Residents of non-European countries: 400 cigarettes or 100 cigars or 500gr. tobacco. 2 lits. alcoholic beverages up to 15% and 1 lit. over 15%.
Syria	200m cigarettes or 50 cigars or 250gr. tobacco. 1 lit. spirits and 1bottle wine. A reasonable quantity of perfume and eau de cologne.
Taiwan	200 cigarettes or 25 cigars or 1lb tobacco. 1 bottle alcoholic beverage.
Tanzania	200 cigarettes or 50 cigars or 250gr. tobacco. 1 lit. wine or 1 lit.spirits. 1/4 lit. perfume.
Thailand	200 cigarettes or 250gr. cigars or tobacco. 1 lit. alcoholic beverages. Goods up to the value of THB100,000.
Togo	100 cigarettes or 50 cigars or 100gr. tobacco. 1 bottle wine and 1 bottle spirits. Reasonable quantity of perfume for personal use.
Tonga	200 cigarettes. 1 lit. alcoholic liquor.
Trinidad & Tobago	200 cigarettes or 50 cigars or 1/2lb tobacco. 1 quart wine. Gifts to value of TTD50.
Tunisia	400 cigarettes or 100 cigars or 500gr. tobacco. 2 lit. alcoholic beverage of less than 25% vol. and 1 lit. alcoholic beverage of more than 25% vol. 1/4 lit. toilet water. Gifts to the value of TND10.
Turkey	200 cigarettes or 50 cigars or 200gr. tobacco and 200 leaves of cigarette papers or 200gr. tumbeki. 5 lits. spirits. 5 bottles of perfume or toilet water or lotions each not exceeding 120ml. 1 kg coffee.

Tuvalu	200 cigarettes or 225gr. tobacco or cigars. 1 lit. spirits and 1 lit. wine. Other goods to value of A$25.
Uganda	200 cigarettes or 1/2lb tobacco. 1 bottle of wine and 1 bottle spirits. 1 pint perfume.
United Arab Emirates	250 cigarettes or 50 cigars or 2kg. tobacco. A reasonable amount of perfume. No alcohol.
Uruguay	Residents, if coming from Argentina, Bolivia, Brazil, Chile or Paraguay: 200 cigarettes or 25 cigars. 1 lit. alcoholic beverage. Whole to maximum value of US$150.
Vanuatu	200 cigarettes or 100 cigarillos or 250gr. tobacco or 50 cigars.1.5lit. spirits and 2 lit. wine. 1/4lit. toilet water and 10cl. perfume. Other articles up to a maximum of VUV6000.
Venezuela	200 cigarettes and 25 cigars. 2 lit. alcoholic beverages. 4 small bottles perfume.
Vietnam	200 cigarettes, 50 cigars or 250gr. tobacco. 1 bottle spirits, reasonable quantity of perfume.
Yemen	200 cigarettes, 50 cigars or 1/2lb tobacco. 2 quarts of alcoholic beverages. 1 pint perfume.
Zaire	100 cigarettes or 50 cigars or the equivalent in tobacco. 1 bottle spirits (opened). A reasonable amount of perfume.
Zambia	200 cigarettes or 250gr. tobacco. 1 bottle alcoholic beverage each, spirits, wine, beer (opened). 1oz. bottle perfume.
Zimbabwe	Cigarettes and tobacco articles for personal use, to be included in the general goods allowance. New articles for personal use (inc.gifts) up to a total value of ZWD500. Incl. 5 lit. alcoholic beverage, of which not more than 2 lit. may be spirits.

CONSUMER ADVICE AND COMPLAINTS

Association of British Travel Agents (ABTA)
55 Newman Street, London W1P 4AH
Tel: **071-637 2444**
Professional body of the British travel industry,with a bond to protect travellers against financial collapse.

Air Transport Users Committee
103 Kingsway, London WC2B 6QX
Tel: **071-242 3882**
Small committee, funded by CAA, but acting independently, to investigate complaints.

Civil Aviation Authority
CAA House, 45 Kingsway, London WC2
Tel: **071-379 7311**
Overall controller of the British airline industry.

From 16 April 1995 UK national dialling codes change. Please see page 587 for details.

WORLDWIDE VOLTAGE GUIDE

In general, all references to 110V apply to the range from 100V to 160V. References to 220V apply to the range from 200V to 260V. Where 110/220V is indicated, voltage varies within country, depending on location.

An adaptor kit may be necessary to provide prongs of various types that will fit into outlets which do not accept plugs from the traveller's own country. A converter is also necessary where the voltage differs from that of the traveller's electrical appliances. Plugging an electrical appliance manufactured to 110V into a 220V outlet without using a converter may destroy the appliance and blow fuses elsewhere in the building. A special adaptor will probably be necessary for electronic items such as computers. Check with the manufacturer. Plugging straight in could wipe the memory.

Afghanistan	220V
Algeria	110/220V
Angola	220V
Anguilla	220V
Antigua	110/220V
Argentina	220V
Aruba	110V
Australia	220V
Austria	220V
Azores	110/220V
Bahamas	110/220V
Bahrain	220V
Bangladesh	220V
Barbados	110/220V
Belgium	110/220V
Belize	110/220V
Benin	220V
Bermuda	110/220V
Bhutan	220V
Bolivia	110/220V
Bonaire	110/220V
Botswana	220V
Brazil	110/220V Y
British Virgin Is	110/220V
Bulgaria	110/220V
Burkina Faso	220V
Burundi	220V
Cambodia	110/220V
Cameroon	110/220V
Canada	110/220V
Canary Islands	110/220V
Cayman Islands	110V
Central African Rep	220V
Chad	220V
Channel Islands	220V*
Chile	220V Y
China	220V
Colombia	110V
Costa Rica	110/220V
Côte d'Ivoire	220V
Cuba	110V
Curacao	110V
Cyprus	220V Y
Czech Republic	110/220V
Denmark	220V
Dominica	220V
Dominican Rep	110/220V
Ecuador	110/220V
Egypt	110/220V
El Salvador	110V
Ethiopia	110/220V
Fiji	220V
Finland	220V
France	110/220V
French Guiana	110/220V
Gabon	220V
Gambia	220V
Germany	110/220V
Ghana	220V
Gibraltar	220V
Greece	110/220V
Greenland	220V
Grenada	220V
Grenadines	220V
Guadeloupe	110/220V
Guatemala	110/220V
Guinea	220V
Guyana	110/220V
Haiti	110/220V
Honduras	110/220V
Hong Kong	220V*
Hungary	220V
Iceland	220V
India	220V Y
Indonesia	110/220V
Iran	220V
Iraq	220V
Ireland	220V
Isle of Man	220V
Israel	220V
Italy	110/220V
Jamaica	110/220V
Japan	110V
Jordan	220V
Kenya	220V
South Korea	220V
Kuwait	220V
Laos	110/220V
Lebanon	110/220V
Lesotho	220V
Liberia	110/220V
Libya	110/220V
Liechtenstein	220V
Luxembourg	110/220V
Macao	110/220V
Madagascar	220V
Madeira	220V Y
Majorca	110V
Malawi	220V

Malaysia	110/220V		Tunisia	110/220V
Mali	110/220V		Turkey	110/220V
Malta	220V		Turks & Caicos	110V
Martinique	110/220V		Uganda	220V
Mauritania	220V		Uruguay	220V
Mexico	110/220V		UAE	220V
Monaco	110/220V		United Kingdom	220V*
Montserrat	220V		USA	110V
Morocco	110/220V		US Virgin Islands	110V
Mozambique	220V		Vanuatu	220V
Myanmar	220V		Venezuela	110/220V
Nepal	220V		Vietnam	110/220V
Netherlands	110/220V		North Yemen	220V
Neth. Antilles	110/220V		South Yemen	220V
Nevis	220V		The Former	
New Caledonia	220V		Yugoslavia	220V
New Zealand	220V		Zaire	220V
Nicaragua	110/220V		Zambia	220V
Niger	220V		Zimbabwe	220V*
Nigeria	220V*			
Norway	220V			
Oman	220V			
Pakistan	220V			
Panama	110V			
Papua New Guinea	220V			
Paraguay	220V Y			
Peru	220			
Philippines	110/220V			
Portugal	110/220V			
Portugal	110V			
Qatar	220V			
Romania	110/220V			
Russia	110/220V			
Rwanda	220V			
St. Barthèlemy	220V			
St. Eustatius	110/220V			
St. Kitts	220V			
St. Maarten	110/220V			
St. Vincent	220V			
Saudi Arabia	110/220V			
Senegal	110V			
Seychelles	220V			
Sierra Leone	220V			
Singapore	110/220V*			
Slovakia	110/220V			
Somalia	110/220V			
South Africa	220V			
Spain	110/220V			
Sri Lanka	220V			
Sudan	220V			
Suriname	110/220V			
Swaziland	220V			
Sweden	110/220V Y			
Switzerland	110/220V			
Syria	110/220V			
Tahiti	110/220V			
Taiwan	110/220V			
Tanzania	220V			
Togo	110/220V			
Tonga	220V			
Trinidad and Tobago	110/220V			

* *Denotes countries in which plugs with 3 square pins are used (in whole or part).*

Y Countries using DC in certain areas.

AWARDS AND GRANTS

Please see under Expedition in section 3 of the Directory. ■

NOTES ON CONTRIBUTORS

Nicholas Barnard specializes in writing on the tribal and folk arts, his books include: *Living with Kilims, Living with Decorative Textiles, Living with Folk Art* and *Traditional Indian Textiles*, published by Thames & Hudson, and *Indian Arts and Crafts*, published by Conran Octopus.

Frank Barrett is Travel Editor of *The Mail on Sunday* and has been named Travel Writer of the Year several times.

John Batchelor is a Fellow of the Royal Geographical Society. He has travelled extensively in Africa, with his wife *Julie Batchelor* who is a teacher, and they have co-authored several books, including *The Congo*.

Dr Nick Beeching is Senior Lecturer in Infectious Diseases at the Liverpool School of Tropical Medicine, and a Consultant at the Regional Infectious Disease Unit at Fazakerly Hospital in Liverpool. He and his young family have travelled widely, and he has worked in India, Australia, New Zealand and the Middle East.

Dr David Bellamy is one of the world's leading environmentalists. Campaigning for the preservation of areas of special interest throughout the world, from Tasmania to the Lake District, he has written countless books, made numerous television programmes and also set up his own charity, The Conservation Foundation.

Col John Blashford-Snell is founder of Operations Drake and Raleigh, and leader of countless expeditions worldwide.

Dominic Boland is past editor of *Practical Photography, British Photographic Industry News*, and *Professional Photographer* magazines and has written, lectured and broadcast extensively in the UK on photography and video. As a travel photographer, recent assignments have included Mexico, the West Indies and The Canary Islands.

Chris Bonington the eminent mountaineer, was the first to climb the Southwest face of Everest in 1975.

Lt. Col Peter Boxhall is an explorer, writer and Arabist. He has worked in the Arab world for many years, including posts as PA to the Mayor of Jeddah, and Director of Save the Children Fund in Jeddah. He writes for many publications, and has led a number of expeditions.

Hilary Bradt divides her time between leading trips in South America, East Africa and Madagascar, and writing and publishing guide books for independent travellers.

Cathy Braithwaite has worked for the Saga Group, which specializes in travel for the elderly.

Caroline Brandenburger is the editor of *Traveller* magazine. She has also written several books including *Establishment Wives* and *Around the World in 80 Ways*.

Roger Bray is Travel Editor of *The Evening Standard*.

Greg Brookes has, since 1963, interspersed periods of full-time study with teaching in Europe and Africa where he is widely travelled.

Tania Brown has a degree in Linguistics from Lancaster University. She speaks fluent German, French and Spanish and worked for two years as an administrator before resigning to join Keith Kimber on a trip round the world. They left in 1983, and were last reported in Cyprus in 1991.

Warren Burton joined Encounter Overland in 1980, having travelled extensively in Asia, Middle East, Europe and North America. He spent 4 years leading expeditions throughout Asia, Africa and South America, before taking on his present position as the Company's Operation Manager.

Tony Bush is editor of *Export Times*, the international trade and finance magazine, and also author of the *Business Travel Planner* (Oyez).

Michael Busselle is a distinguished travel photographer, and author of many books on the art of photography and his great love, France. He contributes a regular column to *Traveller* magazine.

Gill Cairns is a freelance writer and associated with the London Buddhist Centre.

Simon Calder is Travel Correspondent for the Independent. Author of *Hitch-hikers Manual — Britain* and *Europe —a Manual for Hitch-hikers*, plus several guides in the Travellers Survival Kit series.

John Carlton is a keen walker and backpacker. An active member of the YHA for over 36 years, he has worked in the travel trade for the same period. He has visited most countries of Western and Eastern Europe, Morocco, Canada and the USA.

Roy Carter writes on corporate security and risk management for the international business and professional press. He has lectured on related subjects at Loughborough University. He is a former Head of Consultancy for an international group of security companies.

Roger Chapman, MBE, FRGS, was commissioned into the Green Howards after completing a Geography degree at Oxford and a spell at Sandhurst. He has been involved in many expeditions — down the Blue Nile and Zaire Rivers, to Central and South America, to East Greenland with the British Schools Exploration Society, and to Papua New Guinea with Operation Drake to name a few.

David Churchill writes regularly on business travel for *The Times* and *The Sunday Times*.

Trisha Cochrane is a psychologist by training, and ran the Business-woman's Travel Club for two and a half years.

Nicholas Crane has cycled in 29 countries. His charity fund-raising trips *Bicycles up Kilimanjaro* and *Journey to the Centre of the Earth* were undertaken with cousin Richard Crane for Intermediate Technology. He has worked for Afghan Aid in the Hindu Kush mountains, and written and co-written seven books. He also made the TV journey *Atlas Biker* for Central TV and National Geographic Films. He works as a journalist, contributing regularly to *The Sunday Times* and *The Daily Telegraph* newspapers and is President of The Globetrotters Club. He recently walked the length of Europe.

Ingrid Cranfield edited three earlier editions of this book. A freelance writer and broadcaster, she is a Fellow of the Royal Geographical Society.

Quentin Crewe is a writer (author of many books, most recently *A World Guide to Food*), traveller, sometime restaurateur. He has been in a wheelchair since boyhood.

Sheila Critchley is a Canadian journalist now based in London, and has run an airline in-flight magazine.

Dr. Richard Dawood is the author of *How to Stay Healthy Abroad* (OUP). A leading expert on travel health, he contributes a regular column to *Traveller* magazine and is Health Editor of the American magazine *Condé Nast Traveler*.

René Dee was a regular soldier in the Intelligence Corps, serving in Singapore and Malaysia. In 1967, after leaving the army, he travelled overland to India and Nepal, and then led a series of trips to Morocco, specializing in treks by camel and mule.

Christina Dodwell is an inveterate traveller, horsewoman, writer, and microlight pilot. She has written a number of books, most recently *Beyond Siberia*, published by Hodder & Stoughton .

John Douglas, author and photographer, is a former Army officer who has travelled solo and with expeditions through Asia, Africa and the Arctic. He is the author of *Creative Techniques in Travel Photography*, and a director of Geoslides Photo Library.

Doris Dow became a single expatriate in Central Africa, married, and spent 24 years there before returning to the UK. By profession a secretary and teacher, she is actively involved with the Women's Corona Society in London.

Col. Andrew Duncan is the Assistant Director of Information at The International Institute for Strategic Studies.

Tim Ellerby is the Operations Manager of Stanfords, the world's largest map and travel bookshop.

Sir Ranulph Fiennes Bt. was commissioned into the Royal Scots Greys in 1963, and attached to 22 SAS Regiment in 1966. He has led several major expeditions, including the Transglobe Expedition which lasted three years. Author of ten books, he has been awarded the Founders Medal of The Royal Geographical Society and The Polar Medal with Bar from the Queen. Most recently he and Dr Mike Stroud made the longest unsupported journey in polar history across the Antarctic.

Michael Furnell has been involved with property journalism for many years; he edited Homefinder magazine, and in 1963 founded *Homes Overseas*, the monthly specialist periodical for people wishing to buy homes abroad. He is the author of *Living and Retiring Abroad*.

Adrian Furnham is a lecturer in psychology at London University. He holds degrees from the University of London, Strathclyde, and Oxford, and is particularly interested in applied and medical psychology. He is the co-author with Prof. F. Bochner of *Culture Shock: Psychological Consequences of Geographic Movement* (Methuen).

Jon Gardey grew up in California, and has lived in Alaska, Switzerland and England. He is a writer, traveller, and film-maker.

Jan Glen has travelled independently in West Africa, the Sahara, Europe and Asia. She co-wrote *The Sahara Handbook* with her husband.

Sarah Gorman trained as a journalist on provincial newspapers before moving to Hong Kong where she worked as News Editor of the Education Desk on the *Hong Kong Standard*. She has travelled widely and edited *Traveller* magazine between 1989 and 1991. She now lives in New York where she works as a travel writer.

Jan and Rupert Grey have undertaken many journeys to the remoter parts of the world, both before and after having children. They travelled through the interior of Borneo with their two eldest children, and wrote a number of articles about their experiences.

Susan Griffith is a Canadian based in England who writes books for working travellers such as *Work Your Way Around the World* and *Teaching English Abroad*.

Susan Grossman is a former travel editor of *The Telegraph Magazine*, a presenter of the BBC *Food and Drink Programme*, and now editor of BUPAS's *Upbeat* magazine, and *The Best of Britain Guide* (Redwood).

Robin Hanbury-Tenison, OBE, is a well-known explorer, author and broadcaster who has taken part in many major expeditions in South America, Africa and the Far East. He is also founder and President of Survival International, the organization that seeks to prevent the extinction of the world's remaining tribal groups.

Diana Hanks of The Timeshare Council, has worked in consumer relations for many years, particularly in the field of tourism.

Nick Hanna is a freelance journalist and has been travelling in the tropics intermittently for the past 12 years. His features and photographs have appeared in *The Sunday Times, The Guardian, Harpers & Queen* amongst many others. Author of the *BMW Tropical Beach Handbook* (Fourth Estate), and *The Greenpeace Book of Coral Reefs*.

Bryan Hanson is an executive member of The Globetrotters Club and former editor of the club magazine, and has travelled extensively.

Richard Harrington is a widely travelled freelance travel writer.

David Hodgson, AIIP, was senior staff photo-journalist and later picture editor with Features International. His work has featured in many magazines, including *Life, Paris Match* and *Stern.*

Robert Holmes is a traveller, mountaineer, and leading wilderness photographer published in many books and magazines. He teaches photography at the California Academy of Sciences.

Malcolm Irvine is a registered insurance broker, specializing in insurance for adventure and over-land travellers.

Jack Jackson is an experienced expedition leader and overland traveller, explorer, mountaineer, author, photographer, lecturer and diver. He is co-author with Ellen Crampton of *The Asian Highway* (Angus and Robertson) and author of *The Four Wheel Drive Book* (Gentry).

Dr. Jay Kettle-Williams BA, M Litt, FIL, is National Marketing Executive for Richard Lewis Communications, responsible for the Foreign Language Division. He is also Editor of *The Linguist,* the journal of the Institute of Linguists.

Keith Kimber has a degree in Electronics from Southampton University and worked for four years as an electronics engineer before resigning his job and selling everything to travel at the age of 25, with Tania Brown, on a 500cc Honda motorbike.

Robin Knox-Johnston, CBE, RD, was the first man to sail single-handed non-stop around the world in 1968-9, completing the journey in 313 days. He was world class 2 multi hull champion in 1985, and is author of many books on sailing. He recently set the world record for sailing round the world in a catamaran.

Samantha Lee is a freelance journalist and writer, based in London and Scotland.

David Learmount joined the Royal Naval College, Dartmouth, from school in 1965, was briefly an airline steward with British Airways where he learned to fly in his time off, and then joined the RAF for 10 years where he worked as a transport pilot and a flying instructor. He has worked at *Flight International* for 11 years where he is Air Transport Editor, and is an expert on flight safety.

Peter Mason is Senior Lecturer in Geography at Polytechnic South West in Devon. *Author of Tourism: Environment and Development Perspectives* (WWF), and contributor to *The Good Tourist in Britain* (Heinemann), he is also active in Tourism Concern.

Colin McElduff is a Fellow of the Royal Geographical Society, the Royal Anthropological Institute and the Society of Antiquaries (Scotland). In India, Burma and Africa, during the war, he later joined the Colonial Police Service, serving in Malaya, Cyprus, Nigeria and Borneo. In 1965 he returned to the UK and worked for the Royal Automobile Club. He is now retired.

Stephen McLelland is editor of *Telecommunications Magazine.*

Julian McIntosh lived in Africa for several years, and has travelled extensively. His overland experiences prompted him to set up his own specialist tropical equipment firm.

Alex McWhirter has worked in the travel business since he left school, and is now Travel Editor of *Business Traveller* magazine. He has travelled widely in North America, Australia, Europe, the Middle East and Far East.

Paul Melly writes on foreign news, business and travel, for *Export Times, The Guardian, Africa Analysis* and *The Scotsman* amongst others.

Paul Millichip is a successful artist, and author of *The Travelling Painter* (Batsford).

George Monbiot is a writer, broadcaster and campaigner for the environment and threatened tribal peoples. The author of the *Poisoned Arrows, Amazon Watershed* and most recently *No Man's Land,* published by Macmillan. He is a Visiting Fellow of Green College Oxford

Dervla Murphy is a committed independent traveller, and author of many highly successful travel books including *The Road to Coorg*, *Cameroon with Egbert* and *The Ukimwi Road*.

Carey Ogilvie is an experienced traveller, most recently in Kamchatka. She also drove a Fire Engine from Cape North in Norway to Cape Agulhas in South Africa to raise money for the Samaritans. She is co-author of *Around the World in 80 Ways*, published by WEXAS.

David Orchard was a station commander for the British Government in Antarctica, and now leads tours in Africa.

Chris Parrott has lived in France, Singapore, Spain and Brazil, as well as travelling extensively in Europe, the Middle East and the Americas. He is now a director of Journey Latin America.

Tony Pearson has made a serious academic study of outdoor equipment. He worked for several years at Field and Trek Ltd, and is now a freelance consultant to the outdoor equipment trade.

Tony Peisley is a freelance journalist specializing in the cruise industry. He is also a regular contributor for the TV programme *Wish You Were Here*.

Robin Perlstein is a Registered Dietician who has worked at the British Diabetic Association, where she was Assistant in the Diabetes Care Department and was involved in writing and giving advice in many areas relating to diabetes.

Christopher Portway has been a freelance travel writer for nearly 20 years, is the author of several books and recently, aged 70, cycled from the Baltic to the Black Sea.

Paul Pratt has been a ship's radio officer in the British Merchant Navy and an electronics engineer in Britain and Scandinavia. His interest in motor-cycles began with cross-country sporting trials and he now claims the longest continuous journey in motorcycle history which, between 1966 and 1979, took him through 48 countries, a distance of nearly 165,000km. His book of the trip is *World Understanding on Two Wheels*.

John Pullen is Director of Travelmate, the introduction service for travellers.

Philip Ray has been a journalist for the whole of his career, specializing in writing about the airline and travel businesses for the past 21 years. He was Deputy Editor of *Travel News*, the weekly UK travel trade newspaper, until he switched to freelance writing and market research consultancy.

Kent Redding is from Texas, but after travelling through Europe, the Middle East and Africa, now works in London as a journalist.

John Rose was the Principal at the Customs Directorate Division E Branch 4, HM Customs and Excise.

Annie Redmile has been a journalist specializing in aviation subjects for over twenty years.

David Richardson is a freelance journalist specializing in the travel industry.

Martin Rosser is a freelance writer and self-professed vagabond. His writing and travelling have taken him to Africa, Australia and Europe.

Andrew Sanger, journalist and editor, is a frequent contributor to the travel pages of several national newspapers and magazines, among them *The Guardian*, *The Daily* and *Sunday Telegraph*, and the *Sunday Express*. He has written a number of popular guidebooks, including *The Vegetarian Traveller* (Grafton).

Dave Saunders is a freelance journalist in the photographic press, having edited a number of magazines and written and illustrated several books.

Douglas Schatz is Director and General Manager of Stanfords, the world's largest map and travel bookshop.

Gilbert Schwartz, a teacher and veteran traveller, spent over a year researching and compiling his book *The Climate Advisor* (Climate Guide Publications, New York) which has gone into several printings.

Melissa Shales was brought up in Zimbabwe, but returned to Britain to take a degree in History and Archaeology at Exeter University. She edited *Traveller* for five years and since 1987 has worked as a freelance travel writer and editor. Widely travelled in Africa and Europe, she is a Fellow of the Royal Geographical Society and a member of The British Guild of Travel Writers. She is also the editor of two previous editions of this book.

Anne Sharpley now deceased, was a journalist and travel writer, and won awards as Woman Journalist of the Year, and Descriptive Writer of the Year.

James and Sheila Shaw are a husband-and-wife writing team. Their 18-month honeymoon involved four back-to-back freighter trips which took them around Africa and South America.

David Shenkin is the Higher Executive Officer at the Customs Directorate 4D, HM CuStoms.

Ted Simon rode a Triumph 500cc motorcycle round the world, between 1973 and 1977. He travelled extensively in America, Latin America, Australia and Asia, and his book on the journey is *Jupiter's Travels* (Hamish Hamilton).

Anthony Smith is a zoologist by training, and a writer, broadcaster and presenter of television programmes, including the Wilderness series on BBC Television. His first expedition was to Iran with an Oxford University team in 1950. Since then he has ridden the length of Africa on a motorcycle, written an account of the Royal Geographical Society/Royal Society Mato Grosso Expedition of 1967, and built and flown hydrogen-filled balloons and airships. He was co-founder of the British Balloon and Airship Club, and involved with the RGS Expeditions Committee.

Richard Snailham read Modern History at Oxford and was a teacher until 1965, when he became a Senior Lecturer at the Royal Military Academy, Sandhurst. He has been on expeditions to the Middle East, Africa, Asia and South America. He is a co-founder of the Scientific Exploration Society, author of several books, and is actively involved with the Young Explorer's Trust and Operation Raleigh.

Harry Stevens is a businessman running his own engineering and electronics company, which often takes him abroad.

Keith Strickland is a civil servant, and an expert on train travel. He is author of the *Steam Railways Around the World* (Alan Sutton Publishing).

Dr Mike Stroud specializes in the effect of physical extremes on the body and is attached to the Army Personnel Research Establishment at Farnborough. He recently made Polar history with Sir Ranulph Fiennes by completing the longest unsupported journey in the Antarctic,

Mike Thexton is a chartered accountant whose life took an unexpected turn in 1986 when he was trapped on a hi-jacked aeroplane.

Edwina Townsend has worked in the travel trade for twenty years and is now the Customer Relations Officer at WEXAS International.

Tony Bush is editor of *Export Times*, the international trade and finance magazine, and also author of the *Business Travel Planner* (Oyez).

Isabella Tree is travel correspondent on the *Evening Standard*, and is currently writing a book about her travels in Papua New Guinea

Myfanwy Vickers is a traveller, writer and radio producer.

Paul Vickers is a designer and freelance journalist based in Paris.

Debbie Warne is the Sales Support Manager for WEXAS International and has eight years experience of negotiating airline fares.

Steve Weinman is editor of *BBC World Magazine*, the magazine of the World Service.

Stafford Whiteaker is author of *The Good Retreat Guide*, published by Rider Books.

Ralph Whitmarsh is Head of the Passport and Visa Section at Thomas Cook in London.

Arnie Wilson is skiing correspondent of *The Financial Times*, and currently skiing his way round the world.

Nigel Winser is Deputy Director of the Royal Geographical Society and has been responsible for a number of RGS expeditions.

Shane Winser is Information Officer of the Royal Geographical Society and its Expedition Advisory Centre. She studied Zoology and Information Science at London University, before helping her husband to organize scientific expeditions to Sarawak, Pakistan, Kenya and Oman. She writes a regular column, *Frontiers*, for *Geographical Magazine*.

Dr Emma Woolfenden is a lecturer in Travel Medicine at the Liverpool School of Tropical Medicine, and plans to work in the developing world after further experience in Liverpool.

Carol Wright has been a travel writer for over 20 years and has written 30 books including *The Travel Survival Guide*. She is on the committee of the Guild of British Travel Writers.

Pat Yale is an associate lecturer in travel and tourism at a further education college in Bristol, and a freelance travel writer. She is the author of *The Budget Travel Handbook* and *From Tourist Attractions to Heritage Tourism*. She has travelled extensively through Europe, Africa, Asia and Central America, frequently alone, and always on a shoestring. ■

MAP OF THE WORLD

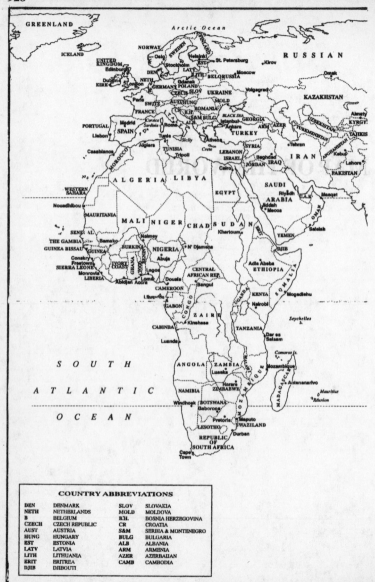

COUNTRY ABBREVIATIONS

DEN	DENMARK	SLOV	SLOVAKIA
NETH	NETHERLANDS	MOLD	MOLDOVA
B	BELGIUM	B.H.	BOSNIA HERZEGOVINA
CZECH	CZECH REPUBLIC	CR	CROATIA
AUST	AUSTRIA	S&M	SERBIA & MONTENEGRO
HUNG	HUNGARY	BULG	BULGARIA
EST	ESTONIA	ALB	ALBANIA
LATV	LATVIA	ARM	ARMENIA
LITH	LITHUANIA	AZER	AZERBAIJAN
ERIT	ERITREA	CAMB	CAMBODIA
DJIB	DJIBOUTI		

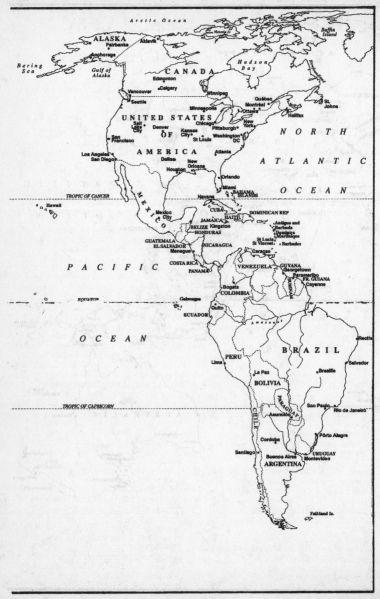

INDEX

934

■